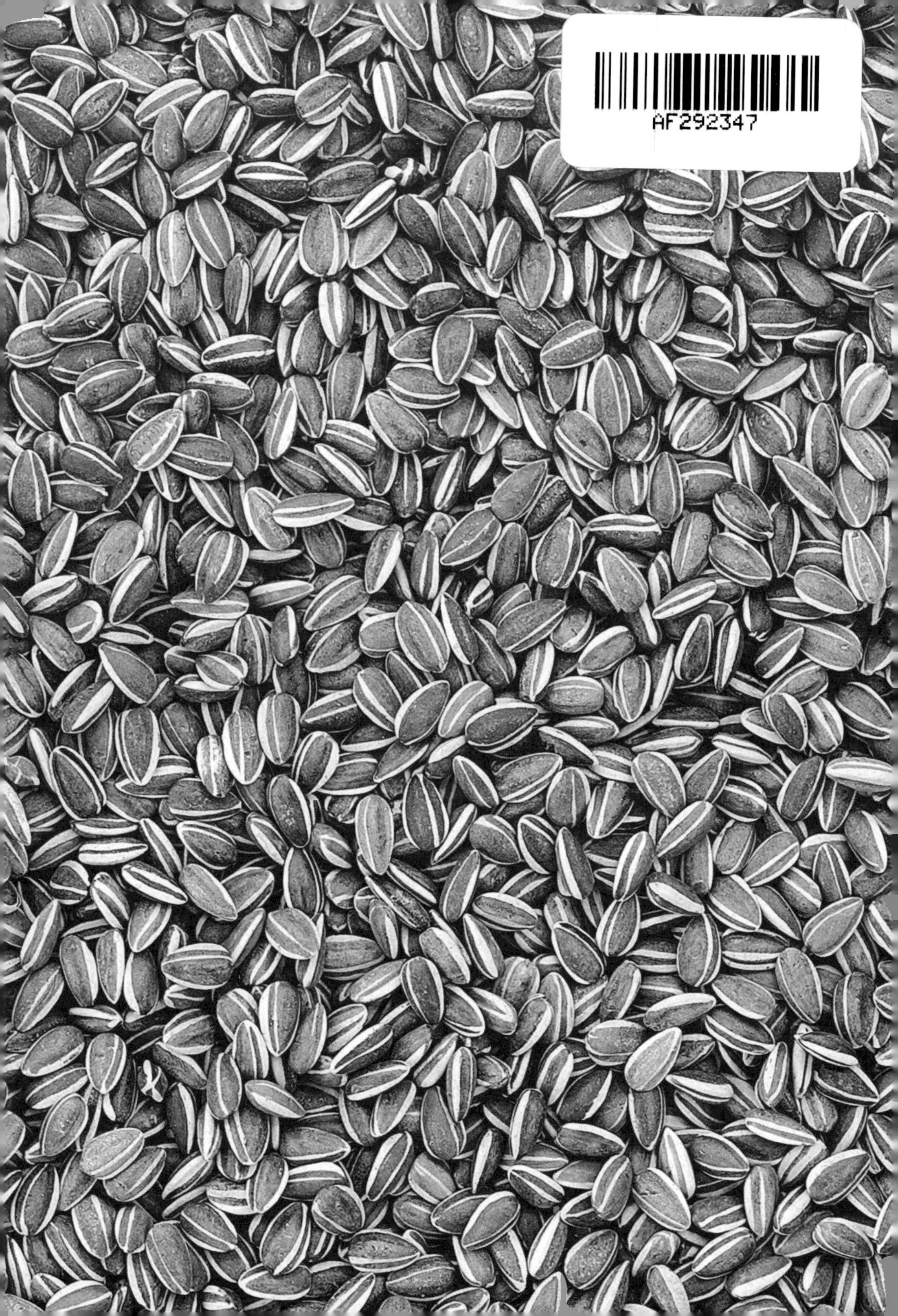
AF292347

AI WEIWEI

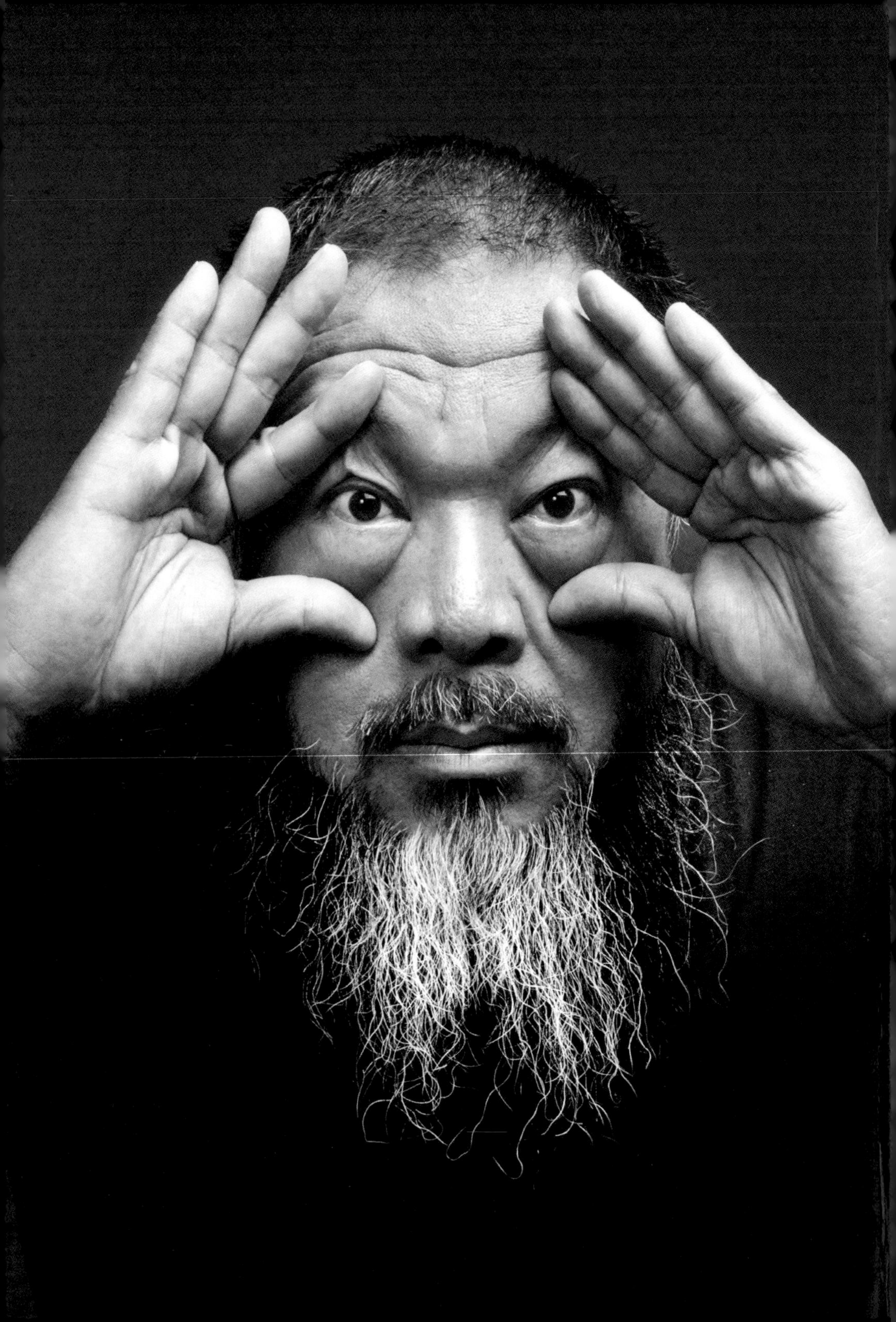

AI WEIWEI

Edited by
Hans Werner Holzwarth

With Texts by
Roger M. Buergel
Uli Sigg

TASCHEN

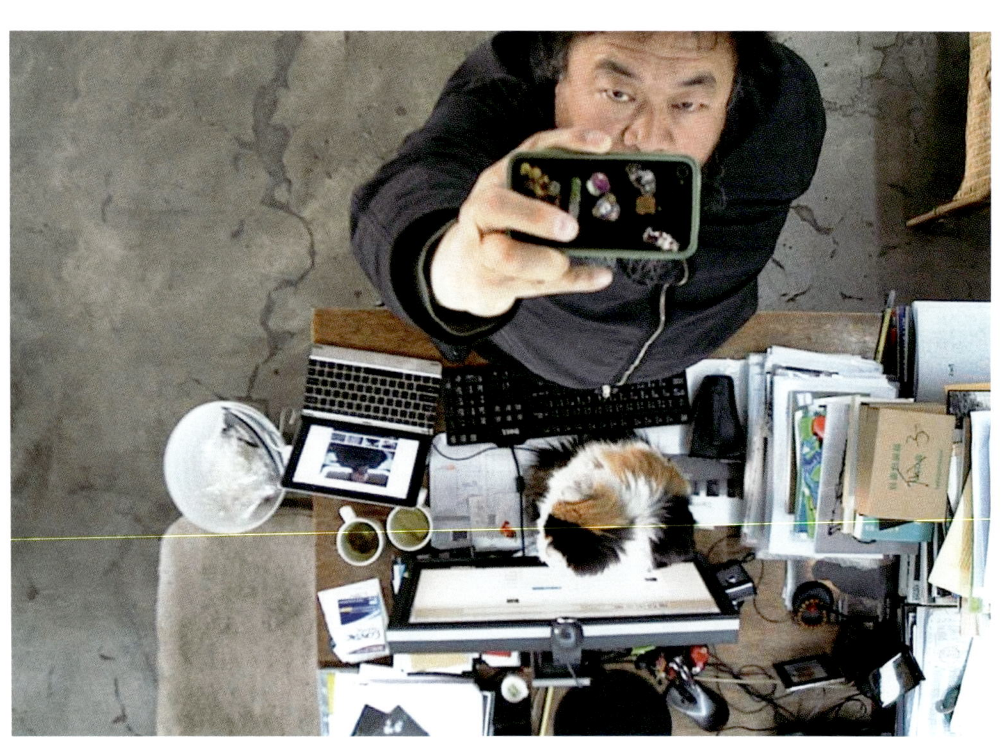

Contents

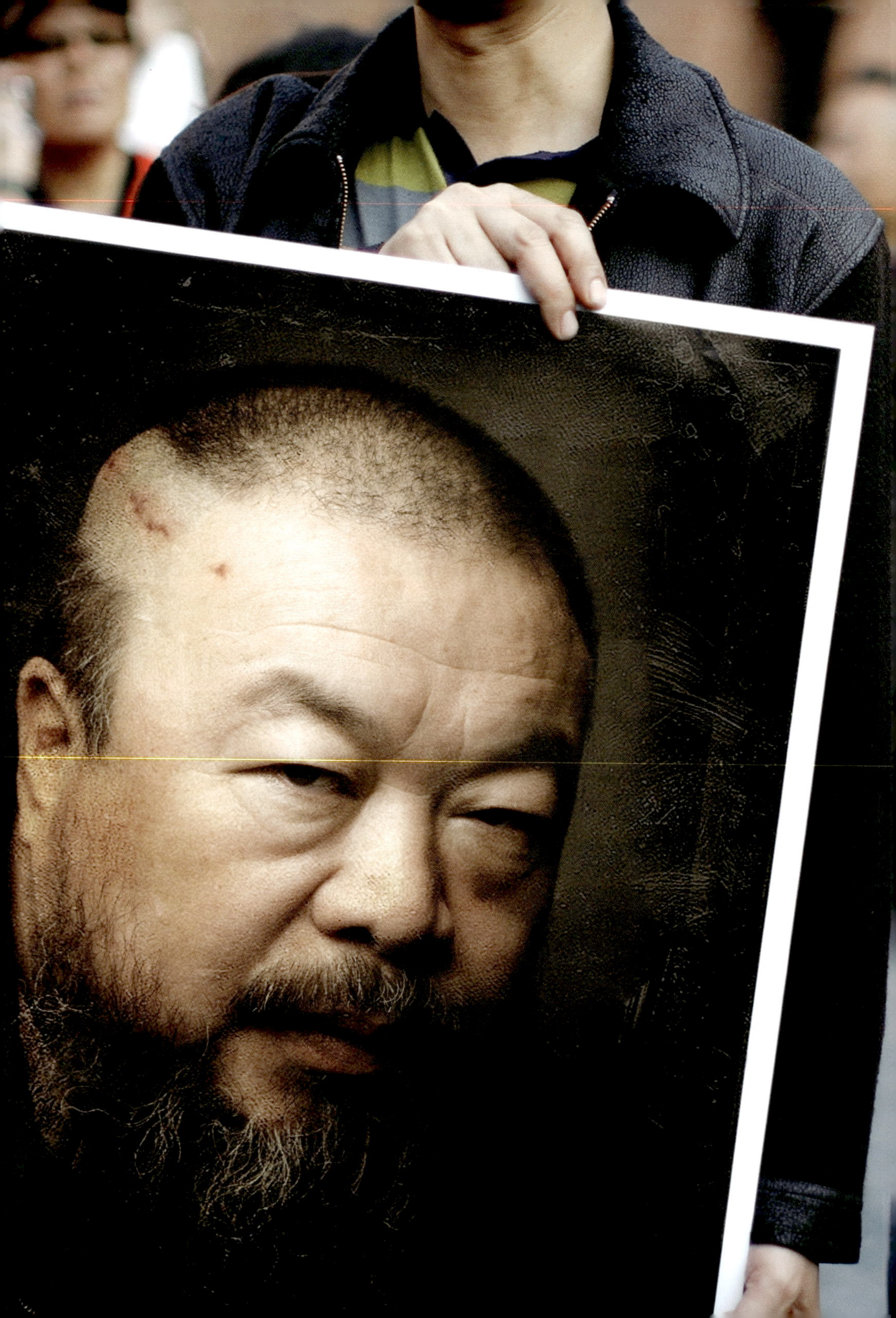

The Better Argument
A Portrait of Ai Weiwei

ULI SIGG

It's become less of a challenge to track down Ai Weiwei these days. He almost perpetually resides in his studio, ever since his passport was unlawfully confiscated after his release from custody in June 2011. A man known to jet around the world a few times a year, who was finally getting in overdose what he would have deserved long ago: worldwide acclaim, interviews, invitations to exhibit, to realize projects, to teach, to clutter China and other parts of the world with buildings, to spend time with established dignitaries, and so on. Now this world comes to his studio. Here he plans and curates his exhibitions, designs magazine covers, tweets, and holds court with as much presence in the global media as ever before. What kind of personality does it take to keep all of this running?

Part of the answer can be extracted from the artist's biography. In the 1950s the writings of his father, a famous poet, had landed the family in exile in China's inhospitable northwest. In 1976 they returned to Beijing, where the young Ai took up studies at the film academy, only to quit soon afterwards, frustrated by the quixotic ideals conveyed there. In 1981 he followed his girlfriend to the United States, a journey the 23-year-old embarked on as a self-declared "postimpressionist" painter: he had been profoundly impacted after chancing upon a van Gogh monograph and a book about impressionism—while, by contrast, he had thrown out a monograph on the incomprehensible concoctions of Jasper Johns. Painting provided Ai with an escape from the Chinese variant of communism, which presented itself to him as a perennial disaster: for incomprehensible reasons, his father had been labeled a dissident "rightist" and thus an enemy of the state. Moreover, major and even very minor decisions in Chinese everyday life invariably ran counter to the official propaganda and defied any attempt to understand them based on reason or human sentiment—on the contrary, neither of those were to be trusted. The only escape into empathy, into emotion and passion, was through painting, where the artist alone was responsible for his choices of line, shading, and color.

A short stay in 1982 at the Parsons School of Design in New York City gave him his first exposure to the concepts of Duchamp and Warhol, which he devoured in one sitting while observing his fellow American students as they painted away wildly, focused on the what and completely bypassing the why—the very central question that would accompany Ai from then on: why should one express oneself as an artist? He subsequently made up his mind to leave painting, or, in his words, a studio full of pictures nobody wanted behind; to turn away from the two-dimensional, finite artwork and toward the ever-expanding universe of conceptual art. For Ai, the most important attribute of the artist's existence would henceforth be reason, which had failed to illuminate most anything in the cultural-revolutionary China of his youth, which again probably explains why he's been practicing it so relentlessly ever since. His discovery of Duchamp had buried the postimpressionist, and in Duchamp's ideas about the artist's existence as a mindset, as a lifestyle, Ai found his identity.

He decided to return to China in 1993, prompted by his father's serious illness. At first he lived in his father's house, where he considered himself a mere guest, and not a particularly respectable one at that, with not a thing to show for all the years spent in the US—no elegant diploma, not even a half-decent art career. So he kept a low profile, limiting his expression to the publishing of three books about Western and experimental Chinese art. His now famous *Han Dynasty Urn with Coca-Cola Logo* from 1994, the photo work *Dropping a Han Dynasty Urn* from 1995 (pp. 85–87), even his first compositions made of deconstructed furniture from 1997 onward (pp. 102–109)—he didn't regard any of it as art. He considered them mere diversions. It wasn't until 1999 that he again faced the challenge of producing art according to his own definition—after being nominated by Harald Szeemann to appear in the Venice Biennale of that year.

Another portion of the answer to the question of Ai's personality can be found in the works he made now that he had found his way back to art. Seen through Western eyes, their gestures consistently produce ambiguity—a very tangible ambiguity. The hardware bears mainly Chinese connotations, while we are left to somehow imagine the software. We sense a personality with a very clear idea of what art is and isn't, and what is needed to grasp or compose a thing and then move it from one sphere into another. But what constitutes this very clear idea—especially when we lack the contextual knowledge of Chinese thoughts and things? Is a cubic meter of tea (*Ton of Tea*, 2006, p. 308) the same on both sides of the world? Of course not: "to drink a cup of tea" is a euphemism often used by the Chinese police when summoning people to preliminary interrogations.

With a more encompassing gaze, now inclusive of Chinese characteristics, we may find another complexity. It is rooted in a specific strength inherent in Chinese culture: the capacity to fuse contradictions into one single proposition. To put it simply: while in a Western mind, according to our Cartesian binary logic, a thing is either this or that, in a Chinese mind that same thing may well be this and that at the same time. Take Ai's work *Whitewash* (1993–2000, pp. 45, 193) as an example: 132 Neolithic vases, each one a beautiful piece of art and a relic, but one fourth of them completely covered or destroyed by white industrial paint. The work fuses two contradictory paradigms of art creation: the Western paradigm of "avant-garde" art, which means a radical destruction of tradition, breaking with the past to create

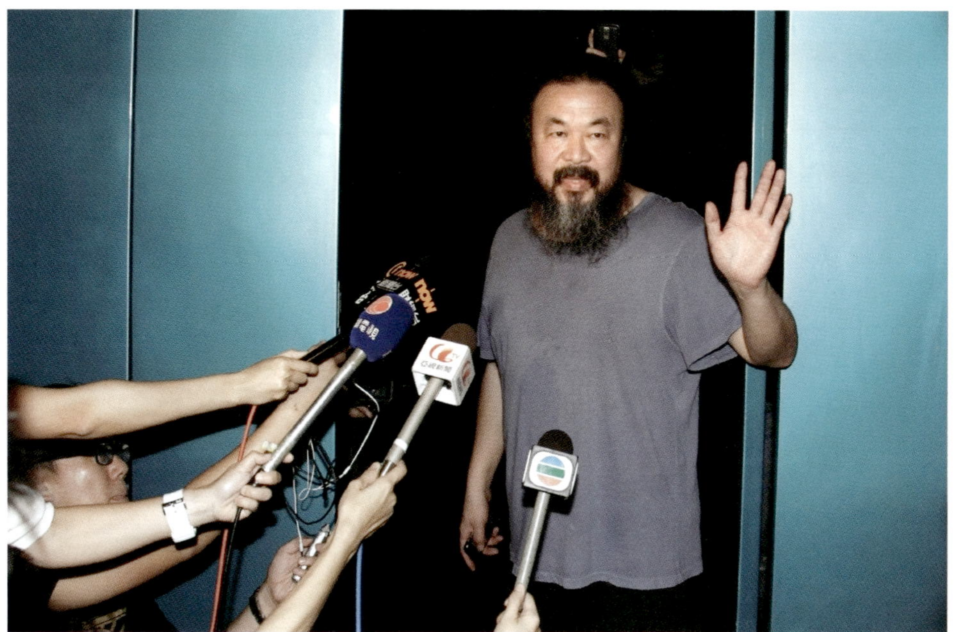

Ai Weiwei in front of his Caochangdi studio after his release from detention, Beijing, June 22, 2011.
Photo: David Gray

space for entirely new thinking; and the classic Chinese paradigm of great respect for tradition and therefore of art creation as an evolving continuum drawing from the wealth of Chinese culture. Add to this scale and Chinese production methods, where factor costs are so low that they enable a bold artist such as Ai to think in big dimensions—and Ai does really think big. In earlier projects, he had already worked with up to 100 people, from laborers to the most skilled and experienced craftsmen China has to offer. Then, in 2007, he chartered the travel of 1,001 Chinese to Documenta 12 in Kassel, involving them as "migrant workers" in a social sculpture. And for his installation *Sunflower Seeds* at the Tate Modern in 2010, he mobilized a workforce of 1,600.

Ai's Documenta piece (*Fairytale*, 2007, pp. 310–327) also revealed an artistic strategy that was to shape his work increasingly. His own greatest strength, the artist says, is "to put himself in an awkward situation"—that's how a contradiction can arise which then calls for resolution or at least control. But this process of gaining control mustn't be easily managed. His art must always also imply the possibility of a major mishap, or else Ai doesn't feel sufficiently challenged. Take *Fairytale:* how do you turn the idea of introducing 1,001 Chinese to a reality entirely different from their own into a work of art? The project posed innumerable logistical difficulties, such as selecting population samples, securing passports, visas, travel and housing arrangements, etc. Then, quite importantly,

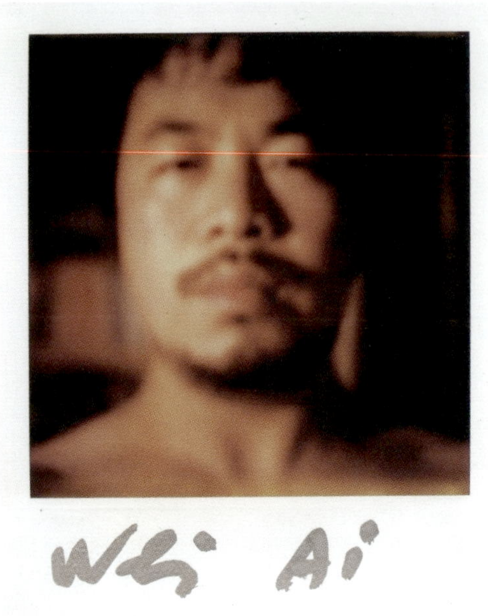

Ai Weiwei, Polaroid, 1983

something had to remain: the myth. Because obviously it was never intended or even possible that anyone would get to see this gigantic *Fairytale* running on a thousand different schedules as a unified whole. What's more, much of it was planned to unfold on the Internet—Ai turned it into a social medium before its hype in China. And finally, something had to take on a physical form, so he made an installation out of 1,001 chairs. They lent a poetic aspect to the work, opening up additional spaces.

Fragments of this strategy are also recognizable in the intensive research actions surrounding the earthquake in Sichuan (e.g. *Namelist,* 2008–2011, pp. 348/349) and in the large-scale installation *Sunflower Seeds* at the Tate Modern (pp. 49, 407–409). These works share the mobilization of massive personnel resources across the entire People's Republic within the shortest of time frames, inconceivable without the Internet. It will hardly be controversial to say that every other artist would have rejected the Tate Modern's request in January 2010 to stage a show in the giant Turbine Hall, not in 2012, as originally scheduled, but much earlier, in October of the same year. If Ai wanted to undertake the physical realization of one of the most prestigious and therefore riskiest engagements in the art world, then transport from China and installing the work would take three months. Which left Ai with six months, counting from January 2010, to develop an idea, draw up a concept, and produce the piece! So 1,600 workers were hired to do the molding, painting, firing, and glazing of more than 100 million *Sunflower Seeds*—it's crazy, if you think about it!

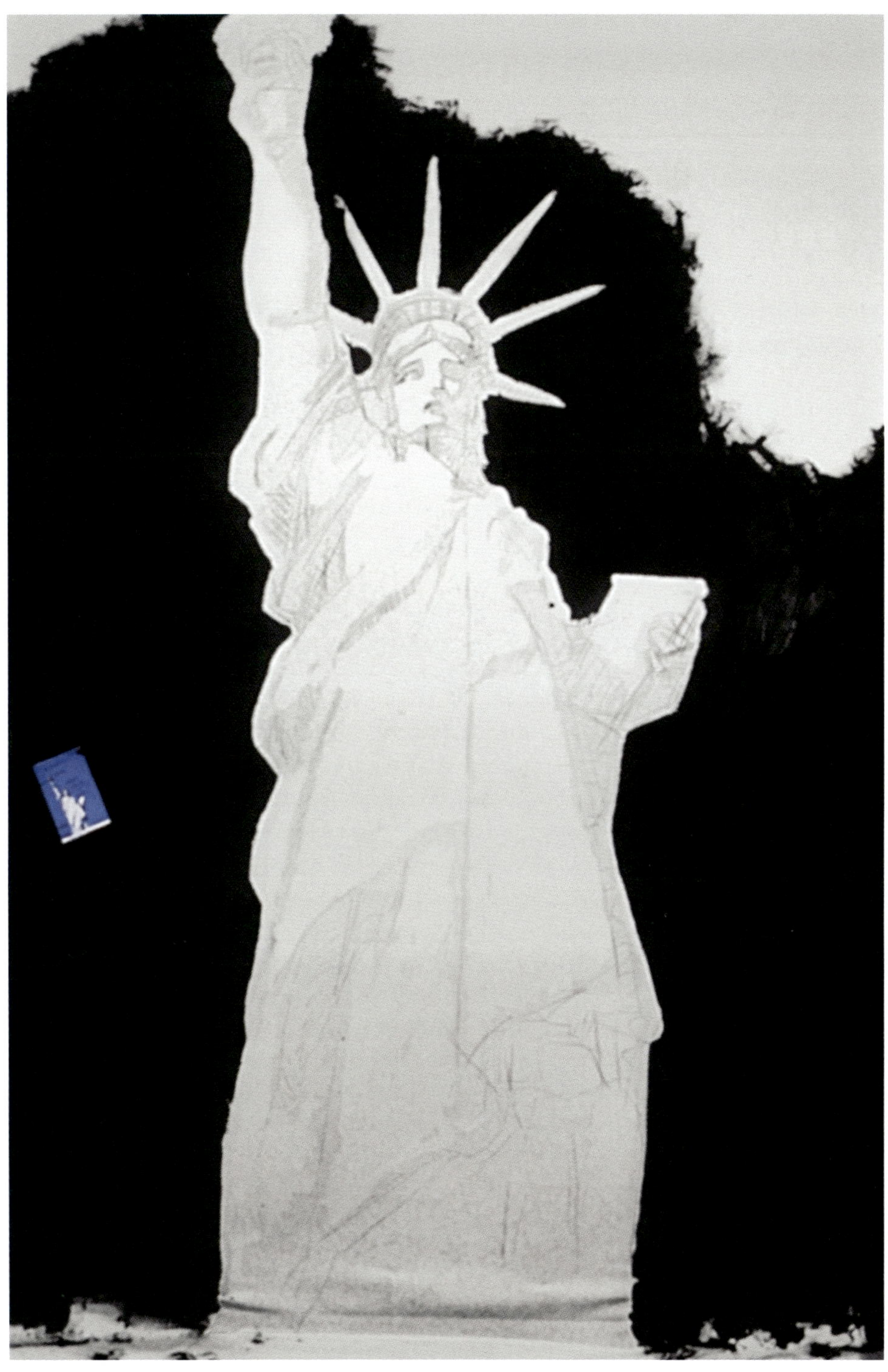

So where did Ai Weiwei get this outsize appetite for risk that drives him to launch such major projects whose basic concepts make them virtually incalculable? It is an aspect of his inner gambler—a no less essential part of Ai's personality than his rationalism—which also had made him leave for the US with $30 in his pocket. It's interesting to note that, back in the 1980s, a limousine sent from an Atlantic City casino drove up to the basement entrance of his and his colleagues' shared abode every weekend. Ai had made a veritable name for himself there as a player of blackjack. The savvy gambler embraces certain routines: to enjoy getting himself into a process whose outcome is determined to be uncertain; to be dead serious about playing the game while knowing that it's only a game; and to be always aware of himself so that he will never overplay his hand. To this day, nothing and no one has been able to break Ai's cool.

It would be surprising if Ai were to accept much of this. He is the born contrarian. He will, just like in his art, turn every argument on its head, or deconstruct it to elegantly prove its inanity—or he'll polish it in an unintelligible transfiguration until it shines brightly. And when he lays down his armor of irony and sarcasm, he can discourse brilliantly on any theme, blessed with not having to unlearn a formal education.

This argumentative brilliance ultimately earned him the most attention, certainly in China. With his blog, begun in 2005, he reached millions of Chinese readers. He never relented in laying bare the weaknesses of the political system of China. He commented without restraint, and in no uncertain terms, on subjects such as the dire consequences of official mismanagement before and after the Sichuan earthquake. He exposed the practices of the Shanghai police in the Yang Jia case, which began with a trifle and escalated to the killing of six police officers. In general he took on a broad spectrum of topics that concerned Chinese civil society. Some of Ai's compatriots have been thrown in jail for less. And were you to remind him where Chinese watchdogs draw the line regarding human-rights activism— where the fun ends in their estimation—this audacious man will graciously thank you for telling him. But it will not affect him or his endeavors to help build a new Chinese society. Many Chinese people will feel exactly the same, but so few of them dare to raise their voices in this way. He writes for them. They will owe him.

But then, on May 28, 2009, the government cut him off from his inland audience of millions: his blog was shut down by the authorities. He subsequently started a series of microblogs on the Chinese Twitter system which were in every case swiftly identified and blocked by the Internet police. Today Ai is active on global Twitter, whose imposed brevity suits his pithy style just fine. These messages, however, are accessible from within China only to those who know how to overcome the "Great Firewall," which prevents Chinese users from navigating the uncensored global space of the Internet.

So what was it that earned Ai Weiwei the de facto charge of subversion (because the investigators never framed it as such in legal terms) against the authority of

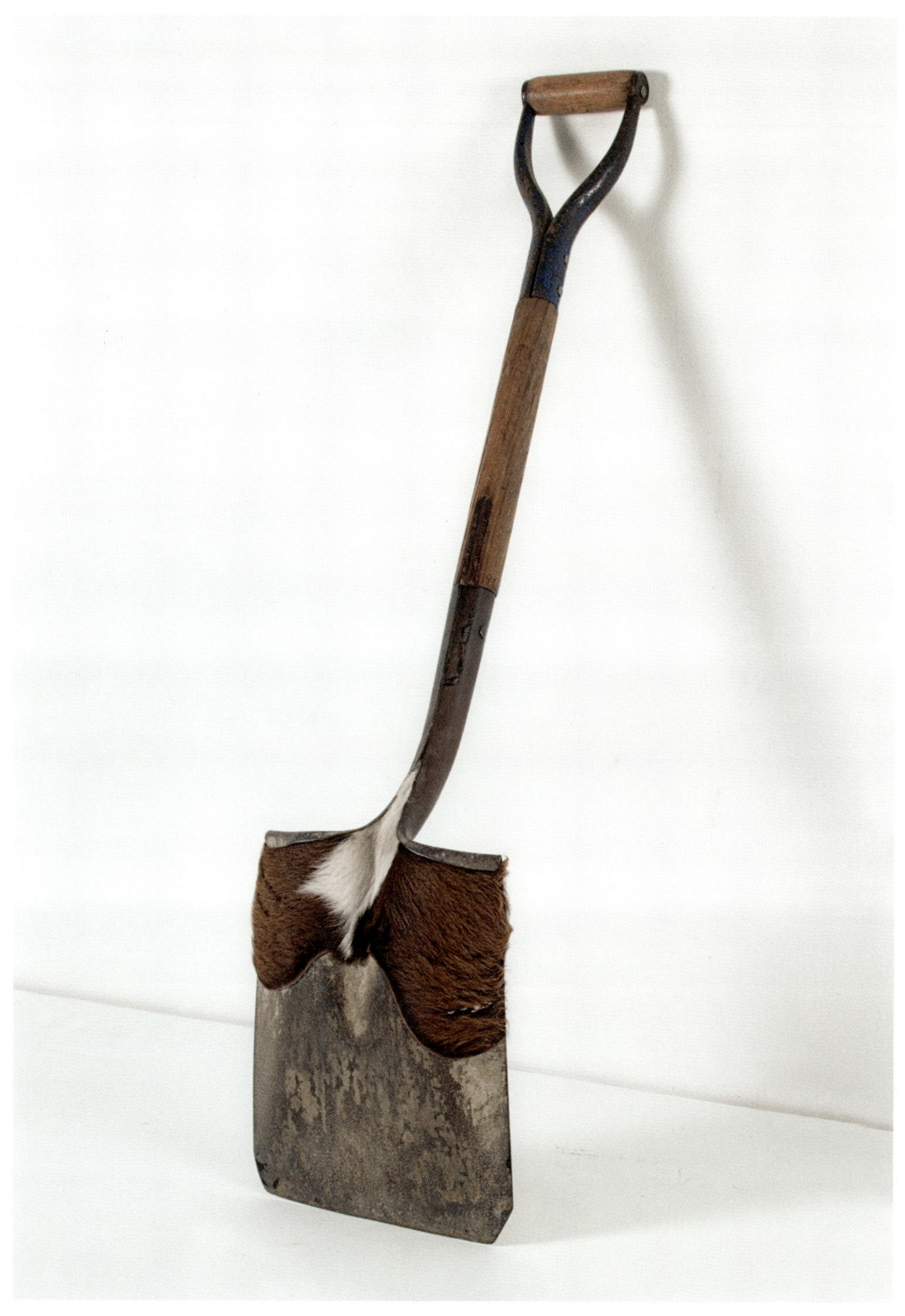

SHOVEL WITH FUR, 1988, shovel, cowhide, height 39 inches
Overleaf: Ai Weiwei with Joan Lebold Cohen outside his East Third Street apartment, New York 1987 | 13

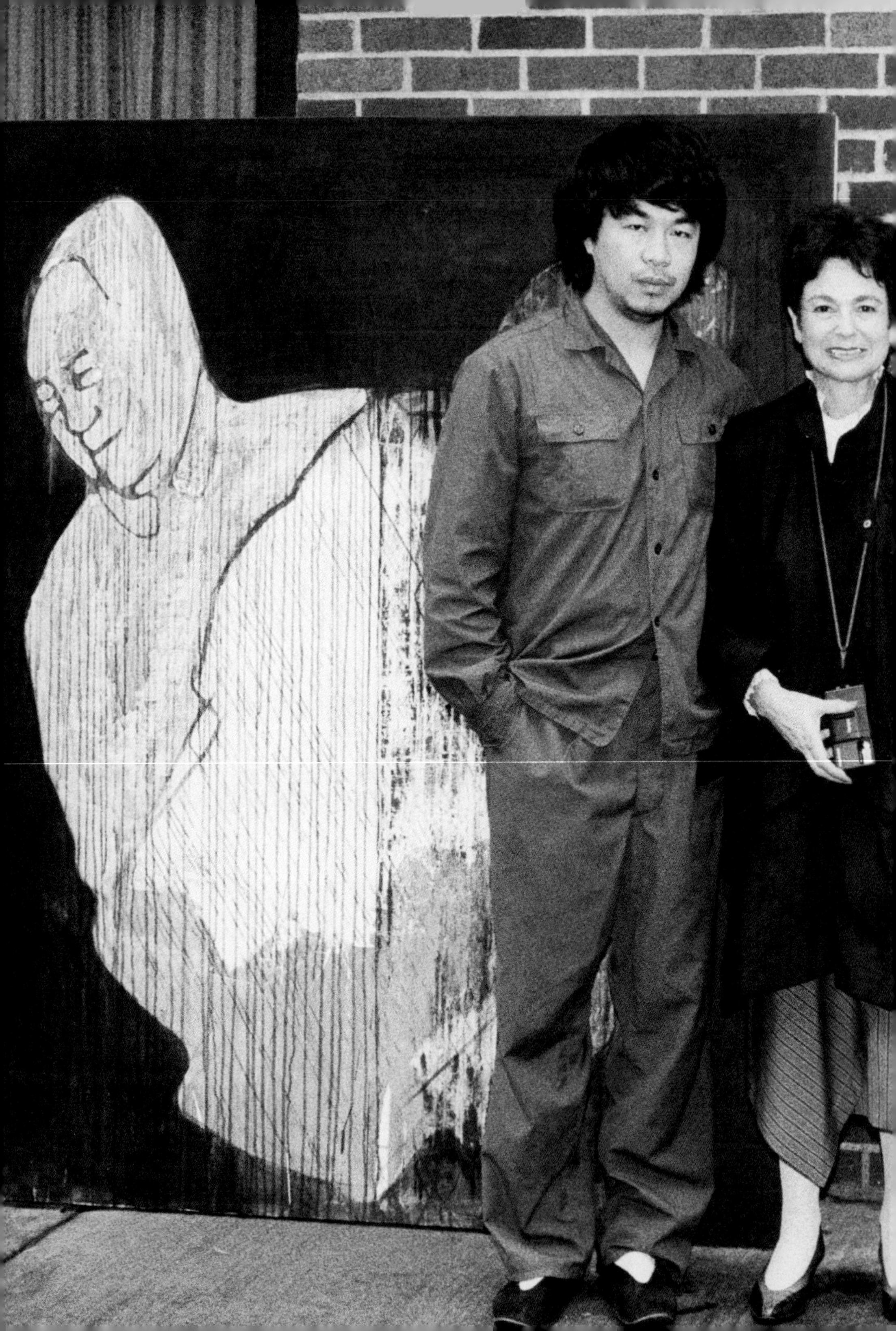

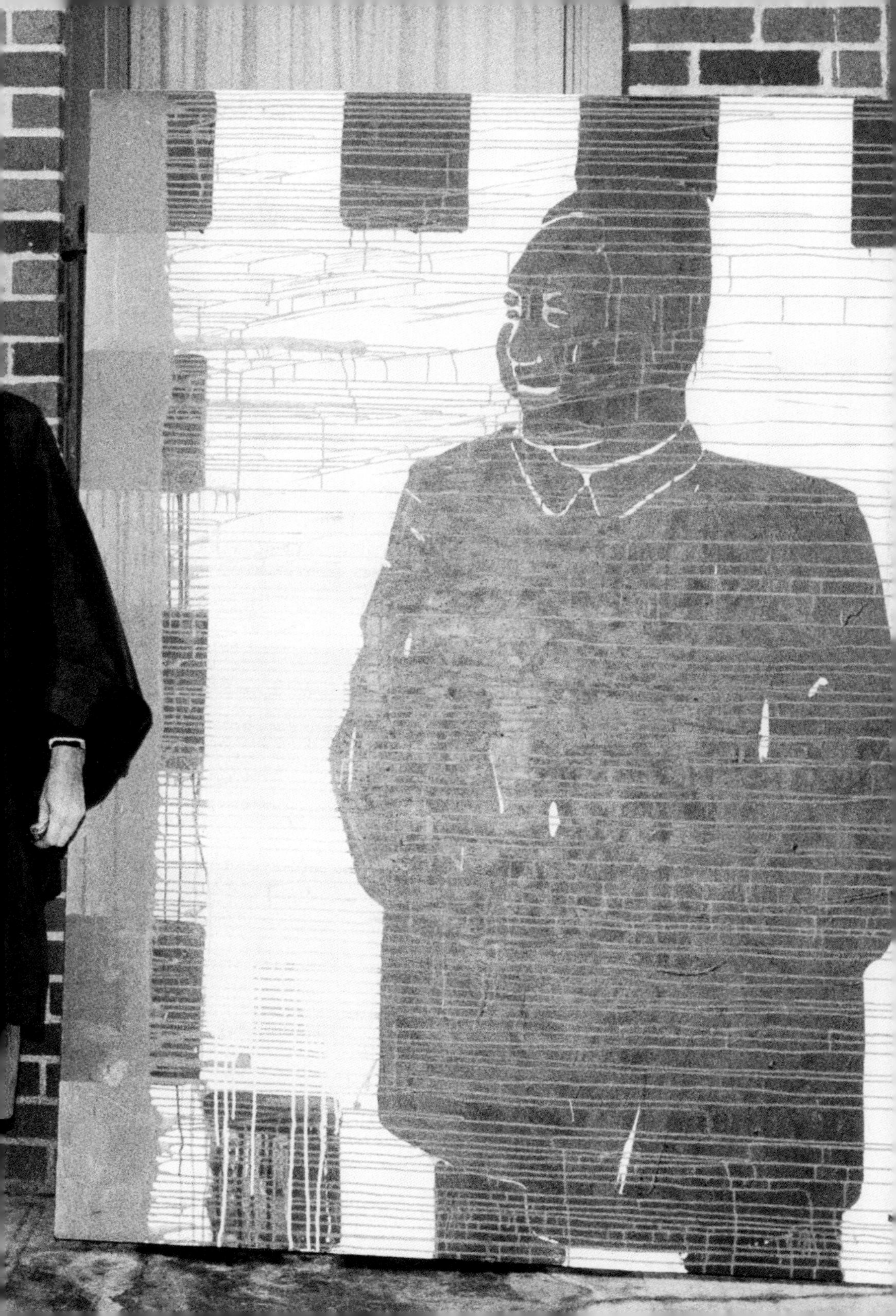

the state? In his texts and overall speech, one word stands out with significant
frequency: argue, argument. Ai says that he lives, quite simply, to argue. A blade
of grass, a tree, everything has its form of existence. And his is to argue. More
specifically, he is all about the rational argument and the better argument. Even
in his art: it is the site of an unintelligible process of transfiguration we may
loosely describe as a sort of short circuit in the apparatus of creative thought;
yet where art succeeds, it will always entail an argument. This argument, however,
can only assert itself in a specific climate, where freedom of opinion prevails.
And this marks the fault line separating Ai's worldview from that of Official China.
To frame it in his terms: the Communists never argue, not even when they appear
to. They decree. Status and decree—as opposed to freedom and democracy's
civil contract—have defined the Chinese system of government for millennia; and
the current "dictatorship of the people" isn't any different. Ai offers the interrogations after his arrest as an example, when the border police marched him
away in the Beijing airport in April 2011 moments before he was to board a flight
to Hong Kong: the investigators acted like chess players, but rather unprofes-
sional ones, decreeing a new set of rules every three moves to make absolutely
sure they would win—and precisely because they always win, they can't learn anything in the game!

Little wonder, then, that the interrogations didn't really address Ai's actions or
methodically explore the different facets of his person. He was to be convicted of tax
fraud, bigamy, and other misdeeds, as the national news agency Xinhua reported,
but Ai himself didn't learn of these accusations until after his release. Instead the
interrogations focused on another question: on behalf of which foreign powers was
he agitating? Money did come up in this context; Ai offered information on the
prices his works fetched as well as what it cost to produce them. The interrogators
simply didn't fathom how such sums could be paid for obsolete and cumbersome
objects and ludicrous ideas. The fact that they showed little interest in other topics
is explained by the peculiarities of the local application of criminal law: the punishment in such cases is not determined based on what is in the files, which might
as well go straight into the archives. In a case as visible as this, Party committees
decree the sentence; the courts are instructed to mete them out. The arguments
submitted by Ai the defendant, but also by Ai the accuser or his legal representative,
were never relevant, if there was ever an opportunity to submit them in the first
place—in Sichuan, for instance, all courts flatly denied jurisdiction, refusing to hear
Ai's complaint that he had suffered battery and assault by the police even though
his unquestionably life-threatening injuries were documented beyond doubt. The
argument of the individual, based on China's constitution and other legislation as
well as fundamental humanist values, standing powerless against this omnipresent
amalgam of arbitrary decisions, ignorance of the law, and transparent and opaque
favors bestowed by all-powerful authorities—these endlessly recurring experiences,
which Ai lived through himself and meticulously researched and recorded in numer-

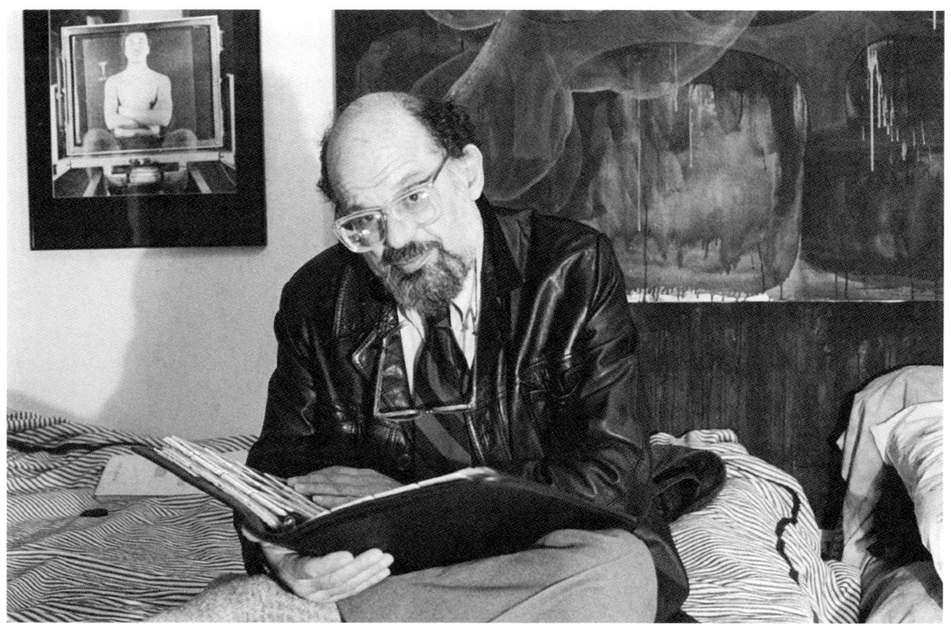

Allen Ginsberg in Ai Weiwei's East Third Street apartment, New York 1986

ous other cases, were what hardened the artist and turned him into an activist. On the day of his arrest in 2011, it was clear that he had stepped over a red line. It put Ai, who had once deliberately fled from Chinese politics and society into the United States, squarely and now officially in the camp of human-rights activism, surely not a term that has a nice ring to it in Official China.

The evolution that turned an artist into an artist-activist and ultimately into an activist-artist took place over the course of three decades and at very different speeds if you compare Ai's own view to that of the outside world. His time in New York, with everything he had experienced there and his insights into the theory and practice of the country's arts scene and the American way of life, had taught him that art must not exhaust itself in aestheticism if it is to be substantial. Truly significant art takes an ethical-moral stand. Having returned in 1993 to an authoritarian system whose Communist ideology had long since started to crumble, a system that even the authorities believed was careening toward a general disintegration of all values, he realized: his art must concern itself with this China, today's China, and assure itself of this reality from a humanist and rational perspective. Simply striking a contemporary note would not suffice. And furthermore, arguing from this rational and humanist perspective, in images or in words, would at some point inevitably bring him into conflict with the authoritarian state, which had a very different priority: maintaining the power of the Party. From 2000 Ai started becoming an object of media attention, first in fashion and design magazines in

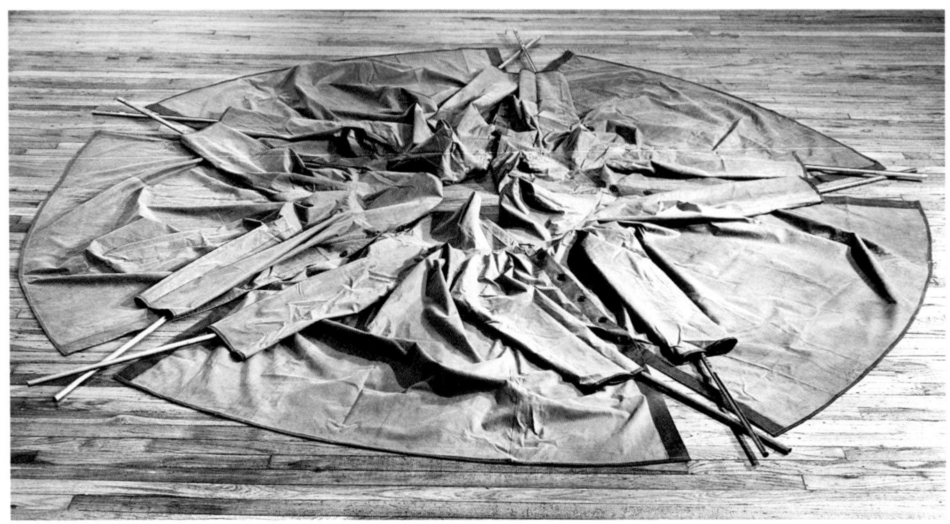

Five Raincoats Holding Up a Star, 1985, raincoats, metal pipes, ø 118 ⅛ inches

his role as the architect of a series of self-designed buildings completed in rapid succession, especially his own utterly spectacular house and studio (pp. 122–139). Then he grew into a public figure through his collaboration with the architects Herzog & de Meuron on the Olympic Stadium in Beijing, begun in 2003 (pp. 385, 387–389). It wasn't until 2005, after starting his blog, that he was first perceived as a political artist. And in 2007 he was finally transformed into an exponent of the opposition, drawing wide media attention for his open antagonism against Official China: the official festivities kicking off the one-year countdown to the opening of the 2008 Olympics shocked him and persuaded him that the Games would be a farce, an authoritarian state's celebration of itself with monarchical pomp as well as distinctly nationalist overtones. From then on, his blogs and interviews on highly diverse topics became increasingly acerbic and confrontational, bolstered by elaborate and precise research into the despotism of government agencies and his experience from his own case. His central demands were always for free speech and the rule of law.

Ai's artistic strategies, for him already one with his life as it was, now coincided entirely with his political activism. In recent years, these overlapping concerns have left him no time for more than occasional forays into the subject of "Chineseness," this nearly boundless cultural trove waiting to be further unearthed, from which he had formerly helped himself with particular gusto—back when he still took delight in the refinement of ancient China and in art-making and toyed with meanings and the interpretations of art audiences. The situation has become more serious, he has become more serious, now that he has resolved to look the beast in the eye every day and confront it, also by means of his art.

Over time, Ai established an online community of committed followers numbering in the millions, people who admired his brazenness in picking fights with the authorities and the way he was willing to spend good money on his activism, sending thousands upon thousands of DVDs to anyone interested free of charge, or throwing parties for like-minded people where defeats on the formal legal terrain, such as the demolition of his Shanghai studio, were celebrated as moral victories. Here, finally, was someone who looked at things that had been exasperating people for a long time and called those things by their rightful name. Sure, he too could not kill the beast—nor does he want to. He simply wants to fight for his own rights and hence, he is quite explicit on this point, also for all others who equally deserve the same rights.

To be sure, his actions also drew vehement opposition on the Internet, and not only government-orchestrated opposition: against his style of argument, which some deemed too confrontational, and against his actions, which denied those he attacked—usually authorities, including uppermost state leadership—any room to save face. That was simply too un-Chinese. Some more insightful commentators focused on his destruction of ancient cultural assets and stoked a sense of incomprehension over how the West could possibly celebrate such a gesture. Ai's art in fact had, with very few exceptions, never been on display in China—the preemptive obedience of Chinese galleries and institutions toward the censors had seen to that for quite some time. Granted, his works initially tend to confuse the untrained Chinese viewer, whose artistic understanding is attuned to the values of traditional Chinese art—most importantly, beauty and harmony. Other critics sought to dismiss Ai as a covert Westerner whose activism, they alleged, was designed to burnish his image and perhaps even to raise his market value in the West, if he wasn't altogether a product, perhaps even a veritable tool, of Western imperialism.

There was so much cause for conflict accumulating, so much potential for political explosion building for so long, that the ideological cleaning staff at the Ministry of Culture had to hand over the matter to the authorities of internal security. Curiously enough, a few weeks before his arrest, a delegation of the city of Beijing approached Ai, offering him a seat in the Chinese People's Political Consultative Conference, the country's second parliament after the National People's Congress. He asked for time to think it over. In the end, the border police resolved his dilemma when they arrested him.

We will probably never know who ordered the Beijing Municipal Public Security Bureau to arrest and interrogate him. True, they cleaned up a critical situation that was getting out of control domestically, but internationally the People's Republic paid, and still pays, a price that those in charge had failed to anticipate. The collateral damage to China's image in the West will remain for a long time. And this very sequence of official measures taken against him over the last few years was what made Ai the living Chinese person most widely known to Western media audiences. In some interviews, he courteously thanked the Chinese government (which has stepped down in the meantime). He knows that he couldn't have achieved his global status on his own. He also owes gratitude to the global visual arts scene, which stood by him with unparalleled solidarity—and with much more leverage than the literary world could build in the case of the Nobel Peace Prize laureate and writer Liu Xiaobo. It's not as though the world of contemporary art carried any weight in the eyes of Official China. But it is very adept at recruiting Western politicians for its purposes by building sufficient media pressure. Ai has secured the highest possible degree of international visibility by role-playing with the international media: by adopting a stance of unrestrained openness, clever and naive at once, sometimes at the risk of exposing himself to ridicule as well, certainly at the price of losing all control over this immense media output—after all, there was no way he was going to get those who wrote about him to clear any quote with him.

No doubt there is disagreement in Official China over how to cope with the phenomenon of Ai Weiwei, this guy who bears the flaw of loving his country and not the Party. Who should accept responsibility for him, and at what official level, and what would be best for the Party's image? Keep him on a short leash at home, or store him abroad, where dissidents have always reliably marginalized themselves—yet this one? Only democracy will no longer make heroes, because it doesn't need them. But that will take time.

Passages of this text first appeared in *Ai Weiwei: Ways beyond Art*, ed. by Elena Ochoa Foster and Hans Ulrich Obrist (London, Madrid: Ivory Press, 2009); these were augmented for my essay "Confusionism and More" in the catalog for the German Pavilion at the Venice Biennale 2013, ed. by Susanne Gaensheimer (Berlin: Gestalten, 2013); and in turn reworked for this portrait of the artist. The most valuable source throughout it all have been the many conversations that Ai Weiwei and I have had for more than 18 years now.

 Ai Weiwei in his East Third Street apartment, New York 1984. Photo: Wendy Lubetkin

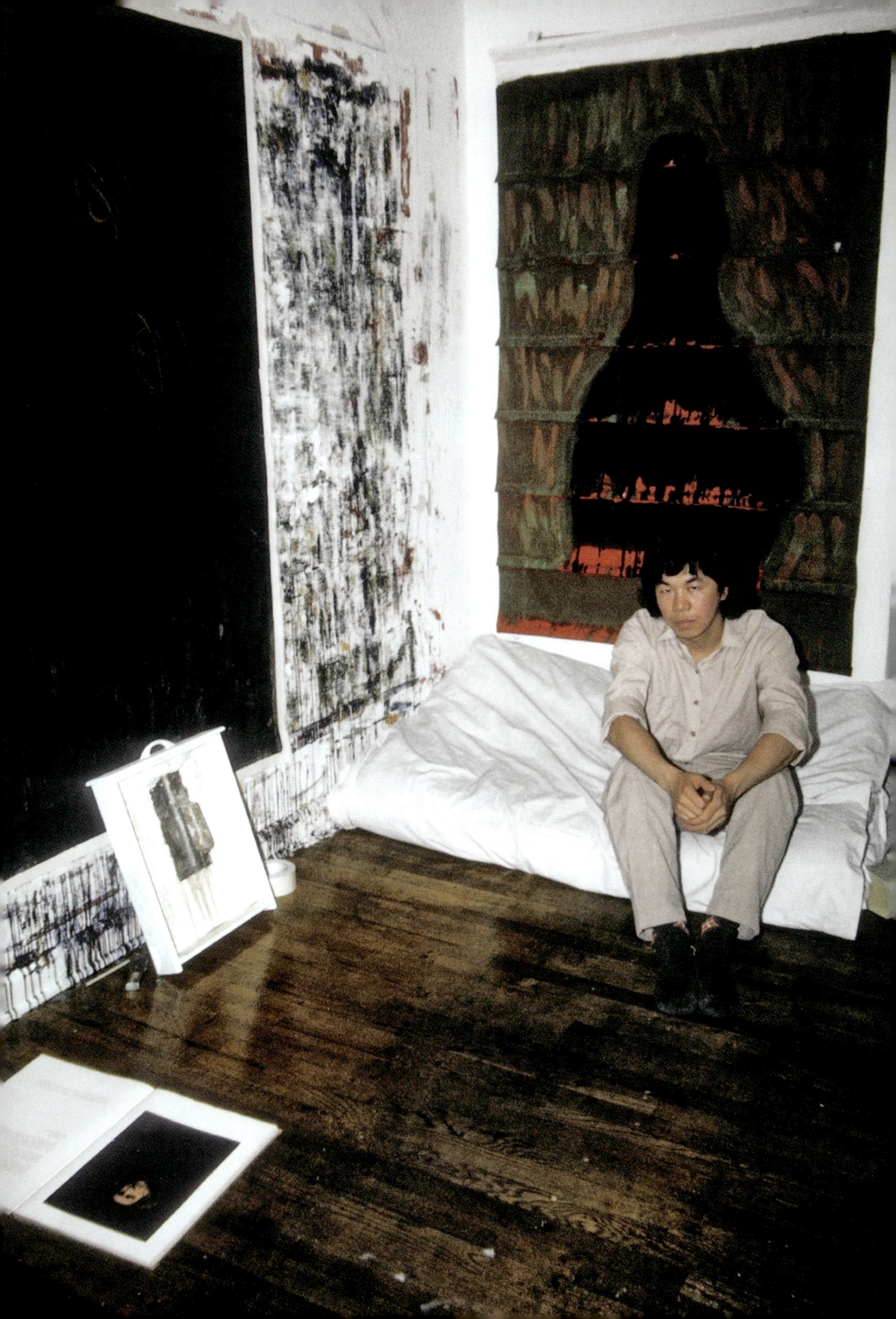

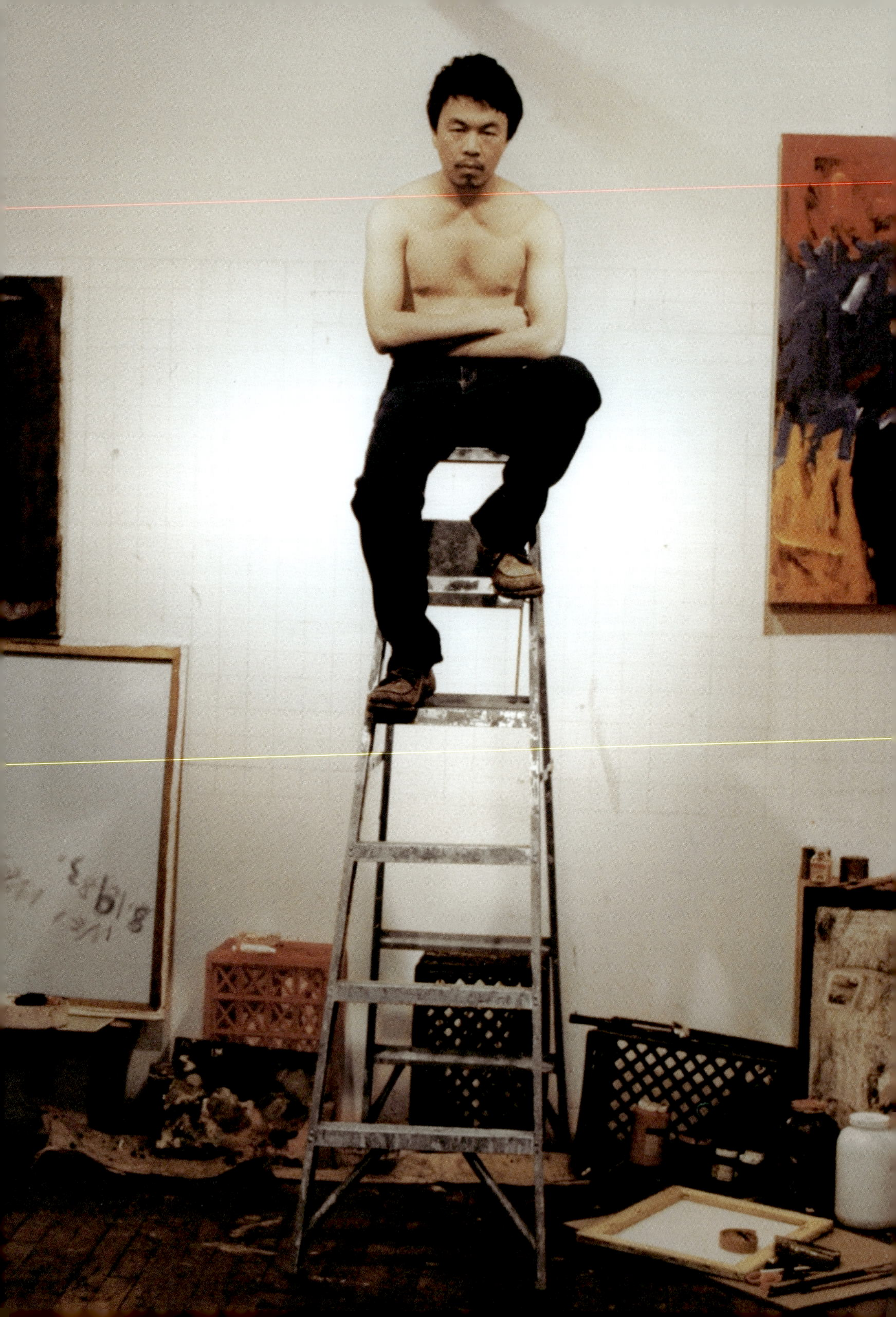
8/19/83.
11/23/

Das bessere Argument
Ein Porträt von Ai Weiwei

ULI SIGG

Es ist heute einfach geworden, diesen Ai Weiwei zu finden, der sich fast unentwegt in seinem Studio aufhält – seit ihm nach seiner Entlassung aus der Haft im Juni 2011 unrechtmäßig der Reisepass vorenthalten wird. Ein Mann, der zuvor pro Jahr einige Male rund um die Welt jettete; einer, der endlich in Überdosis kriegte, was er längst schon verdient hatte: internationale Anerkennung, Interviews, Einladungen für Ausstellungen, für Kunstprojekte, für Lehraufträge, für repräsentative Bauvorhaben in China und anderswo, für Begegnungen mit Würdenträgern und so weiter. Jetzt holt er diese Welt in sein Studio: Hier plant und kuratiert er seine Ausstellungen, gestaltet Titelblätter für Magazine, twittert und hält Hof – so präsent in den Weltmedien als wie zuvor. Welche Art Persönlichkeit braucht es, um all das in Gang zu halten?

Einen Teil der Antwort vermögen wir aus seiner Biografie abzulesen. Der berühmte Vater wurde in den 1950er-Jahren seiner Texte wegen mit der Familie in den unwirtlichen Nordwesten Chinas verbannt, 1976 kehrte die Familie nach Peking zurück. Dort nahm der junge Ai ein Studium an der Filmakademie auf, um es alsbald wieder aufzugeben, frustriert von der Realitätsferne der vermittelten Ideologie. 1981 folgte er seiner Freundin in die USA. Diese Reise trat der damals 23-Jährige laut Selbstdeklaration noch als „postimpressionistischer" Maler an: Ein Buch über Impressionismus und eine Monografie zu van Gogh waren ihm in die Hände geraten und beeindruckten ihn ungemein – eine Monografie über Jasper Johns und dessen unverständliche Machwerke schmiss er indessen fort. Die Malerei bot ihm eine Fluchtmöglichkeit aus dem real existierenden Kommunismus, der sich ihm als fortdauerndes Desaster präsentierte: Der Vater war aus zunächst uneinsehbaren Gründen als „Rechtsabweichler" zum Staatsfeind gestempelt worden, während die großen wie selbst die ganz kleinen Entscheide im chinesischen Alltag stets im Widerspruch zur offiziellen Propaganda standen, weder nachvollziehbar mittels der Vernunft noch durch menschliches Empfinden – ja ganz im Gegenteil, beiden durfte nicht vertraut werden. Flucht in empathisches Empfinden, in Emotion und Leidenschaft, gelang einzig im Malen, mit der selbstverantworteten Wahl der Linie und der Schattierung und der Farbe.

Ein Kurzaufenthalt 1982 an der Parsons School of Design in New York brachte ihn dann erstmals in Kontakt mit den Konzepten von Duchamp und Warhol, die er auf einen Sitz verschlang, während er beobachtete, wie seine amerikanischen

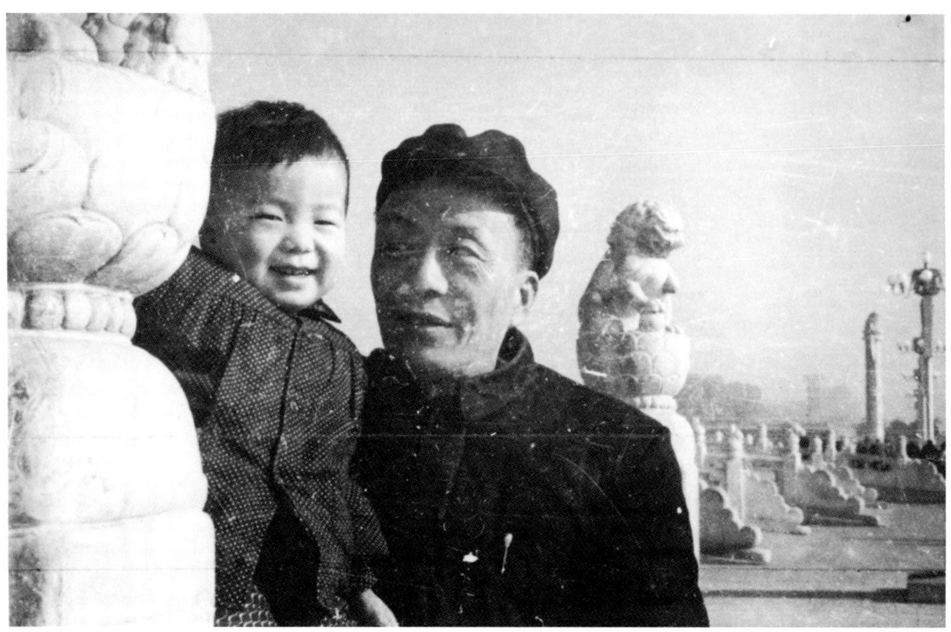

Ai Weiwei with his father Ai Qing at Tiananmen Square, Beijing 1958

Studienkollegen frei und wild drauflosmalten – fokussiert auf das Was und gänzlich
vorbei am Warum, an dieser nunmehr für ihn ganz zentralen Frage, warum denn
einer sich als Künstler ausdrücken soll. Ai Weiwei entschied sich in der Folge, die
Malerei – oder, in seinen Worten, ein Atelier voller Bilder, die niemand wollte – hinter sich zu lassen und sich vom zweidimensionalen, finiten Kunstwerk dem laufend
expandierenden Universum der Konzeptkunst zuzuwenden. Wichtigstes Attribut
des Künstlerdaseins überhaupt war ihm nunmehr der Verstand, der im kulturre-
volutionären China seiner Jugend noch so wenig zu erhellen vermocht hatte und
in dessen Gebrauch er sich seither wohl gerade deshalb so unnachgiebig übt.
Die Rezeption von Duchamp hatte den Postimpressionisten zu Tode gebracht; in
Duchamps Ideen zur Künstlerexistenz als einer Haltung, einem Lebensstil, fand er
zu seiner Identität.

1993 entschied sich Ai zur Rückkehr nach China, der schweren Krankheit seines Vaters wegen. Zunächst wohnhaft in dessen Haus, fühlte er sich in dieser Bleibe
nur als ein Gast, als ein minderer zudem, der den Eltern nach all den Jahren in
den USA gar nichts vorzuzeigen hatte – kein schmuckes Diplom und auch keine
halbwegs passable Künstlerkarriere. So hielt er sich zurück, artikulierte sich nicht
hinaus über den Verlag von drei Büchern über westliche und experimentelle chinesische Kunst. Weder die *Han Dynasty Urn with Coca-Cola Logo* von 1994 noch
die Fotoarbeit *Dropping a Han Dynasty Urn* von 1995 (S. 85–87) und auch nicht
die ersten Kompositionen aus dekonstruierten Möbeln ab 1997 (S. 102–109) wollte

er als Kunst wahrnehmen. Sie galten ihm einzig als Zeitvertreib. Erst 1999 sah er sich wieder herausgefordert, Kunst nach seiner Definition herzustellen – nämlich um der Nominierung als Künstler der Venedig-Biennale durch Harald Szeemann gerecht zu werden.

Aus der Kunst, zu der er nun wieder fand, lässt sich ein anderer Teil der Antwort auf die Frage nach seiner Persönlichkeit ablesen. Mit westlichen Augen betrachtet, ist es eine Geste, die stets Mehrdeutigkeit – eine greifbare Mehrdeutigkeit – produziert. Hardware mit zumeist chinesischer Konnotation ist da, die Software muss man irgendwie imaginieren. Wir spüren eine Persönlichkeit, die eine sehr klare Vorstellung davon hat, was Kunst ist und was nicht und wessen es bedarf, um einen Gegenstand zu greifen oder zu komponieren und ihn von einer Sphäre zur anderen zu befördern. Aber worin besteht diese sehr klare Vorstellung – insbesondere, wenn uns das kontextuelle Wissen über die chinesische Lebenswelt und chinesisches Denken fehlt? Ist ein Kubikmeter Tee (*Ton of Tea*, 2006, S. 308) hüben wie drüben etwa dasselbe? Natürlich nicht: „Eine Tasse Tee trinken" – mit diesem Euphemismus pflegen oftmals chinesische Ordnungshüter zu einer ersten Einvernahme aufzufordern.

Wenn wir Ai Weiwei aus einem weiteren Blickwinkel betrachten, der chinesische Charakteristika einbegreift, dann stoßen wir auf eine zusätzliche Komplexität. Sie wurzelt in einer spezifischen Stärke der chinesischen Kultur: der Fähigkeit, einen Widerspruch in ein und dieselbe Aussage zu verschmelzen. Einfach gesagt: Während für den westlichen, durch die binäre kartesianische Logik geprägten Geist ein Gegenstand entweder dies oder jenes ist, kann derselbe Gegenstand für den Chinesen gleichzeitig dies und jenes sein.

Nehmen wir etwa die Arbeit *Whitewash* (1993–2000, S. 45, 193) – 132 neolithische Gefäße, jedes davon ein wunderbares Kunstwerk und ein Zeugnis vergangener Zeiten, von denen aber ein Viertel mit weißer Industriefarbe übermalt und damit verdorben ist. Das Werk fusioniert zwei konträre Paradigmen der künstlerischen Schöpfung: einerseits das westliche Paradigma der Avantgardekunst, das durch radikale Zerstörung der Tradition und durch den Bruch mit der Vergangenheit Raum für ein ganz neues Denken schaffen will; andererseits das klassische chinesische Paradigma, das der Tradition Respekt zollt und infolgedessen künstlerisches Schaffen als ein sich entwickelndes Kontinuum betrachtet, das aus dem Reichtum der chinesischen Kultur schöpft. Hinzu kommen die chinesischen Produktionsverhältnisse, wo die Kosten derart niedrig sind, dass ein kühner Künstler auch in großen Dimensionen denken kann – und große Dimensionen sind wirklich Ais Sache. Schon früher pflegte er für Projekte schon mal mit bis zu 100 Leuten zu arbeiten, vom Hilfsarbeiter bis zu den sachkundigsten Handwerkern, die China zu bieten hat. Im Jahr 2007 dann verfrachtete er 1001 Chinesinnen und Chinesen zur Documenta 12 nach Kassel, um sie als „Wanderarbeiter" in eine soziale Plastik einzubinden. Und für seine Installation *Sunflower Seeds* in der Tate Modern 2010 mobilisierte er 1600 Arbeitskräfte.

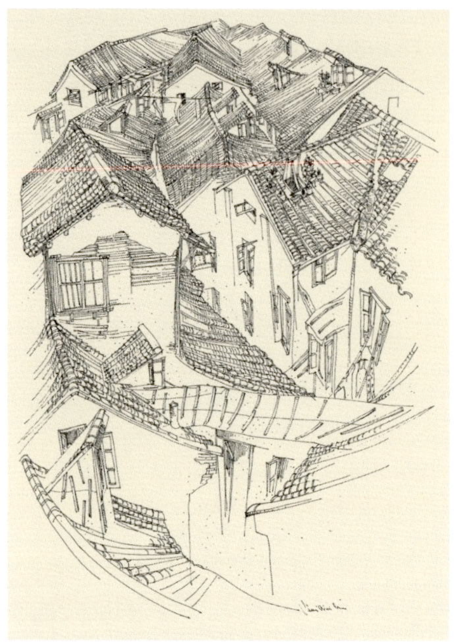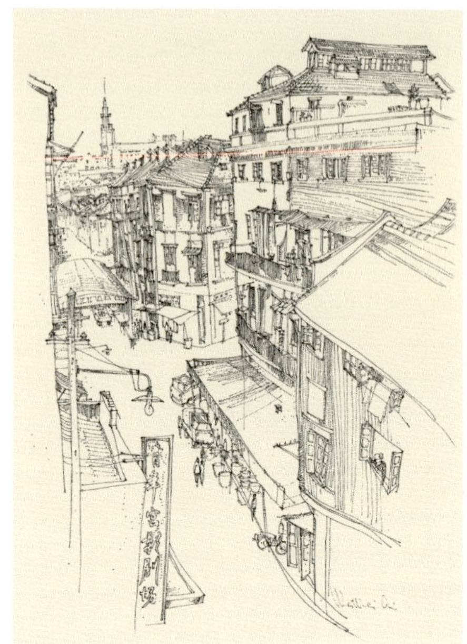

Studies from a trip to Shanghai and Suzhou, 1979

Seine Documenta-Arbeit (*Fairytale*, 2007, S. 310–327) offenbarte auch eine künstlerische Strategie, die Ais Werk immer mehr prägen sollte. Als seine eigene größte Stärke nennt Ai die Fähigkeit, „sich selbst in eine unangenehme Situation zu bringen" – so kann dann ein Widerspruch entstehen, der nun nach Auflösung oder zumindest Kontrolle verlangt. Dieser Kontrollprozess darf allerdings nicht einfach zu bewältigen sein. Denn seiner Kunst muss immer auch Potential zum Unfall eignen. Nur so wird Ai ausreichend gefordert. Am Exempel *Fairytale:* Wie macht man aus der Idee, 1001 Chinesen eine ganz andere Realität als die ihre zu vermitteln, ein Kunstwerk? Da waren ungezählte logistische Schwierigkeiten wie Auswahl des Bevölkerungs-Samples, Pässe, Visa, Reisen, Unterkunft etc. zu überwinden. Dann, ganz wichtig, sollte etwas zurückbleiben: der Mythos. Denn es war gar nicht möglich und eben auch nicht intendiert, dass irgendwer dieses monströse und vieltausendfach getaktete *Fairytale* je als eine Gesamtheit zu Gesicht bekommen konnte. Weiter sollte sehr vieles über das Internet geschehen – es geriet Ai zum *social medium* noch vor dessen Hype in China. Und ferner musste irgendetwas auch physisch Gestalt annehmen, deshalb schuf er eine Installation aus 1001 Stühlen. Sie gaben dem Werk eine gewisse Poesie, hatten weitere Räume zu öffnen.

Fragmente dieser Strategie lassen sich ebenso in den aufwändigen Recherche-Aktionen um das Erdbeben in Sichuan (u. a. *Namelist*, 2008–2011, S. 348/349) und in der Groß-Installation *Sunflower Seeds* in der Tate Modern erkennen (S. 49, 407–409). Allen gemein ist etwa das Mobilisieren größter personeller Ressourcen quer

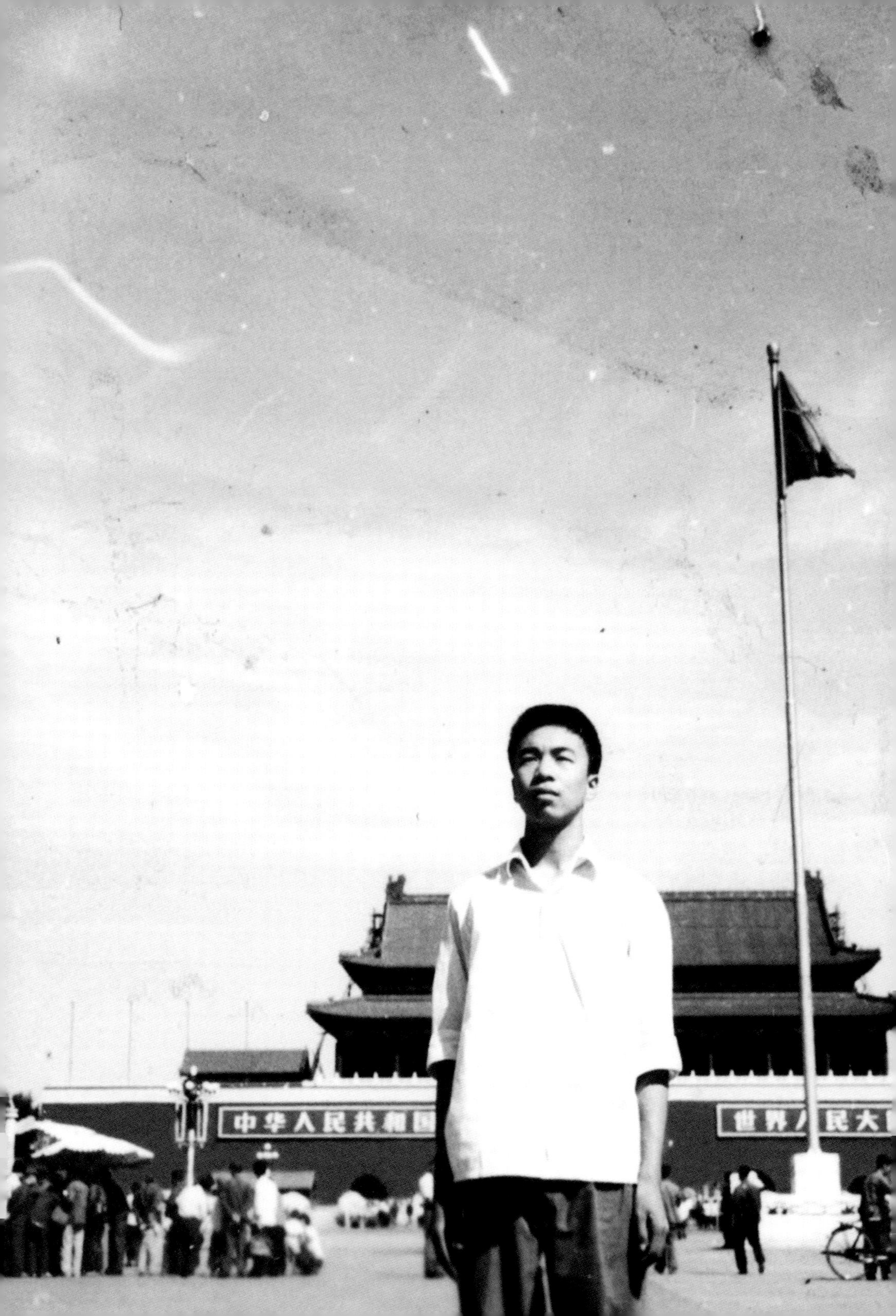
中华人民共和国
世界人民大

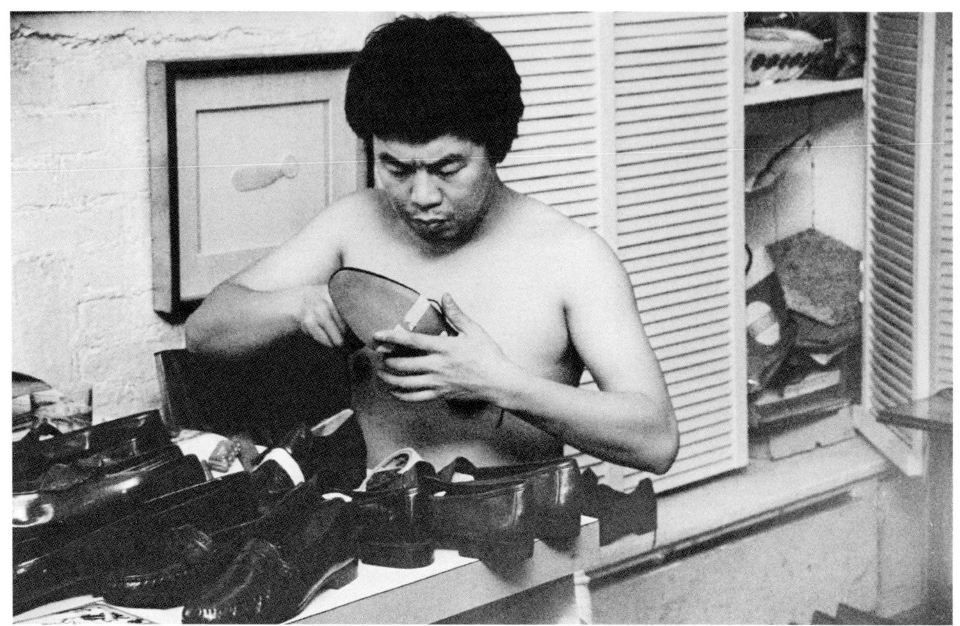

Ai Weiwei working with shoes, New York, 1987

durch die Volksrepublik in jeweils kürzester Zeitspanne, denkmöglich nur dank des Internets. So ist die Behauptung nicht verwegen, dass jeder andere Künstler die Aufforderung der Tate im Januar 2010 zurückgewiesen hätte, die gigantische Turbinenhalle nicht etwa wie vorgesehen 2012 zu bespielen, sondern vorzeitig im Oktober desselben Jahres. Wenn Ai für eine der prestige- und daher risikoreichsten Angelegenheiten in der Kunstwelt die physische Realisierung eines Werks unternehmen wollte, dann beanspruchten allein der Transport ab China und die Installation drei Monate. Blieben für Idee, Konzeption und Produktion ab Januar 2010 sechs Monate! Deshalb mussten also für das Formen, Bemalen, Brennen und Glasieren der mehr als 100 Millionen *Sunflower Seeds* die 1600 Arbeiterinnen und Arbeiter her – im Grunde eine Verrücktheit.

Ai Weiweis ausgeprägter Risikoappetit auf derartige Großprojekte, die in ihrer Anlage kaum kalkulierbar sind, scheint Teil einer Spielernatur, die ihn seinerzeit mit 30 Dollar in der Tasche auch nach den USA aufbrechen ließ und die ihn genauso ausmacht wie seine Rationalität. Dazu ist wissenswert, dass in den 1980er-Jahren jeweils an den Wochenenden die Limousine des Casinos von Atlantic City für ihn und die Kollegen vor dem Kellergeschoss auffuhr, in dem sie gemeinsam hausten. Ai hatte sich da als Blackjack-Spieler einen veritablen Namen gemacht. Ein gewiefter Spieler macht sich bestimmte Routinen zu eigen: etwa sich mit Lust in einen Prozess hineinzubegeben, dessen Ausgang determiniert ungewiss sein soll; das Spiel mit tödlichem Ernst zu betreiben immer im Bewusstsein, dass es nur

Spiel ist; und sich seiner selbst immer gewiss zu bleiben, um die Grenzen seines Blatts nie aus den Sinnen zu verlieren. Bis heute hat es nichts und niemand vermocht, der Coolness von Ai Weiwei den Garaus zu machen.

Es wäre überraschend, wenn Ai viel vom eben Gesagten unterschreiben würde. Er ist der Widerspruch in Person. Genau wie dies in seiner Kunst geschieht, wird er jedes Argument auf den Kopf stellen oder dekonstruieren, um elegant dessen Nichtigkeit zu beweisen – oder er wird es durch einen uneinsehbaren Transfigurationsprozess zu strahlendem Glanz aufpolieren. Und wenn er seinen Panzer aus Ironie und Sarkasmus ablegt, kann er sich brillant zu jeglichem Thema äußern – auch dank dem segensreichen Umstand, dass er von keinerlei standardisierter Bildung beschwert ist.

Diese argumentative Brillanz trug ihm am Ende vielleicht die größte Aufmerksamkeit ein, jedenfalls in China. Mit seinem Blog erreichte er ab 2005 Millionen chinesischer Leser, und er legte unerbittlich den Finger auf die Schwachstellen des politischen Systems. Er äußerte sich ohne jede Zurückhaltung und mit denkbar klaren Worten über die entsetzlichen Folgen von Inkompetenz und Missmanagement vor und nach dem Erdbeben von Sichuan 2008. Er prangerte in dieser Zeit die Praktiken der Shanghaier Polizei im Fall Yang Jia an, der mit einer Bagatelle begann und zur Tötung von sechs Polizisten eskalierte, und nahm sich überhaupt eines breiten Spektrums von Themen an, die Chinas Zivilgesellschaft beschäftigen. Manche von Ais Landsleuten sind für weniger ins Gefängnis geworfen worden. Und erinnert man ihn daran, wo die chinesischen Wachhunde beim Menschenrechtsaktivismus die Grenze ziehen – wo ihrer Ansicht nach der Spaß aufhört –, dann wird dieser mutige Mann freundlichst für den Hinweis danken. Doch bei seinen Bemühungen um den Aufbau einer neuen chinesischen Gesellschaft tangiert ihn derlei nicht. Mehr und mehr Chinesen fühlen und denken gleich, aber nur die wenigsten wagen es, wie er die Stimme zu erheben. Er schreibt für sie. Sie werden ihm etwas schuldig sein.

Dann jedoch markierte der 28. Mai 2009 den gouvernementalen Trennschnitt von seinem inländischen Millionenpublikum: Sein Blog wurde von den Behörden geschlossen. In der Folge eröffnete er eine Serie von Mikroblogs auf dem chinesischen Twitter-System, die stets von der Internet-Polizei rasch identifiziert und blockiert wurden. Heute ist Ai auf dem globalen Twitter aktiv, dessen aufgenötigte Kürze seinem plakativen Stil sehr zupasskommt. Allerdings sind diese Botschaften in China nur denen zugänglich, die die „Great Firewall" zu überwinden wissen. Nur so lässt sich aus China im unzensierten globalen Internet-Raum navigieren.

Was ist es denn, das Ai Weiwei de facto – von den Ermittlern nämlich nie de jure ausformuliert – den Vorwurf der Subversion gegen die Staatsgewalt eingebrockt hat? In Ais Texten und ganz allgemein in seinem Sprachgebrauch findet sich ein Wort signifikant häufiger als jedes andere: argumentieren, Argument. Er lebe schlechthin, um zu argumentieren, sagt er. Ein Grashalm, ein Baum, alles habe seine Existenzform. Und die seine sei eben das Argumentieren. Ganz genau geht es

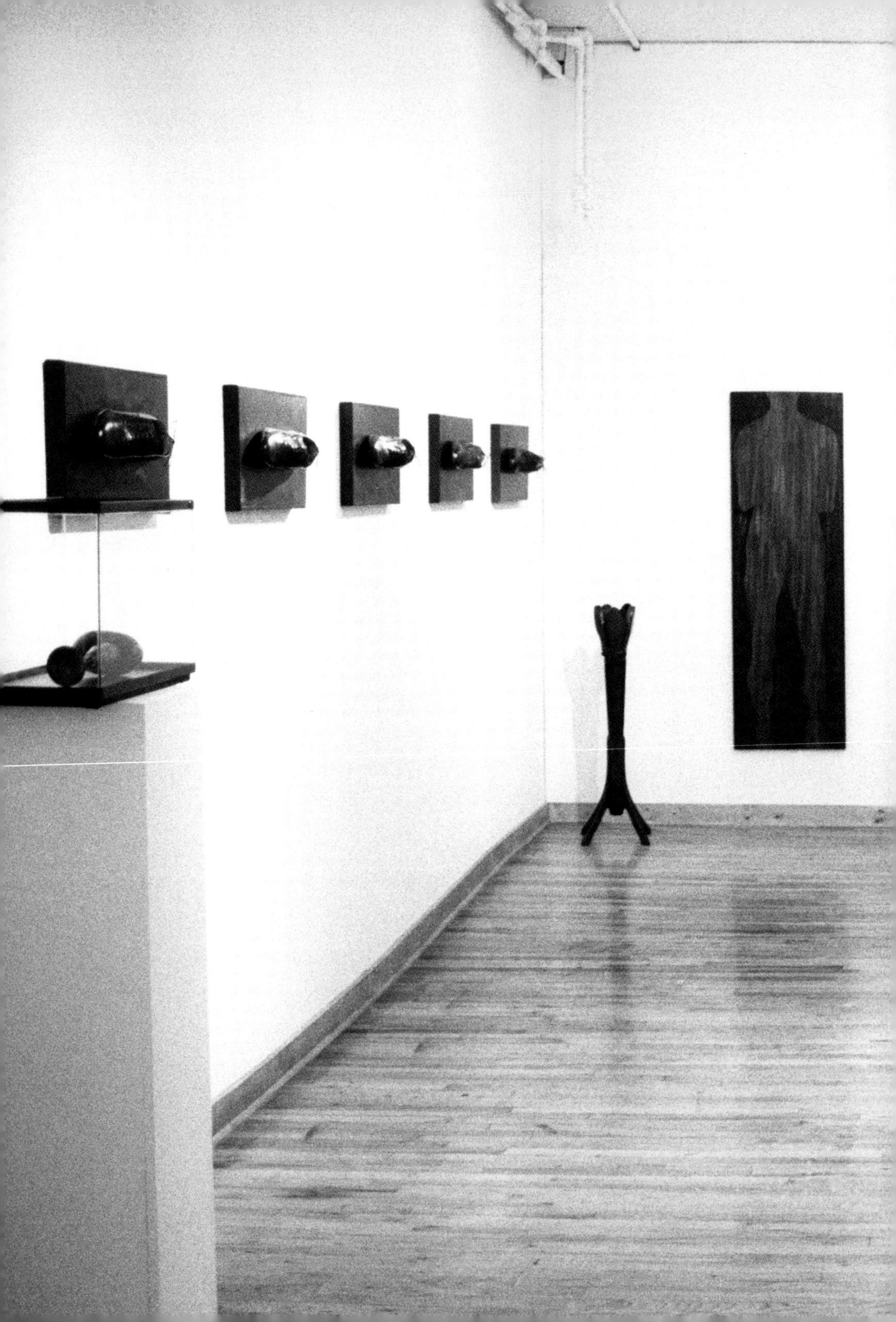

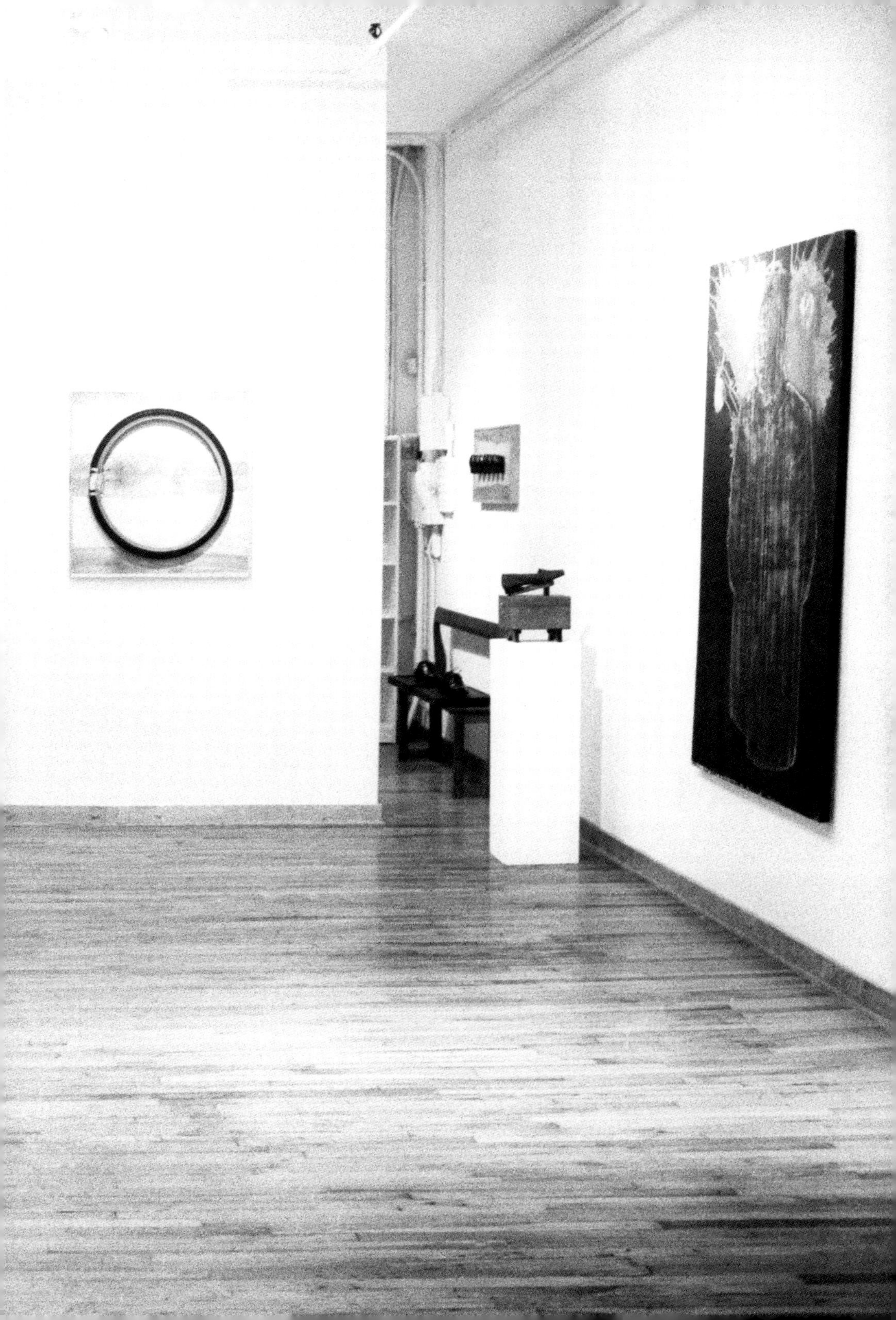

ihm um das rationale Argument und um das bessere Argument. Selbst in seiner Kunst: Dort kommt es zu diesem uneinsehbaren Transfigurationsprozess, den man wohl halbwegs treffend als eine Art Kurzschluss im Denkapparat des Kreativen bezeichnen mag; doch wenn Kunst gelingt, stellt sich immer ein Argument dazu. Das Argument vermag sich allerdings nur in einer ganz bestimmten Ökologie durchzusetzen, in derjenigen der Meinungsfreiheit. Und da ist genau die Bruchstelle, die Ais Weltsicht und diejenige des Offiziellen Chinas trennt. Die Kommunisten, in seiner Diktion, argumentieren nie, auch nicht dann, wenn es scheinbar so daherkommt. Sie ordnen an. Status und Anordnung – gegenüber Freiheit und Bürgervertrag in der Demokratie – definieren das chinesische Herrschaftssystem seit Jahrtausenden; und dito in der gegenwärtigen Epoche der „Diktatur des Volkes". Als persönliches Beispiel dienen Ai die Verhöre nach seiner Festnahme, als er Anfang April 2011 unmittelbar vor dem Abflug nach Hongkong im Pekinger Flughafen von der Grenzpolizei abgeführt wurde. Die Ermittler stellten sich zwar an wie Schachspieler, aber wie Spieler, die einfach nach drei Zügen jeweils neue Regeln anordnen, damit sie auch ganz bestimmt gewinnen – und gerade weil sie stets gewinnen, können sie nichts lernen im Spiel!

Diese Verhöre nahmen nicht wirklich Handlungen und Facetten der Person Ai Weiwei ins Visier. Dass er des Steuerbetrugs, der Bigamie und weiterer Untaten überführt werden sollte, wie es die staatliche Nachrichtenagentur Xinhua verlautbart hatte, wurde Ai erst nach seiner Haftentlassung gewahr. Die Verhöre fokussierten auf die Frage, im Auftrag welcher ausländischen Mächte er seine Agitationen unternehme. Von Geld war zwar die Rede in diesem Zusammenhang, Ai machte Angaben zu Preisen wie auch zu den Produktionskosten für seine Kunst. Den Ermittlern blieb jedoch unverständlich, wie für obsolete und sperrige Gegenstände und skurrile Ideen derartige Summen Geldes fließen konnten. An anderen Themen zeigten sie kaum Interesse. Das erklärt sich aus den Besonderheiten, wie das Strafrecht in China lokal angewendet wird: Die Strafe für derartige Fälle wird nicht aufgrund der Akten bestimmt – die könnten getrost gleich abgeheftet werden. In einem Fall mit dieser Visibilität wird das Strafmaß von Parteigremien für die Gerichte angeordnet. Die Argumente des Angeschuldigten Ai Weiwei, aber auch des Anklägers Ai Weiwei oder seines Rechtsvertreters, hatten nie Relevanz, wo sie denn überhaupt vorgetragen werden konnten – in Sichuan etwa lehnten alle Gerichte eine Zuständigkeit allein schon für die Annahme der Klage auf eine Körperverletzung Ais durch die Polizei rundweg ab, obwohl diese zweifelsfrei dokumentiert lebensbedrohliche Folgen hatte. Das in der chinesischen Verfassung und anderswo in der Rechtsordnung fundierte und überdies auf humanistischen Grundwerten fußende Argument des Individuums, das in seiner Ohnmacht gegenüber diesem allgegenwärtigen Amalgam aus Willkür, Rechtsunkenntnis, durchsichtigen und undurchsichtigen Gefälligkeiten seitens übermächtiger Behörden steht – es sind diese immer wiederkehrenden Erfahrungen, selbst durchlebt und in zahlreichen anderen Fällen von ihm minutiös recherchiert und aufgezeichnet, die den Künstler

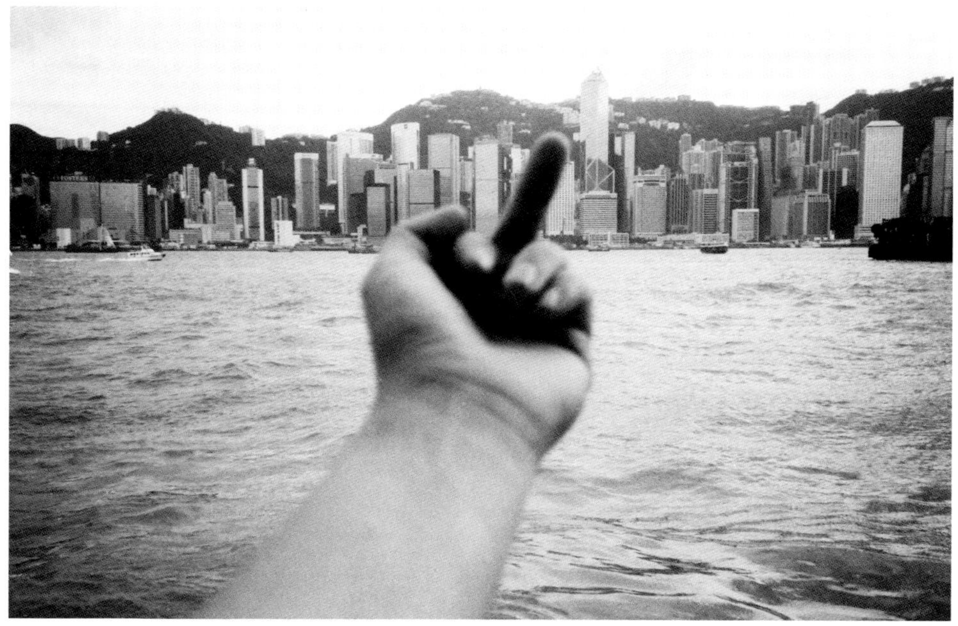

Study of Perspective – Hong Kong, 1995, black-and-white photograph, 35⅜ x 50 inches

zum Aktivisten härteten. Offensichtlich hatte er zum Zeitpunkt der Festnahme 2011 eine rote Linie überschritten. Ai, 1981 noch vorsätzlich der Politik und Gesellschaft Chinas in die USA entwischt, war damit endgültig und amtlich im Menschenrechtsaktivismus angekommen. Und dieser Begriff hat im Offiziellen China nun wirklich keinen guten Klang.

Diese Entwicklung vom Künstler zum Künstler/Aktivisten und schließlich zum Aktivisten/Künstler erfolgte über drei Dekaden und mit ganz unterschiedlichen Geschwindigkeiten in der Innen- und Außenwahrnehmung. Die Zeit in New York mit all den Erfahrungen und Einsichten in Theorie und Praxis der amerikanischen Kunstszene und des *American Way of Life* lehrte ihn, dass bedeutende Kunst sich nicht im Ästhetizismus erschöpfen darf. Ist sie wirklich bedeutend, eignet ihr ein ethisch-moralischer Standpunkt. Ab 1993 wieder zurück in einem autoritären System, dessen kommunistische Ideologie längst am Wegbrechen war und das selbst aus obrigkeitlicher Sicht einem allgemeinen Wertezerfall entgegenschlitterte, wurde ihm dort klar: Seine Kunst musste sich mit diesem China befassen, in dieser Zeit, und sich dieser Realität aus einer humanistisch-rationalen Sicht vergewissern. Einfach nur einen zeitgenössischen Ton anzuschlagen würde nicht hinreichen. Und weiter: Das Argumentieren aus dieser humanistisch-rationalen Sicht, sei es nun in Bild oder Wort, musste irgendwann in den Konflikt mit dem autoritären Staat führen, da der ja einen gänzlich anderen Primat hat, nämlich den Machterhalt der Partei. Mit dem Bau seines eigenen, durchaus spektakulären Wohnhauses

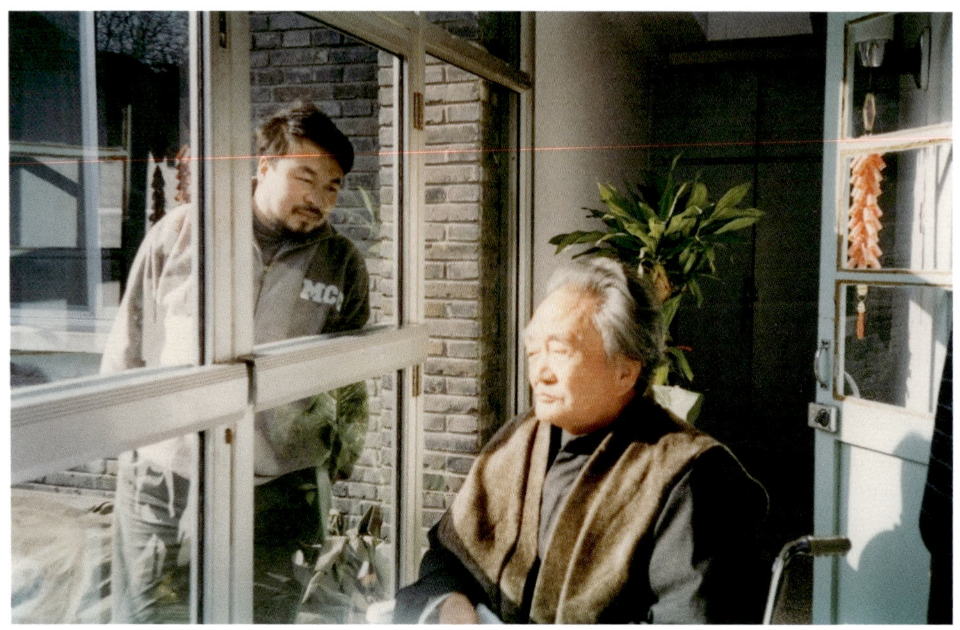

Ai Weiwei with his father Ai Qing in the family courtyard on Dongsishisantiao Alley, Beijing 1994

mit Studio (S. 122–139) und mit weiteren Bauten, in rascher Folge von ihm selbst entworfen, wurde er ab dem Jahr 2000 ganz unvermittelt zum Medienobjekt, dies allerdings für Mode- und Designmagazine in seiner Rolle als Architekt. Das machte ihn zur öffentlichen Person, verstärkt ab 2003 durch die Zusammenarbeit mit den Architekten Herzog & de Meuron für das Olympiastadion in Peking (S. 385, 387– 389). Als ein politischer Künstler erstmals wahrgenommen wurde er 2005, mit dem Eröffnen seines Blogs. Und 2007 mutierte er dann zum Oppositionellen, nun weithin sichtbar. Erstmals machte er medial und offen Front gegen das Offizielle China. Die offizielle Feier des Countdowns zur Olympiade 2008 ein Jahr vor der Eröffnung hatte ihn geschockt – er kam zu dem Schluss, dass die Olympischen Spiele zu einer Farce würden, mit monarchischem Pomp und nationalistisch verbrämter Selbstzelebrierung eines autoritären Staates. Fortan wurden seine Blogs und Interviews zu den verschiedensten Themen immer härter im Ton, schneidender und konfrontativ. Sie waren unterlegt mit aufwändigen und präzisen Recherchen zu Behördenwillkür und auch mit seinen Erfahrungen in der eigenen Causa. Ins Zentrum stellte er stets seine Forderung nach Meinungsfreiheit und Rechtsstaat.

Die künstlerischen Strategien, für ihn ohnehin schon eins mit seinem Leben, deckten sich nun vollständig mit seinem politischen Aktivismus. Über diese Schnittmenge hinaus blieb dann in jüngerer Zeit nur mehr Raum für ein gelegentliches Stochern im Sujet der „Chineseness", dieser fast unendlich weiten kulturellen Fundstätte, an der er sich früher mit besonderer Lust bedient hatte – damals,

als er sich noch an der Raffinesse des alten Chinas und am Kunstmachen delektierte und mit Bedeutungen und Deutungen eines Kunstpublikums spielte. Alles ist jetzt ernster geworden, und er ist jetzt ernster geworden, seit er sich entschieden hat, dem Biest jeden einzelnen Tag in die Augen zu schauen und es zu konfrontieren, auch mit seiner Kunst.

Mittlerweile hatte er eine engagierte Millionengefolgschaft unter den Netizens begründet, die ihn für seine Unverfrorenheit bewunderte, sich unentwegt mit der Staatsmacht anzulegen, sich dies auch einiges Geld kosten zu lassen, etwa mit Abertausenden von DVDs, die er stets unentgeltlich an die Interessierten verschickte, oder mit Partys für Gleichgesinnte, wo Niederlagen auf dem formalrechtlichen Terrain wie der Abbruch seines Studios in Shanghai als moralische Siege gefeiert werden konnten. Endlich war da einer, der jene Dinge schnörkellos beim Namen nannte, an denen auch sie sich schon lange gerieben hatten. Klar, auch er konnte das Biest nicht töten – das will er auch nicht. Will einfach für sein eigenes Recht kämpfen, und damit ganz bewusst auch für all die anderen, denen diese Rechte genauso zustehen.

Freilich, im Netz erhob sich auch Widerspruch, nicht nur gelenkter: etwa gegen sein als zu konfrontativ empfundenes Argumentieren und ohnehin gegen seine Aktionen, die den Angegriffenen, in der Regel Behörden, oberste Staatsführung inklusive, jeglichen Raum zur Gesichtswahrung verweigerten – zu unchinesisch eben. Mancher Kommentar machte sich an seiner Zerstörung alten Kulturguts fest und schürte Unverständnis, wie eine derartige Geste im Westen gefeiert werden könne. Zwar war Ais Kunst mit ganz wenigen Ausnahmen in China gar nie zu Gesicht zu bekommen – dafür hatte ein den Zensurbehörden vorauseilender Gehorsam der chinesischen Galerien und Institutionen schon eine ganze Weile gesorgt. Es ist allerdings einzuräumen, dass sie das Kunstverständnis des ungeschulten chinesischen Betrachters zunächst überfordert, das auf die Werte der traditionellen chinesischen Kunst geeicht ist – vor allem auf Schönheit und Harmonie. Andere Kritik suchte Ai in die Westecke abzudrängen, als einen, der mit seinem Aktivismus sein Profil oder gar seinen Marktwert im Westen aufzupolieren trachte oder überhaupt ein Produkt wenn nicht gar ein Instrument des westlichen Imperialismus sei.

Längst waren so viel Konfliktstoff und so viel politisches Sprengpotential zusammengekommen, dass das ideologische Reinigungspersonal des Kulturministeriums an die Behörden der Inneren Sicherheit übergeben musste. Dabei war kurioserweise wenige Wochen vor seiner Verhaftung eine Abordnung der Stadt Peking an Ai herangetreten und hatte ihm die Mitgliedschaft in der Nationalen Politischen Konsultativen Volkskonferenz angeboten, der zweiten Volkskammer neben dem Nationalen Volkskongress. Er erbat sich Bedenkzeit. Schließlich griff die Grenzpolizei zu, und so löste sich sein Dilemma auf.

Es wird wohl ein Geheimnis bleiben, auf wessen Geheiß das Büro für Innere Sicherheit der Stadt Peking Verhaftung und Verhöre vornahm. Zwar war im Inneren eine ausufernde Situation bereinigt; nach außen zahlt die Volksrepublik jedoch weiterhin einen Preis, den die Auftraggeber so nicht antizipiert hatten: Die Kollateralschäden im Westen für das Image von China sind auf geraume Zeit kaum reparabel. Und es ist ausgerechnet diese Sequenz von behördlichen Maßnahmen über die letzten Jahre, die Ai Weiwei für die Medienkonsumenten im Westen zum bekanntesten lebenden Chinesen gemacht hat. Dafür bedankte er sich in seinen Interviews auch mal artig bei der nun abgetretenen chinesischen Regierung. Er weiß, aus eigener Kraft wäre sein Welt-Status nicht zu schaffen gewesen. Zu danken hat er auch der Globalszene der visuellen Kunst, die mit einer Solidarität ohnegleichen für ihn eingestanden ist – mit sehr viel mehr Hebel als etwa die Welt der Literatur nach der Verhaftung des Friedensnobelpreisträgers und Schriftstellers Liu Xiaobo. Nicht dass die Welt der Gegenwartskunst per se Gewicht hätte in den Augen des Offiziellen Chinas. Aber die westlichen Politiker lassen sich von ihr instrumentalisieren, wenn genügend Mediendruck dies gebietet. Und über sein Rollenspiel mit den internationalen Medien hat Ai sich ein Höchstmaß an Visibilität im Ausland verschafft – mit einer schrankenlosen Offenheit, clever und naiv zugleich, mitunter mit dem Risiko, auch sich selbst bloßzustellen, jedoch um den Preis jeglicher Kontrolle über diesen immensen Medien-Output, den er ja gar nie gegenlesen konnte.

Zweifellos herrscht ein Dissens im Offiziellen China, wie man dem Phänomen Ai Weiwei beikommen soll, diesem Typen mit dem Makel, sein Land und nicht die Partei zu lieben. Wer auf welcher Stufe überhaupt Verantwortung für den zu übernehmen hat und was pfleglicher ist fürs Image: ihn im Inland an kurzer Leine führen oder besser im Ausland aufheben, wo Dissidenten sich noch stets zuverlässig marginalisiert haben – doch der da? Erst die Demokratie macht dann keine Helden mehr, braucht sie nicht. Doch das wird noch dauern.

Passagen dieses Texts erschienen zuerst in *Ai Weiwei: Ways beyond Art,* hrsg. von Elena Ochoa Foster und Hans Ulrich Obrist, Ivory Press, London/Madrid 2009 (die deutsche Übersetzung erschien in der *Neuen Zürcher Zeitung* vom 21. November 2009); diese wurden erweitert für meinen Essay „Konfusionismus und mehr" im Katalog des Deutschen Pavillons auf der Biennale Venedig 2013, hrsg. von Susanne Gaensheimer, Gestalten Verlag, Berlin 2013; und für das vorliegende Porträt noch einmal überarbeitet. Als wichtigste Quelle für alle Versionen dienten die zahllosen Gespräche, die Ai Weiwei und ich über nunmehr als 18 Jahre hinweg führen.

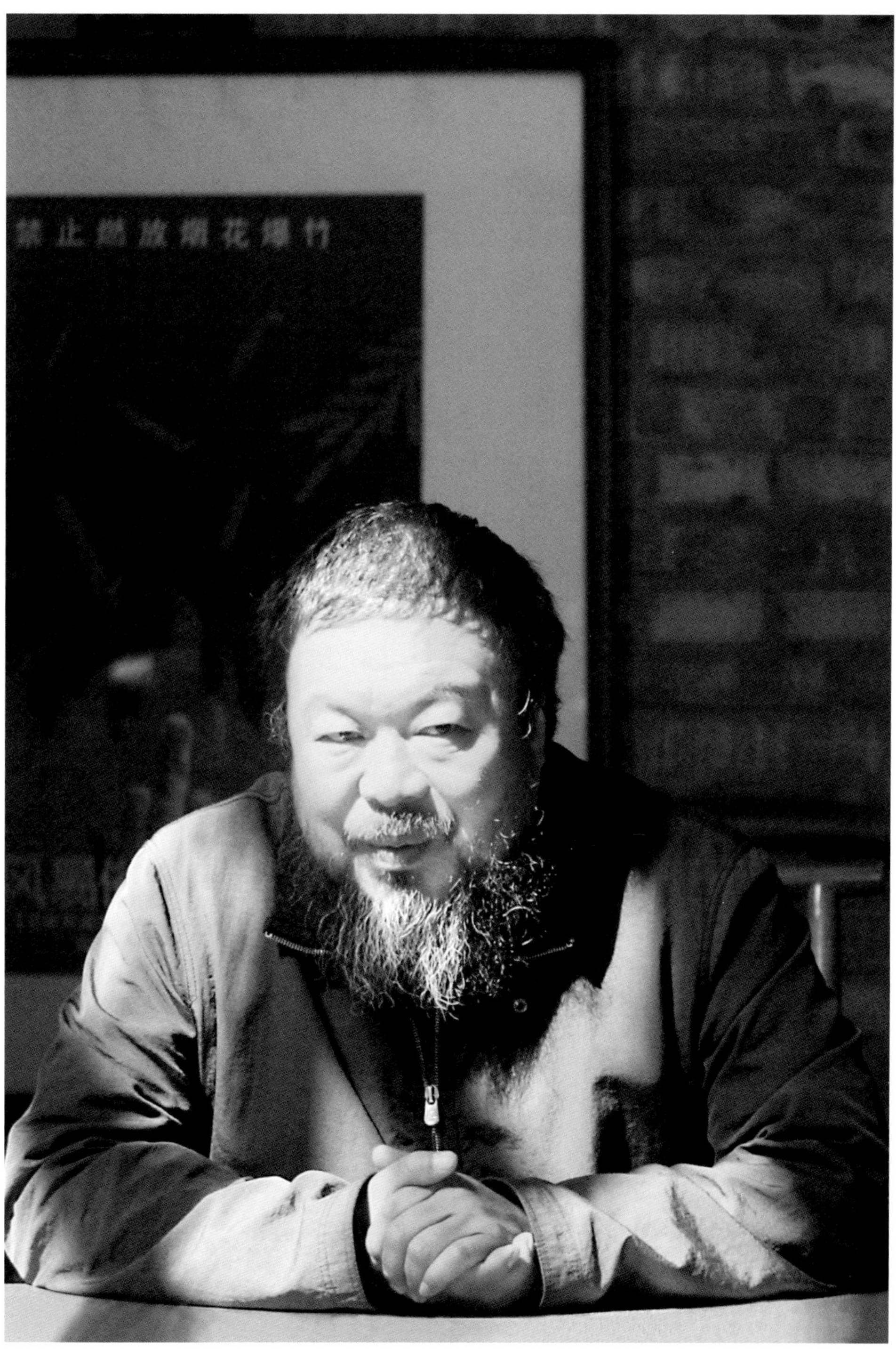

Ai Weiwei in his Caochangdi studio, Beijing 2009. Photo: Stephen Shaver | 37

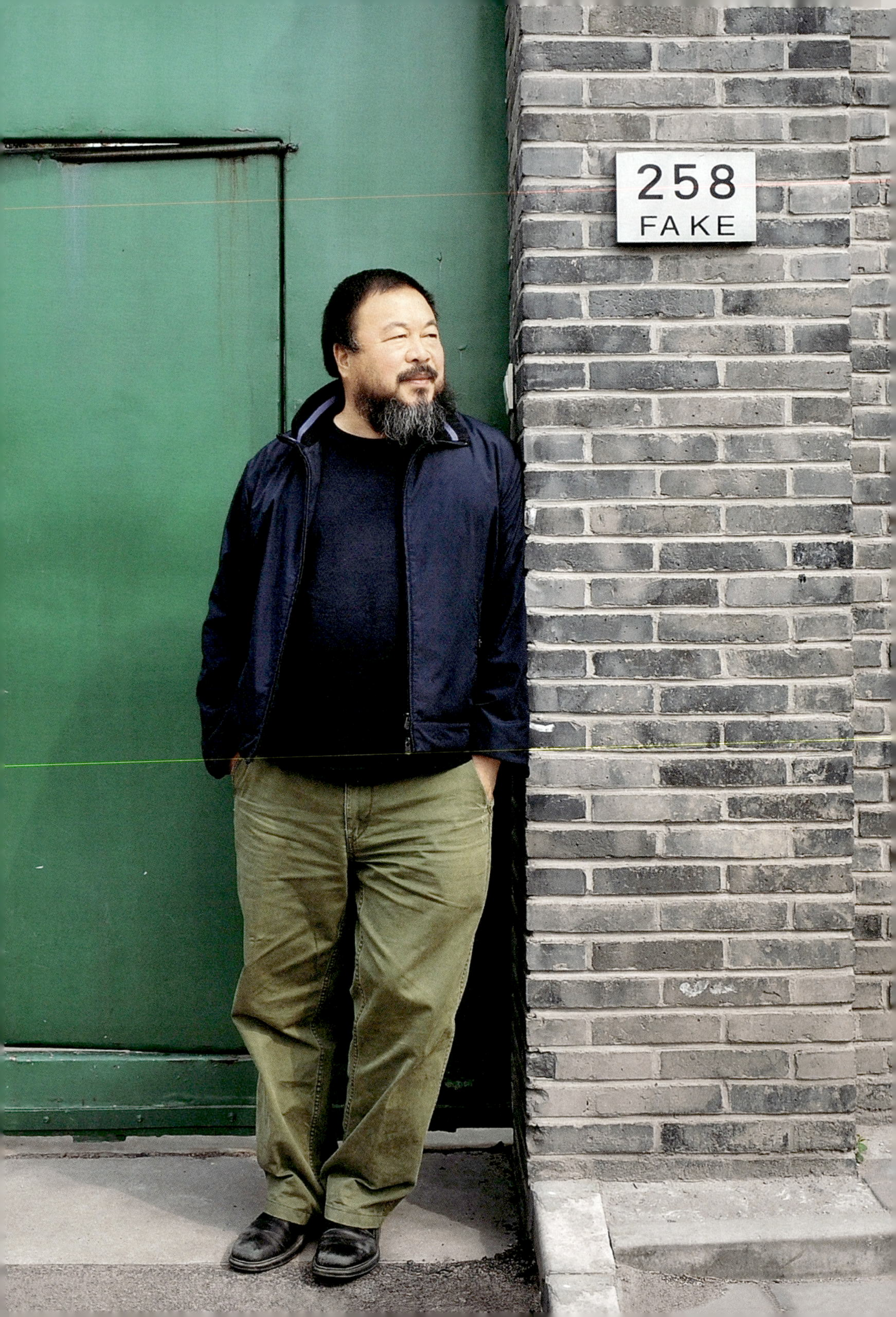
258
FAKE

Le meilleur argument
Un portrait d'Ai Weiwei

ULI SIGG

Aujourd'hui, il n'est pas vraiment difficile de trouver le dénommé Ai Weiwei, qui réside presque continuellement dans son atelier depuis la fin de sa détention en juin 2011, la restitution de son passeport lui étant indûment refusée. Cet homme qui faisait auparavant le tour du monde en avion plusieurs fois par an, cet homme qui recevait enfin ce qui lui revenait de droit depuis longtemps : la reconnaissance internationale, des invitations à des expositions, à des projets artistiques, à des conférences, à de prestigieux projets architecturaux en Chine et ailleurs, à des rencontres avec des dignitaires, etc. Aujourd'hui, il convoque tout ce monde dans son atelier, où, organisateur et commissaire de ses expositions, il conçoit des unes de magazines, twitte et reçoit – plus présent que jamais dans les médias. Quel genre de personnalité faut-il pour maintenir à flot toute cette activité ?

La réponse se trouve en partie dans sa biographie. Dans les années 1950, le père, célèbre, était banni avec sa famille dans les contrées inhospitalières du nord-ouest de la Chine à cause de ses écrits. En 1976, la famille rentre à Pékin, où le jeune Ai commence des études à l'École de cinéma – études qu'il interrompt bientôt, dépité par l'idéologie qu'on y propage, à mille lieues de toute réalité. En 1981, il suit sa compagne aux États-Unis. Selon ses propres déclarations, le jeune homme âgé alors de vingt-trois ans entreprend ce voyage en tant que « peintre postimpressionniste » : un livre sur l'impressionnisme et une monographie sur Van Gogh étaient tombés entre ses mains et l'avaient profondément marqué, alors qu'il jetait à la même époque une monographie sur Jasper Johns et ses croûtes ineptes. La peinture lui offrait une échappatoire à la réalité du communisme, qui n'était pour lui qu'un désastre permanent : pour d'obscures raisons de « dérive droitière », son père avait été déclaré ennemi de l'État, alors que toutes les décisions du quotidien chinois, qu'elles soient d'importance ou non, étaient en perpétuelle contradiction avec la propagande officielle, ne présentant aucun motif intelligible, ni pour la raison ni pour les sentiments – ni l'une ni les autres n'étant considérés comme fiables. La fuite dans des sentiments d'empathie, dans l'émotion et la passion n'étaient possibles qu'en peinture, avec le choix responsable de la ligne, des ombres et des couleurs.

En 1982, un bref passage à la Parsons School of Design à New York le mit pour la première fois en contact avec les concepts de Duchamp et de Warhol dans lesquels il s'immergea, tout en observant ses camarades d'études américains se lancer dans une peinture libre et sauvage, à corps perdu et sans se poser trop de questions – concentrés sur le comment et passant totalement à côté du pourquoi, et de la question cruciale à ses yeux : pourquoi s'exprimer en tant qu'artiste. Peu après, il décida d'abandonner la peinture – d'après ses termes, un atelier plein de tableaux dont personne ne voulait –, de se détourner de l'œuvre plane, finie, pour aborder l'univers expansionniste de l'art conceptuel. Selon lui, l'attribut qui justifiait entre tous l'existence de l'artiste était désormais la raison qui, dans la Chine de la révolution culturelle de sa jeunesse, n'avait pas pu éclairer grand-chose – raison sans doute pour laquelle il l'applique de manière aussi intraitable. La réception de Duchamp avait tué le postimpressionniste ; les idées de ce dernier sur l'existence de l'artiste comme attitude, comme style de vie, lui permirent de trouver son identité.

En 1993, Ai Weiwei décide de rentrer en Chine car son père est gravement malade. Dans un premier temps, il vécut chez son père, mais s'y sentit comme un invité, et même pire, un invité de second rang n'ayant pas la moindre chose à présenter à ses parents après toutes ces années passées en Amérique : ni fringant diplôme, ni carrière d'artiste un tant soit peu présentable. Il fit donc profil bas, passant même sous silence l'édition de trois livres sur l'art occidental et l'art expérimental chinois. Ni l'œuvre *Han Dynasty Urn with Coca-Cola Logo* (1994), ni le travail photographique *Dropping a Han Dynasty Urn* (1995, pp. 85–87), ni même, à partir de 1996, ses premières compositions de meubles déconstruits (pp. 102–109), n'étaient de l'art à ses yeux. Il ne s'agissait pour lui que d'un passe-temps. Ce n'est qu'en 1999 qu'il se met à nouveau au défi de produire un art répondant à sa propre définition pour justifier son invitation à la Biennale de Venise par Harald Szeemann.

L'art dont il retrouve alors le chemin offre une autre perspective sur la question de sa personnalité. D'un point de vue occidental, il s'agit d'une position ambiguë. Pour filer la métaphore informatique, le matériel de base à connotation globalement chinoise est fourni, le logiciel doit en revanche être imaginé. L'on perçoit une personnalité qui a une idée très claire de ce qu'est l'art et de ce qu'il n'est pas, et de ce qu'il faut pour cerner ou composer un objet et le faire passer d'une sphère à une autre. Mais en quoi consiste cette conception très claire – surtout lorsque la connaissance de la pensée et du contexte chinois fait défaut ? Un mètre cube de thé (*Ton of Tea*, 2006, p. 308), représente-t-il la même chose ici qu'en Chine ? Bien sûr que non : « Prendre une tasse de thé » – c'est souvent avec ce doux euphémisme que les gardiens de l'ordre chinois convient à un premier interrogatoire.

Celui qui aborde Ai Weiwei sous un angle prenant en compte les caractéristiques chinoises est confronté à une complexité supplémentaire enracinée dans une force particulière de la culture chinoise : la faculté de fondre une contradiction en une seule et même affirmation. Plus simplement : alors que l'esprit occidental marqué par le fonctionnement binaire de la logique cartésienne considère qu'un objet est soit ceci, soit cela, le même objet peut être pour le Chinois à la fois l'un *et* l'autre. À titre d'exemple, prenons *Whitewash* (1993–2000, pp. 45, 193) – une

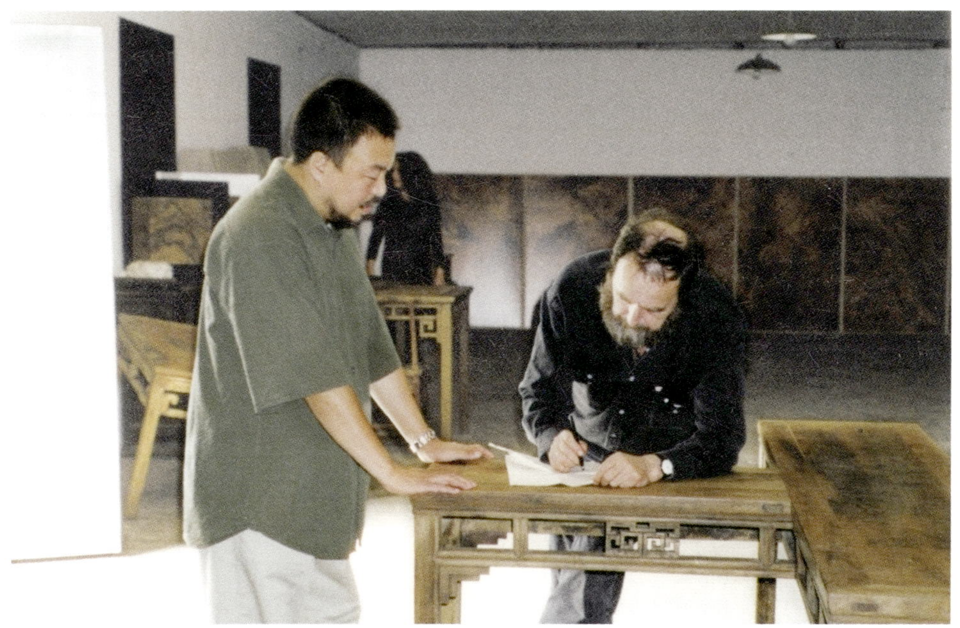

Ai Weiwei with curator Harald Szeemann in the artist's studio, Beijing 1998

œuvre composée de 132 amphores néolithiques, toutes de merveilleuses œuvres d'art témoins d'époques anciennes, mais dont un quart ont été couvertes d'une peinture industrielle blanche les dénaturant. L'œuvre fusionne deux paradigmes antagonistes de la création artistique : d'un côté, le paradigme occidental de l'art d'avantgarde qui, par la destruction radicale de la tradition et la rupture avec le passé, entend ouvrir un espace à une pensée entièrement nouvelle, de l'autre, le paradigme chinois classique qui respecte la tradition et pour lequel la création artistique est une évolution dans la continuité, nourrie de la richesse du fonds culturel chinois. Il convient d'ajouter à cela les conditions de production en Chine, où les coûts sont tellement bas qu'un artiste audacieux peut aussi penser en grandes dimensions – et les grandes dimensions sont vraiment l'affaire d'Ai Weiwei. Dès ses premières années d'activité, l'artiste avait pris l'habitude de travailler avec des équipes pouvant compter jusqu'à 100 personnes – du simple manœuvre aux artisans les plus qualifiés de Chine. En 2007, il emmène alors 1001 Chinoises et Chinois à la Documenta 12 à Cassel pour les intégrer à sa sculpture sociale en tant qu'«ouvriers saisonniers». Et pour l'installation *Sunflower Seeds* réalisée en 2010 à la Tate Modern, il mobilisera 1600 travailleurs.

L'œuvre de la Documenta 12 (*Fairytale*, 2007, pp. 310–327) révéla aussi une stratégie artistique qui allait marquer de plus en plus fortement son travail. Définissant son point fort, Ai Weiwei évoque sa capacité à «se mettre lui-même dans une situation périlleuse» – d'où peut résulter une contradiction qui exige alors une

solution, ou du moins un contrôle. Cette prise de contrôle ne doit pas être facile
à mettre en œuvre. Car son art doit en effet toujours receler la possibilité d'un
accident. C'est seulement ainsi qu'Ai Weiwei se sent suffisamment stimulé. Illus-
tration à l'appui de *Fairytale*: comment transformer en œuvre d'art le projet qui
consiste à communiquer à 1001 Chinois une tout autre réalité que la leur? Il fallut
surmonter pour cela d'innombrables difficultés logistiques: choix d'un échantillon
de population représentatif, passeports, visas, voyages, logement, etc. Et puis, très
important, il fallait que reste une chose: le mythe. Car il n'était absolument pas
possible, ni même espéré, que qui que ce soit puisse jamais embrasser visuellement
la totalité de ce monstrueux *Fairytale* décliné en plusieurs milliers de rythmes. De
plus, bien des choses durent se faire via Internet – Ai Weiwei en fit un média social
avant même que ceux-ci ne connaissent en Chine l'engouement actuel. Et quelque
chose devait aussi prendre une forme physique, c'est pourquoi Ai Weiwei créa
une installation de 1001 chaises qui conféraient à l'œuvre une certaine poésie et
devaient ouvrir d'autres espaces.

Des fragments de cette stratégie se révèlent aussi dans les vastes recherches
menées autour du séisme du Sichuan (notamment *Namelist, 2008–2011,*
pp. 348/349) et dans la monumentale installation *Sunflower Seeds* réalisée à la
Tate Modern (pp. 49, 407–409). Leur point commun est la mobilisation d'immenses ressources humaines issues de toute la République populaire, le tout en
un laps de temps chaque fois très court, chose inenvisageable sans Internet. L'on
ne s'avance donc pas trop en affirmant qu'en janvier 2010, tout autre artiste
aurait décliné la demande de la Tate d'investir l'immense salle des turbines dès
le mois d'octobre de la même année, plutôt qu'en 2012, comme cela avait été
initialement prévu. Alors qu'Ai Weiwei décidait d'entreprendre la réalisation
physique d'une œuvre dans un des cadres les plus prestigieux – et donc les plus
risqués – du monde de l'art, il faut savoir que le transport depuis la Chine et
l'installation devaient prendre à eux seuls trois mois. À compter de janvier 2010,
restaient alors six mois pour l'idée, la conception et la production! C'est la raison
pour laquelle Ai Weiwei dut faire appel à 1600 travailleuses et travailleurs pour
modeler, peindre, cuire et vernir plus de cent millions de graines de tournesol
(Sunflower Seeds) – une pure folie.

Le goût du risque très marqué d'Ai Weiwei, qui le rend friand de ces grands
projets difficilement évaluables en termes d'organisation, semble être une part de
sa personnalité de joueur, qui lui fit notamment décider de tout quitter pour se
rendre en Amérique avec 30 dollars en poche, et qui le caractérise tout autant que
son rationalisme. À cet égard, l'on apprend utilement que dans les années 1980,
chaque weekend, une limousine du casino d'Atlantic City se présentait chez lui et
ses collègues du sous-sol dans lequel ils vivaient en communauté. Ai Weiwei s'était
fait un nom en tant que joueur de black-jack. Un joueur chevronné s'approprie un
certain nombre de routines, notamment celle qui consiste à entrer avec jubilation
dans un processus dont l'issue doit être résolument incertaine, à pratiquer le jeu

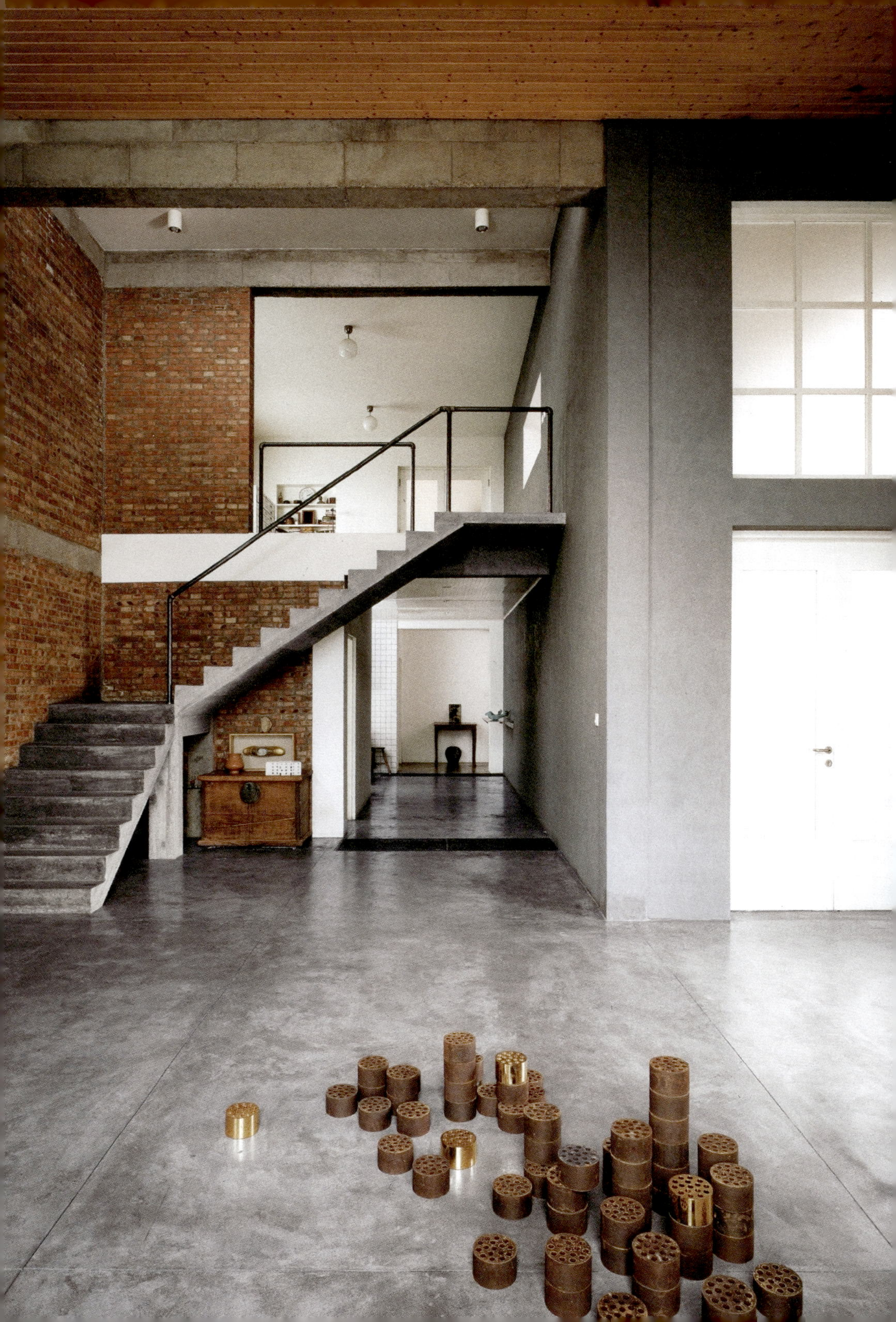

avec un sérieux mortel tout en restant à tout moment conscient qu'il s'agit seulement d'un jeu, à toujours rester suffisamment maître de soi pour ne jamais perdre de vue ses propres limites. À ce jour, rien ni personne n'a pu venir à bout du flegme d'Ai Weiwei.

Il serait étonnant qu'Ai Weiwei souscrive à la majeure partie de ce qui vient d'être dit. Il est la contradiction personnifiée. Comme dans son art, il mettra sens dessus dessous ou déconstruira tout argument pour en démontrer élégamment la futilité – ou le polira à l'excès par un obscur processus de transfiguration. Et lorsqu'il ôte sa cuirasse d'ironie et de sarcasme, il est capable de disserter brillamment sur n'importe quel sujet – notamment grâce à l'heureuse circonstance qui fait qu'il n'est encombré d'aucune culture standardisée.

Finalement, c'est peut-être à cette brillante aptitude à l'argumentation qu'il doit la grande attention dont il bénéficia, notamment en Chine. Dès 2005, il touchait des millions de lecteurs chinois à travers son blog qui pointait implacablement les faiblesses du système politique. Ai Weiwei s'y exprimait alors sans aucune retenue et dans les termes les plus explicites sur les conséquences catastrophiques de l'incompétence et de la gabegie, avant et après le séisme du Sichuan en 2008. Il dénonça les pratiques de la police de Shanghai dans l'affaire Yang Jia, broutille qui aboutit pourtant à l'assassinat de six policiers. Plus généralement, Ai Weiwei se pencha sur un vaste éventail de sujets de préoccupation de la société civile chinoise. Certains de ses concitoyens ont été jetés en prison pour beaucoup moins que cela. Et quand on lui rappelle la ligne rouge tracée par les chiens de garde chinois en matière d'activisme des droits de l'homme – la limite au-delà de laquelle ils n'ont plus du tout envie de rire –, cet homme intrépide vous remercie le plus courtoisement du monde. Mais dans ses efforts pour construire une nouvelle société chinoise, cet aspect des choses le laisse froid. De plus en plus de Chinois sentent et pensent comme lui, mais rares sont ceux qui osent élever la voix. C'est pour cette petite minorité qu'il écrit. Elle lui en sera redevable.

Le 28 mai 2009 marqua la césure gouvernementale d'avec ses millions de lecteurs en Chine : son blog fut fermé par les autorités chinoises. Par la suite, il ouvrit sur le Twitter chinois une série de microblogs bien vite identifiés et bloqués par la police du net. Aujourd'hui, Ai Weiwei est actif sur le Twitter global, dont la concision convient parfaitement à son style lapidaire. Il est vrai qu'en Chine, ses messages ne sont accessibles qu'à ceux qui savent franchir le *Great Firewall*. En Chine, c'est la condition *sine qua non* pour pouvoir surfer dans l'espace du net global non censuré.

Mais quels sont concrètement les faits – jamais formulés *de jure* par les enquêteurs – qui ont valu à Ai Weiwei d'être accusé d'activisme subversif contre le pouvoir de l'État ? Dans les textes de l'artiste, et plus généralement dans son vocabulaire, il est un mot qui revient de manière bien plus fréquente que tout autre : argument, argumentation. Pour lui, sa vie consiste essentiellement à argumenter. Un brin d'herbe, un arbre, toute chose a son mode d'existence. Et le sien

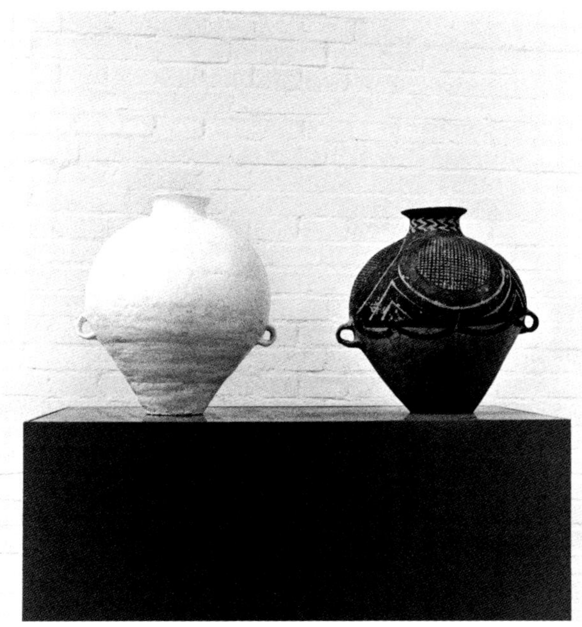

Prototype for *Whitewash*, 1993–2000,
neolithic clay urns, industrial paint,
dimensions variable

est justement l'argumentation. Très précisément, il s'agit pour lui de l'argument rationnel et du meilleur argument. Ceci vaut aussi pour son art : l'on y décèle cet obscur processus de transfiguration qui peut être décrit de manière à peu près pertinente comme une sorte de court-circuit dans le fonctionnement intellectuel du fait créatif ; mais quand l'art réussit, il s'accompagne toujours d'un argument. Cela dit, l'argument ne peut jamais s'imposer que dans le cadre d'une écologie particulière, en l'occurrence la liberté d'opinion. Et c'est bien là le point de rupture qui sépare la vision du monde d'Ai Weiwei de celle de la Chine officielle. Dans sa version, les communistes n'argumentent jamais. Pas même quand il n'y a aucun enjeu. Ils ordonnent. Le statut et l'ordre – face à la liberté et au contrat social en démocratie – définissent le système politique chinois depuis des millénaires, et ceci vaut en particulier à l'époque présente de la « dictature du peuple ». Ai Weiwei en a personnellement fait l'expérience avec les interrogatoires qu'il a subis après son arrestation début avril 2011, lorsqu'il fut embarqué par la police des frontières de l'aéroport de Pékin juste avant son départ pour Hong Kong. Ses enquêteurs se sont évidemment conduits comme des joueurs d'échecs, mais comme des joueurs qui établissent de nouvelles règles tous les trois coups pour être sûrs de gagner – et c'est justement parce qu'ils gagnent à tous les coups qu'ils n'apprennent rien !

Ces interrogatoires ne portaient pas vraiment sur des actes ou des facettes de l'individu Ai Weiwei. Comme le diffusera l'agence de presse nationale Xinhua, il s'agissait de le convaincre d'évasion fiscale, de bigamie et d'autres méfaits, ce qu'Ai Weiwei n'apprit qu'une fois relâché. Les interrogatoires visaient à savoir pour le

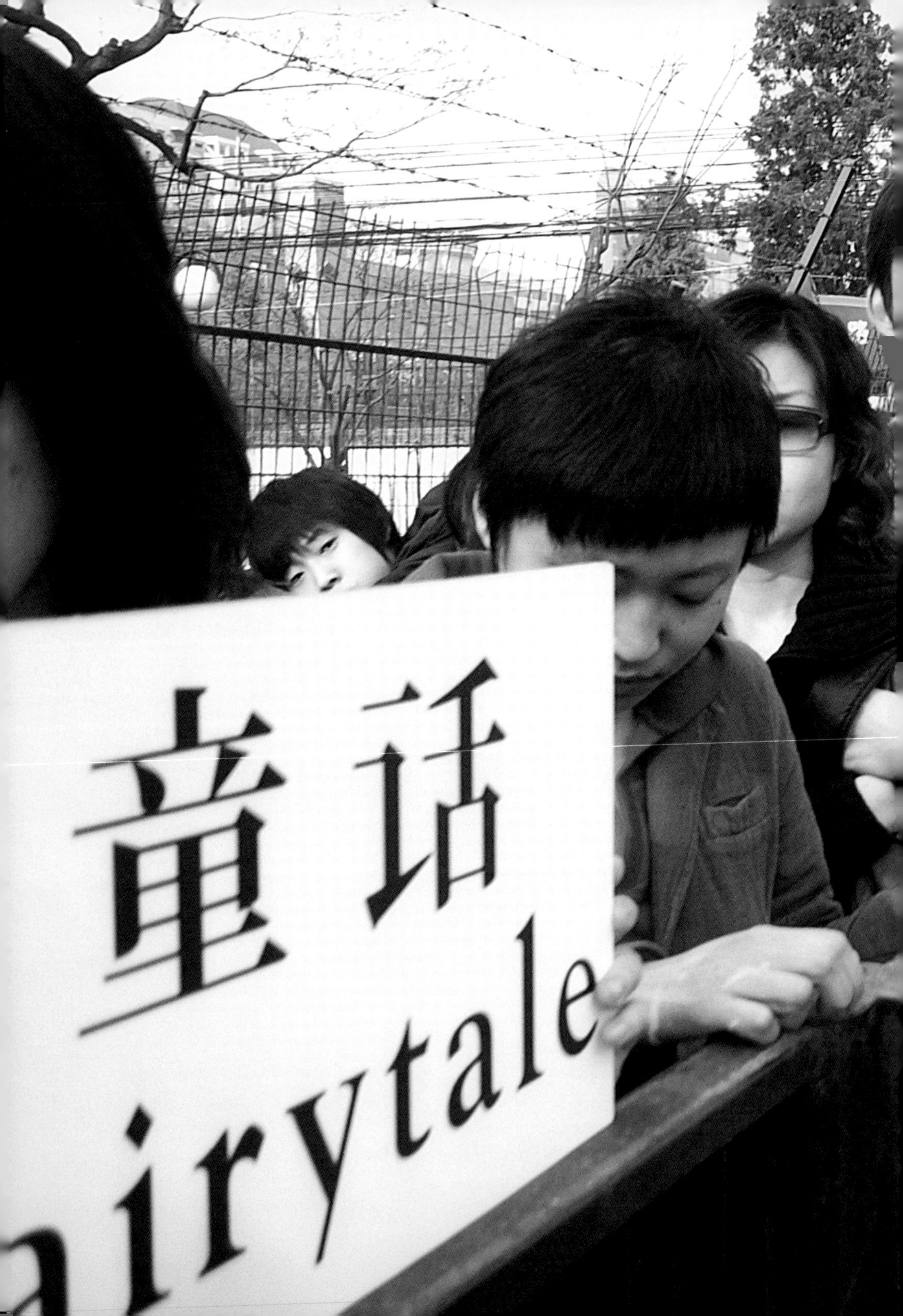

童话
airytale

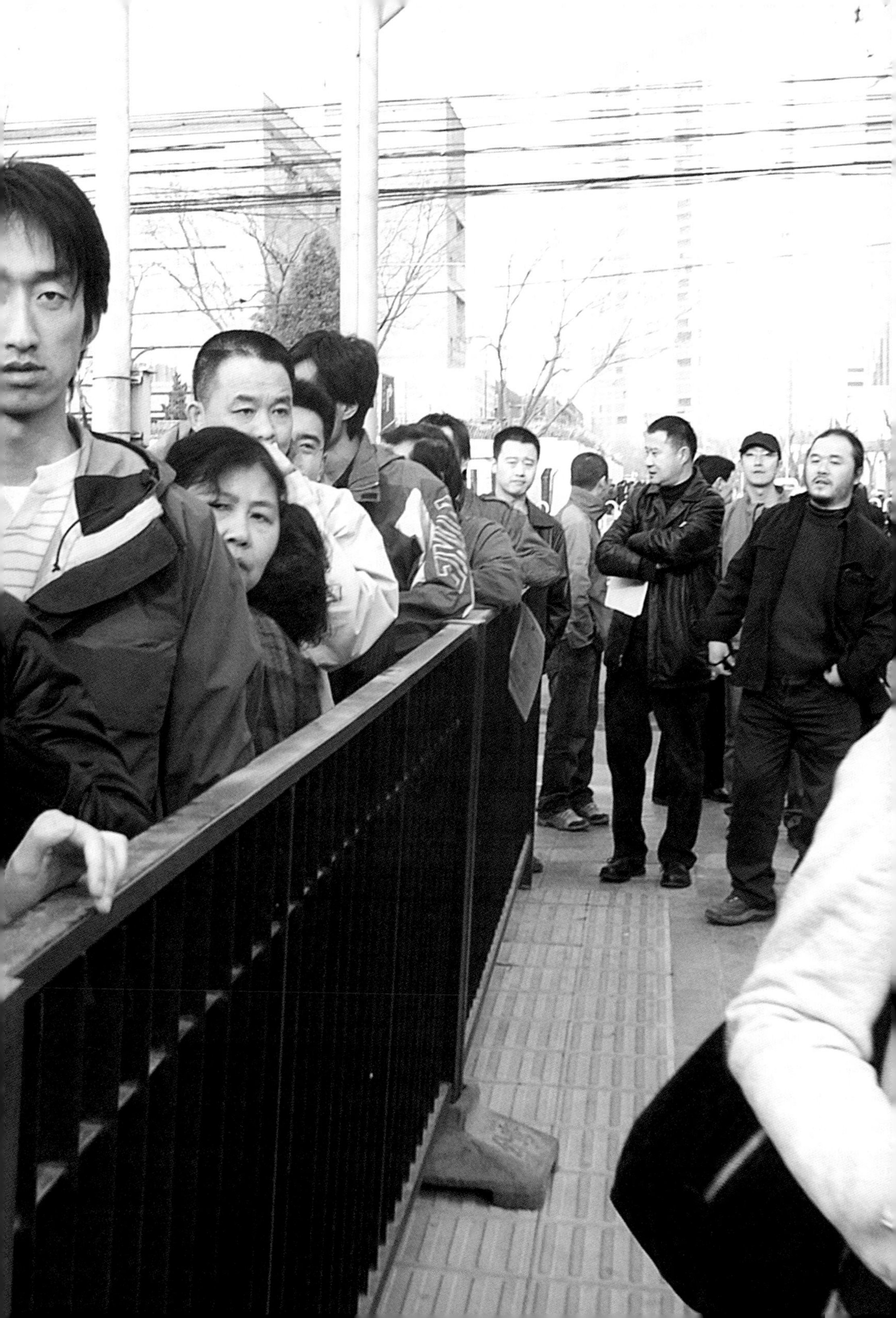

compte de quelles puissances étrangères il menait ses agitations. Dans ce contexte, la question de l'argent fut sans doute évoquée – Ai Weiwei donna des indications sur les prix et les coûts de production de son travail –, mais les enquêteurs ne parvinrent pas à comprendre comment de telles sommes d'argent pouvaient être mobilisées pour des objets aussi futiles qu'encombrants et des idées aussi saugrenues. Ils ne s'intéressèrent guère à d'autres sujets. Cela s'explique aussi par les particularismes dans l'application du droit pénal chinois : pour ce genre de cas, la peine n'est pas en fonction des actes – ceux-ci peuvent être allègrement passés sous silence. Dans un cas présentant une telle visibilité, l'évaluation de la peine dépend des consignes transmises aux tribunaux par les conseils du parti. Les arguments de l'accusé Ai Weiwei, mais aussi de l'accusateur Ai Weiwei ou de ses défenseurs, n'eurent jamais la moindre valeur – quand toutefois ils pouvaient être présentés. Au Sichuan, tous les tribunaux se déclarèrent d'emblée incompétents ne serait-ce que pour enregistrer la plainte d'Ai Weiwei pour coups et blessures par la police, bien que la mise en péril de sa vie eût été dûment documentée. L'argument individuel qui s'appuie sur l'ordre juridique fondé dans la constitution chinoise et ailleurs, mais aussi sur les valeurs fondamentales humanistes, et son impuissance face à ce constant amalgame d'arbitraire, d'ignorance du droit, de complaisances patentes ou opaques de la part d'institutions toutes-puissantes – telles sont les expériences récurrentes, vécues et souvent dûment mises à jour et consignées, qui ont endurci l'artiste jusqu'à en faire un activiste. Lors de son arrestation en 2011, Ai Weiwei avait manifestement franchi une ligne rouge. Lui qui avait encore délibérément déserté la politique et la société chinoises en se rendant aux États-Unis en 1981, était ainsi définitivement et administrativement entré dans le domaine de l'activisme des droits de l'homme. Et dans la Chine officielle, ce terme n'a pas franchement bonne presse.

L'évolution qui a transformé l'artiste en artiste/activiste et pour finir en activiste/artiste, s'est produite sur trois décennies et à des rythmes très différents dans les perceptions chinoise et étrangère. Avec toutes les expériences et prises de conscience concernant la théorie et la pratique de la scène artistique américaine et de l'*American Way of Life,* l'époque new-yorkaise lui a appris que l'art véritable ne saurait se résumer à l'esthétisme. Quand l'art est authentiquement grand, il se caractérise par un point de vue éthique et moral. Après 1993 et son retour au sein d'un système autoritaire dont l'idéologie communiste avait depuis longtemps dépassé le point de rupture et qui, même du point de vue de l'autorité, glissait déjà vers une déchéance générale des valeurs, Ai Weiwei comprit très clairement que son art devait s'occuper de cette Chine, de cette époque, et s'assurer de cette réalité d'un point de vue humaniste et rationnel. Se contenter d'entonner un air contemporain serait insuffisant. À un moment ou à un autre, argumenter du point de vue humaniste et rationnel, par l'image ou par la parole, devait forcément aboutir au conflit avec l'État autoritaire, qui obéit en effet à un tout autre primat : la conservation du pouvoir au profit du parti. À partir de 2000, avec la construction

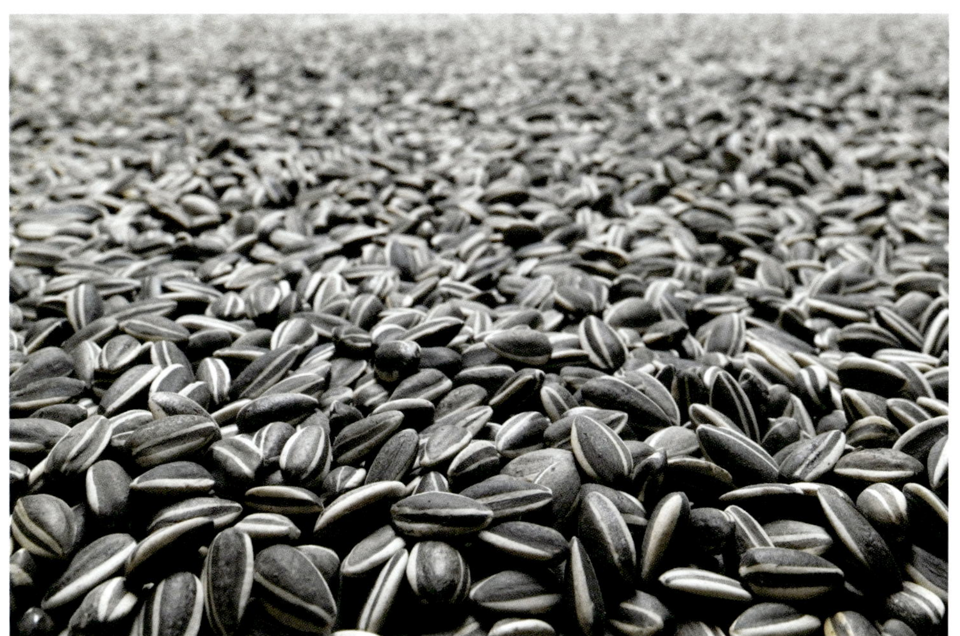

Sunflower Seeds, 2010 (detail), porcelain, paint, 100 million pieces, dimensions variable;
Turbine Hall, Tate Modern, London 2010 (see pp. 407–409)

de sa propre maison, réellement spectaculaire, avec atelier et autres dépendances dessinées en un temps record par l'artiste (pp. 122–139), Ai Weiwei devint inopinément un sujet médiatique, en qualité d'architecte, dans le cadre de magazines de mode et de design, ce qui fit de lui un personnage officiel, notamment et plus fortement encore à partir de 2003 en raison de sa collaboration avec les architectes Herzog & Meuron dans le cadre du stade olympique de Pékin (pp. 385, 387–389). C'est en 2005 que l'ouverture de son blog le fit percevoir pour la première fois comme un artiste politique. Et en 2007, il vira à l'opposant désormais doté d'une large visibilité. Pour la première fois, il affronta alors ouvertement la Chine officielle par la voie des médias. La célébration officielle du compte à rebours des Jeux olympiques de 2008, un an avant leur inauguration, le choqua – il en conclut que les Jeux olympiques allaient être une mascarade, avec toute la pompe monarchique et l'autocélébration pseudo-nationaliste d'un État autoritaire. Peu à peu, ses blogs et ses interviews autour de toutes sortes de sujets durcirent le ton, se firent plus incisifs et frontaux. Ils furent étayés par de vastes et minutieuses recherches sur l'arbitraire du pouvoir, mais aussi par ses expériences dans sa propre cause. Au centre de son propos, Ai Weiwei mit constamment son exigence de liberté d'opinion et d'État de droit.

Les stratégies artistiques avec lesquelles il faisait déjà entièrement corps se fondirent désormais avec son activisme politique. Au-delà de cet ensemble commun, il

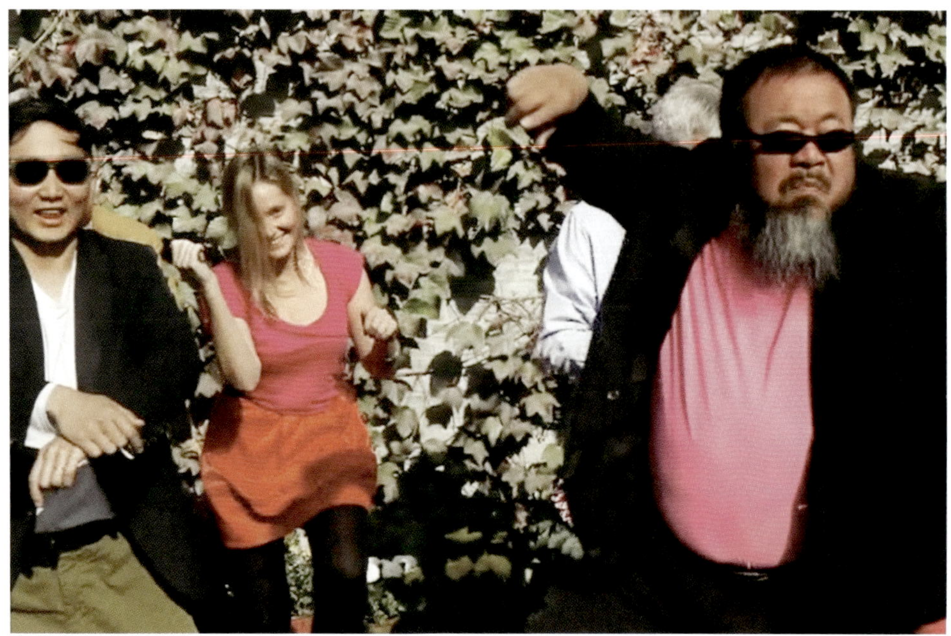

Above and opposite: Stills from the video *Caonima Style*, 2012, Ai's politicized take on South Korean singer Psy's "Gangnam Style"

ne lui restait plus récemment que peu de temps pour des échappées occasionnelles dans la *Chineseness*, ce fonds archéologique et culturel presque infini dans lequel il avait puisé naguère avec une jubilation particulière – à l'époque où il se délectait encore des raffinements de la Chine antique et de la création artistique, où il jouait sur les significations et les interprétations du public de l'art. Aujourd'hui, tout a pris une tournure plus grave ; et lui-même est devenu plus grave depuis qu'il a décidé de regarder chaque jour la bête dans les yeux et de l'affronter, y compris avec son art.

Entre-temps, il a regroupé une communauté de millions de partisans engagés parmi les internautes, qui l'admirent pour son impertinence, ses constants démêlés avec le pouvoir de l'État et l'investissement occasionnel de ses propres deniers dans sa cause – notamment avec les milliers de DVD qu'il envoie gratuitement aux personnes intéressées, ou avec des fêtes organisées pour des frères d'armes, lors desquelles les défaites sur le terrain purement juridique – comme la démolition de son atelier à Shanghai – ont pu être célébrées comme des victoires morales. Enfin, quelqu'un nommait par leur nom les choses auxquelles ils s'étaient eux-mêmes frottés depuis longtemps. Ai Weiwei ne pouvait évidemment pas tuer la bête, et ce n'est d'ailleurs pas son intention. Il entend seulement se battre pour son bon droit, et du même coup pour tous ceux qui eux aussi revendiquent les mêmes droits. Certes, des voix contraires se firent aussi entendre sur le net, et pas seulement des

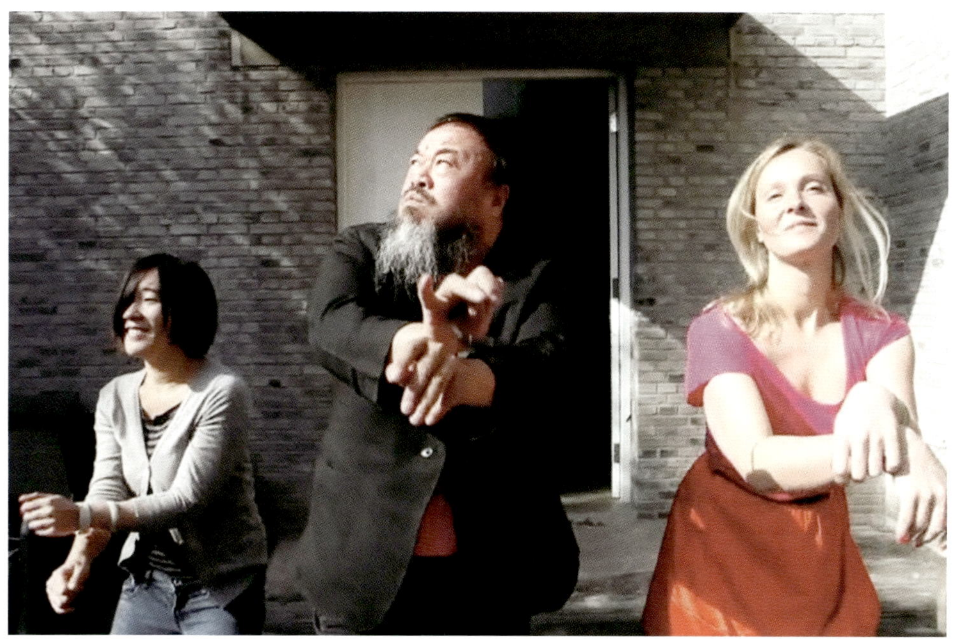

voix téléguidées : entre autres pour critiquer une argumentation jugée trop frontale, et plus généralement contre des actions qui dénient à ses adversaires – le plus souvent les autorités jusqu'au sommet de l'État – toute sortie qui leur éviterait de perdre la face – une attitude jugée bien peu chinoise. Certains commentaires se sont crispés sur la destruction de biens culturels antiques et ont alimenté l'incompréhension à l'égard du fait qu'une telle démarche puisse être célébrée en Occident. Si l'on peut regretter l'impossibilité de voir l'art d'Ai Weiwei en Chine – à de très rares exceptions près, l'obéissance servile des galeries et des institutions chinoises à la censure ayant depuis longtemps pris les devants –, il convient toutefois d'y opposer que l'art d'Ai Weiwei excède largement la faculté de compréhension artistique du spectateur chinois inexpérimenté, formaté par les valeurs de l'art chinois traditionnel, au premier rang desquelles figurent la beauté et l'harmonie. Une autre critique cherchait dès lors à reléguer Ai Weiwei dans la case occidentale, à le présenter comme un artiste dont l'activisme aurait pour but de rehausser son profil, voire sa valeur marchande, et plus généralement comme un produit de l'impérialisme occidental, sinon comme son outil.

La matière à conflit et le potentiel explosif politique avaient atteint un tel degré que le personnel du ministère de la Culture assigné à l'épuration idéologique dut transmettre le cas à la sécurité intérieure. Curieusement, quelques semaines seulement avant son arrestation, une délégation de la Ville de Pékin avait approché

Ai Weiwei pour lui proposer de devenir membre de la Conférence consultative politique du peuple chinois, deuxième chambre parlementaire à côté du Congrès du peuple. L'artiste demanda un temps de réflexion. Pour finir, son dilemme fut résolu par l'action de la police des frontières.

L'on ne saura sans doute jamais à l'initiative de qui le bureau de la sécurité intérieure de la Ville de Pékin décida d'arrêter et d'interroger l'artiste. À l'intérieur, une situation incontrôlable était apurée ; mais vers l'extérieur, la République populaire continue de payer un prix que les commanditaires n'avaient pas anticipé. En Occident, les dommages collatéraux pour l'image de la Chine seront difficilement réparables avant longtemps. Et c'est précisément cette séquence de mesures administratives récentes qui a fait d'Ai Weiwei le Chinois vivant le plus célèbre aux yeux des consommateurs de médias occidentaux. Dans ses interviews, l'artiste en a dûment remercié l'ex-gouvernement chinois. Il sait bien que ses seules forces ne lui auraient jamais permis d'accéder à ce statut mondial. Il doit aussi des remerciements à la la scène artistique mondiale, qui s'est engagée en sa faveur dans un élan de solidarité exemplaire – avec bien plus de leviers que le monde littéraire après l'arrestation du prix Nobel de la paix Liu Xiaobo. Non que le monde de l'art contemporain en soi ait le moindre poids dans la Chine officielle, mais les politiciens occidentaux peuvent être instrumentalisés quand la pression médiatique est trop forte. Et par le truchement de son jeu de rôles avec les médias internationaux, Ai Weiwei s'est donné un maximum de visibilité à l'étranger – avec une sincérité sans bornes, aussi habile que naïve, parfois au risque de se ridiculiser et au prix de la perte de tout contrôle sur cet immense battage médiatique sur lequel il n'eut jamais aucune prise.

Dans la Chine officielle règnent à n'en pas douter des divergences sur la manière dont il convient de traiter le cas Ai Weiwei, cet individu dont le plus grand défaut est d'aimer son pays et non le parti. Qui, et à quel échelon, pourra en prendre la responsabilité et décider de ce qui convient le mieux pour l'image du pays : le tenir en bride au sein des frontières nationales ou le faire garder à l'étranger, où les dissidents ont toujours su finir opportunément marginalisés – mais celui-là ? Seule la démocratie ne produit plus de héros – elle n'en a d'ailleurs pas besoin. Mais il faudra encore bien du temps.

Des extraits de ce texte ont déjà été publiés dans *Ai Weiwei: Ways beyond Art* (Elena Ochoa Foster et Hans Ulrich Obrist, éd., Londres/Madrid, Ivory Press, 2009) ; ils ont été revus pour mon article « Confusionism and more » du catalogue du pavillon allemand pour la Biennale de Venise de 2013 (Susanne Gaensheimer, éd., Berlin, Gestalten, 2013) et retravaillés pour ce portrait de l'artiste. La source principale de toutes ces versions est la série de discussions que j'ai eues avec Ai Weiwei depuis plus de dix-huit ans.

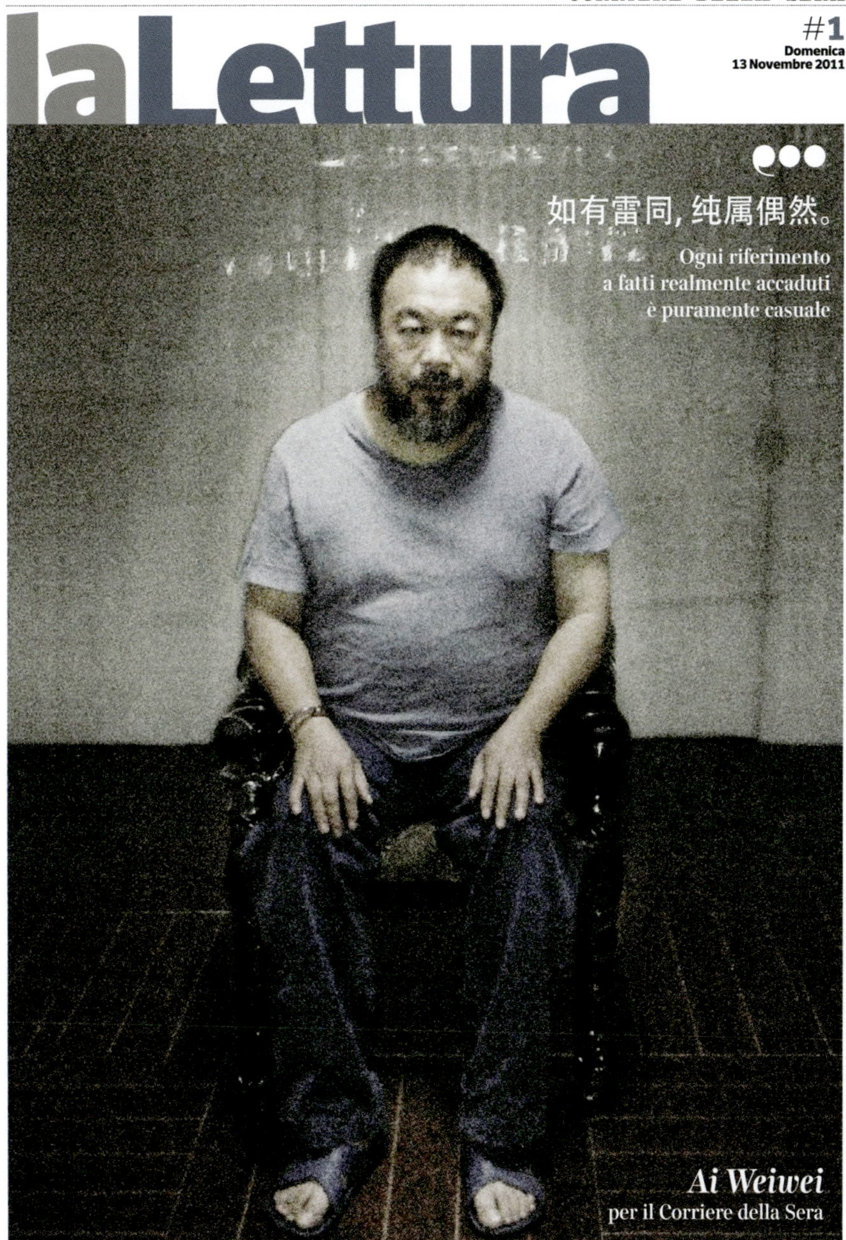

IL DIBATTITO DELLE IDEE ● NUOVI LINGUAGGI ● ARTE ● INCHIESTE ● RACCONTI
CORRIERE DELLA SERA
laLettura
#1
Domenica
13 Novembre 2011
如有雷同, 纯属偶然。
Ogni riferimento
a fatti realmente accaduti
è puramente casuale
Ai Weiwei
per il Corriere della Sera

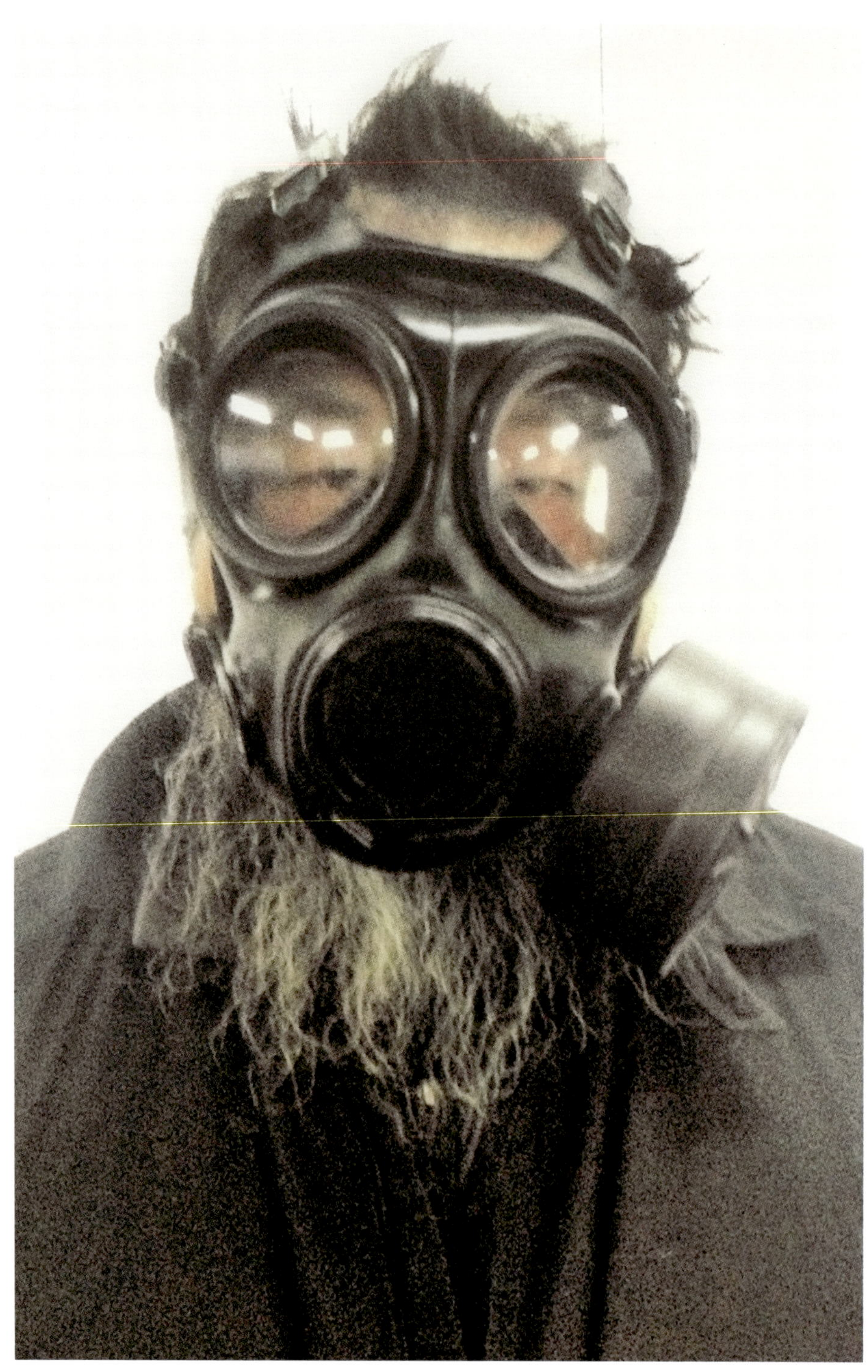

 Self-portrait in response to record-breaking air pollution levels in Beijing, 2013

1983–1993 New York

"I was sure I would spend my whole life in New York. I was so fascinated with
what was going on there. You had to attend those galleries and also the East
Village. And there was such a big mix and also a struggle. You started asking
yourself what kind of artist you wanted to be … I started to take a lot of photos,
thousands of photos, mostly in black and white. I didn't even develop them.
Taking photos is like drawing with a different method. It's an exercise in what
you see and how you record it, in trying to not use your hands but rather your
vision and your mind. Taking photos is like breathing. It becomes a part of you."
— AI WEIWEI

Ich war überzeugt, dass ich mein ganzes Leben in New York verbringen würde. Ich war
fasziniert von der Lebendigkeit der Stadt. Es gab all diese Galerien, die man besuchen
konnte, und das East Village. Es war ein großes Durcheinander und auch ein Kampf. Da fragt
man sich selbst, welche Art von Künstler man sein will … Ich fotografierte sehr viel, machte
Tausende von Fotos, zum größten Teil in Schwarz-Weiß. Ich ließ die Filme nicht einmal entwickeln. Fotografieren ist wie Zeichnen mit anderen Mitteln. Man übt den eigenen Blick und
wie man ihn aufzeichnet, eben nicht mit den Händen, sondern mit einer Vorstellung im Kopf.
Fotografieren ist wie Atmen. Es wird zu einem Teil von dir.

J'étais convaincu que je passerais toute ma vie à New York. J'étais fasciné par ce qui s'y
passait. Il fallait voir ces galeries, et l'East Village. Il y avait là un mélange extraordinaire de
gens, mais aussi une lutte constante. Je me demandais quelle sorte d'artiste je voulais être…
J'ai commencé à prendre plein de photos, des milliers de photos, la plupart en noir et blanc.
Je ne développais même pas mes films. Photographier, c'est un peu comme dessiner, avec
une méthode différente. C'est un exercice qui permet de réfléchir sur ce qu'on voit et sur la
manière dont on l'enregistre, en essayant de ne pas utiliser ses mains, mais plutôt sa vision,
son esprit. Photographier, c'est comme respirer. Au bout d'un moment, ça devient un geste
naturel.

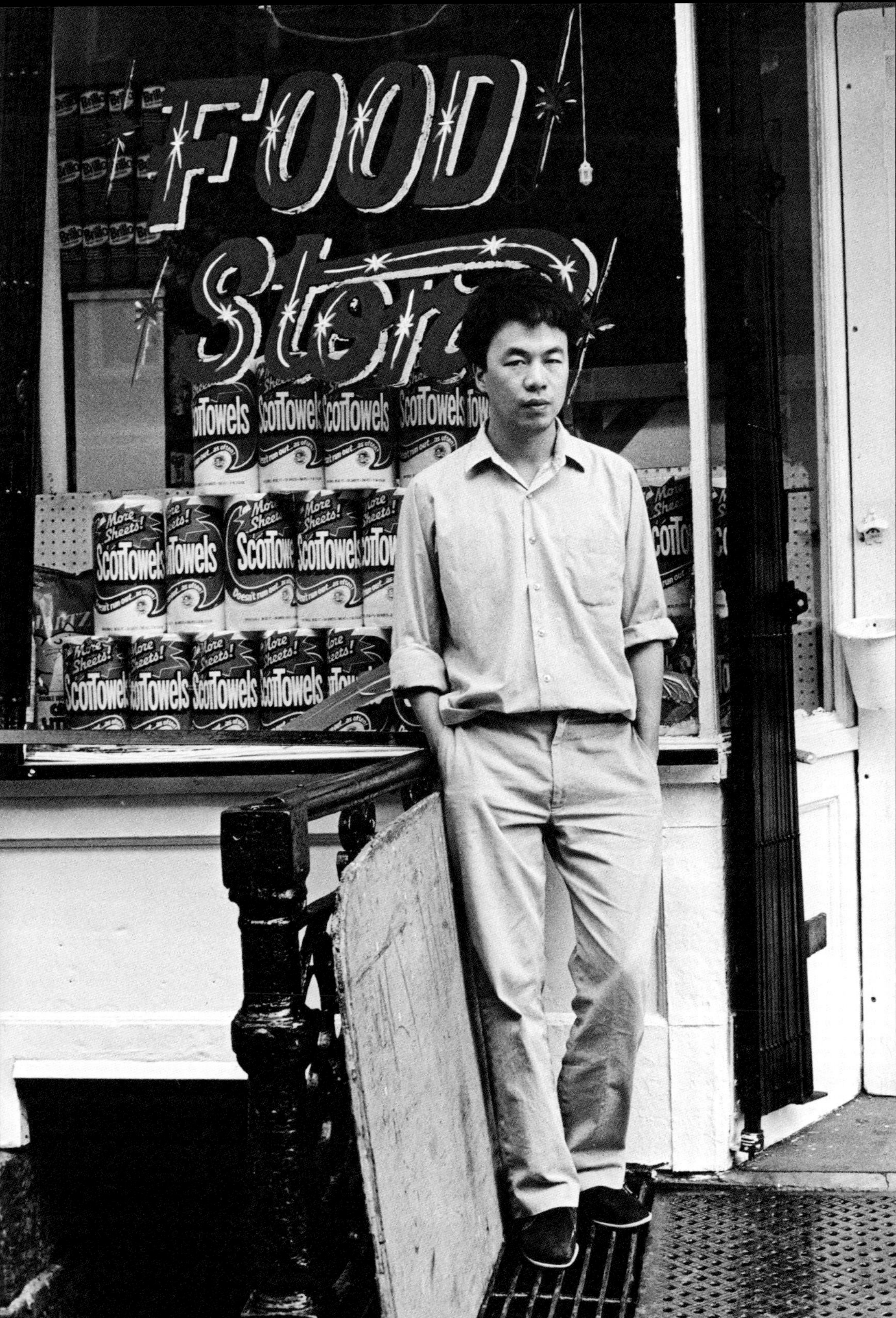

FOOD
STORE
ScotTowels
More Sheets!
ScotTowels
Doesn't run out...as often
Brillo

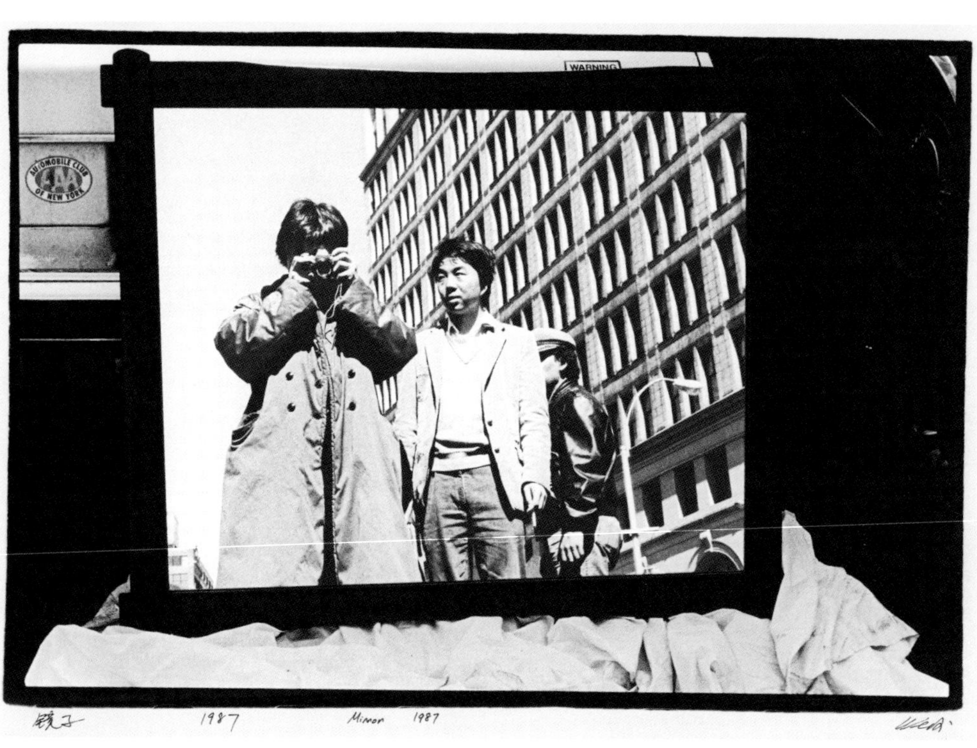

58 | NEW YORK PHOTOGRAPHS, 1983–1993, black-and-white photographs, various dimensions

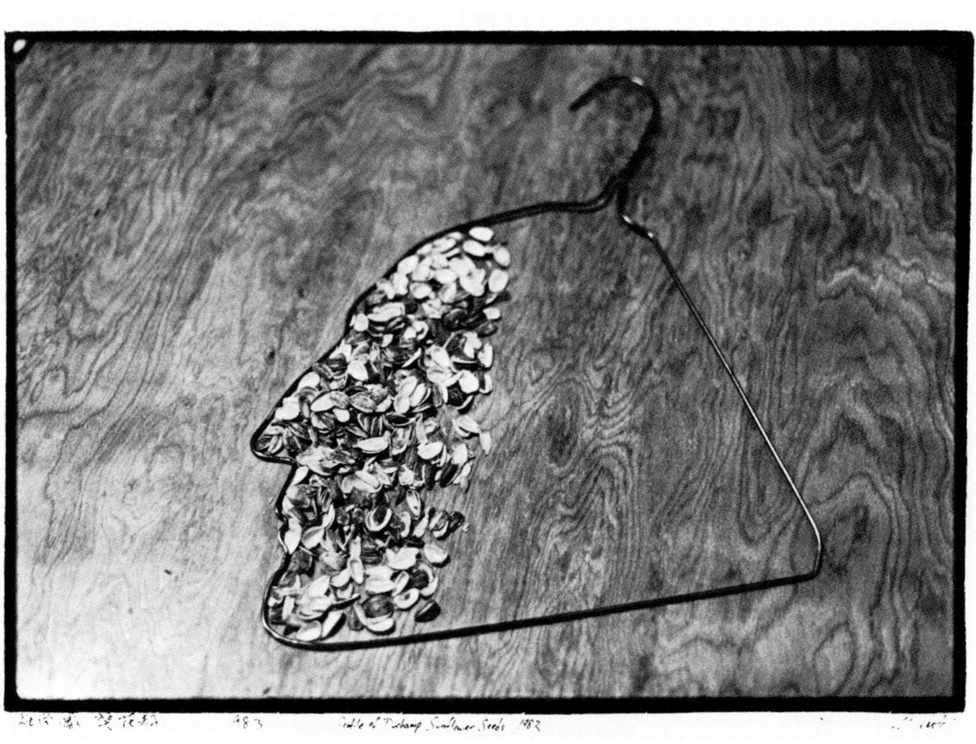
Profile of Duchamp, Sunflower Seeds 1983

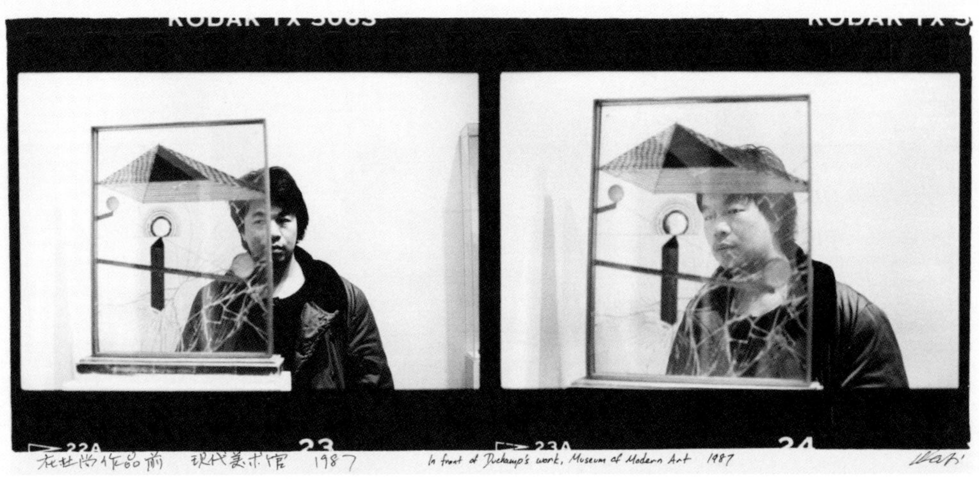

在杜尚作品前　现代美术馆　1987　In front of Duchamp's work, Museum of Modern Art　1987

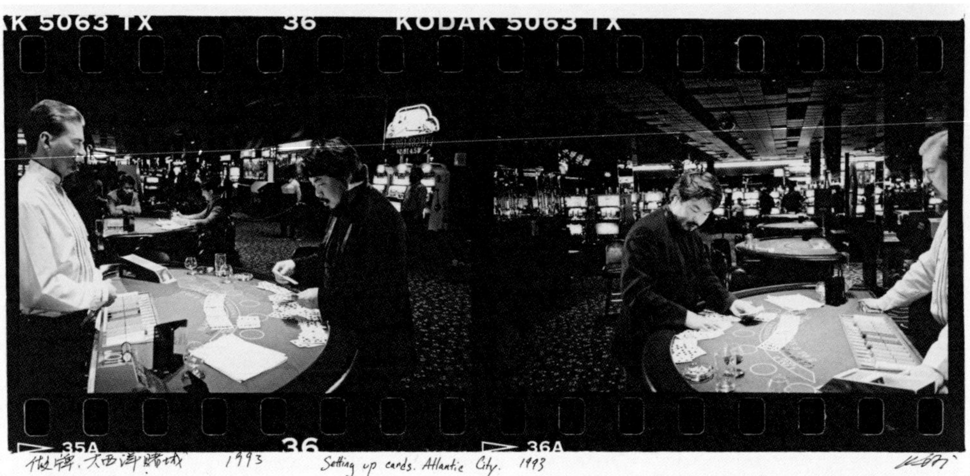

赌博．大西洋赌城　1993　Setting up cards. Atlantic City. 1993

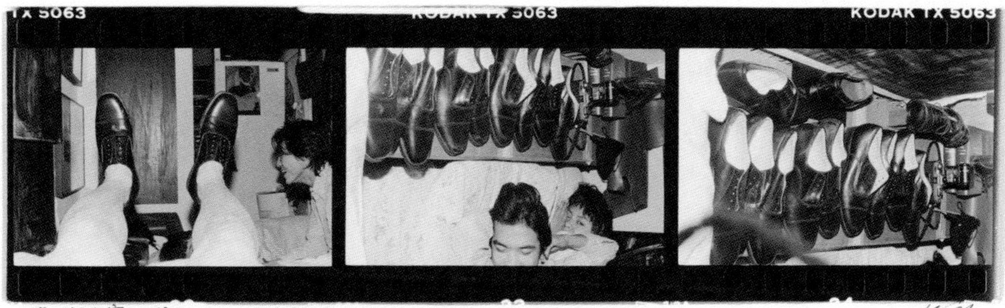

东三街公寓. 1987.   East 3rd Street Apartment. 1987

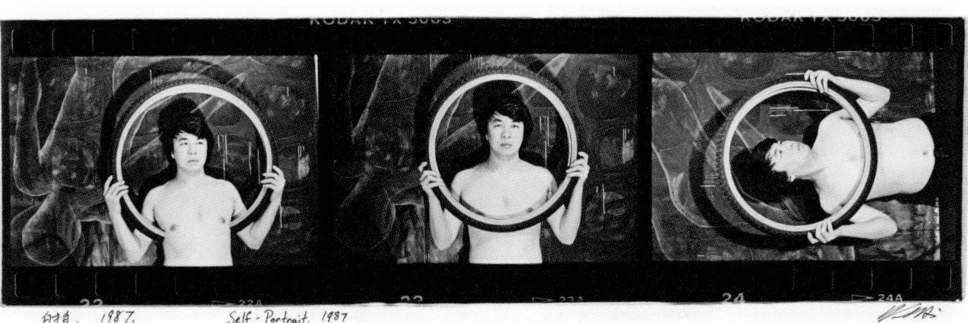

自拍. 1987.   Self - Portrait. 1987

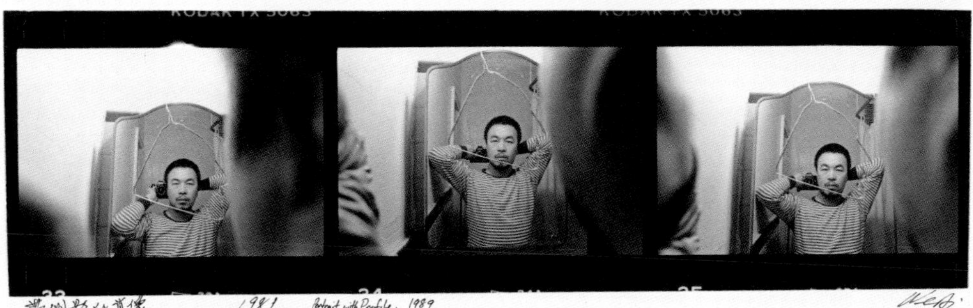

带侧影的肖像   1989   Portrait with Profile. 1989

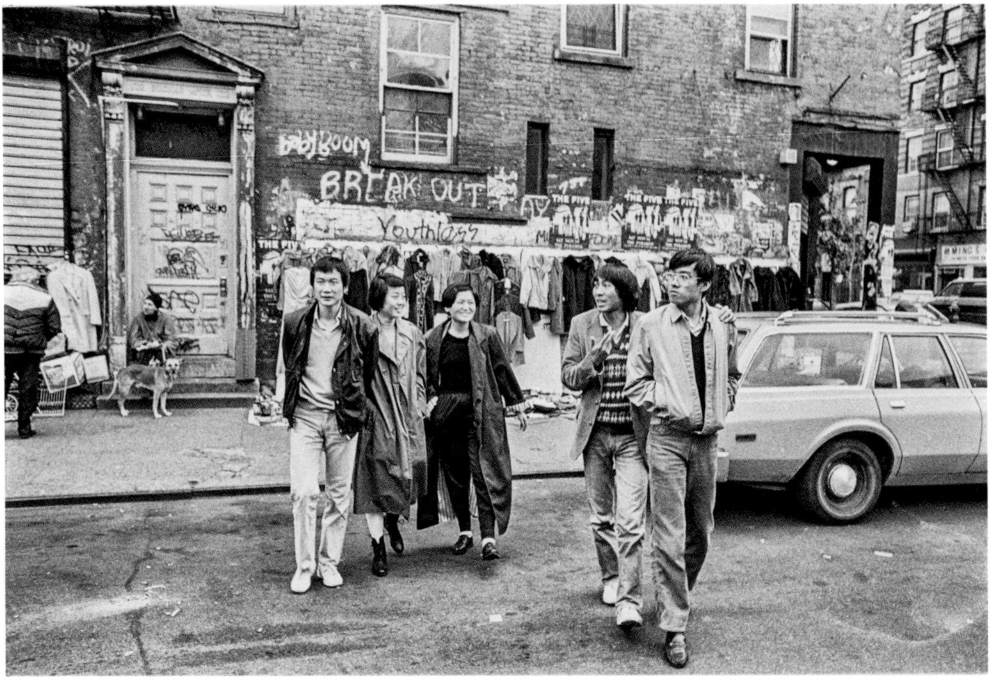

SAFE DE OS T VAUL

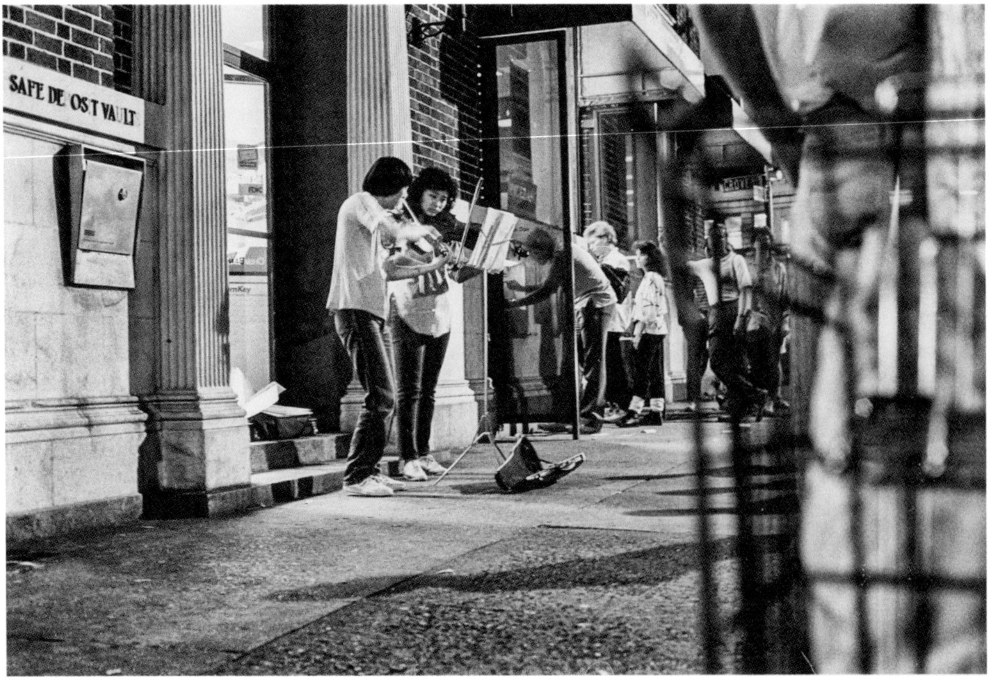

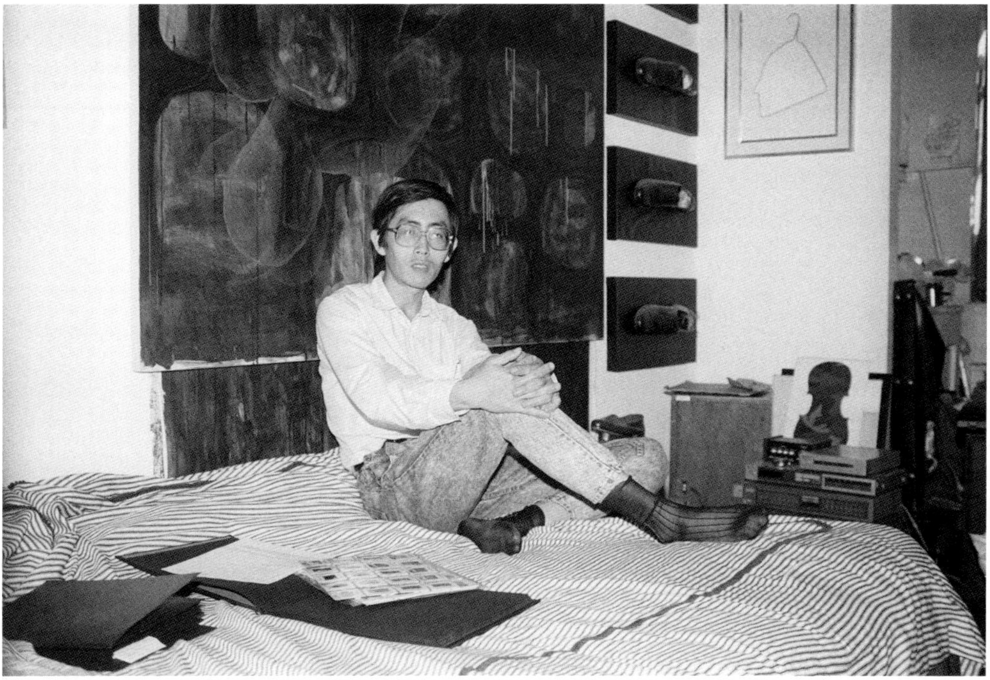

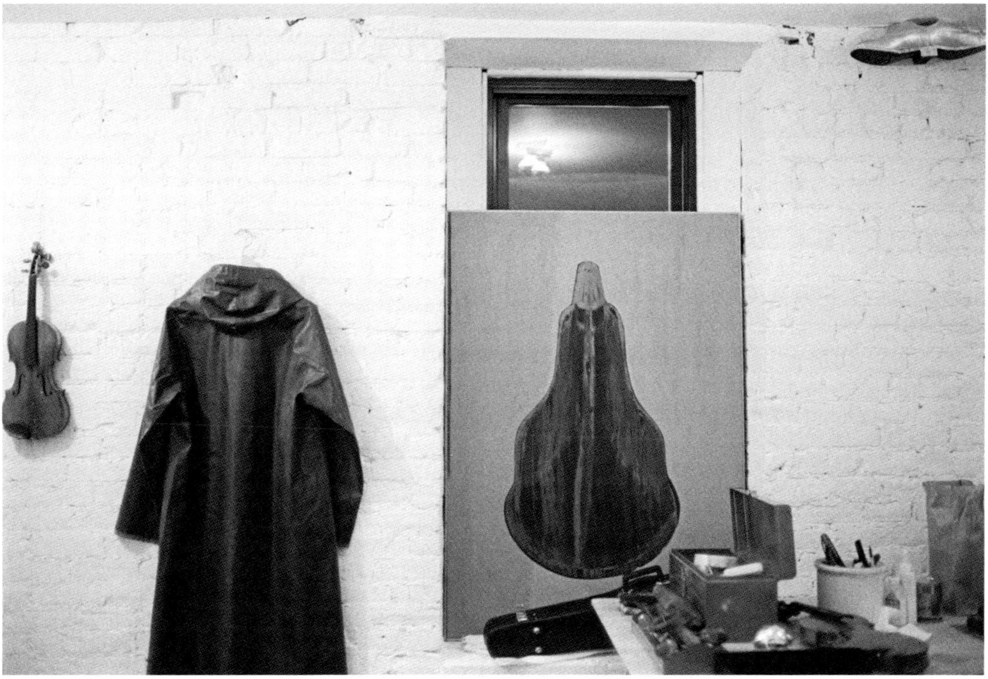

"I started as a painter. My earliest paintings were mostly about landscapes,
in the fashion of Munch—or even in the fashion of Cézanne … The Mao series were
the last paintings I did. I did those Maos, and it was somehow like saying goodbye
to the old times. I did the group over a period, and then I just gave up painting
altogether." — AI WEIWEI

Ich habe als Maler angefangen. Meine frühesten Gemälde waren meistens Landschaften
im Stil von Munch – und manchmal im Stil von Cézanne … Die Mao-Serie waren die letzten
Gemälde, die ich gemacht habe. Ich habe diese Maos gemalt, und es war, als verabschiedete
ich mich von den alten Zeiten. Die Werkgruppe ist über einige Zeit entstanden, und danach
habe ich die Malerei ganz aufgegeben.

À mes débuts, j'étais peintre. Mes premières œuvres étaient souvent des paysages dans
le style de Munch et parfois dans celui de Cézanne… Mes derniers tableaux ont été cette
série de Mao. Lorsque je les ai terminés, c'est comme si je disais adieu au passé. J'ai mis un
certain temps à réaliser cette série, et après j'ai définitivement abandonné la peinture.

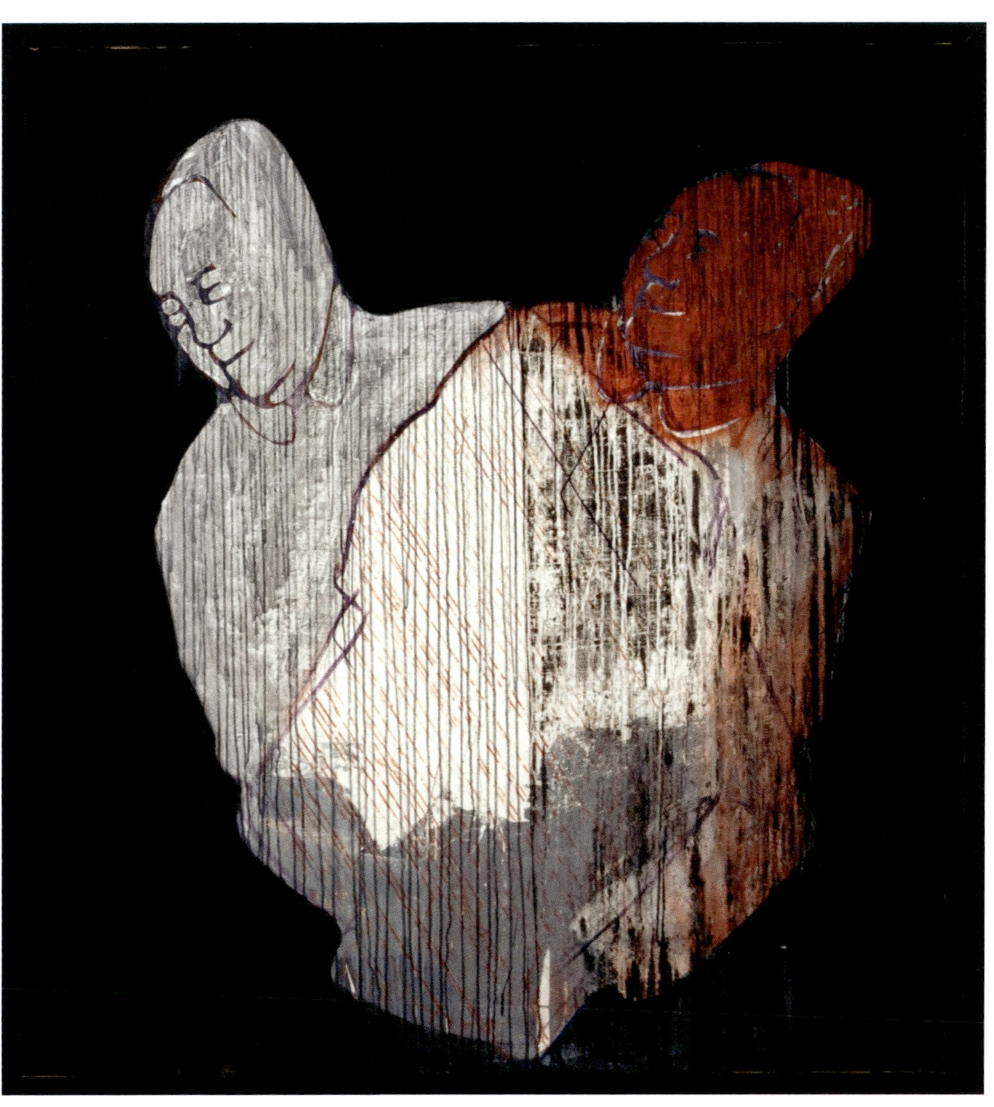

DOUBLE MAO, 1985, acrylic on canvas, 70⅞ x 52¾ inches | 65

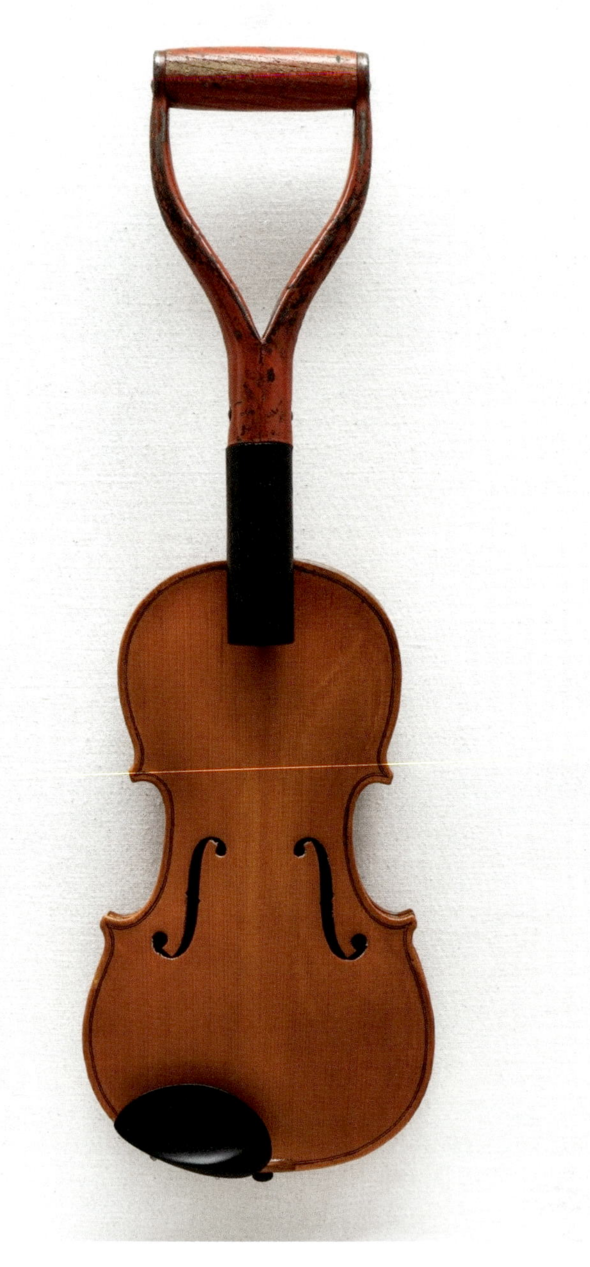

66 | VIOLIN, 1985, handle of a shovel, violin, 24 ¾ x 9 ⅝ x 2 ¾ inches

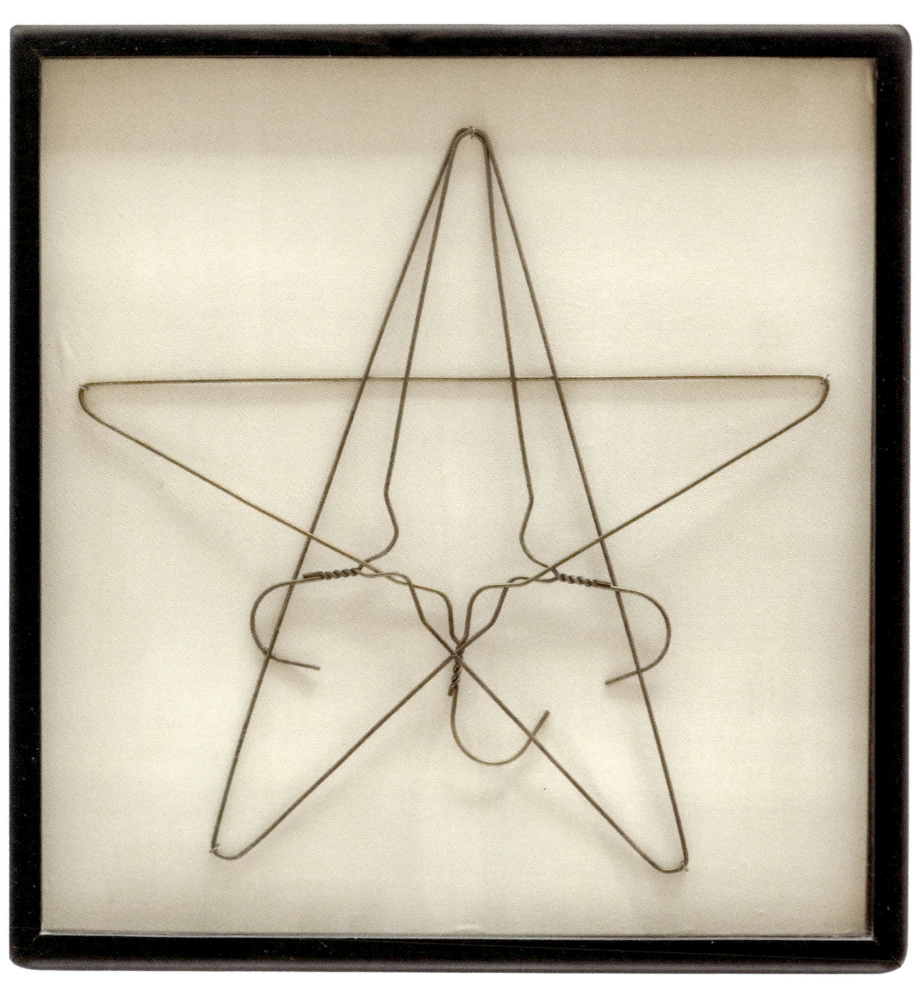

THREE CLOTHES HANGERS AS A STAR, 1987–1988, clothes hangers, wooden frame, ca. 16⅞ x 16⅞ inches | 67

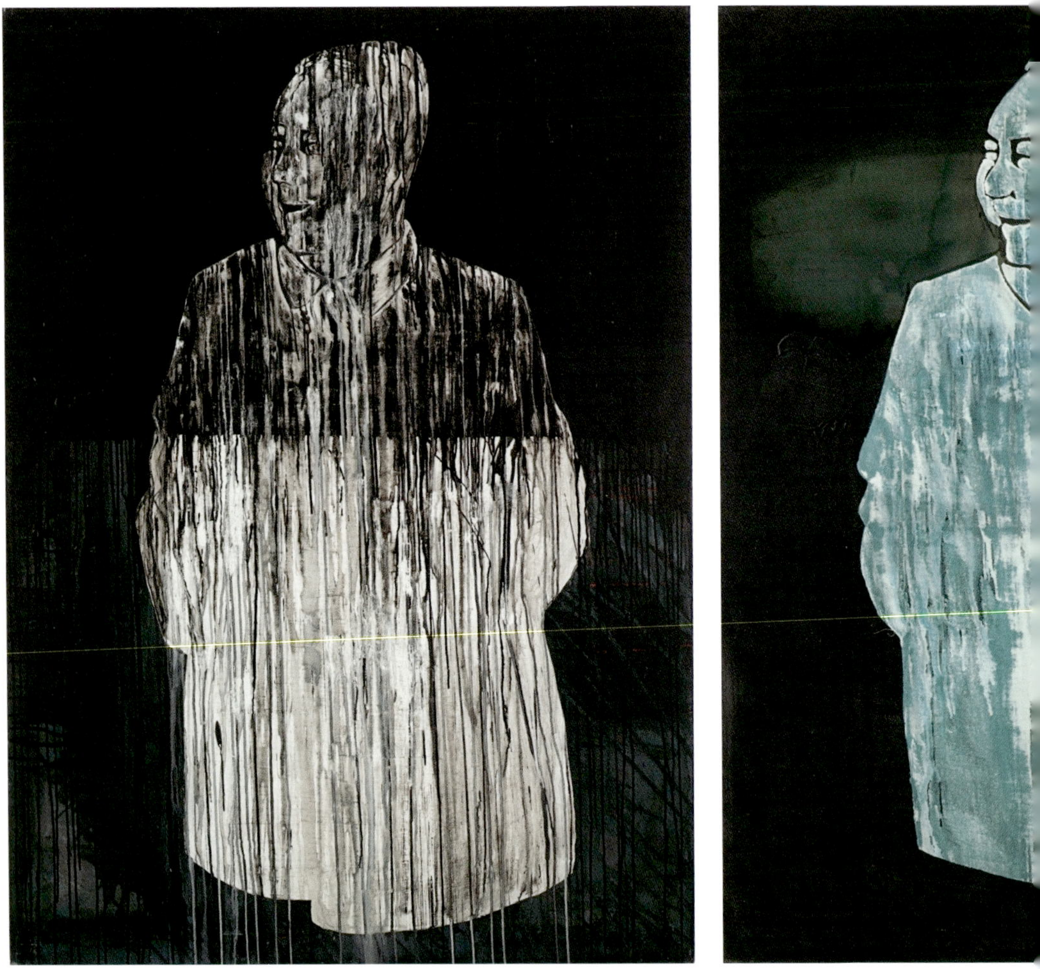

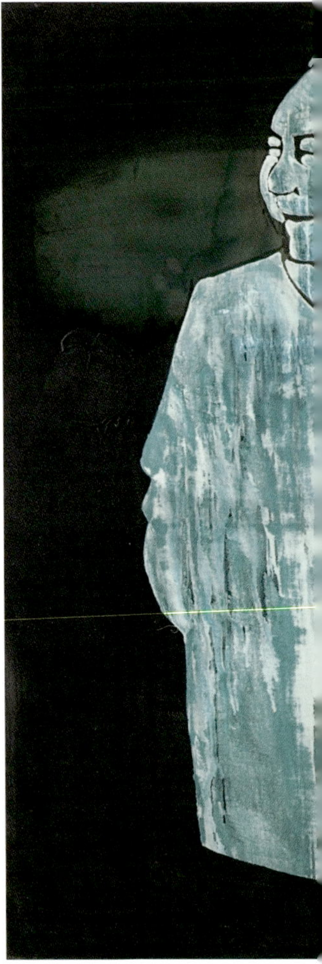

 | MAO 1–3, 1985, acrylic on canvas, each 70⅞ x 53⅛ inches

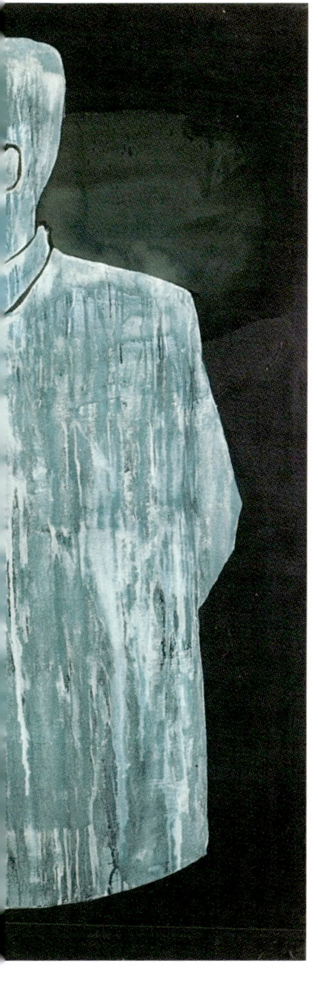

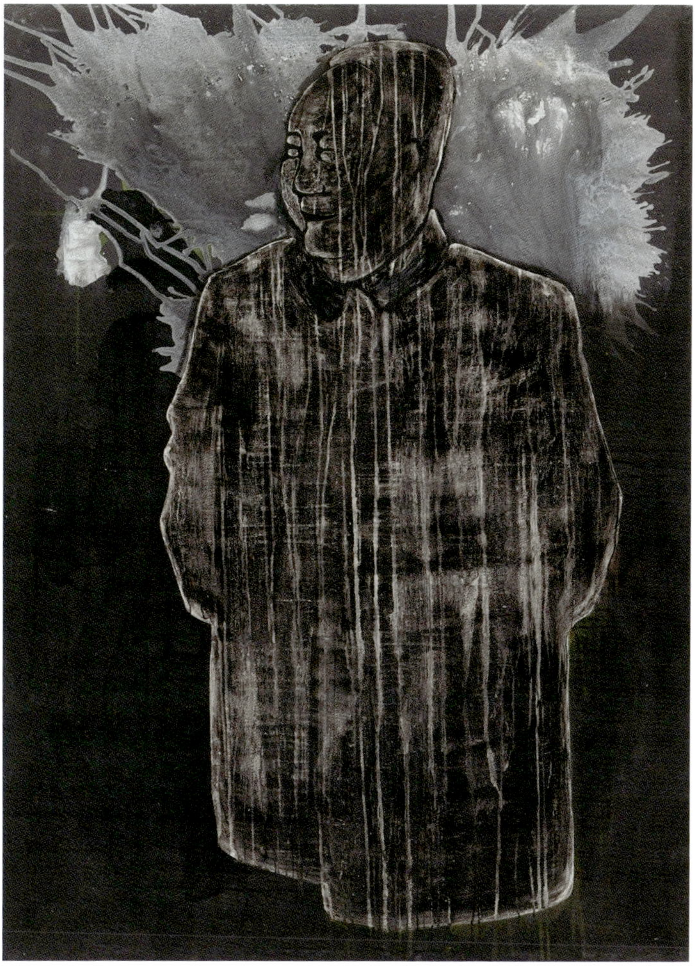

"That time I had attached condoms to an army raincoat. It was about safe sex
because around that time everybody was so scared about AIDS…I really wanted
to work with everyday objects—it was the influence of Dada and Duchamp—but
I didn't do much. There are only a few objects left because every time I moved—
and I moved about ten times in ten years in New York—I had to throw away all the
works." — AI WEIWEI

Dann hatte ich Kondome an einem Armee-Regenmantel befestigt. Es ging um Safe Sex,
weil damals alle Angst vor AIDS hatten … Ich wollte mit Alltagsgegenständen arbeiten – das
war der Einfluss von Dada und Duchamp –, viel habe ich aber nicht gemacht. Heute sind
nur ein paar Objekte übrig, weil ich bei jedem Umzug – und ich bin während meiner zehn
Jahre in New York ungefähr zehnmal umgezogen – alle Arbeiten wegwerfen musste.

Cette fois, j'avais fixé des préservatifs sur un imperméable de l'armée. Je voulais parler
des rapports sexuels protégés, à cette époque, tout le monde avait tellement peur du SIDA…
Je voulais vraiment travailler avec des objets de la vie quotidienne – c'était l'influence du
mouvement Dada et de Duchamp – mais je ne l'ai pas fait tant que ça finalement. Et la plupart de ces objets ont disparu parce qu'à chaque fois que je déménageais – et j'ai déménagé
une dizaine de fois pendant ces dix ans à New York –, il fallait que je jette la plupart de
ces travaux.

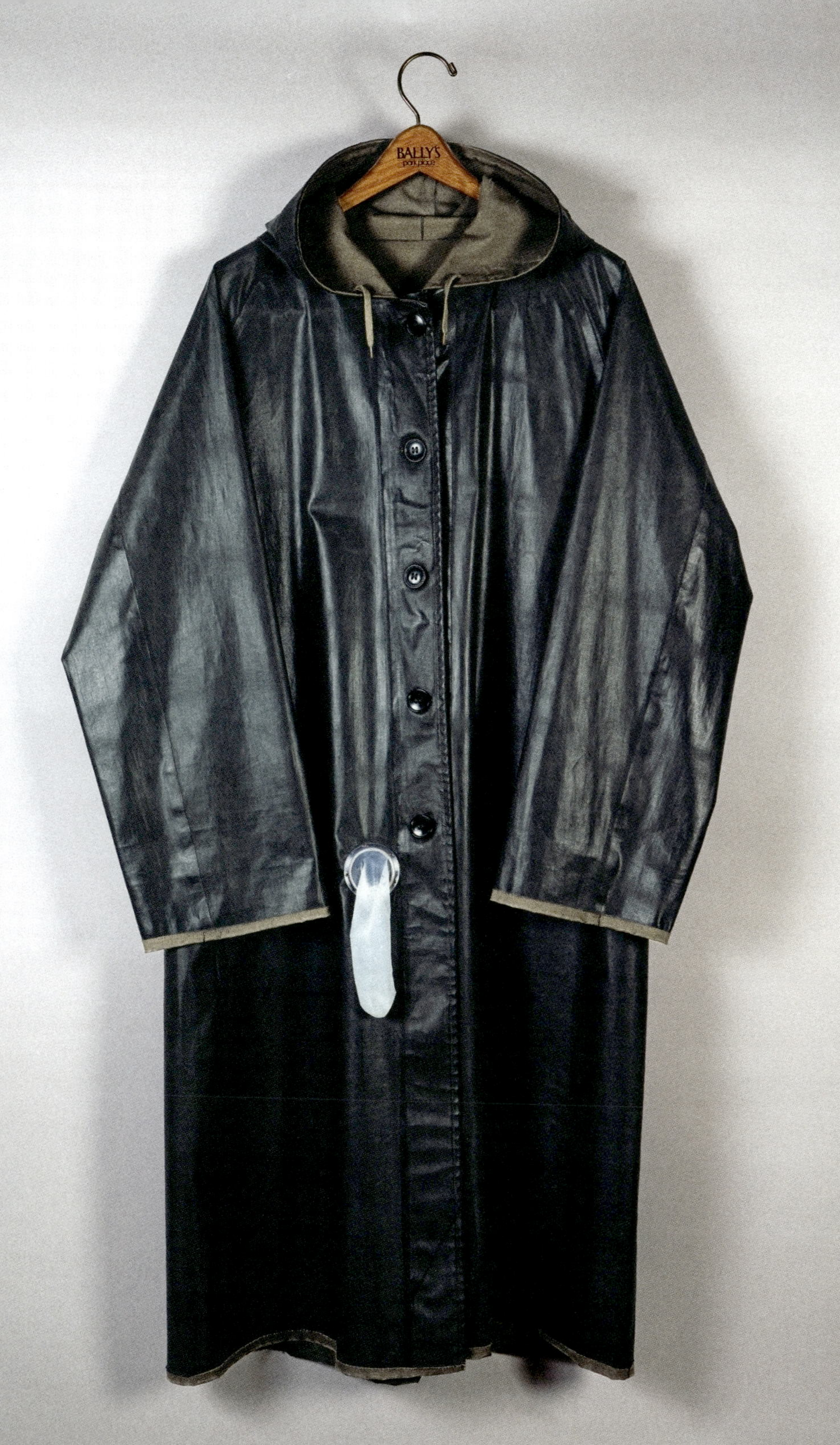
BALLY'S
park place

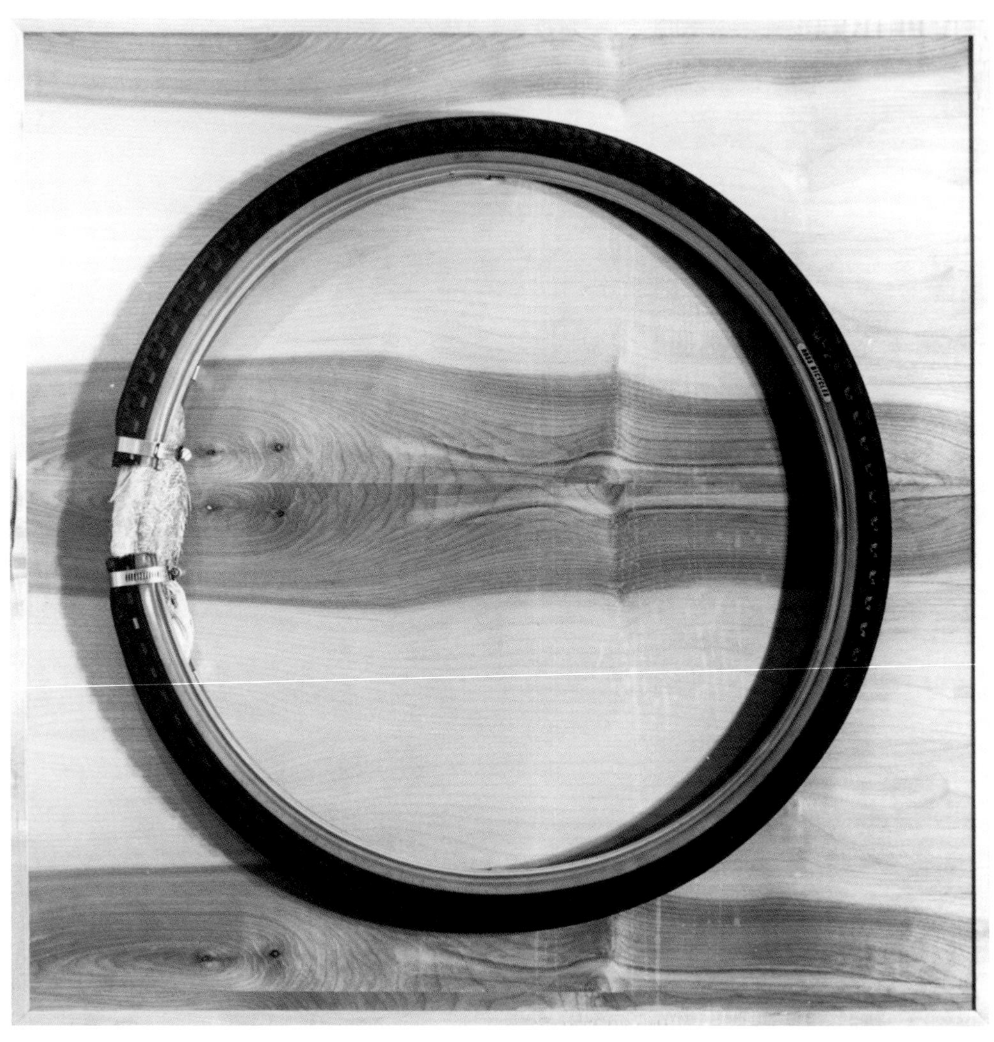

72 | TIRE AND SALTED FISH, 1987, bicycle tire, salted fish, wooden board, 33 ⅞ x 33 ⅞ x 3 ½ inches

UNTITLED, 1987, shoe heels, wood, 55 ⅛ x 31 ½ x 3 ⅞ inches | 73

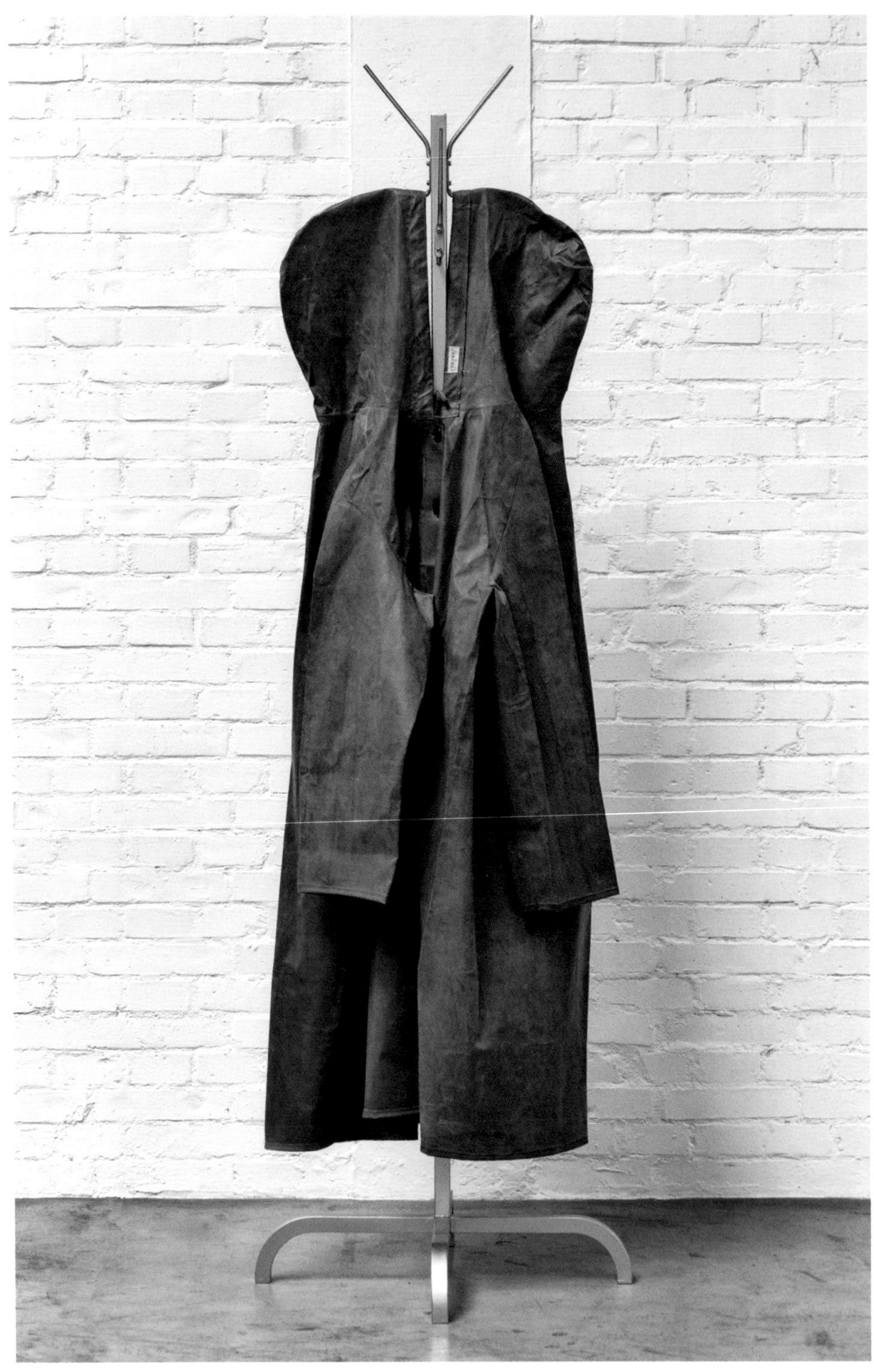

74 | UNTITLED, 1988, raincoats, coat stand, 74¾ x 23⅝ x 23⅝ inches

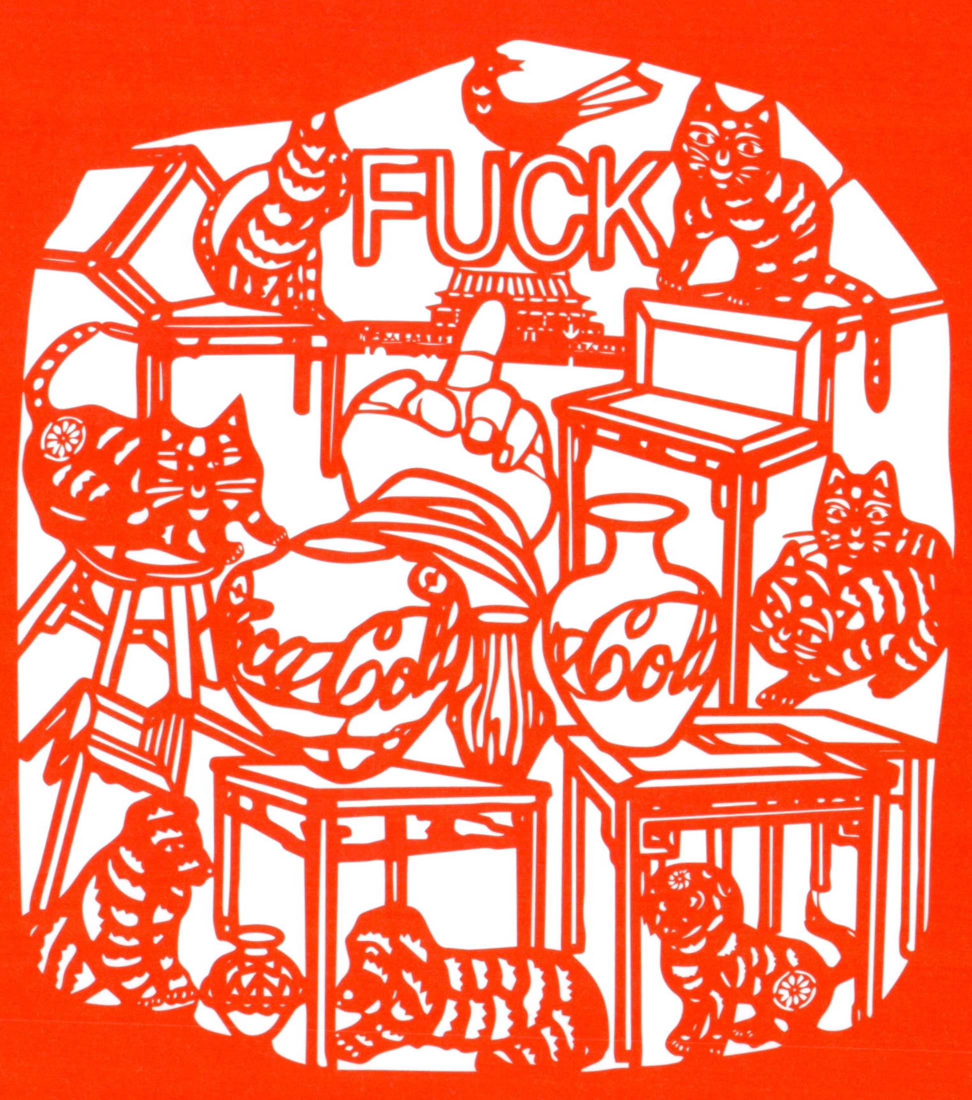

1993–1999 Beijing

"The years after I came back to China were a rather closed era, when all the art events took place underground, when artists were being followed and driven apart like criminals. They were forced to face the facts of being arrested and put into prison. The art events that took place in Beijing's East Village marked the first time that contemporary Chinese art voluntarily took up the theme of existence itself in a sober attitude, focused on the connection between art and existential realities, as well as the spiritual and physical experiences of the artists themselves. I remember how artists would gather in the courtyard where I lived on Alley No. 13 in eastern Beijing to debate concepts and implementations of their works; along with these art discussions, we also talked about preparations to hide or even flee the country." — AI WEIWEI

In den Jahren nach meiner Rückkehr war China eine ziemlich geschlossene Gesellschaft, in der alle Kunstereignisse im Untergrund stattfanden. Künstler wurden überwacht und wie Kriminelle vertrieben. Stets hatte man vor Augen, dass Verhaftung und Gefängnis drohten. Die Veranstaltungen im Pekinger East Village waren das erste Mal, dass sich zeitgenössische chinesische Künstler freiwillig mit dem Thema ihrer Existenz auf nüchterne Art und Weise beschäftigten. Der Blick war auf die Verbindung von Kunst und existentieller Realität gerichtet, auf die eigenen geistigen und körperlichen Erfahrungen. Ich erinnere mich, wie sich die Künstler auf dem Hof bei meiner Wohnung in Gasse Nr. 13 im Osten Pekings versammelten und über Konzepte und Realisierung ihrer Arbeiten diskutierten. Daneben ging es auch darum, in den Untergrund abzutauchen oder sogar aus dem Land zu fliehen.

Quand je suis rentré en Chine, les premières années, la société était vraiment fermée, les événements artistiques étaient tous underground, les artistes étaient poursuivis et séparés comme des criminels. Ils subissaient arrestations et emprisonnements. Avec les manifestations artistiques qui ont eu lieu dans l'East Village de Pékin, c'était la première fois que l'art contemporain chinois envisageait de manière objective le thème de l'existence et se penchait sur les relations entre l'art et les réalités existentielles ainsi que sur les expériences physiques et spirituelles des artistes mêmes. Je me souviens qu'ils se rassemblaient dans ma cour, avenue n° 13, dans l'est de Pékin, pour discuter de leurs concepts et de la réalisation de leurs œuvres, et en marge de ces discussions artistiques, nous parlions aussi de nos préparatifs pour vivre dans la clandestinité ou carrément fuir le pays.

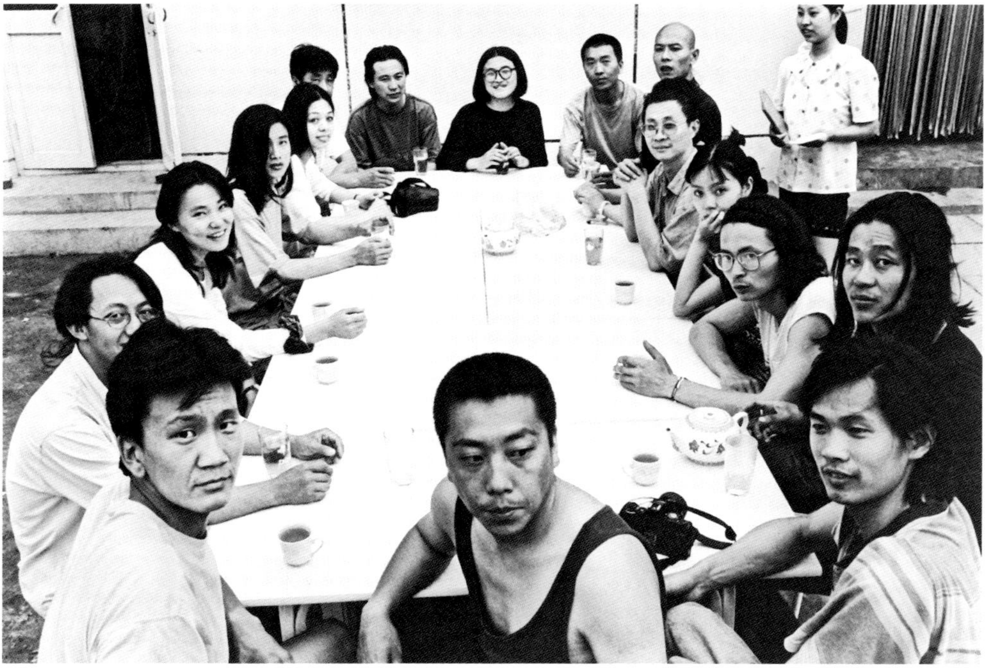

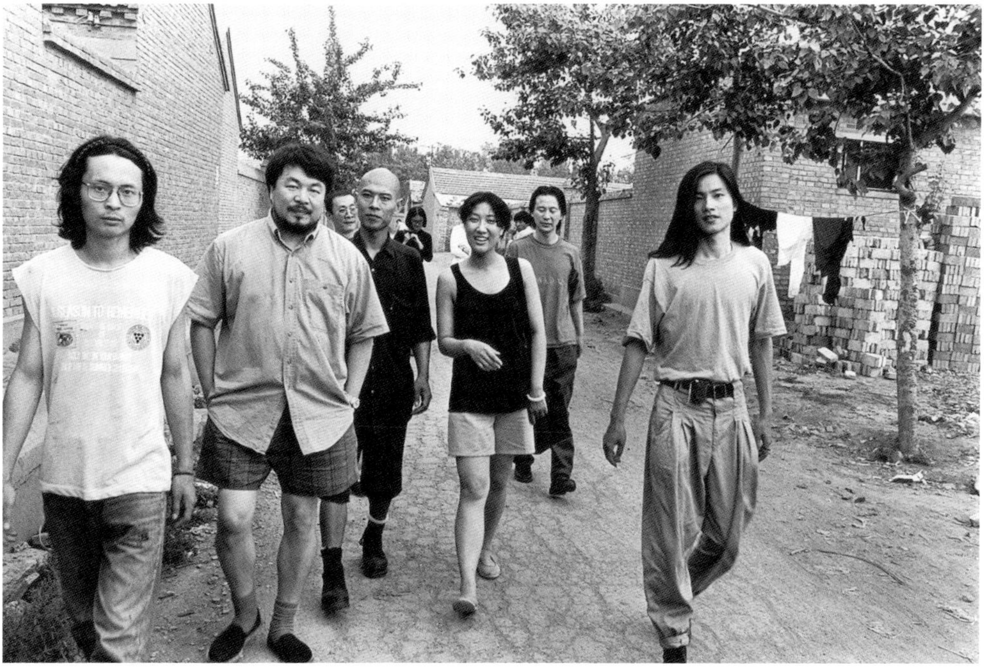

BEIJING PHOTOGRAPHS, 1993–2001, black-and-white photographs, various dimensions:
Last dinner in the East Village, 1994 (top); Last photo in the East Village, 1994 (bottom) | 77

"I saw posters everywhere in Beijing telling people that it was forbidden to set off fireworks. This was right before Spring Festival, when everyone lights fireworks to celebrate. The poster said 'Changing traditions benefits the nation and the people' and I thought it was ironic that a government that had sent tanks to kill students would tell people to change their customs. So I collected some posters and cut pieces out, making a collage so that the finger on one hand became a middle finger on another. This was the first time I used a middle finger in one of my works." — AI WEIWEI

Überall in Peking sah ich Plakate, die den Menschen das Abbrennen von Feuerwerkskörpern verboten. Es war kurz vor dem Frühjahrsfest, das für gewöhnlich jeder mit Feuerwerk feiert. Auf dem Plakat war zu lesen: „Traditionen zu ändern, bringt der Nation und dem Volk Nutzen." Die Ironie war, dass eine Regierung, die Panzer eingesetzt hatte, um Studenten zu töten, ihrem Volk vorschrieb, seine Sitten und Gebräuche zu ändern. Ich sammelte also einige Plakate und schnitt sie derart zurecht, dass der Finger einer Hand zum Mittelfinger an einer anderen wurde. Es war das erste Mal, dass ich einen Mittelfinger in meinen Arbeiten einsetzte.

Partout à Pékin, je voyais des affiches annonçant qu'il était interdit de lancer des feux d'artifice. C'était juste avant le Festival du printemps, où tout le monde lance des feux d'artifice pour célébrer le Nouvel An. L'affiche disait que «modifier certaines traditions était bon pour la nation et les citoyens», et je me suis dit que c'était assez ironique de la part d'un gouvernement qui avait envoyé des chars pour tuer des étudiants de demander aux gens de changer leurs coutumes. J'ai récupéré quelques affiches que j'ai découpées pour en faire un collage sur lequel le doigt d'une main devenait un majeur sur une autre. C'était la première fois que j'utilisais un doigt d'honneur dans mes travaux.

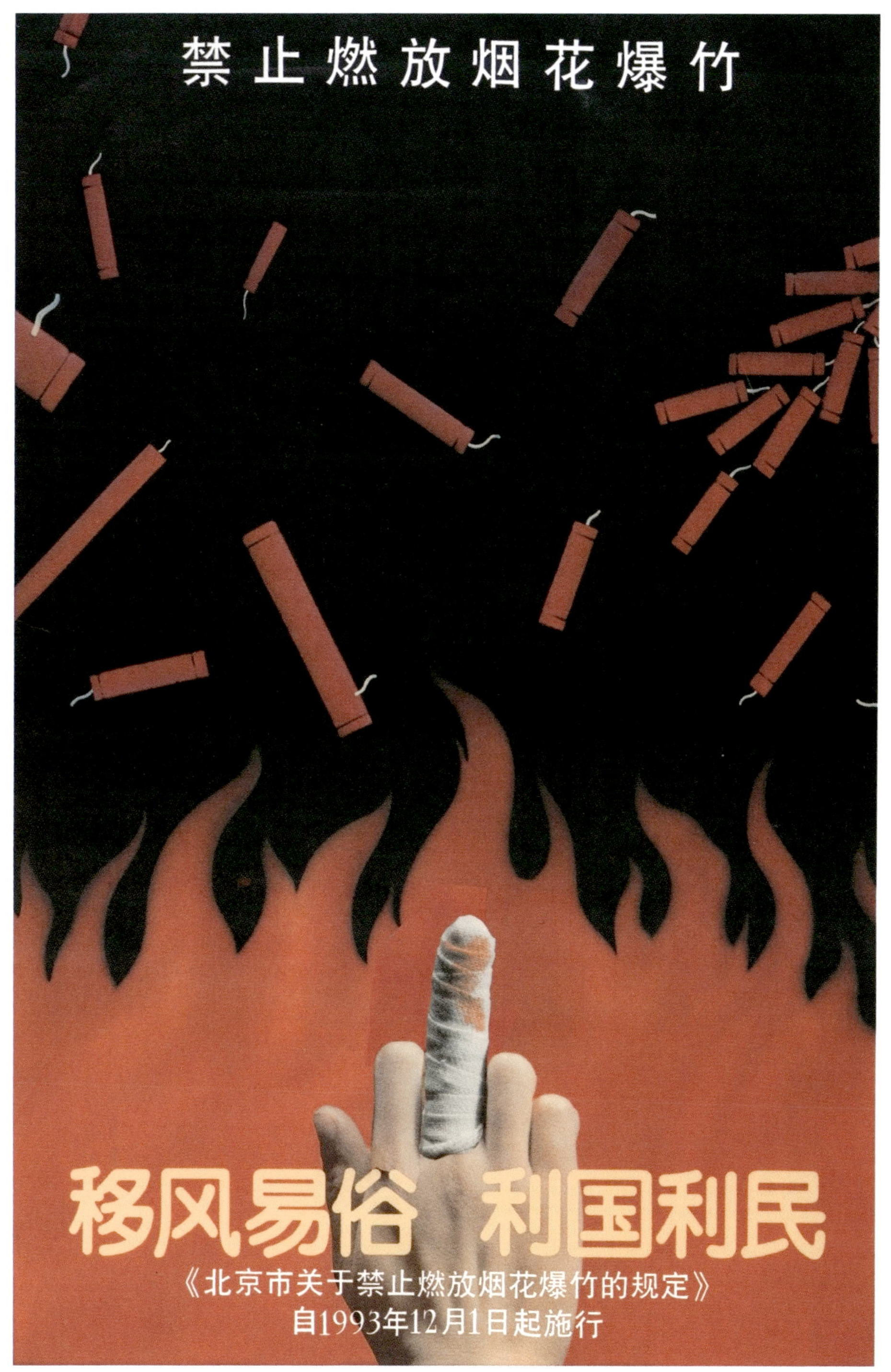

禁止燃放烟花爆竹
移风易俗　利国利民
《北京市关于禁止燃放烟花爆竹的规定》
自1993年12月1日起施行

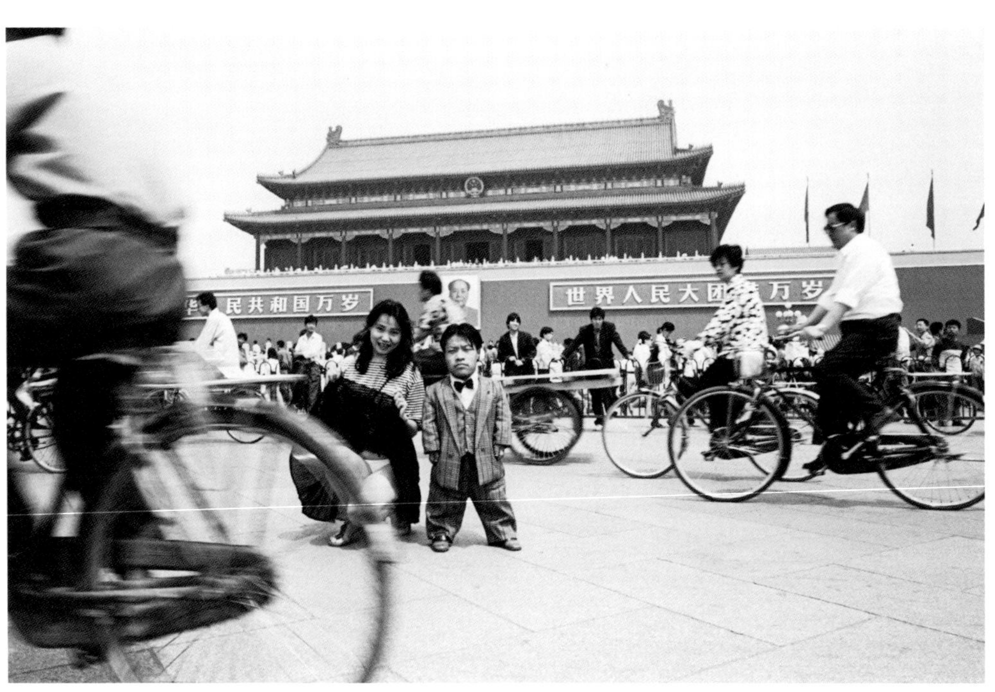

Lu Qing and an unknown tourist at Tiananmen Square, Beijing 1994

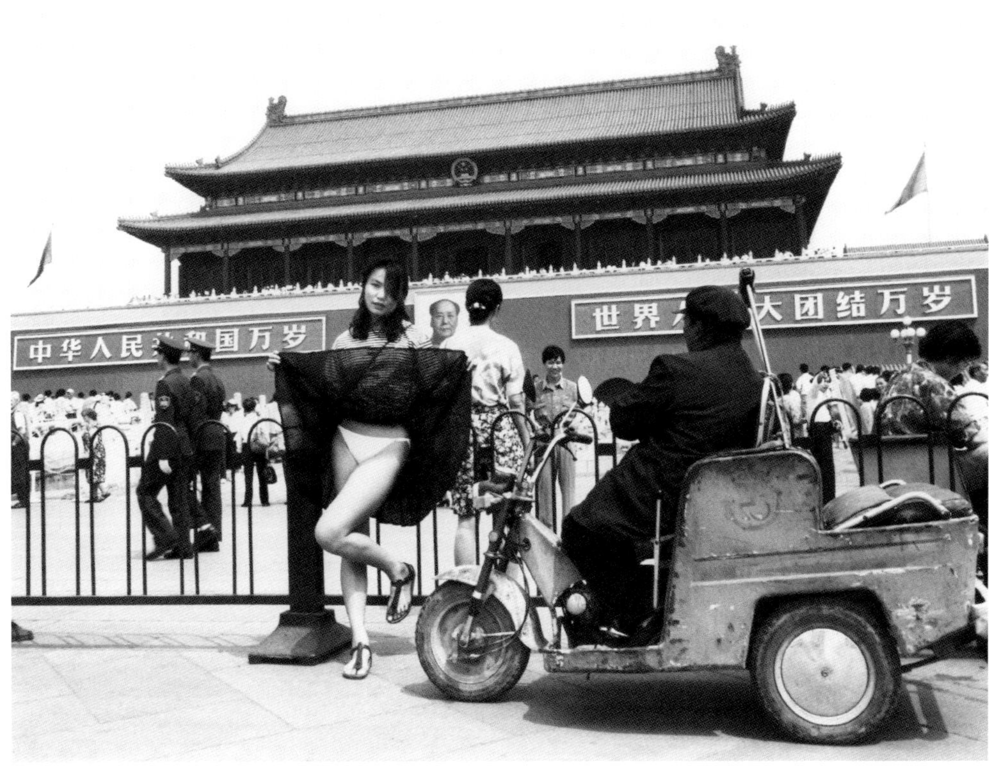

JUNE 1994, 1994, black-and-white photograph, 47⅝ x 61 inches | 81

"Museums in China only serve for propaganda purposes. But they can't
support themselves only on propaganda, so they rent museums out to anybody
who wants to have a show. So I collected all the papers from the National Art
Museum of China about the prices for renting the museum, and the policies you
had to follow if you were going to rent it. And my concept was to rent the whole
space and shut it down for that period. If the museum doesn't function as a
public museum, but rather as an expression of the state's will and power or the
market, my decision was to shut it down." — AI WEIWEI

In China dienen Museen allein Propagandazwecken. Allerdings können sie sich durch
Propaganda nicht finanzieren, und so kann sich jeder, der eine Ausstellung zeigen will,
ein Museum mieten. Ich sammelte also alle Papiere des chinesischen nationalen Kunstmu-
seums, die Informationen über Mietpreise und Nutzungsbedingungen für Mieter enthielten.
Das Konzept der Arbeit bestand darin, das ganze Gebäude zu mieten und für diesen Zeit-
raum zu schließen. Wenn das Museum nicht als öffentliches Museum funktioniert, sondern
nur den Ausdruck des Willens eines Staats oder des Markts darstellt, dann war meine Entscheidung, es einfach zuzumachen.

En Chine, les musées ne sont que des outils de propagande. Mais ils ne peuvent pas vivre
que de ça, alors on loue les musées à des particuliers qui veulent y organiser un événement.
Je me suis procuré les documents du Musée d'Art national de Chine, pour me renseigner
sur les prix et la marche à suivre pour le louer. Mon idée était de le louer et qu'il reste fermé
pendant toute la période de location. Si le musée n'est pas un musée public, mais plutôt
l'expression du pouvoir de l'État ou du marché, alors je fermerai ses portes.

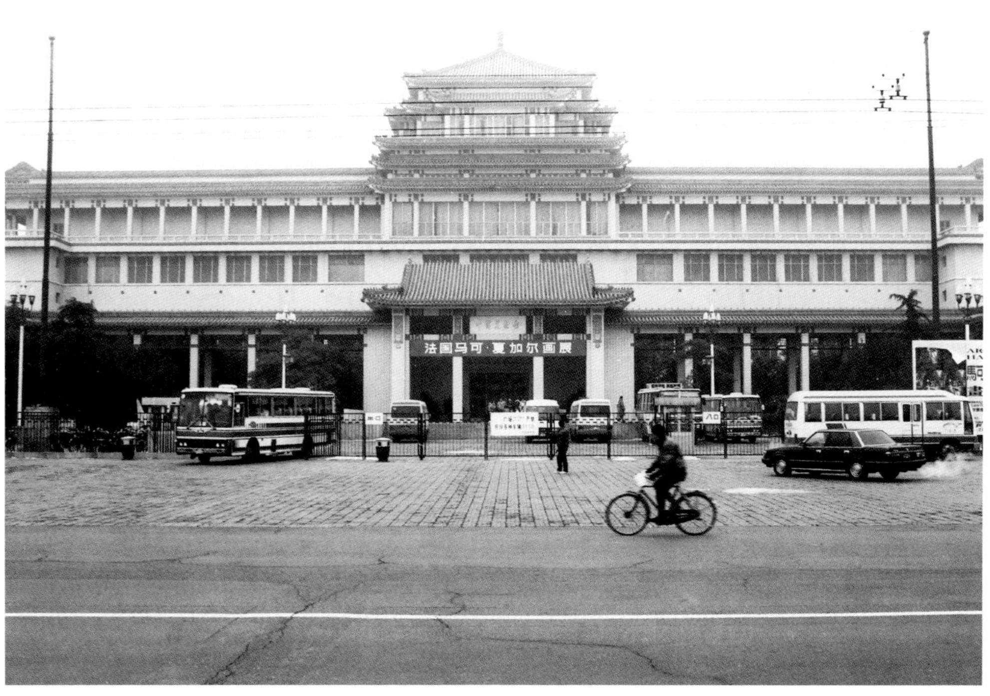

SHUTTING DOWN THE MUSEUM, 1994, black-and-white photograph, dimensions variable | 83

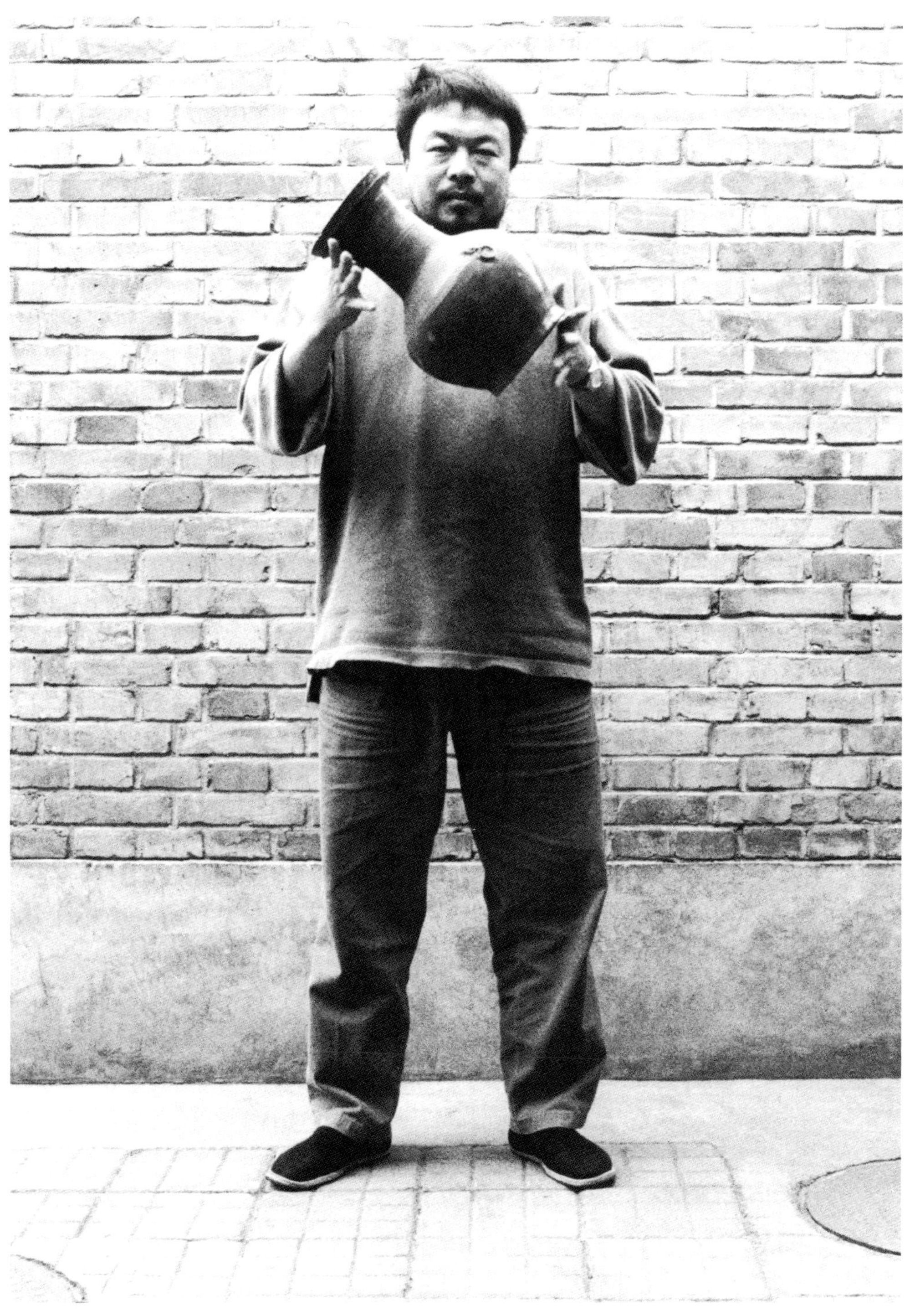

DROPPING A HAN DYNASTY URN, 1995, 3 black-and-white photographs, each 58 ¼ x 47 ⅝ inches (above and overleaf) | 85

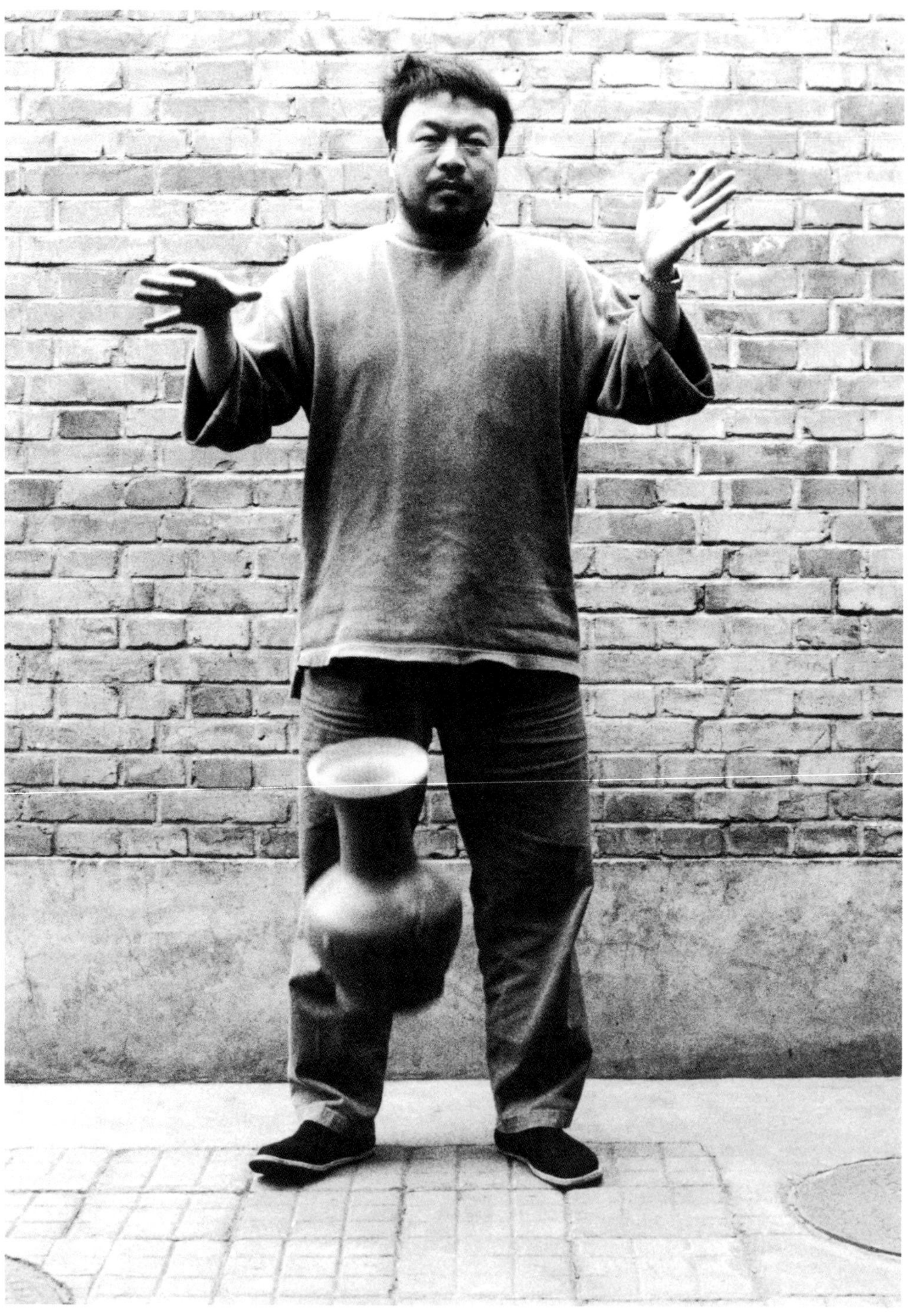

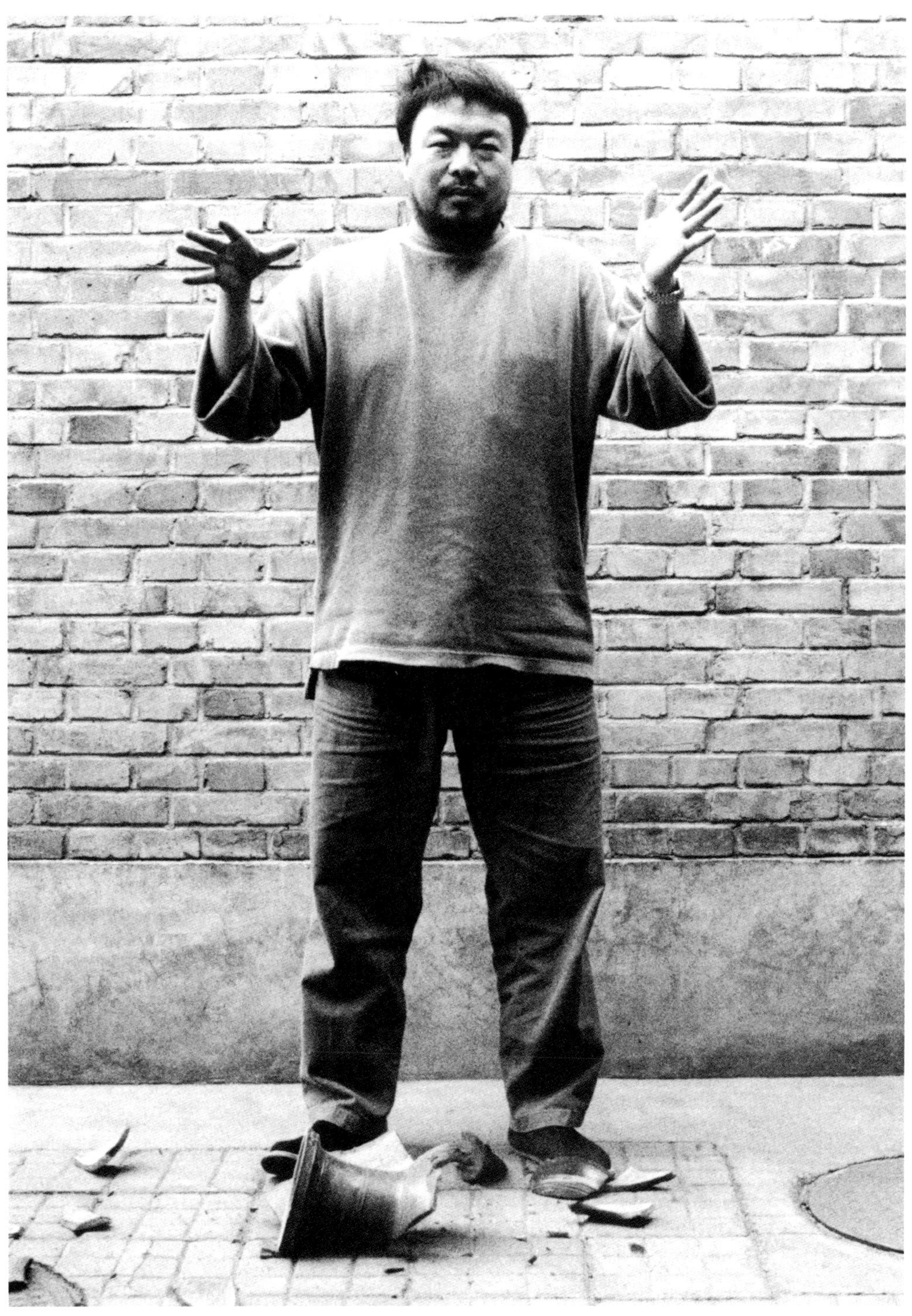

Overleaf: BLUE AND WHITE, 1996, replicas of blue-and-white porcelain from the
Kangxi, Yongzheng, and Qianlong Periods, various dimensions | 87

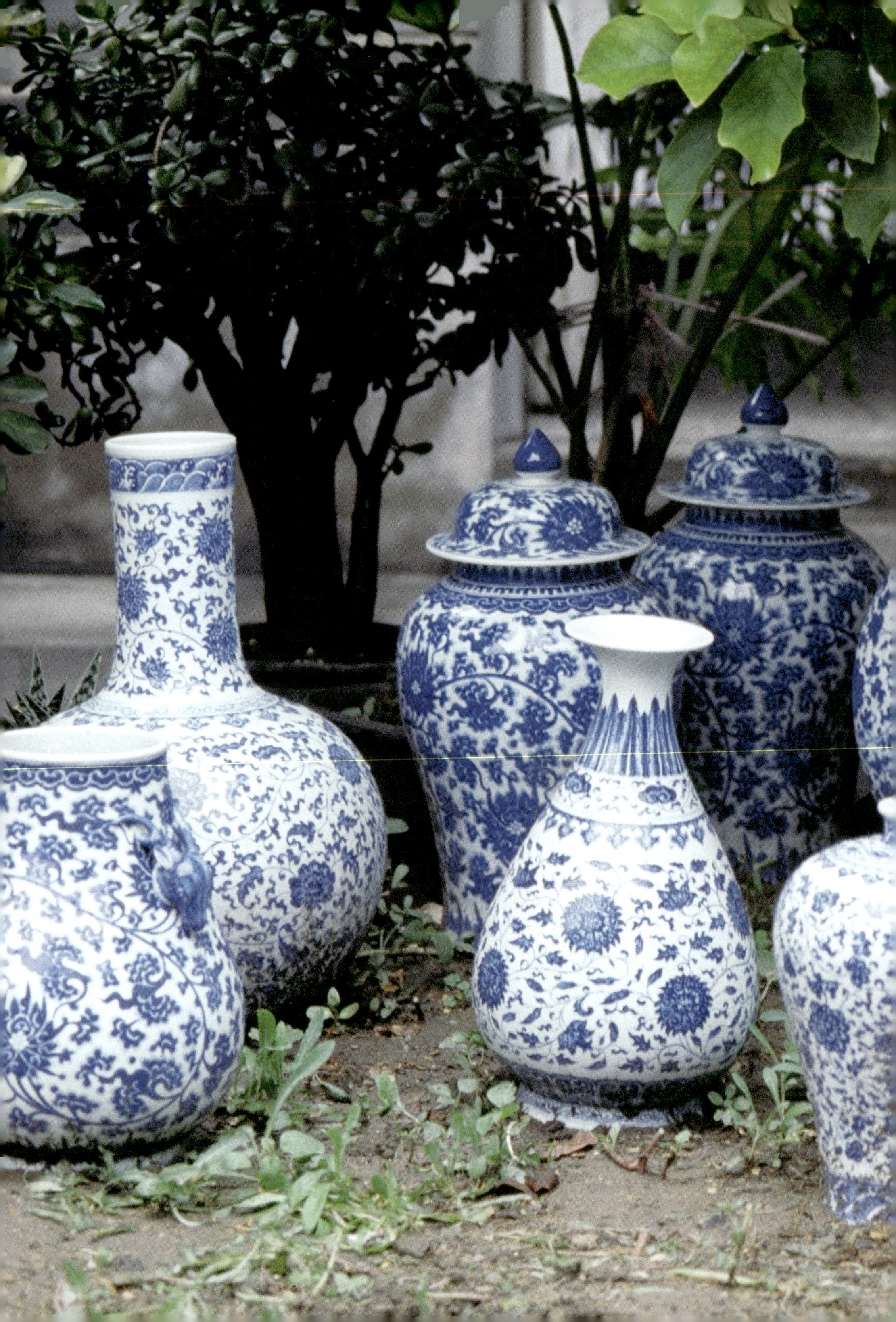

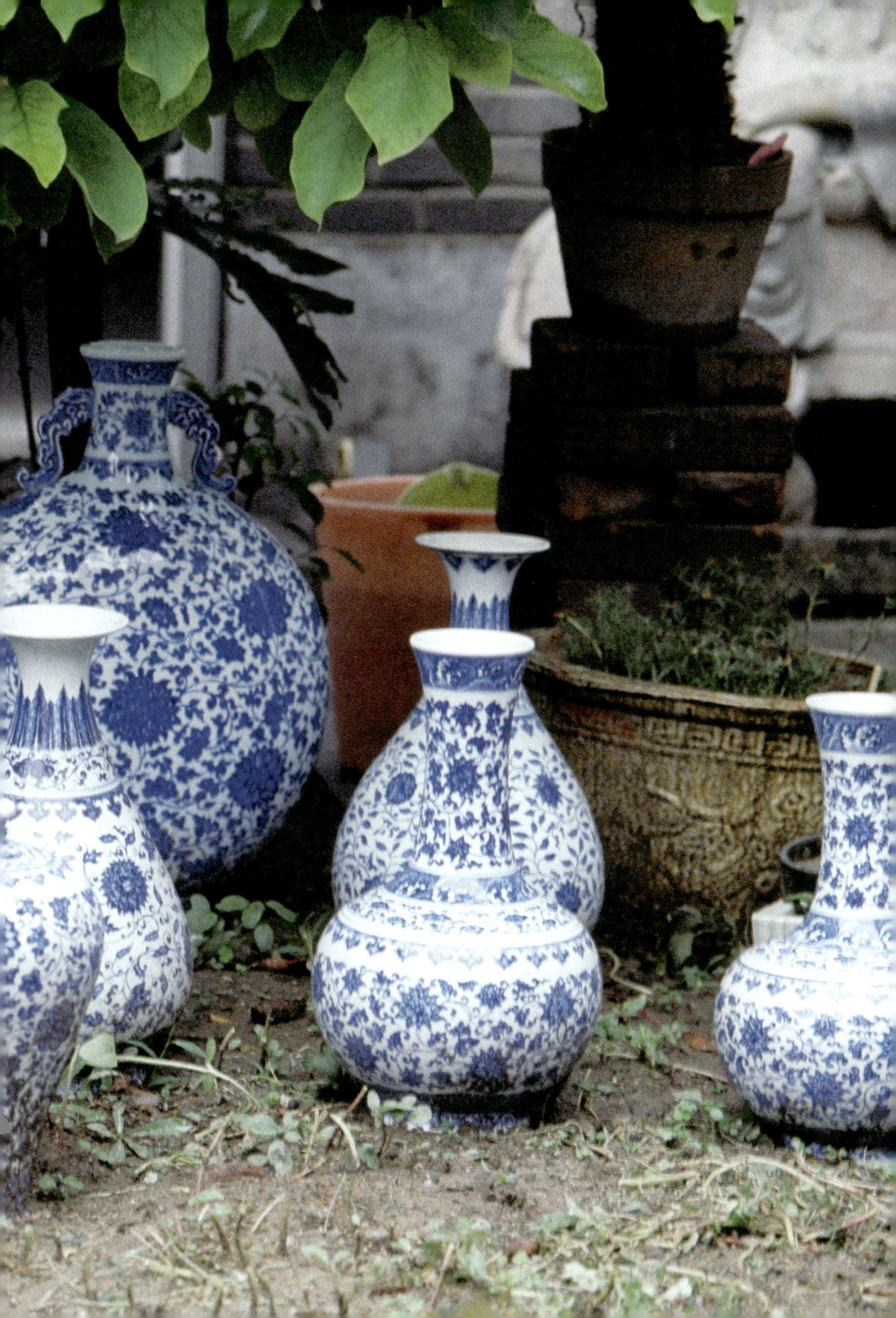

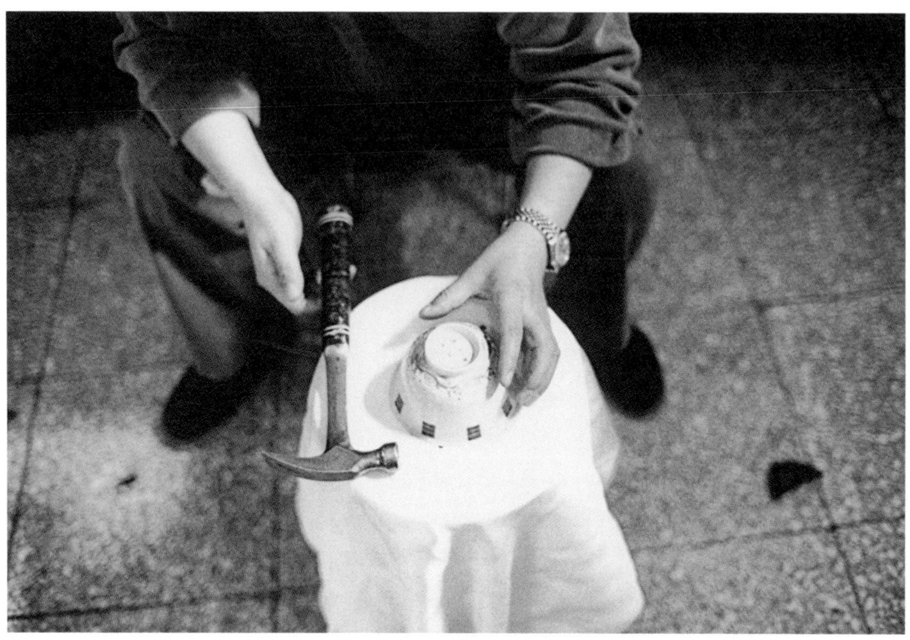

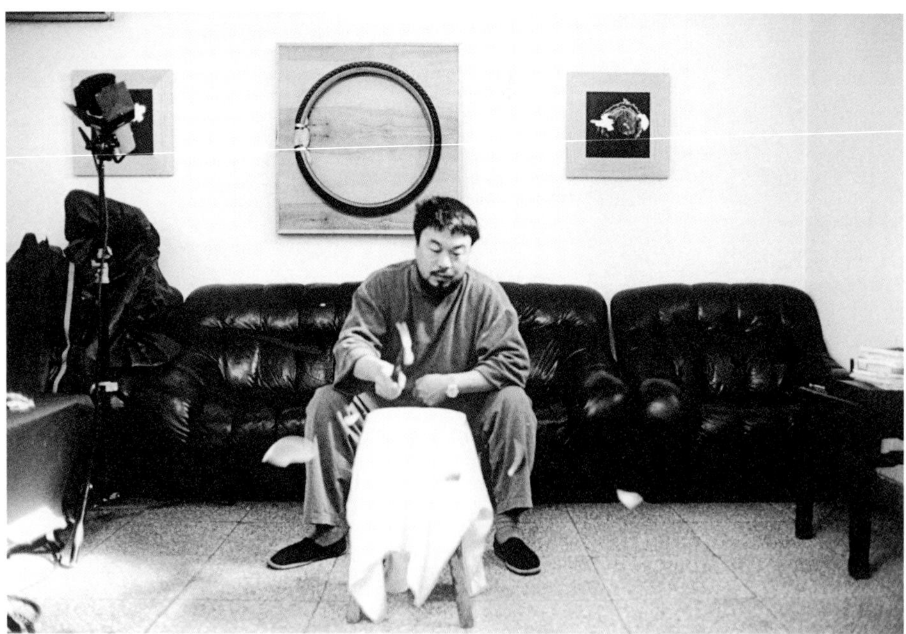

Documentation for *Breaking of Two Blue-and-White Dragon Bowls*, 1996

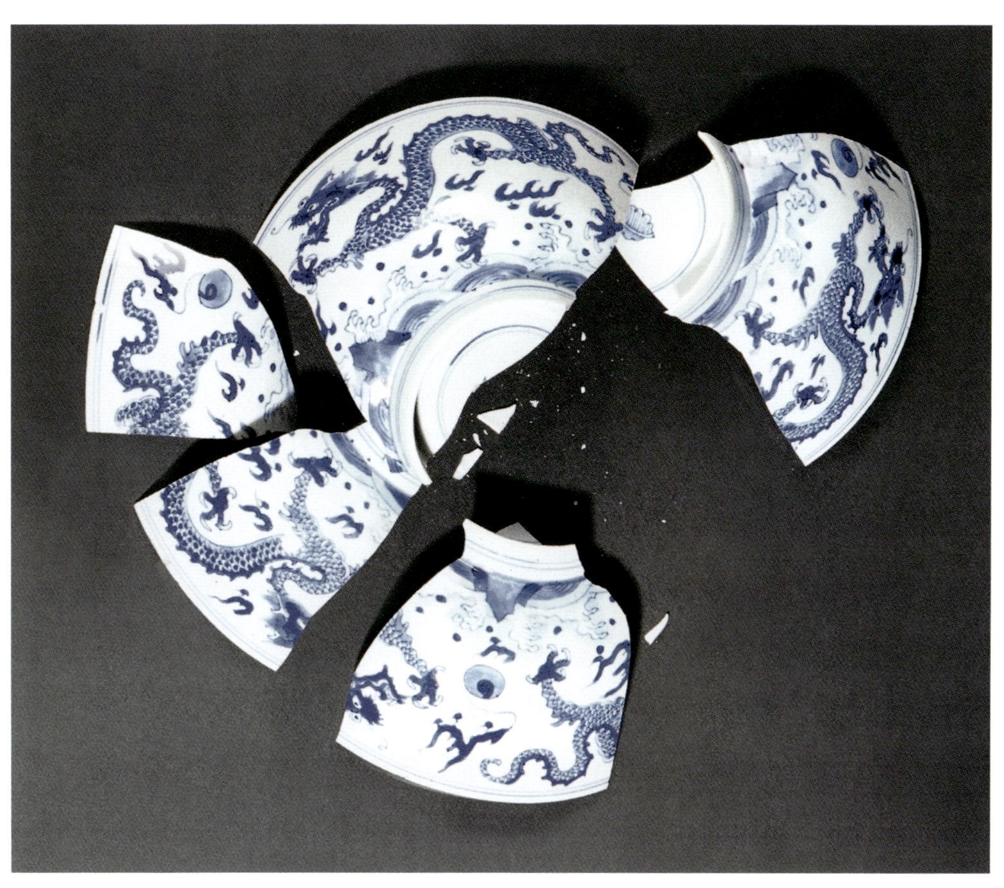

BREAKING OF TWO BLUE-AND-WHITE DRAGON BOWLS, 1996,
blue-and-white dragon bowls, each ø 7 ½ inches | 91

"Most of my activities are about updating or redefining objects. I had this vase for a while, and I admired its shape, but I had nothing to do with it. It just looked so bare, so empty, and I wanted to make it more related to today. To me, the Coca-Cola logo is a clear announcement of property, and of cultural or political identity, but it is also a clear sign to stop thinking. It's full of ignorance, but it's also a redefinition." — AI WEIWEI

In meiner Arbeit geht es meist darum, Objekte zu aktualisieren oder sie neu zu definieren. Diese Vase hatte ich schon eine Weile und bewunderte ihre Form, aber ich wusste nicht, was ich mit ihr tun sollte. Sie sah so kahl aus, so leer, und ich wollte sie irgendwie ins Heute bringen. Für mich ist das Coca-Cola-Logo ein deutlicher Besitzanspruch, ein Zeichen für eine bestimmte kulturelle oder politische Identität, und gleichzeitig ein klares Signal, jetzt das Denken einzustellen. Es ist voller Ignoranz, aber zugleich auch eine Neudefinition.

La plupart de mes travaux tournent autour de l'actualisation ou de la redéfinition de certains objets. Ça faisait un moment que j'avais ce vase, et j'admirais sa forme, mais rien ne me liait à cet objet. Il avait quelque chose de trop simple, de vide, j'avais envie de le rendre plus actuel. Selon moi, le logo de Coca-Cola est une claire revendication de propriété, d'identitié politique ou culturelle, mais c'est aussi une invitation claire à cesser de penser. C'est un symbole d'ignorance, mais aussi une redéfinition.

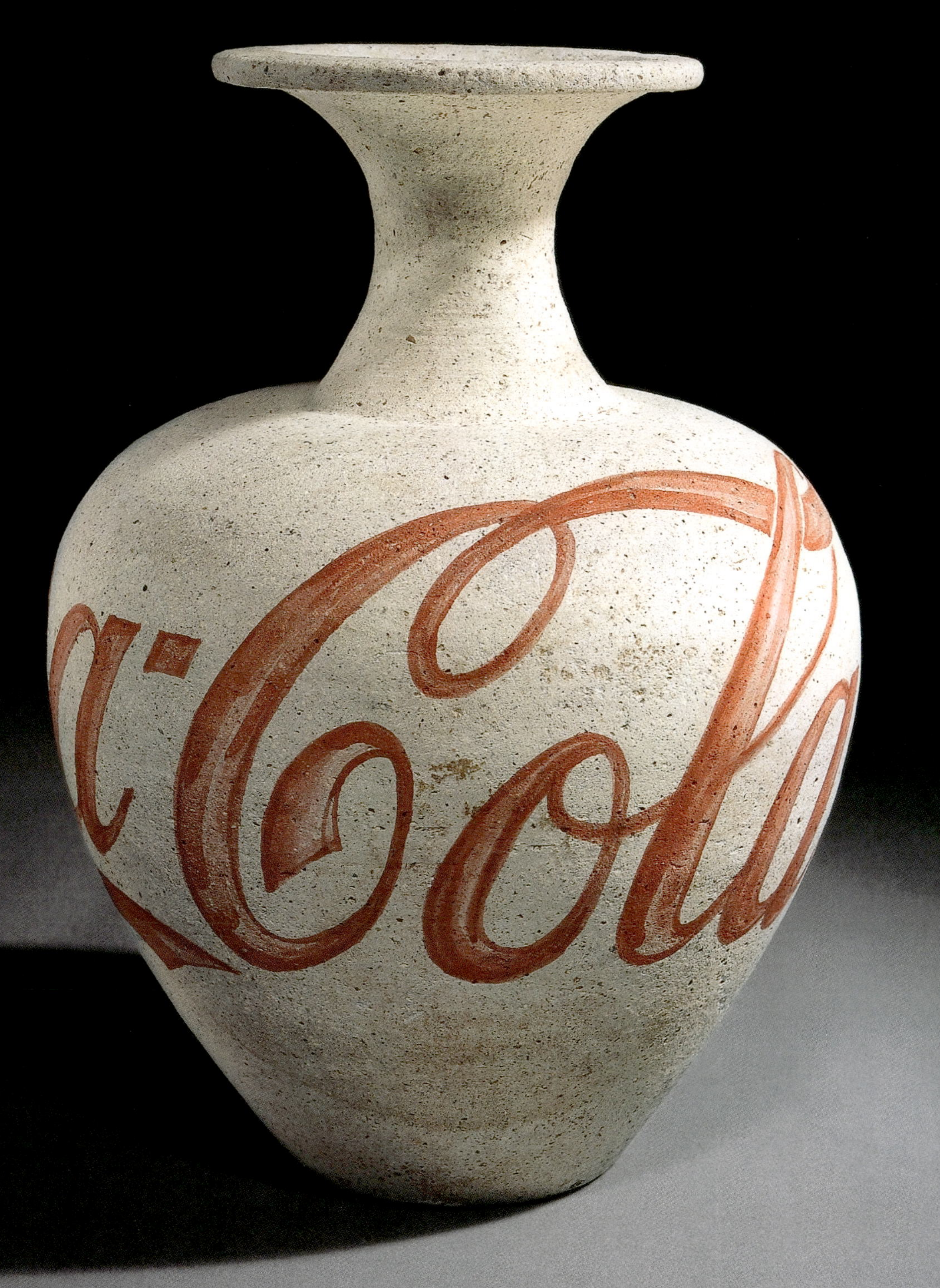

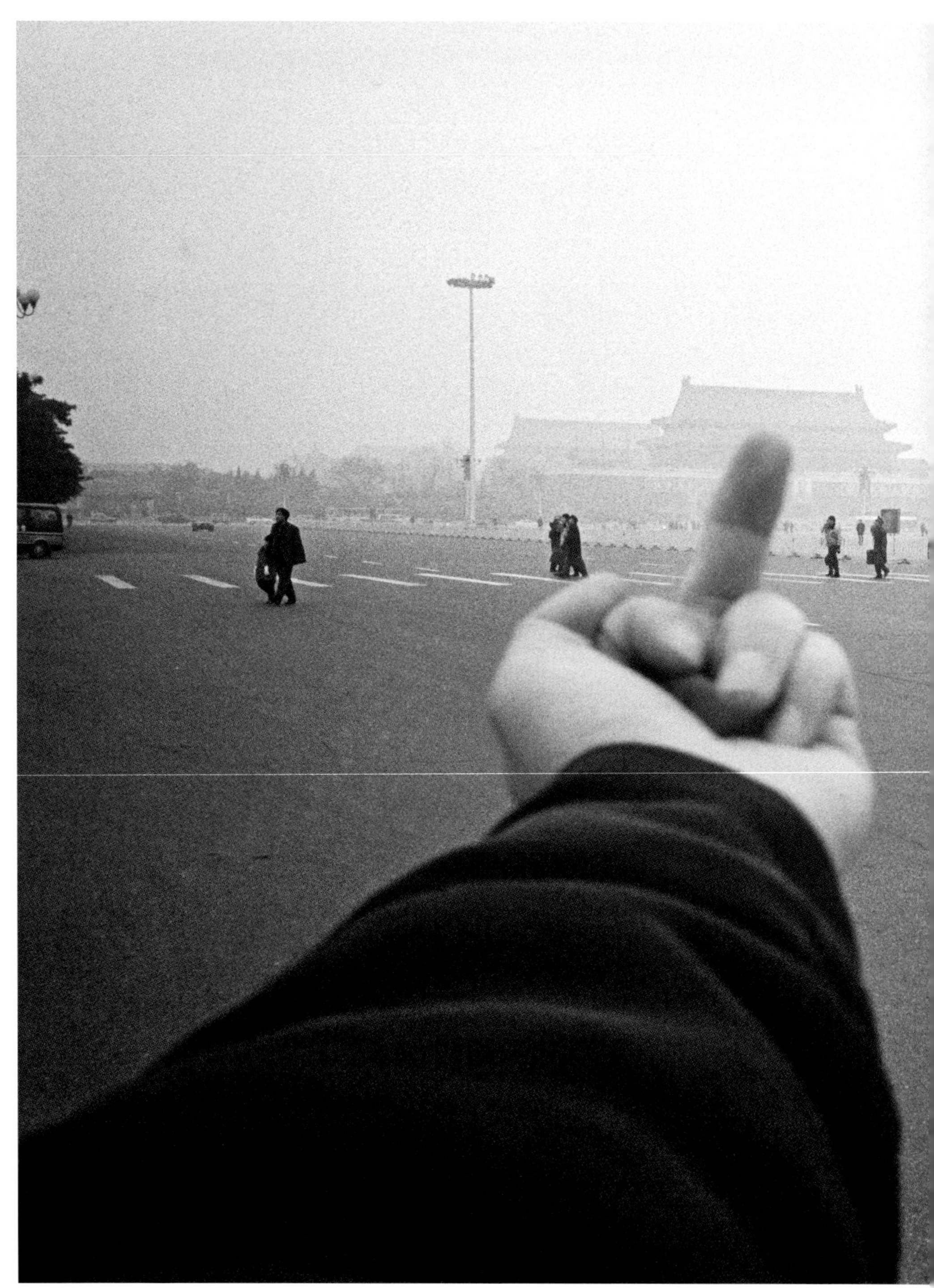

94 | STUDY OF PERSPECTIVE – TIANANMEN, 1995, black-and-white photograph, 35⅜ x 50 inches

广场禁止各种车辆穿行

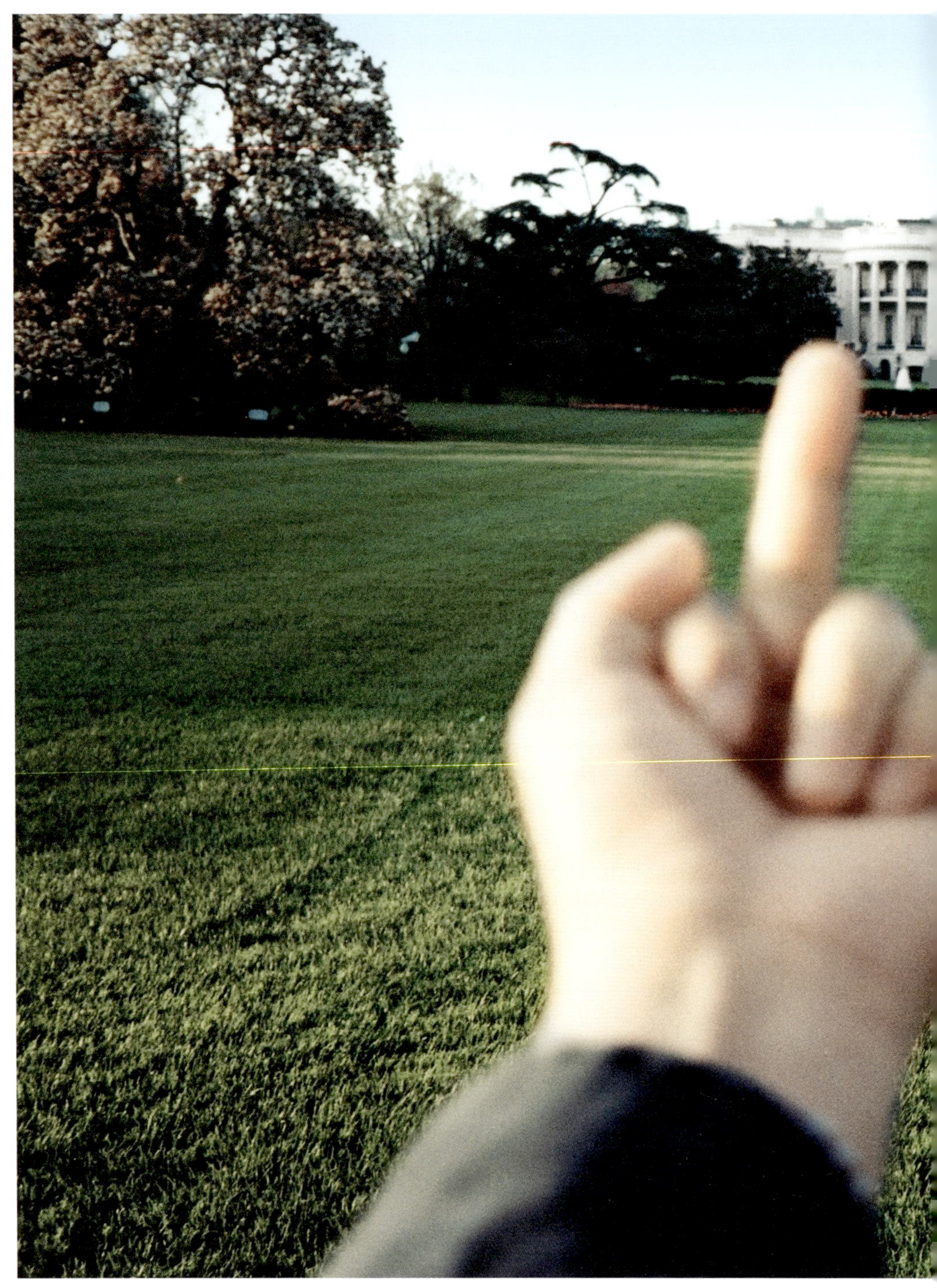

96 | STUDY OF PERSPECTIVE – THE WHITE HOUSE, 1995, color photograph, 35⅜ x 50 inches

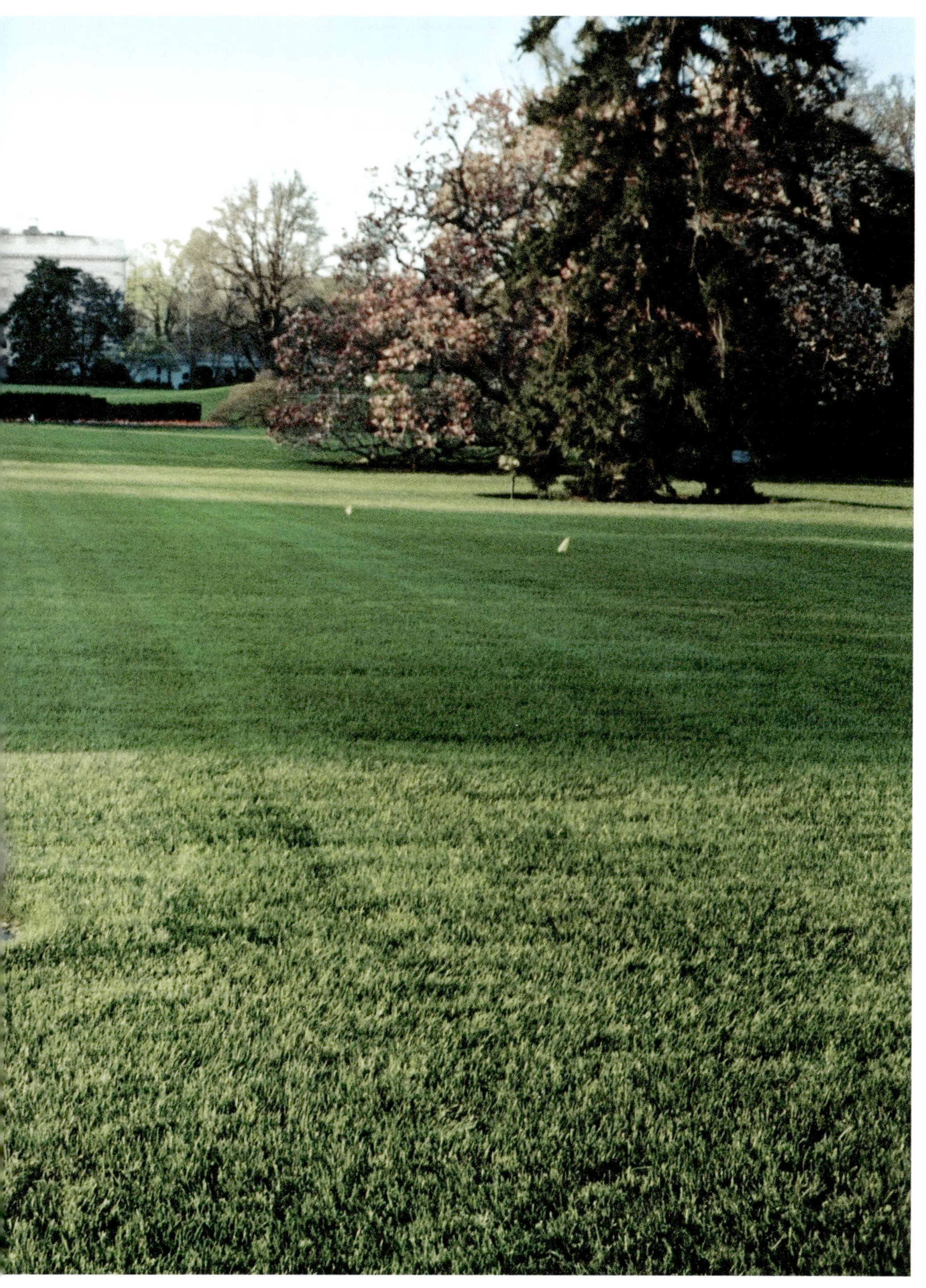

"When I first came back in 1993, the government had tightened control to
the point that there were no galleries and not a single magazine for talking about
art. There were a lot of young artists coming to me who wanted to know what
it's like in New York, why I came back, how we could be recognized. So I thought
I would use my knowledge to create a book for recording that time's activity,
which could be circulated and studied, and could leave us an archive for the future.
First we asked the artists to write about the concept of their works. They all sent
me photos, sculpture; I said none of them can be used. Return everything. Write
down what is in your mind… It was too dangerous to print the books in Beijing.
At that time, you needed your ID just to make photocopies, and all the Xerox
shops had notes saying: 'All copied materials will be submitted to the police.'
We had to make the book secretly in Shenzhen, and eventually printed it in
Hong Kong. In a little motel, Feng Boyi, Lu Qing, and I pasted them together.
So they're basically handmade books." — AI WEIWEI

Als ich 1993 nach China zurückkehrte, hatte die Regierung die Zügel so fest im Griff,
dass es keine Galerien gab und keine einzige Zeitschrift, die über Kunst schrieb. Eine
Menge junger Künstler kamen auf mich zu und wollten wissen, wie es sich in New York lebte,
warum ich zurückgekehrt war, wie wir mehr Anerkennung erlangen könnten. So kam ich
auf die Idee, ein Buch zu machen, das die Aktivitäten jener Zeit aufzeichnen sollte, herum-
gereicht und studiert werden und in Zukunft als Archiv dienen konnte. Zunächst baten wir
die Künstler, über die Konzepte hinter ihren Arbeiten zu schreiben. Alle schickten sie mir
Fotos und Skulpturen. Ich erklärte ihnen, dass wir nichts davon verwenden könnten. Alles
musste zurückgeschickt werden. Sie sollten ihre Gedanken aufschreiben … Es war zu gefährlich, die Bücher in Peking zu drucken. Damals musste man sich ausweisen, wenn man auch
nur fotokopieren wollte. In allen Kopierläden hingen Schilder mit der Aufschrift: „Sämt-
liches Material wird der Polizei vorgelegt." Wir stellten das erste Buch heimlich in Shenzhen
zusammen und ließen es dann in Hongkong drucken. In einem kleinen Motel leimten Feng
Boyi, Lu Qing und ich die Exemplare. Im Grunde sind es handgemachte Bücher.

Quand je suis rentré, en 1993, le gouvernement contrôlait tout, il n'existait plus
une seule galerie, pas un seul magazine qui pouvait parler d'art. Un grand nombre de jeunes
artistes venaient me voir pour me demander comment était New York, pourquoi j'étais rentré, comment faire pour être reconnu. Je me suis dit que j'allais me servir de mes connaissances pour faire un livre retraçant l'activité de cette période, un livre qui pourrait circuler,
qu'on pourrait consulter, et qui serve d'archives pour le futur. Nous avons demandé aux
artistes d'exposer les concepts de leurs travaux. Ils m'ont tous envoyé des photos de leurs
sculptures, etc., mais pour moi il n'y avait rien d'utilisable. J'ai tout renvoyé, je leur ai
dit d'écrire ce qu'ils avaient en tête… Imprimer les livres à Pékin aurait été trop dangereux.
Á l'époque, il fallait présenter sa carte d'identité pour faire de simples photocopies, d'ailleurs toutes les boutiques de photocopies avaient affiché cette note : «Tout matériel photo-
copié sera transmis à la police.» Nous avons dû faire ce livre en secret, à Shenzhen, et nous
l'avons imprimé à Hong Kong. Feng Boyi, Lu Qing et moi avons relié les livres dans un petit
motel. Ce sont vraiment des livres faits main.

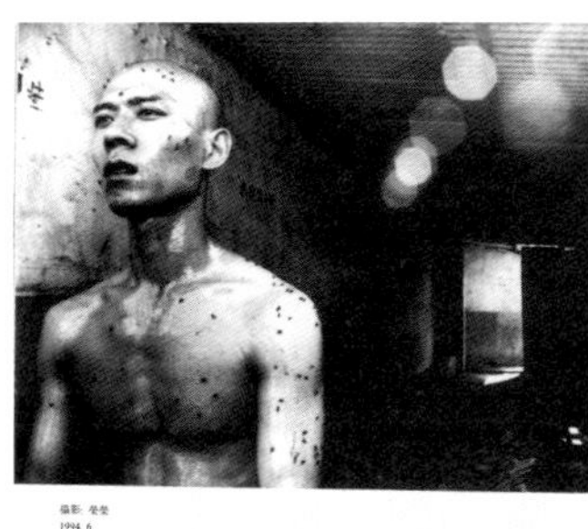

攝影 榮榮
1994. 6.

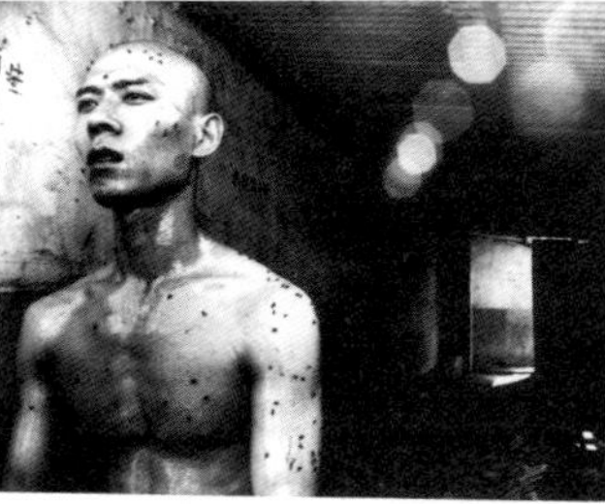

阿 仙

藝術*《正未計劃草案》

1. 媒介：A. 國際聯網電腦系統；
   B. 國際性重要報刊、重要藝術期刊；
   C. 國際性大都市的最主要廣告牌（最好是電子廣告屏幕）。
2. 樣式：以現代廣告模式，通過上述媒介向全世界盡可能多的國家和地區發出邀請，大量的"藝術征求"(ART* WANTED)信息，并收集信息反饋。
3. 實施：A. 選擇確定：
   ① 分布于不同國家和地區的國際重要都市中最主要的巨幅廣告牌，如紐約時代廣場、東京銀座、北京站廣場、于容街、天安門廣場及香港、臺北、悉尼、巴黎、編義、柏林、莫斯科、馬德里、羅馬、威尼斯等；
   ② 若干國際性報刊、藝術期刊，如《TIME》、《NEWS WEEK》、《ASIA WEEK》、《FLASH ART》、《ART IN AMERICA》、《ART AND AUSTRALIA》、《藝術家》等。
   ③ 國際電腦網絡。
   B. 發函咨詢，向廣告公司、報刊、期刊編輯部發函征求：
   ① 巨幅普通/電子廣告牌租用方式和對應價格；
   ② 報紙、期刊對一次全頁廣告的報價；
   C. 作出預算。

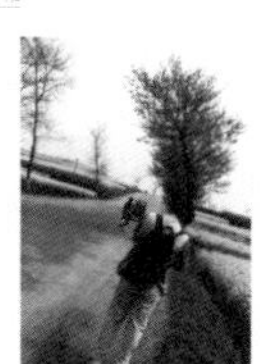

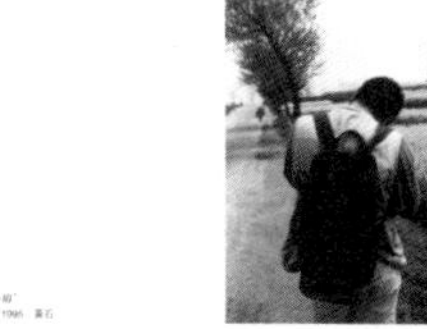

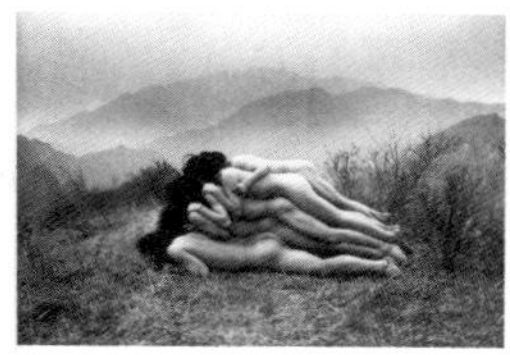

中國北京 · 一九九五

"When I began making furniture works, I was collecting antique furniture
and had learned quite a bit about it. I didn't want to make anything new. I wanted
to use the old, and use its own logic, because antique Chinese furniture has a
very special way of construction. Very clear, very principled about proportion and
structure and always made according to the type of wood. There's no nails, yet
even if the table is used for a hundred years, it will never break. It really reflects
the Chinese understanding of aesthetics and their relation with nature. So I
wanted to reconstruct or to disturb or to destroy the original, but without traces.
We took great care with the cutting and sanding to make sure the patina of the
furniture looked untouched; even an expert would be confused because everything
is so perfect." — AI WEIWEI

Als ich anfing, mit Möbeln zu arbeiten, hatte ich bereits eine Zeitlang antike Stücke
gesammelt und einiges darüber gelernt. Ich wollte nichts Neues machen. Ich wollte das Alte
benutzen, die ihm eigene Logik, weil antike chinesische Möbel eine höchst spezielle Bau-
weise besitzen. Sehr klar, äußerst prinzipientreu in Proportion und Struktur und immer
der Holzsorte gemäß angefertigt. Es gibt keine Nägel, dennoch wird der Tisch auch nach
100 Jahren Gebrauch keinesfalls brechen. Das ist wirklich das chinesische Verständnis von
Ästhetik und Verhältnis zur Natur. Mein Plan war also, Originale neu zu konstruieren oder
ihrer Funktion zu berauben oder zu zerstören, allerdings ohne Spuren zu hinterlassen.
Wir gaben uns die größte Mühe beim Sägen und Schleifen, damit die Patina der Möbel un-
berührt aussah. Selbst Experten sollten verwirrt sein, weil alles so perfekt ist.

Lorsque j'ai commencé à travailler avec des meubles, je collectionnais les meubles
anciens, et j'avais appris pas mal de choses sur le sujet. Je ne voulais pas faire quelque chose
de neuf. Je voulais utiliser l'ancien, et utiliser sa propre logique, car les meubles chinois
anciens étaient fabriqués d'une manière très spéciale. Leur ligne était toujours claire, on se
préoccupait beaucoup des proportions et de la structure, et le mode de fabrication dépen-
dait toujours du type de bois. Dans une table, il n'y avait aucun clou, on pouvait l'utiliser
pendant cent ans sans jamais qu'elle casse. Cela reflète vraiment l'idée que les Chinois ont
de l'esthétique et leur relation à la nature. J'ai voulu reconstruire, déranger ou détruire
l'original, mais sans laisser de traces. Nous avons coupé et poncé avec le plus grand soin
pour faire en sorte que la patine du meuble ait l'air intacte, pour que même un expert soit
troublé par la perfection de notre travail.

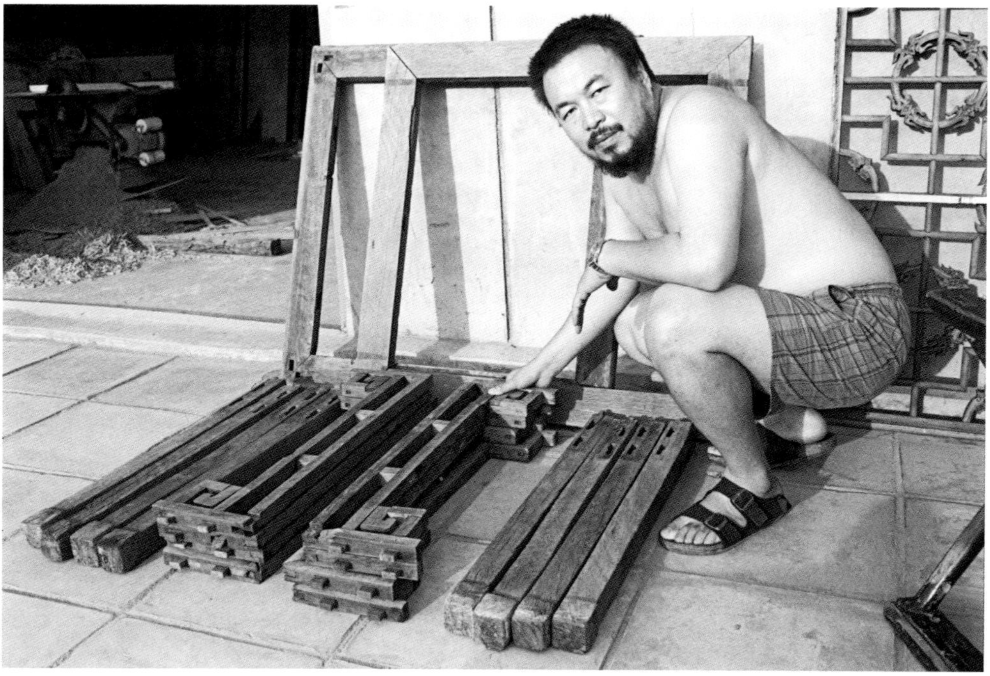

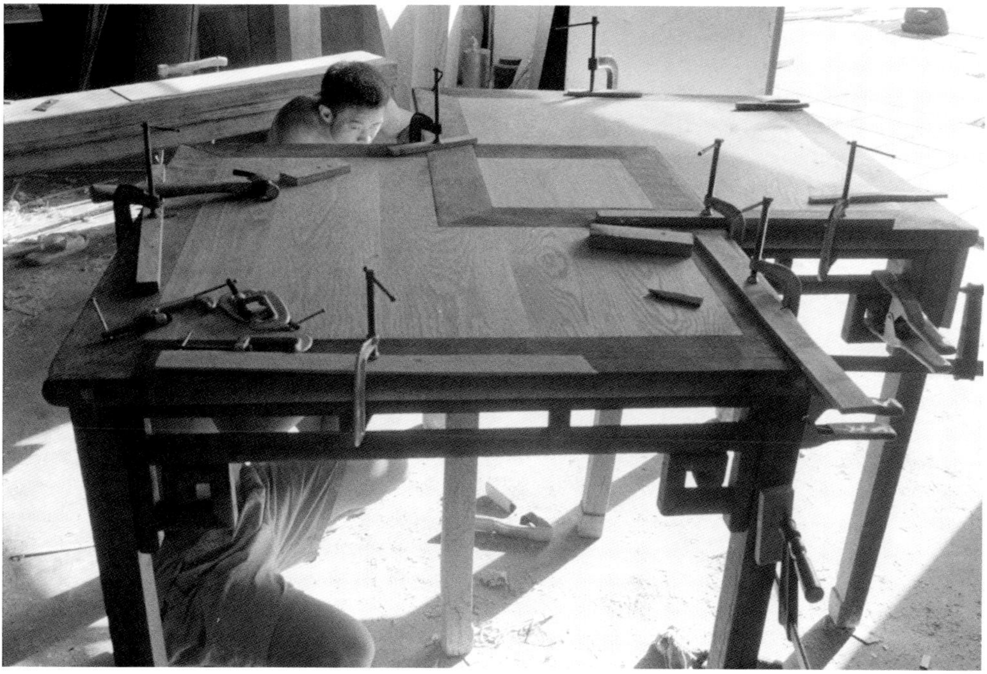

Production views of TABLES WITH CROSSED CORNERS, 1998, Qing Dynasty tables,
31 ½ x 35 ⅜ x 51 ⅛ inches | 101

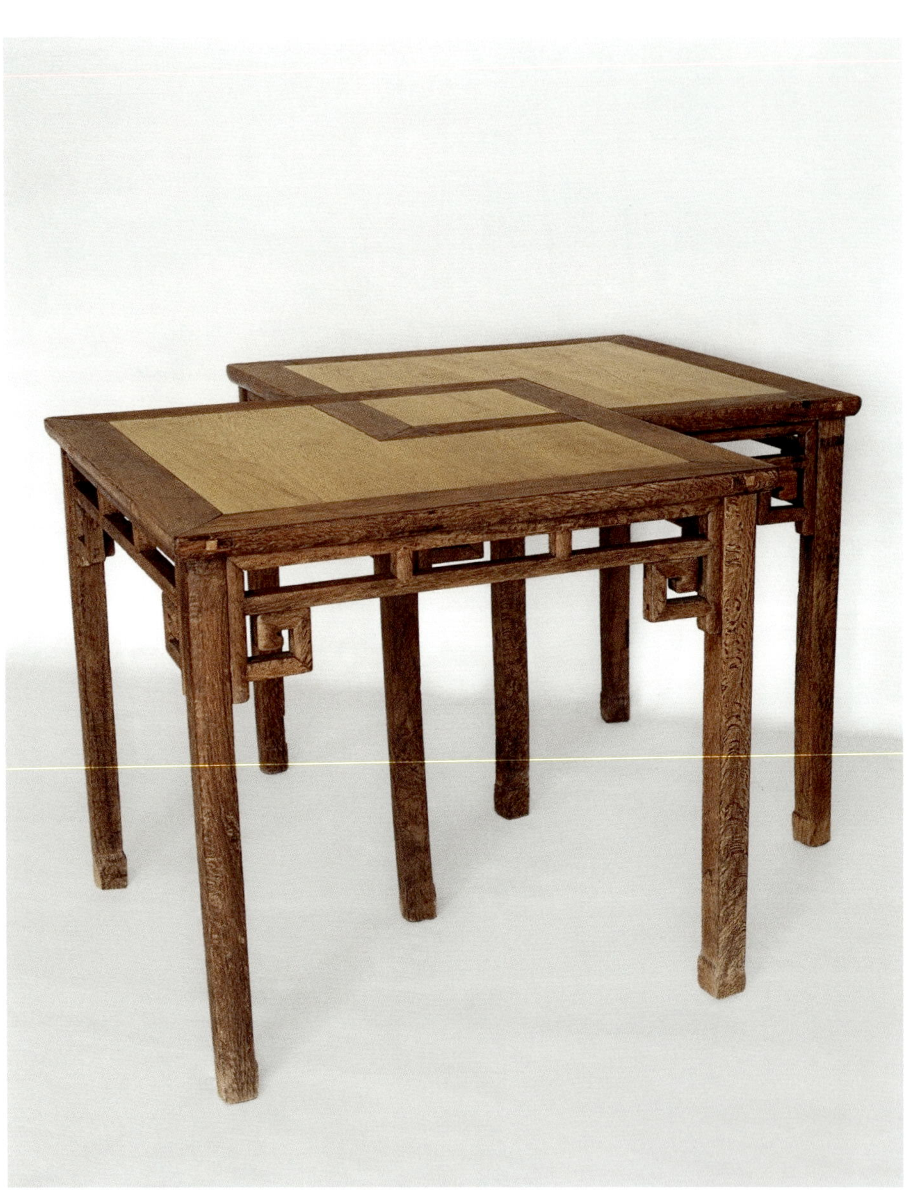

TABLES WITH CROSSED CORNERS, 1998, Qing Dynasty tables, 31 ½ x 35 ⅜ x 51 ⅛ inches
102 | Opposite: TABLE WITH TWO LEGS ON THE WALL, 1997, Qing Dynasty table, 35 ⅝ x 46 ½ x 48 inches

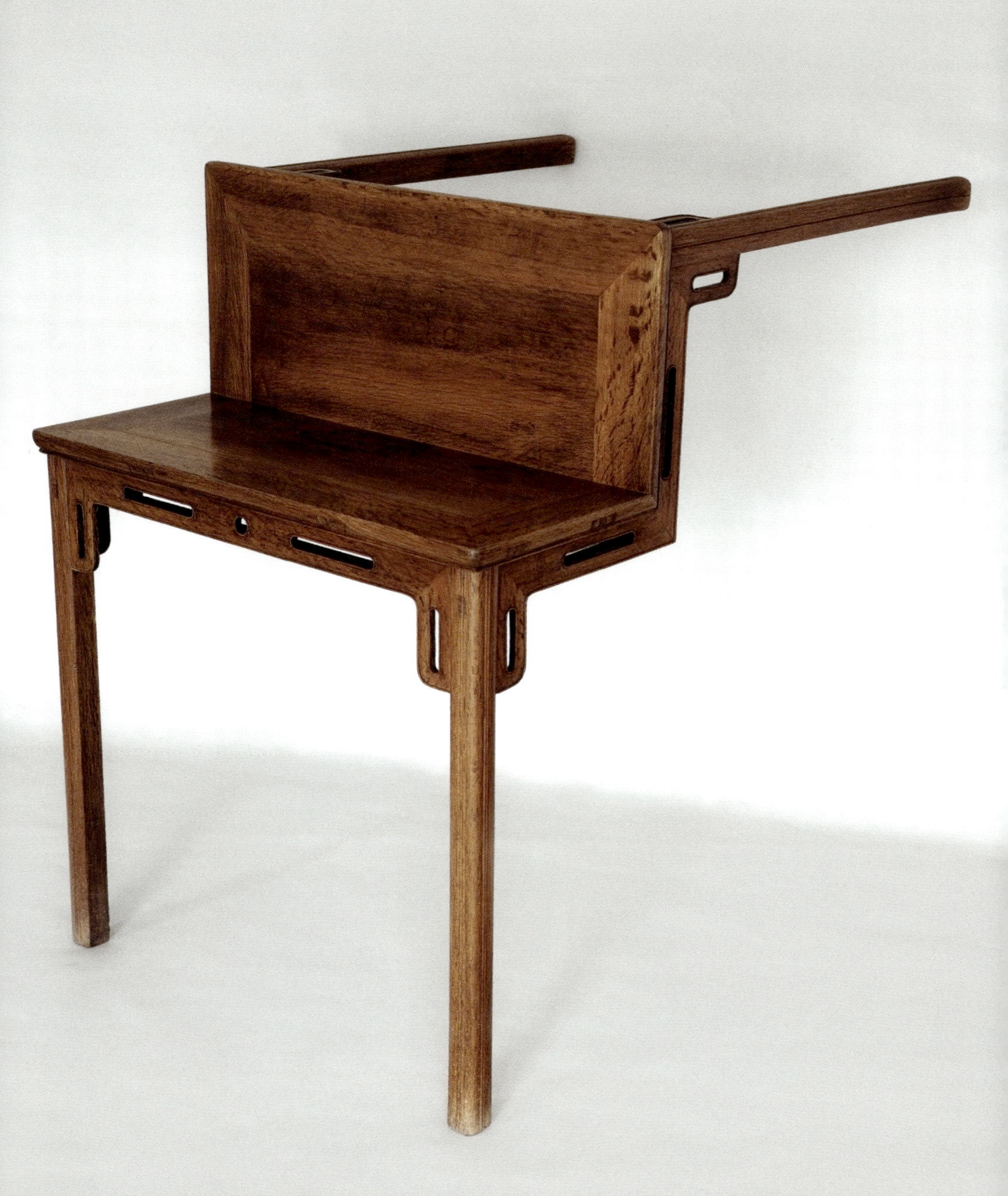

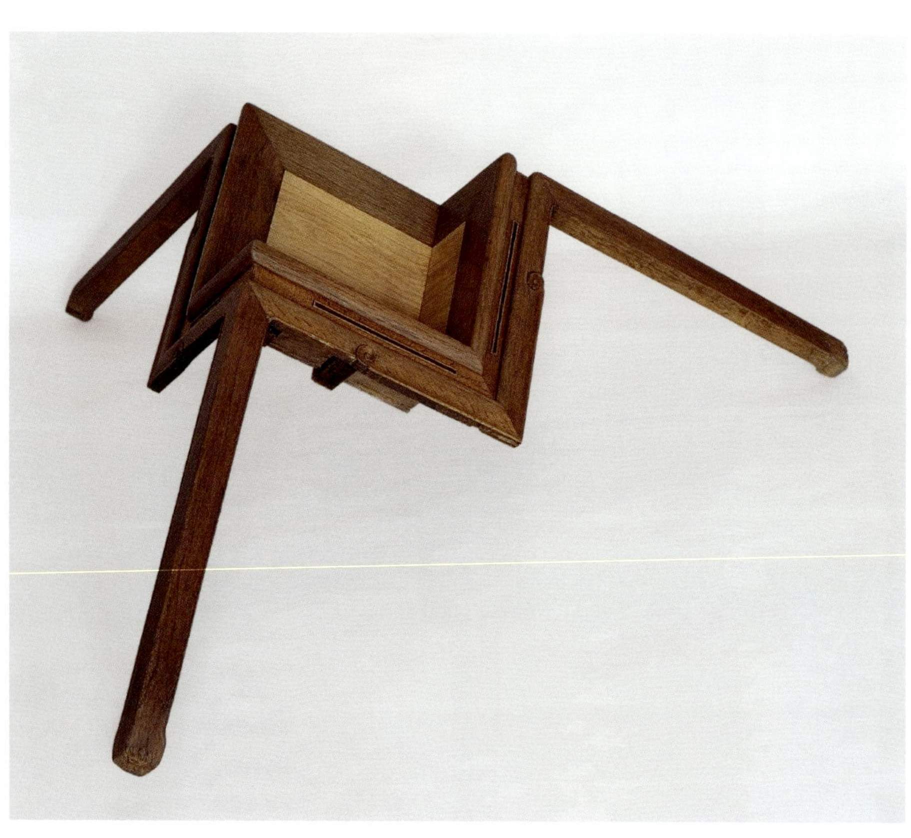

TABLE WITH THREE LEGS, 1998, Qing Dynasty table, 35 ⅞ x 40 ⅛ x 67 ¾ inches
104 | Opposite: TABLES AT RIGHT ANGLES, 1998, Qing Dynasty tables, 68 ⅞ x 49 ⅝ x 68 ½ inches

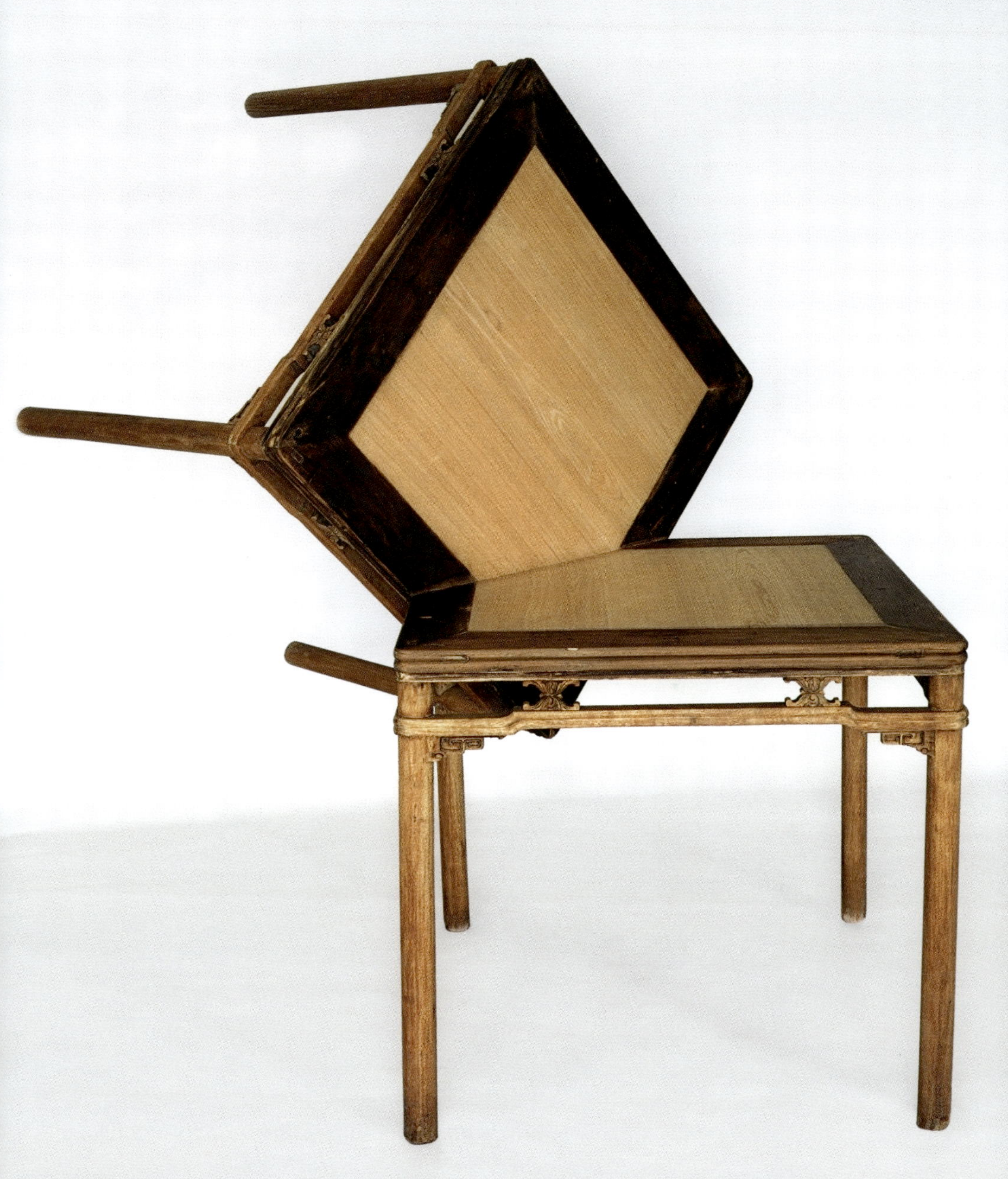

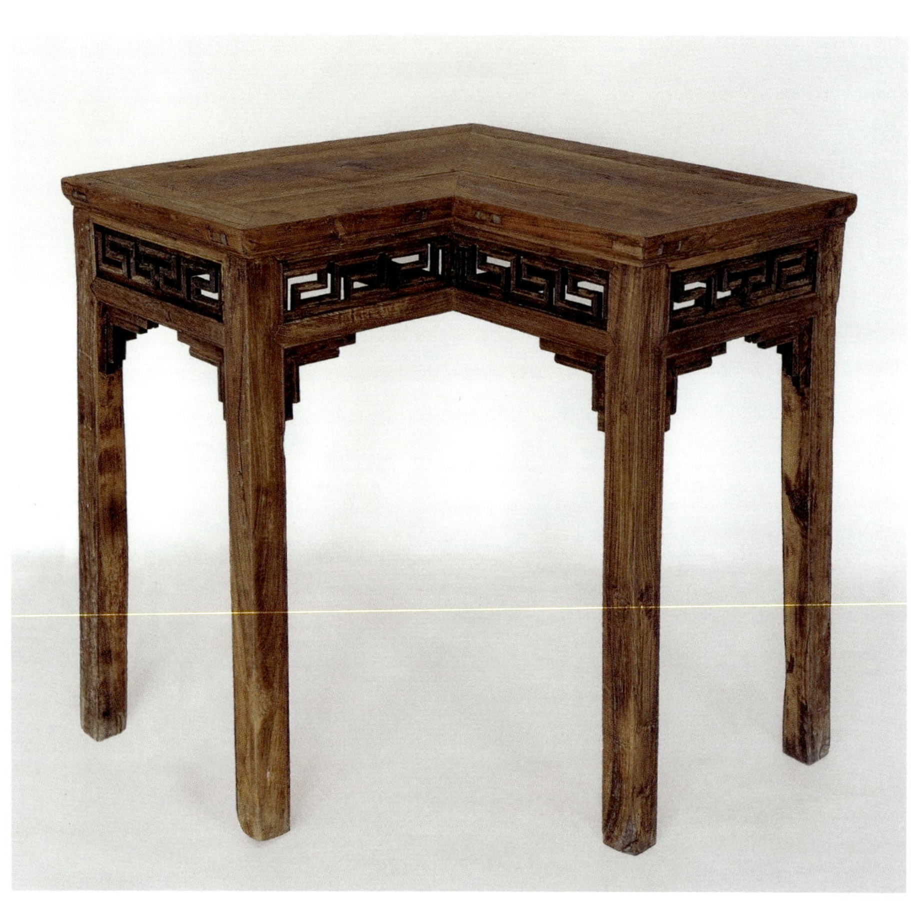

CORNERED TABLE, 1997, Qing Dynasty table, 34 ⅝ x 35 ⅜ x 35 ⅜ inches
Opposite: CROSSED TABLES, 1997, Qing Dynasty tables, 33 ⅞ x 79 ½ x 79 ½ inches (top);
106 | CROSSED TABLES, 1997, Qing Dynasty tables, 33 ⅞ x 44 ½ x 81 ⅛ inches (bottom)

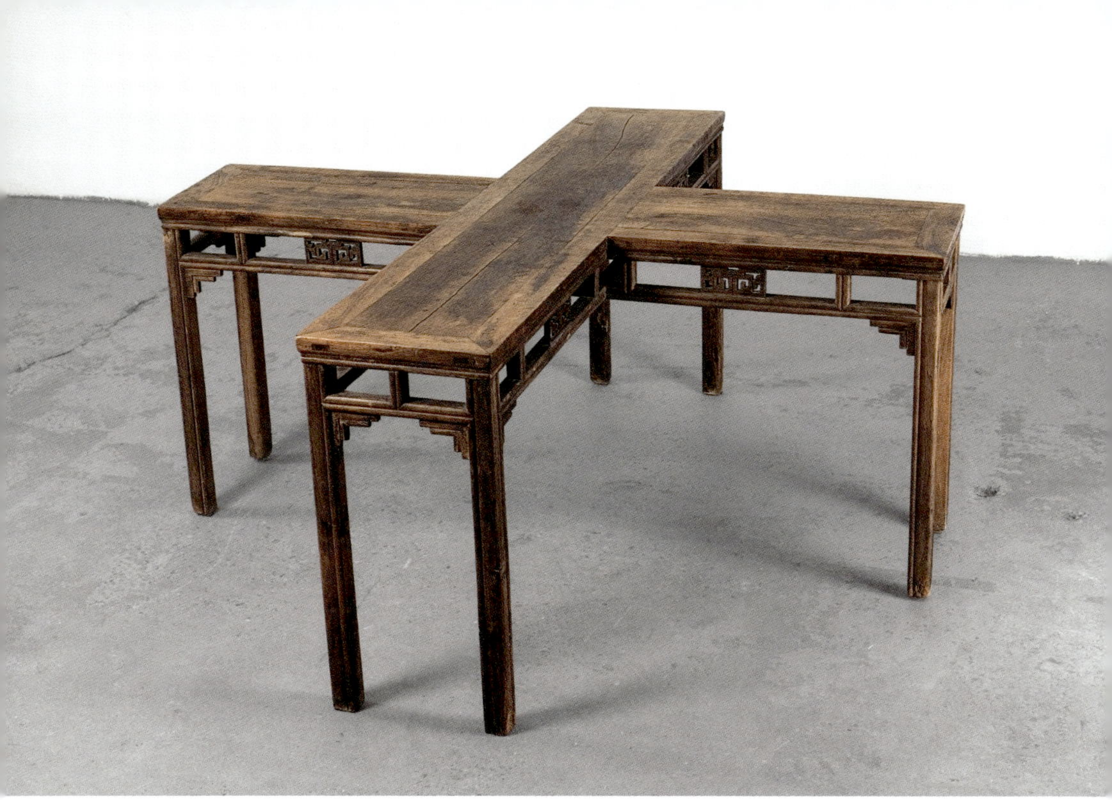

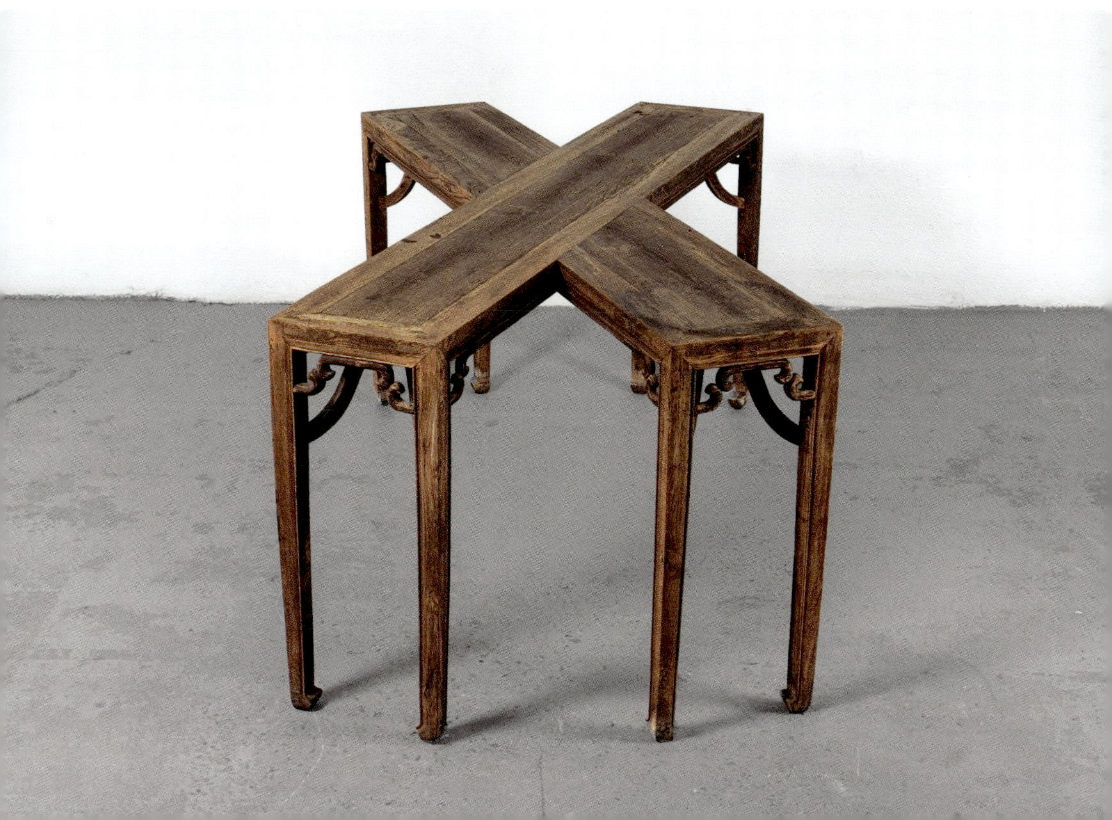

"In the Chinese family, every piece of furniture has a moral meaning. It's a
cultural element. But this kind of stool is really a most liberal type. You can use
it indoors or outdoors, it doesn't associate with hierarchies and classic relations.
It's purely functional, three legs, one surface. So I made two stools that shared
one leg; when put together there were five legs. It's like an on/off situation;
whichever stool you use the other stool is at rest." — AI WEIWEI

Für die chinesische Familie besitzt jedes Möbelstück eine moralische Bedeutung.
Es ist ein Stück Kultur. Nur diese Art Hocker ist davon eher frei. Man kann ihn drinnen wie
draußen benutzen, er hat keine Verbindung zu Hierarchien und klassischen Beziehungen.
Er ist rein funktional: drei Beine, eine Sitzfläche. So habe ich zwei Hocker mit einem ge-
meinsamen Bein gemacht, die also zusammen fünf Beine besitzen. Es ist wie eine An/Aus-
Situation – wenn ein Stuhl benutzt wird, hat der andere Pause.

Dans la famille chinoise, chaque meuble a une signification morale. C'est un élément
culturel. Mais ce type de tabouret incarne une certaine liberté. On peut s'en servir à l'intérieur comme à l'extérieur, il ne rentre dans aucun schéma de hiérarchie ou de relations
classiques. Il est purement fonctionnel. Trois pieds, une assise. J'ai créé deux tabourets qui
partageaient un pied, à eux deux ils n'en avaient que cinq. C'est comme un objet avec un
bouton marche/arrêt, lorsqu'on utilise un tabouret, l'autre se repose.

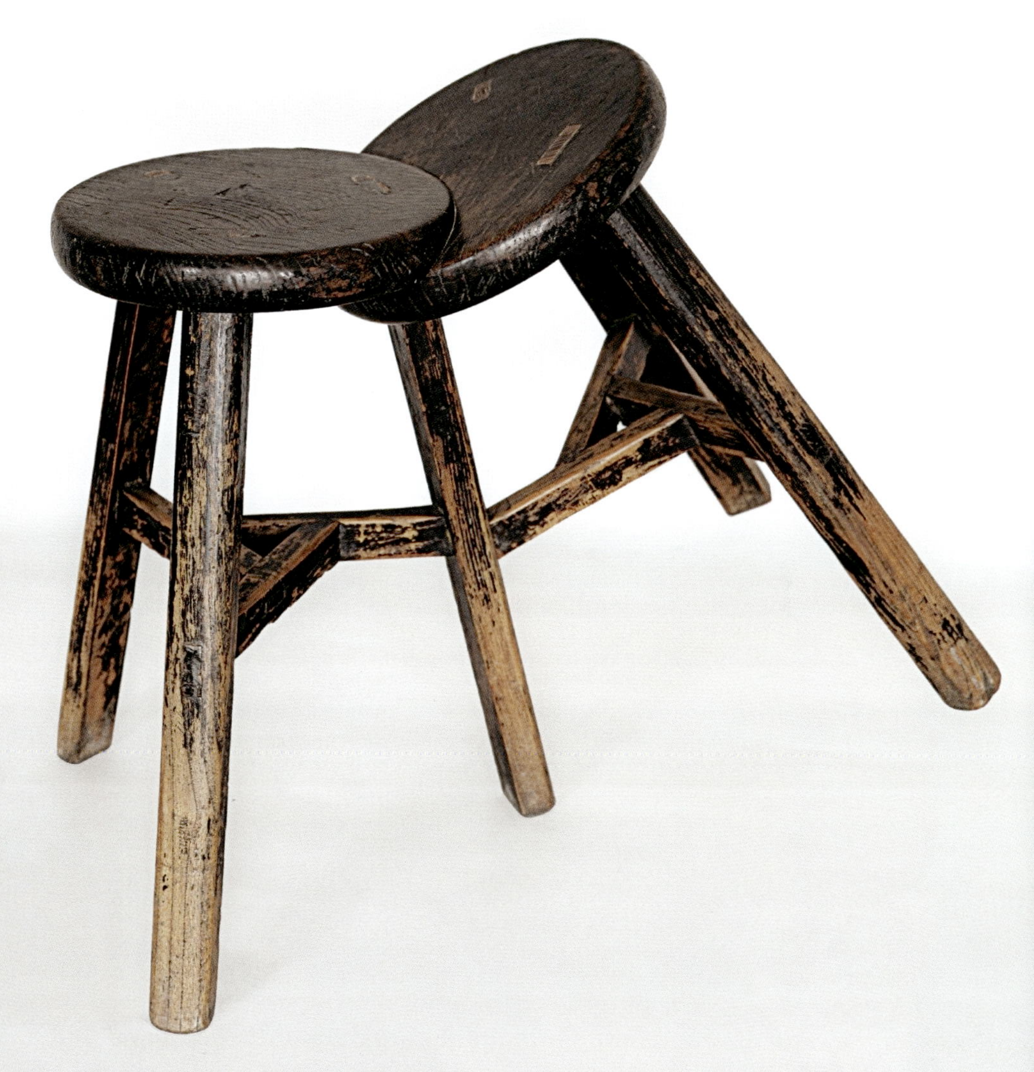

"In 1999, I was part of the Venice Biennale. It was an honor to be chosen by Harald Szeemann, but at the same time I felt a little bit strange because at that time I was not very involved with the art world. So the day before the opening I left. I was at Piazzo San Marco, where all these exchange counters are. I saw they took an exchange fee and I changed US$100 into one currency and then another. My brother took photographs on my Nikon camera. After a few changes, the man working at the first counter got mad at me and refused to change any more money, so I had to go to another counter, and then to another, until finally there was too little money to change." — AI WEIWEI

1999 nahm ich an der Biennale von Venedig teil. Es war eine Ehre, von Harald Szeemann eingeladen zu werden, und doch fühlte ich mich etwas sonderbar, weil ich damals gar nicht viel mit der Kunstwelt zu tun hatte. So reiste ich einen Tag vor der Eröffnung ab. Ich stand auf dem Markusplatz, wo es all diese Wechselstuben gibt, und sah, dass sie eine Provision nahmen. Ich wechselte 100 US-Dollar zunächst in eine, dann in eine andere Währung. Mein Bruder machte Fotos mit meiner Nikon-Kamera. Nach einigen Transaktionen wurde der Mann hinter dem Tresen wütend auf mich und weigerte sich, mir weiterhin Geld zu wechseln, sodass ich zu einem anderen Tresen gehen musste, und dann zu einem weiteren, bis nicht mehr genug Geld zum Wechseln übrig war.

En 1999, j'ai été invité à la Biennale de Venise. C'était un honneur d'avoir été choisi par Harald Szeemann, mais c'était un peu étrange pour moi, parce qu'à cette époque je n'avais pas vraiment de relations avec le monde de l'art. La veille de l'ouverture, j'ai décidé de partir. Je suis allé sur la Place Saint-Marc, où il y a plein de bureaux de change. J'ai vu qu'ils prenaient tous une commission, et j'ai changé 100 dollars US dans une monnaie, puis dans une autre. Mon frère prenait des photos avec mon Nikon. Au bout d'un moment, l'employé du premier bureau s'est fâché, il a refusé de continuer à changer mon argent, alors je suis allé dans un autre bureau, puis un autre, et finalement il n'y avait plus assez d'argent pour le changer.

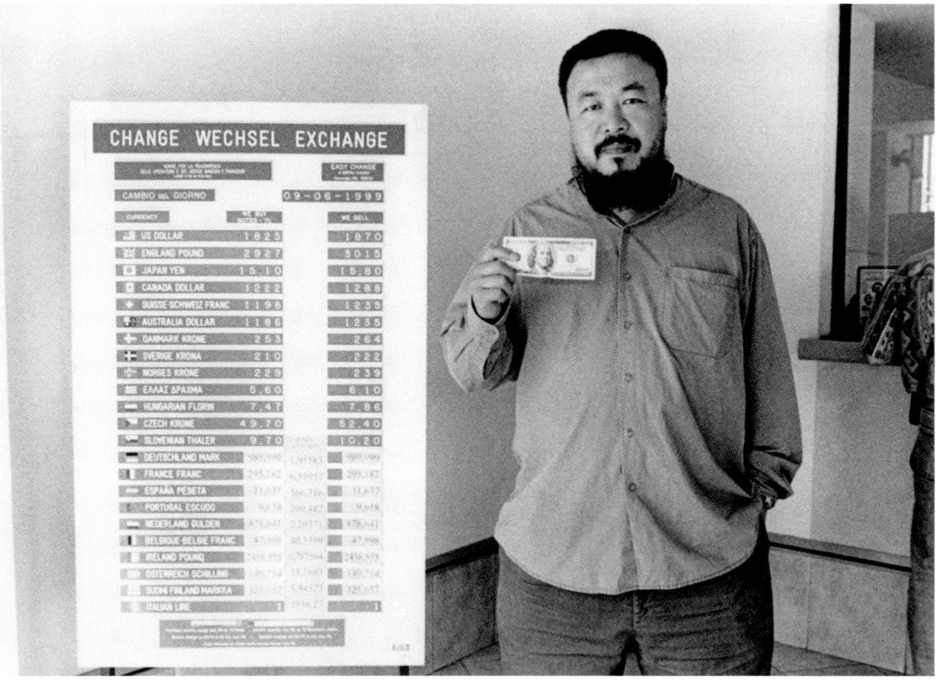

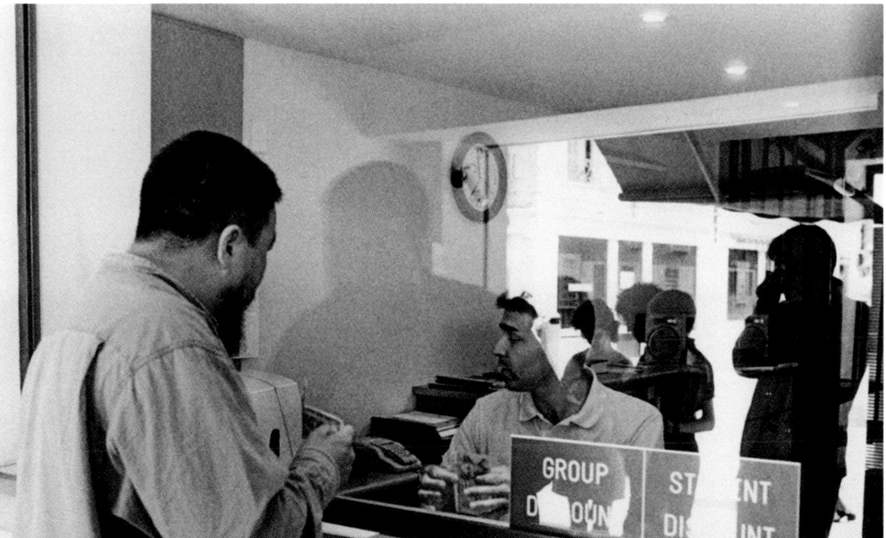

Top and pages 112–115: EXCHANGE, 1998, 11 black-and-white photographs, 2 C-prints,
various dimensions | 111

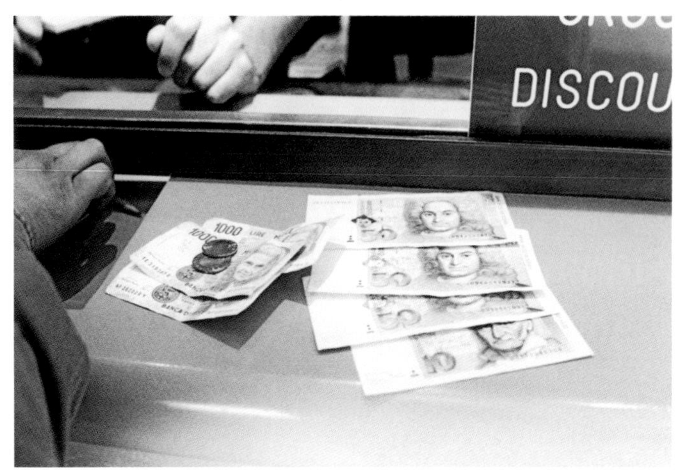

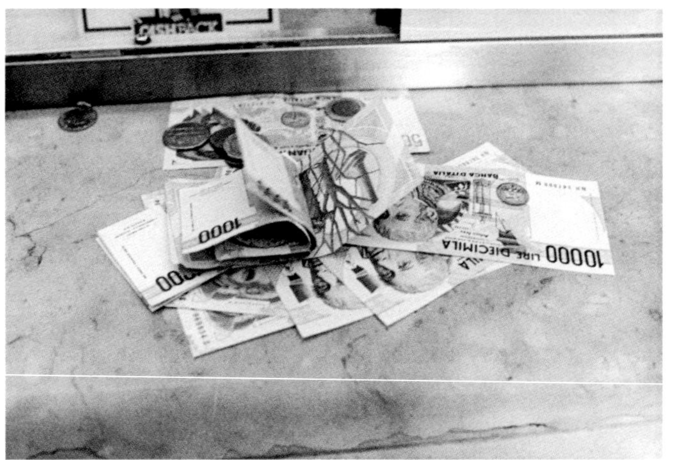

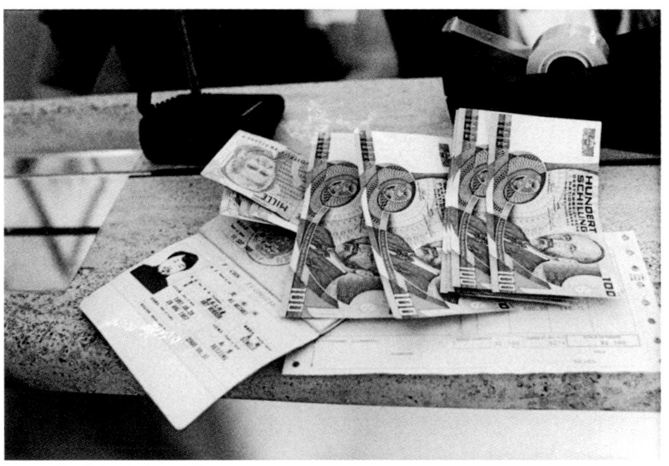

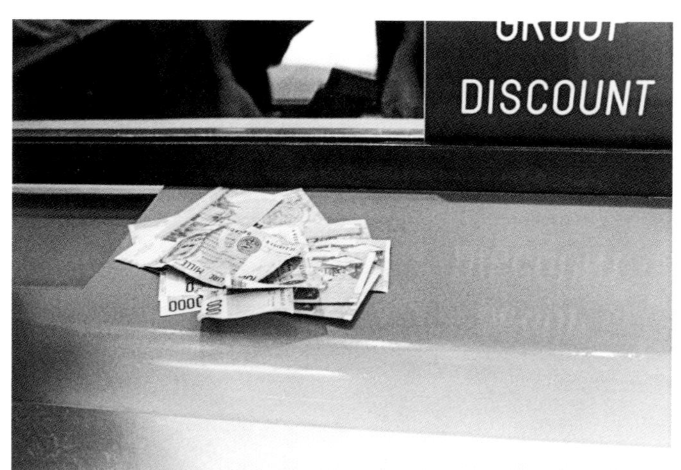
GROUP
DISCOUNT

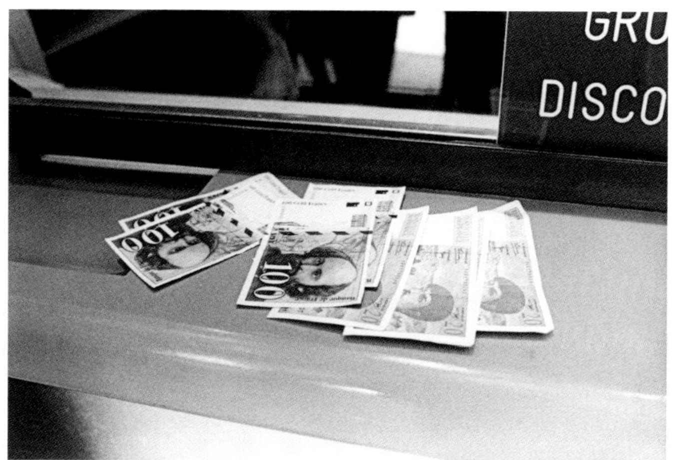
GRO
DISCO
100
100

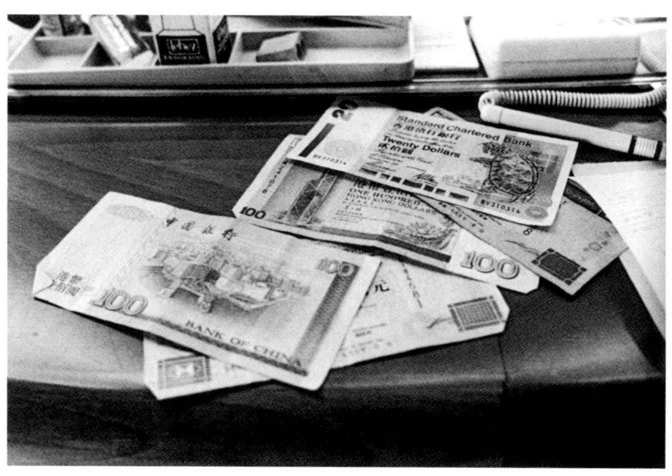
Standard Chartered Bank
Twenty Dollars
BV310314
100
ONE HUNDRED
HONG KONG DOLLARS
BANK OF CHINA
100

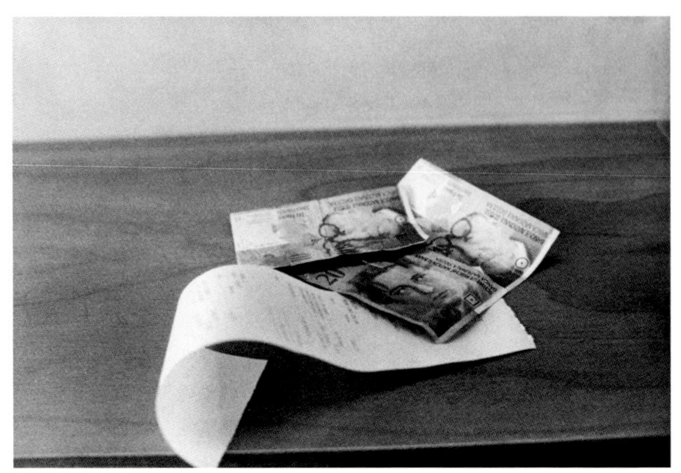

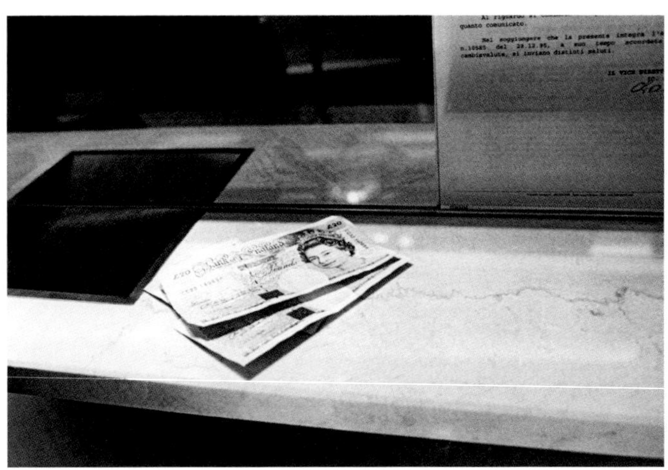
Al riguardo si
quanto comunicato.

Nel aggiungere che la presente integra l'a
n.10585 del 29.12.95, a suo tempo accordata
cambiavaluta, si inviano distinti saluti.

IL VICE DIRETT

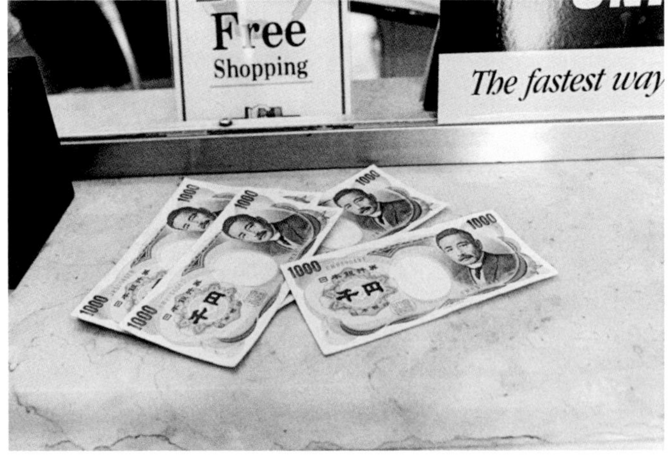
Free
Shopping
The fastest way

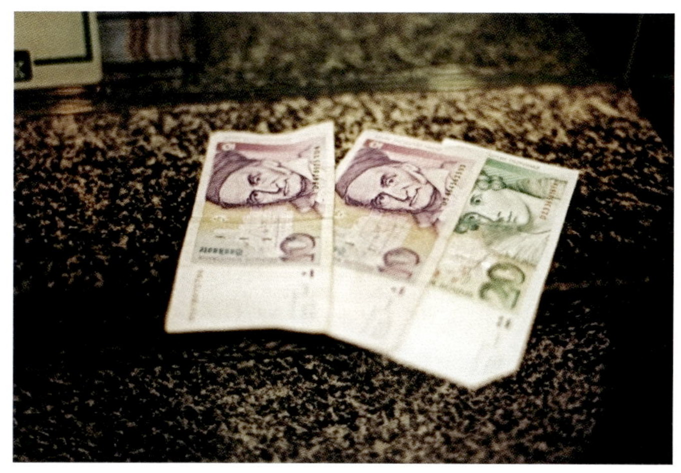

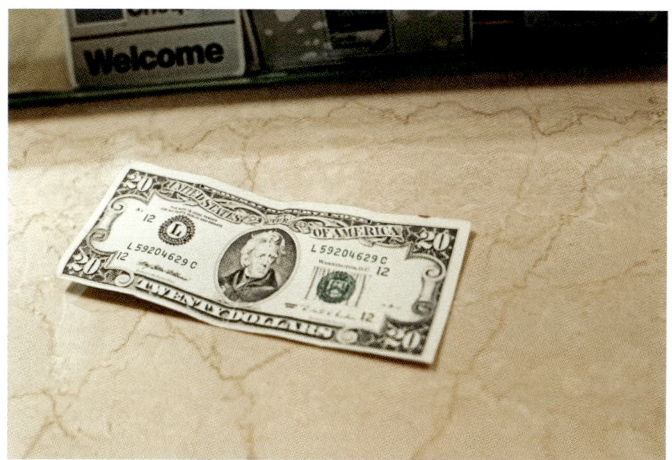

Welcome

"Maybe *Fuck Off* was most important for what it represented. It wasn't necessarily the best show because we had to put it together in a very short time, and the conditions were such that the police could shut it down at any moment and everything could be taken away. But the concept was clear, and we were very clear about what we wanted to say toward the Chinese institutions as well as Western curators and institutions and dealers; their functions are all similar in one way or the other. It's all about the deal, about labor, how to trademark different interests. We had to say some things as individual artists to the outside world and what we said was 'fuck off.'" — AI WEIWEI

Vermutlich war das Wichtigste an *Fuck Off* die Haltung, die wir ausdrückten. Es war nicht unbedingt die beste Ausstellung, da wir sie in kurzer Zeit realisieren und außerdem damit rechnen mussten, dass die Polizei sie jeden Moment schließen und alles beschlagnahmen konnte. Aber das Konzept war sehr klar, und es wurde deutlich, was wir den chinesischen Institutionen, aber auch den westlichen Kuratoren und Kunsthändlern mitteilen wollten. Die sind sich in dem, was sie tun, alle auf die eine oder andere Weise ähnlich. Es geht ums Geschäft, um Arbeit und wie man aus einem Interesse eine Marke macht. Wir hatten als individuelle Künstler der Außenwelt dazu ein paar Dinge zu sagen, und was wir sagten, war: „Fuck off."

L'exposition *Fuck Off* était surtout importante pour ce qu'elle a représenté. Ce n'était pas spécialement ma meilleure exposition : nous avons dû la réaliser en très peu de temps, tout pouvait être interrompu par la police à tout moment, ils pouvaient tout emporter. Mais le concept était clair, et nous lancions un message très clair au pouvoir chinois, mais aussi aux curateurs occidentaux, aux institutions et aux marchands d'art ; finalement, ils ont une fonction semblable. Tout tourne autour du marché, du travail, de comment commercialiser différents intérêts. En tant qu'artistes, nous avions quelque chose à dire au monde extérieur, et ce que nous avions à dire, c'était « fuck off ».

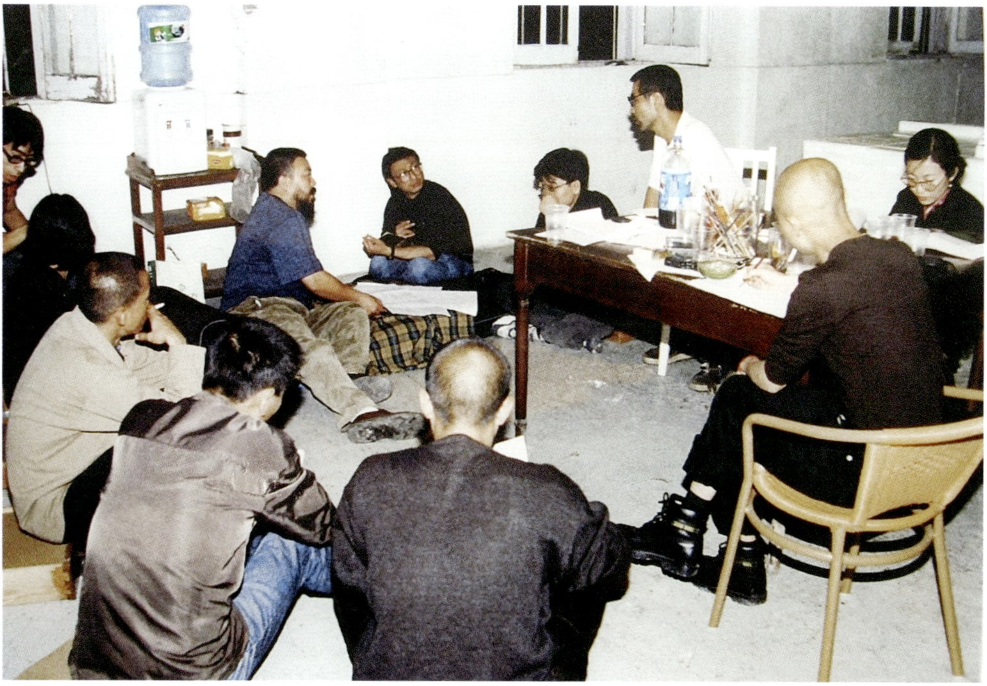

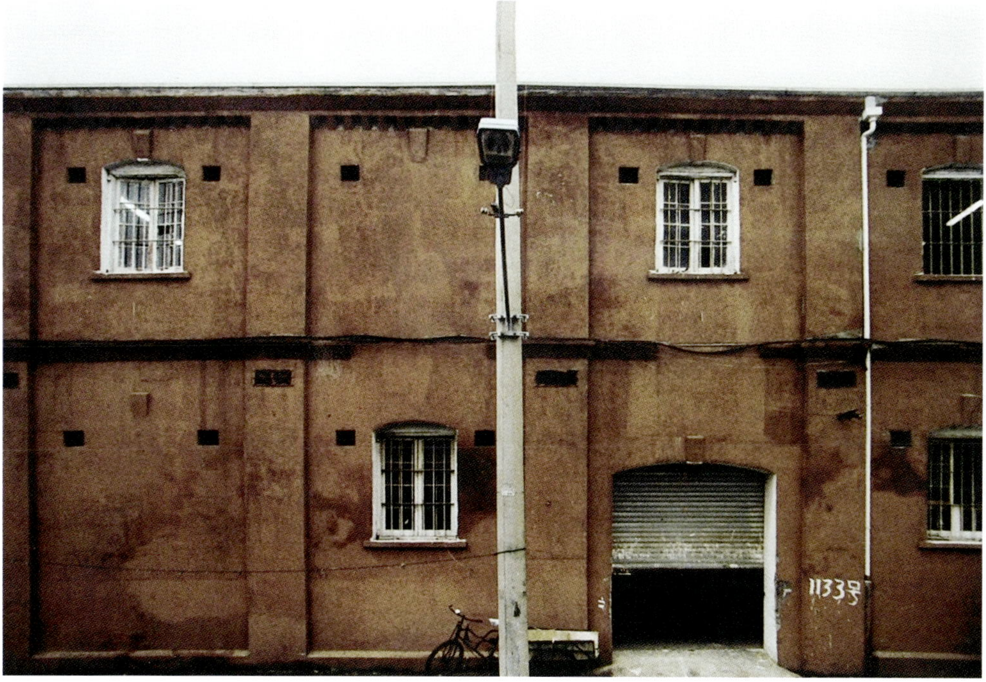

FUCK OFF, group exhibition, Eastlink Gallery, Shanghai 2000 (above and overleaf) |

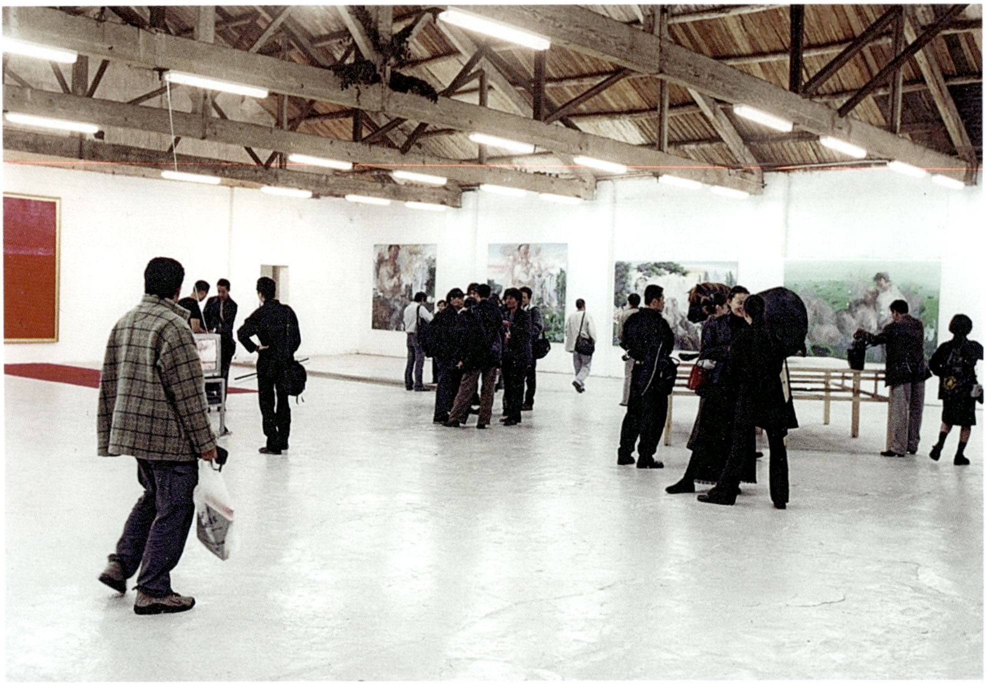

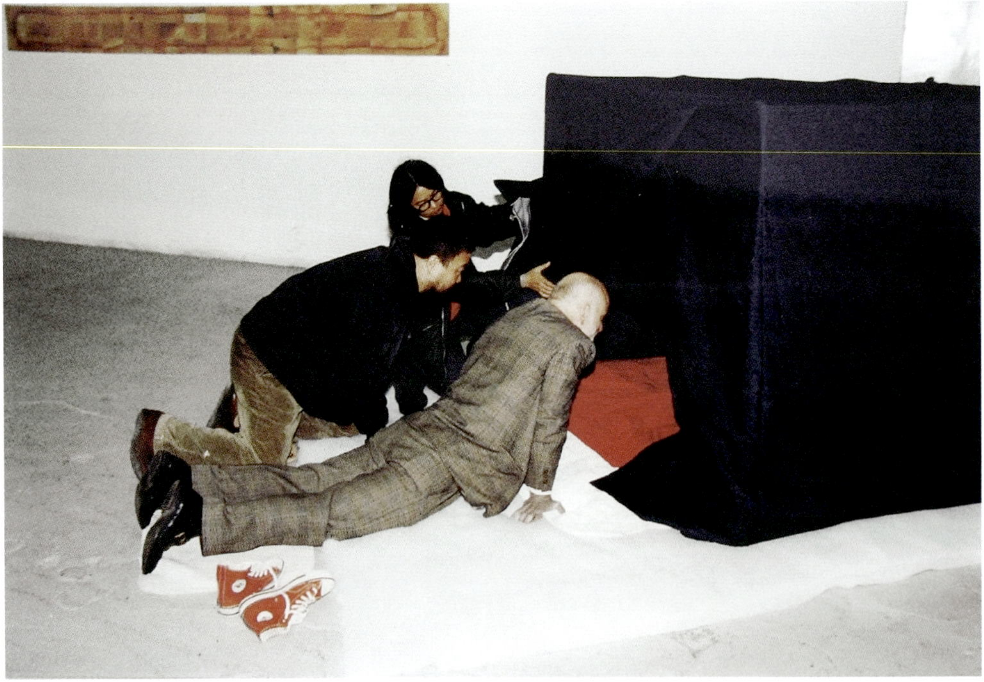

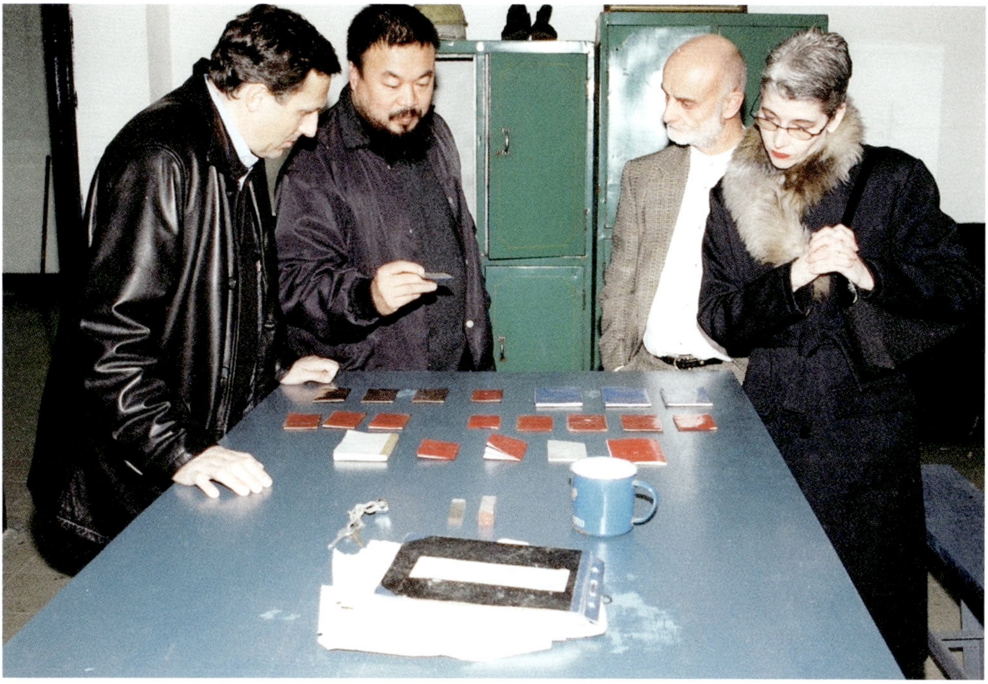

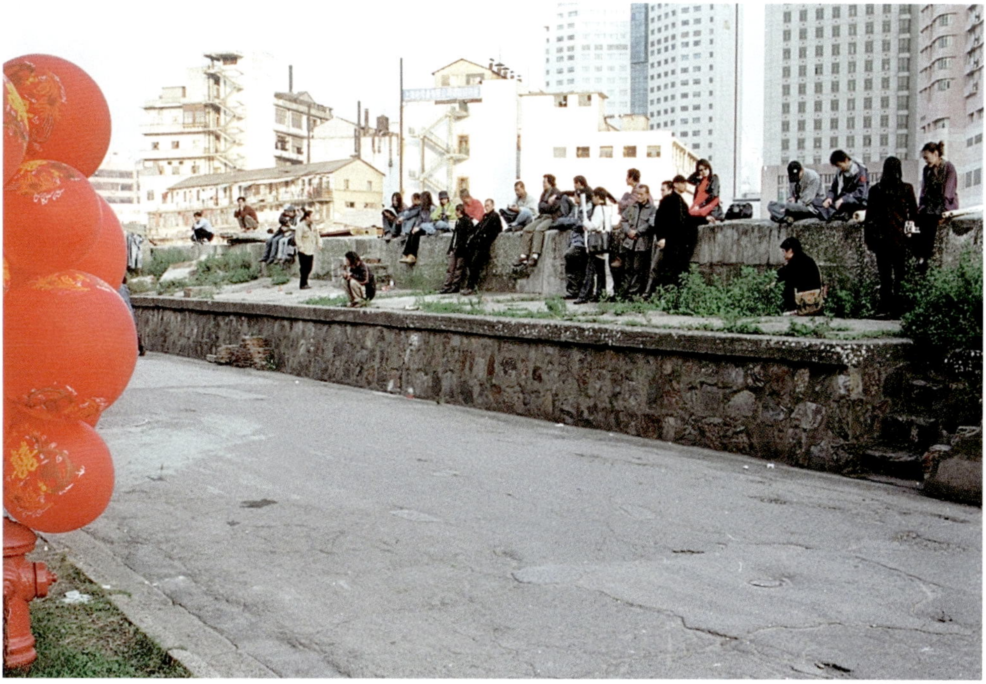

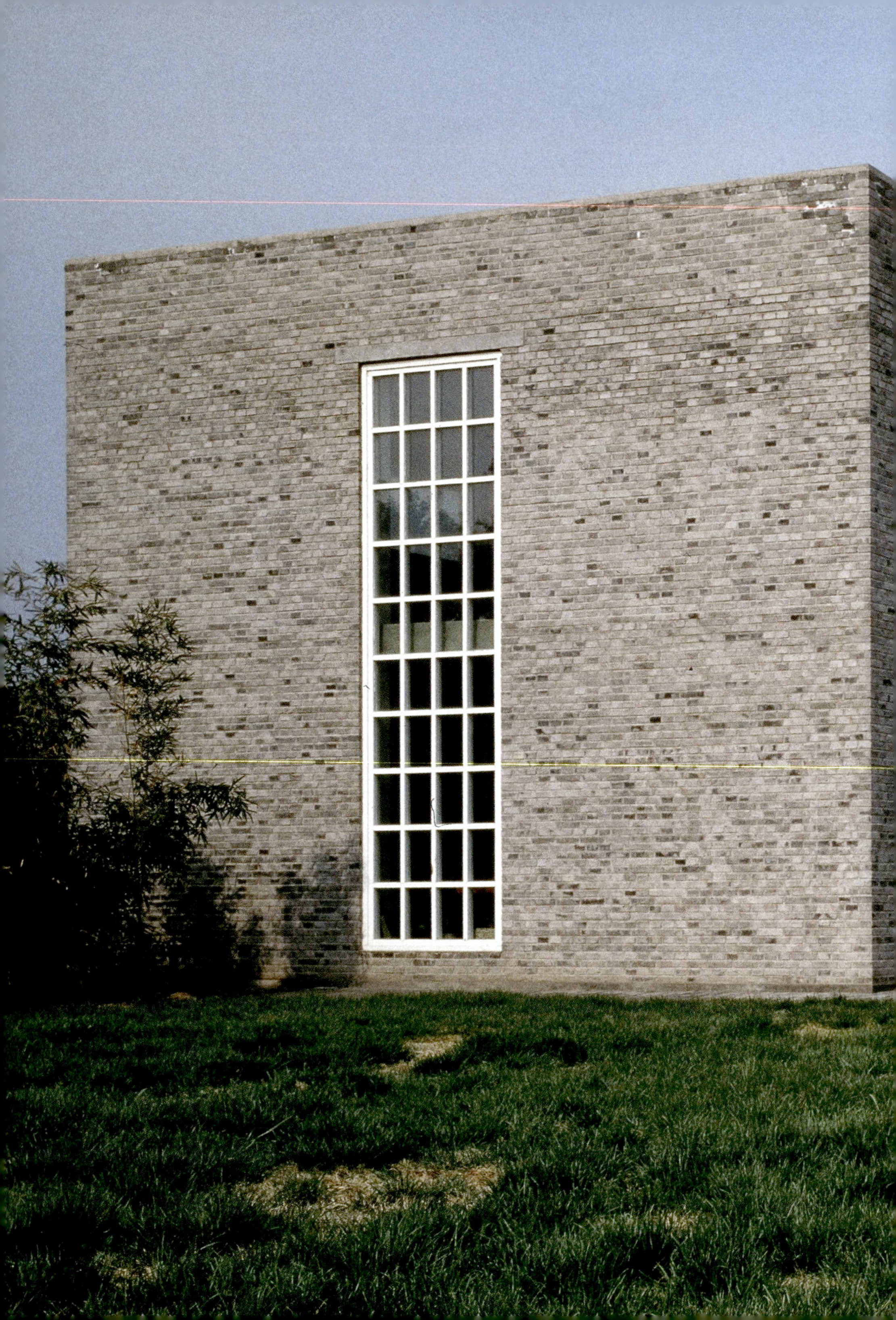

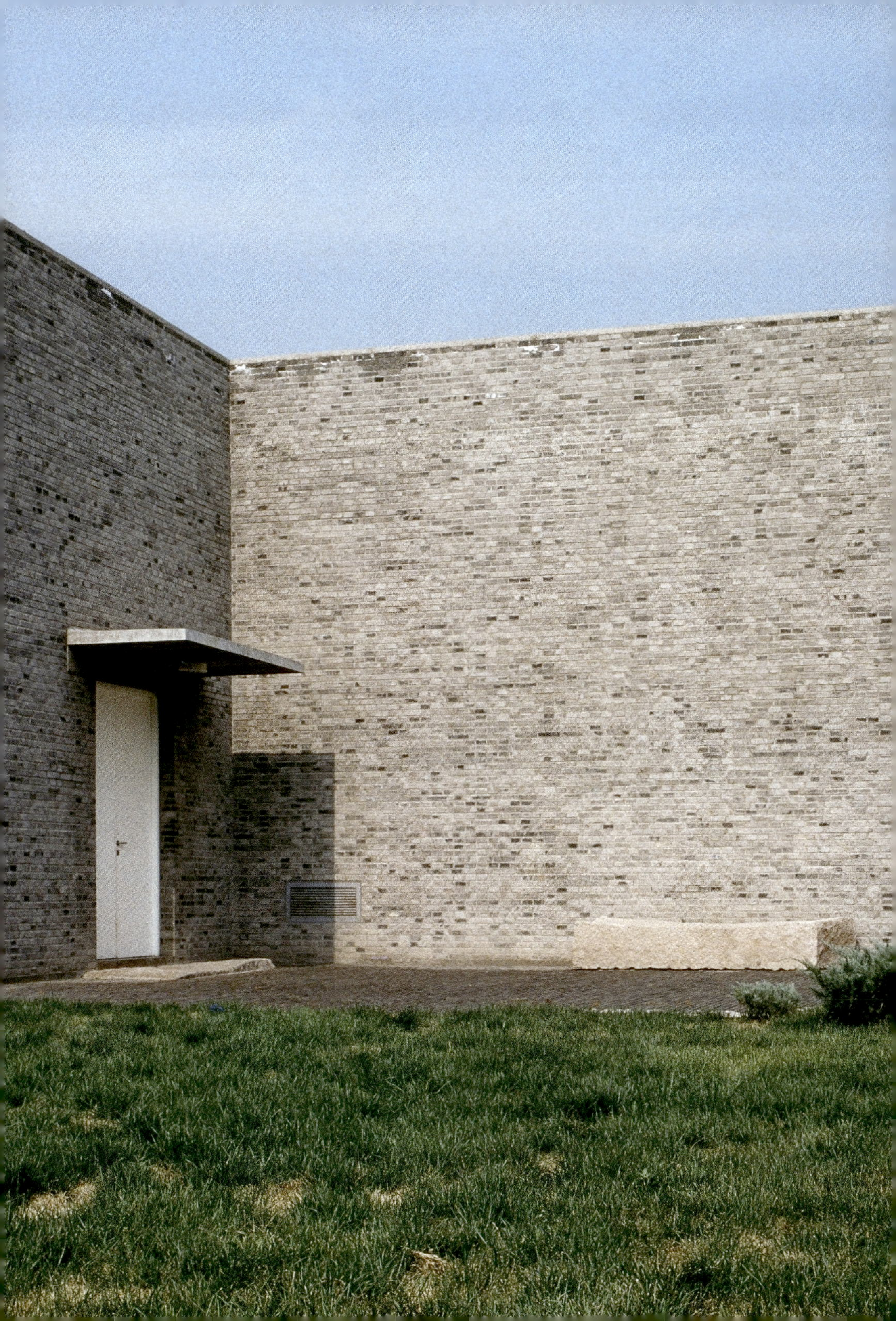

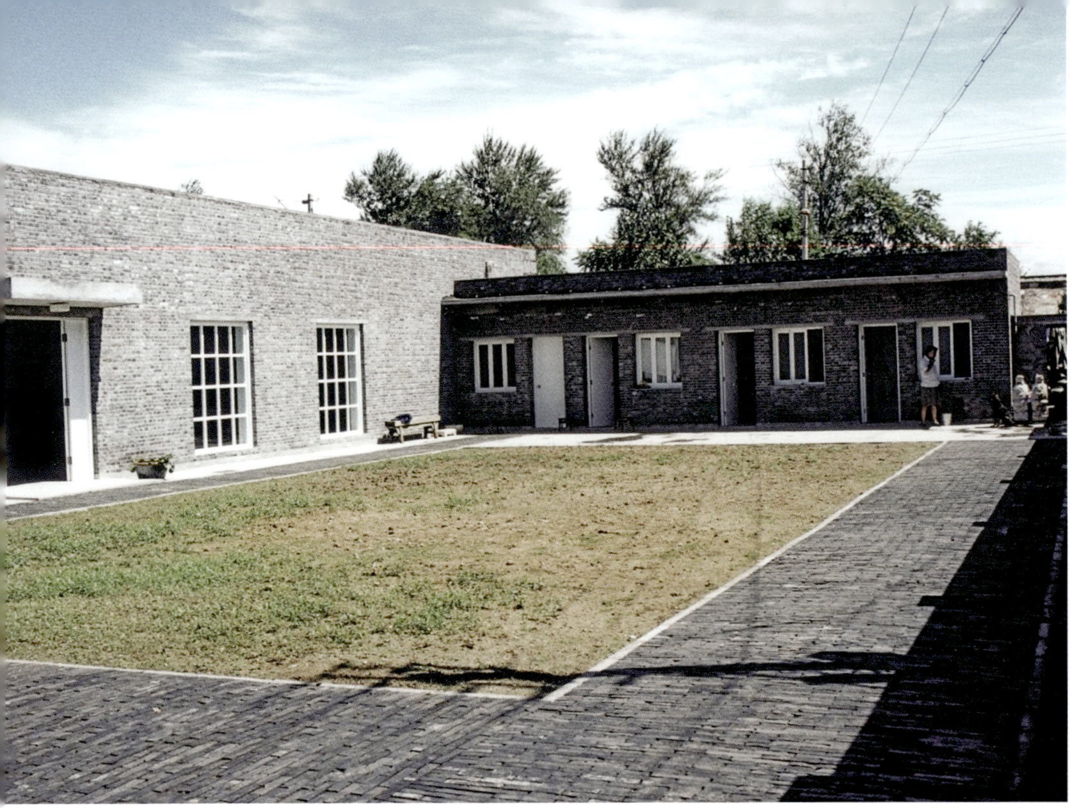

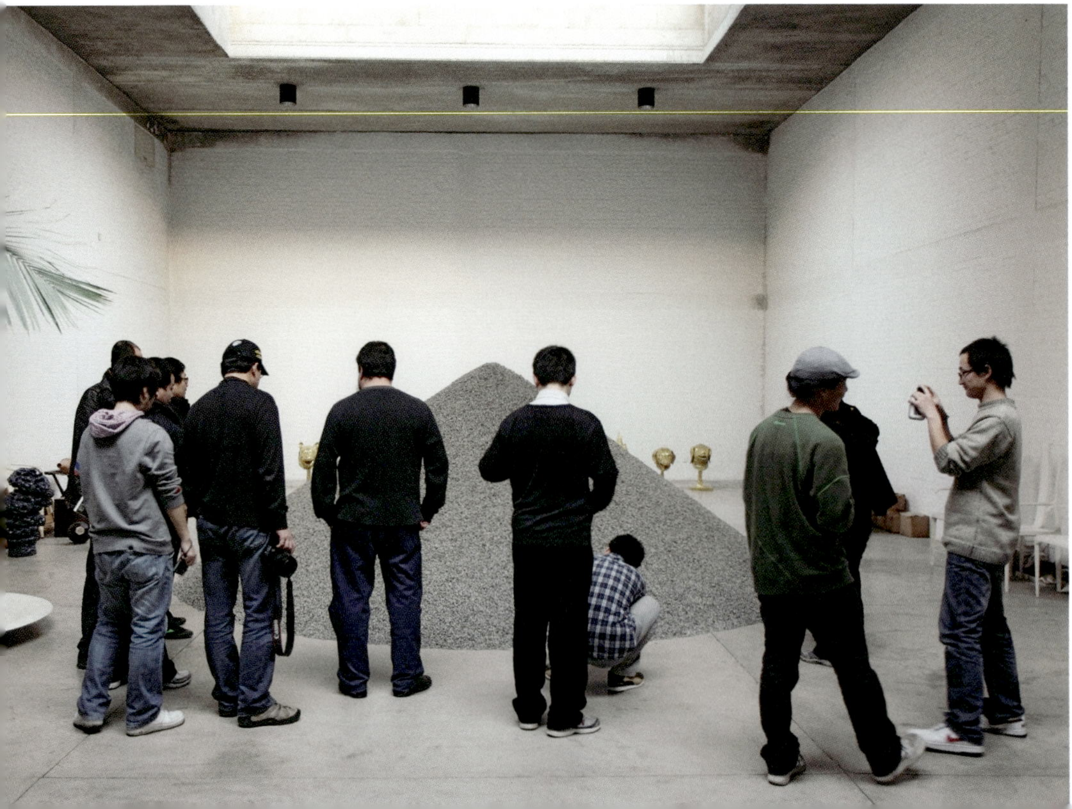

Ai Weiwei Studio, Caochangdi 258, 1999–

CONSTRUCTING THE STUDIO

Ai Weiwei. A few years after I moved back to China from the United States, I decided I wanted to find my own place. When I saw this compound by the side of the Airport Expressway, I liked it. There are lots of taxis coming down the Airport Expressway, so I could always get a cab into town. And the plot of land was near the train tracks, which I thought was great—nobody wants land by train tracks, so there was no danger of the land being reclaimed, and more than that, the railroad authority in China is untouchable, so nobody would dare to propose a development project that interfered with the railroad. Being next to the train tracks didn't bother me, so I made the decision to build. I felt so eager to build something. I knew from the beginning that the studio was to be a temporary building because we didn't have official approval. There was always the possibility it would be destroyed because it's not a legal construction project. But the local authorities told us to go ahead, they didn't care if we built on the land or not. I didn't care about the permits either. Even if I built something only for the authorities to destroy it I would have been satisfied. I wanted to live in something like a loft, a living condition that could give me space to work and engage in different activities. Comfort has never been most important to me—I grew up in the harsh conditions of the Gobi desert. I was more interested in creating a space that reflected my sense of aesthetics. I have never trained as an architect, but I've seen construction and building all around me since I was little. I made my first brick from mud when I was ten; I learned how to cast it and fire it. To me, building is a natural act, like eating. You don't need to be taught. So I made a simple drawing with measurements to show to the workers. Perhaps for a professional architect, it was just a naive sketch, but to the people who were going to build, it was very clear. The design was very simple—just one door, one window, one living quarter, one bathroom, one kitchen, and one staircase. I wanted an adjacent room for installing art that was completely sealed with no windows, only two large skylights. We built the studio with respect for the construction methods, using local material and cheap technology—that's why it's made entirely of concrete and gray brick. There is no decoration, so the inside and outside look the same…

The architectural language isn't trendy. Maybe it's become trendy because you live in it. It has become fashionable, and it's been copied in this area. When it was being constructed, however, the farmers who helped build it thought it wasn't finished. They didn't understand why I didn't want any interior design. I had to tell them I'd run out of money.

Young Architecture of China, 2001. In a little village not far from Beijing airport, the artist Ai Weiwei has designed this house and studio, where he and his wife create and display their work. At first sight it is a simple courtyard ensemble in the local gray brick. But really the house is the result of an artist's performance: within one hundred days local craftsmen from the village were called in to build this spatially refined set of volumes under the supervision of the artist.

Detail Magazine, 2002. Designed for an artist, this studio building has a floor area of 500 m². It consists of a reinforced concrete skeleton-frame structure—left exposed internally—with reddish brick infill panels. An outer skin of gray facing bricks is drawn over the structure and articulated with a few carefully proportioned window openings. The principal element of the scheme is the two-story-high studio space set at right angles to the living tract. The windowless studio receives daylight solely from above via two skylight strips. The number of materials used was reduced to a minimum.

China Radio International, 2004. Here's what Ai Weiwei had when building his house: 130,000 bricks, 180 tons cement, 7.5 tons reinforcing steel bars, 34 prefabricated planks, 45 cubes of sand, and some wood scraps. Construction took 60 days and wall painting 40 days. One of Ai Weiwei's principles of design is being economical. "The best design is also the most money-saving design," said Ai. His home undoubtedly best reflects this idea. In his home the established concept of walls, doors, and a roof has been abandoned. As long as practicability is concerned, all other irrelevant factors in design and decoration are considered unnecessary triviality and repetition, and were given up by Ai without any hesitation.

The most noteworthy part of his home is the washroom on the second floor. It is completely open. The toilet and the wash bowl are much like pieces of furniture, casually positioned around. Now in China many families use a ground glass wall to separate the washroom from other sections. However, none is as bold as Ai Weiwei who challenges traditional definition of privacy by exposing it to visitors. Ai Weiwei holds that the second floor is already a relatively private sector and there is no need to place another wall here. "We are susceptible to established concepts without asking why and how, for example the door, window, wall, and privacy. A good designer shouldn't present what he was taught, but seek to present his original look."

As a result, elements of a home are simplified to the maximum. The walls are crude bricks and the windows are made of frosted glass. As the walls are for display of his works, heating caliducts are embedded in the ground. Staircases are no more than fabricated cement planks. When the house was completed, it also surprised the construction workers: there's no roof. Certainly you can't call the lid a roof. "A house is like a box. It is merely a container. When a certain roof is applied, the building is easily changed into a stylish thing. What I need is just some basic components for the house." That explains why Ai Weiwei just put a lid to the box.

NEIGHBORHOOD DEVELOPMENTS

Ai Weiwei. After my studio was built, people immediately started asking me to build something for them. People thought I had demonstrated a very solid understanding of aesthetics in the construction of my studio. So I started taking on construction projects for friends. My first project was a bar for a writer, and many projects followed after that—studios for other artists, restaurants, all kinds of things. I started to really enjoy it. There was a need for the type of architecture we were doing, there were customers, and the buildings were being put to use.

Jonathan Napack, art critic and writer, 2003. Ai Weiwei has lived in this house for five years now. A constant stream of visitors come through the gate, from early in the morning until late in the afternoon. On this day, there is a factory owner from Shenyang who wants to build a better factory; an actor's son who is creating a chain of cinemas for people in the countryside; a young American filmmaker with an idea for a new documentary. They all have just two things in common: a desire to know something, and a feeling that somehow Ai Weiwei can help them know it.

The New York Times, 2007. Seven years ago, the preeminent Chinese artist Ai Weiwei made a bold move to the outskirts of Beijing. In an area called Caochangdi Village, by the Fifth Ring Road in the city's northeast, he designed a compound for himself, some friends and a gallery called China Art Archives and Warehouse. For a while, they were left alone. This spring, as the 798 District, the epicenter of Beijing's lively contemporary art scene, becomes increasingly crowded with boutiques and tourists, some of China's leading gallery owners are bypassing the district altogether, and heading directly to Caochangdi Village. Or maybe they should call it Ai Weiwei Village.

WORK AT THE STUDIO AND WORKSHOPS

Lao San, project assistant based in Beijing. I had been a carpenter since I was 16. My three brothers were all carpenters. I came

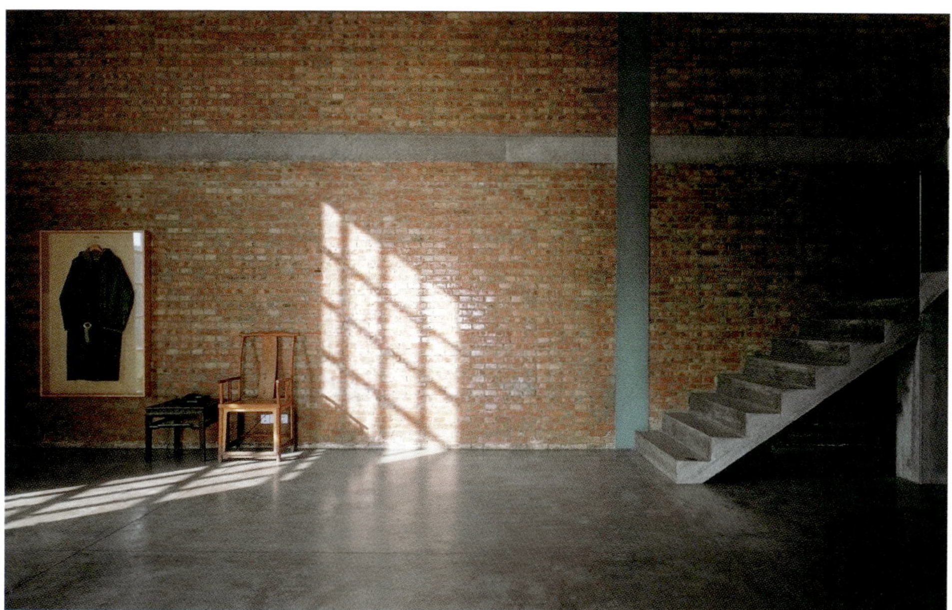

Ai Weiwei Studio, Caochangdi, Beijing 1999, interior view 2000

to Beijing in 1994 when I was 25. Back then there were a lot of factories producing furniture, doors. Teacher Ai's younger brother Ai Dan asked me to make some doors and windows for his house. That's how I met Teacher Ai. I heard he had just returned from the US. Back then it was quite carefree; we'd hang out at his brother's place and eat meals together. After half a year, he asked me to work for him.

The first work I made was the *Table with Two Legs on the Wall* (1997, p. 103). Teacher Ai asked, could you join these two tables so? I said it was possible. In the beginning some details were quite difficult. Every work has its own specific structure so they are all hard to make at first. But I don't think one is harder than another. Every piece takes a different amount of time, and sometimes we need to find a space that's large enough to make the big artworks in. In the beginning we make a model that Teacher Ai approves, then we enlarge it to the actual size. We think about how to take something apart and how to put it back together. There's a lot of trial and error with the wood pieces and their shapes. The *Maps of China* (2003–, pp. 163–166) are each made of at least 500 wood pieces. There are more than 130 on the outer edge of the work, and more than 180 inside. I've made a lot of them. There's a special one with a map-shaped hole in its center made of just eight pieces of wood. When you put them together, there's a hole in the shape of China in the middle. The wooden works based on the cat's toy (2004–, pp. 207, 259) are easier; they're round, like a ball. We carpenters all know how to make this.

Now there are usually about ten carpenters here, more when there are large projects. Many are from my hometown in Anhui. There is a long tradition of carpentry there. I don't judge the artwork itself. Art doesn't have a fixed value. Everyone has a different perspective. It's hard to make something that everyone is happy with.

Liu Weiwei, project assistant based in Jingdezhen. I'm from Beijing. I'd always been involved in antiques and had a shop in the antique market. In the 1990s I had some friends who were in the trade and I grew to like it too. I first got to know Weiwei in the early '90s when he was collecting antiques

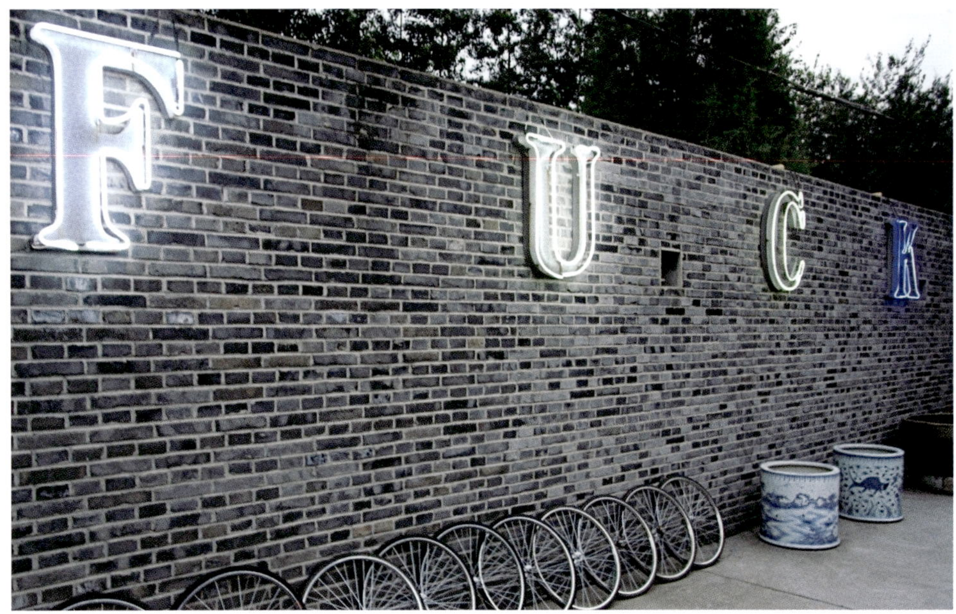

Studio courtyard with *F.U.C.K.*, 2000, neon tubes, metal, dimensions variable

and heard I was making porcelains. The first time we worked on something together was in 2006. He came up with the idea for the *Ruyi* (p. 301) and I helped him make it. He was pretty satisfied.

The workshop in Jiangxi is about 2,100 square meters. If there's nothing special going on, we usually have about 20 people working here. We made our kilns ourselves; we have three of them. They're gas kilns, like all the kilns in Jingdezhen. The hardest thing I made was the porcelain scaffoling for *Field* (2010), where each part was one meter long. It's particularly thin and goes flat when you fire it. I developed this work for four years before I was successful.

Another extremely challenging project was the *Sunflower Seeds* (2010, pp. 49, 407–409). We worked on this for almost three years. In the beginning we experimented slowly, making test works, and finally we completed the entire project. There were so many steps involved in the production. In all, we employed about 1,600 people in Jingdezhen who made 150 tons of seeds. They worked in about ten different locations. Some were in villages, some in city areas.

I rented some factory spaces. It wasn't easy to supervise them. We had a supervisor for each team. I had to oversee all of this and do all the quality control. If the weather wasn't good, the materials remained wet and stuck to the boards.

Zhao Zhao, former studio assistant, artist based in Beijing. I grew up in Xinjiang, in Shihezi, the same place as Ai Weiwei. After I graduated from art school, I decided to move to Beijing in 2004 because Xinjiang just isn't the sort of place that can support independent artists. My plan was to rent a place in the Songzhuang artist community and paint.

I met Weiwei after I'd only been in Beijing for ten days. I told him who I was and about my plans to live in Songzhuang. He told me that Songzhuang was a miserable place and looked through my portfolio.

He called me a few days later and asked me if I knew how to use a Sony camera. I told him I could and went over to his place. He asked me what I thought about giving up painting. I asked him what I would do if I didn't paint. He told me I could film documentaries. He took out a piece of paper and drew a line on it: "This is Chang'an Boulevard," he said. "Start at the east end of it and film it. Every 50 meters, stop and film the road. Film the whole street like that." I didn't understand it right away—what kind of film doesn't have a plot? But once he explained that it was a conceptual video piece, I understood.

It took more than a month to finish filming Chang'an Boulevard, and once I was done, he said: "Okay, now film the Second Ring Road like that." And then once I finished that, he asked me to film the Third Ring Road. Once I'd finish one project, he'd always give me another (pp. 271–273).

Later, things got much busier. Weiwei started working on the Bird's Nest, and asked me to document the process of its construction (pp. 385, 387–389). Every day I'd enter the construction site illegally, using an old CCTV ID that Weiwei had gotten from someone he knew. So I'd put the ID on the dashboard of my car and just drive in. Usually nobody stopped me, and if someone did, I'd just tell them I was working for so-and-so and they'd leave me alone. Then I documented the construction of Terminal 3, designed by Norman Foster (pp. 275–277).

I worked as his assistant when he taught courses and traveled with him to set up exhibitions.

Liu Yanping, volunteer for the Citizens' Investigation, then studio staff member, active blogger based in Beijing. I studied public finance at the Central Finance University, where I got a master's degree. Then I worked for a bank. The work was comfortable but boring. After that I got a PhD from the Central Academy of Social Sciences in the history of modern finance. In 2009 my daughter went to kindergarten, and I felt lucky I had so much time and could surf the Internet. The first time I heard of Ai Weiwei was through his Sina blog in 2007 or 2008. I thought it was great and I liked it a lot. In 2009 when he started to do the Citizens' Investigation of the May 12 earthquake (pp. 344 ff.), he wrote an article on his blog with an interview discussing why it was important to find these names. I thought his point of view was really uncommon. Even though China has more than a million people,

people who can talk about why they have this idea, why they have to find this name list, he said very clearly. And few people can do this. So I wrote to the studio and said if you need help, I can come over.

My first task was to help the volunteers who were going to Sichuan. They would go visit the schools and the parents and write down the names. They would send emails very quickly back to us. We would collect the names from them and enter the data into our forms according to the information we were looking for, and then if there were phone numbers we'd call the parents. Mainly it was organizing the materials. This lasted for a few months.

I think everything really surprised me. The videos that the volunteers sent back from Sichuan, the name lists, the text messages that the parents sent us—it all was stuff I'd never known about before. Before, I felt like my attitude toward the government was unclear, fuzzy. I thought I had no relationship with the government. All I wanted was for the government to steer clear of me, and for me to steer clear of the government. It's also not the government that I chose for myself, right? Now, I think I understand the government a bit better but I still don't know what kind of relationship I have with it. I just know a bit more about reality than I did before.

After the Citizens' Investigation we worked on the applications to the government to release information for half a year. Then, we did a few other things, like looking into past legal precedents. Then Teacher Ai was detained.

When he came out, he hadn't changed at all on the inside. He told me: "Those people, they wanted to change my thinking. But I told them an apple will always be an apple, a pear will always be a pear. You can't make an apple a pear." He really hadn't changed at all!

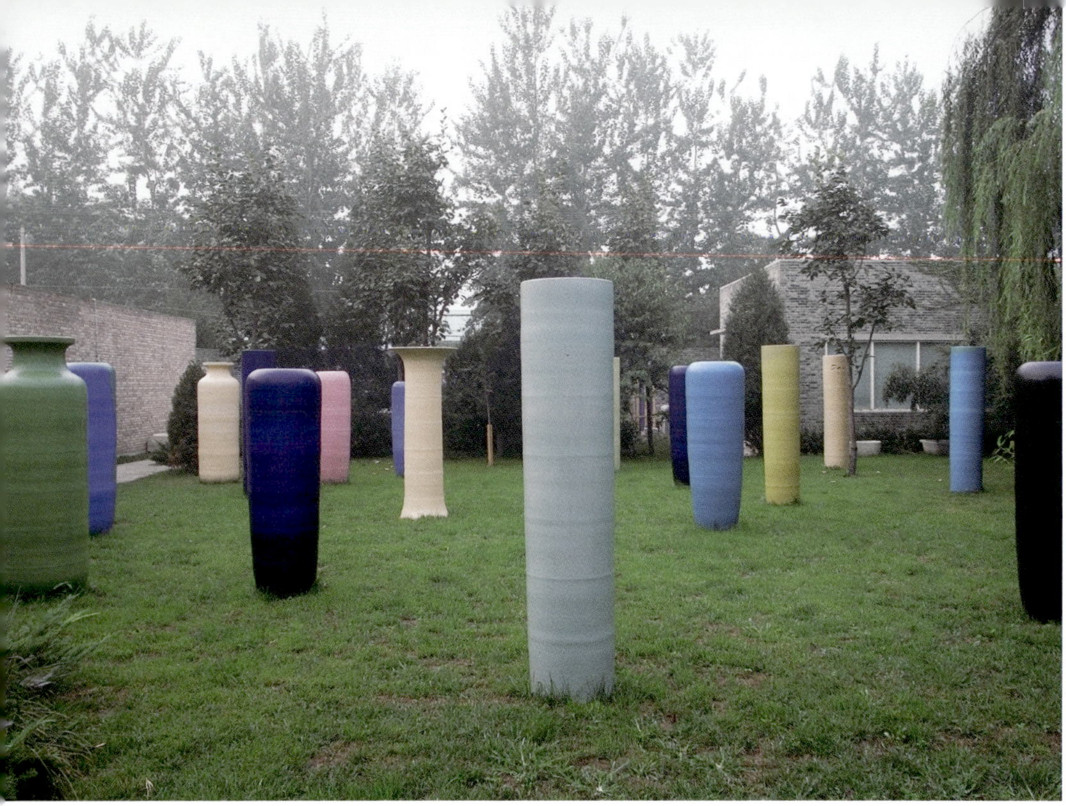

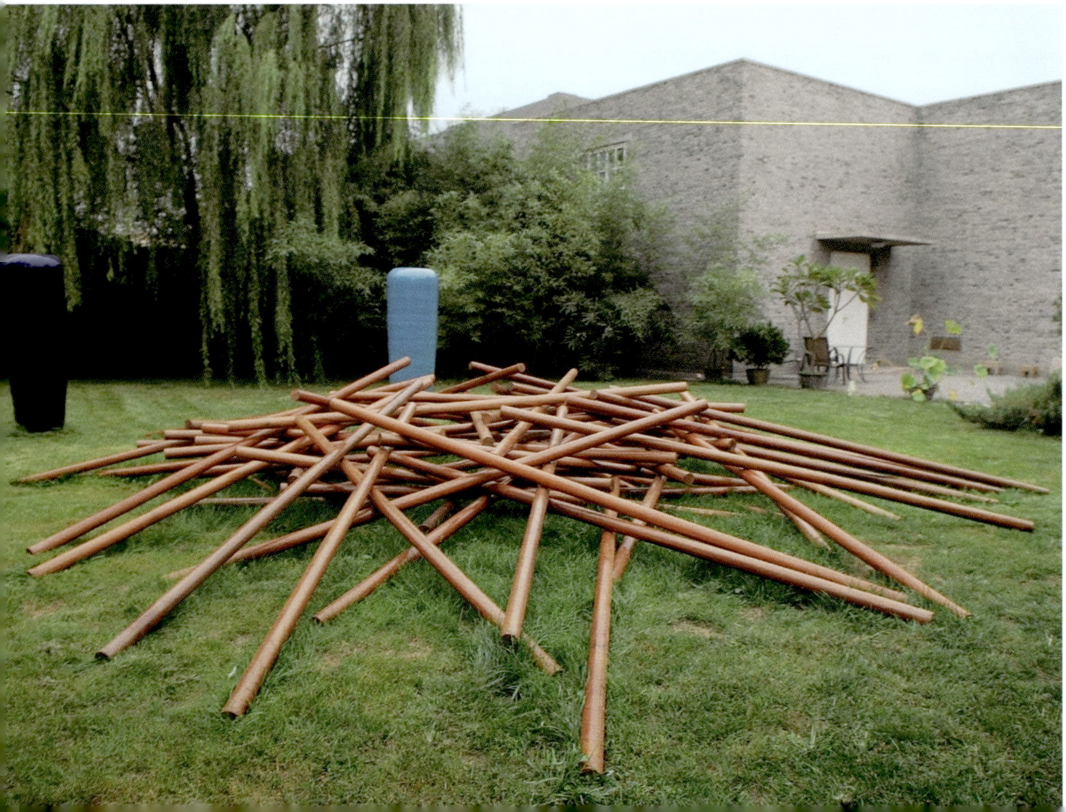

Ai Weiweis Studio, Caochangdi 258, 1999–

BAU DES STUDIOS

Ai Weiwei. Ein paar Jahre nachdem ich aus den USA nach China zurückgekommen war, suchte ich nach einem eigenen Studio. Dieses Grundstück in der Nähe der Autobahn zum Flughafen gefiel mir auf den ersten Blick. Vom Flughafen kommen jede Menge Taxis, und es ist einfach, eine Fahrt ins Stadtzentrum zu bekommen. Außerdem liegt das Gelände nahe an der Eisenbahnstrecke. Ein weiterer Vorteil, dachte ich, niemand will Land in einer solchen Lage kaufen. Es besteht also keine Gefahr, dass die Gegend neu bebaut wird. Die chinesische Bahngesellschaft ist unantastbar. Niemand würde es wagen, ein Projekt vorzuschlagen, das den Zugverkehr behindert. Mich störte die Nähe der Gleise nicht, und ich beschloss zu bauen.

Ich konnte es kaum erwarten. Von Anfang an war klar, dass das Studio ein Provisorium bleiben würde, denn wir hatten keine offizielle Genehmigung. Es bestand immer die Möglichkeit, dass es wieder abgerissen würde. Aber die örtliche Behörde sagte, macht nur. Es war ihr egal, ob wir auf dem Grundstück etwas bauten oder nicht. Ich habe mich auch nicht weiter um die Genehmigung gekümmert. Wenn wir das Studio nur gebaut hätten, damit es der Staat wieder abreißen kann, wäre ich auch zufrieden gewesen.

Ich wollte in einem Loft wohnen, in einem Raum, in dem ich arbeiten kann und der offen ist für alle möglichen Aktivitäten. Auf Komfort habe ich nie besonderen Wert gelegt – ich bin in der Wüste Gobi aufgewachsen und das harte Leben gewohnt. Viel wichtiger war es, dass der Raum meiner Ästhetik entspricht. Ich bin zwar kein ausgebildeter Architekt, aber schon als ich Kind war, wurde überall um mich herum gebaut. Meinen ersten Lehmziegel machte ich, als ich zehn war. Ich habe gelernt, wie man einen Ziegel formt und brennt. Bauen ist eine natürliche Tätigkeit wie Essen, für die man nicht auf die Universität gehen muss.

Ich fertigte eine einfache Maßzeichnung an, die habe ich den Arbeitern gezeigt. Für einen Berufsarchitekten wäre das vielleicht nur eine kindische Skizze gewesen, aber die Arbeiter verstanden sie sehr gut. Nichts Kompliziertes – eine Tür, ein Fenster, ein Wohnbereich, ein Badezimmer, eine Küche und eine Treppe, nicht mehr. Ein anliegender Raum war für die Installation von Kunstwerken vorgesehen. Abgeschlossen, ohne Fenster, nur zwei große Dachfenster. Die Konstruktion bestimmt die Form des Baus. Wir haben lokales Material und billige Produkte verwendet. Deshalb besteht es zur Gänze aus Beton und grauen Ziegeln. Es gibt keine Dekoration. Das Studio sieht innen genauso aus wie außen …

Die Architektursprache ist nicht trendy. Vielleicht ist sie dadurch trendy geworden, dass wir hier das Studio haben. Dadurch ist es wie eine Mode geworden, den Stil hier in der Umgebung zu kopieren. Aber als wir fertig waren, dachten die Bauern aus dem Ort, die mithalfen, da fehlt noch was. Sie verstanden nicht, warum ich keine Innenausstattung wollte. Ich musste ihnen vormachen, dass mir das Geld ausgegangen war.

Young Architecture of China, 2001. In einer Siedlung nicht weit vom Flughafen Peking baute sich der Künstler Ai Weiwei ein Wohnhaus und Studio, in dem er und seine Frau arbeiten und ihre Kunstwerke präsentieren. Auf den ersten Blick handelt es sich um einen einfachen Atrium-Block aus den grauen Ziegeln lokaler Produktion. Aber das Haus ist in Wirklichkeit das Resultat einer Performance des Künstlers: 100 Tage lang arbeiteten die örtlichen Handwerker unter Ais Aufsicht an dieser perfekt abgestimmten Sequenz von Raumvolumen.

Detail Magazine, 2002. Dieses Künstlerstudio hat eine Grundfläche von 500 Quadratmetern. Das Betonskelett ist mit rötlichen Ziegeln ausgefacht und bleibt innen offen. In den äußeren Mantel aus grauen Vormauerziegeln sind wenige wohlproportionierte Fenster eingelassen. Hauptelement der Anlage ist das zwei Etagen hohe Studio, das im rechten Winkel zum Wohntrakt steht. Die Wände sind dort fensterlos, als einzige Lichtquelle dienen zwei lange schmale Dachfenster. Die Zahl der Baumaterialien wurde möglichst gering gehalten.

China Radio International, 2004. Ai Weiwei standen für sein Bauprojekt die folgenden Materialien zur Verfügung: 130.000 Ziegel, 180 Tonnen Zement, 7,5 Tonnen Bewehrungsstäbe, 34 Fertigdielen, 45 Kubikmeter Sand sowie Altholz. Die Bauzeit betrug 60 Tage, das Weißen der Wände nahm weitere 40 Tage in Anspruch. Wirtschaftlichkeit ist eines der grundlegenden Designprinzipien von Ai Weiwei. „Das beste Design ist immer auch das, das am meisten Geld spart", erklärt er. Sein Haus ist der beste Ausdruck dieser Idee. Es kommt ohne Konventionen wie Wände, Türen oder Dach aus. Zweckmäßigkeit hat Priorität, alle anderen Aspekte von Design und Dekor sind unnütze Wiederholungen und wurden von Ai kurzentschlossen eliminiert. Der bemerkenswerteste Teil des Hauses ist das Badezimmer im ersten Stock. Es ist völlig offen. Toilette und Waschbecken stehen wie Möbel frei im Raum. In den meisten chinesischen Häusern neuerer Bauart wird das Badezimmer durch Milchglas abgetrennt. Ai geht einen Schritt weiter und öffnet den traditionellen Privatbereich für den Besucher. Der erste Stock sei ohnehin privat, erklärt er, eine weitere Wand wäre überflüssig. „Wir übernehmen Konventionen, ohne uns zu fragen, warum und wie. Zum Beispiel die Tür, das Fenster, die Wand und die Privatsphäre. Ein guter Designer soll nicht zeigen, was er gelernt hat, sondern eine eigenständige Sprache suchen." Dies führt zu einer radikalen Vereinfachung der Wohnelemente. Wände aus Rohziegeln und Fenster aus Milchglas. Da die Wände zur Präsentation von Kunst dienen, sind die Wärmeleitungen im Boden eingelassen. Treppen bestehen schlicht aus Zementbohlen. Selbst die Arbeiter waren überrascht, als das Haus fertig war: Es hat ja gar kein Dach! So ein Deckel ist doch kein Dach. „Ein Haus ist wie eine Schachtel. Es ist nur ein Behälter. Wenn es so ein richtiges Dach bekommt, verwandelt sich ein Haus sofort in ein Designobjekt. Ich brauche für ein Haus nur die einfachsten Bestandteile." Nur logisch also, dass Ai Weiwei die Schachtel einfach mit einem Deckel zugemacht hat.

WEITERE BAUTEN UND CAOCHANGDI

Ai Weiwei. Nachdem mein Studio fertig war, wollten sofort auch andere Leute, dass ich ihnen etwas baue. Sie meinten, ich hätte beim Bau meines Studios einen starken Sinn für Ästhetik bewiesen. Ich begann, Bauaufträge von Freunden anzunehmen. Mein erstes Projekt war eine Bar für einen Schriftsteller, und viele weitere folgten – Studios für andere Künstler, Restaurants, alles Mögliche. Es fing an, Spaß zu machen. Die Art von Architektur, die wir machten, war gefragt, es gab Kunden, und die Gebäude erfüllten ihren Zweck.

Jonathan Napack, Kunstkritiker und Autor, 2003. Ai Weiwei lebt seit mehr als fünf Jahren in diesem Haus. Ein ständiger Strom von Besuchern kommt durchs Tor, von frühmorgens bis spätabends. Heute sind es: ein Fabrikbesitzer aus Shenyang, der seine Werksanlagen verbessern will, der Sohn eines Schauspielers, der Kinos für die Landbevölkerung baut, und eine junge amerikanische Filmemacherin, die eine Idee für einen Dokumentarfilm hat. Sie alle haben zwei Dinge gemeinsam: Sie wollen etwas wissen, und sie haben das Gefühl, dass Ai Weiwei ihnen weiterhelfen kann.

The New York Times, 2007. Der chinesische Kunststar Ai Weiwei wagte vor sieben Jahren den Sprung an die Peripherie der Hauptstadt. Im Dorf Caochangdi an der Fünften Ringstraße im Nordosten entwarf er einen Komplex für sich selbst, mehrere Bauten für Freunde sowie eine Galerie namens China Art Archives and Warehouse. Eine Zeitlang blieben er und sein Kreis allein. Doch da sich im Kunstbezirk 798, dem Epizentrum der zeitgenössischen Kunstszene Pekings, immer mehr Boutiquen und Touristen drängen, wandern viele führende chinesische Galerien seit Frühling nach Caochangdi ab. Ins Ai-Weiwei-Dorf, wie man mit gutem Recht sagen könnte.

ARBEIT IM STUDIO UND IN DEN WERKSTÄTTEN

Lao San, Projektassistent in Peking. Ich bin seit meinem 16. Lebensjahr Tischler. Meine drei Brüder sind alle Tischler. Ich kam 1994 nach Peking, da war ich 25. Damals gab

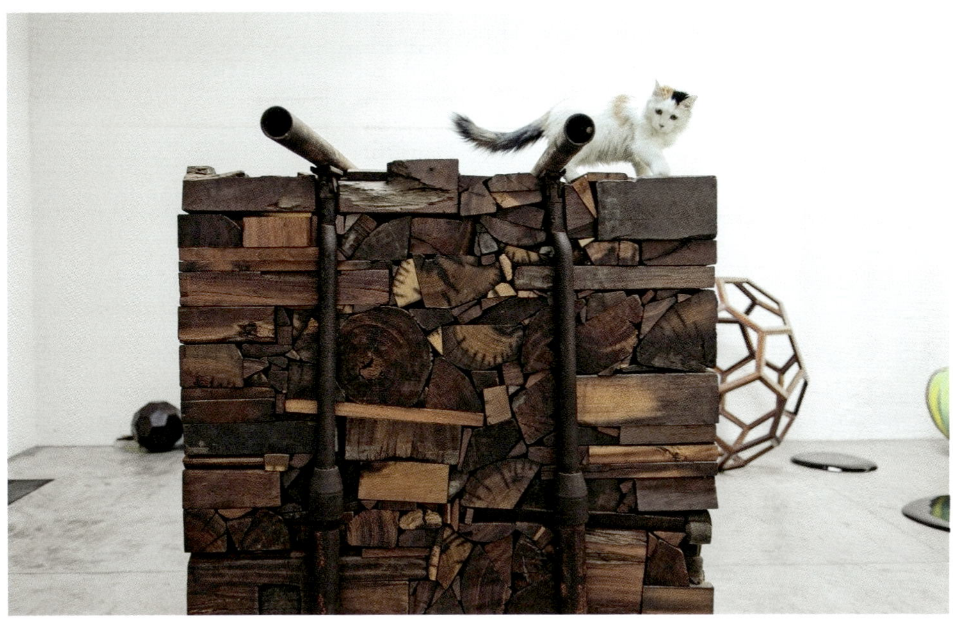

Studio cat with *Kippe*, 2006, tieli wood from dismantled Qing Dynasty temples, iron bars,
71 ⁵⁄₈ x 112 ⁵⁄₈ x 41 ⁷⁄₈ inches (see pp. 280/281)

es hier viele Möbel- und Türfabriken. Ai Weiweis Bruder Ai Dan bat mich, Türen und Fenster für sein Haus zu machen. Durch ihn traf ich Ai, der, wie ich hörte, gerade aus Amerika zurückgekommen war. Das war eine unbeschwerte Zeit. Wir trafen uns im Haus seines Bruders und aßen zusammen. Nach einem halben Jahr fragte er mich, ob ich für ihn arbeiten will.

Das erste Kunstwerk, das ich gemacht habe, war *Table with Two Legs on the Wall* (1997, S. 103). Ai fragte: Kannst du die beiden Tische so zusammenfügen? Ich sagte ja. Anfangs gab es ein paar kleine Schwierigkeiten. Jedes Werk hat seine eigene Struktur und seine eigenen Herausforderungen, wenn man es zum ersten Mal macht. Aber eines ist nicht schwerer als das andere. Jedes braucht seine Zeit. Für Großprojekte müssen wir manchmal erst einen geeigneten Raum finden.

Wir beginnen mit einem Modell. Wenn Ai es genehmigt, vergrößern wir es maßstabsgetreu. Wir überlegen uns, wie man es auseinandernehmen und wieder zusammensetzen kann. In den Holzarbeiten und den Formen stecken viel Versuch und Irrtum, viel Auspro-

bieren. Die *Maps of China* (2003–, S. 163–166) bestehen aus mindestens 500 Holzteilen. Über 130 außen und über 180 innen. Viele davon habe ich gemacht. Eine spezielle Version aus nur acht Holzteilen hat, wenn man sie zusammensetzt, in der Mitte ein Loch in der Form der chinesischen Landesgrenzen. Die Holzskulptur, die einem Katzenspielzeug nachgebaut ist (2004–, S. 207, 259), war einfacher. Rund wie ein Ball. Wir Tischler wissen, wie man so etwas macht.

Normalerweise arbeiten ungefähr zehn Tischler hier, bei großen Projekten auch mehr. Viele sind aus meiner Heimatstadt in Anhui. Es gibt dort eine lange Tischlertradition.Ich beurteile Kunstwerke nicht. Kunst hat keinen festen Wert. Jeder hat seine eigene Meinung. Es ist schwer, etwas zu machen, das allen gefällt.

Liu Weiwei, Projektassistent in Jingdezhen.
Ich komme aus Peking und stieg früh ins Antiquitätengeschäft ein. Freunde von mir waren in den 1990er-Jahren in der Branche, und mir hat es auch sofort zugesagt. Ich hatte einen Laden auf dem Antiquitätenmarkt.

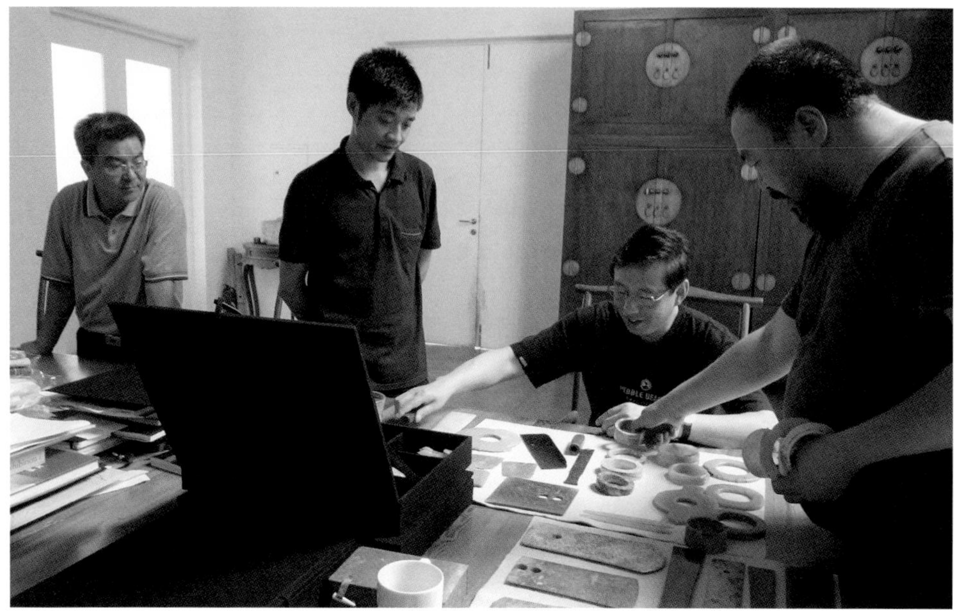

Studio life, Caochangdi, Beijing 2007–2009; work meeting

Ai Weiwei traf ich schon Anfang der 1990er-Jahre. Er sammelte damals Antiquitäten und hörte, dass ich mit Porzellan arbeitete. Unsere Zusammenarbeit begann 2006. Er hatte die Idee für einen *Ruyi* (S. 301), und ich habe ihm geholfen, sie zu realisieren. Er war ziemlich zufrieden.

Die Werkstatt in Jiangxi hat ungefähr 2100 Quadratmeter. Wenn nichts Besonderes anfällt, arbeiten dort ungefähr 20 Leute. Wir haben unsere eigenen Brennöfen gebaut, drei Stück. Gasbrennöfen wie alle in Jingdezhen. Das Schwierigste war das Porzellangerüst für *Field* (2010). Es bestand aus jeweils ein Meter langen Elementen. Die Form war sehr dünn und fiel beim Brennen zusammen. Ich musste vier Jahre lang experimentieren, bis es klappte.

Sunflower Seeds (2010, S. 49, 407–409) stellte uns vor ähnliche Herausforderungen. Wir haben fast drei Jahre lang daran gearbeitet. Anfangs machten wir eine Reihe von Probestücken, und dann haben wir das gesamte Projekt fertiggestellt. Dazu waren viele Schritte notwendig. Insgesamt haben ungefähr 1600 Arbeiter in Jingdezhen 150 Tonnen Porzellansamen erzeugt. Wir hatten zehn verschiedene Standorte, manche in Dörfern, manche in der Stadt. Ich mietete Fabrikräume. Es war nicht einfach, das zu organisieren. Jedes Team hatte einen Aufseher. Ich war für die Projektleitung und die Qualitätskontrolle verantwortlich. Wenn das Wetter schlecht war, wurden die Stücke nicht trocken und klebten am Brett.

Zhao Zhao, ehemaliger Studioassistent, Künstler in Peking. Ich bin in Shihezi aufgewachsen, in der Provinz Xinjiang wie Ai Weiwei. Nach dem Kunststudium beschloss ich, nach Peking zu ziehen, denn Xinjiang ist kein leichtes Pflaster für unabhängige Künstler. Ich plante, einen Raum im Künstlerdorf Songzhuang zu mieten und zu malen.

Ich traf Weiwei 2004 nur zehn Tage nach meiner Ankunft in Peking. Ich stellte mich vor und sagte ihm, dass ich in Songzhuang wohnen wollte. Er meinte, Songzhuang sei schrecklich, und schaute sich meine Mappe an. Ein paar Tage später rief er mich an. Er wollte wissen, ob ich mit einer Sony-Kamera umgehen könne. Ich sagte ja und ging zu ihm. Ai fragte mich, ob ich bereit war, die Malerei aufzugeben. „Was soll ich denn

sonst tun?", antwortete ich. Er sagte, ich
könne Dokumentarfilme machen. Er nahm
ein Blatt Papier und zog eine Linie: „Das ist
die Chang'an-Avenue", sagte er. „Fang am
Ostende an, bleib alle 50 Meter stehen und
filme die Straße. Von einem Ende zum
andern." Ich verstand ihn nicht sofort – ein
Film ohne Handlung? Er erklärte mir, dass es
sich um experimentelle Videokunst handelt,
und dann habe ich begriffen.
Es hat mehr als einen Monat gedauert, die
ganze Chang'an-Avenue zu filmen. Als ich fertig war, sagte er: „Gut, mach jetzt die Zweite
Ringstraße." Dann kam die Dritte Ringstraße
dran. Sobald ich mit einem Projekt fertig war,
kam das nächste (S. 271–273).
Später gab es noch viel mehr zu tun. Als die
Arbeit am Olympiastadion begann, bat mich
Weiwei, die Bauarbeiten zu dokumentieren
(S. 385, 387–389). Jeden Tag fuhr ich ohne
Genehmigung auf die Baustelle. Ai hatte von
einem Bekannten einen alten Ausweis bekommen, den legte ich aufs Armaturenbrett. Meistens hielt mich niemand auf, und wenn doch,
sagte ich einfach, ich arbeite für Soundso,
und die ließen mich durch. Ich habe auch den
Bau des Flughafenterminals 3 fotografiert,
den Norman Foster entworfen hat (S. 275–
277). Ich war sein Assistent bei Lehrvorträ-
gen und sein Reisebegleiter, wenn es Ausstellungen zu organisieren gab.

**Liu Yanping, freie Mitarbeiterin der
Citizens' Investigation und danach
Studioassistentin, Bloggerin in Peking.**
Ich studierte Volkswirtschaftslehre an der
Central University of Finance and Economics.
Nach meinem Master arbeitete ich für eine
Bank. Das war bequem, aber langweilig. Ich
promovierte dann an der Chinese Academy of
Social Sciences im Fach Geschichte des
modernen Finanzwesens. Im Jahr 2009 ging
meine Tochter in den Kindergarten, und ich
war froh, plötzlich so viel Zeit fürs Internet-
Surfen zu haben.
Von Ai Weiwei hörte ich zum ersten Mal 2007
oder 2008 durch seinen Sina-Blog. Den fand
ich sehr interessant. Nach dem Erdbeben vom
12. Mai 2009, als er die Citizens' Investigation startete (S. 344ff.), erklärte Ai in einem
Artikel und Interview für seinen Blog, warum
es so wichtig war, die Namen der Opfer herauszufinden. Das war eine außergewöhnliche

Initiative, die mich sehr berührte. Ai setzte
sehr deutlich auseinander, was ihn motivierte
und warum es notwendig war, eine Opferliste
zusammenzustellen. China hat mehr als eine
Milliarde Einwohner, aber es gibt nur wenige,
die so etwas tun können. Also schrieb ich an
sein Studio: Wenn ihr Hilfe braucht, kann ich
rüberkommen.
Meine erste Aufgabe war, die Helfer vor der
Abfahrt auf ihre Arbeit in Sichuan vorzuberei-
ten. Sie sollten in die Schulen und zu den
Eltern gehen, die Namen der Opfer aufschreiben und sofort per E-Mail an uns senden. Wir
haben die Daten erfasst und in unsere Liste
eingetragen. Wenn es Telefonnummern gab,
riefen wir die Eltern an. Es war in erster Linie
Organisationsarbeit. Das dauerte mehrere
Monate.
Ich war wirklich überrascht. Die Videos, die
die Helfer aus Sichuan schickten, die Namens-
listen, die SMS der Eltern – ich hatte von all
dem nichts gewusst. Meine Beziehung zum
Staat war vorher eher vage gewesen. Ich
dachte, ich und die Regierung, wir haben
nichts miteinander zu tun. Ich wollte, dass
die mich in Ruhe lassen, und ließ sie meiner-
seits auch in Ruhe. Es war ja nicht meine
Regierung, ich hatte sie nicht gewählt. Ich
habe seither viel dazugelernt, aber ich weiß
noch immer nicht genau, welche Beziehung
ich zur Regierung habe. Nur die Realität ver-
stehe ich jetzt ein bisschen besser.
Nach der Citizens' Investigation arbeiteten
wir ein halbes Jahr an unserer Petition an die
Regierung, eine offizielle Aufstellung der
Opfer zu veröffentlichen. Danach versuchten
wir noch ein paar andere Dinge, zum Beispiel
untersuchten wir genau, welche Präzedenz-
fälle es gab. Und dann wurde Ai festgenommen.
Im Inneren war er trotz der Haft derselbe
Mensch geblieben. Er erzählte mir: „Die wollten mir eine Gehirnwäsche verpassen, damit
ich anfange, anders zu denken. Aber ich sagte
ihnen, ein Apfel bleibt ein Apfel, eine Birne
bleibt eine Birne. Ihr könnt aus einem Apfel
keine Birne machen." Er hatte sich überhaupt
nicht verändert!

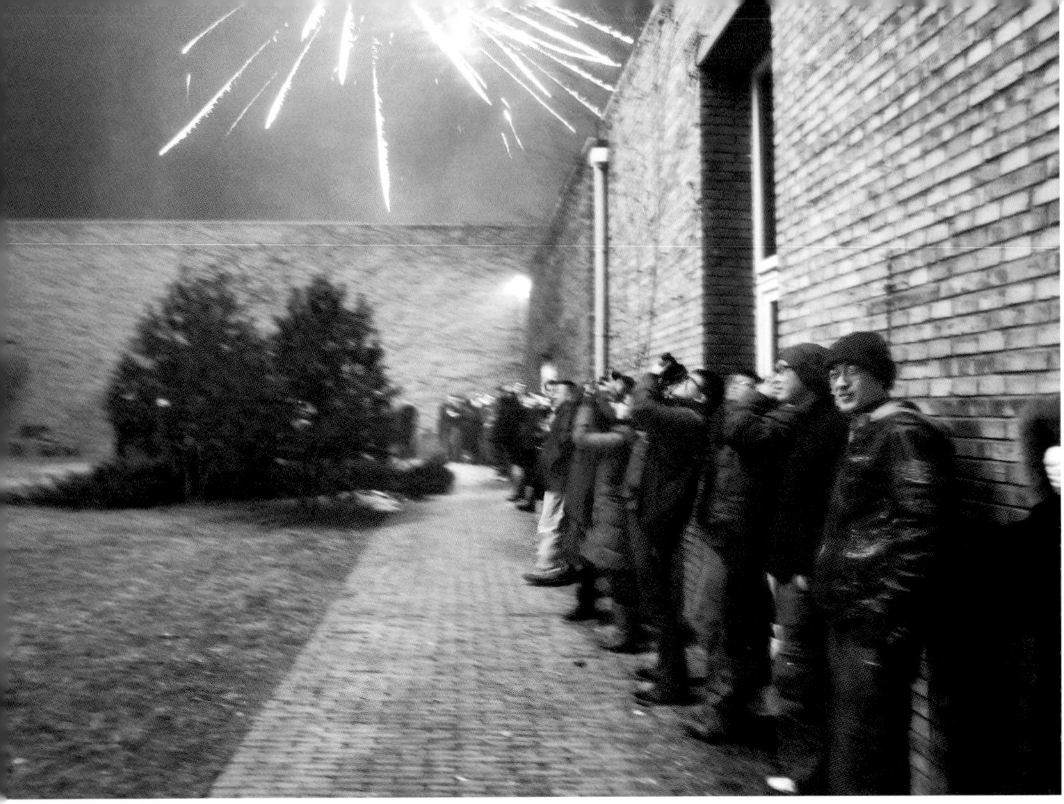

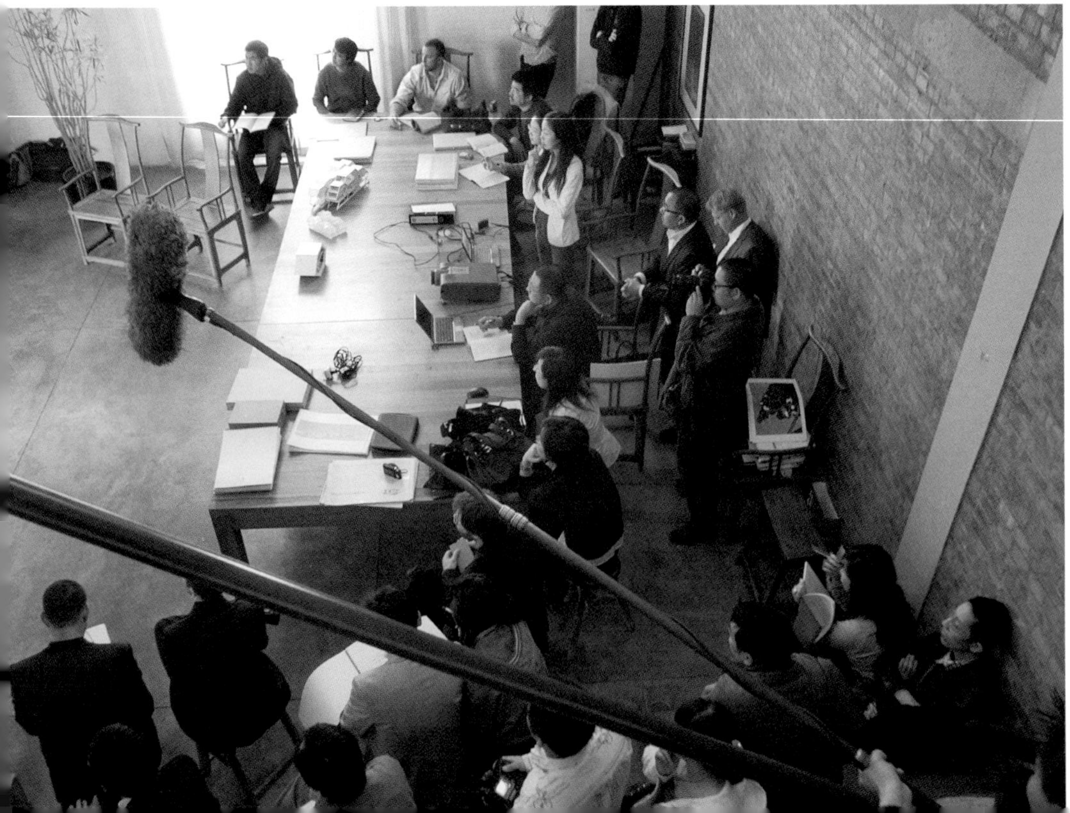

Ai Weiwei Studio, Caochangdi 258, 1999–

LA CONSTRUCTION DU STUDIO

Ai Weiwei. Quelques années après mon retour des États-Unis, j'ai décidé d'avoir un endroit à moi. Quand j'ai vu ce terrain à côté de la voie express qui mène à l'aéroport, il m'a tout de suite plu. Il y a beaucoup de taxis sur cette voie express, je pouvais donc facilement en trouver un à chaque fois que je voulais aller en ville. Et puis ce lopin de terre n'était pas loin des rails de la voie de chemin de fer, ce qui m'a semblé idéal – personne ne veut acheter de terrain près d'une voie de chemin de fer. Il n'y avait donc pas de danger que quelqu'un essaie de récupérer cette terre et, surtout, la direction des chemins de fer étant intouchable en Chine, personne n'oserait proposer un projet de développement qui viendrait remettre en question le tracé des voies. Moi, ça ne me dérangeait pas d'être à côté des voies, j'ai donc décidé de construire. J'avais très envie de construire quelque chose. Je savais dès le début que le studio serait un bâtiment temporaire car nous n'avions pas d'approbation officielle. Il était possible qu'on le détruise parce que ce n'était pas un projet de construction légal. Mais les autorités locales nous ont dit qu'on pouvait se lancer, ça leur était égal qu'on construise sur ce terrain. Je ne me suis pas préoccupé d'avoir un permis. Même si j'avais construit quelque chose que les autorités auraient détruit aussitôt, j'aurais été satisfait.

J'avais envie de vivre dans un espace de type loft, qui pourrait me fournir un espace de travail mais aussi d'activités diverses. Le confort n'a jamais été déterminant pour moi – j'ai grandi dans le désert de Gobi, dans des conditions très rudes. Ce qui m'intéressait, c'était de créer un espace qui reflète mon sens de l'esthétique. Je n'ai aucune formation d'architecte, mais j'ai observé les travaux de construction et les bâtiments qui m'entouraient depuis mon enfance. J'ai fabriqué ma première brique en torchis à l'âge de dix ans ; j'ai appris à mouler et à cuire les briques. Pour moi, construire est un acte naturel, comme manger. Pas besoin de prendre de cours.

J'ai donc fait un dessin tout simple, avec les mesures, que j'ai montré aux ouvriers. Un architecte professionnel n'y aurait peut-être vu qu'une esquisse naïve, mais pour les gens qui allaient m'aider à construire, c'était très clair. Le design était très simple – une porte, une fenêtre, un espace à vivre, une salle de bains, une cuisine, un escalier. Je voulais aussi une pièce attenante pour les œuvres d'art dans laquelle il n'y aurait pas de fenêtre, juste deux grandes verrières. Nous avons construit le studio en respectant les méthodes de construction traditionnelles, en utilisant des matériaux locaux et une technologie bon marché – voilà pourquoi il est entièrement en béton et en briques grises. Il n'y a aucune décoration, le bâtiment est pareil à l'intérieur qu'à l'extérieur…

Le langage architectural n'est pas à la mode. Peut-être qu'il le devient quand on habite le bâtiment. Il est devenu tendance, il a été copié. Mais quand on était en train de construire, les paysans qui nous ont aidés pensaient que ce n'était pas fini. Ils ne comprenaient pas pourquoi je ne voulais pas de décoration intérieure. J'ai dû leur dire que je n'avais plus d'argent.

Young Architecture of China, 2001.
Dans un petit village non loin de l'aéroport international de Pékin, l'artiste Ai Weiwei a conçu cette maison-atelier où sa femme et lui créent et exposent leurs œuvres. À première vue, il s'agit d'un simple ensemble avec cour intérieure construit en briques grises. Mais le bâtiment est vraiment le résultat d'une performance artistique : en cent jours, ce sont des artisans locaux qui ont construit, sous la supervision de l'artiste, ces volumes qui témoignent d'un sens très raffiné de l'espace.

Detail Magazine, 2002. Conçue pour un artiste, cette maison-atelier a une surface au sol de 500 m². La structure est faite de béton armé – laissé nu à l'intérieur – et de panneaux de briques rouges. Une couche extérieure en briques grises a été montée autour de cette structure et est percée de quelques fenêtres

aux proportions soigneusement étudiées.
L'élément principal de cette construction est
le studio de deux étages placé perpendiculai-
rement à l'espace habitable. Dans le studio
sans fenêtres, la lumière du jour pénètre uni-
quement par deux verrières. Le nombre de
matériaux utilisés a été réduit au minimum.

Radio Chine International, 2004. Voici
ce qu'Ai Weiwei a utilisé pour construire
sa maison : 130 000 briques, 180 tonnes de
ciment, 7,5 tonnes de barres de soutènement
en acier, 34 panneaux préfabriqués, 45 m^3
de sable et quelques planches de bois. La
construction a pris soixante jours, la peinture des murs quarante jours. Ai Weiwei a
pour principe d'être économique. Pour lui,
« le meilleur design est aussi le plus économique ». Sa maison reflète sans aucun doute
au mieux cette idée. Chez lui, les concepts
établis de murs, de portes et de toit ont disparu. Les éléments de design et de décoration
qui ne sont pas purement pratiques sont
considérés comme autant de banalités et de
répétitions inutiles, Ai Weiwei les a abandon-
nés sans aucune héstation.
L'élément le plus frappant dans sa maison
est la salle de bains du deuxième étage. Elle
est complètement ouverte. Les toilettes et le
lavabo sont comme des meubles posés dans
la pièce au hasard. En Chine, de nombreuses
familles ont une simple paroi en verre pour
séparer la salle de bains des autres pièces
de la maison. Mais personne encore n'a eu
l'audace d'Ai Weiwei, qui remet en question
la définition traditionnelle de l'intimité en
l'exposant à ses visiteurs. L'artiste considère
que le deuxième étage est déjà un espace
relativement privé et qu'il n'est nul besoin d'y
ajouter une cloison. « Nous avons du mal avec
les concepts établis qu'on ne remet pas en
question, comme la porte, la fenêtre, le mur,
l'intimité. Un bon designer ne devrait pas
reproduire ce qu'on lui a appris, mais présenter son regard original sur les choses. »
Résultat, les éléments architecturaux sont
réduits au maximum. Les murs sont en
briques nues et les fenêtres en verre dépoli.
Comme les murs servent à présenter ses
œuvres, le chauffage a été installé au sol. Les
escaliers ne sont rien de plus que des plaques
préfabriquées en ciment. Une fois le bâtiment
terminé, les ouvriers ont été surpris qu'il n'y

ait pas de toit. Car on ne peut qualifier de toit
le couvercle qui en fait office. « Une maison,
c'est comme une boîte. Ce n'est rien de plus
qu'un container. Il est facile en y ajoutant un
toit de changer le bâtiment en quelque chose
de trop stylé. J'ai juste besoin de composants
de base pour la maison. » Ce qui explique
pourquoi Ai Weiwei s'est contenté de fermer
la boîte par une sorte de couvercle.

LE DÉVELOPPEMENT DU QUARTIER

Ai Weiwei. Dès que j'eus fini de construire
mon studio, des gens m'ont demandé de
construire pour eux. Ils estimaient que j'avais
fait preuve d'un solide sens esthétique dans la
construction de mon studio. J'ai commencé à
accepter des projets de construction pour des
amis. Mon premier projet a été de construire
un bar pour un écrivain, puis de nombreux
autres ont suivi – des studios pour d'autres
artistes, des restaurants, toute sorte de
choses. J'ai commencé à vraiment aimer ça.
Il y avait une demande pour le type d'architecture que nous proposions, il y avait des
clients, et ces bâtiments avaient leur utilité.

**Jonathan Napack, auteur et critique d'art,
2003.** Cela fait cinq ans maintenant qu'Ai
Weiwei vit dans ce bâtiment. Un flot constant
de visiteurs franchit le portail tout au long
de la journée. Parmi eux ce jour-là, le propriétaire d'une usine de Shenyang qui veut
faire construire un bâtiment plus fonctionnel ;
le fils d'un acteur qui monte une chaîne de
cinémas à la campagne ; un jeune réalisateur
américain qui a une idée de documentaire.
Tous ces gens ont deux choses en commun :
le désir d'apprendre quelque chose, et le sentiment qu'Ai Weiwei pourrait les aider dans
ce processus.

The New York Times, 2007. Il y a sept
ans, l'éminent artiste chinois Ai Weiwei a
eu l'audace d'aller s'installer en périphérie
de Pékin. Dans ce qu'on appelle le village de
Caochangdi, près du cinquième périphérique,
au nord-est de la ville, il a conçu un domaine
pour lui-même et quelques amis ainsi qu'une
galerie baptisée China Art Archives and
Warehouse. Ils y ont été tranquilles pendant
un moment. Mais ce printemps, le quartier
798, le centre de la scène d'art contemporain

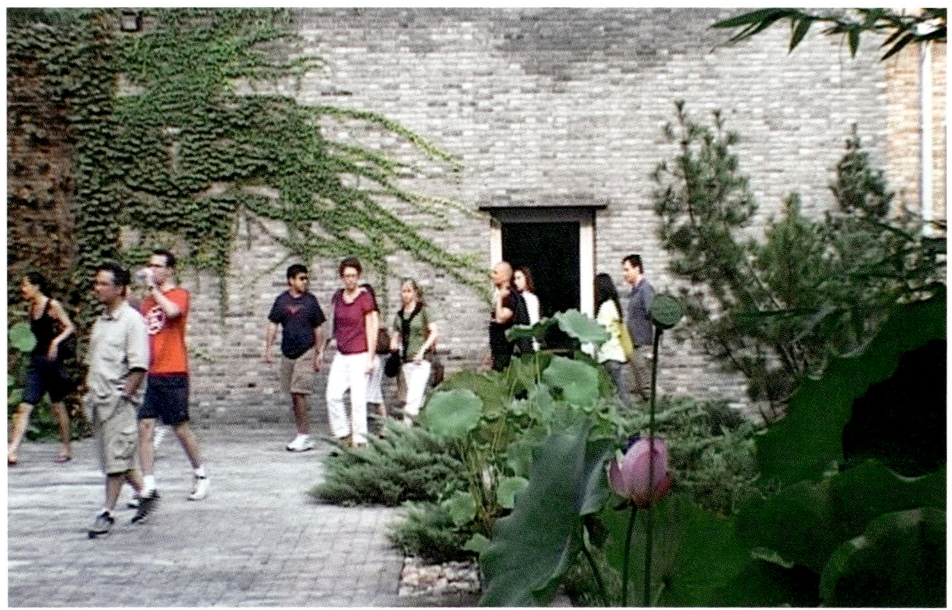

Still from *The MoMA Visit*, 2006, 5 videos, each 50 min

de Pékin, s'est mis à accueillir de plus en plus de boutiques et de touristes, et certains des propriétaires des galeries les plus importantes de Chine commencent à aller s'installer dans le village de Caochangdi. Qu'on devrait peut-être appeler village Ai Weiwei.

LE TRAVAIL AU STUDIO ET DANS LES ATELIERS

Lao San, assistant de projet, Pékin. Je suis menuisier depuis l'âge de seize ans. Mes trois frères sont tous menuisiers. Je suis arrivé à Pékin en 1994 à vingt-cinq ans. À l'époque, il y avait beaucoup d'usines de meubles et de portes. Ai Dan, le jeune frère de maître Ai, m'a demandé de fabriquer les portes et les fenêtres de sa maison. C'est comme ça que j'ai rencontré maître Ai. J'ai appris qu'il rentrait juste des États-Unis. L'ambiance était assez cool ; on passait souvent du temps chez son frère, on mangeait ensemble. Au bout de six mois, il m'a proposé de travailler avec lui. La première œuvre que j'ai réalisée pour lui était *Table with Two Legs on the Wall* (1997, p. 103). Maître Ai m'a demandé si je pouvais assembler deux tables comme ça. Je lui ai dit

que c'était possible. Au début, certains détails ont posé pas mal de difficultés. Chaque œuvre a une structure bien spécifique, et elles sont toutes difficiles à réaliser au début. Mais je ne pense pas qu'il y en ait une qui soit plus difficile qu'une autre. Chaque œuvre a besoin d'un certain temps et parfois il nous faut trouver un espace assez grand pour y fabriquer des œuvres d'envergure.

On commence par faire une maquette, et une fois que maître Ai l'a approuvée, on construit l'objet en taille réelle. On réfléchit à ce qu'on pourrait enlever, et comment le remettre. Il y a beaucoup d'expériences successives avec les pièces en bois et leur forme.

Chacune des *Maps of China* (2003–, pp. 163–166) se compose d'au moins 500 morceaux de bois. Il y en a plus de 130 sur la face extérieure de l'œuvre, et plus de 180 à l'intérieur. J'en ai fabriqué beaucoup. Il y en a une spéciale avec un trou en forme de carte en son centre, qui ne se compose que de huit pièces de bois. Quand on les assemble, il y a un trou qui a la forme de la Chine en son centre. Les travaux en bois inspirés d'un jouet pour chat (2004–, pp. 207, 259) sont plus faciles ; ils sont ronds, comme une balle.

Tous les menuisiers savent fabriquer ce genre de pièces. En temps ordinaire, nous sommes une dizaine de menuisiers ici, plus quand un projet important est en cours. Nombre d'entre eux viennent d'Anhui, ma ville natale. Il y a une longue tradition de menuiserie dans cette région.

Je ne juge pas l'œuvre d'art en elle-même. L'art n'a pas de valeur fixe. Chacun a une perspective différente. Il est difficile de faire quelque chose dont tout le monde soit content.

Liu Weiwei, assistant de projet, Jingdezhen. Je suis originaire de Pékin. J'ai toujours travaillé dans les antiquités, j'avais une boutique au marché des antiquaires. Dans les années 1990, j'avais des amis qui étaient dans le commerce, et je me suis mis à aimer ça moi aussi. J'ai rencontré Ai Weiwei au début des années 1990. Il collectionnait les antiquités et avait entendu dire que je faisais de la porcelaine. C'est en 2006 que nous avons travaillé ensemble pour la première fois. Il avait eu l'idée de *Ruyi* (p. 301) et je l'ai aidé à le réaliser. Il a été très satisfait. L'atelier de Jiangxi fait à peu près 2100 m². Quand on n'est pas sur un projet spécial, on est une vingtaine de personnes à y travailler. Nous avons fabriqué nos fours nous-mêmes ; nous en avons trois. Ce sont des fours à gaz, comme tous les fours à Jingdezhen. La pièce la plus difficile que j'ai réalisée, c'est la structure en porcelaine de *Field* (2010), où chaque section faisait un mètre de long. C'est particulièrement fin, et ça s'aplatit quand on le cuit. J'ai travaillé quatre ans sur ce projet avant d'arriver à un résultat satisfaisant. Le projet des *Sunflower Seeds* (2010, pp. 49, 407–409) a lui aussi été un gros défi. Nous y avons travaillé pendant près de trois ans. Nous avons commencé par expérimenter lentement, nous avons fait pas mal de tests avant de passer à la réalisation du projet. La production comptait un très grand nombre d'étapes. En tout, nous avons employé près de 1600 personnes à Jingdezhen qui ont fabriqué 150 tonnes de graines en porcelaine. La fabrication a eu lieu en une dizaine d'endroits différents. Dans des villages ou en ville. J'ai loué des usines. Ce n'était pas évident de superviser autant de monde. Nous avions un chef pour chaque équipe. Il fallait que je supervise tout ça et que je procède au contrôle de qualité. Quand il ne faisait pas beau, les graines ne séchaient pas et restaient collées aux planches.

Zhao Zhao, ancien assistant au studio, artiste, Pékin. J'ai grandi à Shihezi, dans la province du Xinjiang, comme Ai Weiwei. Après avoir obtenu mon diplôme à l'école d'art, j'ai décidé de m'installer à Pékin en 2004, car la province du Xinjiang n'est pas vraiment un endroit propice aux artistes indépendants. J'avais l'intention de louer une chambre dans la communauté d'artistes de Songzhuang et de peindre.

J'ai rencontré Ai Weiwei dix jours à peine après mon arrivée à Pékin. Je lui ai dit qui j'étais et que j'avais l'intention de vivre à Songzhuang. Il m'a dit que Songzhuang était un endroit épouvantable, et il a regardé mon portfolio. Il m'a appelé quelques jours après en me demandant si je savais me servir d'une caméra Sony. Je lui ai dit que oui et je suis passé chez lui. Il m'a demandé si je pouvais envisager d'abandonner la peinture. Je lui ai demandé ce que je ferais si je ne peignais plus. Il m'a répondu que je pourrais faire des films documentaires. Il a pris une feuille de papier et y a tracé une ligne en disant : « Voici le boulevard Chang'an. Vas à l'extrémité est du boulevard et filme-le. Tous les cinquante mètres, arrête-toi et filme la rue. Filme toute la rue comme ça. » Je n'ai pas compris tout de suite – pourquoi faire un film sans histoire ? Mais quand il m'a expliqué qu'il s'agissait d'une œuvre vidéo conceptuelle, j'ai compris. Il m'a fallu plus d'un mois pour finir de filmer le boulevard Chang'an, et une fois que j'eus fini, il m'a dit : « O.K., maintenant, filme le deuxième périphérique de la même manière. » Une fois que j'eus fini celui-ci, il m'a demandé de filmer le troisième périphérique. À chaque fois que j'avais terminé un projet (pp. 271–273). Il m'en donnait un autre.

Par la suite, il y a eu de plus en plus de travail. Ai Weiwei a commencé à travailler sur le projet du « Nid d'oiseau », et il m'a demandé de filmer le processus de sa construction (pp. 385, 387–389). Chaque jour, je me rendais sur le chantier sans permission, en utilisant un vieux pass de CCTV [Télévision centrale de Chine] qu'une connaissance d'Ai Weiwei lui avait donné. Je mettais le pass en évidence sur le tableau de bord de ma voiture et j'entrais. En principe, personne ne m'arrêtait, et si c'était le cas, je disais que je travaillais pour Untel et on me laissait tranquille. Après ça, j'ai filmé la construction du Terminal 3, conçu par Norman Foster (pp. 275–277). J'ai été son assistant quand il donnait des cours et je l'ai accompagné dans ses voyages quand il allait mettre en place ses expositions.

Liu Yanping, bénévole de l'enquête citoyenne, puis membre du personnel du studio, auteur d'un blog, Pékin. J'ai fait des études de finances publiques à l'Université Centrale des Finances de Pékin, où j'ai obtenu un Master. Ensuite, j'ai travaillé dans une banque. Le travail était confortable, mais ennuyeux. Après ça, j'ai fait un post-doc à l'Académie centrale des sciences sociales, en histoire de la finance moderne. En 2009, ma fille est entrée à l'école maternelle et j'ai eu un peu plus de temps pour surfer sur Internet.

La première fois que j'ai entendu parler d'Ai Weiwei, c'était par son blog Sina, en 2007 ou 2008. Je le trouvais super, je l'aimais beaucoup. En 2009, lorsqu'il a initié cette enquête citoyenne sur le tremblement de terre du 12 mai (p. 344 sqq.), il a écrit un article sur son blog avec une interview dans laquelle il disait pourquoi il était important de trouver ces noms. Je me suis dit que son point de vue était vraiment original. Même s'il y a plus d'un million de personnes en Chine qui ont pu s'exprimer sur le sujet, et dire pourquoi il fallait trouver cette liste de noms, lui l'a fait de manière très claire. Il n'y a pas beaucoup de gens qui savent faire ça. Alors j'ai écrit au studio et j'ai proposé mon aide.

Ma première tâche consistait à aider les bénévoles qui partaient pour le Sichuan. Ils visitaient les écoles, allaient voir les parents, consignaient les noms. Puis ils nous envoyaient tout ça par e-mail. Nous rassemblions les noms et entrions les données dans nos formulaires en fonction de l'information que nous cherchions, et s'il y avait un numéro de téléphone, nous appelions les parents. Il s'agissait donc surtout de classer des documents. Ça a duré pendant quelques mois. Tout ça était vraiment surprenant. Les vidéos que les bénévoles nous faisaient parvenir du Sichuan, les listes de noms, les messages que les parents nous envoyaient – j'ignorais tout ça avant. Je trouve qu'avant, mon attitude envers le gouvernement n'était pas claire. Je pensais que je n'avais aucune relation avec lui. Tout ce que je voulais, c'était ne pas avoir affaire à lui. Après tout, ce n'est pas moi qui l'ai choisi. Aujourd'hui, je crois que je le comprends un peu mieux, mais je ne sais toujours pas quel type de relation j'ai avec lui. J'en sais juste un peu plus sur la réalité qu'avant.

Après l'enquête citoyenne, nous avons passé six mois à travailler sur les demandes adressées au gouvernement pour qu'il rende les informations publiques. Ensuite, nous avons fait d'autres choses, comme étudier les jurisprudences précédentes. Ensuite, maître Ai a été mis en détention.

Quand il est sorti, il n'avait pas du tout changé à l'intérieur. Il m'a dit : « Ces gens ont voulu changer ma façon de penser. Mais je leur ai dit qu'une pomme serait toujours une pomme, et une poire toujours une poire. On ne peut pas changer une pomme en poire. » C'était vrai, il n'avait pas changé du tout !

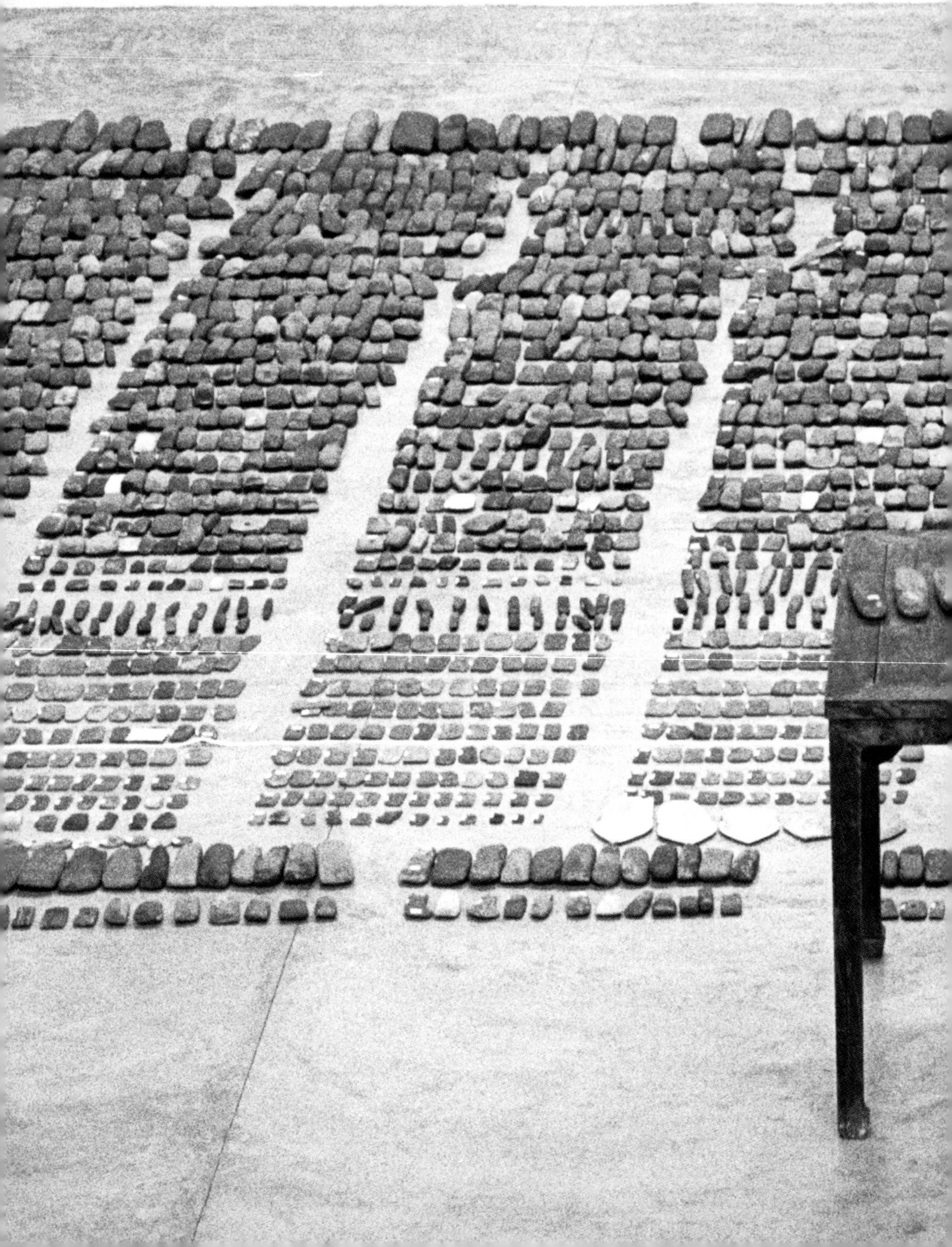

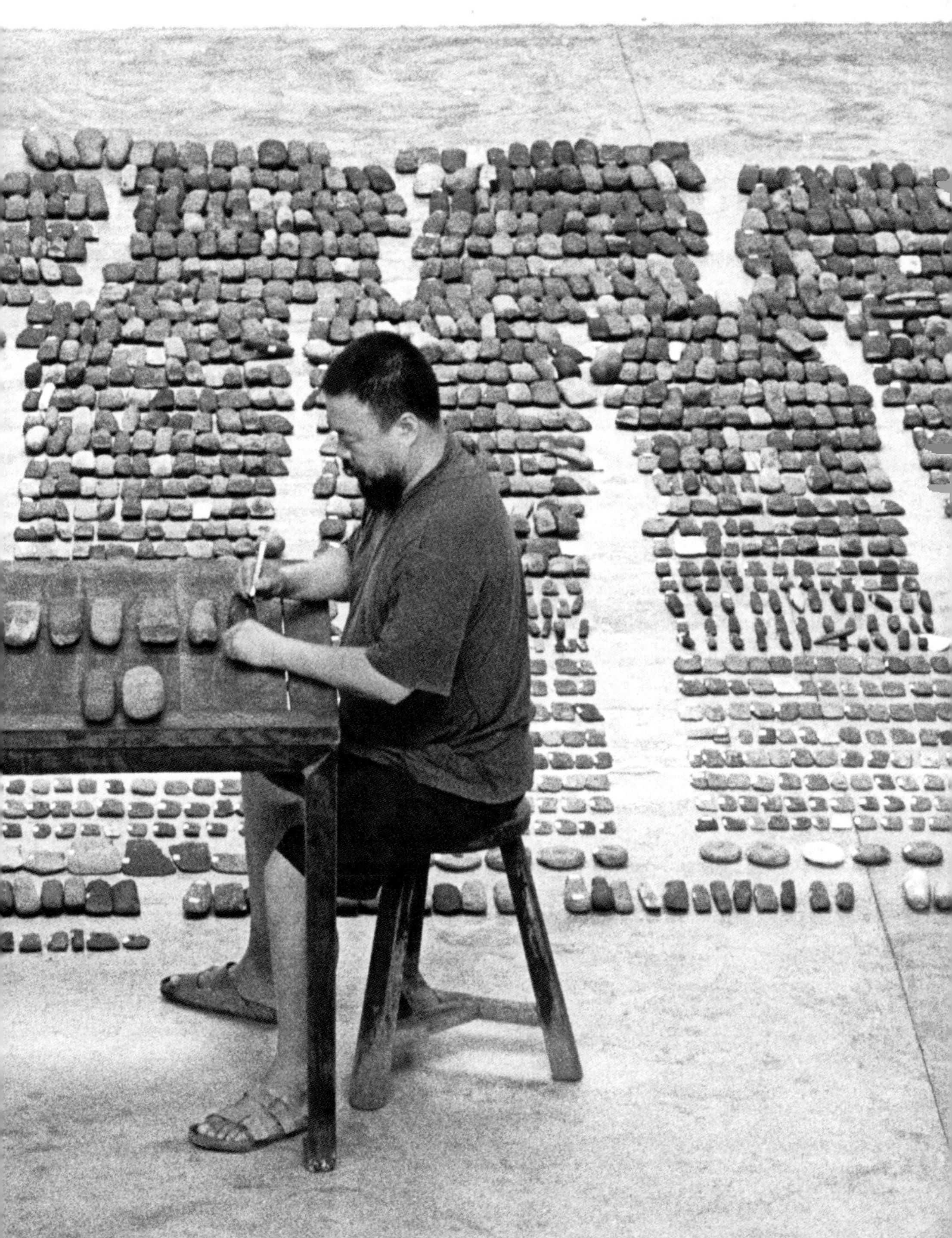

"We founded the China Art Archives and Warehouse in 1998. It was a time when there were no galleries or museums, and most contemporary art was shown in hotel lobbies or in the private apartments of foreigners. Hans van Dijk was interested in showing contemporary activities, but had no space, so we decided to do one together. Both of us shared the directorship, and our financial backing came from Frank Uytterhaegen. We couldn't call it a gallery because then we would have to go through special lessons by the police. That's why we called it a warehouse. Our first space was in a former factory in the Longzhaoshu area in the south of Beijing. I remember one early show of minimalist art. People came in and looked around, and then came back out and asked where the art was. Nobody recognized the canvases on the wall as art. We eventually moved from Longzhaoshu because to get there you had to go past a garbage landfill. I chose a spot in Caochangdi, and built something that couldn't be thrown away so easily." — AI WEIWEI

Wir gründeten die China Art Archives and Warehouse im Jahr 1998. Das war eine Zeit, in der es keine Galerien oder Museen gab und zeitgenössische Kunst meist in Hotellobbys oder Privatwohnungen von Ausländern zu sehen war. Hans van Dijk war interessiert, Zeitgenössisches zu präsentieren, hatte aber keinen Raum, und so entschieden wir uns, etwas zusammen zu machen. Wir teilten uns den Direktorenposten, während die Finanzierung von Frank Uytterhaegen auf die Beine gestellt wurde. Galerie konnten wir es nicht nennen, denn sonst hätten wir uns einer speziellen Schulung durch die Polizei unterziehen müssen. Daher nannten wir es Lagerhalle. Unsere ersten Räumlichkeiten fanden wir in einer ehemaligen Fabrik in Longzhaoshu im Süden Pekings. Ich kann mich gut an eine der ersten Ausstellungen dort erinnern, die minimalistische Kunst zeigte. Die Leute kamen herein, schauten sich um, gingen wieder hinaus und fragten, wo die Kunst zu finden sei. Niemand erkannte die Leinwände an der Wand als Kunst. Schließlich zogen wir aus Longzhaoshu weg, weil man auf dem Weg dorthin an einer Mülldeponie vorbeimusste. Ich entschied mich für einen Standort in Caochangdi und baute etwas, das nicht so leicht entsorgt werden konnte.

Nous avons créé la China Art Archives and Warehouse en 1998. À cette époque, il n'y avait ni galeries ni musées, l'art contemporain était principalement montré dans des hôtels ou dans les appartements privés de particuliers étrangers. Hans van Dijk avait envie de montrer des travaux contemporains, mais il n'avait pas d'espace, alors nous avons décidé d'en créer un ensemble. Nous nous partagions la direction de la CAAW, et Frank Uytterhaegen nous apportait un soutien financier. Nous ne pouvions pas l'appeler galerie, cela nous aurait valu des ennuis avec la police. D'où le terme d'entrepôt. Au début, nous nous sommes installés dans une ancienne usine de Longzhaoshu, au sud de Pékin. Je me souviens d'une des premières expositions d'art minimaliste. Les gens sont entrés faire un tour dans l'entrepôt, puis ils sont ressortis et nous ont demandé où étaient les œuvres d'art. Personne n'avait pensé que les toiles accrochées aux murs étaient des œuvres d'art. Nous avons fini par quitter Longzhaoshu, parce que pour y arriver, il fallait passer à côté d'une décharge. J'ai choisi un endroit à Caochangdi et j'y ai construit quelque chose qu'on ne peut pas jeter à la poubelle aussi facilement.

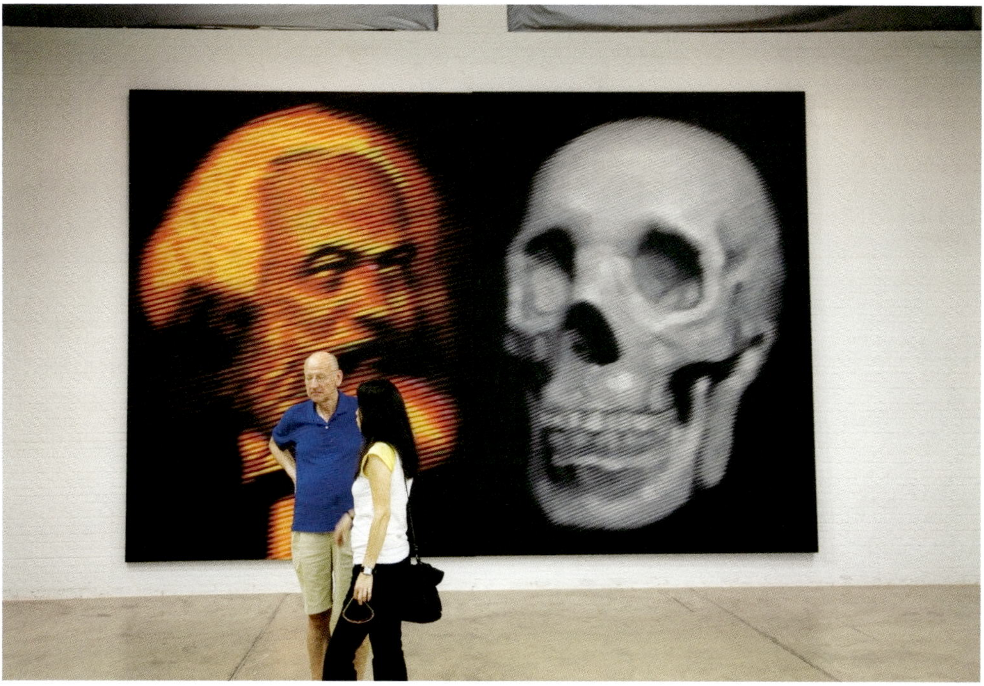

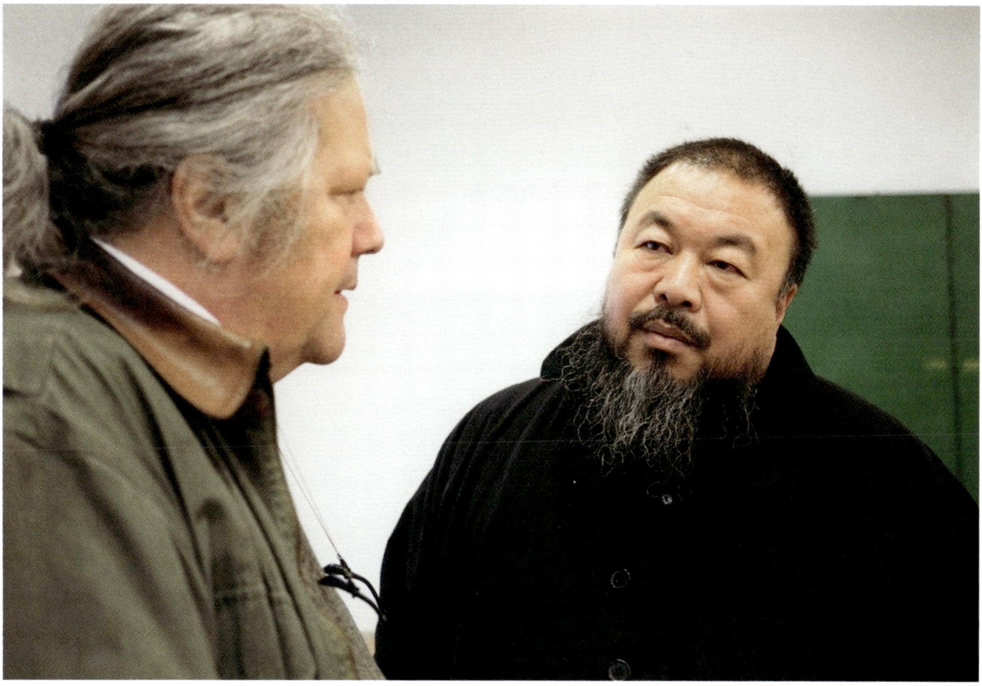

Top and pages 144–146: Views of exhibitions curated by Ai Weiwei
at China Art Archives and Warehouse, Beijing 1999–2006 | 143

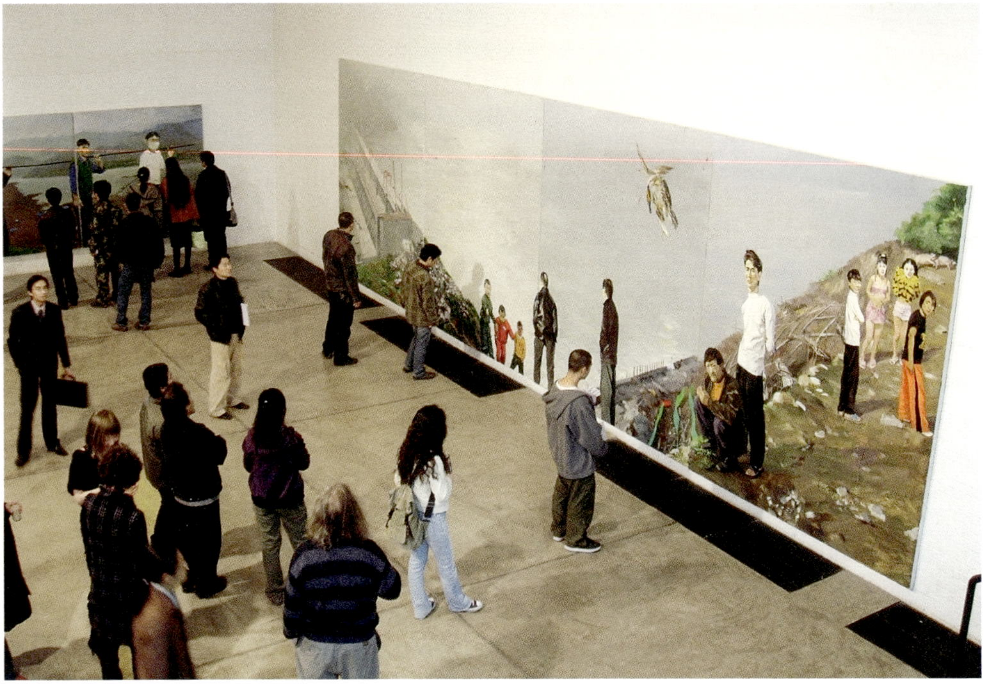

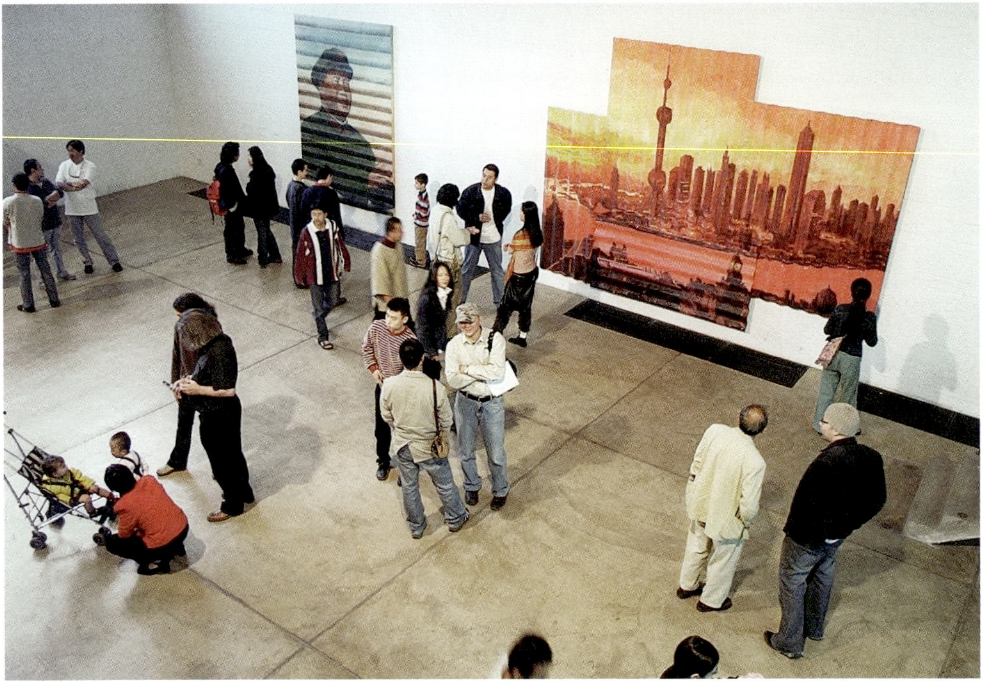

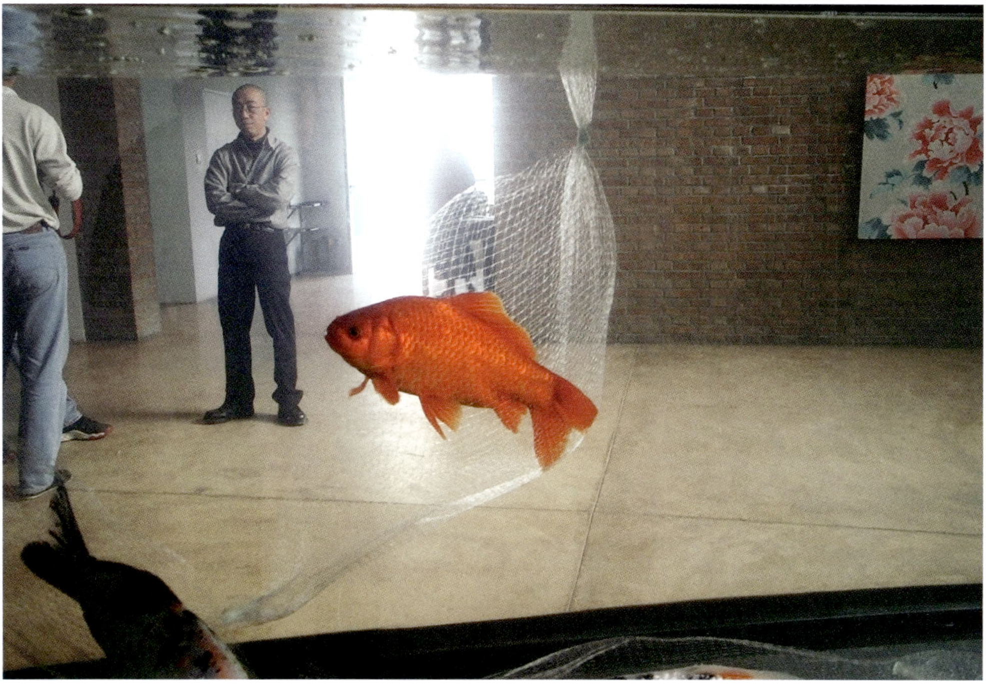

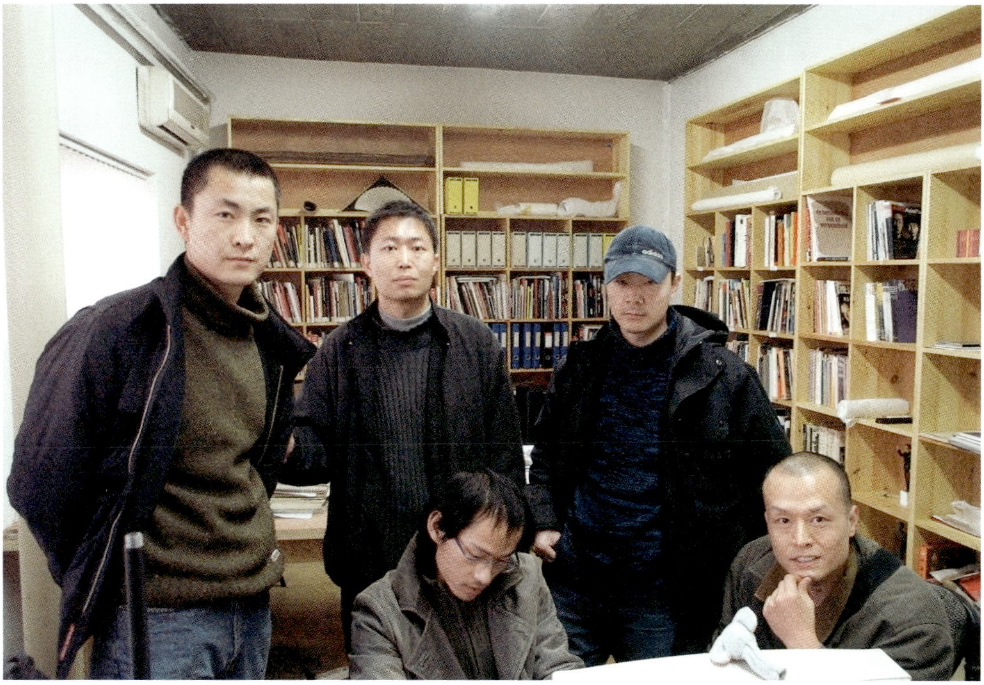

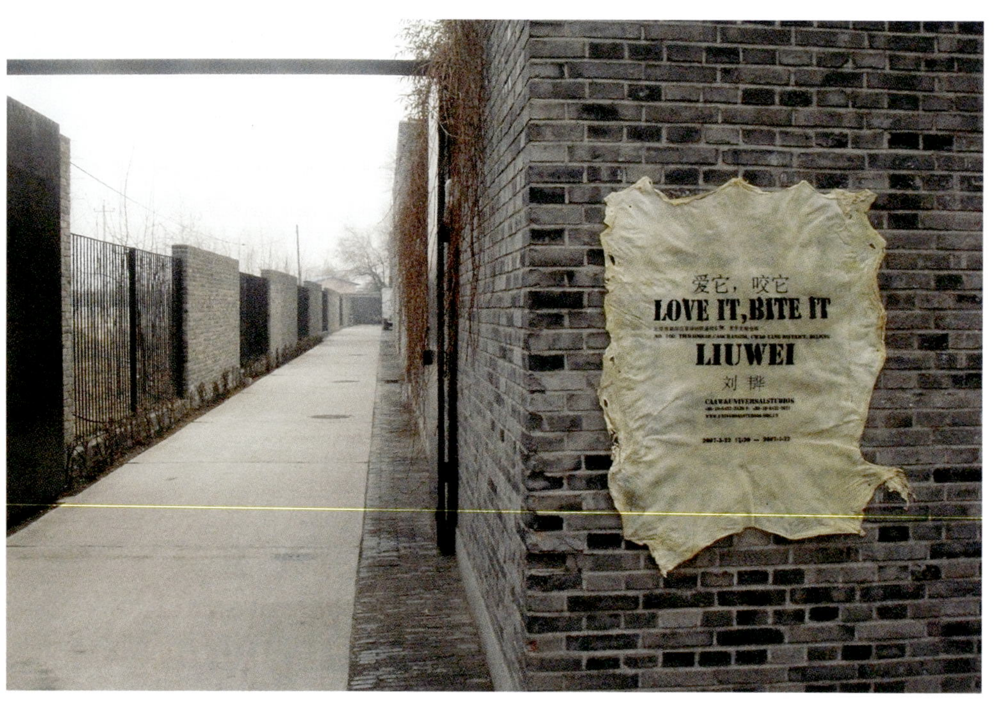

爱它，咬它
LOVE IT, BITE IT
LIUWEI
刘韡
CAAW&UNIVERSALSTUDIOS

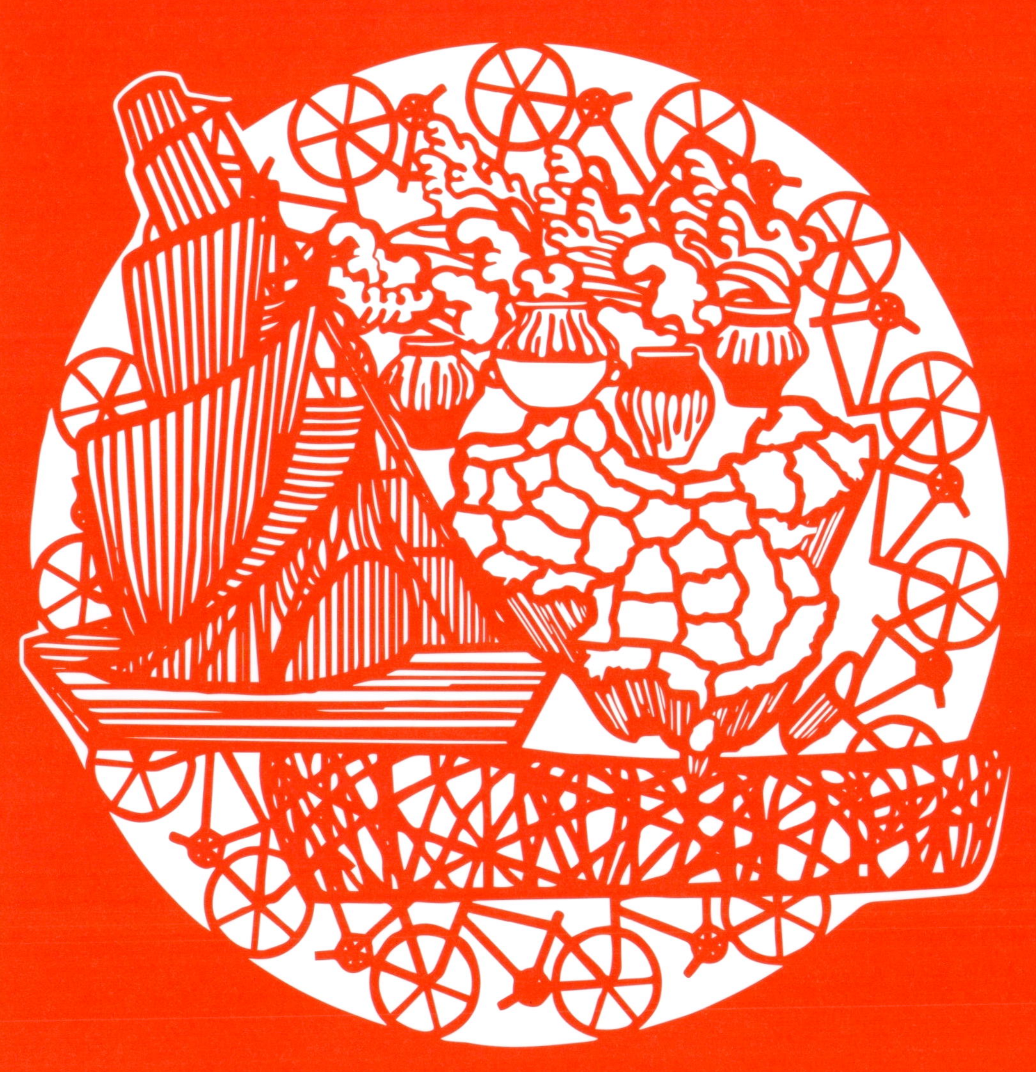

2000–2004

"The pillar is from an old temple—so the pillar represents the thinking of
the temple and religion. The table represents another specific way of thinking, so
Table and Pillar merges these two ways of thinking. It's violent but at the same
time gentle. They both have holes in them but neither one is broken." — AI WEIWEI

Die Säule stammt aus einem alten Tempel – sie repräsentiert also das Denken des
Tempels und der Religion. Der Tisch steht für ein ganz anderes spezifisches Denken, sodass
Table and Pillar diese beiden miteinander verschmelzen lässt. Es ist brutal und zart zugleich.
Beide sind voller Löcher, aber unbeschädigt.

La colonne vient d'un temple ancien – la colonne représente donc l'idée du temple,
la religion. La table représente une autre manière spécifique de penser, donc *Table and Pillar*
fait se rejoindre ces deux manières de penser. Il y a quelque chose de violent mais de doux
à la fois. Toutes deux ont été trouées, mais aucune n'est cassée.

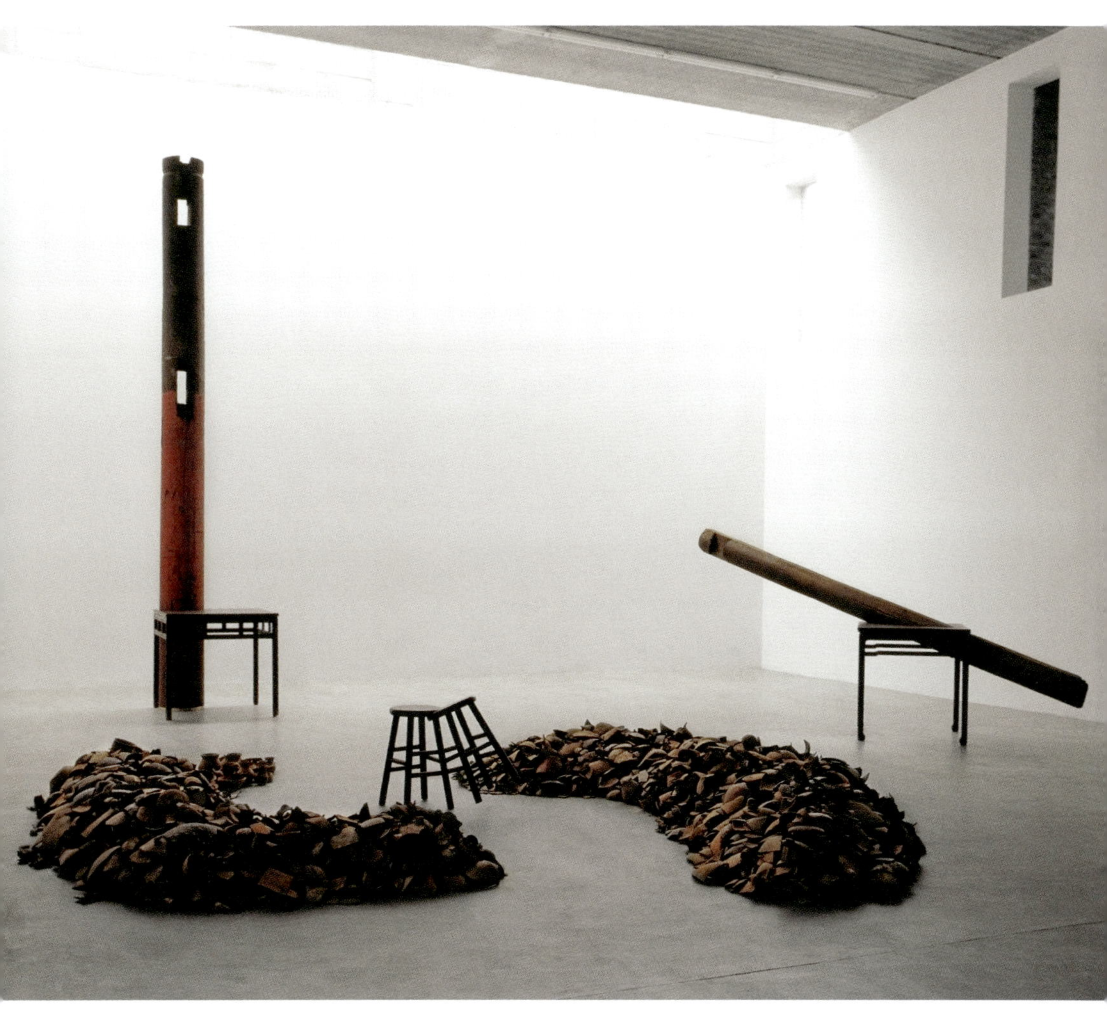

TABLE AND PILLAR, 2002, Qing Dynasty pillar and table, 185 x 35⅜ x 35⅜ inches; STOOL, 2005, wooden Qing Dynasty stools, 17¾ x 25⅝ x 27½ inches; TABLE AND BEAM, 2002, Qing Dynasty table and beam, 63⅛ x 159¾ x 35⅜ inches, Neolithic vase fragments, dimensions variable; installation at Ai Weiwei's studio | 149

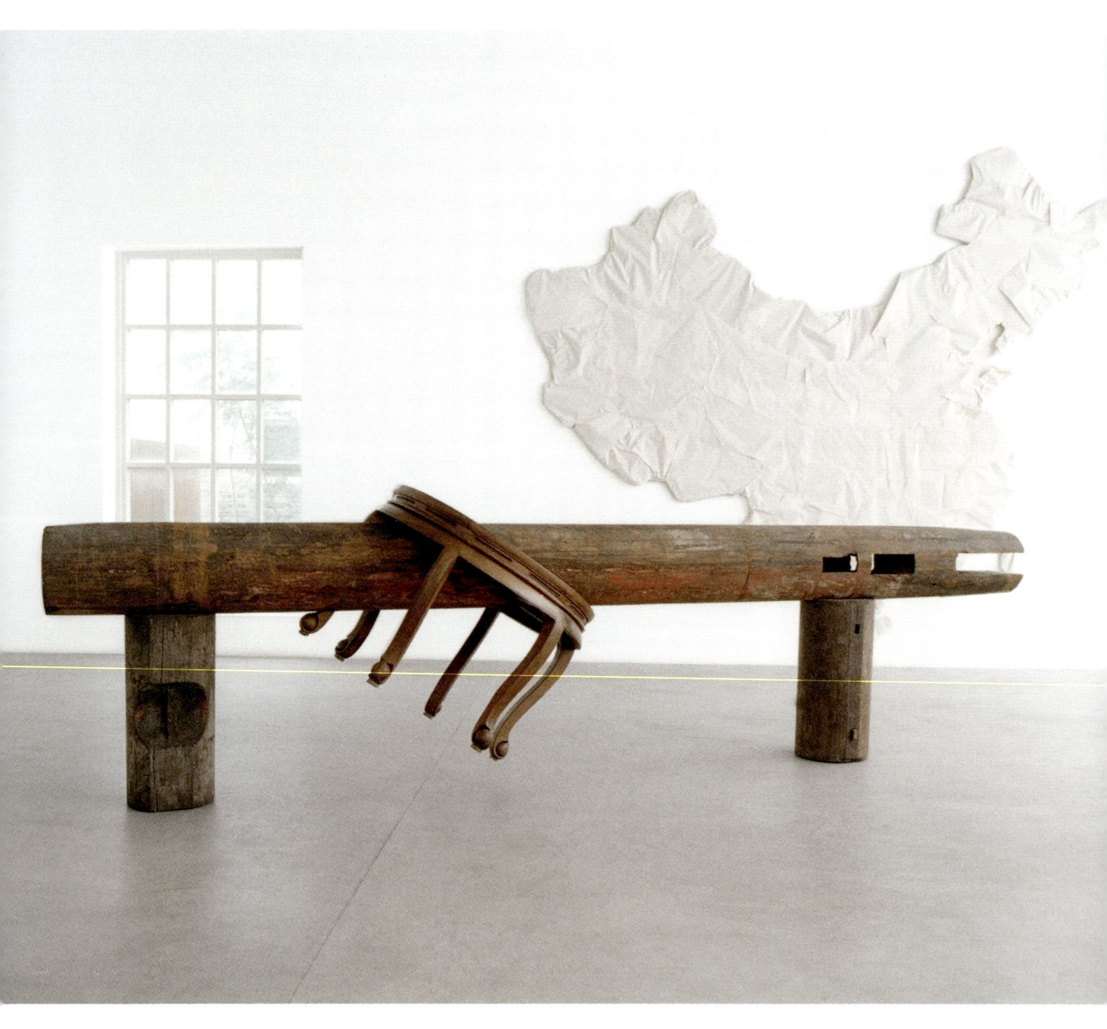

PILLAR THROUGH ROUND TABLE, 2004–2005, pair of Qing Dynasty elm wood half tables,
Qing Dynasty tieli wood pillar and 2 pillar fragments, 55 ⅞ x 202 x 46 inches; China Art Archives
 and Warehouse, Beijing 2004

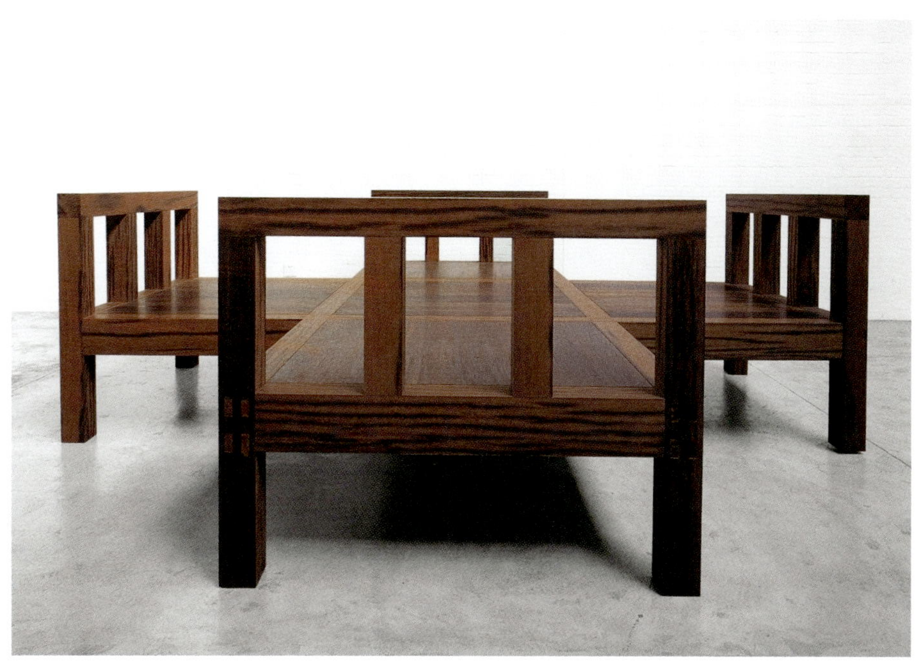

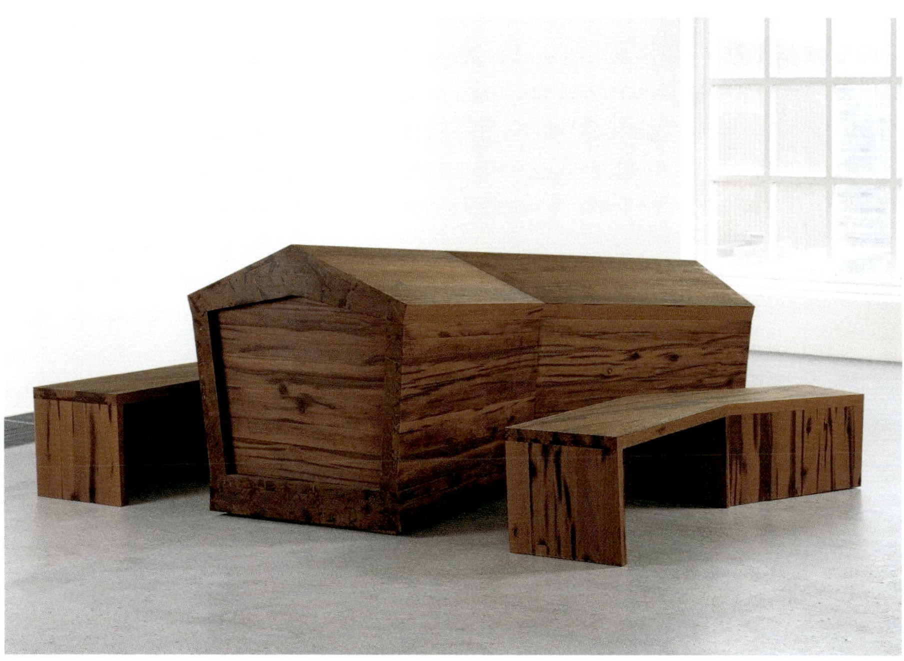

CROSSED BEDS, 2002, tieli wood from dismantled Qing Dynasty temples, 31 ½ x 102 ⅜ x 102 ⅜ inches (top); COFFIN, 2005, tieli wood from dismantled Qing Dynasty temples, 3 pieces, 14 ½ x 73 ⅝ x 27 ½, 38 x 101 ⅛ x 51 ⅛, 15 ⅜ x 109 ½ x 33 ½ inches (bottom) | 151

"I had always heard about Jinhua because it was my father's hometown.
After his death in 1996, I built his tomb. That was probably my first architecture.
It's how they got to know me and later they said, why don't you build this park
we named after your father? Which I found was just a small green area next to
this river, so I built a new embankment and my father's memorial. The next project, the Architectural Park, was a collaboration not only with 17 international
architects, but also with the local government and construction teams, and the
dream was to make something happen for the community being set up there,
bringing culture and attention to an old town. But like most Chinese culture-
related projects the government was trying to raise the value of the real estate.
As a result, the park's concept and construction are high-quality but left for
nothing, nobody uses it." — AI WEIWEI

Ich habe Geschichten über Jinhua gehört, solange ich denken kann, denn es ist die
Geburtsstadt meines Vaters. Nach seinem Tod 1996 hatte ich dort sein Grabmal gebaut.
Das war vermutlich meine erste Architekturarbeit. Dadurch kannten sie mich noch und
fragten mich: Warum baust du nicht diesen Park, den wir nach deinem Vater benennen?
Ich musste feststellen, dass es sich lediglich um eine kleine Grünfläche am Fluss handelte.
Ich baute eine neue Uferbefestigung und das Denkmal für meinen Vater. Das darauffolgende
Projekt, der Architekturpark, war dann eine Zusammenarbeit mit 17 internationalen Archi-
tekturbüros, aber auch mit der Kommunalregierung und den Bautrupps. Unser aller Traum
war es, etwas für die Gemeinschaft zu tun, die dort entstand, und der alten Stadt Kultur und
Aufmerksamkeit zu bringen. Wie bei den meisten kulturellen Projekten in China ging es der
Regierung jedoch nur um die Erhöhung der Immobilienpreise. Konzept und Anlage des Parks
sind erstklassig, aber niemand hat etwas davon, weil man ihn nicht nutzen kann.

Je connaissais Jinhua parce que c'était la ville natale de mon père. Après sa mort en
1996, c'est moi qui ai construit sa tombe. C'était probablement mon tout premier projet
architectural. C'est comme ça que les gens là-bas ont entendu parler de moi, et ils m'ont
proposé d'aménager un parc qui porterait le nom de mon père. Au final, c'était un tout petit
espace vert au bord de la rivière, alors j'ai juste aménagé la berge et construit un mémorial
pour mon père. Le projet suivant, le Parc architectural, s'est fait en collaboration avec
17 architectes internationaux, mais aussi avec le gouvernement et des équipes de construction locale, et mon rêve était de faire quelque chose pour cette communauté, d'apporter
un peu de culture mais aussi d'attention à une vieille ville. Mais comme pour la plupart des
projets culturels en Chine, le seul objectif du gouvernement était de faire monter les prix
de l'immobilier. En fin de compte, le concept et la réalisation du parc sont excellents, mais
il ne sert à rien, personne ne l'utilise.

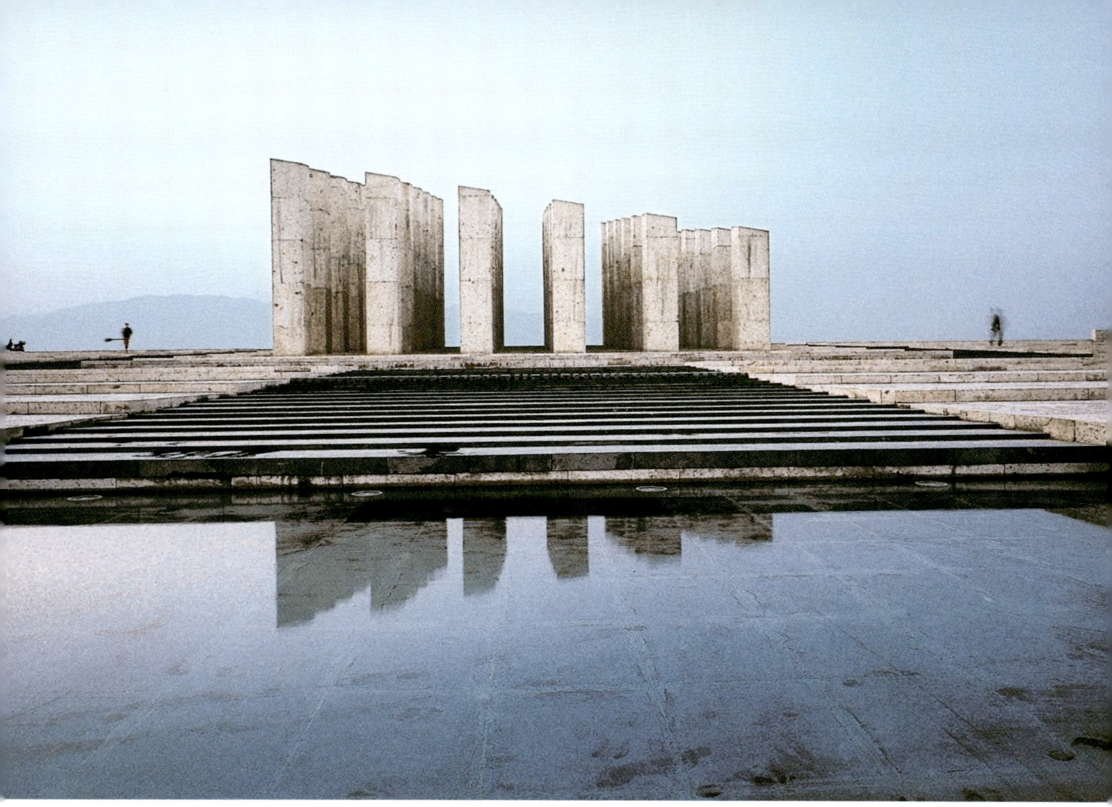

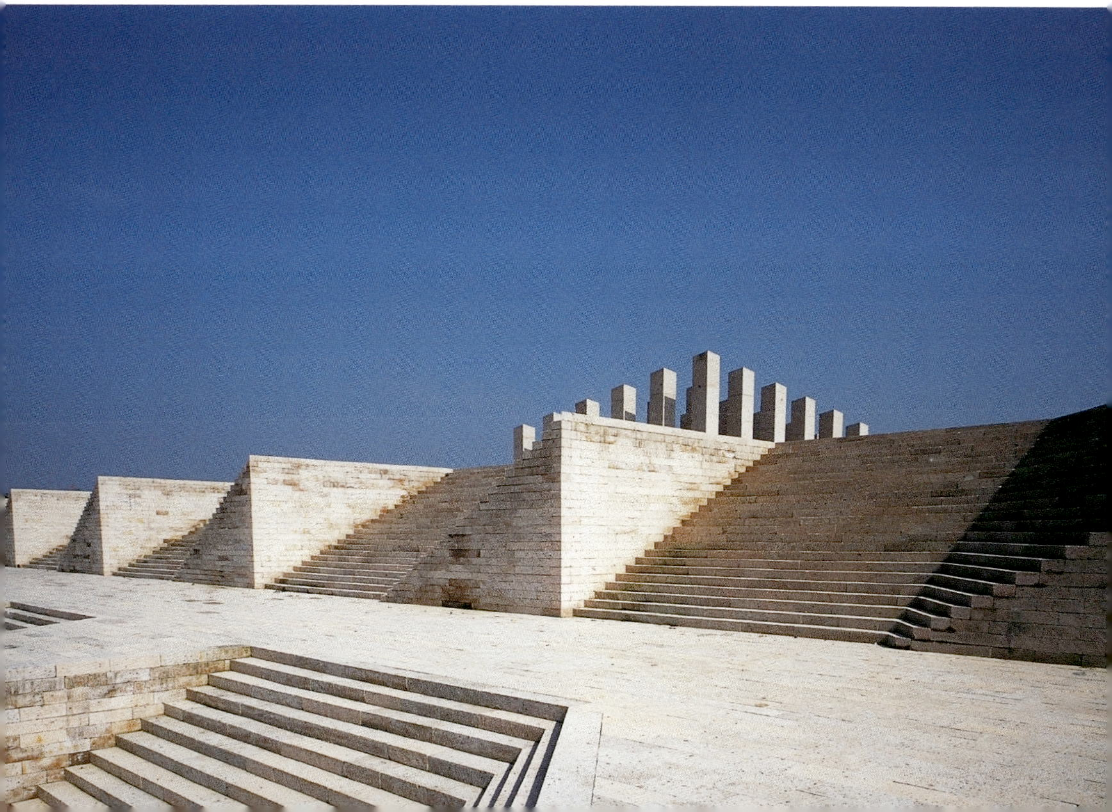

"The Neolithic Pottery Museum is a very bare structure without any decoration. The building is made from concrete only cast once using a special technique that I developed. It uses one language both above ground and below ground and for the surroundings—a hexagonal form developed into a language that fulfills all the needs." — AI WEIWEI

Das Museum für neolithische Töpferkunst ist ein einfacher Bau ohne jede Dekoration. Das Gebäude besteht aus Beton, der in einer von mir entwickelten Technik in einem Durchgang gegossen wurde. Sowohl über als auch unter der Erde sowie für das umgebende Gelände wurde ein und dieselbe Formensprache verwendet: eine sechseckige Form, die allen Anforderungen gerecht wird.

Le musée de poterie du Néolithique est une structure très nue, sans aucune fioriture. Le bâtiment est fait de béton à coffrage unique, réalisé selon une technique spéciale que j'ai développée. Le langage architectural est le même en sous-sol qu'en surface et sur le site du bâtiment. C'est une forme hexagonale transformée en un langage qui répond à tous les besoins.

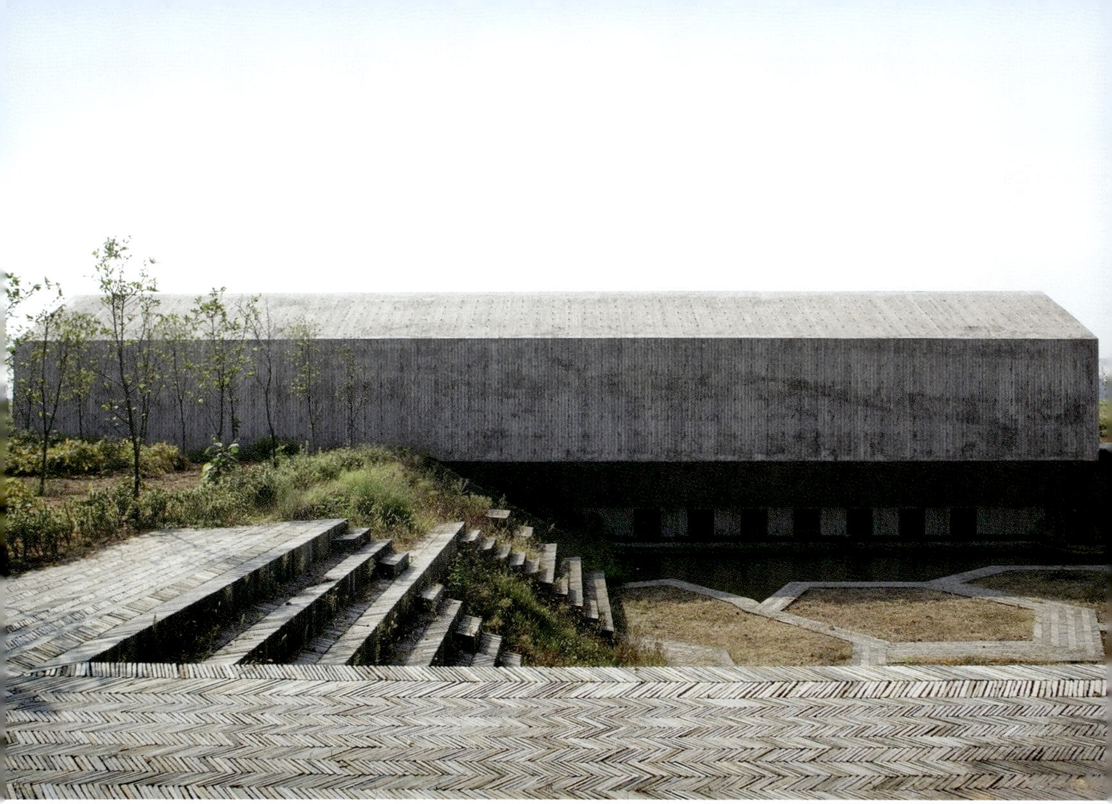

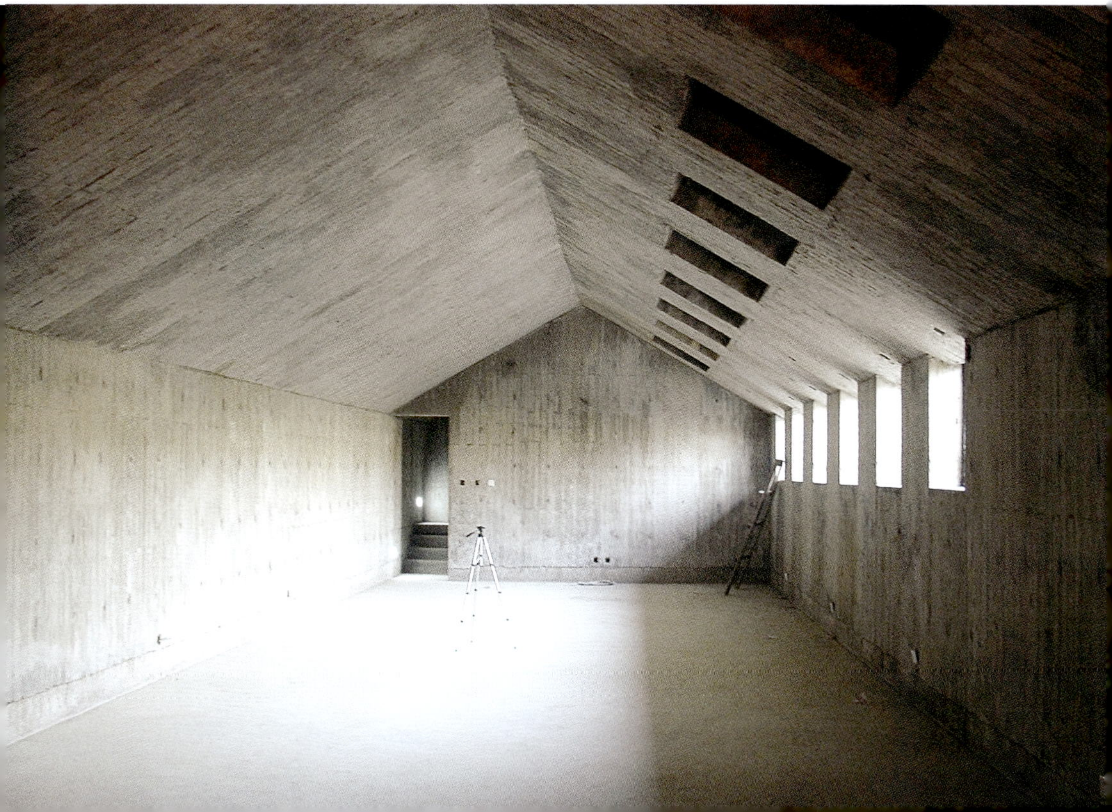

"I became interested in light as an object: both the object that gives off light, but also the form that light creates by itself in the illumination it generates, and how illumination alters the surrounding environment. The first chandelier I made was built into the scaffolding structure. It was important to me that people would experience the work in terms of its physical presence, and its relationship to the human body and scale. So it had to be big. I designed it to hang low, so when people approached it they were forced to walk into the light, which was accentuated by the dark grid of the scaffold bars. The crystals I used come from Zhejiang Province, from the same place that produced the crystals for the chandeliers in the Great Hall of the People. We can trace this back to Deng Xiaoping's decision to let some people get rich first. For me, the crystals represent this wealth."
— AI WEIWEI

Ich fing an, mich für Licht als ein Objekt zu interessieren: als Objekt, das Licht abgibt, aber auch als Form, die aus dem Licht selbst entsteht und dadurch das Umfeld verändert. Meinen ersten Leuchter baute ich in eine Gerüststruktur hinein. Es war mir wichtig, dass die Besucher ihn in seiner ganzen physischen Präsenz erlebten, seine Beziehung zum menschlichen Körper und dessen Proportionen. Dementsprechend groß musste er sein. Ich hängte den Leuchter sehr niedrig auf, damit die Besucher, wenn sie sich näherten, gezwungen waren, ins Licht zu treten, was durch das schwarze Raster der Gerüststreben noch betont wurde. Die Kristalle, die ich verwendete, stammen aus der Provinz Zhejiang, wo auch die Kristalle herkommen, die für die Leuchter in der Großen Halle des Volkes verwendet wurden. Das geht zurück auf die Entscheidung Deng Xiaopings, einige Leute reich werden zu lassen. In meinen Augen stehen diese Kristalle für deren Reichtum.

J'ai commencé à m'intéresser à la lumière en tant qu'objet : l'objet qui éclaire, mais aussi la forme que crée la lumière dans l'illumination qu'elle génère, et comment cette illumination modifie son environnement. Le premier lustre que j'ai construit était intégré à un échafaudage. Il était important pour moi que les gens fassent l'expérience de cette œuvre en termes de présence physique, et qu'ils perçoivent sa relation à l'échelle humaine et au corps humain. Il fallait donc qu'il soit grand. Je l'ai conçu pour qu'il soit suspendu assez bas, si bien que les gens, en s'approchant, étaient obligés de marcher dans la lumière, un effet accentué par la grille sombre de l'échafaudage. J'ai utilisé du cristal de la province du Zhejiang, des ateliers qui avaient produit le cristal des lustres du Palais de l'Assemblée du Peuple. On pense à la manière dont Deng Xiaoping a voulu laisser certaines personnes s'enrichir. Pour moi, le cristal représente cette richesse.

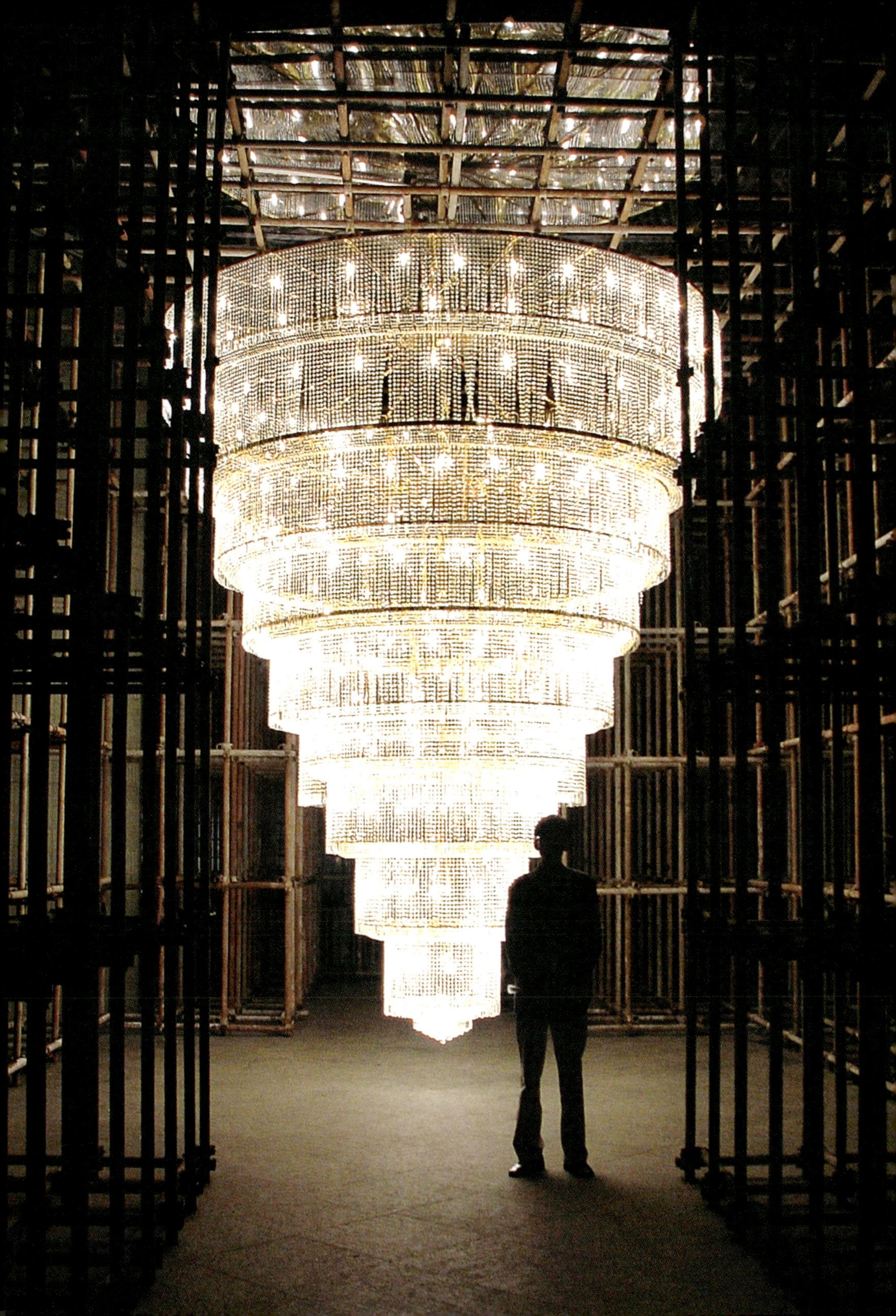

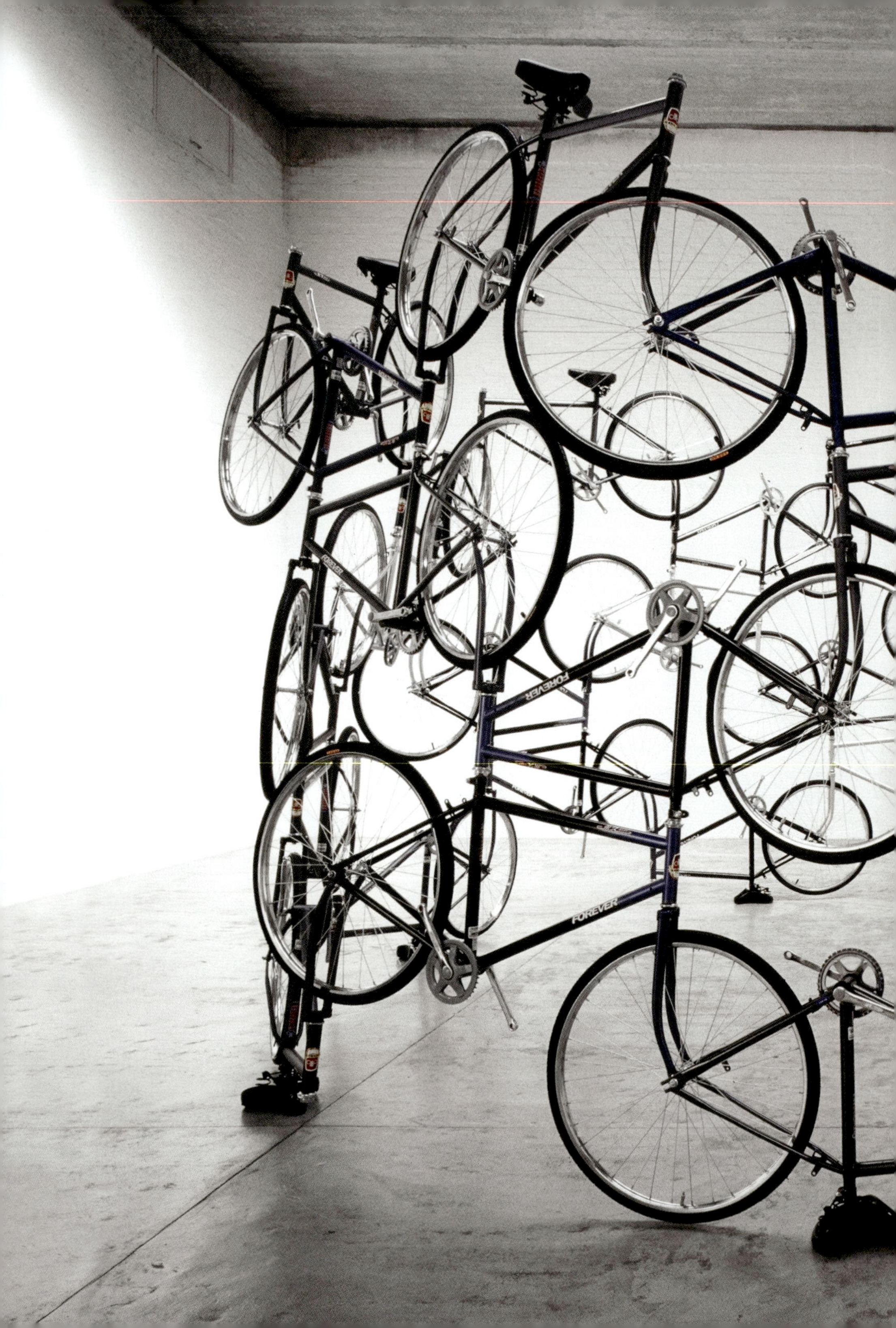

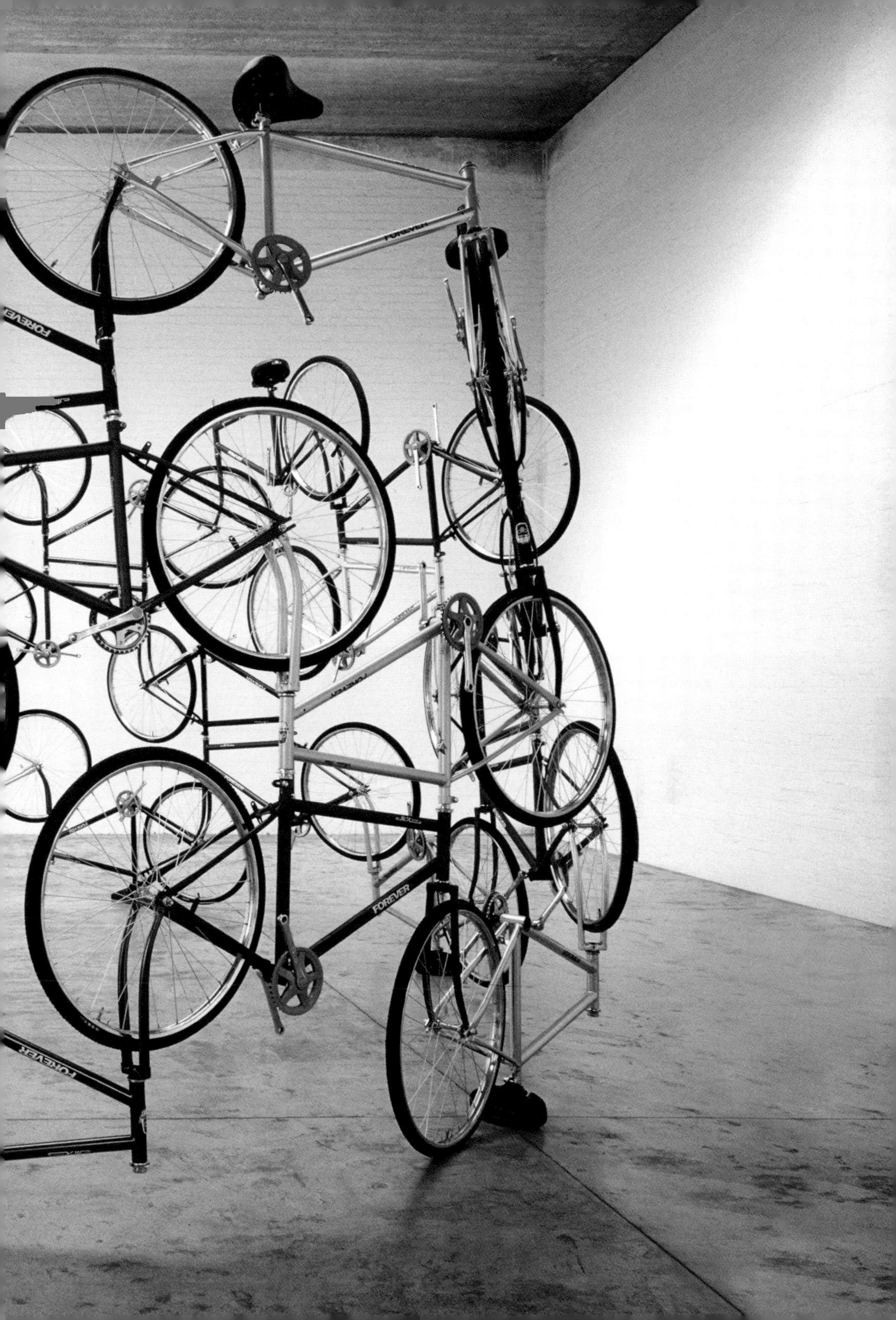

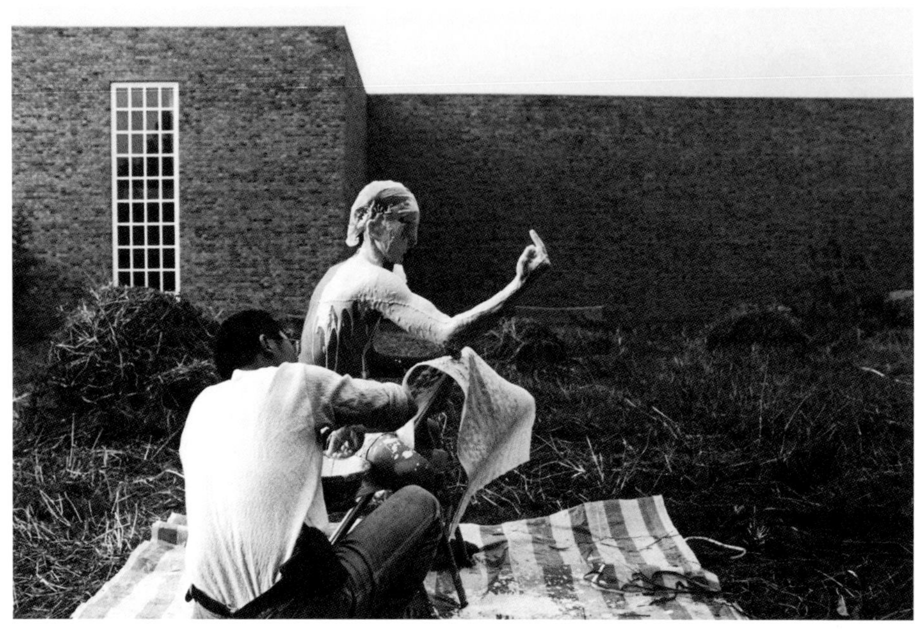

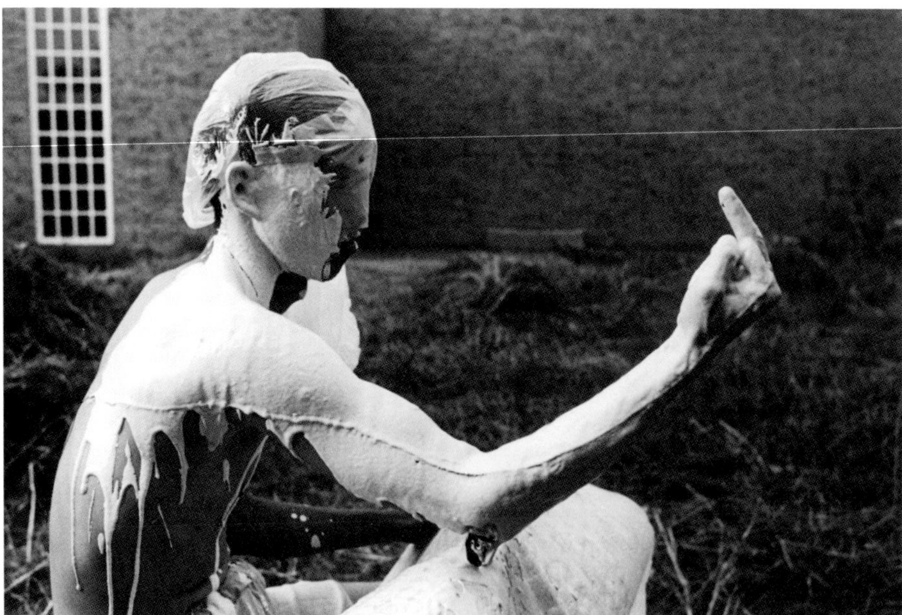

Making of *Arm*, 2004

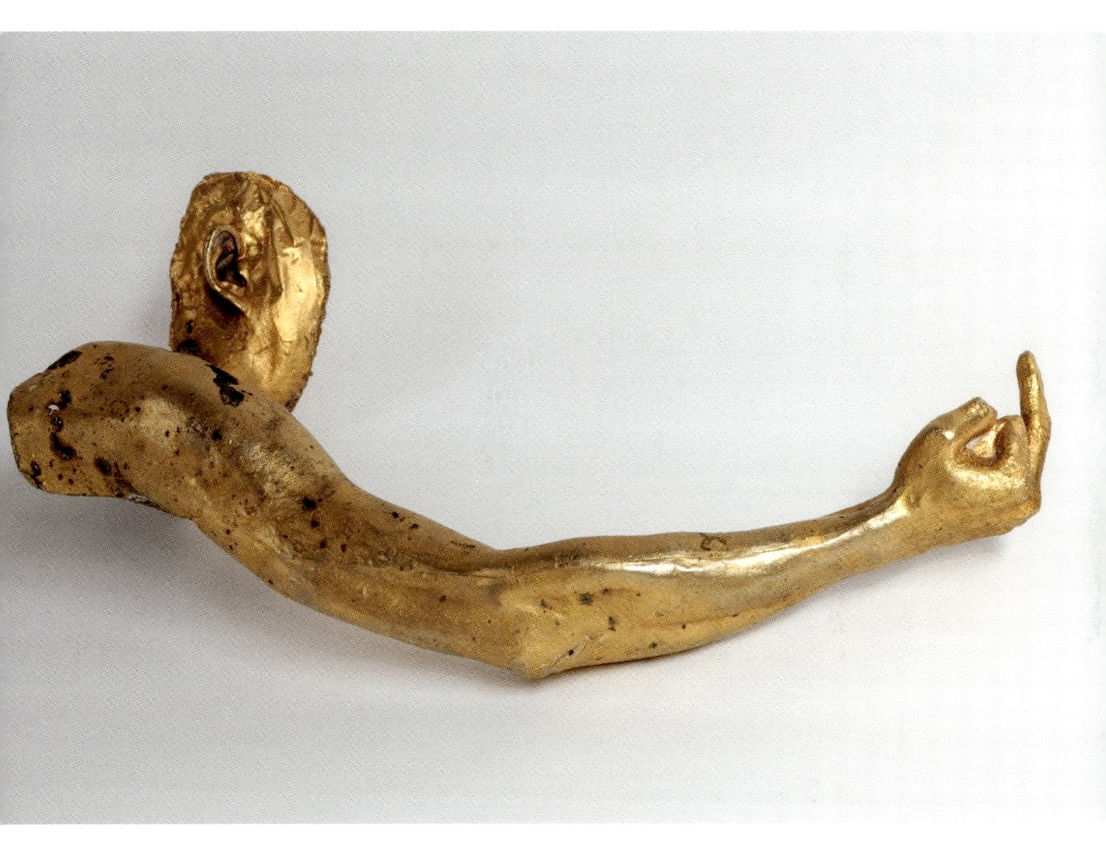

"*Map of China* is made from the wood of an old temple that was torn down for development. People often ask me if there is a political condition represented here, but it was made according to the materials and the possibilities they presented. All joints were made according to each specific shape. The major problem was to resolve how to hold together 100 pieces tightly and precisely. The map is just the shape of it." — AI WEIWEI

Map of China besteht aus dem Holz eines alten Tempels, der für ein neues Bauprojekt abgerissen wurde. Ich werde oft gefragt, ob hier eine politische Situation dargestellt ist, aber bei der Arbeit folgte ich ganz den Möglichkeiten, die das Material bot. Sämtliche Verbindungsstücke wurden entsprechend der jeweiligen Form hergestellt. Die größte Herausforderung, die es zu meistern galt, bestand darin, einhundert Teilstücke fest und präzise zusammenzuhalten. Die Landkarte ist lediglich die äußere Form.

Map of China a été réalisée avec le bois d'un temple ancien détruit pour laisser la place à une nouvelle construction. Les gens me demandent souvent s'il y a un message politique ici, mais cette carte a été réalisée en fonction des matériaux et des possibilités que ces derniers présentaient. Les pièces ont été assemblées en fonction de la forme de chacune. Le plus difficile a été de trouver comment assembler aussi précisément une centaine de pièces. La carte est juste la forme de cet ensemble.

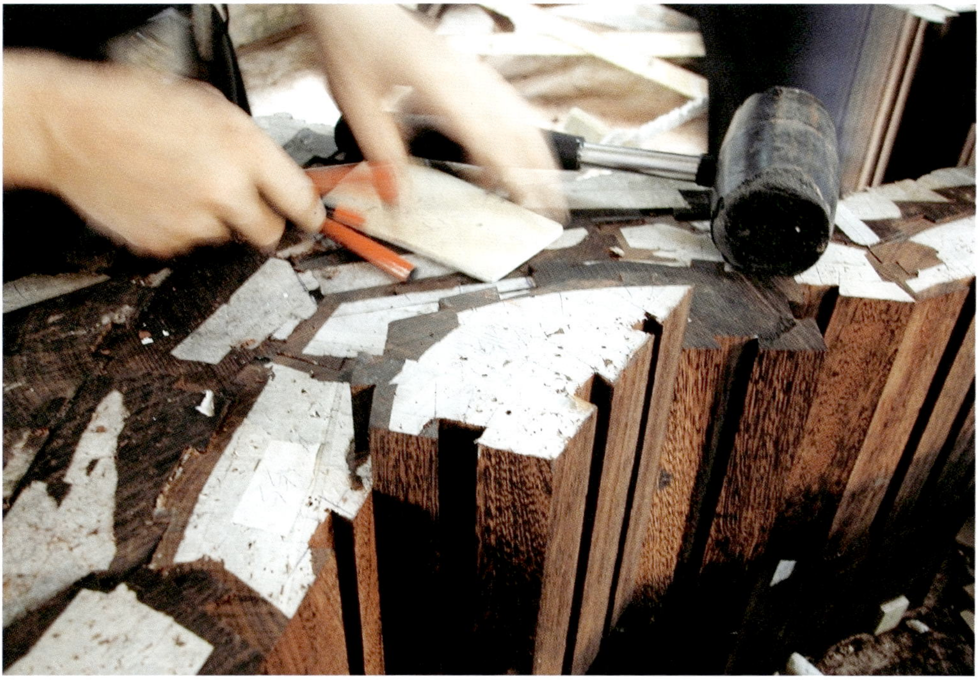

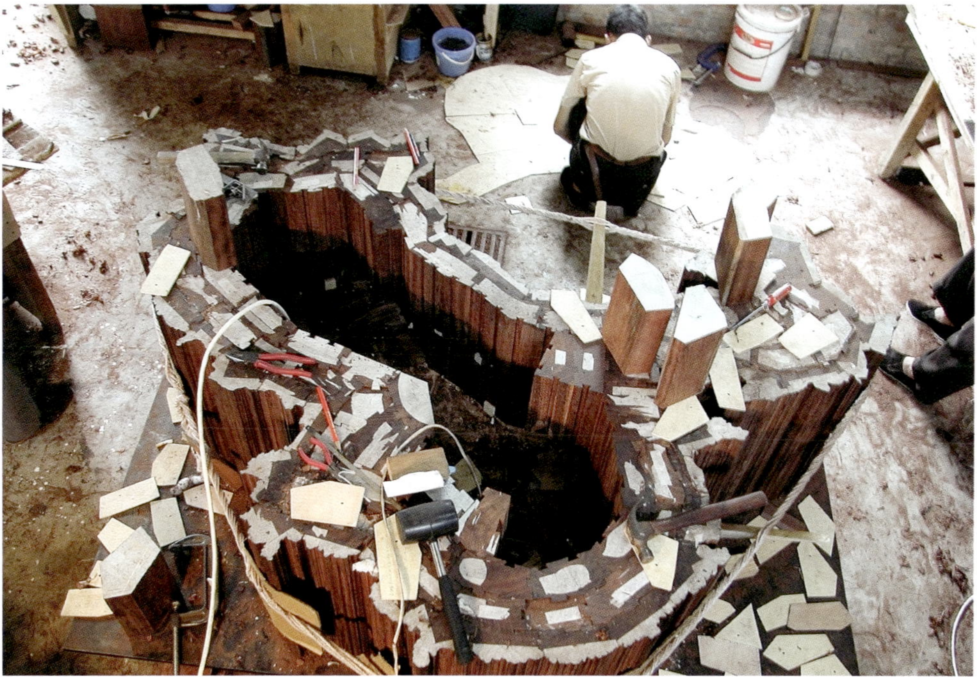

Making of MAP OF CHINA, 2003, tieli wood from dismantled Qing Dynasty temples, 39⅜ x ø 39⅜ inches | 163

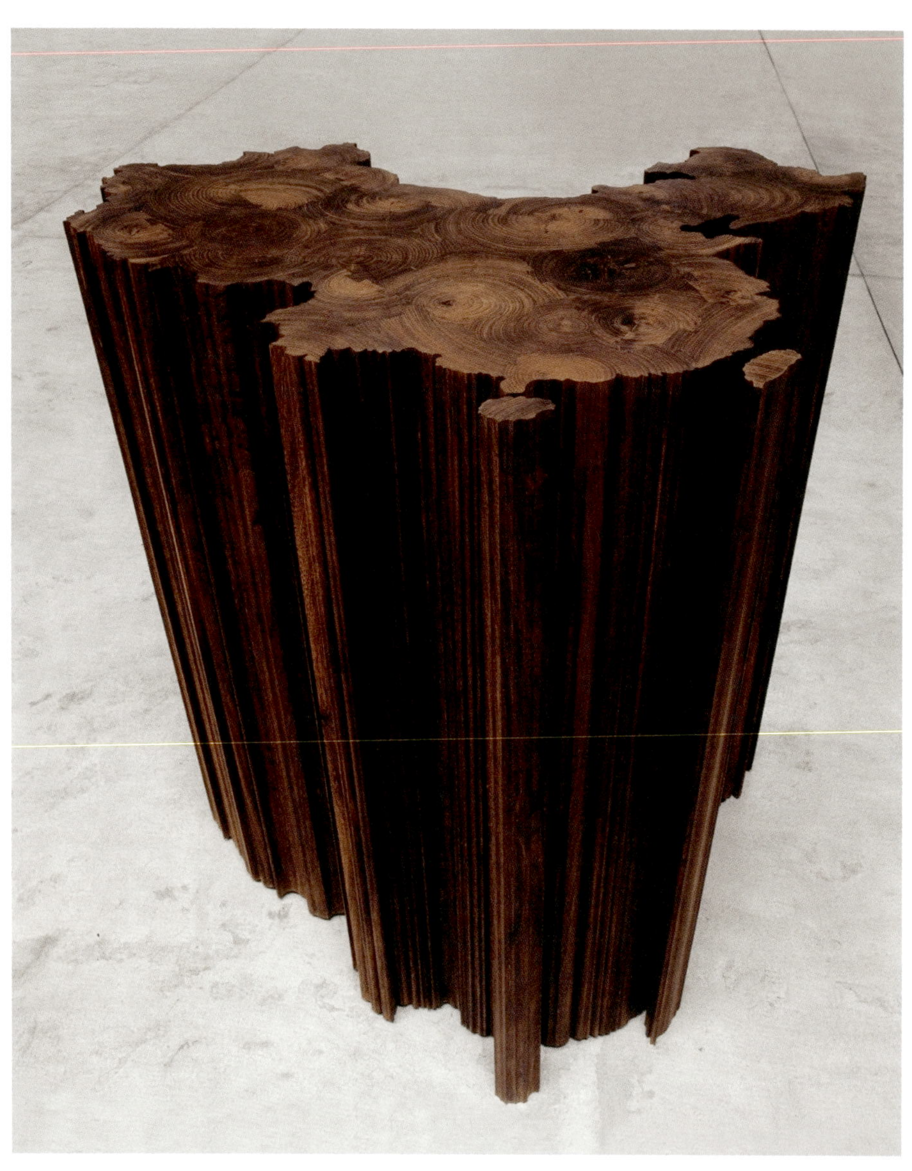

164 | MAP OF CHINA, 2003, tieli wood from dismantled Qing Dynasty temples, 39⅜ x ⌀ 39⅜ inches

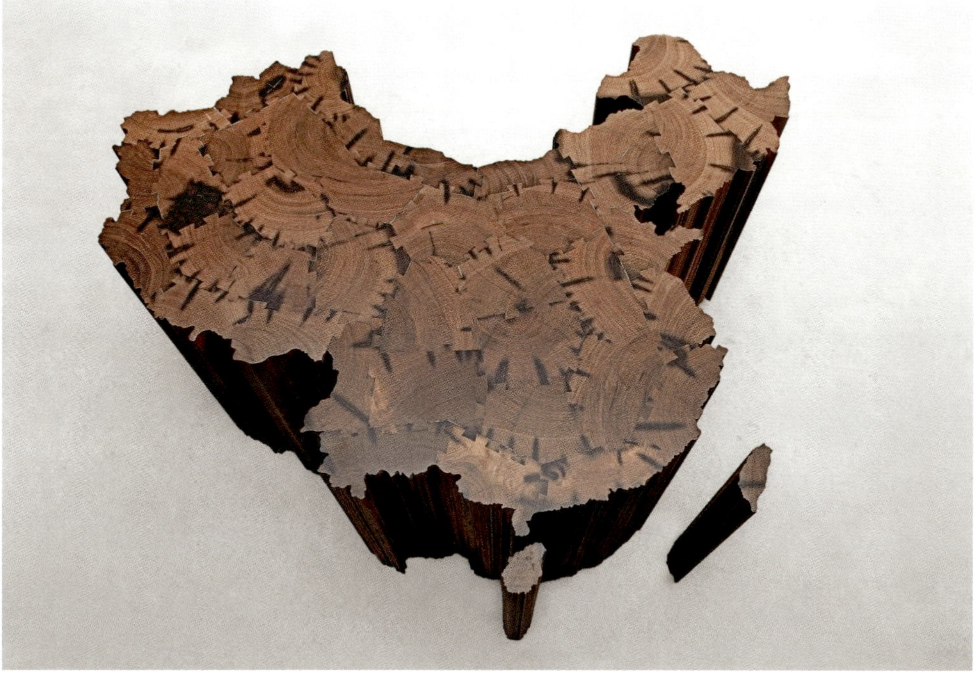

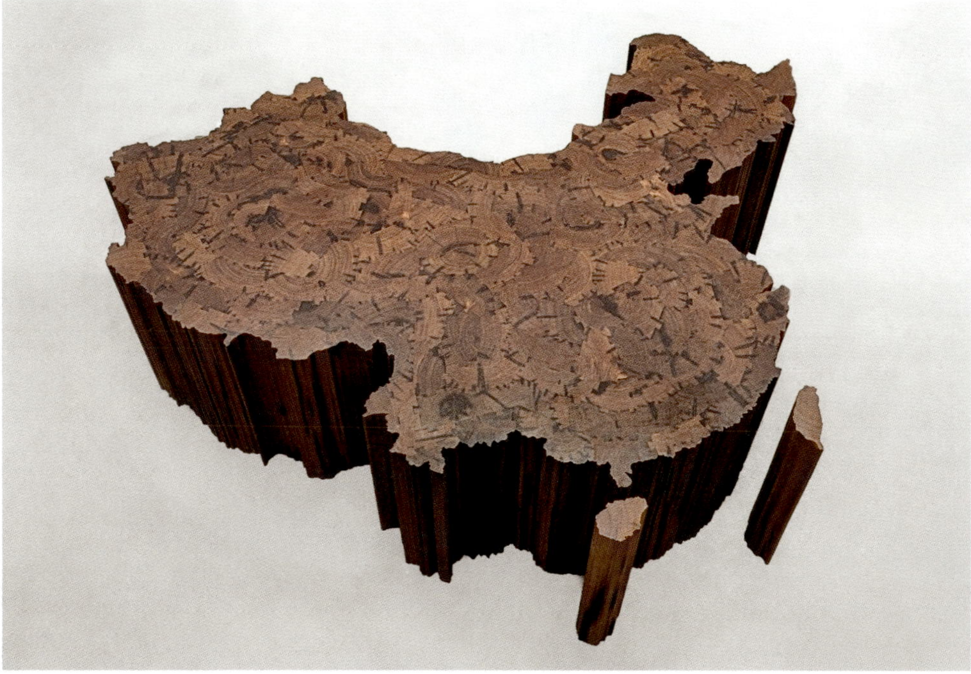

MAP OF CHINA, 2004, tieli wood from dismantled Qing Dynasty temples, 20 ⅛ x ø 78 ¾ inches (top);
MAP OF CHINA, 2006, tieli wood from dismantled Qing Dynasty temples, 15 x ø 38 inches (bottom) | 165

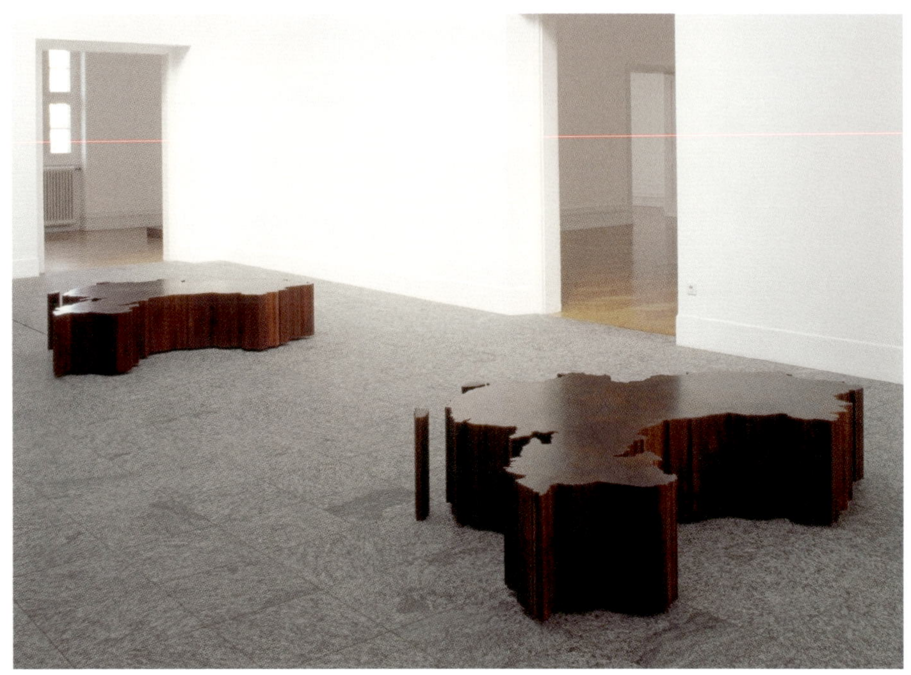

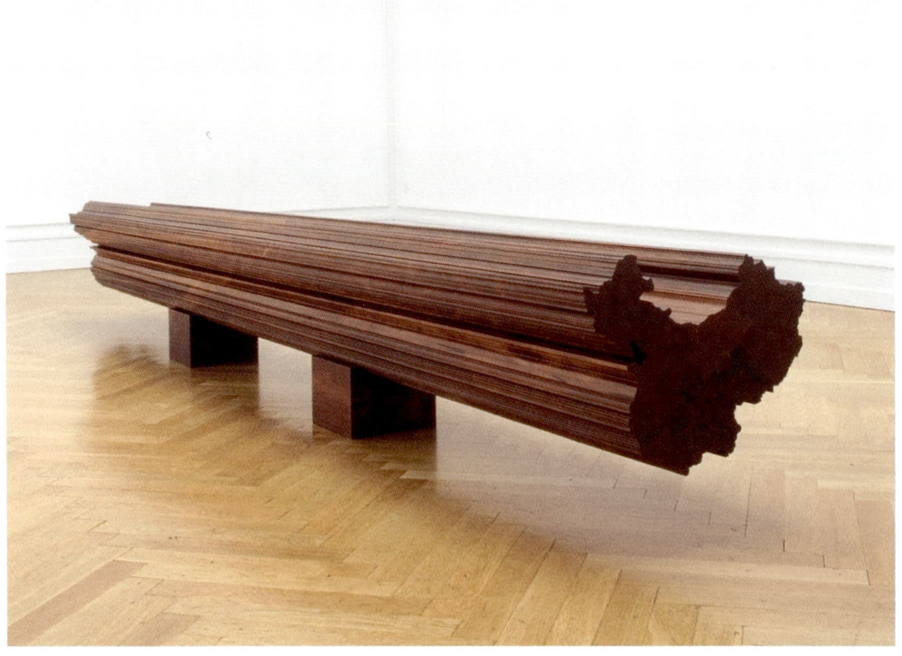

MAPS OF CHINA, 2004, tieli wood from dismantled Qing Dynasty temples, each 15¾ x ø 76¾ inches
(top); BENCH, 2004, tieli wood from dismantled Qing Dynasty temples, 175½ x ø 21⅝ inches (bottom)
Opposite: TABLE, 2004, tieli wood from dismantled Qing Dynasty temples, 34⅝ x 55⅛ x 55⅛ inches;

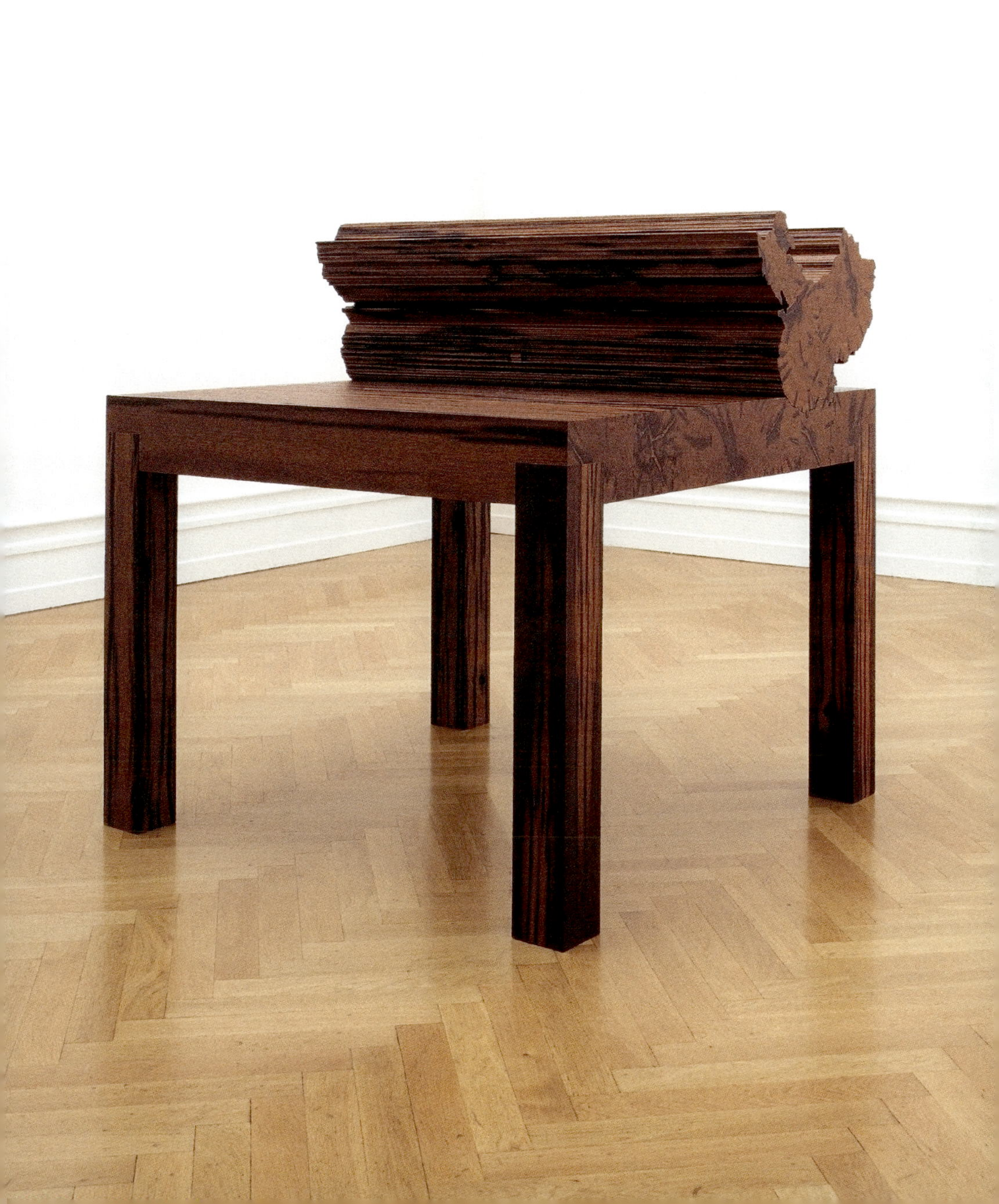

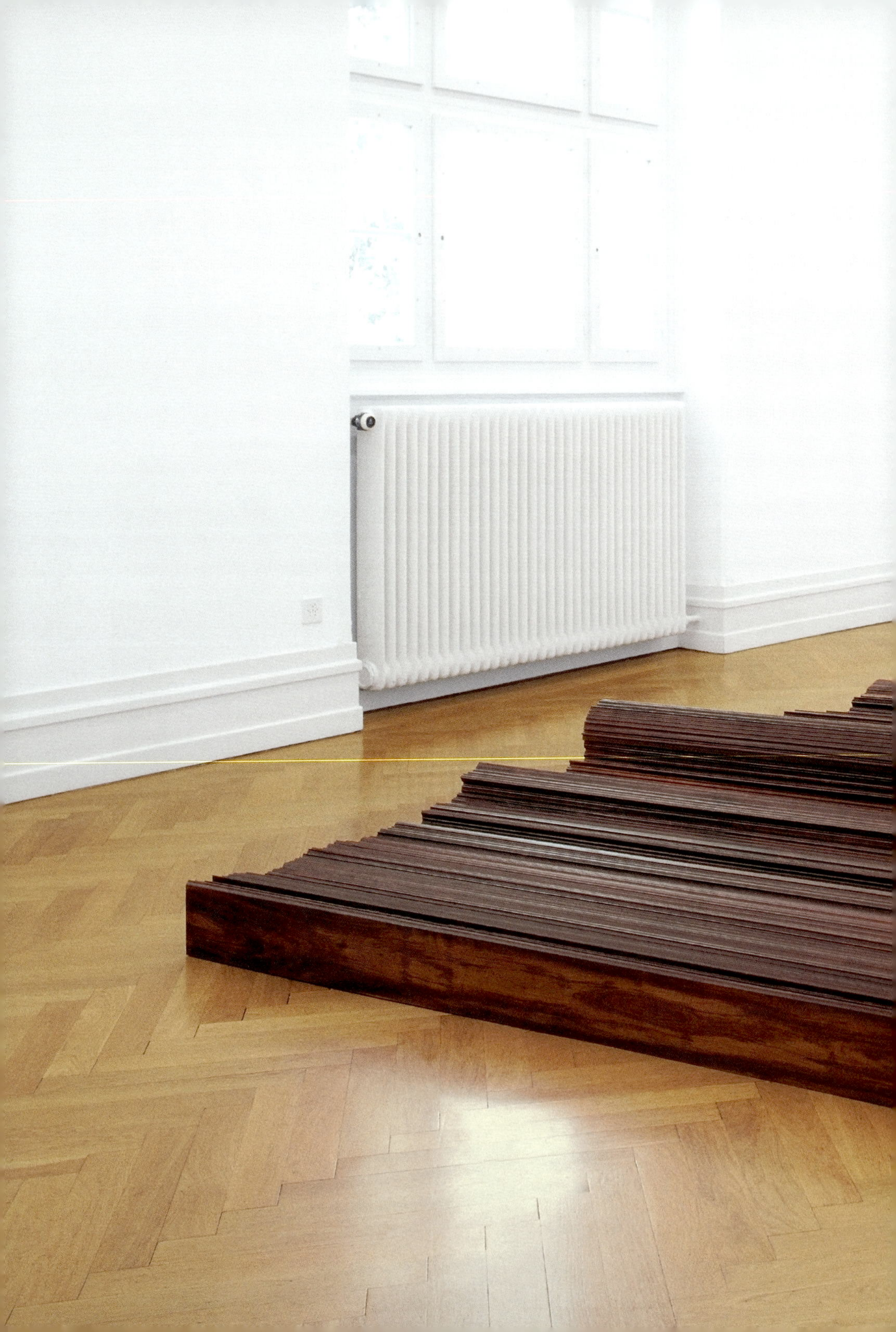

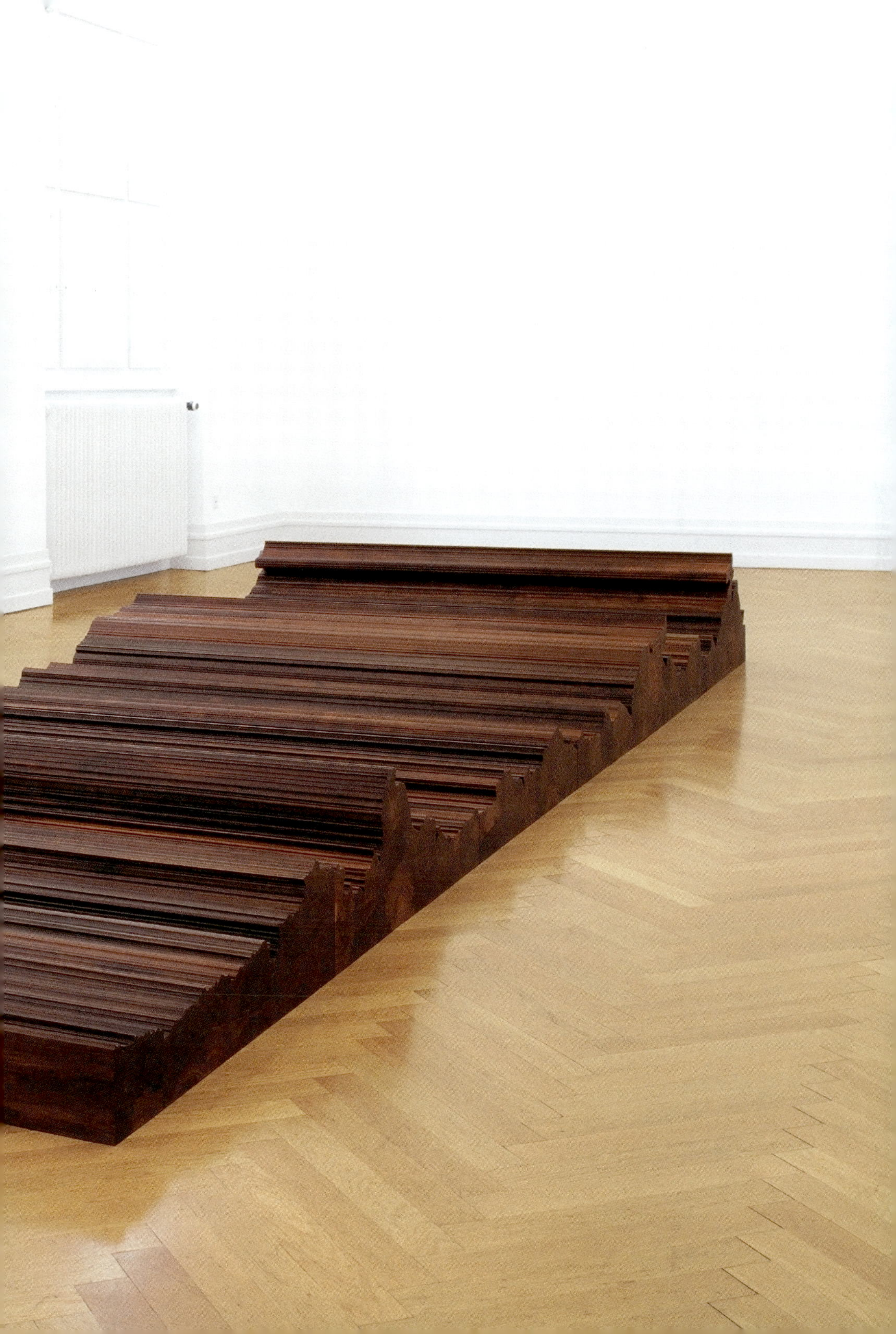

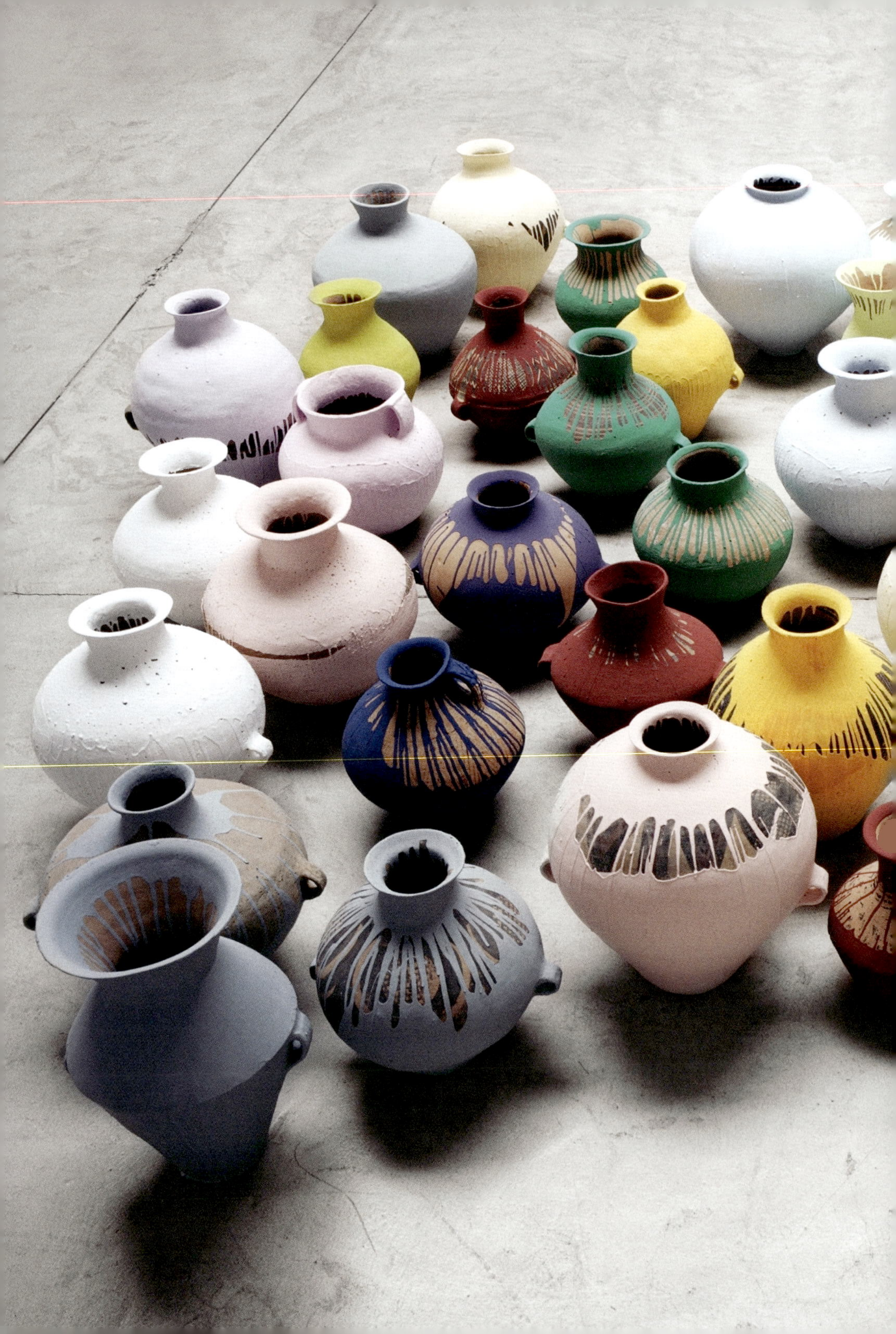

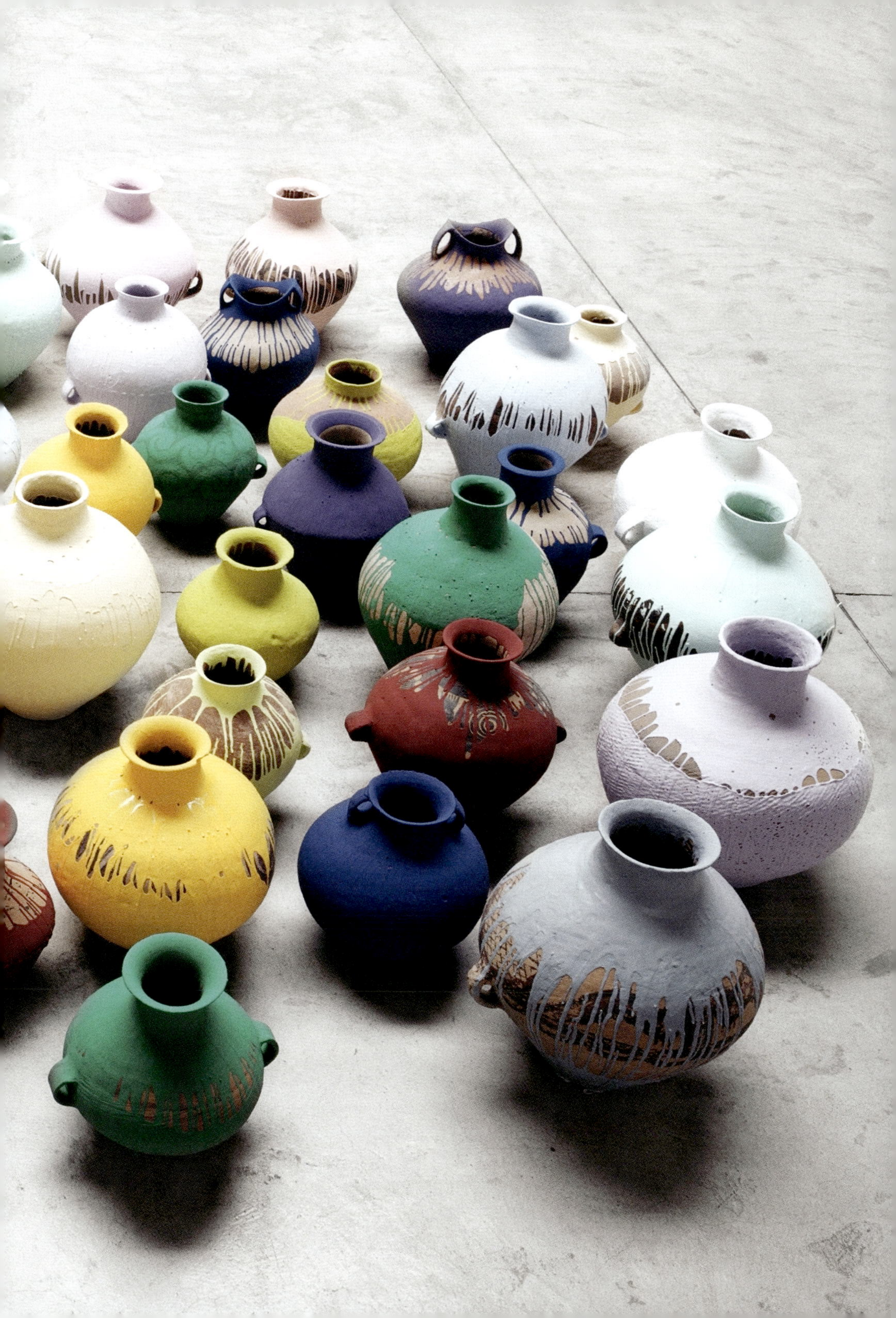

"All those Neolithic vases are from 4,000 years ago and have been dipped
into a Japanese-brand industrial household paint, and they become another image
entirely, with the original image hiding in thin layers of this paint. The act of
changing the understanding and perspective of an object, or reworking an established concept, disrupts its stability. To have other layers of color and images
above the previous ones calls into question both the identity and authenticity of
the object. It makes both conditions non-absolute: you cover something so that
it is no longer visible but is still there underneath, and what appears on the surface is not supposed to be there but is there." — AI WEIWEI

All diese neolithischen Vasen sind um die 4000 Jahre alt und wurden in den Allzweck-
lack eines japanischen Herstellers getaucht. Das verändert ihr Aussehen völlig, da das ursprüngliche Bild unter der dünnen Farbschicht verborgen ist. Wenn man Bedeutung und
Perspektive eines Gegenstandes verändert und das vorhandene Konzept überarbeitet, unter-
gräbt man dessen Geist. Die überdeckenden Farbschichten und neuen Bilder stellen die Identität und Authentizität des Objekts infrage. Sie relativieren beide Zustände: Man bedeckt
etwas, sodass es nicht mehr sichtbar, aber doch noch darunter vorhanden ist, und was auf
der Oberfläche erscheint, gehört dort nicht hin, ist aber trotzdem da.

Ces vases néolithiques fabriqués il y a 4000 ans ont été trempés dans des pots de peinture murale industrielle de marque japonaise, ce qui leur donne une apparence tout autre,
leur apparence d'origine se cachant sous une fine couche de peinture. L'acte de transformer la compréhension et la perspective d'un objet, ou de retravailler un concept établi,
perturbe sa stabilité et le remet en question. Ajouter des couches de peinture et des images
sur celles d'origine remet en question l'identité et l'authenticité de l'objet. On relativise
ces deux qualités : on recouvre quelque chose qui n'est plus visible mais qui est toujours là,
et ce qui apparaît en surface n'est pas censé être là, mais est là quand même.

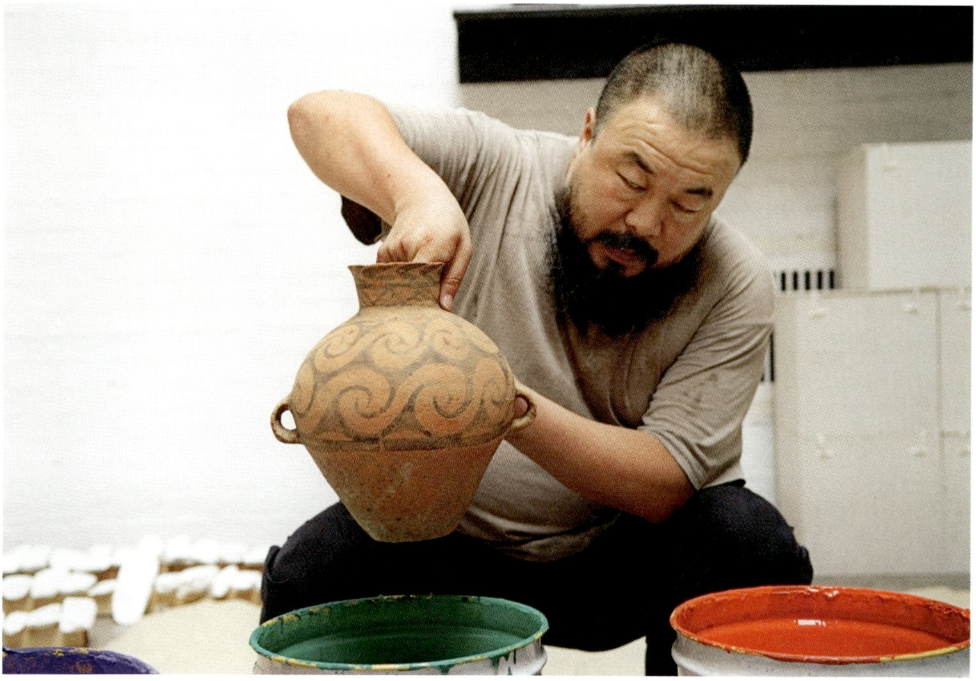

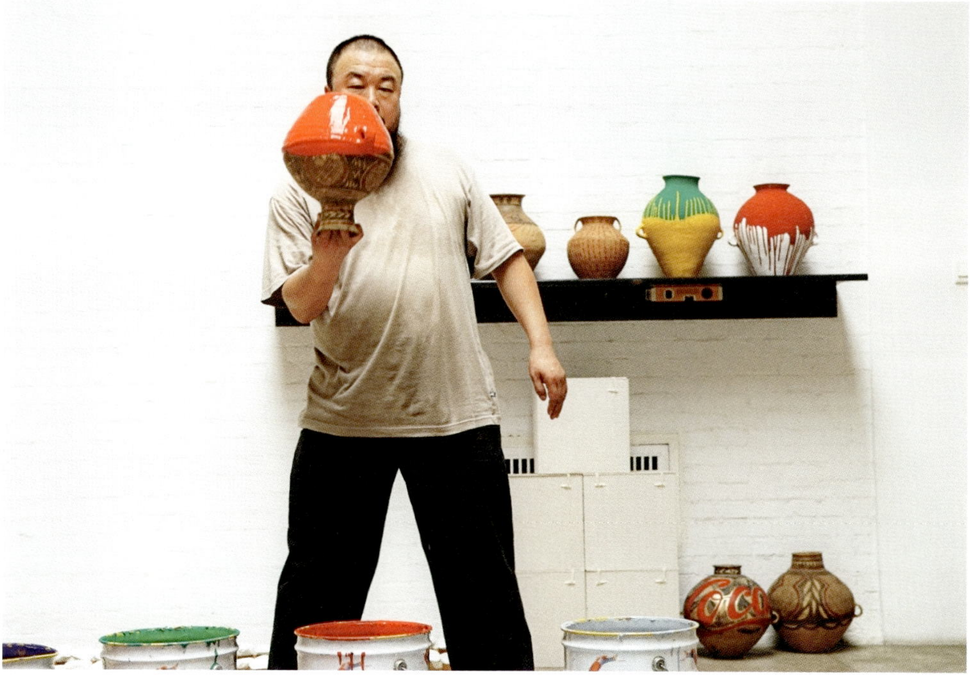

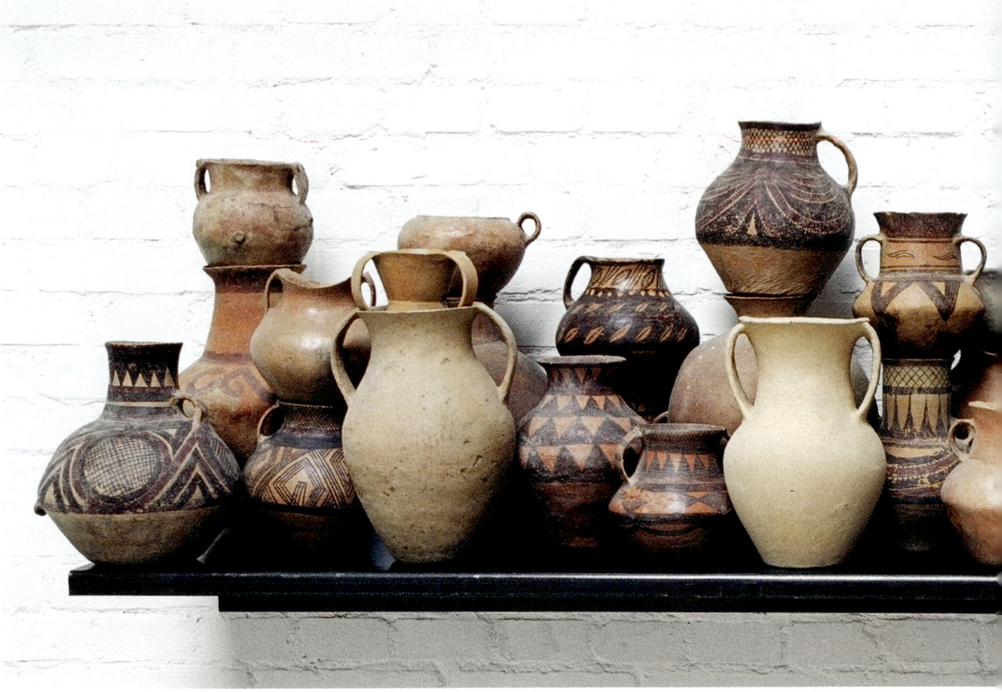

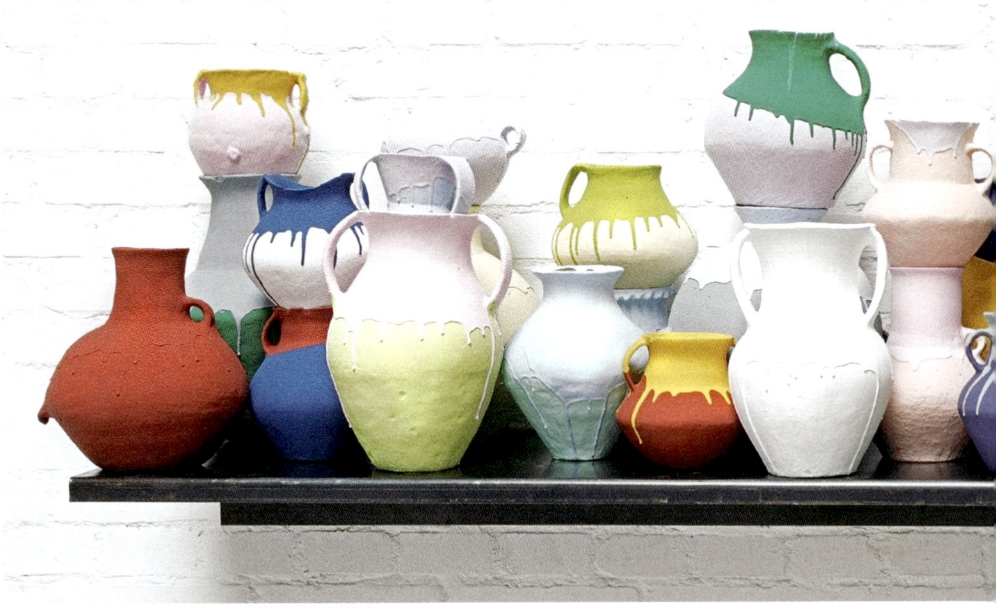

COLORED VASES, 2006, Neolithic vases, industrial paint, 39 pieces, dimensions variable;
before painting (top) and finished work (bottom)

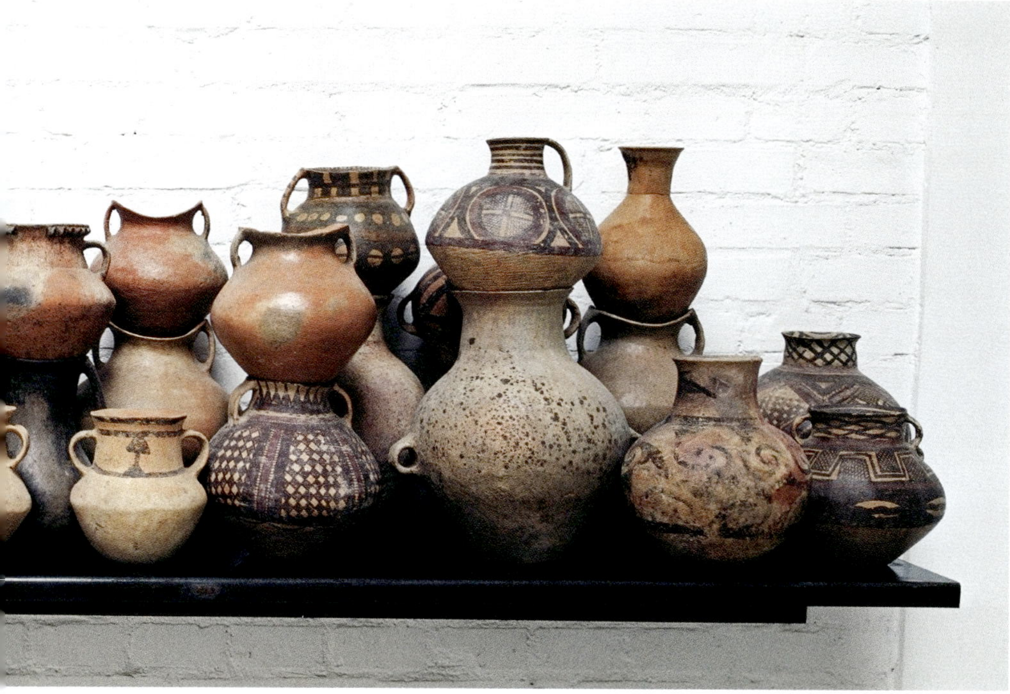

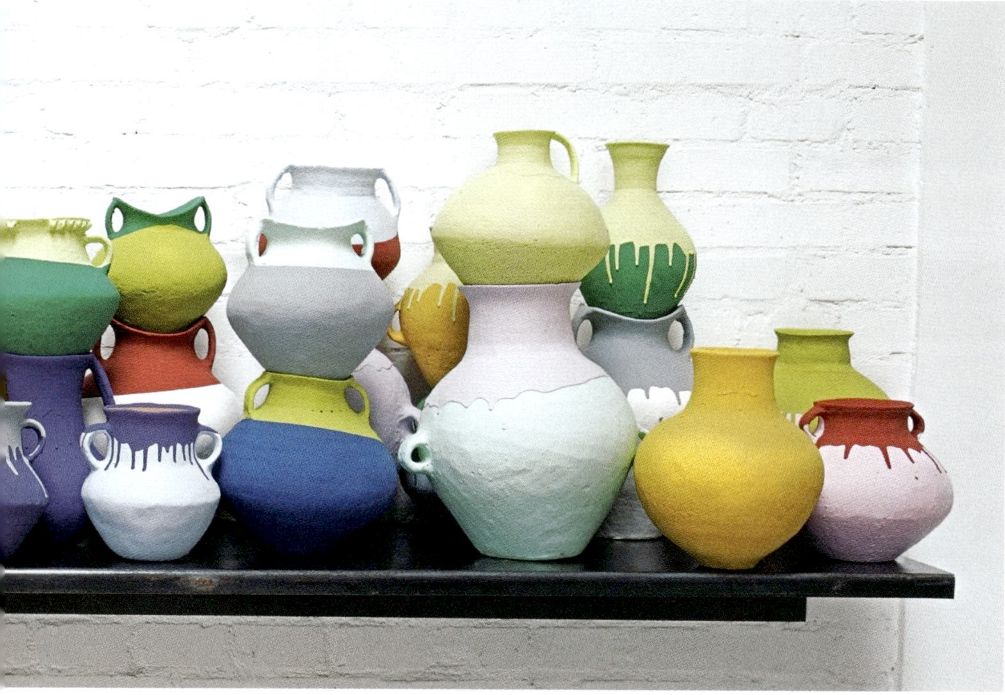

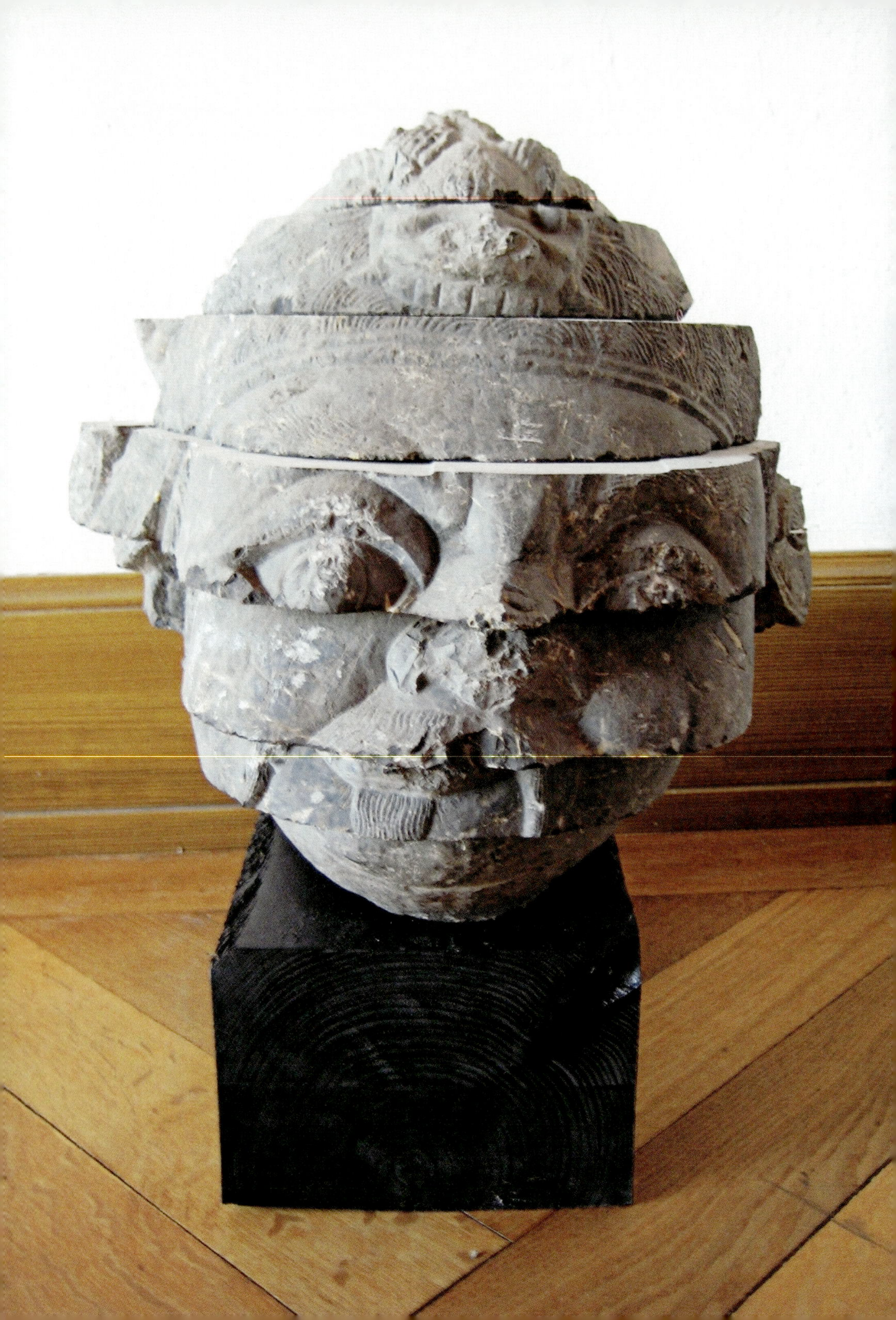

The Mediator's Ways
The Freedom and Art of Ai Weiwei

ROGER M. BUERGEL

I. Just a few days after the opening of Documenta 12, Ai Weiwei's *Template* (2007, pp. 328–330) collapsed following a storm. The structure, around 23 feet tall and one of the festival's key outdoor exhibits, was made of exactly 1,001 door and window frames from the Ming and Qing Dynasties (1368–1911). Ai had acquired the frames, like so many basic components of his work, at Chinese antique markets. The artist assigned his assistants to craft the wooden antiques into four relief-like walls placed upright in the shape of a star around an axis. The way in which the individual walls were assembled accentuated both the ramshackle character of the abandoned frames and the randomness of where they ended up. The fragility of *Template* brought to mind a large house of cards.

But, unlike playing cards, the walls were cut on their inside edges so that a negative space arose from the sum of the recesses in the construction's interior. This negative space had the outline of a traditional temple of the kind seen on a thousand hilltops or other selected sites in China, although they increasingly have to make way for capitalist China's infrastructure projects. It was this "missing temple" that enabled visitors to walk through *Template* and appreciate its ingenious, fragile construction not only by observation but also by physical experience. In this process of experience, which linked the viewer's lines of movement and chains of thought with the willful structure of the non-building, its material consistency and historic texture, something of the original function of the temple was preserved and at the same time radicalized: the creation of a link between the self and the world. Unlike in a "full" temple, however, for *Template* this link no longer appeared stable. The spiritual superstructure had given way to an empty space that was framed by wooden remnants of traditional China.

It would be wrong to interpret Ai's empty space as nothing more than a farewell. Like many of his works, *Template* is a testament of despair about what once was and now is no more. But this is a productive despair. It revives an old Chinese theme: the relationship between emptiness and spirituality. The subject derives from religious beliefs where the heavenly powers, unlike the thundering God of Judeo-Christian tradition, offer no explanation. China's celestial beings do not speak (for there to be light), but manifest themselves in harmonious parallels that require two things to be fully grasped: considerable faculties of abstraction that enable one to ignore what's insignificant, and the capacity and leisure for

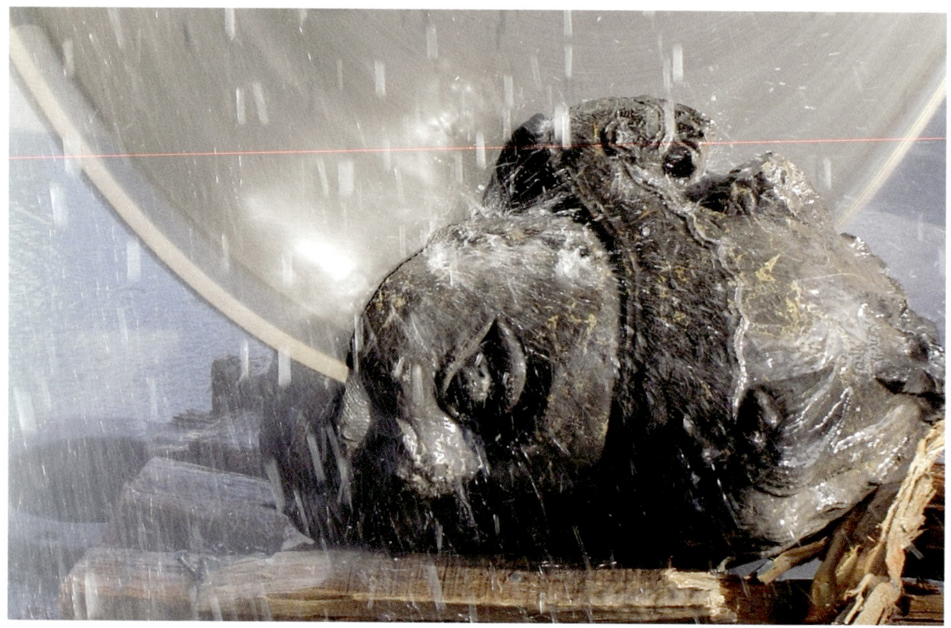

Making of *Head (Warrior)*, 2004

contemplative immersion to divine the laws of celestial harmony in what appears to be the most insignificant detail.[1] In Ai's secular or post-religious spirituality, celestial powers have been replaced by the Chinese governmental system (which also does not offer explanations), and meditative immersion has been replaced by unfettered interaction with one's own creative resources.

If, for him, there is no temple to bless the link between the self and the world, it does not mean that there is no creative imperative to establish such a link or create something out of nothing and the remnants of times gone by.

II. At the opening of Documenta, *Template* was the main attraction. This was due both to the sculpture's aesthetic power and to its location in the middle of Karlsaue Park. The media's tendency to pick out a single work as representative of the whole was another factor, as was the presence of Ai himself, who as a global artist appeared to offer at least two faces, a Chinese and a western one, and who could therefore be profiled as a go-between for Asia and the West against the backdrop of the current geopolitical power shift. But maybe the chief reason for all the media attention was the enormous commotion caused by Ai's *Fairytale* (the visit by 1,001 Chinese people to Documenta) in the run-up to the exhibition. And although the dimensions and implications of this work provided ample food for thought, there was no definable image to latch onto, so *Template* benefited from a kind of displaced attention as a result in addition to the factors outlined above. It was hardly surprising that, out of all the works on show, the German president and a whole range of other dignitaries posed beneath *Template* at the official opening, implanting Ai's highly fragile monument into the short-lived but far-reaching memory of the media.

These fresh media images—together with the public attention enjoyed by every Documenta exhibition, at least in Germany—must have been the reason that the collapse of the work was seen as so newsworthy and why it created a new awareness of the piece. In actual fact, *Template* had only partially collapsed and was, in its new, transformed state, anything but an unarticulated heap of stuff. The iron framing encompassing the old wooden frames had simply yielded to the forces of nature and been oddly twisted in the process. The outcome was a bizarre and very unique configuration that had a poetically disconcerting overall effect enhanced by the fact that the Ming and Qing elements—previously subordinate to the larger form—had to a certain extent been able to emancipate themselves from Ai's sculpture.

It is known that Ai accepted the outcome of the storm, the transformed *Template,* with gratitude. He never considered restoring the work. So the fallen monument lived through Documenta in its new guise and attracted a quite specific public, one that, like most of the 1,001 Chinese whom Ai had invited to Kassel, was not particularly interested in the exhibition or in art as such. These new visitors were disaster tourists; they wanted to see an improbable event for themselves. What exactly did they find in the Karlsaue? Disaster architecture indeed, packaged in an Asian idiom vaguely reminiscent of the media images transmitted around the world after earthquakes or tsunamis. But *Template* was not an image that showed an alien world as "the world of the others." It was something difficult to comprehend, something that transcended the perceptual distance between the realities of China and Kassel. As such, it was the art of a genuine mediator, a wayfarer between worlds.

III. After Documenta came to an end, Ai commissioned his team of craftsmen to recreate the collapsed monument detail for detail. On the one hand, this was a matter of incorporating the work into his oeuvre, which meant repeating both the situative and the coincidental structure, and copying the aesthetic echo of the forces of nature. On the other hand, Ai realized that, thanks to the spectacular performance of *Template,* a crucial dimension had been added to his work: it now had a life of its own. For the artist, this "life of its own" would be difficult to achieve, because it does not allow itself to be planned or programmed. Just like the celestial harmony of Chinese religion, it may obey rules and laws, but these remain concealed. There are, however, factors that the artist can take care of, and in Ai's case this includes interaction with his craftsmen. This interaction is highly permeable: Ai not only depends on their technical competence—as craftsmen creating his designs—but is both respecting and making demands on them as guarantors of the material and its history.

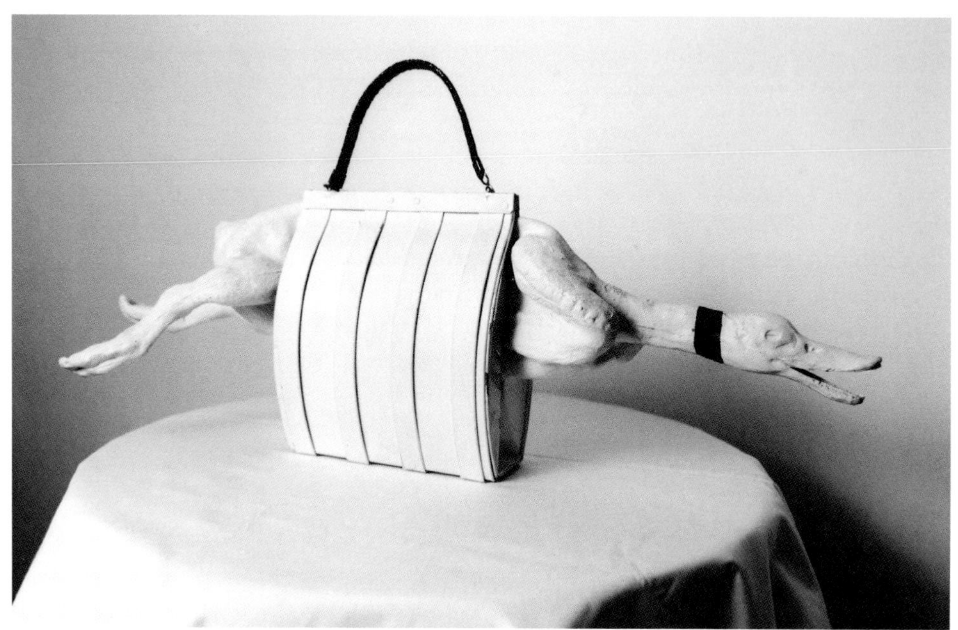

Handbag for Fashion, 1988, leather handbag, rubber duck, dimensions unknown

He begins the process by confronting the craftsmen with a problem: he introduces the material available—in the case of *Template,* the 1,001 antique door and window frames; for *China Log* (2005, pp. 188/189), eight pillars of a ruined temple from the Qing Dynasty (1644–1911)—and asks, what can be done with this? The craftsmen then present suggestions that are discussed, discarded, modified, and put into effect. This kind of artistic collaboration is notable, as it grants the material history of Chinese culture a significant place in the artist's own, contemporary act of creation. On the one hand, Ai confronts himself with this history through the sheer abundance of abandoned artifacts for sale in China, which he acquires for himself and his production. On the other, Ai perceives this material history as embodied in his craftsmen, and it seems to him as though the craftsmen can do more than they (and also Ai himself) know beforehand. So the artistic production aims to trigger a collective process in which the unforeseeable can happen. It is a process that invokes a power and makes a claim on it, a power we might describe as the "material unconscious."

The material unconscious encompasses the experiences that have accumulated over the course of centuries of highly disciplined practice in the manual skills as well as the cultural ways of life. The astonishing achievements of the Chinese can be attributed not only to their ingenuity, but also to an immense, enduring pressure that can only be exerted by a long-established feudal regime with brutally rigid and meticulously organized social hierarchies. Not that the work of craftsmen is exclusively a torment. It does of course yield moments of happiness, for example when a porcelain bowl emerges blemish-free from the kiln and appears almost immaterial. It also enjoys intellectual triumphs such as the 11th-century Fogongsi Pagoda in Yingxian that has withstood any earthquake or storm despite its height of 220 feet.[2] But what is the relationship between these moments of happiness and intellectual triumph and their existential cost, the commitment, even the sacrifice they call for?

The material unconscious is an explosive mix, that much at least is certain—one that spilled over into the Cultural Revolution's orgies of destruction, to which Ai has created an ambivalent memorial in the form of his early performance *Dropping a Han Dynasty Urn* (1995, pp. 85–87). More on that later, for now it should be noted that the material unconscious is just as much alive in the artifacts as in the technical abilities of the craftsmen, who carry a knowledge of how to work with materials acquired and handed down over generations. Contemporary China, which, with the opening of the markets since the 1980s, has committed itself to the imperative of blanket modernization, can see no more use for this treasury of experience, but instead radicalizes the cultural-revolutionary principle of tabula rasa. Accordingly, the traditional handicraft techniques are threatened with extinction, like animals and languages. This lends a profoundly sad character to many of Ai's works that are based on them.

IV. There exists a profound parallelism between the craftsmanship and the artifacts of yore, the urns, the temple columns, the chipped-off feet and hands of Buddha sculptures, the door and window frames, and all that is incorporated into Ai's oeuvre and has been adopted as readymades. The artist does not do much more than link these parallels or even short-circuit them. He is playing with these forces rather than producing something in the conventional sense. The aforementioned permeability as a feature of Ai's work (though it may appear paradoxical in view of his physical presence and charisma) forms a basic prerequisite for the forces to unfold and display the very same independent will that is the artist's ultimate goal and that manifests itself so arrestingly in *Template*.

V. In a different form, this independent will was also a decisive factor of *Fairytale* (2007, pp. 310–327), Ai's second contribution to Documenta 12, which essentially consisted of allowing a broad cross-section of 1,000 Chinese nationals (the 1,001st Chinese was Ai himself) to travel to Kassel. Unlike *Template*, here the work expressed a life of its own due not to the unforeseeable performance of a sculpture but to the improvised nature of a group. Philip Tinari rightly described the entire piece as an "experiment in controlled chaos."[3] *Fairytale* also involved Ai combining various forces, for example the curiosity of Chinese people who would never have otherwise been able to afford such a trip, or the infrastructural and medial possibilities of a large-scale exhibition, as well as the western interest in a panorama of

China that did not reproduce official doctrine. Ai did not create an identifiable art object but rather he marked certain details, including the design of the suitcases and the sleeping quarters, hair cutting, and personal presence on the site. Although the organizational effort and immense costs of *Fairytale* alone appeared to fulfill all the criteria of a large-scale work, the true dynamic of this aesthetic of existence was effected in small and apparently insignificant aspects: for example, in the meeting between Chinese and Hessian farmers, where both talked shop in untranslatable expressions, yet understood each other perfectly well. While *Fairytale* was embedded within a huge institutional exhibition, it was neither about aesthetic experiences in a narrower sense nor about social sculpture. Instead the both open and structured scattering of singular experiences combined to form an aesthetic of existence. Ai's permeability as quasi-uninvolved moderator of the whole undertaking focused on the creation and preservation of the dynamic equilibrium such an aesthetic of existence requires: the interplay between openness and structure. The singular experiences of the participants were not subject to any choreography, let alone any guiding constraints. They partook of the experiences for themselves, although it may well have been the same for them as it was for the disaster tourists—an entry into another, strange perceptual relationship with the world awaited them.[4]

VI. The aesthetic of existence is a theme in Ai's work that can be traced back at least to his time in New York (1982–1993). One can delve even further back into the artist's biography and consider the years in the desert to which Ai's father Ai Qing, probably China's most influential modern poet, had been banished during the purges of the Cultural Revolution to perform menial tasks like cleaning public toilets. Ai Weiwei often makes reference to this story, the precarious living conditions in conjunction with the iron resolution to keep one's own dignity, reminding us that aesthetic quality has just as much to do with beautiful forms as with the naked life.

VII. Ai ended up in New York because, although his father had been rehabilitated, his own situation at home no longer appeared to be tenable. His years in the American metropolis were a time of bohemian hanging out, of indirect learning, and of the incubation of as yet underdeveloped ideas. Ai himself documented everything in countless photos (pp. 57–63)—not deliberately like a diarist who takes himself too seriously, but casually, ironically, in a dandyesque manner. And infused with a healthy dose of nihilism, which one might attribute to Ai's age at the time, his bitter experience with the Chinese system, and a certain disorientation, even isolation in a foreign place, but also to the key lessons of modernist art that he afforded himself in New York and Philadelphia. The body of pictures in his photo archive (only a fraction of the approximately 10,000 negatives has ever been published) covers an encyclopedic spectrum of both the exotic aspects of urban daily

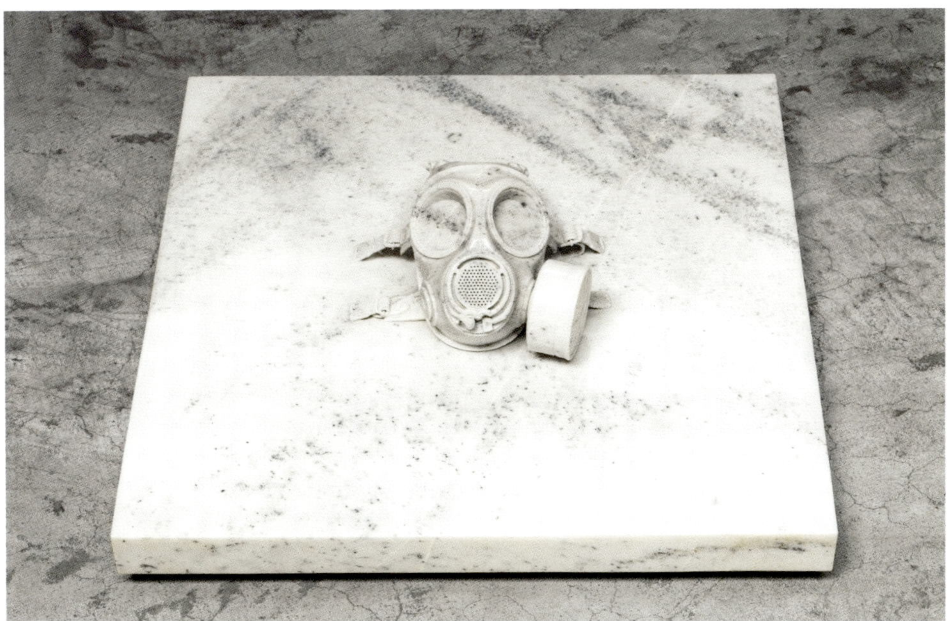

Mask, 2013, marble, 8⅝ x 30¾ x 30¾ inches

life in the East Village and the opulent displays in galleries and museums supported by Reaganomics. Ai documented the AIDS rallies and the bloody clashes between demonstrators and police during the occupation of Tompkins Square Park, while he also photographed new friends such as the poet Allen Ginsberg (p. 17), members of the Chinese diaspora—and himself. The self-portraits show the artist as a young man sometimes struggling to counter his boredom, trying a number of different ways to frame his own face with a bicycle tire, and posing in MoMA alongside one of Andy Warhol's serial self-portraits while coquettishly mimicking the artist's affected hand position. The photos also show peculiar, almost informal artistic experiments in the studio, for example a wire coat hanger that Ai has twisted into the distinctive profile of Marcel Duchamp with a pair of pliers. When one considers that the Chinese have a monopoly on laundromats in New York, this coat hanger could be interpreted as Ai's first transcultural icon—a hunch corroborated by a photo of the coat hanger laid flat and filled with sunflower seeds, a popular snack in China.

VIII. While all the existential and artistic experiments of the New York years with their flowing transitions may have rather playful and unpretentious qualities, one should not be mistaken: here too, the artist was entering into a new, strange perceptual relationship with the world, something that cannot have been easy for him. The artistic act aligns itself with what is available or, to acknowledge Duchamp's

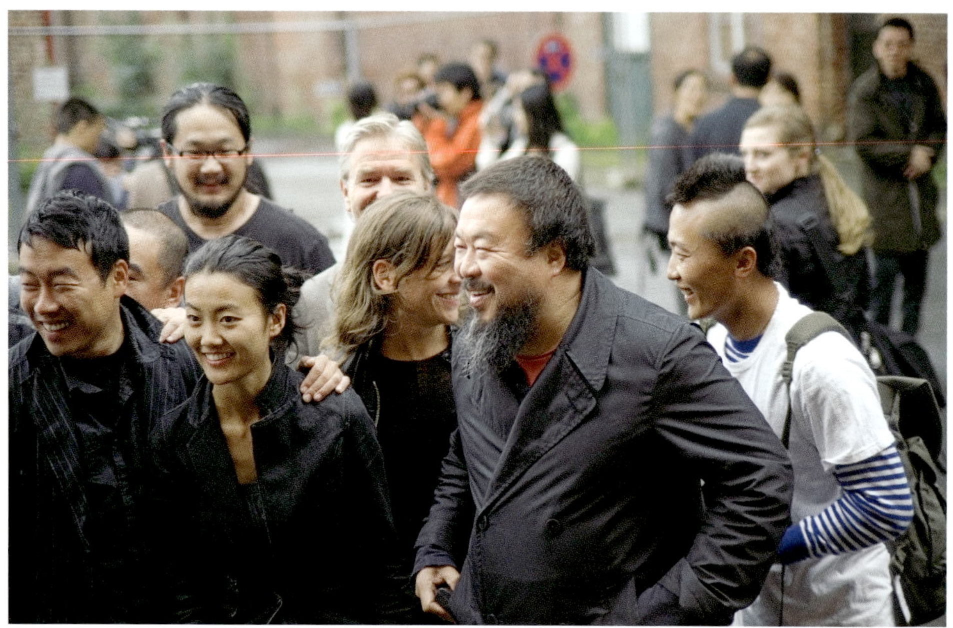

Wishing farewell to the last group of *Fairytale* participants, Kassel 2007

concept, what is "readymade." It is notable that while Ai does not shy away from contact with American culture, he appears bafflingly indifferent to its material products. At a small gallery exhibition in 1988, he presented the floor installation *Five Raincoats Holding Up a Star* (1985, p. 18): five olive-green rubber raincoats, defining symbols of everyday life in China, as well as metal pipes running through the amorphous mass of rubber coats and merged into a five-point star, the symbol of the Chinese Communist Party. Just as in the works of his later, mature period, here he smuggled Chinese textures and systems of reference into the modernist canon, whose language he had usurped—in this case that of minimalism. To this day it has still not become clear whether Ai actually speaks this language with body and soul and deep conviction, or whether he is faking it and deploying it as a vehicle.

IX. In New York, the émigré Marcel Duchamp and Andy Warhol became Ai's artistic guiding lights. Not only were both men present with their own oeuvre, they also played a weighty role as reference points for the conceptual and politically min-ded spectrum of American art at the time. For example, Barbara Kruger sought to further develop Warhol's aesthetics of advertising; Jeff Koons set everyday objects in hermetic displays that made them iconic in reference to Duchamp; and Jenny Holzer utilized hypervisible Times Square billboards to communicate platitudes to which the scale and central location of this public place would lend an ominous

significance. This list of artists and artistic positions is not coincidental.⁵ It comes
from Ai himself, who after his return to China published three anthologies that
introduced readers to western modernist art and the Chinese avant-garde: *Black
Cover Book* (1994, p. 99), *White Cover Book* (1995, p. 99), and *Gray Cover Book*
(1997). Texts by Duchamp and Warhol were translated into Chinese for the anthologies and the abovementioned artists, among others, were presented through their
own words and images. A section titled "Studio" included monographic articles on
the contemporary Chinese art scene. It is typical of Ai that the publications were
not simply a way of processing and conveying his own learning experience, but that
he launched the three anthologies as a platform for a conceptually oriented Chinese scene perceived to be on the cusp of its emergence and for which he was later
to become a mentor.

X. The ideas that Ai drew from Warhol, Duchamp, and their artistic heirs were very
diverse. For his reception of Warhol, the voice of the artist must have played a decisive role. In one of the first publications Ai had acquired in New York, that voice
expounds the following credo: "What's great about this country is that America
started the tradition where the richest consumers buy essentially the same thing
as the poorest. You can be watching TV and see Coca-Cola, and you know that the
President drinks Coca-Cola, Liz Taylor drinks Coca-Cola, and just think, you can
drink Coca-Cola, too. A coke is a coke and no amount of money can get you a better coke than the one the bum on the corner is drinking. All the cokes are the
same and all the cokes are good. Liz Taylor knows it, the President knows it, the
bum knows it, and you know it."⁶
  One may find Warhol's undertone, his radical affirmation of the American Way
of Life, ironic. But what difference does it make whether this total political trav-
esty, which proclaims universal equality on the basis of Coca-Cola, is intended as
serious or tongue-in-cheek? Warhol's explanation is on an equal footing with the
American ideology, and therein lies its diagnostic property and its perverse appeal.
Ai, who from an early age had been forced to listen to Mao's shrill and all-pervasive
propaganda with its shoddy slogans, cannot have failed to notice the affinities
between the social utopias of Communism and consumerism. Young bohemian that
he was, Ai's intent was to cultivate a stance against the system. And what could be
more obvious than to school himself in Warhol's cool sentimentality, which was
anything but unrealistic but, quite to the contrary, coupled with an excessive participation in social agency?
  Of course Ai and Warhol are obviously quite different characters, and Beijing
does not provide an opportunity to operate from behind the cover of a promiscuous
metropolis, not even for party cadres. Still, the sprawling entourage of friends, visitors, journalists, assistants, helpers, and cats that populates Ai's premises around
the clock in Caochangdi may to no small extent owe its inspiration to Warhol's
legendary Factory on Broadway. Also, the Warholian voice makes itself felt in Ai's

blog-political activities, which comment on contemporary life in China with a sarcasm that is difficult to translate yet never bitter—noting on the occasion of the German *Art of the Enlightenment* exhibition on Tiananmen Square: "Those Europeans always have such beautiful things to show."[7]

XI. Ai's reception of Duchamp revolved around the concept of the readymade and that snapshot moment of artistic transformation described by Duchamp as an "inscription," manifested for example in the false signature on the 1917 urinal, when the work's true creator, Duchamp, identified himself as a certain "R. Mutt."[8] While Warhol's universe basically revolved around Warhol, Duchamp operated on a highly intellectual but at the same time witty and quite frivolous level that no longer dwelled on the aesthetic appearance of art, but made its ontological status the issue—in other words, its state of being art in one sense and non-art in another. The full scope of these Duchampian stimuli was presumably felt by Ai in China, where not only idiosyncratic objects such as urinals, bicycle wheels, or bottle racks awaited him; there he was received by a culture both fragmented and monumental, ready to be adopted as artistic material indifferent to meaning. The impact of the European colonial powers, the Japanese occupation, the civil war, and Mao's grandiose and fatal systemic experiments, as well as the current state-capitalist stratification of the country, had knocked this culture out of joint. Duchamp taught Ai how to handle this flotsam of a liquidized history.

Duchamp's reflections on the artistic designation of everyday objects are one thing. The artist blurs the lines between art and non-art to gain room for maneuvering. At the same time, it becomes evident that aesthetic appearance, the visibility of a work, is wholly insufficient to capture its true, conceptual dimension.[9] Quite another aspect is offered by the concrete destiny of Duchamp's works, which existed in defiance of all mental acrobatics and eventually found their way into the museum despite the artist's internal opposition. Or maybe they didn't? As befits Duchamp, at this point the story gets seriously complicated. Decisive works such as the original urinal no longer existed. Duchamp himself only became aware of this in the 1960s, when his work had finally received its due and the original readymades were needed for a big retrospective in Pasadena. Anyone who thinks a urinal is easy to replace is very much mistaken. Industrial production methods had long since changed; technologies only have a limited shelf life. Which meant that the objects Duchamp had deliberately selected as industrial products devoid of any aura had to be artistically reproduced by hand.[10] With his revolutionary designation of 1917, Duchamp had been able to demonstrate that a urinal is not identical with itself. In the context of a gallery presentation, and furnished with a (false) signature, it can gain ontological status as a work of art. But during the preparations for the retrospective, it also became clear that even a readymade is not identical to itself. And later all these trials and tribulations over the destiny of a form were documented in Ai's *Black Cover Book* with photographs of the original 1917 instal-

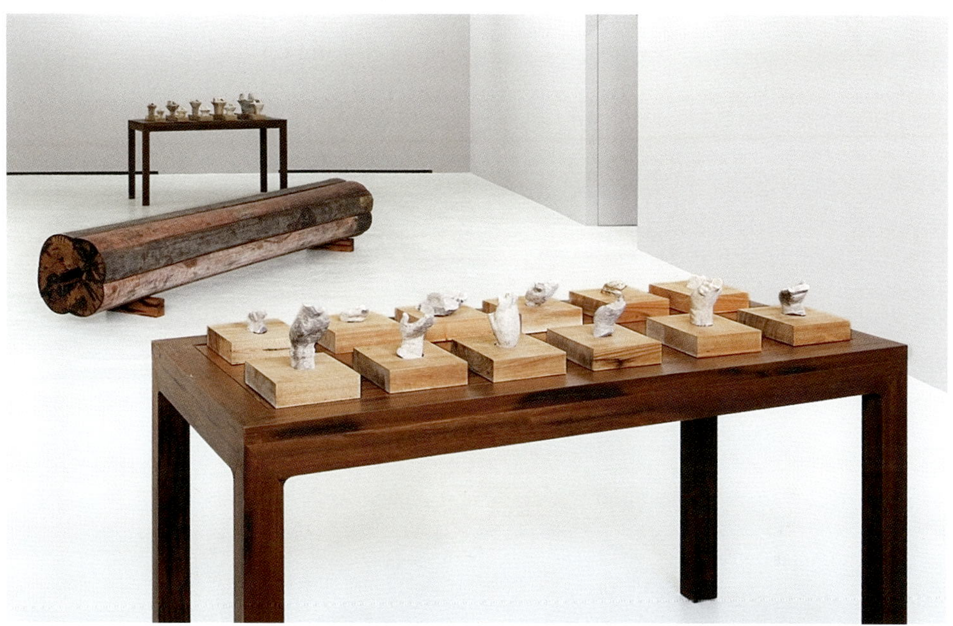

Hands, 2003, 12 fragments of Northern Wei Period stone sculptures, wooden plinths, wooden table,
49 ⅝ x 26 ¾ x 66 ⅛ inches; *China Log,* 2005, tieli wood from destroyed Qing Dynasty temples,
132 ⅝ x ø 22 ⅜ inches; *Feet,* 2003, 10 fragments of Northern Qi Period stone sculptures, wooden plinths,
wooden table, 49 ⅝ x 26 ¾ x 66 ⅛ inches (front to back); Museum DKM, Duisburg 2010

lation, as well as the elevations for the 1964 replica that Duchamp's dealer Arturo
Schwarz commissioned.

XII. This and other lessons drawn from Duchamp had a huge influence on the
New York scene of the 1980s, which Ai studied with great care—he claims to have
seen pretty much every exhibition, and his photos back this up. They appeared to
show ways to move art away from commodity characterization or institutional finishing, but also urged artistic particularity on in its battle against capitalist standardization. Then again, Ai drew his own, rather more Chinese conclusions. The
market or commodity character was never a problem for him—on the contrary,
he viewed the market as a social medium. Capitalist standardization might represent a better opponent, but in the context of a one-party dictatorship, Ai starts
from a different standpoint, that of anti-totalitarian mobilization. A formless work
such as *Fairytale* can serve as an example here, as well as the research into the
Sichuan earthquake that would occupy him on several levels from 2008. The conclusions that Ai draws from Duchamp move him toward a free and easy appropriation process. This does not mean that everything can become art but that it's not
at all relevant whether what you are doing is art or not—indeed there are special
possibilities inherent in this indistinguishability of practices.

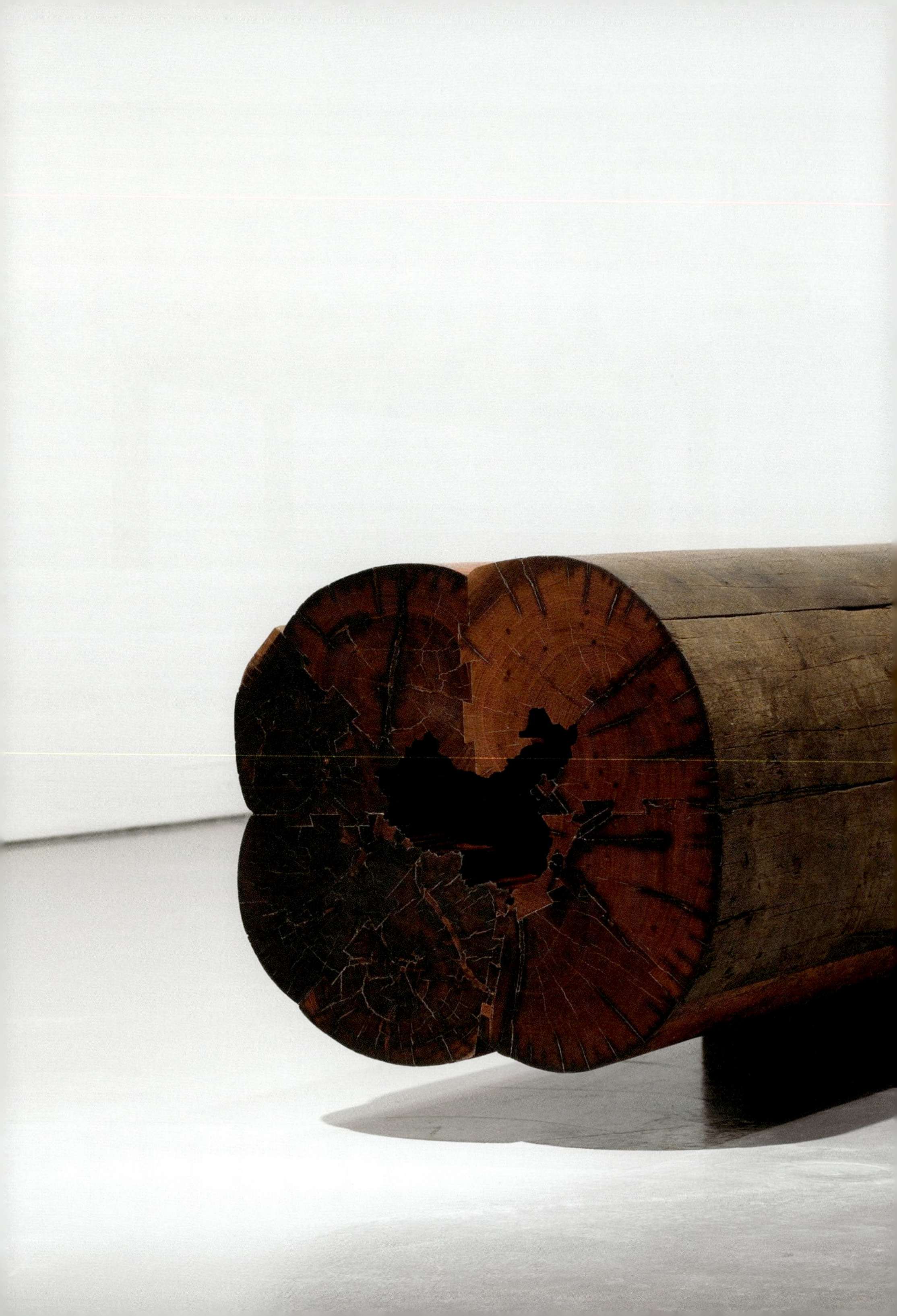

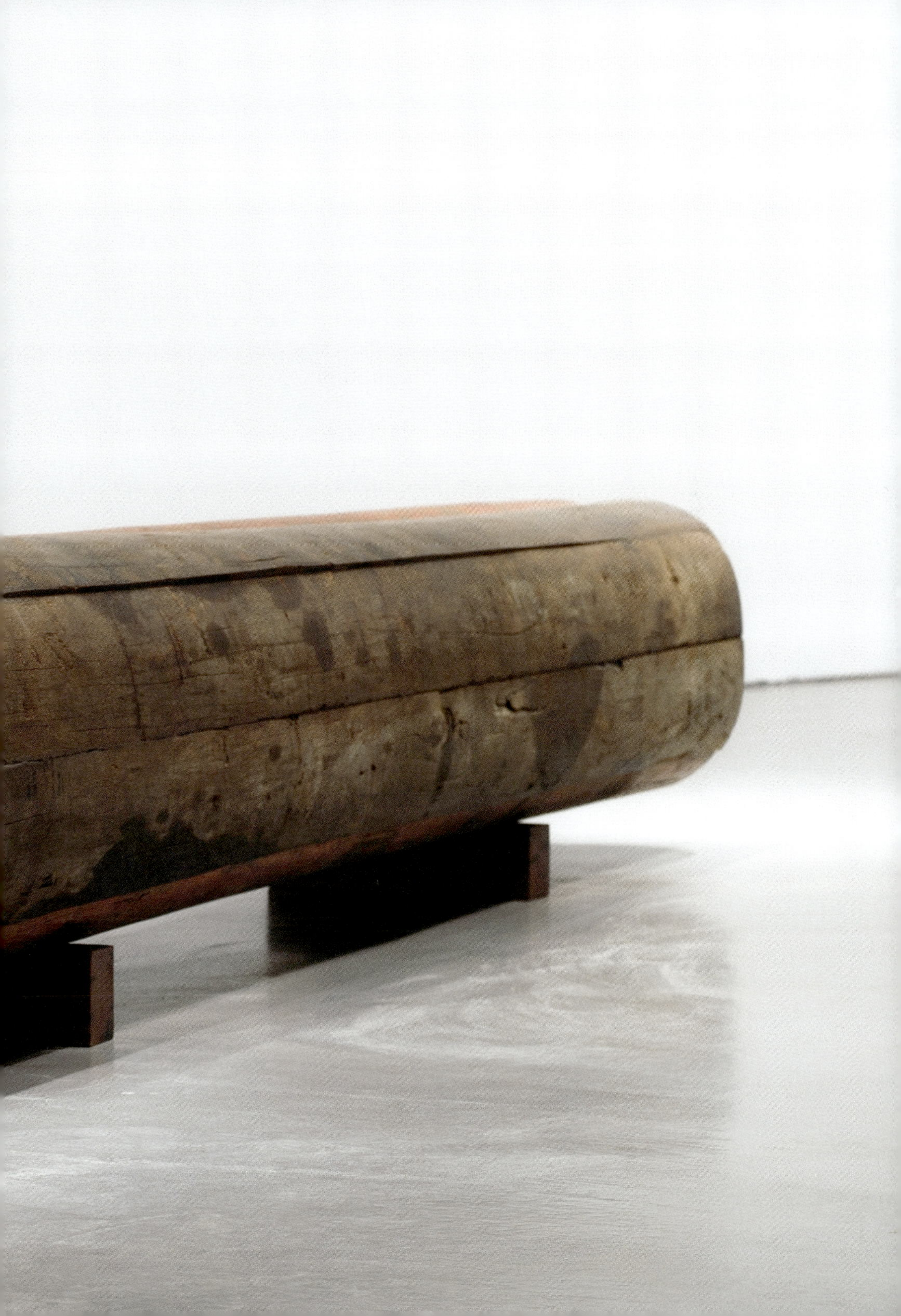

XIII. When Ai returned to China in 1993 because his sick father needed him,
he arrived with a well-equipped box of conceptual tools. The questions and possibilities it contained are indicated by his first mature works. For *Han Dynasty Urn
with Coca-Cola Logo* (1994), Ai marked a circa 2,000-year-old vase with the words
"Coca-Cola."[11]

The vase, disfigured with the logo, reads upon first glance like a memento
mori: a 2,000-year-old piece of historic heritage overwritten and at the same time
devalued by a global brand. On second glance, it turns out that Ai is, apparently
incidentally, exploring the formal parallels that exist between the swirling Spence-
rian font of 1936 and traditional Han paintings. This means his painted logo is not
invasive. While the red appears muted, almost earthy in color, the sweeping letters
are in keeping with the belly-like shape of the urn. Anyone who thinks in long time
frames like Ai does will remember Chinese culture's particular capacity for adaptation—which it proved following the Mongol invasion during the Yuan Dynasty
(1279–1368), for example—appropriating something alien overnight as a way
of remaining the same. If one further extrapolates this thought, it may be that
2,000 years from now Coca-Cola will be perceived as a Chinese brand. This is an
aspect of the abovementioned freedom in the appropriation process (something
that any western entrepreneur in China will understand without any help from
Duchamp).

The legendary performance work *Dropping a Han Dynasty Urn* (1995,
pp. 85–87) shows Ai in simple peasant garb standing in front of a high wall. In his
hand, his fingers ostentatiously splayed, he is holding an urn, again an antique,
that he will drop in the next instant. This performance is distributed over three
photos taken within fractions of a second of each other. Ai is seen holding the urn,
then the urn falls, and finally the shards can be seen lying at the foot of the artist.
It is a shocking scene, not only for the museum-savvy western observer. This may
have something to do with the antique urn and its imaginary value, and yet more
with the indifferent facial expression of the artist, which directly confronts the
observer. The act of allowing the urn to fall is not emotional, but an act of deliberately calculated barbarism that plunges the observer, as powerless witness, into
an ethical-aesthetical dilemma.

Just like the ostensibly disfigured Han vase, *Dropping* suggests a straightforward reading: "Look, China's historic heritage is being shattered." Yet significantly
it is Ai himself who slips into the role of a rustic henchman getting his revenge on
tradition. And indeed, this performance is probably about fathoming that certain
deep layer that links people in post-cultural revolutionary China, including Ai himself, with their Chinese heritage. Instead of making a statement, the performance
throws up the question: "Do we still feel the pain (in the face of destruction)?"
In short, this is less about an urn breaking into pieces than about a relationship,
in which Ai deliberately exposes himself as a partner and as a consequence portrays

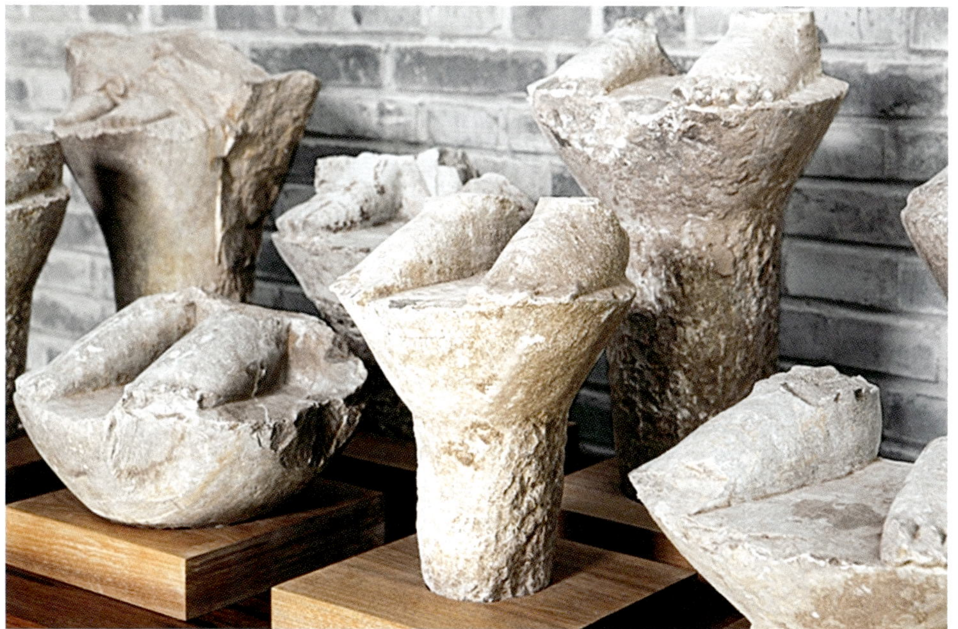

Feet, 2003 (detail), 10 fragments of Northern Qi Period stone sculptures, wooden plinths, wooden table, 49⅝ x 26¾ x 66⅛ inches

himself as a damaged person—an exceptional moment in Chinese contemporary art. He does not simply endure this damage, but actively stages it in performance. One can suppose that this very confident recognition of the damage that he has sustained also contains the seed of the genuine solidarity that facilitates Ai's activist mediations.

XIV. In *Hands* (p. 187) and *Feet* (above, both 2003) this solidarity extends to the forms of damaged people, or more precisely: hands and feet knocked off Buddha statues dating from the Qi Dynasty (550–577), which Ai displays on two large wooden tables. The fragmentation of these pieces of stone (there are a total of twelve hands and ten feet) underlines the almost animated character of the bodily elements and lines that bear witness to the heyday of Buddhism in northern China. But they also bear witness to the violence that would soon be directed against the power and the wealth of the monasteries. In his display, Ai does not treat the stone relicts as historic material but like autonomous pieces à la Rodin. Every single foot and every single hand rests on its own square wooden plinth, demonstrating the individual, even unique form caused by the uniformly violent character of their fragmentation.

While it makes no use of the anthropomorphic, *Rebar* (2012, p. 477) also deals with damaged human beings. Iron girders that reinforce concrete building blocks are twisted in almost calligraphical fashion. Ai picked the deformed girders out of the ruins of school buildings that had been badly hit by the Sichuan earthquake in 2008. As it turned out, local authorities and building firms had calmly cut expenses in the construction of the schools to fill their own pockets. Ai took part in a civilian investigation into the earthquake and the deaths of many schoolchildren, and he also collected the used iron girders that now took the place of the ancient relics in the earlier work.

For an exhibition of the iron bars, Ai had them copied twice. Allowing the originals to circulate within the art system as *art engagé* would have been stupid. But not to exhibit them at all would have been cowardly. Within their triple exposition lies something genuine, and yet this authenticity is absorbed by the plurality—or, more precisely, the authenticity has been displaced. Ai is not concerned with using a piece of iron to attest to a catastrophe, but rather he makes the observer feel an association with the event. Entering into this kind of perceptual relationship comes at a price: it reveals the irreconcilable abyss between the twisted piece of iron from Sichuan and the other two pieces, or between non-art and art.

XV. The shocking experience of *Rebar* is due to an essentially straightforward realization: here is a horrific piece of reality, a twisted iron rod that bears no resemblance to the identical piece of iron beside it—apart from its form, which says nothing as such. This realization does not question the observer's perceptiveness but requires him to activate his powers of imagination because the subject matter of this work cannot be captured aesthetically. A sense of connection with the world develops during the process of observation, where the Sichuan catastrophe does not remain a purely external event one reacts to with sympathy or outrage. Much more, the catastrophe takes on an emotional dimension and is pushed into the interior perspective, provoking the question "How does it affect me?" rather than "What does it have to do with me?" In Chinese, this accessing of emotional resources is described as "nurturing life," but presumably everybody knows the feeling.[12] No one really had to tell the disaster tourist from Kassel what the collapsed *Template* had to do with him (and if he had not known the answer, he would not have traveled there of his own accord). Nevertheless, *Template* did accommodate the observer to the extent that the deformed sculpture had bridged any perceptual distance almost of its own volition and demanded no aesthetic preparatory work. In the case of *Rebar*, this bridging occurs more subtly, namely on the back of the formal modernist canon, and it requires the ability to think abstract. But regardless of the respective form or fate of this and other works, the entity that Ai's artistic conception is addressing becomes apparent: it is the self of the observer, including his or her emotional resources.

Nowhere is this self more unmistakably addressed than in a work created secretly over a number of years, in which Ai processes his traumatic prison experience from early 2011. *S.A.C.R.E.D.* (2011–2013, pp. 218, 221, 223, 481–483)

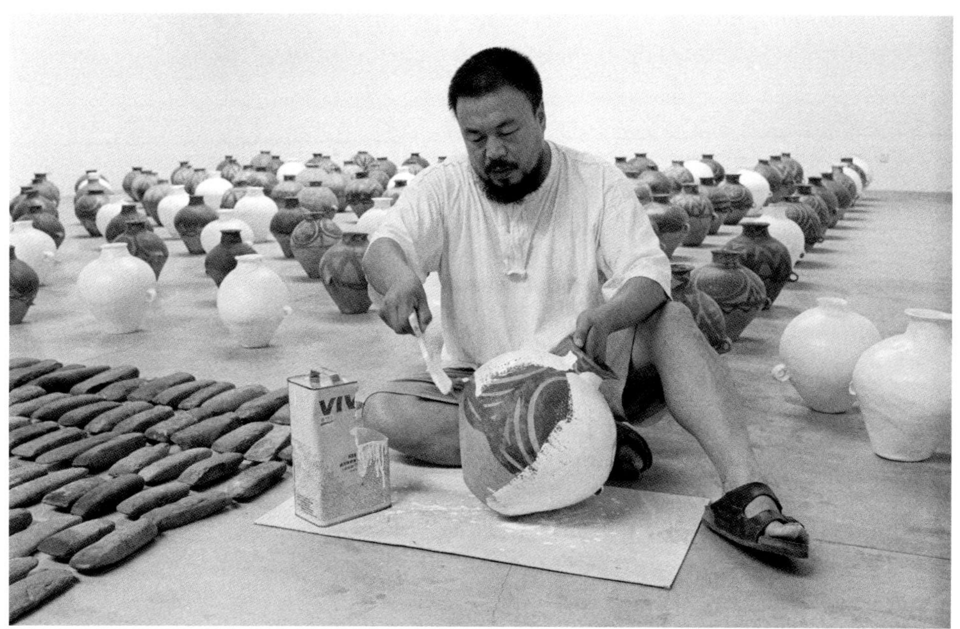

Making of *Whitewash*, 1993–2000, neolithic clay urns, industrial paint, dimensions variable

consists of six dark iron boxes around shoulder height, roughly 13 feet long and
6.5 feet wide. Each of these iron boxes contains a half life-sized diorama modeled
in fiberglass, showing Ai in key situations during his 81-day detention. The title
of the work is an acronym: S. stands for Supper, A. for Accusers, C. for Cleansing,
R. for Ritual (here: defecation), E. for Entropy (here: sleep), and D. for Doubt.
It is clear that the terms vary between those that describe routine activities
and those that characterize emotional states: for example, Entropy characterizes
the sense of personality dissolution that must have crept up on Ai when he had
to sleep under permanent guard in a confined, fully lit space beneath an inadequate blanket. After all, the title of the work—sacred—has nothing to do with
Christianity, but makes reference to the word's ancient meaning of *homo sacer*
as someone without rights, someone excluded from society. This *homo sacer*
belongs to the gods, but in the sinister sense of complete and utter defenseless-
ness. Because he has broken the pact with the gods, he can be killed by anyone
without punishment and this murder will not be judged as a human crime but as
divine retribution.[13]

At the work's first installation in the central nave of the Chiesa di Sant'Antonin
in Venice during the summer of 2013, these ominous, somber blocks from a distance recalled catafalques, while in a White Cube they would be associated with
orthodox-minimalist sculptures. But in contrast to catafalques or minimalist surfaces, Ai's monumental form beckoned with narrative elements. For example, a

half-sized closed door was simulated on the wall of one iron box, while a box standing before it suggested the possibility that the observer might climb up on top to carry out a closer inspection of the form. Indeed, the dioramas could be viewed through a slit; the slits were also mounted on the walls. Just like Duchamp's *Étant donnés* (1946–1966)—which was incidentally also created in secret—where the observer has to spy through a knothole, one does not simply become witness to an obscene spectacle but is deliberately pushed into a voyeuristic position. Put differently, the observer becomes aware of his observer status. While Duchamp's diorama with its naked female holding a lamp illuminating the surreal scene remains to some extent inscrutable, *S.A.C.R.E.D.* is without ambiguity—quite the contrary. The cell interior lit by the light of a bulb, Ai, his two uniformed guards, the security personnel interrogating him, and the sparse furnishings: all are captured with great realism and an almost hallucinatory attention to detail.

The didactic, entirely non-artistic tradition of the diorama aims to depict a reality that makes no reference to the presence of the observer. For example, museums of ethnology have dioramas intended to illustrate how people lived in the Stone Age. In the case of *S.A.C.R.E.D.*, this is different. On the one hand, the observer who peers through the slit is forced to reflect on himself. His own vantage point in conjunction with the insularity of the iron box and the miniaturization of the action creates an insurmountable distance. On the other hand, what is going on inside the cell is all too familiar. The laptop on which the security official is taking down the statement is familiar, just like the handcuffs shackling Ai to the chair during his interrogation, the carefully folded clothes in the cupboard, the plastic dishes with Chinese dumplings, the shower jet, and the brightly colored bottles of shampoo. Everybody knows what it means to sit on the toilet. Above all, Ai himself is familiar—or at least appears to be familiar. Yet the artist's self is not an authentic self. This is not about victim narcissism but, as in Warhol's work, about the image of the artist as a decisive vehicle of identification on the part of the observer.

This text has already touched upon the matter of Ai's role as mediator as well as on his poetic doctrine bridging perceptual distances. In *S.A.C.R.E.D.*, one encounters both the artist and his doctrine in an almost unbearably pure form. This leads the superficial observer to claim that the artist is exploiting his dissident status to propagate his work.[14] He could be answered with the question: "Why not?" Why should anyone whose personal destiny is shaped by a readymade totalitarian system not recreate that destiny in model form and thereby lay himself bare? Above all, when it is evident that this seemingly personal destiny is just as impersonal under dictatorial conditions as the cell interior in *S.A.C.R.E.D.* Each and every Chinese national could potentially disappear behind door 1135 and become *homo sacer*. Ai's compatriots, who sent banknotes in the form of paper airplanes over the high walls of his premises in Caochangdi after it became known that he had been heavily fined for tax evasion, are also aware of this. Wholly in keeping with the artist himself, they developed their own creative way to express solidarity and bridge perceptual distances. In such spontaneous actions, which presage the dynamic of a civil society with its interplay of individual initiative and collective spirit, the mediator disappears and with him the separation of art and non-art. Or we could put it this way: in such a world, Ai would no longer be fixated on the mediator role, because this role could indeed be taken over by many. Only then would Ai's artistic freedom begin in the proper sense—a freedom that would also include the freedom to do nothing.

[1] The role of these parallels as a foundation stone of Chinese culture is discussed by Léon Vandermeersch in *Les deux raisons de la pensée chinoise: Divination et idéographie* (Paris: Gallimard, 2013). [2] See Lothar Ledderose, *Ten Thousand Things: Module and Mass Production in Chinese Art*, The A. W. Mellon Lectures in the Fine Arts (Princeton: Princeton University Press, 1998). [3] Philip Tinari used this term in his essay "Chairs and Visitors" in *Ai Weiwei, Works 2004–2007*, ed. by Urs Meile (Zürich: JRP Ringier, 2008), p. 12. [4] For a more thorough account of the bizarre details surrounding *Fairytale*, see my essay "Meeting Alterity" in *Ai Weiwei: Fairytale, A Reader*, ed. by Lionel Bovier and Salomé Schnetz (Zürich: JRP ingier; Lucerne: Einfache Gesellschaft Fairytale, 2012), pp. 31–42. [5] It is remarkable that two artists are missing in these anthologies who not only had a considerable influence at that time, but whose artistic approach showed corresponding tendencies to Ai's own. One of them was Sherrie Levine. In her reproductions of photos by Walker Evans (*After Walker Evans*, 1981), Levine established a concept of the "copy" that undermined the original's status. The other artist was Allan McCollum, whose installations Ai photographed for his private archives. McCollum's theme in those years was the relation between identity and difference, which he developed in proliferating displays of objects that seemed the same yet were not. [6] Andy Warhol, *The Philosophy of Andy Warhol (From A to B and back again;* New York: Harcourt Brace Jovanovich, 1975), p. 100. [7] *The Art of the Enlightenment* was a collaboration between three major German museums in Berlin, Dresden, and Munich, who staged the exhibition at the Chinese National Museum in Beijing. The aim was to promote cultural exchange between the states. Ironically the exhibition started its way to Beijing just as Ai was detained at the Beijing airport. [8] The best introduction into Duchamp's wonderful complexities is David Joselit, *Infinite Regress: Marcel Duchamp 1910–1941* (Cambridge, MA: MIT Press, 1998). [9] The complete failure of aesthetic criteria in engaging with contemporary art is one of the chief characteristics of post-conceptual art, according to the English philosopher Peter Osborne in *Anywhere or Not at All: Philosophy of Contemporary Art* (London and New York: Verso, 2013). Indeed Ai must be described as a post-conceptual artist who has taken his cue from the productive failure of conceptualism. [10] The story of the re-editioned readymades is told by curator Helen Molesworth in her catalog essay "Duchamp: By Hand, Even" for her exhibition *Part Object, Part Sculpture* (Columbus, OH: Wexner Center for the Arts, 2005), pp. 156–165. [11] Ai during these years did not see himself as making art; the Coca-Cola vase was produced on a whim. This was pointed out to me by Uli Sigg. [12] See Francois Jullien, *Nourrir sa vie* (Paris: Seuil, 2005). [13] In *Homo sacer: Sovereign Power and Bare Life* (Stanford: Stanford University Press, 1995), the Italian philosopher Giorgio Agamben constructs the state of being completely exposed, what he also calls "naked life," as an effect of modern government. While this is not the place to follow the thought in detail, one should still remember that Ai's situation in his cell, stripped of all human rights, was not an exclusively Chinese situation. The democratic western world also keeps its non-spaces, for example in Guantánamo. [14] For instance, Franceso Bonami insinuates that Ai used his "lukewarm dissidence" to boost his market value in the West, whereas "real" dissidents would be locked away by the regime forever; see galleristny.com/2013/06/francesco-bonami-i-hate-ai-weiwei/.

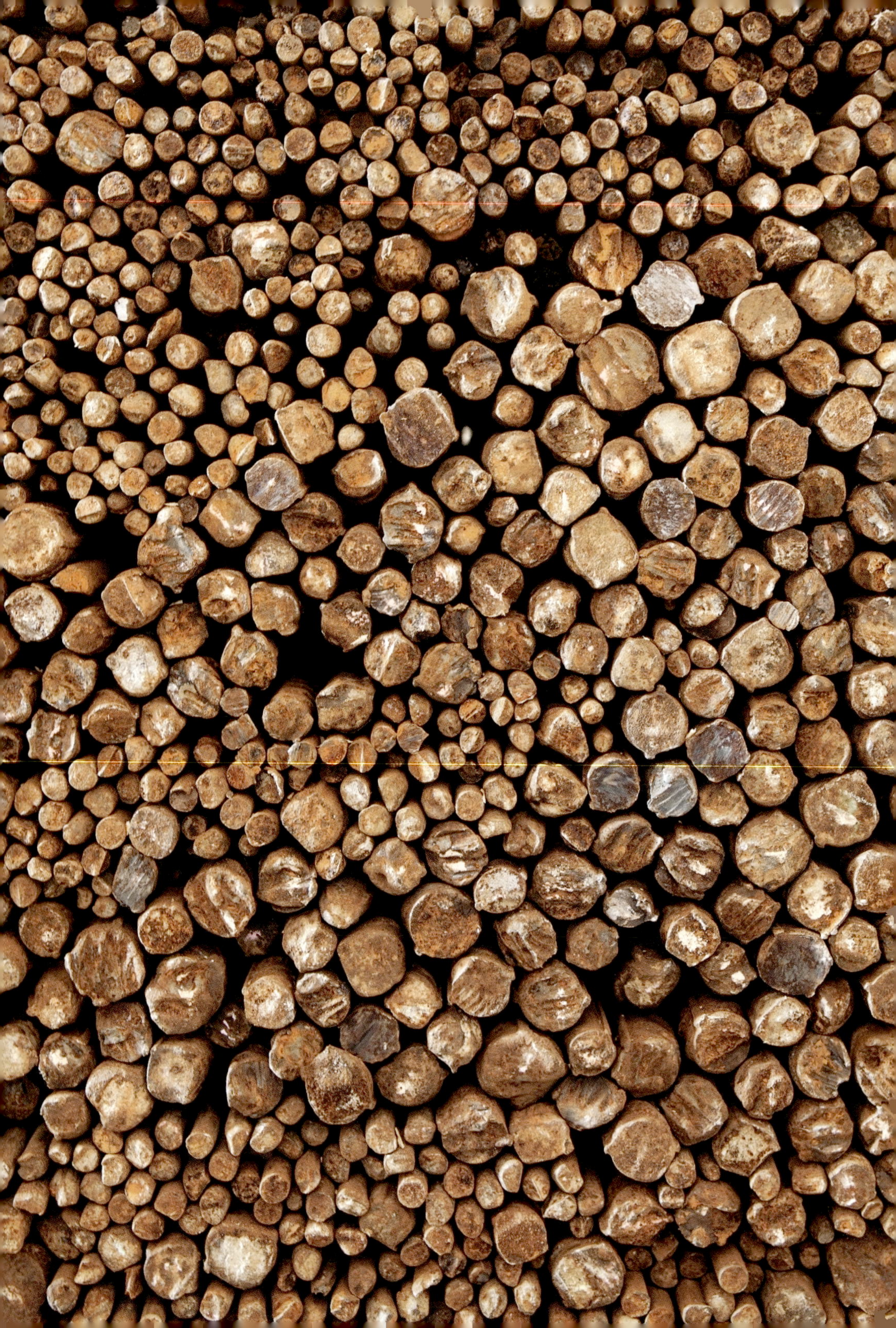

Die Wege des Mittlers
Freiheit und Kunst des Ai Weiwei

ROGER M. BUERGEL

I. Nur einige wenige Tage nach Eröffnung der Documenta 12 krachte Ai Weiweis *Template* (2007, S. 328–330) nach einem Gewitter zusammen. Die rund sieben Meter hohe Struktur, eines der zentralen Werke im Außenraum, bestand aus genau 1001 Tür- und Fensterrahmen der Ming- und Qing-Dynastien (1368–1911), die Ai wie so viele andere Grundbausteine seiner Werke auf chinesischen Antikmärkten erstanden hatte. Aus diesen hölzernen Relikten hatte der Künstler von seinen Handwerkern vier reliefhafte Wände zimmern lassen, die sternförmig um eine Achse herum aufgestellt wurden. Die Art, nach der die einzelnen Wände montiert waren, unterstrich sowohl den klapprigen Charakter der herrenlosen Rahmen als auch das Zufallsmoment, nach dem sie sich kombinierten. In seiner Fragilität ließ *Template* an ein großes Kartenhaus denken.

Anders als Spielkarten waren die Wände an der Innenkante aber angeschnitten, sodass sich aus der Summe der Aussparungen ein negativer Raum im Inneren der Konstruktion ergab. Dieser negative Raum hatte die Umrisslinien eines traditionellen Tempels, wie man ihm in China tausendfach auf Hügeln oder an anderen ausgewählten Orten begegnen kann, obwohl mehr und mehr dieser Tempel den Infrastrukturprojekten des kapitalistischen Chinas zu weichen haben. Es war dieser „fehlende Tempel", der es den Besuchern ermöglichte, durch *Template* hindurchzugehen und die ebenso raffinierte wie gebrechliche Konstruktion nicht nur betrachtend zu erfassen, sondern physisch zu erfahren. Bei diesem Erfahrungsprozess, in dem sich die Bewegungslinien und Gedankenketten des Besuchers mit der eigenwilligen Struktur dieses Nicht-Gebäudes, seiner materiellen Konsistenz und historischen Textur verbanden, blieb etwas gewahrt von der ursprünglichen Funktion des Tempels und wurde zugleich radikalisiert: die Herstellung einer Verbindung zwischen dem Selbst und der Welt. Anders als bei einem „vollen" Tempel erschien diese Verbindung bei *Template* allerdings nicht länger gegeben. Der spirituelle Überbau war einer Leere gewichen, die von den hölzernen Relikten des traditionellen Chinas gerahmt wurde.

Es wäre falsch, Ais Leere lediglich als Abgesang zu deuten. Wie viele Arbeiten Ais zeugt auch *Template* von einer Verzweiflung angesichts dessen, was war und nicht mehr ist. Doch ist es eine produktive Verzweiflung. In ihr erneuert sich ein altes chinesisches Thema: das Verhältnis von Leere und Spiritualität. Dieses Thema entspringt einer Religiosität, in der sich die himmlischen Mächte, anders als der

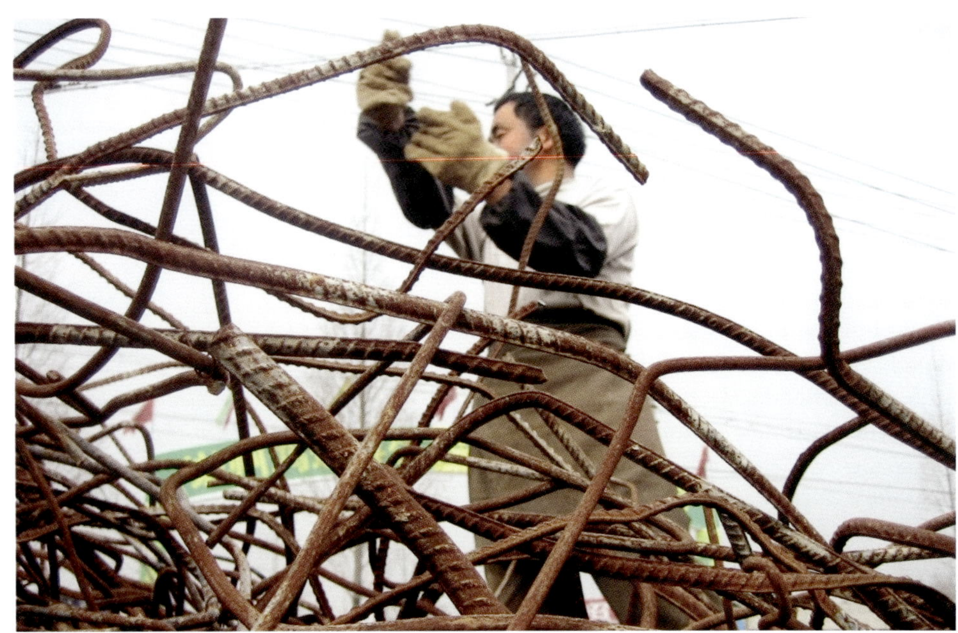

Processing rebar salvaged from Beichuan Middle School, Sichuan 2011

donnernde Gott jüdisch-christlicher Prägung, nicht erklären.[1] Chinas himmlische
Mächte sprechen nicht (auf dass Licht werde), sondern manifestieren sich in har-
monischen Entsprechungen, die zu entdecken zweierlei voraussetzt: ein hohes
Abstraktionsvermögen, das von allem Unwichtigen abzusehen weiß, und die Fähigkeit und Muße zur kontemplativen Versenkung, die noch im scheinbar unwesent-
lichsten Detail die Regeln der himmlischen Harmonie aufspürt. In Ais weltlicher
oder post-religiöser Spiritualität ist an die Stelle der himmlischen Mächte das
chinesische Regierungssystem getreten (das sich ebenfalls nicht erklärt), an die
Stelle der meditativen Versenkung der freie Umgang mit den eigenen kreativen
Ressourcen. Gibt es für ihn keinen Tempel, der die Verbindung zwischen dem
Selbst und der Welt absegnet, so heißt das nicht, dass kein schöpferischer Auftrag
besteht, diese Verbindung herzustellen beziehungsweise aus dem Nichts und den
Resten von früher zu schaffen.

II. Bei der Eröffnung der Documenta war *Template* der Blickfang schlechthin.
Neben der ästhetischen Kraft der Skulptur war das ihrer zentralen Lage inmitten
der Karlsaue geschuldet. Dazu kamen der Hang der Medien, sich ein Werk heraus-
zupicken, das fürs Ganze stehen sollte, sowie die Präsenz von Ai, der als globaler
Künstler wenigstens zwei Gesichter zu haben schien, ein chinesisches ebenso wie
ein westliches, und der vor dem Hintergrund der aktuellen geopolitischen Kräfte-
verschiebung somit als *go-between* zwischen Asien und dem Westen porträtiert

werden konnte. Es lag schließlich am gewaltigen Aufruhr, den Ais *Fairytale* (der Documenta-Besuch von 1001 Chinesen) im Vorfeld der Ausstellung verursacht hatte – ein Werk, dessen Dimensionen und Implikationen zwar die Phantasie beschäftigten, für das es aber kein Bild gab, sodass *Template* neben all den genannten Gründen auch in den Genuss einer Art verschobener Aufmerksamkeit kam. Es war somit kein Wunder, dass der deutsche Bundespräsident neben allerlei anderen Würdenträgern bei der feierlichen Eröffnung der Ausstellung gerade unter *Template* posierte und dadurch Ais hochfragiles Monument in das zwar kurzlebige, aber breit gestreute Mediengedächtnis einschleuste.

Es müssen diese frischen Medienbilder gewesen sein – immer in Verbindung mit der öffentlichen Aufmerksamkeit, welche die Documenta wenigstens in Deutschland ohnedies genießt –, die den Einsturz des Werks als nachrichtenwürdig erscheinen ließen und ihm zugleich einen neuen Wahrnehmungshorizont eröffneten. Dabei war *Template* eigentlich nur bedingt eingestürzt und in seiner neuen, transformierten Gestalt alles andere als ein unartikulierter Materialhaufen. Die eiserne Rahmung, welche die alten Holzrahmen fasste, hatte sich dem Druck der Naturgewalten lediglich gebeugt und dabei sonderbar eingedreht. Das Resultat war eine bizarre, in jedem Fall höchst singuläre Gestalt, zu deren poetisch-beunruhigender Gesamtwirkung beitrug, dass sich die Ming- und Qing-Elemente, die vorher der großen Form untergeordnet waren, von Ais Skulptur ein Stück weit emanzipieren konnten.

Ai hat das Resultat des Sturms, das transformierte *Template*, bekanntlich dankend akzeptiert. Nie war da ein Gedanke, das Werk wieder aufzubauen. So überdauerte das gefallene Monument die Documenta in seiner neuen Gestalt und schuf sich ein durchaus eigenes Publikum – ein Publikum, das wie das Gros der 1001 Chinesen, die Ai nach Kassel eingeladen hatte, mit der Ausstellung oder Kunst als solcher nicht unbedingt etwas am Hut hatte. Diese neuen Besucher waren Katastrophentouristen; sie wollten sich des unwahrscheinlichen Ereignisses vergewissern. Aber was genau fanden sie in der Karlsaue vor? Tatsächlich Katastrophenarchitektur, verpackt in eine asiatische Formensprache, die vage an jene Medienbilder erinnerte, wie sie nach Erdbeben oder Tsunamis um die Welt gehen. *Template* war aber gerade kein Bild, das die Welt der anderen als „die Welt der anderen" zeigte. Es war ein schwer greifbares Ereignis, das die Wahrnehmungsdistanz zwischen chinesischer und Kassler Realität aufgehoben hatte. Als ein solches war es die Kunst eines genuinen Mittlers, eines Wanderers zwischen den Welten.

III. Nach Ende der Documenta hat Ai seine Handwerker beauftragt, das gefallene Monument eins zu eins nachzubauen. Dabei ging es einerseits darum, das Werk dem Œuvre einzuverleiben. Dazu musste dessen situative, auch zufällige Gestalt wiederholt, das ästhetische Echo der Naturgewalt kopiert werden. Andererseits war Ai nicht entgangen, dass sich dank der spektakulären Performance von *Template* sein Œuvre um eine entscheidende Dimension erweitert hatte. Benennen lässt sich diese Dimension am ehesten als „Eigenleben". Für den Künstler ist ein solches Eigenleben schwer zu handhaben, weil es sich nicht planen oder programmieren lässt. Gleich der himmlischen Harmonie der chinesischen Religiosität mag es Regeln und Gesetzen gehorchen, doch bleiben diese verborgen. Es gibt allerdings Faktoren, für die ein Künstler Sorge tragen kann, und dazu gehört bei Ai beispielsweise der Umgang mit seinen Handwerkern. Dieser Umgang ist in hohem Maße durchlässig. Ai setzt bei seinen Handwerkern nicht nur auf deren technische Kompetenz – als Handwerker eben, die seine Entwürfe ausführen –, sondern respektiert und beansprucht sie als Gewährsleute des Materials und dessen Geschichte.

Er beginnt damit, dass er seine Handwerker mit Problemstellungen konfrontiert: Es gibt dieses und jenes Material, bei *Template* waren es die 1001 antiken Tür- und Fensterrahmen, bei *China Log* (2005, S. 188/189) waren es die acht Säulen eines zerstörten Tempels der Qing-Dynastie (1644–1911) – was lässt sich daraus machen? Die Handwerker kommen daraufhin mit Vorschlägen, die diskutiert, verworfen, modifiziert und umgesetzt werden. Dieser Typus von künstlerischer Kollaboration ist insofern bemerkenswert, als er der Materialgeschichte der chinesischen Kultur einen bedeutenden Platz im eigenen, zeitgenössischen Schaffen einräumt. Ai konfrontiert sich mit dieser Geschichte einerseits in Form der schieren Fülle herrenloser Artefakte, die in China feilgeboten werden und die er für sich und seine Produktion sichert. Andererseits findet Ai die Materialgeschichte in seinen Handwerkern verkörpert, und es will ihm scheinen, als ob die Handwerker mehr können, als sie selber (und Ai) wissen. Die künstlerische Produktion besteht also zunächst darin, einen kollektiven Prozess anzustoßen, in dem sich unvorhersehbare Dinge ereignen können. Einen Prozess, der eine Macht adressiert und in Anspruch nimmt, die sich als das Materiell-Unbewusste bezeichnen lässt.

Das Materiell-Unbewusste umfasst im Wesentlichen die Erfahrungen, die sich im Laufe von Jahrhunderten hochdisziplinierter Praxis im handwerklichen Vermögen wie in den Lebensformen einer Kultur abgelagert haben. Die staunenswerten Leistungen der Chinesen verdanken sich nicht allein ihrem Ingenium, sondern einem immensen, dauerhaft ausgeübten Druck, wie ihn vermutlich nur ein eingesessenes Feudalregime mit seinen zugleich brutal-rigiden und pingelig ausdifferenzierten Sozialhierarchien auszuüben vermag. Das soll nicht heißen, dass handwerkliche Arbeit ausschließlich quälerisch ist. Sie kennt selbstverständlich Glücksmomente, etwa wenn eine Porzellanschale dem Brennofen vollkommen makellos entsteigt und geradezu immateriell erscheint. Sie kennt auch intellektuelle Triumphe, so etwa die Fogongsi-Pagode in Yingxian, die, im 11. Jahrhundert erbaut, trotz ihrer 67 Meter Höhe noch jedem Erdbeben oder Sturm zu trotzen wusste.[2] Doch in welchem Verhältnis stehen diese Glücksmomente und intellektuellen Triumphe zum existentiellen Aufwand, zum Einsatz, ja zum Opfer, das sie erfordern? Das Materiell-Unbewusste ist eine explosive Mischung, so viel steht fest. Eine explosive Mischung, die sich in den Zerstörungsorgien der Kulturrevolution entladen hatte, denen wiederum Ai mit seiner frühen Performance *Dropping a Han*

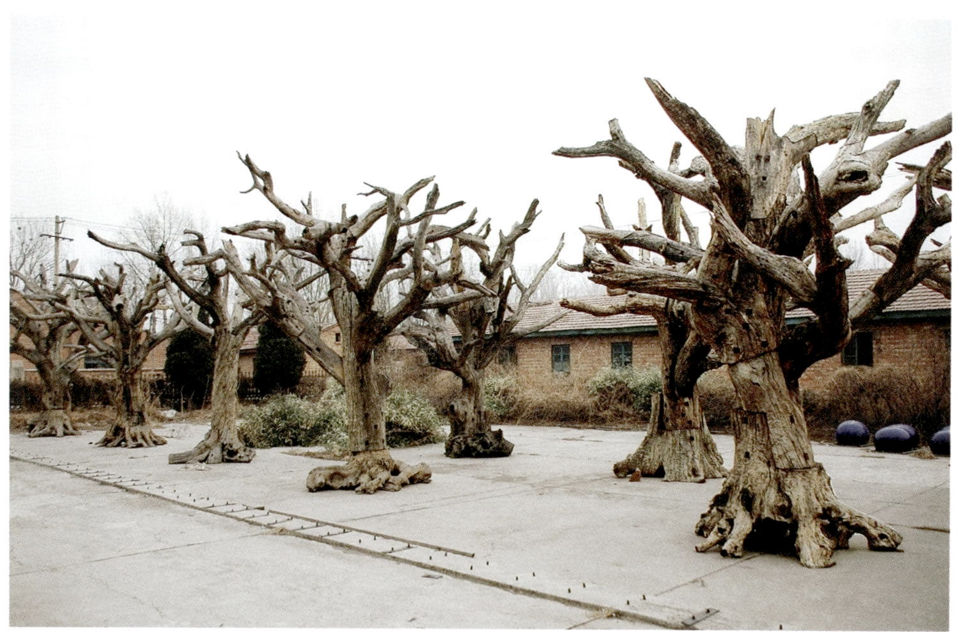

Trees, 2009–2010, wood, steel, dimensions variable, at Ai Weiwei's studio, Beijing 2010

Dynasty Urn (1995, S. 85–87) ein zwiespältiges Denkmal setzte. Doch dazu später mehr. Zunächst gilt es festzuhalten, dass das Materiell-Unbewusste den Artefakten ebenso eingeschrieben ist, wie es fortlebt im technischen Vermögen der Handwerker, die das über Generationen erarbeitete und tradierte Gewusst-Wie des Materialumgangs in sich tragen. Das zeitgenössische China, das sich mit der Marktöffnung seit den 1980er-Jahren zugleich dem Imperativ der flächendeckenden Modernisierung verschrieben hat, kennt keinerlei Verwendung mehr für diesen Erfahrungsschatz, sondern radikalisiert im Grunde das kulturrevolutionäre Prinzip der Tabula rasa. Die traditionellen Handwerkstechniken sind daher nicht anders als Tierarten oder Sprachen vom Aussterben bedroht, wodurch viele der Arbeiten Ais, die auf diesen Techniken basieren, einen tieftraurigen Charakter bekommen.

IV. Zwischen den Artefakten von einst, den Urnen, Tempelsäulen, abgeschlagenen Füßen und Händen von Buddha-Skulpturen, den Tür- und Fensterrahmen und was das Œuvre noch alles kennt – zwischen all diesen verlorenen, von Ai als Readymade adoptierten Artefakten und dem handwerklichen Vermögen besteht ein inniger Parallelismus. Der Künstler tut nicht viel mehr, als diese Parallelen zu verbinden, ja kurzzuschließen. Er spielt also eher mit Kräften, als dass er selbst etwas produziert im konventionellen Sinne. Die erwähnte Durchlässigkeit, die Ai auszeichnet (und die paradox erscheinen mag angesichts seiner physischen Präsenz, auch seines Charismas), bildet die Grundvoraussetzung dafür, dass sich die Kräfte entfalten können

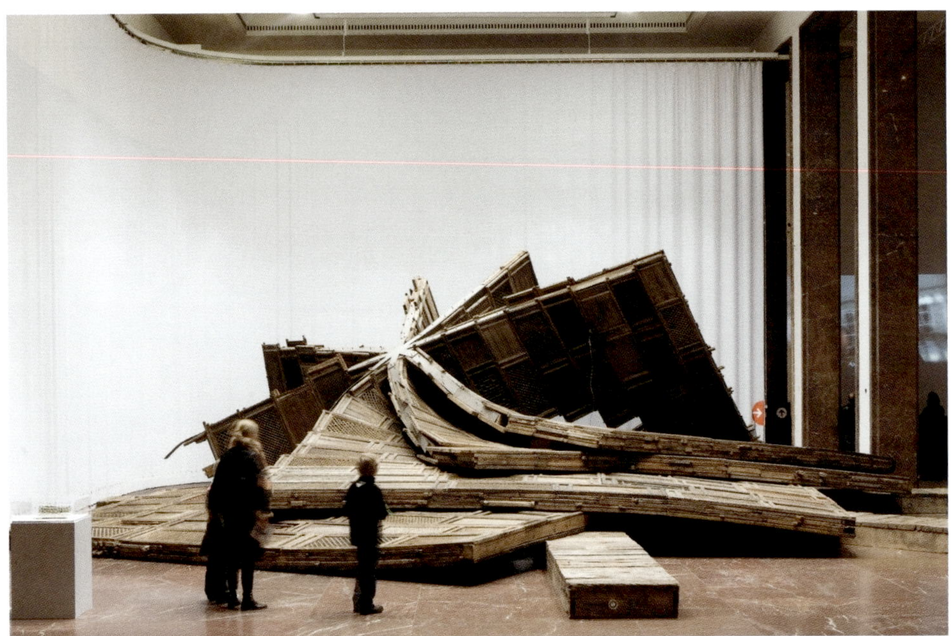

Post-Template, 2007–2009, wooden doors and windows from destroyed Ming and Qing Dynasty houses, 166 ⅛ x 435 ½ x 344 ½ inches; Haus der Kunst, Munich 2009

und eben jenes Eigenleben an den Tag legen, das des Künstlers höchstes Ziel ist und das sich in *Template* so eindrucksvoll manifestiert.

V. In anderer Form war dieses Eigenleben auch bestimmend für *Fairytale* (2007, S. 310–327). Als zweiten Beitrag für die Documenta 12, der im Wesentlichen darin bestand, einem bunt zusammengewürfelten Mix aus 1000 Chinesen (der Chinese +1 war er selbst) die Reise nach Kassel zu ermöglichen. Anders als bei *Template* verdankte sich das Eigenleben hier keiner unvorhersehbaren Performance einer Skulptur, sondern der improvisierten Seinsform einer Gruppe. Philip Tinari hat das Ganze denn auch zu Recht als „Experiment in Sachen kontrolliertes Chaos" bezeichnet.[3] Auch für *Fairytale* hat Ai verschiedene Kräfte verknüpft, etwa die Reiseneugier insbesondere solcher Chinesen, die sich die Reise nie hätten leisten können, die infrastrukturellen und medialen Möglichkeiten einer Großausstellung sowie das westliche Interesse an einem China-Panorama, das nicht die offizielle Doktrin reproduziert. Als gestalterische Aktivität resultierte aber in keinem identifizierbaren Werk, sondern markierte lediglich Punkte, wozu das Design der Reisekoffer, der Schlafstätten, das Haareschneiden und die persönliche Präsenz vor Ort zählten. Obwohl *Fairytale* allein aufgrund des organisatorischen Aufwands und der immensen Kosten den großen Maßstab zu bedienen schien, vollzog sich die eigentliche Dynamik dieser Ästhetik der Existenz im Kleinen und scheinbar

Unwesentlichen, beispielsweise in der Begegnung des chinesischen Bauern mit dem hessischen Bauern, deren beider Fachsimpeleien unmöglich zu übersetzen waren, obwohl sie sich offensichtlich wunderbar verstanden. Trotz der institutionellen Einbettung von *Fairytale* in eine Großausstellung ging es hier weder um ästhetische Erfahrung im engeren Sinne noch um soziale Skulptur, sondern um die einerseits offene, andererseits strukturierte Streuung singulärer Erfahrungen, die sich zu einer Ästhetik der Existenz verbanden. Ais Durchlässigkeit als gewissermaßen unbeteiligter Moderator des Ganzen zielte auf die Herstellung und Bewahrung des dynamischen Gleichgewichts, das eine solche Ästhetik der Existenz bedingt: im Spiel von Offenheit und Struktur. Dabei unterstanden die singulären Erfahrungen keiner Choreografie, geschweige denn Gängelung. Die Chinesen machten die Erfahrungen für sich, wobei es ihnen ähnlich wie den Katastrophentouristen gegangen sein dürfte: Auf sie wartete der Eintritt in ein anderes, fremdes Wahrnehmungsverhältnis zur Welt.[4]

VI. Die Ästhetik der Existenz ist ein Thema Ais, das sich mindestens bis in die New Yorker Jahre (1982–1993) rückverfolgen lässt. Vermutlich kann man sogar noch weiter zurückgehen in der Künstlerbiografie und die Jahre in der Wüste dazunehmen, wohin Ai Qing, der Vater Ais und Chinas wohl bedeutendster moderner Dichter, infolge kulturrevolutionärer Säuberungen verbannt worden war, um öffentliche Latrinen zu putzen. Ai erwähnt diese Geschichte häufig, die prekären Lebensverhältnisse in Verbindung mit dem eisernen Vorsatz, die eigene Würde zu wahren, und erinnert so daran, dass Ästhetik ebenso viel mit schönen Formen wie mit bloßem Leben zu tun hat.

VII. Die New Yorker Jahre – es hatte Ai in die Metropole verschlagen, nachdem der Vater zwar rehabilitiert worden war, es für Ai selbst im eigenen Land aber nicht mehr weiterzugehen schien – waren Jahre des bohemistischen Abhängens, also des indirekten Lernens und des Brütens über unausgegorenen Ideen. Ai selbst hat diese Jahre in unzähligen Fotos genauestens dokumentiert (S. 57–63). Nicht absichtsvoll wie ein Tagebuchschreiber, der sich selbst zu wichtig nimmt, sondern beiläufig, ironisch, dandyesk. Und mit einer kräftigen Portion Nihilismus versehen, die man Ais damaligem Alter, der bitteren Erfahrung mit dem chinesischen System, einer gewissen Desorientiertheit, ja auch Einsamkeit in der Fremde, aber eben auch den Schlüssellektionen der künstlerischen Moderne, die er sich in New York und Philadelphia erteilen ließ, zuschreiben mag. Der Bilderbogen des Fotoarchivs (von den rund 10.000 Negativen ist nur ein Bruchteil publiziert) deckt ein enzyklopädisches Spektrum ab, das von den exotischen Aspekten des urbanen Alltags im East Village ebenso handelt wie von den üppigen Displays der Galerien und Museen zu Zeiten der Reagan'schen Politik des billigen Geldes.

Ai verfolgt die Unruhen und blutigen Zusammenstöße zwischen Demonstranten und Polizisten rund um die Besetzung des Tompkins Square Park, die AIDS-Kundgebungen, fotografiert aber auch neue Freunde wie den Dichter Allen Ginsberg (S.17), die Angehörigen der chinesischen Diaspora – und sich selbst. Diese Selbstporträts zeigen einen Künstler als jungen Mann, der mal vor Langeweile nicht weiter weiß, der sich an den verschiedenen Möglichkeiten versucht, das eigene Gesicht mit einem Fahrradreifen zu rahmen, und der im MoMA neben einem der seriellen Selbstporträts von Andy Warhol posiert, wobei er kokett dessen manierierte Handhaltung kopiert. Die Fotos zeigen aber auch eigene, nahezu informelle künstlerische Experimente im Studio, so einen Kleiderbügel aus Draht, den Ai mit einer Zange zum markanten Profil Marcel Duchamps zurechtgebogen hat. Zieht man in Betracht, dass die New Yorker Wäschereien fest in chinesischer Hand sind, so mag man diesen Bügel als Ais erste transkulturelle Formel deuten. Ein solcher Verdacht erhärtet sich noch, wenn man das Foto zu Rate zieht, auf dem Ai den Bügel auf eine Fläche gelegt hat, um die Innenseite des Profils mit Sonnenblumenkernen, einer beliebten chinesischen Knabberei, aufzufüllen.

VIII. All den existentiellen wie künstlerischen Experimenten der New Yorker Zeit mit ihren fließenden Übergängen haftet zwar etwas Spielerisches und Unprätentiöses an, doch sollte man sich nicht täuschen: Auch hier ging es um den Eintritt in ein anderes, fremdes Wahrnehmungsverhältnis zur Welt, das dem Künstler nicht leichtgefallen sein kann. Der künstlerische Akt selbst richtet sich an dem aus, was vorhanden oder, um Duchamps Konzept zu würdigen, „Readymade" ist. Dabei fällt auf, dass Ai den Kontakt mit der amerikanischen Kultur vielleicht nicht scheut, dass er ihren materiellen Hervorbringungen gegenüber aber verblüffend indifferent erscheint. Bei einer kleinen Galerieausstellung (1988) präsentiert er die Bodeninstallation *Five Raincoats Holding Up a Star* (1985, S. 18): fünf olivgrüne Regenmäntel aus Gummi, wie sie den chinesischen Alltag definieren, sowie Metallrohre, die sich durch die amorphe Gummimantelmasse ziehen und zu einem fünfzackigen Stern, dem Symbol der Kommunistischen Partei Chinas, zusammenschließen. Wie in seinen späteren, reifen Werken schmuggelt er chinesische Texturen und Bezugssysteme in einen modernistischen Kanon ein, indem er sich dessen Sprache, in diesem Fall des minimalistischen Idioms, bedient. Dabei wird nicht klar – und ist bis heute nicht klar geworden –, ob Ai diese Sprache tatsächlich spricht, also mit Leib und Seele und tiefster Überzeugung, oder ob er sie lediglich vortäuscht und als Vehikel einsetzt.

IX. Zu Ais künstlerischen Leitsternen wurden in New York der *émigré* Marcel Duchamp und Andy Warhol. Beide waren nicht nur mit ihrem Œuvre präsent, sondern spielten eine gewichtige Rolle als Referenzfiguren des konzeptuell und politisch gesinnten Spektrums der damaligen amerikanischen Kunstszene. So suchte Barbara Kruger Warhols Werbeästhetik weiterzuentwickeln; Jeff Koons inszenierte Alltagsobjekte in hermetischen Displays, die im Sinne Duchamps den Gegenstand zum Zeichen formten; und Jenny Holzer bediente sich der hypersicht-

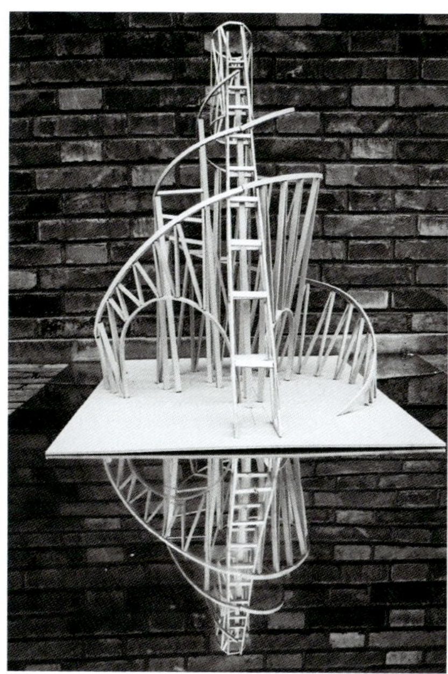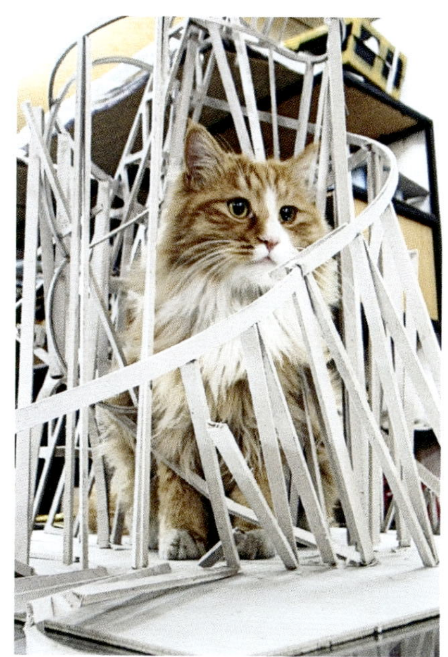

Model for *Fountain of Light*, 2007 (see p. 283)

baren Reklametafeln am Times Square, um Gemeinplätze zu kommunizieren, die hier eine ominöse Bedeutung erhalten mussten. Diese Aufzählung von Künstlern und künstlerischen Arbeitsweisen ist nicht zufällig.[5] Sie stammt von Ai selbst, der nach erfolgter Rückkehr drei Anthologien – *Black Cover Book* (1994, S. 99), *White Cover Book* (1995, S. 99), *Gray Cover Book* (1997) – herausgab, in denen er westliche Moderne und chinesische Avantgarde-Kunst vorstellte. Für diese Anthologien wurden Texte von Duchamp und Warhol ins Chinesische übertragen sowie die oben genannten Künstler, und andere mehr, in Text und Bild vorgestellt. Unter der Rubrik „Studio" erschienen aber auch monografische Beiträge zur aktuellen chinesischen Kunstszene. Es ist charakteristisch für Ai, dass er es nicht bei einer bloßen Aufarbeitung und Weitergabe der eigenen Bildungserfahrung belässt, sondern die drei Anthologien zugleich als Plattform für eine konzeptuell orientierte chinesische Szene lancierte, die eben im Entstehen begriffen war und deren Mentor er werden sollte.

X. Vielfältig sind die Anregungen, die Ai von Warhol, Duchamp und deren künstlerischen Nachlassverwaltern bezog. Bei der Warhol-Rezeption dürfte die Stimme des Künstlers eine wichtige Rolle gespielt haben. In einer der ersten Publikationen, die Ai in New York erworben hatte, lässt sie folgendes Credo vernehmen: „Das ist das Phantastische an diesem Land: In Amerika ist es seit jeher so, dass auch der reichste Verbraucher im Wesentlichen das Gleiche kauft wie der ärmste. Du siehst

Coca-Cola im Fernsehen und kannst sicher sein, dass der Präsident sein Cola trinkt, dass Liz Taylor Cola trinkt – und du selber kannst auch ein Cola trinken! Coca-Cola ist und bleibt Coca-Cola und für kein Geld der Welt kannst du irgendwo ein Cola herkriegen, das besser wäre als das, was der Penner an der nächsten Ecke trinkt. Es ist immer das gleiche Coca-Cola, und es ist immer gleich gut. Das weiß Liz Taylor, das weiß der Penner, und du selber weißt das auch."[6]

Man mag Warhols Unterton, seine radikale Affirmation des *American Way of Life*, ironisch finden. Doch welchen Unterschied macht es, ob diese totale politische Travestie, die universale Gleichheit, auf der Basis von Cola verkündet, ernst oder ironisch gemeint ist? Warhols Apologie weiß sich auf Augenhöhe mit der amerikanischen Ideologie, darin liegt ihr diagnostisches Vermögen und ihr perverser Reiz. Ai, der von klein auf Maos ebenso buntschillernde wie allgegenwärtige Propaganda mit ihren unterkomplexen Slogans über sich ergehen lassen musste, dürften die Affinitäten zwischen Kommunismus und Konsumismus respektive ihrer gesellschaftlichen Utopien nicht entgangen sein. Junger Bohemien, der er war, ging es Ai in jedem Fall darum, dem System gegenüber eine Haltung auszubilden. Und was lag näher, als sich an Warhols cooler Larmoyanz zu schulen, die alles andere als abgehoben war, sondern sich ganz im Gegenteil mit einer exzessiven Anteilnahme am gesellschaftlichen Geschehen paarte? Dabei ist Ai gewiss ein anderer Typ als Warhol. Es gibt in Peking auch nicht die Möglichkeit, aus der Deckung einer promiskuitiven Metropole zu operieren, nicht einmal für Parteikader. Der ausgedehnte Zirkel aus Freunden, Besuchern, Journalisten, Assistenten, Helfern und Katzen, der Ais Anwesen in Caochangdi rund um die Uhr bevölkert, ja die ganze Idee einer solchen Existenzform, die zugleich Produktionsform ist, dürfte ihre Inspiration aber zu einem nicht geringen Teil Warhols legendärer Factory am Broadway verdanken. So wie auch die Warhol'sche Stimme in Ais blog-politischen Aktivitäten nachhallt, die Chinas zeitgenössisches Leben mit einem schwer nur zu übersetzenden, aber nie bitteren Sarkasmus kommentieren (und die deutsche Ausstellung *Die Kunst der Aufklärung* am Platz des himmlischen Friedens mit dem Hinweis, dass „die Europäer immer so schöne Sachen zu zeigen haben").[7]

XI. Ais Duchamp-Rezeption kreiste um das Konzept des Readymade und jenen Schnappschuss-Moment der künstlerischen Transformation, den Duchamp als „Einschreibung" bezeichnet hatte und der sich beispielsweise in der falschen Signatur des Urinoirs von 1917 manifestierte, als dessen eigentlichen Schöpfer Duchamp einen gewissen „R. Mutt" auswies.[8] Während Warhols Universum vornehmlich um Warhol kreiste, operierte Duchamp auf einer hochintellektuellen, dabei witzig-frivolen Ebene, die sich bei der ästhetischen Erscheinung von Kunst nicht länger aufhielt, sondern deren ontologischen Status, also ihr So-Sein als Kunst oder Anders-Sein als Nicht-Kunst, zum Thema machte. Die ganze Tragweite der Duchamp'schen Anregungen erfasste Ai vermutlich in China, wo ihn nicht nur idiosynkratische Objekte wie Urinoirs, Fahrradfelgen oder Flaschentrockner erwar-

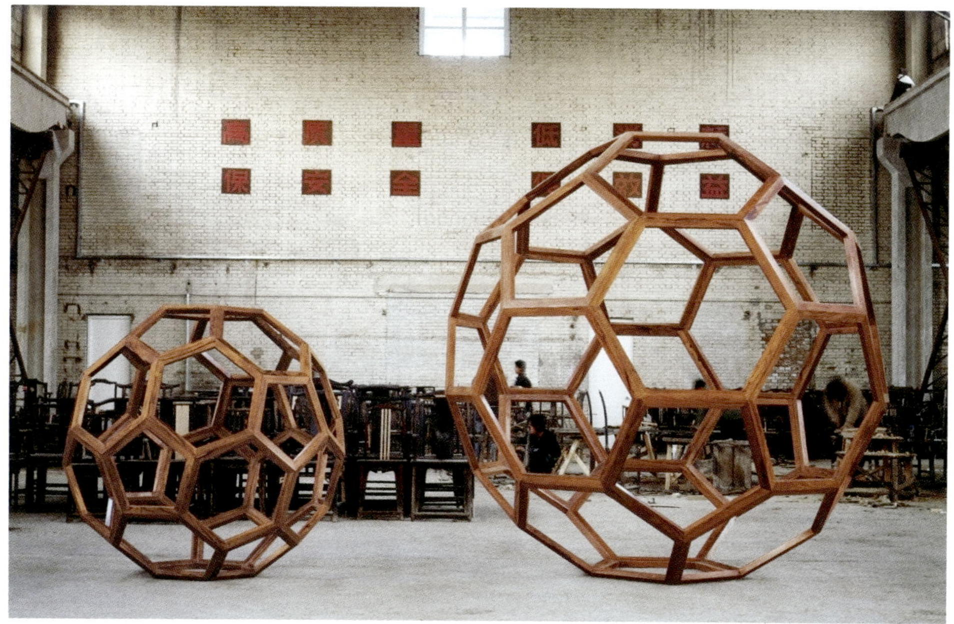

Untitled, 2006, huali wood, 2 pieces, ø 66 ½ and 109 ½ inches; Ai Weiwei's studio, Beijing 2006

teten. Nein, in China empfing ihn eine ebenso fragmentierte wie monumentale Kultur, die bereit war, als bedeutungsindifferentes künstlerisches Rohmaterial adoptiert zu werden. Diese Kultur war unter den Schlägen der europäischen Kolonialmächte, der japanischen Besatzung, des Bürgerkriegs, der ebenso grandiosen wie fatalen Systemexperimente Maos, aber auch der aktuellen staatskapitalistischen Stratifizierung des Reichs der Mitte aus den Fugen geraten. Duchamp lehrte Ai, mit diesem Treibgut einer liquidierten Historie umzugehen.

Duchamps Überlegungen zur künstlerischen Einschreibung von Alltagsdingen sind das eine. Der Künstler verwischt die Grenzen von Kunst und Nicht-Kunst, um Handlungsspielräume zu gewinnen. Zugleich wird evident, dass die allein ästhetische Erscheinung, etwa die Sichtbarkeit eines Werkes, völlig unzureichend ist, um die eigentliche, konzeptuelle Dimension zu erfassen.[9] Das andere ist das konkrete Schicksal der Duchamp'schen Werke, die es ja trotz aller Gehirnakrobatik gab und die allen inneren Widerständen zum Trotz doch irgendwann Einzug ins Museum hielten. Oder etwa nicht? Wie es sich für einen Duchamp ziemt, wird die Geschichte ab dieser Wendung ernsthaft kompliziert. Tatsächlich gab es entscheidende Werke wie das ursprüngliche Urinoir nicht mehr. Das bemerkte Duchamp selbst erst, als in den 1960er-Jahren die eigentlich bahnbrechende Rezeption seines Werkes einsetzte und die Readymades von einst für die große Retrospektive in Pasadena benötigt wurden. Wer meint, ein Urinoir sei leicht zu ersetzen, irrt. Der Stand der industriellen Produktion war längst ein anderer, weil Technologien

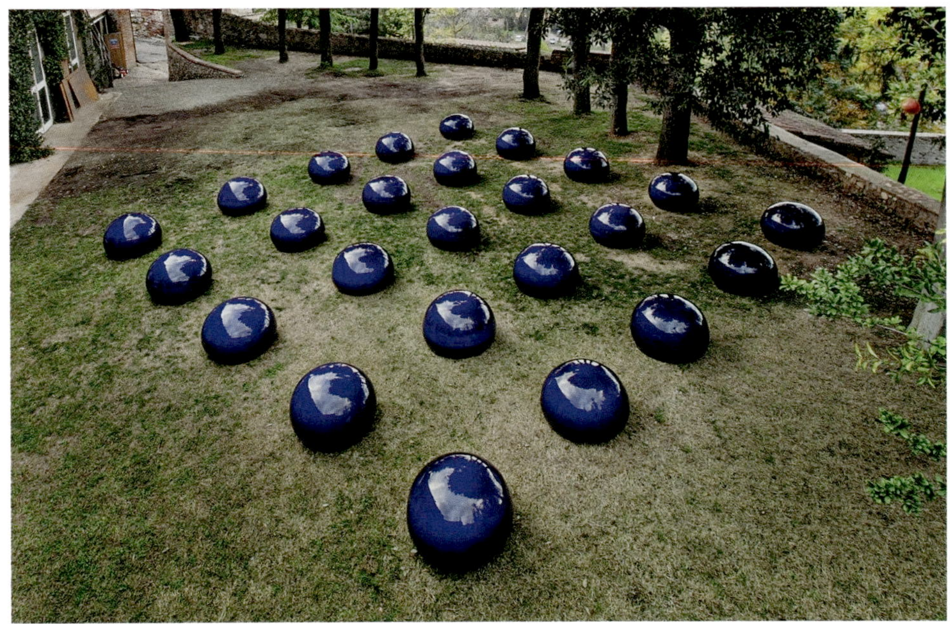

Bubbles, 2008, porcelain, each 19¾ x ø 29½ inches; Galleria Continua, San Gimignano 2012

über einen Zeitkern verfügen. Und so mussten jene Objekte, die Duchamp damals absichtsvoll als Industrieware bar jeglicher Aura gewählt hatte, kunstvoll von Hand reproduziert werden.[10] Zwar hatte Duchamp mit seiner revolutionären Setzung von 1917 demonstrieren können, dass ein Urinoir nicht mit sich identisch ist. Im Rahmen einer Galeriepräsentation und mit (falscher) Signatur versehen, kann es den ontologischen Status eines Kunstwerks erhalten. Im Zuge der Vorbereitungen zur Retrospektive zeigte sich darüber hinaus, dass auch ein Readymade nicht mit sich identisch ist. All diese Irrungen und Wirrungen eines Formenschicksals werden in Ais *Black Cover Book* mit Aufnahmen der ursprünglichen Installation von 1917 belegt sowie den Aufrissen für die Replik von 1964, die Duchamps Händler Arturo Schwarz kommissioniert hatte.

XII. Für das New Yorker Milieu der 1980er-Jahre, das Ai aufmerksam studierte – er behauptet von sich, damals so ungefähr jede Ausstellung gesehen zu haben, und seine Fotos deuten in diese Richtung –, waren diese und weitere Duchamp'schen Lektionen enorm prägend. Sie schienen der Kunst Auswege aus der Warenförmigkeit oder institutionellen Zurichtung zu weisen, forcierten aber auch die künstlerische Partikularität in ihrem Kampf gegen die kapitalistische Standardisierungswalze. Ai wiederum zog seine eigenen, eher chinesischen Schlüsse. Der Markt oder Warenförmigkeit waren für ihn nie ein Problem, im Gegenteil. Ihm ist der Markt ein *social medium* unter anderen. Die kapitalistische Standardisierungswalze wäre

schon eher eine Gegnerin, doch setzt Ai unter Bedingungen der Ein-Parteien-
Diktatur woanders an: bei der antitotalitären Mobilisierung, für die ein Werk
ohne Form wie *Fairytale* ebenso ein Beispiel darstellt wie die Sichuan-Recherche,
die ihn auf mehreren Ebenen ab 2008 beschäftigen wird. Die Schlüsse, die Ai
für sich aus der Erfahrung mit Duchamp zieht, gehen in Richtung Freiheit beim
Aneignungsprozess. Das bedeutet nicht, dass alles Kunst werden kann, sondern
dass es bei dem, was man tut, gar nicht darauf ankommt, ob das jetzt Kunst ist
oder nicht, ja dass gerade in dieser Ununterscheidbarkeit von Praktiken Möglichkeiten liegen.

XIII. Als Ai 1993 zurück nach China ging, weil sein kranker Vater ihn brauchte,
kam er mit einer konzeptuell gut ausgestatteten Werkzeugkiste. Was diese an
Fragestellungen und Möglichkeiten barg, deuten die ersten reifen Arbeiten an:
Für *Han Dynasty Urn with Coca-Cola Logo* (1994) hat Ai eine rund 2000 Jahre
alte Vase mit dem Schriftzug „Coca-Cola" versehen.[11] Die mit dem Logo verschan-
delte Urne liest sich auf den ersten Blick wie ein Memento mori: 2000 Jahre altes
historisches Erbe wird zugleich überschrieben und entwertet durch ein globales
brand. Auf den zweiten Blick erweist sich, dass Ai wie beiläufig den Entsprechungen folgt, die zwischen der geschwungenen Buchhalterschrift von 1936 und traditionellen Han-Malereien ohnedies bestehen. So ist sein gemaltes Logo nicht
invasiv. Während das Rot zurückgenommen, fast erdfarben wirkt, harmoniert der
Schwung der Schrift mit dem bauchigen Körper der Urne. Wer wie Ai in langen
Zeiträumen denkt, erinnert sich des besonderen Adaptionsvermögens der chinesischen Kultur, die sich wie nach der Mongoleninvasion in der Yuan-Dynastie
(1279–1368) Fremdes über Nacht zu eigen machen kann – um sich gleich zu
bleiben. Spinnt man den Gedanken weiter, so ist nicht ausgeschlossen, dass in
2000 Jahren von heute gerechnet Coca-Cola als chinesisches Label gelten wird.
Das ist ein Aspekt der oben erwähnten „Freiheit beim Aneignungsprozess" (und
jeder westliche Unternehmer in China versteht das auch ohne Duchamp).

Die legendäre Performance *Dropping a Han Dynasty Urn* (1995, S. 85–87)
zeigt Ai in der schlichten Aufmachung eines Bauern vor einer hohen Mauer. In
seinen Händen hält er mit ostentativ gespreizten Fingern eine Urne, erneut ein
antikes Stück, die er im nächsten Moment fallen lassen wird. Gebannt ist diese
Performance auf drei Fotos, die in Sekundenbruchteilen aufgenommen wurden.
Man sieht Ai die Urne halten, dann fällt die Urne, und schließlich sieht man
die Scherben zu Füßen des Künstlers liegen. Das Geschehen ist schockierend,
nicht nur für den museal getrimmten westlichen Betrachter. Das hat etwas mit
der antiken Urne und ihrem ideellen Wert zu tun, mehr aber noch mit dem
unbeteiligten Gesichtsausdruck des Künstlers, der den Betrachter frontal konfrontiert. Das Fallenlassen ist keine Affekthandlung, sondern ein Akt bewusst
kalkulierter Barbarei, der den Betrachter als ohnmächtigen Zeugen in ein
ethisch-ästhetisches Dilemma stürzt.

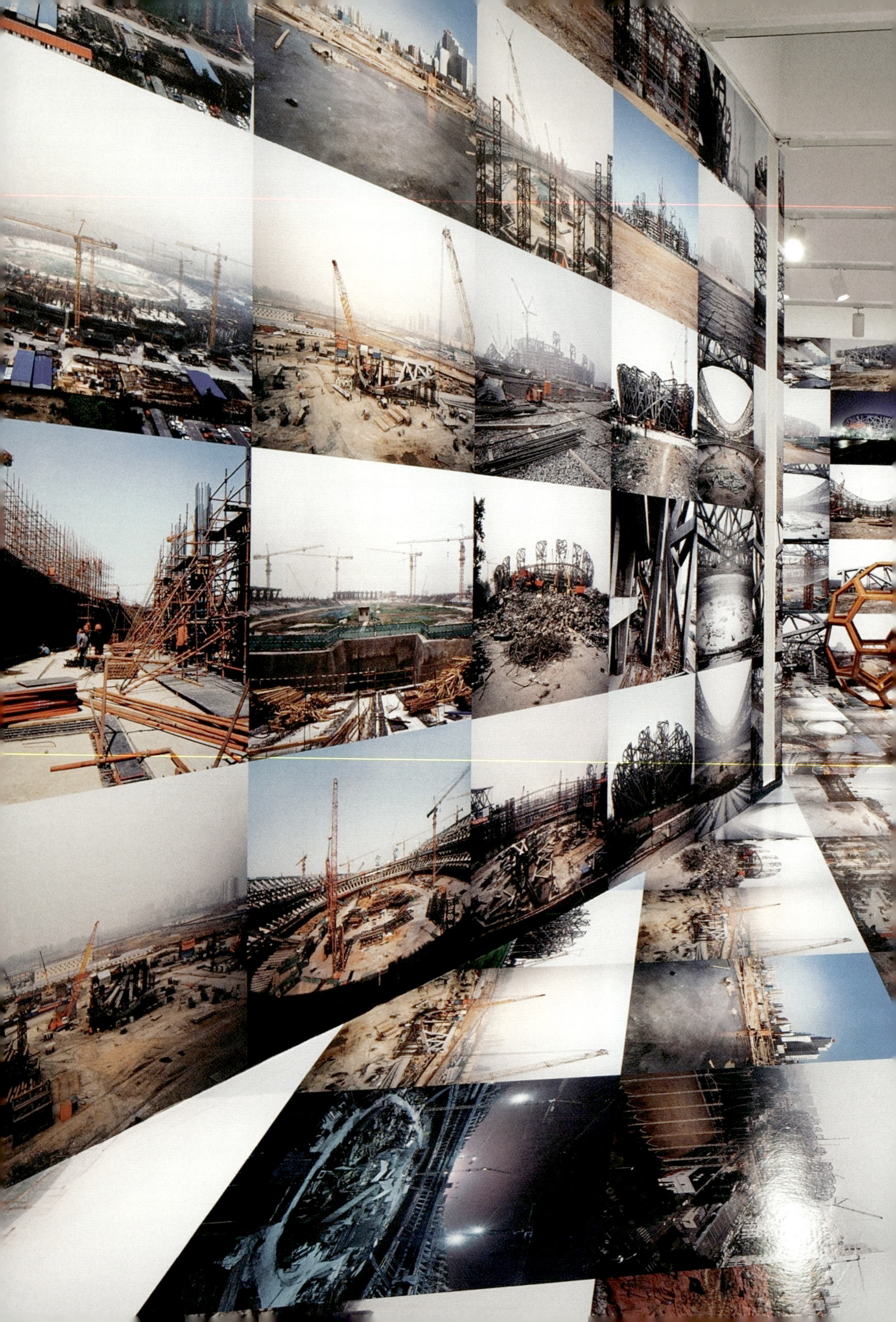

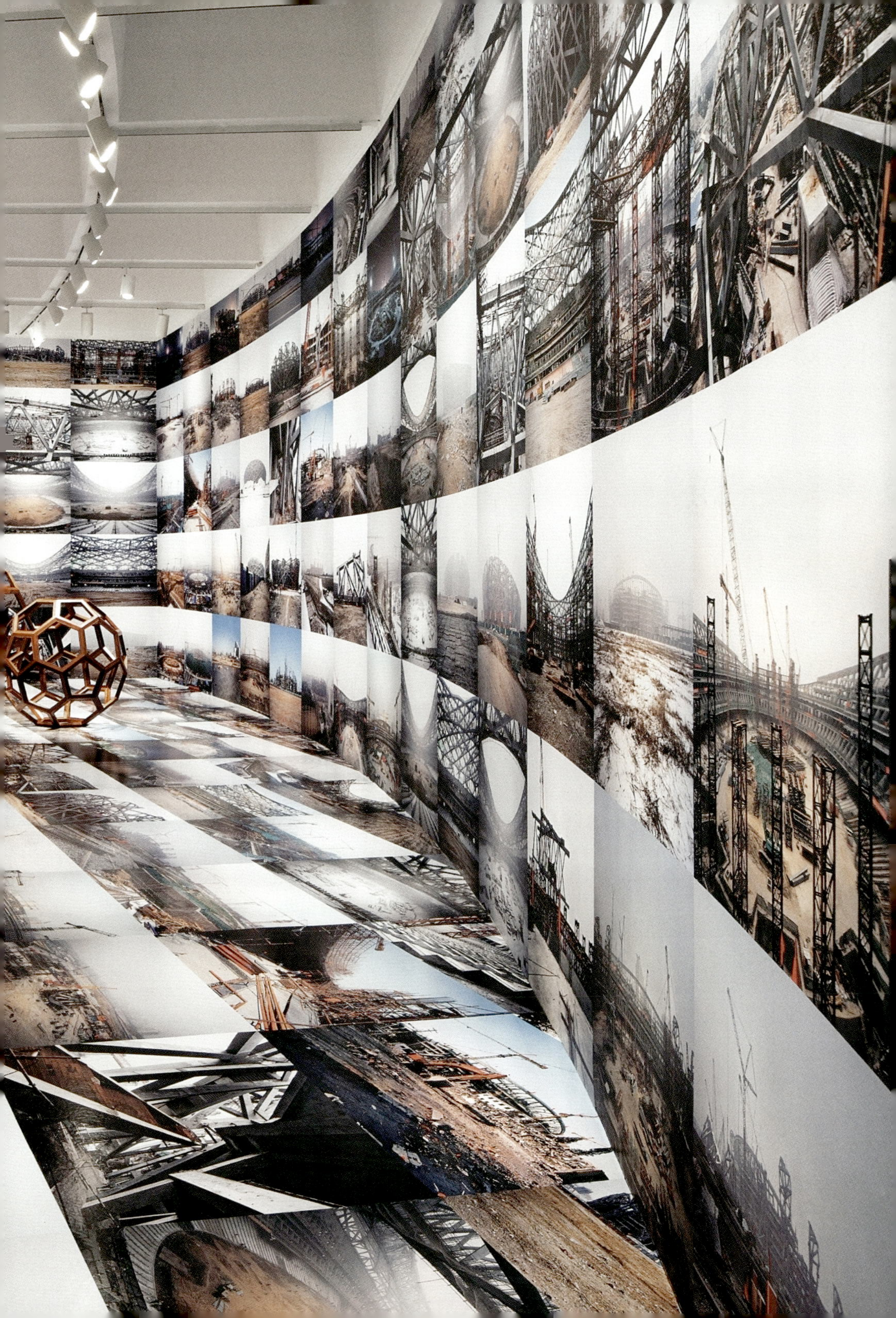

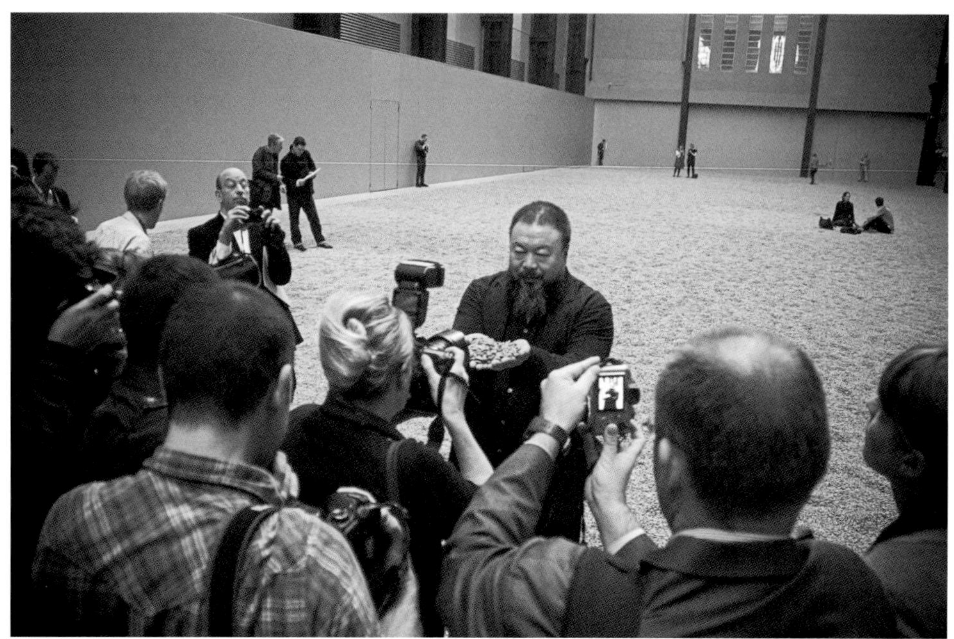

Ai Weiwei with *Sunflower Seeds*, 2010, porcelain, paint, 100 million pieces, dimensions variable;
Turbine Hall, Tate Modern, London 2010 (see pp. 407–409)

Wie bei der vorgeblich verschandelten Han-Vase legt *Dropping* eine einfache
Lesart nahe: „Seht her, Chinas historisches Erbe wird zerschlagen." Bezeichnen-
derweise schlüpft Ai aber selbst in die Rolle eines bäuerlichen Schergen, der sich
an der Tradition rächt. Und tatsächlich geht es bei dieser Performance wohl vor
allem um die Auslotung jener Tiefenschicht, welche die post-kulturrevolutionären
Chinesen, Ai eingeschlossen, mit dem chinesischen Erbe verbindet. Statt eine
Aussage zu treffen, wirft die Performance eher die Frage auf: „Wird da noch ein
Schmerz spürbar (angesichts der Zerschlagung)?" Kurzum, hier geht nicht so
sehr eine Urne in die Brüche als eine Beziehung, in der sich Ai bewusst als Partner
outet, und das heißt: als beschädigten Menschen porträtiert – ein innerhalb der
chinesischen Gegenwartskunst exzeptioneller Moment. Er erleidet diese Beschädigung aber nicht einfach, sondern setzt sie aktiv in Szene. Es lässt sich vermuten,
dass in genau dieser souveränen Anerkennung der eigenen Beschädigung der Keim
zu jener genuinen Solidarität steckt, die Ai seine aktivistischen Brückenschläge
ermöglicht.

XIV. Bei *Hands* und *Feet* (S. 187, 191, beide 2003) erstreckt sich diese Solidarität
auf die Formen beschädigter Menschen, genauer: abgeschlagene Hände und Füße
von Buddha-Statuen der Qi-Dynastie (550–577), denen Ai auf zwei großen Holz-
tischen einen Ort gibt. Der Fragmentcharakter dieser steinernen Stücke (insge-

samt zwölf Hände und zehn Füße) unterstreicht den nahezu beseelten Charakter
der Körpervolumina oder Handlinien, die von der Blütezeit des Buddhismus im
nördlichen China zeugen. Sie zeugen aber auch von der Gewalt, die sich bald gegen
die Macht und den Reichtum der Klöster richten sollte. In seinem Display behandelt Ai die steinernen Relikte nicht als historisches Material, sondern à la Rodin
wie autonome Stücke. Jeder einzelne Fuß, und jede Hand, ruht auf einem eigenen
quadratischen Holzsockel und demonstriert so die eigene, singuläre Form, die sich
aber der stets gleichen gewaltförmigen Zurichtung verdankt.

Bei *Rebar* (2012, S. 477), drei nahezu kalligrafisch verbogenen Armiereisen,
wie sie zur Festigung von Beton dienen, entdeckt man zwar keinerlei Anthropomor-
phien, doch auch hier geht es um beschädigte Menschen. Ai hat solche deformier-
ten Träger aus den Trümmern von Schulgebäuden geklaubt, die beim Erdbeben von
Sichuan (2008) auffallend stark in Mitleidenschaft gezogen worden waren. Wie sich
herausstellte, hatten Behörden und Baufirmen einträchtig gespart, um die Gelder
in die eigenen Taschen umzuleiten. Ai hat sich an der zivilen Recherche über dieses
Erdbeben und die toten Schulkinder beteiligt, aber eben auch jene Eisenstangen
an sich genommen, die diesmal keine antiken Relikte waren. Um die Eisenstangen
auszustellen, ließ er sie zweimal kopieren. Das Original als *art engagé* im Kunst-
system zirkulieren zu lassen, wäre dumm. Es nicht auszustellen, wäre feige. In der
Verdreifachung existiert etwas, das echt ist, doch wird diese vorgebliche Authentizität durch die Häufung geschluckt. Genauer wäre es, zu sagen, dass die Authentizität verschoben wird. Es geht Ai nicht darum, dass ein Stück Eisen die Katastrophe bezeugt, sondern dass sich der Betrachter mit dem Geschehen verbindet. Der
Eintritt in ein solches Wahrnehmungsverhältnis hat klarerweise seinen Preis. Dieser
besteht im Aufzeigen des unüberbrückbaren Abgrunds, der zwischen dem verbogenen Eisenstück aus Sichuan und den anderen beiden Stücken, oder zwischen
Nicht-Kunst und Kunst, klafft.

XV. Die schockierende Erfahrung von *Rebar* verdankt sich einer im Grunde simplen
Erkenntnis: Hier ist ein grausames Stück Realität, ein verbogenes Armiereisen, das
einem identischen Stück Eisen in nichts gleicht – außer eben seiner Form, die als
solche aber nichts besagt. Diese Erkenntnis stellt das Wahrnehmungsvermögen des
Betrachters nicht infrage, nötigt ihn aber, sein Vorstellungsvermögen zu aktivieren,
denn das, worauf es hier ankommt, ist ästhetisch nicht zu erfassen. So entwickelt
sich im Prozess der Betrachtung ein Weltbezug, in dem die Sichuan-Katastrophe
kein bloß äußerliches Ereignis bleibt, auf das man mit Mitleid oder Empörung
reagiert. Der Katastrophe wächst vielmehr eine seelische Dimension zu, sie wird in
die Innenperspektive gerückt und provoziert die Frage „Was macht das mit mir?"
eher als „Was hat das mit mir zu tun?". Im Chinesischen heißt diese Erschließung
seelischer Ressourcen „das Leben nähren", aber vermutlich weiß jeder Mensch, was
damit gemeint ist.[12] Dem Katastrophentouristen von Kassel musste tatsächlich
niemand erzählen, was das eingestürzte *Template* mit ihm zu tun hatte (und hätte

er es nicht gewusst, wäre er kaum aus freien Stücken angereist). Allerdings war *Template* dem Betrachter auch insofern entgegengekommen, als die deformierte Skulptur jegliche Wahrnehmungsdistanz nahezu im Alleingang überbrückt hatte und eigentlich keiner ästhetischen Vorbildung bedurfte. Bei *Rebar* erfolgt der Brückenschlag subtiler, nämlich auf dem Rücken des modernistischen Formenkanons, und erfordert eine Abstraktionsleistung. Unabhängig von der jeweiligen Gestalt oder dem Schicksal dieser und weiterer Arbeiten wird aber deutlich, welche Instanz Ais künstlerische Konzeption adressiert: Es ist das Selbst des Betrachters einschließlich seiner seelischen Ressourcen.

Dieses Selbst wird nirgendwo unmissverständlicher adressiert als in jenem über die Jahre heimlich entstandenen Werk, mit dem Ai seine traumatische Gefängniserfahrung im Frühjahr 2011 durcharbeitet. *S.A.C.R.E.D.* (2011–2013, S. 218, 221, 223, 481–483) besteht aus sechs dunklen, etwa schulterhohen Eisenkästen im Umfang von knapp vier Metern Länge und zwei Metern Breite. Jeder dieser Eisenkästen birgt ein Diorama in halber Lebensgröße, das aus Fiberglas modelliert wurde. Es zeigt Ai in Schlüsselsituationen seiner 81 Tage währenden Haft. Der Werktitel ist ein Akronym; S. steht für *Supper* (Abendessen), A. für *Accusers* (Ankläger), C. für *Cleansing* (Waschen), R. für *Ritual* (hier: Stuhlgang), E. für *Entropy* (hier: der Schlaf) und D. für *Doubt* (Zweifel). Die Bezeichnungen, so viel wird deutlich, variieren zwischen der Bezeichnung gewöhnlicher Tätigkeiten und der Charakterisierung seelischer Zustände, so bei *Entropy* des Gefühls von Persönlichkeitsauflösung, das Ai beschlichen haben muss, als er unter ständiger Bewachung auf engstem Raum und bei brennendem Licht unter einer knapp bemessenen Decke schlafen musste. Der Werktitel schließlich – *S.A.C.R.E.D.* – hat nichts mit der christlichen Bedeutung von „heilig" zu tun, sondern geht zurück auf die antike Bedeutung des Homo sacer als eines rechtlosen, von der Gesellschaft ausgeschlossenen Menschen. Dieser Homo sacer gehört den Göttern, aber im üblen Sinne völliger Schutzlosigkeit. Weil er den Pakt mit den Göttern gebrochen hat, kann er von jedermann straflos getötet werden, und dieser Mord wird nicht als menschliches Verbrechen, sondern als Rache der Götter gewertet.[13]

Bei ihrer ersten Installation im Hauptraum der Chiesa di Sant'Antonin im Sommer 2013 in Venedig erinnerten diese ominösen dunklen Blöcke von ferne an Katafalke; in einem White Cube würde man sie mit orthodox-minimalistischen Skulpturen assoziieren. Im Gegensatz zu Katafalken oder minimalistischen Oberflächen lockte Ais monumentale Form aber mit narrativen Elementen. So war an der Wand des Eisenkastens eine verschlossene Tür in halber Größe nachgebildet, während eine Kiste dem Betrachter die Möglichkeit zum Draufsteigen und genaueren Inspizieren der Form suggerierte. Tatsächlich ließen sich die Dioramen durch einen Sehschlitz in Aufsicht betrachten; solche Schlitze waren auch an den Wänden angebracht. Wie bei Duchamps übrigens ebenfalls heimlich entstandenen *Étant donnés* (1946–1966), wo der Betrachter durch ein Astloch spähen muss, wird man nicht bloß Zeuge eines obszönen Spektakels, sondern vorsätzlich in eine

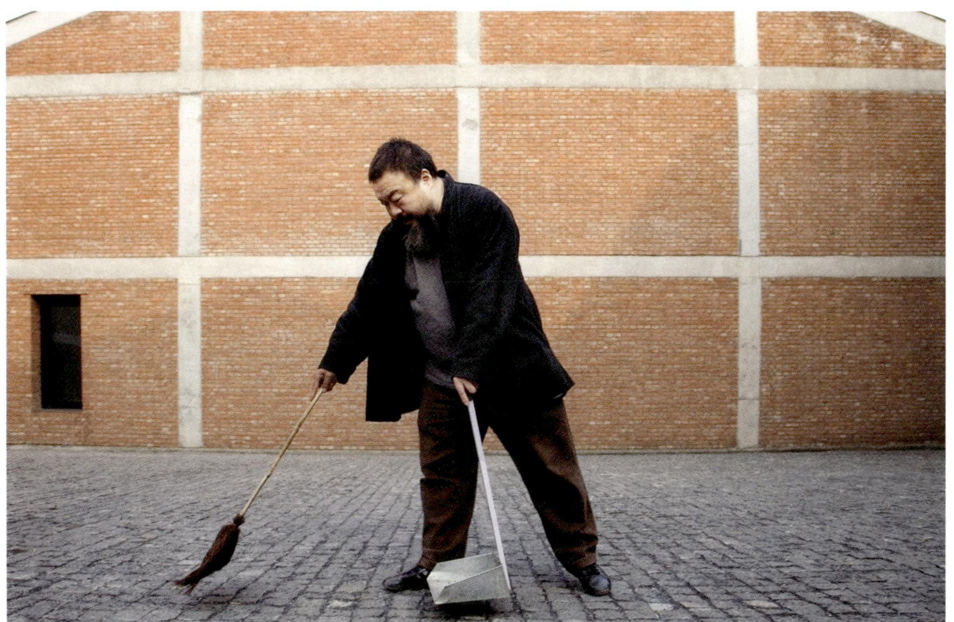

Ai Weiwei at his newly built studio, Shanghai 2010

voyeuristische Position gerückt. Anders formuliert, wird sich der Betrachter seiner Betrachterposition bewusst. Während Duchamps Diorama mit seinem nackten Frauenkörper, der eine Lampe hält, die Licht auf die unwirkliche Szenerie wirft, einigermaßen rätselhaft bleibt, kennt *S.A.C.R.E.D.* keinerlei Zweideutigkeiten, ganz im Gegenteil. Das von einer Glühbirne ausgeleuchtete Zelleninterieur mit Ai, seinen beiden uniformierten Bewachern, den Sicherheitsleuten, die ihn verhören, aber auch dem spärlichen Mobiliar ist in einem Darstellungsrealismus gehalten, dessen Detailtreue nahezu halluzinatorischen Charakter aufweist.

Es liegt in der didaktischen, gänzlich außerkünstlerischen Tradition des Dioramas begründet, eine Wirklichkeit anschaulich zu machen, die keinen Bezug zur Gegenwart des Betrachters hat. So findet man beispielsweise in Völkerkundemuseen Dioramen, die veranschaulichen sollen, wie die Menschen in der Steinzeit lebten. Bei *S.A.C.R.E.D.* ist das anders. Einerseits wird der Betrachter, der durch den Schlitz blickt, auf sich zurückgeworfen. Die eigene Blickposition in Verbindung mit der Abgeschlossenheit des Eisenkastens und der Miniaturisierung des Geschehens schafft eine unüberwindliche Distanz. Andererseits erscheint das, was sich in der Zelle tut, nur allzu vertraut. Man kennt den Laptop, auf dem der Sicherheitsbeamte mitschreibt, ebenso wie die Handschellen, mit denen Ai während des Verhörs am Stuhl gefesselt wird. Man kennt die sorgsam gefaltete Wäsche im Schrank, die Plastikschalen mit den chinesischen *dumplings,* den Duschstrahl und die bunten Shampooflaschen. Jeder weiß, was es heißt, auf dem Klo zu sitzen. Vor allem aber

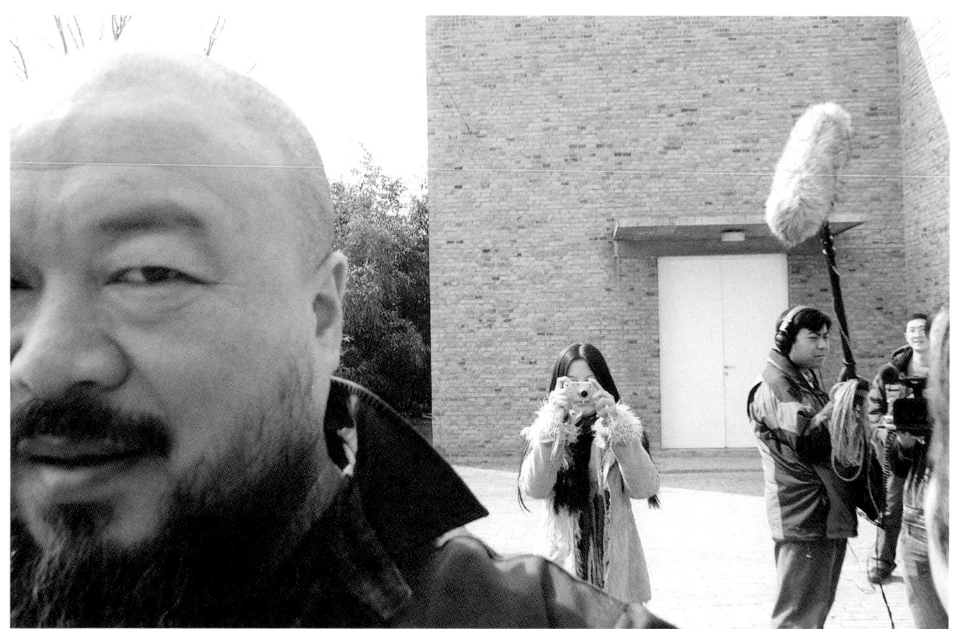

Studio life, Caochangdi, Beijing 2007–2009; meeting with journalists

kennt man Ai selbst – oder meint ihn zu kennen. Das Selbst des Künstlers ist aber kein authentisches Selbst. Es geht hier nicht um Opfernarzissmus, sondern wie bei Warhol um das *Image* des Künstlers als entscheidendes Vehikel der Identifikation seitens des Betrachters.

Es war in diesem Text schon die Rede von Ais Rolle als Mittler sowie von seiner poetischen Doktrin, Wahrnehmungsdistanzen zu überbrücken. Bei *S.A.C.R.E.D.* begegnet man sowohl dem Künstler wie auch seiner Doktrin in nahezu unerträglicher Reinform. Oberflächliche Betrachter verführt das zu der Behauptung, wonach der Künstler sein Dissidentenschicksal ausbeutet, um sein Werk zu propagieren.[14] „Warum nicht?", ließe sich dem entgegenhalten. Wem sein persönliches Schicksal von einem totalitären System *ready-made* zugerichtet wird, warum soll der dieses Schicksal nicht modellhaft nachgestalten und sich damit seiner entäußern? Vor allem wenn klar ist, dass dieses vorgeblich persönliche Schicksal unter diktatorischen Bedingungen ebenso unpersönlich ist wie bei *S.A.C.R.E.D.* das Zelleninnere. Potentiell kann jeder Chinese hinter der Tür 1135 verschwinden und zum Homo sacer werden. Das wissen auch jene Landsleute Ais, die nach Bekanntwerden des Vorwurfs der Steuerhinterziehung Geldscheine in Gestalt von Papierfliegern über die hohen Mauern seines Anwesens in Caochangdi segeln ließen. Ganz im Sinne des Künstlers entwickelten sie dabei ihre eigene, ebenso schöpferische wie solidarische Form der Überbrückung von Wahrnehmungsdistanzen. In solchen spontanen Aktionen, welche die Dynamik einer Zivilgesellschaft mit ihrem Wechselspiel von individueller Initiative und kollektivem Geist vorzeichnen, verschwindet der Mittler und mit ihm die Trennung von Kunst und Nicht-Kunst. Oder sagen wir so: Ai wäre in einer solchen Welt nicht mehr auf die Mittlerrolle fixiert, weil sie tatsächlich von vielen übernommen werden könnte. Dann erst würde Ais künstlerische Freiheit im eigentlichen Sinne beginnen, die auch die Freiheit einschließen würde, nichts zu tun.

[1] Der Rolle der Entsprechungen als einer der Grundlagen der chinesischen Kultur widmet sich Léon Vandermeersch in *Les deux raisons de la pensée chinoise: Divination et idéographie*, Gallimard, Paris 2013. [2] Siehe hierzu Lothar Ledderose, *Ten Thousand Things: Module and Mass Production in Chinese Art*, The A. W. Mellon Lectures in the Fine Arts, Princeton University Press, Princeton 1998. [3] Diese Wendung prägte Philip Tinari in seinem Aufsatz „Chairs and Visitors", in: *Ai Weiwei, Works 2004–2007*, hrsg. von Urs Meile, JRP Ringier, Zürich 2008, S. 12. [4] Für eine eingehende Darstellung der Bizarrerien von *Fairytale* siehe meinen Aufsatz „Meeting Alterity", in: *Ai Weiwei: Fairytale, A Reader*, hrsg. von Lionel Bovier und Salomé Schnetz, JRP Ringier, Zürich, und Einfache Gesellschaft Fairytale, Luzern 2012, S. 31–42. [5] Es fällt auf, dass in den drei Anthologien zwei Künstler fehlen, die damals nicht nur einen entscheidenden Einfluss ausübten, sondern ganz unmittelbar mit Ais Methoden korrespondieren. Da ist zum einen Sherrie Levine. Mit ihren Reproduktionen der Fotos von Walker Evans (*After Walker Evans*, 1981) etablierte sie ein Konzept von „Kopie", das den Status des Originals unterminierte. Der andere Künstler ist Allan McCollum, dessen Installationen Ai für sein privates Archiv fotografierte. McCollums Thema war damals das Verhältnis von Identität und Differenz, das er in raumgreifenden Displays von Objekten entwickelte, die gleich schienen, dies aber nicht waren. [6] Andy Warhol, *The Philosophy of Andy Warhol (From A to B and back again)*, Harcourt Brace Jovanovich, New York 1975, S. 100. Deutsche Ausgabe: *Die Philosophie des Andy Warhol von A bis B und zurück*, übers. von Regine Reimers, Knaur, München 1991, S. 105. [7] *Die Kunst der Aufklärung* war eine Kollaboration dreier großer deutscher Museen (Berlin, Dresden, München) im chinesischen Nationalmuseum, die den Anspruch hatte, auf staatlicher Ebene kulturellen Austausch zu fördern. Ironischerweise wurde Ai zu dem Zeitpunkt auf dem Beijinger Flughafen verhaftet, als der offizielle Tross nach Deutschland abreiste. [8] Als Einführung in Duchamps wundersame Komplexitäten empfiehlt sich David Joselit, *Infinite Regress: Marcel Duchamp 1910–1941*, MIT Press, Cambridge, Mass., 1998. [9] Der englische Philosoph Peter Osborne definiert in *Anywhere or Not at All: Philosophy of Contemporary Art* (Verso, London und New York 2013) das völlige Ungenügen ästhetischer Kriterien bei der Beurteilung zeitgenössischer Kunst als eines der Hauptmerkmale post-konzeptueller Kunst. Tatsächlich ist Ai ein post-konzeptueller Künstler, der seine Schlüsse aus dem produktiven Scheitern des Konzeptualismus gezogen hat. [10] Die Geschichte der Neuauflage der Readymades beschreibt Helen Molesworth im Katalogbeitrag „Duchamp: By Hand, Even" der von ihr kuratierten Ausstellung *Part Object, Part Sculpture*, Wexner Center for the Arts, Columbus, Ohio 2005, S. 156–165. [11] Ai hatte in dieser Zeit nicht den Anspruch, Kunst zu machen; die Coca-Cola-Vase entstand beiläufig. Diesen Hinweis verdanke ich Uli Sigg. [12] Siehe François Jullien, *Nourrir sa vie*, Seuil, Paris 2005. Deutsche Ausgabe: *Sein Leben nähren: Abseits vom Glück*, Merve, Berlin 2005. [13] In *Homo sacer: Sovereign Power and Bare Life* (Stanford University Press, Stanford 1995) rekonstruiert der italienische Philosoph Giorgio Agamben den Zustand völliger Ausgesetztheit, den er auch als „bloßes Leben" bezeichnet, als Effekt der modernen Regierungstechnik. Ohne dem Gedanken an dieser Stelle nachgehen zu können, sei doch erwähnt, dass Ais Zellensituation beziehungsweise sein Zustand völliger Rechtlosigkeit keine rein chinesische Angelegenheit ist. Auch der demokratische Westen unterhält solche legalen Nicht-Räume, beispielsweise in Guantánamo. [14] Ein Beispiel ist Francesco Bonami, der Ai unterstellt, sein „falsches" Dissidententum nutzen zu wollen, um seinen Marktwert zu erhöhen, während „wahre" Dissidenten vom Regime liquidiert würden; siehe galleristny.com/2013/06/francesco-bonami-i-hate-ai-weiwei/.

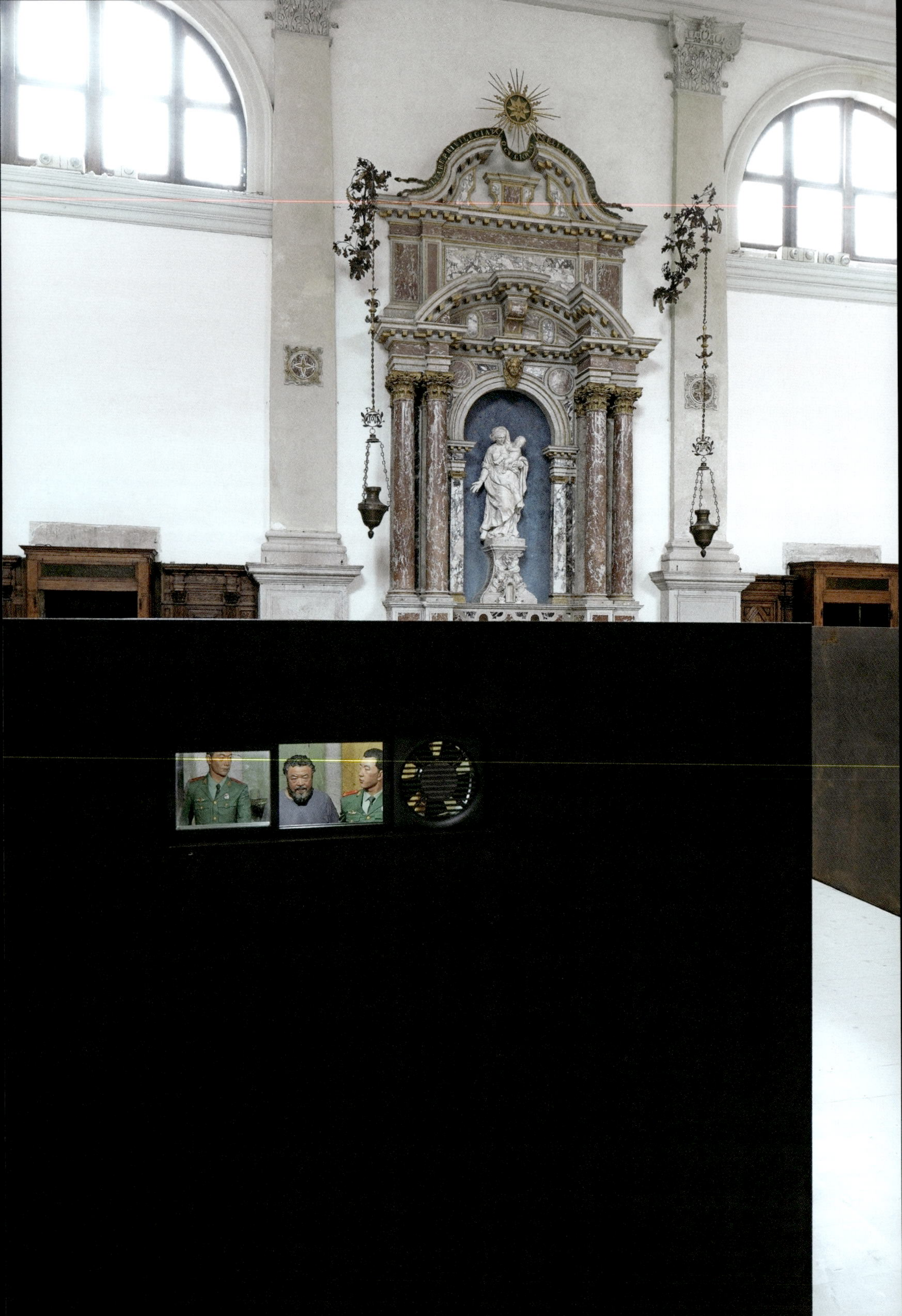

Les voies du médiateur
La liberté et l'art d'Ai Weiwei

ROGER M. BUERGEL

I : Quelques jours seulement après l'inauguration de la Documenta 12, l'œuvre d'Ai Weiwei *Template* (2007, pp. 328–330) s'effondrait sous les coups d'un orage. La structure d'environ sept mètres de haut, une des œuvres centrales présentées en plein air, était composée de 1001 bâtis de portes et de fenêtres des dynasties Ming et Qing (1368–1911) achetés sur les marchés d'antiquités chinois par Ai Weiwei – comme tant d'autres éléments de construction de ses œuvres. Partant de ces vestiges en bois, l'artiste avait fait réaliser à des artisans quatre murs en relief qui furent ensuite montés en étoile autour d'un axe vertical. La manière dont les différents murs étaient assemblés soulignait à la fois le caractère précaire des bâtis orphelins et le facteur aléatoire de leur ordonnancement. Dans sa fragilité, *Template* faisait songer à un grand château de cartes.

Contrairement aux cartes à jouer, les murs avaient été découpés autour du bord intérieur de telle sorte que la somme des ouvertures produisait un espace en négatif à l'intérieur de la construction. Cet espace en négatif reprenait les contours d'un temple traditionnel comme il s'en trouve des milliers en Chine – posés sur des collines ou en d'autres endroits choisis –, même si un nombre croissant de ces temples doivent céder la place aux projets infrastructurels de la Chine capitaliste. C'était ce « temple absent » qui permettait aux spectateurs de traverser *Template* non seulement en en embrassant visuellement la construction fragile et raffinée, mais également en l'appréhendant physiquement. Dans l'expérience vécue qui reliait les cheminements et les enchaînements d'idées du spectateur à la structure velléitaire de ce non-bâtiment, de sa consistance physique et de sa matière historique, il subsistait quelque chose de la fonction originelle du temple, qui se voyait en même temps radicalisé : la création d'un lien entre le moi et le monde. Mais dans le cas de *Template* et contrairement au cas d'un temple « en dur », il est vrai que ce lien n'était plus matérialisé. La superstructure spirituelle avait cédé la place à un vide encadré par les vestiges en bois de la Chine traditionnelle.

Il serait faux toutefois d'interpréter le vide d'Ai Weiwei comme un adieu. Comme tant d'autres œuvres de l'artiste, *Template* est empreint d'un désespoir face à ce qui fut et n'est plus. Mais il s'agit d'un désespoir productif qui revivifie une vieille thématique chinoise : le rapport entre vide et spiritualité. Ce thème participe d'une religiosité dans laquelle les puissances célestes – contrairement au dieu tonnant du monde judéo-chrétien – ne s'expliquent pas[1]. Les puissances célestes de la Chine ne parlent pas (Que la lumière soit!), mais se manifestent à travers des correspondances harmonieuses dont la découverte suppose deux choses: une forte capacité d'abstraction capable d'ignorer tout aspect accessoire, ainsi que la faculté et le loisir d'une immersion contemplative qui perçoit les règles de l'harmonie céleste jusqu'en ses détails les plus insignifiants. Dans la spiritualité profane ou postreligieuse d'Ai Weiwei, les puissances célestes ont cédé la place au système gouvernemental chinois (qui ne s'explique pas davantage), l'immersion méditative dans ses propres ressources créatives. S'il n'existe pas pour lui de temple capable de sanctifier le lien entre le moi et le monde, cela ne signifie nullement qu'il n'existe aucun mandat créatif pour instaurer ce lien, ou plutôt pour le créer *ex nihilo* à partir des vestiges du passé.

II : Le jour de l'inauguration de la Documenta, *Template* fut le centre absolu de l'attention générale. Indépendamment de sa force esthétique, cela s'expliquait par la place centrale occupée par la sculpture au milieu de la grande pelouse. À cela vinrent s'ajouter la tendance des médias à se focaliser sur une œuvre représentative de l'ensemble et la présence d'Ai Weiwei, artiste global qui semblait présenter au moins deux visages, l'un chinois, l'autre occidental – dont on pouvait donc faire le portrait sous forme d'un trait d'union entre l'Asie et l'Occident sur fond de changements actuels dans les rapports de forces géopolitiques. Cela se devait enfin à toute l'agitation que *Fairytale* (la visite de la Documenta par 1001 Chinois) avait suscitée en amont de l'exposition – une œuvre dont les dimensions et les implications étaient dans tous les esprits sans qu'il y en eût aucune image, de sorte que *Template,* en plus des autres raisons évoquées ci-dessus, bénéficia d'une sorte d'attention décalée. L'on ne s'étonne donc pas que, lors de l'inauguration de l'exposition, ce soit précisément sous *Template* que le Président allemand prit la pose, entouré de toute une série de dignitaires, faisant ainsi entrer clandestinement le monument hautement précaire d'Ai Weiwei dans une mémoire médiatique aussi éphémère que largement diffusée.

Ce sont sûrement ces images médiatiques encore toutes fraîches – toujours associées à l'attention publique que la Documenta suscite pour elle-même, du moins en Allemagne – qui firent de l'effondrement de l'œuvre un sujet d'actualité tout en lui ouvrant de nouveaux horizons de perception. L'effondrement de *Template* n'avait pourtant été que partiel, et sous sa nouvelle forme, la sculpture était tout autre chose qu'un tas de matériaux inarticulé. Le cadre métallique qui enchâssait les vieux bâtis de bois avait seulement ployé sous la pression des puissances naturelles, tout en se tordant d'étrange façon. Le résultat était une forme bizarre, en tous cas hautement singulière, dont l'effet général poétique et inquiétant était encore renforcé par le fait que les éléments Ming et Qing, précédemment subordonnés à la forme générale, purent s'émanciper un peu de la sculpture d'Ai Weiwei.

L'on sait qu'Ai Weiwei a salué avec gratitude le résultat de la tempête, le nouveau *Template.* L'idée n'a jamais surgi de reconstruire l'œuvre ; le monument

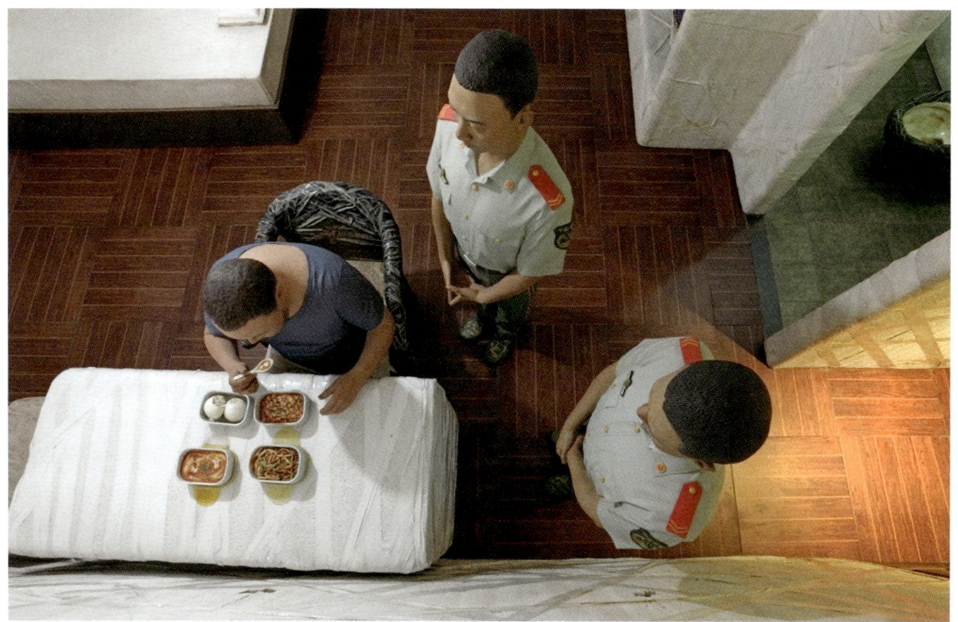

Detail from *S.A.C.R.E.D.*, 2011–2013, showing the diorama for S. = Supper

sinistré survécut donc à la Documenta sous sa nouvelle forme tout en attirant un nouveau public – public qui, tout comme la majorité des 1001 Chinois qu'Ai Weiwei avait invités à Cassel, n'avait pas forcément beaucoup d'atomes crochus avec l'exposition ou l'art en tant que tel. Ces nouveaux visiteurs étaient des amateurs de catastrophes qui voulaient voir l'improbable événement *de visu*. Mais que trouvèrent-ils exactement sur la pelouse de la Documenta? Une architecture de catastrophe, drapée dans un langage formel asiatique évoquant vaguement les images médiatiques qui font le tour du monde après un séisme ou un tsunami. Mais *Template* n'était justement pas une image montrant le monde des autres comme «le monde des autres». C'était un événement lourdement tangible qui avait aboli la distance perceptive entre les réalités chinoise et casseloise. En tant que tel, c'était l'art d'un authentique médiateur, d'un promeneur entre les mondes.

III : Après la fin de la Documenta, Ai Weiwei a chargé ses artisans de reconstruire le monument effondré en grandeur nature. Il s'agissait d'intégrer la sculpture dans l'œuvre général : sa forme situative, mais aussi fortuite, devait donc être reproduite, l'écho esthétique de la puissance naturelle copié. Cependant, il n'avait pas échappé à Ai Weiwei que grâce à la performance spectaculaire de *Template,* son œuvre s'était élargi d'une dimension cruciale. Le meilleur terme pour définir au mieux cette dimension est celui de «vie propre». Pour l'artiste, ce genre de vie propre est difficile à gérer parce qu'on ne peut la planifier, et moins encore la programmer. Tout comme l'harmonie céleste de la religiosité chinoise, elle peut obéir à des règles et à des lois, mais celles-ci restent cachées. Il est vrai qu'il existe des facteurs sur lesquels un artiste peut agir, et parmi ceux-ci, on trouve chez Ai Weiwei la relation avec ses artisans. Cette relation est au plus haut point perméable. Ai Weiwei ne mise pas seulement sur leurs compétences techniques – celles d'exécutants de ses projets –, mais les respecte et les mobilise comme garants du matériau et de son histoire.

Il commence par confronter ses artisans à des problématiques. Nous avons tel ou tel matériau – dans le cas de *Template*, les 1001 anciens bâtis de portes et de fenêtres, pour *China Log* (2005, pp. 188/189), les huit colonnes d'un temple détruit de la dynastie Qing (1644–1911) –, que peut-on faire de tout ça? Les artisans soumettent alors des propositions qui sont débattues, rejetées, modifiées, réalisées. Ce genre de collaboration artistique a ceci de remarquable que, dans sa propre création contemporaine, elle accorde une place importante à l'histoire du matériau dans la culture chinoise. Ai Weiwei se confronte à cette histoire, d'une part dans l'aspect de surabondance d'artefacts orphelins vendus en Chine, qu'Ai Weiwei met de côté pour lui-même et pour sa production artistique. Par ailleurs, Ai Weiwei voit l'histoire du matériau incarnée dans ses artisans: tout se passe pour lui comme si ses artisans avaient plus de capacités que ce qu'eux-mêmes (et Ai Weiwei) imaginaient. La production artistique consiste donc d'abord à lancer un processus collectif dans lequel peuvent se produire des choses imprévisibles, un processus qui invoque et revendique une puissance que l'on peut définir comme l'inconscient matériel.

L'inconscient matériel englobe essentiellement la somme d'expériences qui se sont déposées pendant des siècles de pratique hautement disciplinée dans les aptitudes artisanales et les formes de vie d'une civilisation. Les stupéfiantes capacités des Chinois ne viennent pas seulement de leur génie propre, mais de l'immense et durable pression que seul un régime féodal profondément incrusté, avec ses hiérarchies sociales aussi brutales et rigides dans les manières que mesquines et pinailleuses dans les formes, est sans doute à même d'exercer. Cela ne veut pas dire que le travail manuel et artisanal soit seulement une torture. Il connaît évidemment des moments de bonheur, par exemple quand un bol en porcelaine sort du four sans la moindre imperfection et présente un aspect résolument immatériel. Il connaît aussi des triomphes intellectuels comme la pagode de Fogongsi à Yingxian qui, bien que construite au XIᵉ siècle et haute de 67 mètres, a su résister à tous les séismes et à toutes les intempéries[2]. Mais quel est le juste rapport entre ces moments de bonheur, ces triomphes intellectuels et l'investissement existentiel, l'engagement, voire le sacrifice qu'ils exigent? L'inconscient matériel est un mélange explosif, c'est un fait. Un mélange explosif qui s'était déchargé dans les orgies destructrices de la révolution culturelle, auxquelles Ai Weiwei avait élevé un monument ambigu avec sa performance *Dropping a Han Dynasty Urn* (1995, pp. 85–87), que nous évoquerons plus loin. Dans un premier temps, il importe de garder à l'esprit que l'inconscient matériel survit tout autant dans les artefacts que

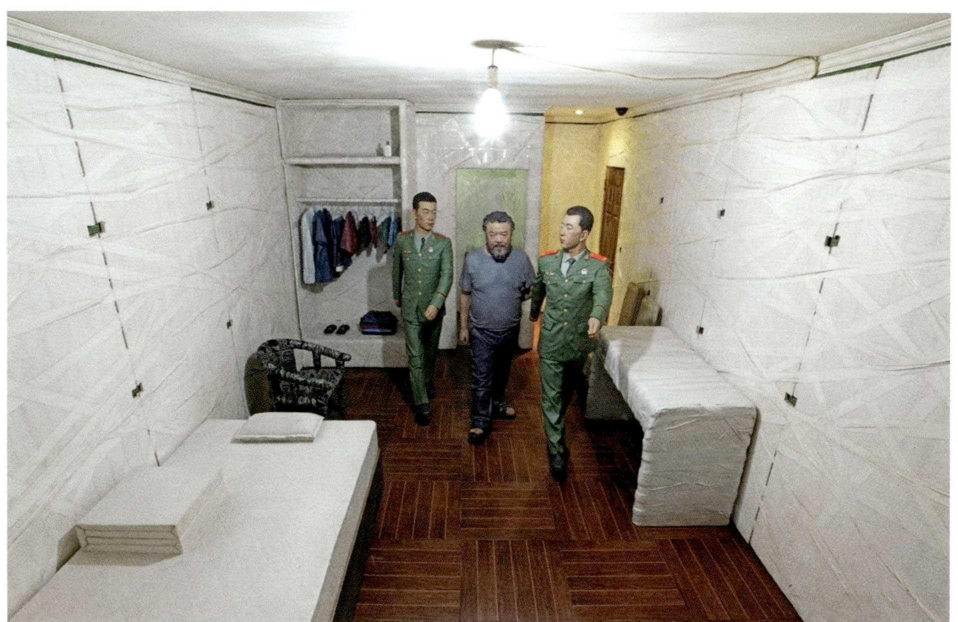

Detail from *S.A.C.R.E.D.*, 2011–2013, showing the diorama for D. = Doubt

dans les aptitudes techniques des artisans qui recèlent en eux le savoir-faire dans le maniement du matériau élaboré et transmis pendant des générations. La Chine contemporaine qui, avec l'ouverture du marché depuis les années 1980, a aussi souscrit sans réserves à l'impératif de la modernisation à outrance, ne voit plus d'utilité à ce trésor d'expérience acquise, mais radicalise en fait le principe de la révolution culturelle, celui de la *tabula rasa*. Les techniques artisanales traditionnelles ne sont donc que des espèces ou des langages en voie de disparition, raison pour laquelle beaucoup d'œuvres d'Ai Weiwei qui reposent sur ces techniques se chargent d'un caractère profondément triste.

IV : Entre les artefacts d'autrefois, les urnes, colonnes de temples, pieds et mains brisées de statues de Bouddhas, bâtis de portes et de fenêtres et tout ce que l'œuvre d'Ai Weiwei comprend par ailleurs, entre tous ces artefacts orphelins adoptés par l'artiste sous forme de *ready-made* d'une part, et les aptitudes artisanales d'autre part, il existe un étroit parallélisme. L'artiste ne fait guère plus que relier ces parallèles, voire les court-circuiter. Il joue donc avec les forces plutôt que de produire quelque chose au sens conventionnel. La perméabilité déjà évoquée qui caractérise Ai Weiwei (et qui peut sembler paradoxale au regard de sa présence physique et de son charisme) constitue la condition fondamentale pour que ces forces puissent se déployer et révéler cette vie propre, but suprême de l'artiste et qui se manifeste de manière si impressionnante dans *Template*.

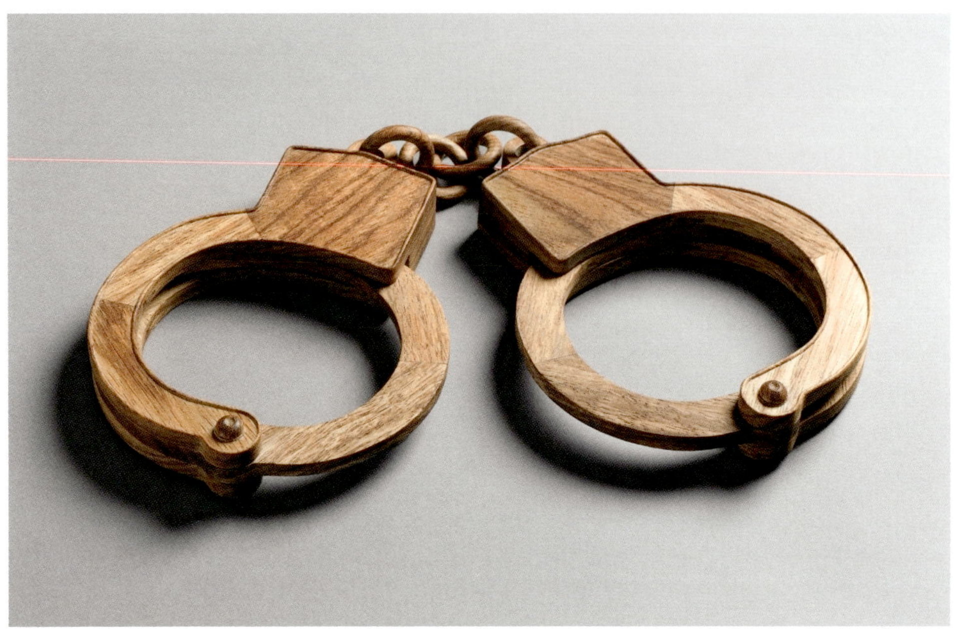

Handcuffs, 2012, huali wood, 5 ⅛ x 15 ¾ x ¾ inches

V : Sous un autre aspect, cette vie propre a aussi été déterminante pour *Fairytale* (2007, pp. 310–327), la deuxième contribution d'Ai Weiwei à la Documenta 12, contribution qui consistait en substance à faire venir à Cassel un mélange improbable de 1000 Chinois (le 1001ᵉ n'étant autre que lui). Contrairement à ce qui se passait avec *Template*, la vie propre de l'œuvre n'était pas due à la performance imprévue d'une sculpture, mais à l'existence improvisée d'un groupe. Philip Tinari a très justement qualifié l'entreprise d'« expérience en matière de chaos contrôlé »[3]. Pour *Fairytale* aussi, Ai Weiwei connectait entre elles différentes forces, notamment la curiosité touristique – particulièrement de la part de Chinois n'ayant pas les moyens de s'offrir un tel voyage –, les possibilités infrastructurelles et médiatiques d'une grande exposition et l'intérêt de l'Occident pour une vision de la Chine qui ne soit pas calquée sur la doctrine officielle. Néanmoins, l'activité créatrice d'Ai Weiwei ne produisait pas une œuvre identifiable, mais elle se bornait à s'inscrire dans certains aspects comme le design des valises et des logements, les coupes de cheveux et les présences individuelles sur place. Bien que *Fairytale* ait semblé sacrifier aux grandes dimensions, ne serait-ce que par la logistique et les coûts immenses, la dynamique concrète de cette esthétique de l'existence se fit sentir dans des détails apparemment insignifiants, par exemple dans la rencontre du paysan chinois avec le paysan hessois, dont les banalités du métier s'avérèrent intraduisibles alors que la compréhension semblait parfaite. En dépit de l'insertion institutionnelle de *Fairytale* dans une grande exposition, il ne s'agissait là ni d'expérience esthétique au sens restreint, ni de sculpture sociale, mais d'une diffusion à la fois ouverte et structurée d'expériences singulières s'associant pour former une esthétique de l'existence. La perméabilité d'Ai Weiwei comme modérateur, en quelque sorte hors circuit de toute l'opération, visait à la production et au maintien de l'équilibre dynamique qui détermine une telle esthétique de l'existence : dans l'interaction entre ouverture et structure. En l'occurrence, les expériences singulières n'étaient pas soumises à une chorégraphie, et moins encore à une gestion autoritaire. Les Chinois faisaient leurs expériences pour eux-mêmes, sachant qu'ils durent éprouver à peu près la même chose que les touristes amateurs de catastrophes : ce qui les attendait était l'entrée dans un rapport de perception au monde différent, étranger[4].

VI : L'esthétique de l'existence est un thème d'Ai Weiwei sur lequel on peut retrouver des traces jusque dans ses années new-yorkaises (1982–1993). L'on peut sans doute remonter encore plus loin dans la biographie de l'artiste et y ajouter les années de traversée du désert pendant lesquelles Ai Qing, père d'Ai Weiwei et sans doute le plus grand poète chinois de l'époque moderne, fut banni dans le cadre des purges de la révolution culturelle pour aller nettoyer des latrines publiques. Ai Weiwei évoque souvent cette histoire, les conditions de vie précaires doublées de la résolution inébranlable de conserver sa dignité, et rappelle ainsi que l'esthétique à autant à voir avec les belles formes qu'avec la vie crue.

VII : Ai Weiwei s'est retrouvé à New York – même si son père venait d'être réhabilité, il lui semblait impossible de rester dans son pays. Ces années passées dans la métropole américaine furent synonyme de vie de bohème, une période d'apprentissage indirect, de mûrissement d'idées nouvelles. Ai Weiwei a documenté ces années avec une grande précision dans d'innombrables photos (pp. 57–63). Pas avec une intention précise se prenant très au sérieux, mais comme accessoirement, de manière ironique, dandyesque. Et avec une bonne dose de nihilisme que l'on attribuera volontiers à son âge d'alors, à l'expérience cruelle du système chinois, à une certaine désorientation, voire à la solitude en terre étrangère, mais précisément aussi aux leçons clés de modernité artistique qu'il prend à New York et à Philadelphie. L'album photo de ses archives (des quelque 10 000 négatifs, seule une infime partie a été publiée) couvre un spectre encyclopédique qui traite aussi bien d'aspects exotiques du quotidien urbain d'East Village, que des luxueuses vitrines des galeries et musées à l'époque de la politique reaganienne de l'argent facile. Ai Weiwei suit de près les troubles et les confrontations sanglantes entre manifestants et policiers autour de l'occupation de Tompkins Square Park, les apparitions du SIDA, mais photographie aussi de nouveaux amis comme le poète Allen Ginsberg (p. 17), les membres de la diaspora chinoise – et lui-même. Ces autoportraits montrent l'artiste comme un jeune homme qui s'ennuie jusqu'au désœuvrement, qui s'essaie à toutes sortes de possibilités d'encadrer son visage avec un

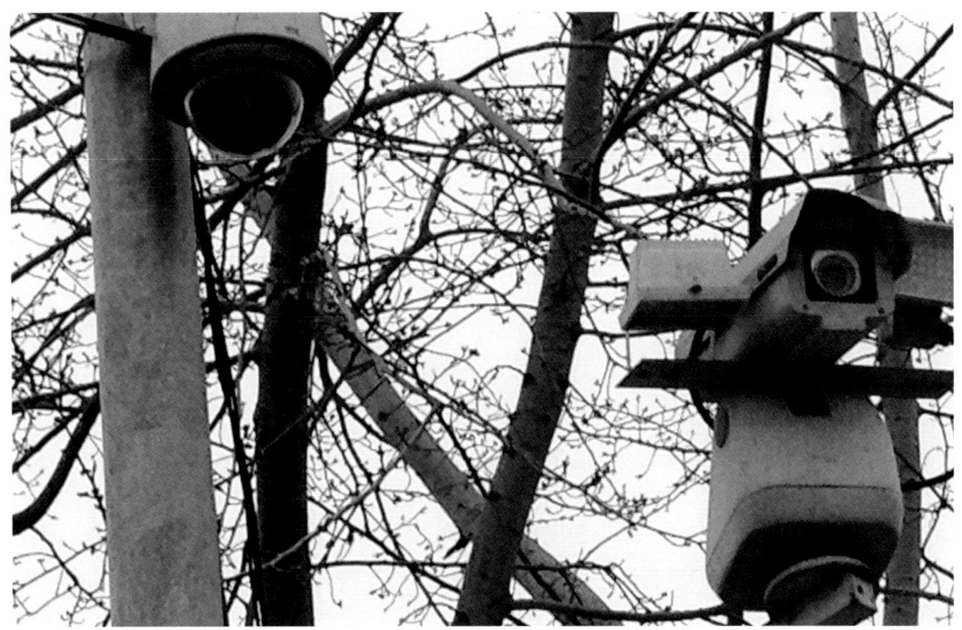

Surveillance cameras outside Ai Weiwei's studio, Caochangdi, Beijing 2011–2012

pneu de vélo et qui pose au MoMA à côté d'un autoportrait sériel d'Andy Warhol, non sans copier coquettement la pose maniérée du *pop artist*. Mais ses photos montrent aussi des expériences personnelles et presque informelles à l'atelier, comme un cintre en fil de fer qu'Ai Weiwei a tordu avec une pince pour en faire un profil frappant de Duchamp. Sachant qu'à peu près toutes laveries de New York appartiennent à des Chinois, on peut interpréter ce cintre comme la première formule transculturelle d'Ai Weiwei. Cette supposition se confirme encore un peu plus quand on se penche sur la photo dans laquelle Ai Weiwei a posé le cintre sur une surface pour emplir l'intérieur du profil de graines de tournesol, aliment volontiers grignoté par les Chinois.

VIII : Toutes les expériences existentielles et artistiques de la période new-yorkaise, avec leurs transitions fluides, ont quelque chose de ludique et d'ingénu, mais ne nous trompons pas : ici aussi, il s'agissait d'entrer dans un rapport de perception au monde différent, étranger, chose qui n'a pas dû être facile pour l'artiste. L'acte artistique lui-même s'oriente sur ce qui existe, ou pour faire honneur au concept de Duchamp, sur ce qui est « *ready-made* ». Il est stupéfiant de voir qu'Ai Weiwei ne craint peut-être pas le contact avec la culture américaine, mais qu'il semble étonnamment indifférent à ses productions matérielles. Lors d'une petite exposition dans une galerie (1988), il présente l'installation au sol *Five Raincoats Holding Up a Star* (1985, p. 18) : cinq imperméables en caoutchouc caractéris-

tiques du quotidien chinois et des tubes métalliques s'étirant le long de la masse
caoutchouteuse des manteaux s'allient pour former une étoile à cinq branches,
symbole du Parti communiste chinois. Comme dans les œuvres ultérieures de sa
maturité artistique, Ai Weiwei fait passer en douce des textures et des systèmes
référentiels chinois dans un canon moderniste, dont il a usurpé la langue, ici
l'idiome minimaliste. Impossible de discerner clairement – et ce n'est pas plus clair
aujourd'hui – si Ai Weiwei parle réellement cette langue, c'est-à-dire s'il l'utilise
corps et âme avec la plus entière conviction, ou s'il se contente de la mimer et de
s'en servir comme d'un véhicule.

IX : À New York, les artistes qui deviennent des références pour Ai Weiwei sont
l'émigré Marcel Duchamp et Andy Warhol. Tous deux n'étaient pas seulement pré-
sents avec leur œuvre, mais jouaient alors un rôle de premier plan comme figures
tutélaires d'une scène artistique américaine tendanciellement conceptuelle et politique : Barbara Kruger cherchait à faire progresser l'esthétique publicitaire de
Warhol, Jeff Koons mettait en scène des objets quotidiens dans des vitrines hermé-
tiques qui transformaient l'objet en signe au sens duchampien, Jenny Holzer utili-
sait les panneaux publicitaires hypervisibles de Times Square pour faire passer des
lieux communs, qui, à cet emplacement, ne pouvaient manquer de prendre un
sens angoissant. Cette liste d'artistes et de modes de travail n'est pas fortuite, elle
vient d'Ai Weiwei lui-même, qui publia après son retour en Chine trois anthologies
chinoises – *Black Cover Book* (1994, p. 99), *White Cover Book* (1995, p. 99),
Gray Cover Book (1997) – présentant l'art moderne occidental et l'avant-garde
artistique chinoise. Pour ces anthologies, des textes de Duchamp et de Warhol
furent traduits en chinois, tandis que les artistes cités plus haut étaient présentés
par des textes et des illustrations[5]. Dans la rubrique « Studio » parurent aussi des
contributions monographiques sur la scène artistique chinoise contemporaine.
On reconnaît une caractéristique majeure d'Ai Weiwei dans le fait qu'il ne se soit
pas cantonné à une simple assimilation et transmission de sa propre expérience
formatrice, mais que les trois anthologies aient servi en même temps de plate-
forme de lancement à la scène chinoise d'orientation conceptuelle qui était en
train d'émerger, et dont Ai Weiwei allait devenir le mentor.

X : Les inspirations qu'Ai Weiwei a pu tirer de Warhol, de Duchamp et de leurs
héritiers artistiques sont multiples. Pour la réception de Warhol, la voix de l'artiste
a sans doute joué un rôle important. Dans une des premières publications qu'il
acheta à New York, Ai Weiwei put lire le credo suivant : « Ce qu'il y a de formidable
dans ce pays, c'est que l'Amérique a créé la tradition où les plus riches consommateurs achètent la même chose que les plus pauvres. Vous pouvez regarder la télévision et voir Coca-Cola, et vous pouvez savoir que le président boit du Coca, Liz
Taylor boit du Coca-Cola, et pensez donc, vous aussi, vous pouvez boire du Coca.
Un Coca est un Coca, aucune somme d'argent au monde ne peut vous procurer un

meilleur Coca que celui du clochard au coin de la rue. Tous les Cocas sont pareils, et tous les Cocas sont bons. Liz Taylor le sait, le président le sait, le clochard le sait, et vous le savez. »[6]

Dans l'affirmation radicale de l'*American way of life* de Warhol, on peut noter une pointe d'ironie. Mais quelle différence cela fait-il que cette parodie politique absolue qui proclame une égalité universelle fondée sur le Coca soit sérieuse ou ironique ? L'apologie d'Andy Warhol sait qu'elle se situe à hauteur d'yeux de l'idéologie américaine, et c'est là que résident son pouvoir diagnostique et son charme pervers. Ai Weiwei, qui depuis sa plus tendre enfance, avait été obligé d'entendre une propagande maoïste aussi insaisissable qu'omniprésente avec ses slogans infracomplexes, n'aura pas manqué de percevoir les affinités entre communisme et consumérisme et leurs utopies sociétales. Pour le jeune bohémien qu'était alors Ai Weiwei, rien ne comptait plus que de développer une position face au système. Quoi de plus naturel alors que de se former à l'école de la larmoyance décontractée de Warhol, qui n'avait rien d'irréaliste, mais qui s'accompagnait au contraire d'une participation excessive au fait social ? Cela dit, Ai Weiwei est un tout autre type que Warhol, et à Pékin, l'on n'a pas non plus la possibilité d'opérer sous le couvert d'une métropole promiscuitaire, pas même quand on est cadre du parti. Le vaste cercle d'amis, de visiteurs, de journalistes, d'assistants et de chats qui peuplent jour et nuit la maison d'Ai Weiwei, et même toute l'idée d'une telle forme d'existence, doit sans doute une part non négligeable de son inspiration à la légendaire *Factory* de Warhol à Broadway. De même d'ailleurs que la voix de Warhol résonne dans les activités du blogueur politique Ai Weiwei, qui commente l'actualité chinoise avec un sarcasme difficilement traduisible, mais jamais amer – tout comme l'exposition allemande *Die Kunst der Aufklärung* (L'art au temps des Lumières) présentée place Tiananmen, accompagnée du commentaire : « Les Européens ont toujours de si belles choses à montrer. »[7]

XI : La réception de Duchamp par Ai Weiwei tournait autour du concept de *ready-made* et de celui de l'instantané de la transformation artistique que Duchamp avait qualifié d'« inscription », et qui s'est notamment manifesté dans la fausse signature de l'urinoir de 1917, pour lequel Duchamp avait indiqué un créateur du nom de « R. Mutt »[8]. Alors que l'univers de Warhol était essentiellement centré autour de Warhol, Duchamp opérait sur un plan hautement intellectuel, mais en même temps humoristico-frivole qui ne s'attardait pas sur la manifestation esthétique de l'art, mais qui prenait pour thème son statut ontologique, c'est-à-dire son existence en tant qu'art ou en tant que non art. C'est sans doute en Chine qu'Ai Weiwei a saisi toute la portée des idées lancées par Duchamp, en Chine où ne l'attendaient pas seulement des objets aussi idiosyncratiques que des urinoirs, des roues de bicyclettes ou des porte-bouteilles. Non, en Chine, il était accueilli par une culture aussi morcelée que monumentale, une culture prête à être adoptée comme matière première artistique sémantiquement indifférenciée. Sous les coups des puissances

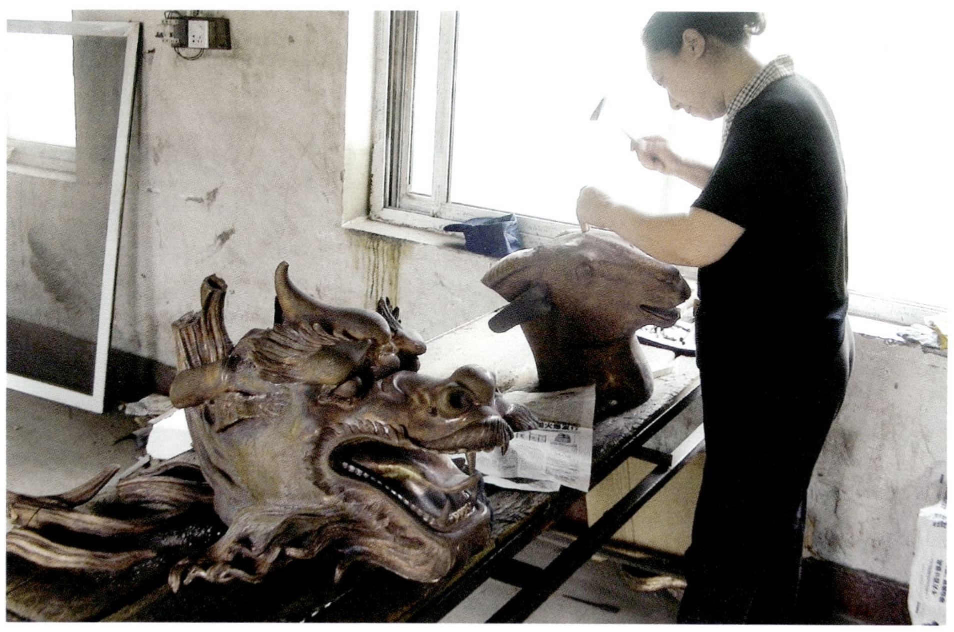

Making of *Circle of Animals*, 2012, bronze with gold plating, 12 pieces, various dimensions (see pp. 411–415)

coloniales européennes, de l'occupation japonaise, de la guerre civile, des expériences systémiques aussi grandioses que fatales de Mao, mais aussi de la stratification actuelle du capitalisme d'État dans l'Empire du Milieu, cette culture était en
voie de désagrégation. Duchamp montrait à Ai Weiwei comment travailler avec les
épaves d'une histoire liquidée.

Les réflexions duchampiennes sur l'inscription artistique d'objets du quotidien
sont un aspect. L'artiste brouille les limites entre art et non art pour se donner des
marges de manœuvre. En même temps s'impose l'évidence que la manifestation
purement esthétique – la visibilité d'une œuvre par exemple – s'avère totalement
insuffisante pour embrasser la véritable dimension conceptuelle[9]. L'autre aspect
est le sort concret des œuvres de Duchamp, qui ont existé indépendamment de
toutes les acrobaties cérébrales et qui, nonobstant toutes les résistances internes,
sont quand même entrées un jour au musée – n'est-ce pas ? Comme il sied à un
Duchamp, l'histoire se complique fortement à partir de ce tournant. Concrètement,
des œuvres aussi décisives que l'urinoir original avaient disparu. Duchamp lui-même
ne s'en aperçut que dans les années 1960, quand débuta la réception proprement
révolutionnaire de son œuvre et que l'on eut besoin des *ready-made* d'antan pour la
grande rétrospective de Pasadena. Facile de remplacer un urinoir ? Aucunement !
La production industrielle était depuis longtemps passée à autre chose parce que
les technologies bénéficient d'une fenêtre de tir plutôt restreinte. Et c'est ainsi que
les objets que Duchamp avait naguère délibérément choisis comme des produits

industriels dénués de toute aura durent être reproduits à la main comme de l'artisanat d'art[10]. Si son acte de 1917 avait permis à Duchamp de démontrer qu'un urinoir n'était pas identique à lui-même, et que présenté dans le cadre d'un salon d'art, pourvu d'une (fausse) signature, il pouvait prendre le statut ontologique d'œuvre d'art, indépendamment de cela, dans le cadre des préparatifs d'une rétrospective, il s'avéra qu'un *ready-made* n'était pas non plus identique à lui-même. Toutes ces tribulations sont documentées dans le *Black Cover Book* d'Ai Weiwei, clichés de l'installation originale de 1917 à l'appui, et avec les croquis pour la réplique de 1964 qu'Arturo Schwarz, le marchand de Duchamp, avait commandée.

XII : Pour le milieu new-yorkais des années 1980, qu'Ai Weiwei étudia soigneusement – il affirma avoir vu à l'époque à peu près toutes les expositions, et ses photos tendent à le prouver –, cette leçon et d'autres leçons de Duchamp furent extraordinairement marquantes. Elles semblaient indiquer à l'art des issues hors de la marchandisation ou de l'ajustement institutionnel, mais poussaient aussi la particularité artistique dans sa lutte contre le rouleau compresseur de la standardisation capitaliste. Ai Weiwei pour sa part en tira ses propres conclusions plutôt chinoises. Le marché ou la marchandisation ne lui ont jamais posé aucun problème : pour lui, le marché est un média social parmi d'autres. Comme adversaire, il y aurait plutôt le rouleau compresseur de la standardisation capitaliste, mais dans les conditions de la dictature du parti unique, Ai Weiwei se place ailleurs : dans la mobilisation anti-totalitaire, dont une œuvre sans forme comme *Fairytale* est un tout aussi bon exemple que l'enquête sur le séisme du Sichuan, qui va l'occuper à de multiples niveaux à partir de 2008. Les conséquences qu'Ai Weiwei tire pour lui-même de sa fréquentation de Duchamp vont dans le sens de la liberté dans le processus d'appropriation. Cela ne veut pas dire que tout peut devenir de l'art, mais que ce qui compte dans ce que l'on fait n'est absolument pas de savoir si c'est vraiment de l'art ou pas, et que c'est précisément dans cette indifférenciation des pratiques que résident des possibilités.

XIII : En 1993, quand Ai Weiwei revient en Chine à l'appel de son père malade, il arrive avec une boîte à outils conceptuelle bien dotée. Ce qu'elle recelait de questionnements et de possibilités s'annonce dès les premières œuvres mûres : pour *Han Dynasty Urn with Coca-Cola Logo* (1994), Ai Weiwei a peint les mots « Coca-Cola » sur une urne d'environ 2000 ans[11]. L'urne ainsi défigurée se lit de prime abord comme un *memento mori* : un objet historique vieux de 2000 ans est non seulement défiguré par une écriture, mais aussi dévalorisé par une marque globale. À y regarder de plus près, il s'avère qu'Ai Weiwei suit presque accessoirement les correspondances, qui existent indépendamment de cette œuvre, entre l'écriture administrative de 1936 et les peintures traditionnelles de l'ère Han. Et son logo peint n'est pas intrusif : tandis que le rouge est d'un effet réservé, presque terreux, les pleins et déliés de la graphie s'harmonisent avec le corps pansu de l'urne.

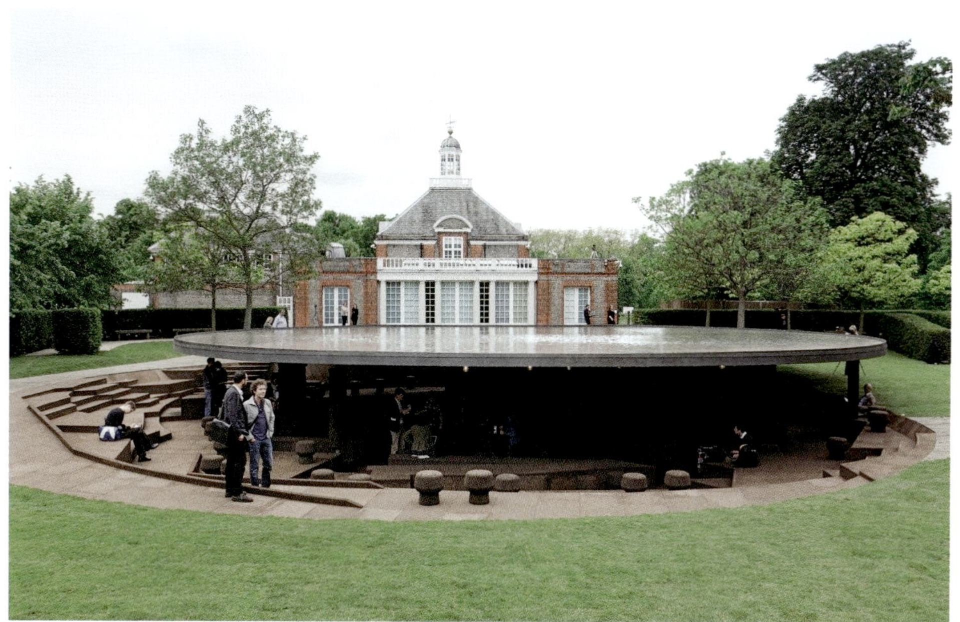

Serpentine Gallery Pavilion, London 2012 (collaboration with Herzog & de Meuron)

Quelqu'un dont la pensée embrasse de longues périodes temporelles, comme c'est le cas d'Ai Weiwei, se rappelle la faculté d'adaptation particulière de la culture chinoise, qui après l'invasion mongole, s'appropria du jour au lendemain une culture étrangère sous la dynastie Yuan (1279–1368) – pour rester elle-même. En poussant l'idée un peu plus loin, il n'est pas exclu que dans 2000 ans à dater d'aujourd'hui, Coca-Cola sera considéré comme une marque chinoise. C'est un aspect de la « liberté dans le processus d'appropriation » évoquée plus haut (voilà quelque chose que tout entrepreneur occidental travaillant en Chine comprend sans avoir besoin de Duchamp).

La légendaire performance *Dropping a Han Dynasty Urn* (1995, pp. 85–87) nous montre Ai Weiwei sous l'habit sobre d'un paysan, debout devant un haut mur. Entre ses mains aux doigts ostensiblement écartés, il tient une urne – à nouveau une pièce antique – qu'il est sur le point de laisser tomber. Cette performance a été fixée dans trois photos prises en quelques fractions de seconde. On voit Ai Weiwei tenir l'urne, puis l'urne tomber, et pour finir, les tessons jonchant le sol aux pieds de l'artiste. L'acte est choquant, pas seulement pour le muséophile occidental. Cela a quelque chose à voir avec l'urne antique et sa valeur idéale, mais plus encore avec l'expression indifférente de l'artiste, qui aborde frontalement le spectateur. La chute de l'objet n'est pas une action chargée d'affect, mais un acte de barbarie froidement calculé qui plonge le spectateur dans un dilemme éthico-esthétique en tant que témoin impuissant.

Overleaf: BABY FORMULA, 2013, 1,815 full cans of milk powder, dimensions variable; Sheung Wan Civic Centre, Hong Kong 2013 | 231

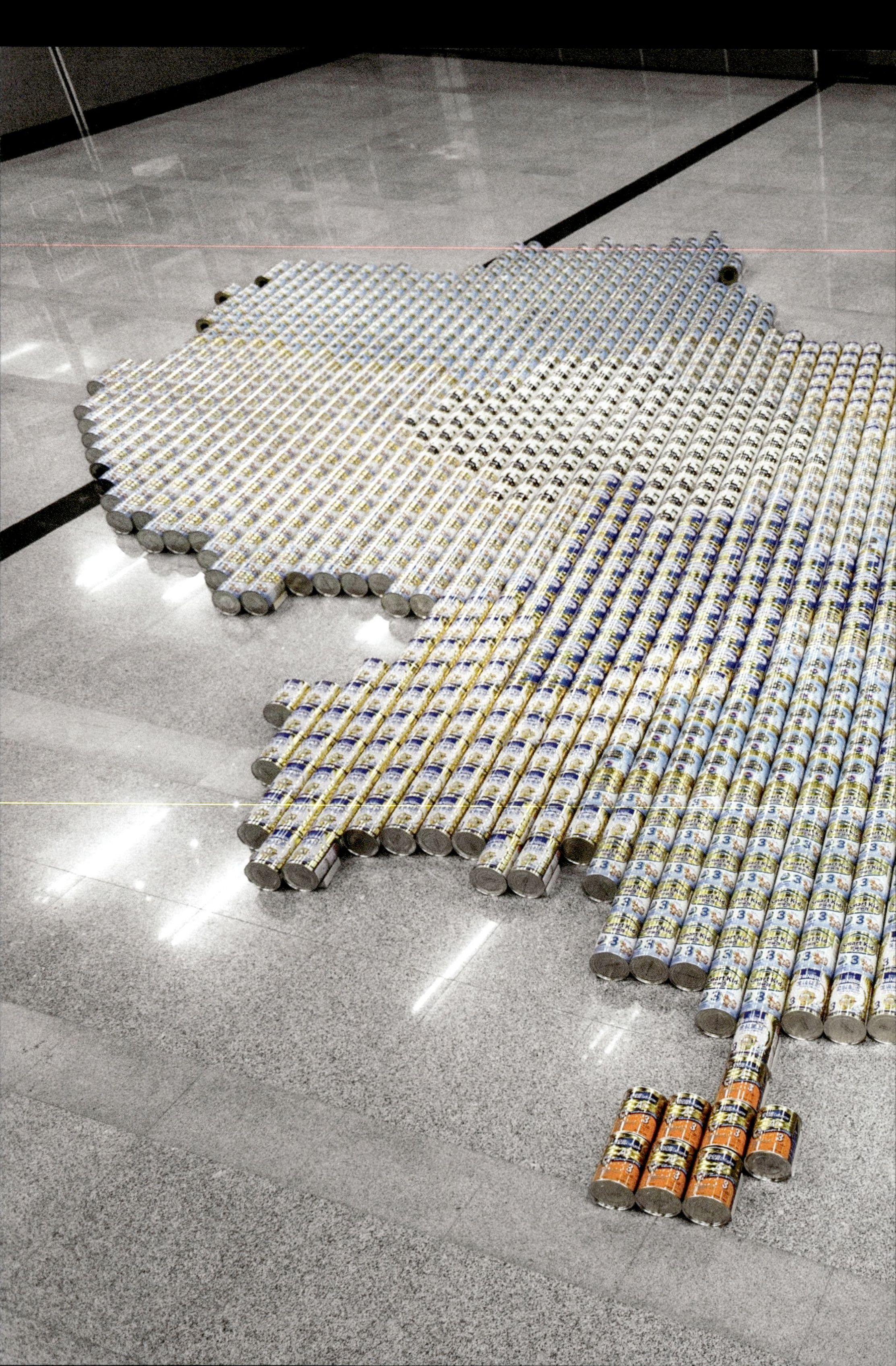

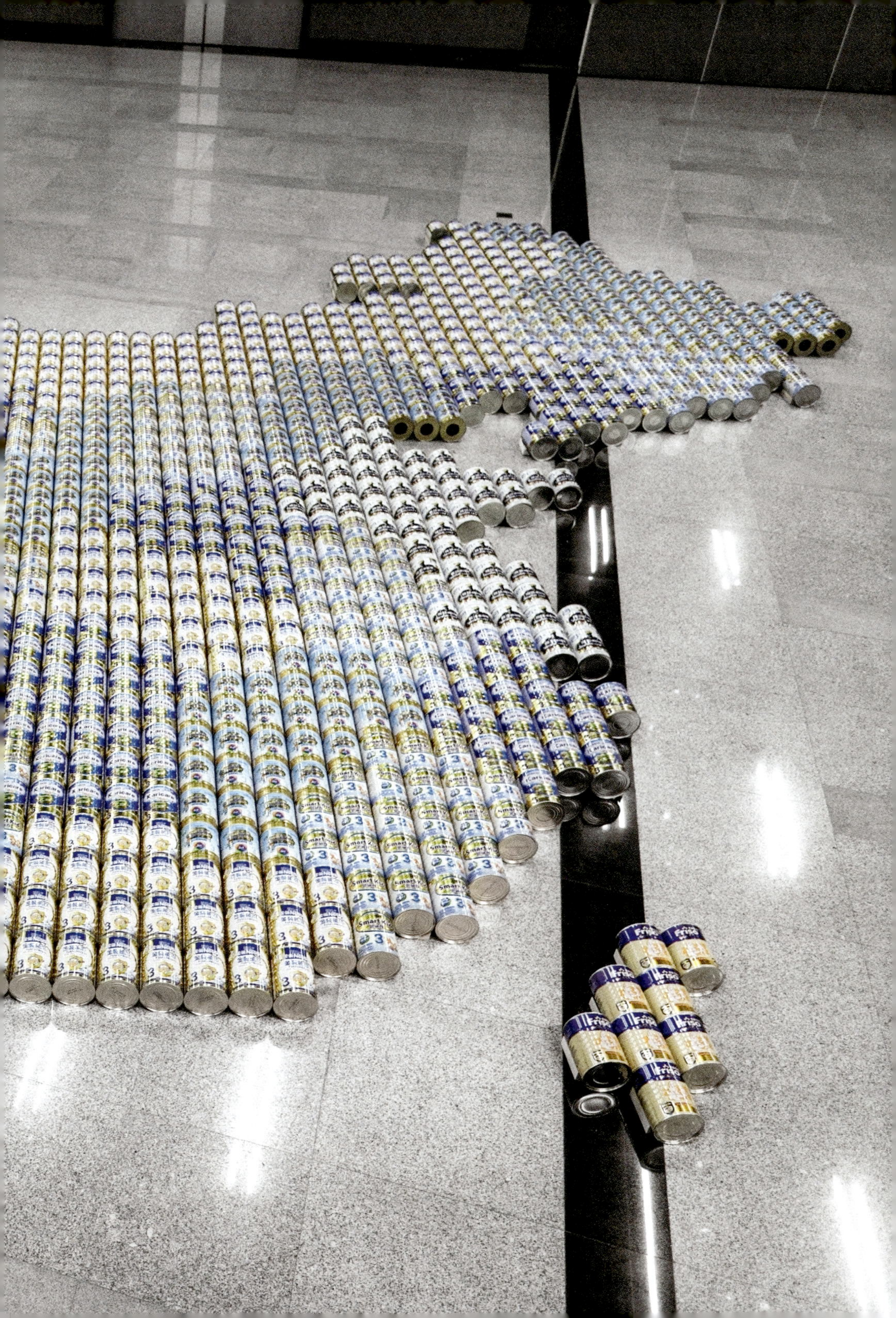

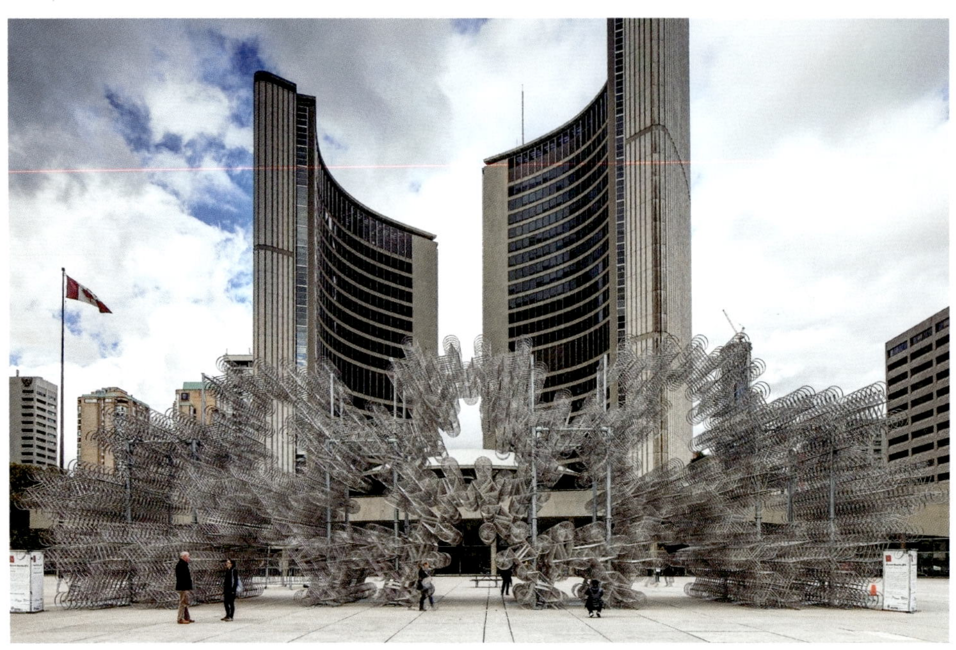

Forever Bicycles, 2013, 3,144 Forever bicycles, 319 x 1,240 x 375 inches; Nathan Phillips Square, Toronto 2013

Comme le vase Han prétendument défiguré, *Dropping* est ouvert à une lecture simple : « Regardez, on détruit l'héritage historique de la Chine. » Fait significatif, Ai Weiwei se glisse lui-même dans le rôle du sbire rustique qui se venge sur la tradition. Et de fait, dans cette performance, il est sans doute surtout question de sonder cette strate enfouie qui relie les Chinois d'après la révolution culturelle – Ai Weiwei compris – à l'héritage chinois. Au lieu d'émettre une déclaration, la performance soulève plutôt la question : « Peut-on encore percevoir ici une souffrance (au regard de la destruction) ? » Bref, ce n'est pas tant une urne qui se brise qu'une relation dont Ai Weiwei s'affirme délibérément comme partenaire, c'est-à-dire : se représente lui-même comme homme meurtri – un moment exceptionnel dans l'art chinois contemporain. Mais il ne se contente pas de subir cette meurtrissure, il la met activement en scène. L'on peut supposer que c'est précisément dans cette souveraine reconnaissance de sa propre meurtrissure que réside le germe de l'authentique solidarité qui permet à Ai Weiwei de jeter ses ponts activistes.

XIV : Dans *Hands* et *Feet* (pp. 187, 191, tous 2003), cette solidarité s'étend aux formes humaines meurtries, en fait aux mains et aux pieds brisés de statues de Bouddha de la dynastie Qi (550–577), auxquels Ai Weiwei donne un emplacement sur deux grandes tables en bois. L'aspect fragmentaire de ces pièces en pierre (au total, douze mains et dix pieds) souligne le caractère presque vivant des volumes corporels ou des lignes des mains, témoins de l'apogée du bouddhisme dans le nord de la Chine. Mais elles témoignent aussi de la violence qui s'abattra bientôt sur la puissance et la richesse des monastères. Dans son dispositif, Ai Weiwei ne traite pas les vestiges de pierre comme un matériau historique, mais à la Rodin comme des pièces autonomes. Chaque pied, chaque main, repose sur son propre socle en bois et démontre ainsi sa forme singulière, qui se doit toutefois toujours au même acte de violence.

Dans *Rebar* (2012, p. 477), trois fers à béton tordus de manière presque calligraphique, normalement utilisés pour renforcer le béton armé, on ne trouve sans doute pas de traces anthropomorphes, mais il y est une fois de plus question d'hommes meurtris. Ai Weiwei a récupéré ces fers déformés dans les ruines de bâtiments scolaires irrémédiablement détruits lors du séisme du Sichuan (2008). Comme il s'avéra par la suite, les autorités et les entreprises de construction s'étaient entendues pour construire à bas prix et empocher les économies ainsi réalisées. Ai Weiwei a participé à la recherche civile sur le séisme et les écoliers tués, mais a aussi récupéré ces barres de fer qui cette fois-ci ne sont pas des reliques antiques.

Pour exposer ces fers, il en fit réaliser deux copies. Injecter l'original dans le circuit artistique sous forme d'art engagé serait bête. Ne pas les exposer serait une lâcheté. Leur triple existence recèle une authenticité, mais cette authenticité affichée est réabsorbée par l'accumulation. Il serait plus juste encore de dire que l'on assiste à un déplacement de l'authenticité. Le propos d'Ai Weiwei n'est pas qu'un morceau de fer témoigne de la catastrophe, mais que le spectateur se relie à l'événement. L'entrée dans un tel rapport de perception a évidemment son prix, qui réside dans la mise en évidence du fossé infranchissable qui bée entre le fer du Sichuan et les deux autres pièces, ou entre le non art et l'art.

XV : L'expérience choquante de *Rebar* est due en fait à la compréhension d'une vérité très simple : voici un cruel morceau de réalité, un fer à béton tordu qui n'a rien de commun avec un bout de fer identique – hormis précisément sa forme, qui toutefois ne dit rien en tant que telle. Cette vérité ne remet pas en cause la perception du spectateur, mais l'oblige à activer son imagination, car ce dont il s'agit ici ne peut être appréhendé sur un mode esthétique. Dans le processus de la contemplation apparaît donc un rapport au monde dans lequel la catastrophe du Sichuan ne reste pas un événement purement extérieur entraînant la commisération ou l'indignation. La catastrophe prend davantage une dimension qui relève de l'âme, elle est poussée vers une perspective intérieure et suscite la question « Qu'est-ce que cela fait avec moi ? », plutôt que la question « Qu'est-ce que cela a à voir avec moi ? ». En chinois, cette mobilisation des ressources de l'âme s'appelle « nourrir la vie ». Mais tout homme sait sans doute ce que cela veut dire[12]. De fait, personne n'avait besoin d'expliquer au touriste amateur de catastrophes de Cassel ce que la sculpture effondrée *Template* avait à voir avec lui (s'il ne l'avait pas su, il n'aurait

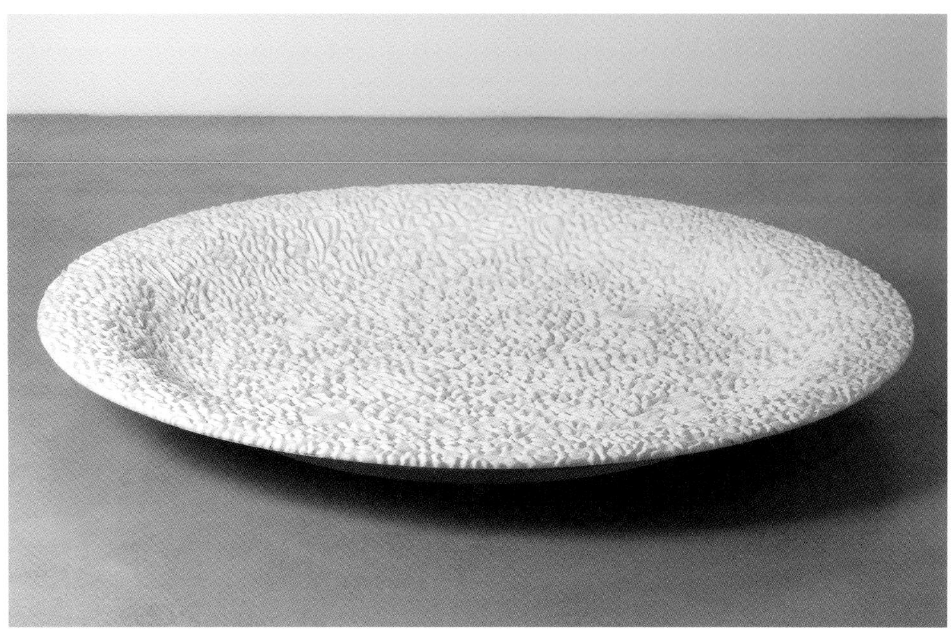

Plate, 2010, marble, 3 ⅛ x ø 39 ⅜ inches

sûrement pas décidé de venir la voir). Il est vrai que *Template* avait fait un bout du chemin vers le spectateur dans la mesure où la sculpture déformée avait pratiquement enjambé à elle seule le fossé perceptif et ne requérait en définitive aucune préparation esthétique de la part du spectateur. Dans le cas de *Rebars*, l'enjambement se produisait de manière plus subtile, en l'occurrence sur le dos du canon formel moderniste, et demandait un effort d'abstraction. Indépendamment de la forme respective ou du sort de cette œuvre et des œuvres à venir, on voit toutefois clairement à quelle instance s'adresse la conception artistique d'Ai Weiwei. Il s'agit du moi du spectateur, et sa capacité d'interprétation émotionnelle.

Ce moi n'est visé nulle part de manière plus claire que dans l'œuvre réalisée secrètement sur plusieurs années à travers laquelle Ai Weiwei travaille sur son expérience traumatique de la prison au printemps 2011. *S.A.C.R.E.D.* (2011–2013, pp. 218, 221, 223, 481–483) est composé de six caissons en fer sombre arrivant à peu près à hauteur d'épaule, et dont le pourtour mesure un peu moins de 2 x 4 mètres. Chaque caisson abrite un diorama à l'échelle 1/2 modelé en fibre de verre et montrant Ai Weiwei dans des situations clés de ses 81 jours de détention. Le titre de l'œuvre est un acronyme ; S. renvoie à *Supper* (dîner), A. à *Accusers* (accusateurs), C. à *Cleansing* (laver), R. à *Ritual* (rituel, ici, la défécation), E. à *Entropy* (ici, le sommeil), et D. à *Doubt* (doute). Le champ de ces dénominations, ou ce que l'on en comprend dans un premier temps, va de la désignation d'activités courantes à la caractérisation d'états d'âme, comme avec *Entropy* le sentiment de dissolution de la personnalité qui dut s'immiscer en Ai Weiwei quand il lui fallut dormir sous constante surveillance, dans un espace plus que réduit, sous une ampoule allumée en permanence et avec une couverture aussi sommaire que possible. Le titre de l'œuvre enfin – *sacred* – n'a rien à voir avec le « sacré » au sens chrétien, mais remonte à l'antique signification de l'*homo sacer*, l'homme privé de droits, l'exclu de la société. Cet *homo sacer* est la propriété des dieux, mais au sens funeste d'une perte de toute forme de protection. Parce qu'il a rompu le pacte avec les dieux, il peut être impunément tué par le premier venu, et ce meurtre n'est pas considéré comme un crime humain, mais comme une vengeance des dieux[13].

À l'été 2013, lors de leur première installation dans la nef principale de la Église Sant' Antonin à Venise, ces sinistres blocs évoquaient de loin des catafalques – dans un *white cube*, on aurait pu les associer à des sculptures dans la plus pure tradition minimaliste. Contrairement aux catafalques ou aux surfaces minimalistes, la forme monumentale d'Ai Weiwei attirait toutefois le spectateur avec des éléments narratifs. Sur le mur de chaque caisson était reproduite une porte close à l'échelle 1/2, tandis qu'une caisse invitait le spectateur à monter dessus pour procéder à une inspection approfondie de la forme. Et de fait, une lucarne permettait de regarder à l'intérieur des dioramas en vue plongeante. De telles lucarnes étaient aussi aménagées sur les parois latérales. Comme pour *Étant donnés* (1946–1966), œuvre de Duchamp également réalisée en secret où le spectateur doit regarder à travers le trou laissé dans le bois par un nœud, le spectateur ne devient pas seulement le témoin d'un spectacle obscène, il est volontairement placé en position de voyeur. Autrement dit, le spectateur prend conscience de sa position de spectateur. Alors que le diorama de Duchamp, avec son corps de femme nue tenant une lampe qui éclaire la scène irréelle, conserve une certaine part de mystère, *S.A.C.R.E.D.* ne connaît aucune ambiguïté, bien au contraire. Éclairés par une ampoule à incandescence, l'intérieur des cellules, Ai Weiwei, ses deux gardes en uniforme, ses interrogateurs, mais aussi le mobilier succinct, sont traités avec un réalisme dont la fidélité dans les moindres détails produit une impression presque hallucinatoire.

La tradition didactique, entièrement étrangère à l'art, du diorama, veut que soit visualisée une réalité qui n'a aucun rapport avec le présent du spectateur. Dans les musées d'ethnographie, on trouve ainsi des dioramas censés montrer la manière dont vivaient les hommes préhistoriques. Il en va autrement dans le cas de *S.A.C.R.E.D.* D'un côté, le spectateur qui regarde par la lucarne est renvoyé à lui-même. Sa propre position de spectateur associée au caisson hermétiquement clos et la miniaturisation de l'événement instaurent une distance infranchissable. D'un autre côté, ce qui se déroule dans la cellule ne semble que trop familier. On connaît l'ordinateur portable sur lequel le policier consigne l'interrogatoire, de même que les menottes avec lesquelles Ai Weiwei est attaché à sa chaise pendant son interrogatoire. On connaît le linge soigneusement plié dans l'armoire, les bols en plastique avec des boulettes chinoises, le jet d'eau de la douche et les bouteilles

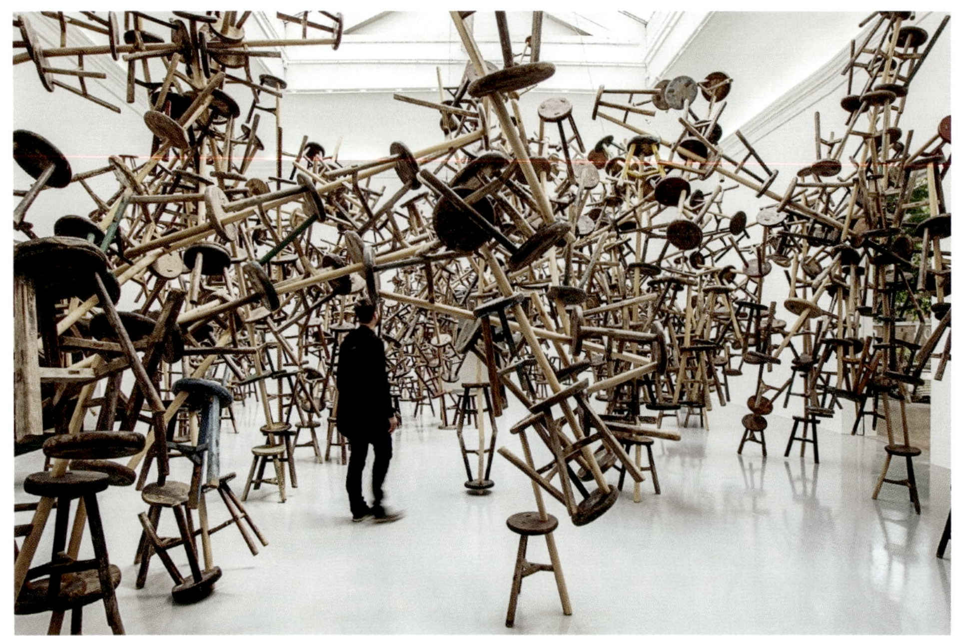

Bang, 2013, 886 stools, dimensions variable; German contribution in the French Pavilion, 55th Venice Biennale, Venice 2013

de shampoing bariolées. Chacun sait ce que c'est qu'être assis aux toilettes. Mais on connaît surtout – ou on croit connaître – Ai Weiwei lui-même. Cela dit, le moi de l'artiste n'est pas un moi authentique. Il ne s'agit pas ici de narcissisme sacrificiel, mais comme chez Warhol, de l'image de l'artiste en tant que véhicule d'identification décisif pour le spectateur.

Dans notre texte, il a déjà été question du rôle de médiateur d'Ai Weiwei et de sa doctrine poétique d'enjambement des distances de perception. Dans le cas de *S.A.C.R.E.D.*, l'on rencontre l'artiste aussi bien que sa doctrine sous une forme si brute qu'elle en est presque insupportable. Cela expliquant que les spectateurs superficiels se réfugient dans l'affirmation selon laquelle l'artiste exploite son sort de dissident pour diffuser son œuvre[14]. « Pourquoi pas ? », pourrait-on leur répondre. Quand un homme voit son destin personnel transformé en *ready-made* par un système totalitaire, pourquoi devrait-il s'interdire de recréer et se défaire de ce destin sous forme de maquette ? Surtout quand on sait que dans des conditions dictatoriales, ce destin soi-disant personnel est tout aussi impersonnel que l'intérieur d'une cellule dans *S.A.C.R.E.D.* Potentiellement, tout Chinois peut disparaître derrière la porte 1135 et devenir *homo sacer*. Tout le monde le sait, même les concitoyens d'Ai Weiwei qui, après avoir appris l'accusation de fraude fiscale, lui ont fait parvenir des billets de banque sous forme d'avions en papier envoyés par dessus les hauts murs de sa maison à Caochangdi. Dans l'esprit même de l'artiste, ils développaient ainsi leur propre forme créatrice et solidaire d'enjambement des distances de perception. Dans ce type d'actions qui dessinent la dynamique d'une société civile avec son interaction entre initiative individuelle et esprit collectif, le médiateur disparaît et avec lui la séparation entre art et non art. En d'autres termes : dans un monde ainsi fait, Ai Weiwei n'aurait plus à tenir le rôle du médiateur, car celui-ci pourrait être adopté par une multitude de gens. Alors seulement, la liberté artistique d'Ai Weiwei pourrait commencer au sens propre en incluant celle de ne rien faire.

1 Le rôle des correspondances en tant qu'un des fondements de la culture chinoise est abordé par Léon Vandermeersch dans *Les deux raisons de la pensée chinoise. Divination et idéographie*, Gallimard, Paris, 2013. 2 Voir à ce sujet Lothar Ledderose : *Ten Thousand Things: Module and Mass Production in Chinese Art*, The A. W. Mellon Lectures in the Fine Arts, Princeton University Press, Princeton, 1998. 3 La formule est de Philip Tinari, qui l'emploie dans son essai « Chairs and Visitors », in *Ai Weiwei, Works 2004–2007*, Urs Meile (dir.), JRP Ringier, Zurich, 2008, p. 12. 4 Pour une description détaillée des bizarreries de *Fairytale*, voir mon essai « Meeting Alterity », in *Ai Weiwei: Fairytale, A Reader*, Lionel Bovier et Salomé Schnetz (dir.), JRP Ringier, Zurich ; Einfache Gesellschaft Fairytale, Lucerne, 2012, pp. 31–42. 5 Dans ces trois anthologies, on relève l'absence notoire de deux artistes qui n'avaient pas seulement une influence décisive à l'époque, mais dont le travail était directement lié aux méthodes d'Ai Weiwei. Il s'agit d'une part de Sherrie Levine : avec ses reproductions de photographies de Walker Evans (*After Walker Evans*, 1981), elle inaugurait un concept de « copie » qui sapait le statut de l'original. D'autre part Allan McCollum, dont Ai Weiwei photographia les installations pour ses propres archives. À l'époque, McCollum s'intéressait au thème du rapport entre identité et différence, qu'il développait dans d'immenses présentoirs d'objets apparemment identiques, mais qui ne l'étaient pas. 6 Andy Warhol : *Ma philosophie de A à B et vice versa*, Flammarion, Paris, 2007, pp. 89–90. 7 L'exposition *Die Kunst der Aufklärung* était une collaboration de trois grands musées allemands (Berlin, Dresde, Munich) au Musée national de Chine, qui entendait favoriser les échanges culturels au niveau de l'État. Ironiquement, Ai Weiwei fut arrêté au moment même où le cortège officiel repartait en Allemagne. 8 En guise d'introduction aux complexités duchampiennes, nous recommandons la lecture de David Joselit : *Infinite Regress: Marcel Duchamp 1910–1941*, MIT Press, Cambridge, Mass., 1998. 9 Dans *Anywhere or Not at All: Philosophy of Contemporary Art*, Verso, Londres ; New York, 2013, le philosophe anglais Peter Osborne définit l'insuffisance totale des critères esthétiques pour le jugement artistique comme une des caractéristiques principales de l'art postconceptuel, qui a tiré les leçons de l'échec productif du conceptualisme. 10 L'histoire de la réédition du *ready-made* est décrite par Helen Molesworth dans « Duchamp: By Hand, Even », sa contribution au catalogue de l'exposition *Part Object, Part Sculpture* dont elle fut la commissaire, Wexner Center for the Arts, Columbus, Ohio, 2005, pp. 156–165. 11 À l'époque, Ai Weiwei ne prétendait pas faire de l'art : l'urne au logo Coca-Cola fut réalisée incidemment. Je remercie Uli Sigg pour cette indication. 12 Voir François Jullien : *Nourrir sa vie*, Seuil, Paris, 2005. 13 Dans *Homo Sacer : le pouvoir souverain et la vie nue*, Seuil, Paris, 1998, le philosophe italien Giorgio Agamben reconstitue l'état d'exposition totale qu'il caractérise aussi comme « vie nue », en tant qu'effet de la technique de gouvernement moderne. Bien que la place manque ici pour nous pencher sur cette idée, notons tout de même que la situation d'Ai Weiwei dans sa cellule, plus précisément son état de totale privation de droits, n'est pas un sujet purement chinois. L'Occident démocratique cultive lui aussi ce genre de non-espaces légaux, par exemple à Guantánamo. 14 Par exemple Franceso Bonami, qui fait à Ai Weiwei le procès d'intention de vouloir exploiter sa « fausse » situation de dissident pour faire monter sa valeur marchande, alors que les « vrais » dissidents seraient liquidés par le régime. Cf. galleristny.com/2013/06/francesco-bonami-i-hate-ai-weiwei/.

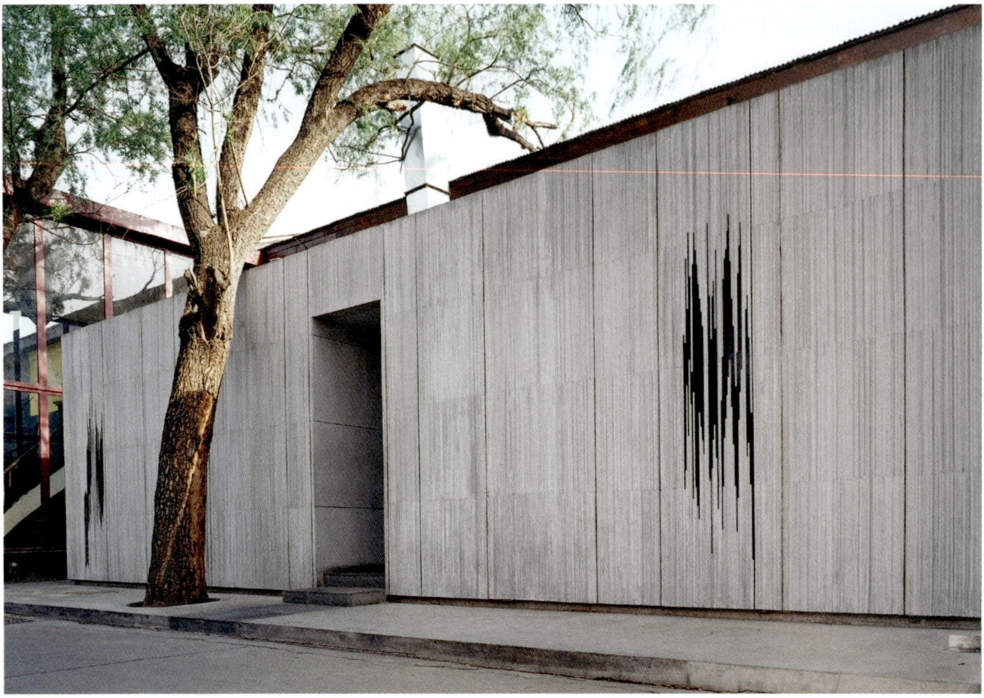

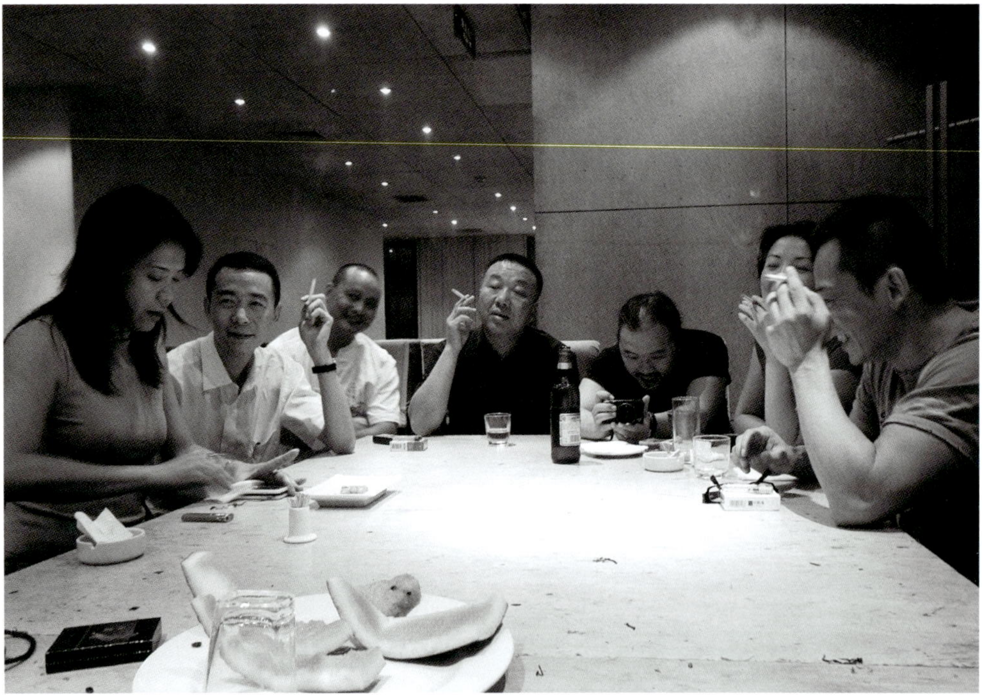

240 | GO WHERE? RESTAURANT, Beijing 2004, facade and interior view

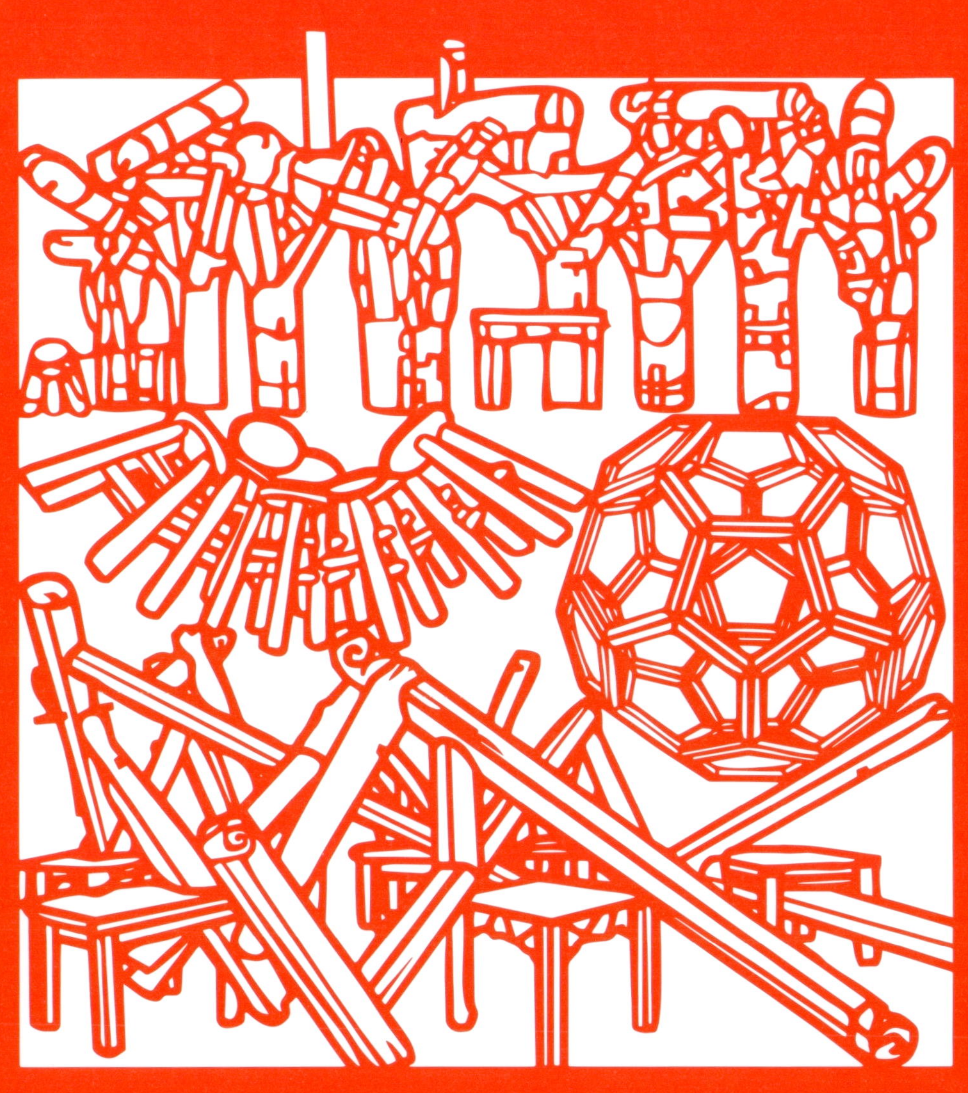

2005–2007

"When I found a location in Caochangdi in 1999 after a long search for a place to build my studio, I couldn't imagine there would be others moving here, or that it would later become one of the most lively and culturally oriented areas for contemporary activities. Around 2004 or 2005 people started coming and I had clients asking me to build the same type of studio space for different artists and cultural facilities. So this whole thing was like a silent, culturally quite loose start that I was part of. And I quickly designed a total of at least 20 houses in red brick. The best thing about Caochangdi is that the newcomers live among the original villagers, there's not much segregation here. The villagers are profiting from people renting and using the space. We have to coexist." — AI WEIWEI

Als ich nach langer Suche 1999 den Ort für mein Studio in Caochangdi fand, konnte ich mir nicht vorstellen, dass andere auch dorthin ziehen würden und dass dort im Lauf der Jahre einer der lebendigsten Bezirke für zeitgenössische Kultur entstehen würde. Um 2004 oder 2005 fingen die Leute an herzuziehen, und Bauherren traten an mich heran, damit ich für sie dieselbe Art Atelierraum für andere Künstler und Kultureinrichtungen baute. So wurde ich Teil dieser anfangs ganz leisen und kulturell eher unbestimmten Entwicklung. Rasch entwarf ich mindestens 20 Häuser aus roten Ziegeln. Das Beste an Caochangdi ist, dass Neuankömmlinge unter den ursprünglichen Dorfbewohnern leben. Es gibt hier nicht viel Abgrenzung. Die Dorfbewohner profitieren davon, dass Leute kommen und den vorhandenen Raum mieten und nutzen. Wir müssen alle miteinander leben.

Lorsque j'ai fini par trouver un endroit à Caochangdi pour construire mon studio, en 1999, je n'imaginais pas que d'autres gens viendraient s'y installer aussi ni que le quartier deviendrait l'un des plus vivants et des plus riches en activités culturelles. Les gens se sont mis à arriver en 2004 ou 2005, et des clients m'ont demandé de construire le même type de studio pour différents artistes et pour des installations culturelles. Tout ça a donc été comme le point de départ silencieux de quelque chose dont je faisais partie. Très rapidement, j'ai conçu au moins une vingtaine de maisons en brique rouge. Ce qui est formidable, à Caochangdi, c'est que les nouveaux arrivants se mélangent aux villageois, il n'y a guère de ségrégation ici. Les villageois profitent des loyers que paient les gens et l'espace est utilisé. Nous devons tous vivre ensemble.

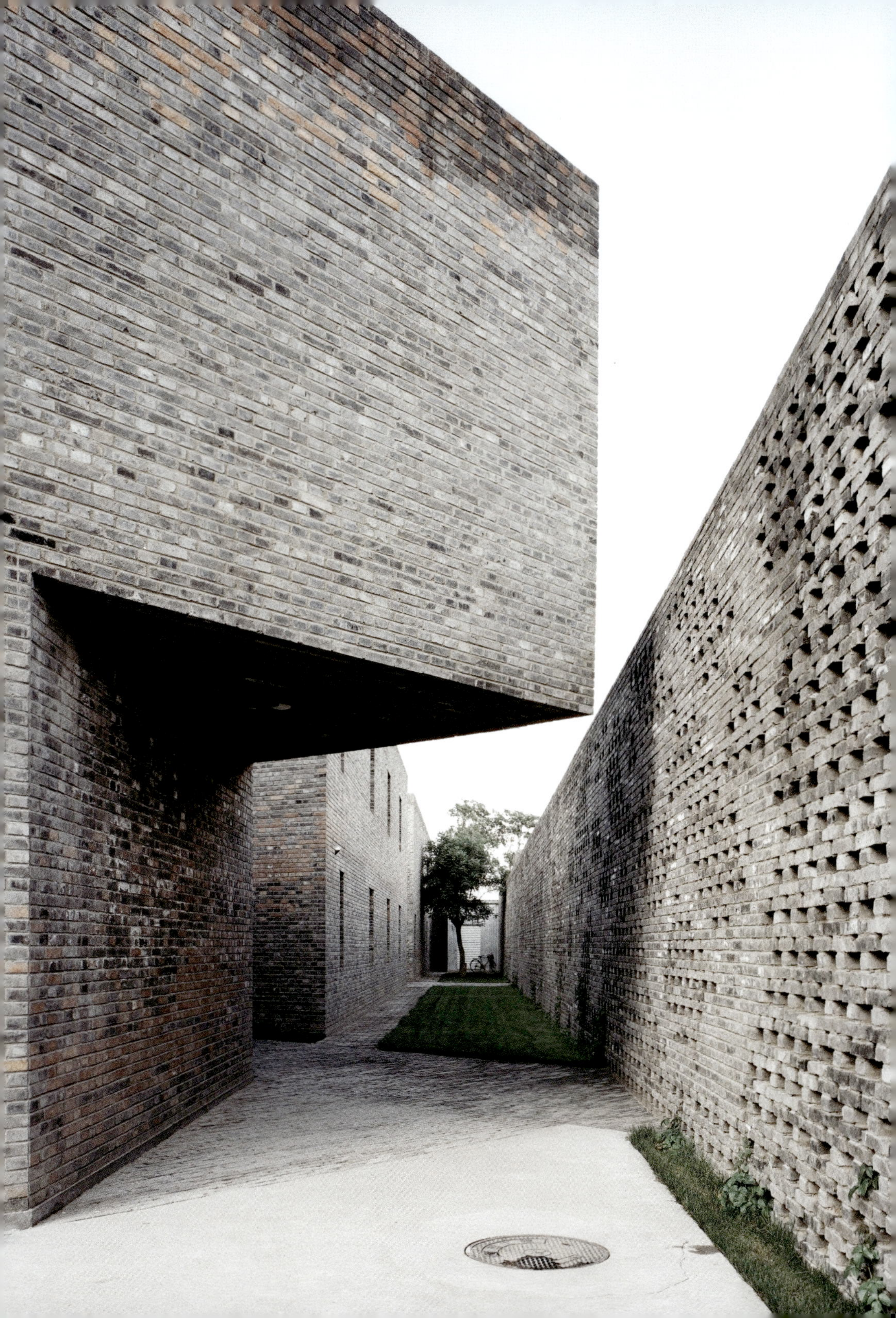

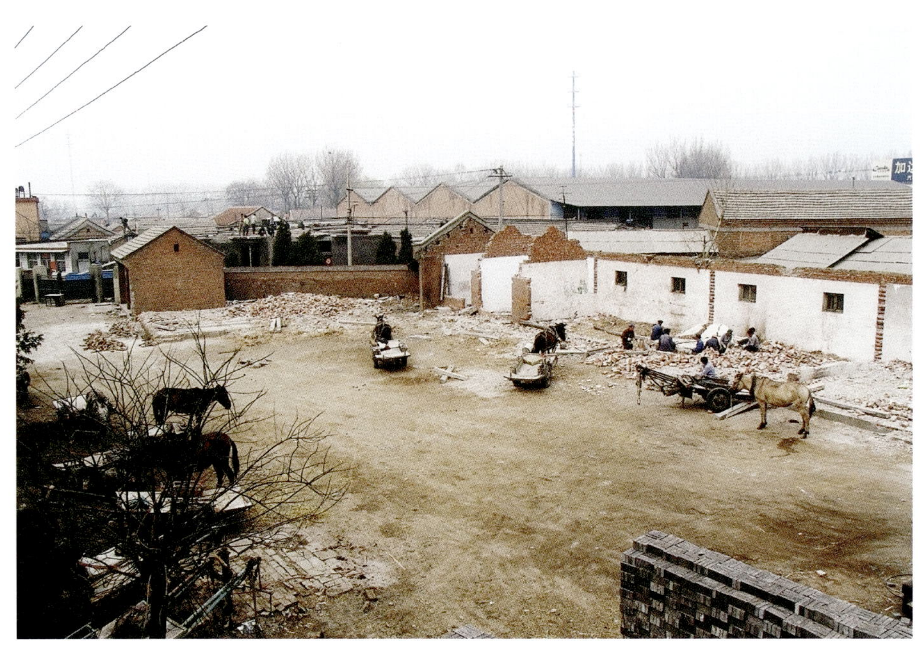

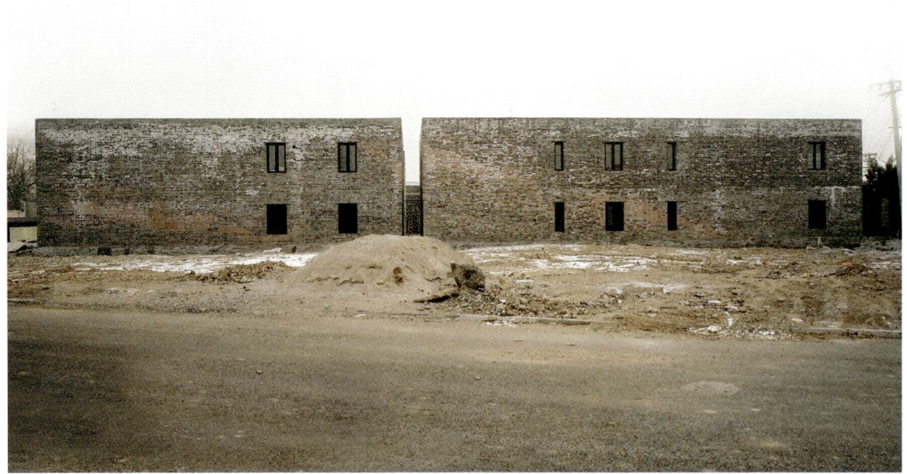

Site of *Courtyard 105* before and during construction

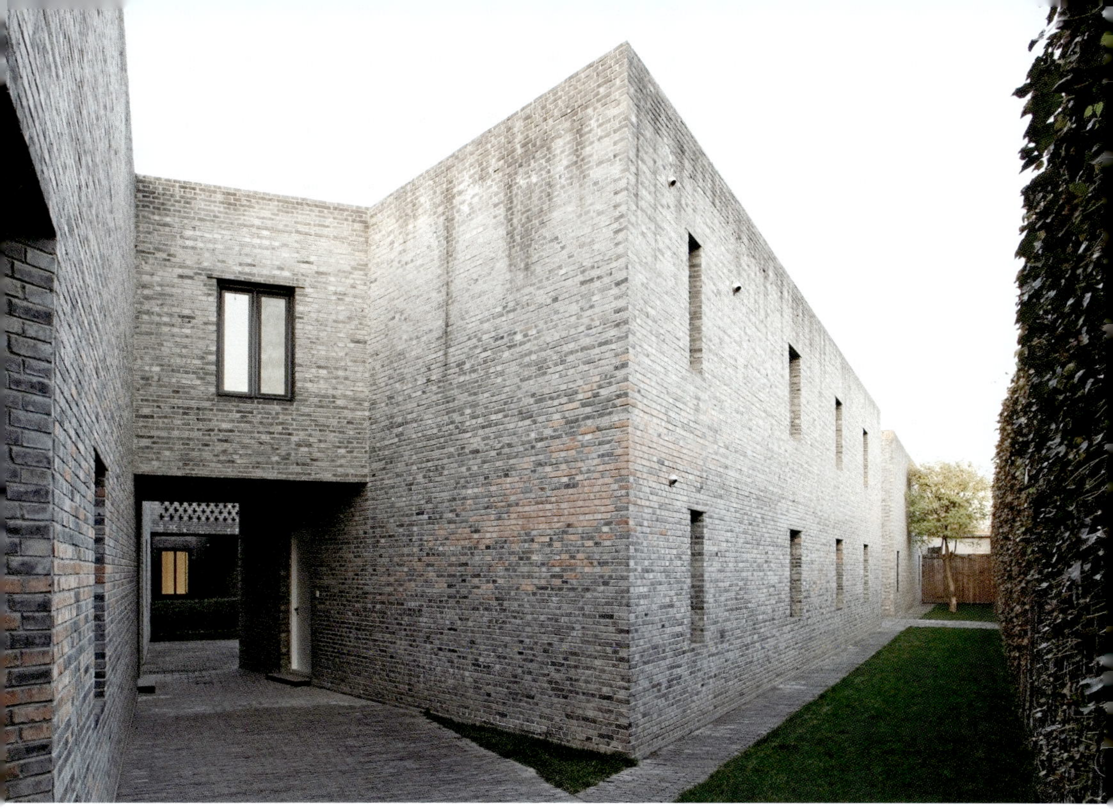

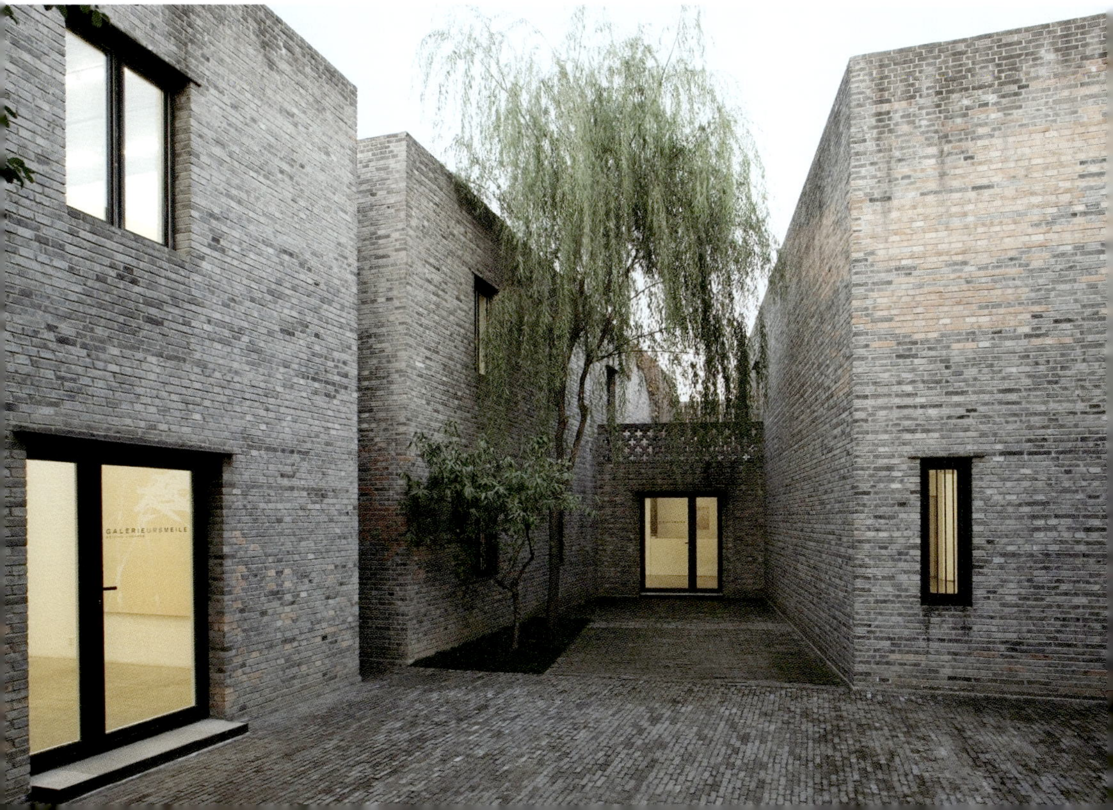

GALERIE URSMEILE

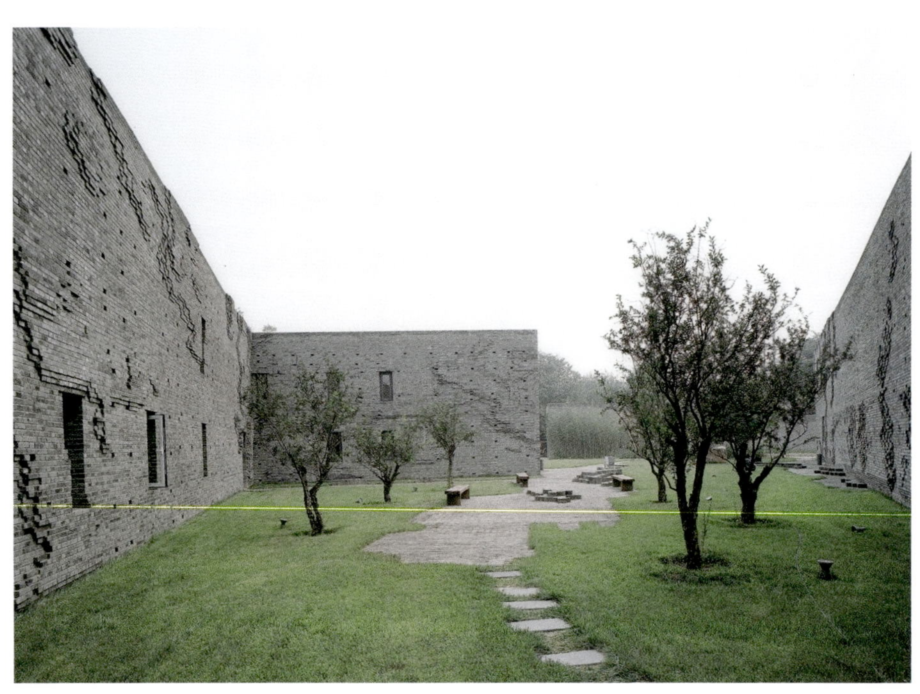

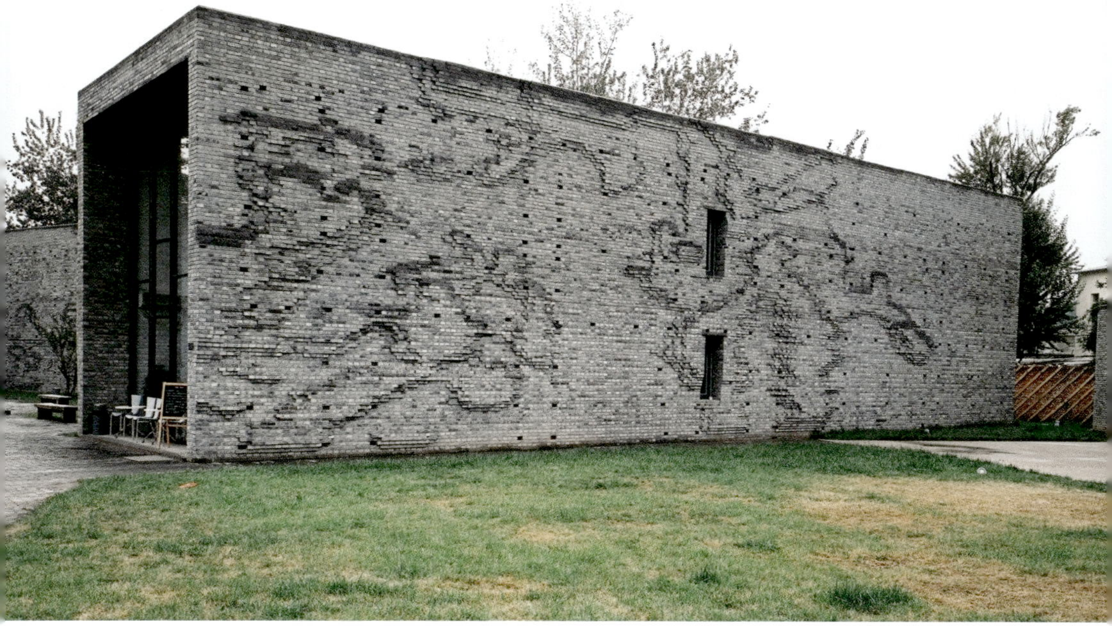

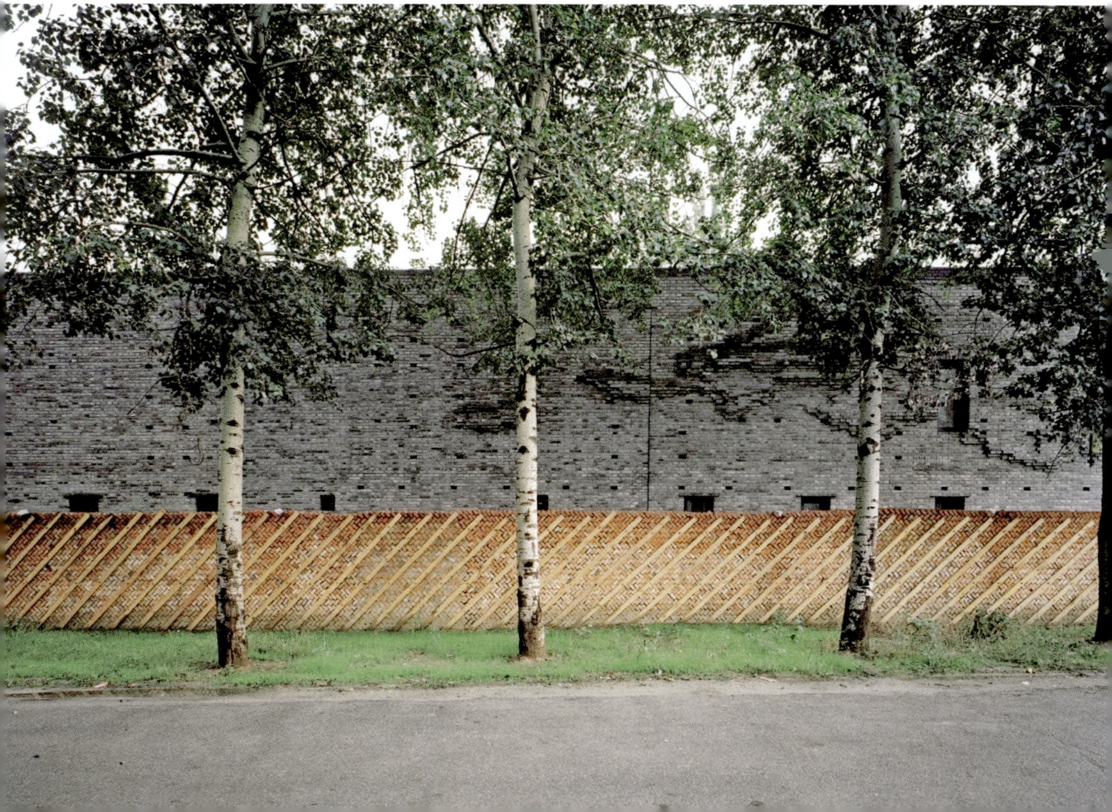

"The fragments I used in my installation are from three or four different temples, so everything is misfit and connected wrongly. Each piece is joined differently, each is a different size, and each has a different angle. None of them have any rational need to be connected to one another, but at the same time, each one is precisely joined to the next to resemble a map of China. It requires craftsmanship to shape them so expertly." — AI WEIWEI

Die Holzstücke, die ich für diese Installation verwendet habe, stammen von drei oder vier verschiedenen Tempeln. Daher passt nichts zusammen, und alle Stücke sind jeweils unterschiedlich aneinandergesetzt, jedes besitzt ein anderes Format, steht in einem anderen Winkel. Es gibt keinen erfindlichen Grund, der sie miteinander verknüpft, zugleich jedoch sind sie präzise so verfugt, dass sie einer Landkarte von China ähneln. Es war viel handwerkliches Geschick vonnöten, um sie derart kunstvoll zu formen.

Les fragments que j'ai utilisés dans cette installation viennent de trois ou quatre temples différents, donc rien n'est assemblé correctement. Chacune de ces pièces est assemblée différemment, chacune a une taille différente, chacune un angle différent. Aucune d'entre elles n'a un besoin rationnel d'être reliée à une autre, mais en même temps, chacune d'entre elles est assemblée précisément à sa voisine et l'ensemble forme une carte de la Chine, il s'agit là du résultat du travail expert des artisans.

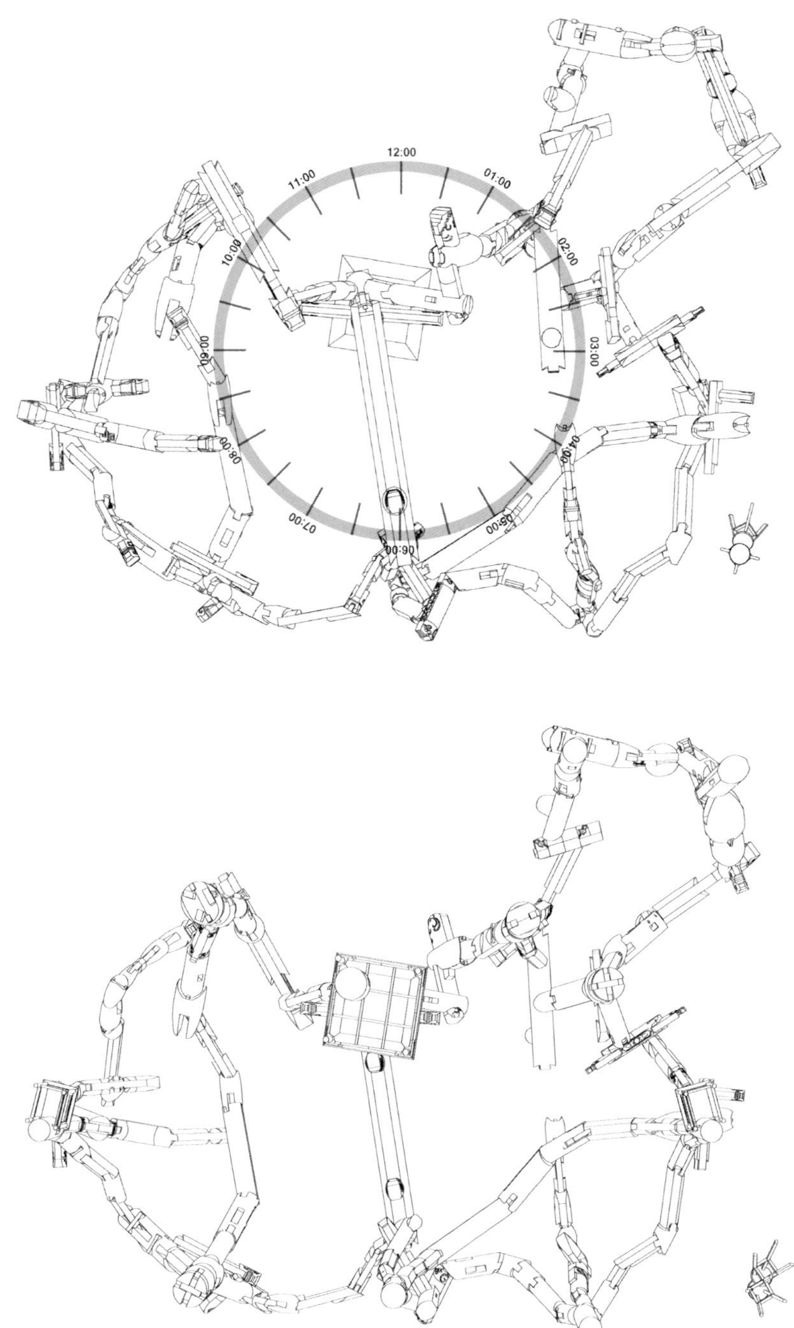

FRAGMENTS, 2005, table, chairs, parts of beams and pillars from dismantled Qing Dynasty temples, 196 ⅞ x 334 ⅝ x 275 ⅝ inches, plan drawings (above); Galerie Urs Meile, Beijing 2006 (overleaf) | 249

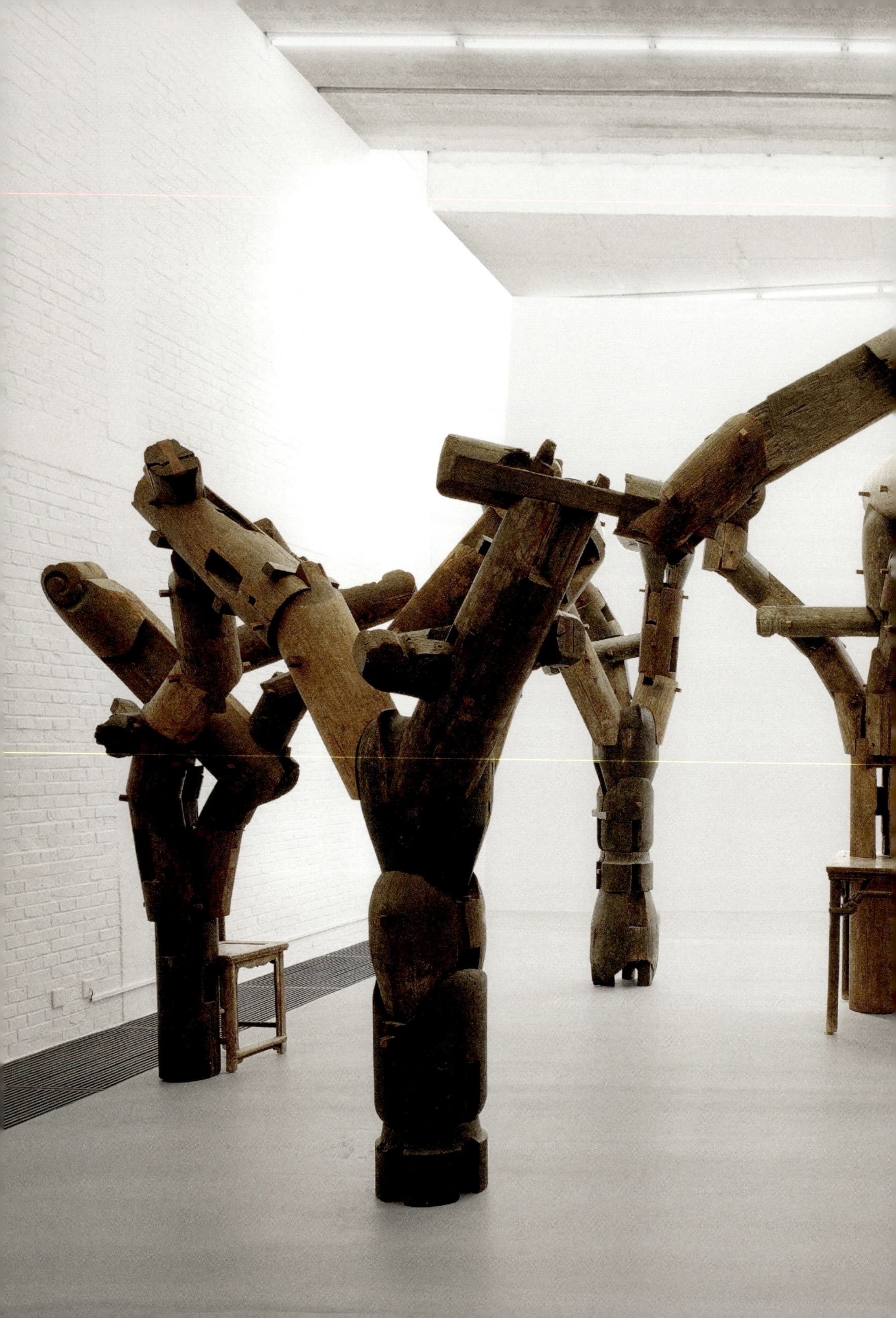

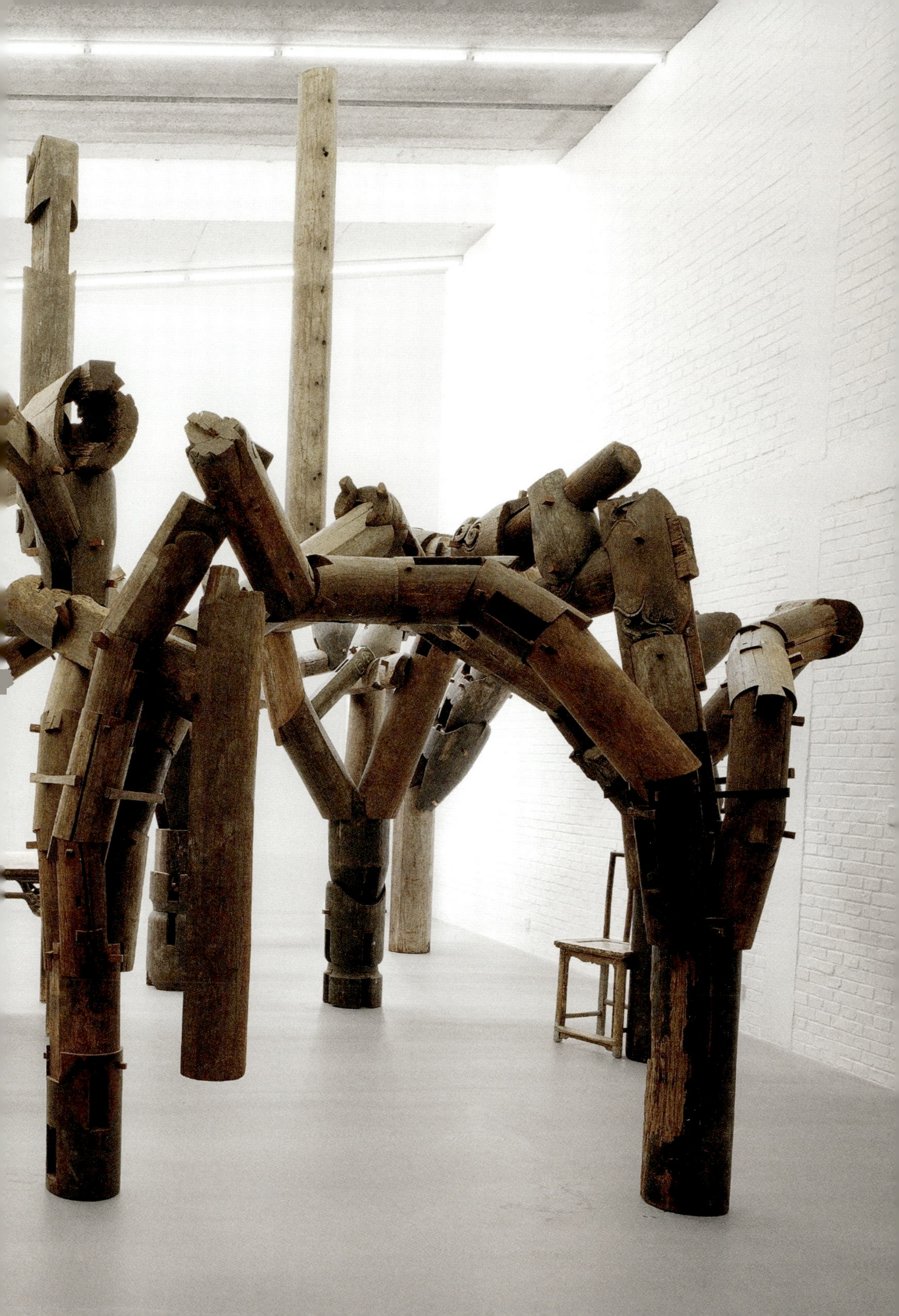

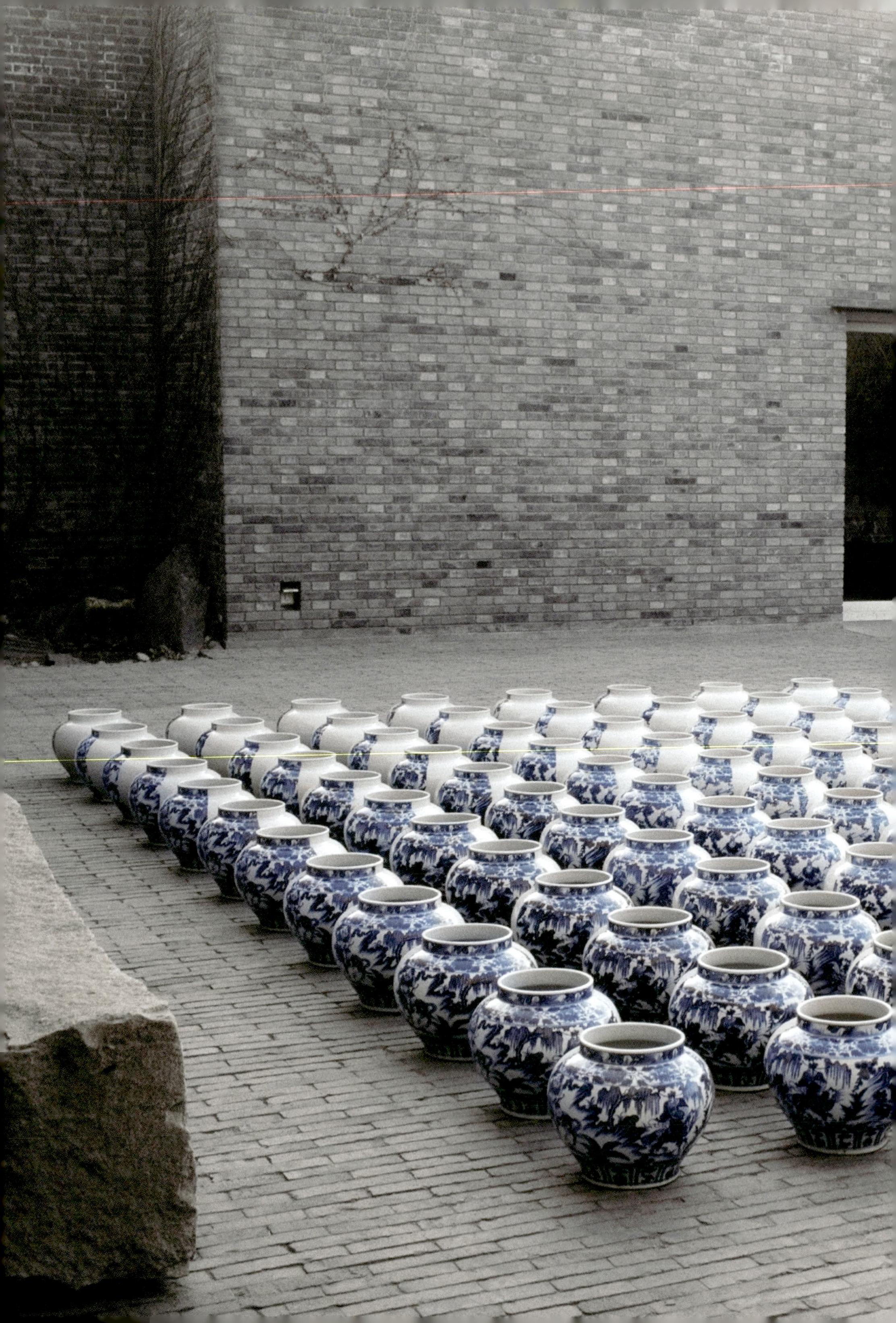

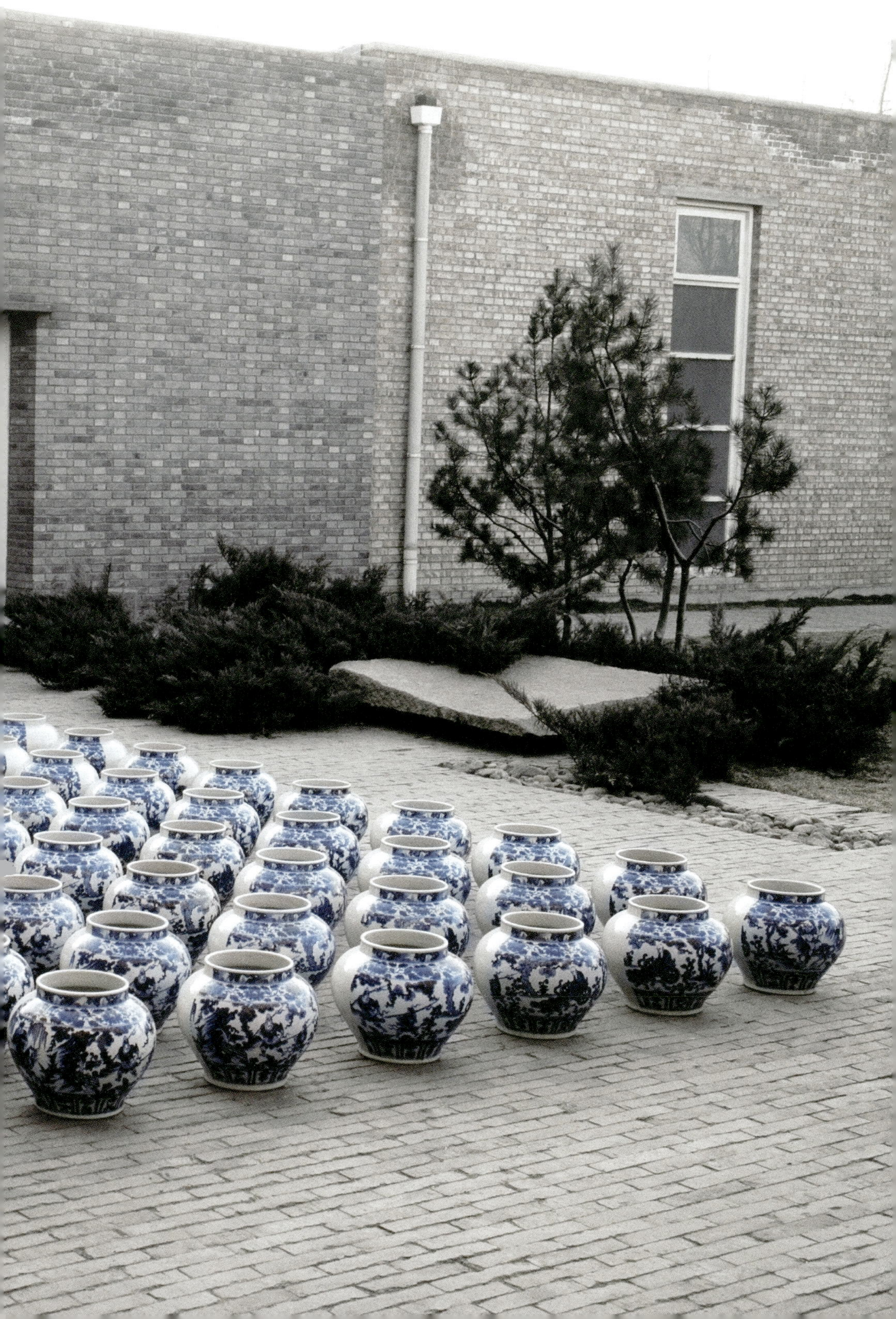

"I was trying to use Chinese porcelain skills in the contemporary field. I took traditional forms and motifs of objects from the Yuan Dynasty; these are really the most famous stories, everybody knows them. I wanted to show how Ghost Gu was coming down from the mountain in a conceptual language one could still decipher. So I made this collaboration with Serge Spitzer. We divided up the motifs on design paper, which we gave to the painter. Some covered exactly half the jar, some only a part, or the inside, while the rest remained blank. The title is from the painting on a famous porcelain jar, which at that time held the highest price for an Asian artwork at auction." — AI WEIWEI

Ich wollte das chinesische Porzellanhandwerk in die zeitgenössische Kunst bringen. Dafür wählte ich traditionelle Formen und Motive von Objekten aus der Yuan-Dynastie. Es sind einfach die berühmtesten Geschichten, jedes Kind kennt sie. Ich wollte zeigen, wie der Geist Gu aus den Bergen herabkam, jedoch in einer konzeptuellen Sprache, die gerade noch zu entziffern ist. Dafür arbeitete ich mit Serge Spitzer zusammen. Wir unterteilten die Motive auf Skizzenblättern gaben sie an einen Maler – manchmal wurde der Krug zur Hälfte bemalt, manchmal weniger oder nur das Innere. Der Rest blieb leer. Der Titel stammte von unserer Vorlage: dem Gemälde auf einem berühmten Porzellankrug, der damals den Höchstpreis für ein versteigertes asiatisches Kunstwerk erzielt hatte.

Je voulais utiliser les propriétés de la porcelaine chinoise dans le champ contemporain. J'ai repris des formes et des motifs traditionnels d'objets de la dynastie Yuan ; ce sont vraiment les histoires les plus célèbres, tout le monde les connaît. Je voulais raconter l'histoire de Gu, l'esprit qui descend de la montagne, dans un langage conceptuel qu'on puisse tout de même déchiffrer sans problème. J'ai travaillé à ce projet avec Serge Spitzer. Nous avons reproduit les motifs sur du papier à dessin et nous les avons donnés au peintre. Certains d'entre eux couvrent la moitié du vase, d'autres seulement une partie, ou l'intérieur, tandis que le reste est uni. Le titre de l'œuvre est celui d'une peinture sur un célèbre vase de porcelaine qui, à cette époque, était l'œuvre d'art asiatique la plus chère jamais vendue aux enchères.

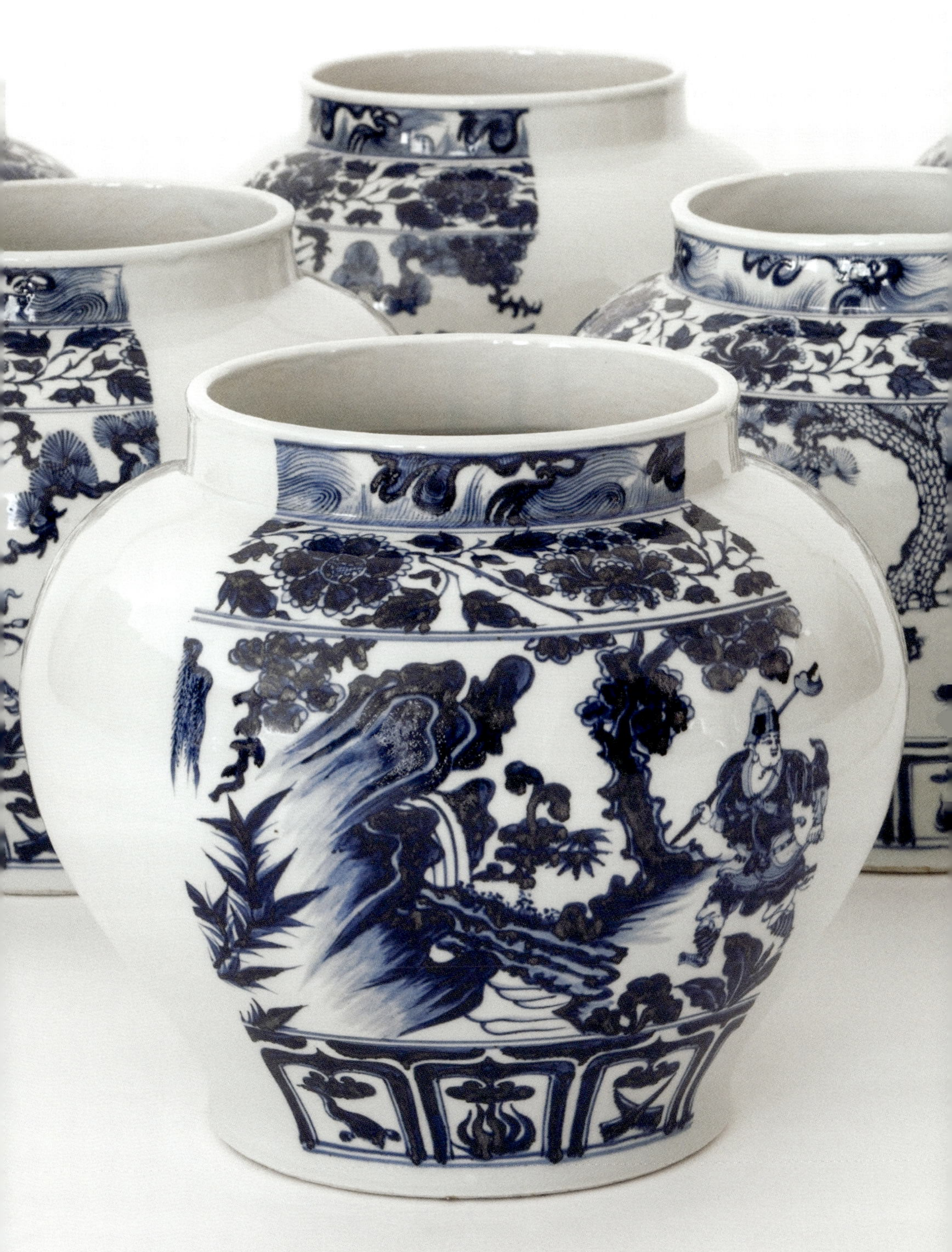

"There are many references here. For example to paintings from the Yuan
Dynasty that are just about water, ten different kinds of water, very beautiful. And
of course Japanese woodblock also. And then I had a dream where the sea rose,
and the image of the ocean and the waves was fascinating me. And I think two
weeks later, the big tsunami happened. So I worked with a porcelain maker, trying to find a way to fire this form so it would keep its shape; and we failed many
times. Porcelain is an ancient and beautiful language, but because the process of
creating it is so complicated, involving many different steps, it's impossible to
have complete control over the material." — AI WEIWEI

Die Arbeit bietet eine Vielzahl von Bezügen, zum Beispiel zu Malereien aus der Yuan-
Dynastie, in denen es nur um Wasser geht, zehn verschiedene Sorten von Wasser, wunder-
schön, aber auch zu japanischen Holzschnitten. Außerdem hatte ich einen Traum, in dem
die Meere aufstiegen, und dieses Bild vom Ozean und den Wellen faszinierte mich. Zwei
Wochen später, glaube ich, kam dann der große Tsunami. Ich arbeitete mit einem Porzellanhersteller zusammen, um herauszufinden, wie man das Objekt brennen musste, damit es
seine Form behielt. Viele Versuche sind uns erst einmal misslungen. Porzellan ist eine alte
und schöne Sprache, aber der Herstellungsprozess ist derart kompliziert, mit vielen unterschiedlichen Schritten, dass man das Material nicht vollständig kontrollieren kann.

Il y a beaucoup de références dans cette œuvre. Par exemple aux tableaux de la dynastie
Yuan qui ne représentent que de l'eau, dix sortes différentes d'eau, et qui sont magnifiques.
Et bien sûr aussi aux estampes sur bois japonaises. Et puis j'ai fait un rêve dans lequel la
mer montait et où j'étais fasciné par les vagues. À peu près deux semaines plus tard, le grand
tsunami s'est produit. J'ai travaillé avec un porcelainier, et nous avons essayé de trouver
le moyen de cuire cette forme en la conservant; et nous avons échoué de nombreuses fois.
La porcelaine est un langage ancien et magnifique, mais son processus de fabrication est
si complexe, il comprend tellement d'étapes, qu'il est impossible de contrôler totalement
la matière.

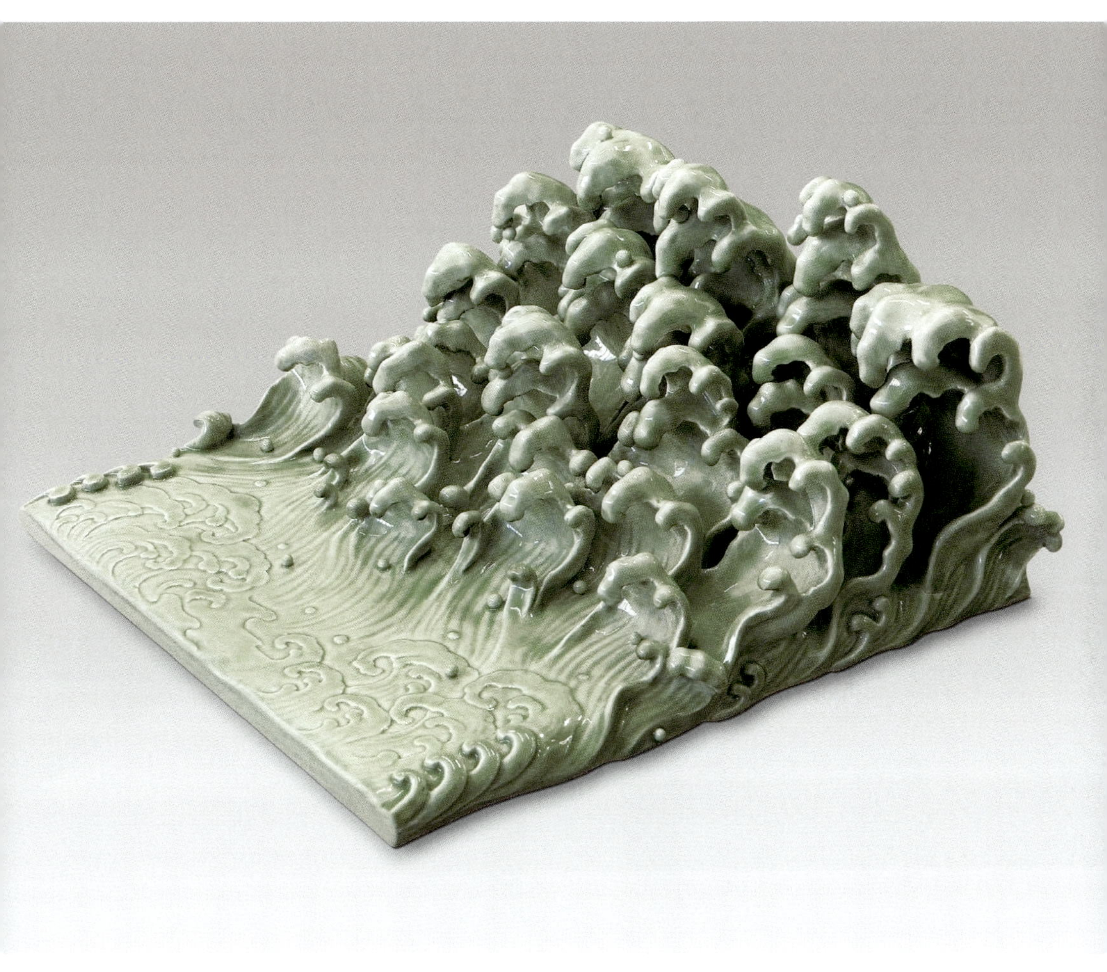

THE WAVE, 2005, porcelain, 9 ⅞ x 15 ¾ x 15 ¾ inches
Overleaf: TWO JOINED SQUARE TABLES, 2005, Qing Dynasty tables, 53 ½ x 65 ½ x 36 inches | 257

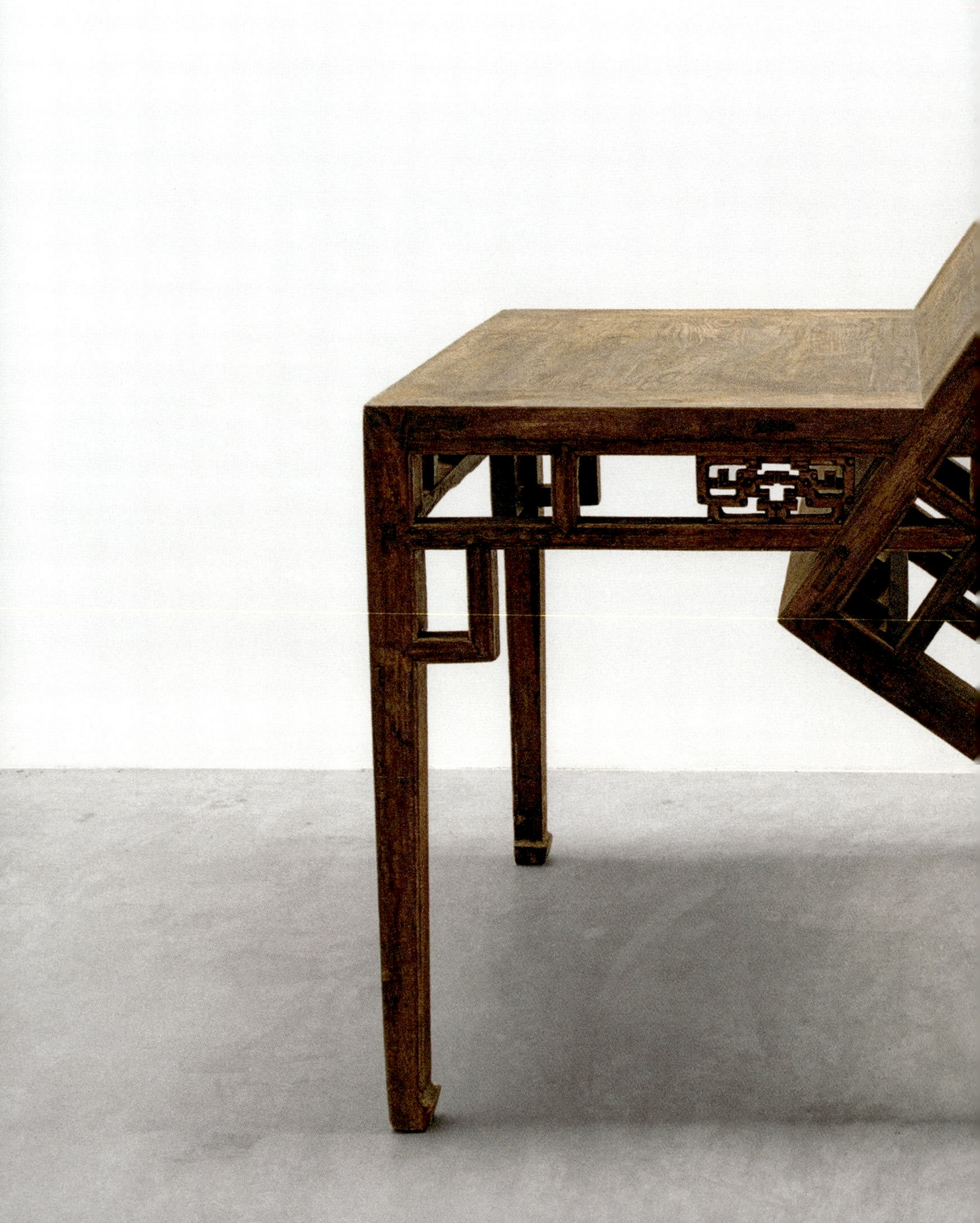

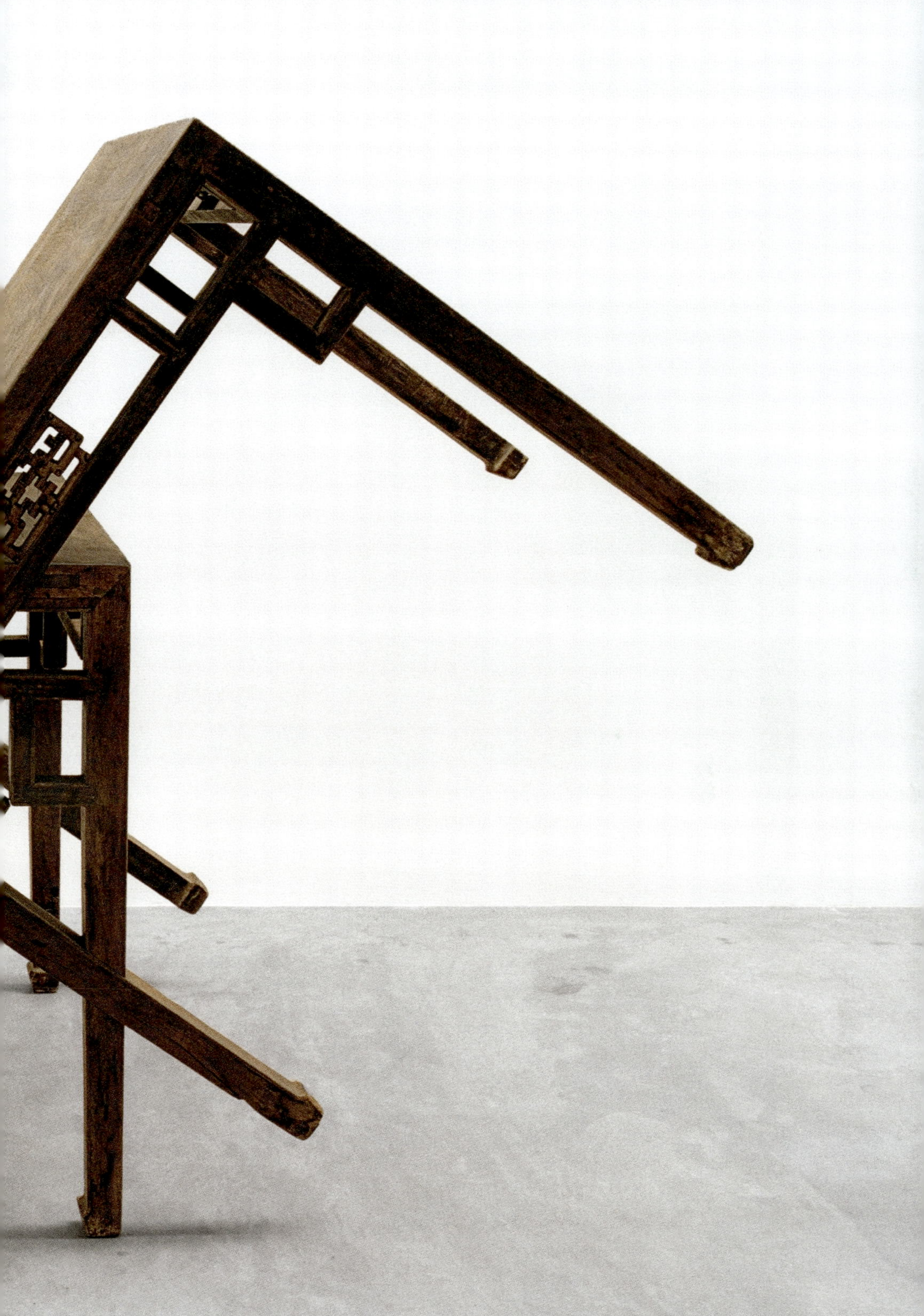

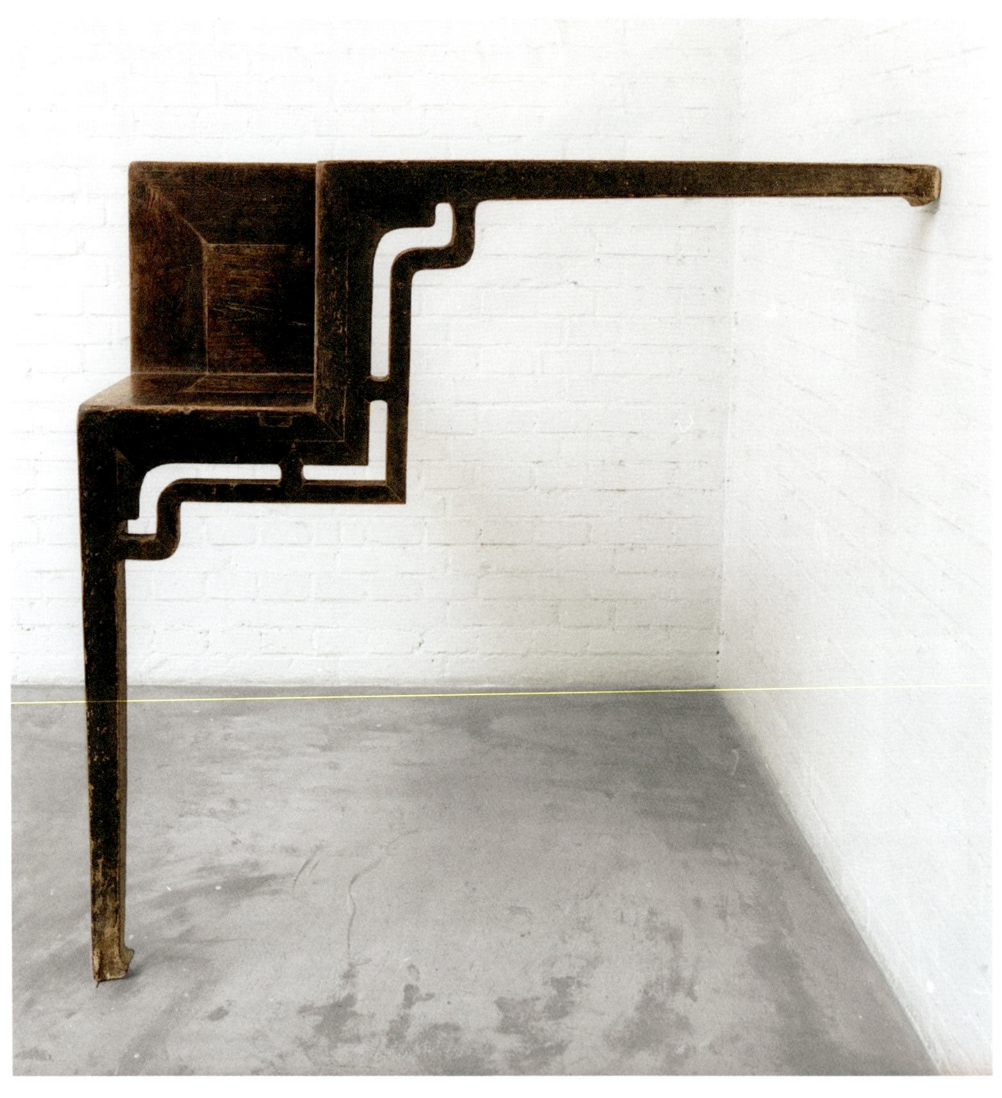

260 | TABLE WITH THREE LEGS, 2008, Qing Dynasty table, 44 ⅞ x 44 ⅞ x 44 ⅞ inches

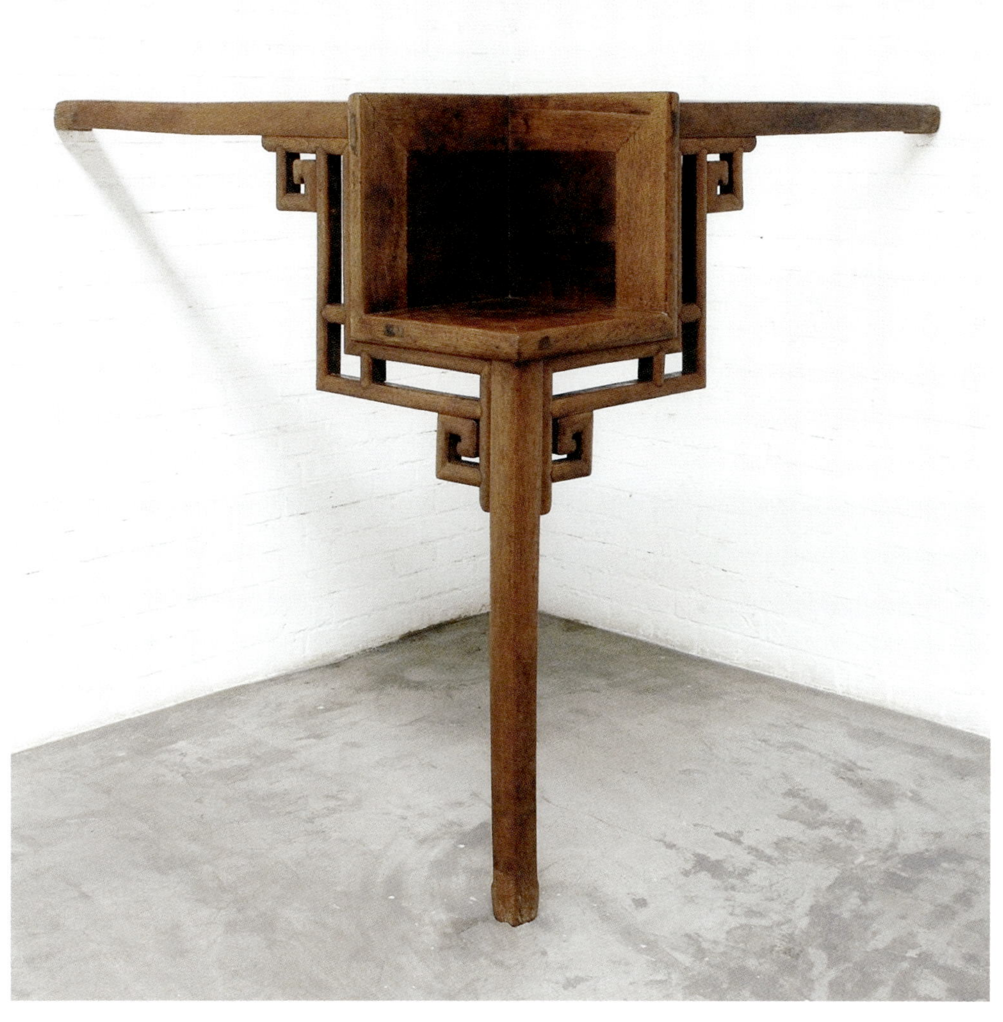

"We made a plan and divided Beijing into 16 parts. Then my students and I
spent 16 days on the bus, and each day the bus would go through all the streets in
one of the sections of the city. I put a video camera in front of the bus. In those
16 days, I completed a 150-hour-long video. It's a visual map of Beijing, recording
every *hutong* and street that cars could reach. Of course, during and after the
recording, the city and its streets had already changed or disappeared."
— AI WEIWEI

Wir machten einen Plan und teilten Peking in 16 Stücke auf. 16 Tage lang fuhren meine
Studenten und ich mit dem Bus durch sämtliche Straßen in jeweils einem der 16 Abschnitte
der Stadt. Vor den Bus montierte ich eine Kamera. Während der 16 Tage drehten wir ein
Video von 150 Stunden Länge. Jeden *Hutong* und jede Straße, die der Bus erreichen konnte,
haben wir aufgezeichnet, wie auf einer visuellen Karte von Peking. Aber schon während der
Aufnahmen und natürlich danach veränderten sich die Straßen der Stadt, und manche
verschwanden völlig.

Nous avons divisé Pékin en 16 sections, puis mes étudiants et moi avons passé 16 jours
dans un bus qui, chaque jour, sillonnait toutes les rues d'une des sections de la ville. J'avais
placé une caméra vidéo à l'avant du bus. Au bout de ces 16 jours, j'avais 150 heures de vidéo.
C'est une carte visuelle de Pékin, témoignant de chaque *hutong* (ruelle ancienne), et de
chaque rue accessible en voiture. Bien entendu, depuis cet enregistrement vidéo, et même
pendant l'enregistrement, la ville n'a cessé de se modifier et certaines de ses rues de
disparaître.

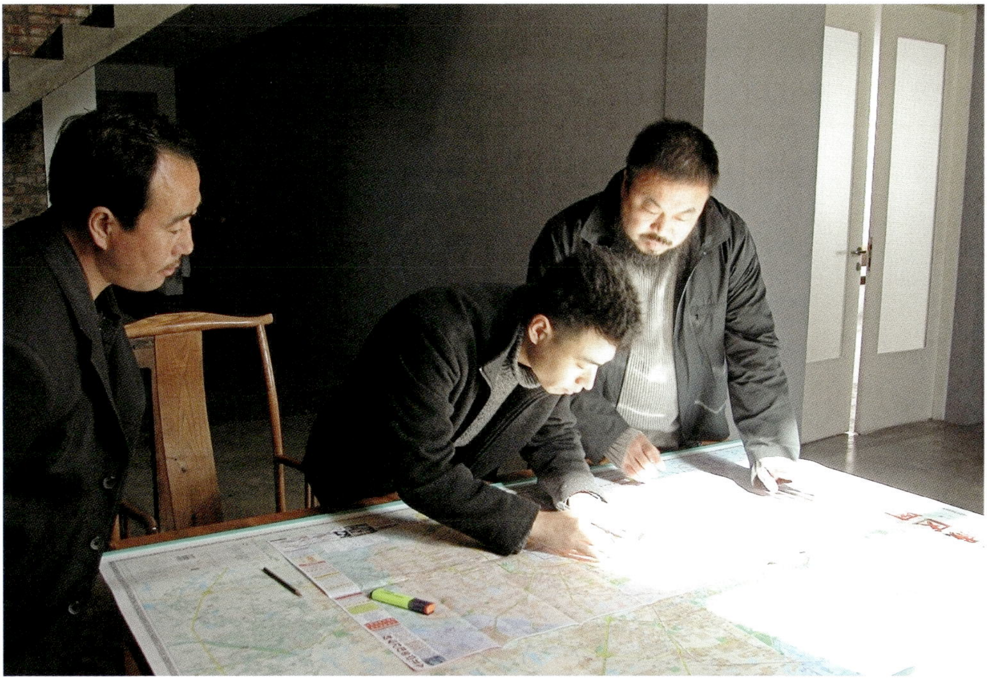

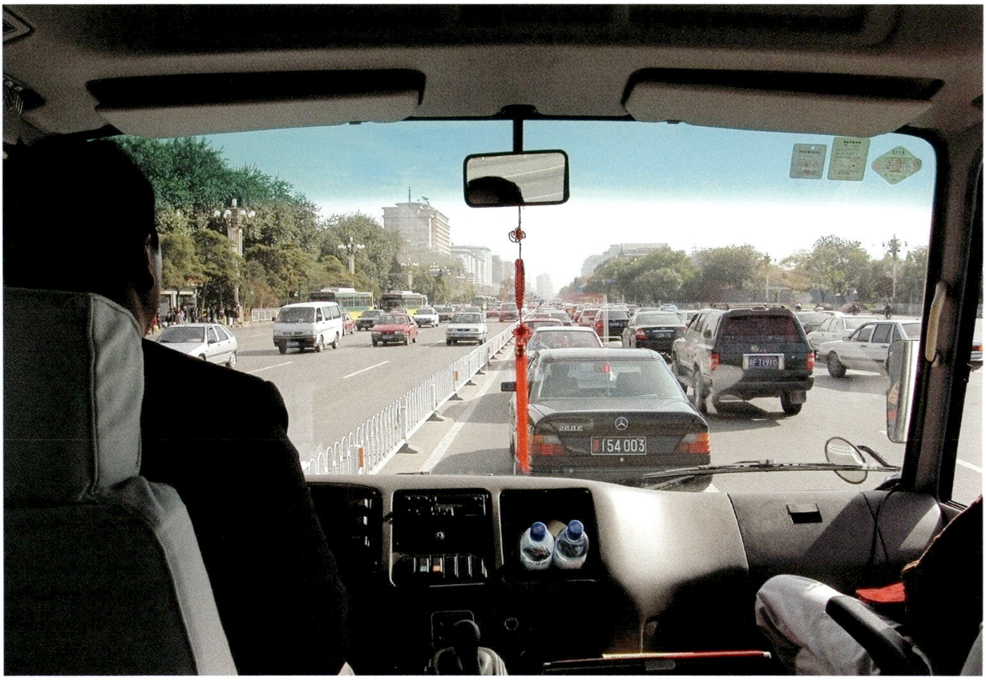

Production views of BEIJING 2003, 2003, video, 1 h 50 min |

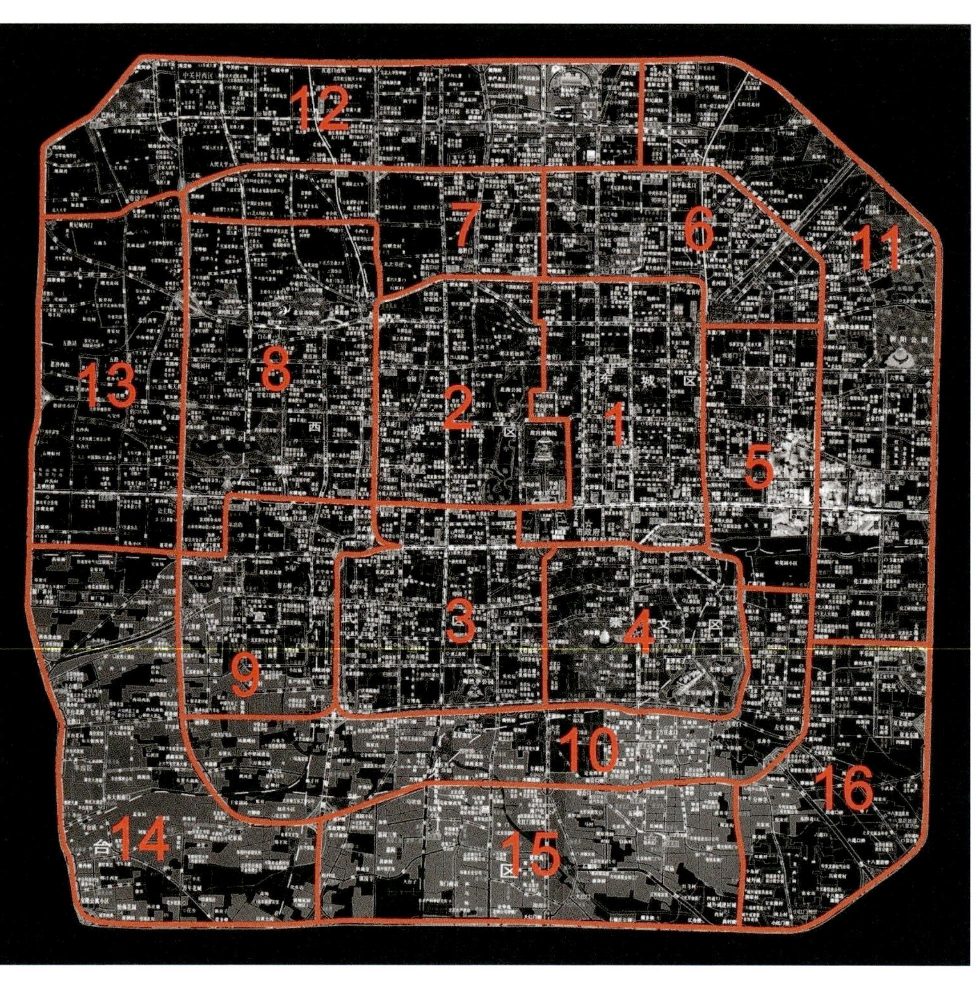

264 | BEIJING 2003, 2003, video, 1 h 50 min; plan map (above); video stills (opposite)

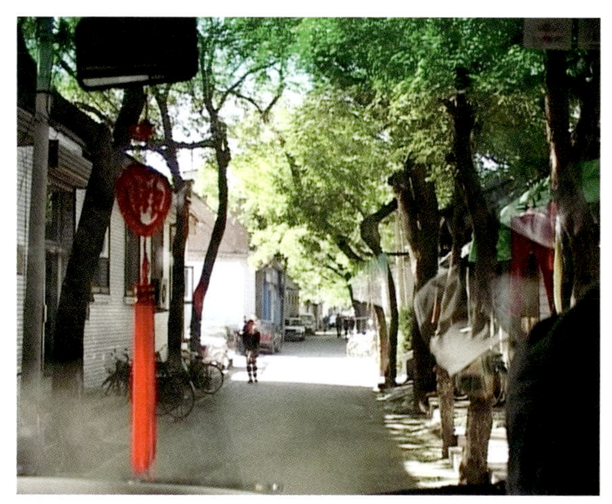

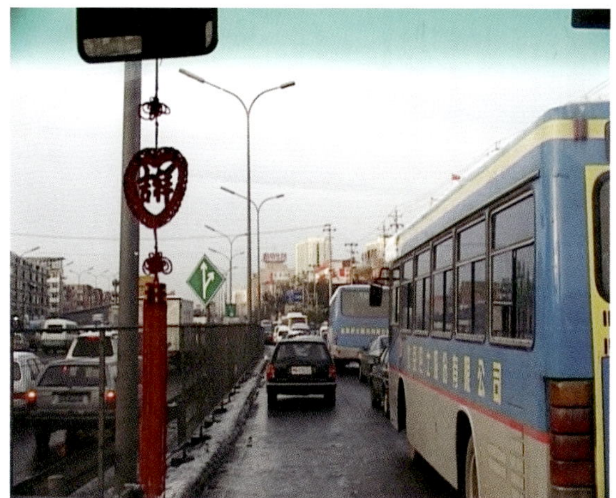

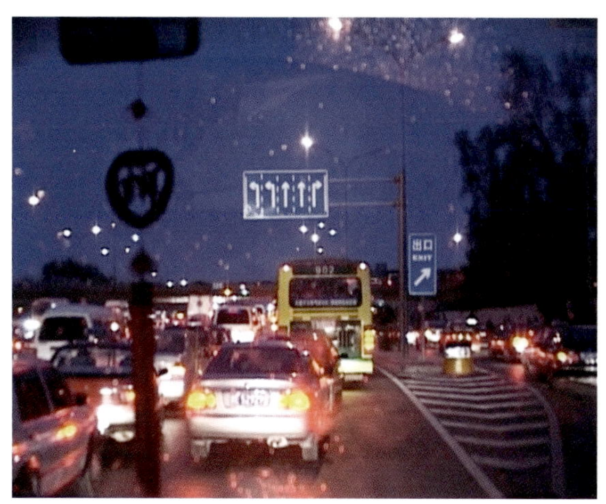

"I started the work with the intention to become very conscious about our
time. The whole of our life, it's just shifting from one thing to another. Most
people only recognize the before and after, but they don't pay attention to the
change in between, and for me the details in those photographs are about that."
— AI WEIWEI

Ich nahm die Arbeit mit der Absicht auf, ein schärferes Bewusstsein für unsere Zeit zu
entwickeln. Unser gesamtes Leben lang ändern sich die Dinge und werden zu etwas anderem. Die meisten Menschen erkennen nur das Davor und das Danach, aber sie richten ihre
Aufmerksamkeit nicht auf den Wandel dazwischen, und genau darum geht es in den Einzelheiten auf diesen Fotografien.

J'ai commencé ce travail dans l'intention d'être plus conscient du temps présent. Dans
la vie, la plupart du temps, on ne fait que passer d'une chose à la suivante. La plupart des
gens sont conscients de l'avant et de l'après, mais ils ne prêtent pas attention aux changements qui se produisent entre les deux, et pour moi les détails de ces photographies
montrent exactement cela.

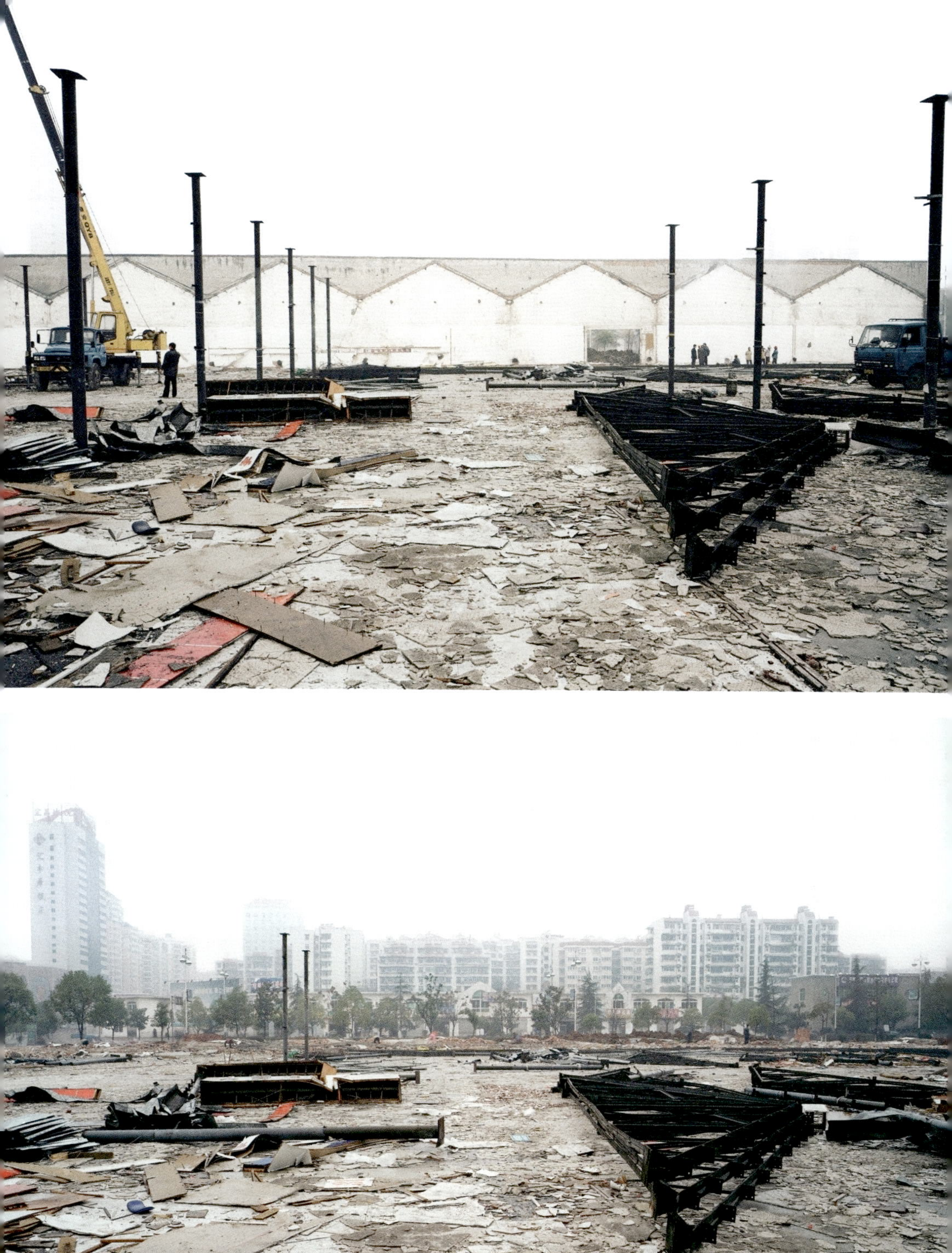

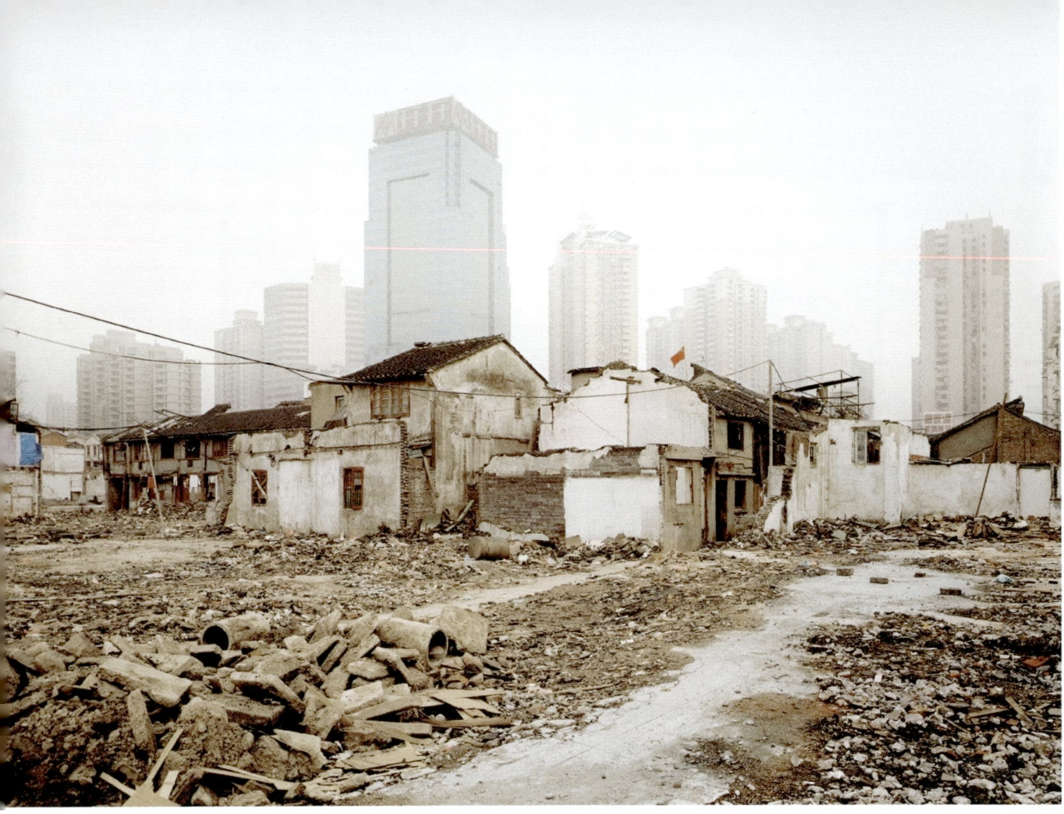

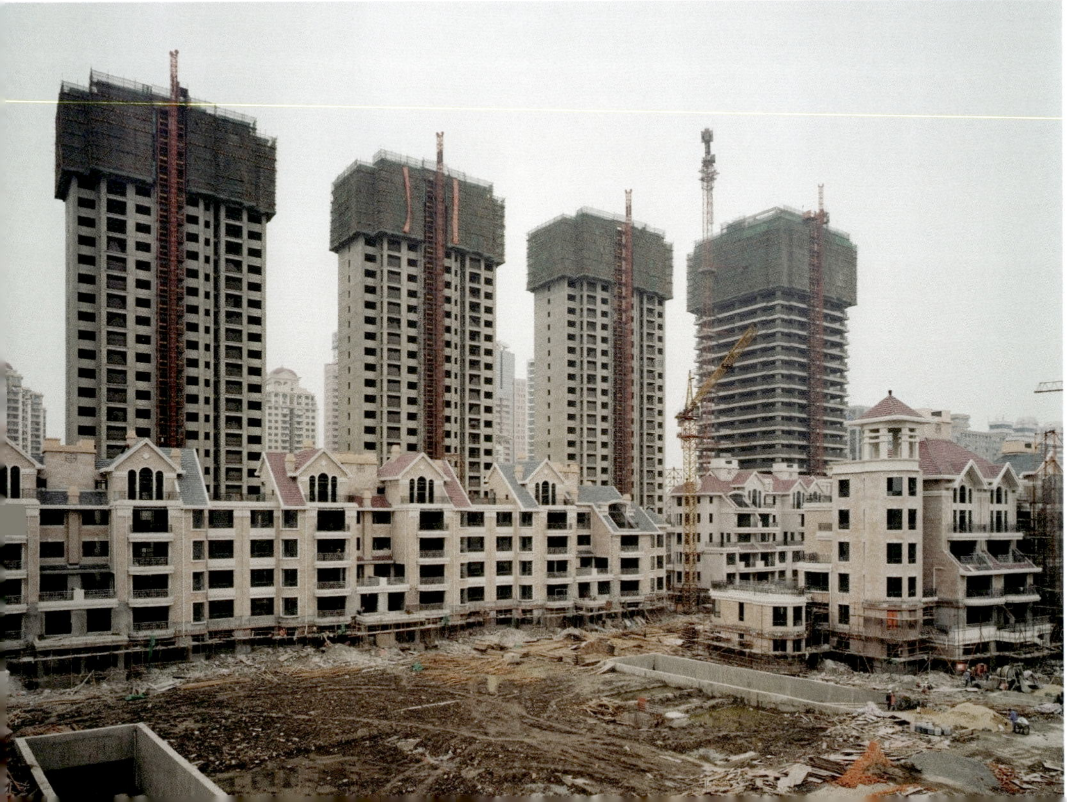

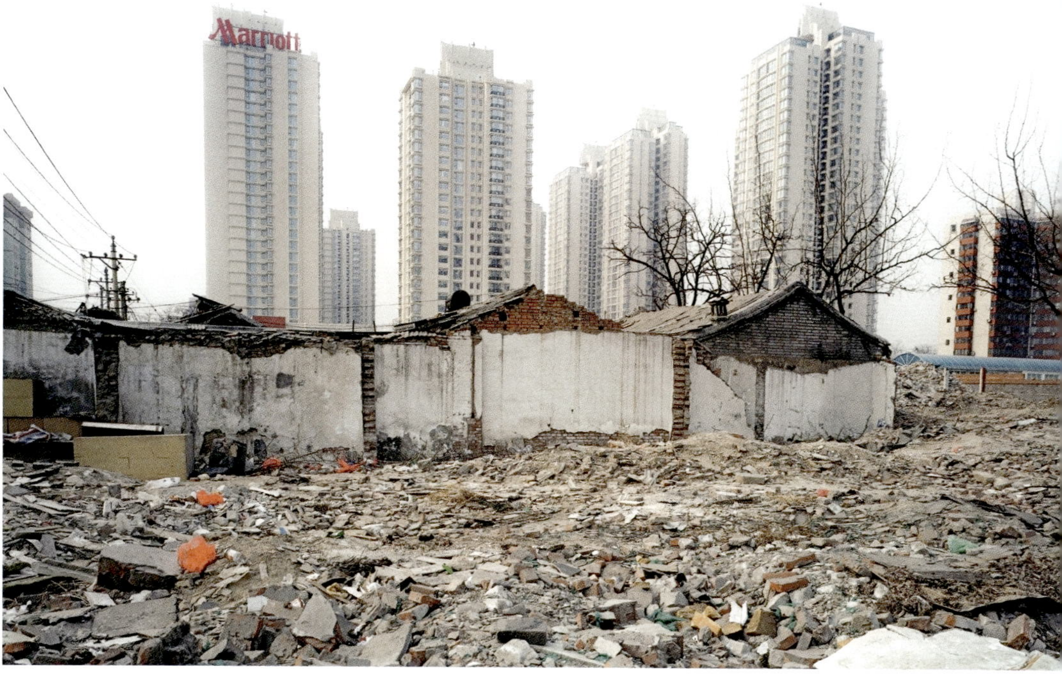

Marriott

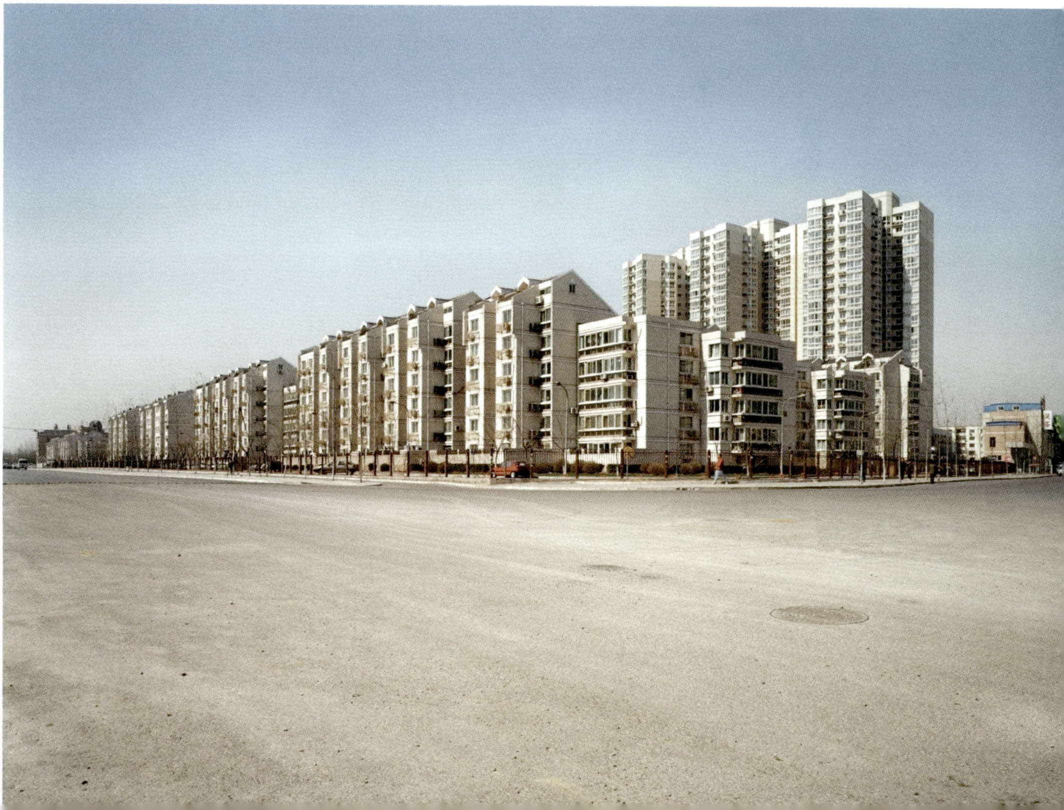

"Along Chang'an Boulevard, the distance between the east and west perimeters of the Sixth Ring Road is 43 kilometers. I took a one-minute video every 50 meters. So connecting them all made a video a little longer than ten hours. It records the complete Beijing, from the rural area, to the commercial district, to the political center Tiananmen Square. Then I made *Second Ring* and *Third Ring* immediately following that. There are more than 30 pedestrian walkovers on the Second Ring. I shot one minute of video in both directions of each bridge, making 60 minutes all together. There are more than 50 bridges on Third Ring Road, and I shot the video the same way. It's very boring, but nevertheless it records the condition at the time." — AI WEIWEI

Entlang dem Chang'an-Boulevard beträgt der Abstand zwischen dem östlichen und westlichen Ende der Sechsten Ringstraße 43 Kilometer. Alle 50 Meter nahm ich eine Minute mit der Videokamera auf. Die Aufnahmen wurden aneinandergeschnitten und ergaben einen Film von etwas über zehn Stunden Laufzeit. Ganz Peking ist hier aufgezeichnet, von den ländlichen Vororten über den Bankenbezirk bis hin zum politischen Zentrum am Tiananmen-Platz. Unmittelbar danach drehte ich *Second Ring* und *Third Ring*. Auf dem Zweiten Ring gibt es mehr als 30 Fußgängerübergänge. Ich filmte auf jeder Brücke für eine Minute in beide Richtungen, insgesamt 60 Minuten. Dasselbe tat ich auf allen 50 Brücken, die es entlang der Dritten Ringstraße gibt. Die Videos sind ziemlich langweilig, aber sie zeichnen den Zustand zu einer bestimmten Zeit auf.

Si on suit le boulevard Chang'an, la distance entre les extrémités est et ouest du sixième périphérique est de 43 kilomètres. J'ai fait une vidéo d'une minute tous les 50 mètres. Au total, cela donne un peu plus de dix heures de vidéo. C'est un témoignage de toutes les facettes de Pékin, des zones rurales au quartier du commerce et au centre politique, la place Tiananmen. Juste après j'ai fait *Second Ring* et *Third Ring*. Il y a plus d'une trentaine de passerelles piétonnes qui traversent le deuxième périphérique. J'ai fait une minute de vidéo dans les deux directions sur chacune d'entre elles, ce qui fait 60 minutes en tout. Il y a plus d'une cinquantaine de ponts sur le troisième périphérique, et j'ai fait cette vidéo sur le même principe. Ce n'est pas très passionnant, mais c'est un témoignage d'une situation à un moment donné.

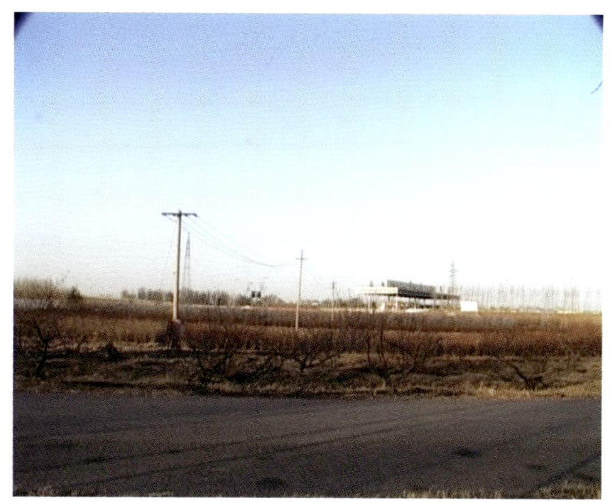

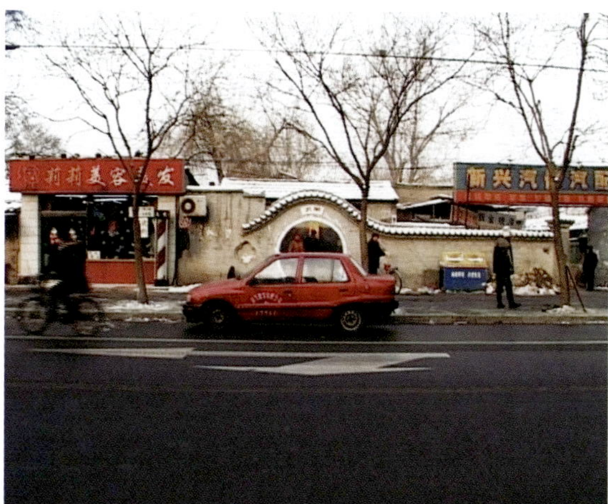

莉莉美容美发
新兴汽修汽配

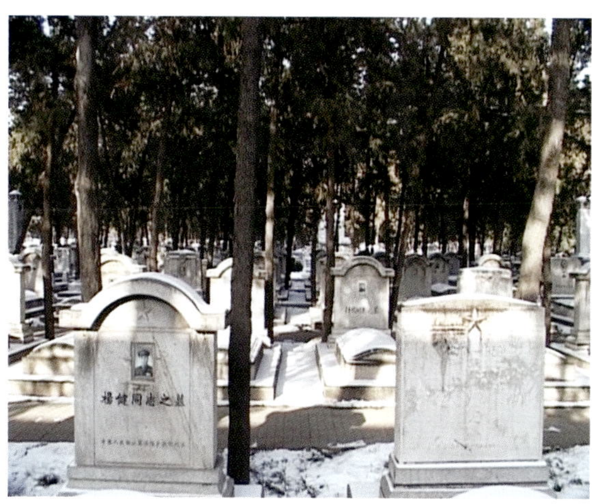

杨镜同志之墓

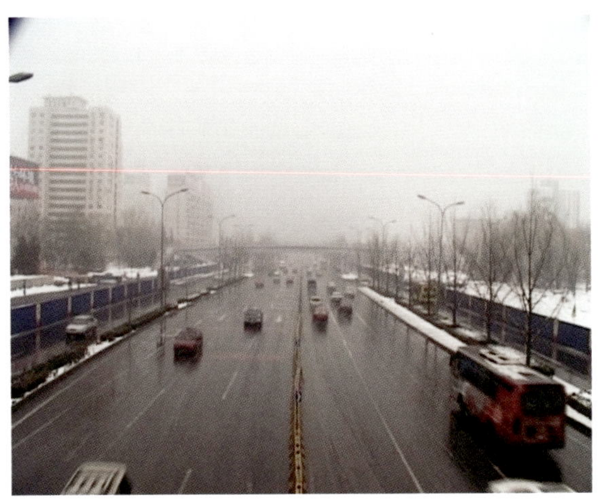

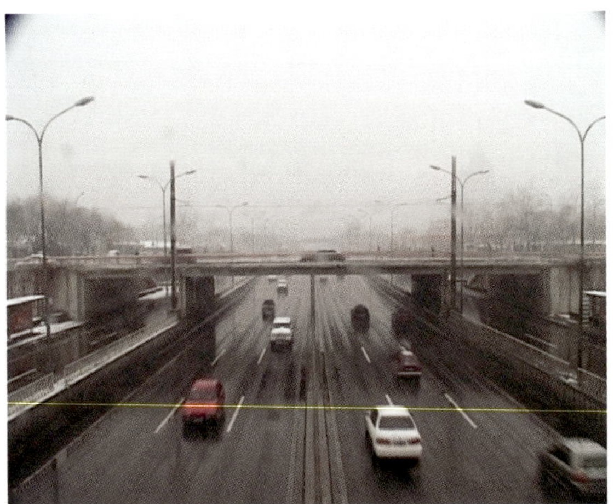

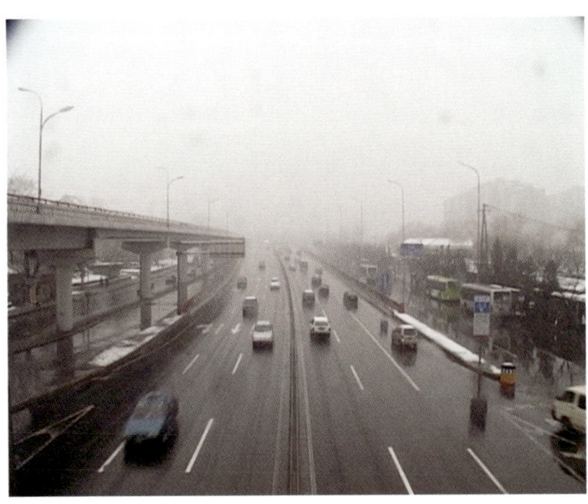

 BEIJING: THE SECOND RING, 2005, video, 1 h 16 min; video stills

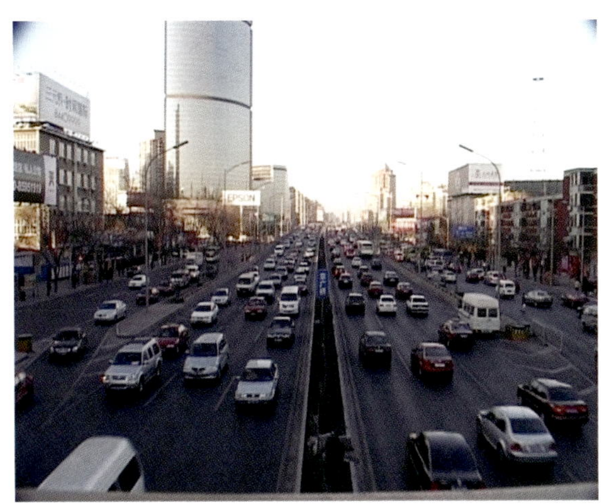

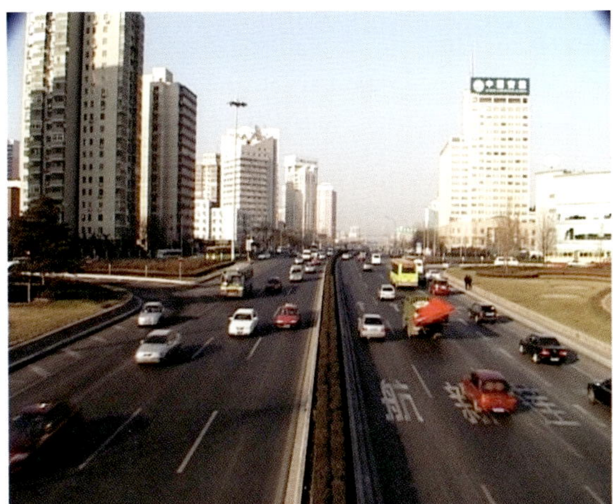

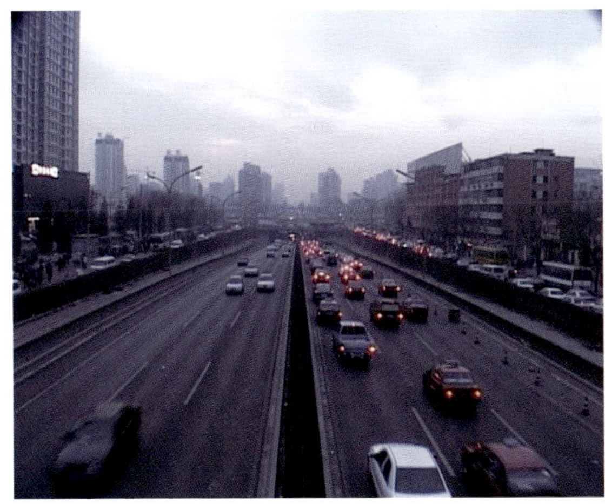

"At the moment China is facing a great time. At the same time, people have
no interest in this process. They only want the glamour, the final result. So I
asked my assistant to help me to take pictures of the Beijing airport construction
site after they had destroyed the old buildings there. These photos show a very
objective view. It seems like they've been taken by a construction worker, there is
no artistic interest in them. That way they give a clear definition of the time and
the situation and the place. You can gain something from looking at the process
of construction. Without those photos, there wouldn't be any." — AI WEIWEI

Im Moment geht China goldenen Zeiten entgegen. Zugleich interessieren sich die
Menschen überhaupt nicht für diesen Prozess. Sie wollen nur den schönen Schein, das End-
ergebnis. Ich bat also meinen Assistenten, mir dabei zu helfen, Aufnahmen an der Baustelle
des Flughafens von Peking zu machen, nachdem dort die alten Gebäude zerstört worden
waren. Die Fotografien zeigen einen sehr objektiven Blick. Es scheint, als hätte ein Bauar-
beiter sie aufgenommen, sie besitzen nicht den geringsten künstlerischen Ehrgeiz. So bieten
sie eine klare Definition der Zeit, der Situation und des Orts. Man hat schon etwas davon,
diesen Prozess des Bauens zu betrachten. Ohne diese Fotografien gäbe es ihn nicht.

La Chine traverse une période très intéressante. Mais les gens ne s'intéressent pas du
tout à ce processus. Tout ce qu'ils veulent, c'est le glamour, le résultat final. Alors j'ai
demandé à mon assistant de m'aider à prendre des photos du chantier de l'aéroport de Pékin
après la destruction des anciens bâtiments. Ces photos témoignent d'une vision très objective. On dirait qu'elles ont été prises par un ouvrier du chantier, elles n'ont aucune préten-
tion artistique. Elles donnent une définition claire du moment, de la situation, de l'endroit.
Observer le processus de construction peut nous apporter quelque chose. Sans ces photos,
il n'existerait pas.

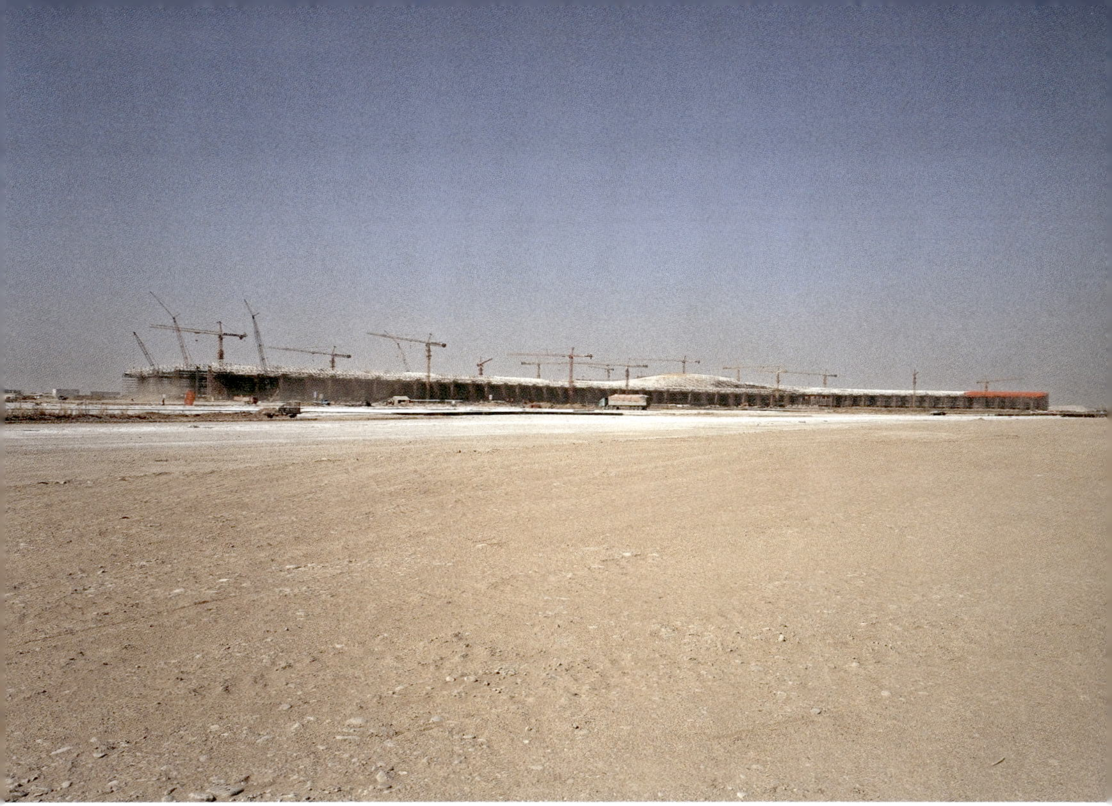

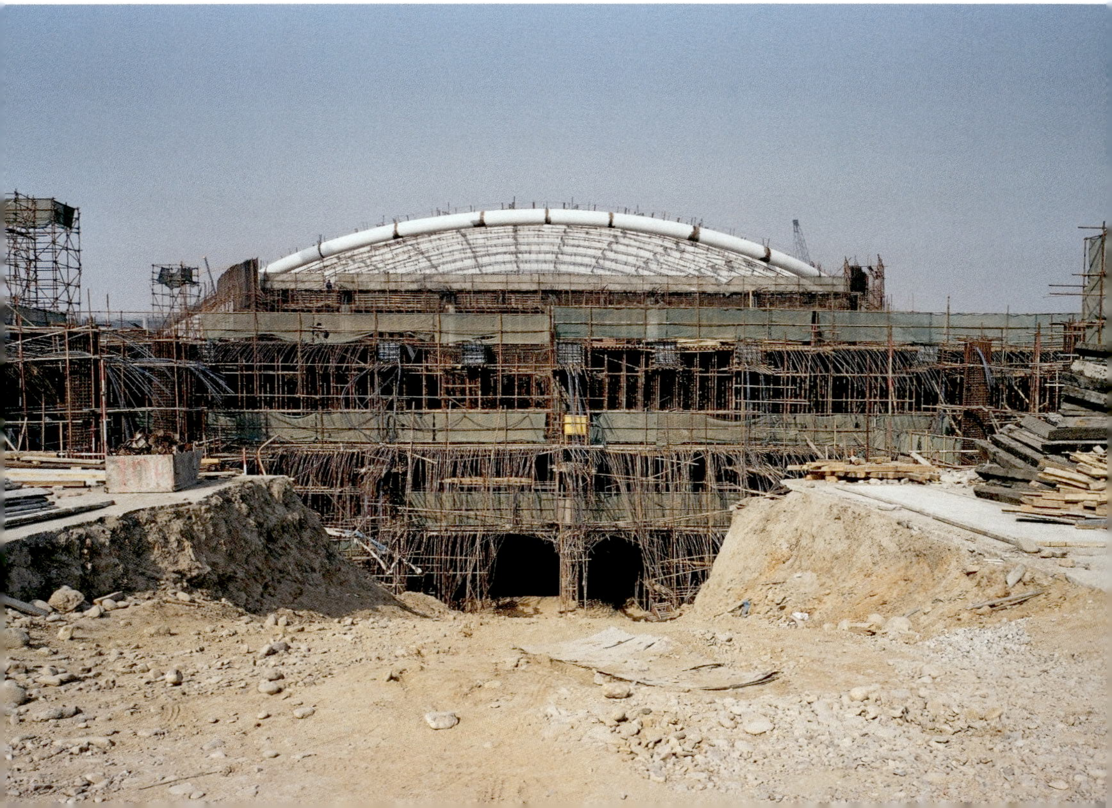

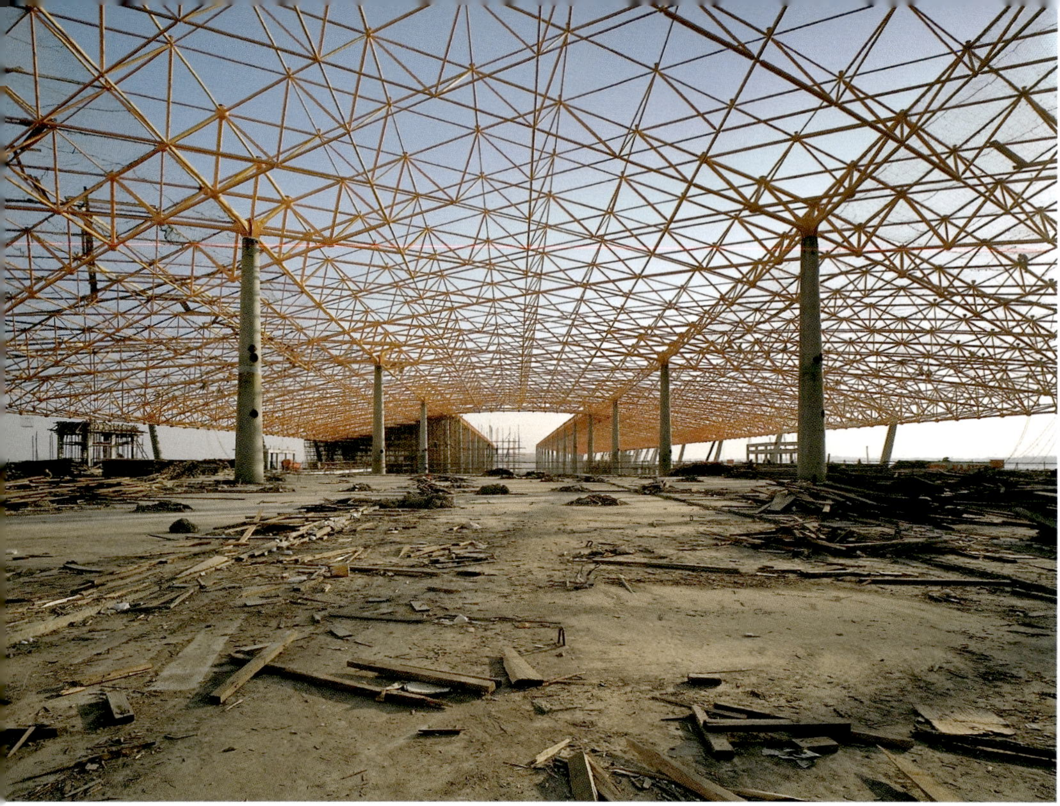

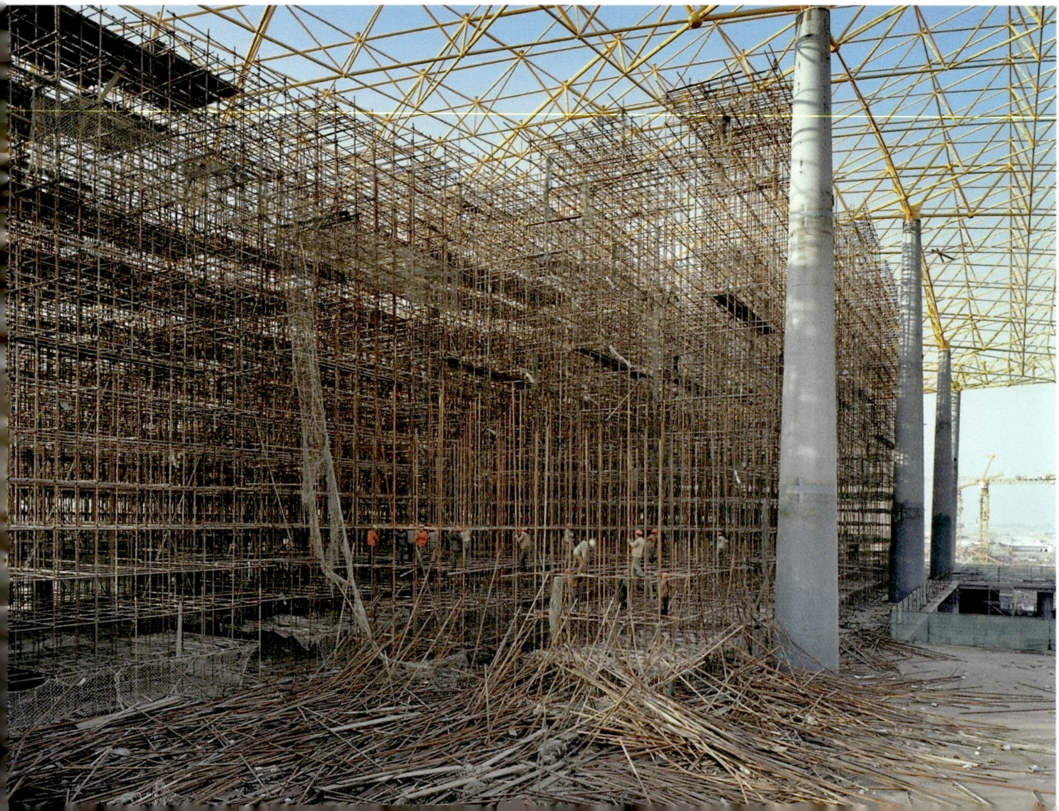

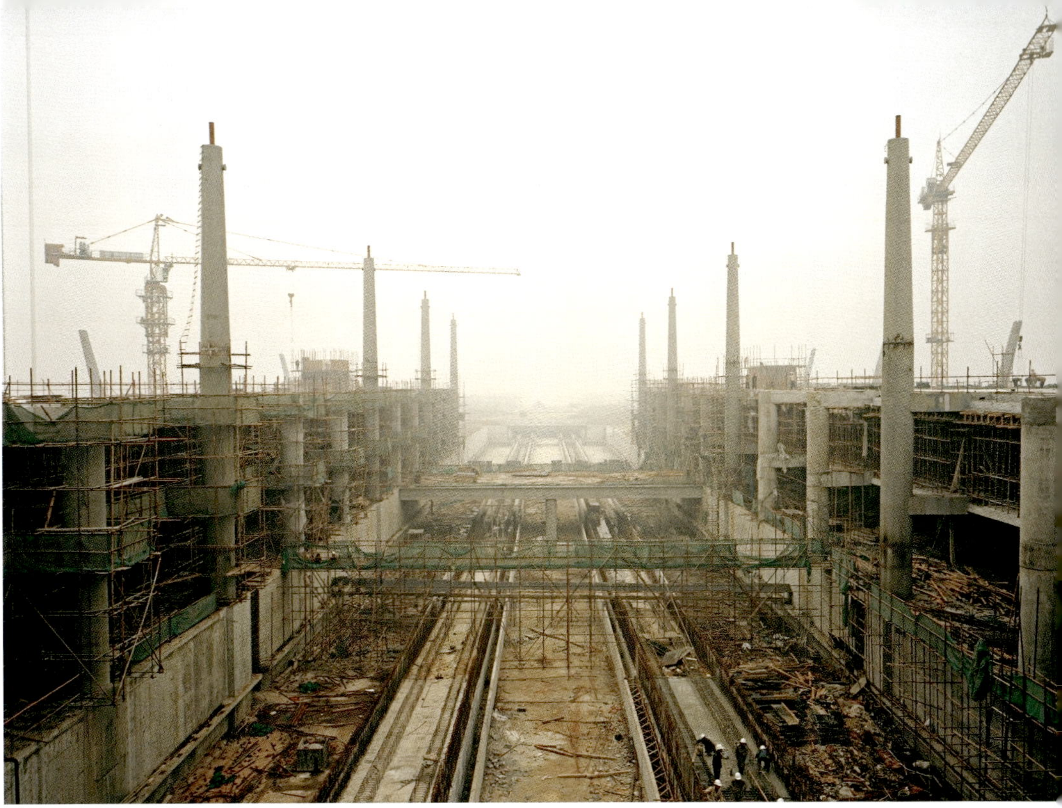

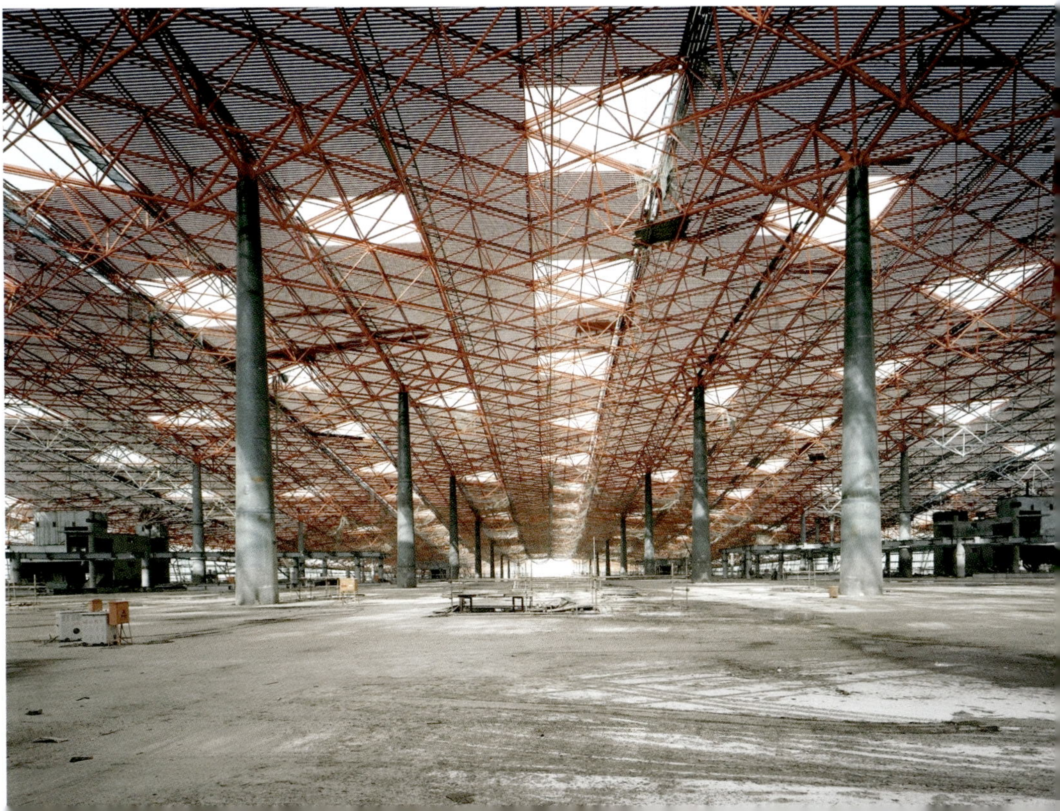

"The idea originally came from a little plastic colored ball for cats to play with. So I discussed with my carpenter if we could start to structure it in the classic Chinese way, which means a Ming-style structure, with purely wooden joints without any nails. The technical and aesthetic challenge of the piece took us one or two years to figure out. To me, it's about art as much as it is a conversation with my carpenters." — AI WEIWEI

Die Idee zu diesem Werk kam durch einen kleinen bunten Plastikball, mit dem Katzen spielen. Ich erörterte mit meinem Tischler, ob wir dieselbe Struktur auf die klassische chinesische Weise konstruieren könnten, im Ming-Stil mit allein hölzernen Verbindungsstücken, ohne Nägel. Die technische und ästhetische Herausforderung der Skulptur beschäftigte uns ein oder zwei Jahre lang. Für mich geht es hier neben der Kunst ebenso sehr um den Austausch mit den Tischlern.

L'idée de cette œuvre est venue d'une petite balle en plastique coloré, un jouet pour chats. J'ai demandé à mes menuisiers si nous pouvions en fabriquer une à la manière chinoise classique, c'est-à-dire dans le style Ming, en assemblant des pièces de bois sans utiliser aucun clou. C'était un défi technique et esthétique, et nous avons mis un ou deux ans à trouver. Pour moi, c'est autant de l'art qu'un dialogue avec mes menuisiers.

UNTITLED, 2010, huali wood, ø 27 ½ inches; F-SIZE, 2011, huali wood, ø 51 ⅛ inches; Galleria Continua, San Gimignano 2012 (top); 81 WOODEN BALLS, 2012, huali wood, 81 pieces, each ø 16 ⅛ inches, dimensions variable; KODE Kunstmuseer, Bergen 2012 (bottom) | Overleaf: KIPPE, 2006, tieli wood from dismantled Qing Dynasty temples, iron bars, 71 ⅝ x 112 ⅝ x 41 ⅞ inches; Hirshhorn Museum, Washington, D.C. 2012

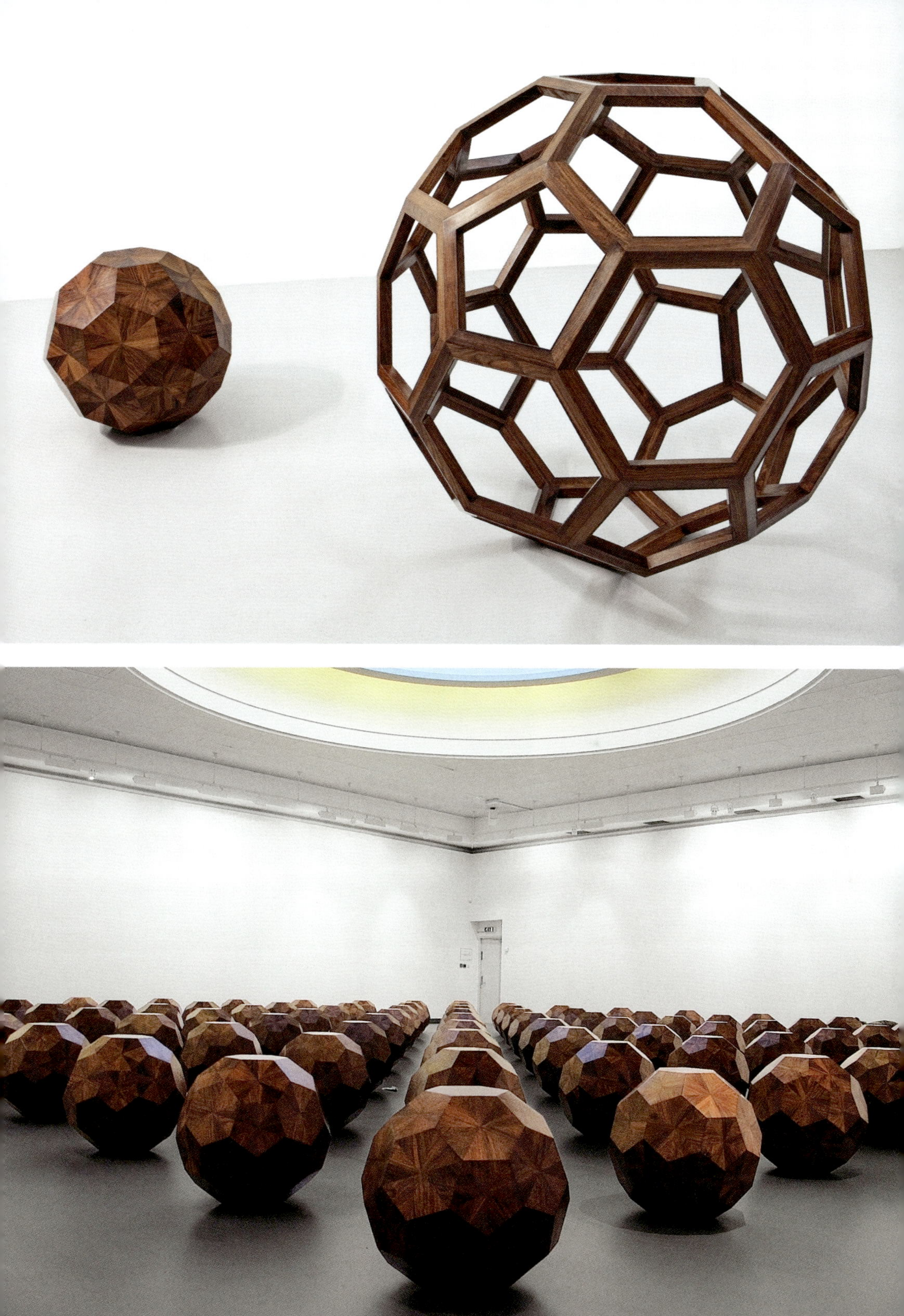

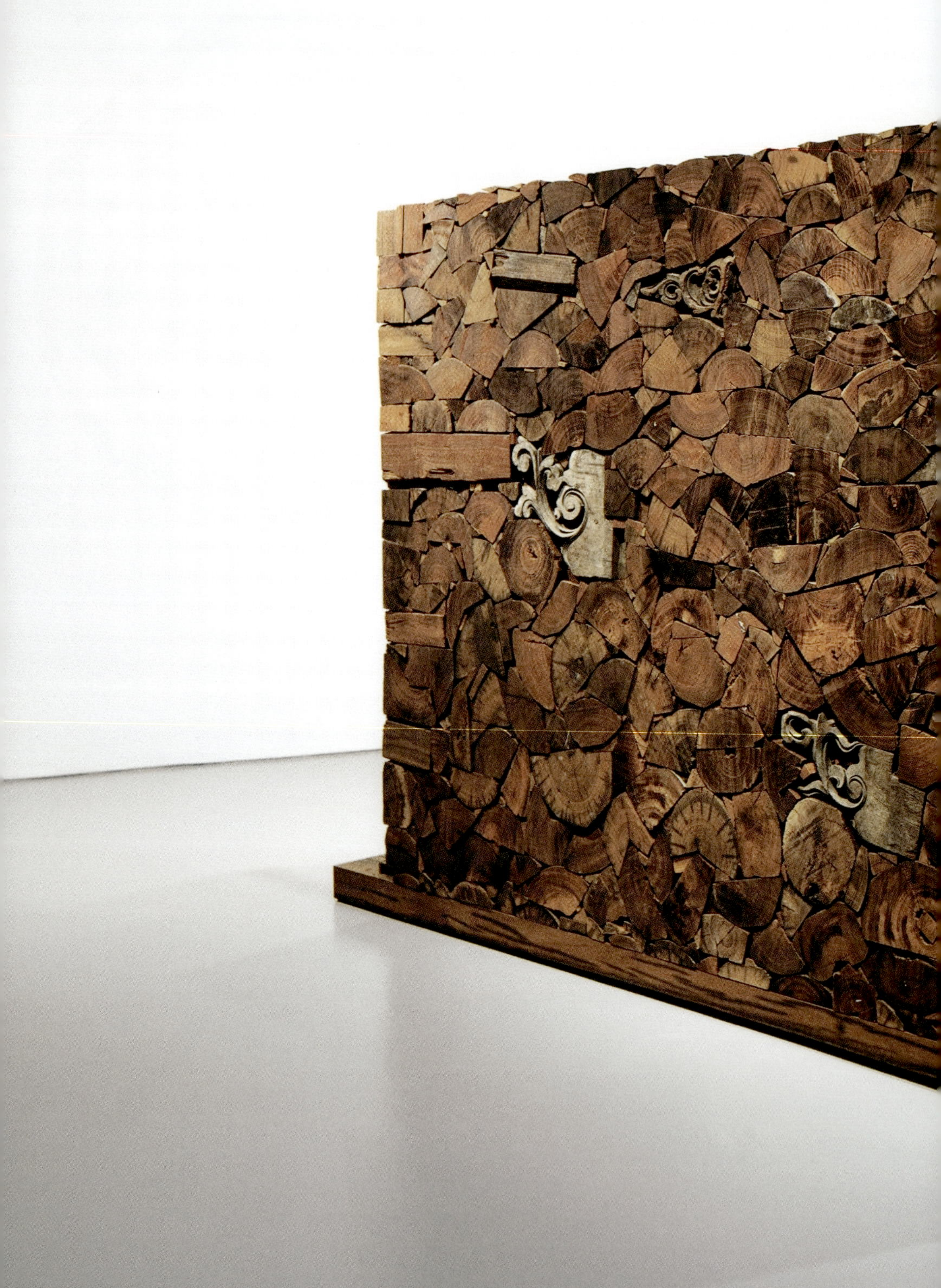

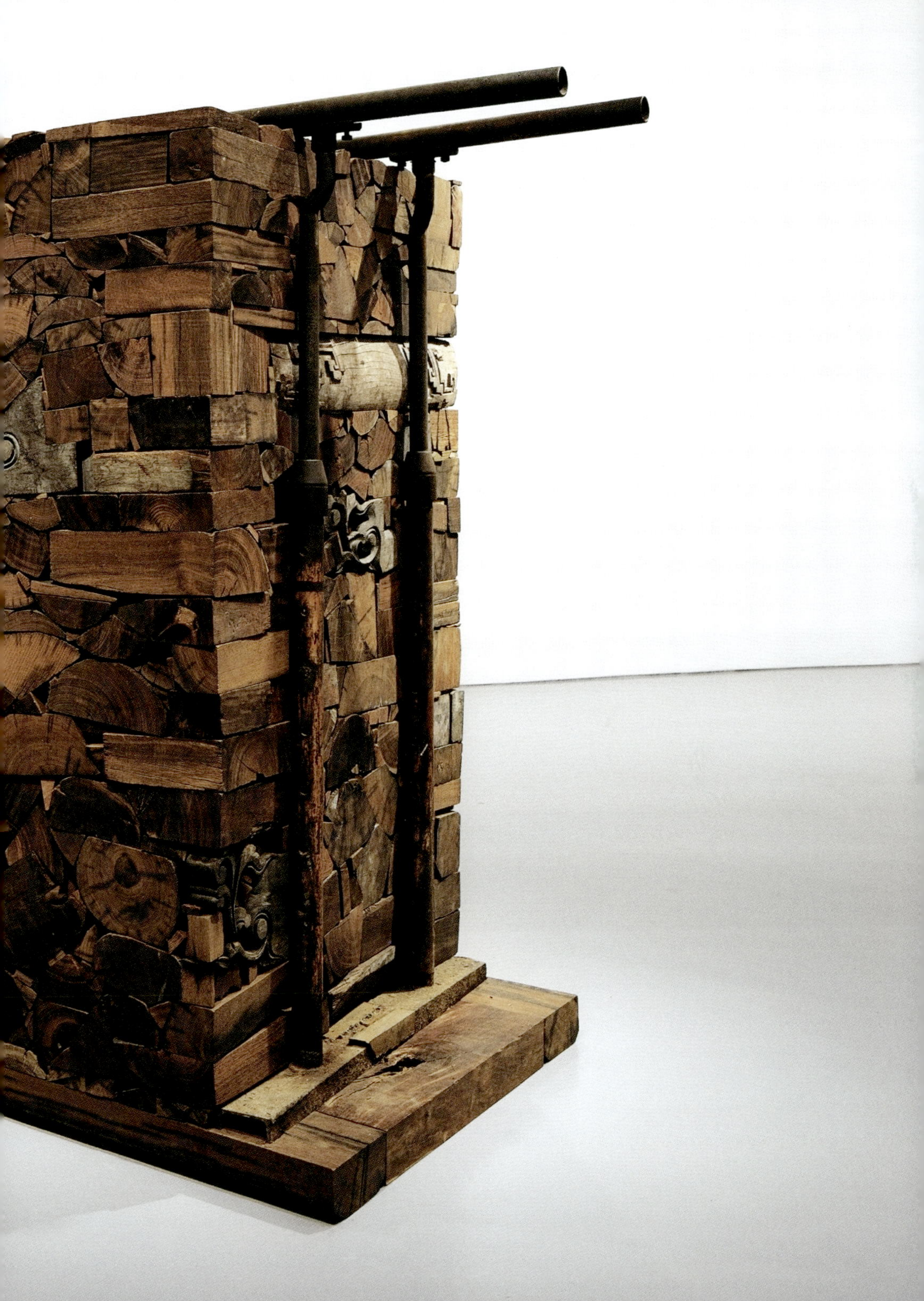

"I like the shape of the spiral, which is so common in nature, but almost impossible to use in architecture. What is fascinating about it is that the dynamic upward motion ultimately goes nowhere: no matter how big you start at the bottom, a spiral always moves in ever smaller concentric circles. This is the shape that defines Vladimir Tatlin's *Monument to the Third International*. It seems to contradict the intellectual ideal it was meant to symbolize, and instead it implies the way in which power ultimately collapses in upon itself. The original building was to be made of glass and steel, which are the same materials used for most chandeliers. Tatlin intended the glass to emphasize the clear, enlightened thinking behind the ideal social system put forward in Lenin's theories. But as we see again and again in history, whenever men experience a bout of revolutionary thinking, they end up boxing themselves in. *Fountain of Light* was just my thinking about these things as they remain relevant today." — AI WEIWEI

Ich mag die Spiralform, die es in der Natur so häufig gibt, in der Architektur jedoch nahezu unmöglich zu verwenden ist. Mich fasziniert die dynamische Aufwärtsbewegung, die letztlich nirgendwohin führt: Gleichgültig, wie groß man unten anfängt, bewegt sich die Spirale in immer kleiner werdenden konzentrischen Zirkeln. Es ist die Form von Vladimir Tatlins Entwurf für das *Monument der Dritten Internationale* und scheint dort dem intellektuellen Ideal zu widersprechen, das sie eigentlich symbolisieren soll. Sie impliziert stattdessen, dass jede Macht letztlich in sich zusammenfällt. Der geplante Bau sollte aus Stahl und Glas gefertigt werden, Materialien, die oft auch für Kronleuchter verwendet werden. Tatlin wollte, dass das Glas das klare, aufgeklärte Denken im idealen Gesellschaftssystem Lenins betonte. Aber wie die Geschichte immer wieder zeigt, legen sich Menschen bei jedem Anfall revolutionären Denkens nur eine Zwangsjacke an. *Fountain of Light* stellt meine Gedanken zu diesen Themen dar, die heute unvermindert relevant sind.

J'aime la forme de la spirale, qu'on trouve partout dans la nature mais qu'il est presque impossible d'utiliser en architecture. Ce qui me fascine, c'est que ce mouvement dynamique vers le haut ne va finalement nulle part : peu importe quelle taille elle a à sa base, une spirale se développe toujours en cercles concentriques de plus en plus petits. C'est cette forme qui a présidé au *Monument à la Troisième Internationale* de Vladimir Tatlin. Il semble en contradiction avec l'idée qu'il est censé incarner, et sous-entendre au lieu de cela que le pouvoir finit toujours par s'effondrer sur lui-même. La construction devait être réalisée en verre et en acier, les mêmes matériaux qu'on utilise souvent pour construire des lustres. Pour Tatlin, le verre devait souligner la clarté, la pensée éclairée contenue dans la théorie léniniste du système social idéal. Mais comme nous avons pu le voir à maintes reprises au cours de l'Histoire, lorsque les hommes vivent une expérience révolutionnaire, ils finissent par s'enfermer. *Fountain of Light* est ma réflexion sur ces problèmes qui sont toujours d'actualité.

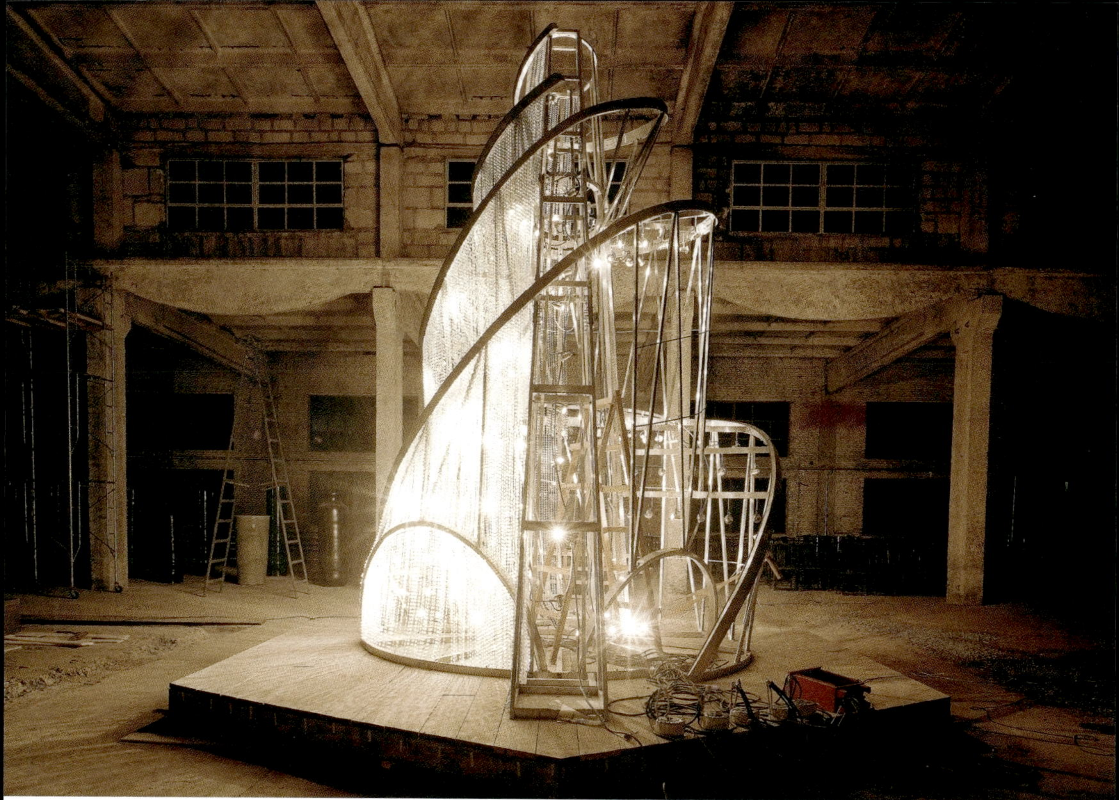

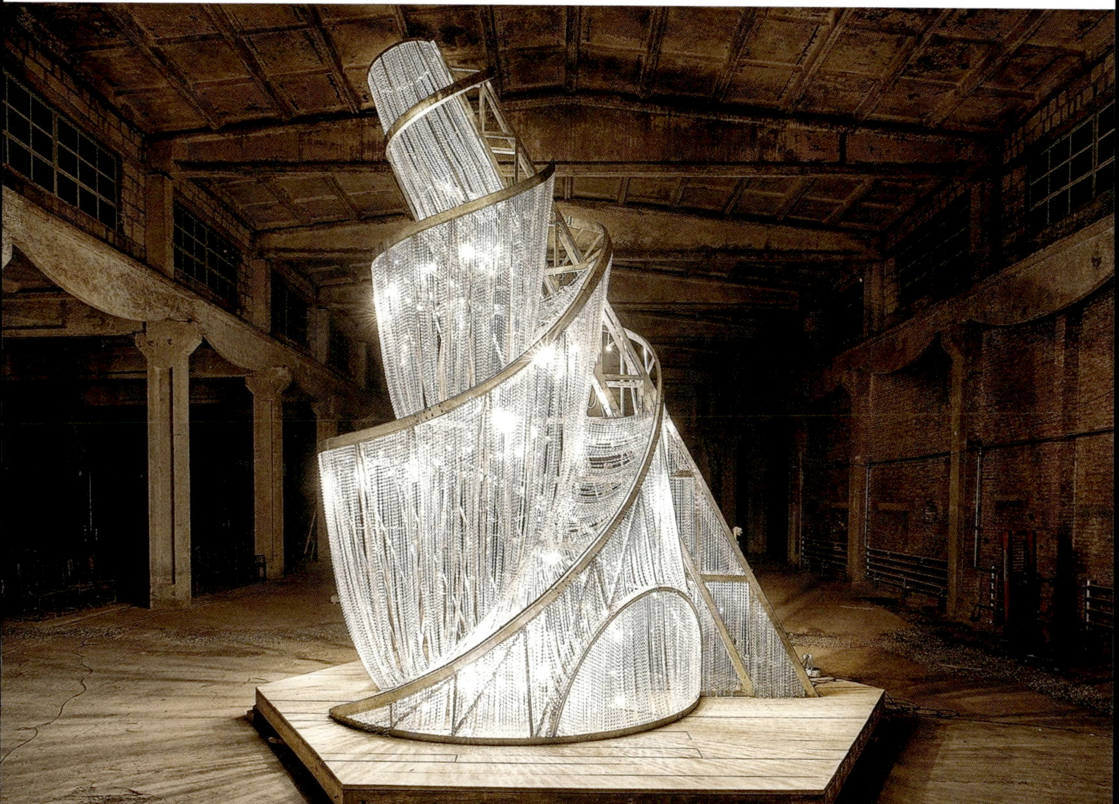

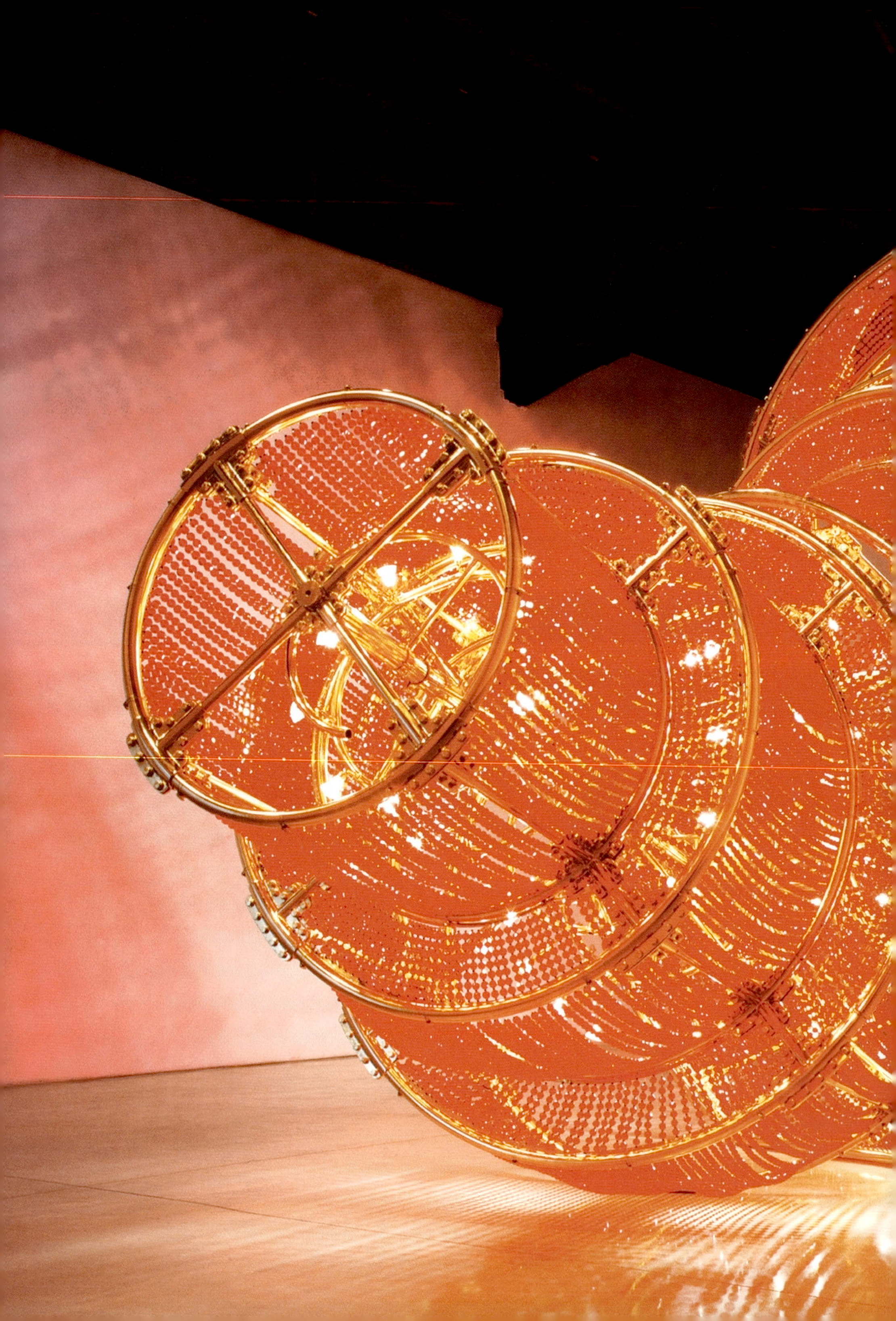

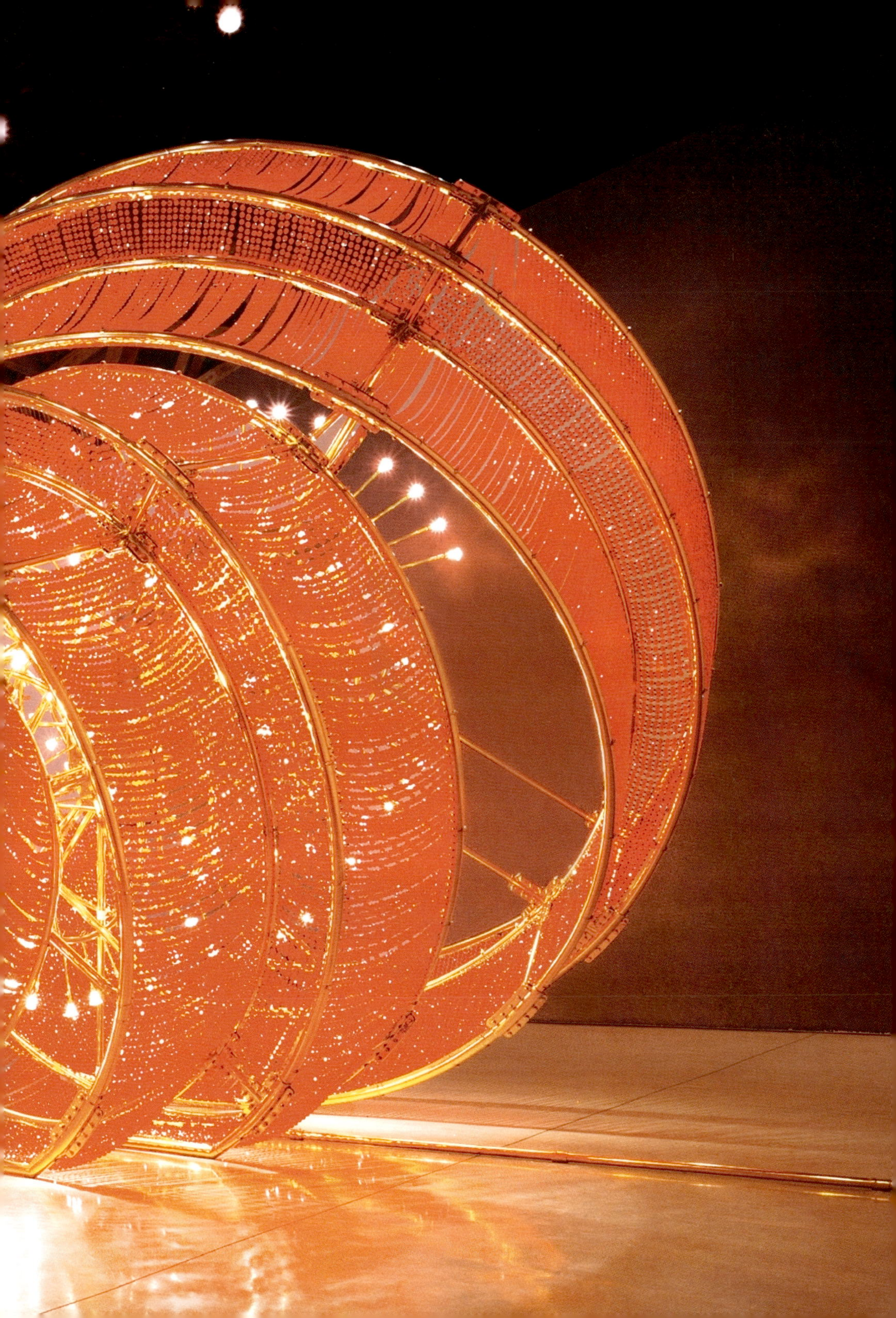

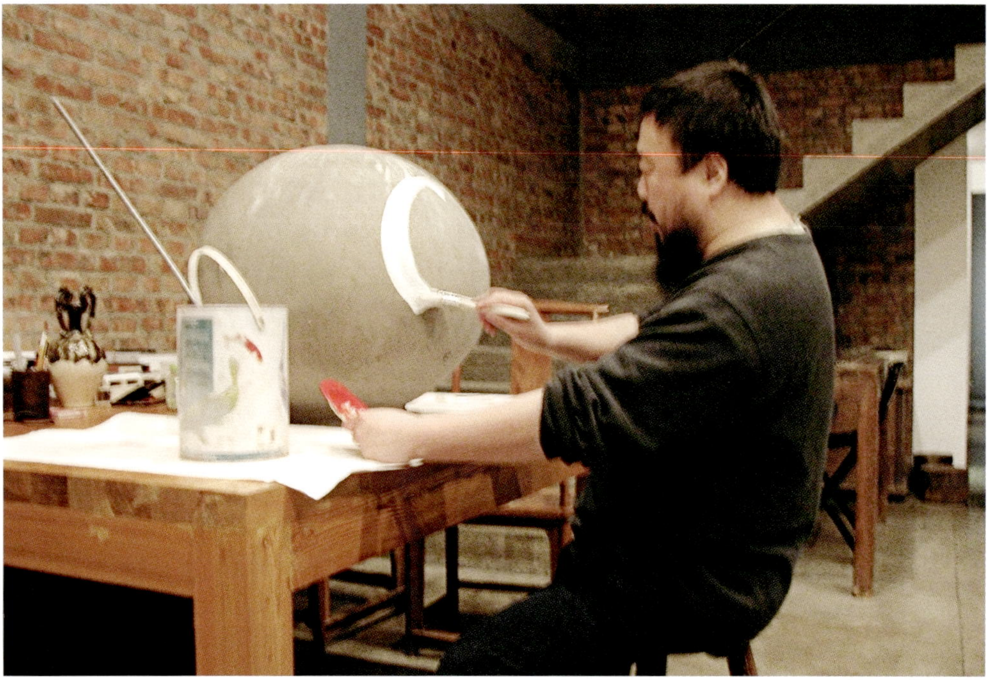

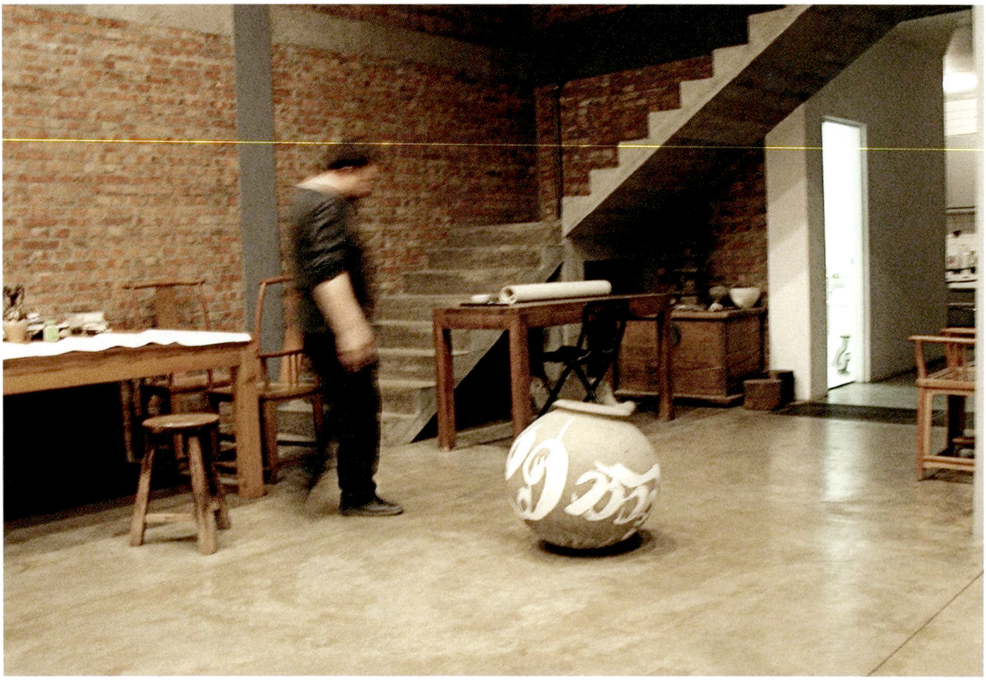

286 | Production views of URN, 2004, urn, paint, 23⅝ x ø 23⅝ inches

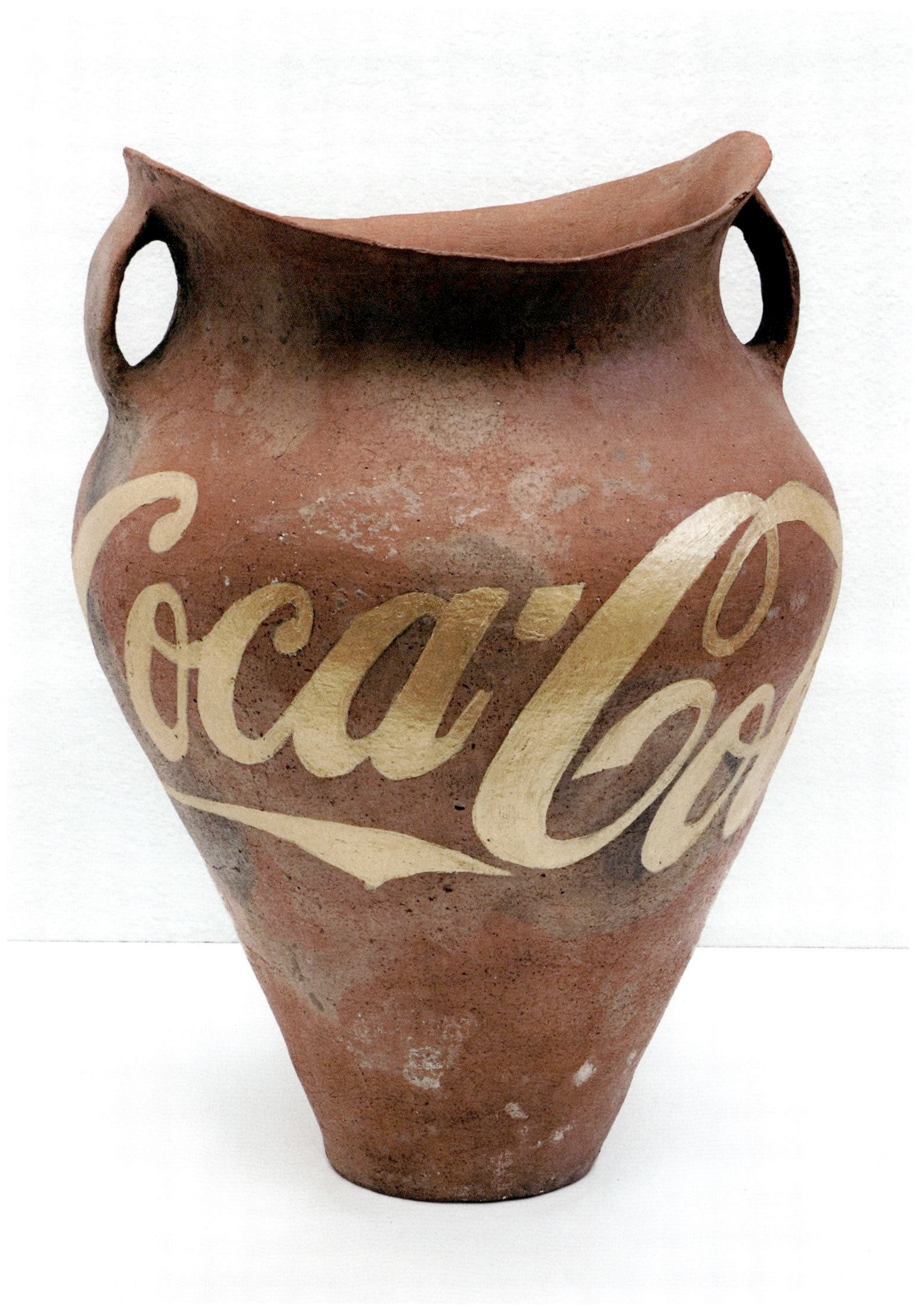

COCA-COLA VASE, 2008, Neolithic vase, paint, 17⅞ x ⌀ 14⅛ inches | 287

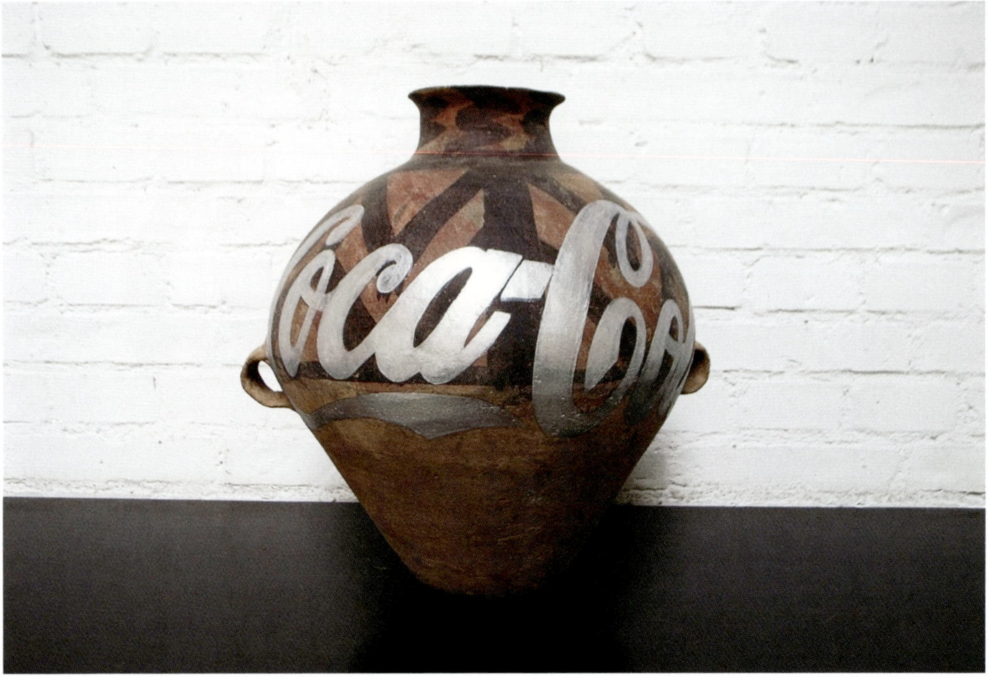

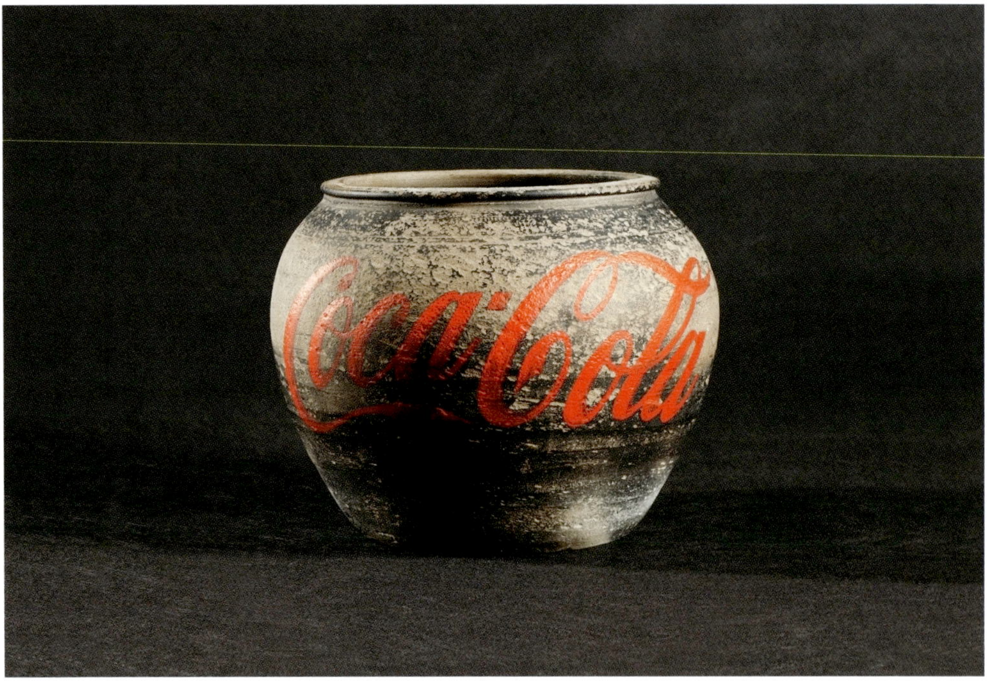

COCA-COLA VASE, 2007 Neolithic vase, paint, 11 x ø 9⅞ inches (top);
288 | COCA-COLA VASE, 2011, Neolithic vase, paint, 11 x ø 13¾ inches (bottom)

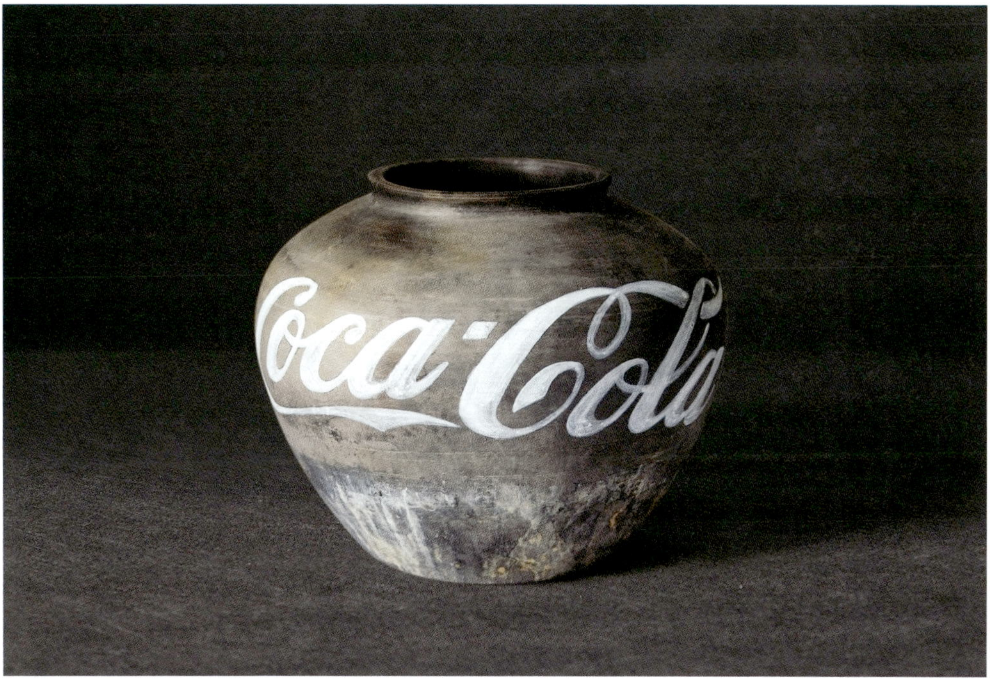

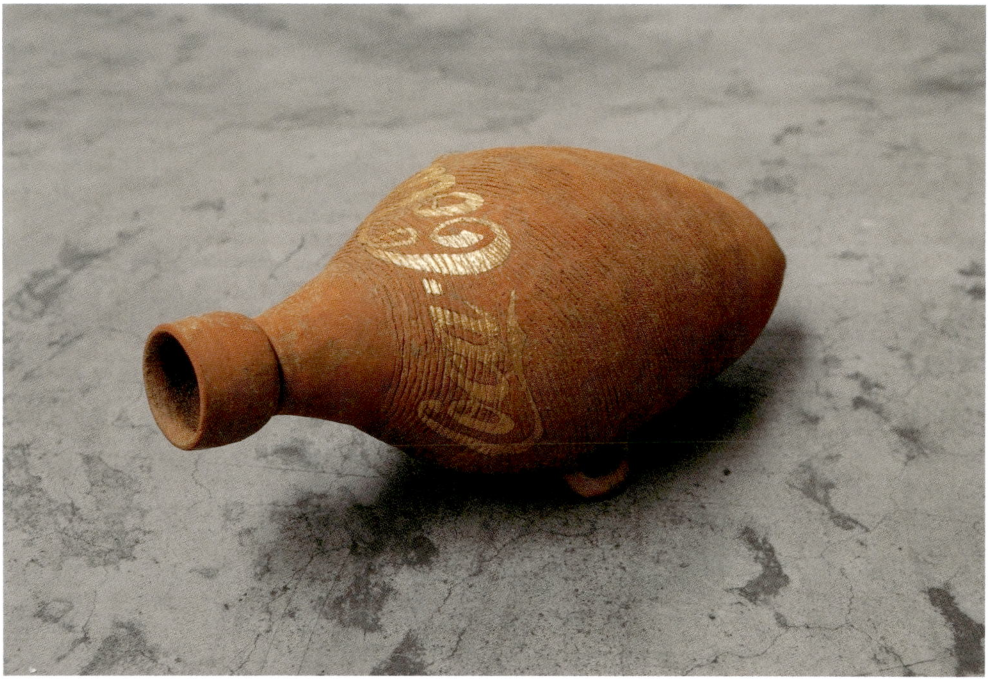

COCA-COLA VASE, 2010, Han Dynasty vase, paint, 10¼ x ø 13 inches (top); COCA-COLA
VASE, 2009, Neolithic amphora from the Yangshao culture, paint, 19¾ x 7½ x ø 9½ inches (bottom) | 289

"Jingdezhen is a town that used to produce high-quality porcelain for emperors, which also filled the treasuries through foreign export. Now it's a city for fakes, counterfeits, and the low-end ugly type of decorations. The traditions are all in ruin, it's very sad. Still we mostly work in a very traditional way. We try to use the highest quality possible; we do have people and knowledge to achieve that. Porcelain is probably the first high-quality material for practical use, which also appeals to an upper-class appreciation of good craft, because it's about the composition of the chemical change during the firing, the color texture, the fineness of the shape. Nothing else ever can really replace it even today. So that's why I'm so fascinated with it." — AI WEIWEI

In der Stadt Jingdezhen wurde früher das hochwertige Porzellan für die Kaiserhäuser hergestellt, dessen Export auch die kaiserlichen Schatztruhen füllte. Heute ist es die Hauptstadt der Fälschungen, Nachahmungen und der billigsten, hässlichsten Form der Dekoration. Die Tradition liegt in Scherben; es ist sehr traurig. Dennoch arbeiten wir dort zum größten Teil auf traditionelle Art. Wir streben nach der höchstmöglichen Qualität und haben Fachkräfte und das Know-how, sie zu erreichen. Porzellan ist wahrscheinlich der erste hochwertige Werkstoff, der zu praktischen Zwecken eingesetzt wurde, was wiederum der Oberklasse mit ihrer Vorliebe für gutes Handwerk gefiel. Es geht um die genauen chemischen Veränderungen während des Brennens, um die Farbtextur, die Feinheit der Form. Bis heute kommt dem Porzellan kein anderes Material gleich – darum fasziniert es mich.

Jingdezhen est une ville où l'on produisait de la porcelaine d'excellente qualité pour les empereurs, et l'exportation de ces produits a rempli les caisses de l'État. Aujourd'hui, c'est la ville de la contrefaçon et des décorations de mauvaise qualité et de mauvais goût. Les traditions se perdent, et c'est bien triste. Nous continuons à travailler avec des méthodes traditionnelles. Nous nous efforçons d'utiliser des produits de la meilleure qualité possible ; nous avons les artisans et les connaissances qui le permettent. La porcelaine est probablement le premier matériau de qualité dédié à un usage pratique, et les classes les plus aisées apprécient la qualité de cet artisanat. Tout est fonction de la modification de la composition chimique pendant sa cuisson, la texture de sa couleur, la finesse de sa forme. Aujourd'hui encore, rien ne peut vraiment la remplacer. C'est pour cela que la porcelaine me fascine autant.

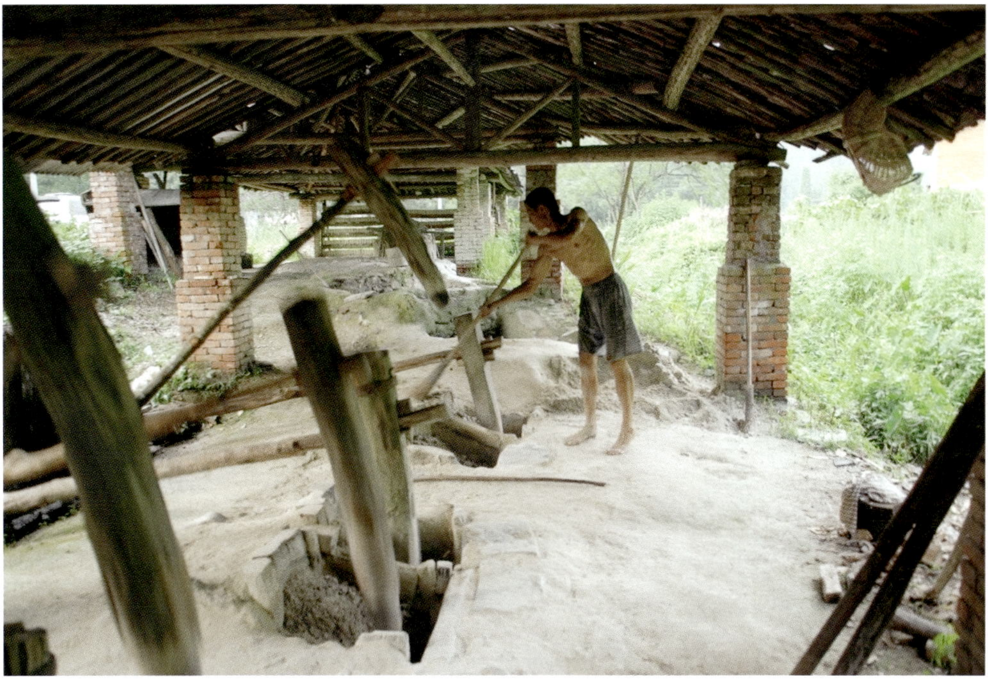

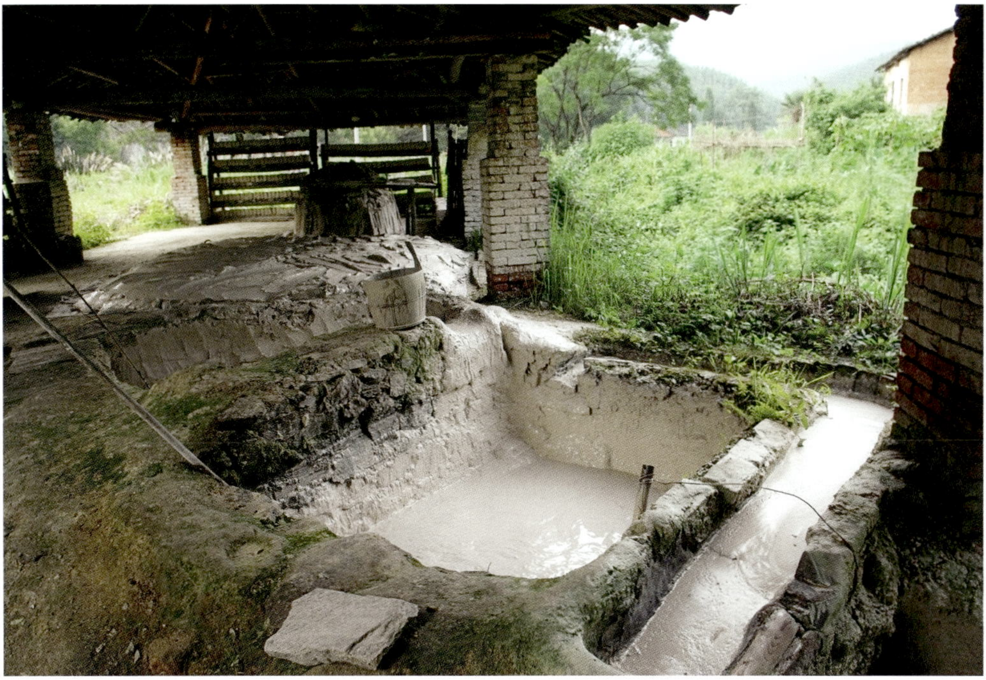

Porcelain production for Ai Weiwei, Jingdezhen, Zhejiang Province, 2006 |

"In the beginning I just wanted to test out how the craftsmen's skill was. So we went to this local dress shop. I bought this dress for little girls and said: Can you just try to find a way to make this one? The result was fine, though it's like you have to know it. It was like practice. All my work is like practice for nothing." — AI WEIWEI

Anfangs wollte ich nur das Können des Handwerkers testen. Wir gingen also in einen kleinen Kleiderladen, wo ich ein Mädchenkleid kaufte, und ich bat ihn: Versuch einmal, ob du das irgendwie machen kannst. Die Ergebnisse waren gut, aber vielleicht muss man dazu das Originalkleid kennen. Es war wie eine Übung. Mein gesamtes Werk ist wie eine Übung ohne Zweck.

Au début, je voulais juste tester le savoir-faire des artisans. Je suis allé dans cette boutique de robes de fabrication industrielle. J'en ai acheté une pour petite fille et j'ai demandé aux artisans de refaire cette robe. Le résultat était très satisfaisant, mais c'était comme s'il fallait que je m'assure que c'était possible. C'était comme un entraînement. Toute mon œuvre est un entraînement pour rien.

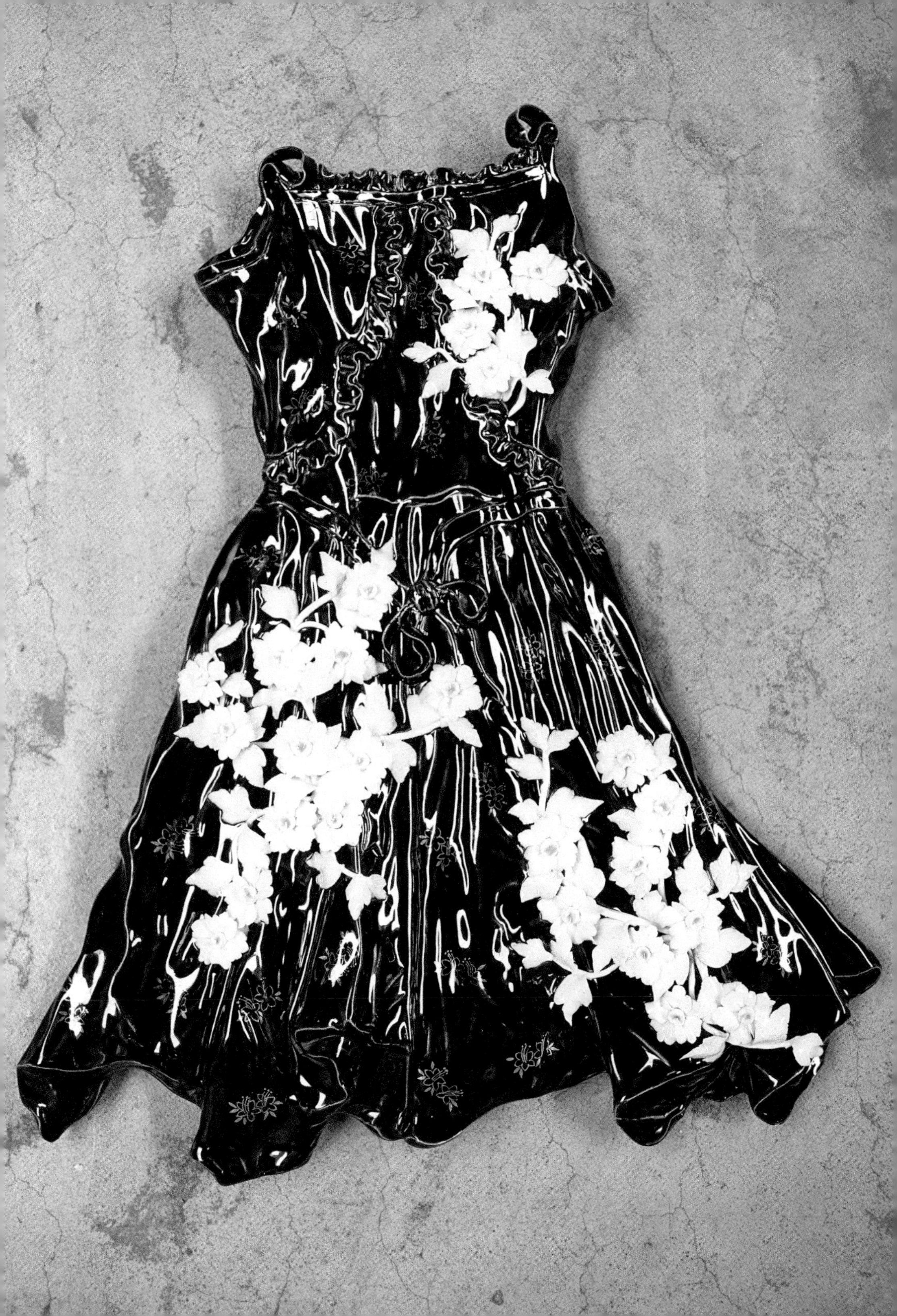

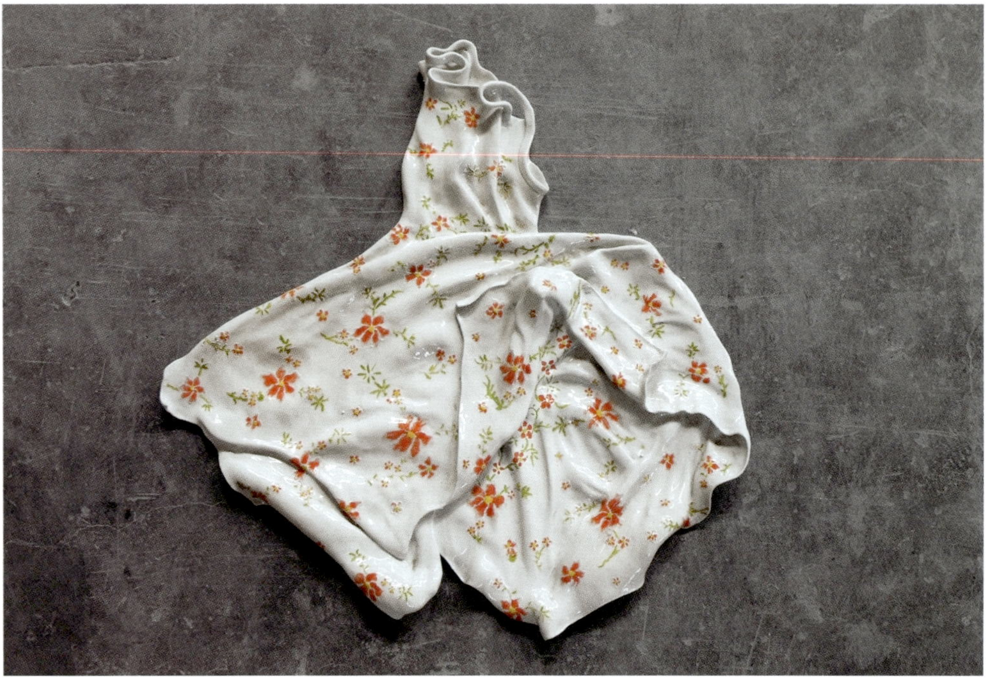

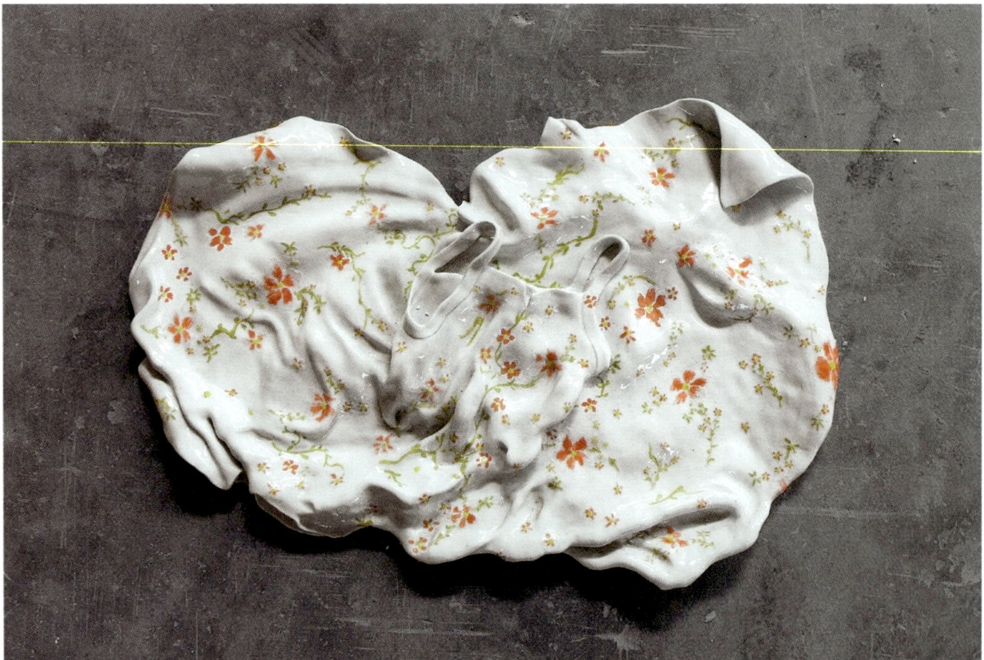

DRESS WITH FLOWERS, 2007, porcelain, 3 ⅛ x 26 x 25 ¾ inches (top);
294 | DRESS WITH FLOWERS, 2004, porcelain, 2 ⅜ x 26 ⅗ x 18 ⅛ inches (bottom)

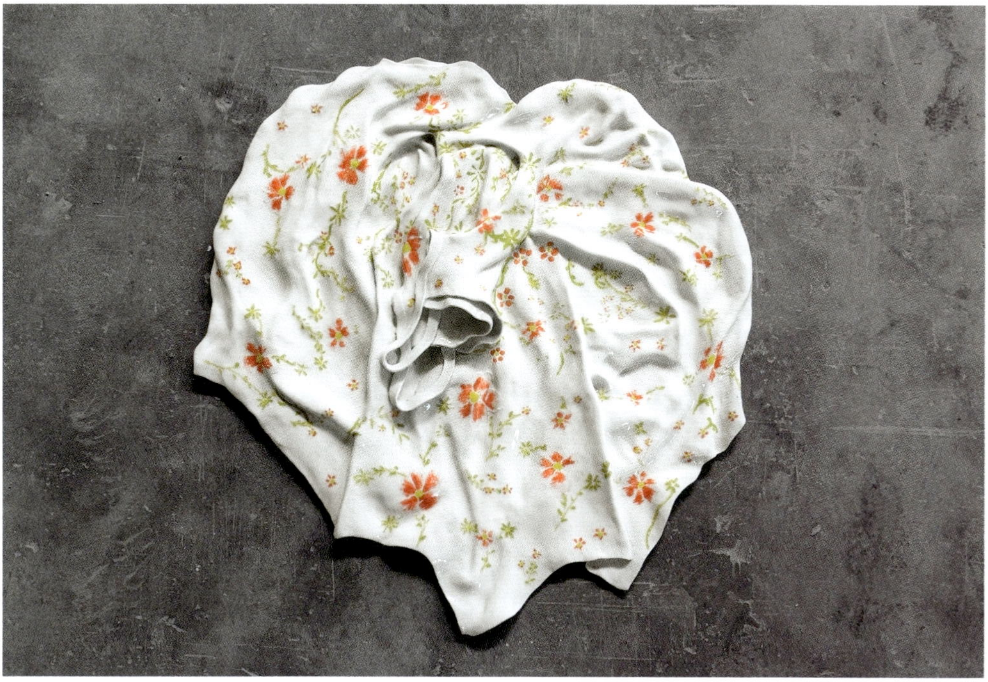

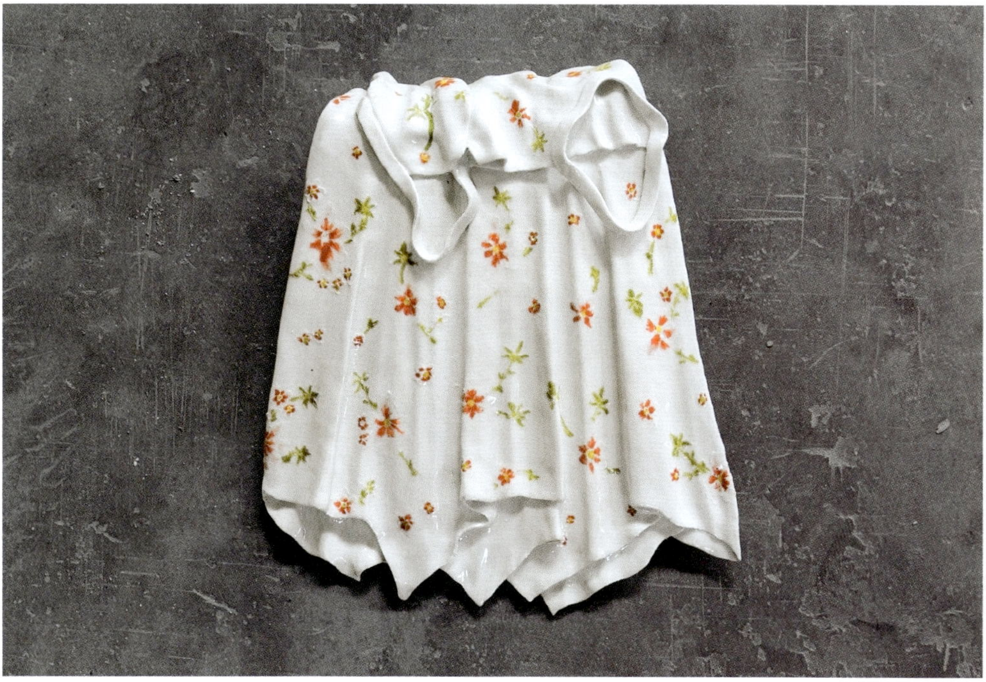

DRESS WITH FLOWERS, 2007, porcelain, 2⅜ x 22 x 22 inches (top);
DRESS WITH FLOWERS, 2007, porcelain, 8⅛ x 15⅜ x 13¾ inches (bottom) | 295

"We were trying to find out the limit of porcelain making. In the old
temples, the vases were made for practical purposes. So to make something huge
like this was really ridiculous. We had to build a special kind of kiln to fire it.
That became a technical challenge, because in the high temperature the pieces
often collapsed, hundreds of them, often also destroying the kiln. So for me it
was that challenge: this is the largest object in one piece that you can make in
porcelain." — AI WEIWEI

Wir wollten die Grenzen der Porzellanherstellung austesten. In alten Tempeln waren
die Vasen immer für praktische Zwecke gemacht. Es war eigentlich lächerlich, sie zu solch
gewaltigen Ausmaßen zu vergrößern. Wir mussten eine spezielle Art von Ofen bauen, um
sie zu brennen. Das wurde zu einem technischen Problem, denn bei den hohen Tempera-
turen fielen die Stücke oft in sich zusammen, Hunderte von ihnen, und oft ging dabei
auch der Ofen zu Bruch. Darin bestand die Herausforderung für mich: Das ist das größte
Objekt, das man in einem Stück aus Porzellan machen kann.

Nous nous demandions quelles étaient les limites de la fabrication de la porcelaine.
Dans les vieux temples, les vases avaient une utilité pratique. Fabriquer des objets aussi
grands était vraiment ridicule. Il nous a fallu construire un four spécial pour pouvoir les
cuire. C'est devenu un défi technique, car à haute température, les objets s'effondraient
souvent sur eux-mêmes, par centaines, endommageant aussi le four. Pour moi, c'était
un défi : voilà le plus grand objet d'un seul tenant qu'on peut fabriquer en porcelaine.

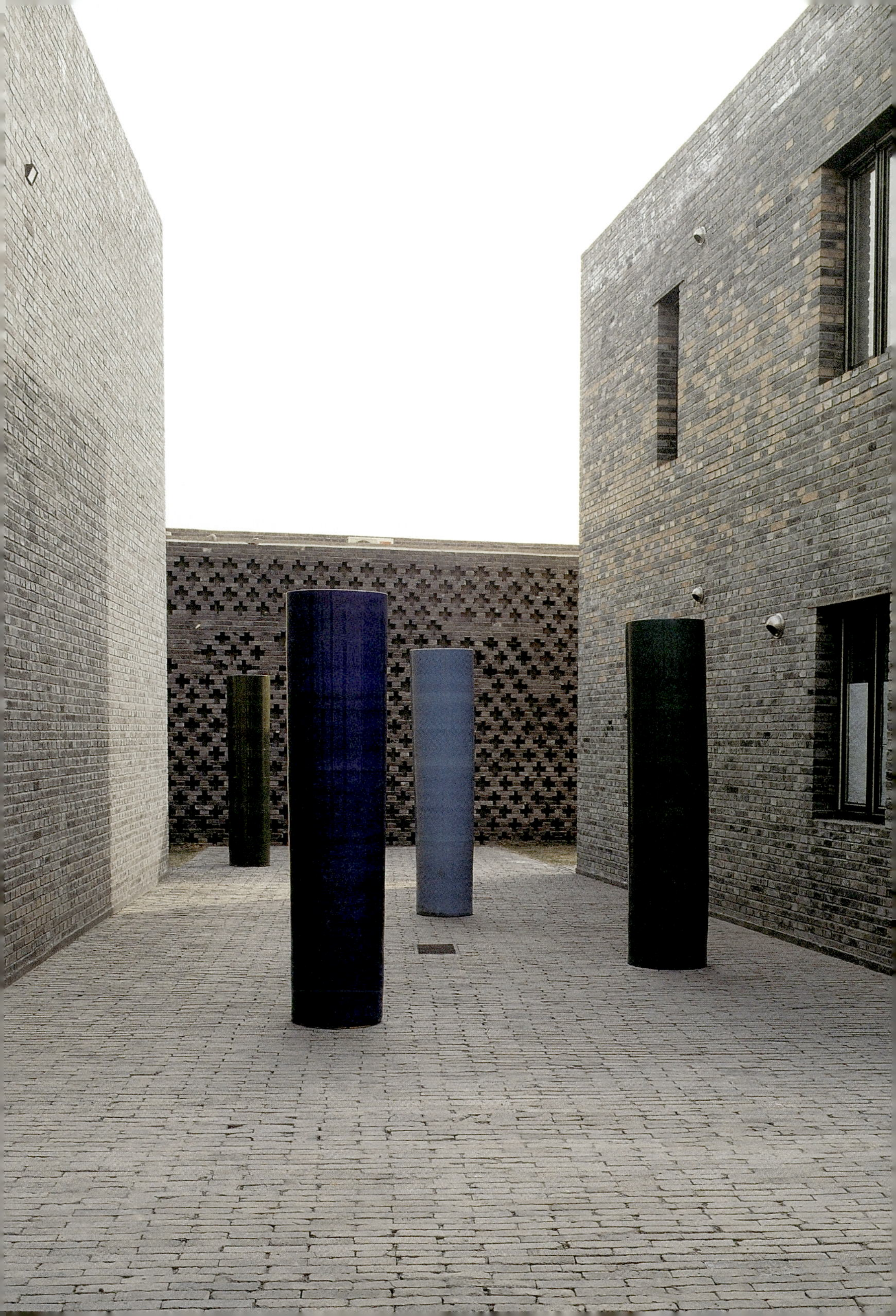

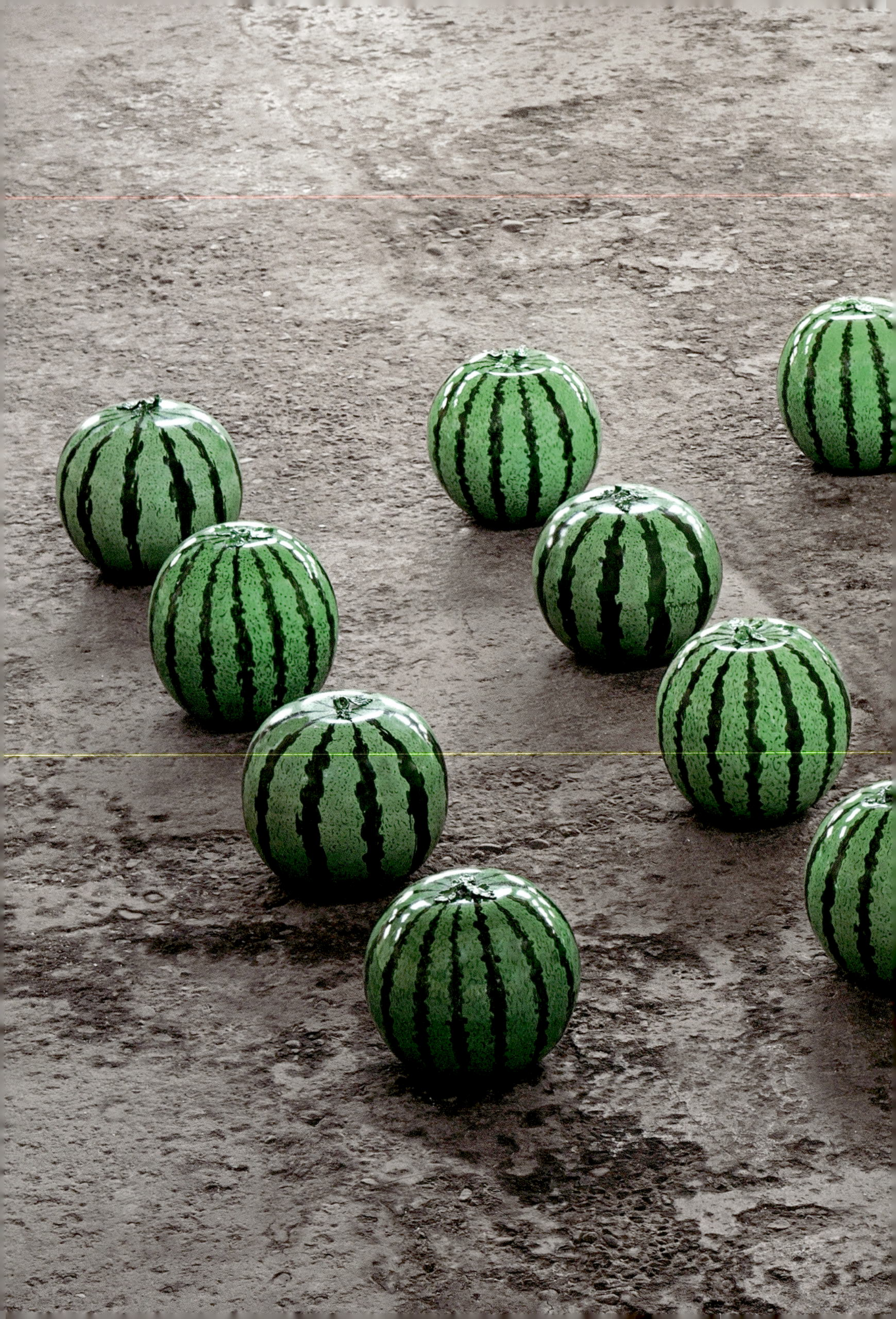

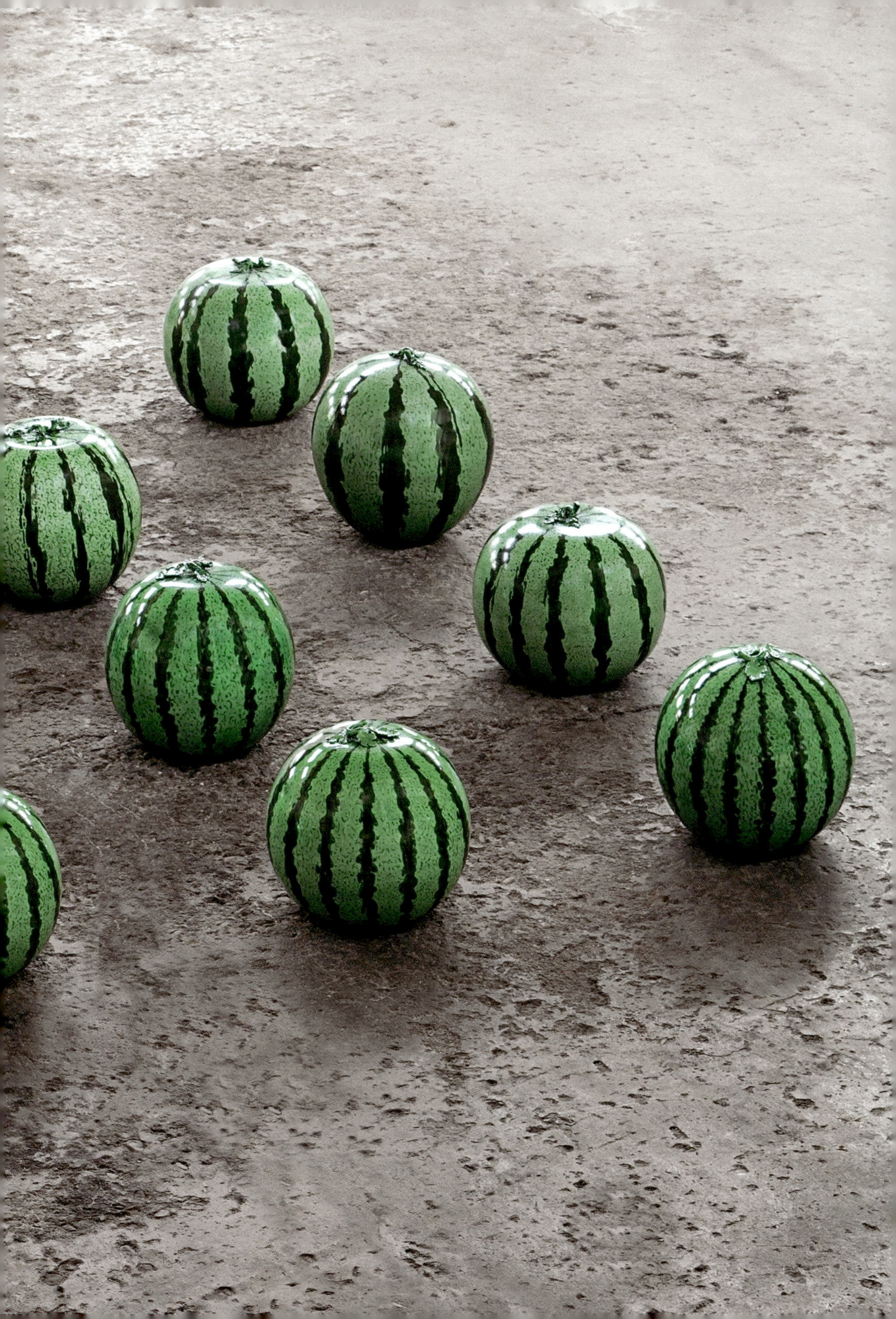

"This work relates to several things. The ruyi scepter was an object which belonged to the imperial courts and then later also to scholars or as a talisman to the people. But we used the language of porcelain, which is really the finest language China has ever created. And then there are the organs. I have often written about this in my blogs: China has become the world's most active market for human organs. It's not because the Chinese people are cheap; even though you live cheaply doesn't mean you'll become cheap after you die. You will discover that, as an average person, once you are disassembled and sold, you will become very expensive. If someone opens you and sells your spare parts once you've departed, you become much more valuable than you were as a complete living and breathing organism." — AI WEIWEI

Diese Arbeit weist mehrere Bezüge auf. Das Ruyi-Zepter war ursprünglich ein Gegenstand des kaiserlichen Hofs. Später wurde es an Gelehrte vergeben und zu einem Talisman des Volkes. Wir wählten für unsere Version die Sprache des Porzellans – die feinste Sprache, die China hervorgebracht hat. Dann sind da noch die Organe. Ich habe häufig in meinem Blog darüber geschrieben: China ist mittlerweile der aktivste Handelsplatz für menschliche Organe. Das liegt nicht etwa daran, dass die Chinesen billig sind. Auch wenn man billig lebt, heißt das nicht, dass man nach dem Tod billig ist. Es zeigt sich, dass der Durchschnittsmensch, einmal zerlegt und verkauft, sehr teuer ist. Wenn Sie jemand nach Ihrem Tod aufschneidet und Ihre Einzelteile verkauft, so werden Sie sehr viel wertvoller sein, als Sie es zu Lebzeiten waren.

Cette œuvre fait référence à plusieurs choses. Le ruyi était un sceptre qu'on trouvait dans les cours impériales, puis chez les érudits, et il fait office de talisman pour le peuple. Pour réaliser cette œuvre, nous avons utilisé le langage de la porcelaine, qui est le plus délicat que la Chine ait créé. Quant aux organes : je l'ai souvent évoqué dans mon blog, la Chine est devenu le marché d'organes humains le plus actif au monde. Pas parce que c'est moins cher ; ce n'est pas parce qu'on vit modestement qu'on ne vaudra pas grand-chose après sa mort. Apprenez qu'une personne moyenne, une fois désassemblée, vaut beaucoup d'argent. Une fois mort, si quelqu'un vend vos organes comme des pièces détachées, vous vaudrez bien plus que lorsque vous étiez vivant.

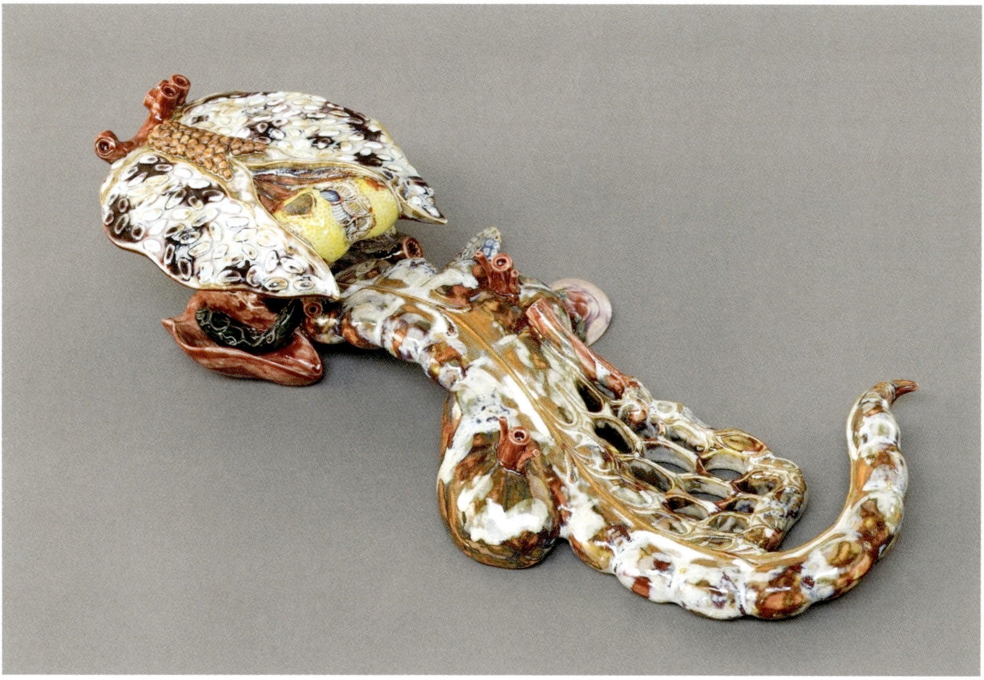

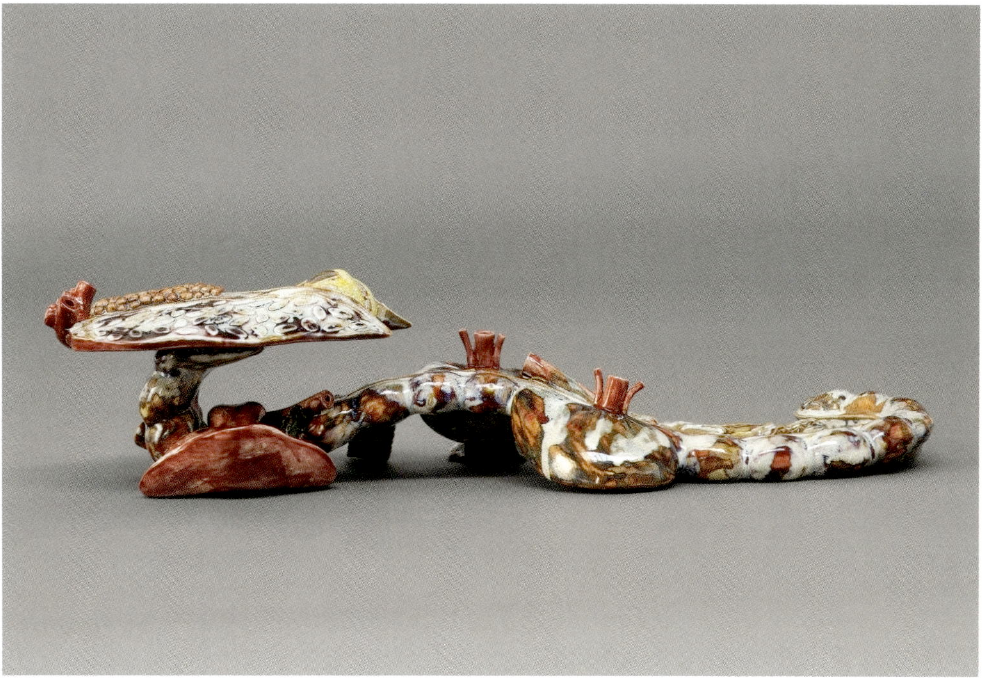

RUYI, 2006, porcelain, 5 ⅛ x 30 ¼ x 9 ⅝ inches |

"Over the past decade China would have thousands of people vanishing in the mines every year because of the bad safety standards. And there were environmental incidents. So I wrote a lot of blog articles. And I wanted to use coal for this work. The coal is actually cast in fiberglass and painted with a Chinese lacquer, which looks very similar. When people see the arrangement of the pieces, they will also think of Richard Long, so at the same time I make fun of that." — AI WEIWEI

In den letzten zehn Jahren sind aufgrund mangelnder Sicherheitsvorkehrungen jedes Jahr Tausende von Bergleuten in Minen verschüttet worden. Auch gibt es immer wieder Umweltskandale. Ich schrieb viele Blogartikel darüber. Und ich wollte dieses Werk realisieren, in dem ich Kohle verwendete. Die Kohle aber ist in Glasfaser gegossen und mit einem chinesischen Lack bemalt, sodass die Ähnlichkeit verblüffend ist. Wenn Betrachter die Installation sehen, müssen sie unwillkürlich an Richard Long denken, darüber mache ich mich auch ein bisschen lustig.

Au cours des dix dernières années, des milliers de personnes ont disparu chaque année dans les mines chinoises en raison des mauvaises conditions de sécurité. À cela s'ajoutent les accidents environnementaux. J'ai posté de nombreux articles sur mon blog à ce sujet. Et j'ai voulu utiliser du charbon pour cette œuvre. En fait, le charbon est ici entouré de fibre de verre et peint à la laque de Chine, mais c'est très ressemblant. Quand les gens verront la disposition des morceaux de charbon, cela va aussi les faire penser à Richard Long, c'est un peu une parodie.

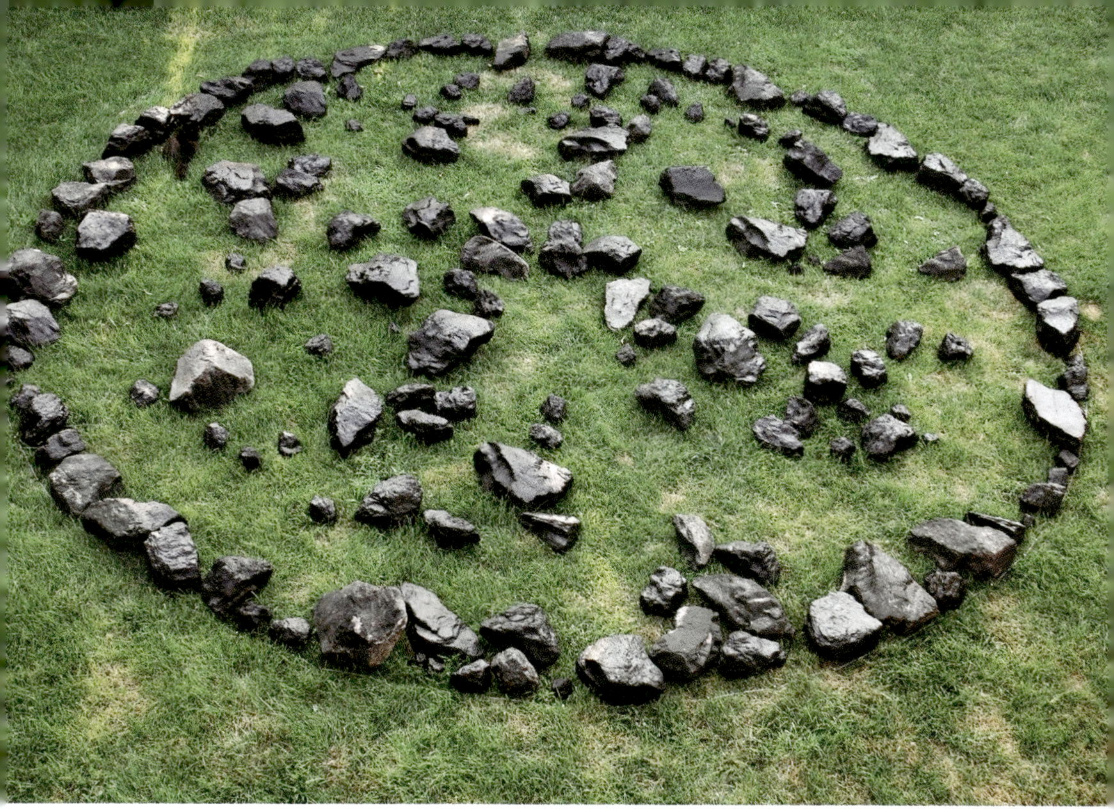

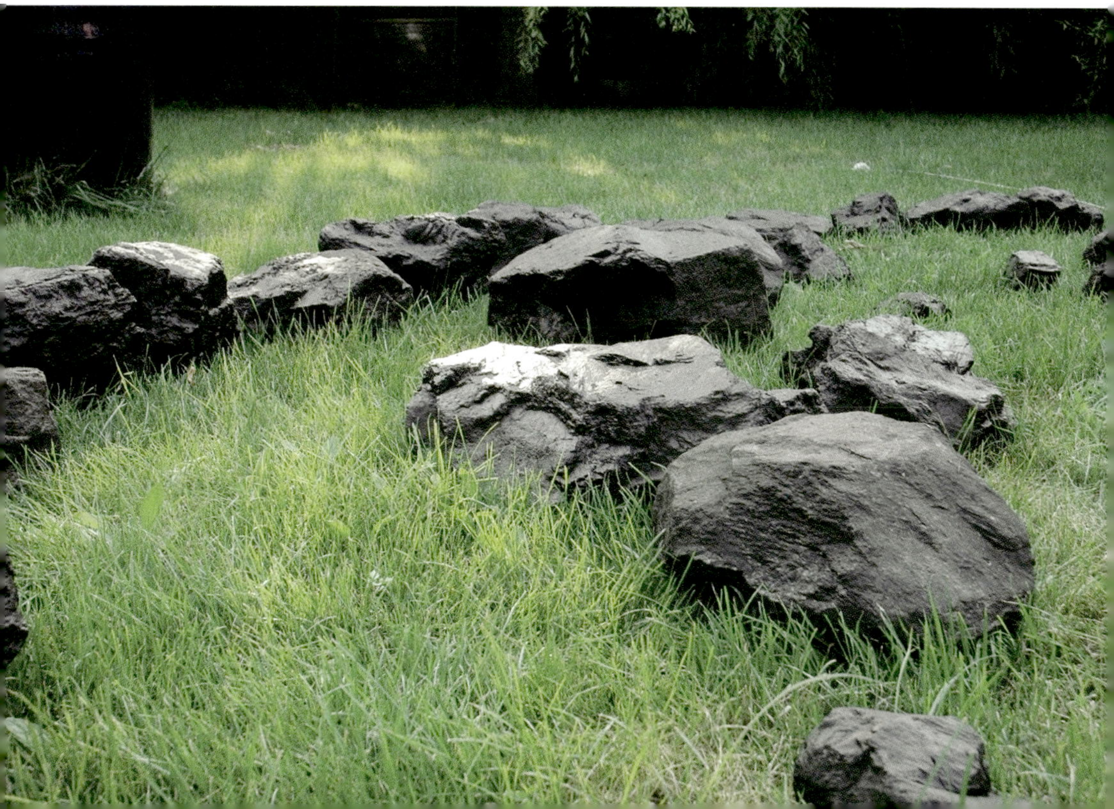

"In China there is a lot of appreciation for natural materials. If there's a
defect in any object, it is regarded as a unique quality, because it shows that some
kind of incident has happened in nature. So those defects are used to make
beautiful things. Every surface in these marble doors is different. The dimensions
of the doors are all based on mathematics, like conceptual art or minimalism.
But, at the same time, each has very beautiful stains in the stone that look like
a special fog or air." — AI WEIWEI

In China werden natürliche Materialien überaus geschätzt. Weist ein Gegenstand
Schadstellen oder Fehler auf, so wird dies als eine einzigartige Qualität betrachtet, die das
Walten der Natur zeigt. Also werden diese Mängel dazu benutzt, besonders schöne Dinge zu
fertigen. Bei den Marmortüren hier sind alle Oberflächen verschieden. Die Abmessungen
der Türen basieren auf mathematischen Verhältnissen, wie bei Konzeptkunst oder Mini-
malismus. Dabei hat jede Marmorplatte sehr schöne Verfärbungen, die wie Nebelschleier
oder ein besonderer Himmel erscheinen.

En Chine, on apprécie beaucoup les matériaux naturels. Si un objet présente un
défaut, celui-ci est considéré comme une qualité unique, le témoignage d'un incident qui
s'est produit dans la nature. Ces défauts sont donc utilisés pour fabriquer des belles choses.
La surface de chacune de ces portes en marbre est différente. Ses dimensions ont été
mesurées, calculées mathématiquement, comme dans une œuvre d'art conceptuel ou minimaliste. Mais chacune d'entre elles présente de magnifiques défauts qui font penser au
ciel ou à la brume.

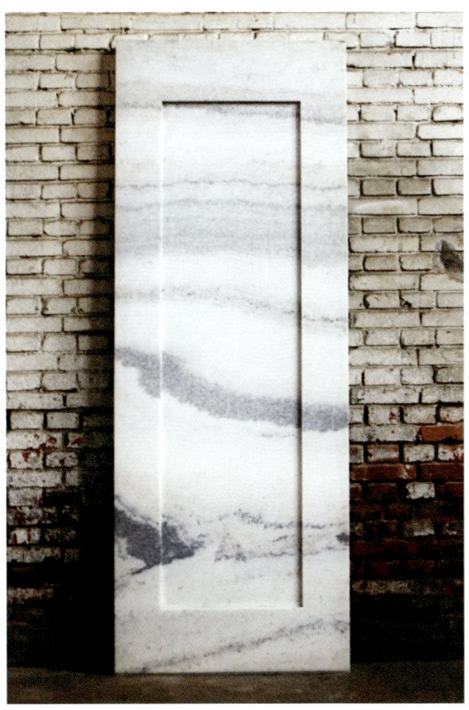
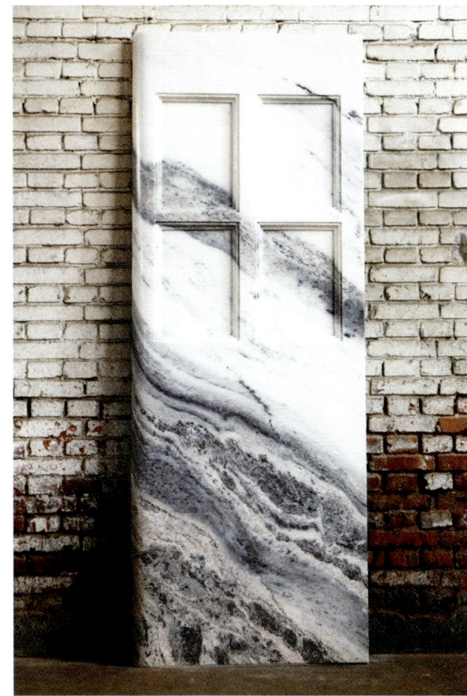
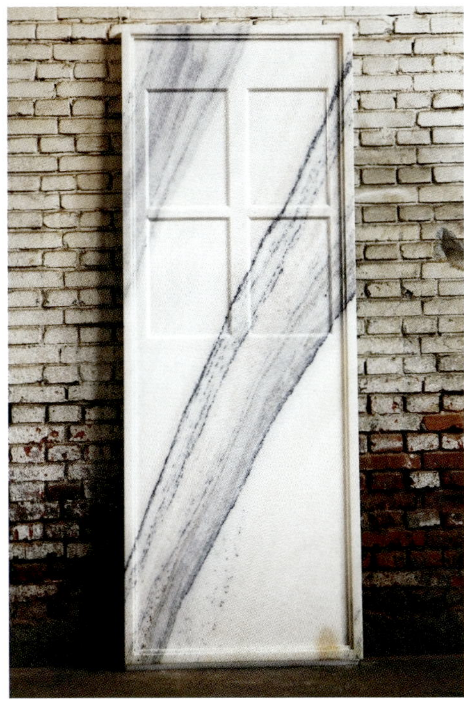
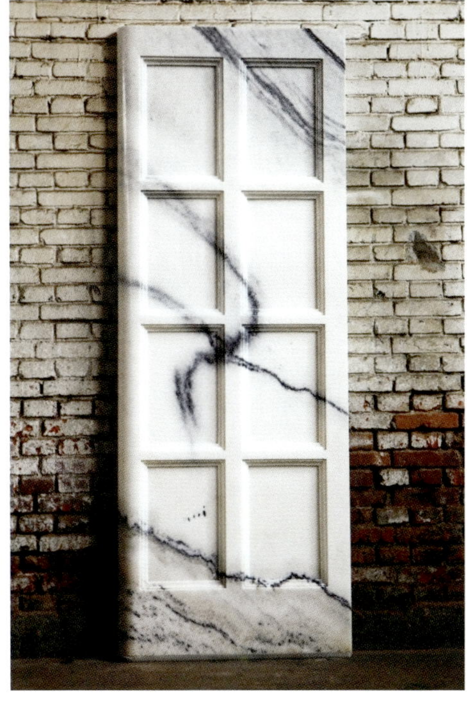

MARBLE DOORS, 2007, marble, each 82 ⅝ x 31 ½ x 2 ⅜ inches | 305

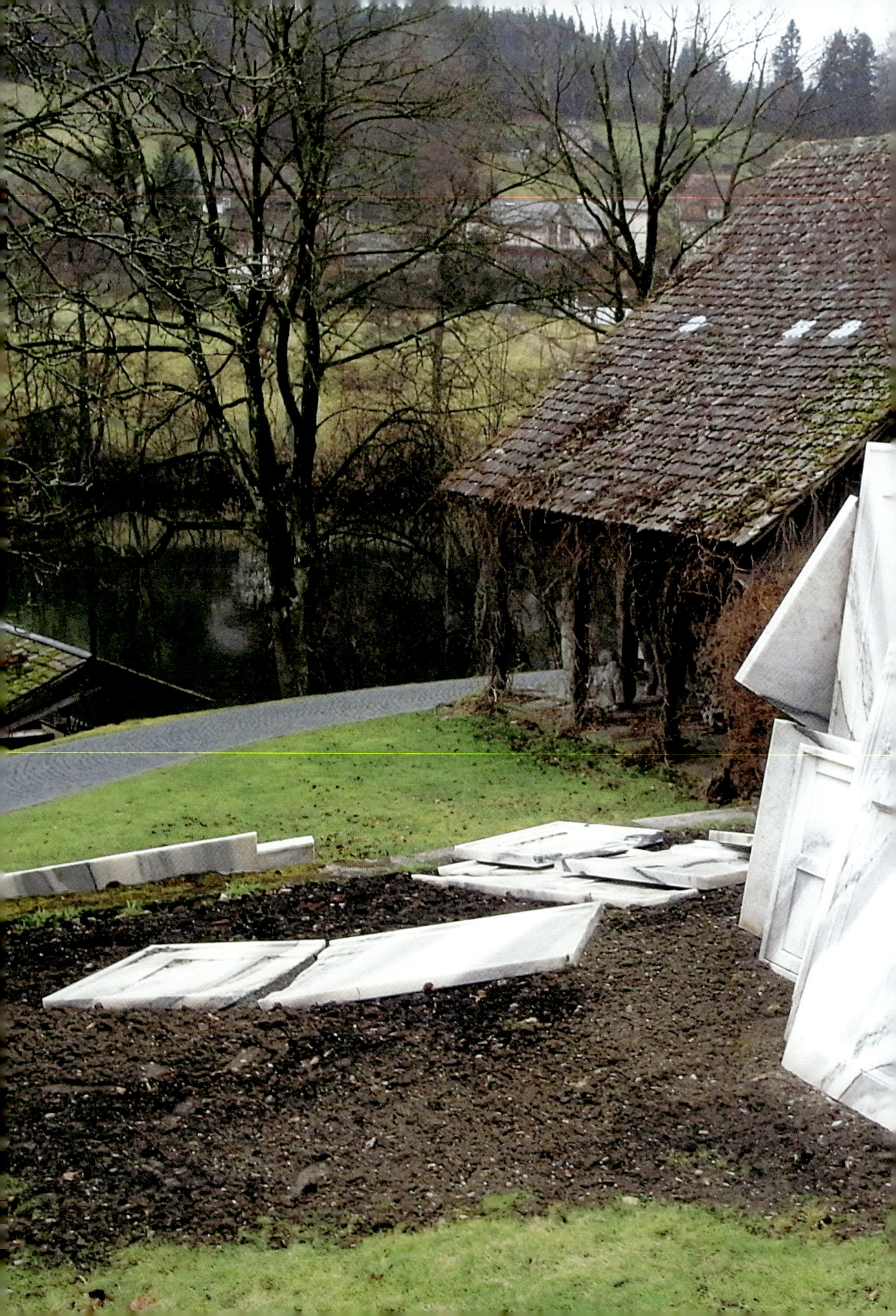

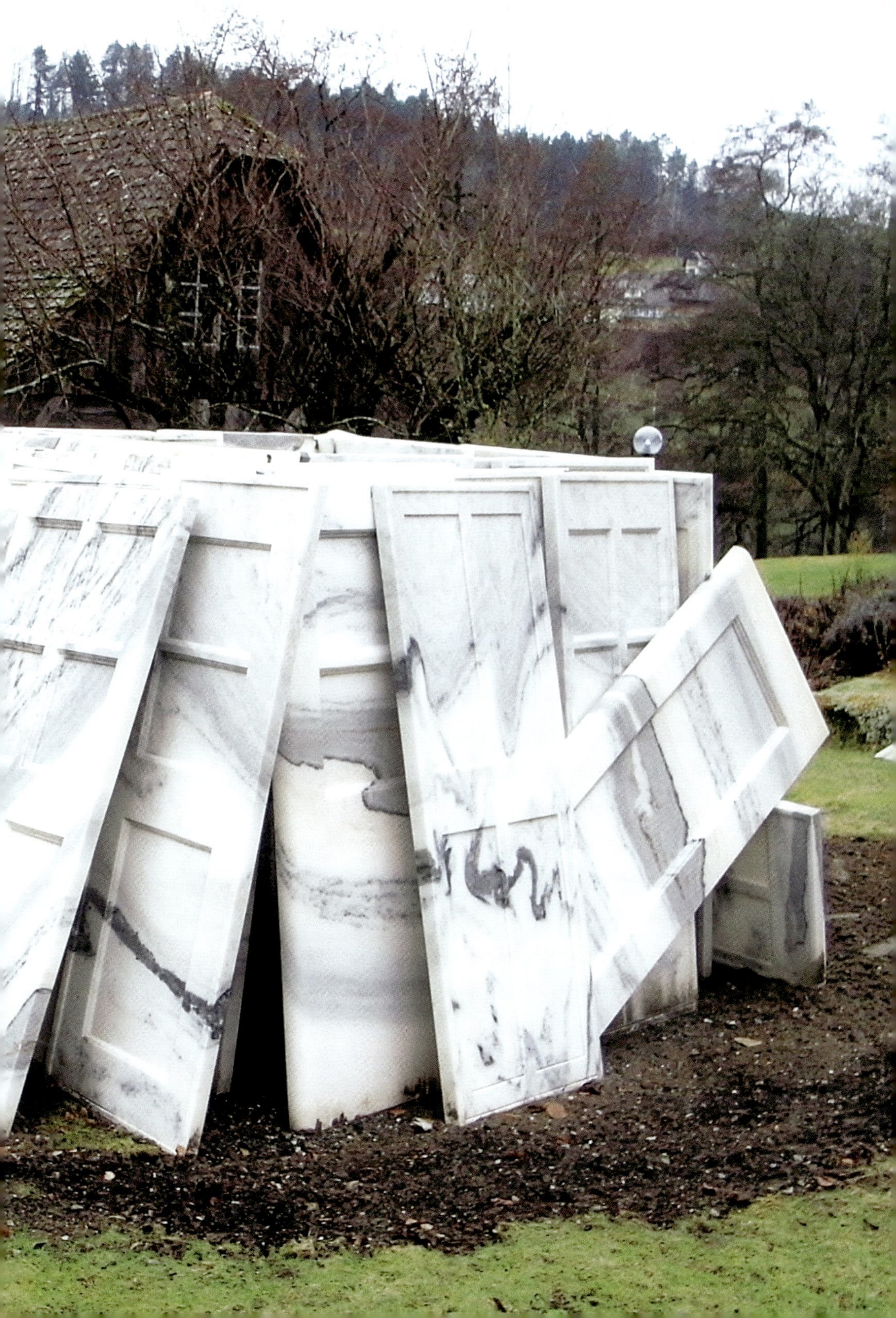

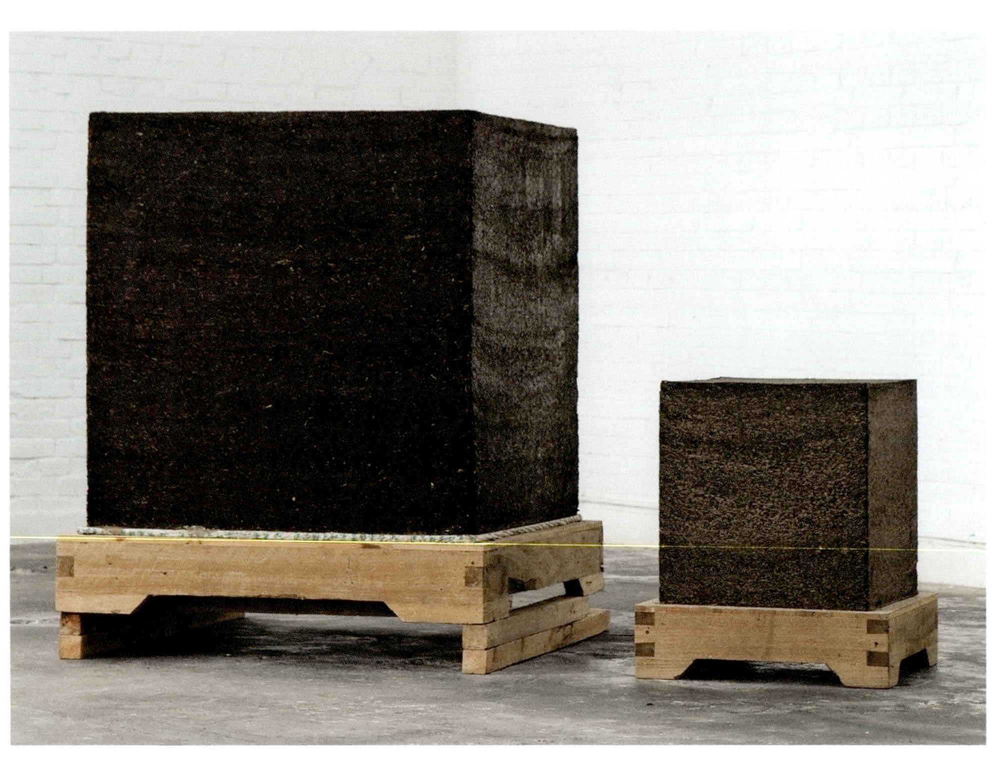

TON OF TEA, 2006, 1 ton of compressed tea, 39 ⅜ x 39 ⅜ x 39 ⅜ inches; TEA CUBE, 2008, compressed tea, 19 ¾ x 19 ¾ x 19 ¾ inches | Previous spread: MONUMENTAL JUNKYARD, 2007, marble, 40 pieces, each 83 ⅞ x 35 ⅞ x 2 ⅜ inches, 20 pieces, each 82 ⅝ x 31 ½ x 2 ⅜ inches; Uli Sigg residence, Schloss Mauensee

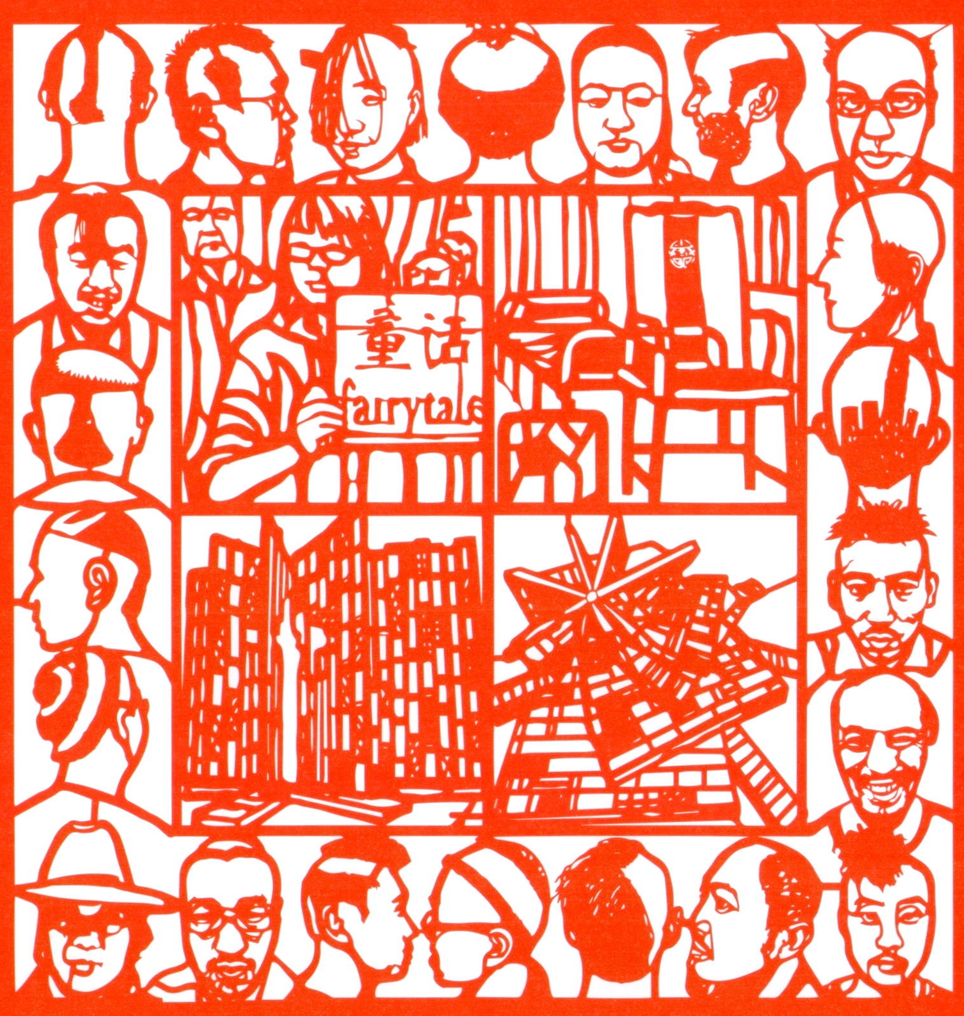

Documenta 2007

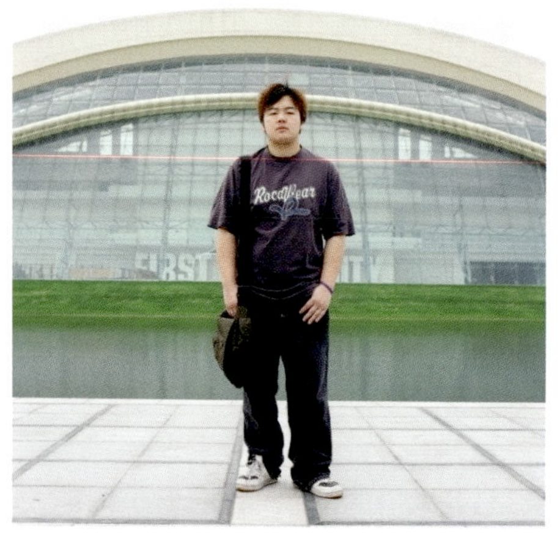 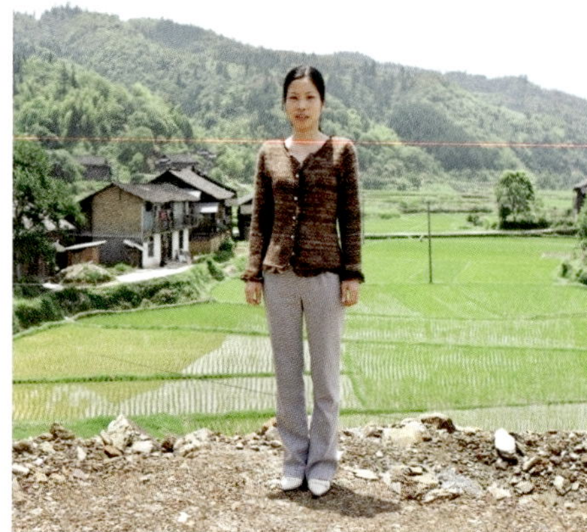

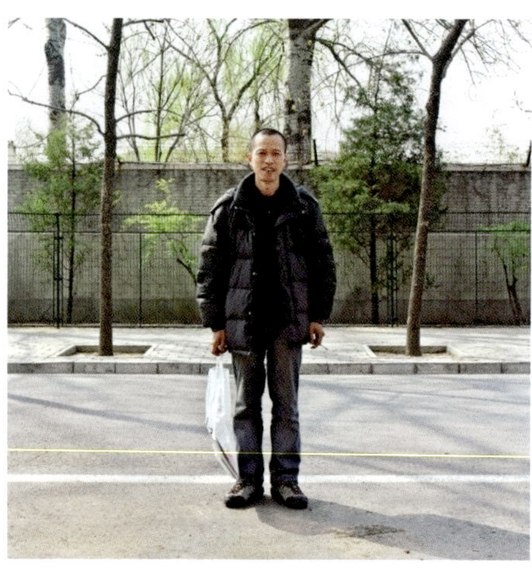 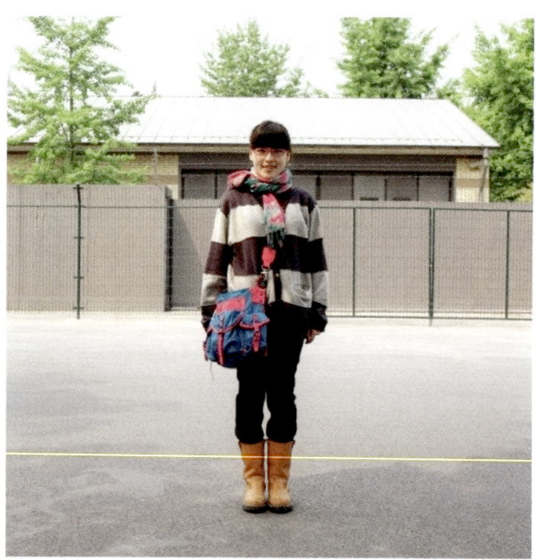

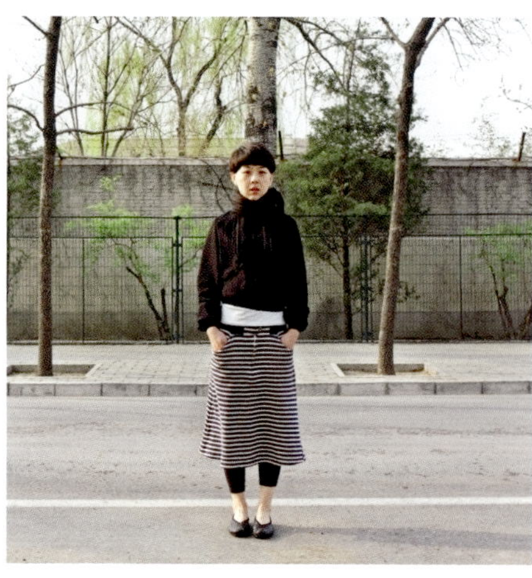 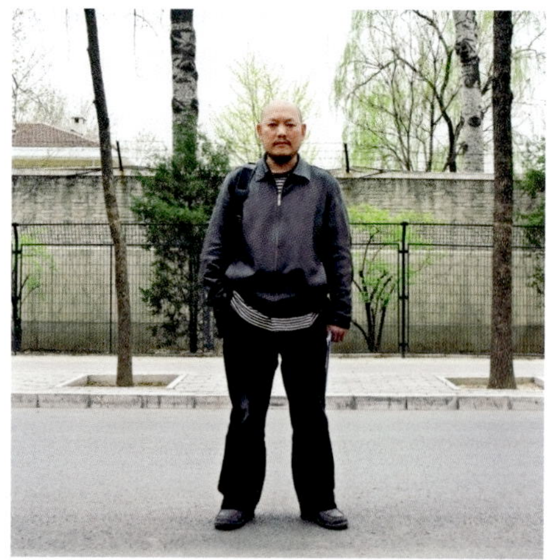

310 | FAIRYTALE PORTRAITS, 2007, C-prints, each 39⅜ x 39⅜ inches

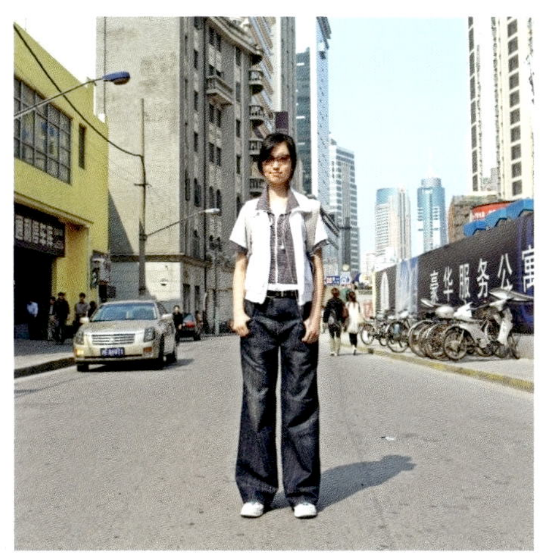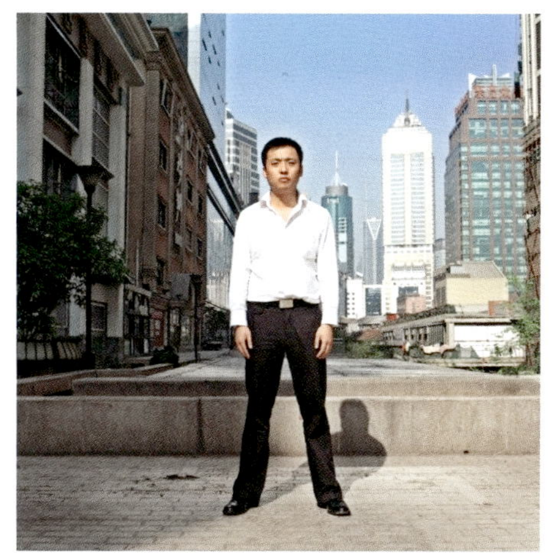

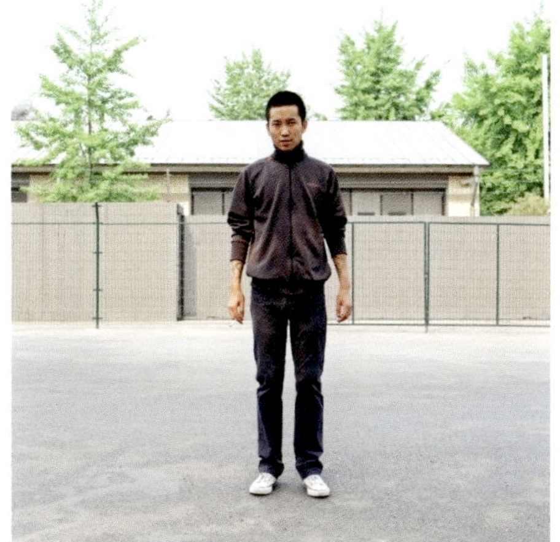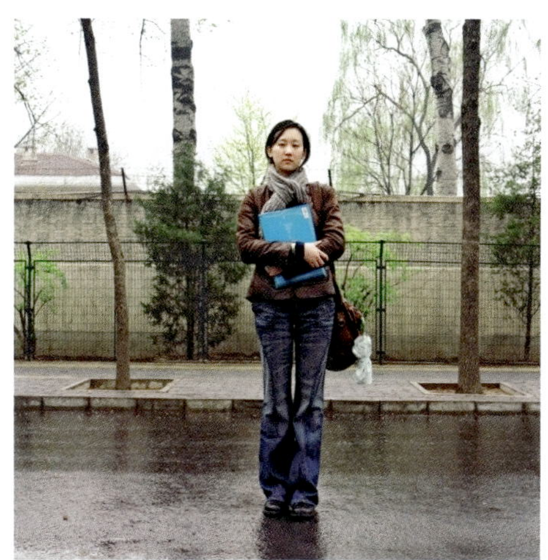

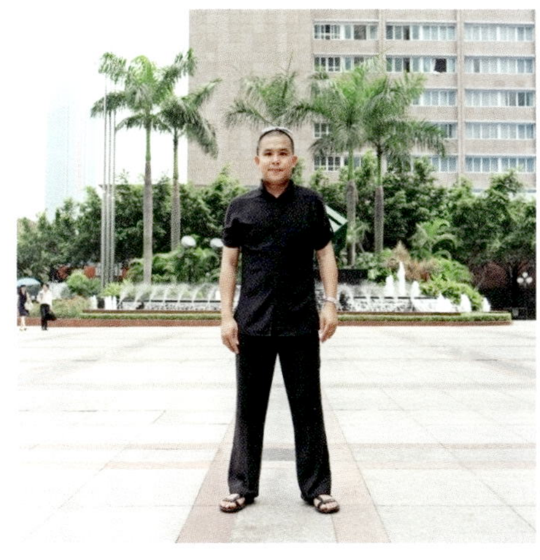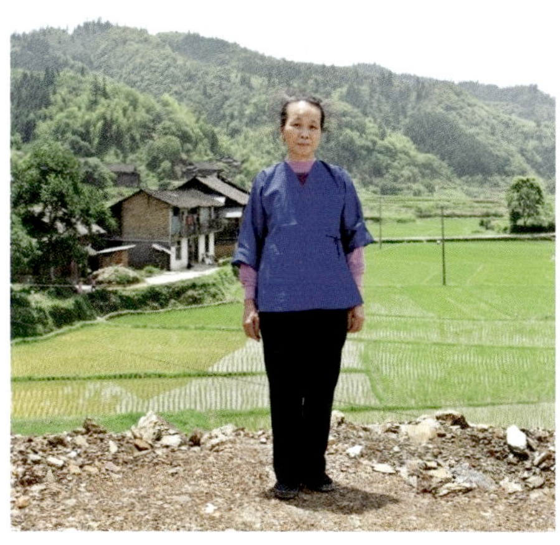

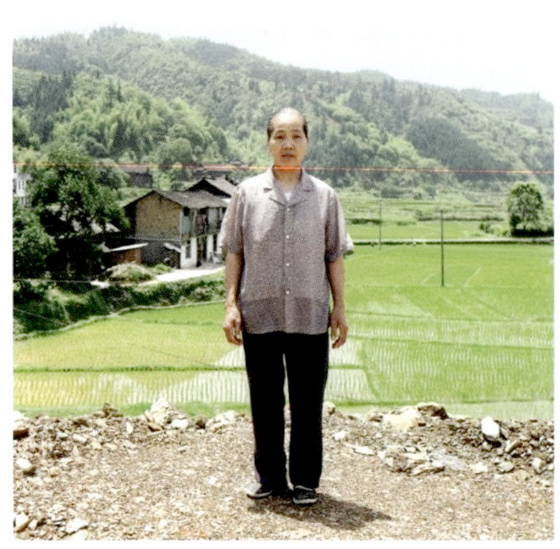
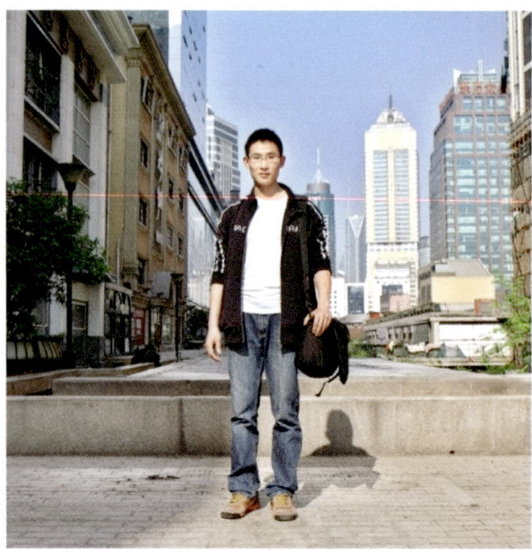
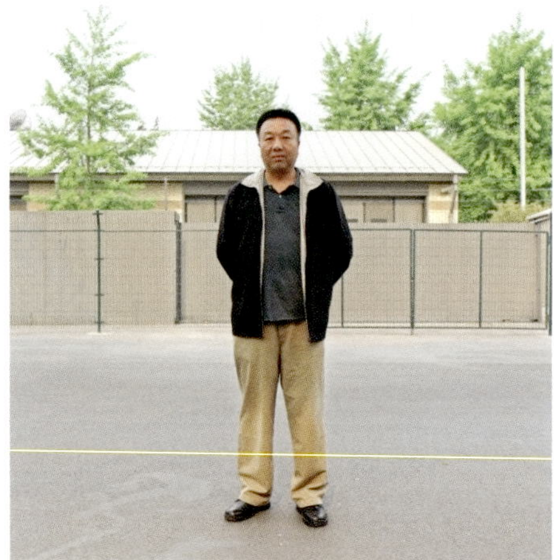
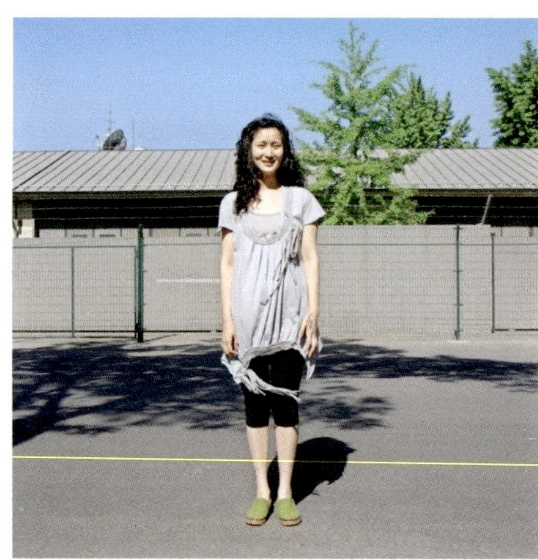
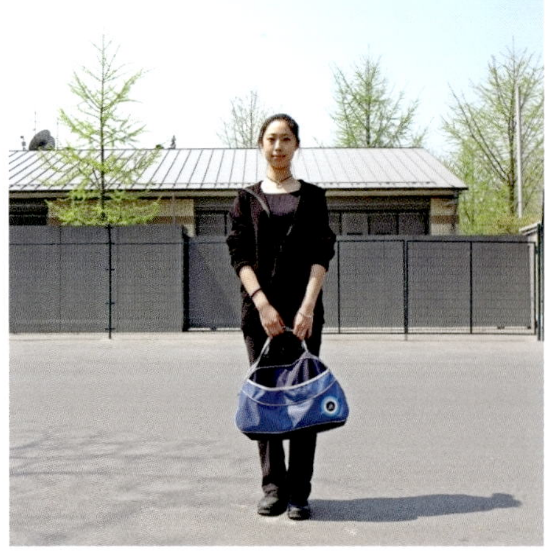
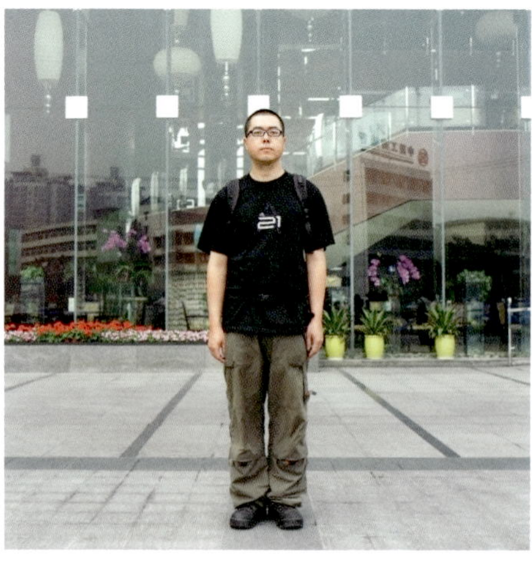

312 | FAIRYTALE PORTRAITS, 2007, C-prints, each 39⅜ x 39⅜ inches

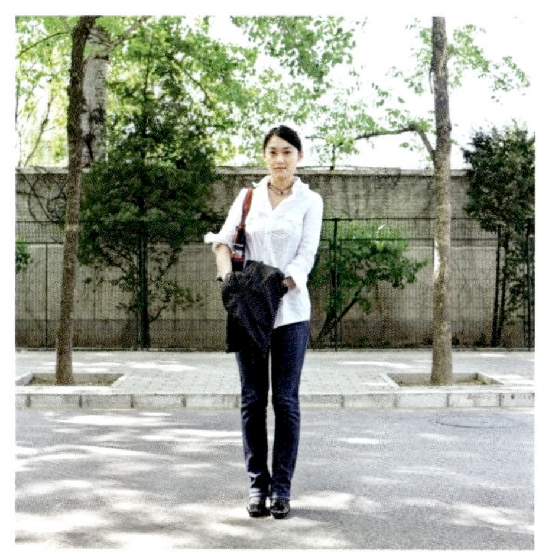
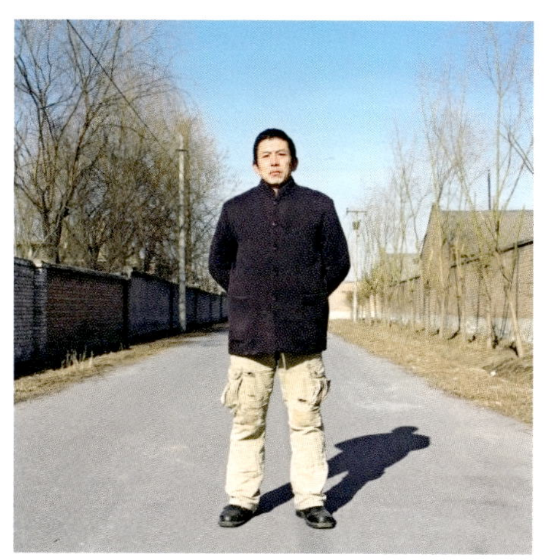
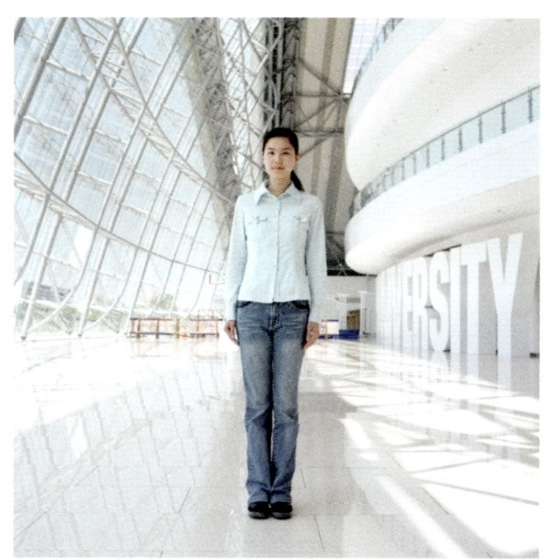
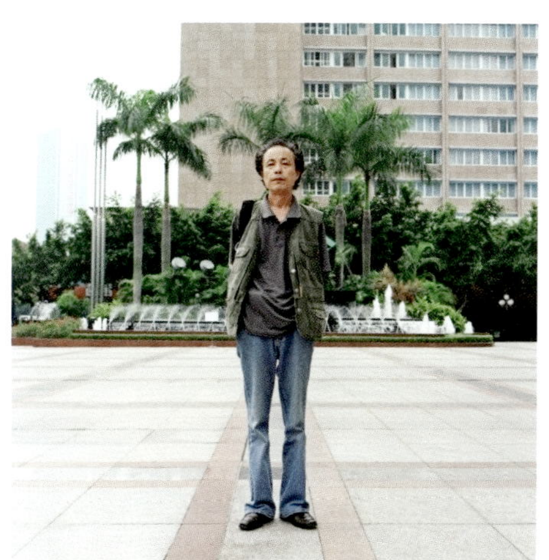
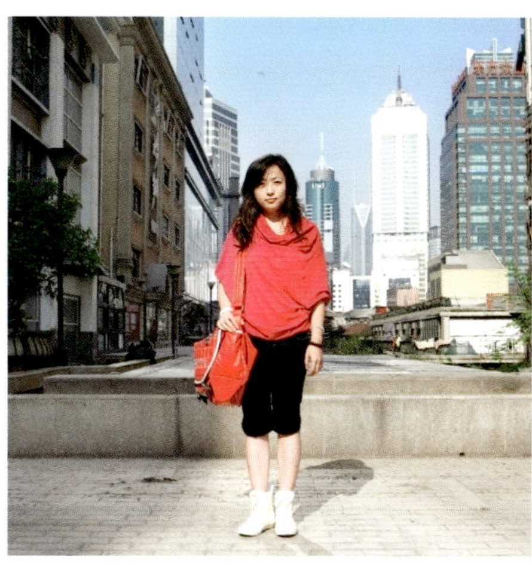
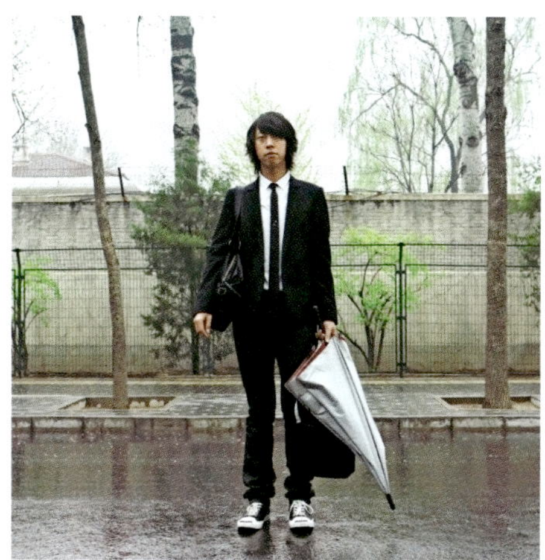

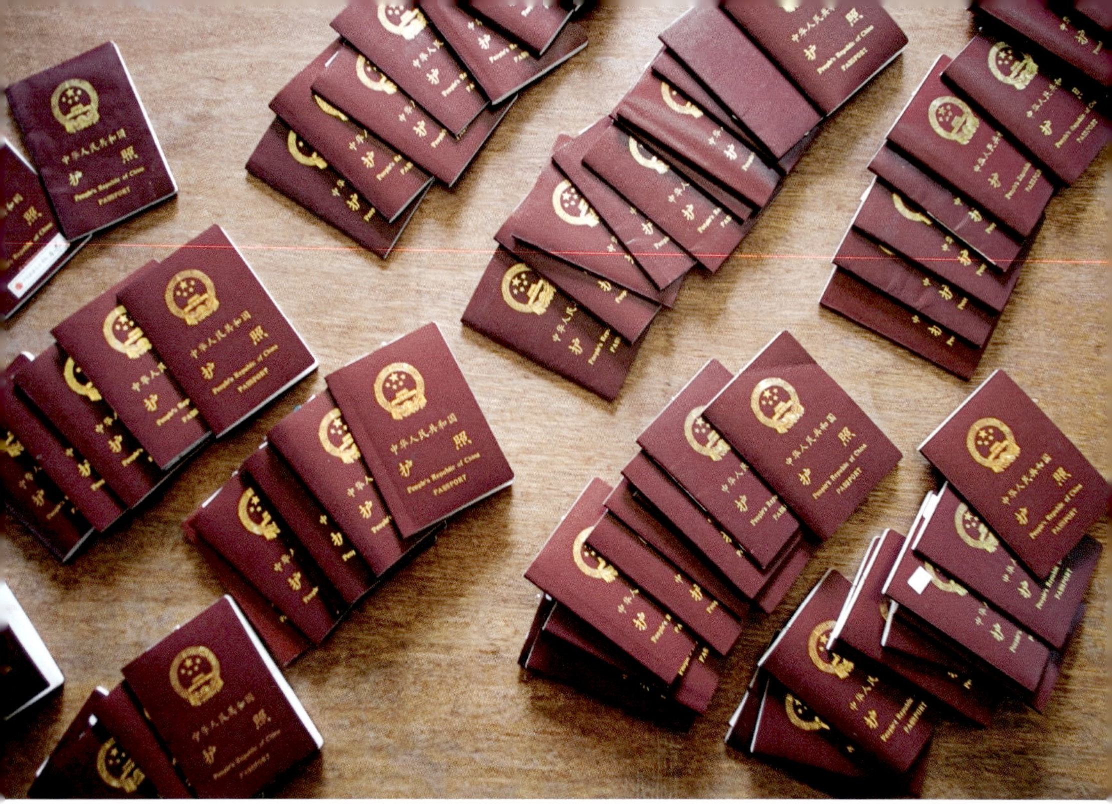
中华人民共和国
护 照
People's Republic of China
PASSPORT

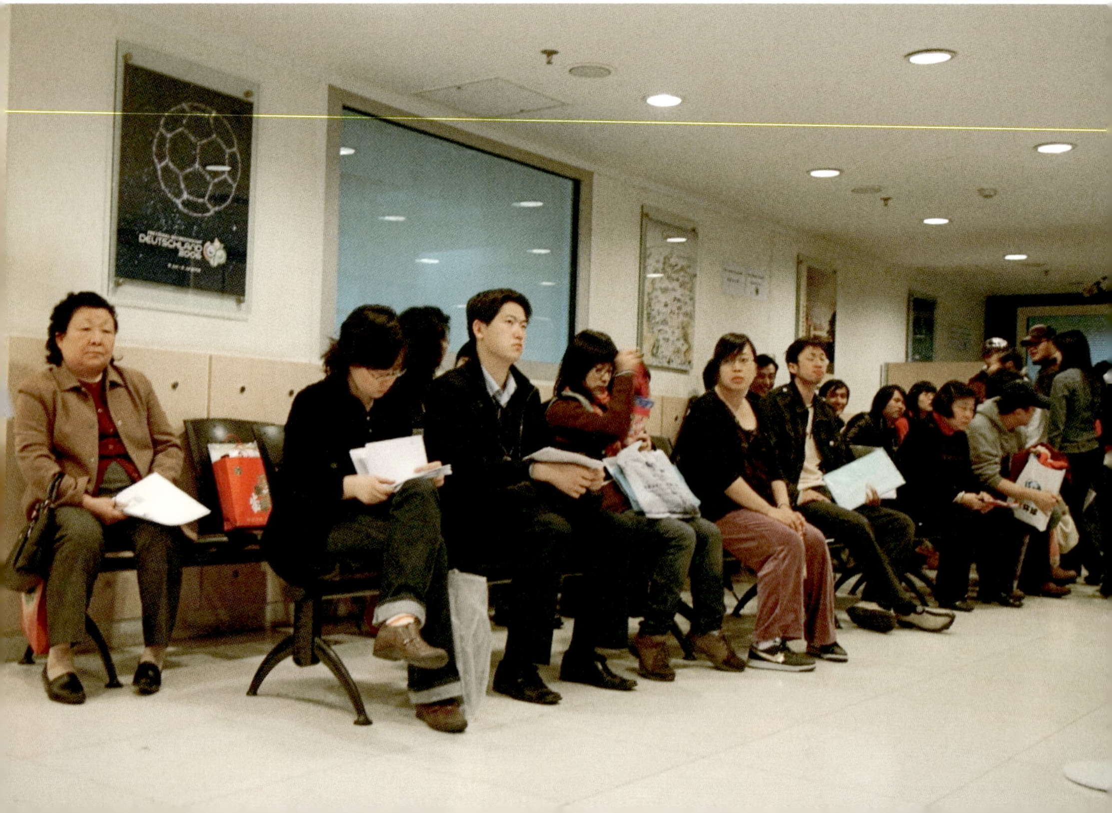
DEUTSCHLAND 2006

Fairytale, Documenta, 2007

AUGUST 1, 2006

Ai Weiwei views the Documenta exhibition venue in Kassel.

AUGUST 7, 2006

In Val Roseg, Switzerland, Ai encounters an Italian hiking group and is inspired to the basic concept of *Fairytale,* for which he will invite 1,001 Chinese citizens to travel to the Documenta site as part of the exhibition. "I was mountain climbing in Switzerland, and watched a huge number of Italian tourists pass by, dragged down by their small children. It made me think of taking a group of high-strung Chinese on a journey. That seemed like a more complete slice of cake, and such a slice would include all the special elements of the cake itself. This was also the reason why I didn't choose 50 or 100; the amount had to achieve a specified quantity." Besides *Fairytale,* Ai is planning to show the work *Template,* a 40-foot-high outdoor sculpture made from wooden doors and window frames of destroyed Ming and Qing Dynasty houses.

FEBRUARY 22, 2007

In a first step, a film crew is selected to begin shooting a *Fairytale* documentary. Ai would later describe the process: "With the participation of almost 20 directors from China and overseas, we completed a documentary that follows some of the interesting characters in *Fairytale.* We recorded their life, work, and daily experiences in China, and the various mental and physical efforts and costs that they expended over the course of their participation. This included their collective life experiences, their expectations and anxieties, their goals and present conditions, education, and families. The source material is already in excess of one 1,000 hours."

FEBRUARY 26, 2007

Recruitment information for *Fairytale* is published on Ai's blog. "At the beginning I did not want to announce my project through traditional media such as newspapers, television, but since I have been doing my personal blog for one year and I use it as a vehicle to express myself and to have direct communication with somebody unknown, somebody whom I would otherwise never have the chance to meet, I thought that maybe it would have been a good idea in order to help me to select people randomly. That's why I announced it through my blog."

Applicants have to fill out a questionnaire: "The questionnaire was an interim practical procedure. I want to affirm to these people that we are earnestly at work, we aren't joking around. Leading them in by beginning to think about issues of Western cultural background and their own personal situations was related to the nature of the entire artwork. The farmers just wrote, 'I don't know,' but as long as they complete the entire questionnaire and sign their name at the bottom, that illustrates that they are identifying with the activity."

FEBRUARY 26–MARCH 1, 2007

Ai visits luggage, bamboo pillow, and mat factories in Jiangsu, Zhejiang, and Shanghai. "We also designed some products. I don't want this to become a big art display, which would be paradoxical to the entire significance of the work. I want to disturb the day-to-day life as little as possible, preserving original habits and rhythms. At the same time, there should also be a feeling of consensus among the participants. There are a few necessities, such as beds, sheets, blankets, pillows, partitions, and we want to make the room into small private spaces. Living in this unfamiliar city, certain tools that constitute historical memory and special status are important; for example, 1,001 chairs, suitcases, and USB bracelets. These symbols that attest to their status are linked to a definite self-confidence and sense of pride. The details aren't important, but without them it would fall apart, there will be no identical experiences on this collective journey."

MARCH 2, 2007
Ai visits the antique markets and selects 1,001 Ming and Qing Dynasty chairs that he will distribute at the Documenta site as a tangible part of the work.

MARCH 7, 2007
Since over 3,000 people have already applied, the original deadline for applications of March 31 is changed to March 8. "I did not want to disappoint the people who were not chosen, so I closed the blog temporarily. The fact that this many people can communicate by my blog surprised me. Checking the profile and personal history of the individuals who had applied, I chose one out of every three. There were applicants from about 20 provinces who had various jobs such as police officers, toll gate ticketing staff, public service personnel, students, teachers, farmers, and so on. Surprisingly, I found out that all the residents of one small village in Guangxi Province applied. They were living under primitive conditions and most of them did not even have a name. They needed to have names registered in the family register to get a visa and a passport. Three generations of a family from Gansu Province had also applied. Some of them have never been out of their town, not to mention out of the nation."

MARCH 16, 2007
A preliminary list of 1,100 participants is published on the blog. "I am really very thankful to anybody who does not know me well, does not know the program well and said: 'Yes, we want to participate in it because we believe this is a project for imagination and possibility.' Of course later they had to pay a lot of money, as they had to go back to their hometowns, to apply for a passport … sometimes it turned out to be very difficult, many were even denied, but for many others it was much easier. Many people said: 'Oh, it is already a miracle for us, it is already a fairy tale … even if I cannot go, this will help me to think differently for the rest of my life.' It is very encouraging when you hear some ordinary people saying that."

MARCH 19–20, 2007
An acceptance notice is sent to each selected participant by email.

MARCH 20–APRIL 9, 2007
The *Fairytale* working team starts compiling information regarding passports, visas, and related issues for 1,004 participants and assists them in completing electronic visa application forms, applying for individual insurance, and booking flights.

APRIL 10–MAY 10, 2007
The *Fairytale* staff and participants arrive in groups at the German consulates in Beijing, Shanghai, Guangzhou, and Chengdu to apply for 1,004 German visas. There is a total of three rejections.

MAY 10, 2007
Production of suitcases, kitchen appliances, clothing, pillow covers and blankets, F1001 wristbands and flash drives, and curtain dividers for the dormitory have all been confirmed.

MAY 21, 2007
The preparatory staff team departs for Germany, among them 17 *Fairytale* participants.

JUNE 11, 2007
taz. *A DIFFERENT KIND OF FAIRY TALE.*
"The most formative fairy tale in my life was the myth of communism. When I was ten, I had to learn the Communist Manifesto by heart," says artist, curator, critic, and architect Ai Weiwei when asked after the title of his ambitious work. No less than 1,001 Chinese citizens of different ages and professions, coming from all of the country's provinces, will arrive at the Documenta in about five groups. A former textile mill serves as a home for the roughly ten days each group will spend in Kassel. Catering to specific cultural idiosyncrasies, bedding and cooks have been brought over from China. A special survival kit has been designed to help through all foreseeable accidents, since most of the art immigrants do not speak a foreign language. All other details of the performance, which Ai Weiwei labels a "socio-political readymade," still remain a surprise.
One thing that is certain, though, is that the work will not be like a fairy tale. "I'm interested in fairy tales as a category with a strict separation between good and evil, the relation between truth and fantasy. These dualisms can also be found in the relations

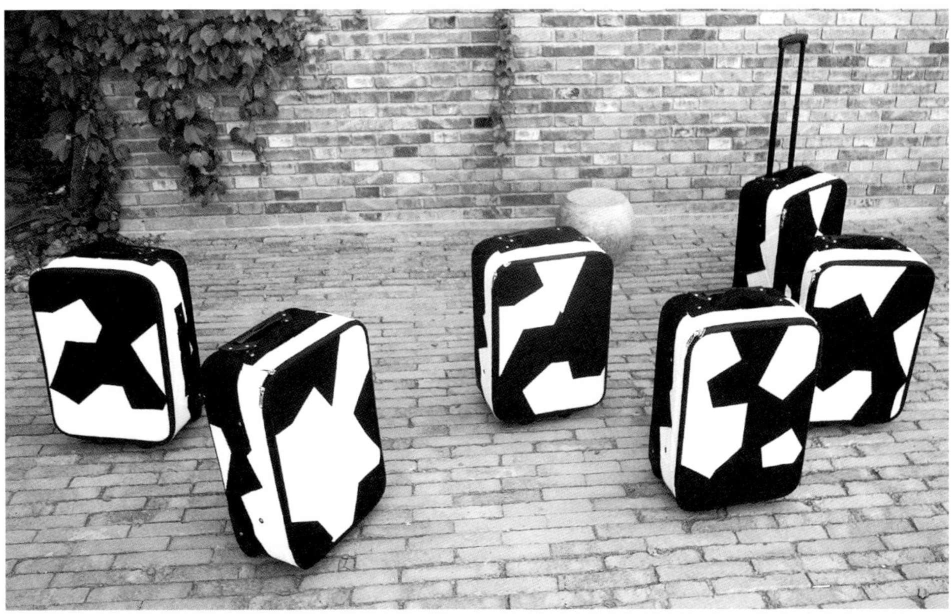

Fairytale suitcases, Beijing 2007

between China and the West. But the title also refers to the city of Kassel. After all, the brothers Grimm lived there," Ai Weiwei says. "At the center of *Fairytale* we have a meeting of cultures. By calling the work a fairy tale and introducing the number 1,001 we have already addressed two different cultures, since the story of the 1,001 nights comes from Arabia. You also have to remember that the genre doesn't exist in China at all. We tell our children fables and myths, fairy tales are purely a Western import."

JUNE 12–20, 2007
The first group of 184 *Fairytale* participants arrives in Germany and stays at Documenta.

JUNE 16, 2007
Official opening of the Documenta exhibition. Press coverage includes many images of the outdoor sculpture *Template* as one of the exhibition's most visually striking pieces. Ai explains the work: "The windows and doors for *Template* used to belong to destroyed houses located in the Shanxi area, Northern China, where entire old towns have been pulled down. We bought the fragments from different quarters, and these are probably the last pieces of that civilization. I like to use these leftovers as part of … not a sentiment, but evidence of our past activity. I like to carry these pieces into a completely contemporary context and I think it works well. It really is a mixed, troubled, questioning context, and a protest for its own identity. To me the temple itself—you know I'm not religious—means a station where you can think about the past and the future, it's a void space. The selected area—not the material temple itself—tells you that the real physical temple is not there, but constructed through the leftovers of the past."

JUNE 19–25, 2007
Second group of 228 *Fairytale* participants stays at Documenta.

JUNE 20, 2007
Frankfurter Allgemeine Zeitung.
AI WEIWEI'S TEMPLATE COLLAPSED AFTER STORM. Template, the Documenta piece of Chinese artist Ai Weiwei, has collapsed. The 40-foot wooden tower broke apart after a short rainstorm over Kassel

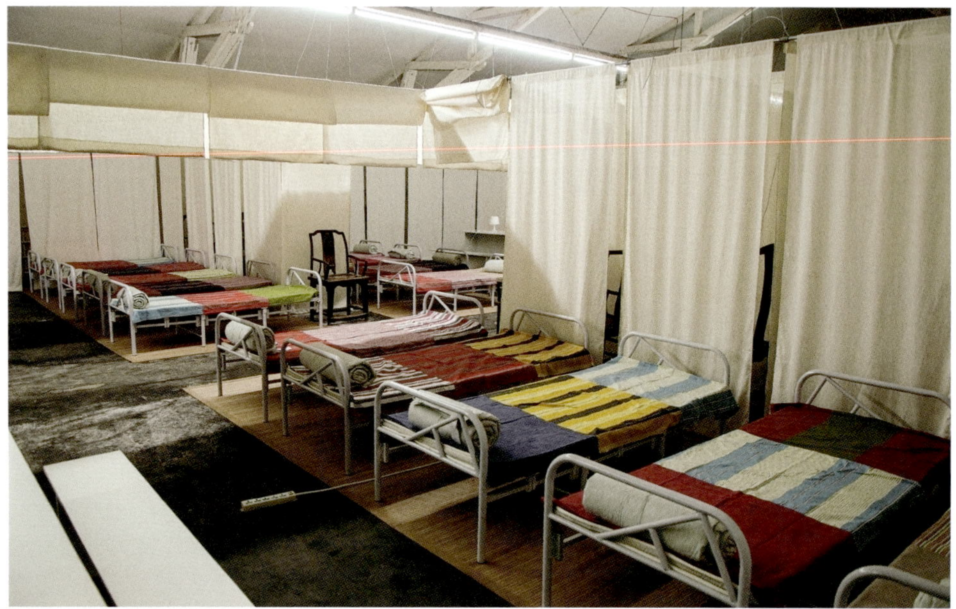

Women's dormitory, Gottschalk-Halle, Kassel 2007

on Wednesday. According to a Documenta spokesperson, the object will be rebuilt shortly. *Template* is made from the doors and windows of antique houses that fell victim to the building boom in China. On the previous Saturday, Federal President Horst Köhler had visited the work.

JUNE 21, 2007
Focus. Ai Weiwei, best known for inviting 1,001 fellow Chinese citizens to Documenta, does not consider rebuilding the work. "It's better than before," the 50-year-old artist says. "Now you can see the force of nature. Art becomes more beautiful through these kind of emotions." For Documenta chief curator Buergel, standing barefoot in a big puddle in front of *Template*, the collapse was "logically consistent … The rubble now allows a wide range of associations. And this is what art is aiming for: to make propositions." President Köhler had not been in any danger. "It needed a rainstorm for the work to collapse, strong enough to put the bravest president to flight." For the next day, a prospective buyer for *Template* had been expected. Directly after the collapse,

Ai Weiwei still remained his optimism: "The prize has just doubled," he said.
Ai Weiwei. *Template* was really made for indoors, it was not prepared for the German weather and wind. So it collapsed after six days of showing there. I was a little surprised, but not very surprised, because I knew it was not strong. When I saw how the site had collapsed—not totally, it has turned into some other shape—I thought it is now really like a ruin. I was quite impressed. It comes from ruins and now it's really a ruin … After the collapse, we asked engineers at Kassel University to make a complete calculation of the measurements. We're thinking about the possibilities of removing and rebuilding the structure in its present condition. It's more interesting than it was. I think of it as dealing with change and remaking a miracle.

JUNE 24–30, 2007
Third group of 192 *Fairytale* participants stays at Documenta.

JUNE 29–JULY 5, 2007
Fourth group of 185 *Fairytale* participants stays at Documenta.

JULY 4–JULY 10, 2007
Fifth group of 189 *Fairytale* participants stays
at Documenta.

JULY 11, 2007
All of the 995 participants who eventually
managed the trip to Kassel have returned
to China.
Fairytale Documentary. Interviewer: What
would you do if some of the participants, or
even one, wouldn't come back? You know
this happened quite often when artists, as
long as Germany was separated, had the
allowance to go to a concert, or whatever
professionally doing, to the other side, and
then they say, no, I don't come back. They
just hid and… What would you do? / Ai Weiwei: As a work itself, of course, I set it up
that people come and go back to China as
one group. In reality, I cannot limit anybody from their free will. I cannot even pre-
dict the reason I cannot do it. I don't even
know if I'll go back. The decisions are
made each day. All our decisions are ques-
tionable, because we are human. The con-
sciousness… it's always dangerous to try
to see the world as not dangerous. If everything is planned, it's mistaken, I think. So
my answer is very clear: I don't really know.

SEPTEMBER 1, 2007
With the editing of the *Fairytale* documentary, the work is completed.
Ai Weiwei. Talking about the scale and the
way in which it works, *Fairytale* is apparently
different from my previous works, as it deals
with living individuals, their lives, as well as
their hope and imagination. I think that it
is all these things that give a strong character to this project… The point is: how to
make everybody feel that all this is made for
him or her, for each individual, and to enable
the participants to have a very detailed and
carefully planned trip that is free? How to
make sure that they have the absolutely cor-
rect conditions for traveling and being in
this Documenta as viewers and at the same
time as part of the work? I see the whole
process as the work itself. I see what kind
of hopes, what kind of worries, what kind of
frustrations… and waiting, and anticipat-
ing… then the dream, then imagination,
then… maybe surprise.

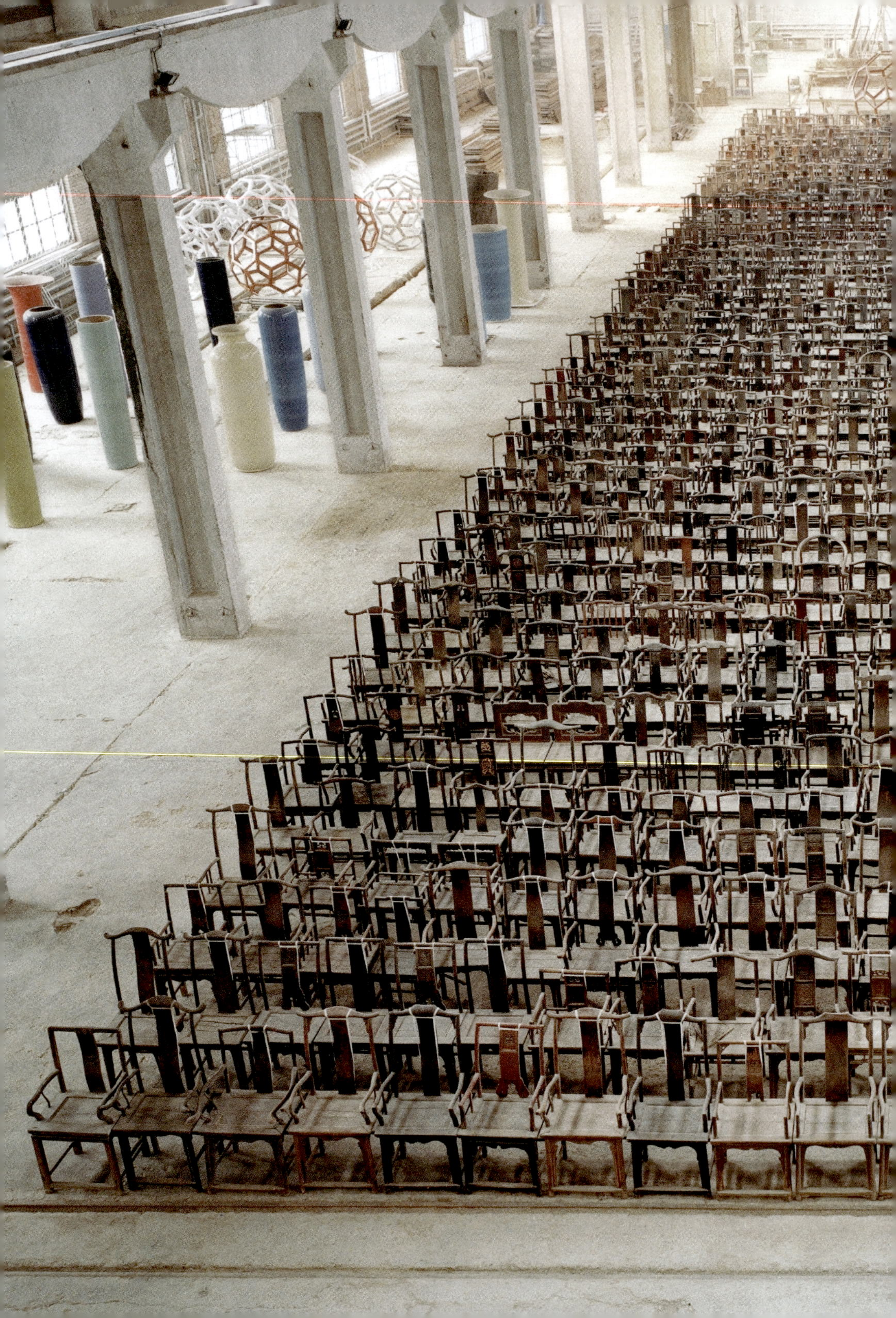

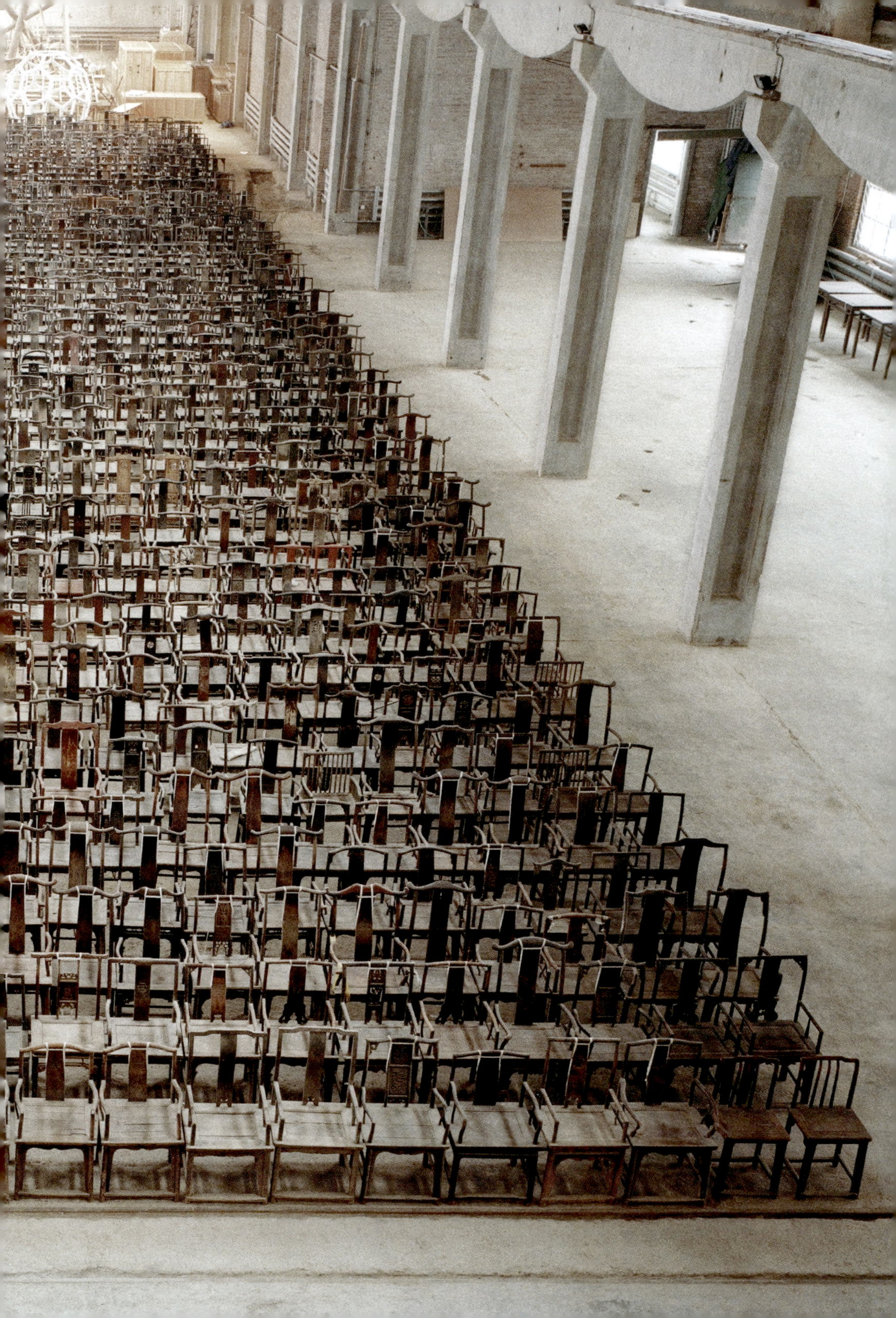

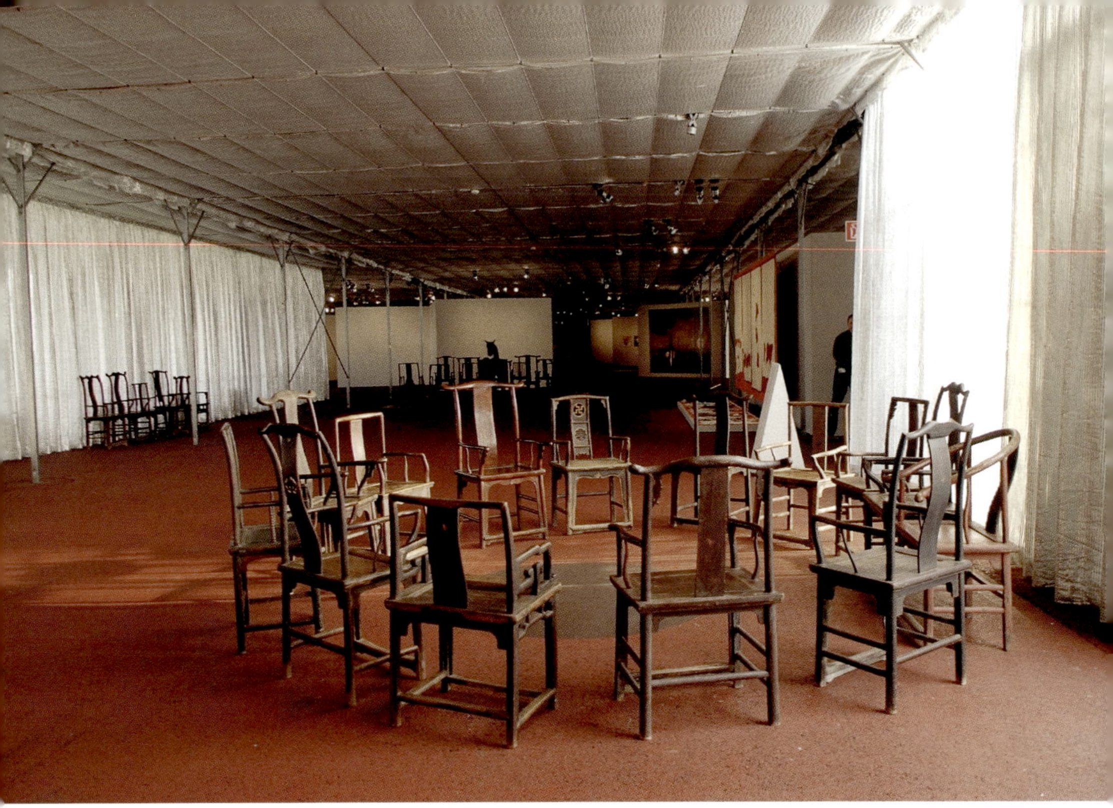

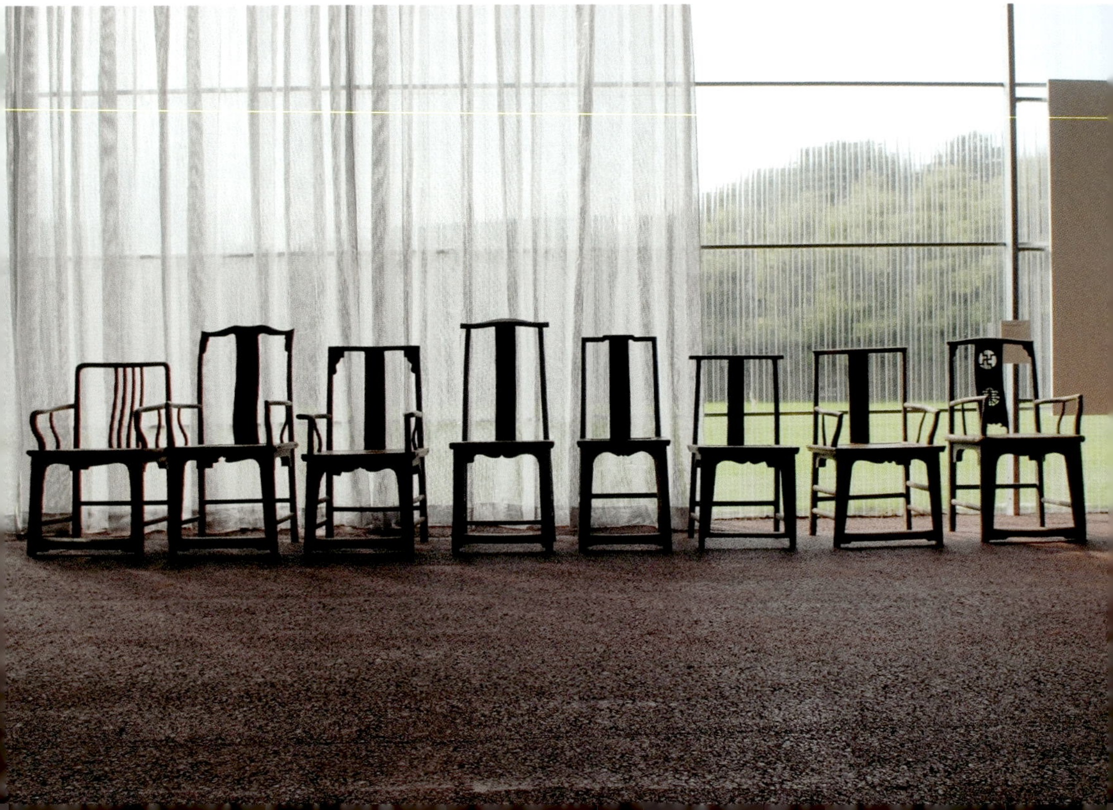

Fairytale, Documenta, 2007

1. AUGUST 2006
Ai Weiwei besucht Kassel und besichtigt das
Ausstellungsgelände der Documenta.

7. AUGUST 2006
Im Schweizer Val Roseg trifft Ai Weiwei auf
eine Gruppe italienischer Wanderer und hat
die Idee für das Ausstellungsprojekt *Fairytale:*
Er wird 1001 chinesische Bürger einladen,
die Documenta zu besuchen. „Beim Klettern
in den Schweizer Alpen traf ich eine riesige
Gruppe italienischer Touristen, die schlepp-
ten da ihre Kinder an uns vorbei. Ich hatte
den Einfall, mit einer Gruppe eigenwilliger
Chinesen auf Reisen zu gehen. Das schien mir
eine komplettere Mischung, wie ein Stück
eines Kuchens, das alle besonderen Zutaten
des kompletten Kuchens enthielt. Aus diesem Grund habe ich nicht 50 oder 100 ausgewählt, wir brauchten schon eine kritische
Masse." Neben *Fairytale* plant Ai die Präsentation des Werks *Template,* einer zwölf Meter
hohen Außenskulptur aus den Holztüren
und Fensterrahmen zerstörter Häuser aus
der Ming-Dynastie.

22. FEBRUAR 2007
Als erster Schritt wird ein Filmteam zusam-
mengestellt, um mit den Dreharbeiten für
den Dokumentarfilm *Fairytale* zu beginnen.
Ai beschreibt später den Entstehungsprozess:
„Fast 20 Kameraleute aus China und anderen
Ländern waren beteiligt. Der Dokumentar-
film zeigt, wie einige der *Fairytale*-Teilnehmer
leben und arbeiten, ihren Alltag in China,
sowie auch die geistigen und körperlichen
Mühen und Kosten, die sie im Laufe des
Projekts in Kauf nehmen mussten. Dazu
zählen ihre kollektiven Erlebnisse, ihre
Hoffnungen und Ängste, ihre Ziele und ihre
Lebensumstände, ihre Bildung und ihre
Familien. Das gefilmte Material ist bereits
mehr als 1000 Stunden lang."

26. FEBRUAR 2007
Ai veröffentlicht auf seinem Blog die Teilnah-
mebedingungen für *Fairytale*. „Ich wollte das
Projekt nicht in traditionellen Medien wie
Presse oder Fernsehen ankündigen. Da ich
bereits seit einem Jahr einen Blog hatte – als
Ausdrucksventil und als direkte Verbindung
zu Unbekannten, die ich sonst nie getroffen
hätte –, dachte ich, vielleicht ist das der
richtige Weg, um ganz willkürlich Kandidaten
auszuwählen. Ich beschloss, das Projekt auf
meinem Blog anzukündigen."
Die Kandidaten müssen einen Fragebogen
ausfüllen. „Der Fragebogen erfüllte einen
praktischen Zweck. Ich wollte den Leuten
klarmachen, dass unser Projekt kein Witz,
sondern eine ernste Sache war. Sie sollten
sich eingangs Gedanken über die Kultur
des Westens und über ihre eigene Situation
machen, das war Teil des Kunstwerks. Manche
Bauern schrieben einfach: ‚Ich weiß nicht.'
Aber dass sie den ganzen Fragebogen ausfüll-
ten und ihren Namen daruntersetzten, bewies
an sich schon, dass sie bereit waren, sich auf
die Sache einzulassen."

26. FEBRUAR–1. MÄRZ 2007
Ai besucht Fabriken in Jiangsu, Zhejiang
und Shanghai, die Koffer, Bambuskissen
und Matten herstellen. „Wir haben einige
Produkte selbst entworfen. Aber ich möchte
nicht, dass aus dem Werk ein großes Kunst-
spektakel wird, das würde seinen Sinn ad
absurdum führen. Das tagtägliche Leben
soll so wenig wie möglich gestört werden,
die Gewohnheiten und Rhythmen sollen
ungestört weiterlaufen. Zugleich möchten
wir, dass unter den Teilnehmern ein Gefühl
der Gemeinsamkeit entsteht. Es gibt ein
paar notwendige Dinge wie Betten, Laken,
Decken, Kissen und Trennwände, die den
Raum in kleine private Bereiche aufteilen.
In einer fremden Stadt braucht man bestimmte Kennzeichen, die unsere historische
Erinnerung und unsere Sonderstellung mar-
kieren, zum Beispiel 1001 Stühle, Koffer und
USB-Armbänder. Diese Kennzeichen verleihen
dem Träger Selbstvertrauen und machen ihn
stolz. Die Einzelheiten sind nicht so wichtig,
aber ohne dieses verbindende Element fällt

das Projekt auseinander, es gibt dann keine
übereinstimmenden Erfahrungen auf unserer
gemeinsamen Reise.“

2. MÄRZ 2007
Ai besucht Antiquitätenmärkte und erwirbt
1001 Stühle aus den Ming- und Qing-
Dynastien als materielle Komponenten des
Documenta-Projekts.

7. MÄRZ 2007
Da sich bereits Anfang März mehr als 3000
Freiwillige gemeldet haben, von denen nur
1100 in die engere Auswahl kommen können,
wird die Anmeldefrist vom 31. März auf den
8. März vorgezogen. „Ich wollte diejenigen,
die nicht ausgewählt wurden, nicht enttäu-
schen und habe den Blog vorübergehend
geschlossen. Dass sich so viele Leute über
meinen Blog melden, hat mich überrascht.
Wir haben die Angaben und Biografien der
Kandidaten geprüft und einen von drei
genommen. Es gab Freiwillige aus ungefähr
20 Provinzen mit allen möglichen Berufen –
Polizisten, Mautkontrolleure, Beamte,
Studenten, Lehrer, Bauern und so weiter.
Zu meiner Überraschung stellte ich fest,
dass alle Einwohner eines Dorfs in der Provinz
Guangxi sich gemeldet hatten. Die leben dort
unter sehr einfachen Bedingungen. Manche
hatten nicht einmal einen Namen und mussten sich erst ins Familienregister eintragen
lassen, um einen Pass und ein Visum zu
bekommen. Drei Generationen einer Familie
aus der Provinz Gansu wollten auch mitma-
chen. Einige sind nie aus ihrem Dorf heraus-
gekommen, von fremden Ländern ganz zu
schweigen.“

16. MÄRZ 2007
Eine vorläufige Liste mit 1100 Namen wird
auf dem Blog veröffentlicht. „Ich danke allen,
die mich gar nicht richtig kennen und nicht
genau wissen, was wir vorhaben, und trotzdem
sagen: ‚Ja, ich will bei diesem Projekt mitma-
chen, bei dem es um unsere Phantasie und
um neue Möglichkeiten geht.‘ Später mussten
sie teilweise eine Menge Geld bezahlen, sie
mussten an ihrem Wohnort einen Pass beantragen … das war manchmal außerordentlich
schwierig, einige wurden abgewiesen, bei
anderen ging es leichter. Viele sagten: ‚Das
ist schon ein Wunder für mich, das ist schon

ein Märchen … auch wenn ich nicht mitfah-
ren kann, ich werde viele Dinge jetzt anders
sehen als vorher.‘ Wenn ich so etwas von einfachen Menschen höre, empfinde ich das als
starke Ermutigung.“

19.–20. MÄRZ 2007
Alle ausgewählten Kandidaten werden per
E-Mail benachrichtigt.

20. MÄRZ–9. APRIL 2007
Das *Fairytale*-Team beginnt, die Pass-, Visa-
und Personaldaten aller 1004 Teilnehmer zu
erfassen, und hilft ihnen, Anträge für Visa,
Versicherungen und Flugtickets zu stellen.

10. APRIL–10. MAI 2007
Das *Fairytale*-Team und die Teilnehmer
besuchen gruppenweise die deutschen Kon-
sulate in Peking, Shanghai, Guangzhou
und Chengdu, um 1004 Visa zu beantragen.
Drei davon werden abgelehnt.

10. MAI 2007
Die Herstellung von Koffern, Küchengeräten,
Kleidungsstücken, Kissenbezügen, Decken,
F1001-Armbändern mit USB-Sticks und
Vorhängen für den Schlafraum wird bestätigt.

21. MAI 2007
Das *Fairytale*-Team fliegt mit den ersten
17 Teilnehmern nach Deutschland.

11. JUNI 2007
taz. *MÄRCHEN MAL ANDERS.* „Das prä-
gendste Märchen in meinem Leben war der
Mythos vom Kommunismus. Als Zehnjähriger
musste ich das kommunistische Manifest
auswendig lernen“, beantwortet der Künstler,
Kurator, Kunstkritiker und Architekt Ai Weiwei die Frage nach der Intention des Titels
für das kühne Projekt. Nicht weniger als
1001 Chinesen unterschiedlichen Alters,
Berufs und aus den verschiedenen Provinzen
des Landes werden in ca. fünf Schüben beim
Kunst-Event Documenta eintreffen. Eine
ehemalige Kasseler Zeltfabrik dient als Bleibe
für den rund zehntägigen Aufenthalt jeder
Gruppe. Betten und Köche werden gleich aus
China mitgebracht, um den kultureigenen
Empfindlichkeiten entgegenzukommen.
Ein spezielles Survival-Paket soll den zumeist
keine Fremdsprache beherrschenden Kunst-

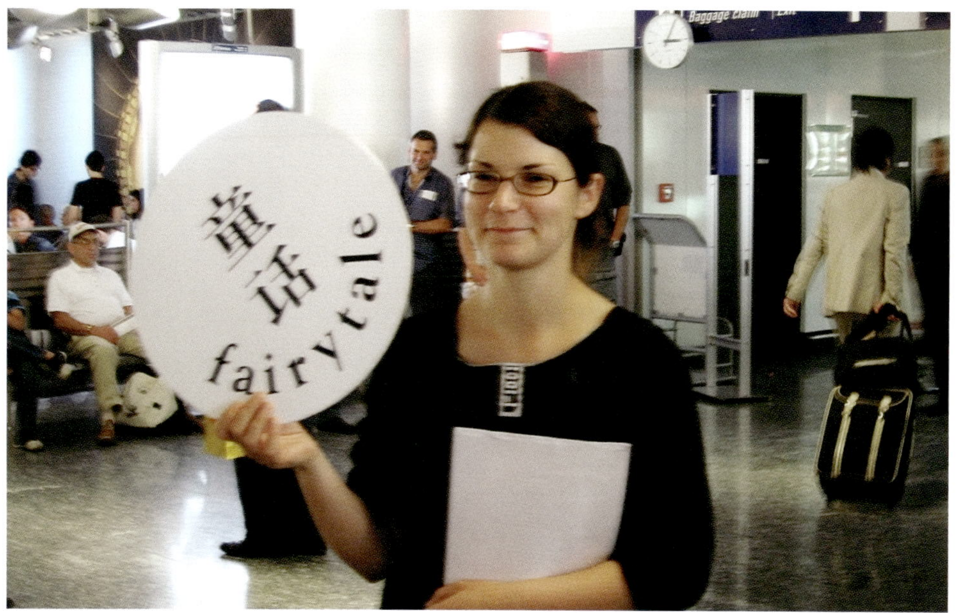

Personal photo from *Fairytale* participant, welcome at the airport, Kassel 2007

Immigranten bei den berechenbaren Irrungen und Wirrungen helfen. Was die Performance, die Ai Weiwei kurz als „sozio-politisches Readymade" bezeichnet, im Einzelnen beinhaltet, bleibt weiterhin Überraschung. Eines steht allerdings fest, *Fairytale* soll nicht märchenhaft werden. „Mich interessiert die Kategorie des Märchens in erster Linie als Dachbegriff für die Trennung zwischen dem Bösen und dem Guten, dem Verhältnis von Wahrheit und Phantasie. Diese Dualismen gibt es ebenso im Verhältnis zwischen China und dem Westen. Der Titel nimmt aber auch konkret Bezug auf den Ort Kassel. Immerhin haben dort die Gebrüder Grimm gelebt", so Ai Weiwei. „Im Zentrum von *Fairytale* steht das Aufeinanderprallen unterschiedlicher Kulturen. In dem Moment, wo wir das Ganze Märchen nennen und die Zahl 1001 ins Spiel bringen, haben wir schon zwei Kulturen angesprochen. Immerhin kommt ja die Erzählung ‚Tausendundeine Nacht' aus dem arabischen Raum. Wenn man dann noch mitdenkt, dass es diese Formen des Erzählens in China gar nicht gibt. In China erzählt man den Kindern Fabeln und Mythen, Märchen sind ganz klar Westimport."

12.–20. JUNI 2007

Ankunft und Aufenthalt der ersten *Fairytale*-Gruppe mit 184 Teilnehmern auf der Documenta in Kassel.

16. JUNI 2007

Offizielle Eröffnung der Documenta. Viele Pressefotos zeigen die Außenskulptur *Template*, eines der visuellen Merkzeichen der Ausstellung. Ai erläutert die Arbeit: „Die Fenster und Türen von *Template* stammen aus abgerissenen Häusern in der Provinz Shanxi im Norden Chinas, wo ganze alte Dörfer dem Boden gleichgemacht wurden. Wir haben Trümmer aus verschiedenen Gegenden gekauft. Das sind vielleicht die letzten Überreste dieser Zivilisation. Ich verwende sie als Teil … nicht einer sentimentalen Stimmung, sondern als Evidenz unserer historischen Aktivität. Ich stelle diese Stücke gerne in einen zeitgenössischen Kontext, und ich glaube, das funktioniert gut. Es ist wirklich ein gemischter, gestörter, kritischer Kontext, ein Protest für eine eigene Identität. Der Tempel – wie Sie wissen, bin ich nicht religiös – ist ein Ort, wo man über die Vergangenheit und die Zukunft nachdenken kann,

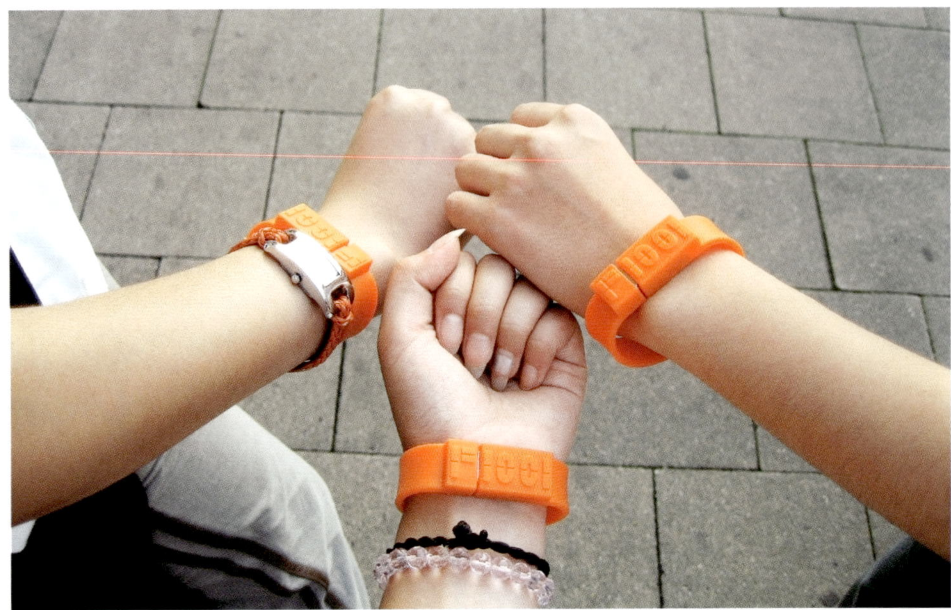

Personal photo from *Fairytale* participant, *Fairytale* USB bracelets, Kassel 2007

ein leerer Raum. Der gewählte Platz – nicht der materielle Tempel selbst – teilt dir mit, dass da kein wirklicher, physischer Tempel existiert, sondern nur ein Bau aus Überresten der Vergangenheit."

19.–25. JUNI 2007
Aufenthalt der zweiten *Fairytale*-Gruppe mit 228 Teilnehmern auf der Documenta.

20. JUNI 2007
Frankfurter Allgemeine Zeitung.
AI WEIWEIS TEMPLATE NACH UNWETTER EINGESTÜRZT. Der zwölf Meter hohe Holzturm brach am Mittwoch nach einem kurzen Unwetter über Kassel zusammen. Laut Documenta soll das Objekt wieder aufgebaut werden. *Template* besteht aus Türen und Fenstern alter Häuser, die dem Bauboom in China zum Opfer gefallen sind. Erst am Samstag hatte Bundespräsident Horst Köhler das Werk besucht.

21. JUNI 2007
Focus. Doch Ai, vor allem durch seine Einladung an 1001 seiner Landsleute zur Documenta bekannt, denkt nicht an Wiederaufbau.

„Das ist besser als vorher", sagt der 50-Jährige. „Jetzt wird die Kraft der Natur sichtbar. Und Kunst wird durch solche Emotionen erst schön." Documenta-Chef Buergel, barfuß in einer großen Pfütze vor *Template*, sah den Einsturz als „nur konsequent ... Die Trümmer lassen jetzt jede Menge Assoziationen zu. Und genau das will Kunst ja: anregen." Für Köhler habe keine Gefahr bestanden. „Für den Einsturz war ein solches Unwetter nötig, bei dem selbst der mutigste Bundespräsident das Weite gesucht hätte." Für den nächsten Tag hatte sich ein Käufer für *Template* angekündigt. Ai Weiwei zeigte sich direkt nach dem Einsturz dennoch optimistisch: „Der Preis hat sich soeben verdoppelt."
Ai Weiwei. *Template* war eigentlich für den Innenraum gemacht und nicht dafür, Wind und Wetter in Deutschland standzuhalten. Sechs Tage, nachdem wir die Skulptur aufgestellt hatten, brach sie zusammen. Ich war ein wenig überrascht, aber nicht sehr, denn ich wusste, dass sie nicht besonders stabil war. Als ich sah, wie sie eingestürzt war – nicht ganz, sie hatte eine andere Form angenommen –, dachte ich, jetzt ist sie wie eine Ruine. Das hat mich beeindruckt.

Sie war aus Ruinen entstanden und wieder zur Ruine geworden ... Wir baten Ingenieure der Universität Kassel, die eingestürzte Struktur genau zu vermessen, damit die Möglichkeit bestand, sie an einem anderen Ort in ihrem jetzigen Zustand neu zu errichten. Sie ist durch den Einsturz interessanter geworden. Es geht darum, mit Veränderungen umzugehen, und um das Remake eines Wunders.

24.–30. JUNI 2007
Aufenthalt der dritten *Fairytale*-Gruppe mit 192 Teilnehmern auf der Documenta.

29. JUNI–5. JULI 2007
Aufenthalt der vierten *Fairytale*-Gruppe mit 185 Teilnehmern auf der Documenta.

4.–10. JULI 2007
Aufenthalt der fünften *Fairytale*-Gruppe mit 189 Teilnehmern auf der Documenta.

11. JULI 2007
Alle der tatsächlich 995 Teilnehmer, die am Ende die Reise nach Kassel wirklich antreten konnten, sind wieder nach China zurückgekehrt.
Fairytale-Dokumentarfilm. Journalistin: Was würden Sie tun, wenn sich Teilnehmer weigern, nach China zurückzukehren? Als Deutschland noch geteilt war, geschah das häufig. Künstler hatten die Genehmigung für ein Konzert oder irgendeinen anderen Termin. Sie überquerten die Grenze und sagten, nein, ich gehe nicht zurück, und versteckten sich irgendwo ... Was machen Sie in einem solchen Fall? / Ai Weiwei: Wir haben natürlich geplant, dass alle als Gruppe aus China kommen und wieder zurückfliegen. Andererseits kann ich realistisch gesehen niemandem, der eine freie Entscheidung trifft, Vorschriften machen. Die Gründe, die so eine Entscheidung auslösen, lassen sich nicht vorhersehen. Ich weiß selbst nicht, ob ich zurückgehe. Solche Entscheidungen fallen jeden Tag, und sie können nie zu 100 Prozent richtig sein, weil wir Menschen sind. Das Bewusstsein ... es ist gefährlich, sich vorzustellen, dass die Welt nicht gefährlich ist. Alles planen zu wollen, wäre meiner Ansicht nach falsch. Meine Antwort ist klipp und klar: Ich weiß nicht, was ich tun würde.

1. SEPTEMBER 2007
Mit dem Schnitt des Dokumentarfilms *Fairytale* endet das Projekt.
Ai Weiwei. Im Hinblick auf Dimension und Funktion unterscheidet sich *Fairytale* deutlich von meinen früheren Arbeiten. Es geht hier um lebendige Menschen, deren Leben, Hoffnungen und Phantasien. Ich glaube, all diese Dinge geben dem Projekt einen starken Charakter ... Wir fragten uns: Was müssen wir tun, damit jeder Teilnehmer das Gefühl hat, dass alles eigens für sie oder ihn gemacht wird, für jede Einzelperson, und damit jeder Teilnehmer eine gut durchgeplante, kostenlose Reise erhält? Wie können wir den Teilnehmern optimale Bedingungen für ihre Reise und für ihren Documenta-Aufenthalt als Besucher und als Teil des Werks garantieren? Für mich gehört das direkt zum Prozess des Werks. Ich sehe, welche Hoffnungen es gibt, welche Sorgen, welche Frustrationen ... das Warten und Erwarten ... dann die Träume, die Phantasien, dann ... vielleicht auch Überraschungen.

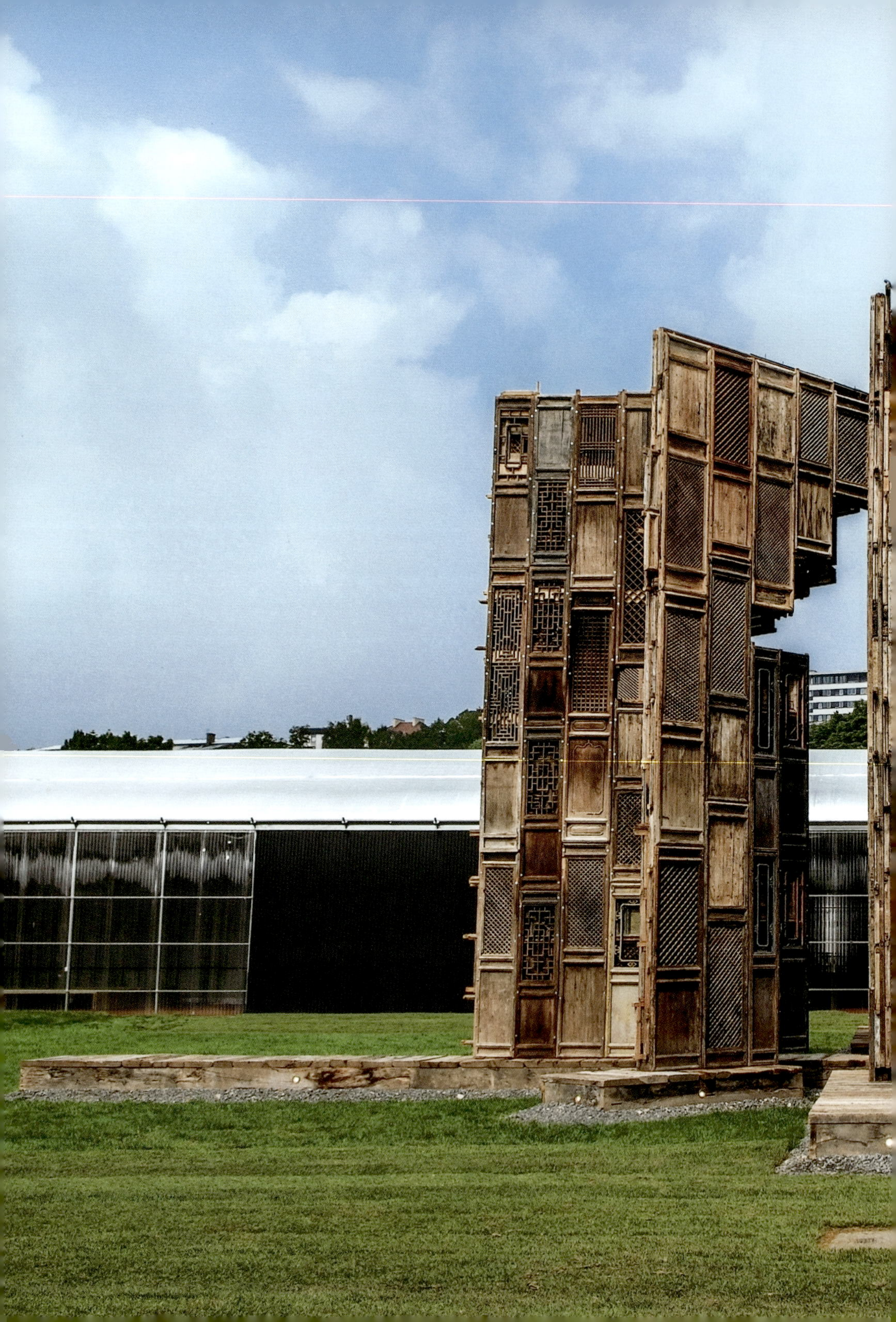

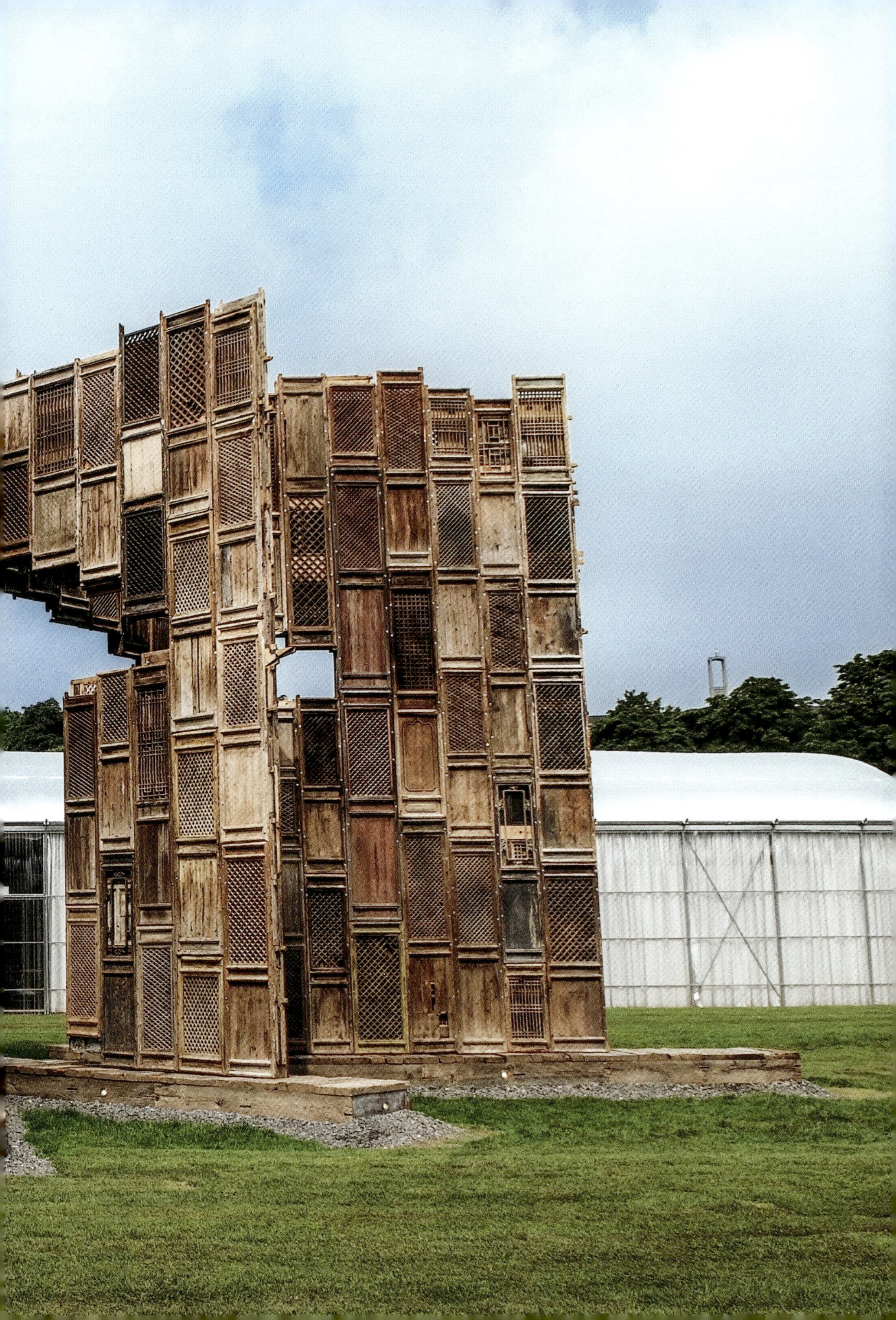

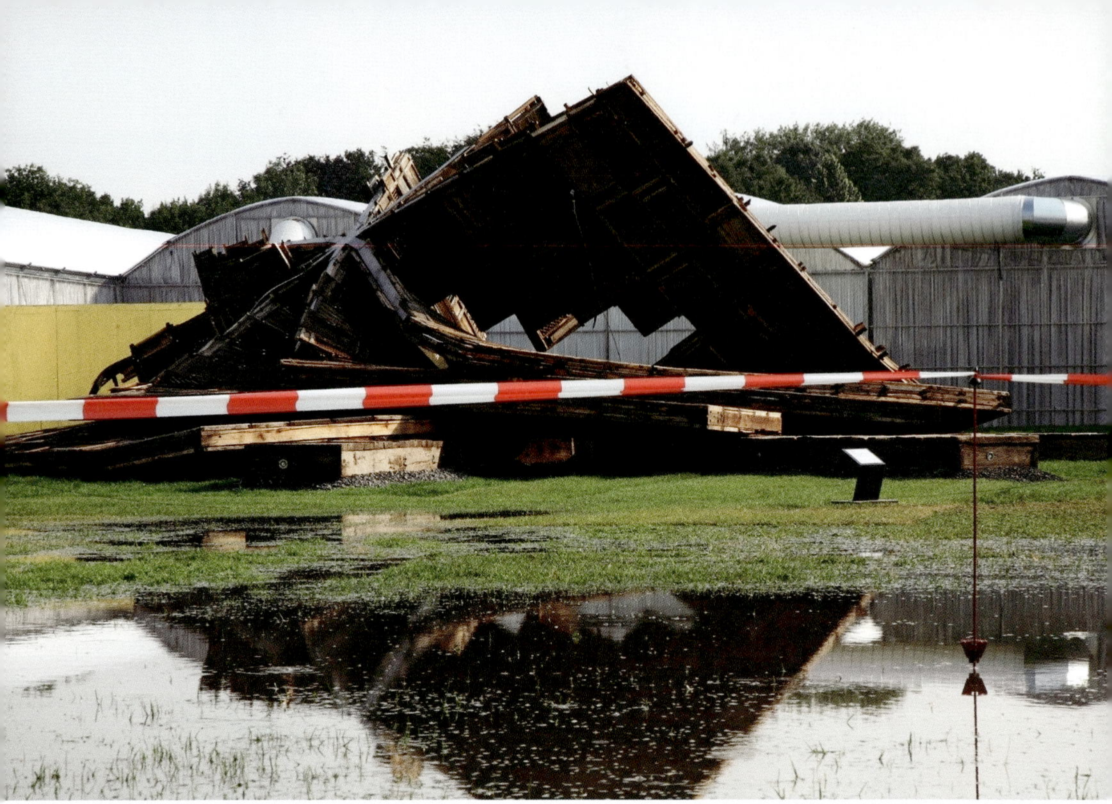

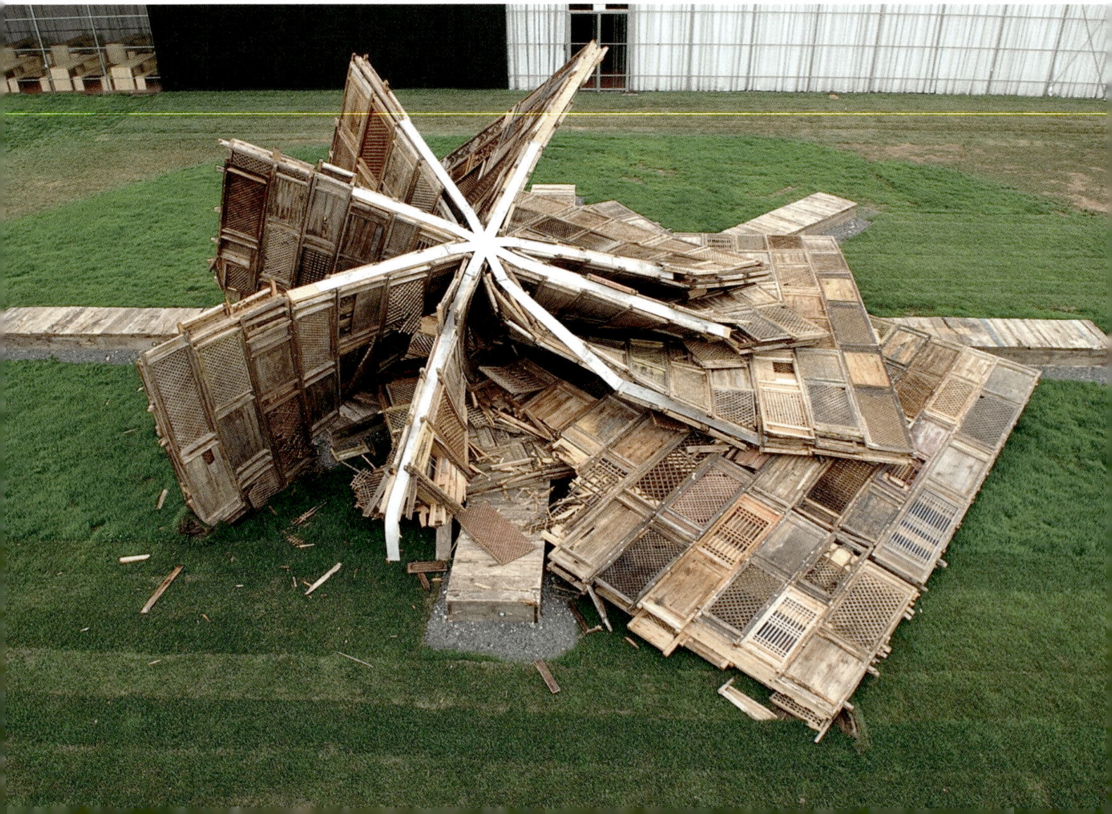

Fairytale, Documenta, 2007

1ᴱᴿ AOÛT 2006
Ai Weiwei visite l'aire d'exposition de la
Documenta à Cassel.

7 AOÛT 2006
À Val Roseg, en Suisse, Ai Weiwei croise
un groupe de randonneurs italiens qui lui
inspirent le concept fondamental de
Fairytale, œuvre pour laquelle il va inviter
1001 compatriotes chinois à faire partie
de l'exposition.
« Je faisais de l'alpinisme en Suisse et j'ai
vu passer un immense groupe de touristes
italiens entraînés vers la vallée par leurs
petits enfants. Cela m'a fait penser à emme-
ner en voyage un groupe de fringants
Chinois. C'était comme une part de gâteau
plus complète, une part qui allait inclure
tous les ingrédients du gâteau. C'est aussi
la raison pour laquelle je n'ai pas voulu en
inviter cinquante ou cent ; le nombre devait
représenter une certaine quantité. »
Parallèlement, Ai Weiwei projette d'exposer
Template, sculpture de douze mètres de
haut faite de bâtis de portes et de fenêtres
provenant de maisons détruites remontant
aux dynasties Ming et Qing.

22 FÉVRIER 2007
La première étape fut de rassembler une
équipe pour commencer le tournage du
documentaire *Fairytale*. Par la suite, Ai
Weiwei décrira ce processus de la manière
suivante : « Avec une petite vingtaine de
réalisateurs chinois et étrangers, nous
avons tourné un documentaire qui suit
quelques-uns des personnages les plus inté-
ressants de *Fairytale*. Nous avons consigné
leur vie, leur travail, leurs expériences quo-
tidiennes en Chine, ainsi que les différents
efforts mentaux et physiques et les dépen-
ses qu'ils ont engagés pour ce projet. Ceci
incluait leurs expériences de vie collective,
leurs attentes, leurs inquiétudes, leurs ob-
jectifs, leurs conditions actuelles, leur
éducation et leur famille. Le matériau ainsi
obtenu dépasse déjà mille heures. »

26 FÉVRIER 2007
Sur le blog d'Ai Weiwei, publication d'une
information sur le recrutement pour
Fairytale : « Je ne voulais pas annoncer mon
projet par la voie des médias traditionnels
comme les journaux ou la télévision. Comme
je tenais mon blog personnel depuis un an et
que je l'utilise pour m'exprimer et communiquer directement avec des inconnus que je
n'aurais aucune chance de rencontrer autrement, j'ai pensé que ce pourrait être une
bonne idée pour m'aider à choisir les gens
aléatoirement. C'est pourquoi je l'ai annoncé
sur mon blog. »
Les candidats doivent remplir un formulaire :
« Le questionnaire était une procédure intéri-
maire répondant à des considérations pratiques. Je veux dire à ces gens que nous
sommes sérieux : nous ne sommes pas en
train de rigoler. Les intégrer dans ce projet
en menant une réflexion sur la toile de fond
culturelle du monde occidental et leur situation personnelle était dans la nature de
l'œuvre. Les paysans répondaient simplement : « Je ne sais pas ». Mais s'ils rempli-
saient tout le questionnaire et signaient leur
nom en dernière page, cela montrait qu'ils
s'identifiaient au projet. »

26 FÉVRIER–1ᴱᴿ MARS 2007
Ai Weiwei visite des usines de bagages,
d'oreillers et de nattes dans le Jiangsu, le
Zhejiang et à Shanghai. « Nous avons aussi
conçu quelques produits. Je ne veux pas que
tout cela devienne une grande vitrine artistique, ce serait contraire au sens de ce travail.
Je veux perturber le moins possible la vie
quotidienne et préserver les habitudes et les
rythmes originaux. En même temps, il serait
bon qu'un consensus se dessine parmi les
participants. Il y a des besoins basiques
comme des lits, des draps, des couvertures,
des oreillers, des séparations – nous voulons
diviser l'espace en petites unités privées. Pour
vivre dans cette ville inconnue, certains outils
qui constituent une mémoire historique et
qui ont un statut spécial sont importants,

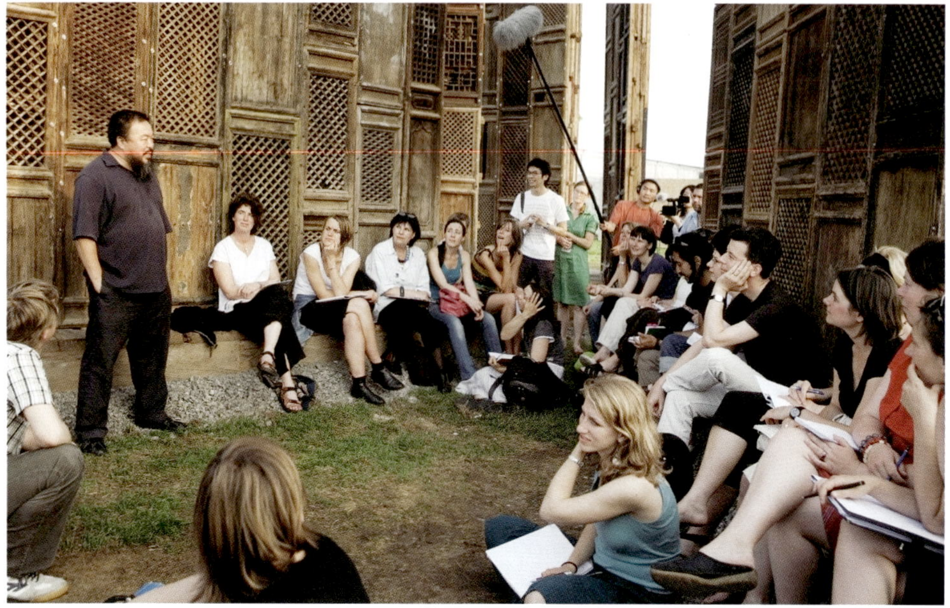

Ai Weiwei with exhibition guides and his film team in front of *Template*, Documenta 12, Kassel 2007

par exemple, 1001 chaises, des valises, des bracelets USB. Ces symboles statutaires sont liés à une confiance en soi et une fierté bien définies. Les détails importent peu, mais sans eux, tout éclaterait ; il n'y aura pas deux expériences identiques pendant cette aventure collective. »

2 MARS 2007

Ai Weiwei visite les marchés aux puces chinois et choisit 1001 chaises des dynasties Ming et Qing qui seront réparties sur le site de la Documenta comme éléments tangibles de ce travail.

7 MARS 2007

3000 candidatures ayant été recensées, dont seules 1100 seront retenues, le délai fixé au 31 mars pour postuler est ramené au 8 mars. « Je ne voulais pas décevoir les gens qui n'ont pas été choisis, j'ai donc temporairement fermé mon blog. Le fait qu'autant de gens puissent communiquer à travers mon blog m'a surpris. J'ai passé en revue le profil et l'histoire personnelle des individus qui avaient postulé – j'en ai choisi un sur trois. Les candidats venaient d'une vingtaine de provinces et exerçaient toutes sortes de métiers : policiers, agents de poste de péage, petits fonctionnaires, étudiants, enseignants, paysans, etc. Fait étonnant, tous les habitants d'un petit village du Guangxi avaient postulé. Ils vivaient dans des conditions primitives et la plupart n'avaient même pas de nom. Il leur fallait des noms pour se faire enregistrer dans le livret de famille et obtenir un passeport et un visa. Et trois générations d'une même famille du Gansu avaient également postulé. Certains d'entre eux n'étaient jamais sortis de leur ville et encore moins du pays. »

16 MARS 2007

Une liste provisoire de 1100 participants est publiée sur le blog d'Ai Weiwei. « Je remercie vraiment tous ceux qui ne me connaissent pas bien, qui ne savent pas grand-chose du programme et qui disent : "Oui, nous voulons y participer parce que nous croyons que c'est un projet qui sert l'imagination et les possibilités." Après bien sûr, ils ont dû dépenser beaucoup d'argent pour rentrer chez eux et demander un passeport… parfois c'était très difficile, beaucoup ont essuyé un refus, mais pour beaucoup, ça a été bien plus facile.

Beaucoup m'ont dit : "Pour nous, c'est déjà
un miracle, c'est déjà un conte de fées…
même si je ne peux pas partir, cela m'aidera
à penser autrement pour le reste de ma vie."
C'est très motivant quand on entend des gens
simples dire cela. »

19–20 MARS 2007
L'acceptation de sa candidature est notifiée
par email à chaque participant.

20 MARS–9 AVRIL 2007
L'équipe de *Fairytale* commence à compiler
les informations sur les passeports, les visas
et les problèmes que rencontrent les 1004
participants, qu'elle aide à remplir le formulaire de demande de visa en ligne, à souscrire
des assurances individuelles et à réserver
des vols.

10 AVRIL–10 MAI 2007
L'équipe et les participants de *Fairytale*
arrivent en groupes au consulat allemand de
Pékin, Shanghai, Canton, Chengdu pour
demander 1004 visas allemands. Il y aura en
tout trois refus.

10 MAI 2007
Production de valises, d'ustensiles de cuisine,
de vêtements, de taies d'oreillers et de couvertures. Les 1001 bracelets et clés USB et
les séparations du dortoir ont été intégralement confirmés.

21 MAI 2007
L'équipe des organisateurs part en Allemagne
avec dix-sept participants de *Fairytale*.

11 JUIN 2007
taz. *CONTE DE FÉES D'UN AUTRE GENRE :*
« Le conte de fées le plus marquant de ma vie
a été le mythe du communisme. À l'âge de
dix ans, j'ai dû apprendre par cœur le manifeste communiste », nous explique l'artiste,
commissaire d'expositions, critique d'art et
architecte Ai Weiwei à propos du titre de
ce projet audacieux. 1001 Chinois de tous
âges, de toutes professions, originaires de
différentes provinces de Chine, vont venir
s'intégrer à l'événement artistique de la
Documenta en cinq groupes. Une ancienne
usine de toile de tentes servira de logement
pendant la dizaine de jours que durera le

séjour de chaque groupe. Pour respecter les
différentes sensibilités culturelles, les lits et
les cuisiniers viennent directement de Chine.
En cas de perte ou de confusion, un kit de
survie aidera les immigrés artistiques, dont la
plupart ne parlent aucune langue étrangère.
Ce que cette performance, succinctement
qualifiée de «ready-made sociopolitique» par
Ai Weiwei, recouvre dans les détails, ménage
encore des surprises.
Une chose est sûre, *Fairytale* n'aura rien
d'un conte de fées. «La catégorie du conte
de fées m'intéresse avant tout comme terme
générique recouvrant la distinction entre le
bien et le mal, le rapport entre la vérité et
l'imaginaire. Ces dualismes existent aussi
entre la Chine et l'Occident. Mais le titre
se réfère aussi très concrètement au site de
Cassel. C'est quand même là qu'ont vécu les
frères Grimm », explique Ai Weiwei. «Au
centre de *Fairytale*, il y a le choc entre différentes cultures. Dès lors que nous parlons de
conte et que nous introduisons le nombre
1001, nous avons déjà une référence à deux
cultures. Car le conte des *Mille et une nuits*
vient de l'espace arabe. Il faut ajouter que
ces formes de récit n'existent pas en Chine.
En Chine, on raconte aux enfants des fables
et des mythes, les contes de fées sont une
importation purement occidentale. »

12–20 JUIN 2007
Arrivée et séjour à la Documenta du premier
groupe de 184 participants à *Fairytale*.

16 JUIN 2007
Inauguration officielle de la Documenta.
La couverture de presse comprend de nombreuses vues de la sculpture extérieure *Template*, visuellement une des œuvres les plus
frappantes de l'exposition. Ai donne les ex-
plications suivantes sur son œuvre : «Les
fenêtres et les portes utilisées pour *Template*
faisaient partie de maisons détruites dans
le Shanxi, dans le nord de la Chine, où d'anciennes villes ont été entièrement rasées.
Nous avons acheté les fragments de différents
quartiers, et ce sont probablement les dernières pièces de cette civilisation. J'aime
utiliser ces reliquats comme une partie…
pas d'un sentiment, mais comme une preuve
de notre activité passée. J'aime transposer
ces pièces dans un contexte résolument

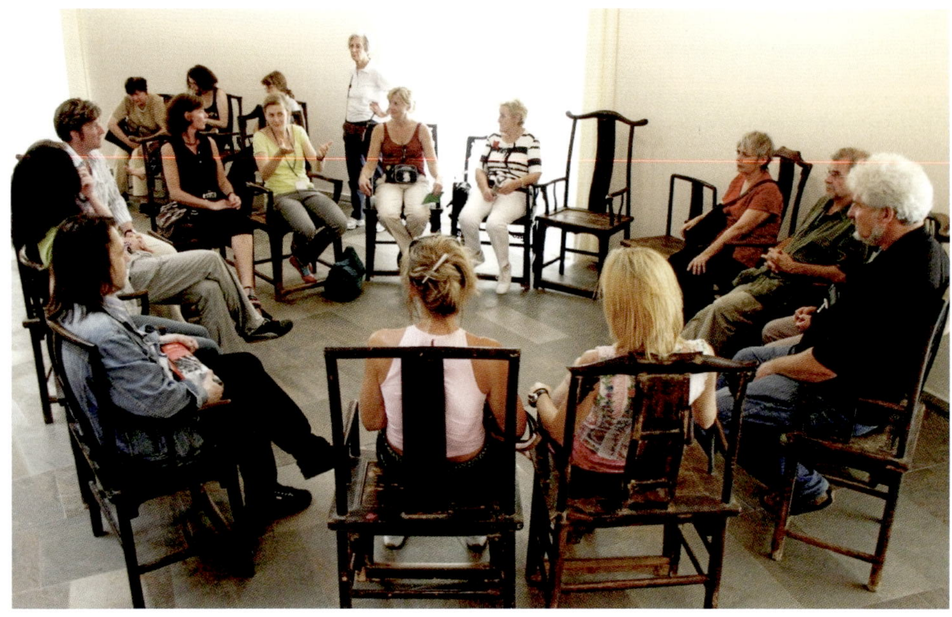

Documenta guide with a group of visitors on chairs from the *Fairytale* project, Kassel 2007

contemporain et je pense que cela fonctionne bien. C'est vraiment un contexte mixte, troublé, qui interpelle, qui revendique sa propre identité. Pour moi, le temple lui-même – vous savez que je ne suis pas religieux – est une situation dans laquelle on peut penser au passé et au futur, un espace vide. La zone sélectionnée – pas le temple matériel – vous dit que le temple physique réel n'est pas là, mais qu'il est construit par les reliquats du passé. »

19–25 JUIN 2007
Séjour à la Documenta du deuxième groupe de 228 participants à *Fairytale*.

20 JUIN 2007
Frankfurter Allgemeine Zeitung.
TEMPLATE, LA SCULPTURE D'AI WEIWEI, S'EFFONDRE APRÈS UN VIOLENT ORAGE.
Template, l'œuvre de l'artiste chinois Ai Weiwei s'est effondrée. La tour en bois de douze mètres s'est effondrée mercredi à Cassel après un court épisode orageux. Selon la Documenta, la pièce va être reconstruite. *Template* est composé de portes et de fenêtres d'anciennes maisons victimes du boom immobilier en Chine. Le président fédéral Horst Köhler avait visité l'œuvre samedi dernier.

21 JUIN 2007
Focus. Ai Weiwei, connu pour avoir invité 1001 compatriotes chinois à la Documenta, n'envisage pas de reconstruire l'œuvre. « Elle est bien mieux qu'avant », nous dit l'artiste âgé de cinquante ans. « Maintenant, on peut y lire les forces de la nature. C'est ce genre d'émotions qui fait la beauté de l'art. » Pieds nus dans une grande flaque d'eau devant *Template*, Buergel, le commissaire de la Documenta, juge l'effondrement « très logique… Les vestiges permettent désormais toutes sortes d'associations. Et c'est exactement ce que l'art entend susciter. » Selon lui, le président Köhler ne risquait absolument rien. « L'effondrement ne pouvait se produire sans cet orage lors duquel même le plus intrépide des présidents fédéraux aurait pris le large. » La visite d'un acheteur potentiel était prévue pour le lendemain. Mais même après l'effondrement, Ai Weiwei ne s'est pas départi de son optimisme en déclarant: « Le prix de l'œuvre vient de doubler. »

Ai Weiwei. En fait, *Template* avait été conçu pour un espace clos, pas préparé pour la météo allemande. L'œuvre s'est donc effondrée après six jours. J'ai été un peu surpris, mais pas tout à fait, parce que je savais qu'elle n'était pas extrêmement solide. Quand j'ai vu comment elle s'était effondrée – pas entièrement, elle a seulement pris une autre forme –, j'ai pensé qu'elle était désormais vraiment comme une ruine. J'ai été assez impressionné. Elle vient de ruines, et maintenant, elle est vraiment une ruine… Après l'effondrement, nous avons demandé aux ingénieurs de l'université de Cassel d'en calculer intégralement les mesures. Nous réfléchissons à la possibilité de démonter et de reconstruire la structure en l'état. Elle est plus intéressante qu'avant. Je la considère désormais comme une pièce qui travaille sur le changement et qui reproduit un miracle.

24–30 JUIN 2007
Séjour à la Documenta du troisième groupe de 192 participants à *Fairytale*.

29 JUIN–5 JUILLET 2007
Séjour à la Documenta du quatrième groupe de 185 participants à *Fairytale*.

4–10 JUILLET 2007
Séjour à la Documenta du cinquième groupe de 189 participants à *Fairytale*.

11 JUILLET 2007
L'ensemble des 995 participants venus à Cassel sont rentrés en Chine.

Fairytale Documentaire. Intervieweur : Que feriez-vous si quelques participants, ou un seul, ne rentraient pas en Chine ? Vous savez, c'est arrivé bien souvent à l'époque où l'Allemagne était divisée : un artiste obtenait l'autorisation de se rendre à un concert ou de faire autre chose professionnellement, et puis, une fois de l'autre côté, il refusait de revenir. Il se cachait et… Que feriez-vous ? / AW : En tant qu'artiste et pour l'œuvre aussi bien sûr, j'ai organisé la venue et le retour de ces gens en Chine en tant que groupe uni. Cela dit, je ne peux empêcher qui que ce soit d'exercer son libre arbitre. Et je ne peux même pas prédire la raison qui m'en empêcherait. Je ne sais même pas si je vais moi-même rentrer. Ces décisions se prennent au jour le jour. Toutes nos décisions sont sujettes à interrogation parce que nous sommes humains. La conscience… c'est toujours dangereux d'essayer de voir le monde comme quelque chose qui ne serait pas dangereux. Quand tout est planifié, à mon avis, c'est une erreur. Donc ma réponse est très claire : je n'en sais rien.

1ER SEPTEMBRE 2007
Avec la production finale du documentaire *Fairytale*, l'œuvre est achevée.

Ai Weiwei. Concernant l'échelle et le fonctionnement de l'œuvre, *Fairytale* est une œuvre apparemment différente de mes précédentes œuvres parce qu'elle travaille avec des individus vivants, avec leurs vies, aussi bien qu'avec leurs espoirs et leur imagination. Je pense que ce sont toutes ces choses qui confèrent son fort caractère à ce projet… Plus précisément : comment faire que chacun ressente que tout ceci est fait pour lui ou elle, pour chaque individu, et permettre aux participants de vivre un voyage tout à la fois très détaillé, soigneusement planifié et libre ? Comment faire pour qu'ils aient des conditions de voyage tout à fait correctes et qu'ils soient à la Documenta à la fois comme spectateurs et comme partie intégrante de l'œuvre ? Je considère l'ensemble du processus comme l'œuvre elle-même. Je vois le genre d'espoirs, d'inquiétudes, de frustrations… et d'expectatives, et d'anticipations… puis le rêve, puis l'imagination, puis… peut-être, la surprise.

Overleaf: POST-TEMPLATE, 2007–2009, wooden doors and windows from destroyed Ming and Qing Dynasty houses, 166 ⅛ x 435 ½ x 344 ½ inches | 335

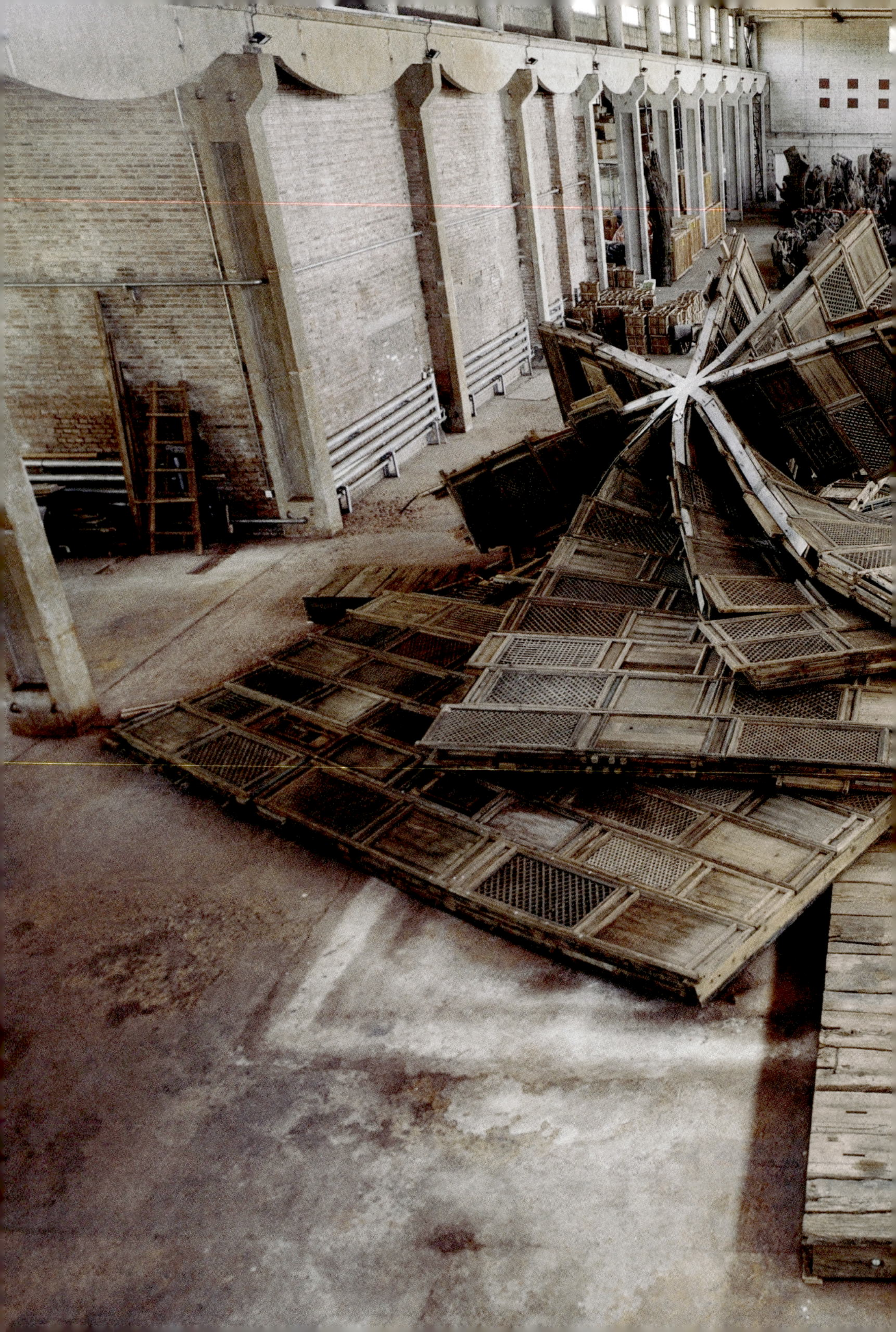

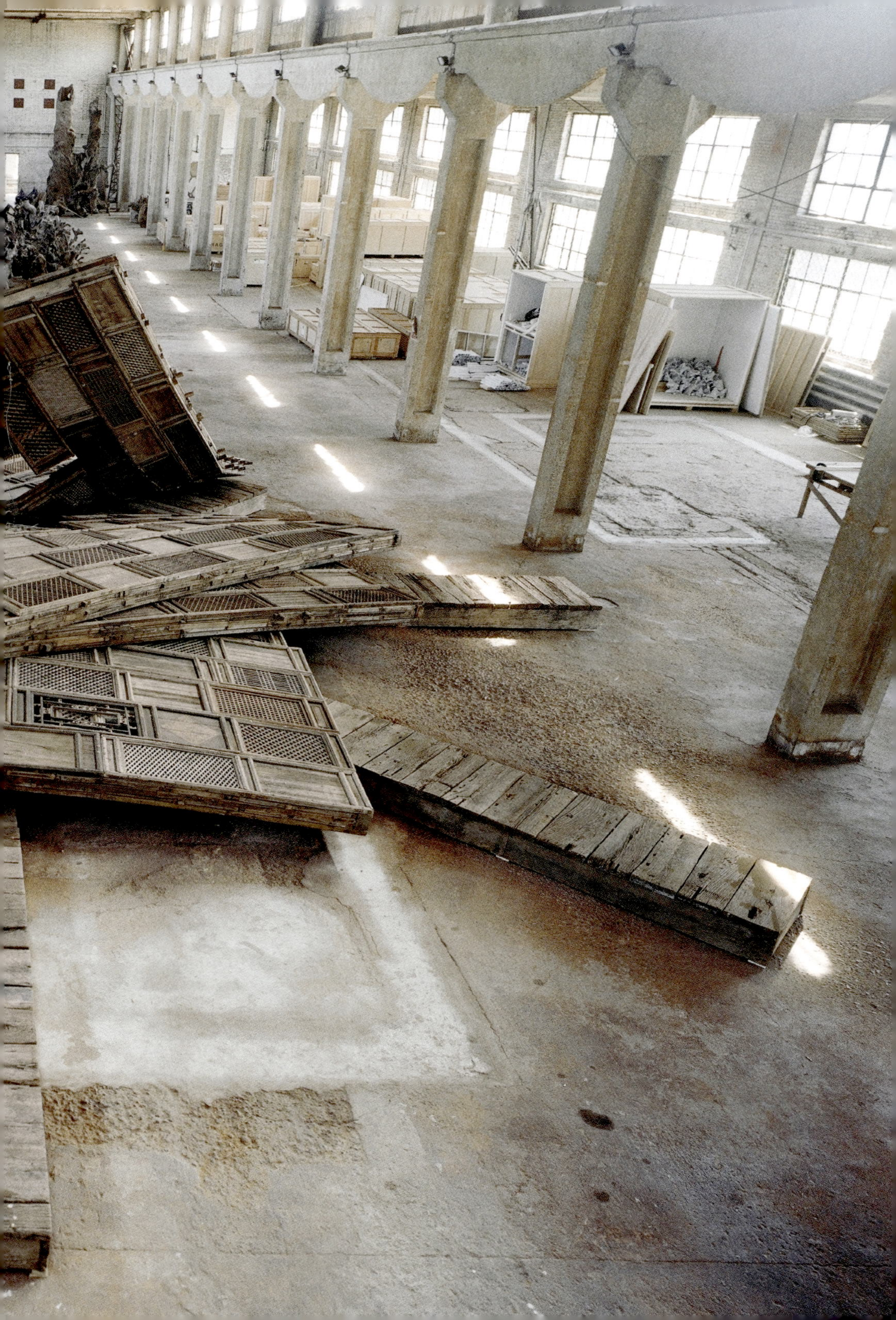

"Each time I cut someone's hair it's a challenge because I don't know what
I'm going to do. Only when my scissors touch their hair do I decide what to do.
The first haircuts happened when I was bored in the office and started to cut
the hair of people working there. Then we put photos of the haircuts on my blog,
and many people thought it was funny—more and more people started coming
just to get their hair cut. Haircutting is a practice now, as serious as any other.
It's not a joke, or maybe life is a joke." — AI WEIWEI

Jeder Haarschnitt ist eine neue Herausforderung für mich, denn ich weiß nie, was
ich tun werde. Erst wenn die Schere die Haare berührt, entscheide ich, was nötig ist. Ich
fing mit dem Haareschneiden aus Langeweile im Büro bei den Leuten an, die dort arbeiteten. Dann stellten wir Fotografien der Frisuren in meinen Blog, und viele Leute fanden
das lustig. Immer mehr Menschen kamen im Büro vorbei, um sich die Haare schneiden
zu lassen. Haareschneiden ist eine Tätigkeit, die so seriös ist wie jede andere. Es ist kein
Witz, oder vielleicht ist das Leben ein Witz.

Chaque fois que je coupe les cheveux de quelqu'un, c'est un défi : je ne sais jamais
ce que je vais faire. Ce n'est que lorsque mes ciseaux touchent les cheveux de la personne
que je décide de ce que je vais faire. Mes premières coupes de cheveux, je les ai faites
lorsque je m'ennuyais dans un bureau et que j'ai commencé à couper les cheveux des gens.
Puis nous avons posté des photos sur mon blog, beaucoup de gens ont trouvé ça drôle – et
de plus en plus de gens sont venus me voir pour que je leur coupe les cheveux. Couper les
cheveux est devenu un métier pour moi, aussi sérieux qu'un autre. Ce n'est pas une blague,
ou alors peut-être que la vie est une blague.

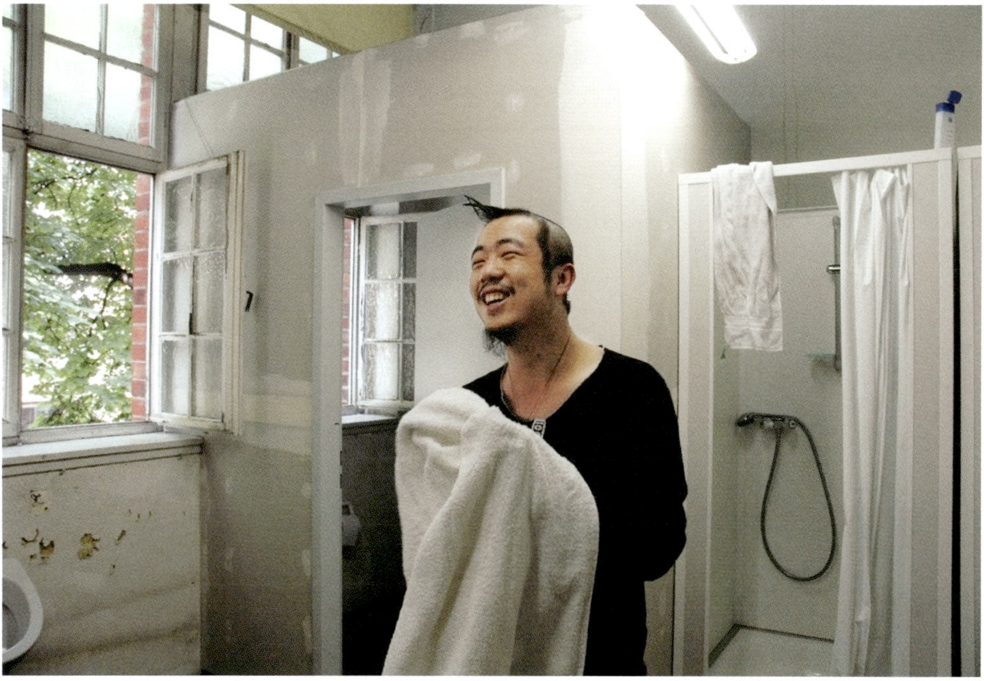

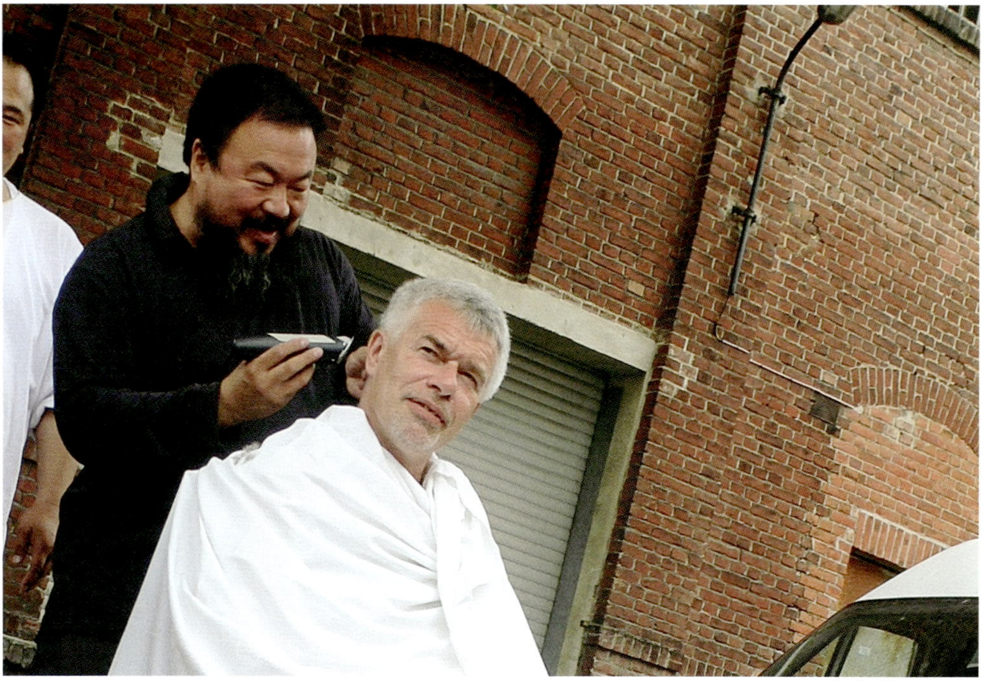

Ai Weiwei giving haircuts to Chris Dercon, studio employees, and
Fairytale participants, Kassel 2007 (above and overleaf) | 339

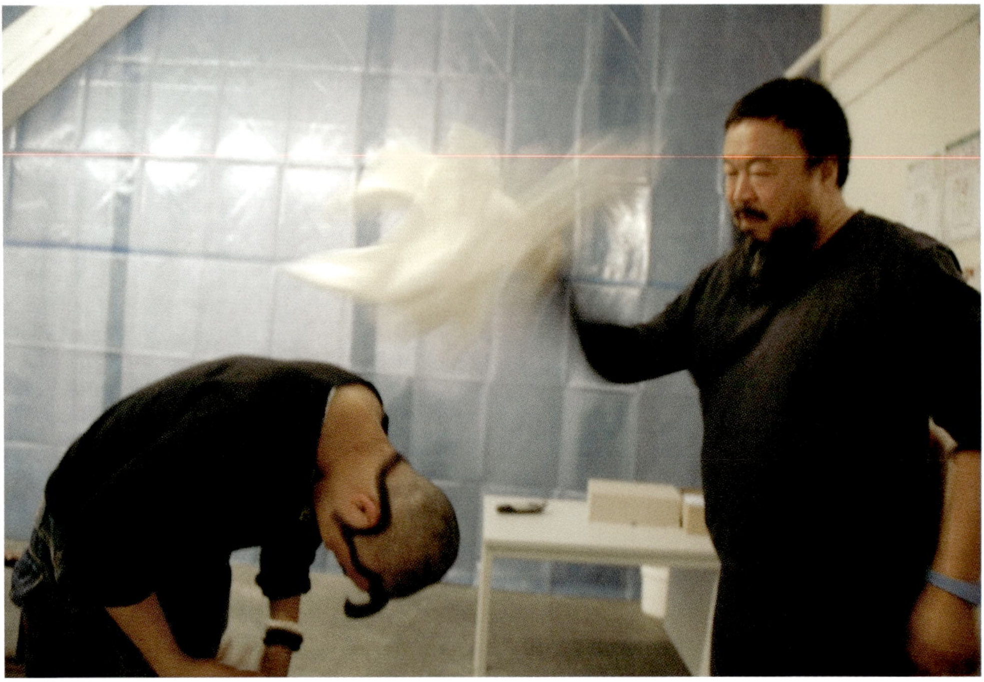

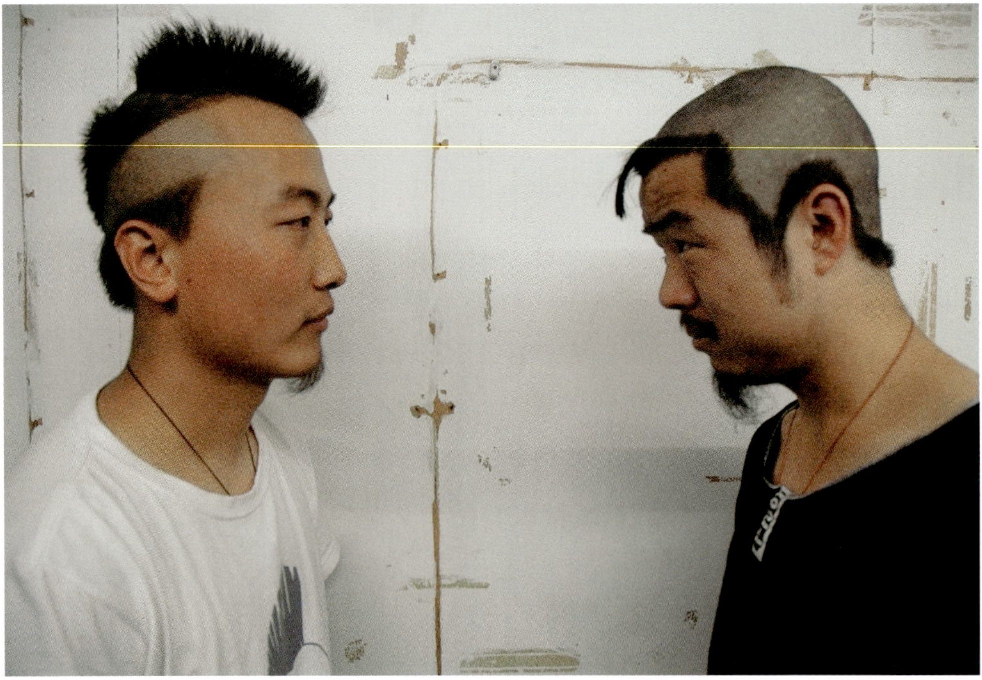

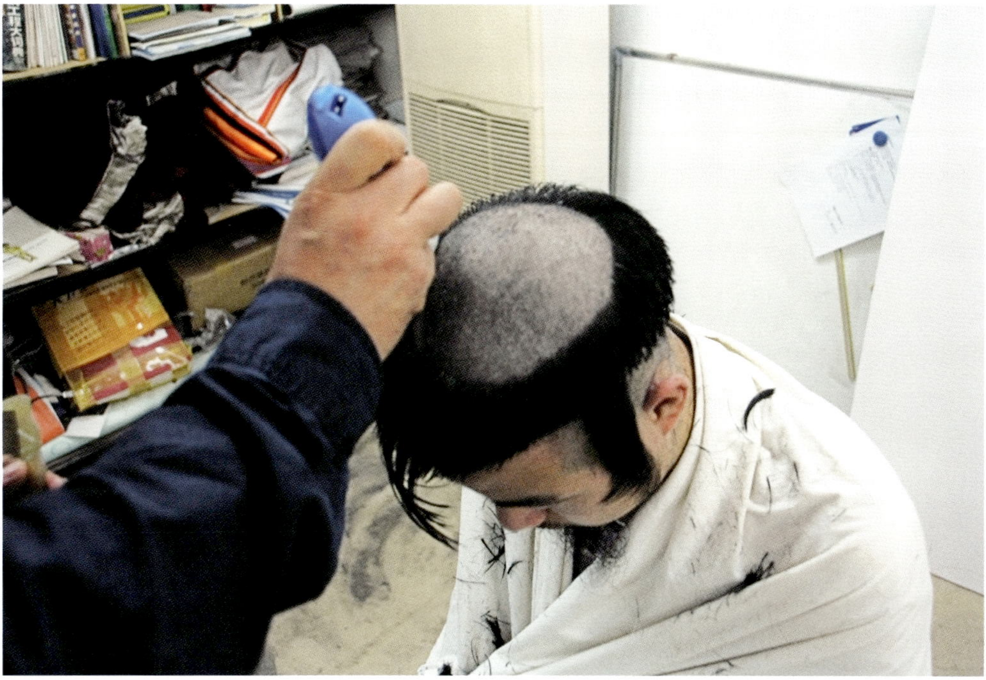

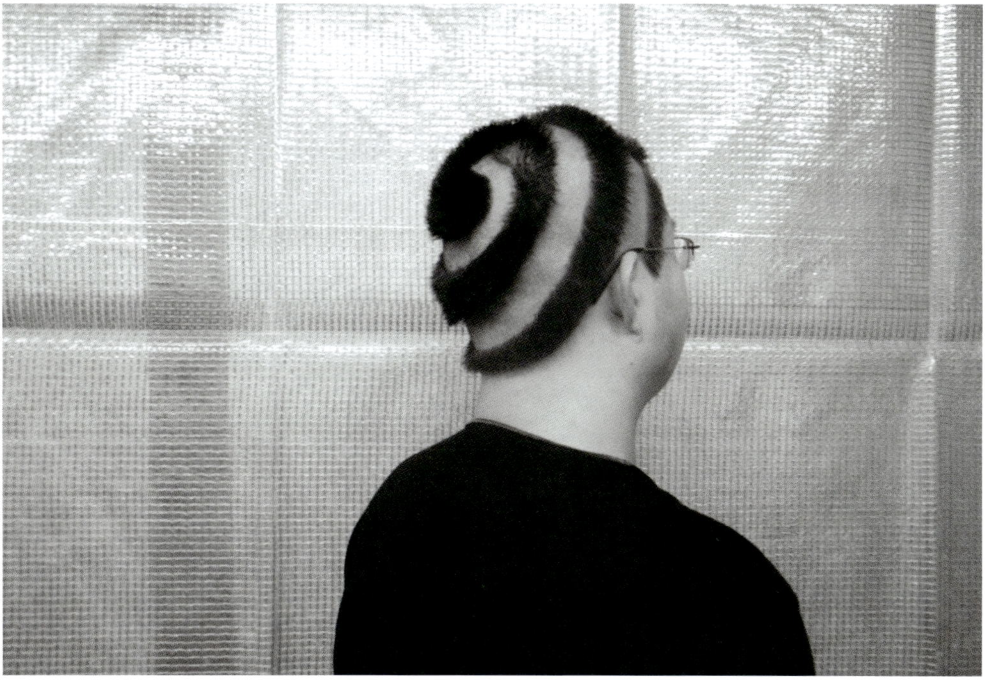

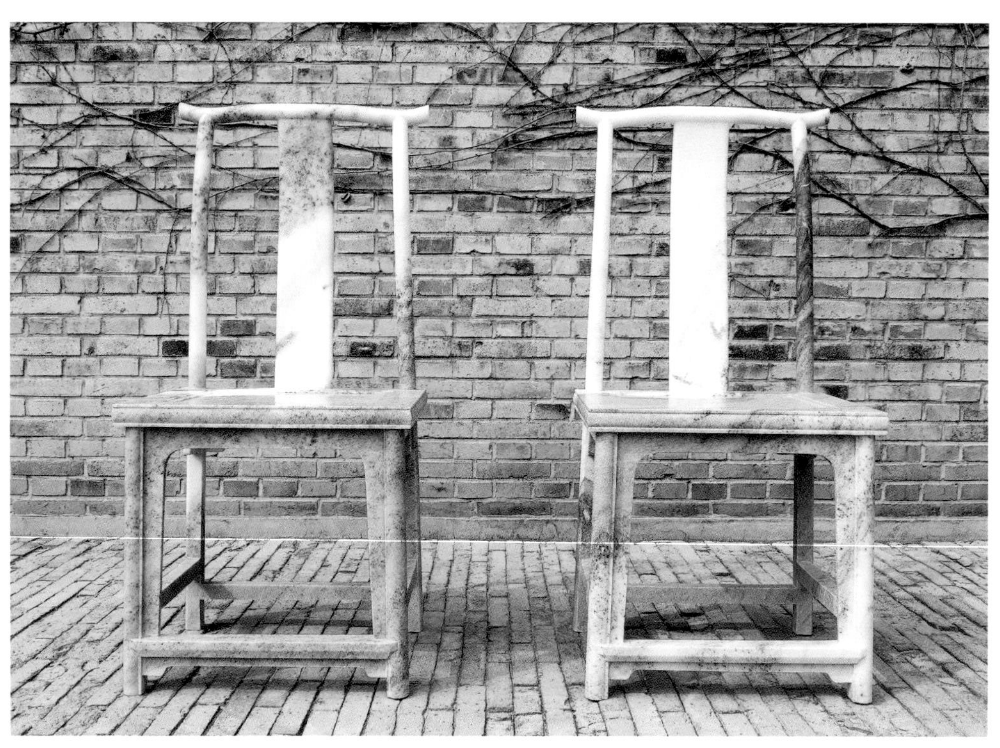

342 | MARBLE CHAIRS, 2008, marble, each 47 ¼ x 22 x 18 ⅛ inches

2008–2011

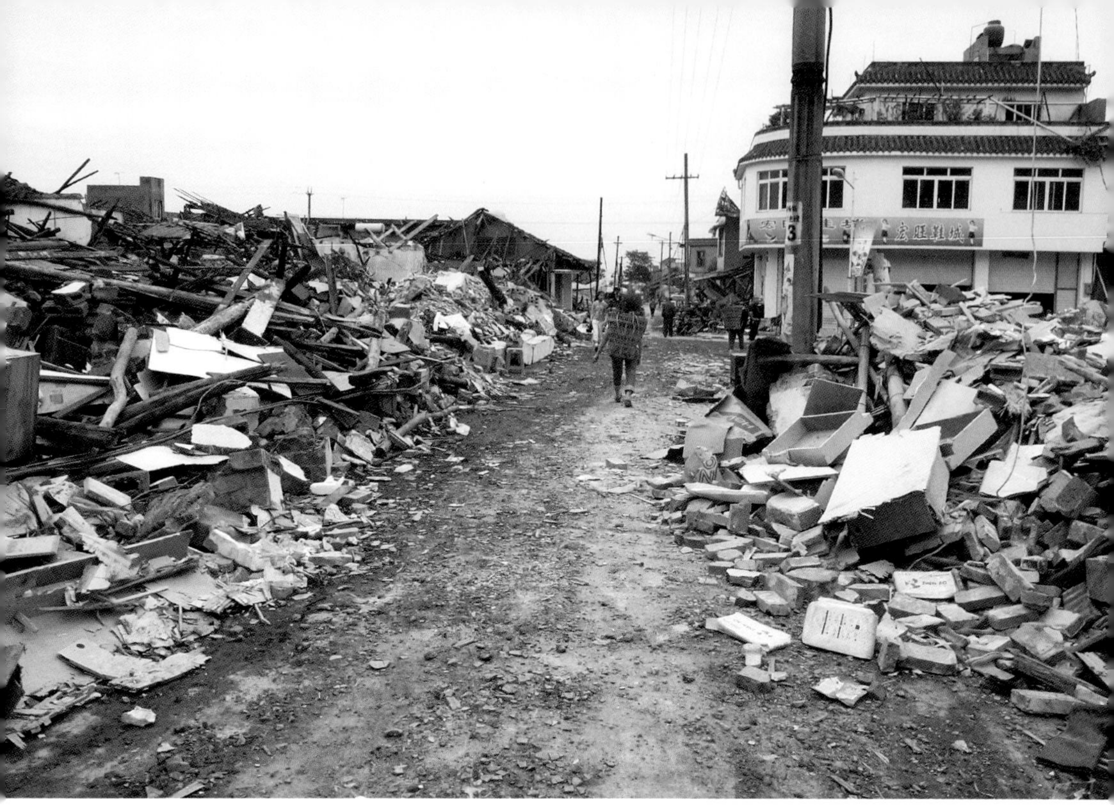

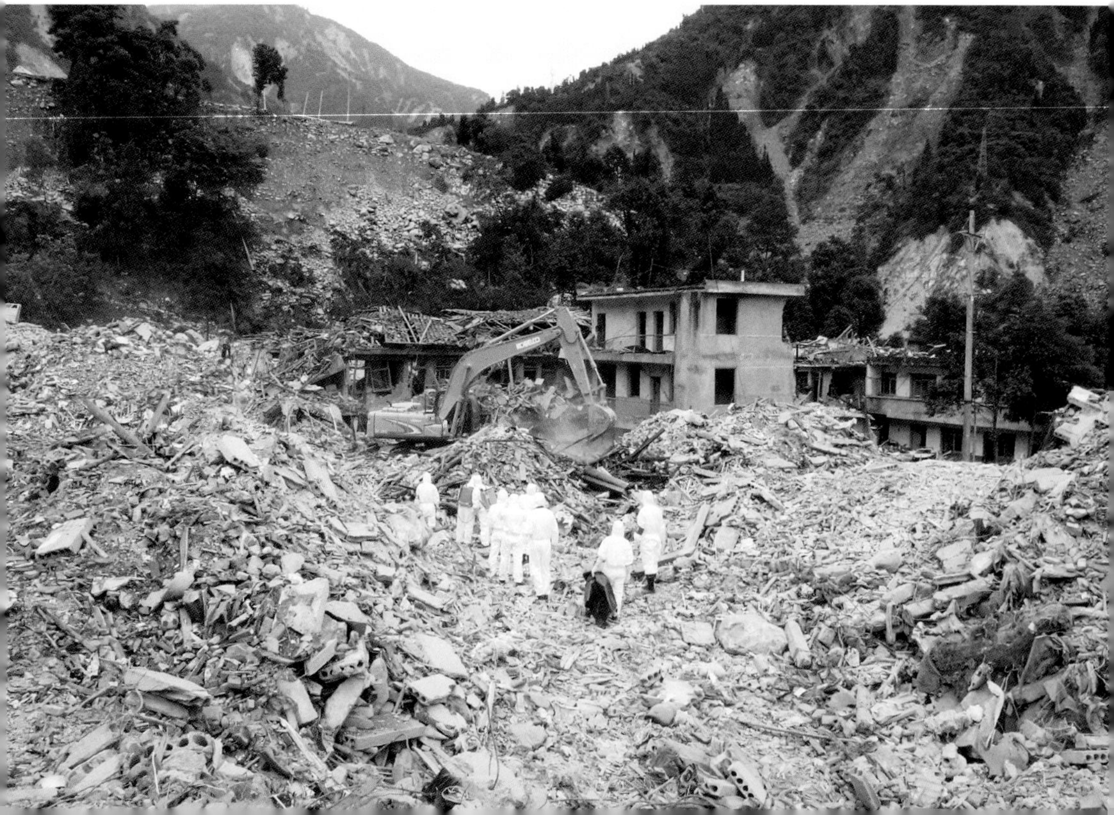

Sichuan Earthquake and Citizens' Investigation

MAY 12, 2008
BBC News. *THOUSANDS DEAD IN CHINESE QUAKE.* A powerful earthquake has killed at least 10,000 people in China's southwestern Sichuan province, up to 5,000 of them in just one county. Many more have been killed and injured in other parts of the country after the 7.8-magnitude quake struck at 14:28 local time. At least 50 bodies have been recovered from the rubble of a school where an estimated 900 students were buried. President Hu Jintao has urged "all-out" efforts to rescue victims. Search teams were sent to the area but struggled to get through because routes were blocked. With communication links down, he says there is still no real indication of the death toll at the epicenter, in Wenchuan county, about 57 miles from Chengdu, Sichuan's provincial capital.

MAY 13, 2008
The New York Times. *"NO HOPE" FOR CHILDREN BURIED IN EARTHQUAKE.*
One of the most jarring tragedies of the disaster was the school collapse in a suburb of Dujiangyan. At least several hundred children were killed, perhaps as many as 900. Prime Minister Wen Jiabao flew here on Monday to survey the destruction, but he was powerless to ease the suffering of the survivors…
The children who were considered fortunate escaped with a broken bone or a severed limb. The others, hundreds of them, were carried out to be buried, and their remaining classmates lay crushed beneath the rubble of the schoolhouse. "There's no hope for them," said Lu Zhiqing, 58, as she watched uniformed rescue workers trudge through mud and rain toward the mound of bricks and concrete that had once been a school. "There's no way anyone's still alive in there." Little remained of the original structure of the school. No standing beams, no fragments of walls. The rubble lay low against the wet earth. Dozens of people gathered around in the schoolyard, clawing at the debris, kick-ing it, screaming at it. Soldiers kept others from entering.

MAY 22, 2008
Ai Weiwei's blog. Extending a hand to those caught in trouble, rescuing the dying and helping the injured is a form of humanitarianism, unrelated to love of country or people. Do not belittle the value of life; it commands a broader, more equal dignity. Throughout these days of mourning, people do not need to thank the Motherland and her supporters, for she was unable to offer any better protection. Nor was it the Motherland, in the end, who allowed the luckier children to escape from their collapsing schoolhouses. There is no need to praise government officials; for the lives that are fading just as we speak need effective rescue measures far more than they need sympathetic speeches and tears. There is even less need to thank the army, as doing so would be to say that in responding to this disaster, soldiers offer something other than the fulfillment of their sworn duty.

MAY 25, 2008
The New York Times. *CHINESE ARE LEFT TO ASK WHY SCHOOLS CRUMBLED.*
There is no official figure on how many children died at Xinjian Primary School, nor on how many died at scores of other schools that collapsed in the powerful May 12 earthquake in Sichuan Province. But the number of student deaths seems likely to exceed 10,000, and possibly go much higher, a staggering figure that has become a simmering controversy in China as grieving parents say their children might have lived had the schools been better built. The Chinese government has enjoyed broad public support for its handling of the earthquake, and in Sichuan on Saturday, Secretary General Ban Ki-moon of the United Nations praised the government's response. But as parents at different schools begin to speak out, the question of whether official negligence, and possibly corruption,

contributed to the student deaths could turn public opinion. The government has launched an investigation, but censors, wary of the public mood, are trying to suppress the issue in state-run media and online. An examination of the collapse of Xinjian Primary School offers a disturbing picture of a calamity that might have been avoided. Engineers and earthquake experts who examined photographs of its wreckage concluded that the structure had many failings and one critical flaw: inadequate iron reinforcing rods running up the school's vertical columns. One expert described the unstable concrete floor panels as "time bombs."

JUNE 1, 2008
Ai Weiwei's blog. Twenty days have passed since the earthquake, and still there is no roster clearly listing the names of missing children, and there are no accurate counts of the dead. The public still doesn't know who these departed children are, who their families are, who neglected to reinforce the schools with steel, and who mixed inferior concrete in their foundations and concrete supports when they were constructed.
Reuters. About 25 miles down the valley in Dujiangyan, some 200 parents and relatives of pupils killed in the quake gathered on Sunday for a Children's Day commemoration in the rubble-strewn grounds of what used to be Xinjian primary school. Thousands of children died in the quake when their schools crumpled like packs of cards, arousing suspicions among parents that building standards had been flouted because of corruption. Responding to the fury of parents is one of the stiffest political challenges for the ruling Communist Party in the aftermath of the quake. Angry and tearful, they wore white T-shirts with the name of the school on the front and, in huge red characters on the back, the slogan "Severely Punish Corrupt Tofu Dregs Construction"—a reference to the remnants left when making tofu, or beancurd, a common Chinese term for shoddy workmanship and poor materials.

JULY 28, 2008
Ai Weiwei's blog. The headlines this morning read: "Wenchuan has announced it will establish an earthquake memorial." The Vietnam War had a profound effect on the United States; it caused the kind of pain that cuts deep; and ten years after the conclusion of the war, they erected a memorial bearing the engraved names of more than 58,000 departed soldiers on a field of grass in Washington, D.C. As for the affairs here, all we get is a statement from the top such as the one above, and the excited clamoring of a pack of expert bastards kicking up a fuss. As you can imagine, this memorial isn't preparing to accurately record the actual events. Historical facts were altered even before they were allowed to run their full course. Even more impossible would be holding a memorial service for those who died as a result of carelessness... How many people were actually killed and wounded in the Wenchuan earthquake? How did they perish, and who should shoulder the blame? Confronted with this question, the responsible Ministry of Education and Ministry of Architecture are refusing to answer, they want to eternally play dead.

MARCH 13, 2009, 10:01 A.M.
Phone call to the Beichuan County Stability Maintenance Group. Ai Weiwei Studio: Hello, is Supervisor Sun there? Is this the "Stability Maintenance Group"? / Beichuan Stability Maintenance Group: Yes, this is he. / Studio: I'm someone calling from Chaoyang District in Beijing, my group is investigating the death toll and names of students who died in Beichuan during the May 12 earthquake. / Beichuan: Where is your group from? / Studio: Beijing. / Beichuan: What work unit or public security branch in Beijing? / Studio: We're self-organized by citizens. / Beichuan: I'm sorry, we can't give our death toll to you, and we can't release it to the public. / Studio: Why is that? / Beichuan: It's not a matter of why, it's a matter of discipline. / Studio: What sort of discipline? / Beichuan: National discipline. / Studio: Does our state have such a provision? Is it written somewhere? / Beichuan: What group are you? / Studio: We are a group of citizens. / Beichuan: Why does a group of citizens need to know this? / Studio: We're all fellow countrymen, everybody is concerned about this. / Beichuan: Do you mean to say we don't know how to be concerned about our own comrades? / Studio: That's not what I meant, everybody is con-

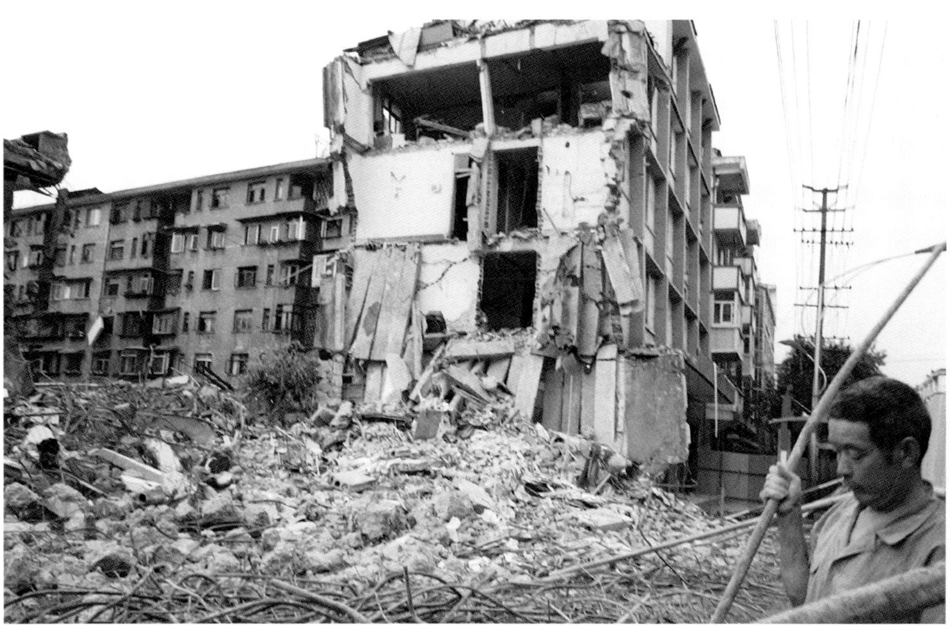

Earthquake, 2008–2010, C-print, 14⅝ x 21¾ inches; in the earthquake disaster zone, Beichuan County, May 2008

cerned, but this is how we're expressing it. / Beichuan: Let me tell you, this whole thing isn't really clear. / Studio: Why isn't it clear? Isn't your division given information from your superior in charge? / Beichuan: Who said that? / Studio: An employee, but the domestic media have already publicized it, so we're making an inquiry with you. / Beichuan: I'm sorry. / Studio: This is your job, isn't it the responsibility of the "Stability Maintenance Group" to respond to the people when they have inquiries? / Beichuan: It's our duty to release the materials that you want? / Studio: This isn't a law, it's a basic thing! / Beichuan: Which law? / Studio: You're government employees. / Beichuan: We make reports to the government, and we've reported to the government everything that we're expected to. Which work unit we're supposed to report to, that's for the government to decide. / Studio: Your responsibility is to report to the government? Then what about the people? You're the government, or at least a part of it! / Beichuan: Also, I don't know who you are, you haven't told me clearly what group you're calling from. / Studio:

We're not from some organization, we're citizens! / Beichuan: Citizens? Citizens like you are supposed to make your inquiries with the government. / Studio: So now you're government again? / Beichuan: I'm government, and I report to my superiors. How do I know who you are? What if you have ulterior motives? / Studio: What do you mean ulterior motives? What do you mean by that? If a citizen makes a phone call about something all citizens should know, does that mean I have ulterior motives? / Beichuan: How can you prove you don't have something else in mind? That's just how it is! (hangs up)

MARCH 20, 2009
Ai Weiwei's blog. Three hundred days ago I traveled to the earthquake zone in Wenchuan county. There I witnessed infinite suffering and terror. Today, we still cannot know who left us in the earthquake, why those children left us, and how they were taken. We will never know what they were feeling as they lay under the rubble waiting. During that disaster, I did not extend my hand. I honestly could not find the strength. They say the

death of the students has nothing to do with them. They say it was inevitable, unavoidable, and that experts have demonstrated this. They close their mouths and do not discuss corruption, they avoid the tofu-dregs engineering. They conceal the facts, and in the name of "stability" they persecute, threaten, and imprison the parents of these deceased children who are demanding to know the truth. They flagrantly violate the constitution and trample on people's fundamental rights. Those children who perished in the earthquake are not an unknown figure, they are not the result of a "stabilized" nation. Those children have parents, dreams, and they could smile, they had a name that belonged to them. That name will belong to them three years from now, five years, eighteen or nineteen years later; it is everything about them which may be remembered, it is everything that might be evoked. Reject the failure to remember, reject lies. To remember the departed, to show concern for life, to take responsibility, and for the potential happiness of the survivors, we are initiating a "Citizens' Investigation." We will seek out the names of each departed child, and we will remember them. People interested in the Citizens' Investigation, please leave your contact information: xuesheng512@gmail.com. Your actions create your world.

MARCH 24, 2009
Ai Weiwei's blog. Q: Online searches reveal the headline: "Wenchuan earthquake has disclosed a list of 19,065 names; the death toll is still being investigated." This means that the government is doing similar work. Why do you still want to create a new list of names? / AWW: We made more than 150 phone calls, hoping that we could obtain a list of the 19,065 names. All we obtained was procrastination, stalling, and unclear answers. Not a single person knows where this list of names was published or how it was published, and the list has never appeared on any official websites. More than three hundred days have passed, and we have yet to see a figure that inspires people's belief. The government should clearly display the names of these people, their ages, and the cause of their deaths, as well as the place they were killed and the area in which they were registered. This kind of basic information, no matter in life or in death, can only be completed under the auspices of the government, and it should be readily available at any moment. We undertook this investigation under the premise of official opacity. Our reasoning behind this investigation is to achieve the very lowest level of respect for the deceased. The most fundamental worth and civil right of any person is their right to their name; this name is the smallest, most basic unit that helps us attest to an individual's existence.

MARCH 2009
Interview with Liu Yanping (volunteer for the Citizens' Investigation and later member of Ai Weiwei's studio). My main job was to stay here and collect the information that they sent back. At the time the government had released the names of the districts that were hit the hardest, the county names. And we'd divide that up amongst ourselves to research. The second group of people went to the areas that hadn't been visited yet. Basically all of the hardest hit areas, we went to. In the beginning, we got a lot of names at once, but as the investigation went on, it became harder and harder to learn new names. You'd only get a few names out of a trip. For example, at this school everybody said there were about one hundred students that died. It was relatively easy to get the names of those students, because everybody knew. And some of it was online. But after that, it was harder and harder to get information. Some of the names that were given to you were names that you already had. So finding the rest of them was hard. You'd have to go to more remote areas, where maybe the parents weren't too willing to interact with the outside world, people who don't use the internet or stuff like that. Those names were really difficult to get. I did make phone calls to a lot of parents. And we'd ask if they knew of anyone else who had died. I think they were mostly really surprised to hear from us. They were very moved. They'd say that nobody else had asked about their child. The time that we spent on the ground wasn't that long. We started working on the applications for freedom of information to different government bureaus. Because this is supposed to be their responsibility, to release to the public

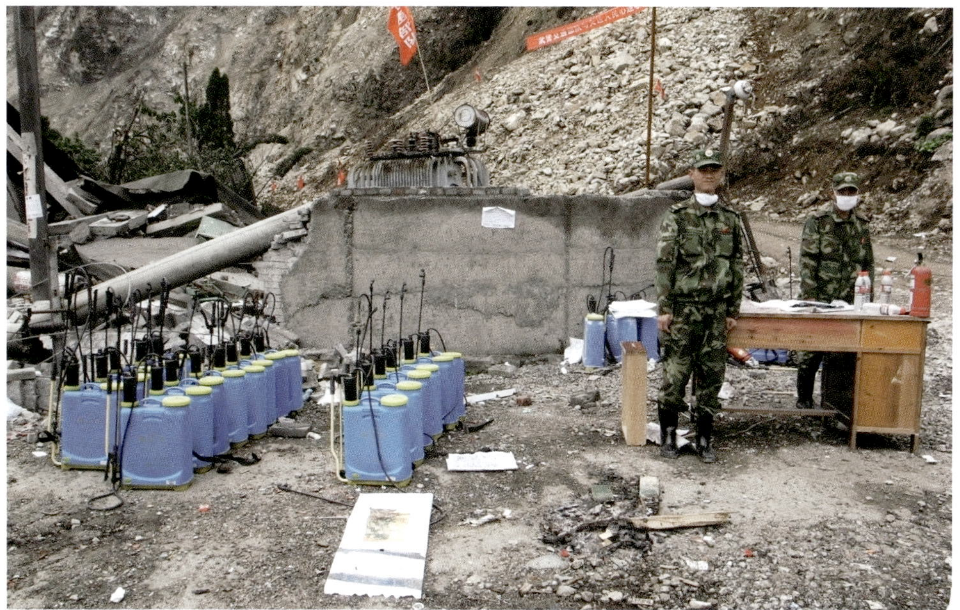

Earthquake, 2008–2010, C-print, 14⅝ x 21¾ inches; in the earthquake disaster zone, Beichuan County, May 2008

information about the victims, the state of the construction of the schools—they're supposed to tell us about this. So we prepared for this. All told, we prepared I think more than 10,000 questions.

APRIL 18, 2009
Phone call to the Sichuan Ministry of Education. Representative of the Ministry of Education: This name list, first we want to say that the government will certainly release it to the public. / Ai Weiwei: Yes, I was happy to hear the State Council's promise yesterday. / MoE: Our province has already made this promise. / AWW: Then where's the name list? / MoE: Don't worry, all in good time, this has to happen step by step. The name list is definitely going to be released, if it isn't released that'll be a problem, then the government will have broken its promise. Second, the student victims, they're a part of the total group of people who died, so if we confirm that the name list will be released, then the students' names will be on that list. / AWW: Your logic is clear. / MoE: You say that you haven't seen the name list yet, that we haven't compiled it, but I want to tell you that we are working on it right now. / AWW: Okay, then that is also clear. / MoE: If this is clear, then how are we going about it? At the time, the State Council had a provision that provincial level governments or local governments should determine the way in which they release the information. They should do this, they should verify the names of the victims. Now up until now, we have been working on this, and we've already released the names of some of the disaster victims. So where did we release this name list? In our county government and subdistrict offices, they posted it on their announcement boards. / AWW: Let me interrupt you— this isn't what it means to release this information to the public. If this is what you think it means to release information to the public, you're not understanding it right. / MoE: If this isn't releasing information to the public then what is? / AWW: Of course this isn't. Making information public means making it available to anybody who pays taxes— anybody has the right and ability to access this name list. That's what it means to make information available to the public. You

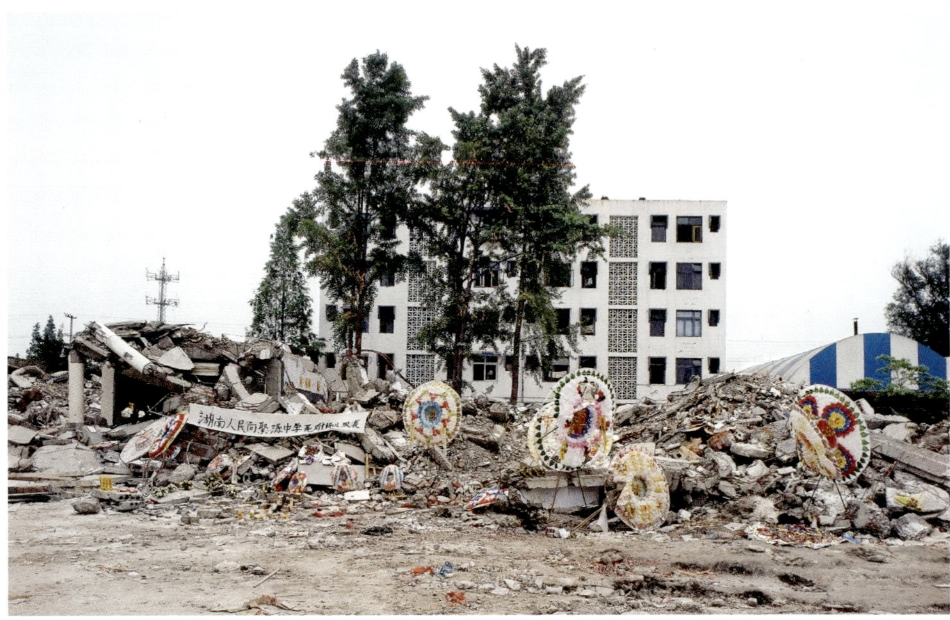

Earthquake, 2008–2010, C-print, 14 ⅝ x 21 ¾ inches; in the earthquake disaster zone, Beichuan County, May 2008

should understand this. / MoE: Put it like this, right now… / AWW: If you can't get this straight, then we can't talk about even more fundamental things. If you announce something by writing it on a chalkboard and then you wipe it off and nobody's seen it, this isn't releasing information to the public. Making information public means that anybody in this society, at any time they wish, can get ahold of this information, that's what it means.

MAY 7, 2009
Ai Weiwei's blog. The Sichuan government indicated once again that it would not pursue the issue of quality construction in the schools that collapsed during the earthquake. Their reasoning is that, in earthquakes of magnitudes exceeding the earthquake-proofing standards of the collapsed buildings, all losses are natural.

The seemingly rational grounds to this argument are enough to allow those behind the tofu-dregs engineering to collectively exhale a sigh of relief—in the name of "scientific development" and "shouldering the power to build a party that serves the interests of the

people," more than 2,000 Chinese architectural experts wrote down some of their wise assessments in a marvelous document… What has never been clearly explained is: of more than one hundred schools scattered around the severe disaster area, only fourteen schools could claim a death toll in excess of one hundred due to collapse. Even though this was an earthquake of magnitude 8, the remaining ninety schools did not topple. Yet, among the fourteen schools that did, there was no unified pattern of destruction: rooms with larger widths collapsed, and while some of the classroom buildings were left unharmed, the dormitory buildings fell. Towers that had fallen into disrepair for many years remained standing, but newer buildings had collapsed. Identical teaching buildings came down, but not administrative buildings. Surrounding the areas where the most students were killed, at the Beichuan and Juyuan Middle Schools, many buildings were left standing. Thus, interpreting a magnitude 8 earthquake as a "spicy hot pot" (where everything has a different flavor going in, but comes out tasting the same) is evidently a crude explanation.

MAY 8, 2009

Ai Weiwei's blog. Automatically generated messages published in place of deleted blog postings: "Your article X was deleted by the administrator. Deepest regrets for the inconvenience." 2009-05-08 17:48

MAY 28, 2009

Ai Weiwei's blog. Just the day before, I had called 110 twice, and sent two domestic security officers who had forgotten to bring their identification to the Public Security Bureau. Today, I called 110 three times to file a report, sending those two plainclothes cops who were trailing me to the PSB. What I want to illustrate is: as a human, I feel compelled to uphold my rights. No one should provoke me. I've tolerated your deleting my blog, I've tolerated your wiretapping my phone, I've tolerated your monitoring my residence. However, I am unable to tolerate your charging into my home and threatening me in front of my 76-year-old mother. I am unable to tolerate plainclothes officers secretly trailing me and threatening my safety.

AUGUST 12, 2009

Audio recording from Ai Weiwei's video camera as police break into the hotel room where Ai and his volunteers are staying, Ease & Comfort Hotel, Chengdu, 3:15 am. Police Officer: Open the door! / AWW (on the phone): I'm in Room 513. / PO: Open up! Police! / AWW: We're in the 158 Ease & Comfort Hotel. Yes. They've already broken in. (Sounds of a struggle) What are you doing? / PO: I'm not doing anything. / AWW: You're hitting me? / PO: I didn't know who you are! / AWW: Why can't I call 110? You can hit people with so many police. / PO: Take the phone away. / AWW: Go ahead! You brought all these cops to beat me? He hit me. / PO: Who hit you? Who saw it? / AWW: Is this how police officers behave? Is this how police behave? / PO: Prove it. / AWW: Is this how police behave? / PO: Where's your evidence? Who hit you? Where? Where's the wound? Don't speak without evidence. / AWW: 7998, I'm taking your badge number. What's your name? / PO: None of your business! / AWW: You broke into my room! Show me your badge! / PO: Did I enter your room? Am I in your room? / AWW: Did you break in? /

PO: Is this your room? What do you mean by "break in"? It's a routine inspection, not a break-in. / AWW: It's routine to beat people? How did my clothes get torn? / PO: You did it yourself. / AWW: I tore my own clothes and beat myself? / PO: Right. / AWW: You insist on saying that? / PO: It's the only explanation. Because I didn't see anyone hit you. We're just doing our jobs.

The Guardian. *CHINESE POLICE DETAIN 11 WHO PLANNED TO ATTEND ACTIVIST'S TRIAL.* Chinese police are holding 11 people who planned to attend today's trial of an activist who investigated the death of schoolchildren in last year's Sichuan earthquake, a high-profile artist and government critic among the detainees said. Ai Weiwei, a contemporary artist who designed the Olympics Bird's Nest stadium, said he and six others were detained at their hotel, while four others were taken to a police station. Police punched him on the jaw and roughed up another man, he said. They were in Chengdu to attend this morning's trial of Tan Zuoren, a Sichuan activist charged with subversion, apparently in connection to his inquiry into how many children died when school buildings collapsed due to the earthquake and essays he wrote about 1989's student-led demonstrations in Tiananmen Square. Ai, who has led a group of volunteers attempting to list the names of all the students who died, said Tan's lawyer had asked him to give evidence about the deaths and poor building work. When the court barred him from appearing as a witness, he decided to watch the trial anyway, along with 10 volunteers. Speaking from his hotel, he said: "I wanted to show my support for Mr. Tan. I feel nowadays less and less people stand up for truth and justice [and] it is hurting the truth and dignity of the law. At around midnight, about 20 or 30 policemen and plainclothes officers came shouting and knocking at the door. I did not open it at first and asked how they could prove their identities. But [several] forced the door open and told me that's how they proved it. I insisted on them showing me their police identification and during the chaos I was punched on my chin." Police originally told him and other volunteers they could leave at noon but as the deadline passed they remained in detention.

SEPTEMBER 16, 2009
Der Spiegel. *OPERATION IN MUNICH: CHINESE ARTIST ACCUSES GOVERNMENT FOR INJURY.* Surgeons at a clinic in Munich on Monday performed surgery on 51-year-old Chinese artist Ai Weiwei, after diagnosing a cerebral hemorrhage on the right side of his brain. Ai told *Spiegel* in August that secret police had attacked him in his hotel room in southern China's Sichuan province on August 12. The head injury now being treated is presumed to be connected to the attack. On Monday, Ai underwent a check-up at the hospital. Sources close to Ai told *Spiegel* on Tuesday that the surgery had gone smoothly. (The artist himself has since posted a photo of himself recovering via Twitter.) However, doctors have ordered the patient to remain in the hospital to recover for the next few days. If the suspicion that the injury was caused by blows to his head by police in August can be backed up with more evidence, Ai says he will consider taking legal action.

OCTOBER 11, 2009
Focus. *REMEMBERING THE DEAD CHILDREN.* When you look at the facade of the Haus der Kunst in Munich from afar, you might think it was covered by a gigantic, cheerily colorful placard. But on closer inspection the many-hued patches reveal themselves as an arrangement of differently colored backpacks. Chinese conceptual artist Ai Weiwei had 9000 of these manufactured for his piece *Remembering.* The bags are arranged over a width of 100 meters to form the sentence "She lived happily on this earth for seven years" in Chinese characters. These were the words of a mother in memory of her daughter, who had lost her life in the devastating May 2008 earthquake in the Chinese Sichuan province.

NOVEMBER 20, 2009
Ai Weiwei's blog. What can they do to me? Nothing more than to banish, kidnap, or imprison me. Perhaps they could fabricate my disappearance into thin air, but they don't have any creativity or imagination, and they lack both joy and the ability to fly. This kind of political organization is pitiful.

FEBRUARY 10, 2010
The Wall Street Journal. *CHINA SENTENCES EARTHQUAKE ACTIVIST.* A court in the provincial capital of Chengdu on Tuesday found Tan Zuoren guilty of inciting subversion of state power for writings that commemorated the 1989 Tiananmen Square crackdown, according to his lawyer, Pu Zhiqiang. However, Mr. Pu, along with human rights groups and other supporters, say they believe the underlying reason for Mr. Tan's prosecution was his investigations into the collapse of school buildings during the May 2008 earthquake and the resulting deaths of thousands of schoolchildren. Previous charges against Mr. Tan included references to his activism on the earthquake, a sensitive matter for authorities. But Tuesday's verdict did not mention the earthquake, and Mr. Pu said the issue was not raised during Mr. Tan's trial, which took place last August.

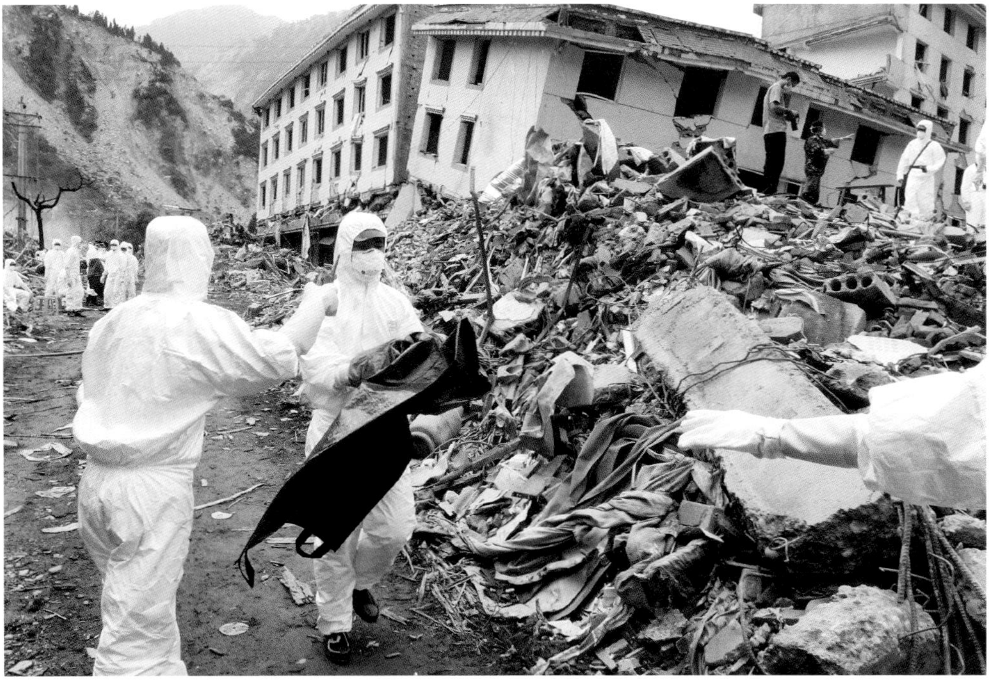

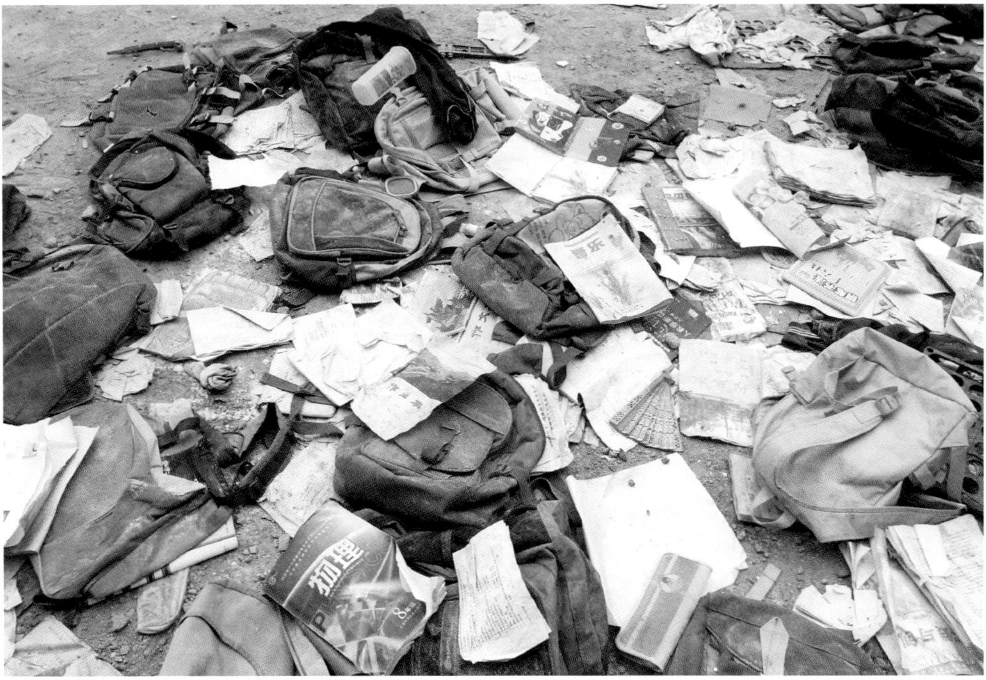

EARTHQUAKE, 2008–2010, C-prints, each 14⅝ x 21¾ inches; in the
earthquake disaster zone, Beichuan County, May 2008 | 355

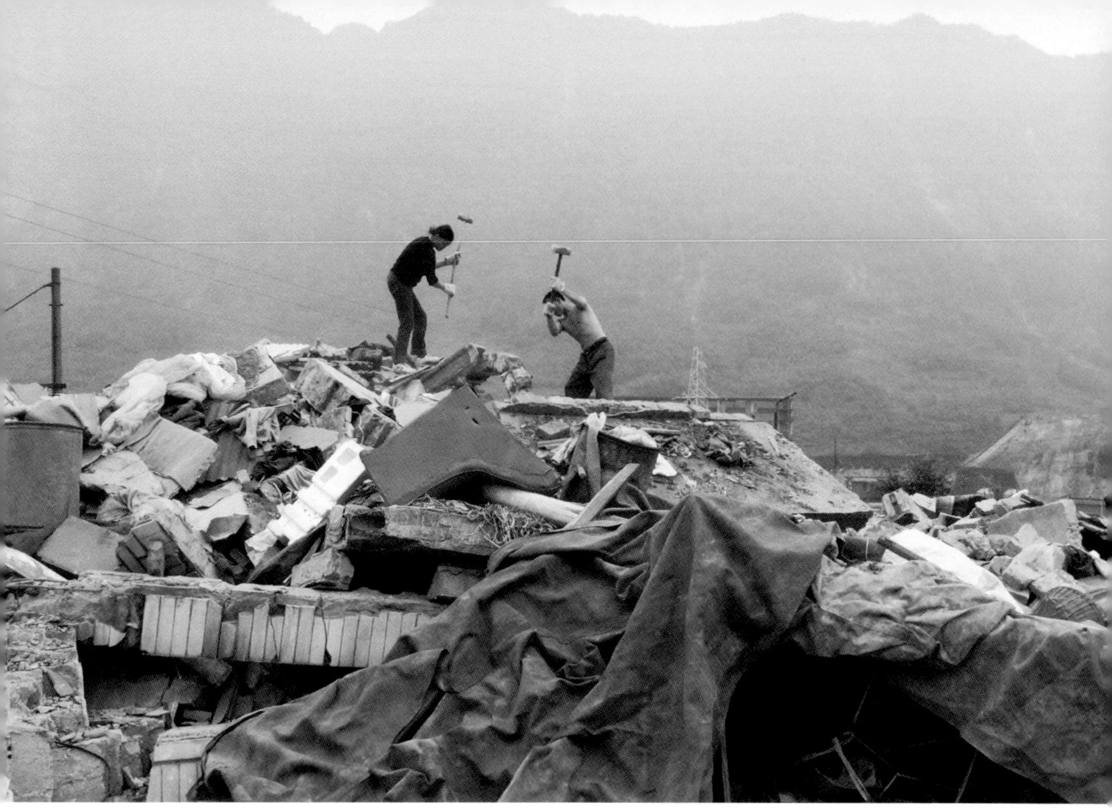

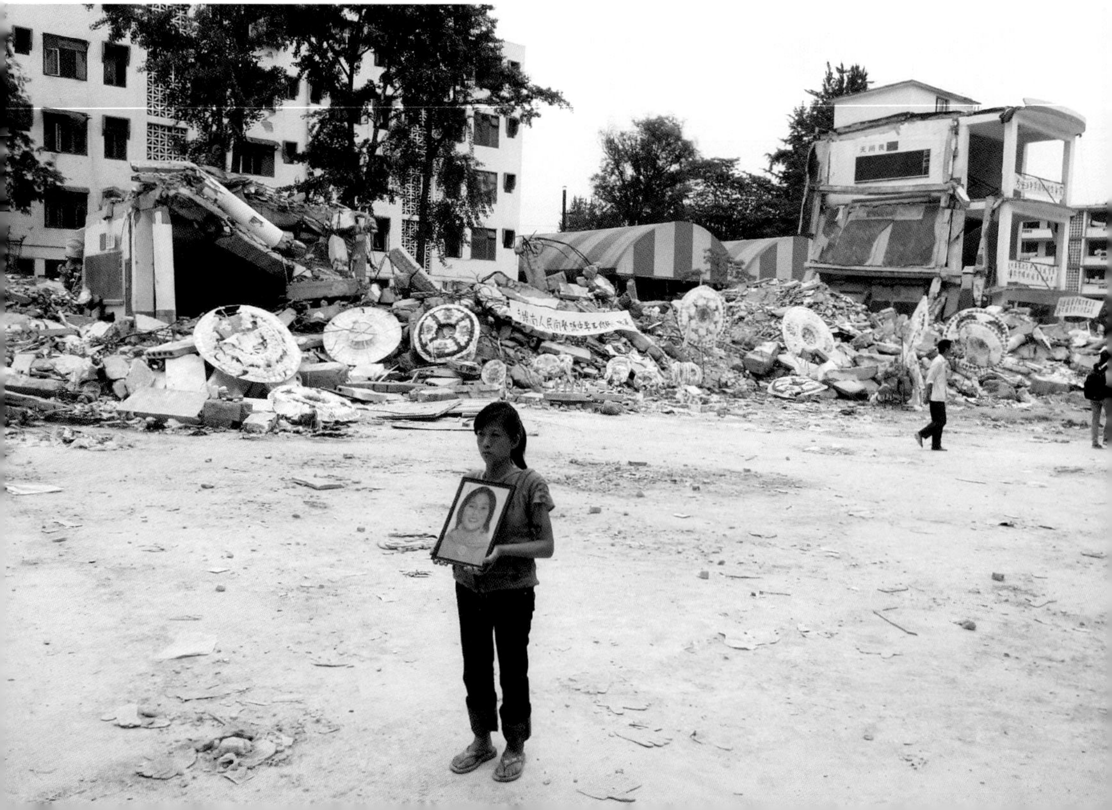

Erdbeben von Sichuan und Citizens' Investigation

12. MAI 2008
BBC News. *TAUSENDE TOTE NACH ERD-BEBEN IN CHINA.* Ein starkes Erdbeben in der südwestchinesischen Provinz Sichuan hat mindestens 10.000 Menschenleben gefordert, bis zu 5000 in einem einzigen Bezirk. Auch in anderen Landesteilen wurde eine große Zahl von Menschen getötet oder verletzt, als das Beben der Stärke 7,8 um 14:28 Uhr Ortszeit eintrat. Mindestens 50 Leichen wurden aus den Trümmern einer Schule geborgen, in der schätzungsweise 900 Schüler und Schülerinnen verschüttet worden waren. Präsident Hu Jintao hat „uneingeschränkte" Anstrengungen zur Rettung der Opfer gefordert. Suchmannschaften wurden in die betroffene Region entsendet, hatten jedoch aufgrund von gesperrten Straßen Mühe durchzukommen. Durch den Zusammenbruch von Nachrichtenverbindungen gibt es Hu zufolge noch keine genauen Anhaltspunkte zu Opferzahlen am Epizentrum des Bebens im Bezirk Wenchuan, das etwa 90 Kilometer von der Provinzhauptstadt Chengdu entfernt liegt.

13. MAI 2008
The New York Times. *„KEINE HOFFNUNG" FÜR IM ERDBEBEN VERSCHÜTTETE SCHULKINDER.* Eine der erschütterndsten Tragödien der Katastrophe war der Einsturz eines Schulgebäudes in einem Vorort von Dujiangyan. Mindestens einige 100 Schulkinder kamen ums Leben, möglicherweise bis zu 900. Premierminister Wen Jiabao flog am Montag ein, um sich ein Bild von der Zerstörung zu machen, aber er konnte das Leid der Überlebenden nicht lindern ... Von Kindern, die mit Knochenbrüchen oder abgetrennten Gliedmaßen davonkamen, wird gesagt, sie hätten Glück gehabt. Hunderte andere wurden aus den Trümmern getragen und beerdigt, während weitere Klassenkameraden zermalmt unter den Trümmern des Schulgebäudes zurückblieben. „Für sie besteht keine Hoffnung", sagt Lu Zhiqing

(58) mit Blick auf die Kolonne der uniformierten Rettungskräfte, die sich durch Schlamm und Regen ihren Weg zu dem Hügel aus Ziegelsteinen und Beton bahnt, der einst eine Schule gewesen ist. „Es ist unmöglich, dass da drinnen noch jemand am Leben ist." Vom ursprünglichen Gebäude der Schule steht so gut wie nichts mehr. Keine Säulen, nicht einmal Mauerreste. Der Schutt liegt platt auf dem nassen Erdboden. Dutzende Menschen versammeln sich auf dem Schulhof, durchwühlen die Brocken mit bloßen Händen und Füßen, manchmal schreien sie in den Trümmern. Anderen verwehren Soldaten den Zutritt.

22. MAI 2008
Ai Weiweis Blog. Den Notleidenden die Hand zu reichen, den Sterbenden beizustehen und den Verletzten zu helfen, sind humanitäre Handlungen, die nichts mit patriotischer Liebe zu einem Land oder einem Volk zu tun haben. Schmälert den Wert des Lebens nicht; ihm eignet eine allgemeinere, für alle gleiche Würde. Die Menschen brauchen in diesen Tagen der Trauer nicht dem Vaterland und seinen Helfern zu danken, denn das Vaterland konnte sie nicht besser schützen. Es war letzten Endes auch nicht sein Verdienst, dass die Glücklicheren unter den Kindern aus den einstürzenden Schulgebäuden entkommen konnten. Auch die Regierungsbeamten brauchen nicht gelobt zu werden, denn die dahinsiechenden Menschen benötigen wirksame Hilfsmaßnahmen viel dringender als Beileidsbekundungen und Tränen. Noch weniger braucht der Armee gedankt zu werden, denn das hieße ja, die Soldaten hätten bei ihrem Einsatz etwas anderes getan, als ihre Pflicht zu erfüllen.

25. MAI 2008
The New York Times. *IN CHINA FRAGT MAN SICH, WARUM DIE SCHULEN EIN-STÜRZTEN.* Es gibt keine offizielle Zahl der Kinder, die in der Grundschule von

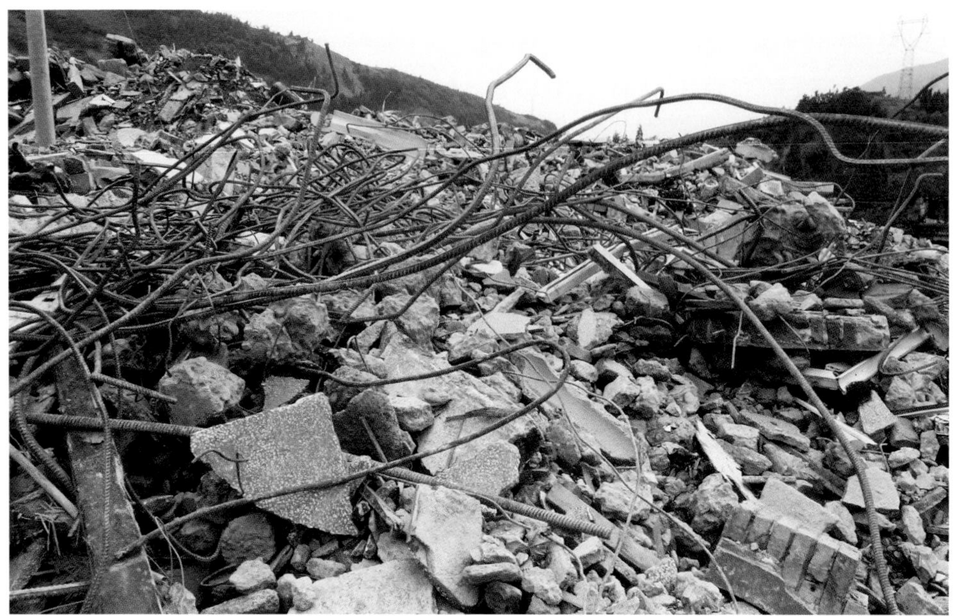

Earthquake, 2008–2010, C-print, 14 ⅝ x 21 ¾ inches; in the earthquake disaster zone, Beichuan County, May 2008

Xinjian ums Leben gekommen sind, noch für die anderen Schulen, die am 12. Mai vom starken Erdbeben in der Provinz Sichuan betroffen waren. Wahrscheinlich übersteigt die Zahl der toten Schüler jedoch 10.000 und liegt möglicherweise noch viel höher. Um diese erschütternde Zahl hat sich in China eine wachsende Kontroverse an Aussagen trauernder Eltern entzündet, nach denen ihre Kinder noch am Leben sein könnten, wenn die Schulen nur besser gebaut worden wären. Die chinesische Regierung erhielt breiten Zuspruch für ihre Reaktion auf das Erdbeben. Auch der UN-Generalsekretär Ban Ki-moon lobte am Samstag in Sichuan die Maßnahmen der Regierung. Es mehren sich jedoch die kritischen Stimmen der Eltern von Opfern aus mehreren Schulen. Die Frage, ob Nachlässigkeit seitens der Regierung und möglicherweise Korruption zu der Zahl der Toten Schüler beigetragen hat, könnte für einen Umschwung in der öffentlichen Meinung sorgen. Die Regierung hat eine Untersuchung eingeleitet. Ihre Zensoren sind jedoch besorgt um die Stimmung in der Öffentlichkeit und versuchen daher, das Thema in den staatlichen Medien wie auch im Internet zu unterdrücken. Nachforschungen zum Einsturz der Grundschule von Xinjian fördern das beunruhigende Bild einer Katastrophe zutage, die hätte verhindert werden können. Ingenieure und Erdbebenfachleute, die Fotos von dem Trümmerhaufen geprüft haben, kamen zu dem Schluss, dass das Gebäude zahlreiche Mängel und eine entscheidende Schwachstelle aufwies: unzureichende Stahlstäbe in den vertikalen Pfeilern des Schulgebäudes. Ein Experte beschrieb die instabilen Bodenplatten aus Beton als „Zeitbomben".

1. JUNI 2008

Ai Weiweis Blog. 20 Tage sind seit dem Erdbeben vergangen, und es gibt immer noch keine Liste mit den Namen der vermissten Kinder und keine genaue Statistik über die Opfer. Die Öffentlichkeit weiß immer noch nicht, wie die Kinder heißen, wer ihre Familien sind, wer es versäumt hat, die Schulen mit Stahl zu verstärken, und wer beim Bau minderwertigen Beton für Fundamente und Stützpfeiler verwendet hat.

Reuters. Ungefähr 40 Kilometer talabwärts in Dujiangyan versammeln sich um die 200 Eltern und Verwandte von Schülern, die bei dem Erdbeben umgekommen sind, zum Gedenken am Tag des Kindes auf dem mit Schutt übersäten Gelände der ehemaligen Grundschule von Xinjian. Tausende von Kindern starben, als ihre Schulen wie Kartenhäuser einstürzten. Unter den Eltern ist der Verdacht aufgekommen, dass Korruption die Einhaltung der Bauvorschriften verhindert habe. Der Umgang mit der Wut der Eltern nach dem Erdbeben erweist sich als eine der unbequemsten politischen Aufgaben für die Partei. Wütende und verweinte Eltern tragen weiße T-Shirts mit dem Namen der Schule auf der Brust und einem Slogan in riesigen roten Schriftzeichen auf dem Rücken: „Strenge Strafen für korrupten Tofu-Bau" – ein Verweis auf die Reste der Herstellung von Tofu beziehungsweise Sojaquark und eine geläufige Metapher für minderwertige Werkstoffe und Pfusch bei der handwerklichen Arbeit.

28. JULI 2008
Ai Weiweis Blog. Die Schlagzeile heute Morgen lautete: „Wenchuan will ein Denkmal des Erdbebens schaffen." Der Vietnamkrieg erschütterte die Vereinigten Staaten schwer und hinterließ tiefe, schmerzhafte Wunden. Zehn Jahre nach seinem Ende wurde auf einer Wiese in Washington, D. C., eine Gedenkstätte mit den Namen von über 58.000 gefallenen oder vermissten Soldaten errichtet. Bei uns gibt es in einem solchen Fall nur eine Verlautbarung von oben wie die eben zitierte und das aufgeregte Geschrei eines Haufens von Experten. Wie man sich denken kann, wird dieses Denkmal nicht an das erinnern, was wirklich passiert ist. Die historischen Fakten wurden verfälscht, noch bevor sie vollständig dokumentiert waren. Noch undenkbarer wäre es, einen Gedenkgottesdienst für die Opfer abzuhalten, die als Folge der Schlamperei ums Leben gekommen sind. Wie viele Menschen wurden bei dem Erdbeben von Wenchuan tatsächlich getötet und verletzt? Wie kamen sie ums Leben und wer ist daran schuld? Diese Fragen wollen die zuständigen Ministerien für Bildung und Architektur nicht beantworten, lieber stellen sie sich bis in alle Ewigkeit tot.

13. MÄRZ 2009, 10:01 UHR
Telefongespräch mit der Stabilitätserhaltungsgruppe des Bezirks Beichuan. Studio Ai Weiwei: Hallo, spreche ich mit Aufsichtsperson Sun? Spreche ich mit der „Stabilitätserhaltungsgruppe"? / Stabilitätserhaltungsgruppe Beichuan: Ja, am Apparat. / Studio: Ich rufe aus dem Bezirk Chaoyang in Peking an, meine Gruppe untersucht die Opferzahlen und Namen der Schüler, die während des Erdbebens in Beichuan am 12. Mai umgekommen sind. / Beichuan: Woher kommt Ihre Gruppe? / Studio: Peking. / Beichuan: Welche Arbeitsgruppe oder Zweigstelle der öffentlichen Sicherheit in Peking? / Studio: Wir sind eine von Bürgern selbst organisierte Gruppe. / Beichuan: Es tut mir leid, wir können Ihnen die Opferzahlen nicht geben und wir können sie nicht öffentlich machen. / Studio: Warum? / Beichuan: Es ist keine Frage von warum, es ist eine Frage der Disziplin. / Studio: Welche Disziplin? / Beichuan: Die nationale Disziplin. / Studio: Gibt es in unserem Staat eine solche Vorschrift? Ist sie irgendwo aufgeschrieben? / Beichuan: Was für eine Gruppe sind Sie? / Studio: Wir sind eine Gruppe Bürger. / Beichuan: Warum muss eine Gruppe Bürger das wissen? / Studio: Wir sind alles Landsleute, wir sind darüber besorgt. / Studio: Wollen Sie damit sagen, dass wir nicht wissen, wie wir für unsere Genossen Sorge tragen? / Studio: Das habe ich nicht gemeint, jeder macht sich Sorgen, aber wir drücken unsere so aus. / Beichuan: Hören Sie zu, diese Sache ist alles andere als klar. / Studio: Was ist nicht klar? Erhält Ihre Abteilung keine Informationen von Ihren Vorgesetzten? / Beichuan: Wer sagt so etwas? / Studio: Ein Mitarbeiter, aber es kam bereits in den Medien, also machen wir eine Anfrage bei Ihnen. / Beichuan: Tut mir leid. / Studio: Das ist doch Ihre Aufgabe, oder liegt es nicht in der Verantwortung der „Stabilitätserhaltungsgruppe", Bürgern Antworten zu geben, wenn diese Fragen stellen? / Beichuan: Es soll unsere Pflicht sein, Ihnen Informationen herauszugeben? / Studio: Das ist kein Gesetz, es ist eine grundsätzliche Frage! / Beichuan: Welches Gesetz? / Studio: Sie sind Angestellte der Regierung. / Beichuan: Wir unterstehen der Regierung, und wir haben der Regierung über all das Notwendige Bericht erstattet. Welcher Arbeitsgruppe wir Bericht erstatten sollen, ist etwas, das die Regierung

entscheidet. / Studio: Ihre Verantwortung besteht darin, der Regierung Bericht zu erstatten? Wie steht es dann mit dem Volk? Sie sind doch die Regierung oder wenigstens Teil von ihr! / Beichuan: Außerdem weiß ich gar nicht, wer Sie sind. Sie haben mir nicht deutlich gesagt, im Auftrag welcher Gruppe Sie anrufen. / Studio: Wir sind von keiner Organisation, wir sind Bürger! / Beichuan: Bürger? Bürger wie Sie sollten Ihre Anfragen an die Regierung stellen. / Studio: Sind Sie jetzt doch wieder Regierung? / Beichuan: Ich bin Teil der Regierung, und ich unterstehe meinen Vorgesetzten. Woher weiß ich, wer Sie sind? Was, wenn Sie irgendwelche Hintergedanken haben? / Studio: Was meinen Sie mit Hintergedanken? Was soll das heißen? Wenn ein Bürger aus Gründen anruft, über die alle Bürger Bescheid wissen sollten, heißt das, dass ich Hintergedanken habe? / Beichuan: Wie können Sie beweisen, dass Sie nicht etwas anderes im Sinn haben? So ist das! (Legt auf.)

20. MÄRZ 2009
Ai Weiweis Blog. Vor 300 Tagen reiste ich in das Erdbebengebiet im Kreis Wenchuan in der Provinz Sichuan. Dort sah ich schreckliche Zustände und unendliches Leid. Noch heute wissen wir nicht, wie viele Menschen bei dem Erdbeben gestorben sind. Wir wissen nicht, warum all diese Kinder gestorben sind und wie sie gestorben sind. Wir werden nie erfahren, was sie empfanden, als sie unter dem Schutt lagen und warteten. Während der Katastrophe streckte ich meine Hand nicht zu ihnen aus. Ich muss gestehen, dass es über meine Kräfte ging. Sie sagen, sie hätten nichts mit dem Tod der Schulkinder zu tun. Sie sagen, die Katastrophe sei unvermeidlich gewesen, die Experten hätten es bewiesen. Sie vertuschen die Wahrheit und sprechen nicht über die Korruption, sie vermeiden es, sich zu den Tofu-Konstruktionen zu äußern. Sie verbergen die Fakten, und im Namen der „Stabilität" verfolgen, bedrohen und verhaften sie die Eltern der toten Kinder, weil diese Menschen die Wahrheit wissen wollen. Sie verstoßen offen gegen die Verfassung und treten die Grundrechte der Menschen mit Füßen. Die Kinder, die bei dem Erdbeben starben, sind keine unbekannte Masse, sie sind nicht das Ergebnis der „Stabilisierung" einer Nation. Diese Kinder hatten Eltern, sie hatten

Träume, sie konnten lächeln. Jedes von ihnen hatte einen Namen, der ihm gehörte. Ihre Namen werden ihnen auch noch in drei, in fünf, in 18 oder 19 Jahren gehören; ihre Namen sind das Einzige, was von ihnen bleiben wird, das Einzige, was in Erinnerung gerufen werden kann. Wehrt euch gegen das Unvermögen zu erinnern, wehrt euch gegen die Lügen. Um der Toten zu gedenken, Sorge um die Lebenden zu zeigen, Verantwortung zu übernehmen und die Möglichkeit des Glücks für die Überlebenden aufrechtzuerhalten, leiten wir eine „Citizens' Investigation" ein. Wir werden die Namen aller verschwundenen Kinder herausfinden, und wir werden dieser Kinder gedenken. Wer Interesse an dieser Untersuchung durch die Bürger hat, kann unter folgender Adresse seine Kontaktdaten hinterlassen: xuesheng512@gmail.com. Deine Handlungen erschaffen deine Welt.

24. MÄRZ 2009
Ai Weiweis Blog. Frage: Bei einer Online-Suche findet man folgende Schlagzeile: „Die Liste der Erdbebenopfer in Wenchuan enthält 19.065 Namen. Die Zahl der Toten wird noch untersucht." Das bedeutet, dass die Regierung eine ähnliche Arbeit macht. Warum wollen Sie immer noch eine Liste der Namen erstellen? / Ai Weiwei: Wir haben mehrere Regierungsstellen in Sichuan kontaktiert und mehr als 150 telefonische Anfragen gemacht, um eine Liste der 19.065 Namen zu erhalten. Wir werden hingehalten und haben immer nur unklare Antworten erhalten. Niemand weiß, wo diese Liste der Opfernamen veröffentlicht oder wie sie erstellt wurde, und sie ist nie auf einer offiziellen Website erschienen. Mittlerweile sind mehr als 300 Tage vergangen, und wir haben immer noch keine Zahl, die den Menschen glaubwürdig scheint. Die Regierung sollte die Namen der Opfer, ihr Alter, ihren Wohnort sowie Todesursache und Ort des Todes veröffentlichen. Diese grundlegenden Informationen können für Lebende und Tote nur unter Aufsicht der Regierung gesammelt werden und sollten jederzeit verfügbar sein. Wir begannen unsere Untersuchung, weil die Vorgehensweise der Regierung undurchsichtig war. Unser Ziel ist es, den Verstorbenen ein Mindestmaß an Respekt zu zollen. Das fundamentalste Bürgerrecht ist das Recht jedes Menschen auf einen Namen,

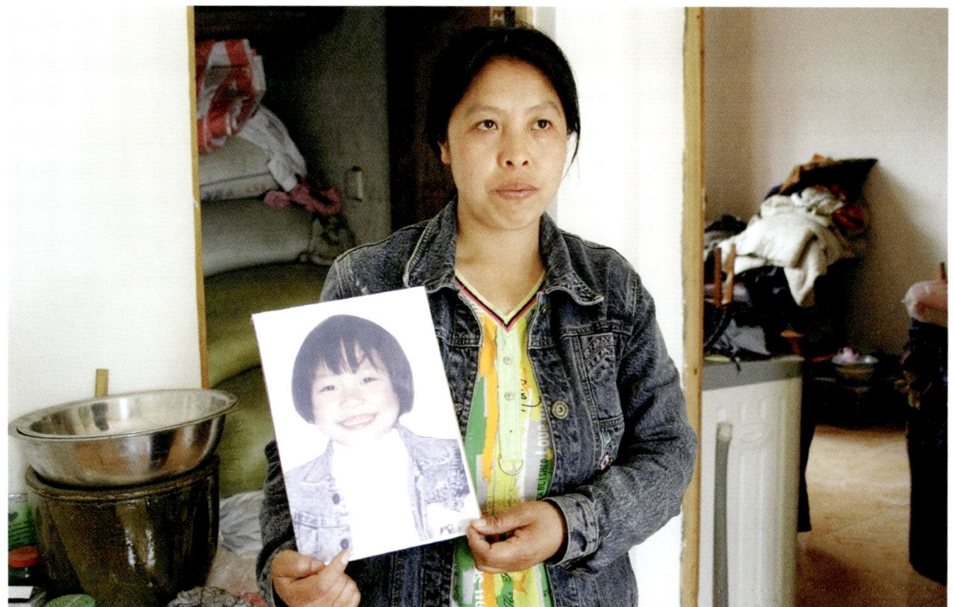

Earthquake, 2008–2010, C-print, 14 ⅝ x 21 ¾ inches; Citizens' Investigation gathering names of deceased students, Sichuan 2008

der ihm einen Wert verleiht. Der Name ist die kleinste, grundlegendste Einheit, die das Dasein einer Person bestätigt.

MÄRZ 2009

Interview mit Liu Yanping (freie Mitarbeiterin der Citizens' Investigation und danach Assistentin in Ai Weiweis Studio). Zuerst bestand meine Hauptaufgabe darin, zentral die Informationen zu sammeln, die wir zusammentrugen. Damals hatte die Regierung die Namen der Bezirke veröffentlicht, die besonders stark in Mitleidenschaft gezogen waren. Wir teilten sie unter uns für die Nachforschungen auf. Eine zweite Gruppe fuhr in Gebiete, in denen noch niemand gewesen war. Eigentlich waren wir in allen stark betroffenen Regionen. Zunächst erhielten wir eine Menge Namen, alle auf einmal, aber im Laufe der Untersuchung wurde es zunehmend schwerer, an neue zu kommen. Eine ganze Reise lieferte dann nur eine Handvoll Namen. Zum Beispiel gab es diese Schule, wo alle sagten, dass ungefähr 100 Schüler gestorben wären. Erst war es leicht, die Namen zu ermitteln, da alle Bescheid wussten. Manches war auch im Internet zu finden. Später wurde es immer schwieriger, an Informationen zu kommen. Viele Namen hatten wir schon. An die übrigen war schwer heranzukommen. Wir mussten in entlegene Gegenden, wo die Leute nur ungern Kontakt mit der Außenwelt hatten, keinen Internetzugang, solche Sachen. An diese Namen war schwer heranzukommen. Ich habe mit unzähligen Eltern telefoniert. Wir fragten, ob sie noch andere Opfer kannten. Ich glaube, sie waren vor allem überrascht, von uns zu hören. Das hat sie tief bewegt. Oft sagten sie, dass sich sonst niemand nach ihrem Kind erkundigt hatte. Wir waren nicht sehr lang vor Ort. Dann begannen wir, Auskunftsanträge gemäß dem Gesetz zur Informationsfreiheit bei den unterschiedlichen Regierungsbehörden einzureichen. Es lag schließlich in ihrer Verantwortung, Informationen über die Opfer und den baulichen Zustand der Schulgebäude der Öffentlichkeit zugänglich zu machen. Sie sollten einem eigentlich darüber Auskunft geben. Daran arbeiteten wir. Alles in allem haben wir, denke ich, mehr als 10.000 Anfragen verfasst.

18. APRIL 2009
**Telefongespräch mit dem Bildungsminis-
terium der Provinz Sichuan.** Vertreter des
Ministeriums für Bildung: Diese Namensliste
– zunächst möchten wir sagen, dass die Regierung sie gewiss für die Öffentlichkeit freige-
ben wird. / Ai Weiwei: Ja, ich war sehr froh,
als ich gestern das Versprechen des Staatsrats
gehört habe. / MfB: Unsere Provinz hat dieses
Versprechen bereits gegeben. / AWW: Wo ist
dann die Namensliste? / MfB: Machen Sie sich
keine Sorgen, alles zu seiner Zeit, das wird
Schritt für Schritt geschehen. Die Namensliste wird definitiv veröffentlicht. Würde sie
nicht veröffentlicht, so wäre das ein Problem,
weil dann die Regierung ihr Versprechen brechen würde. Zweitens, die Opfer unter den
Schülern sind ein Teil der Gesamtzahl aller
Toten. Also werden die Namen der Schüler
auf der veröffentlichten Liste sein. / AWW:
Ihre Logik ist bezwingend. / MfB: Sie sagen,
Sie haben die Liste noch nicht gesehen,
dass wir sie nicht erstellt haben. Ich möchte
Ihnen jedoch mitteilen, dass wir in diesem
Moment daran arbeiten. / AWW: O.k, dann
ist das auch klar. / MfB: Wenn das klar ist,
wie sind wir dann vorgegangen? Zuerst hatte
der Staatsrat eine Vorschrift erlassen, dass
die Provinzregierungen oder die kommunalen
Regierungsstellen die Art und Weise festlegen
sollten, wie diese Informationen freigegeben
werden. Sie sollten dies tun; sie sollten die
Namen der Opfer prüfen. Bis heute arbeiten
wir daran, und wir haben bereits die Namen
einiger Opfer der Katastrophe freigegeben.
Wo wir diese Liste veröffentlicht haben? In
unseren Büros der Bezirksregierung und
Unterbezirken. Sie hängten sie an die Verlaut-
barungstafeln. / AWW: Lassen Sie mich kurz
unterbrechen – das ist nicht, was es heißt,
Informationen an die Öffentlichkeit zu geben.
Wenn Sie denken, dass man so Informationen
an die Öffentlichkeit gibt, dann verstehen Sie
es nicht richtig. / MfB: Wenn das nicht die
Freigabe von Informationen an die Öffentlichkeit ist, was dann? / AWW: Selbstverständlich
ist es das nicht. Informationen zu veröffentlichen, heißt, sie jedem zugänglich zu machen,
der Steuern zahlt – jeder hat das Recht und
die Möglichkeit, Zugang zur Liste zu erhalten.
Das versteht man darunter, Informationen
der Öffentlichkeit zugänglich zu machen.
Das sollten Sie wissen. / MfB: So formuliert,

gerade jetzt … / AWW: Wenn Ihnen das nicht
einleuchtet, dann hat es keinen Sinn, über
noch grundlegendere Dinge zu sprechen.
Wenn Sie etwas verkünden, indem Sie es auf
eine Tafel schreiben, es dann wieder auswi-
schen, und niemand hat es gesehen, dann ist
das keine Freigabe von Informationen an die
Öffentlichkeit. Informationen zu veröffentlichen, heißt, dass alle in dieser Gesellschaft,
wann immer sie es wünschen, Zugang zu
ihnen erhalten, das und nichts anderes.

7. MAI 2009
Ai Weiweis Blog. Die Regierung der Provinz
Sichuan hat erneut erklärt, dass sie die bauli-
che Qualität der Schulgebäude, die bei dem
Erdbeben einstürzten, nicht untersuchen
wird. Die Begründung lautet, dass bei Erdbeben von einer Stärke, die über die Belastbar-
keit der eingestürzten Gebäude hinausgeht,
alle Schäden auf natürliche Ursachen zurückzuführen seien. Diese scheinbar vernünftige
Begründung erlaubt jenen, die für die Tofu-
Konstruktionen verantwortlich sind, einen
kollektiven Seufzer der Erleichterung auszu-
stoßen – im Namen der „wissenschaftlichen
Entwicklung" und der „Übernahme der Macht
zum Aufbau einer Partei, die den Interessen
des Volkes dient", haben mehr als 2000 chinesische Architekturexperten ihr weises Urteil
in einem wunderbaren Dokument niederge-
schrieben. Folgendes ist nie erklärt worden:
Nur in 14 von mehr als 100 über das zentrale
Katastrophengebiet verstreuten Schulen starben mehr als 100 Kinder. Obwohl es sich um
ein Erdbeben der Stärke 8 auf der Richter-
skala handelte, stürzten die übrigen 90 Schulen nicht ein. Bei den 14 Schulen, die zerstört
wurden, war kein einheitliches Muster von
Schäden festzustellen: Größere Räume stürzten ein, und während einige Klassenzimmer
nicht beschädigt wurden, stürzten die Schlaf-
säle ein. Türme, die seit vielen Jahren nicht
instandgesetzt worden waren, blieben stehen,
während neuere Gebäude den Erdstößen
nicht standhielten. Baugleiche Unterrichtsge-
bäude brachen ein, während Verwaltungsge-
bäude stehen blieben. In der Umgebung der
Mittelschulen von Beichuan und Juyuan, in
denen die meisten Schüler getötet wurden,
blieben viele Gebäude intakt. Daher ist die
Erklärung, ein Erdbeben der Stärke 8 sei eine
„scharf gewürzte Suppe" (die Zutaten, die in

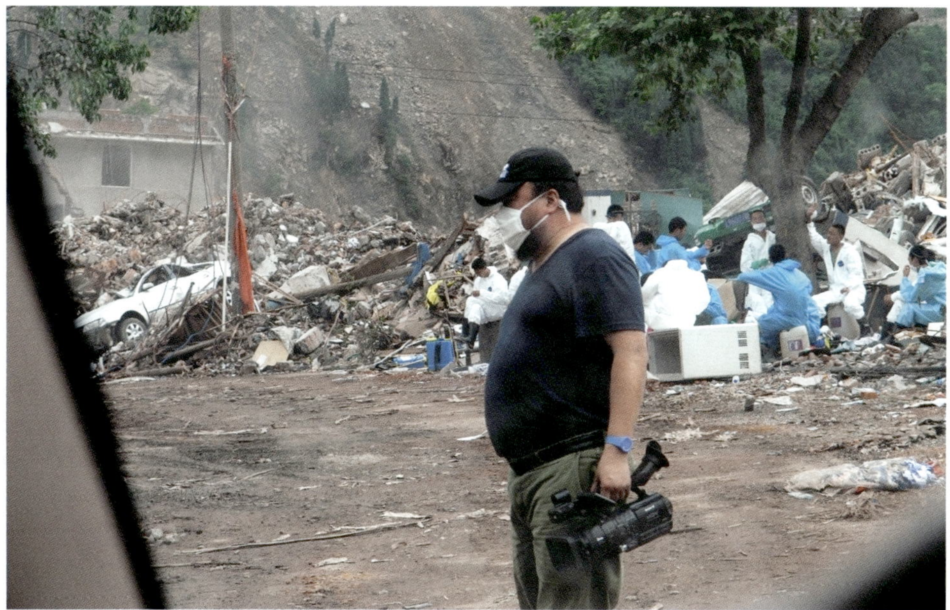

Earthquake, 2008–2010, C-print, 14 ⅝ x 21 ¾ inches; in the earthquake disaster zone, Beichuan County, May 2008

den Topf kommen, haben unterschiedliche Aromen, aber in der scharfen Suppe schmecken sie alle gleich), wenig überzeugend.

8. MAI 2009
Ai Weiweis Blog. Automatisch generierte Nachricht anstelle von gelöschten Postings: „Ihr Artikel X wurde vom Administrator gelöscht. Wir bedauern die Unannehmlichkeit." 2009-05-08 17:48.

28. MAI 2009
Ai Weiweis Blog. Es war nur einen Tag her, dass ich zweimal die 110 angerufen und zwei Beamte des Sicherheitsdienstes, die ihre Ausweise vergessen hatten, zur Polizeidienststelle geschickt habe, damit sie sich dort identifizierten. Heute habe ich dreimal die 110 angerufen, um Anzeige zu erstatten und die beiden Polizisten in Zivil, die mich beschatteten, zur Polizeidienststelle zu schicken. Was ich sagen will, ist Folgendes: Als Mensch muss ich meine Rechte verteidigen. Niemand sollte mich provozieren. Ich habe hingenommen, dass ihr meinen Blog gelöscht habt, ich habe hingenommen, dass ihr mein Telefon ange-

zapft habt, ich habe hingenommen, dass ihr mein Haus überwacht. Doch ich kann nicht hinnehmen, dass ihr in mein Haus eindringt und mich vor den Augen meiner 76-jährigen Mutter bedroht. Ich kann nicht dulden, dass mich Beamte in Zivil beschatten und meine Sicherheit bedrohen.

12. AUGUST 2009
Tonmitschnitt von Ai Weiweis Videokamera, während Polizeikräfte in das Hotelzimmer eindringen, in dem Ai und seine freiwilligen Helfer abgestiegen sind, Ease & Comfort Hotel, Chengdu, 3:15 Uhr morgens. Polizist: Öffnen Sie die Tür! / AWW (am Telefon): Ich bin auf Zimmer 513. / Polizist: Öffnen Sie! Polizei! / AWW: Wir sind im 158 Ease & Comfort Hotel. Ja. Sie haben schon die Tür aufgebrochen. (Geräusche eines Handgemenges) Was tun Sie? / Polizist: Ich tue überhaupt nichts. / AWW: Sie schlagen mich? / Polizist: Ich wusste nicht, wer Sie sind! / AWW: Warum kann ich nicht 110 anrufen? Mit so vielen Polizisten können Sie jeden verprügeln. / Polizist: Nehmen Sie das Telefon weg. / AWW: Na los! Sie haben all diese Polizisten

mitgebracht, um mich zu schlagen? Er hat mich geschlagen. / Polizist: Wer hat Sie geschlagen? Wer hat das gesehen? / AWW: Benehmen sich Polizisten jetzt so? Verhält sich die Polizei so? / Polizist: Beweisen Sie das. / AWW: Benimmt sich die Polizei so? / Polizist: Wo sind Ihre Beweise? Wer hat Sie geschlagen? Wo? Wo ist die Wunde? Sagen Sie nichts ohne Beweise. / AWW: 7998, ich notiere mir Ihre Dienstnummer. Wie heißen Sie? / Polizist: Geht Sie nichts an! / AWW: Sie sind in mein Zimmer eingedrungen! Zeigen Sie mir Ihre Marke! / Polizist: Bin ich in Ihr Zimmer eingedrungen? Halte ich mich in Ihrem Zimmer auf? / AWW: Sind Sie eingebrochen? / Polizist: Ist das Ihr Zimmer? Was meinen Sie mit „einbrechen"? Dies ist eine routinemäßige Inspektion, kein Einbruch. / AWW: Es gehört zur Routine, Menschen zu schlagen? Wie kommt es, dass meine Kleidung zerrissen ist? / Polizist: Das haben Sie selbst getan. / AWW: Ich habe meine Kleider zerrissen und mich selbst geschlagen? / Polizist: Genau. / AWW: Sie bestehen darauf, das zu sagen? / Polizist: Das ist die einzige Erklärung. Denn ich habe nicht gesehen, dass irgendjemand Sie geschlagen hat. Wir tun nur unsere Arbeit.

The Guardian. *CHINESISCHE POLIZEI VERHAFTET 11 BESUCHER VOR AKTIVISTENPROZESS.* Die chinesische Polizei hat elf Personen in Gewahrsam, die dem heute stattfindenden Prozess gegen einen Aktivisten beiwohnen wollten, der den Tod von Schulkindern im letztjährigen Erdbeben in Sichuan untersuchte, wie ein berühmter Künstler und Regierungskritiker unter den Festgenommenen angab. Ai Weiwei, zeitgenössischer Künstler und Designer des Olympiastadions in Peking, erklärte, dass er und sechs weitere Personen in ihrem Hotel festgesetzt worden seien, während sechs andere auf ein Polizeirevier gebracht wurden. Ein Polizist hätte ihn mit der Faust auf den Kiefer geschlagen und einen anderen Mann misshandelt. Sie befanden sich in Chengdu, um am heutigen Prozess gegen Tan Zuoren teilzunehmen, einen Aktivisten aus der Provinz Sichuan, der subversiver Handlungen angeklagt ist. Diese stehen anscheinend mit seinen Nachforschungen in Zusammenhang, wie viele Kinder gestorben sind, als Schulgebäude während des Erdbebens einstürzten, sowie mit Artikeln, die er über die Studentenproteste des Jahres 1989 auf dem Tiananmen Platz schrieb. Ai, der selbst mit einer Gruppe Freiwilliger die Namen der Todesopfer aufzulisten versucht, gab an, Tans Verteidiger habe ihn gebeten, als Zeuge zu den Todesfällen und den Baumängeln auszusagen. Als das Gericht ihn als Zeugen ablehnte, entschloss Ai sich, den Prozess dennoch zusammen mit zehn Mitarbeitern zu beobachten. Von seinem Hotelzimmer aus erklärte er: „Ich wollte Herrn Tan meine Unterstützung bekunden. Mir kommt es so vor, als stünden heute immer weniger Menschen für Wahrheit und Gerechtigkeit ein, und das schadet der Wahrheit und der Würde des Gesetzes. Gegen Mitternacht kamen etwa 20 oder 30 Polizisten, sie schrien und hämmerten an die Tür. Ich machte zunächst nicht auf, sondern verlangte von ihnen, sich auszuweisen. Einige jedoch öffneten die Tür gewaltsam und sagten mir, das wäre ihr Ausweis. Ich beharrte darauf, dass sie mir ihre Polizeiausweise zeigen sollten, und in dem Chaos bekam ich einen Faustschlag auf mein Kinn." Die Polizei hatte ihm ursprünglich zugesichert, dass er mit den anderen um 12 Uhr mittags gehen könnte, aber die Frist verstrich, und alle blieben in Gewahrsam.

16. SEPTEMBER 2009
Der Spiegel. *OP NACH POLIZEIÜBERGRIFF: CHINESISCHER KÜNSTLER AI WEIWEI KLAGT REGIME AN.* Der chinesische Künstler Ai Weiwei, 51, musste sich nach *Spiegel*-Informationen am Montag im Münchner Klinikum Großhadern einer Operation unterziehen. Er litt zuvor unter Kopfschmerzen in Folge eines Hämatoms auf der rechten Schädelseite. Im August war Ai nach eigenen Angaben in einem Hotelzimmer in der chinesischen Provinz Sichuan von Geheimpolizisten überfallen und geschlagen worden, wie er in einem *Spiegel*-Interview ausführte. Vermutlich ist die Kopfverletzung nun eine Folge dieser Schläge. Am Montag ließ er sich im Krankenhaus untersuchen. Die Operation sei gut verlaufen, heißt es aus Ais Umfeld (Bilder nach der OP twitterte der Künstler selbst). Der Patient müsse aber auf Weisung der Ärzte erst einmal im Krankenhaus bleiben und sich mehrere Tage erholen. Falls sich der Verdacht erhärte, dass die Verletzung auf die Schläge

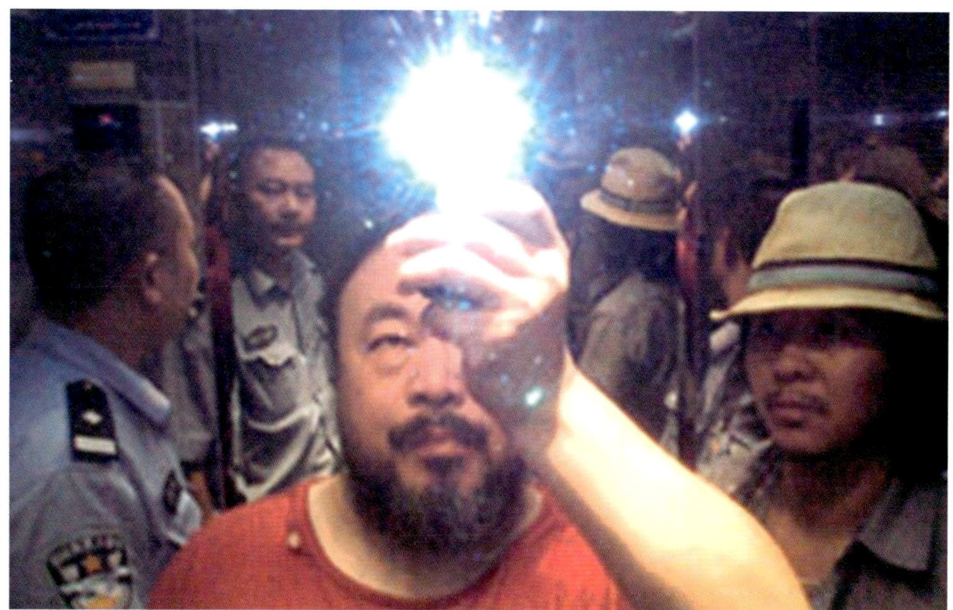

Ai Weiwei and Zuoxiao Zuzhou in an elevator as the police take them into custody, Chengdu, August 2009

der Polizei zurückzuführen sei, wolle Ai sich überlegen, rechtliche Schritte einzuleiten.

11. OKTOBER 2009
Focus. *ERINNERUNG AN TOTE KINDER.*
Wer das Haus der Kunst in München aus der Ferne sieht, könnte denken, die Fassade sei mit einem riesigen fröhlich-bunten Plakat bespannt. Bei näherem Hinsehen entpuppen sich die Farbflächen als ein Arrangement aus Rucksäcken in verschiedenen Farben. 9000 dieser Rucksäcke ließ der chinesische Konzeptkünstler Ai Weiwei für das Werk *Remembering* anfertigen. Über eine Länge von 100 Metern hat er die Taschen so ange-ordnet, dass sie in chinesischen Schriftzei-chen den Satz „Sieben Jahre lebte sie glück-lich in dieser Welt" ergeben. Worte, mit denen eine Mutter ihrer Tochter gedachte, nachdem die bei dem verheerenden Erdbeben in der chinesischen Provinz Sichuan im Mai 2008 ums Leben gekommen war.

20. NOVEMBER 2009
Ai Weiweis Blog. Was können sie mir schon antun? Sie können mich ausweisen, entführen oder einsperren, auch dafür sorgen, dass ich mich in Luft auflöse. Aber sie haben keine Phantasie oder Kreativität. So eine politische Clique ist erbärmlich.

10. FEBRUAR 2010
The Wall Street Journal. *CHINA SETZT STRAFMASS FÜR ERDBEBEN-AKTIVISTEN FEST.* Ein Gericht in der Provinzhauptstadt Chengdu sprach Tan Zuoren am Dienstag schuldig, durch Schriften im Gedenken an die Niederschlagung der Demonstrationen auf dem Tiananmen Platz 1989 zur Untergrabung der Staatsmacht aufgerufen zu haben, wie sein Anwalt Pu Zhiqiang erklärte. Herr Pu und Vertreter von Menschenrechtsorganisationen glauben jedoch, dass der wahre Grund für die Verfolgung Tan Zuorens in seiner Untersu-chung der Einstürze von Schulgebäuden liegt, die während des Erdbebens von 2008 die Leben von Tausenden Schulkindern forder-ten. Frühere Anklagepunkte gegen Tan ent-hielten Bezüge auf seinen Erdbeben-Aktivis-mus, ein heikles Thema für die Obrigkeit. Das Urteil vom Dienstag erwähnte das Erdbe-ben jedoch nicht, und Herr Pu gab an, dass das Thema während des Prozesses im vergan-genen August, nicht angeschnitten wurde.

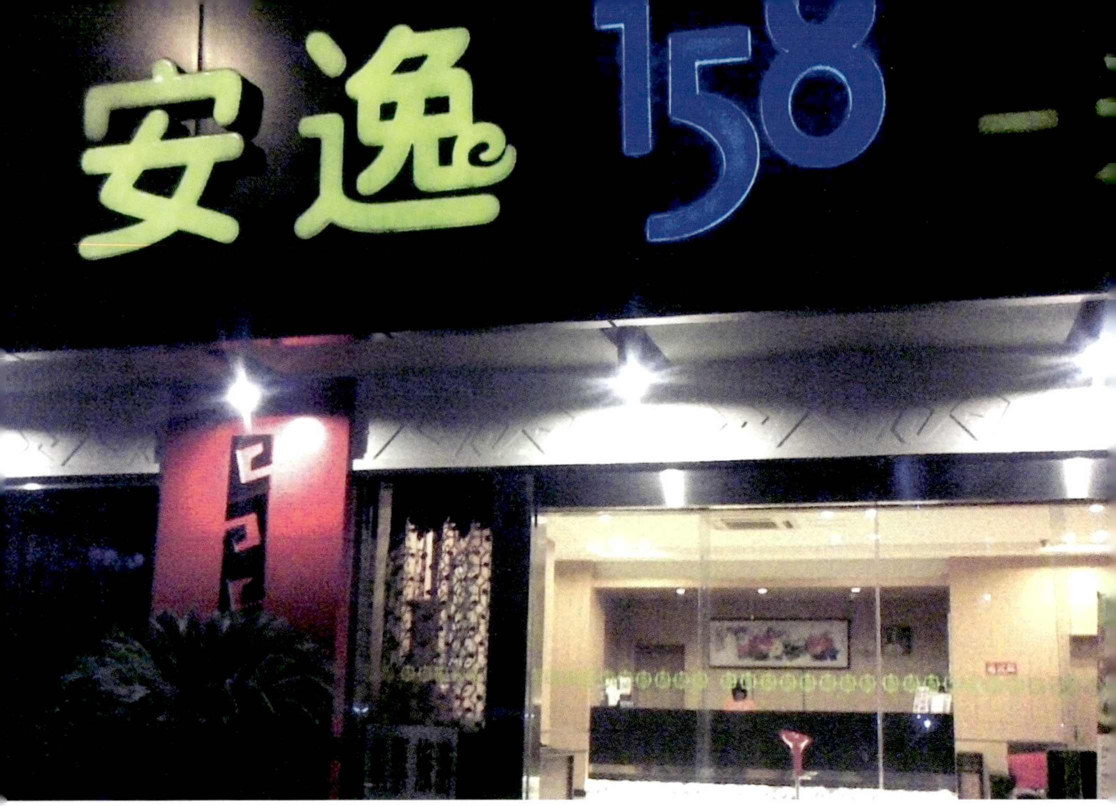

安逸158

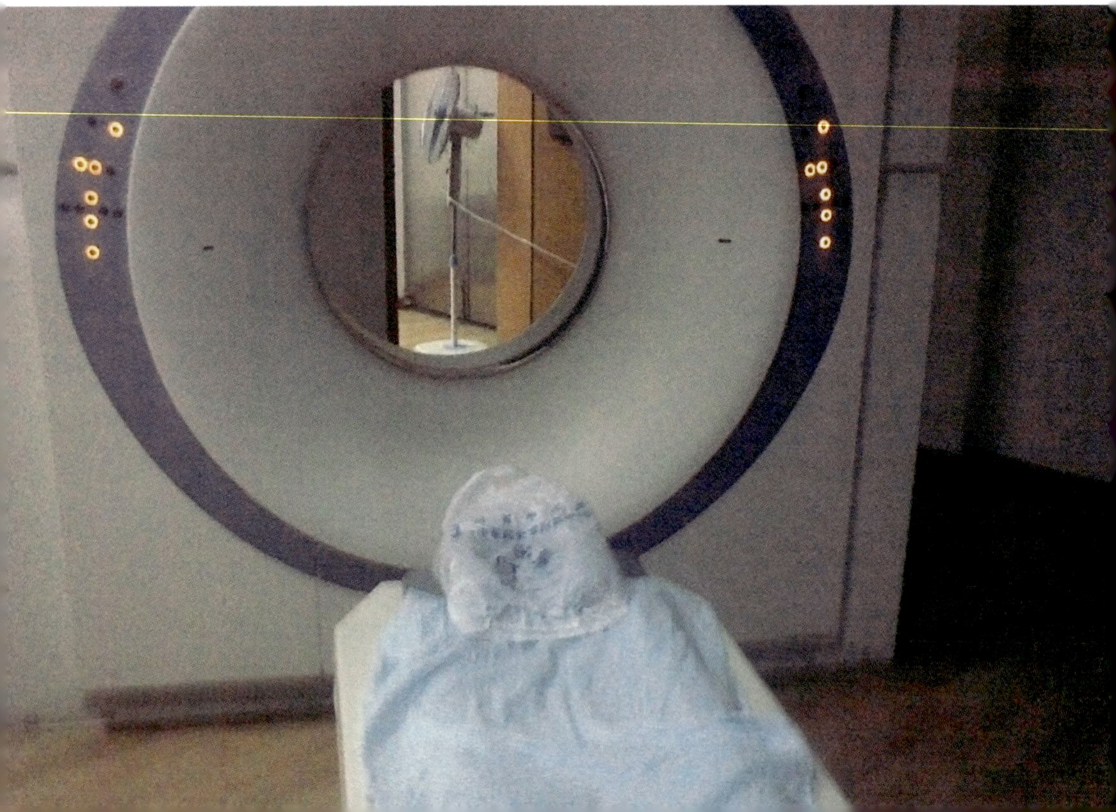

Séisme du Sichuan et Enquête Citoyenne

12 MAI 2008
BBC News. *UN TREMBLEMENT DE TERRE FAIT PLUSIEURS MILLIERS DE VICTIMES EN CHINE.* Un important séisme a fait au moins 10 000 victimes dans la province du Sichuan, dans le sud-ouest de la Chine, dont près de 5000 dans un seul district. De nombreuses personnes ont été tuées ou blessées dans d'autres régions du pays après le séisme de magnitude 7,8 dont la secousse initiale s'est produite à 14h28 heure locale. Une cinquantaine de corps au moins ont été retrouvés dans les décombres d'une école où l'on estime que 900 écoliers ont été enterrés vivants. Le président Hu Jintao a décrété un effort « total » pour venir en aide aux victimes. Des équipes de recherche ont été envoyées sur les lieux mais sont ralenties en raison des routes bloquées. Les liens de communication étant perturbés, il a déclaré qu'on ne disposait pas encore d'une estimation précise du nombre de victimes à l'épicentre du séisme, dans le district de Wenchuan, à quelque 57 miles de Chengdu, la capitale de la province du Sichuan.

13 MAI 2008
The New York Times. *« PLUS AUCUN ESPOIR » POUR LES ENFANTS ENSEVELIS LORS DU TREMBLEMENT DE TERRE.* L'une des plus grandes tragédies liées à ce désastre a été l'effondrement d'une école de la banlieue de Dujiangyan. Plusieurs centaines d'enfants ont été tués, le chiffre de 900 enfants morts a été avancé. Le Premier ministre Wen Jiabao s'est rendu sur les lieux ce lundi pour constater l'ampleur des destructions, mais il a été impuissant à apaiser les souffrances des survivants… Les enfants qui ont « eu de la chance » s'en tirent avec une fracture ou un membre amputé. On en a tiré plusieurs centaines d'autres des décombres pour les inhumer, mais certains de leurs camarades sont toujours ensevelis sous les ruines de l'école.
« Il n'y a plus aucun espoir pour eux », a déclaré Lu Zhiqing, 58 ans, en observant une équipe de sauveteurs en uniforme avancer avec peine dans la boue et la pluie jusqu'à l'amas de briques et de béton qui était, hier encore, une école. « Il est impossible que quelqu'un soit encore en vie là-dedans. »
Il ne reste presque plus rien de la structure d'origine de l'école. Pas une poutrelle intacte, pas un pan de mur. Les décombres ne s'élèvent pas bien haut au-dessus de la terre mouillée. Des dizaines de personnes se sont rassemblées dans la cour de l'établissement, s'agrippant aux débris, leur donnant des coups de pied, hurlant. Les soldats ont empêché d'autres personnes d'accéder au site de l'ancienne école.

22 MAI 2008
Blog d'Ai Weiwei. Tendre la main à ceux qui sont dans le besoin, essayer de sauver les mourants et venir en aide aux blessés est une forme d'humanitarisme qui n'a rien à voir avec l'amour porté à un pays ou à une personne. Il ne faut pas dénigrer la valeur de la vie ; elle participe d'une idée plus vaste et plus égalitaire de la dignité humaine. En ces jours de deuil, les gens n'ont pas besoin de remercier la patrie et ses défenseurs, car elle a été incapable de leur offrir une meilleure protection. Ce n'est pas non plus la patrie qui a permis aux enfants les plus chanceux de s'échapper à temps de leurs écoles en train de s'effondrer. Nul besoin de féliciter les fonctionnaires du gouvernement ; car les vies qui s'achèvent en ce moment même auraient davantage eu besoin de mesures de sauvetage efficaces que de discours compatissants et de larmes. Nul besoin non plus, et encore moins, de remercier l'armée, car les soldats ne font rien d'autre, en réaction à ce désastre, que respecter le serment qu'ils ont prêté.

25 MAI 2008
The New York Times. *LES CHINOIS SE DEMANDENT POURQUOI LES ÉCOLES SE SONT EFFONDRÉES.* On ne dispose encore d'aucun chiffre officiel concernant le nombre d'enfants morts dans les décombres de l'école primaire de Xinjian, et on ignore également

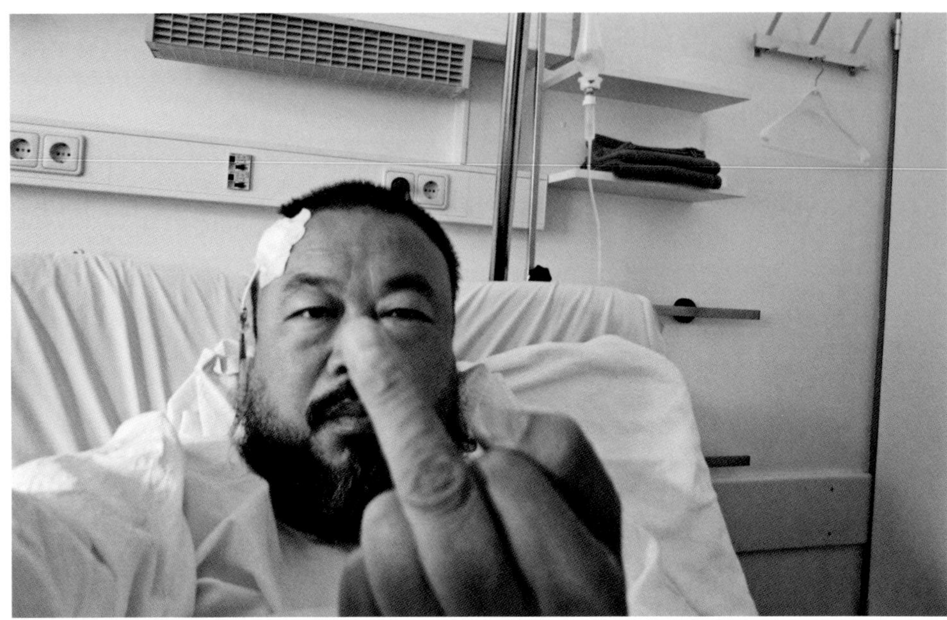

Ai Weiwei in hospital for an emergency brain surgery two months after his beating in Chengdu, Munich 2009

combien de victimes le fort tremblement de terre du 12 mai dans la province du Sichuan a fait dans les autres établissements qui se sont effondrés. Mais il est probable que le nombre d'écoliers tués dans cette catastrophe dépasse les 10 000, et ce chiffre pourrait encore être revu fortement à la hausse. Un chiffre stupéfiant qui a déclenché une polémique en Chine, les parents en deuil affirmant que leurs enfants auraient peut-être survécu au séisme dans des écoles mieux construites. Le gouvernement chinois a bénéficié d'un vaste soutien de la population pour sa réaction au tremblement de terre, et dans la province du Sichuan ce samedi, le Secrétaire général des Nations Unies, Ban Ki-moon, a lui aussi loué la réponse du gouvernement face à cette catastrophe. Cependant, les parents d'enfants tués dans différentes écoles commencent à affirmer qu'il y aurait eu négligence de la part du gouvernement, peut-être même corruption, et l'opinion publique pourrait se rallier à cet avis. Le gouvernement a ordonné une enquête, mais la censure, qui se méfie du jugement du public, essaie de faire disparaître ce sujet sur Internet et dans

les journaux d'État. L'étude de l'effondrement de l'école primaire de Xinjian donne une image inquiétante d'une catastrophe qui aurait peut-être pu être évitée. Les ingénieurs et sismologues qui ont examiné les photographies des décombres en ont conclu que la structure de l'école avait de nombreuses faiblesses et un défaut critique : ils ont déploré l'insuffisance des tiges d'acier qui renforçaient les structures porteuses du bâtiment. Un expert a qualifié les panneaux de béton instables qui formaient le sol de « bombes à retardement ».

1ᴱᴿ JUIN 2008
Blog d'Ai Weiwei. Vingt jours ont passé depuis le séisme et il n'y a toujours ni liste détaillée des noms des enfants disparus, ni décompte exact du nombre de morts. L'opinion publique ne sait toujours pas qui sont ces enfants décédés, ni qui sont leurs familles, qui a omis de renforcer les structures des écoles avec des tiges d'acier ni qui s'est servi de béton de mauvaise qualité pour construire ses fondations et les structures porteuses de l'école.

Reuters. Environ 25 miles plus en aval dans la vallée, à Dujiangyan, quelque 200 parents et proches des écoliers tués lors du séisme se sont rassemblés dimanche pour une journée de commémoration à l'emplacement jonché de décombres de l'ancienne école primaire de Xinjian. Des milliers d'enfants sont morts dans un tremblement de terre qui a vu leurs écoles s'effondrer comme des châteaux de cartes, amenant les parents à penser que, pour des raisons de corruption, les standards de construction n'avaient pas été respectés. Après le séisme, faire face à la colère de ces parents est un des défis politiques les plus durs pour le Parti communiste au pouvoir. En colère, le visage baigné de larmes, les parents portaient des t-shirts blancs imprimés du nom de l'école sur le devant et marqués sur le dos du slogan «Punissez sévèrement la corruption et les constructions en résidus de tofu» en grandes lettres rouges – en référence aux produits résiduels de la fabrication du tofu, une expression courante en chinois pour désigner un travail bâclé ou des matériaux de mauvaise qualité.

28 JUILLET 2008
Blog d'Ai Weiwei. Titres des journaux du matin : «Le Wenchuan a annoncé la construction d'un mémorial du tremblement de terre.» La guerre du Vietnam a eu un effet durable aux États-Unis, elle a provoqué une douleur profonde ; et dix ans après la fin du conflit, sur une pelouse de Washington D.C., on a érigé un mémorial sur lequel sont gravés les noms de plus de 58 000 soldats morts pendant cette guerre. Concernant ce qui se passe ici, tout ce que nous obtenons, c'est une déclaration de l'État comme celle citée plus haut et les vociférations excitées d'une poignée de salauds d'experts qui brassent du vent. Vous pouvez l'imaginer, ce mémorial ne fait en rien avancer le compte-rendu précis de ce qui s'est produit. Les faits historiques ont été modifiés avant même de pouvoir être pleinement diffusés. Il est encore plus impensable d'organiser un service à la mémoire de ceux qui sont morts en raison d'une négligence… Quel est le nombre exact de personnes tuées et blessées lors du tremblement de terre du Wenchuan ? Comment les victimes sont-elles mortes, et sur qui doit-on en rejeter la faute ? Confrontés à cette question, le ministre de l'Éducation et le ministre de l'Architecture ont refusé de répondre, ils font et feront toujours les morts.

13 MARS 2009, 10H01
Conversation téléphonique avec le Groupe de maintien de la stabilité du district de Beichuan. Ai Weiwei Studio : Allô, est-ce que je pourrais parler au directeur Sun ? Je suis bien au «Groupe de maintien de la stabilité» ? / Groupe de maintien de la stabilité du Beichuan : Oui, c'est moi, je vous écoute. / Studio : Je vous appelle du district de Chaoyang à Pékin, mon équipe enquête sur le nombre des victimes et les noms des écoliers qui sont morts dans le tremblement de terre du 12 mai au Beichuan. / Beichuan : D'où vient votre équipe ? / Studio : De Pékin. / Beichuan : Et de quel groupe de travail ou de quel service de sécurité publique à Pékin ? / Studio : Il s'agit d'une initiative citoyenne indépendante. / Beichuan : Je suis désolé, mais je ne peux vous donner aucun chiffre, nous ne pouvons pas communiquer de chiffres au public. / Studio : Et pourquoi cela ? / Beichuan : Comment cela, pourquoi ? C'est une question de discipline. / Studio : Quel genre de discipline ? / Beichuan : Discipline nationale. / Studio : Notre État a prévu ce genre de disposition ? Est-ce que cela figure quelque part ? / Beichuan : De quel groupe êtes-vous ? / Studio : Nous sommes un groupe de citoyens. / Beichuan : Et pourquoi un groupe de citoyens a besoin de savoir ça ? / Studio : Nous sommes tous compatriotes, tout le monde est touché par ça. / Beichuan : Vous voulez dire que nous ne sommes pas touchés par le sort de nos propres camarades ? / Studio : Ce n'est pas ce que je voulais dire, tout le monde est touché, mais c'est notre manière à nous de l'exprimer. / Beichuan : Je vais vous dire une chose, tout ça n'est pas très clair. / Studio : Qu'est-ce qui n'est pas clair ? Votre service n'a pas reçu d'informations de ses supérieurs ? / Beichuan : Qui vous a dit ça ? / Studio : Un employé, mais les journaux nationaux ont déjà publié cette information, c'est pourquoi nous nous adressons à vous. / Beichuan : Je suis désolé. / Studio : C'est votre métier, n'est-il pas de la responsabilité du «Groupe de maintien de la stabilité» de donner des

Brain Inflation, 2009 (detail),
poster, 78¾ x 39⅜ inches

réponses aux gens quand ils vous adressent leurs questions? / Beichuan: Il serait de notre devoir de communiquer les informations que vous voulez avoir? / Studio: Il ne s'agit pas d'une loi, mais d'un principe de base! / Beichuan: Quelle loi? / Studio: Vous êtes employés du gouvernement. / Beichuan: Nous travaillons sous la direction du gouvernement, et nous avons rapporté au gouvernement tout ce que nous avions à lui rapporter. C'est le gouvernement qui décide à quelle unité de travail nous répondons. / Studio: Votre responsabilité est de répondre au gouvernement? Et qu'en est-il des citoyens? Vous êtes le gouvernement, ou du moins vous en faites partie! / Beichuan: Bon, je ne sais pas qui vous êtes, vous ne m'avez pas vraiment dit clairement pour quel groupe vous appelez. / Studio: Nous ne faisons pas partie d'une organisation, nous sommes des citoyens! / Beichuan: Des citoyens? Les citoyens comme vous sont censés s'adresser au gouvernement. / Studio: Alors maintenant vous représentez à nouveau le gouvernement? / Beichuan: Je représente le gouvernement, et je réponds à mes supérieurs. Comment est-ce que je peux savoir qui vous êtes? Et si vous aviez des arrière-pensées? / Studio: Comment ça, des arrière-pensées? Qu'est-ce que vous entendez par là? Alors si un citoyen passe un coup de téléphone pour savoir quelque chose que tous les citoyens devraient savoir, ça veut dire qu'il a des arrière-pensées? / Beichuan: Comment pouvez-vous prouver que vous n'avez pas une autre idée en tête? C'est comme ça, c'est tout! (Il raccroche).

20 MARS 2009

Blog d'Ai Weiwei. Il y a 300 jours, je me suis rendu dans la région du séisme, dans le district de Wenchuan, dans la province du Sichuan. J'y ai été témoin d'une souffrance mais aussi d'une terreur infinies. Nous ne savons toujours pas qui nous a quittés lors de ce tremblement de terre, pourquoi ces enfants nous ont quittés, ni comment ils ont péri. Nous ne saurons jamais ce qu'ils ont ressenti pendant leur attente sous les dé-combres. Pendant ce désastre, je n'ai pas tendu ma main. Je n'en ai franchement pas trouvé la force. Ils disent qu'ils ne sont pas responsables de la mort de ces écoliers. Ils disent que c'était inévitable, que des experts l'ont démontré. Ils ferment leur bouche, refusent de parler de la corruption, des malfaçons. Ils cachent les faits, et au nom de la « stabilité », ils persécutent, menacent et incarcèrent les parents de ces enfants décédés qui veulent connaître la vérité. Ils violent la constitution de manière flagrante et piétinent les droits fondamentaux des citoyens. Ces enfants qui ont péri dans le tremblement de terre ne sont pas un chiffre indéterminé, ils ne sont pas le résultat d'une nation « stabilisée ». Ces enfants ont des parents, des rêves, ils souriaient, ils avaient un nom à eux. Et ce nom sera toujours à eux trois ans, cinq ans, dix-huit ou dix-neuf ans après le drame ; c'est la seule chose d'eux dont on peut se souvenir, la seule chose qui puisse être évoquée. / Rejetons l'oubli, rejetons le mensonge. En mémoire des défunts, pour montrer notre amour de la vie, pour nous montrer responsables et essayer de rendre la joie de vivre aux survivants, nous avons créé une enquête citoyenne. Nous trouverons le nom de chacun des enfants décédés, et nous nous souviendrons. Si vous souhaitez participer à cette enquête citoyenne, merci d'envoyer vos coordonnées à l'adresse suivante : xuesheng512@gmail.com. Vos actions créent votre monde.

24 MARS 2009

Blog d'Ai Weiwei. Q : En faisant des recherches sur Internet, j'ai trouvé cette une : « Liste de 19 065 victimes du séisme du Wenchuan ; l'enquête sur le nombre total de victimes se poursuit. » Cela veut dire que le gouvernement fait un travail similaire au vôtre. Pourquoi voulez-vous une nouvelle liste de noms ? / AWW : Nous avons passé plus de 150 coups de téléphone dans l'espoir d'obtenir une liste de ces 19 065 noms. Tout ce que nous avons obtenu, c'est de la procrastination, des réponses évasives pour gagner du temps. Nul ne sait où ni comment cette liste de noms a été publiée, et cette liste n'est jamais apparue sur aucun site internet officiel. Il s'est passé plus de 300 jours depuis le séisme, et nous n'avons toujours pas de chiffre crédible. Le gouvernement devrait diffuser les noms des victimes, leur âge, la cause et le lieu du décès, ainsi que le district dans lequel elles étaient déclarées. Ce genre d'informations de base, concernant la vie ou la mort des gens, ne peuvent être complétées

que sous les auspices du gouvernement, et devraient être disponibles à tout moment. Nous avons entrepris cette enquête en raison de l'opacité du gouvernement. Si nous faisons cela, c'est pour témoigner aux défunts le minimum de respect auquel tout le monde a droit. La valeur la plus fondamentale, le droit civique le plus fondamental de toute personne est celui d'avoir un nom ; ce nom est le plus petit élément qui nous permet de témoigner de l'existence d'un individu.

MARS 2009

Entretien avec Liu Yanping (bénévole de l'enquête citoyenne puis membre du studio d'Ai Weiwei). Ma tâche principale consistait à rester ici et à rassembler les informations qu'ils m'envoyaient. Le gouvernement venait de publier la liste des districts les plus sévèrement touchés. Nous nous les étions répartis entre nous pour faire nos recherches. La deuxième équipe s'est rendue dans les régions qui n'avaient pas encore été visitées. Nous nous sommes rendus dans pratiquement toutes les zones les plus touchées. Au début, nous avons obtenu un grand nombre de noms d'un coup, mais à mesure que l'enquête avançait, il est devenu de plus en plus difficile d'apprendre de nouveaux noms. Un voyage ne nous apportait que quelques noms supplémentaires. Par exemple, tout le monde disait qu'il y avait eu une centaine d'élèves tués dans cette école. Il a été relativement facile d'obtenir le nom de ces élèves, parce que tout le monde était au courant. Et certaines informations étaient en ligne. Mais après cela, il a été de plus en plus difficile d'obtenir des informations. Certains des noms qu'on nous donnait étaient des noms que nous avions déjà. Trouver le reste d'entre eux était difficile. Il a fallu aller dans des régions plus reculées, où les parents étaient peut-être moins disposés à interagir avec le monde extérieur, ce sont des gens qui n'utilisent pas Internet, ou ce genre de choses. J'ai téléphoné à de nombreux parents. Nous leur avons demandé s'ils connaissaient d'autres gens qui étaient morts. Je crois que la plupart d'entre eux étaient très surpris que nous les appelions. Ils étaient très émus. Ils nous ont dit que personne d'autre ne leur avait demandé de parler de leur enfant. Nous n'avons pas passé tant de temps que ça sur le terrain. Nous

nous sommes mis à préparer des formulaires sur la liberté de l'information destinés à différents bureaux du gouvernement. Parce que c'est censé être leur responsabilité, de communiquer au public les informations concernant les victimes, l'état de construction des écoles – ils sont supposés nous parler de ça. Alors nous nous sommes préparés pour notre enquête. Je pense qu'en tout nous avons préparé plus de 10 000 questions.

18 AVRIL 2009
Conversation téléphonique avec le ministère de l'Éducation du Sichuan. Représentant du ministère de l'Éducation : Premièrement, nous tenons à dire que cette liste de noms, le gouvernement la communiquera au public. / Ai Weiwei : Oui, j'ai été heureux d'entendre la promesse qu'en a fait le Conseil d'État hier. / ME : Notre province a déjà fait cette promesse. / AWW : Alors où est-elle, cette liste de noms ? / ME : Ne vous inquiétez pas, chaque chose en son temps, il faut que tout cela se passe étape par étape. La liste de noms sera publiée, c'est sûr, car si elle ne l'est pas, cela posera un problème, cela voudra dire que le gouvernement n'a pas tenu sa promesse. Deuxièmement, les victimes parmi les écoliers font évidemment partie du groupe plus vaste des victimes de ce séisme, donc si nous confirmons que cette liste sera publiée, les noms des écoliers se trouveront sur cette liste. / AWW : Votre logique est claire. / ME : Vous dites que vous n'avez pas encore vu cette liste de noms, que nous ne l'avons pas encore dressée, mais je tiens à vous dire que nous y travaillons en ce moment même. / AWW : Ok, donc cela est clair aussi. / ME : Comment procédons-nous ? Après le séisme, le Conseil d'État a pris une disposition stipulant que c'était aux gouvernements locaux et à ceux des provinces de décider de quelle manière ils souhaitaient communiquer l'information. C'est à eux de le faire, à eux de vérifier les noms des victimes. Jusqu'à maintenant, nous y travaillons, et nous avons déjà communiqué les noms de certaines des victimes de ce désastre. Comment avons-nous communiqué cette liste de noms ? Dans les bureaux du gouvernement de notre district et dans les bureaux des villes, elle a été affichée sur les tableaux d'annonces. / AWW : Permettez-moi de vous interrompre – ce n'est pas

ce que j'appelle communiquer l'information au public. Si c'est ce que vous entendez par là, vous n'avez pas bien compris ce que je veux dire. / ME : Si ce n'est pas communiquer l'information au public, alors qu'est-ce que c'est ? / AWW : Bien sûr que non. Rendre ces informations publiques signifie les rendre disponibles à quiconque paie des impôts – tout le monde a le droit d'avoir accès à cette liste de noms. Voilà ce que c'est, mettre ces informations à la disposition du public. Vous devriez comprendre. / ME : Dites-le clairement, alors… / AWW : Si vous ne comprenez pas ça, ce n'est pas la peine d'essayer de parler de choses encore plus fondamentales. Annoncer quelque chose en l'écrivant sur un tableau noir que vous effacerez alors que personne ne l'aura vu, ce n'est pas communiquer une information au public. Rendre une information publique signifie que tout le monde dans cette société peut trouver cette information à tout moment, voilà ce que ça veut dire.

7 MAI 2009
Blog d'Ai Weiwei. Le gouvernement du Sichuan a répété qu'il n'ordonnera pas d'enquête sur la qualité des matériaux de construction des écoles qui se sont effondrées durant le séisme. Leur raisonnement est le suivant : lors de séismes dont la magnitude n'est pas prévue par les normes de résistance aux séismes des bâtiments qui se sont effondrés, toutes les pertes humaines sont naturelles. Cet argument rationnel en apparence permet aux responsables de la malfaçon des bâtiments de pousser un soupir de soulagement – au nom du « développement scientifique » et du « soutien à un parti qui sert les intérêts des gens », plus de 2000 experts chinois ont rédigé leur sage évaluation dans un merveilleux document… Ce qui n'a jamais été clairement expliqué, c'est que sur plus d'une centaine d'écoles situées dans la zone la plus sévèrement touchée par la catastrophe, seules quatorze d'entre elles déplorent un nombre de victimes supérieur à cent dû à l'effondrement du bâtiment. Malgré le séisme de magnitude 8, les quatre-vingt-dix autres écoles ne se sont pas effondrées. Toutefois, parmi les quatorze écoles qui se sont effondrées, on ne trouve pas un schéma de destruction unique : certaines grandes

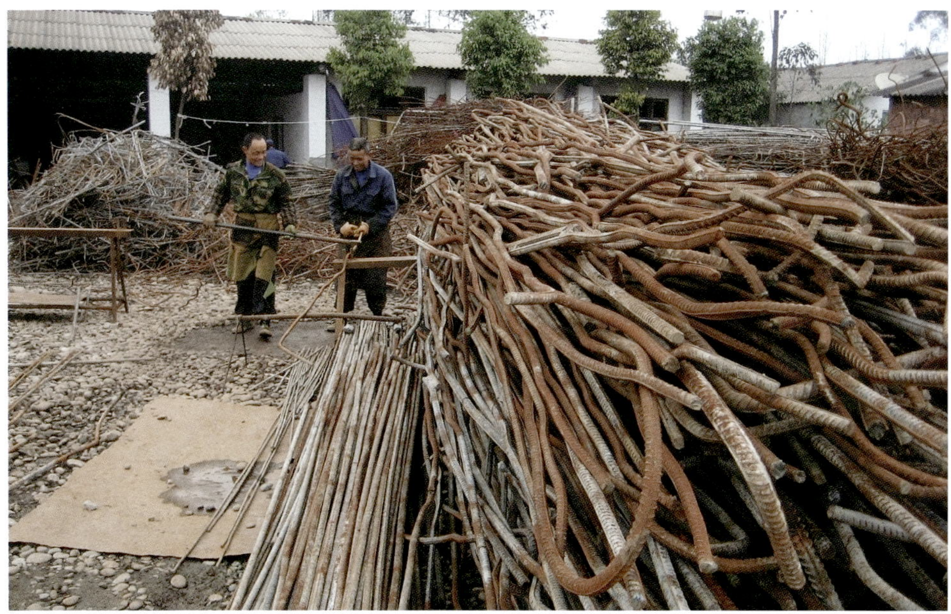

Processing rebar salvaged from Beichuan Middle School, Sichuan 2011

salles se sont effondrées, mais d'autres
parties des bâtiments abritant les salles de
classe sont restées intactes, tandis que les
bâtiments de l'internat se sont écroulés. Des
tours qui étaient dans un état de délabrement
avancé depuis plusieurs années sont restées
debout, tandis que des bâtiments plus récents
n'ont pas résisté. Des bâtiments abritant
des salles de classe se sont effondrés, mais
pas les bâtiments administratifs semblables.
Autour des zones où l'on dénombre le plus
de victimes, les écoles de premier cycle de
Beichuan et de Juyuan, de nombreux bâtiments sont restés debout. Ainsi, comparer
ce séisme de magnitude 8 à une « fondue
chinoise » (dans laquelle tous les ingrédients
ont une saveur différente au départ, mais finalement tous le même goût) est visiblement
une explication trop simpliste.

8 MAI 2009
Blog d'Ai Weiwei. Messages automatiques
apparaissant à la place des articles effacés :
« Votre article X a été effacé par l'administra-
teur. Veuillez nous excuser pour ces désagré-
ments. » 08.05.2009 17h48

28 MAI 2009
Blog d'Ai Weiwei. La veille, j'avais appelé
deux fois le 110 et renvoyé au BSP deux
officiers de la Sécurité intérieure qui avaient
oublié leurs identifiants. Aujourd'hui, j'ai
appelé le 110 trois fois pour porter plainte,
renvoyant ces deux flics en civil qui m'avaient
pris en filature au BSP. Ce que je veux dire
par là, c'est qu'en tant qu'être humain, je
me sens obligé de veiller au respect de mes
droits. Je ne conseille à personne de me
provoquer. J'ai toléré que vous effaciez les
articles de mon blog, j'ai toléré que vous
mettiez mon téléphone sur écoute, j'ai toléré
que vous placiez mon lieu de résidence sous
surveillance. Mais je ne puis tolérer que vous
débarquiez chez moi et me menaciez devant
ma mère, une vieille femme de soixante-seize
ans. Je ne puis tolérer que des officiers en
civil me prennent secrètement en filature et
menacent ma sécurité.

12 AOÛT 2009
**Enregistrement sonore réalisé avec
la caméra d'Ai Weiwei** lors de l'entrée
par effraction d'officiers de police dans la
chambre d'hôtel d'Ai Weiwei et de ses béné-

voles à Chengdu, 3h15 du matin. Officier : Ouvrez cette porte ! / AWW (au téléphone) : Je suis dans la chambre 513. / O : Police ! Ouvrez ! / AWW : Nous sommes au 158 Ease & Comfort Hotel. Oui. Ils sont déjà entrés. (Bruits de lutte). Qu'est-ce que vous faites ? / O : Je ne fais rien. / AWW : Vous me frappez ? / O : Je ne savais pas qui vous étiez ! / AWW : Pourquoi est-ce que je ne peux pas appeler le 110 ? Vous êtes tellement nombreux, vous pouvez frapper les gens. / O : Posez ce téléphone. / AWW : Allez-y ! Vous avez emmené tous ces flics pour me taper dessus ? Eh bien allez-y, tapez. / O : Qui vous a frappé ? Qui l'a vu ? / AWW : C'est comme ça que se comportent des officiers de police ? C'est comme ça que la police se comporte ? / O : Prouvez-le. / AWW : C'est comme ça que la police se comporte ? / O : Où est votre preuve ? Qui vous a frappé ? Où ? Où est la plaie ? Ne parlez pas sans preuve. / AWW : 7998, je prends votre numéro d'insigne. Votre nom ? / O : Ça ne vous regarde pas ! / AWW : Vous êtes entré dans ma chambre par effraction ! Montrez-moi votre insigne ! / O : Est-ce que je suis entré dans votre chambre ? Est-ce que je suis dans votre chambre ? / AWW : Êtes-vous entré par effraction ? / O : C'est votre chambre ? Qu'est-ce que vous entendez par entrer par effraction ? Il s'agit d'une inspection de routine, pas d'une effraction. / AWW : C'est la routine de taper sur les gens ? Comment se fait-il que mes vêtements soient déchirés ? / O : Vous l'avez fait vous-même. / AWW : J'ai déchiré mes propres vêtements et je me suis donné des coups tout seul ? / O : Exactement. / AWW : Vous maintenez cette version ? / O : C'est la seule explication. Je n'ai vu personne vous frapper. Nous faisons seulement notre boulot.

The Guardian. *LA POLICE CHINOISE DÉTIENT 11 PERSONNES POUR LES EMPÊCHER D'ASSISTER AU PROCÈS D'UN MILITANT.* La police chinoise a arrêté onze personnes projetant d'assister ce matin au procès d'un militant qui avait enquêté sur la mort d'écoliers dans le tremblement de terre du Sichuan de l'année dernière ; parmi eux, un artiste en vue, critique envers le gouvernement. L'artiste contemporain Ai Weiwei, qui avait dessiné le nouveau stade olympique de Pékin, a déclaré que six personnes et lui-même étaient détenues à leur hôtel et que quatre autres personnes avaient été emmenées dans un poste de police. Il a ajouté qu'un officier de police l'avait frappé à la mâchoire et avait malmené un autre homme. Ils s'étaient rendus à Chengdu pour assister ce matin au procès de Tan Zuoren, un militant du Sichuan accusé de subversion, apparemment en lien avec l'enquête qu'il a menée pour déterminer le nombre d'enfants morts en raison de l'effondrement de bâtiments scolaires durant le séisme, ainsi qu'avec les articles qu'il a écrits sur les manifestations d'étudiants de la place Tiananmen en 1989. Ai Weiwei, qui a dirigé un groupe de bénévoles tentant d'établir la liste de tous les écoliers décédés, a déclaré que l'avocat de M. Tan lui avait demandé d'apporter des preuves du lien entre les morts et la malfaçon des bâtiments. Lorsque le tribunal lui a demandé de comparaître en tant que témoin, il s'est dit qu'il allait venir assister au procès et a emmené dix bénévoles avec lui. Il a déclaré depuis son hôtel : « Je voulais témoigner de mon soutien à M. Tan. J'ai le sentiment qu'aujourd'hui, de moins en moins de gens se battent pour défendre la vérité et la justice [et] cela porte préjudice à la vérité et à la dignité de la loi. » « Vers minuit, une vingtaine ou une trentaine de policiers en civil et d'officiers de police sont venus tambouriner à notre porte en nous criant d'ouvrir. Je n'ai pas ouvert tout de suite, je leur ai demandé de prouver leur identité. Mais [plusieurs d'entre eux] ont forcé la porte et m'ont dit que cela suffisait à prouver leur identité. J'ai insisté pour voir leur insigne et dans la confusion on m'a frappé au menton. » Alors que les officiers de police leur avaient annoncé qu'ils seraient libres de partir à midi, ils sont restés assignés dans leur chambre d'hôtel bien plus longtemps.

16 SEPTEMBRE 2009

Der Spiegel. *OPÉRATION À MUNICH : UN ARTISTE CHINOIS ACCUSE LE GOUVERNEMENT DE COUPS ET BLESSURES.* Les chirurgiens d'une clinique de Munich ont opéré lundi l'artiste chinois Ai Weiwei, 51 ans, après avoir diagnostiqué une hémorragie cérébrale dans l'hémisphère droit de son cerveau. En août, Ai Weiwei avait déclaré au magazine *Der Spiegel* que la police secrète l'avait molesté dans sa chambre d'hôtel de la province du Sichuan, dans le sud de la Chine, le 12 août. La blessure à la tête qui a justifié son opération pourrait être liée à cette agression. Lundi, Ai Weiwei a passé un bilan de santé à l'hôpital. Ce mardi, des sources proches d'Ai Weiwei ont déclaré au *Spiegel* que l'opération s'était bien passée. (L'artiste lui-même a publié sur Twitter une photo de lui convalescent.) Les médecins ont toutefois demandé au patient de rester encore quelques jours à l'hôpital pour se remettre. Ai Weiwei a déclaré qu'il envisageait d'aller en justice s'il parvenait à prouver que cette blessure était la conséquence des coups au visage infligés par les officiers de police en août dernier.

11 OCTOBRE 2009
Focus. *EN MÉMOIRE DES ENFANTS MORTS.* De loin, on pourrait croire que la façade de la Haus der Kunst de Munich a été recouverte d'une gigantesque affiche aux couleurs gaies. Mais en y regardant de plus près, on s'aperçoit que le patchwork de couleurs est en fait un assemblage de sacs à dos. L'artiste conceptuel chinois Ai Weiwei en a fait fabriquer 9000 pour son œuvre *Remembering.* Les sacs ont été disposés de manière à former, sur plus de cent mètres de large, la phrase « Elle a vécu heureuse sur cette Terre pendant sept ans » en caractères chinois : les paroles d'une mère en mémoire de sa fille décédée lors du séisme dévastateur qui avait touché la province chinoise du Sichuan en mai 2008.

20 NOVEMBRE 2009
Blog d'Ai Weiwei. Que peuvent-ils me faire ? Ils peuvent seulement me bannir, m'enlever ou me mettre en prison. Ils pourraient peut-être me faire disparaître comme par magie, mais ils n'ont ni créativité ni imagination, ils n'ont ni la joie, ni le pouvoir de voler. Ce genre d'organisation politique est lamentable.

10 FÉVRIER 2010
The Wall Street Journal. *LA CHINE CONDAMNE UN MILITANT ENQUÊTANT SUR LE SÉISME.* Selon son avocat, Mᵉ Pu Zhiqiang, ce mardi, un tribunal de Chengdu, la capitale de la province, a déclaré Tan Zuoren coupable d'incitation à la subversion envers le pouvoir de l'État pour des articles qui commémoraient le massacre de la place Tiananmen en 1989. Mᵉ Pu a cependant ajouté que comme certains groupes de défense des droits de l'homme et d'autres défenseurs, il estimait que la raison sous-jacente des poursuites lancées contre M. Tan était l'enquête que celui-ci avait menée dans le cadre de l'effondrement de bâtiments scolaires durant le séisme de mai 2008, qui avait causé la mort de milliers d'enfants. Des charges précédentes contre M. Tan faisaient référence à son militantisme en lien avec le tremblement de terre, un sujet sensible pour les autorités. Le verdict de mardi ne mentionne toutefois pas le séisme, et Mᵉ Pu a déclaré que ce sujet n'avait pas été abordé au cours du procès de M. Tan, qui avait commencé au mois d'août dernier.

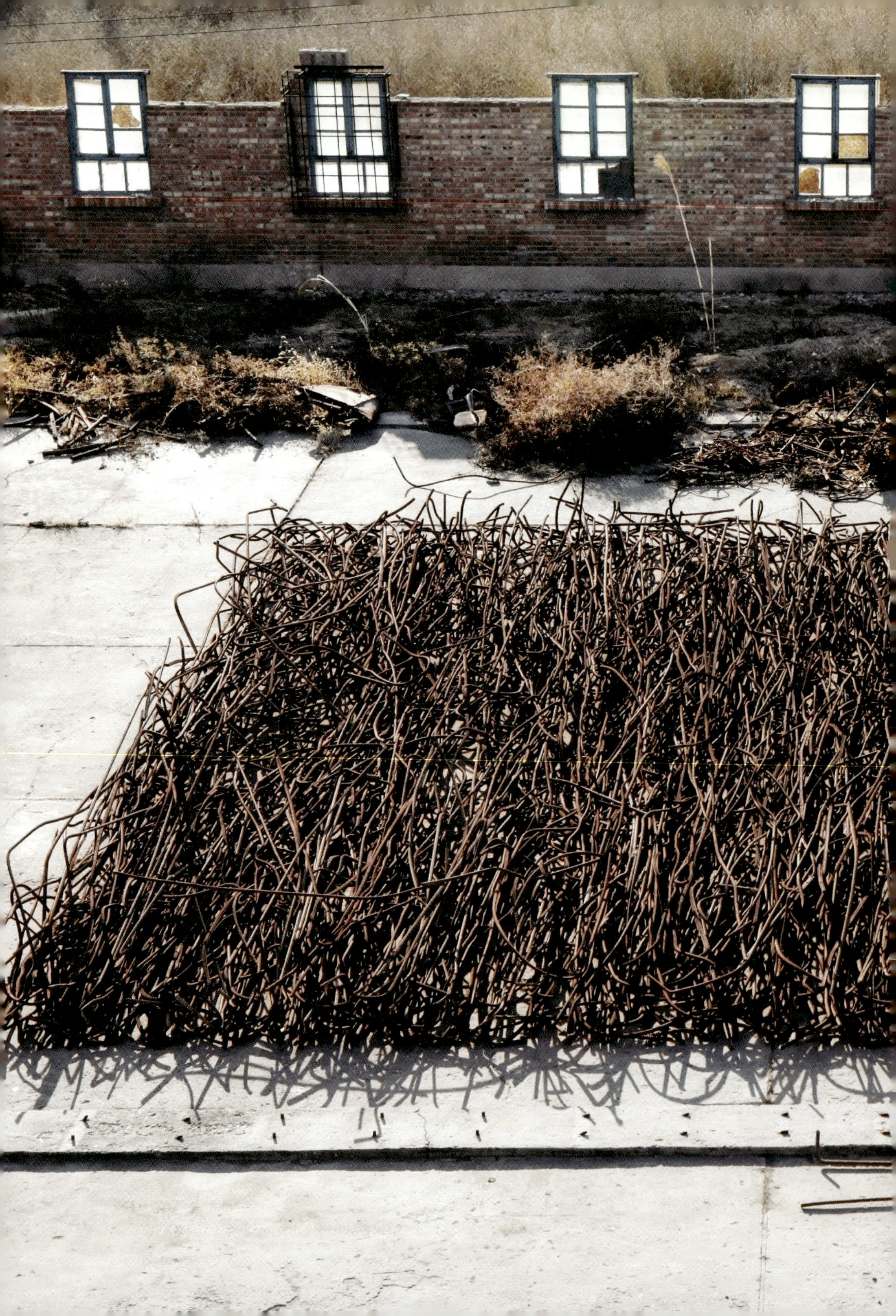

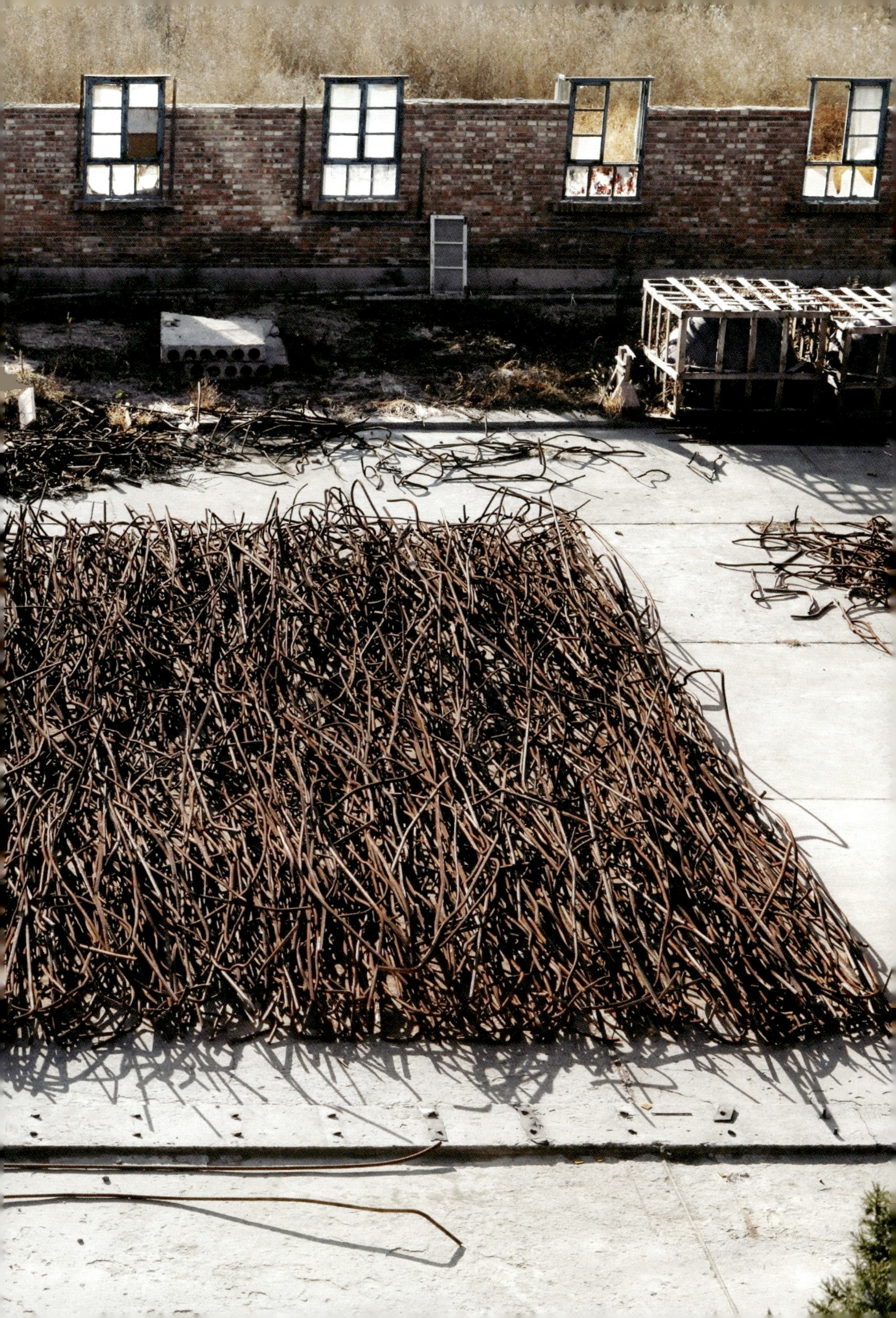

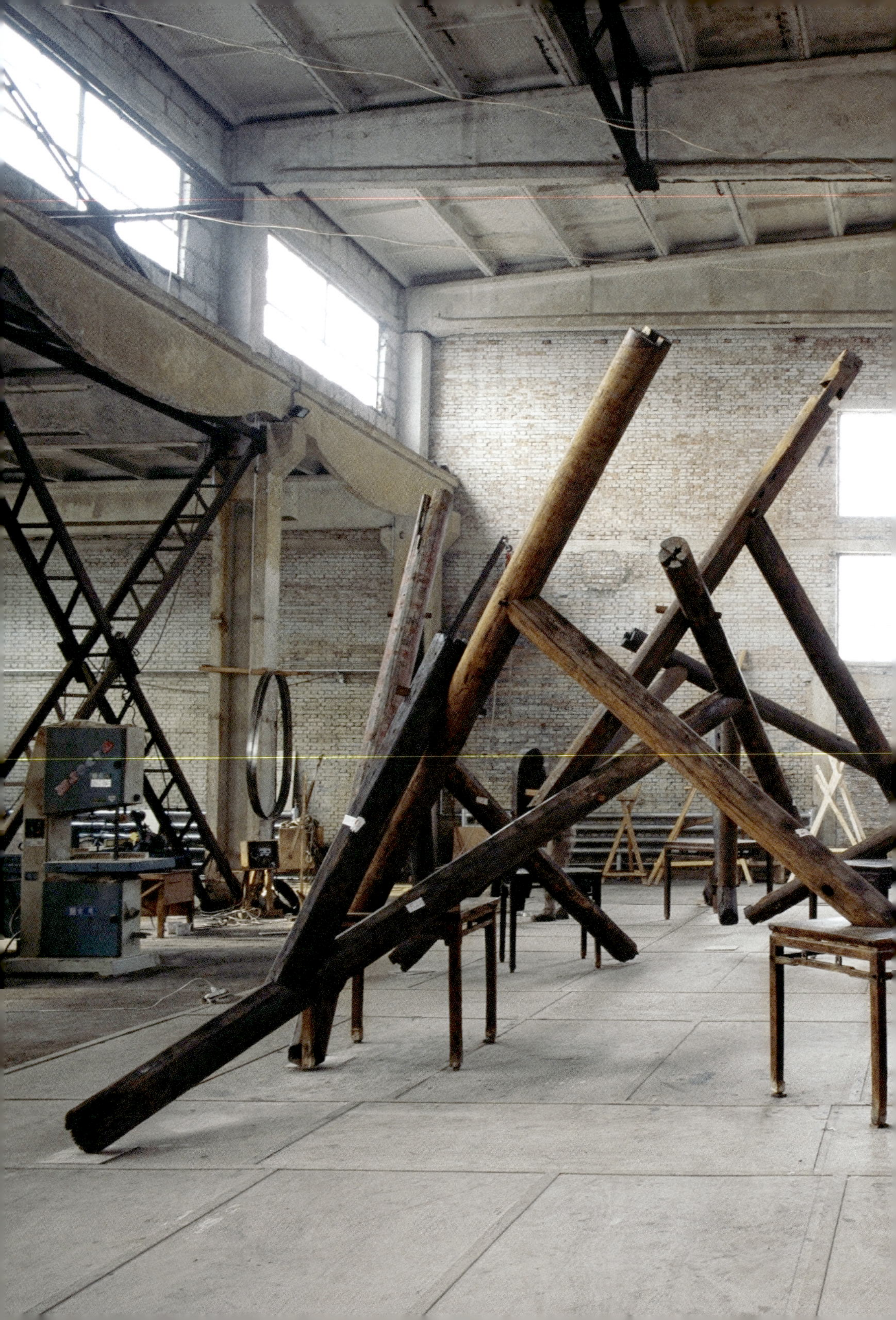

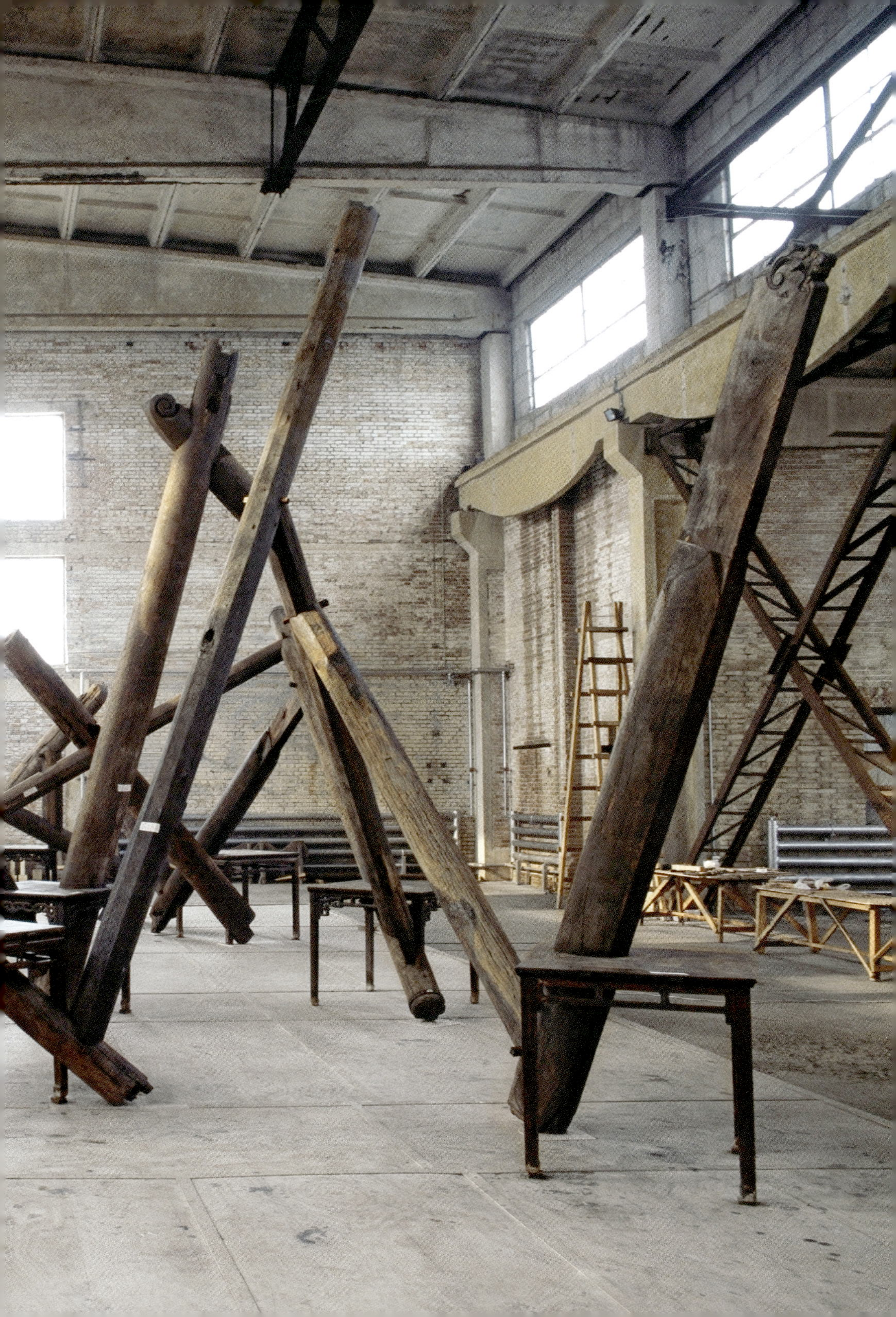

"In Chinese tables, like in architecture or any artifacts, the usage of materials and the basic measurements are relating to very precise moral and aesthetic conditions. That comes from both the clear rationality of philosophy and aesthetics and at the same time a very strong sensitivity about proportions and the right way of dealing with materials. Which involves the judgment of many craftsmen. It takes a lot of study and practice to construct a separate set of logic with these parts of building structure and the table, to make them clash in a way that it looks like a highly skilled arrangement. And when it clashes, or when it's built together, it's like a fine-designed disaster or ruin." — AI WEIWEI

Bei chinesischen Tischen, wie auch in der Architektur oder überhaupt allen Artefakten, nehmen die Auswahl des Materials und die grundlegenden Maße Bezug auf sehr spezifische moralische und ästhetische Vorstellungen. Diese stammen aus einer rationalen Philosophie und Ästhetik und zugleich einer tiefen Sensibilität für Proportionen und den Umgang mit dem jeweiligen Material. Das erfordert die Kenntnisse von vielen Handwerkern und eine lange Lehrzeit. Sehr viel Übung ist notwendig, um diese jeweils eigene Logik für die Strukturelemente und den Tisch zu konstruieren, sie so aufeinandertreffen zu lassen, dass der Eindruck eines höchst kunstfertigen Arrangements entsteht. Wie die Teile dann aufeinandertreffen, also wie sie zusammengebaut sind, gleicht einer feinsinnig entworfenen Katastrophe oder Ruine.

Les tables chinoises, comme c'est le cas en architecture ou pour n'importe quel artefact, sont construites avec des matériaux et selon des mesures qui correspondent à des règles esthétiques et morales très précises. Cela vient du rationalisme de la philosophie et de l'esthétique, mais aussi d'une sensibilité toute particulière pour les proportions et la manière appropriée d'utiliser les matériaux. Tout cela nécessite l'appréciation de nombreux artisans. Il a fallu beaucoup de réflexion et d'essais pour construire une logique particulière à partir de ces éléments de construction et de cette table, pour les faire se heurter comme si on les avait minutieusement disposés. Leur choc ou leur assemblage ressemble à une destruction, un désastre soigneusement préparé.

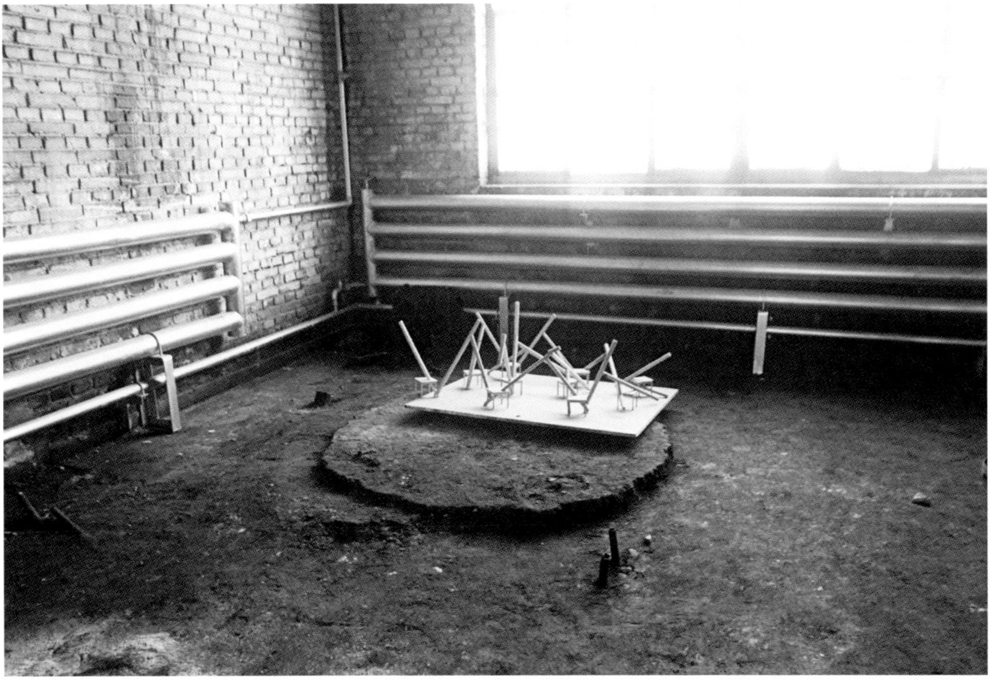

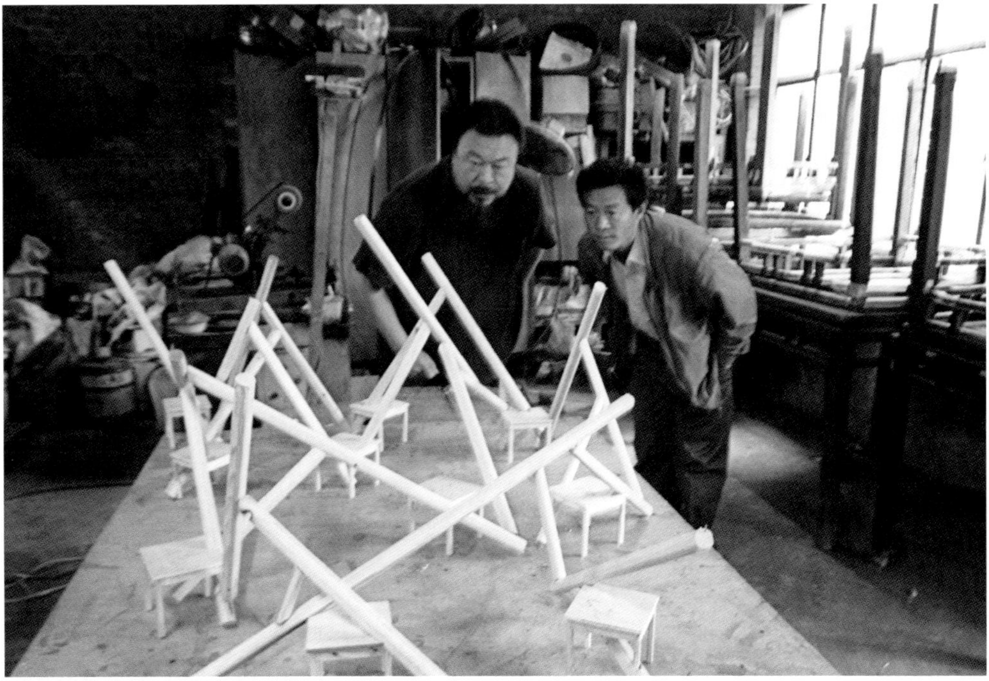

THROUGH, 2007–2008, Qing Dynasty tieli wood tables, parts of beams and pillars from dismantled Qing Dynasty temples, 216 ½ x 334 ⅝ x 543 ¼ inches; Ai Weiwei's studio, Beijing 2008 (previous spread), model (above) | 381

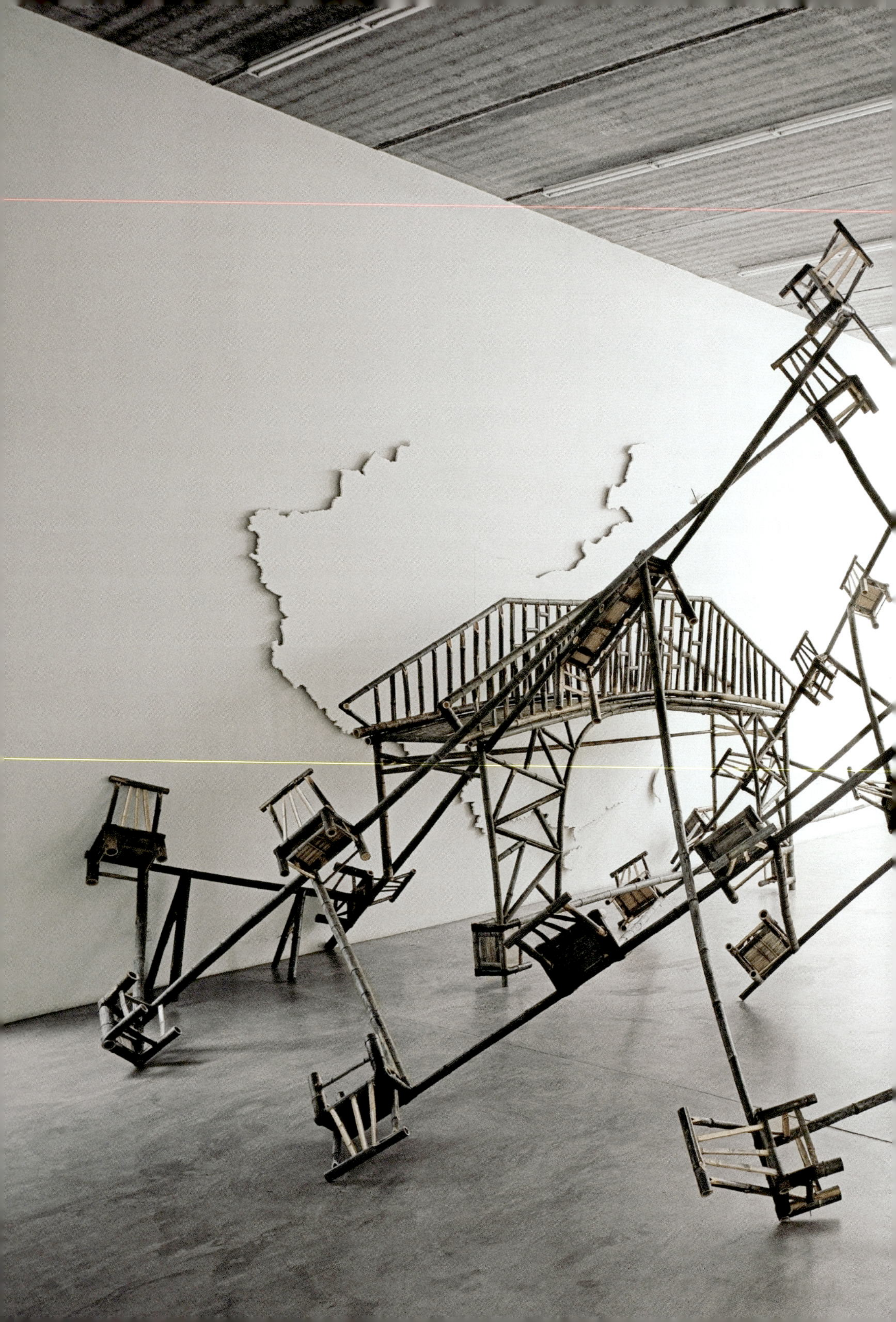

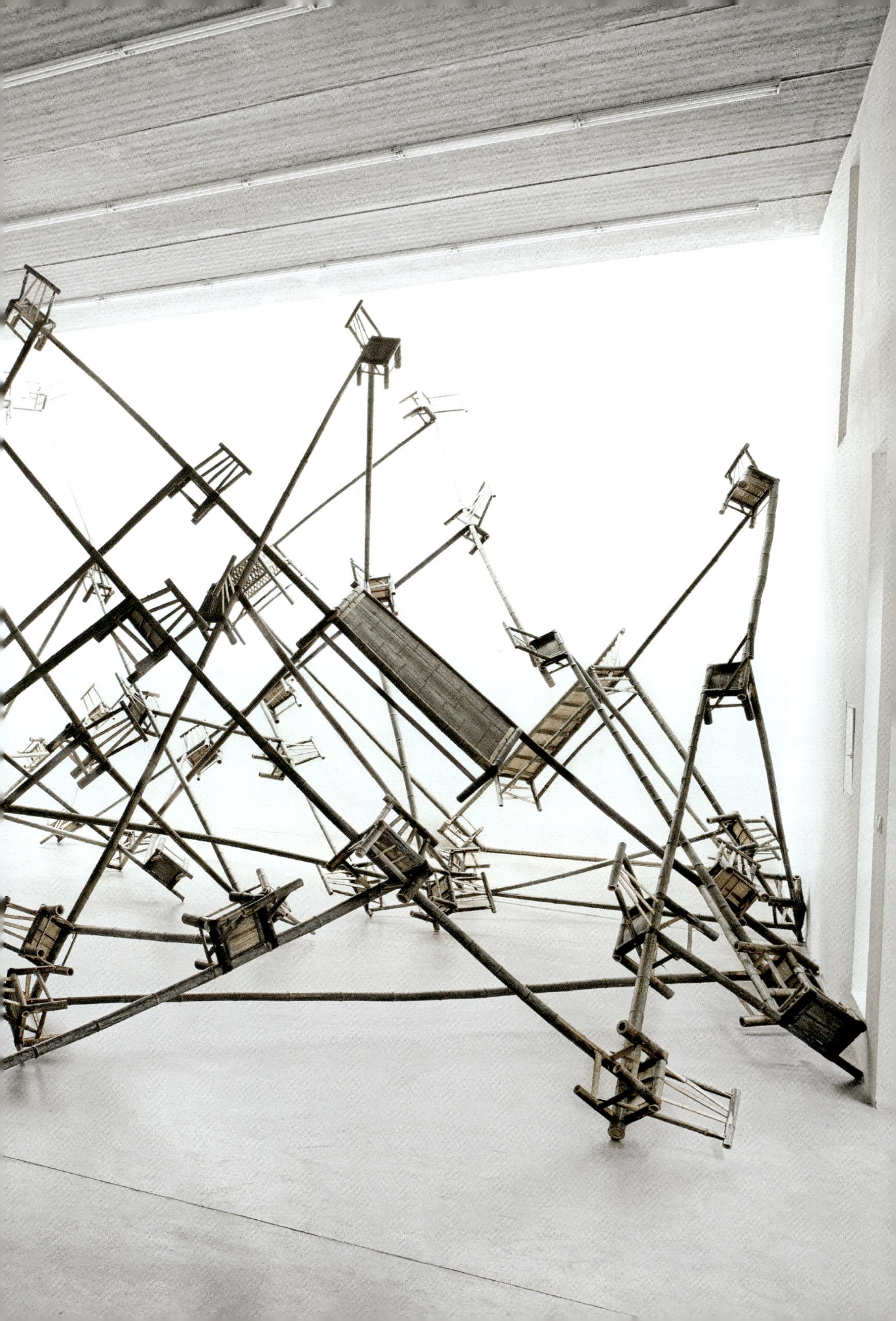

"The National Stadium is called the Bird's Nest, which originated from
the proposal's bid: 'Similar to a bird's nest, its outer appearance and structure
are unified.' Now everyone is used to calling it the Bird's Nest. Its greatest
breakthrough is expressed in its integrity; this feature makes it different from
other stadiums. There were many objections, and the government was hesitating
in their decision-making. I remember the day the Beijing Party Secretary said:
'On the issue of Olympic architecture, the principles of opening and reform
will not be altered.' The final result was to omit the retractable roof featured
in the original design. The original plan has been continuously altered; the
reasons for altering it arise from the need to balance national-interest parties
and appeals from politicians. The Bird's Nest has become a platform for finding balance." — AI WEIWEI

Das Nationalstadion wird „Vogelnest" genannt. Der Name stammt aus unserem Pro-
jektentwurf: „Äußere Erscheinung und Struktur werden ähnlich wie bei einem Vogelnest
vereinheitlicht." Mittlerweile haben sich alle an den Namen gewöhnt. Die wichtigste
Neuerung des Stadions ist seine Integrität, das unterscheidet es von anderen Stadien.
Es gab viele Einwände, und die Regierung zögerte in ihren Entscheidungen. Ich erinnere
mich an den Tag, an dem der Parteisekretär von Peking sagte: „Anlässlich der Frage einer
olympischen Architektur werden die Prinzipien zum Thema Öffnung und Reform nicht
geändert." Das Ergebnis bestand letztlich darin, das verschließbare Dach wegzulassen,
welches im ursprünglichen Entwurf vorgesehen war. Die Planung wurde immer wieder
abgeändert, um die Interessen der beteiligten Parteien auszugleichen. Das „Vogelnest"
ist zu einer Plattform für die Suche nach Gleichgewicht geworden.

Le stade national est surnommé le «Nid d'oiseau» en raison de sa description dans
notre dossier de candidature: «Pareil à un nid d'oiseau, son apparence extérieure et sa
structure ne font qu'un.» Aujourd'hui, tout le monde l'appelle le «Nid d'oiseau». Ce qui
le rendunique, c'est son intégrité; une particularité qui le distingue des autres stades.
Les objections ont été nombreuses, et le gouvernement a hésité avant de prendre sa
décision. Je me rappelle le jour où le secrétaire du Parti de Pékin a déclaré: «En matière
d'architecture olympique, les principes d'ouverture et de réforme ne seront pas remis
en question.» Finalement, on a omis de construire le toit rétractable qui était prévu par
les plans d'origine. Ceux-ci ont été continuellement modifiés pour ménager l'intérêt
national et satisfaire les politiciens. Le «Nid d'oiseau» est devenu l'archétype du compromis.

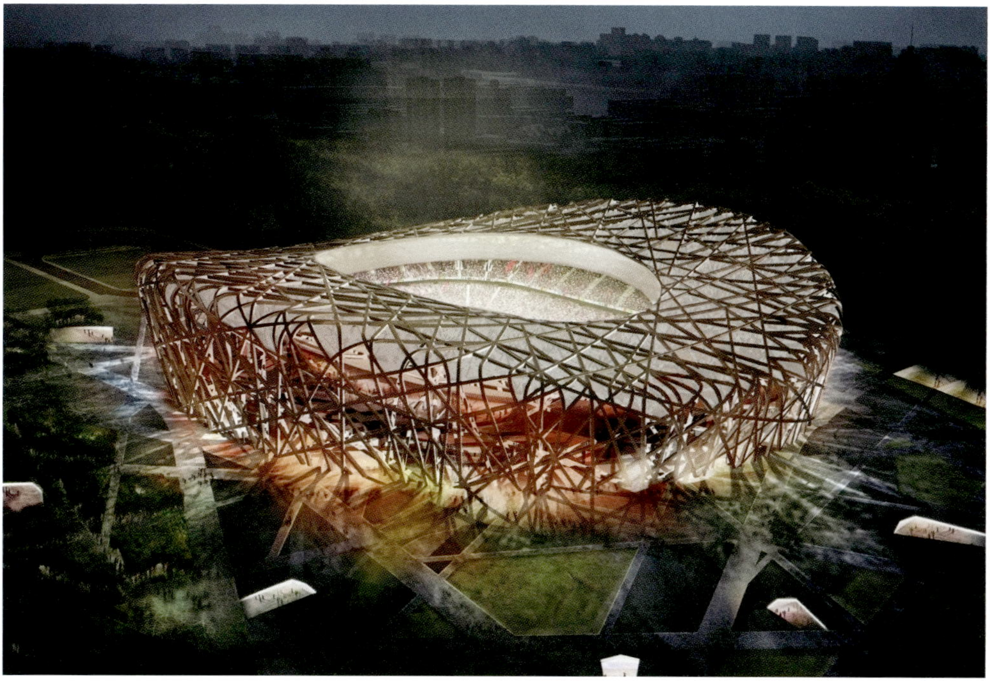

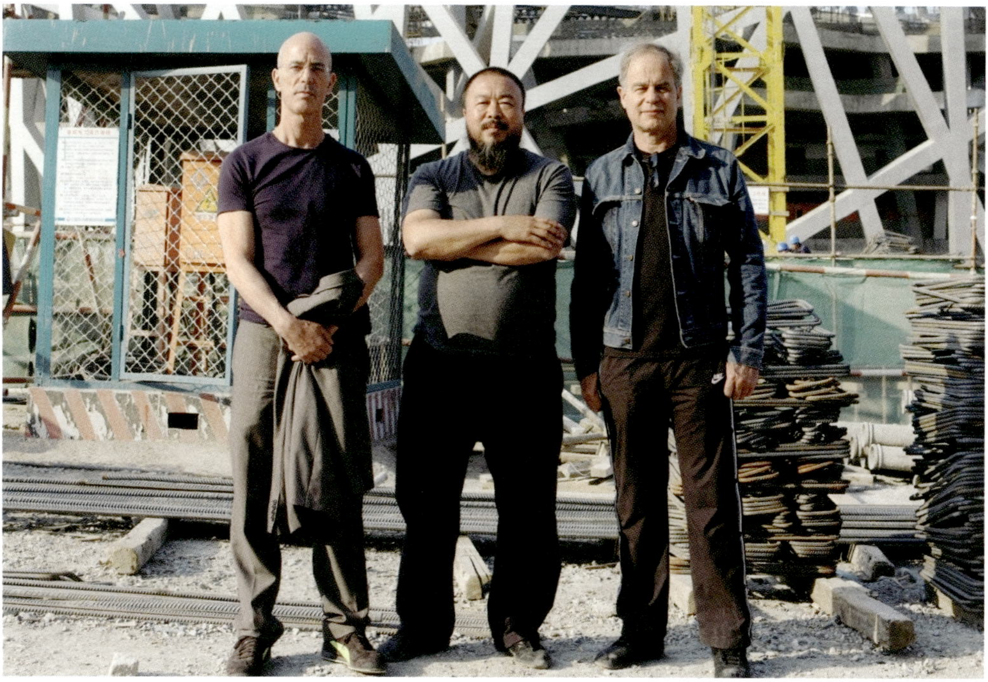

NATIONAL STADIUM, Beijing 2002–2008 (collaboration with Herzog & de Meuron); project visualization (top); Jacques Herzog, Ai Weiwei, and Pierre de Meuron at the construction site, 2008 (bottom) | 385

"I see the Beijing National Stadium as an architectural project. I accepted
Herzog & de Meuron's invitation to collaborate on the design, and our proposal
won the competition. From beginning to end, I stayed with the project. I am
committed to fostering relationships between a city and its architecture. I am
also keen on encouraging participation and exchange during mass events that are
meaningful for humankind. I have no regrets about the role I played; the stadium
is a work of great quality and design. I only withdrew from participating in fake
performances laden with propaganda. I disagreed with the approach, and did not
want my name associated with it. The Beijing opening ceremony had no sensitivity
for the Chinese people; it even had the police force dancing on the fields. This is
the fantasy of a totalitarian society. It was a nightmare… The Beijing Olympics
were a fake smile, an elaborate costume party with the sole intention of glorifying
the country." — AI WEIWEI

Ich sehe das Nationalstadion von Peking als reines Architekturprojekt. Ich nahm die
Einladung von Herzog & de Meuron an, mit ihnen an dem Entwurf zusammenzuarbeiten.
Unser Vorschlag gewann den ausgeschriebenen Wettbewerb. Ich war von Anfang bis Ende des
Projekts daran beteiligt. Ich setze mich stets für eine Architektur ein, die enge Beziehun-
gen zur Stadt hat. Ich bin sehr daran interessiert, dass die Menschen an für sie bedeutsamen
Großveranstaltungen teilnehmen und ihre Gedanken austauschen. Die Rolle, die ich beim
Bau gespielt habe, bedauere ich also nicht: Das Stadion ist ein Werk von hoher Qualität
und gutem Design. Ich habe mich lediglich von der Teilnahme an verlogenen Auftritten zu
Propagandazwecken zurückgezogen. Ich war mit den Inhalten nicht einverstanden und
wollte nicht, dass mein Name damit in Verbindung gebracht wird. Die Eröffnungszeremonie
der Spiele von Peking zeigte keinerlei Sensibilität gegenüber dem chinesischen Volk; sogar
Polizeikräfte tanzten dabei auf dem Feld herum. Das ist die Phantasie einer totalitären
Gesellschaft. Es war ein Albtraum … Die Olympischen Spiele von Peking waren ein falsches
Lächeln, ein aufwändiger Kostümball, der als einzige Absicht die Glorifizierung des Landes
verfolgte.

Je considère le stade national de Pékin comme un projet architectural. J'ai accepté
la proposition que m'ont faite Herzog & de Meuron de créer avec eux le design du stade,
et c'est notre projet qui a gagné le concours. J'ai accompagné ce projet du début à la fin.
Je suis convaincu qu'il faut stimuler la relation qui existe entre une ville et son architecture.
Je tiens également à encourager les phénomènes de participation et d'échange générés par
ces grands événements importants pour l'humanité. Je n'ai aucun regret quant au rôle que
j'ai joué dans ce projet; le design du stade est très réussi, c'est une construction de grande
qualité. J'ai seulement refusé de m'associer à des performances fausses organisées à des
fins de propagande. Je désapprouve cette approche et ne voulais pas que mon nom y soit
associé. La cérémonie d'ouverture des Jeux de Pékin n'a témoigné d'aucune empathie
envers le peuple chinois; parmi les danseurs, il y avait même des représentants des forces
de l'ordre. C'est le fantasme d'une société totalitaire. C'était un cauchemar… Les Jeux
olympiques de Pékin ont été comme un sourire faux, une minutieuse mascarade seulement
destinée à glorifier le pays.

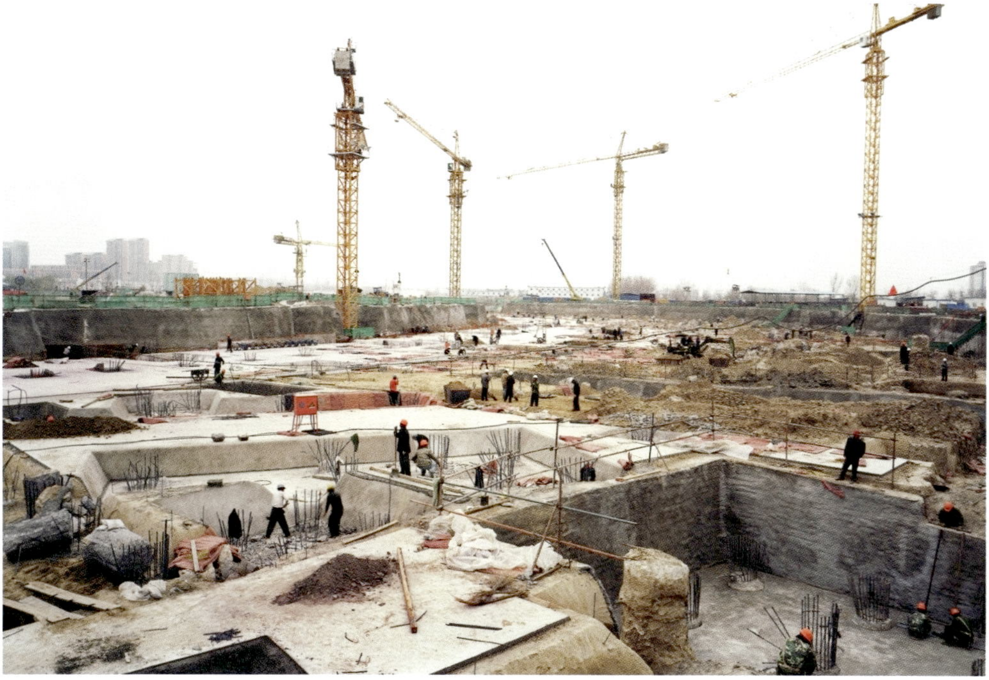

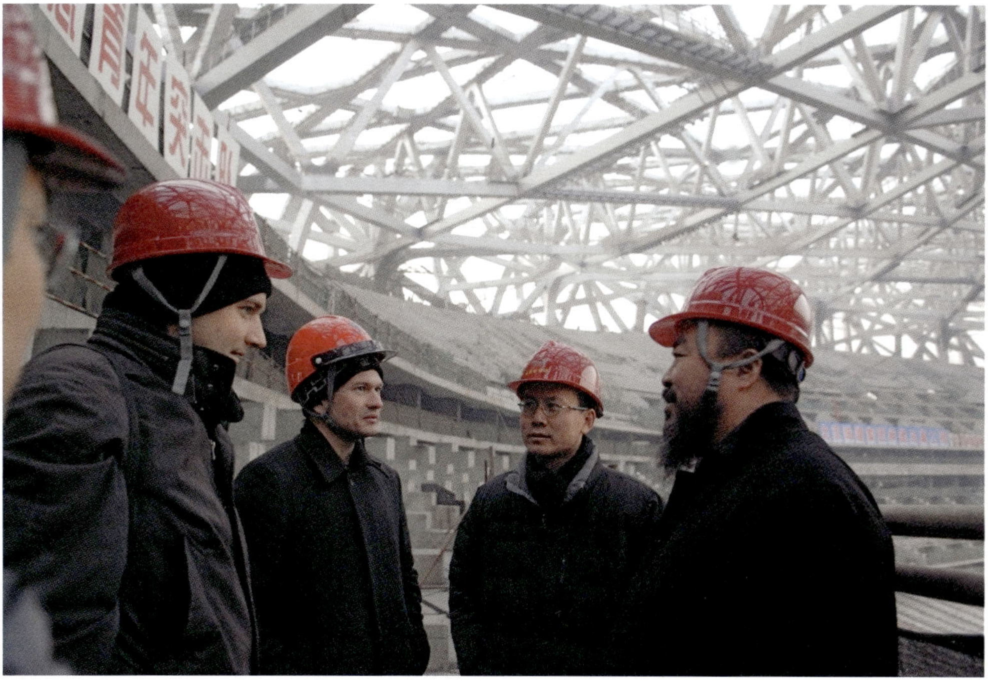

BIRD'S NEST, 2005–2008, C-prints, various dimensions (above and overleaf)

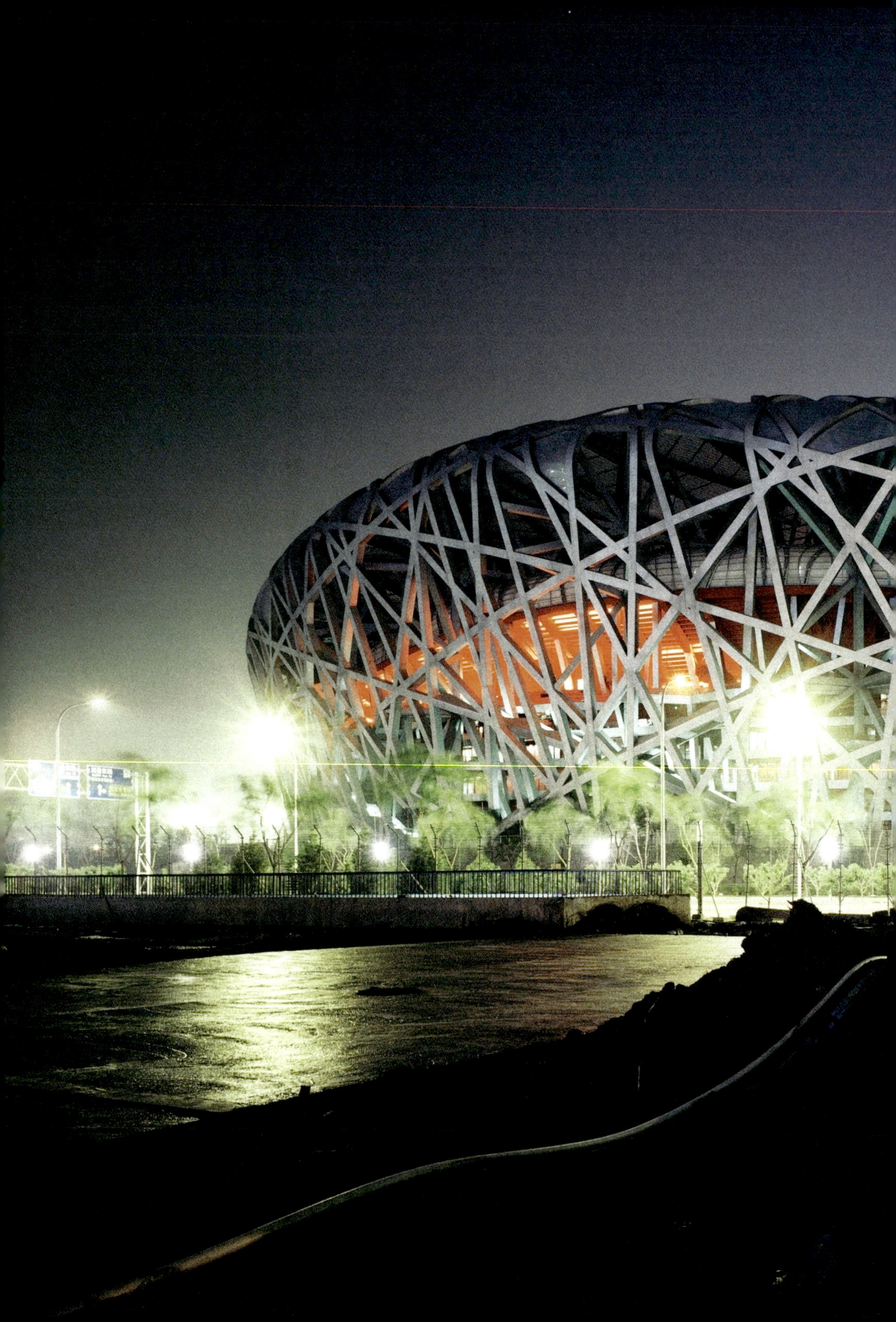

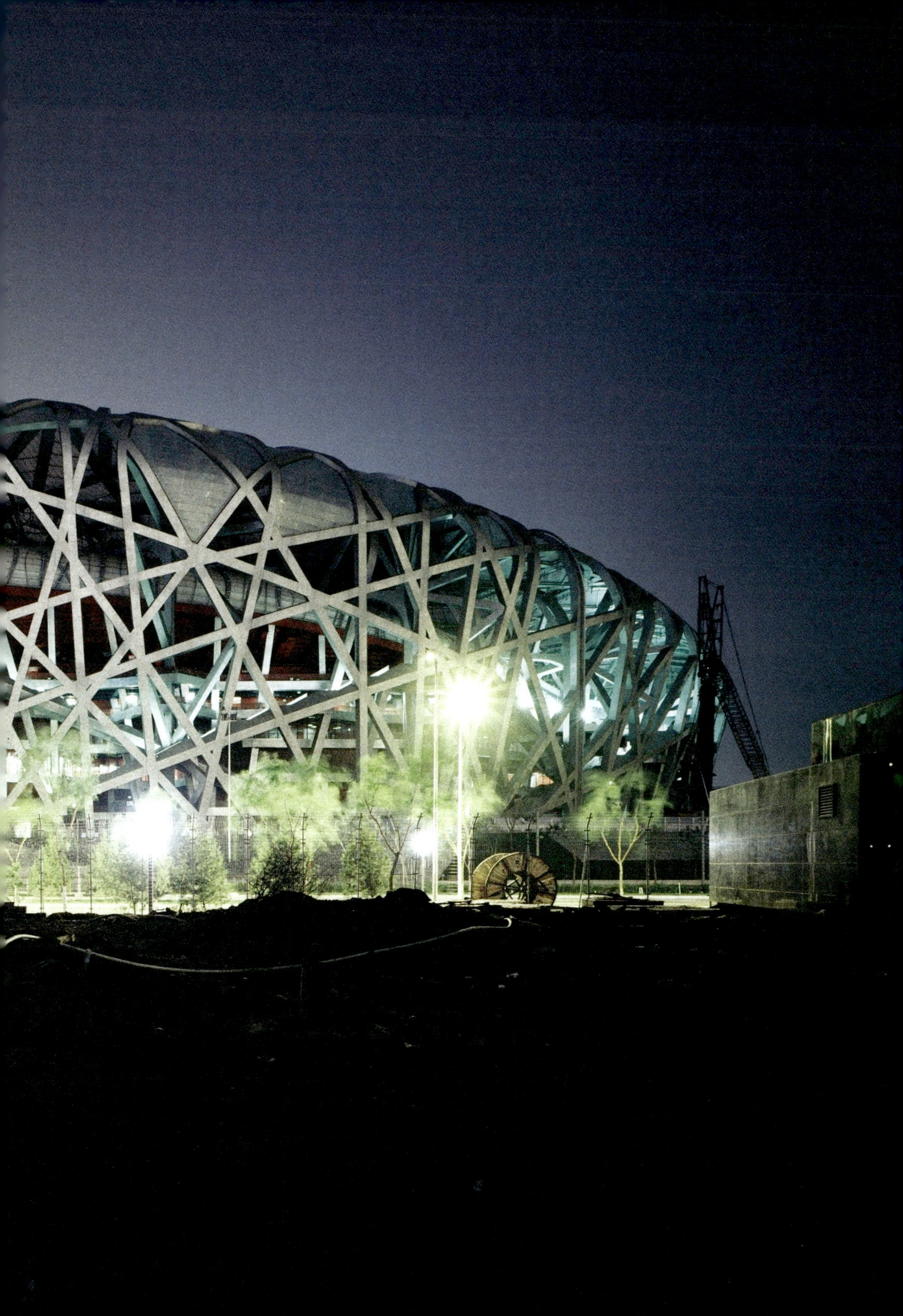

"When we were young we all rode Forever bicycles when we went to forage
for kindling, and it had a reputation for being a very sturdy bicycle. My work with
them started from the question of how can the bicycle use its structure to grow
according to its own logic. *Very Yao* consists of 90 Forever bicycles, but it's very
much like just throwing a pile of bikes together. The title comes from the name
of the blog of Yang Jia, who was arrested and violated by Shanghai police after
they had suspected his rented bicycle was stolen. The judicial system is so brutal,
they do not recognize the individual's cry, so after his appeals were fruitless, he
decided to claim justice by violence himself. He killed six policemen at Zhabei
police station, and in November 2008 he was executed." — AI WEIWEI

Als Kinder fuhren wir auf Fahrrädern der Marke Forever und suchten nach Feuerholz.
Das waren sehr stabile Fahrräder. Meine Arbeit dazu ging von der Fragestellung aus, wie ich
die Struktur des Fahrrads nutzen könnte, um es seiner eigenen Logik gemäß wachsen zu
lassen. *Very Yao* besteht aus 90 Forever-Rädern, aber es sieht eher so aus, als hätte man sie
zusammengeworfen. Der Titel bezieht sich auf den Blog eines Mannes namens Yang Jia, der
von der Polizei in Shanghai verhaftet und misshandelt wurde, weil sie ihn verdächtigten, sein
Mietfahrrad gestohlen zu haben. Die Justiz ist derart brutal, dass sie den Hilfeschrei eines
Individuums nicht hört. Nachdem seine Appelle auf taube Ohren gestoßen waren, beschloss
er, sich sein Recht mit Gewalt zu verschaffen. Er tötete sechs Polizisten auf dem Polizeirevier
in Zhabei und wurde im November 2008 hingerichtet.

Quand nous étions jeunes, nous avions tous des vélos Forever avec lesquels nous allions
chercher du petit bois, ces vélos étaient connus pour leur solidité. Je suis parti du question-
nement sur la manière dont on peut utiliser la structure du vélo et sa logique pour en faire
quelque chose de plus grand. *Very Yao* est composé de 90 vélos Forever, c'est comme une
montagne de vélos. Le titre de l'œuvre est une référence au blog de Yang Jia, qui a été arrêté
et maltraité par la police de Shanghai qui croyait que son vélo de location était volé. Le système judiciaire est très violent, il n'écoute pas les individus. Yang Jia ayant fait appel en vain,
il a finalement décidé de se faire justice lui-même, par la violence. Il a tué six policiers à la
gare de Zhabei et a été exécuté en novembre 2008.

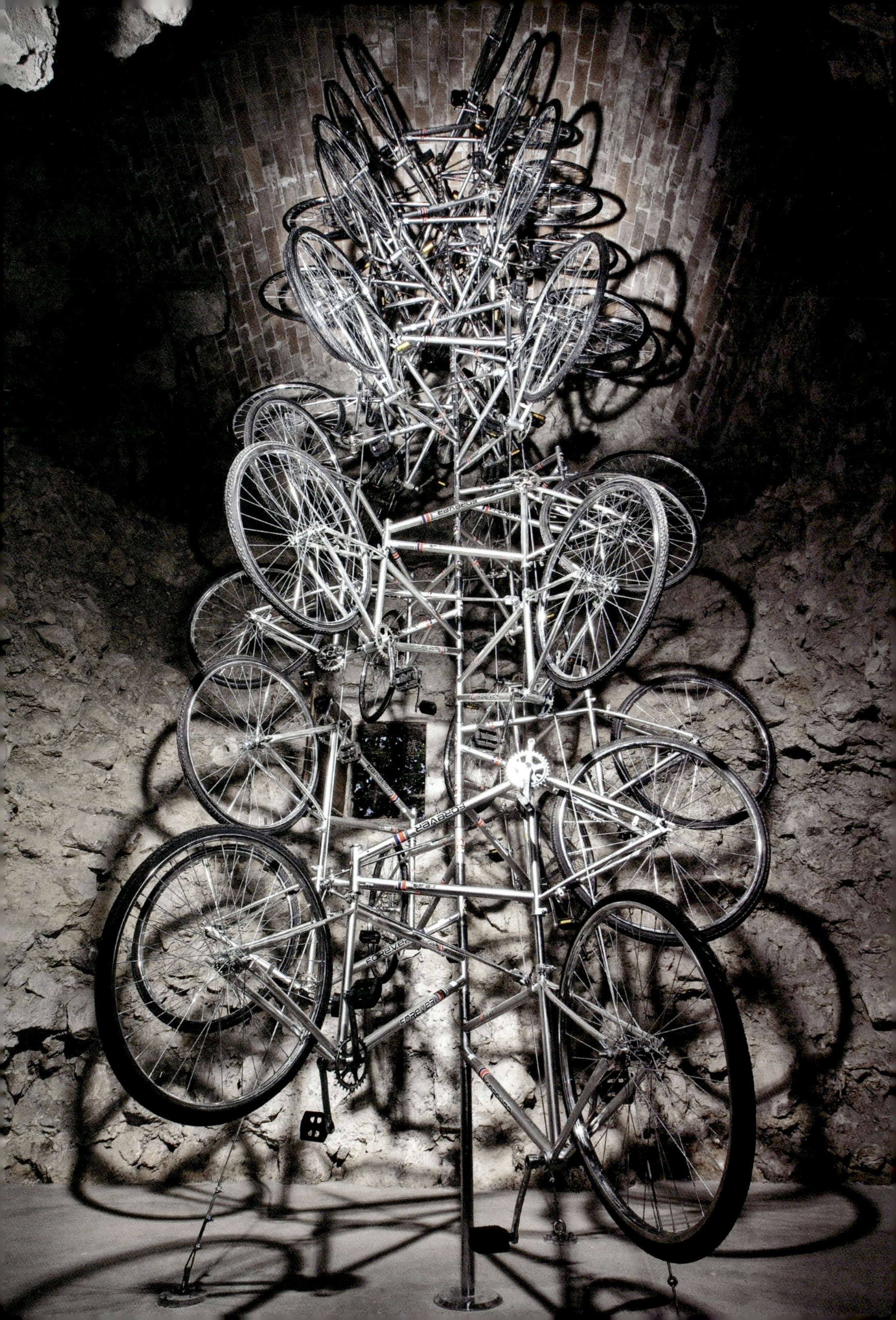

"All the stools are from families in the northern provinces. They're from different ages, a few hundred years apart, all collected by antique dealers. And those stools have traces of the earlier usage. Some were originally used in the temple and are now worth more; the rest are simply from households. Most of them have been through the Cultural Revolution, because stools are so practical and they show no traces of any specific culture. So they survived." — AI WEIWEI

Alle Hocker kommen von Familien aus den nördlichen Provinzen. Sie stammen aus unterschiedlichen Zeiten quer durch die Jahrhunderte und wurden von Antiquitäten-händlern gesammelt. Diese Hocker zeigen Spuren ihrer vormaligen Benutzer. Manche wurden ursprünglich in Tempeln benutzt, was ihren Wert steigert, die übrigen kommen aus einfachen Haushalten. Die meisten von ihnen haben die Kulturrevolution überstanden, weil Hocker so praktisch sind und auf keine spezifische Kultur hinweisen. Darum haben sie überlebt.

Tous ces tabourets appartenaient à des familles des provinces du nord. Ils datent de différentes époques, sur une période de quelques siècles, et ont tous été récupérés par des antiquaires. Tous ces tabourets présentent des traces de leur utilisation antérieure. Certains proviennent de temples et valent davantage d'argent aujourd'hui ; d'autres ont simplement été utilisés par des familles. La plupart d'entre eux ont traversé la révolution culturelle, car ces tabourets sont très pratiques et ne présentent la marque d'aucune culture spécifique. Ils ont donc survécu.

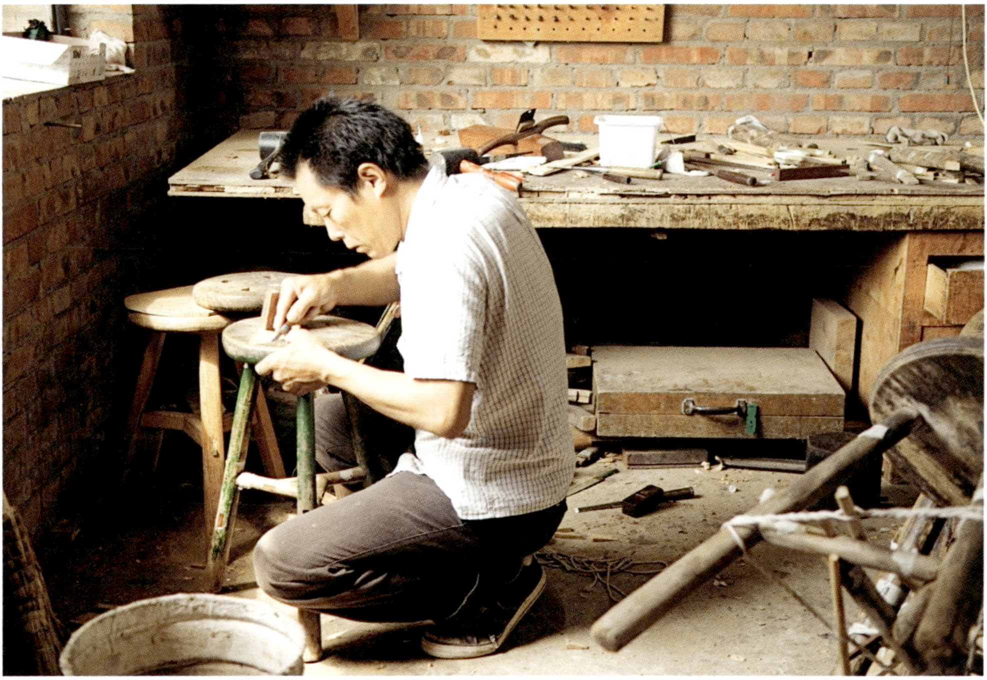

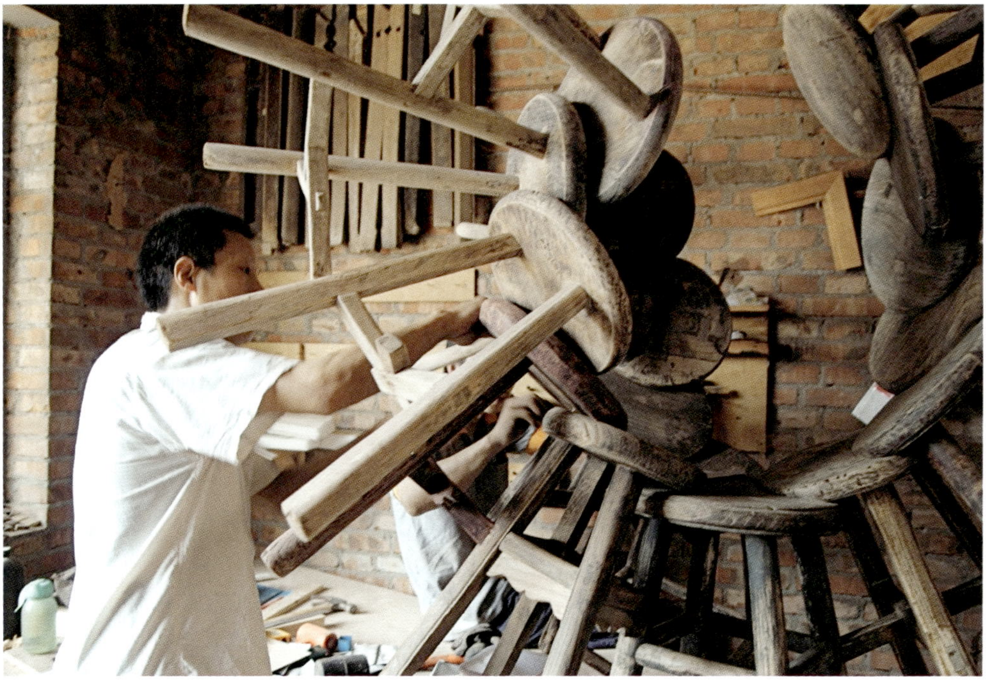

Production views of GRAPES, 2008, 16 wooden Qing Dynasty stools, each 65¾ x 70⅞ x 61¾ inches | 393

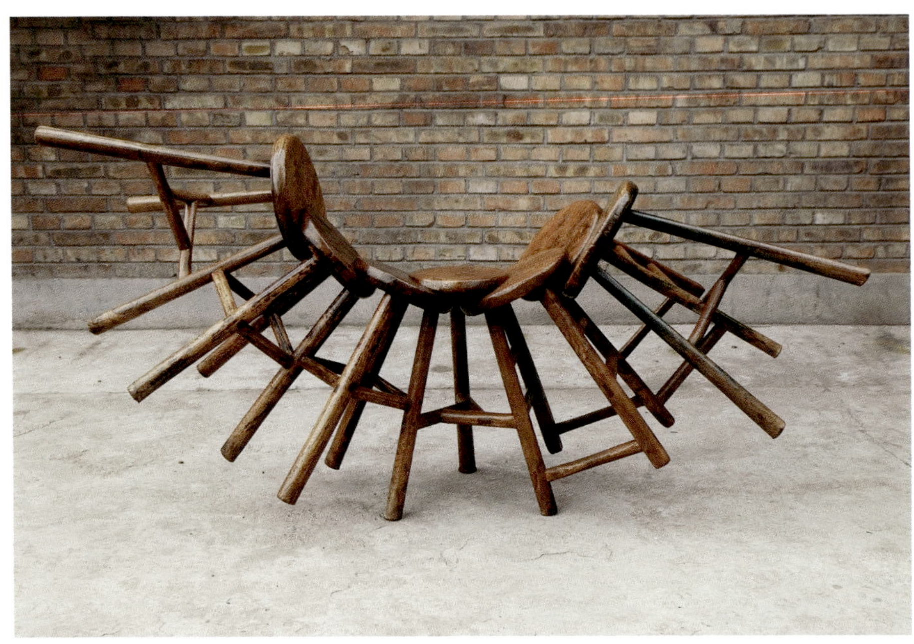

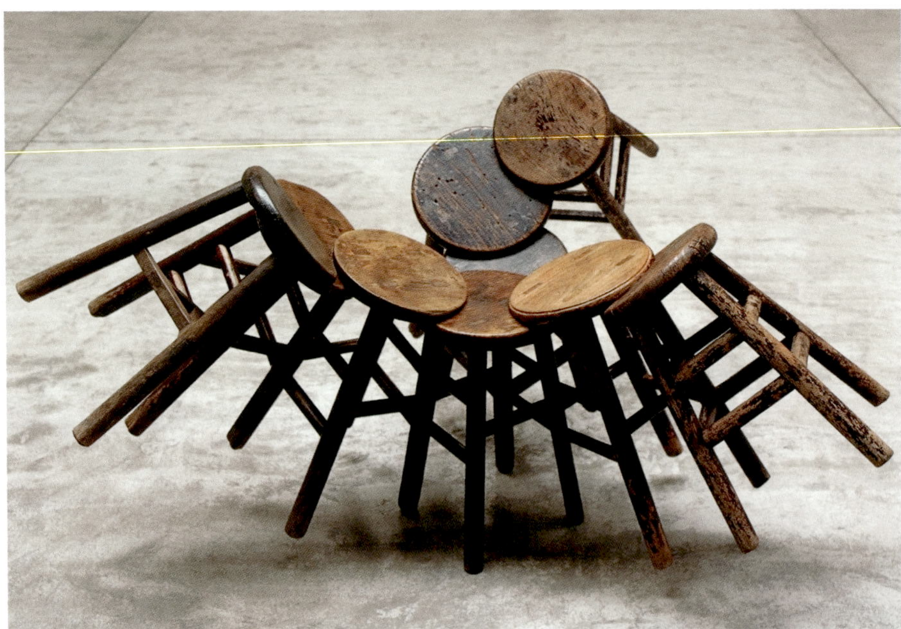

GRAPES, 2008, 7 wooden Qing Dynasty stools, 32¾ x 70⅛ x 27½ inches (top); GRAPES, 2007,
9 wooden Qing Dynasty stools, 31⅛ x 53⅞ x 63 inches (bottom) | Opposite: GRAPES, 2010,
40 wooden Qing Dynasty stools, 87¾ x 73¼ x 74¾ inches; | Overleaf: BOWLS OF PEARLS, 2006,
porcelain, freshwater pearls, 2 pieces, each 15 x 38½ inches (foreground); TEAHOUSE, 2009,
compressed tea, 70⅞ x 47¼ x 70⅞ inches (background); Mori Art Museum, Tokyo 2009 |

 Pages 398/399: SNAKE CEILING, 2009, backpacks, dimensions variable; Mori Art Museum, Tokyo 2009

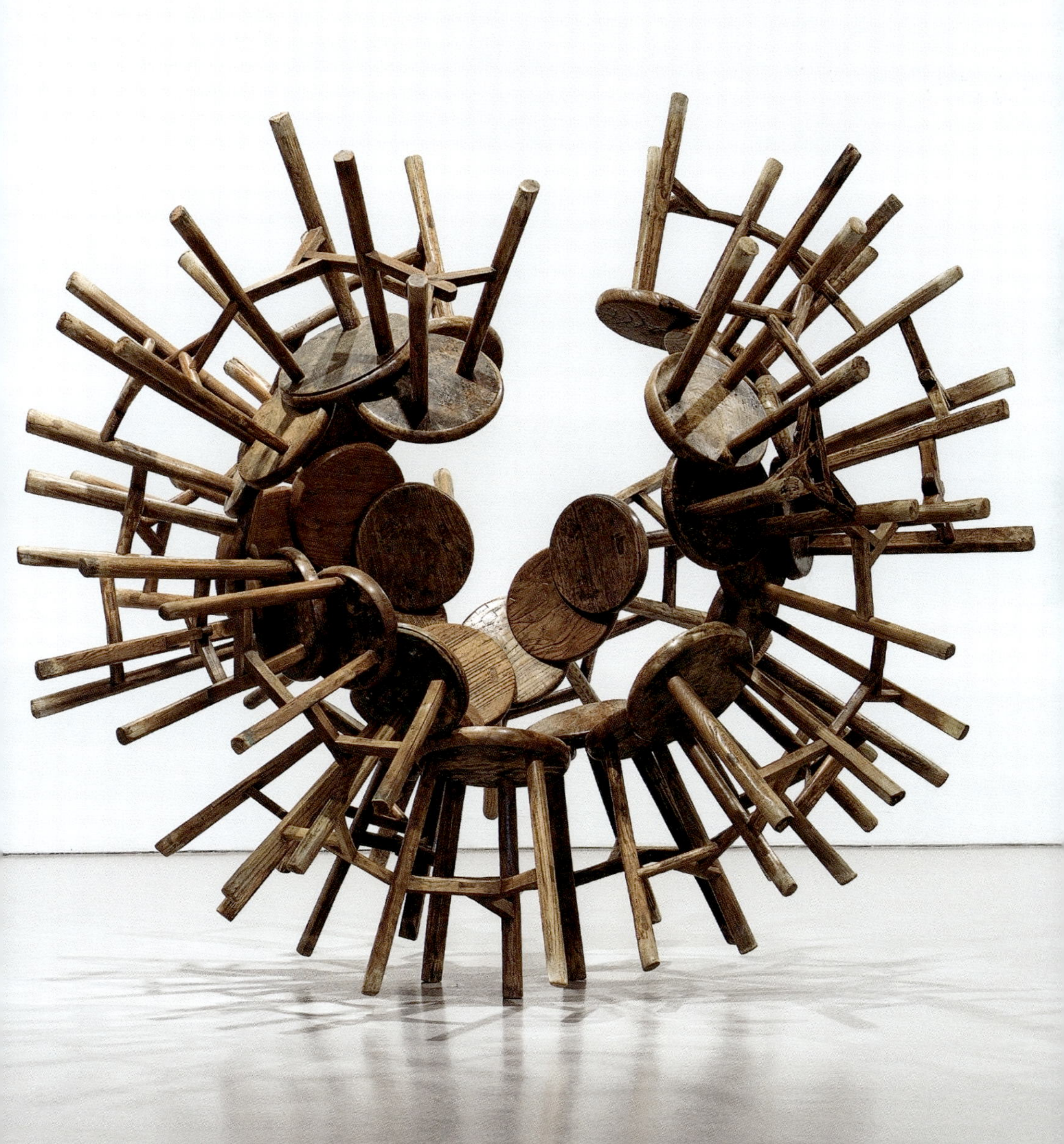

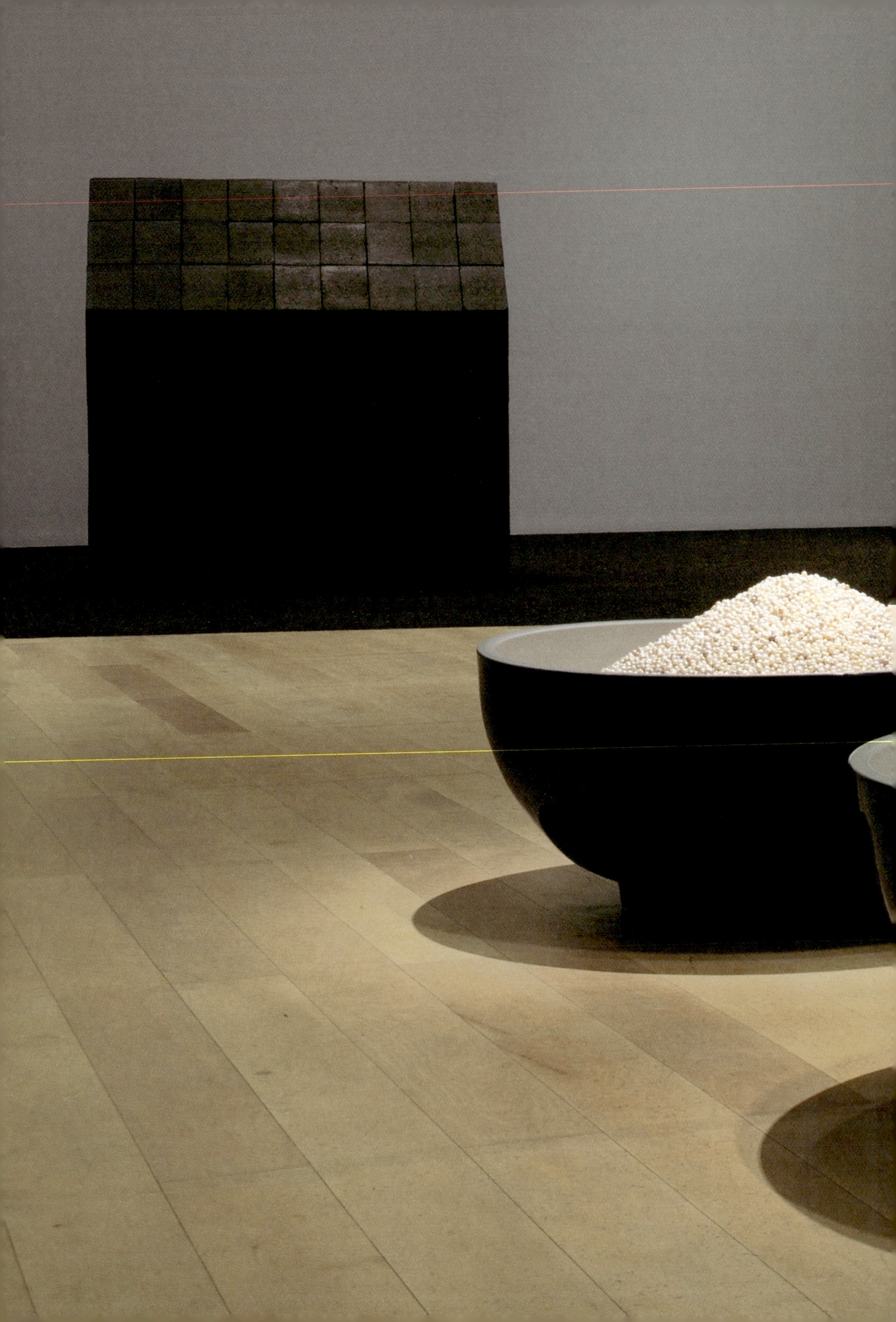

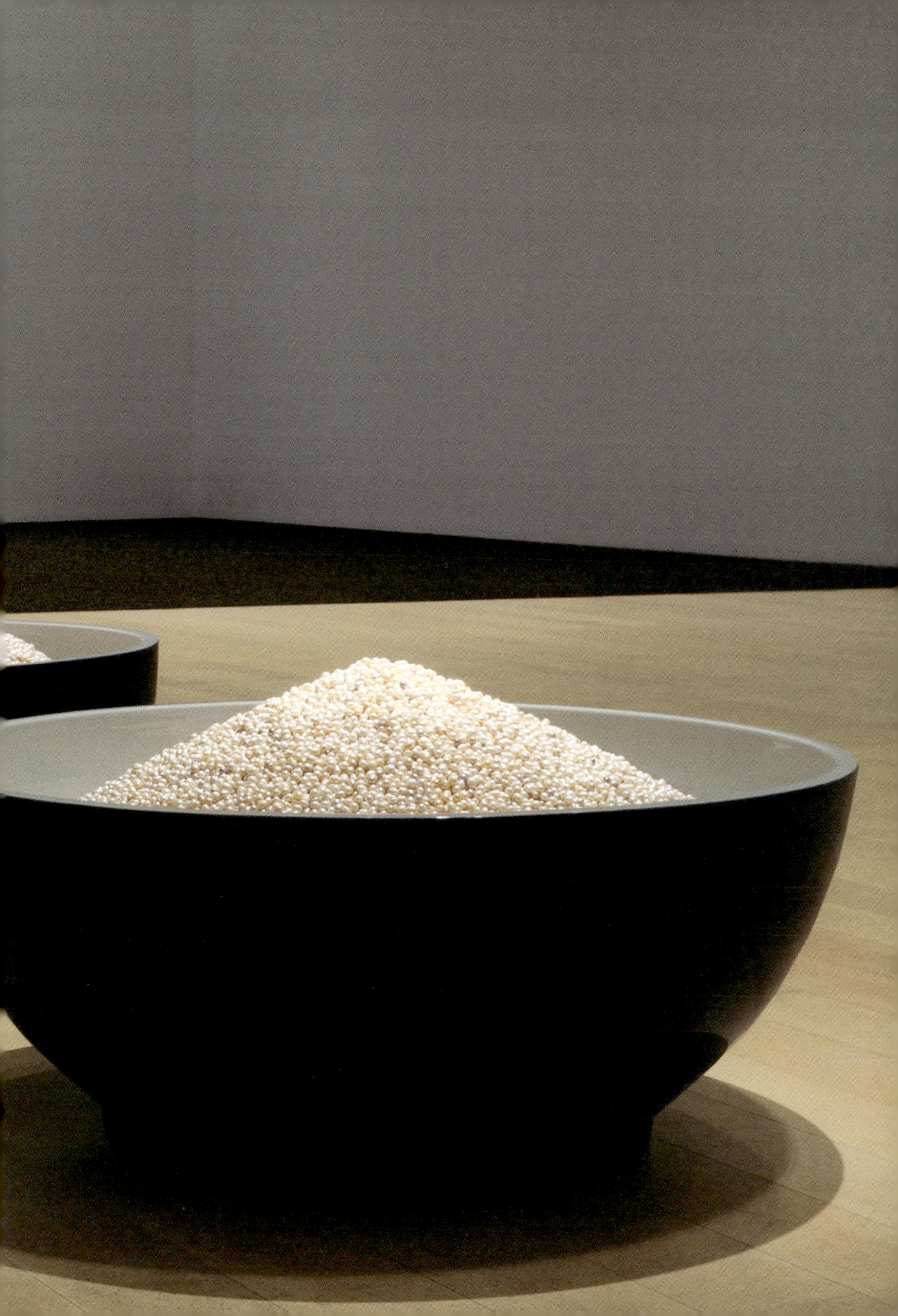

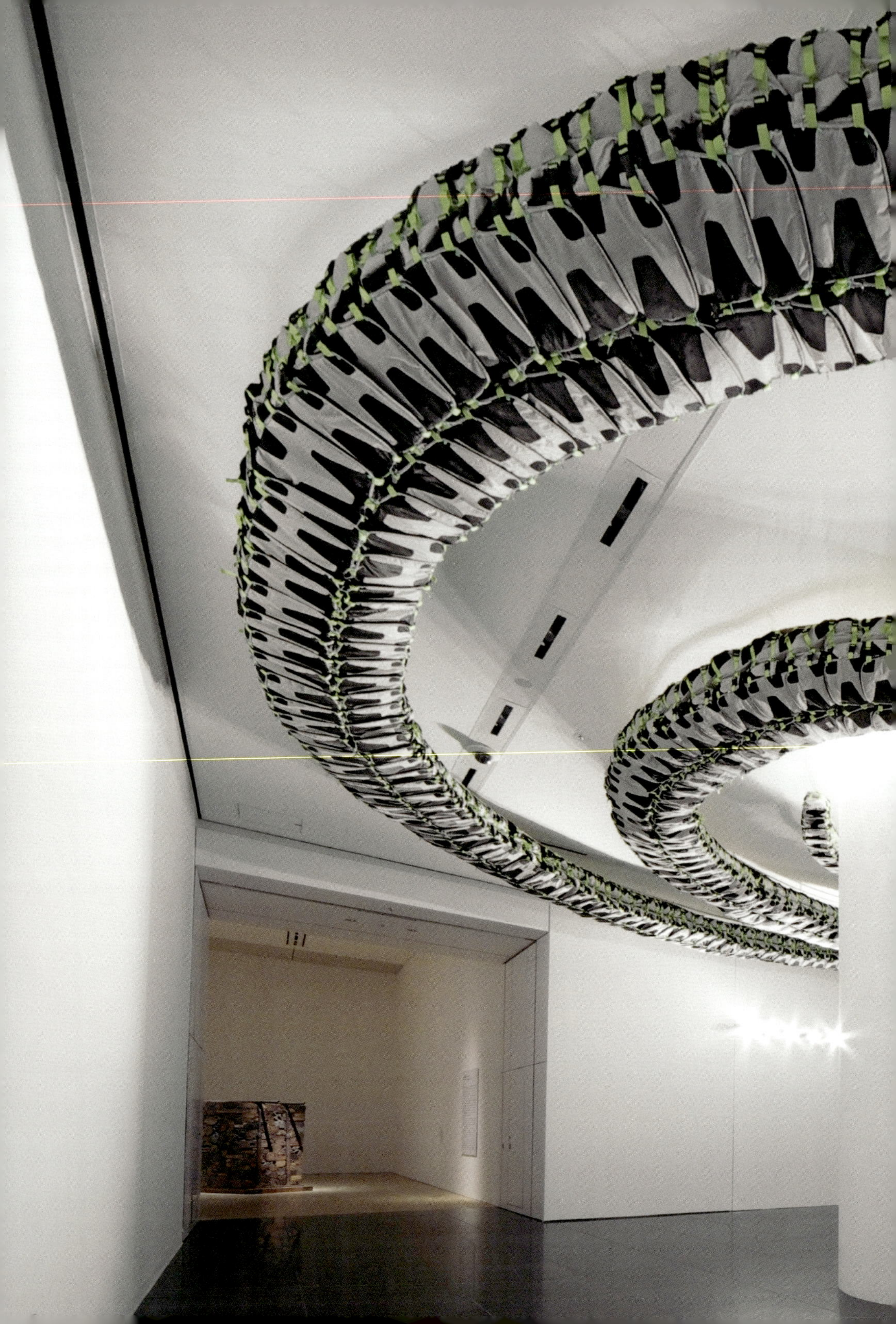

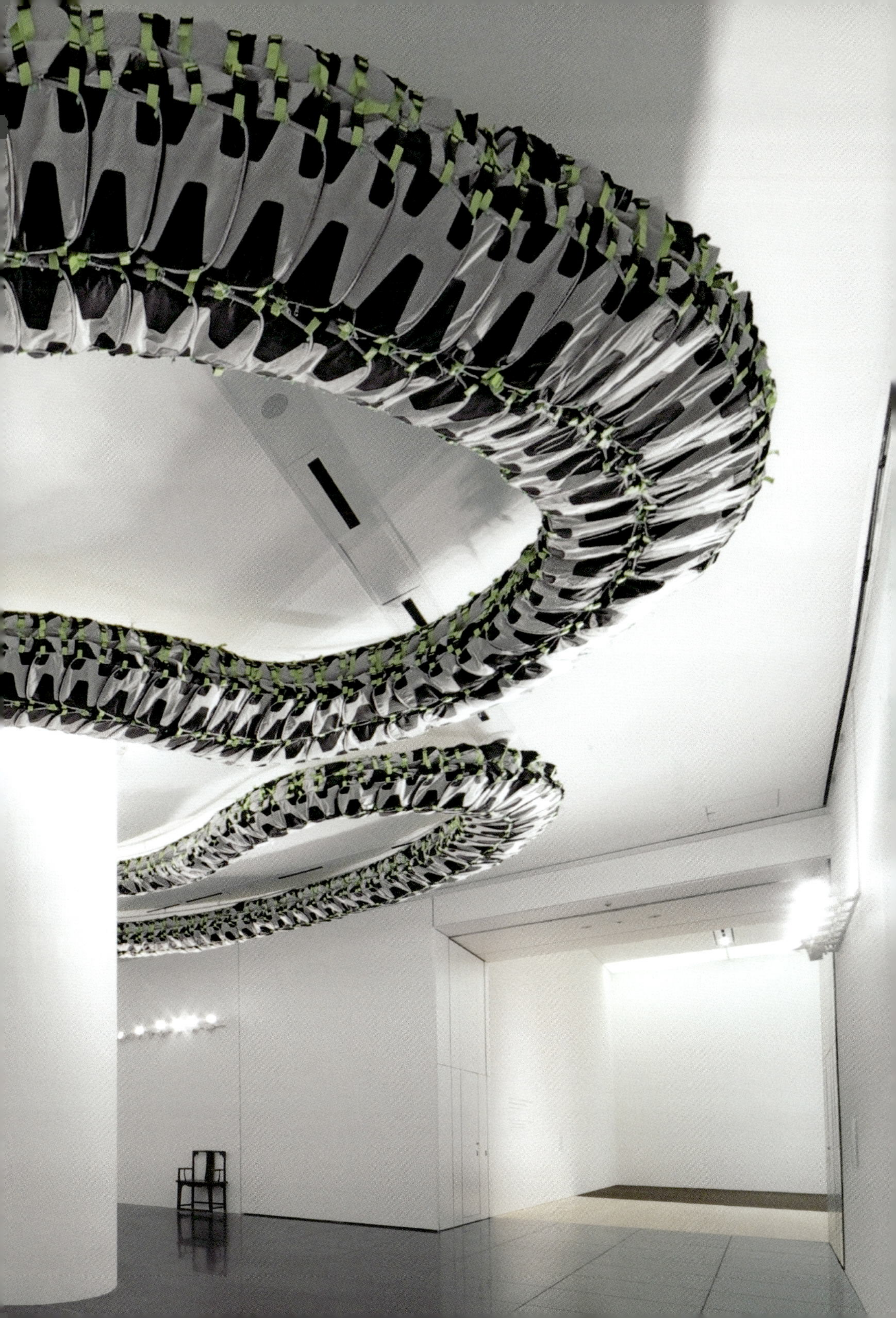

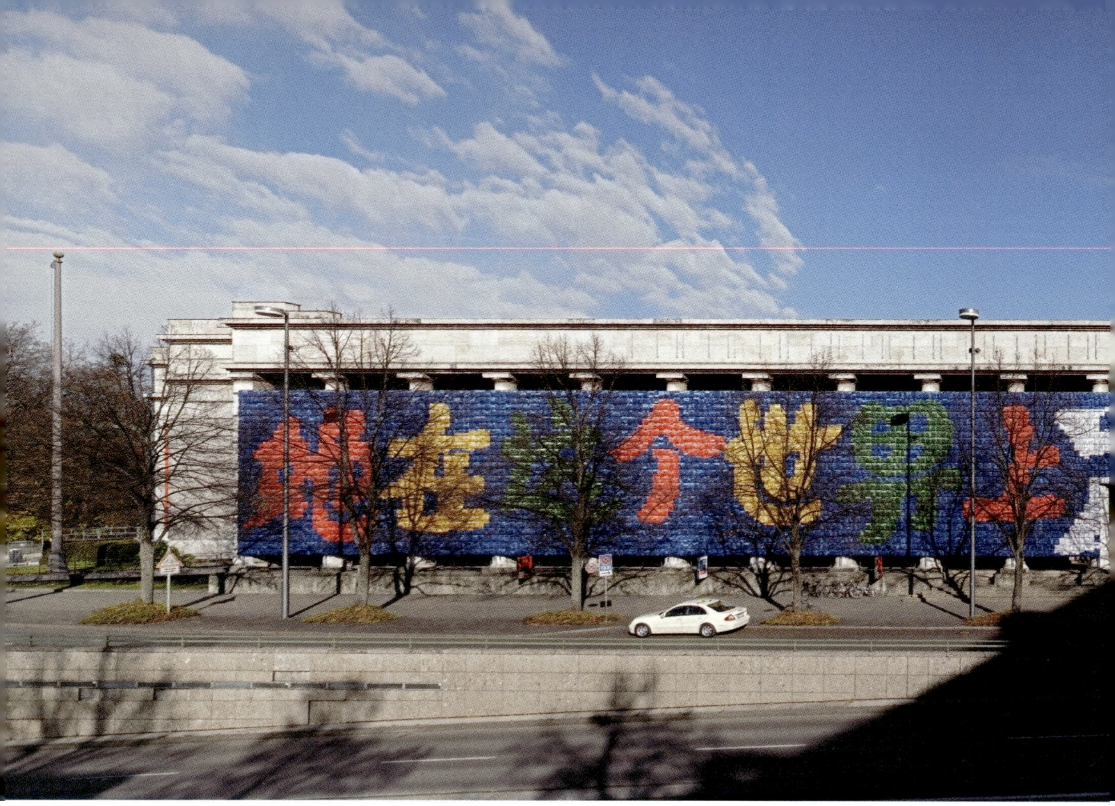

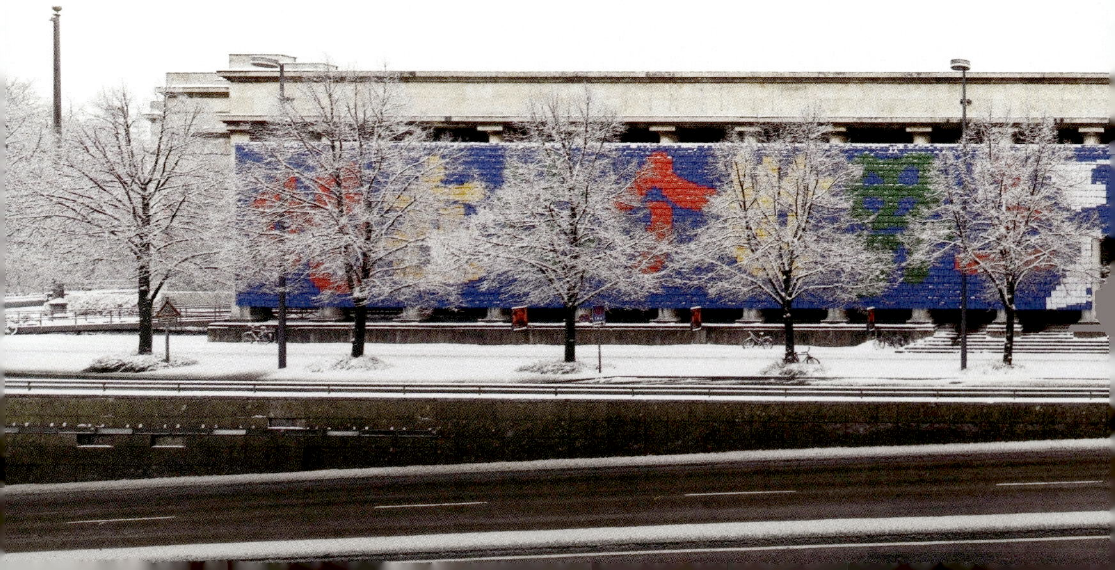

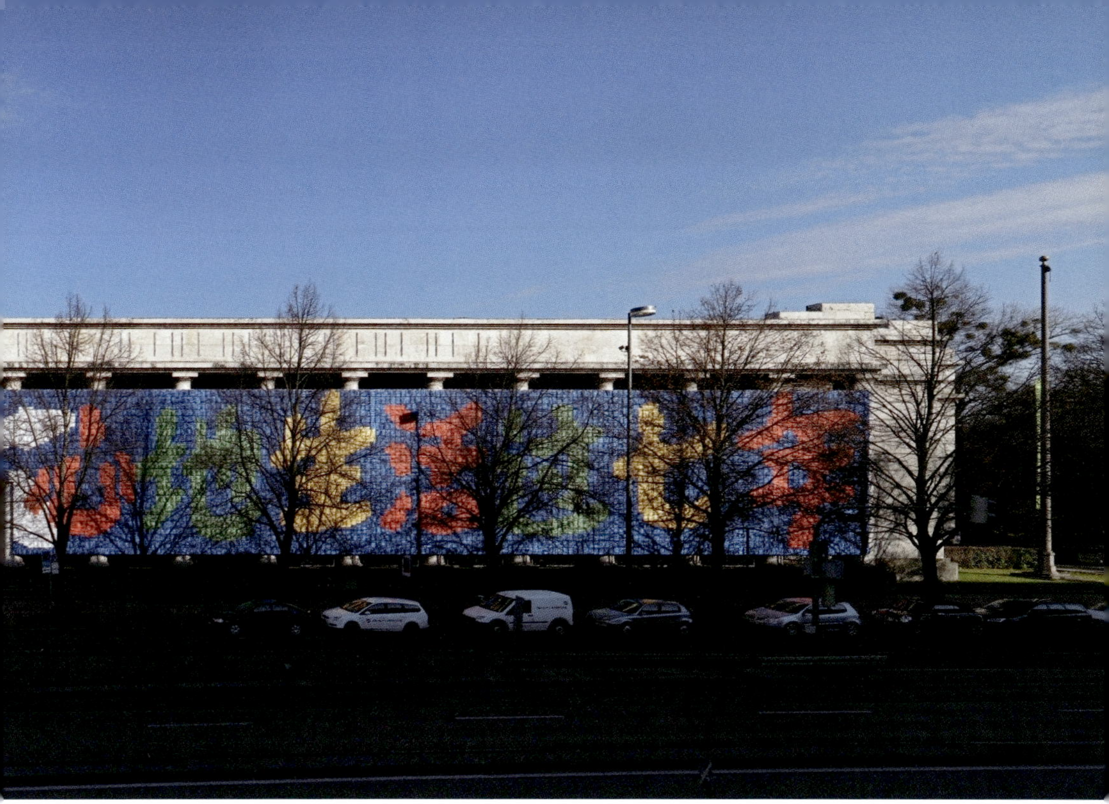

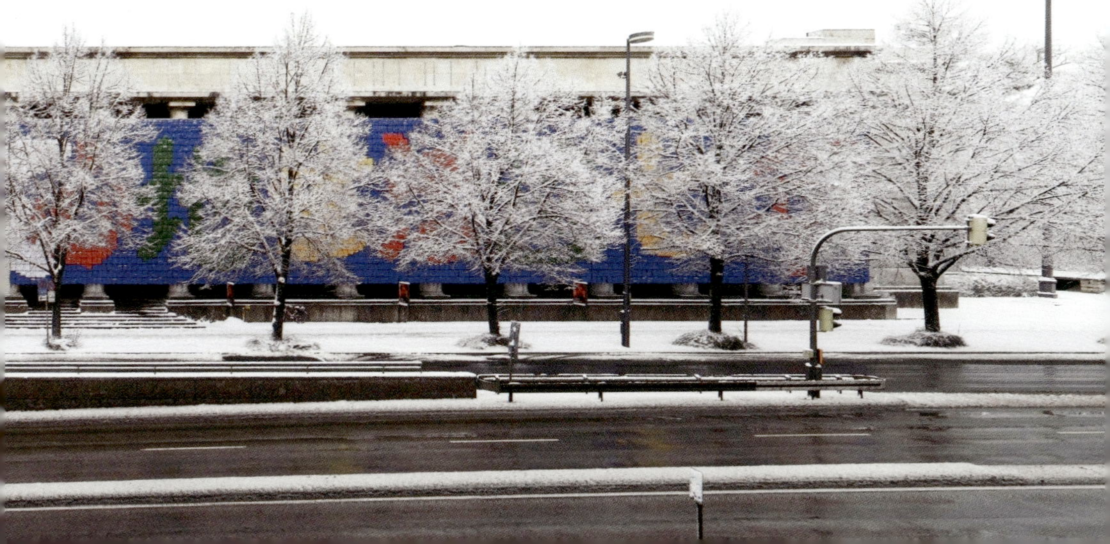

"The idea to use backpacks for *Remembering* came from my visit to Sichuan after the earthquake in May 2008. During the earthquake many schools collapsed. Thousands of young students lost their lives, and you could see bags and study material everywhere … The sentence on the backpacks is from a letter by the mother of a girl who died in the earthquake, who wrote: 'She lived happily in this world for seven years.' … *Rooted Upon* is like a map pointing to the events and people who have been occupying the floor of the Haus der Kunst from 1937 to today, transforming the historical architecture into a soft comfortable condition." — AI WEIWEI

Der Gedanke, für *Remembering* Rucksäcke zu verwenden, kam mir, als ich nach dem Erdbeben im Mai 2008 Sichuan besuchte. Bei dem Erdbeben waren viele Schulgebäude eingestürzt. Tausende von jungen Schülern hatten ihr Leben verloren, und überall lagen ihre Schultaschen und Unterrichtsmaterialien verstreut … Die Rucksäcke bilden einen Satz, der aus dem Brief einer Mutter stammt, deren kleine Tochter bei dem Erdbeben ums Leben gekommen ist: „Sie lebte sieben Jahre lang glücklich auf dieser Welt." … *Rooted Upon* ist wie eine Landkarte, welche die Spuren der Menschen und Ereignisse auf diesem Fußboden im Haus der Kunst von 1937 bis heute zeigt. Die historische Architektur wird dabei in einen weichen, gemütlichen Zustand versetzt.

L'idée d'utiliser des sacs à dos pour *Remembering* m'est venue en me rendant dans le Sichuan après le séisme, en mai 2008. De nombreuses écoles s'étaient effondrées. Des milliers d'écoliers ont perdu la vie, et, partout, on voyait des sacs à dos et du matériel scolaire… La phrase formée par les sacs à dos vient d'une lettre qu'une mère a écrite après avoir perdu sa fille dans le tremblement de terre : « Elle a vécu heureuse sur cette terre pendant sept ans. » … *Rooted Upon* est comme une carte mettant en lumière les traces des hommes et des événements ayant occupé le sol de la Haus der Kunst de 1937 à aujourd'hui. L'architecture historique est ainsi transposée dans une ambiance de douceur et de confort.

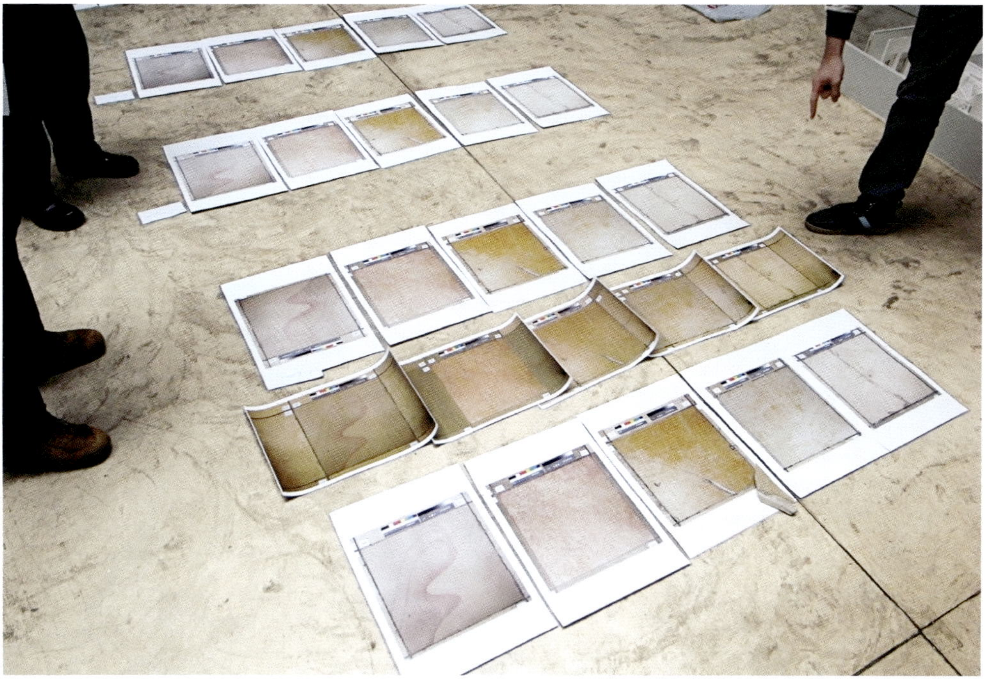

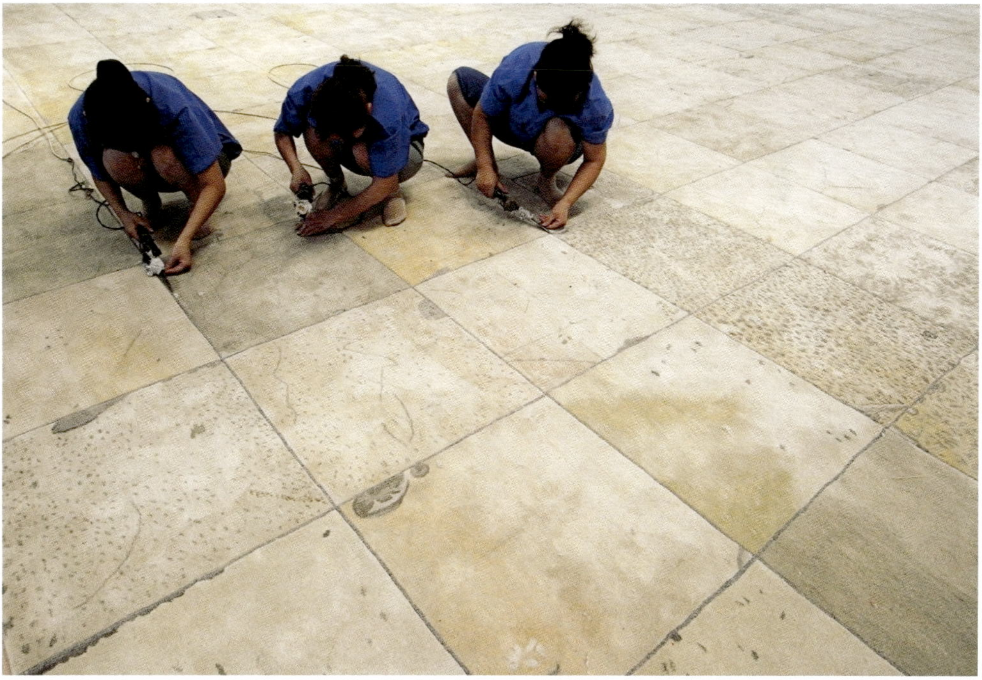

Production and installation of SOFT GROUND, 2009, wool,
417 ¼ x 401 ⅝ inches, Haus der Kunst, Munich 2009 | 403

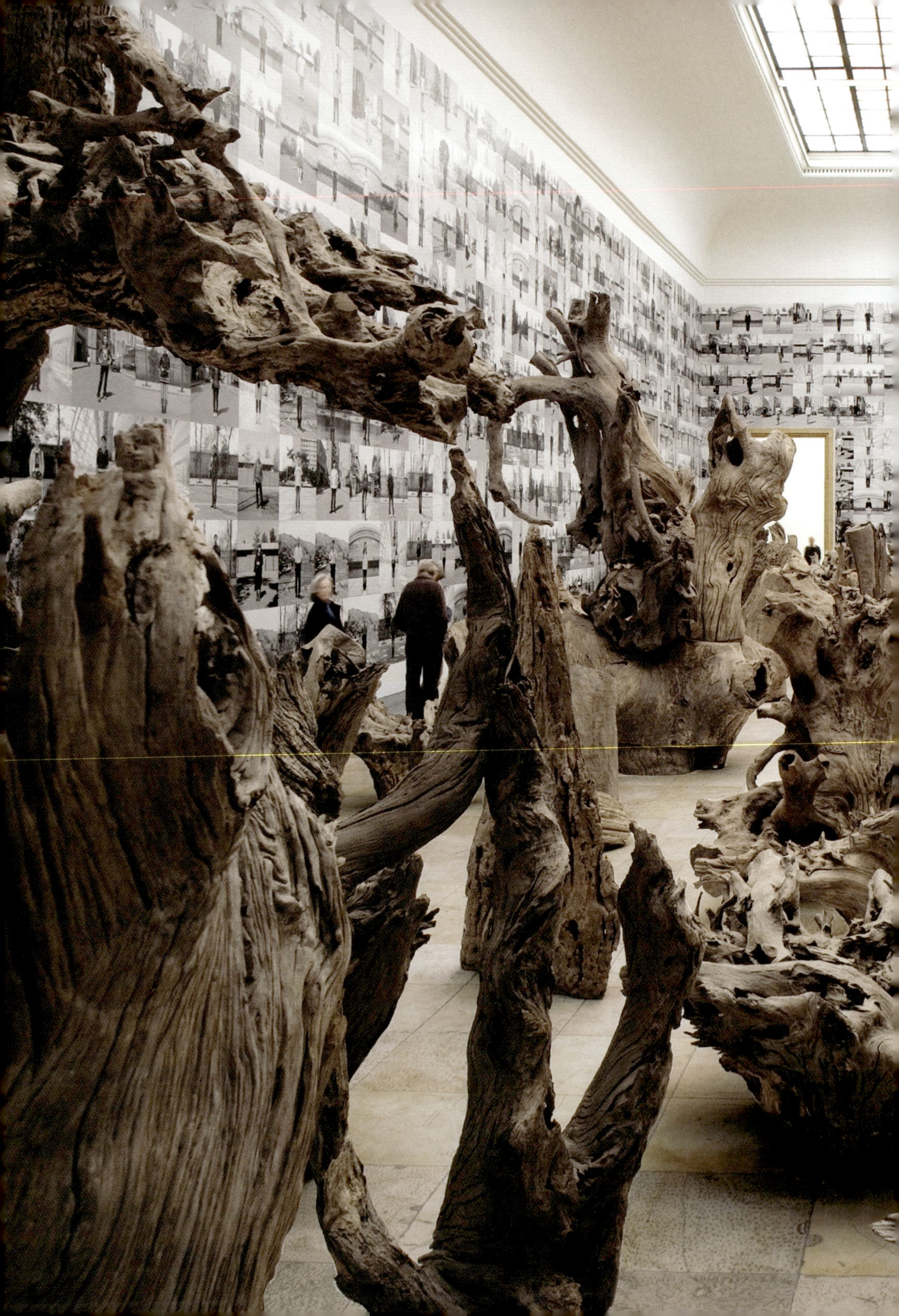

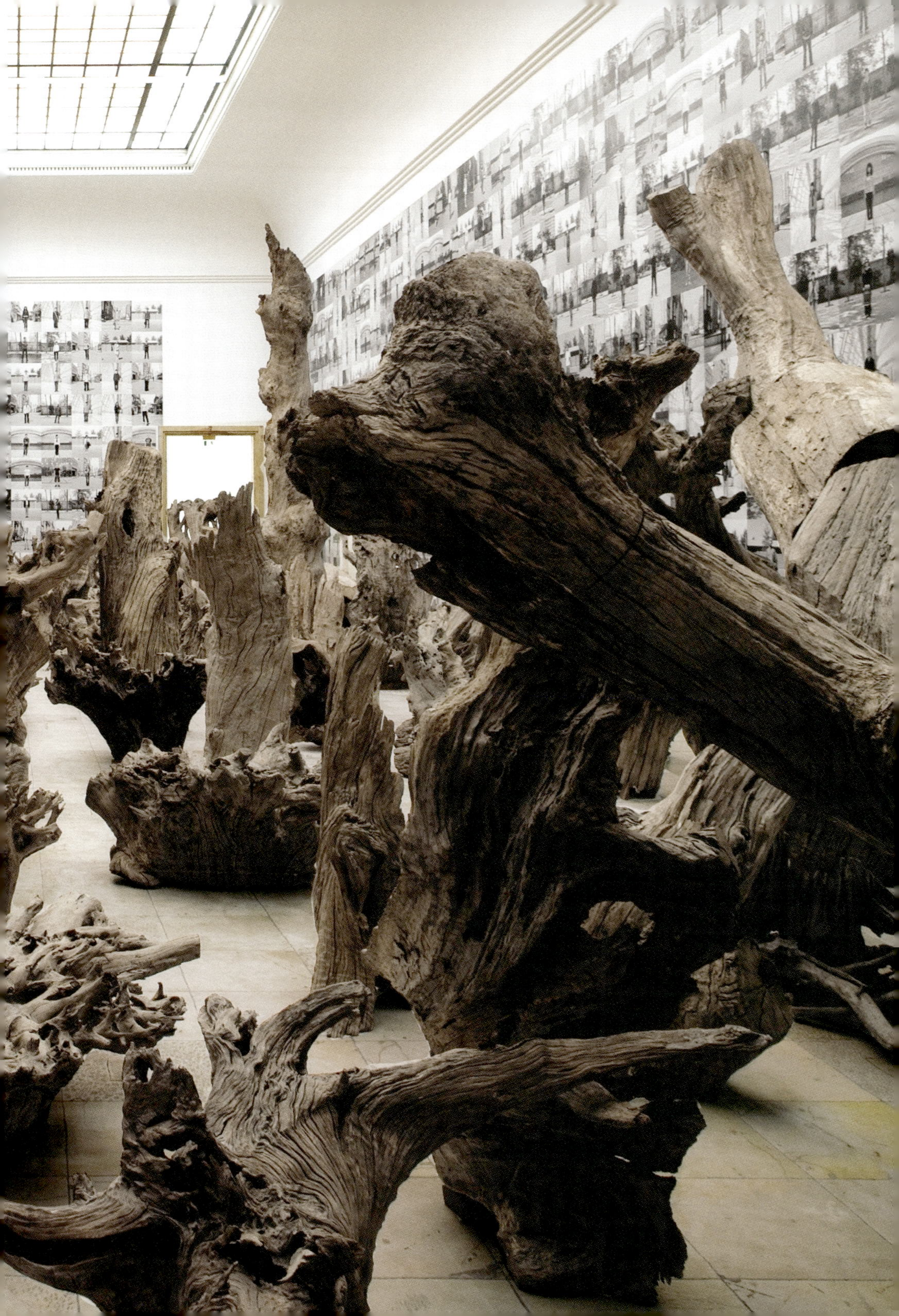

"Each seed appears as this kind of beautiful gray, with the details of the
white lines and the evenly shaded gray color. And each seed is individual yet at
the same time looks identical to the others. When they're accumulated in this
large number, they become something else. People will try to understand how it's
been made and then what's behind those numbers. You see it and you don't see
it because it disappears through this massiveness. But the meaning of the work
has nothing at all to do with its appearance. And the understanding of the process
also goes against its appearance. So what you see is not what it means. And if
what you see is not what it means, then there's a struggle there." — AI WEIWEI

Jeder einzelne Sonnenblumenkern hat dieses wunderbare Grau, mit den Details der
weißen Linien auf dem gleichmäßig grauen Grund. Jeder Kern ist individuell gestaltet und
doch mit allen anderen identisch. Wenn sie in so großer Zahl zusammengehäuft werden,
kommt etwas ganz anderes dabei heraus. Die Menschen versuchen erst einmal, zu verstehen, wie die Kerne gemacht sind, und dann fragen sie nach der Bedeutung dieser riesigen
Menge. Man sieht sie und sieht sie wieder nicht, weil sie in der Masse verschwindet.
Aber die Bedeutung der Arbeit hat nichts mit ihrer Erscheinung zu tun. Und wenn man
den Entstehungsprozess kennt, widerspricht das im Grunde der äußeren Erscheinung.
Was man sieht, ist nicht das, was es bedeutet. Und wenn das, was man sieht, nicht das ist,
was es bedeutet, dann gibt es da einen Widerstreit.

Chacune de ces graines est d'un gris magnifique, au dégradé parfait, paré de lignes
blanches. Chacune est unique, et a pourtant l'air identique aux autres. L'accumulation de
ces graines en fait quelque chose d'autre. Les gens vont essayer de comprendre le pourquoi
de cette œuvre et ce qui se cache derrière ces chiffres. On voit, et en même temps on ne
voit pas, car tout disparaît derrière cette masse. Mais la signification de l'œuvre n'a rien à
voir avec son apparence. La compréhension du processus s'oppose elle aussi à son apparence.
Ce qu'on voit n'a rien à voir avec ce que ça veut dire. Et si ce qu'on voit n'est pas ce que ça
veut dire, il y a un conflit.

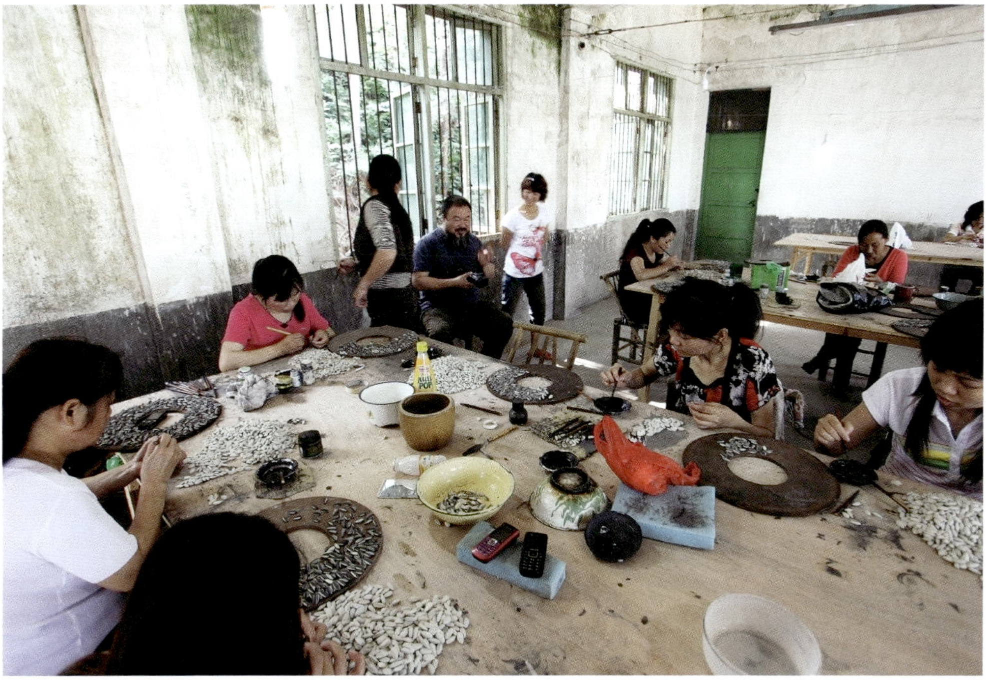

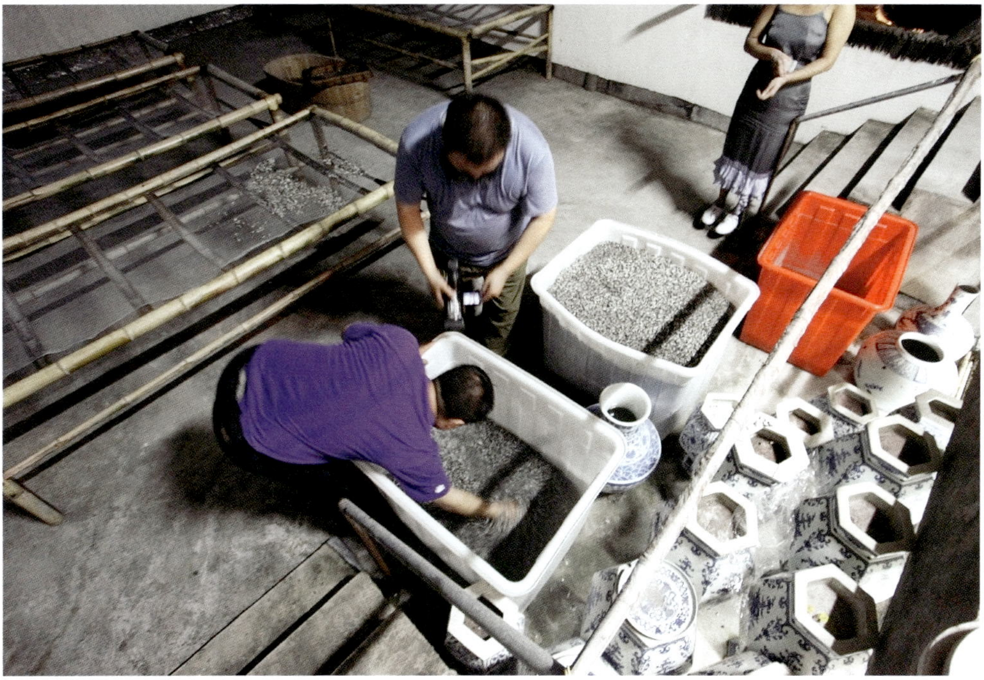

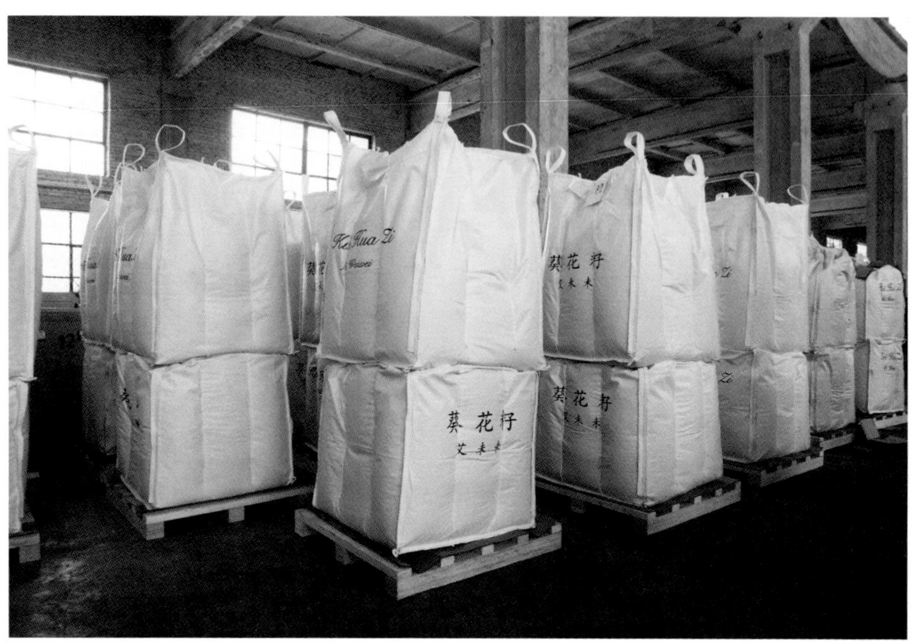

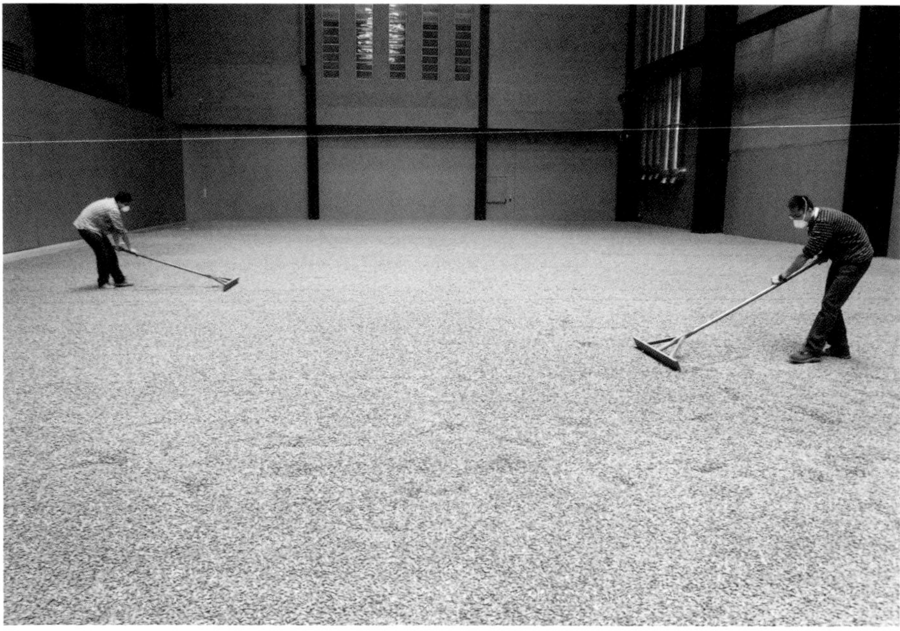

SUNFLOWER SEEDS, 2010, porcelain, paint, 100 million pieces, dimensions variable; transportation from Beijing and installation at Tate Modern, London 2010 (above); Turbine Hall, Tate Modern, London 2010 (opposite)

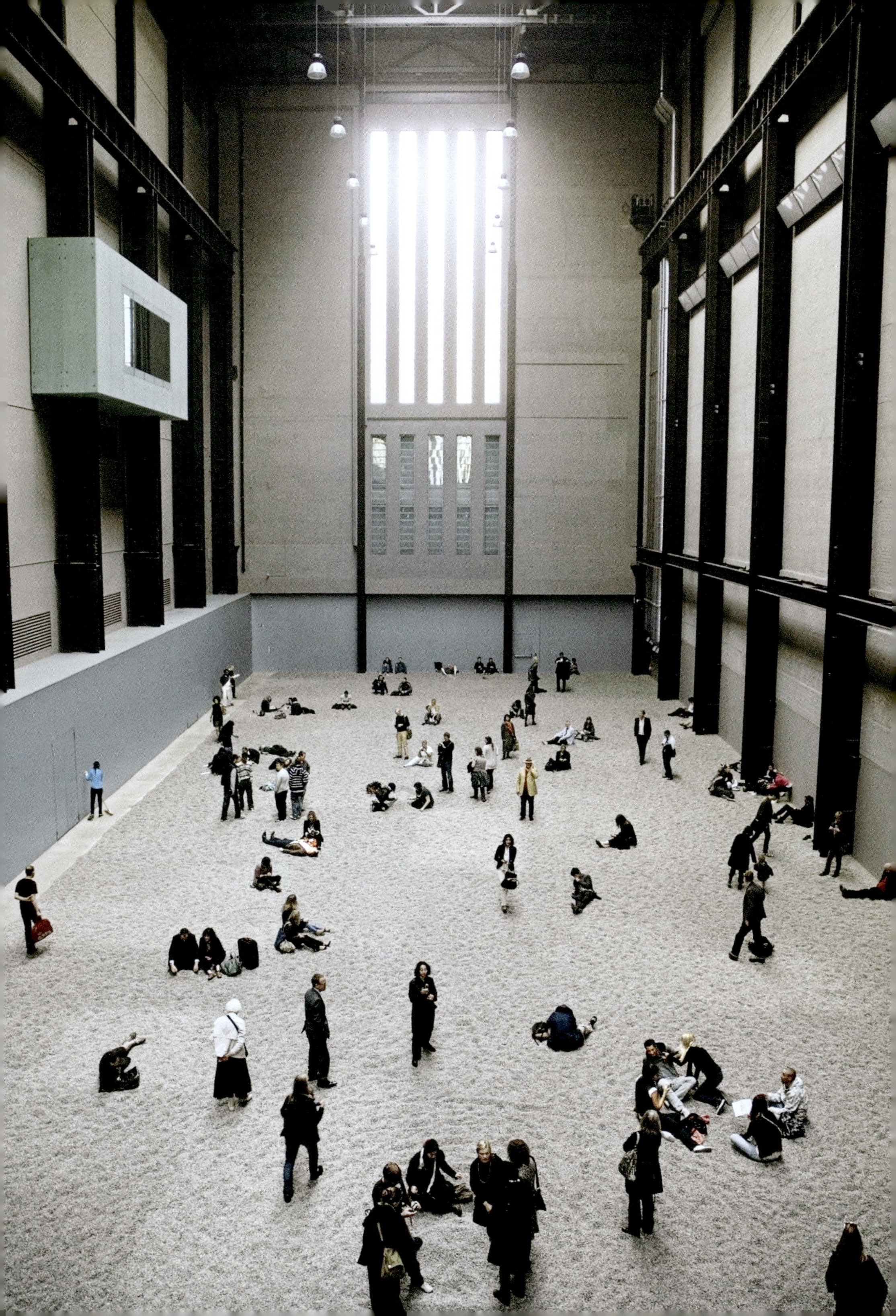

"*Circle of Animals* relates to some very complicated issues. Who made the original zodiac fountain at the Old Summer Palace, for what reason? And why were the heads lost? Are they truly lost, or at the auction house? One of the missing zodiac heads may just show up next season, so we will see how it compares with our version of it. I think it's a good idea to have a complete set: these seven that exist and the five that are unknown. Without twelve it's not a zodiac. So the idea was first, to complete it, and more important, to complete it the way I think it should be." — AI WEIWEI

Circle of Animals nimmt auf einige sehr komplexe Themen Bezug. Wer hat den ursprünglichen Brunnen mit den Figuren der Tierkreiszeichen im Alten Sommerpalast gebaut und aus welchem Grund? Wie sind die Köpfe verloren gegangen? Sind sie wirklich verloren oder im Auktionshaus? Einer der verlorenen Tierköpfe könnte dort gut in der nächsten Saison wieder auftauchen, dann könnte man unsere Version damit vergleichen. Ich hielt es für eine gute Idee, den kompletten Satz zu haben: die sieben, die existieren, und die fünf, deren Verbleib ungeklärt ist. Gibt es keine zwölf, ist es auch kein Tierkreis. Zunächst bestand die Idee also darin, den Tierkreis zu vervollständigen, wichtiger noch, ihn so zu vervollständigen, wie er meiner Meinung nach sein sollte.

Circle of Animals fait référence à des problèmes complexes. Qui a construit la fontaine du zodiaque de l'ancien Palais d'été, et pourquoi? Pourquoi les têtes ont-elles disparu? Ont-elles vraiment disparu ou sont-elles dans une société de vente aux enchères? Peut-être qu'une de ces têtes manquantes fera son apparition au printemps prochain et que nous pourrons la comparer à la version que nous en avons faite. Je crois que c'est une bonne idée de les avoir toutes les douze : les sept existantes et les cinq qui nous sont inconnues. Il faut avoir les douze signes du zodiaque. L'idée était donc de compléter cette série, et surtout de le faire d'une manière qui me paraissait appropriée.

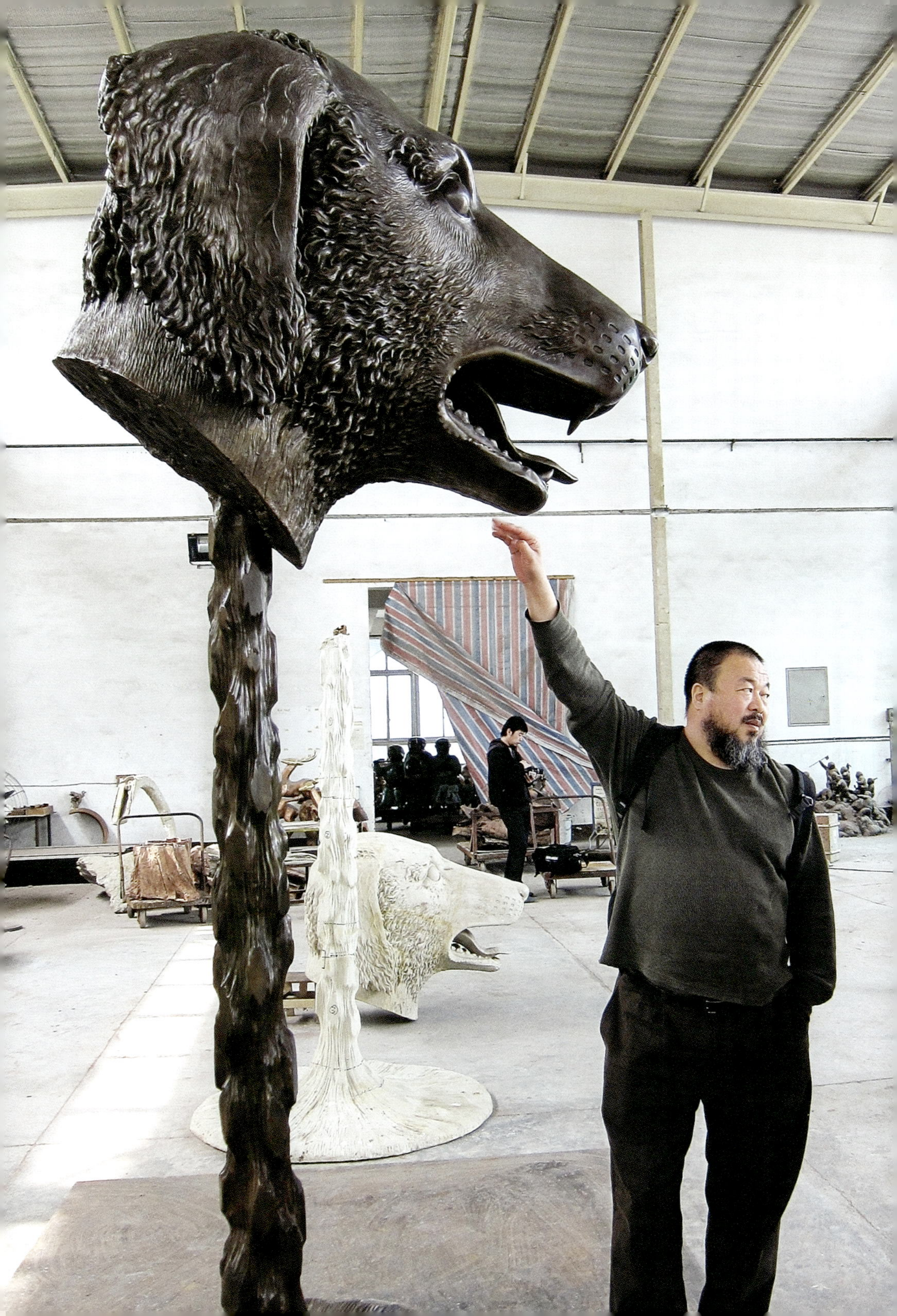

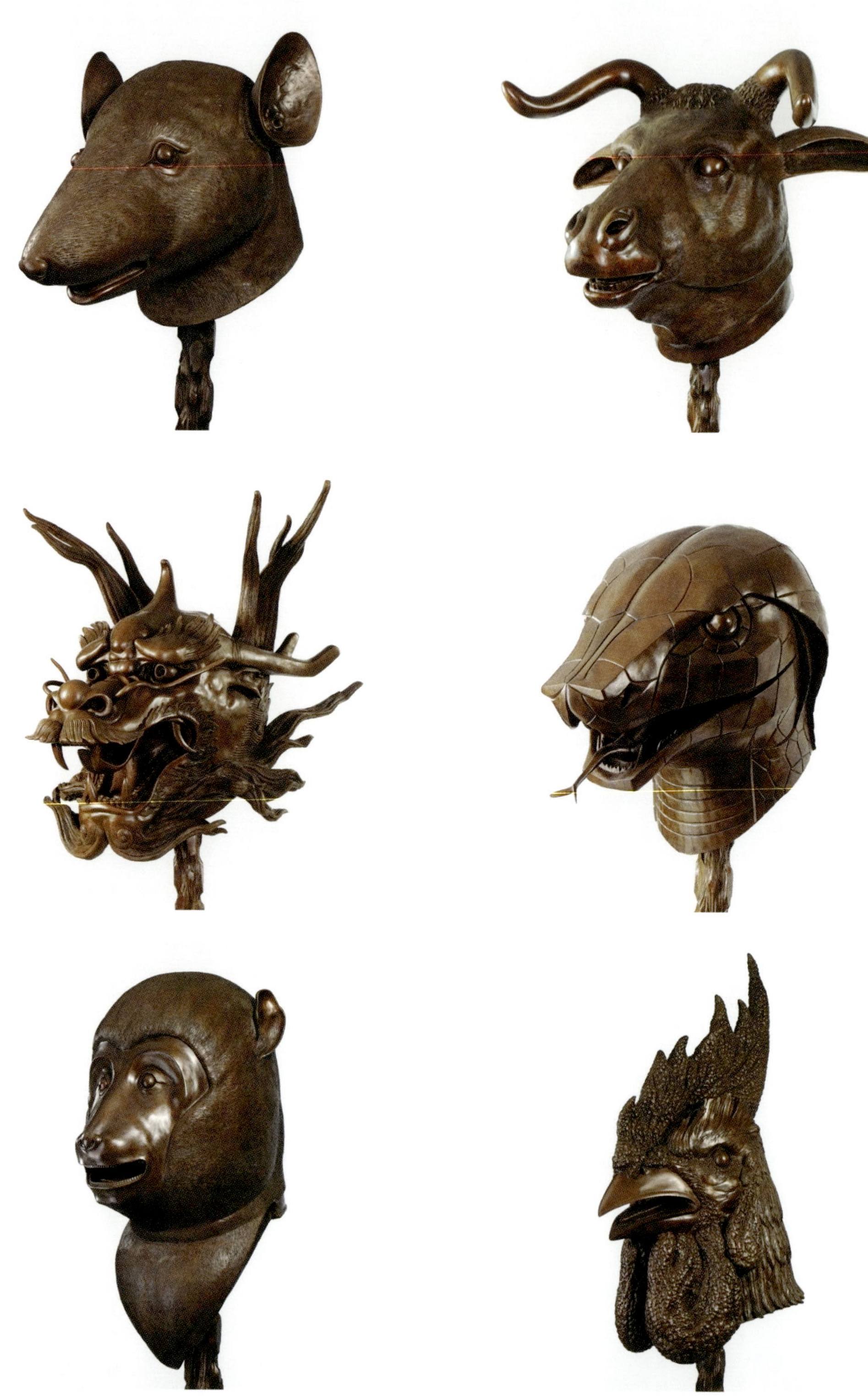

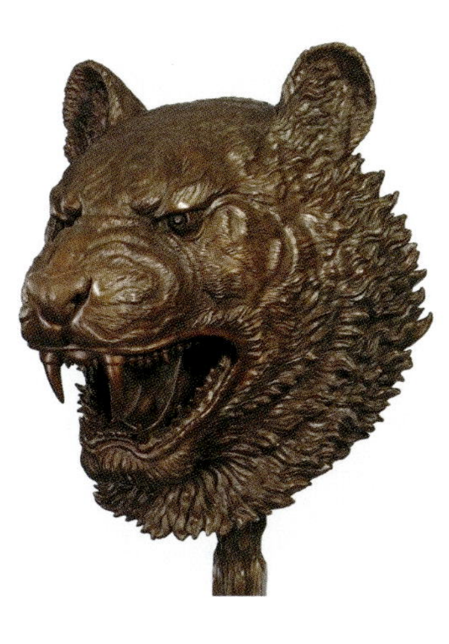
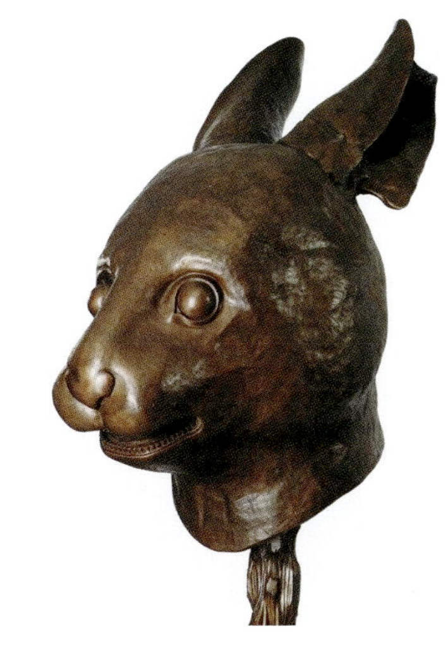
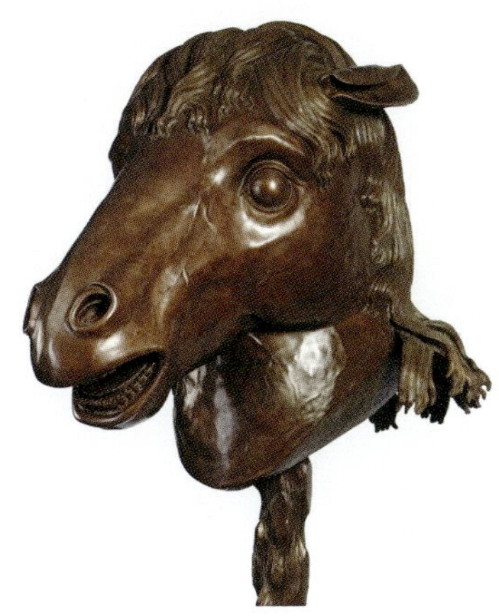
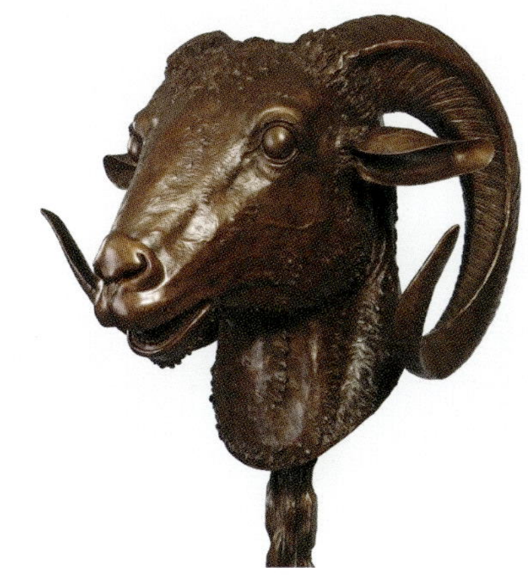
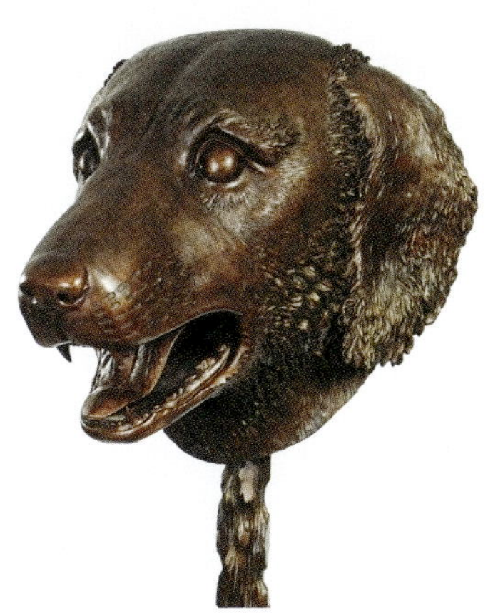
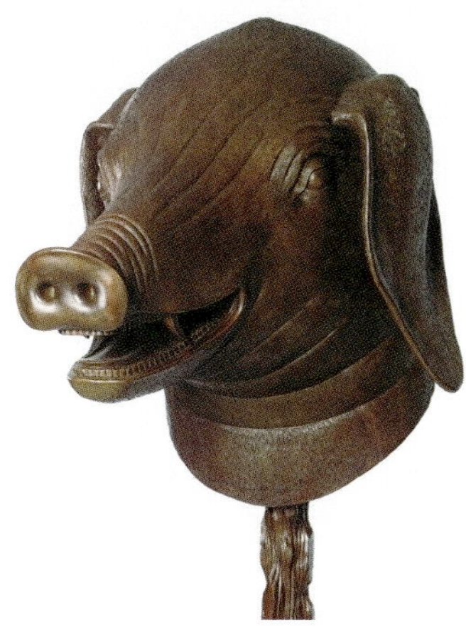

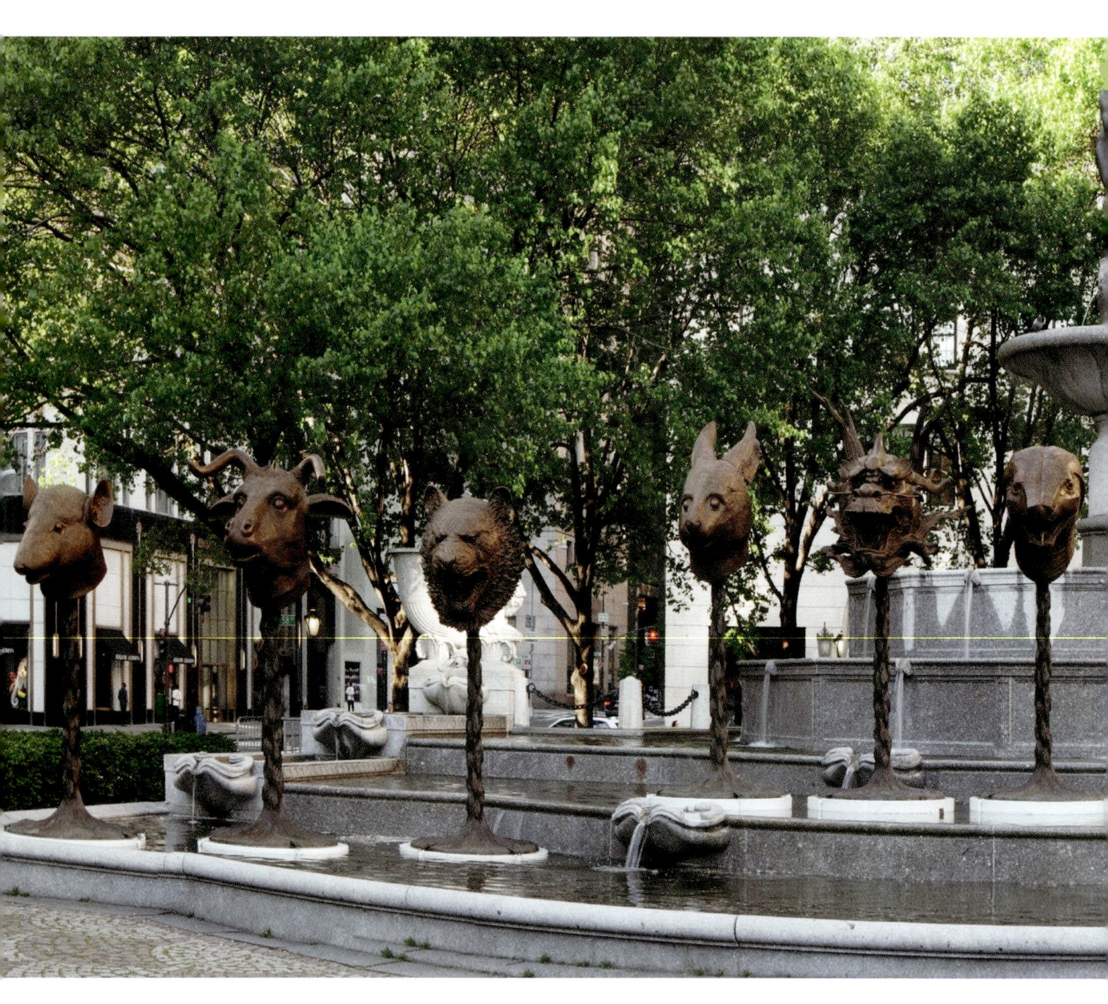

CIRCLE OF ANIMALS, 2010; installation view, *Circle of Animals/Zodiac Heads*, Pulitzer Fountain, Grand Army Plaza, New York 2011

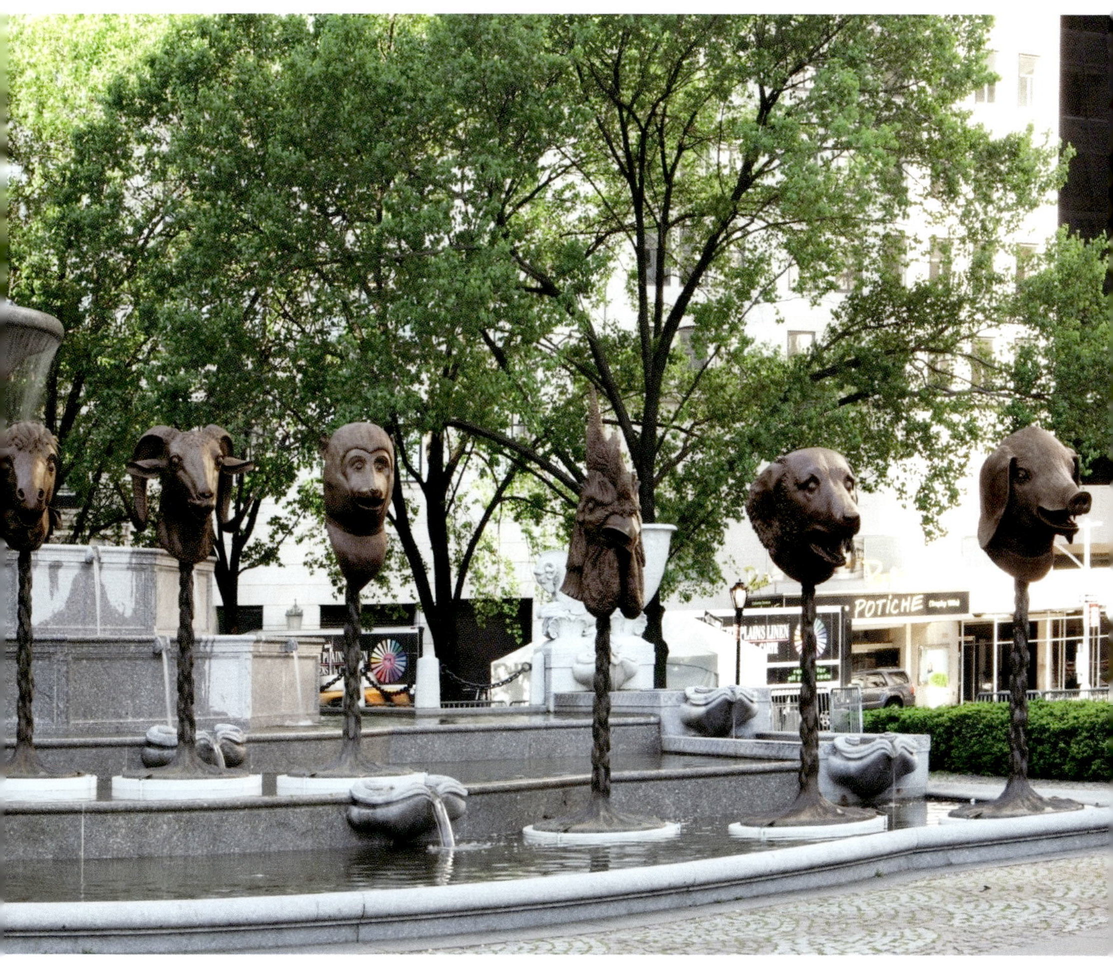

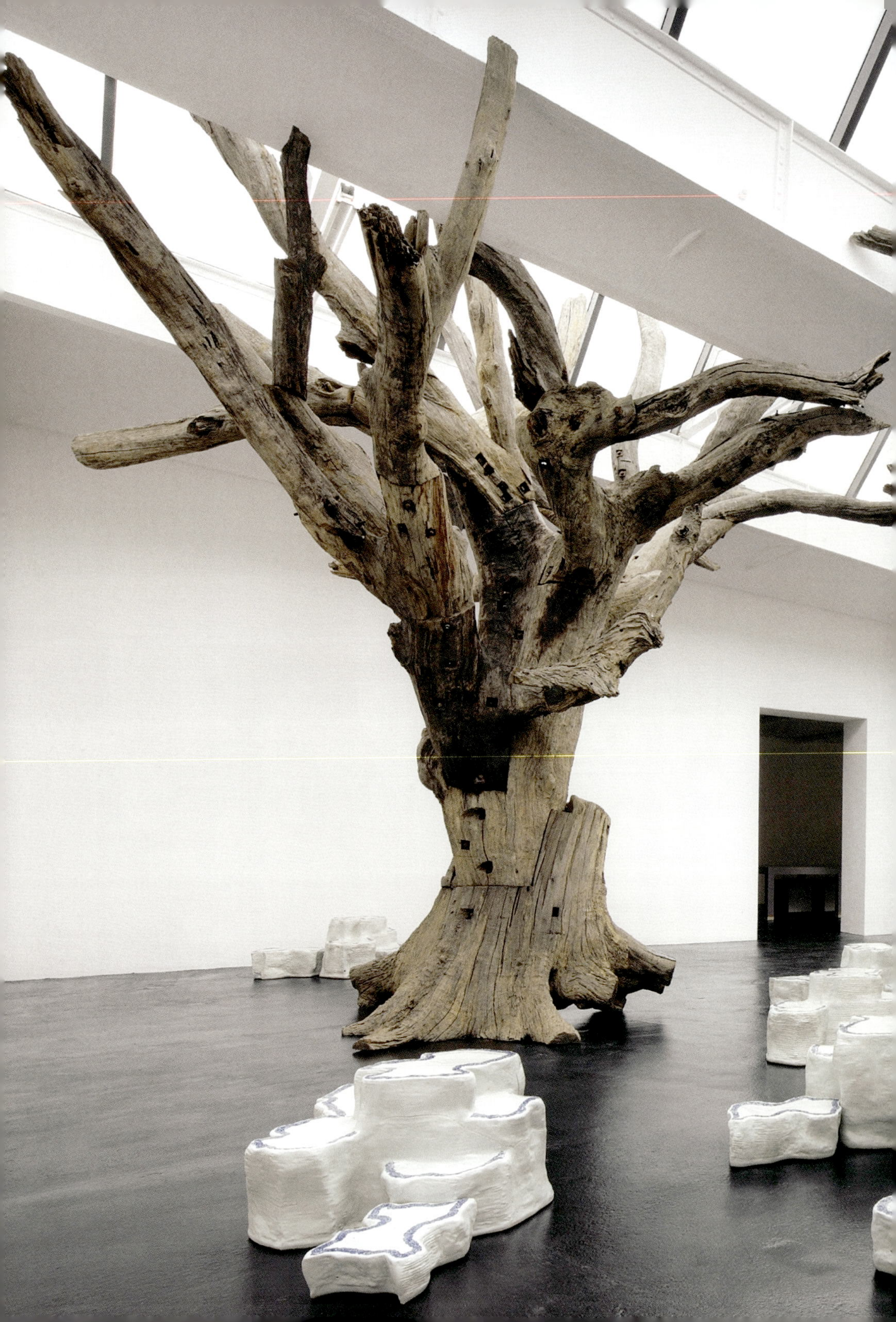

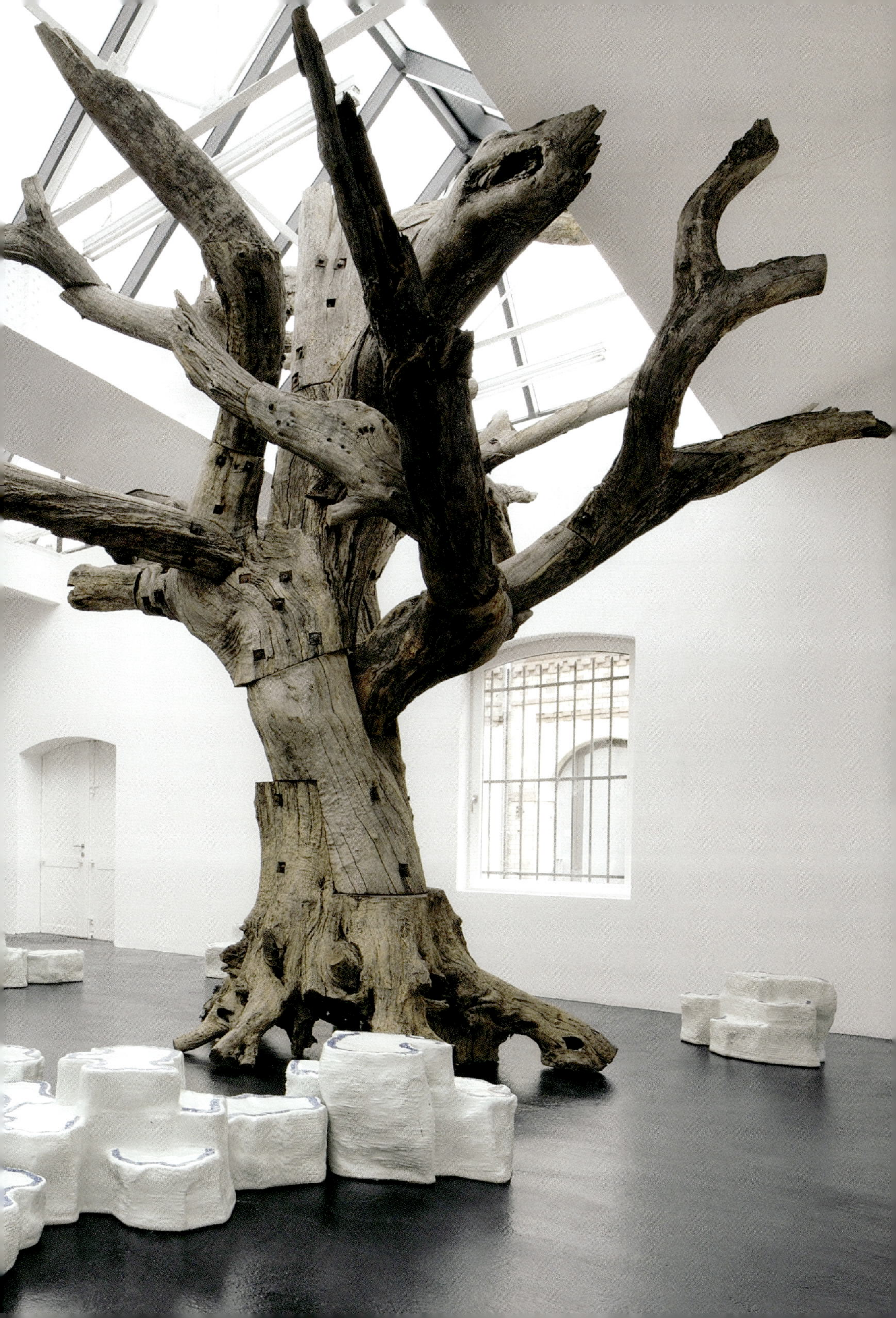

"The trees are dead wood from the mountain ranges in Jiangxi. Those branches were struck by lightning or they simply got too old and had been left abandoned for decades. So I thought it would be nice to put it back together as one tree, but from 100 different locations and belonging to different types of trees. We assembled them together to have all the details of a normal tree. At the same time, you're not comfortable, there's a strangeness there, an unfamiliarness. And it's just like trying to imagine what the tree was like." — AI WEIWEI

Die Bäume sind abgestorbenes Holz aus den Bergen von Jiangxi. Diese Stämme wurden entweder vom Blitz getroffen oder waren schlicht zu alt, und deswegen wurden sie jahrzehntelang einfach liegen gelassen. Also dachte ich, dass es interessant wäre, sie wieder zu einem Baum zusammenzusetzen, jedoch aus unterschiedlichen Baumarten von 100 verschiedenen Stellen. Wir montierten die Stücke zu sämtlichen Details eines gewöhnlichen Baums. Aber dennoch fühlt man sich nicht wohl, etwas Fremdes haftet ihnen an, etwas Unbekanntes. Es ist, als stelle man sich nur vor, wie der Baum gewesen sein könnte.

Ces arbres sont du bois mort des montagnes de Jiangxi. Ces branches ont été frappées par la foudre ou étaient simplement trop vieilles et ont été abandonnées là pendant des décennies. Je me suis dit que ce ne serait pas mal de s'en servir pour reconstruire un arbre, mais avec des bois différents provenant d'une centaine d'endroits différents. Nous avons assemblé ces morceaux de bois pour recréer tous les détails d'un arbre normal. Mais cet arbre nous met mal à l'aise, il dégage quelque chose d'étrange, d'inhabituel. C'est comme si on imaginait à quoi cet arbre pouvait ressembler.

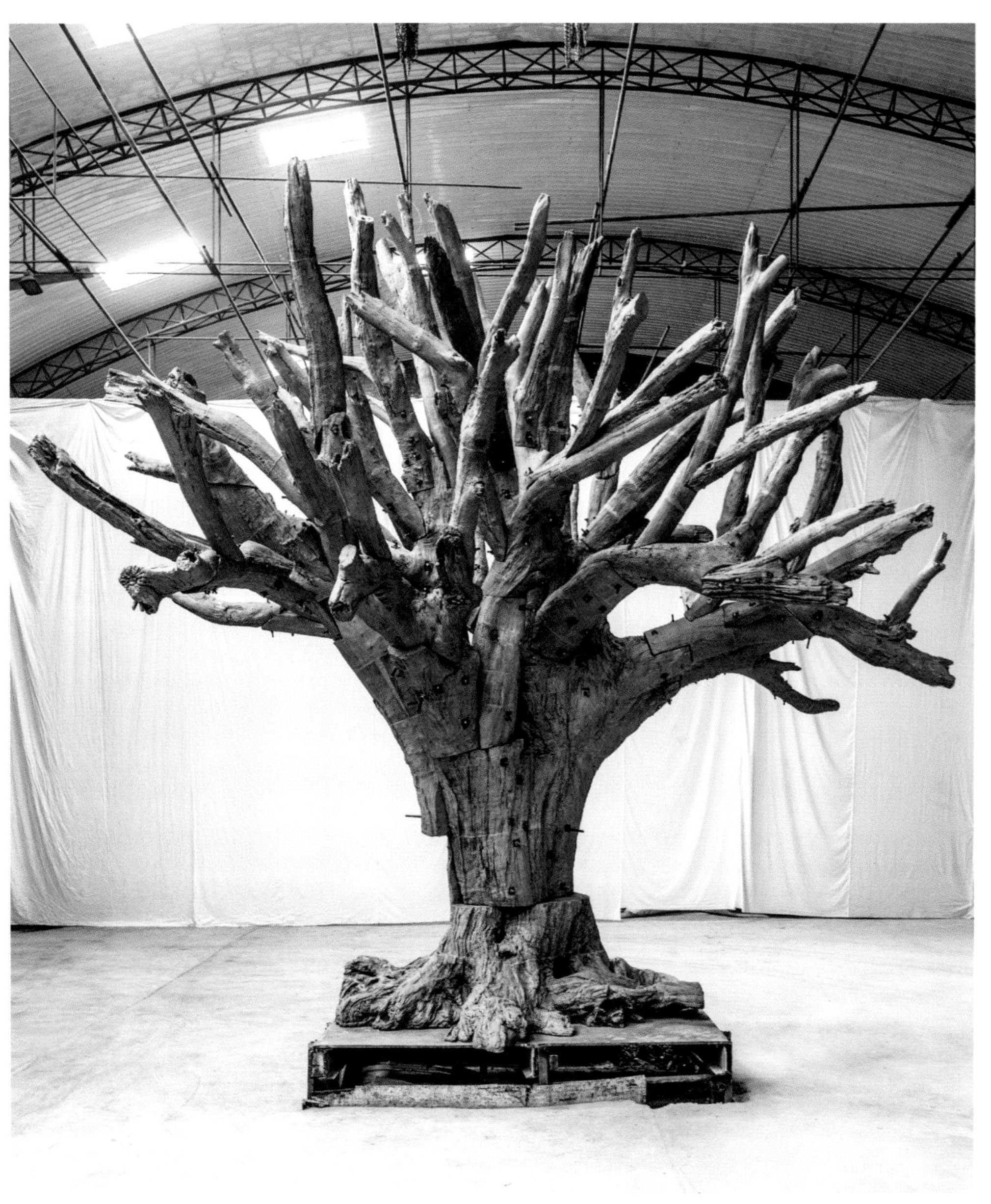

IRON TREE, 2012, iron, 247 ¼ x 279 ½ x 279 ½ inches, Ai Weiwei's studio, Beijing | 419

"When I was invited to build a studio in Shanghai by the district mayor in 2008, I said we were not going to do it. Because we completely have no trust in the government. So he personally came to Beijing to talk to me and convince me. Then two years later they told me they would have to destroy it; the same person who asked us to build now told us this was not legal. The government offered us to pay our money back, a very good price, all in cash. No receipt. When I invited people to a party to celebrate the planned demolition of my studio over Twitter, I was put under house arrest. My intention was to cancel the party, but it still went on. Over a whole week, 3,000 people appeared. It's one of the first instances of civil disobedience in China." — AI WEIWEI

Als ich vom Bezirksbürgermeister 2008 eingeladen wurde, ein Studio in Shanghai zu bauen, sagte ich erst: Das machen wir nicht. Weil wir der Regierung einfach nicht über den Weg trauten. Also kam er für Gespräche persönlich nach Peking und überzeugte mich schließlich. Zwei Jahre später eröffneten sie mir dann, dass sie das Studio wieder abreißen müssten. Dieselbe Person, die mich damals überredet hatte, erzählte mir jetzt, es wäre illegal gewesen. Die Regierung bot uns an, das Geld zurückzuzahlen, und machte einen guten Preis. In bar, ohne Quittung. Als ich dann die Leute über Twitter zu einer geplanten Abrissparty in mein Studio einlud, wurde ich unter Hausarrest gestellt. Also wollte ich die Party wieder absagen, aber die Sache nahm dennoch ihren Lauf. 3000 Gäste erschienen im Lauf einer ganzen Woche. Das war einer der ersten Fälle von zivilem Ungehorsam in China.

Lorsque le maire du district m'a invité à construire mon studio à Shanghai en 2008, j'ai d'abord refusé. Nous ne faisons pas du tout confiance au gouvernement. Il a donc fait le déplacement jusqu'à Pékin pour venir me parler et me convaincre. Deux ans plus tard, on m'a dit qu'on allait être obligé de le détruire ; la personne qui nous avait demandé de le construire nous disait à présent que le bâtiment était illégal. Le gouvernement a offert de nous dédommager, il nous a proposé un très bon prix, en liquide, sans trace écrite. Lorsque j'ai ensuite fait circuler une invitation sur twitter pour une fête pour la démolition de l'atelier, j'ai été assigné à résidence. J'ai d'abord voulu annuler la fête mais elle a finalement eu lieu. Pendant une semaine, 3000 personnes se sont déplacées. Ce fut l'un des premiers cas de désobéissance civile en Chine.

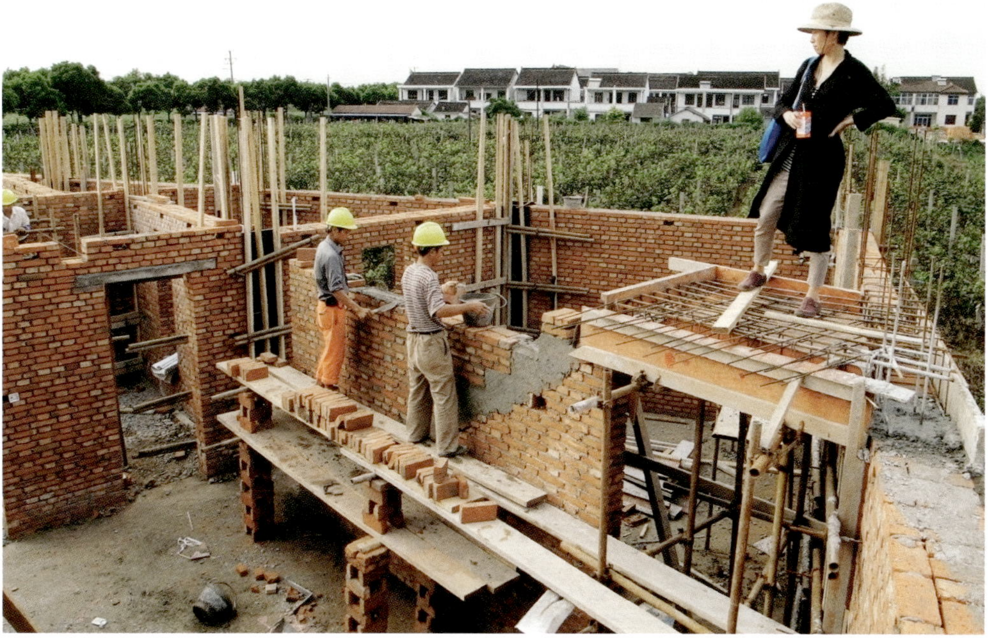

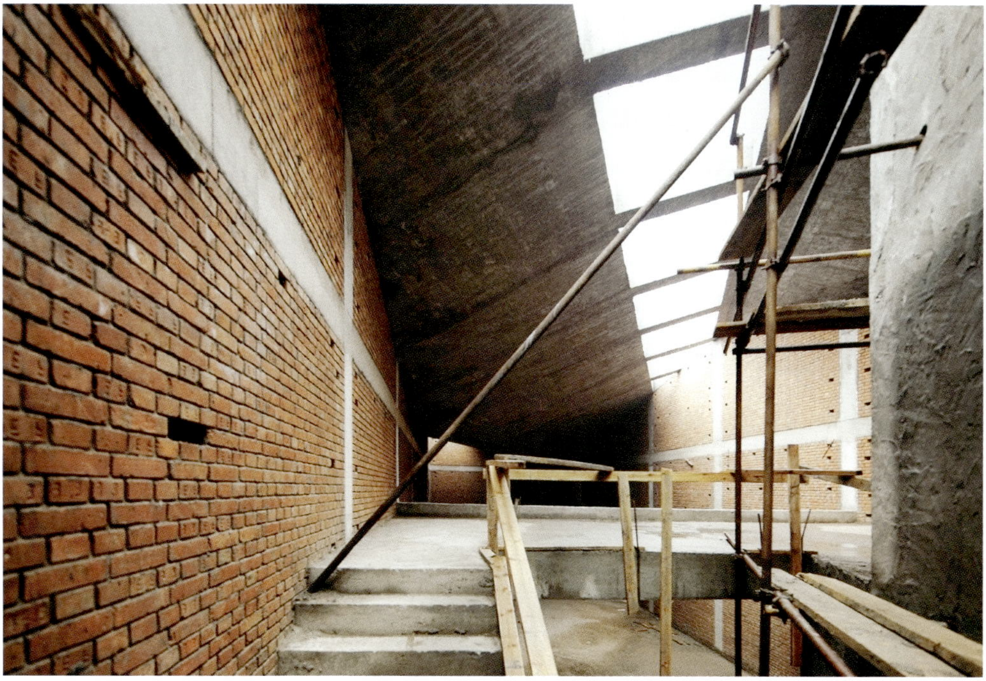

JIADING MALU (SHANGHAI STUDIO), Shanghai 2008–2010,
construction and view (above and overleaf) | 421

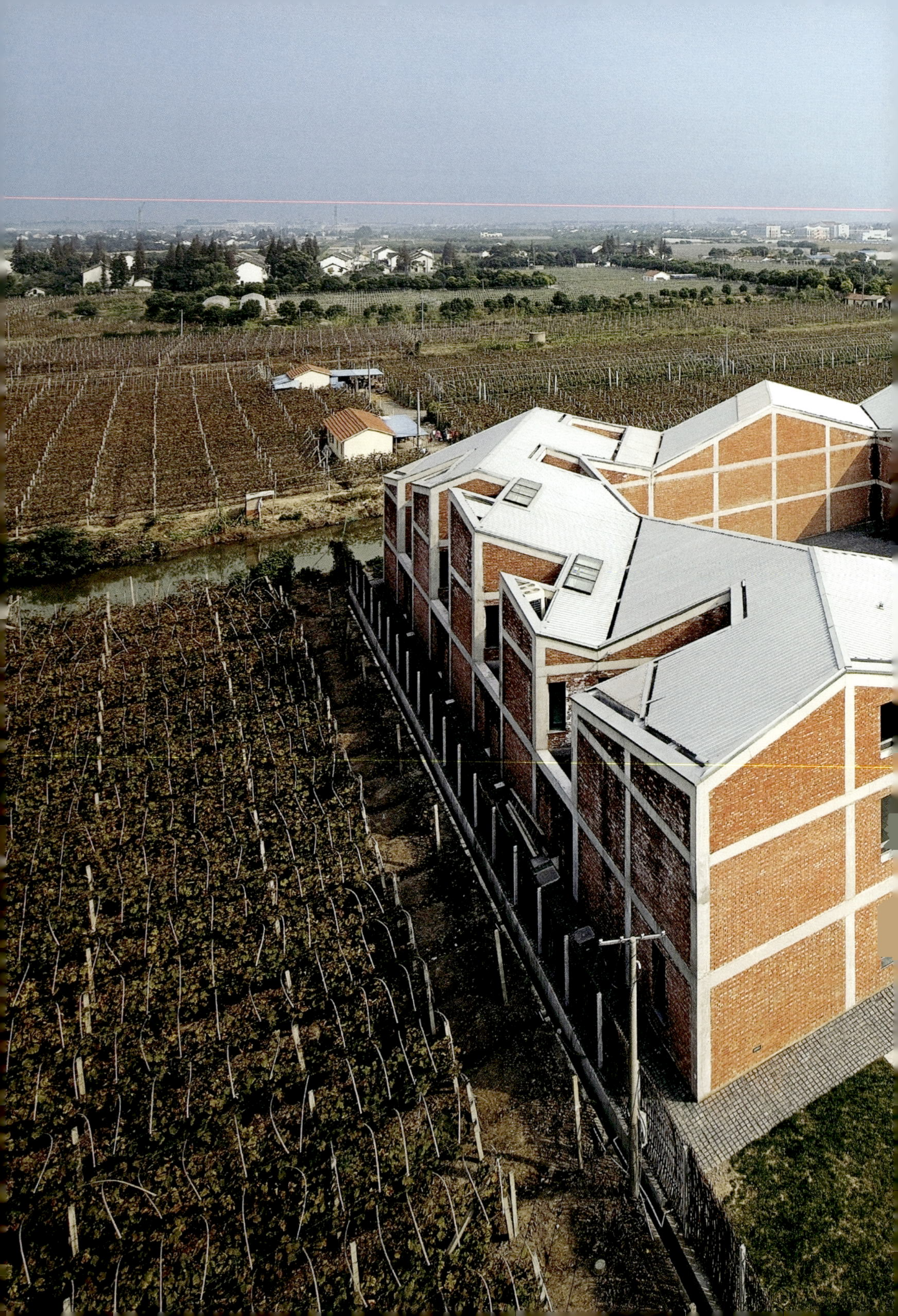

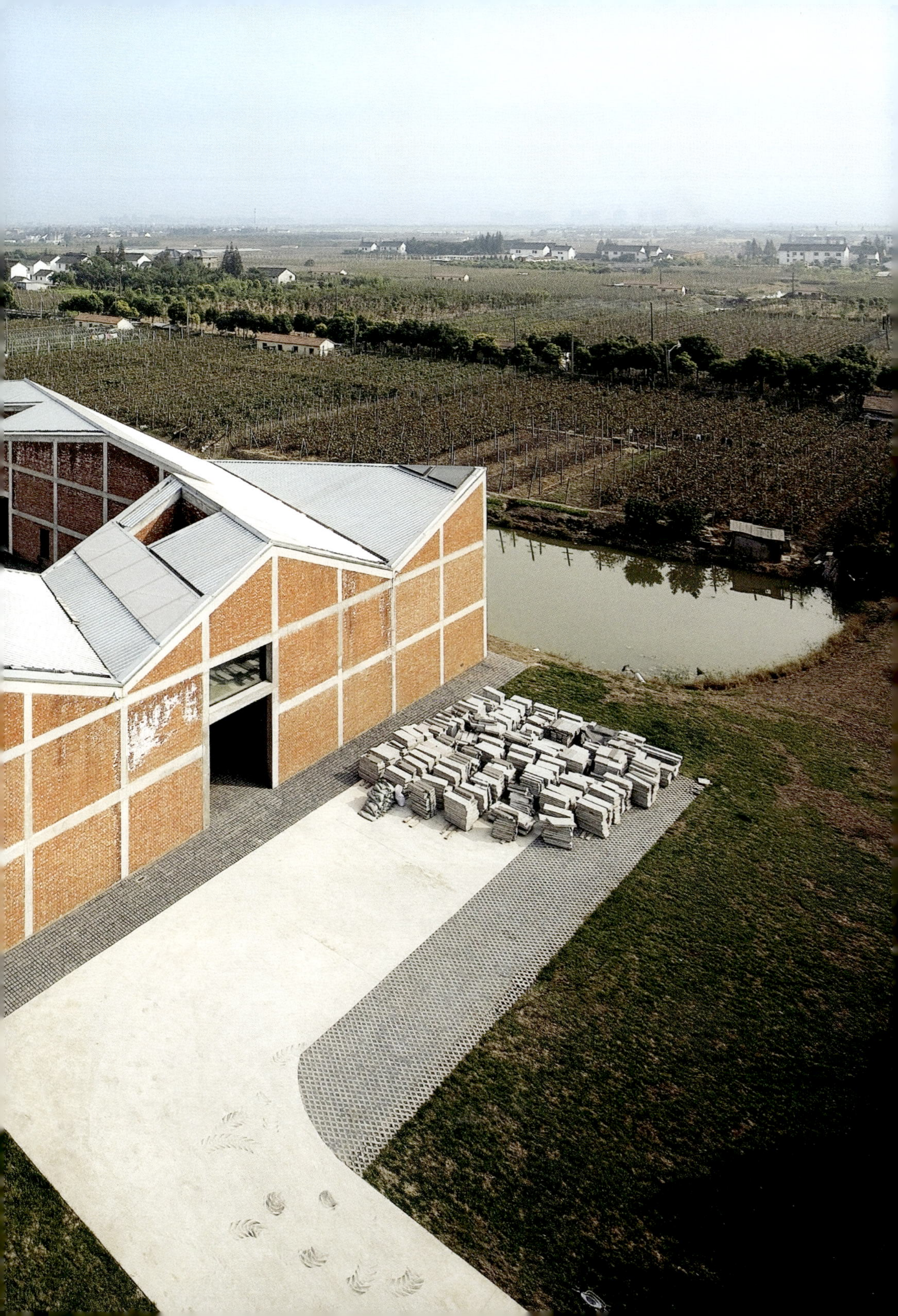

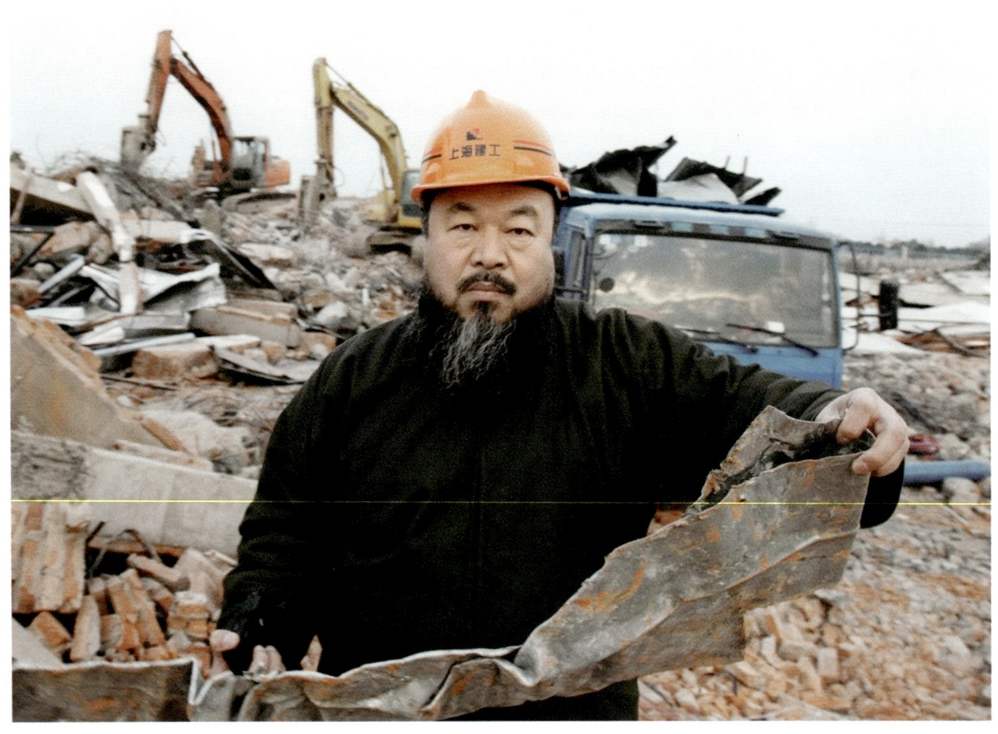

Ai Weiwei during the demolition of his Shanghai studio, January 11, 2011

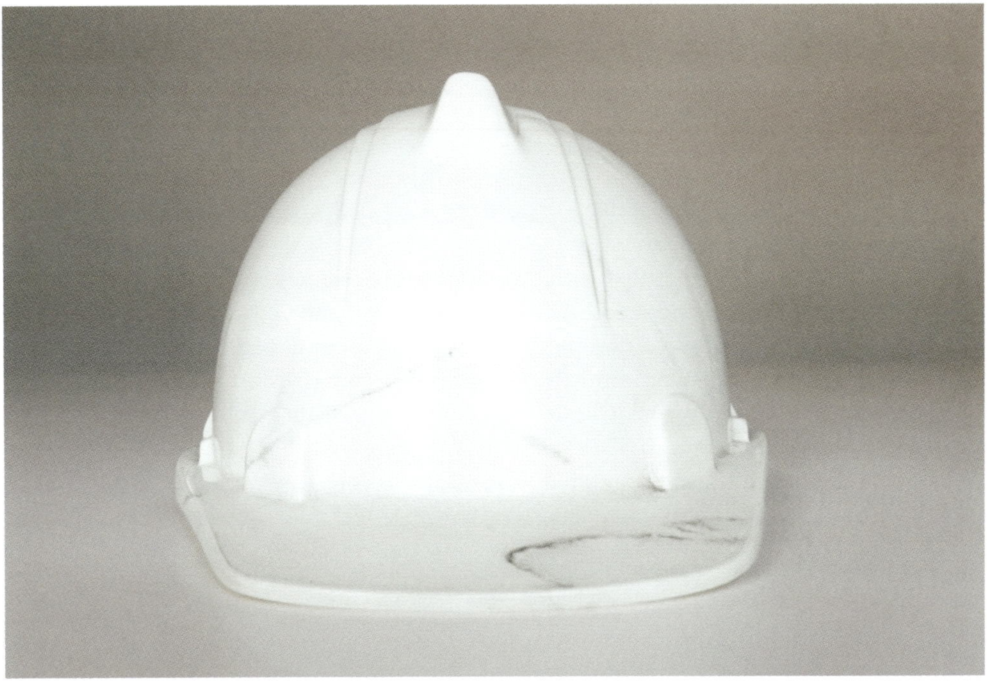

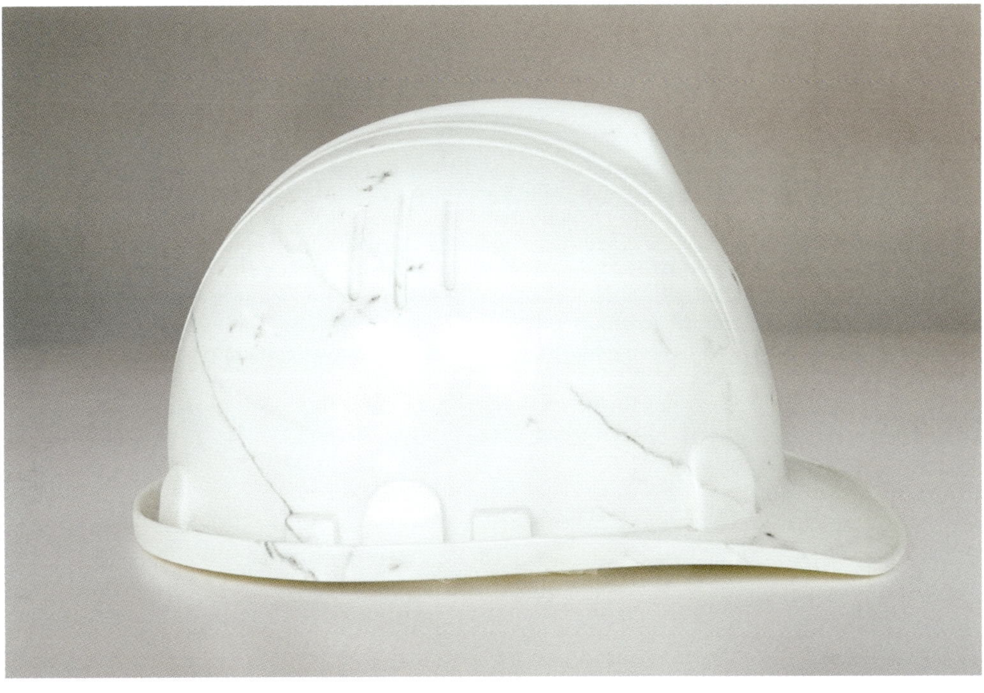

MARBLE HELMET, 2010, marble, 11 ¾ x 9 ⅞ x 5 ⅞ inches |

"In Chinese, 'harmonious' (a code word for state censorship popular among netizens) also sounds like 'crab,' so I asked my porcelain makers to make crabs to bring the irony of the political situation into a physical, everyday visual language that people can understand. Later I realized that the crab had a long history as an object in China—different dynasties made them in jade, or bamboo or onyx. In contemporary times, after the Gang of Four was arrested in 1976, many artists even painted crabs to celebrate. So people painted themselves eating four crabs with wine. The crabs are made of porcelain, and they exploit the best aspects of the craft. They are sculpted so carefully, colored and glazed so nicely— all these details are highly controlled." — AI WEIWEI

Im Chinesischen klingt „harmonisch" (ein Codewort für staatliche Zensur, das sich im Netz großer Beliebtheit erfreut) genau wie „Krabbe", also ließ ich meine Porzellanhersteller Krabben anfertigen, um so die Ironie der politischen Situation in eine materielle, alltägliche visuelle Sprache zu übersetzen, die jeder versteht. Später wurde mir klar, dass die Krabbe in China eine lange Tradition als Kunstobjekt hat. In vielen Dynastien wurde sie aus Jade, Bambus oder Onyx geschnitzt. In jüngerer Zeit, etwa 1976, nach der Verhaftung der Viererbande, malten Künstler Krabben, um das wichtige Ereignis zu feiern. Sie malten sich beispielsweise selbst bei einem Festmahl, das aus vier Krabben und Wein bestand. Meine Krabben sind aus Porzellan und haben alle Vorzüge dieses Materials. Sie sind so sorgsam gefertigt, so schön koloriert und glasiert – alle Details sind in höchstem Maß kontrolliert.

En chinois, «harmonieux» (un code pour la censure d'État populaire parmi les citoyens du net) ressemble au mot «crabe», j'ai donc demandé à mes porcelainiers d'exprimer l'ironie de la situation politique en un langage visuel quotidien, physique, que tout le monde puisse comprendre. Par la suite, j'ai réalisé que les objets en forme de crabe avaient une longue histoire en Chine – pendant plusieurs dynasties, on en a fabriqué en jade, en bambou ou en onyx. Plus récemment, après l'arrestation de la Bande des Quatre, de nombreux artistes ont peint des crabes pour fêter l'événement. Ils se peignaient en train de manger quatre crabes et de boire du vin. Ces crabes sont en porcelaine et exploitent au mieux les possibilités de cet artisanat. Leur forme est extrêmement délicate, et ils ont été peints et vernis si joliment – autant de détails soigneusement contrôlés.

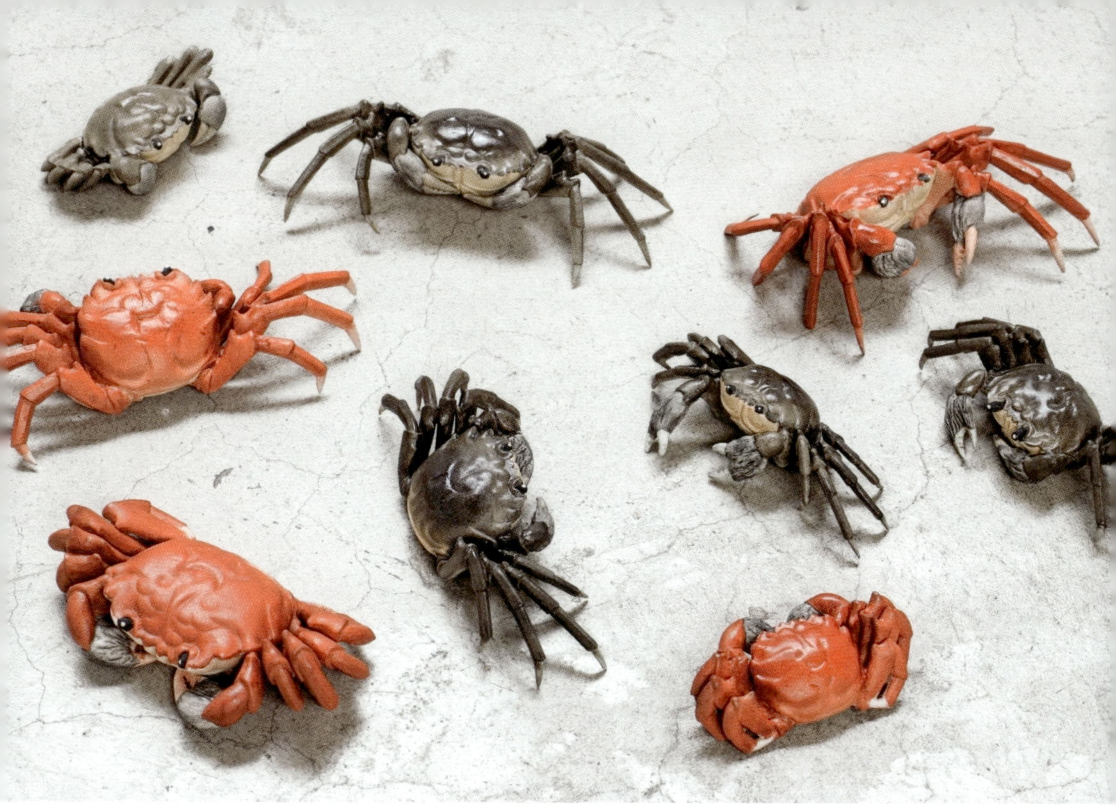

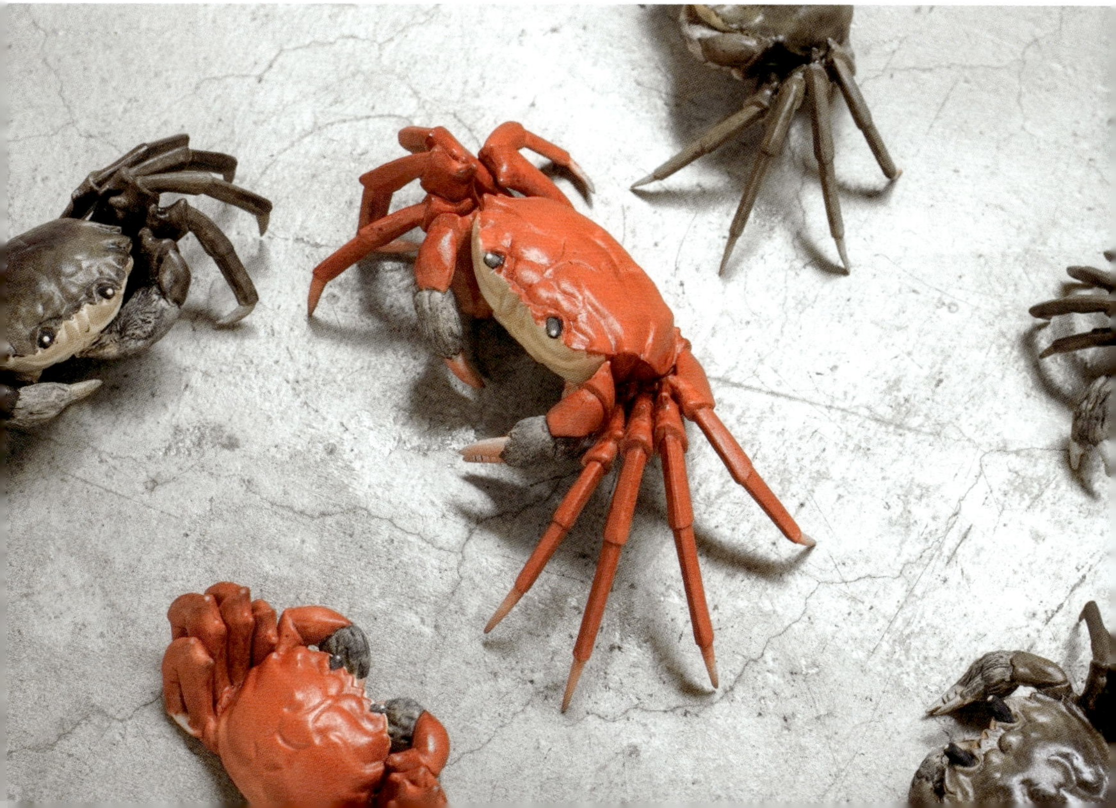

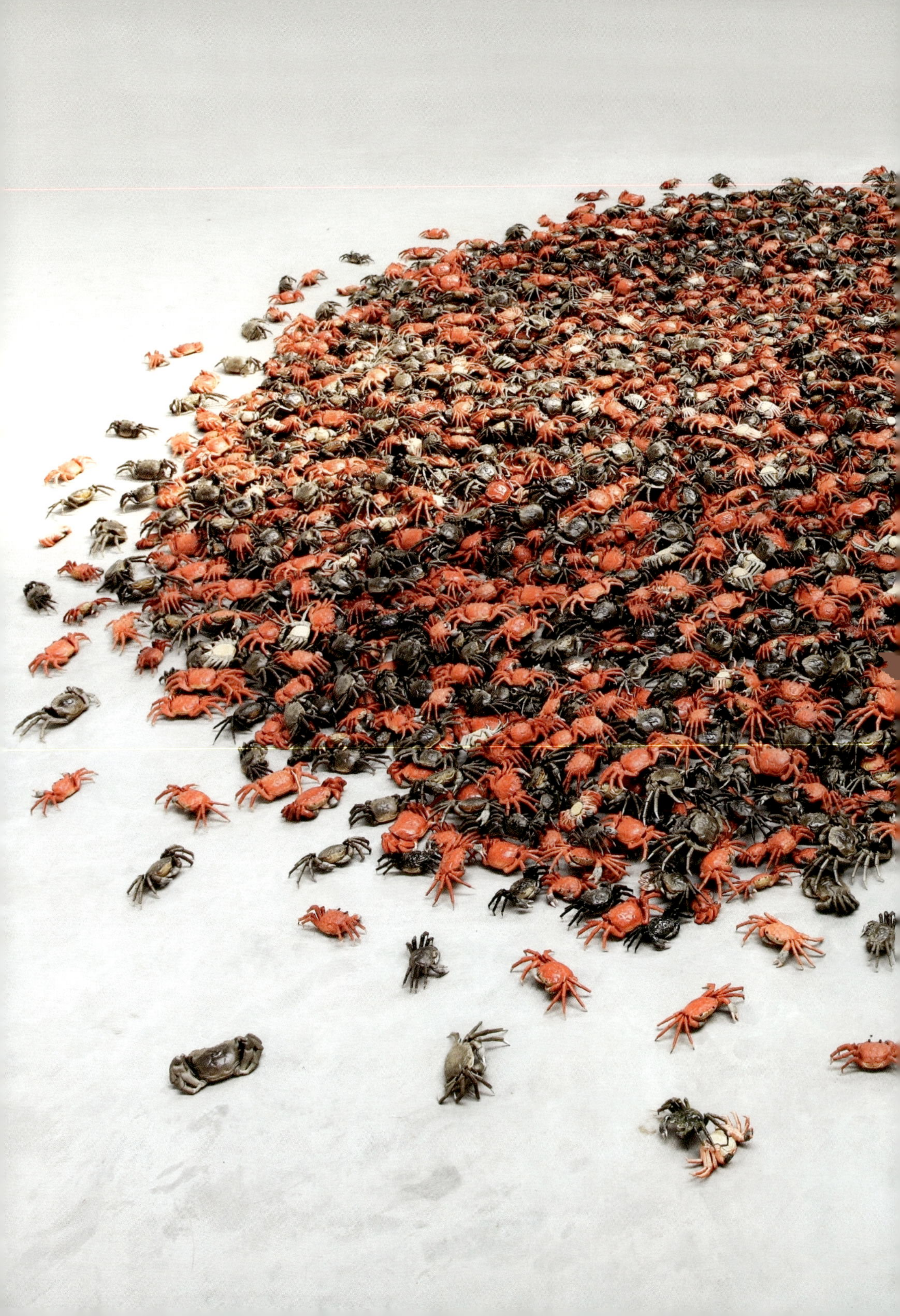

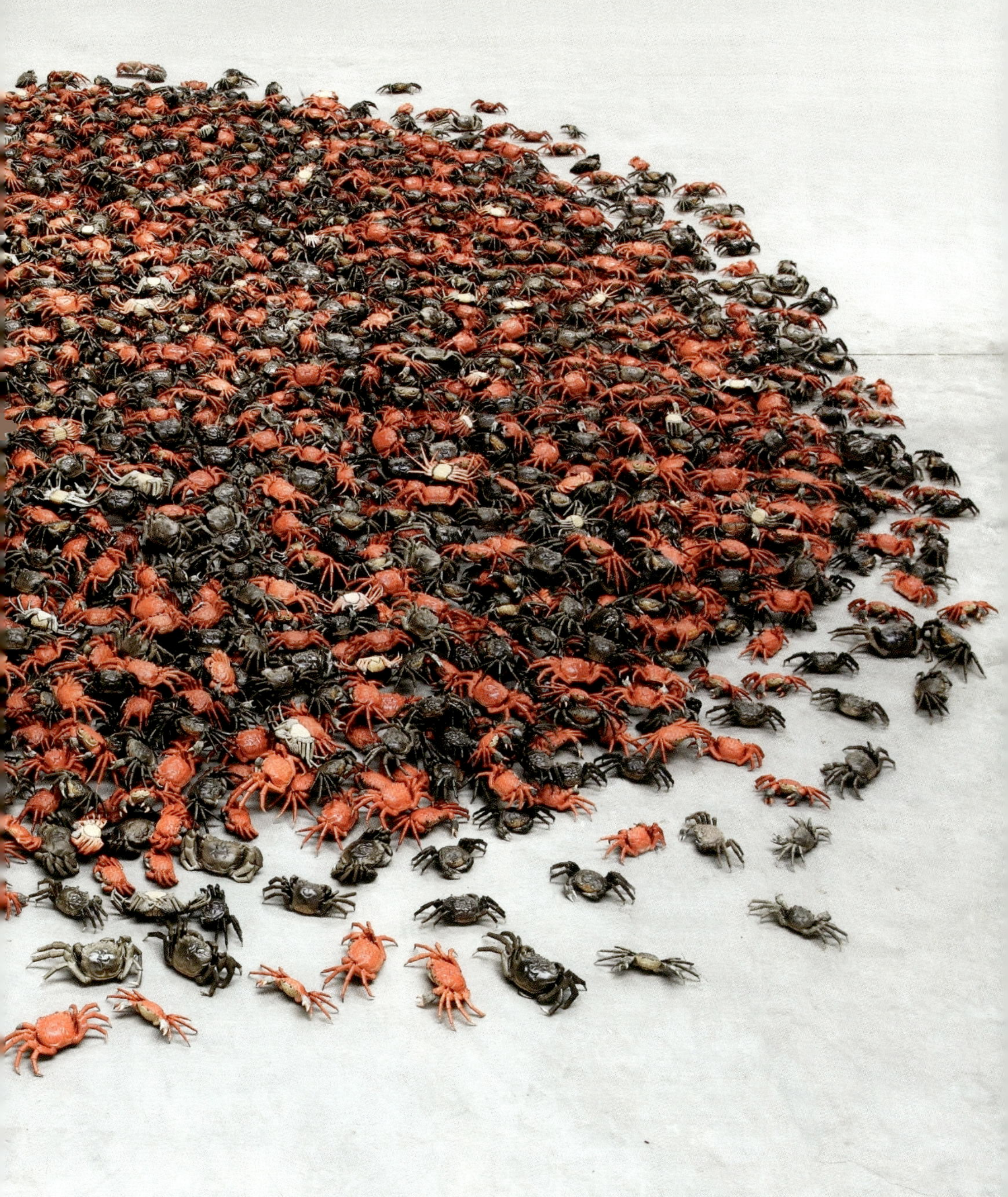

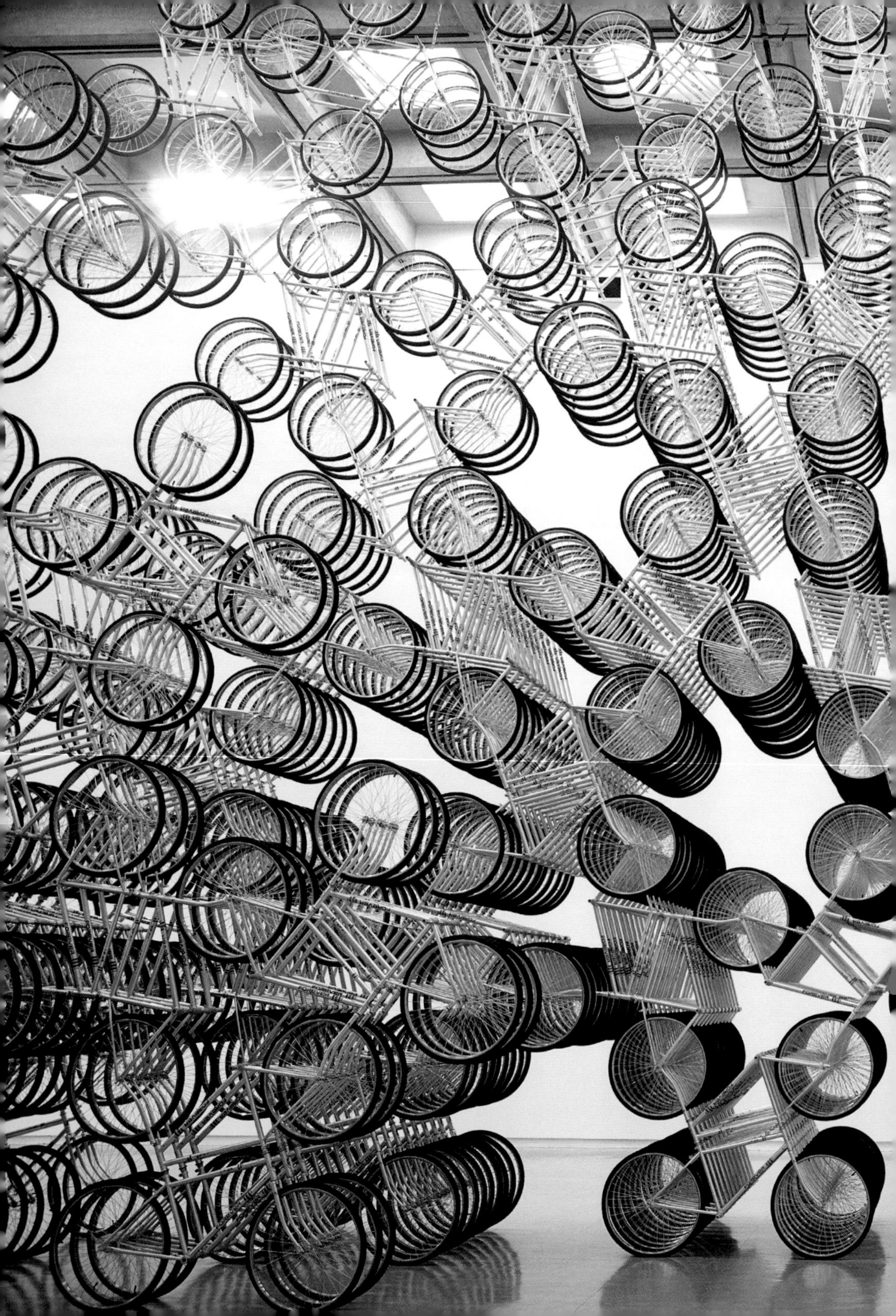

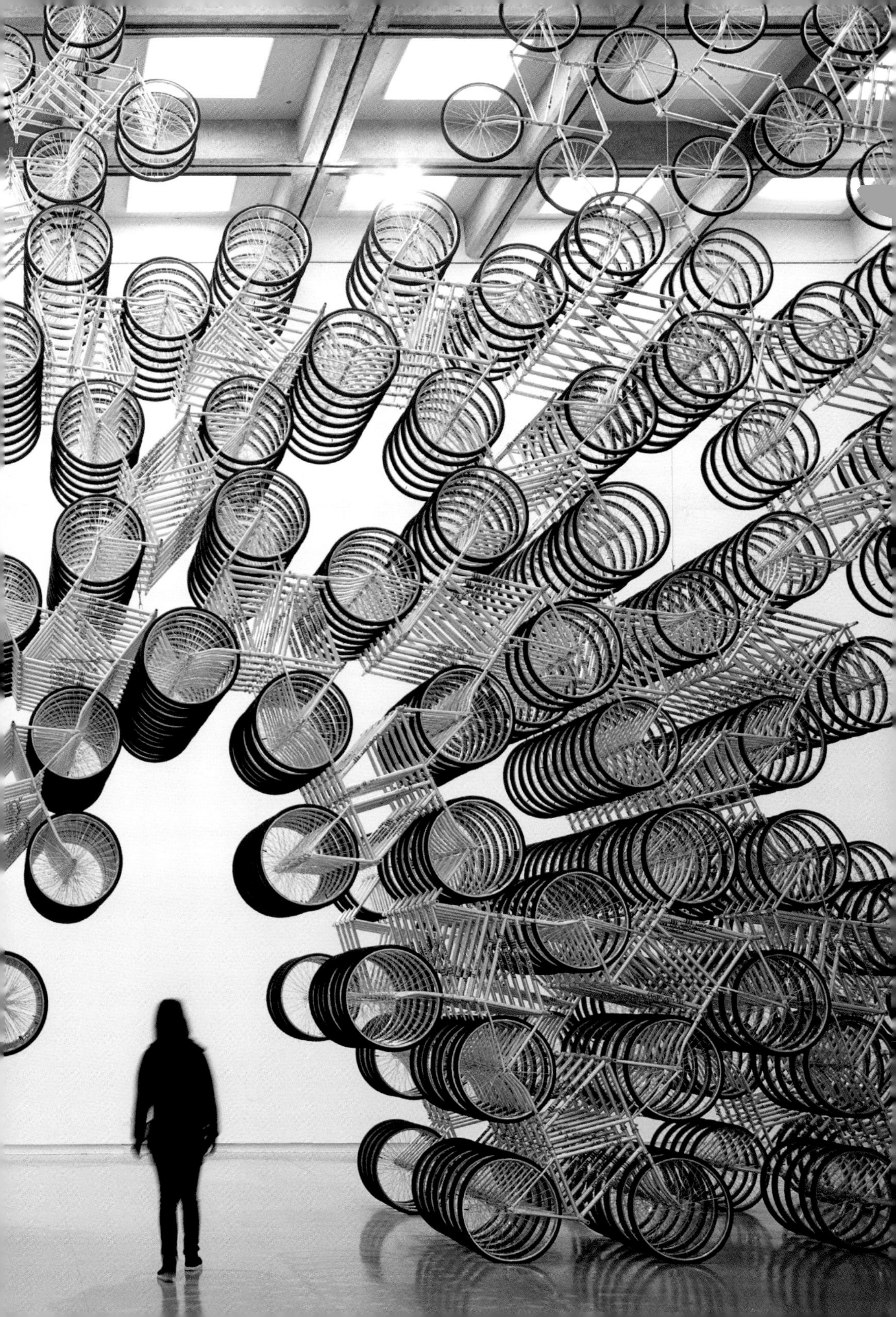

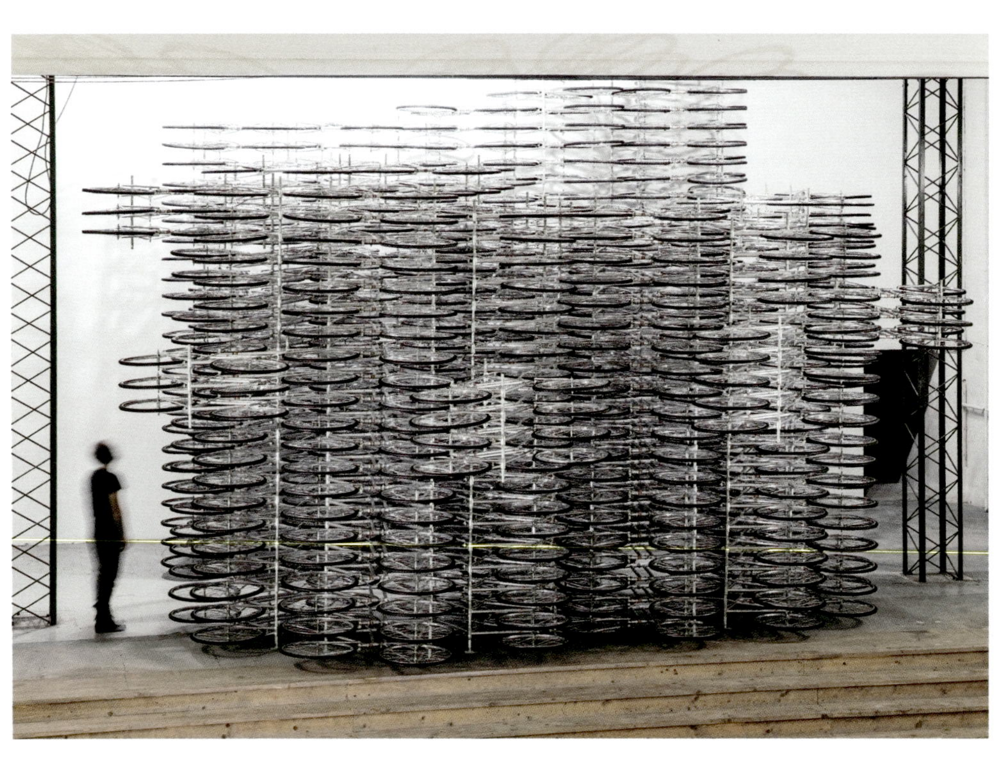

STACKED, 2012, 760 Forever bicycles, dimensions variable; Galleria Continua,
San Gimignano 2012 │Previous spread: FOREVER BICYCLES, 2011, 1,200 Forever bicycles,
432 │ dimensions variable; Taipei Fine Arts Museum 2011

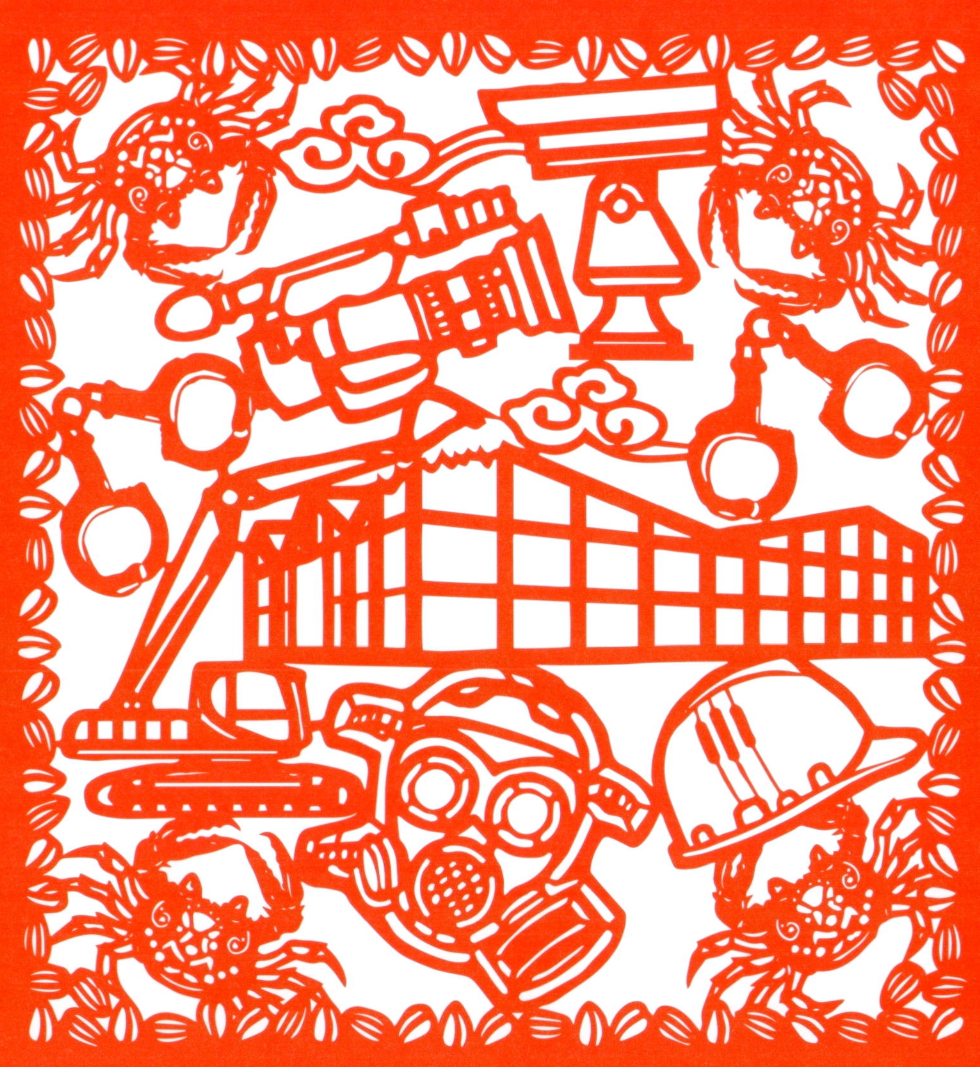

2011–Now

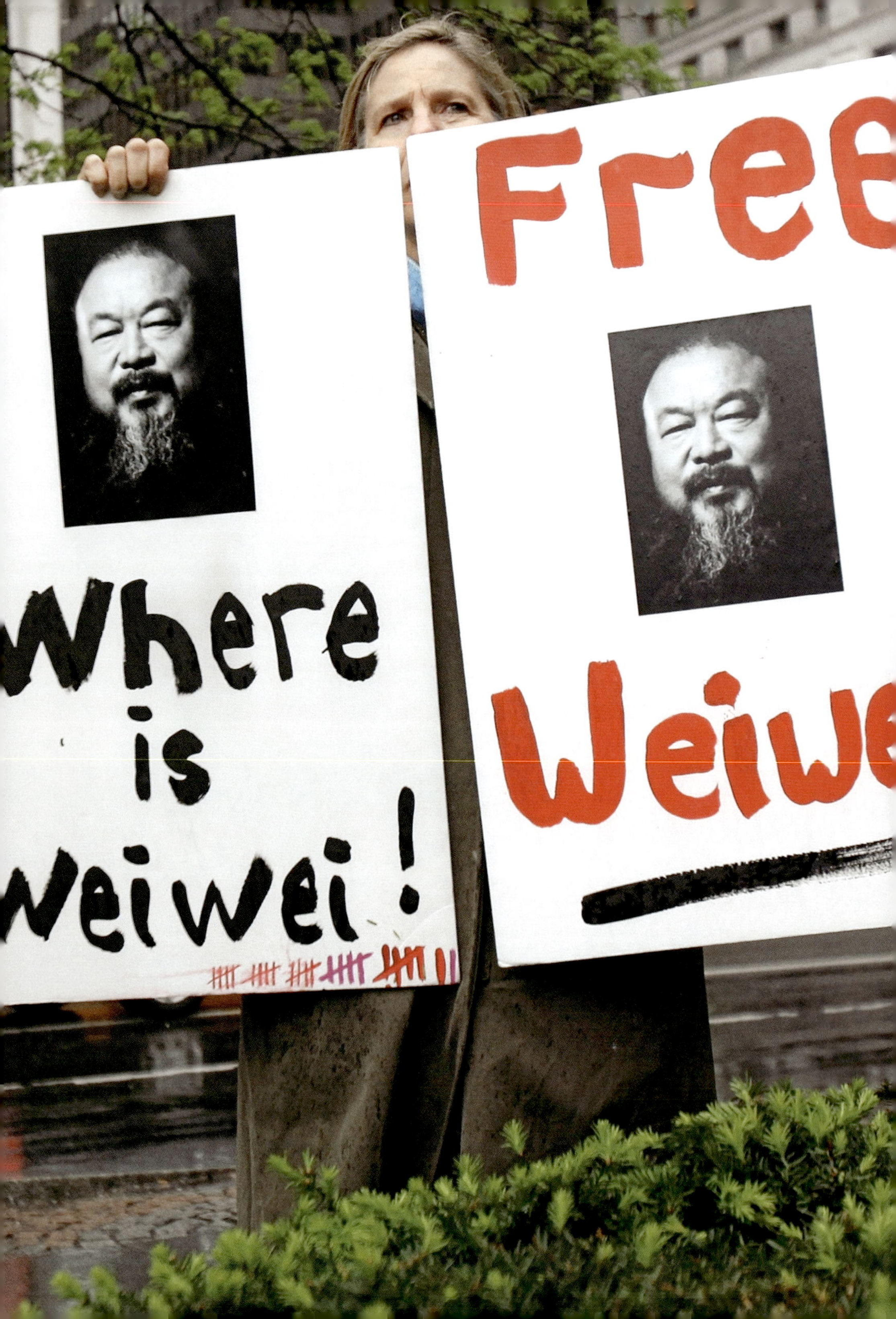

Where
is
Weiwei !
Free
Weiwe

Detention and the FAKE Case

FEBRUARY 22, 2011
@aiww. Yesterday, two people squatted the whole day inside the surveillance van at Caochangdi.

FEBRUARY 23, 2011
The Telegraph. *CHINA FACING NEW CALLS FOR JASMINE REVOLUTION.* Despite the apparent solidity of its powerbase, China's ruling Communist Party has shown signs of growing nervousness in recent weeks as street protests sweep away autocratic regimes across the Middle East. As well as the massive deployment of uniformed police, China's pervasive state security apparatus has worked to neuter the spread of dissent online as well as placing as many as 100 activists and potential organizers under house arrest.

FEBRUARY 27, 2011
@aiww. The Public Security Bureau officers selling flowers outside my place are sleeping through the snowfall.

FEBRUARY 28, 2011
@aiww. It's different this time as the two surveillance vehicles have been outside several days and the men sleep in the cars. Probably because of the upcoming *lianghui* [meeting of both sections of the Chinese national congress].

MARCH 7, 2011
The Telegraph. *AI WEIWEI: "GROWING FORCE BEHIND JASMINE REVOLUTION VERY STRONG."* The controversial activist-artist, whose *Sunflower Seeds* is currently on display at Tate Modern, said he was now under constant surveillance, accusing the Chinese authorities of stifling all opinions "like Chinese parents from olden times." … "In the past two weeks, over 100 people have been arrested. Some are longtime writers, scholars, lawyers; some are just one-time students saying 'let's meet on a certain corner, a certain street.' It's very strong," Mr. Ai said.

MARCH 8, 2011
@aiww. The two police surveillance vehicles outside have vanished. Didn't even come in to offer greetings.

MARCH 31, 2011
@aiww. Police entered my home to conduct an investigation.
@aiww. Forcibly taking down details of staff's ID cards.
@aiww. 14 policemen all decked out with cameras. Said they were spot-checking my foreign assistants' status. Tonight wasn't convenient, they'll return tomorrow.

APRIL 1, 2011
@aiww. Chaoyang District police came again to check the IDs of my staff. It's the third time, looks like something big is on the horizon.
@aiww. Over ten people came to check fire-fighting equipment. Caochangdi must be the underpants of CCTV [reference to Beijing's China Central Television headquarters, which caught fire on February 9, 2009]. Ten armed officers barging in in the middle of the night. Our "stability maintenance fees" aren't paid in vain.

APRIL 3, 2011
@aiww. (tweet by Ai's assistant). On April 3, 2011, Ai Weiwei was detained by two immigration officials at Beijing's international airport. Ai's assistant was separated from him. Ai's mobile phone has been turned off and he has lost contact for 30 minutes; the situation is unclear.
@aiww (tweet by Ai's assistant). An hour ago a group of police officers showed up with a search warrant to Ai Weiwei's studio at 258 Caochangdi. They took away eight studio members to the Beijing Nangao Police Station for interrogation: Xu Ye, Qian Feifei, Dong Jie, Xiao Wei, Xiao Xie, Xing Rui, Jiang Li, and Xiao Pang the nephew. Lu Qing is alone at home with the police. The studio's front and back entrances are barricaded by police

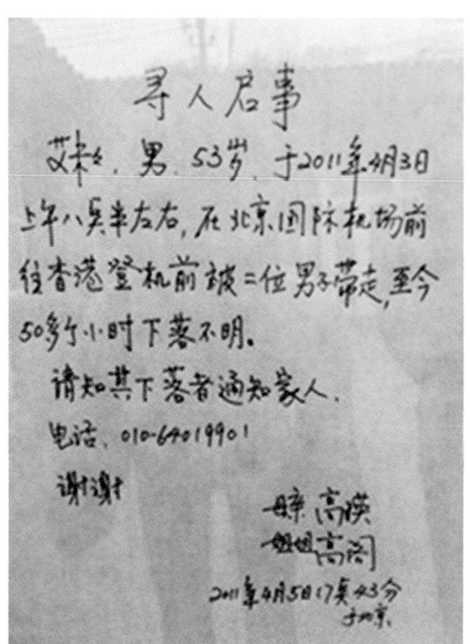

Missing person notice written
by Ai Weiwei's mother, April 5, 2011

with no way to enter or exit. Ai Weiwei has been detained at the Beijing airport for 3 hours and has not been reachable.

BBC News. *CHINA ARTIST AI WEIWEI STOPPED FROM BOARDING FLIGHT.* Prominent Chinese artist and activist Ai Weiwei has been stopped by the authorities from leaving the Chinese capital, Beijing, reports say. There has been no contact with him since, and no comment from the police. One of his assistants told the BBC he had been held by border guards as he tried to get on a flight to Hong Kong. She says police have searched his Beijing home, which is also his studio. Ai Weiwei's compound in Beijing has now been cordoned off. It is not clear whether the 53-year-old artist has been detained or why he was barred from taking the flight from Beijing Capital International Airport.

APRIL 4, 2011

AFP. *POLICE REMAIN SILENT ON AI WEI-WEI DETENTION.* "As he was being detained, police came here with a search warrant and searched everywhere," his wife Lu Qing said by telephone. "They took the computer, computer disks, and other materials. They refused to say why the search warrant was issued or why Ai Weiwei was taken away." Several of Ai's assistants were also detained for questioning on Sunday, but later released, said Lu, adding that she was not under house arrest.

The New York Times. The United States, France, Britain, and Germany on Monday called on China to release Ai Weiwei, an internationally known artist and increasingly vocal government critic. A State Department spokesman, Mark Toner, said the United States was "deeply concerned by the trend of forced disappearances, extralegal detentions, arrests and convictions of human rights activists for exercising their internationally recognized human right for freedom of expression." The German foreign minister, Guido Westerwelle, said, "I appeal to the Chinese government to urgently provide clarification, and I expect Ai Weiwei to be released immediately." Britain and France issued similar statements.

APRIL 5, 2011

Deutsche Welle. Gao Ying, Ai Weiwei's mother, the wife of renowned poet Ai Qing, announced a "missing person notice" with her daughter, Gao Ge, in the evening of April 5 to look for Ai Weiwei, who has been detained at customs in the Beijing Airport on April 3 and whose whereabouts remain unknown as of now. This is a handwritten notice, it states: "Ai Weiwei, male, 53 years old, was taken away by two men at around 8:30am on April 3, 2011 at the Beijing Capital Airport before boarding his flight to Hong Kong. He has now been missing for over fifty hours. Shall you have information of him, please contact his family. Mother Gao Ying, Sister, Gao Ge. 17:43, April 5, 2011, Beijing." Immediately, the missing person notice went viral on the Internet.

APRIL 6, 2011
Global Times (China). *LAW WILL NOT CONCEDE BEFORE MAVERICK.* Ai Weiwei, known as an avant-garde artist, was said to have been detained recently. Some Western governments and human rights institutions soon called for the immediate release of Ai Weiwei, claiming it to be China's "human rights deterioration" while regarding Ai Weiwei as "China's human rights fighter." It is reckless collision against China's basic political framework and ignorance of China's judicial sovereignty to exaggerate a specific case in China and attack China with fierce comments before finding out the truth. The West's behavior aims at disrupting the attention of Chinese society and attempts to modify the value system of the Chinese people … Ai Weiwei will be judged by history, but he will pay a price for his special choice, which is the same in any society. China as a whole is progressing and no one has power to make a nation try to adapt to his personal likes and dislikes, which is different from whether rights of the minority are respected.

APRIL 7, 2011
Washington Post. *AI WEIWEI HELD FOR "ECONOMIC CRIMES."* A foreign ministry spokesman said Ai, an outspoken critic of the government, was being investigated for "economic crimes" and warned other countries not to meddle in the case. "China is a country ruled by law and will act according to law," said Hong Lei, the foreign ministry spokesman, at a regularly scheduled press briefing. "We hope that the countries concerned will respect China's decision … This has nothing to do with human rights or freedom of expression."

APRIL 8, 2011
The New York Times. *MUSEUMS PRESS FOR THE RELEASE OF AI WEIWEI.* The Solomon R. Guggenheim Foundation is leading an international effort to call for the release of Ai Weiwei, the Chinese conceptual artist who was taken into police custody in Beijing after he was detained on Sunday while trying to board a flight for Hong Kong. It has gathered the support of the museum community, including the Museum of Modern Art in New York, the Los Angeles County Museum of Art, the Minneapolis Institute of Arts, and the Tate in London along with the American Association of Art Museum Directors.

APRIL 10, 2011
The Wall Street Journal. *HONG KONG RALLIES FOR AI WEIWEI.* The march was led by members of the Hong Kong Alliance in Support of Patriotic Democratic Movements, including legislators Lee Cheuk-Yan and Albert Ho. The crowd repeatedly yelled out in English, "Release Ai Weiwei," and in Cantonese, "No to political persecution."
BZ Berlin. *DEMO FOR AI WEIWEI IN BERLIN.* Human rights activists in Berlin on Saturday expressed their solidarity with the Chinese artist Ai Weiwei, who has disappeared after his arrest in Beijing. At the Brandenburg Gate, they held up placards with a portrait of the contemporary artist and the question "Where is Ai Weiwei?" At the demonstration, they also collected signatures for the release of Nobel Peace Prize winner Liu Xiaobo and other Chinese dissidents. A spokesman for Amnesty International said Ai Weiwei was symbolic of the thousands of people whose human rights are restricted in the People's Republic.

APRIL 12, 2011
The Guardian. Chinese tax officials have summoned the wife of detained artist Ai Weiwei for questioning, bolstering the theory that authorities may bring tax-related charges against him. Lu Qing spent about an hour at the tax office in Beijing. She was asked to take documents with her, but was unable to do so as they had already been confiscated by police, according to Radio Television Hong Kong.

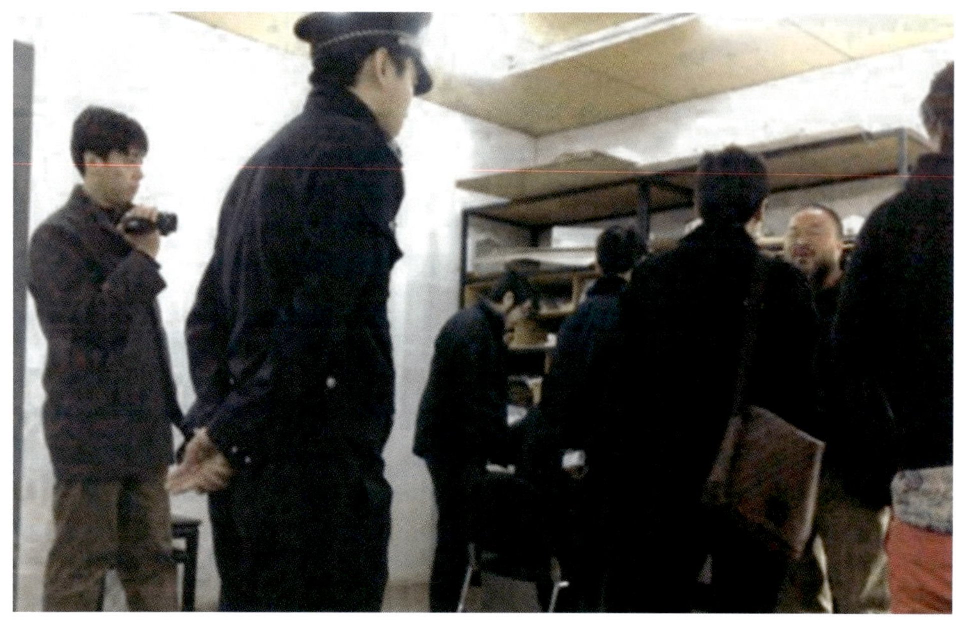

Chaoyang District police at Ai Weiwei's studio, Caochangdi, Beijing, April 1, 2011

APRIL 17, 2011
The Guardian. *AI WEIWEI ARREST PRO-
TESTS AT CHINESE EMBASSIES WORLD-
WIDE.* Demonstrators all over the world were
sitting outside Chinese embassies on Sunday
demanding the release of the detained Chinese artist Ai Weiwei. Hundreds of protestors
brought chairs onto the street to call for the
immediate release of Ai, and in support of the
rights of all Chinese artists. In Hong Kong
there were scuffles as 150 protestors came up
against lines of police, with reports of at least
one detention. In Berlin, about 200 people
took part in a largely silent protest. There was
also a gathering outside the Chinese embassy
in London.

APRIL 19, 2011
PBS. *CRACKDOWN ON AI WEIWEI
EXTENDS TO FAMILY, FRIENDS, AND
ASSOCIATES.* While the world-famous artist's disappearance has been widely covered
and discussed, fewer have taken note that his
friends and associates have also been targeted. Four of Ai's associates are also missing:
journalist Wen Tao, Ai's driver Xiao Pang,
FAKE Design company accountant Hu Ming-

fen and FAKE designer Liu Zhenggang. Earlier
today, Liu Xiaoyuan, a rights lawyer who had
represented Ai in the past and had said he
was willing to do so again, "reappeared" after
a five-day disappearance.

APRIL 20, 2011
Der Spiegel. The imprisoned dissident artist
Ai Weiwei has been offered a visiting professorship at the University of the Arts (UdK)
in Berlin. Ai, 53, would teach at the newly
founded Graduate School for the Arts and
Sciences. He would also work with students
from Danish artist Olafur Eliasson's Institute
for Spatial Experiments. UdK president Martin Rennert says he hopes "Ai Weiwei may
soon begin his work here" but has not men-
tioned a specific time.

APRIL 23, 2011
Reuters. *THOUSANDS MARCH IN HONG
KONG TO DEMAND RELEASE OF CHINA'S
AI.* The rally—the largest in a string of protests across the city in recent weeks—has
underscored Hong Kong's growing role as a
hotbed of support for Ai with local pro-democ-
racy activists and artists ratcheting up pres-

sure on Beijing over its heavy crackdown on dissidents, human rights lawyers and protesters challenging Communist Party controls and censorship. While the event was largely peaceful, brief skirmishes with police broke out as tempers flared.

APRIL 27, 2011
BBC News. *CHINA AND US BEGIN HUMAN RIGHTS TALKS IN BEIJING.* The US is expected to urge China to ease a severe government crackdown on dissent, which activists say has been the most extensive in years. Government critics including lawyers, bloggers and activists—among them artist Ai Weiwei—have been targeted.

MAY 4, 2011
The New York Times. The Chinese artist Ai Weiwei began his second month of detention this week, and still the Chinese government has given an increasingly outraged and anxious world no satisfactory answers to questions about his whereabouts, his condition or the charges against him. But business as usual can sometimes be its own quiet form of defiance. Despite Mr. Ai's absence, his plans for exhibiting his art in the West have been proceeding on schedule. Last weekend an exhibition of new work opened at the neugerriemschneider gallery in Berlin, which displayed an immense white banner printed in black with the words "Where is Ai Weiwei" on the front of its building. A larger exhibition will open next week at the Lisson Gallery in London. And in Manhattan *Circle of Animals/ Zodiac Heads*, which is being termed Mr. Ai's first public sculpture, was proclaimed open on Wednesday morning in a drizzle at the Pulitzer Fountain in front of the Plaza Hotel.

MAY 15, 2011
Associated Press. *DETAINED CHINESE ARTIST ALLOWED VISIT BY WIFE.* The sister of detained Chinese artist Ai Weiwei says he's been allowed his first family visit in 43 days. Beijing police took Ai's wife, Lu Qing, to an undisclosed location Sunday night where she was able to see and talk briefly with Ai. His sister Gao Ge says Lu reported that Ai seemed healthy and was being given access to medication that he needs. Gao says police have still not told the family where Ai is being held. She said Monday that the family is relieved to know he is well, but hope the government can clarify what is going on with his case.

MAY 20, 2011
BBC News. *CHINESE ARTIST AI WEIWEI'S COMPANY "EVADED TAXES."* The Chinese authorities have alleged that a company owned by the detained artist, Ai Weiwei, evaded a "huge amount" of tax, state media report. Beijing Fake Cultural Development— which handles the business aspects of Mr. Ai's art career—"was found to have evaded 'a huge amount' of tax" and also to have "intentionally destroyed accounting documents," Xinhua reported, citing unnamed police in the capital. The agency also said Mr. Ai was being held "under residential surveillance," which usually means detainees are confined to their homes.

JUNE 22, 2011
Xinhua News Agency (China). *AI WEIWEI RELEASED ON BAIL.* The Beijing police department said Wednesday that Ai Weiwei has been released on bail because of his good attitude in confessing his crimes as well as a chronic disease he suffers from…The decision comes also in consideration of the fact that Ai has repeatedly said he is willing to pay the taxes he evaded, police said.
The Guardian. After 81 days in detention, China's best-known artist, Ai Weiwei, returned home a considerably thinner and noticeably quieter man. "I'm fine. I'm out," the 54-year-old artist told the *Guardian* in a telephone call shortly after his release on bail. "I'm back with my family. I'm very happy."

JUNE 23, 2011
The Wall Street Journal. Mr. Ai said his health was fine and thanked reporters for their support as he returned to his studio late Wednesday with his mother and his wife, according to witnesses. He added that he wasn't able to say more under the conditions of his bail. "I can't say much. I can say I'm out. I'm on bail. But I can't say anything more under the conditions of my release," he told *The Wall Street Journal* by telephone. Asked how long the media ban was in place, Mr. Ai said: "One year, at least." He also

confirmed that the ban applied to social media such as Twitter, on which he has a following of more than 88,000. Mr. Ai used to send dozens of tweets daily, many of them criticizing the Chinese government, until his detention in April.

The Guardian. *AI WEIWEI'S COUSIN FREED BUT OTHERS FROM HIS CIRCLE STILL MISSING.* Ai's mother, Gao Ying, said her nephew Zhang Jinsong, who had worked as the artist's driver, returned home in a good mental state but had lost around 9 kg (20 lb). Zhang went missing a few days after his cousin. Three other associates who went missing shortly after Ai remain unaccounted for.

AUGUST 5, 2011

@aiww. Just saying hello.

@aiww. Had ten dumplings for lunch; regained 3 kg.

AUGUST 8, 2011

@aiww. Saw Liu Zhenggang tonight; he talked about the detention for the first time. He raised his right hand and said: reporting to monitor, I request water. Then this tough guy started to weep … His heart condition had flared up while in detention, and several times he was near death.

AUGUST 9, 2011

Global Times (China). *AI WEIWEI BREAKS HIS SILENCE.* Despite the sensitive issues surrounding his case and his release, Ai talked openly about his emotions, ideas, and his thoughts while in custody. "I was cut off from the outside world. No one told me when I would be released. It felt like I had fallen heavily into a collapsed pit," said Ai, sitting comfortably with his legs folded under him on his new couch. "I will never avoid politics, none of us can. We live in a politicized society." Ai crossed his arms and looked serious. He paused for a thought and continued: "You give up your rights when you dodge them. Of course you might live an easier life if you abandon some rights. But there are so many injustices, and limited educational resources. They all diminish happiness. I will never stop fighting injustice." Contingent on his being allowed to leave China, Ai has accepted a teaching offer at the Berlin University of the Arts. Even though the terms of his release restrict him to Beijing for a year, Ai said he would never consider permanently leaving the country. "People with black hearts should be exiled, I will never leave," Ai said with a laugh.

@aiww. They were illegally detained because of me. Liu Zhenggang, Hu Mingfen, Wentao, Zhang Jinsong, innocently they suffered huge mental devastation and physical torture.

NOVEMBER 1, 2011

@aiww. Just now, two employees of the Beijing Tax Bureau tried to deliver an invoice for 15.22 million RMB to 258 Caochangdi. Lu Qing, the company's legal representative, said that the company has not seen its accounting books to this day; that the penalty is without basis; and refused to accept.

AFP. *CHINA ARTIST AI WEIWEI GETS MULTI-MILLION TAX BILL.* Chinese authorities on Tuesday ordered artist Ai Weiwei to pay 15 million yuan ($2.36 million) in alleged back taxes in what the vocal rights activist called an effort to "crush" him. "They gave a written notice today … there was no explanation whatsoever. We questioned where this figure came from—they couldn't give a clear answer," Ai told AFP. "The notice said I have 15 days to pay. That's about one million a day … if you don't pay they could put you in jail, maybe up to seven years. I really have no idea."

Reuters. Ai told Reuters he received the notice from the tax authorities that described his title as the "actual controller" for Beijing Fake Cultural Development Ltd., which has helped produce Ai's internationally renowned art and designs. The company is owned by his wife, Lu Qing, who is the firm's legal representative. "They made up this new title," Ai said. "I'm a designer for the company. I'm not a director, or even a manager."

NOVEMBER 4, 2011

Christian Science Monitor. *IN DEFIANT GESTURE, CHINESE SURGE FORWARD TO HELP AI WEIWEI PAY TAX BILL.* The online public subscription drive began earlier this week, when several prominent supporters of Ai's proposed the idea. It appears to have really taken off since Hu Jia, a well known human rights activist who was released in June after a 40-month sentence

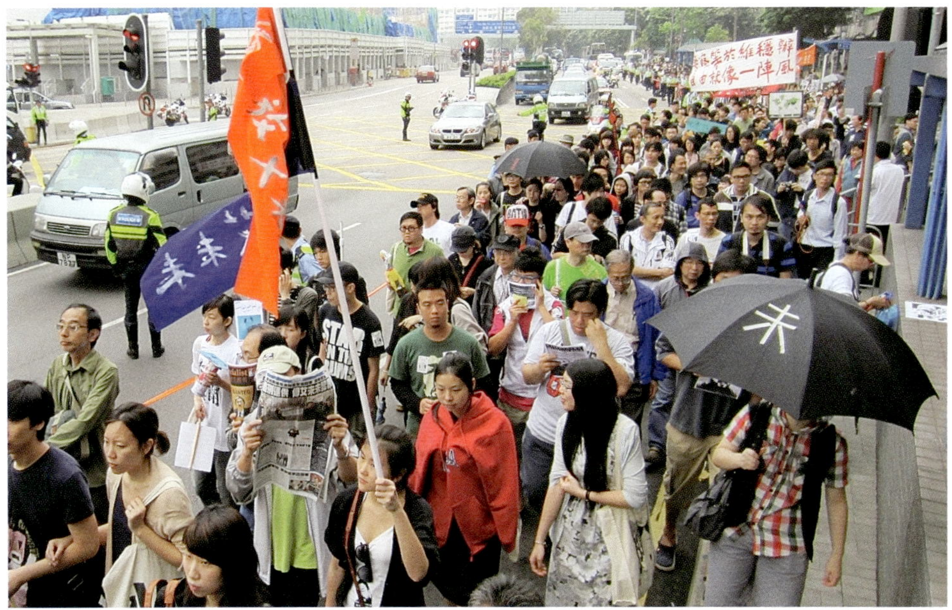

2,000 people protest Ai Weiwei's detention, Hong Kong, April 23, 2011

for "inciting subversion of state power," announced on his Twitter account on Thursday that he had donated 1,000 RMB ($158) to Ai … "We are doing performance art with him to mock the autocratic state machine," said one lender in a message signed @ihnsfa on Ai's microblog. "I hope our slight power can help you win a splendid victory," read another message, accompanying a donation of 1,000 RMB.

NOVEMBER 7, 2011
The New York Times. *ONLINE AND BY PAPER AIRPLANE, CONTRIBUTIONS POUR IN TO CHINESE DISSIDENT.* More than 20,000 people have together contributed at least $840,000 since Tuesday, when tax officials gave Mr. Ai 15 days to come up with an amount that was more than three times the sum he was accused of evading in taxes. On Sunday, after his Weibo account was disabled, dozens of people began arriving at the gate of Mr. Ai's studio on the outskirts of the capital. He said a number of people had folded 100-renminbi notes into airplanes and tossed them over the walls of his compound.

NOVEMBER 14, 2011
The Wall Street Journal. *AI WEIWEI DONATIONS HIT 1.37 MILLION, ENOUGH TO CHALLENGE TAX CHARGES.* "I feel that this is the beginning of civil society in China," he said. "Young people have their own knowledge and don't believe state media or the government's accusations against me. This shows people care. They don't only care, but they take action."

NOVEMBER 15, 2011
BBC News. Chinese artist Ai Weiwei has handed over a $1.3 million bond to the government in order to begin an appeal against a massive tax bill. He said the tax bureau insisted he put the money into its bank account or face police prosecution.

JANUARY 6, 2012
The Guardian. *AI WEIWEI GIVEN HOPE OF TAX REPRIEVE.* The Chinese artist Ai Weiwei has said Beijing tax authorities are reviewing their ruling that he pay a multimillion dollar penalty for alleged tax evasion … The internationally acclaimed conceptual artist said officials told him of the

decision on Wednesday by telephone. They said the review would be completed within two months. Ai said he was hopeful the case would be handled earnestly and transparently.

MARCH 29, 2012
Reuters. *CHINA TELLS AI WEIWEI NO PUBLIC TRIAL FOR TAX CASE.* Chinese authorities have told dissident artist Ai Weiwei he will not be given a public hearing to reconsider a 15 million yuan tax evasion penalty allegedly due from the company he works for, Ai said on Thursday, a move he denounced as "inconceivable." Ai, 54, told Reuters by telephone he received the notice, dated March 23, from tax authorities on Tuesday. It said Beijing Fake Cultural Development Ltd., which has helped produce Ai's internationally renowned art and designs, will only be given "a written hearing" and not a public trial.

MARCH 31, 2012
@aiww. Today, the Beijing Tax Bureau finally permitted FAKE to inspect photocopies of the records illegally seized by police a year ago. Photos and scans are not permitted, but photocopying is. As the Tax Bureau's photocopiers were of very poor quality, we wanted to buy a new photocopier but were not permitted to do so. In fact, the originals of the documents should have been returned long ago. FAKE's manager and accountant still remain in a state of disappearance, enforced by the Public Security Bureau.

APRIL 13, 2012
The Wall Street Journal. *CHINA DISSIDENT ARTIST SUES OVER TAX.* Dissident Chinese artist Ai Weiwei said he filed suit against local Beijing tax authorities for the way they are pursuing their claim against him for $2.4 million in back taxes and penalties. "They don't even try to give us a proper procedure or play right," Mr. Ai said in an interview on Friday. "The only possibility is to sue them in court."

MAY 8, 2012
BBC News. *CHINA SAYS ARTIST AI WEIWEI CAN CHALLENGE $2.4 MILLION TAX BILL.* A court in Beijing has now said it will hear the case. It is not yet clear whether Ai will actually appear at the hearing. He is a designer for Fake Cultural Development Ltd, but is not the company's legal representative. The world-renowned artist told the BBC that he was surprised the authorities had agreed to let him challenge the case.

JUNE 20, 2012
@aiww. This afternoon, FAKE's tax case will be heard in the Chaoyang court. As plaintiff's agent, I am being controlled by the police and cannot go. This magical land, where one is able to go into space, but not to buy a seat to make a statement of innocence with 15.22 million RMB. Not a single seat is kept for the plaintiff in the public gallery. The reality is that the party of justice is forever absent.

The Wall Street Journal. *AI WEIWEI BLOCKED FROM COURT.* Ai Weiwei, the Chinese dissident artist, accused authorities Wednesday of blocking him from attending a hearing on his lawsuit against the Beijing tax bureau. He also said that police had detained his legal adviser. Mr. Ai told *China Real Time* he was notified to attend a hearing on his lawsuit Wednesday, but was then told he couldn't register for a seat in the courtroom, and was finally ordered by police not to attend. He said about 40 police cars had blocked the road outside his house since early Wednesday morning—the strongest police presence since his release from detention last year.

The New York Times. On Wednesday, after the police told Mr. Ai that he could not attend the proceedings and blocked scores of other dissidents from leaving their homes in the capital, hundreds of supporters gathered outside the Chaoyang District Court in Beijing despite a small army of police officers, some of whom videotaped the crowd and led several people away. While Mr. Ai's wife and legal advisers sat in on the hearing, Mr. Ai took to Twitter, sending out messages that ridiculed the authorities and condemned an assault by the police on one of his videographers as he filmed outside the gates of Mr. Ai's studio on Wednesday morning. Mr. Ai posted a photograph of the filmmaker's injuries and a portrait of himself wearing a mischievous grin and an ill-fitting police uniform.

JUNE 21, 2012
Reuters. *CHINA'S AI WEIWEI THREAT-ENED WITH BIGAMY, PORNOGRAPHY CHARGES.* Chinese police told dissident artist Ai Weiwei on Thursday he could face bigamy and pornography charges and barred him from travel, despite lifting strict bail conditions imposed after his detention. Ai, who left his house on Thursday for the first time in a year without having to report his whereabouts to police, was held for 81 days without charge in April 2011 mainly in solitary confinement until his conditional release last year. "If getting back half of my freedom means I'm free, then I'm a free person," Ai said. "But they're restricting my ability to travel and still trying to fabricate crimes."

July 20, 2012
Time. *CHINESE ACTIVIST AI WEIWEI LOSES APPEAL ON TAX CHARGE.* A Beijing court rejected activist artist Ai Weiwei's appeal against a multimillion-dollar penalty the Chinese government says his company owes for evading taxes. Ai, who was blocked from attending the hearing on Friday morning in the Chaoyang District Court in eastern Beijing, says the case against him is politically motivated, and he plans to continue to challenge the government's charge. "We know we can't win. We know the tax bureau, the police, the courts, they are all the same," Ai told TIME after the ruling. "But we will continue to fight to show what this system is like."
@aiww. We will continue to appeal, until that day when we cannot lose arrives.

SEPTEMBER 27, 2012
The Wall Street Journal. *AI WEIWEI: I WON'T PAY.* Artist Ai Weiwei said he would refuse to pay the remainder of a $2.4 million fine for tax evasion after a Beijing court rejected his appeal on Thursday, setting the stage for another possible showdown between the media-savvy dissident and Chinese authorities. "We're not going to pay the fine because we don't recognize the charge," he said. "And I think they're probably too embarrassed to come and ask for it."

OCTOBER 1, 2012
The Guardian. *AI WEIWEI FIRM TO BE CLOSED DOWN BY CHINESE AUTHORI-TIES.* Chinese authorities are closing down the firm handling Ai Weiwei's affairs, the outspoken artist said on Monday, possibly saving him from paying the remainder of a 15 million yuan (£1.5 million) tax fine … Officials said this weekend they were removing Fake Cultural Development's business license because it had not met annual registration requirements. The company has been unable to do so because police confiscated all its materials and its stamp when they detained Ai last year. "I think it could be an excuse not to give us a fine," the artist added.

OCTOBER 2, 2012
@aiww. FAKE Design is no more; "the actual controller" is still here.

OCTOBER 31, 2012
The Guardian. *AI WEIWEI RETURNS MONEY TO SUPPORTERS.* Dissident Chinese artist Ai Weiwei has started returning money to his supporters after exhausting all legal channels to fight a massive tax bill that his backers saw as punishment for his activism. "We have no more options to keep trying. We've done what we could, and the court's decision has been made. So we should repay the money," Ai said in a phone interview.

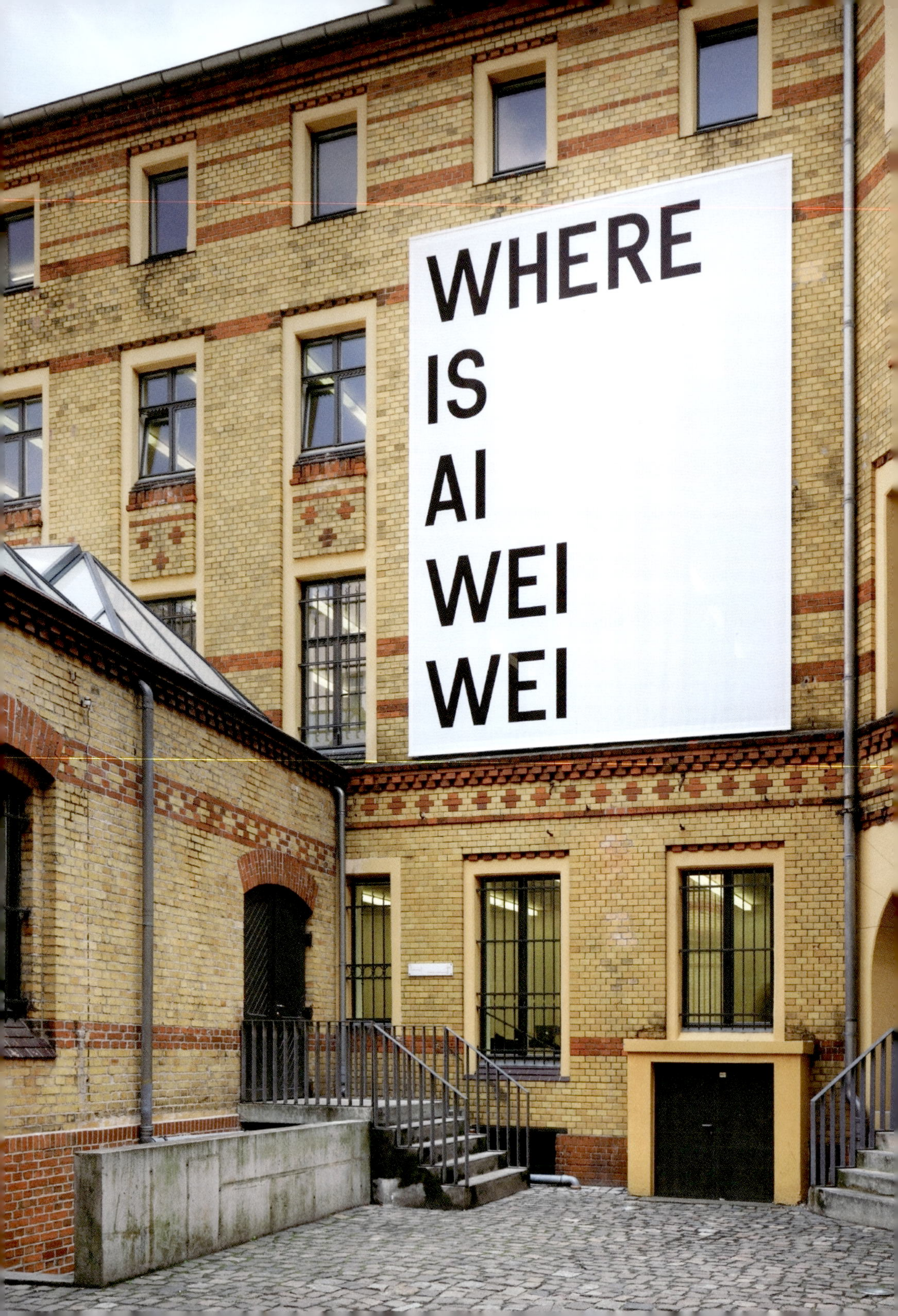
WHERE
IS
AI
WEI
WEI

Verhaftung und Prozess gegen FAKE Design

22. FEBRUAR 2011
@aiww. Gestern hockten zwei Leute den ganzen Tag in einem Überwachungsbus in Caochangdi.

23. FEBRUAR 2011
The Telegraph. *RUFE NACH JASMIN-REVOLUTION IN CHINA.* Die um sich greifenden Proteste im Nahen Osten scheinen China nervös zu machen. Nicht nur durch ein massives Aufgebot auf der Straße, sondern auch durch Internet-Zensur versucht die Polizei, kritische Stimmen zum Schweigen zu bringen. Bis zu 100 Aktivisten und Protestorganisatoren wurden unter Hausarrest gestellt.

27. FEBRUAR 2011
@aiww. Die Sicherheitsleute, die vor meinem Haus Blumen verkaufen, schlafen, während der Schnee fällt.

28. FEBRUAR 2011
@aiww. Irgendwas ist anders diesmal. Die zwei Überwachungsautos stehen seit mehreren Tagen vor der Tür. Die Beamten schlafen sogar im Auto. Vielleicht wegen der bevorstehenden *lianghui* [Konferenz beider Teile des Nationalkongresses].

7. MÄRZ 2011
The Telegraph. *AI WEIWEI: „JASMIN-REVOLUTION IM AUFWIND."* Der politisch engagierte Künstler, dessen *Sunflower Seeds* in der Tate Modern zu sehen sind, steht laut eigenen Angaben unter ständiger Überwachung. Er beschuldigt China, die freie Meinungsäußerung „wie chinesische Eltern alter Zeiten" zu unterdrücken. ... „In den letzten zwei Wochen sind über 100 Personen verhaftet worden. Etablierte Schriftsteller, Wissenschaftler, Anwälte, aber auch einfache Studenten, die sagen: ‚Treffen wir uns an einer bestimmten Ecke, in einer bestimmten Straße.' Es wird hart durchgegriffen", berichtet der Künstler.

8. MÄRZ 2011
@aiww. Die zwei Überwachungsautos sind verschwunden. Haben nicht mal an die Tür geklopft, um sich zu verabschieden.

31. MÄRZ 2011
@aiww. Wir haben Polizisten im Haus, die Fragen stellen.
@aiww. Sie verlangen die Ausweisnummern aller Mitarbeiter.
@aiww. 14 Polizisten, alle mit Kameras bewaffnet. Sie behaupten, sie wollen den Status meiner ausländischen Assistenten prüfen. Heute Abend hat nicht gereicht, die kommen morgen wieder.

1. APRIL 2011
@aiww. Die Bezirkspolizei von Chaoyang ist wieder zurückgekommen, um die Ausweise meiner Mitarbeiter zu prüfen. Das war das dritte Mal. Sieht aus, als hätten die was Größeres vor.
@aiww. Mehr als zehn Beamte kamen, um die Feuerlöscher zu kontrollieren. Caochangdi ist wohl die Unterwäsche von CCTV [das chinesische Staatsfernsehen, in dessen Zentrale am 9. Februar 2009 ein Brand ausbrach]. Zehn bewaffnete Beamte mitten in der Nacht. Die „Stabilitätsaufrechterhaltungsgebühren" rentieren sich also.

3. APRIL 2011
@aiww (Tweet einer Assistentin von Ai). Ai Weiwei wurde am 3. April 2011 auf dem Flughafen Peking von zwei Grenzbeamten aufgehalten und von seiner Assistentin getrennt. Sein Mobiltelefon wurde ausgeschaltet, und er ist seit 30 Minuten nicht erreichbar. Wir haben gegenwärtig keine klaren Informationen.
@aiww (Tweet der Assistentin). Vor einer Stunde erschienen Polizeibeamte mit einem Haussuchungsbefehl in Ai Weiweis Atelier, Caochangdi Nr. 258. Sie brachten acht Mitarbeiter zum Verhör in die Polizeistation Peking-Nangao: Xu Ye, Qian Feifei, Dong Jie, Xiao Wei, Xiao Xie, Xing Rui, Jiang Li

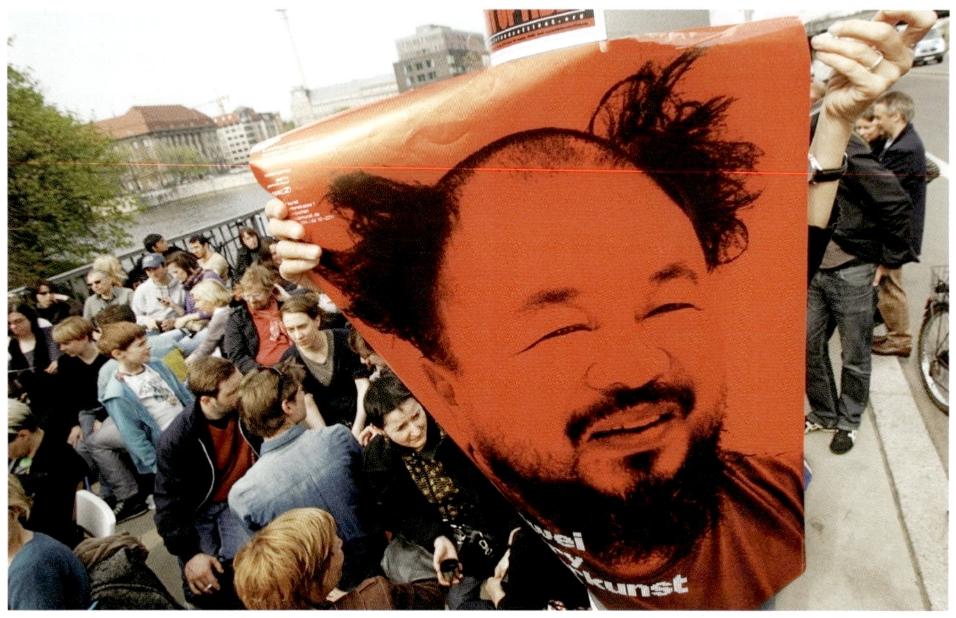

Protest in front of the Chinese embassy in Berlin, April 17, 2011

und Ais Neffen Xiao Pang. Lu Qing ist alleine mit der Polizei im Haus. Die Vorder- und Hintereingänge des Ateliers sind verbarrikadiert. Man kann weder rein noch raus. Ai Weiwei wurde auf dem Flughafen von Peking festgenommen, und bisher gibt es keinen Kontakt.
BBC News. *KÜNSTLER AI WEIWEI AN AUSREISE GEHINDERT.* Laut Berichten wird der bekannte chinesische Künstler Ai Weiwei auf dem Flughafen Peking festgehalten. Es besteht keine Möglichkeit, ihn zu erreichen, und es gibt bisher keine offizielle Stellungnahme. Eine Assistentin teilte der BBC mit, Ai sei von Grenzbeamten am Besteigen einer Maschine nach Hongkong gehindert worden. Sie sagte, die Polizei habe das Haus und Atelier des Künstlers durchsucht und den gesamten Gebäudekomplex abgesperrt. Bisher ist unklar, ob der 53-jährige Künstler verhaftet wurde und aus welchem Grund er nicht ausreisen durfte.

4. APRIL 2011
AFP. *KEINE STELLUNGNAHME ZU AI WEIWEIS VERHAFTUNG.* „Während Ai festgehalten wurde, kam die Polizei mit einem Haussuchungsbefehl und hat hier alles durch-

sucht", teilte Lu Qing, die Frau des Künstlers, telefonisch mit. „Sie haben Computer und andere Dinge mitgenommen. Den Grund für die Hausdurchsuchung und die Verhaftung Ai Weiweis konnten wir nicht erfahren." Mehrere Mitarbeiter Ais wurden am Sonntag verhört und später allerdings freigelassen, berichtete Lu. Sie selbst stehe nicht unter Hausarrest.
The New York Times. Die Vereinigten Staaten, Frankreich, Großbritannien und Deutschland forderten am Montag die chinesische Regierung auf, den international bekannten Künstler und Regimekritiker Ai Weiwei freizulassen. Wie Mark Toner, der Sprecher des US-Außenministeriums, betonte, beobachten die USA „mit Besorgnis die steigende Zahl illegaler Festnahmen und Verurteilungen von Menschenrechtlern, die ihr international anerkanntes Recht auf freie Meinungsäußerung ausüben". Der deutsche Außenminister Guido Westerwelle erklärte: „Ich erwarte von der chinesischen Regierung eine klare Stellungnahme und rechne damit, dass Ai Weiwei binnen kurzer Zeit auf freien Fuß gesetzt wird." Großbritannien und Frankreich gaben ähnliche Erklärungen ab.

Deutsche Welle. Gao Ying, Ai Weiweis Mutter und Frau des bekannten Dichters Ai Qing, veröffentlichte am Abend des 5. April zusammen mit ihrer Tochter Gao Ge eine handgeschriebene Vermisstenmeldung für Ai Weiwei, von dem es seit seiner Festnahme auf dem Flughafen Peking kein Lebenszeichen gibt: „Ai Weiwei, männlich, 53 Jahre alt, wurde am 3. April 2011 um ca. 8:30 Uhr von zwei Männern am Flughafen Peking festgenommen, ehe er seinen Flug nach Hongkong antreten konnte. Er wird seit mehr als 50 Stunden vermisst. Bitte kontaktieren Sie mit weiterführenden Informationen die Familie. Gao Ying, Mutter, und Gao Ge, Schwester, 17:43 Uhr, 5. April 2011, Peking." Die Meldung verbreitete sich schnell über das Internet.

6. APRIL 2011
Global Times (China). *GESETZE GELTEN AUCH FÜR ANDERSDENKENDE.* Kürzlich wurde berichtet, der Avantgardekünstler Ai Weiwei sei festgenommen worden. Einzelne westliche Regierungen und Menschenrechtsorganisationen forderten seine sofortige Freilassung. China „verstoße gegen die Menschenrechte" und Ai sei ein „Verfechter der Menschenrechte in China". Die Übertreibung eines Einzelfalls sowie die Verurteilung unseres Landes ohne Prüfung der Fakten verstößt gegen die politische und rechtliche Souveränität Chinas. Ziel des Westens ist es, Unruhe in die chinesische Gesellschaft zu bringen und ihr Wertsystem zu verändern ... Die eigenmächtigen Handlungen Ai Weiweis werden von der Geschichte beurteilt werden. Sicher wird er für sie den Preis bezahlen, den jede Gesellschaft fordert. Dass die Volksrepublik China Fortschritte macht, ist unbestritten, doch keine Einzelperson kann eine Nation dazu zwingen, sich nach ihren persönlichen Vorlieben und Abneigungen zu richten. Die Frage des Minderheitenrechts hat damit nichts zu tun.

7. APRIL 2011
Washington Post. *AI WEIWEI WEGEN „WIRTSCHAFTSKRIMINALITÄT" INHAF-TIERT.* Ein Sprecher des chinesischen Außenministeriums erklärte, dass gegen den Regimekritiker Ai Weiwei eine Untersuchung wegen Verdachts auf Wirtschaftskriminalität eingeleitet worden sei, und warnte andere Länder davor, sich einzumischen. „China ist ein Rechtsstaat und wird sich dementsprechend verhalten", sagte der Sprecher Hong Lei auf einer Pressekonferenz. „Wir hoffen, dass alle betroffenen Länder die Entscheidung Chinas respektieren ... Es geht in diesem Fall nicht um Meinungsfreiheit oder Menschenrechte."

8. APRIL 2011
The New York Times. *MUSEEN FORDERN DIE FREILASSUNG VON AI WEIWEI.* Die Solomon R. Guggenheim Foundation hat eine internationale Initiative für die Freilassung des chinesischen Konzeptkünstlers Ai Weiwei gestartet, der am Sonntag vor Antritt eines Flugs nach Hongkong festgenommen wurde. Zahlreiche Museen haben die Petition unterzeichnet, darunter das Museum of Modern Art in New York, das Los Angeles County Museum of Art, das Minneapolis Institute of Arts, die Londoner Tate und die American Association of Art Museum Directors.

10. APRIL 2011
The Wall Street Journal. *DEMONSTRATION FÜR AI WEIWEI IN HONGKONG.* Der Protestmarsch wurde von der Hong Kong Alliance in Support of Patriotic Democratic Movements organisiert. Die Demonstranten, darunter die Abgeordneten Lee Cheuk-Yan und Albert Ho, riefen auf Englisch „Freiheit für Ai Weiwei" und auf Kantonesisch „Nein zur politischen Verfolgung in China".

BZ Berlin. *DEMO FÜR AI WEIWEI IN BERLIN.* Menschenrechtsaktivisten haben am Sonnabend in Berlin ihre Solidarität mit dem nach seiner Festnahme in Peking verschwundenen chinesischen Künstler Ai Weiwei bekundet. Am Brandenburger Tor stellten sie auf Plakaten mit dem Konterfei des Gegenwartskünstlers die Frage „Wo ist Ai Weiwei?". Dort sollten Unterschriften auch für die Freilassung des Friedensnobelpreisträgers Liu Xiaobo und anderer chinesischer Dissidenten gesammelt werden. Ai Weiwei stehe symbolisch für Tausende, deren Menschenrechte in der Volksrepublik eingeschränkt würden, sagte ein Sprecher von Amnesty International.

12. APRIL 2011

The Guardian. Lu Qing, die Frau des inhaftierten Künstlers Ai Weiwei, wurde zu einer etwa einstündigen Befragung ins Pekinger Finanzamt geladen. Damit bestärkt sich die Vermutung, dass es ein Steuerverfahren gegen Ai geben wird. Lu Qing war außerstande, die geforderten Dokumente vorzulegen, da diese von der Polizei konfisziert worden waren, berichtet Radio Television Hong Kong.

17. APRIL 2011

The Guardian. *WELTWEITE BOTSCHAFTSPROTESTE FÜR AI WEIWEI.* Am Sonntag fanden vor chinesischen Botschaften in aller Welt Sitzproteste für den inhaftierten Künstler Ai Weiwei statt. Hunderte Demonstranten stellten Stühle auf, um Freiheit für Ai und Menschenrechte für alle chinesischen Künstler zu fordern. In Hongkong kam es zu einem Handgemenge zwischen der Polizei und 150 Demonstranten. Es soll mindestens eine Festnahme gegeben haben. Die Kundgebung in Berlin mit ca. 200 Teilnehmern verlief ohne Zwischenfälle. Auch vor der chinesischen Botschaft in London gab es Proteste.

19. APRIL 2011

PBS. *ANGEHÖRIGE VON KAMPAGNE GEGEN AI WEIWEI BETROFFEN.* Das Verschwinden des Kunststars machte Schlagzeilen. Weniger bekannt ist hingegen, dass auch seine Freunde und Bekannten Ziel staatlicher Repressalien sind. Vier Mitarbeiter gelten als vermisst: der Journalist Wen Tao, der Fahrer Xiao Pang, die Buchhalterin von FAKE Design, Hu Mingfen, und der FAKE-Designer Liu Zhenggang. Der Anwalt Liu Xiaoyuan, der Ai bereits mehrmals vertreten hat und auch diesmal seine Dienste anbot, ist heute nach fünftägiger Abwesenheit wieder „aufgetaucht".

20. APRIL 2011

Der Spiegel. Der inhaftierte regimekritische Künstler Ai Weiwei soll Gastprofessor an der Universität der Künste (UdK) in Berlin werden. Lehren soll Ai Weiwei, 53, an der neugegründeten Graduiertenschule für die Künste und die Wissenschaften. Außerdem soll er mit den Studenten des Instituts für Raumexperimente des dänischen Künstlers Olafur Eliasson arbeiten. UdK-Präsident Martin Rennert sagte dazu, er hoffe, dass „Ai Weiwei in Kürze seine Arbeit hier aufnehmen kann", einen konkreten Zeitpunkt nannte er aber nicht.

23. APRIL 2011

Reuters. *TAUSENDE FORDERN FREIHEIT FÜR AI WEIWEI IN HONGKONG.* Die Demonstration – die größte mehrerer solcher Kundgebungen im Laufe der letzten Wochen – unterstreicht die Schlüsselrolle Hongkongs im Kampf um die Befreiung Ais. Lokale Aktivisten und Künstler kritisieren immer schärfer die Unterdrückung von Dissidenten, Menschenrechtlern und Rechtsanwälten, die sich offen gegen Kontrolle und Zensur aussprechen, durch die Kommunistische Partei Chinas. Abgesehen von kurzen Konfrontationen mit der Polizei verlief die Veranstaltung friedlich.

27. APRIL 2011

BBC News. *MENSCHENRECHTSGESPRÄCHE ZWISCHEN USA UND CHINA IN PEKING.* Es wird erwartet, dass die USA die chinesische Regierung darauf drängen werden, ihre Kampagne gegen Regimekritiker, laut Beobachtern die schärfste seit Jahren, einzustellen. Betroffene Regierungskritiker sind Anwälte, Blogger und Aktivisten – unter anderem auch der Künstler Ai Weiwei.

4. MAI 2011

The New York Times. Die Inhaftierung des chinesischen Künstlers Ai Weiwei geht diese Woche in den zweiten Monat. Die chinesische Regierung schuldet der zunehmend besorgten Weltöffentlichkeit eine Antwort auf die Frage, wo und warum Ai festgehalten wird. Trotz der Abwesenheit des Künstlers werden seine Ausstellungen im Westen wie geplant stattfinden – auch dies eine Form der Kritik an der Handlungsweise Chinas. Bei der Eröffnung einer Ausstellung neuer Arbeiten in der Berliner Galerie neugerriemschneider am vergangenen Wochenende hing an der Fassade ein Transparent mit der Aufschrift „Wo ist Ai Weiwei". Eine größere Schau eröffnet kommende Woche in der Lisson Gallery, London. Und am Pulitzer Fountain vor dem Plaza Hotel in Manhattan wurde am Mittwochmorgen bei Nieselregen Ais „erste Skulptur im öffentlichen Raum" *Circle of Animals/Zodiac Heads* enthüllt.

15. MAI 2011
Associated Press. *AI WEIWEIS FRAU ERHÄLT BESUCHSERLAUBNIS.* Wie seine Schwester Gao Ge mitteilte, erhielt der inhaftierte chinesische Künstler Ai Weiwei zum ersten Mal seit 43 Tagen die Erlaubnis, Familienbesuch zu empfangen. Die Pekinger Polizei brachte Ais Frau Lu Qing an einen unbekannten Ort, wo ein kurzes Gespräch stattfand. Der Künstler machte einen gesunden Eindruck und schien alle nötigen Medikamente zu erhalten. Die Familie besitzt aber weiterhin keine Informationen über seinen Aufenthaltsort. Es sei erleichternd, zu wissen, dass Ai wohlauf ist, versicherte Gao, aber die Familie hoffe, bald offizielle Gründe für seine Verhaftung zu erfahren.

20. MAI 2011
BBC News. *FIRMA VON AI WEIWEI „HINTERZOG STEUERN".* Laut Berichten im staatlichen Rundfunk wird der inhaftierte Künstler Ai Weiwei beschuldigt, „große Steuersummen" hinterzogen zu haben. Die Firma Beijing Fake Cultural Development, die Ais Kunstaktivitäten organisiert, „hat nachweisbar große Steuersummen hinterzogen", zitiert die Nachrichtenagentur Xinhua ungenannte Quellen in der chinesischen Hauptstadt. Ai werde „an seinem Wohnsitz überwacht", gewöhnlich ein Hinweis auf Hausarrest.

22. JUNI 2011
Xinhua (China). *AI WEIWEI GEGEN KAUTION FREIGELASSEN.* Die Pekinger Polizei gab am Mittwoch bekannt, dass Ai Weiwei gegen Kaution freigelassen wurde. Als Gründe wurden ein geleistetes Schuldbekenntnis sowie sein Gesundheitszustand genannt ... Mildernd wirkte zudem Ais Bereitschaft, seine Steuerrückstände zu begleichen, teilte die Polizei mit.
The Guardian. Der chinesische Kunststar Ai Weiwei kehrte nach 81-tägiger Haft merklich schlanker und schweigsamer nach Hause zurück. „Ich bin heraus, mir geht's gut", versicherte der 54-jährige Künstler dem *Guardian* in einem Telefongespräch kurz nach seiner Entlassung auf Kaution. „Ich bin wieder mit meiner Familie vereint. Ich bin sehr glücklich."

23. JUNI 2011
The Wall Street Journal. Er befinde sich bei guter Gesundheit und danke der Presse für ihre Unterstützung, könne aufgrund der Kautionsauflagen jedoch keine weiteren Kommentare abgeben, erklärte Ai Weiwei, als er Mittwochabend mit seiner Frau und seiner Mutter in sein Studio zurückkehrte. „Ich darf nicht viel sagen. Nur so viel: Ich bin gegen Kaution frei", teilte er dem *Wall Street Journal* telefonisch mit. Auf die Frage, wie lange die Schweigepflicht gelte, antwortete Ai: „Mindestens ein Jahr." Sie betreffe auch Social Media wie Twitter, wo er über 88.000 Follower hat. Vor seiner Verhaftung im April postete Ai täglich Dutzende Tweets, viele mit kritischem Inhalt.
The Guardian. *COUSIN VON AI WEIWEI FREI.* Die Mutter Ai Weiweis, Gao Ying, teilte mit, dass ihr Neffe Zhang Jinsong, der Fahrer des Künstlers, in guter geistiger Verfassung, jedoch neun Kilo leichter nach Hause zurückgekehrt sei. Zhang war wenige Tage nach Ai Weiweis Verhaftung mit drei weiteren Mitarbeitern verschwunden.

5. AUGUST 2011
@aiww. Ich sag nur mal hallo.
@aiww. Hatte zehn Klößchen zu Mittag, gleich drei Kilo zugelegt.

8. AUGUST 2011
@aiww. Habe heute Abend Liu Zhenggang getroffen. Er sprach zum ersten Mal über die Haft. Wie er sich mit erhobenem Arm bei der Wache gemeldet hatte und um Wasser gebeten. Dann fing dieser harte Bursche an zu weinen ... Sein Herzleiden hat sich im Gefängnis verschlimmert, er wäre ein paar Mal fast gestorben.

9. AUGUST 2011
Global Times (China). *AI WEIWEI BRICHT SEIN SCHWEIGEN.* Trotz der schwierigen Auflagen, die er seit seiner Entlassung einzuhalten hat, spricht Ai Weiwei offen über seine Gefühle, Gedanken und Ideen während der Haftzeit. „Ich war von der Außenwelt abgeschnitten. Niemand sagte mir, wann ich wieder freikomme. Es war, als wäre ich in eine tiefe Grube gefallen." Ai macht es sich mit übergeschlagenen Beinen auf seiner neuen Couch bequem. „Ich werde die Politik nicht vermeiden. Niemand kann sie ausblenden,

wir leben in einer politisierten Gesellschaft."
Er verschränkt die Arme und blickt ernst.
Nach einer Pause setzt er fort: „Wenn du nicht
auf deinem Recht bestehst, verlierst du es.
Klar, unter Umständen lebt man leichter,
wenn man ein paar Rechte aufgibt. Aber es
gibt so viel Ungerechtigkeit, und es wird zu
wenig für die Bildung getan. All das verringert
das Glück in der Welt. Ich werde nie aufhö-
ren, gegen Ungerechtigkeit zu kämpfen."
Für seine Gastprofessur an der Berliner Universität der Künste benötigt er eine Ausreise-
erlaubnis. Gegenwärtig ist er verpflichtet, ein
Jahr in Peking zu bleiben. Daran, China auf
immer zu verlassen, denkt er allerdings nicht:
„Menschen mit schwarzen Herzen sollen ins
Exil. Ich bleibe", lacht er.
@aiww. Liu Zhenggang, Hu Mingfen, Wen
Tao und Zhang Jinsong wurden wegen mir
illegal festgehalten. Sie waren schweren geistigen Belastungen und körperlicher Folter
ausgesetzt.

1. NOVEMBER 2011
@aiww. Zwei Beamte des Finanzamts Peking
versuchten eben, eine Rechnung über 15,22
Millionen Yuan an unserer Haustür abzuge-
ben. Unsere Anwältin Lu Qing verweigerte die
Annahme mit dem Argument, dass uns noch
immer die Geschäftsbücher fehlen und dass
die Strafe nicht gerechtfertigt sei.
**AFP. *AI WEIWEI ERHÄLT MILLIONEN-
STRAFE.*** Die chinesischen Behörden forder-
ten den Künstler Ai Weiwei am Dienstag auf,
Steuerrückstände in Höhe von 15 Millionen
Yuan zu zahlen. Der Menschenrechtler und
Dissident sieht darin den Versuch, ihn zu
„zerstören". „Ich erhielt heute eine schriftli-
che Mitteilung ... ohne irgendeine Erklärung.
Wir wollten wissen, wie sie auf den Betrag
kamen, erhielten aber keine klare Antwort",
teilte er AFP mit. „Auf dem Bescheid steht,
ich habe 15 Tage Zeit, um zu zahlen. Das
macht ungefähr eine Million pro Tag ... wer
nicht zahlt, bekommt Gefängnis, bis zu sieben Jahre. Ich weiß wirklich nicht, was jetzt
geschieht."
Reuters. Ai berichtete Reuters, er habe einen
Bescheid des Finanzamts erhalten, der ihn
als „Geschäftsführer" der Firma Beijing Fake
Cultural Development Ltd. ausweist. Die
Firma, die Ais renommierte Kunstprojekte
realisiert, gehört seiner Frau Lu Qing.

„Die haben den Titel einfach erfunden",
erklärte Ai. „Ich arbeite als Designer für die
Firma und habe nichts mit der Geschäftslei-
tung zu tun."

4. NOVEMBER 2011
**Christian Science Monitor. *MUTIGE
CHINESISCHE BÜRGER HELFEN AI WEI-
WEI, SEINE STEUERSTRAFE ZU ZAHLEN.***
Die Anfang der Woche von Unterstützern
gestartete Online-Initiative erhielt verstärk-
ten Zulauf, als der bekannte Menschenrechtler Hu Jia, der erst im Juni seine 40-monatige
Haft wegen „Anstiftung zur Untergrabung der
Staatsgewalt" abgebüßt hatte, am Dienstag
eine Spende von 1000 Yuan auf Twitter postete ... „Wir machen mit ihm eine Performance zur Verhöhnung des Staats", schrieb
ein anderer Spender namens @ihnsfa auf Ais
Microblog. „Ich hoffe, das bisschen Macht,
das wir haben, wird am Ende gewinnen",
lautete ein anderer Beitrag, gepaart mit einer
Spende von 1000 Yuan.

7. NOVEMBER 2011
**The New York Times. *SPENDEN AN CHINE-
SISCHEN DISSIDENTEN KOMMEN ONLINE
UND PER PAPIERFLIEGER.*** Die Geldstrafe,
die Ai Weiwei am Dienstag erhielt, ist dreimal so hoch wie die mutmaßlich von ihm
hinterzogenen Steuern. Seither gingen über
20.000 Spenden in Gesamthöhe von mindestens 840.000 US-Dollar ein. Als Ais Weibo-
Account am Sonntag deaktiviert wurde,
kamen viele Spender zur Tür seines Studios
am Rande Pekings. Manche, erzählte Ai,
haben Papierflieger aus 100-Yuan-Noten gefal-
tet und über die Mauern segeln lassen.

14. NOVEMBER 2011
**The Wall Street Journal. *1,37 MILLIONEN
GESPENDET – AI WEIWEI GEHT IN BERU-
FUNG.*** „Ich glaube, wir sehen die Anfänge
einer Zivilgesellschaft in China", sagte Ai.
„Die jungen Menschen sind informiert und
glauben nicht, was ihnen die Staatsmedien
über mich erzählen. Sie interessieren sich
dafür, was passiert, nicht nur das, sie enga-
gieren sich."

15. NOVEMBER 2011
BBC News. Der chinesische Künstler Ai Weiwei hinterlegte eine Kaution von 1,3 Millionen

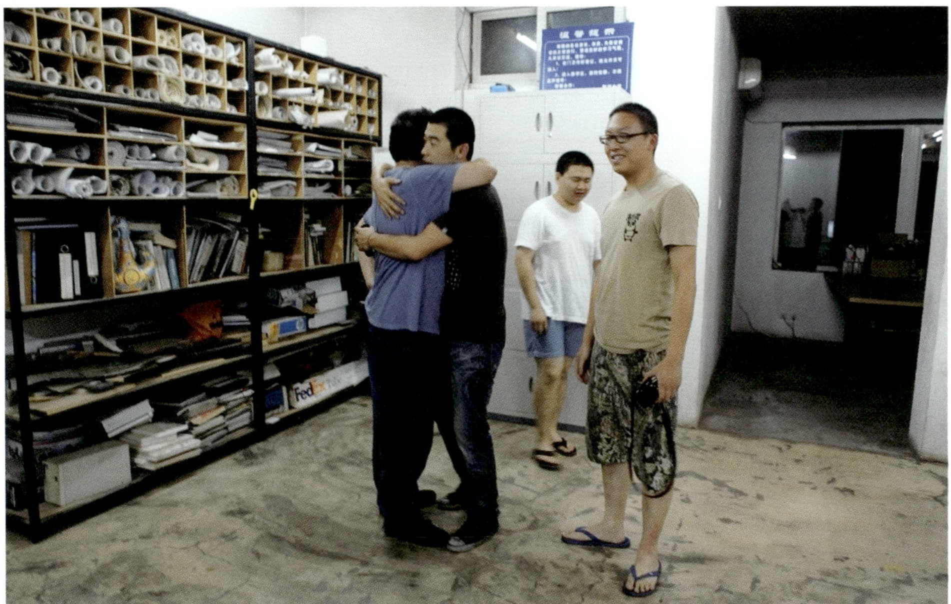

Ai Weiwei returning to his studio, Caochangdi, Beijing, June 22, 2011

US-Dollar und geht nun gegen die Steuerstrafe in Berufung. Er gab an, das Finanzamt
hätte unter Strafandrohung auf Überweisung
der Summe bestanden.

6. JANUAR 2012
The Guardian. *AI WEIWEI KANN AUF
STEUERERLASS HOFFEN.* Der chinesische
Künstler Ai Weiwei teilte mit, dass seine
Millionenstrafe wegen Steuerhinterziehung
gegenwärtig vom Finanzamt Peking geprüft
wird ... Er sei davon am Mittwoch telefonisch
in Kenntnis gesetzt worden, berichtete der
weltbekannte Konzeptkünstler. Die Prüfung
solle zwei Monate dauern. Ai sagte, er hoffe
auf ein faires und transparentes Verfahren.

29. MÄRZ 2012
Reuters. *KEIN ÖFFENTLICHES VERFAH-
REN FÜR AI WEIWEI.* Wie der chinesische
Künstler Ai Weiwei von staatlichen Stellen
erfuhr, wird es keine öffentliche Anhörung zur
mutmaßlichen Steuerhinterziehung der
Firma, für die er arbeitet, in Höhe von 15
Millionen Yuan geben. Ai erklärte am Don-
nerstag, er finde diesen Schritt „unfassbar".
Der 54-jährige Künstler teilte Reuters tele-

fonisch mit, dass er am Dienstag einen vom
23. März datierten Bescheid des Finanzamts
erhalten habe, der besagt, es werde für Ais
Designfirma Beijing Fake Cultural Development Ltd. nur ein „schriftliches Verfahren"
und keine öffentliche Anhörung geben.

31. MÄRZ 2012
@aiww. FAKE erhielt heute endlich die
Erlaubnis, Fotokopien der vor einem Jahr
illegal beschlagnahmten Unterlagen auf dem
Pekinger Finanzamt zu prüfen. Kopieren ist
erlaubt, fotografieren und scannen nicht. Das
Amt hat miese Kopierer. Dementsprechend
unleserlich waren die Kopien. Wir wollten
einen neuen Kopierer kaufen, aber das ging
nicht. Eigentlich hätten sie die Originale
schon längst zurückgeben müssen. Der Leiter
und die Buchhalterin von FAKE sind nach wie
vor verschwunden, dank der Maßnahmen des
Büros für öffentliche Sicherheit.

13. APRIL 2012
The Wall Street Journal. *CHINESISCHER
DISSIDENT IN STEUERSTREIT.* Der chinesische Künstler Ai Weiwei teilte mit, dass er
gegen das Pekinger Finanzamt, das von ihm

Steuerrückstände in Höhe von 2,4 Millionen US-Dollar fordert, Klage eingereicht hat. „Die versuchen nicht einmal, uns ein ordnungsgemäßes Verfahren zu geben", erklärte Ai in einem Interview am Freitag. „Da bleibt nur mehr der Gang zum Gericht."

8. MAI 2012
BBC News. *AI WEIWEI DARF GEGEN MILLIONENSTRAFE KLAGEN.* Ein Pekinger Gericht hat Ai Weiweis Klage stattgegeben. Ob er persönlich vor Gericht erscheinen wird, steht noch nicht fest. Ai ist ein Designer der Firma Fake Cultural Development Ltd., jedoch nicht deren Rechtsvertreter. Der weltbekannte Künstler teilte der BBC mit, er sei überrascht, dass die Behörden seine Klage überhaupt angenommen haben.

20. JUNI 2012
@aiww. Der FAKE-Steuerfall wird diesen Nachmittag im Gericht von Chaoyang verhandelt. Als Vertreter des Klägers stehe ich unter Polizeibewachung und darf nicht hingehen. In diesem Wunderland kann man ins Weltall fliegen, aber man kann sich keinen Sitz kaufen, um in einem Steuerstreit um 15,22 Millionen Yuan seine Unschuld zu beteuern. Es gibt in der Besuchergalerie keinen einzigen Sitz für die Kläger. In Wahrheit ist die Partei der Gerechtigkeit für immer abwesend.
The Wall Street Journal. *AI WEIWEI VON VERFAHREN AUSGESCHLOSSEN.* Der chinesische Künstler Ai Weiwei beschuldigte die Behörden am Mittwoch, seine Teilnahme an seinem Prozess gegen das Pekinger Finanzamt mit allen Mitteln zu verhindern. Auch sein Anwalt sei festgenommen worden. Ai teilte *China Real Time* mit, er sei am Mittwoch schriftlich aufgefordert worden, dem Verfahren beizuwohnen, konnte dann aber keinen Sitz reservieren, und schließlich wurde ihm die Teilnahme polizeilich verboten. Er gab an, ca. 40 Polizeiautos hätten am frühen Mittwochmorgen die Straße vor seinem Haus blockiert – das größte Polizeiaufgebot seit seiner Haftentlassung im Vorjahr.
The New York Times. Nachdem die Polizei Ai Weiwei vom Prozess ausschloss und andere Dissidenten daran hinderte, ihr Haus zu verlassen, versammelten sich am Mittwoch Hunderte Demonstranten vor dem Bezirksgericht Chaoyang in Peking. Die zahlreich ausge-

rückte Polizei machte Videoaufnahmen und nahm einige Verhaftungen vor. Während seine Frau und seine Anwälte im Gerichtssaal saßen, postete Ai Meldungen auf Twitter, die sich über die Behörden lustig machten und die Polizei beschuldigten, am Mittwochmorgen vor seinem Atelier einen seiner Kameraleute angegriffen zu haben. Ai veröffentlichte ein Foto des verletzten Kameramanns und ein grinsendes Selbstporträt in einer zu engen Polizeiuniform.

21. JUNI 2012
Reuters. *BIGAMIE- UND PORNOGRAFIE-VORWÜRFE GEGEN AI WEIWEI.* Wie die chinesische Polizei am Donnerstag mitteilte, droht dem Künstler Ai Weiwei eine Anklage wegen Bigamie und Pornografie. Er erhielt erneutes Reiseverbot, gerade zu einem Zeitpunkt, als die strengen Auflagen nach seiner Entlassung ausgelaufen waren. Am Donnerstag konnte Ai zum ersten Mal seit einem Jahr sein Haus ohne polizeiliche Meldepflicht verlassen. Nach seiner Festnahme ohne Anklage im April 2011 hatte er 81 Tage vorwiegend in Einzelhaft verbracht. „Wenn man mir die Hälfte meiner Freiheit zurückgibt und mir sagt, ich bin frei, dann bin ich frei", sagte Ai. „Aber meine Bewegungsfreiheit ist noch immer eingeschränkt, und die erfinden schon wieder neue Verbrechen."

20. JULI 2012
Time. *BERUFUNGSKLAGE DES CHINE-SISCHEN AKTIVISTEN AI WEIWEI ABGE-LEHNT.* Ein Pekinger Gericht wies den Einspruch Ai Weiweis gegen seine Steuerstrafe in Millionenhöhe zurück. Der Künstler und Aktivist durfte der Verhandlung am Freitagmorgen im Bezirksgericht Chaoyang in Ost-Peking nicht beiwohnen. Ai, der angibt, die Anschuldigungen gegen ihn seien politisch motiviert, will diese Entscheidung erneut gerichtlich anfechten. „Wir wissen natürlich, dass wir nicht gewinnen können. Finanzamt, Polizei, Gericht – die stecken doch alle unter einer Decke", teilte er TIME nach dem Urteil mit. „Wir werden trotzdem weiterkämpfen, damit die Leute sehen, wie das System funktioniert."
@aiww. Wir werden so lange vor Gericht gehen, bis der Tag kommt, an dem es unmöglich ist, dass wir verlieren.

27. SEPTEMBER 2012
The Wall Street Journal. *AI WEIWEI: ICH ZAHLE NICHT.* Der Künstler Ai Weiwei erklärte, er weigere sich, den Rest seiner Steuerstrafe in Höhe von 2,4 Millionen US-Dollar zu zahlen, nachdem ein Pekinger Gericht am Donnerstag seine Berufung abgelehnt hatte. Eine neue Konfrontation des mediengewandten Künstlers mit dem chinesischen Staat scheint unausweichlich. „Wir werden nicht zahlen, weil wir den Klagegrund nicht anerkennen", sagte Ai. „Und die schämen sich wahrscheinlich, danach zu fragen."

1. OKTOBER 2012
The Guardian. *AI WEIWEIS FIRMA DURCH CHINESISCHE BEHÖRDEN GESCHLOS-SEN.* Der kontroverse chinesische Künstler Ai Weiwei berichtete am Montag, seine Design-firma werde von den Behörden aufgelöst. Damit entfällt möglicherweise auch die Ver-pflichtung, den Rest der Steuerstrafe in Höhe von 15 Millionen Yuan zu zahlen ... Der Firma Fake Cultural Development wurde die Lizenz entzogen, da sie, so heißt es von öffentlicher Seite, ihrer jährlichen Registrierungspflicht nicht nachgekommen sei. Dies war jedoch nicht möglich gewesen, da die Polizei nach Ais Verhaftung im Vorjahr die nötigen Unter-lagen konfisziert hatte. „Ich glaube, das könnte eine Ausrede dafür sein, dass sie uns die Strafe erlassen", mutmaßte der Künstler.

2. OKTOBER 2012
@aiww. FAKE Design gibt's nicht mehr. Nur der „Geschäftsführer" ist noch da.

31. OKTOBER 2012
The Guardian. *AI WEIWEI ZAHLT SPEN-DEN ZURÜCK.* Der chinesische Künstler und Dissident Ai Weiwei begann mit der Rücker-stattung der von Unterstützern gespendeten Gelder, nachdem er in seinem Prozess gegen die Steuerstrafe in Millionenhöhe, die viele als Einschüchterungsversuch Chinas gegen den unliebsamen Kritiker werteten, alle Rechtsmittel ausgeschöpft hatte. „Wir haben alles versucht. Das Gericht hat sein Urteil gefällt. Jetzt bleibt nichts mehr übrig, als das Geld zurückzuzahlen", teilte Ai in einem Telefongespräch mit.

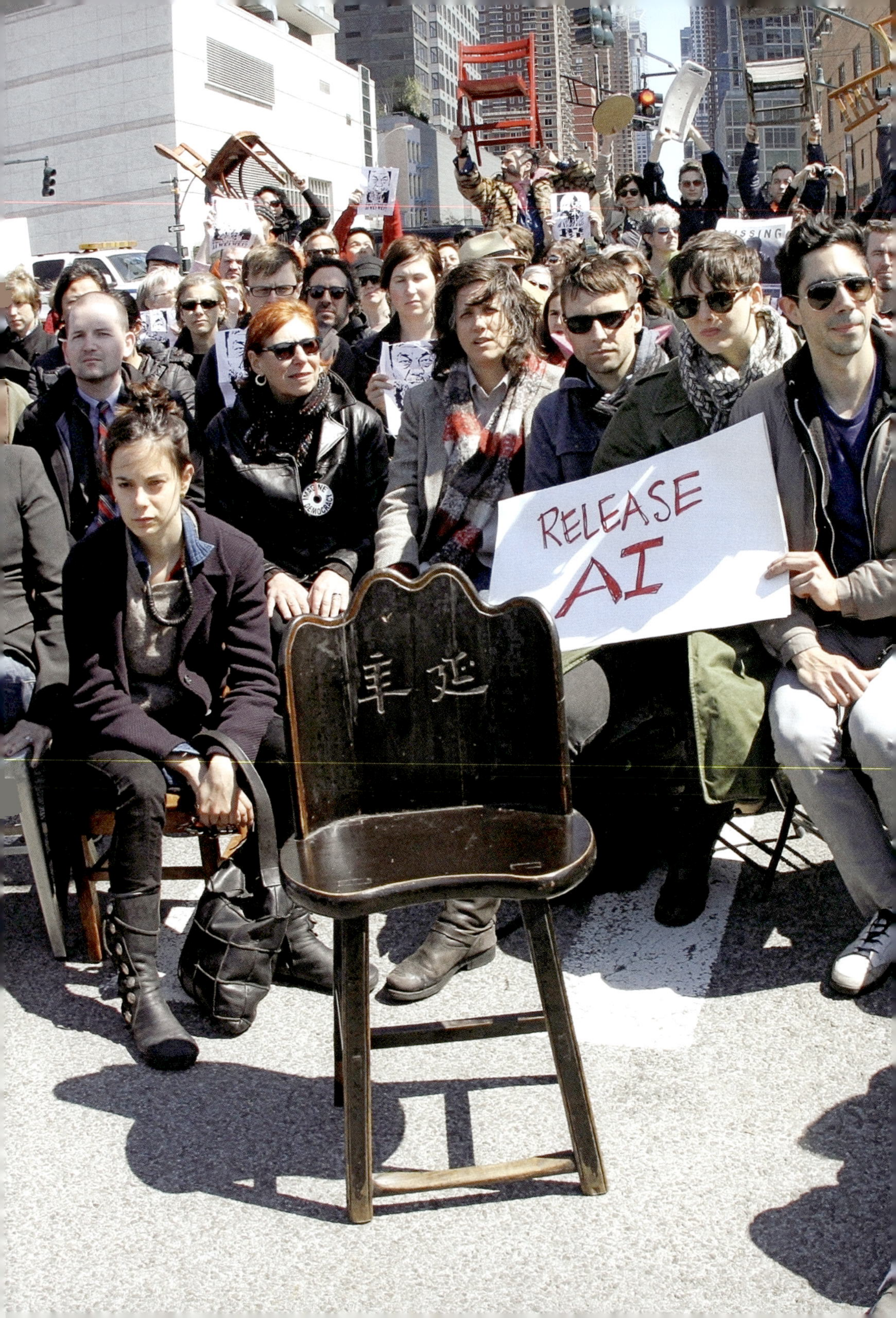

RELEASE
AI

Détention et accusation contre FAKE Design

22 FÉVRIER 2011
@aiww. Hier, deux personnes ont passé la journée dans un mini-van de surveillance à Caochangdi.

23 FÉVRIER 2011
The Telegraph. *DE NOUVEAUX APPELS À UNE RÉVOLUTION DU JASMIN EN CHINE.* Malgré la solidité apparente de son pouvoir, le parti communiste chinois montre des signes de nervosité croissante ces dernières semaines alors qu'au Moyen-Orient des manifestations balayent les régimes dictatoriaux. Outre le déploiement massif de policiers, le dispositif tentaculaire de la sécurité d'État s'est efforcé de neutraliser la propagation de la dissidence sur Internet et a placé une centaine de militants et de meneurs potentiels en résidence surveillée.

27 FÉVRIER 2011
@aiww. Les agents du Bureau de la sécurité publique qui vendent des fleurs devant chez moi dorment pendant que la neige tombe.

28 FÉVRIER 2011
@aiww. Cette fois, c'est différent : deux voitures de surveillance sont garées devant chez moi depuis plusieurs jours et les hommes y dorment. Probablement à cause du prochain *lianghui* [conférence des deux sections du congrès national chinois].

7 MARS 2011
The Telegraph. *AI WEIWEI : «L'ÉLAN VERS UNE RÉVOLUTION DU JASMIN PREND FORCE ET AMPLEUR.»* L'artiste et militant des droits de l'homme, dont les *Sunflower Seeds* sont exposées en ce moment à la Tate Modern, a déclaré qu'il était sous surveillance constante. Il accuse les autorités chinoises de réprimer toute opinion, «comme des parents chinois de jadis». «Ces deux dernières semaines, plus de cent personnes ont été arrêtées. Certaines sont des écrivains, des universitaires, des avocats, opposants de longue date, d'autres des étudiants qui un jour se sont dit "rendez-vous à tel endroit, dans telle rue". C'est très important», dit M. Ai.

8 MARS 2011
@aiww. Dehors, les deux voitures de police ont disparu. Ils ne sont même pas venus me saluer.

31 MARS 2011
@aiww. La police est rentrée chez moi pour une enquête.
@aiww. Employés forcés de sortir leurs papiers qui sont copiés.
@aiww. Quatorze policiers couverts d'appareils photo. Disent qu'ils vérifient tous les détails du statut de mon assistant étranger. Pas pratique ce soir, reviendront demain.

1ᴱᴿ AVRIL 2011
@aiww. La police de Chaoyang revient vérifier les papiers de mon équipe. Pour la troisième fois. Quelque chose de gros semble se préparer.
@aiww. Plus de dix personnes sont venues vérifier l'équipement anti-incendie. Caochangdi doit être aussi inflammable que CCTV [référence aux bureaux de la Télévision centrale de Chine à Pékin qui ont brûlé le 9 février 2009]. Dix policiers armés qui débarquent au milieu de la nuit. Nos «taxes pour le maintien de la stabilité» ne sont pas payées pour rien.

3 AVRIL 2011
@aiww (tweet d'un assistant). Le 3 avril 2011, Ai Weiwei a été arrêté par deux agents de l'immigration à l'aéroport de Pékin. Son assistant et lui ont été séparés. Le portable d'Ai est éteint et le contact est rompu depuis trente minutes, on ne sait pas ce qu'il se passe.

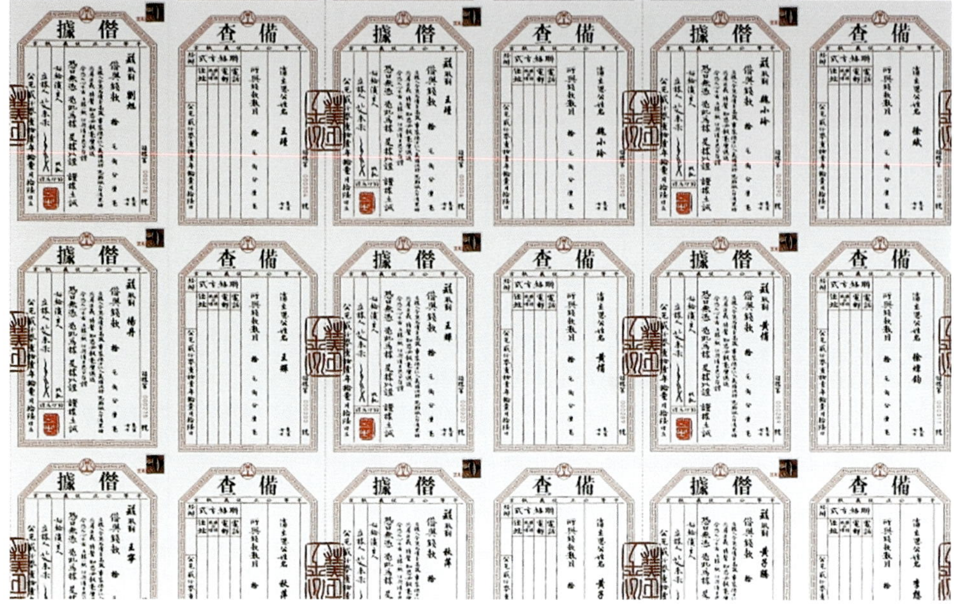

Promissory Notes, 2011 (detail), wallpaper, dimensions variable

@aiww (tweet d'un assistant). Il y a une heure, des officiers de police se sont présentés avec un mandat de perquisition au studio d'Ai Weiwei, 258 Caochangdi. Ils ont emmené huit membres du studio au poste de police de Nangao, à Pékin, pour les interroger : Xu Ye, Qian Feifei, Dong Jie, Xiao Wei, Xiao Xie, Xing Rui, Jiang Li et Xiao Pang, son neveu. Lu Qing est restée seule avec la police. La porte de devant et celle du fond sont barricadées par la police, il est impossible d'entrer ou de sortir. Ai Weiwei est détenu à l'aéroport de Pékin depuis trois heures et est injoignable.

BBC News. *L'ARTISTE CHINOIS AI WEIWEI ARRÊTÉ À L'EMBARQUEMENT.* Les autorités chinoises auraient empêché le célèbre artiste militant Ai Weiwei de quitter Pékin. Il est injoignable depuis et la police se refuse à tout commentaire. Un de ses assistants a dit à la BBC qu'il a été arrêté par des gardes aux frontières alors qu'il allait embarquer sur un vol pour Hong Kong. Il a ajouté que la police avait fouillé sa maison à Pékin, qui est aussi son studio. L'habitation d'Ai Weiwei est maintenant sous scellés. On ne sait pas si l'artiste de cinquante-trois ans est en détention, ni pourquoi on lui a interdit de prendre ce vol depuis l'aéroport international de Pékin.

4 AVRIL 2011
AFP. *LA POLICE RESTE SILENCIEUSE SUR LA DÉTENTION D'AI WEIWEI.* « Pendant qu'on l'arrêtait, la police est venue avec un mandat et a fouillé partout », a déclaré sa femme Lu Qing au téléphone. « Ils ont pris l'ordinateur, les disques durs et d'autre matériel. Ils refusent de dire pourquoi le mandat a été délivré et Ai Weiwei arrêté. » Plusieurs assistants d'Ai Weiwei ont aussi été arrêtés dimanche, puis relâchés, a précisé Lu, ajoutant qu'elle n'était pas assignée à résidence.

The New York Times. Lundi, les États-Unis, la France, la Grande-Bretagne et l'Allemagne ont appelé la Chine à libérer Ai Weiwei, artiste de renommée internationale et opposant de plus en plus virulent au régime. Un porte-parole du Département d'État, Mark Toner, a déclaré que les États-Unis étaient « très préoccupés par cette vague de disparitions forcées, de détentions extralégales, d'arrestations et de condamnations de militants alors qu'ils exercent leur droit internationalement reconnu à la liberté d'expression ». Guido Westerwelle, le ministre allemand des Affaires étrangères, « appelle le gouvernement chinois à clarifier au plus vite la situation et [l']invite à relâcher Ai Weiwei immédiatement ». La France et la Grande-Bretagne ont fait des déclarations similaires.

5 AVRIL 2011
Deutsche Welle. Gao Ying, épouse du célèbre poète Ai Qing et mère d'Ai Weiwei, et Gao Ge, sœur de l'artiste, déclarent avoir lancé un avis de recherche dans la soirée du 5 avril, pour retrouver Ai Weiwei, arrêté à la douane de l'aéroport de Pékin le 3 avril et dont on est sans nouvelles depuis. On peut lire sur cet avis rédigé à la main : « Ai Weiwei, homme, 53 ans, enlevé par deux hommes aux alentours de 8h30 le 3 avril 2011 à l'aéroport de Pékin juste avant d'embarquer pour Hong Kong. Cela fait maintenant plus de 50 heures qu'il a disparu. Si vous avez des informations à son sujet, prière de contacter sa famille. Signé : sa mère, Gao Ying, sa sœur, Gao Ge, à 17h43 le 5 avril, Pékin. » Cet avis de recherche a immédiatement fait le buzz sur Internet.

6 AVRIL 2011
Global Times (Chine). *LA LOI NE CÉDERA PAS FACE AU DISSIDENT.* Ai Weiwei, célèbre artiste d'avantgarde, aurait récemment été arrêté. Certains gouvernements occidentaux et organisations de défense des droits de l'homme ont appelé derechef à sa libération immédiate, soutenant qu'il s'agissait là d'une « détérioration des droits de l'homme » et présentant Ai Weiwei comme le « défenseur de [ces] droits en Chine ». C'est une atteinte imprudente au système politique chinois et la preuve d'un mépris total envers la souveraineté judiciaire de la Chine que de faire une généralité d'un cas particulier et de publier des commentaires acerbes sur la Chine avant d'avoir découvert la vérité. Le comportement de l'Occident cherche à déstabiliser la société chinoise et tente de modifier son système de valeur... C'est l'histoire qui jugera Ai Weiwei, mais il devra payer pour ses choix comme dans toute société. La Chine avance dans son ensemble et personne n'a le pouvoir de forcer une nation à s'adapter à ses préférences personnelles, ce qui est différent de la question du respect des droits des minorités.

7 AVRIL 2011
Washington Post. *AI WEIWEI DÉTENU POUR « CRIMES ÉCONOMIQUES ».* Hong Lei, porte-parole du ministère des Affaires étrangères, a déclaré qu'Ai Weiwei était sous le coup d'une enquête pour « crimes économiques » et a conseillé aux autres pays de ne pas s'en mêler. « La Chine est un pays de droit et agira selon le droit », a dit le porte-parole lors d'une conférence de presse régulière. « Nous espérons que les pays concernés respecteront la décision de la Chine [...] Cela n'a rien à voir avec les droits de l'homme ou la liberté d'expression. »

8 AVRIL 2011
The New York Times. *LES MUSÉES FONT PRESSION POUR LA LIBÉRATION D'AI WEIWEI.* La Fondation Solomon R. Guggenheim mène une action internationale pour un appel à la libération d'Ai Weiwei. Elle a obtenu le soutien de tout un ensemble de musées, parmi lesquels le Museum of Modern Art à New York, le Los Angeles County Museum of Art, le Minneapolis Institute of Arts, la Tate de Londres, ainsi que celui de l'Association américaine des directeurs de musées.

10 AVRIL, 2011
The Wall Street Journal. *HONG KONG SE MOBILISE POUR AI WEIWEI.* La manifestation était menée par des membres de l'Alliance de Hong Kong pour le soutien des mouvements démocratiques patriotes, dont les députés Lee Cheuk-Yan et Albert Ho. La foule scandait en anglais : « Libérez Ai Weiwei », et en cantonais : « Non aux persécutions politiques ».
BZ Berlin. *MANIFESTATION POUR AI WEIWEI À BERLIN.* Les militants des droits de l'homme à Berlin ont exprimé samedi leur solidarité envers l'artiste Ai Weiwei qui a disparu depuis son arrestation à Pékin. À la porte de Brandebourg, ils brandissaient la photo de l'artiste accompagnée de la question « Où est Ai Weiwei ? ». Ils faisaient également signer une pétition pour la libération du

lauréat du Prix Nobel de la paix Liu Xiaobo et
d'autres dissidents chinois. Un porte-parole
d'Amnesty International a déclaré que le cas
d'Ai Weiwei était symbolique de ce que vivent
des milliers de personnes dont les droits sont
restreints en Chine.

12 AVRIL 2011
The Guardian. Le fisc chinois a convoqué
la femme d'Ai Weiwei pour l'interroger,
renforçant l'hypothèse que les autorités
chercheraient à l'accuser de fraude fiscale.
Lu Qing a passé environ une heure dans les
bureaux du fisc de Pékin. On lui avait demandé d'apporter des documents, ce qu'elle n'a
pu faire puisqu'ils ont été confisqués par la
police, selon la Radio Télévision de Hong
Kong.

17 AVRIL 2011
The Guardian. *ARRESTATION D'AI
WEIWEI : DES MANIFESTATIONS DEVANT
LES AMBASSADES CHINOISES PARTOUT
DANS LE MONDE.* Dimanche, partout
dans le monde, des manifestants se sont
rassemblés devant les ambassades chinoises.
Des centaines de personnes se sont installées
sur des chaises pour réclamer la libération
immédiate d'Ai Weiwei et exprimer leur soutien à la liberté d'expression de tous les
artistes chinois. Quelques accrochages ont
eu lieu à Hong Kong quand 150 manifestants
se sont opposés aux forces de l'ordre. On
rapporte une arrestation. À Berlin, environ
200 personnes ont participé à une marche
silencieuse. Il y avait également un rassemblement devant l'ambassade chinoise de
Londres.

19 AVRIL 2011
PBS. *LA RÉPRESSION À L'ENCONTRE
D'AI WEIWEI S'ÉTEND À SA FAMILLE,
SES AMIS ET SES COLLABORATEURS.*
Alors que la disparition de l'artiste a été
largement couverte et discutée dans les
médias, peu ont remarqué que ses amis et
ses collaborateurs sont aussi visés. Quatre
d'entre eux ont également disparu : Xia Pang,
son chauffeur, Hu Mingfen, comptable de
FAKE Ldt., Liu Zhenggang, designer chez
FAKE, et Wen Tao, journaliste. Plus tôt dans
la journée, Liu Xiaoyuan, un avocat des droits
de l'homme qui avait défendu l'artiste dans

le passé et déclaré être prêt à recommencer,
a « réapparu » après une disparition de cinq
jours.

20 AVRIL 2011
Der Spiegel. L'artiste militant Ai Weiwei
s'est vu offrir un poste de professeur invité
à l'université des Arts de Berlin (UdK). Ai
Weiwei, cinquante-trois ans, enseignerait à
l'école supérieure des Arts et des Sciences.
Il travaillerait aussi avec des étudiants de
l'Institut d'expérimentation spatiale de l'artiste danois Olafur Eliasson. Martin Rennert,
président de l'UdK, a déclaré espérer qu'« Ai
Weiwei puisse bientôt commencer son travail
ici », sans préciser de date.

23 AVRIL 2011
Reuters. *DES MILLIERS DE PERSONNES
MANIFESTENT À HONG KONG POUR LA
LIBÉRATION D'AI.* La manifestation – la
plus grosse de ces dernières semaines dans
la ville – a mis en évidence le rôle croissant
de Hong Kong, foyer des mouvements de soutien à l'artiste où les militants locaux pour la
démocratie et des artistes mettent la pression
sur Pékin pour sa lourde répression contre les
dissidents, les avocats des droits de l'homme
et les manifestants qui contestent le contrôle
et la censure du parti communiste. L'événement s'est déroulé dans le calme pour sa
majeure partie, même si, les esprits s'échauf-
fant, de brèves altercations avec la police
ont éclaté.

27 AVRIL 2011
BBC News. *À PÉKIN, LA CHINE ET LES
ÉTATS-UNIS ENTAMENT UNE DISCUSSION
SUR LES DROITS DE L'HOMME.* Les États-
Unis devraient pousser la Chine à assouplir la
sévère répression envers les dissidents politiques, que les militants des droits de l'homme
décrivent comme la plus forte depuis des
années. Des opposants politiques – avocats,
blogueurs et militants, dont l'artiste Ai
Weiwei – ont été visés.

4 MAI 2011
The New York Times. Ai Weiwei a entamé
son deuxième mois de détention cette semaine. À un monde de plus en plus scandalisé
et inquiet, la Chine n'a toujours pas répondu
de façon satisfaisante quant au lieu où il se

trouve, aux conditions de sa détention ni aux faits qui lui sont reprochés. Mais comme d'habitude, le monde des affaires offre ses propres moyens d'opposition silencieuse. En dépit de l'absence de M. Ai Weiwei, ses projets d'exposition en Occident sont réalisés dans le respect des plannings. Le weekend dernier, une exposition d'œuvres inédites s'est ouverte à la galerie berlinoise neugerriemschneider. Accrochée sur la façade de l'immeuble, une immense banderole blanche demandait «Où est Ai Weiwei?». Une exposition plus importante va ouvrir la semaine prochaine à la Lisson Gallery, à Londres. Et à Manhattan, *Circle of Animals/Zodiac Heads*, qui est considéré comme la première œuvre sculptée urbaine d'Ai Weiwei, a été inaugurée mercredi matin sous le crachin, devant la fontaine Pulitzer, au pied du Plaza Hotel.

15 MAI 2011
Associated Press. *L'ARTISTE CHINOIS DÉTENU REÇOIT LA VISITE DE SA FEMME.* Gao Ge, la sœur d'Ai Weiwei, déclare que pour la première fois en quarante-trois jours sa femme a pu le rencontrer. Dimanche soir, la police de Pékin a emmené Lu Qing vers une destination secrète où elle a pu voir son mari et lui parler brièvement. D'après Gao Ge, Lu Qing a rapporté qu'Ai Weiwei est en bonne santé et qu'il a pu prendre les médicaments dont il a besoin. Gao Ge ajoute que la police n'a toujours pas indiqué à sa famille où il est détenu. Lundi, elle a dit que la famille était soulagée de savoir qu'il allait bien, mais souhaitait que le gouvernement puisse clarifier la situation.

20 MAI 2011
BBC News. *«L'ÉVASION FISCALE» DU STUDIO D'AI WEIWEI.* Les autorités chinoises prétendent qu'une entreprise dont l'artiste est propriétaire aurait organisé une évasion fiscale d'«un montant colossal», d'après les médias d'État. «On a découvert que FAKE Ldt. [basée à Pékin et qui gère la partie commerciale de sa carrière artistique] a évadé fiscalement "un montant colossal"» et a également «détruit intentionnellement ses documents comptables», rapporte Xinhua, citant des policiers anonymes de la capitale.

L'agence ajoute que M. Ai est détenu en «résidence surveillée», ce qui veut généralement dire que les prisonniers ne peuvent pas quitter leur domicile.

22 JUIN 2011
Xinhua News Agency (Chine). *AI WEIWEI LIBÉRÉ SOUS CAUTION.* La police de Pékin a déclaré mercredi qu'Ai Weiwei avait été libéré sous caution, grâce à sa bonne conduite qui l'a poussé à avouer ses crimes, et aussi à cause d'une maladie chronique dont il souffre [...] Selon la police, le fait qu'Ai Weiwei ait répété être disposé à payer les impôts auxquels il s'était soustrait a aussi été pris en compte.

The Guardian. Après quatre-vingt-un jours de détention, Ai Weiwei est rentré chez lui, considérablement amaigri et bien moins bavard. «Je vais bien, je suis sorti», a déclaré par téléphone au *Guardian* l'artiste de cinquante-trois ans, peu de temps après sa libération. «Je suis de nouveau en famille, je suis très heureux.»

23 JUIN 2011
The Wall Street Journal. Selon des témoins, M. Ai Weiwei a déclaré que sa santé était bonne et remercié les journalistes de leur soutien, alors qu'il regagnait son studio avec sa mère et sa femme, tard dans la journée de mercredi. Il a ajouté qu'il ne pouvait pas en dire plus sur les conditions de sa caution. «Je ne peux pas dire grand-chose. Je peux juste dire que je suis sorti et sous caution. Mais je ne peux rien ajouter sur les conditions de ma libération», a-t-il dit par téléphone au *Wall Street Journal*. Interrogé sur la durée de son silence médiatique imposé, il a répondu: «Un an au moins». Il a également confirmé que ce silence s'appliquait aux réseaux sociaux, tel Twitter où il a plus de 88 000 abonnés. Avant son arrestation en avril, M. Ai Weiwei postait des douzaines de tweets par jour, la plupart critiquant le gouvernement chinois.

The Guardian. *APRÈS AVOIR ACCORDÉ UNE LIBÉRATION SOUS CAUTION À L'ARTISTE, LA POLICE A LIBÉRÉ SON COUSIN.* Gao Ying, la mère de l'artiste, a déclaré que son neveu Zhang Jinsong, le chauffeur d'Ai Weiwei, était rentré chez lui avec le moral mais qu'il avait perdu environ

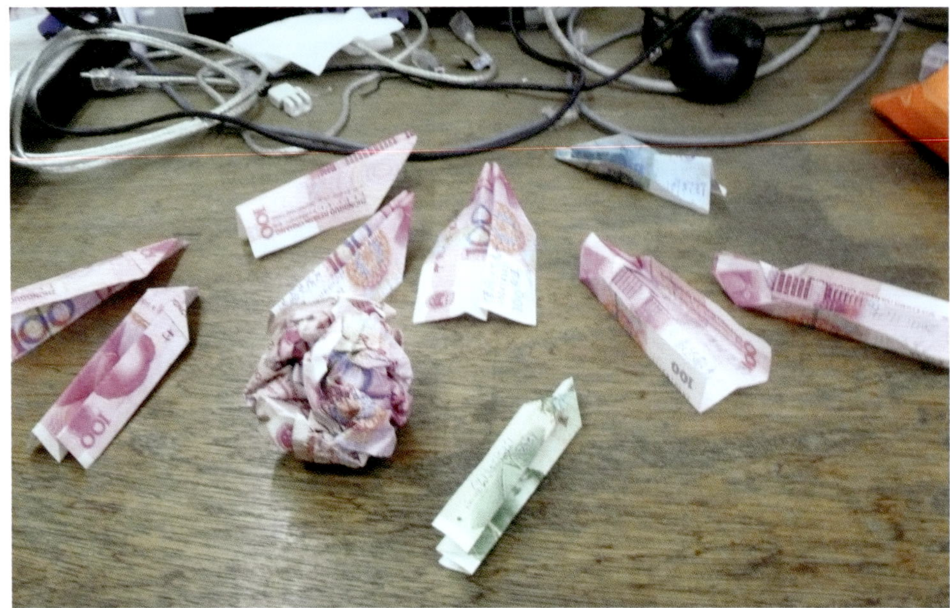

Donations from supporters sent over the studio walls, Caochangdi, Beijing, November 2011

neuf kilos. Zhang avait disparu quelques jours après son cousin. On est toujours sans nouvelles de trois autres collaborateurs, disparus juste après Ai Weiwei.

5 AOÛT 2011
@aiww. Juste pour dire bonjour
@aiww. J'ai mangé dix raviolis au déjeuner, et repris trois kilos

8 AOÛT 2011
@aiww. Ai vu Liu Zhenggang ce soir, il a parlé de sa détention pour la première fois. Il a levé sa main droite, comme s'il s'adressait à une caméra de surveillance, et a dit : j'ai besoin d'eau... Et puis ce dur à cuire s'est mis à pleurer... Son cœur s'est affaibli pendant sa détention et il a failli mourir plusieurs fois.

9 AOÛT 2011
Global Times (Chine). *AI WEIWEI SORT DE SON SILENCE.* Malgré la situation délicate autour de son cas et de sa libération, Ai a ouvertement exprimé ses émotions, ses idées et ses pensées lorsqu'il était détenu. « J'étais coupé du monde extérieur. Personne ne me disait quand je serais libéré. J'avais l'impression d'être tombé dans un trou sans fin », nous a-t-il déclaré, confortablement assis sur son nouveau canapé. « Je ne pourrai jamais éviter la politique, aucun de nous ne le peut. Nous vivons dans une société politisée. » Ai a croisé les bras. Il semblait sérieux. Après une pause pour rassembler ses idées, il a continué : « On abandonne ses droits quand on les évite. Bien sûr, on vit certainement mieux en abandonnant certains droits. Mais il y a tant d'injustice, et si peu de ressources pour l'éducation. Tout cela diminue le bonheur. Je n'arrêterai jamais de combattre l'injustice. » Après avoir reçu l'autorisation de quitter la Chine, Ai a accepté un poste de professeur à l'UdK de Berlin. Même si les conditions de sa libération lui imposent de rester à Pékin un an, Ai dit qu'il n'envisagera jamais de quitter définitivement le pays. « Les gens au cœur noir doivent être exilés, je ne partirai jamais », a-t-il dit en riant.

@aiww. Ils étaient détenus illégalement à cause de moi. Liu Zhenggang, Hu Mingfen, Wentao, Zhang Jinsong, innocents, ils ont souffert, moralement brisés et physiquement torturés.

1ᵉʳ NOVEMBRE 2011
@aiww. À l'instant, deux employés du fisc de Pékin ont voulu envoyer au 258 Caochangdi une facture de 15,22 millions de yuans. Lu Qing, la représentante légale, a répondu qu'à ce jour notre entreprise n'a toujours pas pu consulter ses livres de comptes, que cette somme n'est pas justifiable, et elle a refusé de l'accepter.
AFP. *UN REDRESSEMENT FISCAL DE PLUSIEURS MILLIONS POUR AI WEIWEI.* Mardi, les autorités chinoises ont ordonné à l'artiste de payer quinze millions de yuans ($2,36 millions) pour un prétendu redressement fiscal, dans le but, selon l'éloquent dissident politique, de le « détruire ». « Il m'ont envoyé un courrier officiel aujourd'hui [...] sans aucune explication. Nous avons demandé d'où venait ce montant, ils n'ont pas pu nous répondre clairement », a-t-il déclaré à l'AFP. « Ils me donnent quinze jours. Ça fait environ un million par jour [...] Si on ne paie pas, ils peuvent nous mettre en prison, jusqu'à sept ans. Vraiment, je ne sais pas quoi faire. »
Reuters. Ai Weiwei a déclaré à l'agence Reuters qu'il avait reçu un courrier du fisc dans lequel on lui donne le titre de « gestionnaire actuel » pour FAKE Ltd., basée à Pékin, qui a participé à la production des célèbres œuvres de l'artiste. C'est Lu Qing, sa femme, qui est propriétaire de l'entreprise, dont elle est aussi la représentante légale. « Ils ont inventé ce nouveau titre, dit Ai. Je ne suis qu'un designer dans cette entreprise. Je ne suis pas directeur ou même manager. »

4 NOVEMBRE 2011
Christian Science Monitor. *DANS UN GESTE DE CONTESTATION, DES CHINOIS SE MANIFESTENT POUR AIDER AI WEIWEI À PAYER SES IMPÔTS.* Une souscription publique a été lancée sur Internet en début de semaine, suivant l'idée de plusieurs soutiens importants de l'artiste. Il semble qu'elle ait décollé depuis que Hu Jia – un militant des droits de l'homme célèbre, libéré en juin après une peine de quarante mois pour « incitation à la subversion du pouvoir d'État » – a annoncé un don de 1 000 yuans ($158)... « Nous faisons des performances artistiques avec lui pour moquer la machine d'État autoritaire », a déclaré un souscripteur dans un message signé @ihnsfa sur le microblog d'Ai Weiwei. « J'espère que notre maigre pouvoir pourra vous aider à obtenir une splendide victoire », disait un autre message accompagné d'une donation de 1000 yuans.

7 NOVEMBRE 2011
The New York Times. *SUR INTERNET OU PAR AVION DE PAPIER, LES DONATIONS À AI WEIWEI AFFLUENT.* Plus de 20 000 personnes ont contribué à rassembler au moins $840 000 depuis que, mardi, le fisc a donné quinze jours à l'artiste pour payer un montant trois fois supérieur aux sommes qu'il aurait évadées fiscalement. Dimanche, après la fermeture de son compte Weibo, des douzaines de personnes sont arrivées aux portes du studio de M. Ai Weiwei, dans la banlieue de la capitale. Il a déclaré que de nombre d'entre elles ont lancé par dessus les murs des avions en papier, en billets de cent yuans.

14 NOVEMBRE 2011
The Wall Street Journal. *LES DONATIONS POUR AI WEIWEI S'ÉLÈVENT À 1,37 MILLION, ASSEZ POUR CONTESTER LE REDRESSEMENT FISCAL.* « J'ai l'impression que c'est le début d'une société civile en Chine, a dit l'artiste. Les jeunes ont leurs propres informations et ne font pas confiance aux médias d'État ni aux accusations du gouvernement contre moi. Cela montre que les gens se sentent concernés. Non seulement ça, mais ils agissent aussi. »

15 NOVEMBRE 2011
BBC News. Ai Weiwei a déposé une caution de plus de 1,3 million de yuans pour la révision du redressement fiscal dont il fait l'objet. Il a déclaré que le fisc a insisté pour qu'il leur transfère l'argent, sinon il aurait affaire à la police.

6 JANVIER 2012
The Guardian. *ESPOIRS D'UN RÉPIT FISCAL POUR AI WEIWEI.* Selon l'artiste, le fisc de Pékin est en train de revoir sa décision d'un redressement de plusieurs millions de dollars pour une prétendue évasion fiscale... L'artiste rapporte qu'il en a été informé mercredi, par téléphone. Selon les autorités, la révision prendrait deux mois. Ai Weiwei a déclaré qu'il avait bon espoir

que cette affaire soit traitée avec sérieux et transparence.

29 MARS 2012
Reuters. *LA CHINE ANNONCE À AI WEIWEI QU'IL N'Y AURA PAS DE PROCÈS PUBLIC.* Selon l'artiste, les autorités lui auraient annoncé qu'il ne bénéficierait pas d'une audition publique pour la révision de la pénalité de quinze millions de yuans pour l'évasion fiscale dont se serait rendue coupable l'entreprise dans laquelle il travaille. Une décision que l'artiste a qualifiée d'«inimaginable». Ai Weiwei, cinquante-quatre ans, a expliqué par téléphone à l'agence Reuters qu'il avait reçu mardi un courrier du fisc daté du 23 mars. Ce courrier stipule que FAKE Ldt. ne pourra bénéficier que «d'une audition écrite» et non d'un procès public.

31 MARS 2012
@aiww. Aujourd'hui, le centre des impôts de Pékin a enfin autorisé FAKE à inspecter les photocopies des comptes illégalement saisis par la police il y a un an. Photo et scan sont interdits, mais pas la photocopie. Comme leurs photocopieurs sont en mauvais état, nous avons proposé d'acheter un nouvel appareil, mais on nous l'a refusé. En fait, les originaux auraient dû nous avoir été rendus depuis longtemps. Le manager et le comptable de Fake sont toujours introuvables, certainement retenus par le Bureau de sécurité publique.

13 AVRIL 2012
The Wall Street Journal. *L'OPPOSANT ET ARTISTE CHINOIS CONTESTE SES PÉNALITÉS.* Ai Weiwei a déclaré avoir déposé une plainte contre les autorités locales du fisc à Pékin pour la façon dont elles continuent de lui réclamer $2,4 millions d'impayés et de pénalités. «Ils n'essayent même pas de suivre la procédure ou les règles du jeu, a dit M. Ai Weiwei dans une interview vendredi. La seule issue, c'est de les attaquer en justice.»

8 MAI 2012
BBC News. *LA CHINE DÉCLARE QU'AI WEIWEI PEUT CONTESTER LE REDRESSEMENT DE $2,4 MILLIONS.* À Pékin, une cour a annoncé qu'elle entendrait l'affaire. On ne sait pas encore si Ai Weiwei lui-même sera présent à l'audience. Il est designer pour le studio FAKE, mais ne représente pas légalement l'entreprise. L'artiste mondialement connu a dit à la BBC qu'il était surpris que les autorités l'aient laissé contester l'affaire.

20 JUIN 2012
@aiww. Cet après-midi, le cas du redressement de FAKE sera entendu devant la cour de Chaoyang. En tant que partisan du plaignant, je suis surveillé par la police et je ne peux pas m'y rendre. Ce pays magique où on peut aller dans l'espace mais où on ne peut pas se payer un siège pour clamer son innocence avec 15,22 millions de yuans. Il n'y a pas un seul siège de libre pour l'accusation dans la galerie publique. La réalité, c'est que le parti de la justice est absent à jamais.

The Wall Street Journal. *AI WEIWEI INTERDIT DE COUR.* Mercredi, l'artiste militant chinois a accusé les autorités de l'empêcher d'assister à l'audience de son procès contre le bureau du fisc de Pékin. Il a également déclaré que la police retenait son conseiller juridique. M. Ai Weiwei a dit au *China Real Time* avoir été convoqué à l'audience de son procès mercredi, puis informé qu'il ne pouvait pas réserver de place à la cour. La police lui aurait finalement ordonné de ne pas se présenter. Il a déclaré qu'environ quarante voitures de police bloquaient la route devant chez lui depuis mercredi au petit matin – la présence policière la plus forte depuis sa libération l'an dernier.

The New York Times. Mercredi, à Pékin, après que la police a informé M. Ai Weiwei qu'il ne pouvait pas se rendre à l'audience, et empêché de nombreux autres opposants de quitter leur domicile, des centaines de manifestants se sont rassemblés devant la cour de justice du district de Chaoyang, malgré la présence d'une petite armée de policiers, parmi lesquels certains ont filmé la foule et emmené plusieurs personnes. Tandis que sa femme et ses avocats assistaient à l'audience, Ai Weiwei s'est exprimé sur Twitter, envoyant des messages ridiculisant les autorités et condamnant l'attaque par la police de l'un de ses cameramen qui filmait les portes de son studio mercredi matin. M. Ai Weiwei a posté une photo des blessures de cet homme et un portrait de

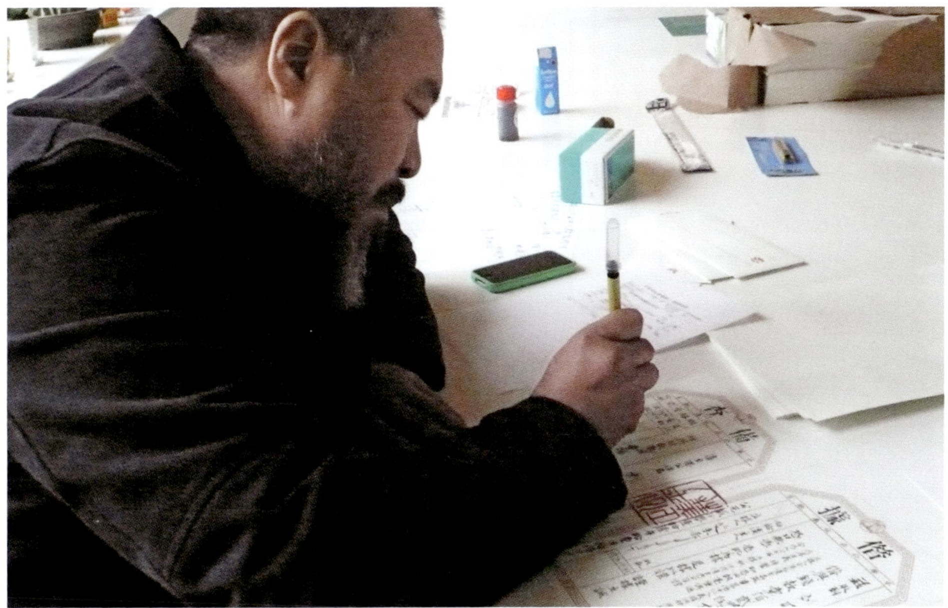

Ai Weiwei writing debt notes to donors, Caochangdi, Beijing, November 2011

lui-même un sourire narquois aux lèvres et vêtu d'un uniforme de police trop petit.

21 JUIN 2012
Reuters. *AI WEIWEI MENACÉ D'ACCU-SATION DE BIGAMIE ET DE PORNO-GRAPHIE.* La police chinoise a fait savoir à l'artiste qu'il pourrait être accusé de biga-mie et de pornographie, et qu'il lui était interdit de quitter le territoire, malgré l'as-souplissement des conditions imposées à sa libération. Ai Weiwei, qui a quitté jeudi pour la première fois depuis un an sa maison sans devoir en informer la police, avait été détenu en avril 2011 pendant quatre-vingt-un jours sans chef d'accusation, à l'isolement principa-lement, avant d'être libéré sous condition l'année dernière. «Si retrouver la moitié de ma liberté veut dire que je suis libre, alors je suis un homme libre, a déclaré Ai Weiwei. Mais ils restreignent mes déplacements et essayent encore de fabriquer des crimes.»

20 JUILLET 2012
Time. *L'OPPOSANT CHINOIS AI WEIWEI PERD EN APPEL.* Une cour de Pékin a rejeté l'appel de l'artiste concernant le redressement de plusieurs millions de dollars que le gouver-nement chinois réclame à son studio pour évasion fiscale. Ai Weiwei, qu'on a empêché de se rendre à l'audience vendredi matin, a déclaré que cette affaire était politique et qu'il entendait continuer à contester les accu-sations du gouvernement. «Nous savons que nous ne gagnerons pas. Nous savons que le fisc, la police, la justice, c'est la même chose, a dit Ai Weiwei au *Time* après le jugement. Mais nous continuerons à nous battre pour montrer à quoi ressemble ce système.» **@aiww.** Nous allons continuer à faire appel, jusqu'à ce qu'arrive le jour où nous ne pour-rons plus perdre.

27 SEPTEMBRE 2012
The Wall Street Journal. *AI WEIWEI: «JE NE PAIERAI PAS.»* L'artiste a déclaré qu'il refusait de payer le solde d'une pénalité pour évasion fiscale de $2.4 millions après qu'une cour de Pékin a rejeté son appel jeudi, annonçant une probable nouvelle épreuve de force entre les autorités et l'opposant, expert en communication médiatique. «Nous n'al-lons pas payer la pénalité car nous n'accep-tons pas les accusations, a-t-il dit. Et je pense

qu'ils sont probablement trop gênés pour
venir la réclamer. »

1ᴱᴿ OCTOBRE 2012
The Guardian. *LE STUDIO D'AI WEIWEI
FERMÉ PAR LES AUTORITÉS.* Les autorités
chinoises sont en train de fermer l'entreprise
qui gère ses affaires, a déclaré lundi l'artiste
au franc-parler, l'empêchant probablement
de payer le solde d'un redressement fiscal de
15 millions de yuans (£1,5 million)... Les
autorités ont annoncé ce weekend qu'elles
allaient rayer FAKE Ldt. du registre du commerce pour n'avoir pas suivi la procédure
d'enregistrement annuel. L'entreprise n'a
pu le faire parce que tous ses documents et
ses cachets ont été confisqués par la police
pendant la détention d'Ai Weiwei l'an dernier.
« Je pense que ça pourrait être une bonne
excuse pour nous faire payer une amende »,
a ajouté l'artiste.

2 OCTOBRE 2012
@aiww. FAKE Design n'existe plus, « le gestionnaire actuel » est toujours là.

31 OCTOBRE 2012
The Guardian. *AI WEIWEI REND LEUR
ARGENT À SES PARTISANS.* L'artiste militant a entrepris de rendre leur argent à ses
partisans après avoir épuisé tous les moyens
légaux de contester un redressement fiscal
très élevé que ses soutiens voyaient comme
une punition pour son militantisme. « Nous
n'avons pas d'autre option que de continuer
à essayer. Nous avons fait ce que nous pouvions, et la cour a rendu sa décision. Alors
nous devons rendre l'argent », a déclaré
Ai Weiwei dans une interview téléphonique.

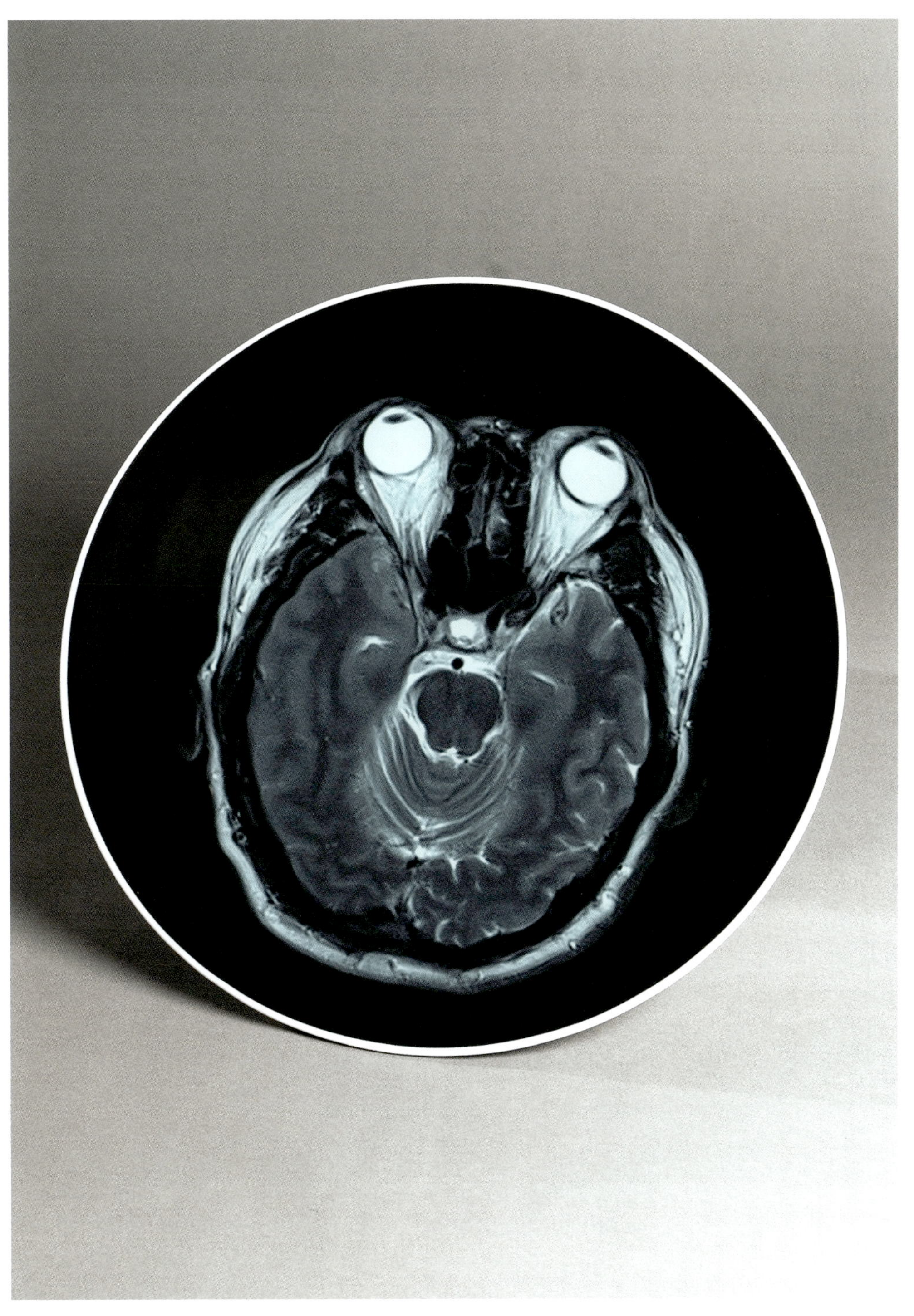

BRAIN SCAN IMAGE ON PLATE, 2012, porcelain, 1¾ x ø 15¾ inches | 465

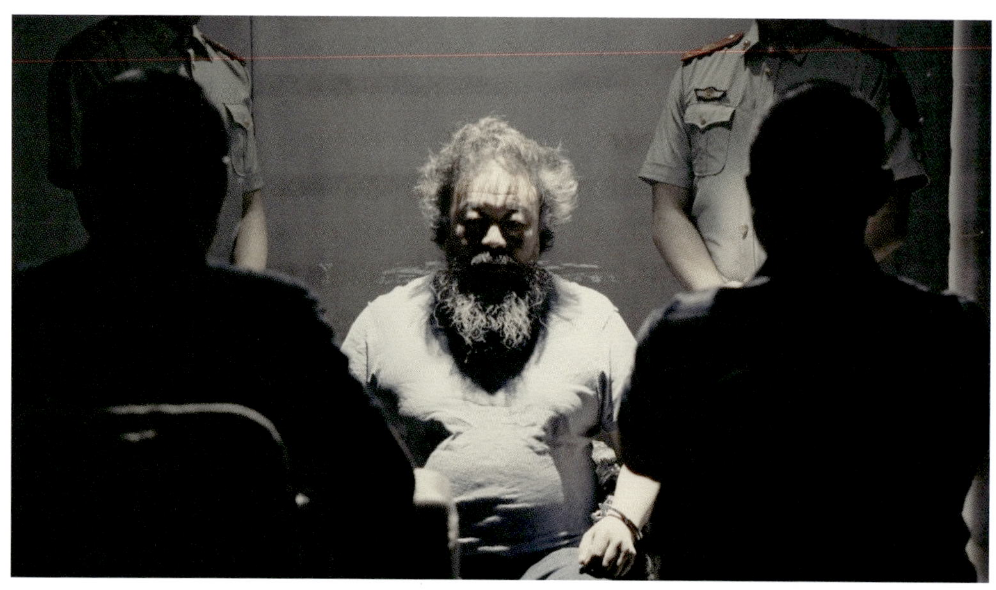

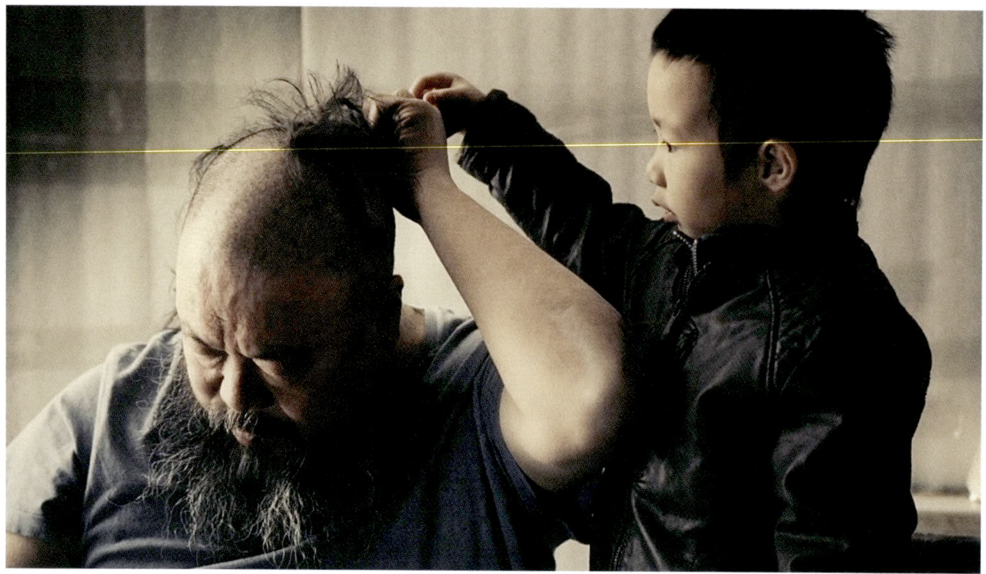

Stills from the music video "Dumbass," 2013, 5 min 13 sec, cinematography by Christopher Doyle
 | Opposite: SURVEILLANCE CAMERA, 2010, marble, 15 ⅜ x 15 ⅝ x 7 ½ inches

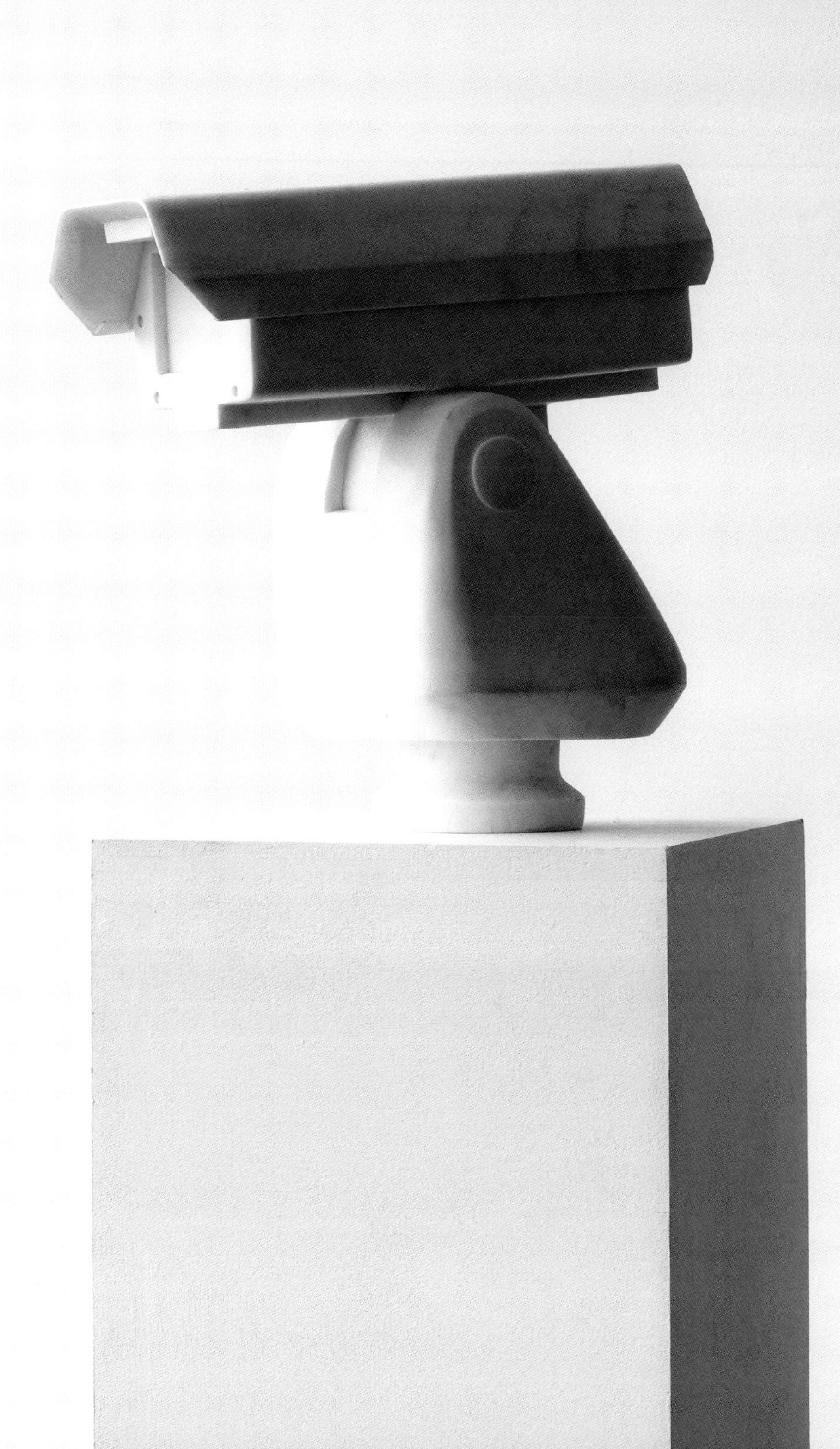

"After I was released from detention, I was under a lot of pressure because the
regulations said that wherever I went I had to report my activities to the police.
And there were 15 cameras placed around my home. At the same time, there were
so many people in the public who wanted to know what was really going on. So I
thought I would do them all a favor and put a camera in front of my desk, my
computer, and in my bedroom, so for 24 hours a day I could inform the authorities and the public about my activities. It's my longtime gesture to say: I can be
transparent, but can you?" — AI WEIWEI

Nach meiner Haftentlassung stand ich unter enormem Druck, weil die Auflagen besag-
ten, dass ich meine sämtlichen Bewegungen und Unternehmungen der Polizei melden
müsste. Außerdem waren 15 Überwachungskameras rund um mein Haus angebracht worden.
Gleichzeitig gab es eine große Zahl von Menschen in der Öffentlichkeit, die wissen wollten,
was wirklich vor sich ging. So dachte ich mir, ich würde allen einen Gefallen tun, wenn ich
Kameras an meinem Schreibtisch, meinem Computer und in meinem Schlafzimmer anbrin-
gen würde, um damit 24 Stunden am Tag die Behörden und die Öffentlichkeit wissen zu lassen, was ich so tat. Es handelt sich da um eine Frage, die ich immer wieder stelle: Ich kann
transparent sein, wie steht es mit euch?

Une fois remis en liberté, j'ai subi une pression énorme car j'étais censé faire le rapport
de toutes mes activités et de tous mes déplacements à la police. Il y avait quinze caméras
disposées autour de ma maison. En même temps, tant de gens voulaient savoir ce qui se passait vraiment. Je me suis dit que je rendrais service à tout le monde en installant une caméra
en face de mon bureau, de mon ordinateur, et dans ma chambre, pour que les autorités et
le public soient informés de mes activités 24 heures sur 24. C'est ma manière à moi de dire :
je peux être transparent, et vous, vous pouvez l'être ?

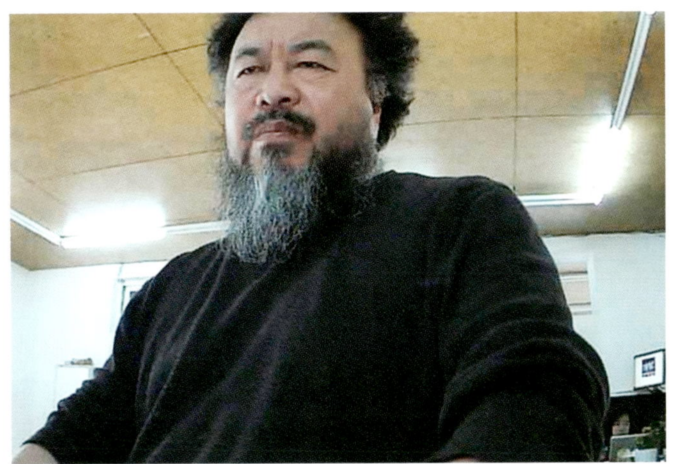

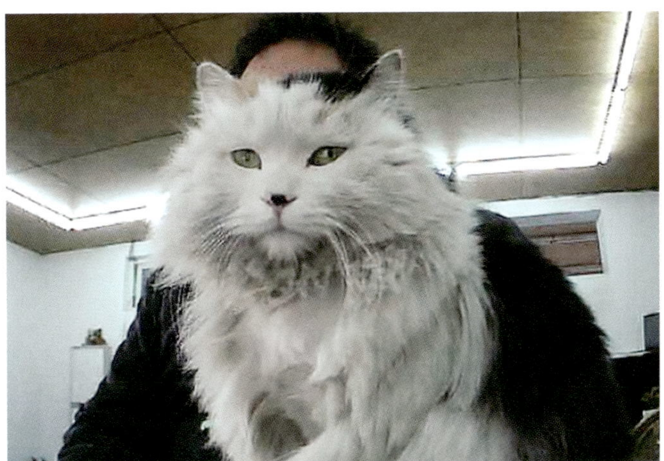

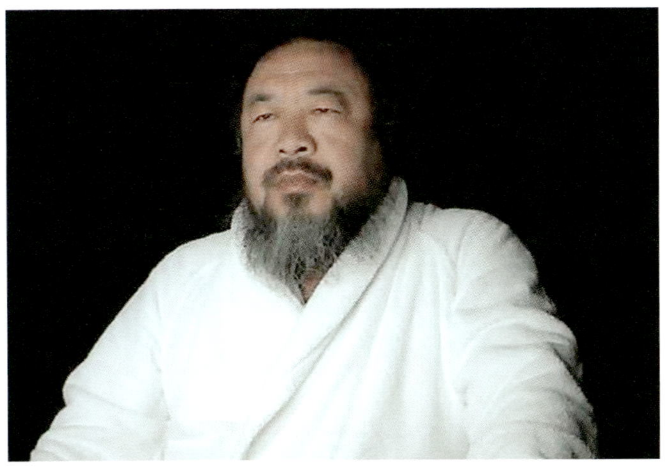

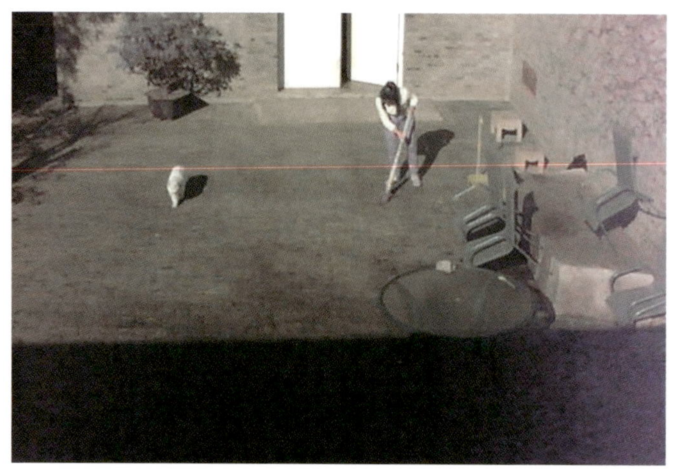

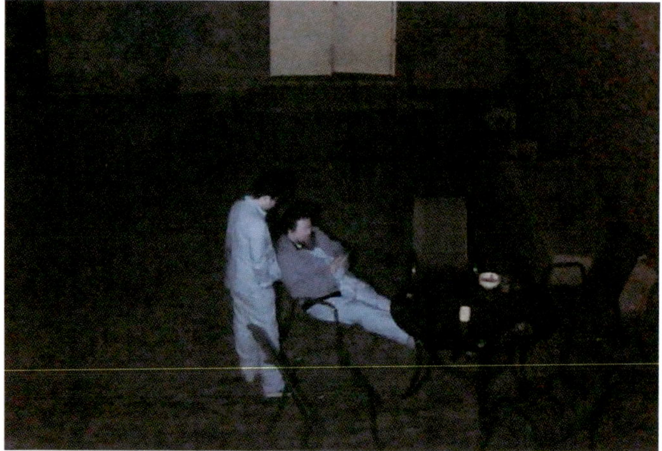

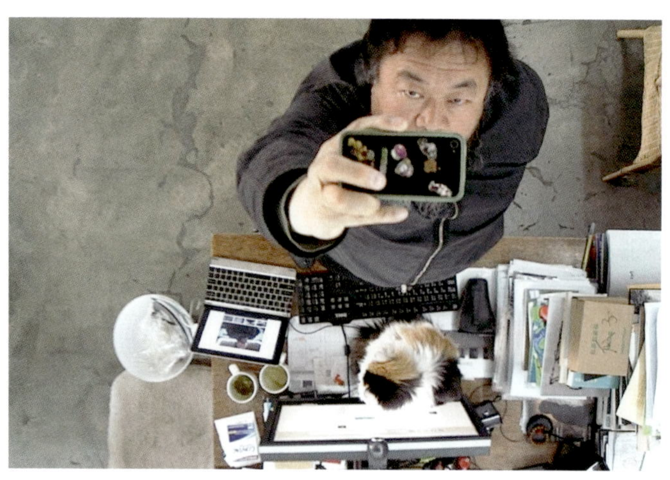

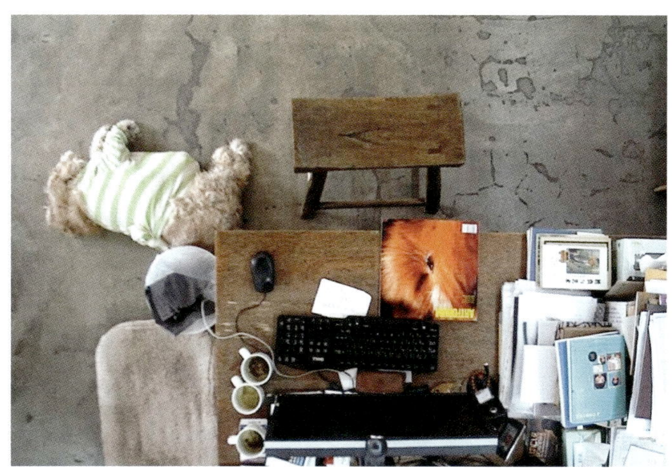

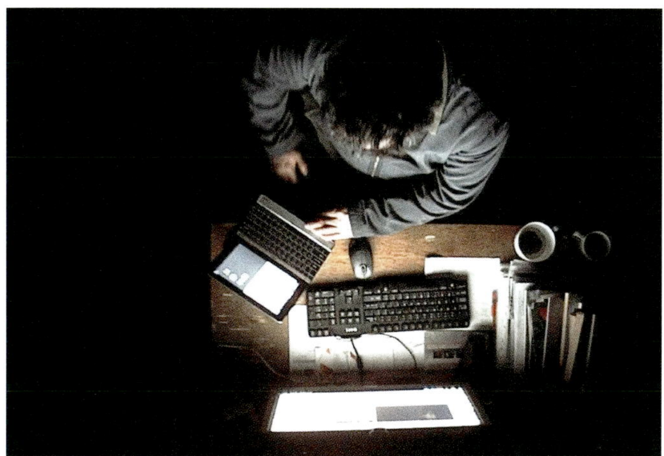

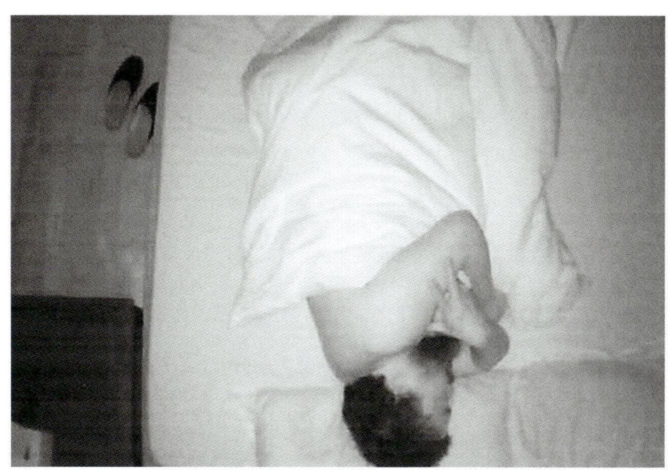

Overleaf: STRAIGHT, 2008–2012, steel reinforcing bars, 236 ⅛ x 472 ½ inches;
Complesso delle Zitelle, Venice 2013 | 471

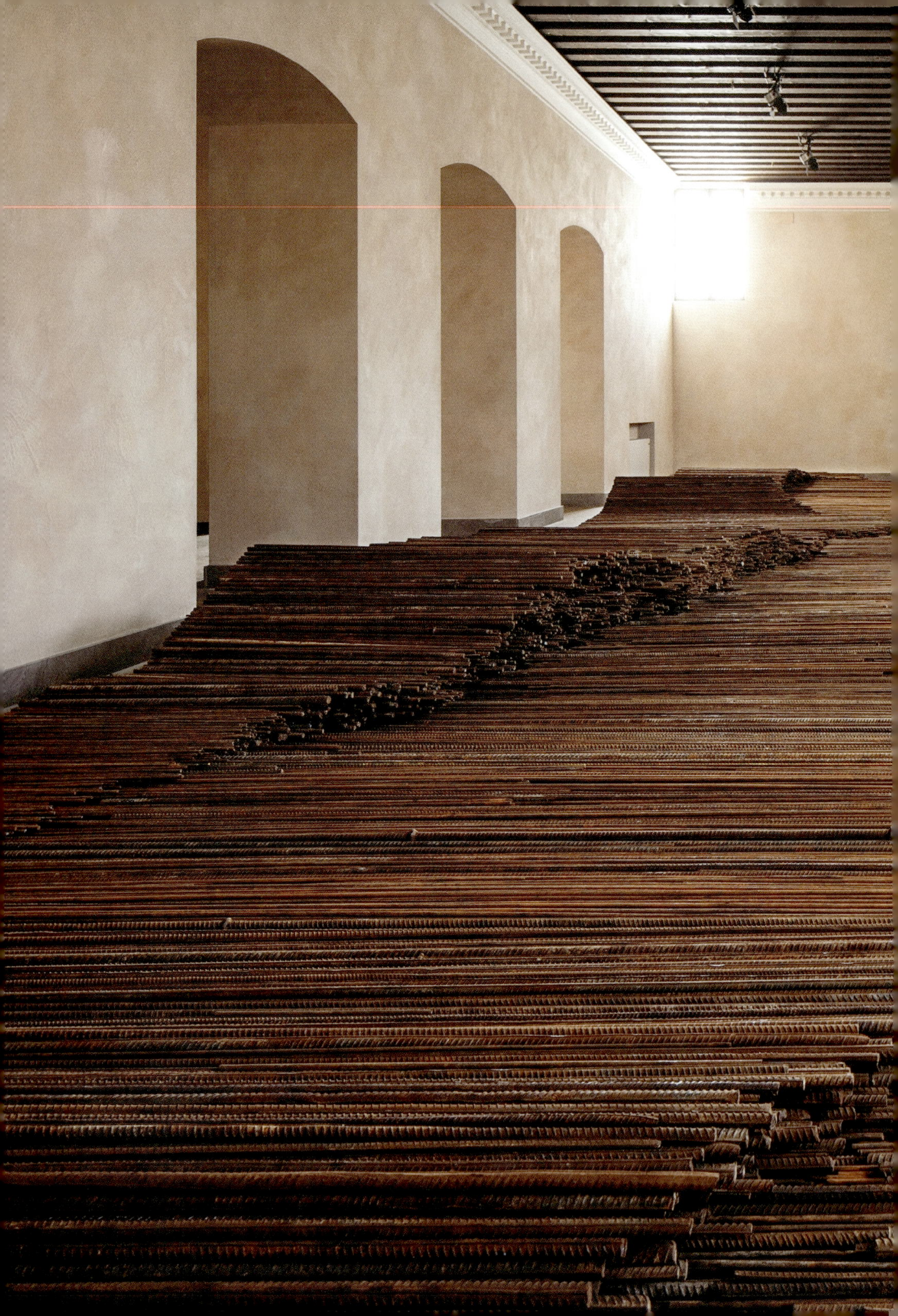

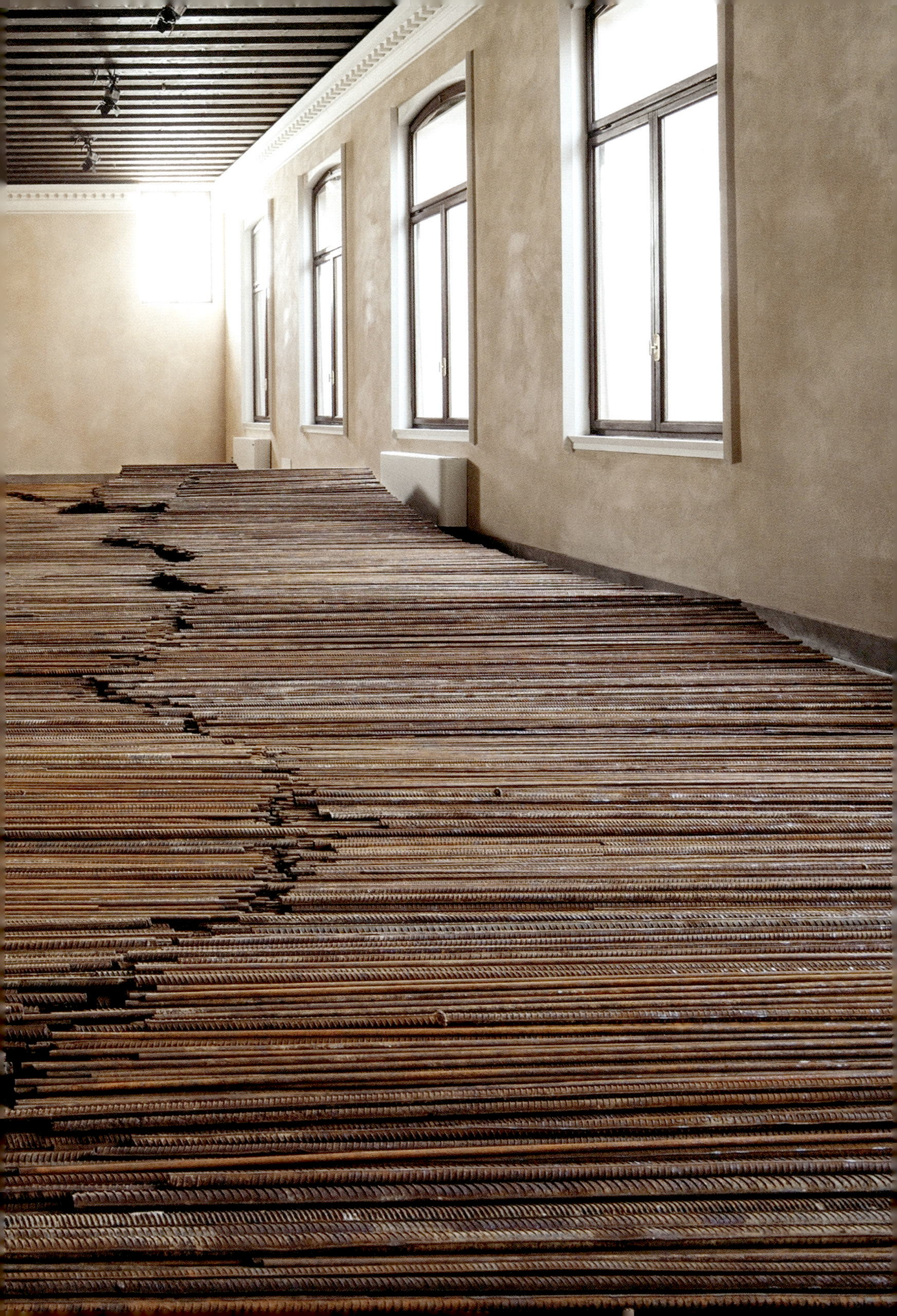

"The works in rebar are the most difficult work, emotionally and physically,
that I have ever made. It's not really made by me—it's made by history, individual
stories, blood, tears, and labor. I just directed it into its current state. Most of
the rebar we collected comes from one area, the Wenchuan Middle School, where
over 1,000 students were killed. It took a long time to collect it, but after visiting
the earthquake disaster zones and seeing ruins everywhere, I knew I needed to
do something with them, to create something from this unspeakable situation.
My first decision was to make all the rebar straight again, to make it look like it
just came out of a factory and nothing ever happened. But of course something
happened to those bars, and it took over 200 corrections to make each bar perfectly straight again." — AI WEIWEI

Die Arbeiten mit Armiereisen sind meine schwierigsten bislang, in emotionaler wie
materieller Hinsicht. Nicht ich habe diese Arbeiten gemacht – sie entstanden aus der
Geschichte, aus individuellen Geschichten, Blut, Tränen und körperlicher Arbeit. Ich habe
ihnen lediglich diese Form gegeben. Den größten Teil des Stahls haben wir an einem einzigen Ort gesammelt, der Mittelschule in Wenchuan, wo mehr als 1000 Schüler beim Erdbeben ums Leben gekommen sind. Das Einsammeln war zeitaufwändig, aber nachdem wir
das Katastrophengebiet besucht und die Ruinen gesehen hatten, wusste ich, dass ich etwas
damit anfangen, etwas Neues aus dieser unbeschreibbaren Situation machen musste. Meine
erste Entscheidung war, alle Stäbe wieder gerade biegen zu lassen, so als kämen sie frisch
aus der Fabrik, als sei nichts geschehen. Doch selbstverständlich war etwas geschehen,
und wir benötigten oft über 200 Korrekturen, damit jeder einzelne Stab wieder absolut
gerade wurde.

Cette œuvre en barres d'acier est la plus difficile que j'aie jamais réalisée, aussi bien
physiquement qu'émotionnellement. Ce n'est pas vraiment moi qui l'ai faite – c'est l'Histoire
qui l'a faite, les histoires individuelles, le sang, les larmes, le travail. J'ai seulement décidé
de sa forme. La plupart des barres que nous avons récupérées proviennent du même endroit,
l'école Wenchuan, où plus d'un millier d'écoliers ont trouvé la mort. Cela nous a pris du
temps de les rassembler, mais lorsque je me suis rendu dans les zones sinistrées par le
séisme, en voyant ces ruines partout, j'ai su qu'il me faudrait en faire quelque chose, pour
créer quelque chose à partir de cette situation indicible. J'ai tout de suite décidé de redresser toutes ces barres, comme si elles sortaient de l'usine et qu'il ne s'était rien passé. Mais
il s'était passé quelque chose, évidemment, et il a fallu plus de deux cent corrections pour
redresser parfaitement chacune de ces barres.

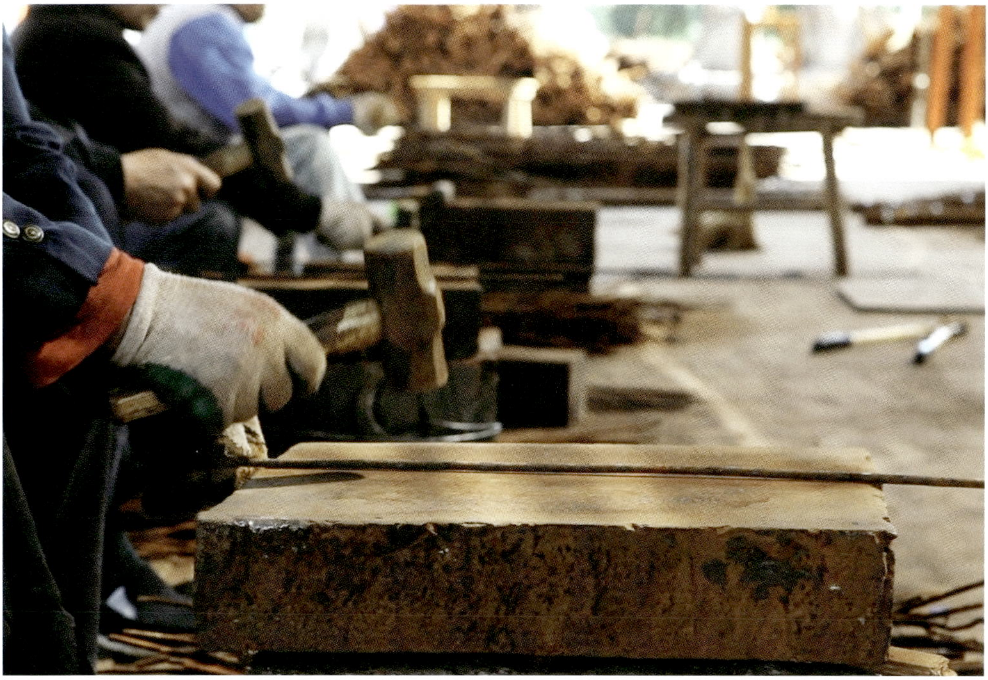

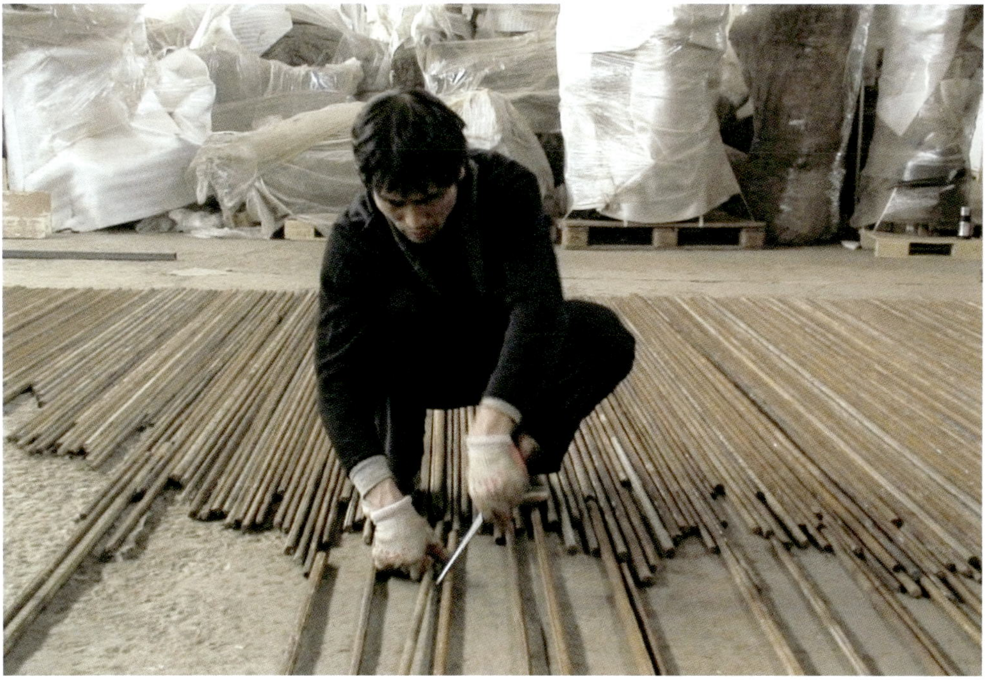

Production views of STRAIGHT, 2008–2012, steel reinforcing bars, 236 ⅛ x 472 ½ inches | 475

"I created another rebar piece where the bent form of one bar was copied twice. I later found that Carl Andre had made a similar work, but I think he was just interested in its minimalist intent, whereas I wanted to double and triple this form created by unknown forces. The first act may have been accidental, but the second and third are very intentional. It's not about recreating beauty or capturing the accidental, but an intentional embrace of a condition." — AI WEIWEI

Ich schuf eine weitere Arbeit aus Armiereisen, bei der die Verbiegungen eines Stahlstabs noch zweimal kopiert wurden. Später fand ich heraus, dass Carl Andre eine ähnliche Arbeit gemacht hatte, doch ich denke, er verfolgte nur eine minimalistische Absicht, wohingegen ich die Form, die unbekannte Kräfte hervorgebracht hatten, verdoppeln und verdreifachen wollte. Der erste Akt mag ein zufälliger gewesen sein, aber beim zweiten und dritten Stab ist es Absicht. Es geht nicht darum, hier etwas Schönes zu kopieren oder den Zufall zu zähmen, sondern um das bewusste Wahrnehmen einer Gegebenheit.

J'ai créé une autre œuvre avec des barres d'acier, dans laquelle la courbe d'une barre est répétée deux fois. Par la suite, je me suis rendu compte que Carl Andre avait fait un travail similaire, mais je crois que ce qui l'intéressait, c'était l'intention minimaliste, alors que pour ma part je voulais copier et copier encore une forme créée par des forces inconnues. Le premier acte a peut-être été accidentel, mais le deuxième et le troisième sont très intentionnels. Il ne s'agit pas de recréer quelque chose de beau ou de fixer l'accidentel, mais d'accepter intentionnellement une certaine condition.

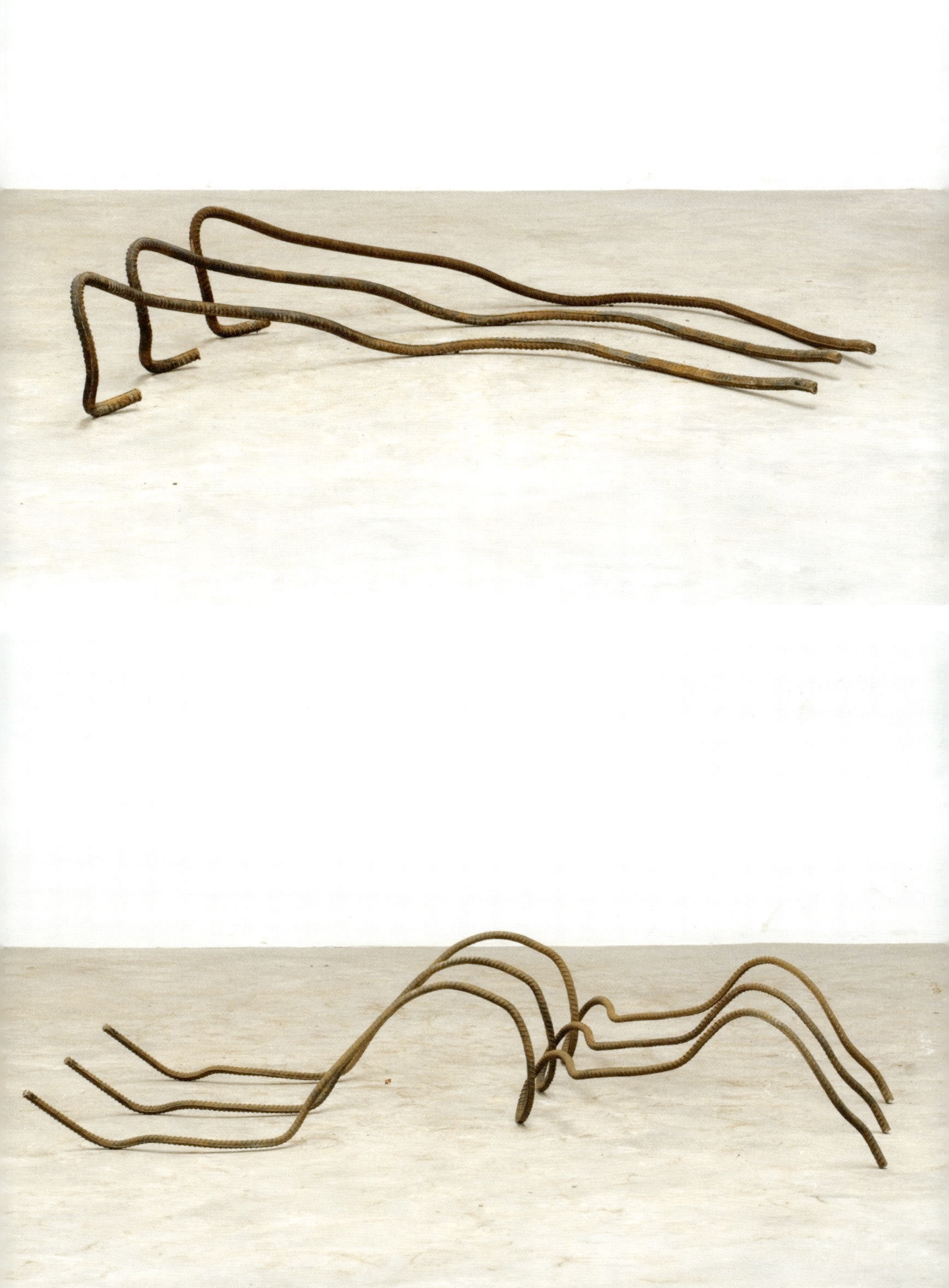

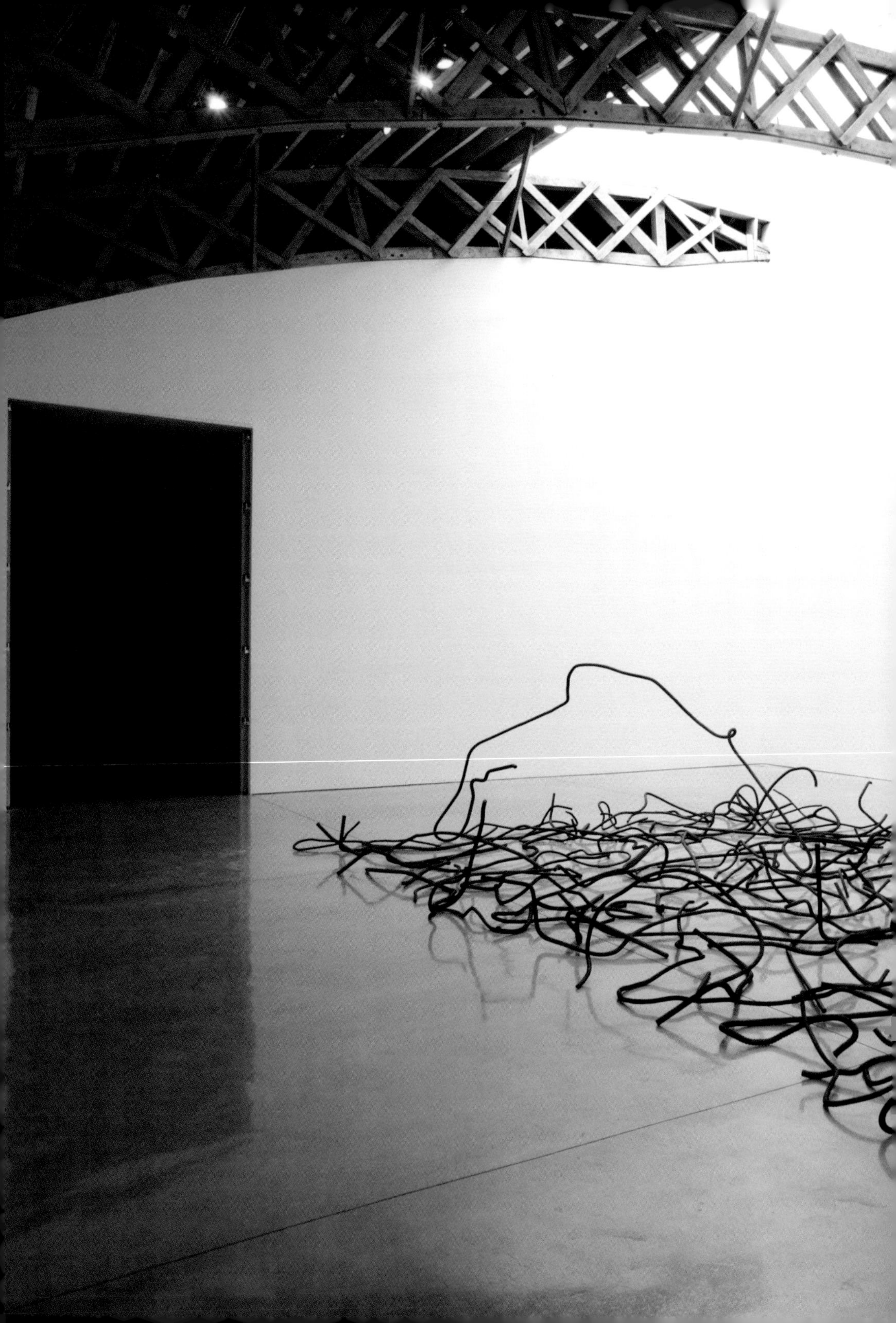

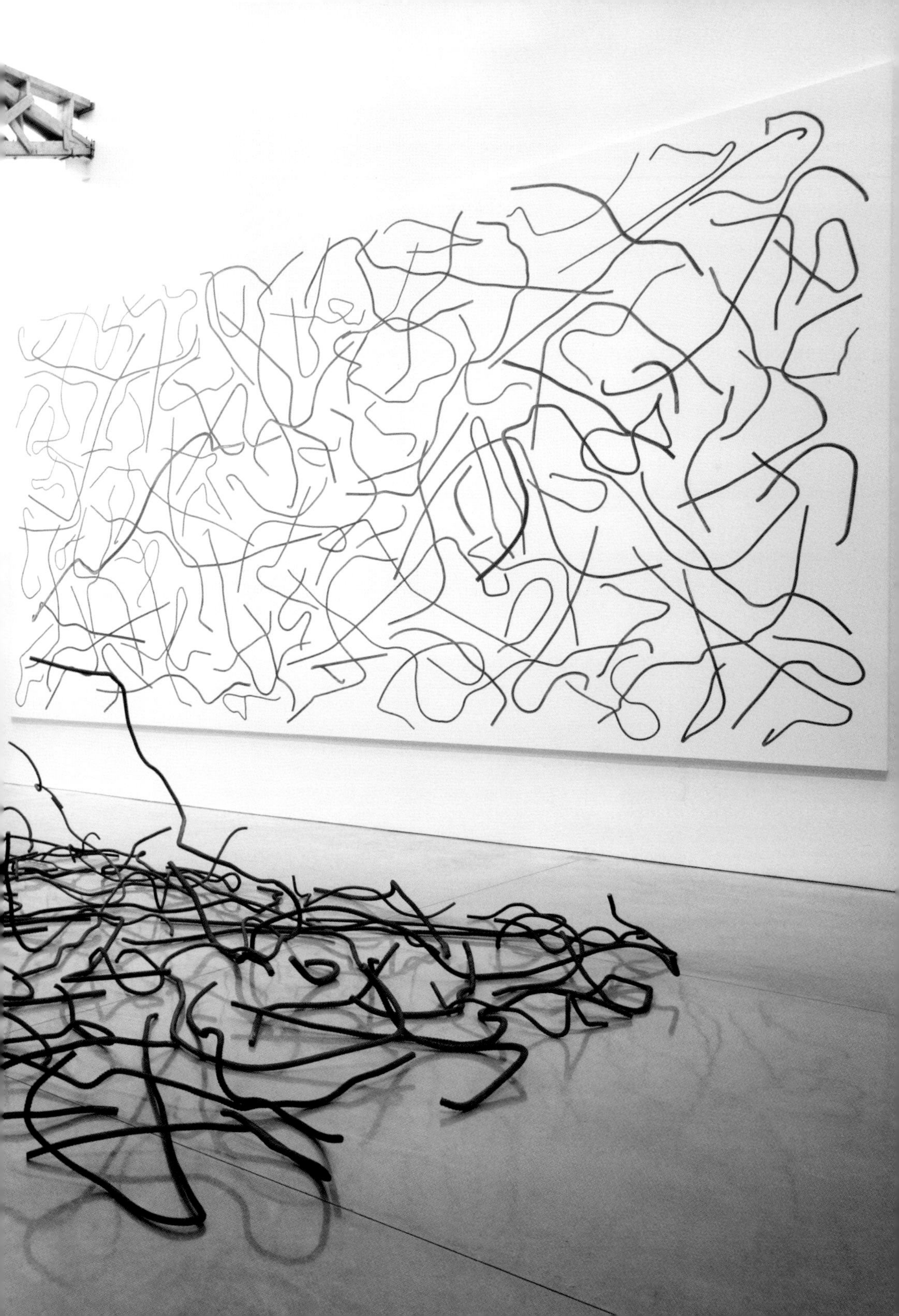

"When I arrived in detention, I was put in a facility for what is called *shuanggui,* a form of detention mostly reserved for high-level party officials who are either political prisoners or people accused of committing economic crimes. The police told me that many people had been here before, but that detention only goes in one direction. Nobody ever comes out, and nobody outside knows what happens inside. Once I got out, I realized I had the privilege to recreate that scene, to represent to society what kind of condition *shuanggui* is…Then I remembered reading my father's books about religion when I was little. At the time, I felt it had nothing to do with my life growing up in the Gobi desert, but when I was deciding on how to depict detention, I thought of those religious images. I chose six scenes: eating, interrogation, showering, sleeping, walking in the room, and using the bathroom. With each scene, I create a frozen moment like in a natural history museum, that could be integrated into our image world and become part of reality." — AI WEIWEI

Als ich in Haft kam, wurde ich in eine Einrichtung für sogenanntes *Shuanggui* gebracht, eine Form des Gewahrsams für meist hochrangige Parteifunktionäre, die entweder politische Gefangene oder ökonomischer Verbrechen angeklagt sind. Die Polizei sagte mir, dass hier schon viele Menschen gewesen wären, und Inhaftierung sei nun einmal eine Einbahnstraße. Niemand kommt heraus, und niemand, der draußen ist, weiß, was drinnen vor sich geht. Sobald ich freikam, wurde mir klar, welches Privileg es sein würde, die Situation neu zu inszenieren und der Öffentlichkeit zu zeigen, welcher Art die Bedingungen von *Shuanggui* sind … Dann erinnerte ich mich daran, wie ich als Kind religiöse Bücher meines Vaters gelesen hatte. Damals schien das nichts mit meinem Leben in der Wüste Gobi zu tun zu haben, doch als ich mir überlegte, wie ich diese Haft darstellen könnte, erinnerte ich mich an diese religiösen Bilder. Ich wählte sechs Szenen aus: Essen, Verhör, Duschen, Schlafen, Auf-und-ab-Gehen im Zimmer, die Nutzung der Toilette. In jeder Szene schaffe ich einen eingefrorenen Moment, wie ein Schaukasten in einem naturhistorischen Museum, der Teil unserer Bildwelt und somit Teil unserer Wirklichkeit werden kann.

Quand j'ai été placé en détention, c'était dans le cadre de ce qu'on appelle le *shuanggui,* réservé en principe aux hauts dignitaires du parti qui sont prisonniers politiques ou accusés d'avoir commis des délits économiques. Les policiers m'ont dit que beaucoup de gens étaient passés par là avant moi, et que le mouvement n'allait que dans un seul sens. On est placé en détention, et personne n'en sort jamais, personne à l'extérieur ne sait ce qui se passe à l'intérieur. Quand j'ai été libéré, je me suis rendu compte que j'avais le privilège de pouvoir recréer cette scène, de montrer à la société quelles sont les conditions de détention en *shuanggui*… Puis je me suis souvenu des livres de religion de mon père que je lisais quand j'étais petit. À l'époque, j'avais l'impression que cela n'avait rien à voir avec ma vie, moi qui vivais dans le désert de Gobi, mais quand je me suis demandé comment représenter la détention, j'ai pensé à ces images religieuses. J'ai choisi six scènes différentes : le repas, l'interrogatoire, la douche, le sommeil, la promenade et les toilettes. Avec chaque scène, j'ai créé comme un moment figé qu'on peut intégrer dans notre monde d'images et qui fait désormais partie de notre réalité.

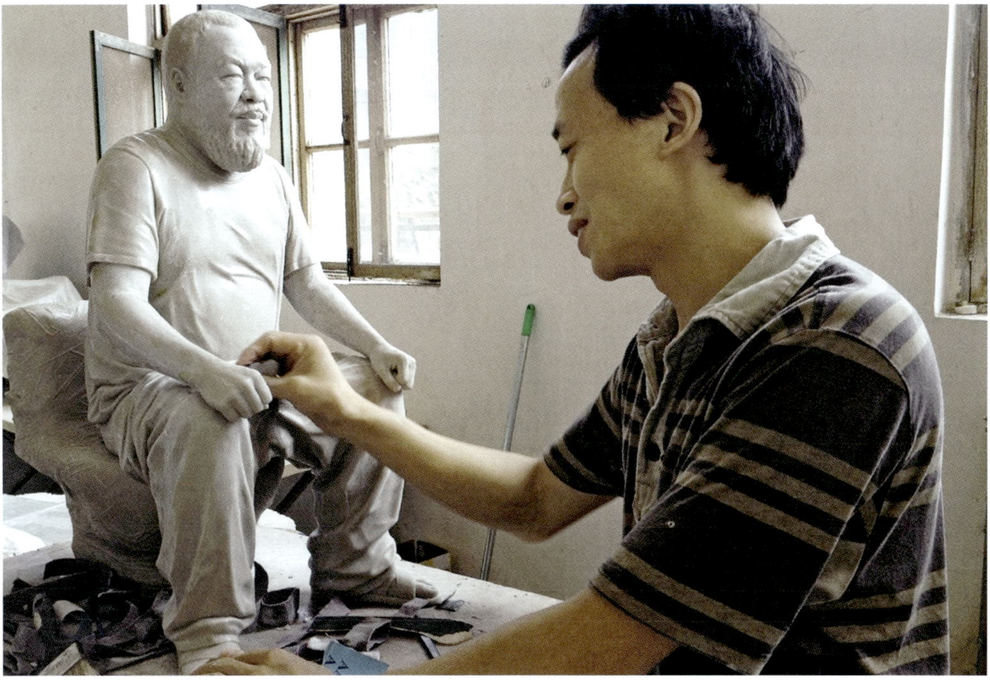

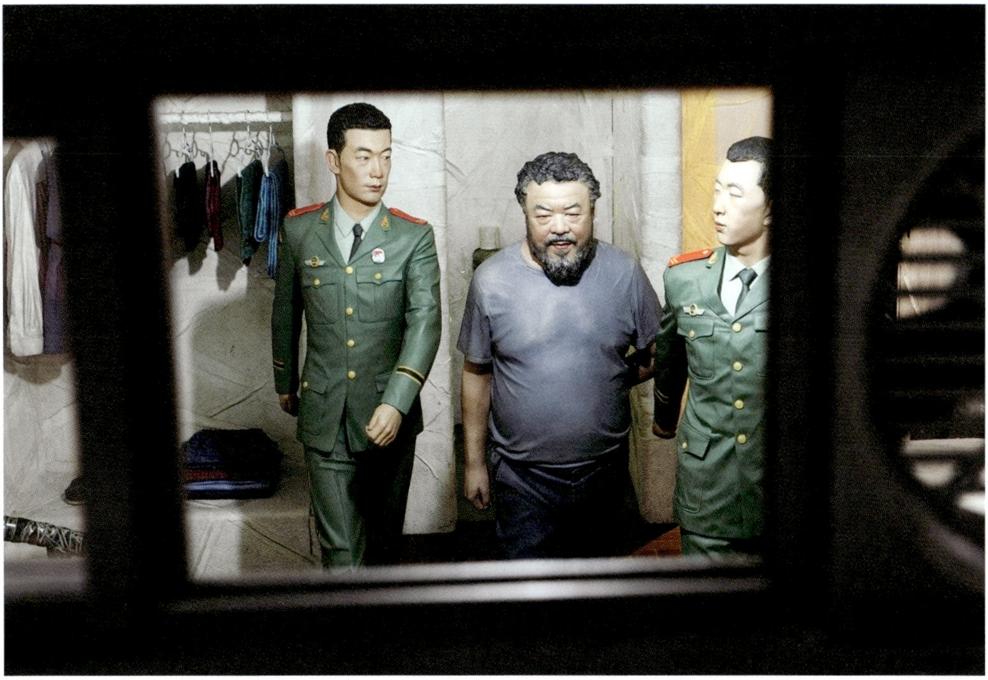

S.A.C.R.E.D., 2011–2013, 6 dioramas, fiberglass, iron, each 148⅜ x 78 x 60¼ inches;
production view (top); detail (bottom); installation view, Chiesa di Sant'Antonin, Venice 2013 (overleaf) | 481

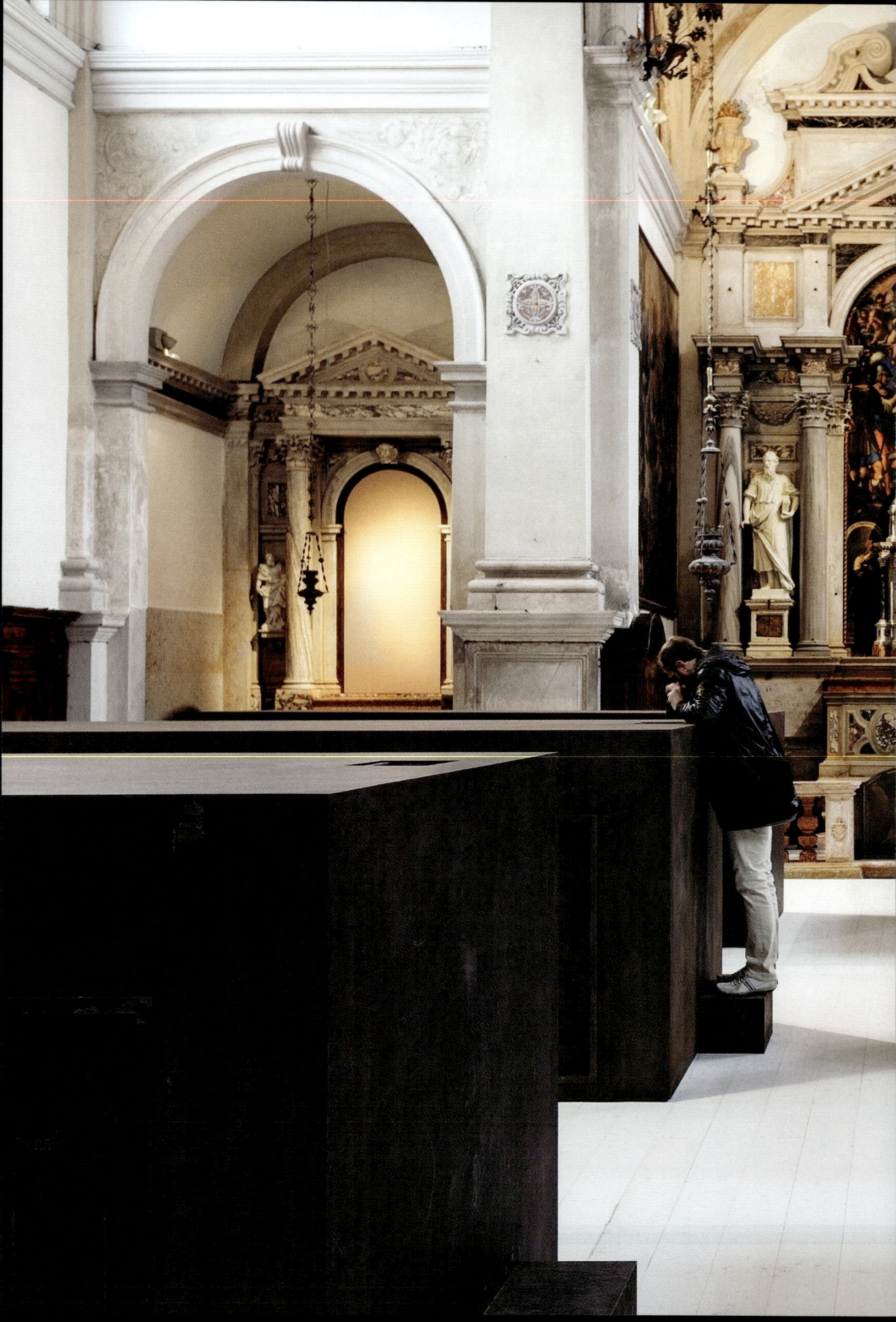

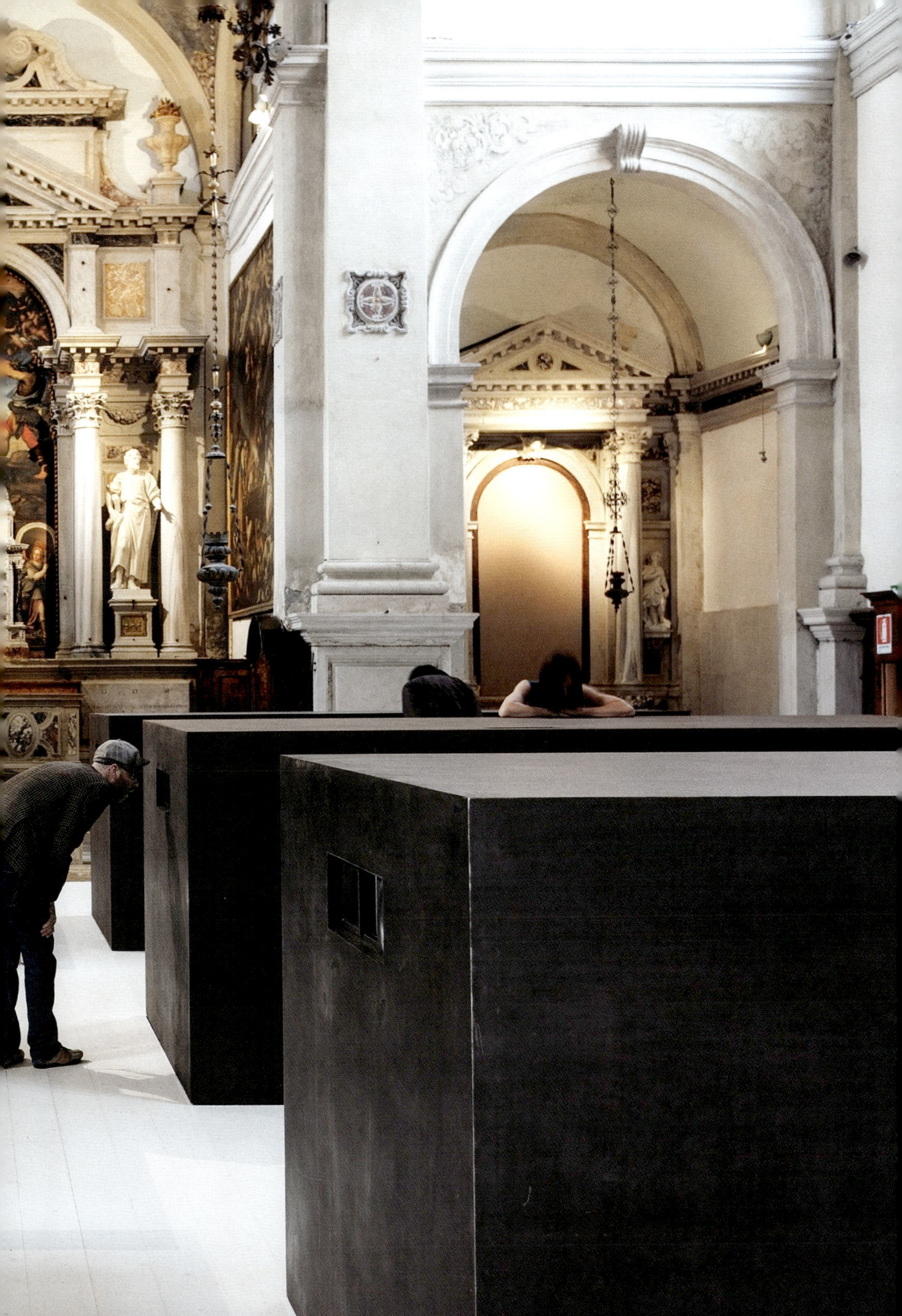

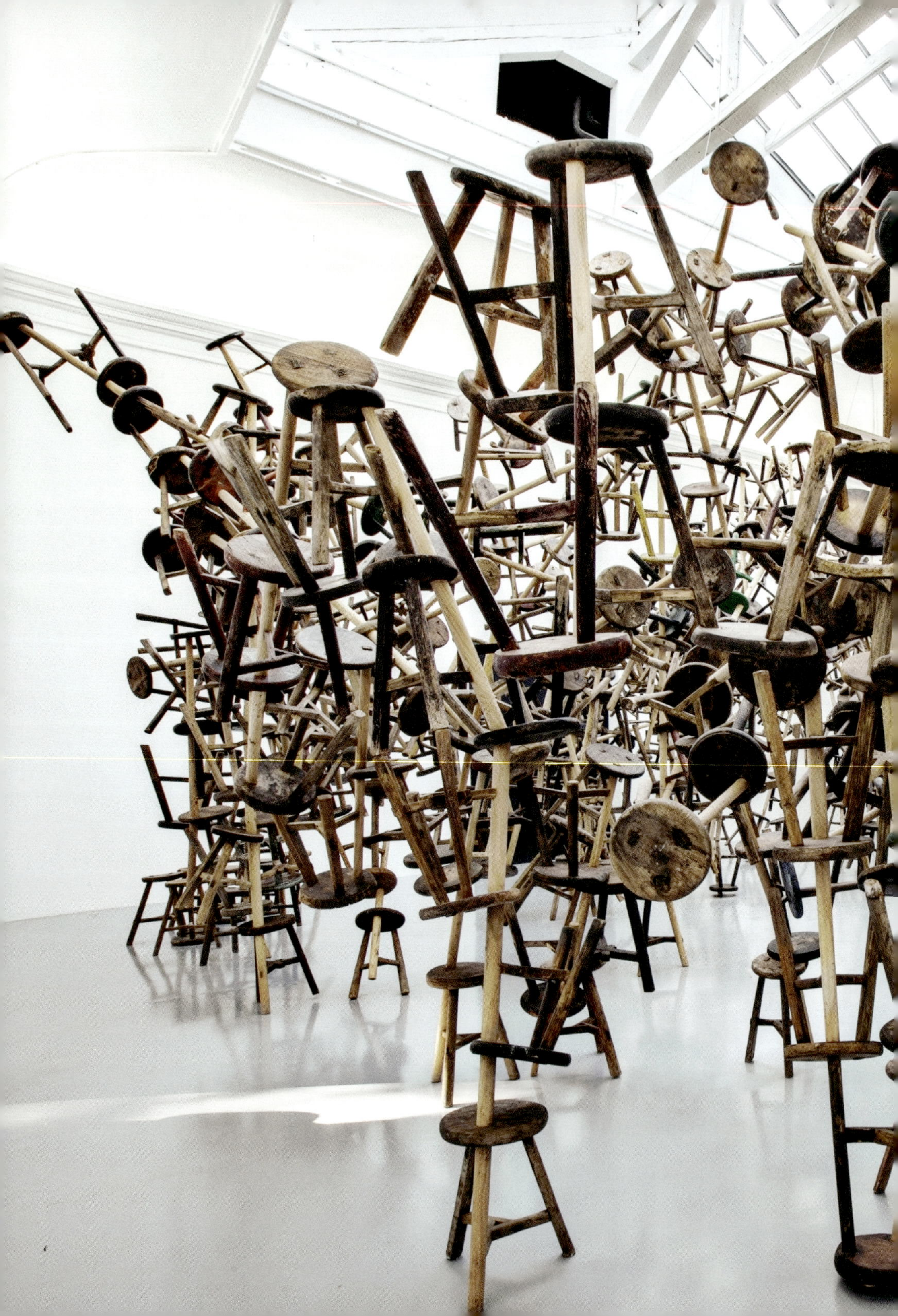

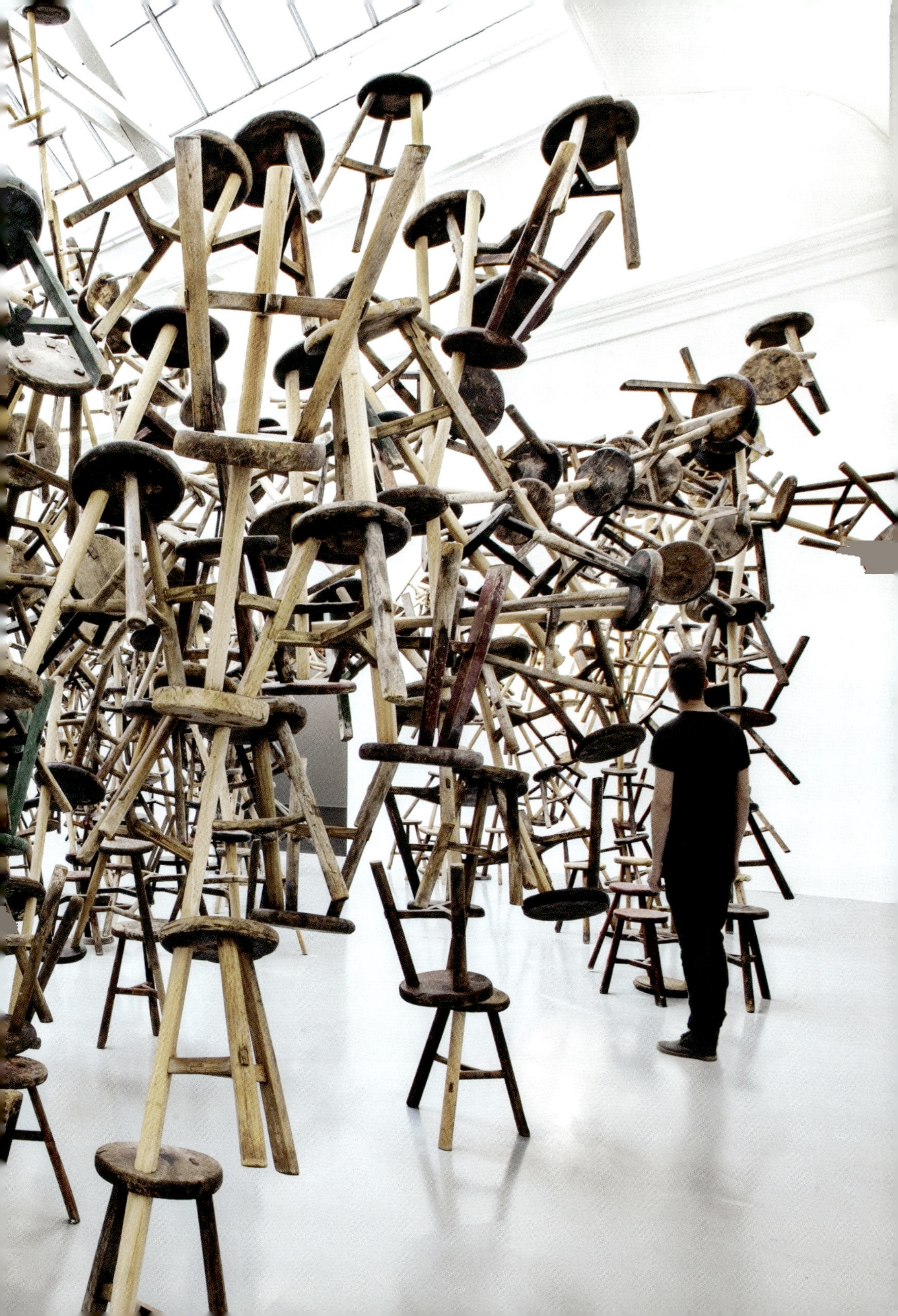

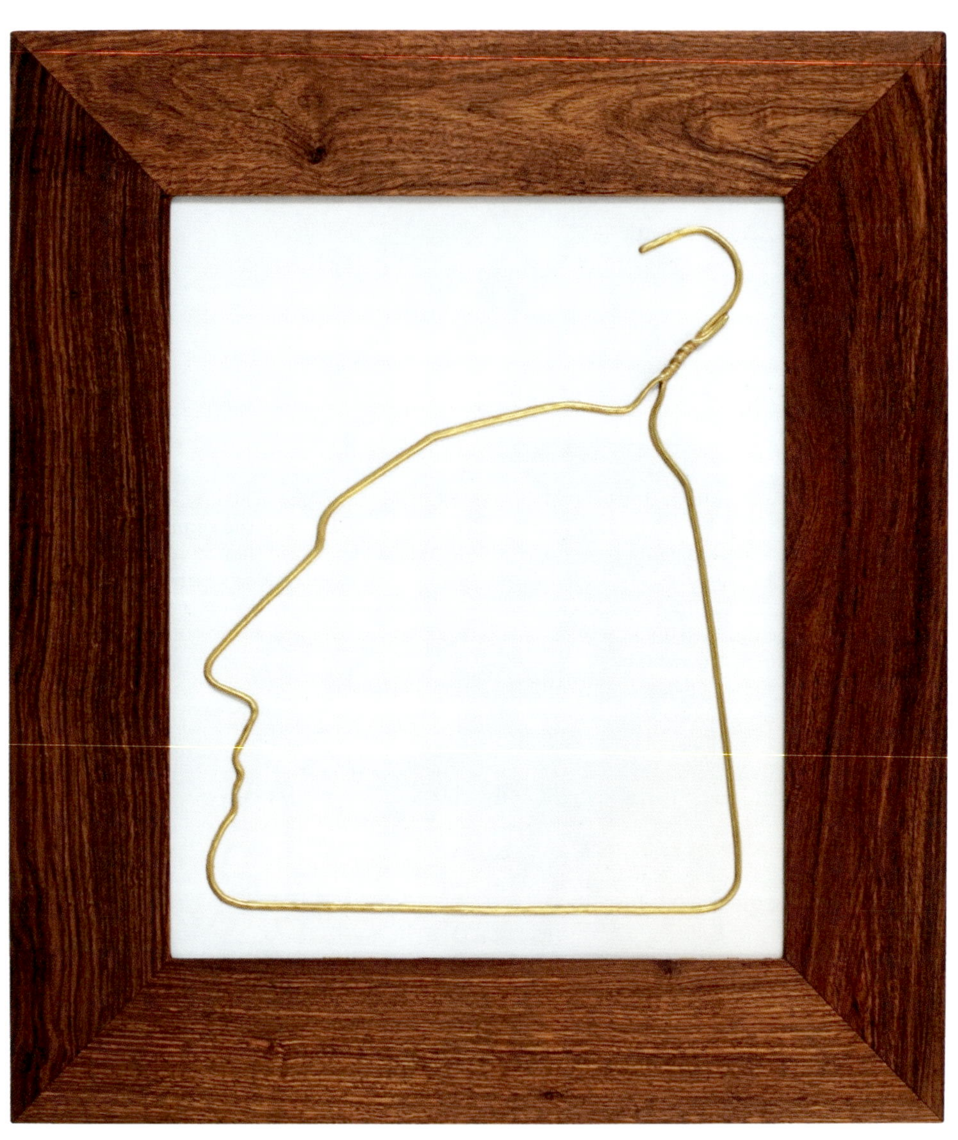

HANGING MAN IN PORCELAIN, 2009, porcelain in huali wood frame, 14 ¼ x 11 ¾ x ⅜ inches
Previous spread: BANG, 2013, 886 stools, dimensions variable; German contribution in the French Pavilion,
 55th Venice Biennale, Venice 2013

Ai Weiwei: Life and Work

1957 Born in Beijing on August 28 as the second son of Gao Ying and poet Ai Qing. His father is a literary celebrity in Communist China, but now targeted in one of Mao's campaigns accusing many intellectuals of "rightist" tendencies.

1958 As a consequence of the purges, Ai Qing's family is relocated to Beidahuang in the Heilongjiang Province in the far northeast near the Russian border.

1960 The family is relocated to Shihezi,a small city in the Xinjiang Province of north-western China, in the middle of the Gobi Desert.

1967 While the Cultural Revolution, which started in May of the previous year, is in full swing, the family is moved again to a more remote village. The conditions are dismal and the family has to live in an underground shed: "Four or five of our family members in twelve square meters. We all slept in the same bed. Very low, no light. We had to dig one shovel deeper so that we could stand straight. The bed was just a big piece of earth. When we dug the hole we left that piece as a bed. At night we often heard the rats. In the morning I checked all my rattraps. Often I found more than ten rats. I lived in those circumstances for five years." Ai Qing is assigned hard labor such as scrubbing the toilets every day.

1972 The family is allowed to move back to Shihezi.

1975 In summer, Ai Weiwei is on his first visit to Beijing, as Ai Qing is allowed medical treatment in the city.

1976 Ai Qing is rehabilitated. Ai Weiwei graduates from No. 1 Shihezi High School in May, and later in the year the family returns to Beijing for good, arriving two days after the devastating Tangshan earthquake. Since their old home has been allotted to others, they move from place to place around the capital as guests. Ai Weiwei studies privately with teachers from the art academies, as universities nationwide have been closed for nearly a decade.

1978 Ai Weiwei enrolls in the Beijing Film Academy, which is the first class to take up students after the Cultural Revolution. Among his classmates are Zhang Yimou and Chen Kaige, who will become internationally famous film directors. He takes the first of his study trips through China, which by 1981 will enable him to see Dunhuang, Shanghai, and Suzhou. Images of his work appear in the monthly magazine *Renmin Huabao* (*China Pictorial*).

1979 Ai leaves the academy to become a founding member of the seminal "Stars" artists group. Since their applications for exhibition space are never granted, they hold a first unauthorized group show on the side-walk outside China's National Art Museum. The exhibition, often seen as the birth of a new Chinese avant-garde, is closed by the Security Police after only three days. On October 1, the 30th anniversary of the People's Republic of China, the Stars march through central Beijing renewing their appeal for exhibition space and are granted 10 days at the Hua Fang Zhai studio in Beihai Park. Most of the works on show are expressionist paintings; Ai contributes some landscape watercolors.

1980 The Stars are granted a show at the National Art Museum in Beijing from August 20 to September 7. It is the first such con-temporary art exhibition in a leading museum and creates a sensation with almost 200,000 visitors by official count.

1981 Together with his girlfriend, who has relatives overseas, Ai leaves China for the United States. He briefly studies English at the University of Pennsylvania in Philadel-phia, then spends a semester in Berkeley, California.

1982–1993 Ai has his first one-man exhibition of 30 paintings executed in China at the Asia Foundation Gallery in San Francisco. He moves to New York and enrolls at the Parsons School of Design, which he attends for one semester. After that he supports himself through work as a street and housepainter, waiter, babysitter, and through other odd jobs. He uses various shops and stores around town as work places and moves often: first he lives in a studio in Long Island City in Queens, then in Brooklyn, and finally the Lower East Side of Manhattan. His residences serve as gathering places for Chinese expatriates, including artists Xu Bing and Tehching Hsieh and musician Tan Dun, as well as other friends like beat poet Allen Ginsberg. On the weekends, Ai gambles at the blackjack tables in Atlantic City. He constantly visits museums and gallery openings, taking in the modern classics from Duchamp to Warhol and the thriving contemporary New York scene, of which Ai later recalls he must have visited every single exhibition. Of his own work as an artist, he says: "I did very little. In twelve years I may have spent one year on art. My economic condition and my communication with the art world did not allow me to become very active. So I became more of a thinking artist, not willing to produce because to whom could I show and sell? I am very happy I never really spent much time thinking about it." He takes thousands of photographs, mostly not even bothering to develop them before his eventual return to China.

1988 Ai has his only solo show during the New York years, *Old Shoes, Safe Sex* at Art Waves/Ethan Cohen. His habit of taking photographs and his interest in social concerns lead him to photo reportage, documenting the Tompkins Square Park riots in August, where police take violent measures against squatters and sympathetic protesters.

1989 Ai participates in a hunger strike in front of the UN building in response to the Tiananmen Square massacre in Beijing on June 4, where Chinese troops have inflicted heavy casualties on unarmed protesters.

1990 A new series of works consists of paintings that are poured over to gradually obscure and finally erase the subjects. Ai puts them into crates before his return to China a few years later and they are never shown or even unpacked.

1992 Ai's basement apartment on East Seventh Street in New York, something like an unofficial embassy for the avant-garde in exile, serves as the set of the post-Tiananmen telenovela *Beijingers in New York* produced by the Chinese state television channel CCTV.

1993 When his father falls ill with a heart condition, Ai faces a decision: "My relatives all told me just to come back and visit him, but I knew that it was either go back to China for good or stay in New York for good." He returns to Beijing, where he lives with his parents, without much to show for himself, neither a career nor a wife. To learn about Chinese traditions after his decade-long exploration of Western art, he browses the antique markets and starts collecting furniture and pottery. Without any great ambition to produce high art, Ai begins series like *Still Life* (1993–2000) and *Whitewash* (1993–2000). He frequently visits a group of young artists, including Zhang Huan and Rong Rong, who have gathered in a village on the eastern fringes of Beijing. They put on performances for one another and discuss their work, dubbing the neighborhood "East Village" in reference to New York.

1994 Together with the critic Feng Boyi, Ai puts together a book introducing the latest Chinese avant-garde art as well as modern and recent Western art to a Chinese audience, the *Black Cover Book*. He also produces the first *Han Dynasty Urn with Coca-Cola Logo*. He meets his future wife, Lu Qing.

1995 Ai begins the series *Studies of Perspective,* snapshots where political or culturally important sites, starting with Tiananmen Square and the White House in Washington, D.C., are measured against his outstretched middle finger. He edits a second art book, this time with a more political bent, the *White Cover Book.*

1996 His father, the poet Ai Qing, dies.

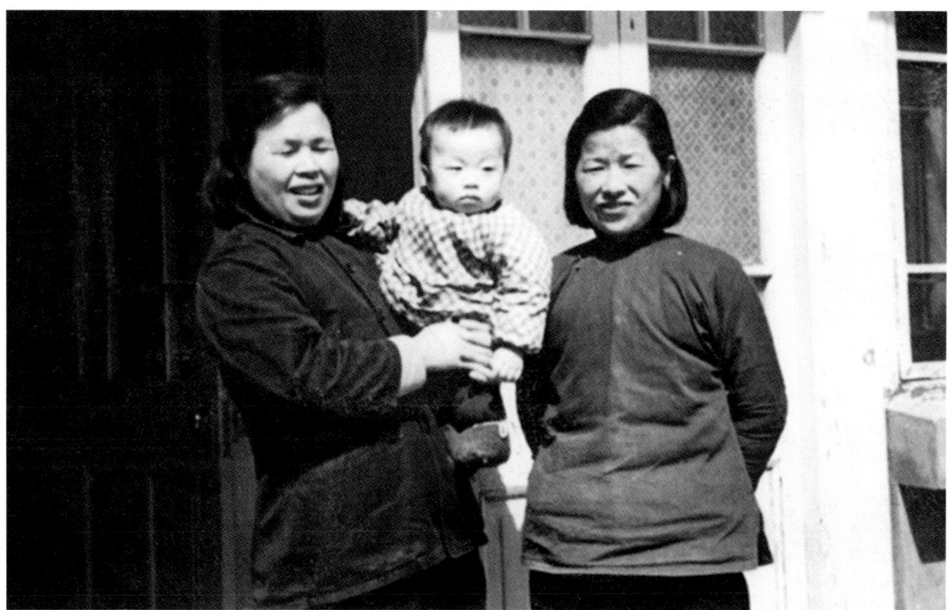

Ai Weiwei and caretakers outside the family home in Beijing, early 1958

1997 Ai edits the *Gray Cover Book* with artist Zhuang Hui. He begins his work with furniture, using traditional Chinese joining and finishing techniques to make tables that contain strange angles or two stools sharing a leg.

1998 With art historian Hans van Dijk and collector Frank Uytterhaegen, Ai founds the nonprofit space China Art Archives and Warehouse. He starts curating exhibitions of contemporary art and editing the accompanying catalogs for CAAW. He also becomes a jury member for the Chinese Contemporary Art Awards established by his close friend, the Swiss collector Uli Sigg. When Ai sends *Coca-Cola Vase* (1997) to Max Protetch Gallery in New York for an exhibition, the authenticity of the antique vessel used for the work is put in doubt, after the urn has broken in transport, a thermoluminescence analysis proves its antiquity.

1999 Ai moves to the Caochangdi village in northeast Beijing near the airport expressway, where he builds his own home and studio from gray bricks. "I just did the drawing in one afternoon. And in 60 days we built it. Then after 100 days I lived in there." Other buildings in the district follow soon; this proves to be the beginning of an international career as an architect. In the autumn, Ai, together with 18 other Chinese artists, takes part in the Venice Biennale curated by Harald Szeemann. This first mark of international recognition encourages Ai to work more self-consciously as an artist, though many of his biggest projects in the coming years will still be architectural.

2000 With Feng Boyi, Ai curates the landmark exhibition *Fuck Off* (the Chinese title *Bu hezuo fangshi* translates as "uncooperative behavior") in a warehouse in Shanghai. Opposed to the commercialized Shanghai Biennale, the show features Chinese avant-garde artists from all major cities. In Caochangdi, Ai designs the new CAAW headquarters.

2001 For the opening of Beijing's SOHO NewTown, a prefab development of more Western-style flexible buildings, Ai contributes *Tong*, a massively unmovable poured-concrete C-shaped sculpture.

2002 Ai produces his first chandelier work nearly 20 feet high for the premiere of the Guangzhou Triennial. He becomes curator of the project Ai Qing Cultural Park in Jinhua, his father's hometown in the eastern province of Zhejiang, for which he designs the south embankment of the Yangtze River. For the associated Architecture Park, he invites 17 architects from seven countries, and designs a memorial to his father and a museum for ancient pottery. Meanwhile he continues his furniture works and wood sculpture on a larger scale, incorporating huge pillars salvaged from demolished ancient temples.

2003 Ai founds FAKE Design, a studio with which to organize his proliferating architectural practice. The name contains a play on the two romanized syllables fake, which is the common Chinese pronunciation of the English word "fuck." Architects Jacques Herzog and Pierre de Meuron, whom Ai met during their visit to his studio in the previous autumn, take him on as a consultant for their proposal of an Olympic Stadium for the 2008 games in Beijing. Together they completely overhaul the plans and submit a design early in the year. It wins the competition and groundwork begins on December 24.

2004 On July 31, construction of the stadium is halted due to a spiraling budget and only resumes in December. Ai has his first big institutional solo exhibition in Europe at Kunsthalle Bern in Switzerland. In Jinhua, construction work on the 17 pavilions in the Architecture Park begins, never to be finished.

2005 In October, Ai agrees to write a blog for the popular Chinese web portal Sina.com. It quickly attracts a large audience and is read by young people from all over the country. The contents vary between texts and everyday snapshots from the studio and Ai's many cats, to highly political posts with a clearly oppositional stance.

2006 Beside numerous architectural projects and the furniture works, Ai starts creating porcelain pieces manufactured in China's old porcelain capital, Jingdezhen.

2007 Ai is invited to Documenta 12 in Kassel, for which he conceives *Fairytale*, a work that organizes a trip to Germany for 1,001 Chinese citizens with considerable logistical effort. His other contribution, the outdoor installation *Template*, collapses during a severe thunderstorm. In August, *The Guardian* publishes an article in which Ai announces his boycott of the Olympic Games as long as there is no freedom of expression in his country. In subsequent interviews he says that the stadium he helped build is now used as a "pretend smile," stressing: "I would feel ashamed if I just designed something for glamour or to show some kind of fake image." These articles establish him as a leading critic of the Chinese government in the Western media.

2008 In January and April, Ai chairs an international architects symposium in the remote city of Ordos in Inner Mongolia and FAKE Design invites Herzog and de Meuron to select 100 architects from 27 countries around the globe to each design a 1,000-square-meter villa there. The project is scheduled to be completed by the end of the year but will never be completely realized. Ai is invited by the Shanghai authorities to build a studio for himself near the city and begins building. On May 12, a disastrous earthquake hits Sichuan Province, killing 70,000 people, a disproportionate number of whom are young students who die in the poorly built schools. Ai visits the affected regions and blogs about the event and the lack of information offered by the authorities. He also blogs extensively about the case of Yang Jia, a man arrested for the murder of six policemen in July and executed in November. There is public controversy over the case, as Yang has been arrested over a supposedly stolen bicycle, mistreated by the police in custody, and all his appeals have been unreasonably rejected.

2009 Ai starts the Citizens' Investigation to research the names of student victims of the Sichuan earthquake after the authorities fail to produce such a list. With numerous volunteers he moves to the area to do field work, interviewing relatives and the local authorities. By April, the list has grown to 5,385

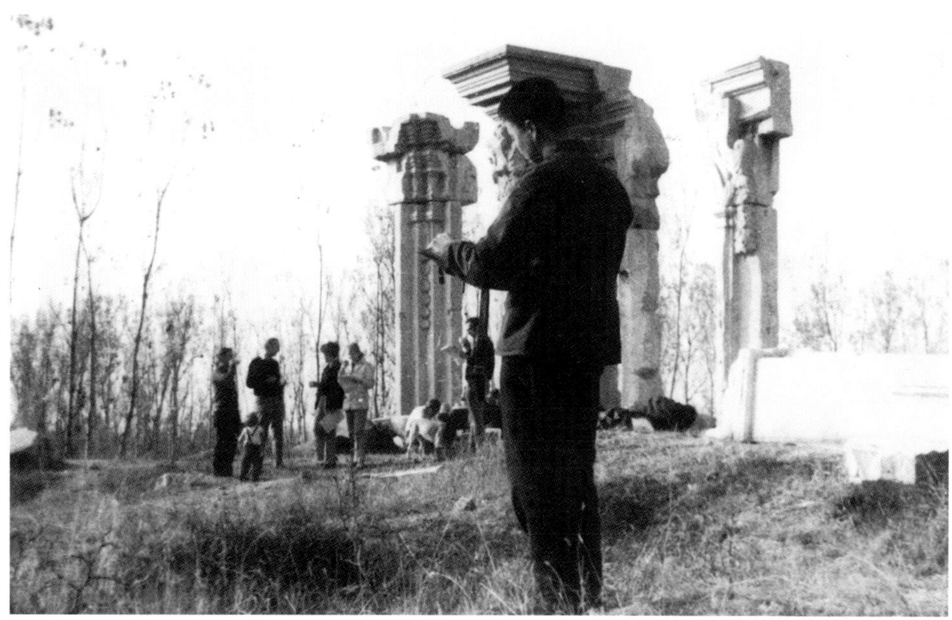

Sketching at the Old Summer Palace at the site of the original *Circle of Animals*, Beijing 1976

names and Ai's studio releases two documentary videos about the incidents and their research. To protest against the Chinese government's proposal to install Green Dam censorship software on every computer sold in China, Ai calls for an "Internet Blackout Day" on July 1—the software installation is eventually canceled. In Tokyo, Ai stages *According to What?*, his first retrospective exhibition, at the Mori Art Museum. Back in China, he agrees to testify at the trial of Tan Zuoren, a fellow activist who has been accused of "subversion of state power" after publishing his own investigation into the deaths of 5,000 students during the Sichuan earthquake. On August 12, the evening before Tan's trial, Ai is beaten by the police in his hotel room and prevented from testifying. Later, while in Munich to prepare his exhibition *So Sorry* at Haus der Kunst, Ai consults a doctor for his headaches and the scans reveal internal cranial bleeding that can be linked back to the police beating. On September 14 Ai has to undergo an emergency operation. This year Ai joins the microblog Twitter, where he will tweet over 104,000 times to 234,000 followers over the next four years.

2010 Ai's *Sunflower Seeds* at Tate Modern's Turbine Hall proves a huge hit with both audiences and critics. Originally visitors are allowed to walk over the millions of porcelain seeds, but after a couple of days the seeds are cordoned off for health concerns. In China, Ai is informed by the authorities that his newly built Shanghai studio will have to be demolished, an abrupt reversal of favor likely caused by Ai's outspoken criticism of the government. Ai announces a "demolition party," to which all his Twitter followers are invited. The police place Ai under house arrest for two days to prevent him from traveling to Shanghai. Over 3,000 followers still show up and the party takes place without him.

2011 On January 11, the Shanghai studio is abruptly demolished without warning. Three days later Ai's planned retrospective at UCCA in Beijing is cancelled. On April 3 Ai is detained at the Beijing Capital International Airport, while his studio is searched by police and all the computers' hard drives are confiscated. Ai is imprisoned without official charges in a secret place, closely surveyed and interrogated. Neither his family nor the public know where he is, and a huge wave of solidarity rises up, involving many artists' actions, official letters of protest, and popular demonstrations, mostly in the West but also in Hong Kong and elsewhere. During his detention, Ai receives honorary memberships of the Berlin Academy of the Arts and the London Royal Academy of Arts, while his art is shown in galleries and museums, including a first public sculpture, *Circle of Animals* in New York. On May 15, his wife Lu Qing is allowed a brief, heavily supervised visit. Finally, after 81 days of illegal detention, Ai is released on bail on June 22. Under the terms of his release he is prohibited from leaving Beijing for one year, and not allowed to give interviews or speak freely to the press or on social media. Subsequently he is asked to pay 12 million RMB ($2.36 million) in back taxes and fines for the company FAKE Design without any evidence or justification. Ai's lawyers file for administrative review before the tax authorities. Followers donate nine million RMB to Ai as gifts or "loans" so he can meet the tax demand. Ai's international role as a public figure is reflected in his number-one ranking on the Power 100 of *ArtReview* and a place in the Time 100 for 2011, among other recognitions.

2012 On the anniversary of his detention, Ai starts the self-surveillance project *Weiwei-Cam*, a live 24-hour online feed from his house and studio, which is shut down by Chinese authorities 46 hours after the site goes live. The tax case is reviewed without public trial and Ai is prevented from attending the closed hearing altogether. After FAKE Design has been officially closed and the fine upheld by the court, Ai begins to repay his lenders their money in November. The government still retains his passport. At the Sundance Film Festival the documentary *Ai Weiwei: Never Sorry* by American filmmaker Alison Klayman receives the Special Jury Prize for Spirit of Defiance. On occasion of an exhibition at Magasin 3 Stockholm Konsthall Ai is elected as a Foreign Member of the Royal Swedish Academy of Fine Arts.

2013 Ai releases his first music single, "Dumbass," singing his own lyrics to music by his friend, the Chinese rock singer Zuoxiao Zuzhou. The accompanying video, with cinematography by Christopher Doyle, shows scenes from the detention that escalate into the surreal. This is followed by a complete mini album, *Divine Comedy,* and two more music videos. At the Venice Biennale Ai is presented in two showcases: an official installation at the German pavilion, and a collateral event inside the church of Sant'Antonin, for which he exhibits *S.A.C.R.E.D.*, a sculpture restaging in diorama-like displays six scenes from the room where he was detained in 2011.

2015 Ai is allowed to leave China and he settles in Berlin, where he is offered a professorship at the University of the Arts (UdK). His art and activism come to focus on the global refugee crisis, especially in the **2017** documentary *Human Flow*, which is selected for the competition of the Venice Film Festival. **Today**, Ai Weiwei lives and works between Cambridge, Berlin, and on travels worldwide.

Ai Weiwei: Leben und Werk

1957 Am 28. August in Peking als zweiter Sohn von Ai Qing und Gao Ying geboren. Der Vater, ein bekannter Dichter, wird in einer politischen Kampagne Mao Tsetungs wie viele andere Intellektuelle „reaktionärer Tendenzen" beschuldigt.

1958 In der nun folgenden Säuberungswelle muss die Familie nach Beidahuang übersiedeln, eine Stadt in der nordöstlichen Provinz Heilongjiang nahe der russischen Grenze.

1960 Die Familie wird nach Shihezi umgesiedelt, eine Kleinstadt in der nordwestlichen Provinz Xinjiang in der Wüste Gobi.

1967 Inmitten der Kulturrevolution, die im Mai des Vorjahrs begonnen hat, muss die Familie erneut in ein noch entlegeneres Dorf umziehen, wo sie in ärmlichen Verhältnissen in einer Erdgrube lebt: „Vier oder fünf Familienmitglieder auf zwölf Quadratmetern. Wir alle schliefen im selben Bett. Sehr niedrig, kein Licht. Wir mussten tiefer schaufeln, damit wir aufrecht stehen konnten. Das Bett war einfach ein Erdhaufen, den wir beim Graben übrig gelassen hatten. Nachts hörten wir Ratten. In der Früh kontrollierte ich meine Fallen. Oft fand ich mehr als zehn Stück. So lebten wir fünf Jahre lang." Ai Qing muss täglich harte Arbeiten wie Toilettenreinigung verrichten.

1972 Die Familie darf nach Shihezi zurückkehren.

1975 Im Sommer besucht Ai Weiwei erstmals Peking, wo sein Vater ärztlich behandelt wird.

1976 Die Anschuldigungen gegen Ai Qing werden fallen gelassen. Ai Weiwei macht im Mai in Shihezi seinen Schulabschluss, ehe die Familie nach Peking zurückkehrt, wo sie zwei Tage nach dem schweren Erdbeben von Tangshan eintrifft. Da ihre Wohnung an andere Mieter vergeben ist, wohnt die Familie abwechselnd bei Freunden und Verwandten.

Ai erhält Privatstunden von Kunstprofessoren, denn die Universitäten Chinas sind seit fast zehn Jahren geschlossen.

1978 Ai besucht an der Pekinger Filmakademie den ersten Jahrgang seit Ende der Kulturrevolution. Zu seinen Studienkollegen zählen Zhang Yimou und Chen Kaige, die später als Regisseure Weltruf erlangen. Er unternimmt erste Studienreisen durch China, die ihn bis 1981 nach Dunhuang, Shanghai und Suzhou führen. Abbildungen seiner Gemälde erscheinen in der Monatszeitschrift *Renmin Huabao* (*China im Bild*).

1979 Ai verlässt die Akademie und wird Gründungsmitglied der progressiven Künstlergruppe „Stars". Da alle Anträge abgelehnt werden, veranstaltet die Gruppe ihre erste, nicht genehmigte Gruppenausstellung auf dem Gehsteig vor dem National Art Museum of China in Peking. Diese Veranstaltung, die als Geburtsstunde der chinesischen Avantgarde gilt, wird nach drei Tagen von der Polizei aufgelöst. Am 1. Oktober, dem Tag des 30. Staatsjubiläums der Volksrepublik, erneuern die „Stars" mit einem Marsch durch das Stadtzentrum ihre Forderung nach Ausstellungsraum. Diesmal erhalten sie zehn Tage im „Studio des bemalten Bootes" im Beihai-Park. Ein Großteil der Exponate sind expressionistische Gemälde. Ai zeigt einige Landschaftsaquarelle.

1980 Die „Stars" erhalten eine Ausstellung im National Art Museum (20. August– 7. September), die erste Präsentation zeitgenössischer chinesischer Kunst in einem Nationalmuseum. Der Erfolg ist sensationell, laut offiziellen Angaben kommen fast 200.000 Besucher.

1981 Ai reist mit seiner Freundin, die dort Verwandte hat, in die Vereinigten Staaten. Er studiert kurze Zeit Englisch an der University of Pennsylvania, Philadelphia, und verbringt ein Semester an der University of California, Berkeley.

1982–1993 In seiner ersten Einzelausstellung zeigt Ai 30 in China entstandene
Gemälde in der Asia Foundation Gallery,
San Francisco. Er zieht nach New York und
besucht ein Semester lang die Parsons School
of Design. Ai bestreitet seinen Lebensunter-
halt mit Gelegenheitsjobs wie Anstreicher,
Kellner oder Babysitter und benutzt Geschäfts-
lokale als Werkstätten. Zuerst wohnt er in
einem Atelier in Long Island City, Queens,
dann in Brooklyn und schließlich an der
Lower East Side, Manhattan. In seinen Woh-
nungen treffen sich chinesische Einwanderer,
darunter Künstler wie Xu Bing und Tehching
Hsieh und der Komponist Tan Dun, und
Freunde wie Beat-Poet Allen Ginsberg. An den
Wochenenden spielt Ai Blackjack in den Casinos von Atlantic City. Er besucht Museen und
Vernissagen, macht sich mit den Klassikern
der Moderne von Duchamp bis Warhol vertraut und mischt sich in die vitale New Yorker
Kunstszene. Wie er später anmerkt, ist ihm
damals keine Ausstellung entgangen. Über
seine eigene künstlerische Arbeit sagt er:
„Ich habe nicht viel gemacht. Von den zwölf
Jahren habe ich vielleicht eines für meine
Kunst verwendet. Meine materiellen Verhält-
nisse und der Dialog mit der Kunstwelt ließen
nicht zu, dass ich etwas Eigenes machte.
Ich entwickelte mich zu einem denkenden
Künstler, dem es weniger auf die Produktion
ankam. Es bestand ohnehin keine Gelegen-
heit, meine Werke auszustellen oder zu
verkaufen. Ich bin froh, dass ich nie viele
Gedanken darüber verschwendet habe.“
Ai nimmt Tausende von Fotografien auf, die
er großteils erst nach seiner Rückkehr nach
China entwickelt.

1988 *Old Shoes, Safe Sex,* Ais einzige Einzelausstellung während seines Aufenthalts
in New York, findet in der Galerie Art Waves/
Ethan Cohen statt. Seine Leidenschaft für
die Fotografie und sein soziales Interesse
führen ihn zur Fotoreportage. Er dokumentiert die Unruhen am Tompkins Square Park
im August, bei denen die Polizei mit Gewalt
gegen Hausbesetzer und deren Sympathisan-
ten vorgeht.

1989 Ai nimmt an einem Hungerstreik vor
dem UN-Hauptquartier in New York teil,
eine Solidaritätsaktion mit den Opfern des
Tiananmen-Massakers in Peking vom 4. Juni,
bei dem chinesische Truppen mit Waffenge-
walt gegen friedliche Protestanten vorgegangen sind.

1990 In einer neuen Serie von Gemälden
wird das Motiv teilweise und schließlich völlig
durch Farbgüsse überdeckt. Vor seiner Rückkehr nach China einige Jahre später packt Ai
diese Werke in Kisten, ohne sie je zu zeigen
oder auch nur auszupacken.

1992 Ais Kellerwohnung an der East Seventh
Street in New York ist zur inoffiziellen Exil-
botschaft der Avantgarde geworden und dient
als Drehort der Post-Tiananmen-Telenovela
Beijingers in New York, produziert vom chinesischen Staatsfernsehen CCTV.

1993 Ein Herzleiden des Vaters zwingt Ai,
sich zu entscheiden: „Meine Verwandten wollten, dass ich zurückkomme und ihn besuche.
Aber ich wusste, dass ich entweder für immer
nach China gehen oder für immer in New York
bleiben würde.“ Ai kehrt nach Peking zurück
und lebt bei seinen Eltern, ohne im Ausland
etwas erreicht zu haben, weder beruflich noch
privat. Um sich nach seiner zehnjährigen
Beschäftigung mit westlicher Kunst besser
mit der chinesischen Tradition vertraut zu
machen, frequentiert er Antiquitätenmärkte
und erwirbt Möbel und Keramiken. Ohne die
Absicht, hohe Kunst zu schaffen, beginnt Ai
Serien wie *Still Life* (1993–2000) und *Whitewash* (1993–2000). Er besucht regelmäßig
eine Gruppe junger Künstler um Zhang Huan
und Rong Rong, die sich am Ostrand Pekings
niedergelassen haben. Die Mitglieder zeigen
sich dort ihre Performances und kritisieren
gegenseitig ihre Werke. In Anlehnung an das
New Yorker Viertel nennen sie ihre Siedlung
„East Village“.

1994 Mit dem Kritiker Feng Boyi stellt Ai
das Buch *Black Cover Book* zusammen, das
die chinesische Kunstöffentlichkeit mit der
neuesten einheimischen Avantgarde sowie mit
der modernen und zeitgenössischen Kunst
des Westens vertraut machen soll. Das erste
Keramik-Werk, *Han Dynasty Urn with Coca-
Cola Logo*, entsteht. Ai trifft seine spätere
Frau Lu Qing.

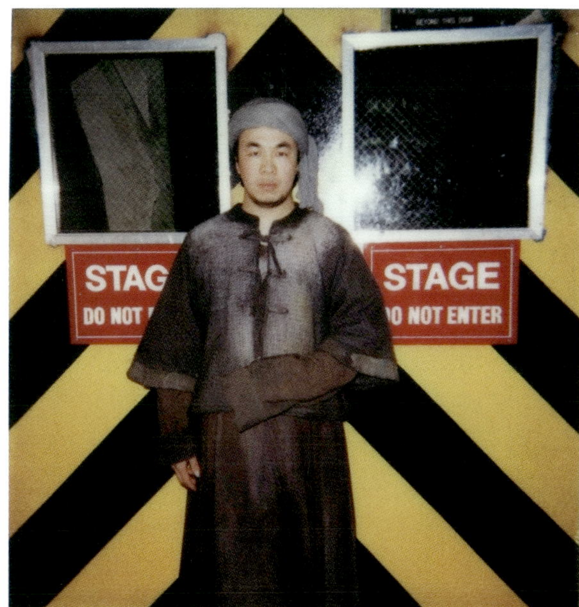

Ai Weiwei backstage at
the Metropolitan Opera before
appearing as an extra in the
opera *Turandot*, New York 1987

1995 Ai beginnt die Serie *Studies of Perspective*, Schnappschüsse von politischen oder kulturellen Wahrzeichen, denen er den ausgestreckten Mittelfinger zeigt. Erste Motive sind der Platz des himmlischen Friedens in Peking und das Weiße Haus in Washington. Ai gibt ein zweites, stärker politisch orientiertes Kunstbuch heraus, das *White Cover Book*.

1996 Tod des Vaters Ai Qing.

1997 In Zusammenarbeit mit dem Künstler Zhuang Hui entsteht das *Gray Cover Book*. Ai beginnt, Möbel nach alten chinesischen Handwerksmethoden anzufertigen, etwa Tische mit ungewöhnlichen Winkeln oder durch ein gemeinsames Bein verbundene Schemel.

1998 Mit dem Kunsthistoriker Hans van Dijk und dem Sammler Frank Uytterhaegen gründet Ai den Non-Profit-Kunstraum China Art Archives and Warehouse (CAAW). Dort kuratiert er Ausstellungen zeitgenössischer Kunst und gibt die Begleitkataloge heraus. Ai wird Juror des Chinese Contemporary Art Award, den sein enger Freund, der Schweizer Sammler Uli Sigg, ins Leben gerufen hat. Beim Transport nach New York für eine Ausstellung in der Max Protetch Gallery zerbricht das Werk *Coca-Cola Vase* (1997). Die angezweifelte Authentizität der Vase wird durch einen Thermolumineszenz-Test bestätigt.

1999 Ai errichtet ein Wohn- und Atelierhaus aus grauen Ziegeln im Dorf Caochangdi, das im Nordosten Pekings an der Autobahn zum Flughafen liegt. „Den Plan habe ich an einem Nachmittag gezeichnet. Nach 60 Tagen stand der Rohbau. Nach 100 zogen wir ein." Er entwirft weitere Gebäude in der Umgebung – der Beginn seiner internationalen Architektenlaufbahn. Im Herbst beteiligt sich Ai mit 18 weiteren chinesischen Künstlern an der von Harald Szeemann kuratierten Biennale von Venedig. Dieses erste Zeichen weltweiter Anerkennung führt in den Folgejahren zu einem intensivierten Kunstschaffen. Viele von Ais größten Projekten bleiben jedoch im Bereich der Architektur.

2000 In einem Lagerhaus in Shanghai organisiert Ai mit Feng Boyi die Ausstellung *Fuck Off* (der chinesische Titel *Bu hezuo fangshi* bedeutet „unkooperative Haltung"). Alternativ zur kommerzialisierten Shanghai-Biennale vereint die Schau chinesische Avantgarde-

Künstler aus allen Großstädten Chinas. Ai entwirft das neue CAAW-Gebäude in Caochangdi.

2001 Zur Eröffnung der Pekinger Siedlung SOHO NewTown, die aus flexiblen Wohn- und Büroeinheiten nach westlichem Muster besteht, errichtet Ai die massiv und unverrückbar wirkende, C-förmige Betonplastik *Tong*.

2002 Ai entwirft seine erste, sechs Meter hohe Lüster-Arbeit für die 1. Triennale in Guangzhou. In Jinhua, der Heimatstadt seines Vaters in der Ostprovinz Zhejiang, wird Ai Kurator des Projekts Ai Qing Cultural Park, für den er das Südufer des Jangtsekiang gestaltet. Ai lädt 17 Architekten aus sieben Ländern in den angegliederten Architecture Park ein. Zudem zeichnet er Pläne für ein Denkmal seines Vaters und ein Museum antiker Töpferkunst. Ai setzt die Arbeit mit Möbel- und Holzskulpturen in größerem Maßstab fort, unter anderem mit Pfeilern abgerissener Tempel.

2003 Ai gründet das Büro FAKE Design, das die steigende Zahl der Architekturprojekte organisiert. Der Name enthält ein Wortspiel: „Fuck" wird von Chinesen meist wie „fake" ausgesprochen. Nach einem Atelierbesuch im Vorherbst bitten die Architekten Jacques Herzog und Pierre de Meuron den Künstler, sie bei ihrem Stadionentwurf für die Olympischen Sommerspiele 2008 in Peking zu beraten. Die Pläne werden komplett überarbeitet und Anfang des Jahres eingereicht. Das Team gewinnt den Wettbewerb, und die Bauarbeiten beginnen am 24. Dezember.

2004 Aufgrund explodierender Kosten bleibt die Baustelle des Stadions vom 31. Juli bis Dezember geschlossen. Ais erste große internationale Einzelausstellung findet in der Kunsthalle Bern statt. In Jinhua beginnt der Bau der 17 Pavillons des Architecture Park, der nie vollendet wird.

2005 Im Oktober beginnt Ai, einen Blog für das beliebte chinesische Webportal Sina.com zu schreiben. Der Blog erfreut sich schnell großer Beliebtheit und wird von jungen Menschen in ganz China gelesen. Sein Inhalt reicht von privaten Texten und Schnapp-

schüssen, die Ais Atelier und seine vielen Katzen zeigen, bis zu brisanten regimekritischen Statements.

2006 Neben Architektur- und Möbelprojekten beginnt Ai die Arbeit mit Porzellan, die er in Jingdezhen, der alten chinesischen Porzellan-Hauptstadt, produzieren lässt.

2007 Ai wird zur Documenta 12 in Kassel eingeladen. Das organisatorisch aufwändige Projekt *Fairytale* bringt 1001 chinesische Besucher nach Deutschland. Ein weiterer Documenta-Beitrag, die Freiskulptur *Template*, stürzt nach einem Unwetter ein. Im August erklärt Ai im britischen *Guardian*, er werde die Olympischen Spiele boykottieren, weil in seinem Land nach wie vor keine Meinungsfreiheit herrsche. In folgenden Interviews bezeichnet er das von ihm mitgestaltete Stadion als „falsches Lächeln": „Ich muss mich schämen, wenn etwas, das ich entworfen habe, als Protzbau dient und ein falsches Bild im Ausland vermittelt." Diese Artikel machen Ai zum Wortführer der chinesischen Dissidenten in den westlichen Medien.

2008 Im Januar und April leitet Ai ein internationales Architektensymposium in der Stadt Ordos in der Inneren Mongolei. FAKE Design bittet Herzog und de Meuron, 100 Architekten aus 27 Ländern weltweit auszuwählen, die jeweils eine 1000 Quadratmeter große Villa entwerfen sollen. Das bis Jahresende geplante Projekt wird nie vollendet. Von der Stadt Shanghai erhält Ai die Einladung, für sich ein Atelier zu errichten, und er beginnt mit dem Bau. Am 12. Mai erschüttert ein schweres Erdbeben die Provinz Sichuan. Ein unverhältnismäßig großer Anteil der 70.000 Todesopfer sind in schlecht gebauten Schulen verschüttete Schüler. Ai besucht die betroffene Region und schreibt in seinem Blog über die Katastrophe und die schlechte Informationspolitik der Behörden. Außerdem nimmt er sich des umstrittenen Falls von Yang Jia an, der nach seiner Festnahme wegen eines angeblich gestohlenen Fahrrads durch die Polizei misshandelt wird. Als seine offiziellen Proteste abgewiesen werden, ermordet Yang Jia sechs Polizisten und wird dafür im Juli hingerichtet.

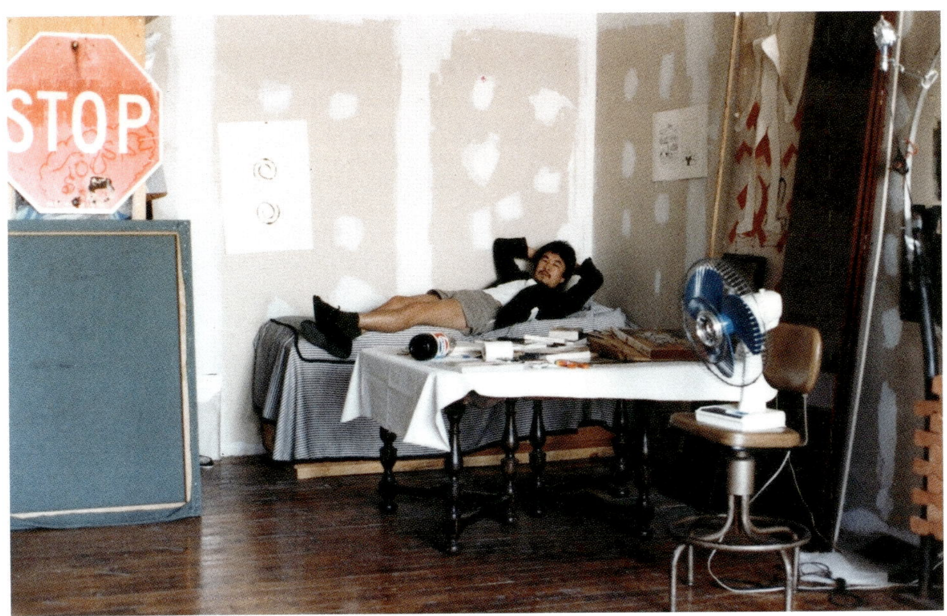

Ai Weiwei at his Long Island City studio apartment, New York 1983

2009 Nachdem von offizieller Seite keine Liste mit den Namen der durch das Erdbeben getöteten Schüler veröffentlicht wird, startet Ai die Citizens' Investigation. Er zieht mit Freiwilligen in die Region, um Feldstudien und Interviews mit Verwandten und Beamten durchzuführen. Im April liegen die Namen von 5385 Opfern vor. Ais Studio gibt zwei Dokumentarvideos über die Lage im Erdbengebiet und die Nachforschungen seines Teams heraus. Als Protest gegen die Absicht der Regierung, in China auf jedem Computer die Contentfilter-Software Green Dam Youth Escort vorzuinstallieren, ruft Ai zu einem „Internet Blackout Day" auf. Die Regierung verschiebt ihren Plan ins Ungewisse. Im Mori Art Museum, Tokio, findet die erste Ai-Retrospektive, *According to What?*, statt. Ai erklärt sich bereit, im Prozess gegen Tan Zuoren als Zeuge auszusagen. Der Aktivist wird der „Untergrabung der Staatsgewalt" beschuldigt, weil er eigene Nachforschungen über den Tod der 5000 Schüler im Sichuan-Erdbeben angestellt hat. Am 12. August, dem Abend vor der Gerichtsverhandlung, wird Ai von Polizeibeamten in seinem Hotelzimmer geschlagen und an der Teilnahme am Prozess

gehindert. Während der Vorbereitungen für seine Ausstellung *So Sorry* im Münchner Haus der Kunst besucht Ai, der unter Kopfschmerzen leidet, einen Arzt. Scans zeigen eine Hirnblutung als Folge des Polizeiübergriffs. Der Künstler unterzieht sich am 14. September einer Notoperation. Ai wird Nutzer des Microblogs Twitter. Während der nächsten vier Jahre sendet er über 104.000 Tweets an 234.000 Follower.

2010 Ais Ausstellung *Sunflower Seeds* in der Turbinenhalle der Tate Modern, London, findet großen Anklang bei Besuchern und Kritikern. Die Millionen auf dem Boden ausgelegten Porzellan-Samen sind anfangs frei begehbar, werden nach einigen Tagen jedoch aus Gesundheitsgründen abgesperrt. Ein Bescheid der Stadtverwaltung informiert Ai, dass sein neues Atelier in Shanghai wieder abgerissen werden muss. Der plötzliche Sinneswandel ist vermutlich auf Ais regimekritische Äußerungen zurückzuführen. Ai kündigt eine „Abrissparty" an, zu der er alle Twitter-Follower einlädt. Um seine Anwesenheit in Shanghai zu verhindern, wird er für zwei Tage unter Hausarrest gestellt. Mehr als

3000 Follower kommen zur Party, die ohne
ihn stattfindet.

2011 Das Atelier in Shanghai wird am
11. Januar unangekündigt abgerissen. Drei
Tage später folgt die Absage einer geplanten
Retrospektive im Ullens Center for Contemporary Art (UCCA), Peking. Am 3. April
nehmen Grenzbeamte den Künstler auf dem
Flughafen Peking fest. Die Polizei durchsucht
sein Atelier und konfisziert alle Festplatten.
Ai wird ohne offizielle Anklage an einem
unbekannten Ort festgehalten und verhört.
Weder seine Familie noch die Öffentlichkeit
wissen, wo er sich aufhält. Ais Festnahme löst
eine Welle von Solidaritätskundgebungen
aus – Künstleraktionen, Protestschreiben und
Demonstrationen, größtenteils im Westen,
aber auch in Hongkong und anderen asiati-
schen Städten. Während seiner Haft wird Ai
zum Mitglied der Akademie der Künste, Berlin, und der Royal Academy of Arts, London,
gewählt. Neben zahlreichen Museums- und
Galerieausstellungen ist seine erste Außenskulptur, *Circle of Animals,* in New York zu
sehen. Seine Frau Lu Qing darf ihn am
15. Mai unter strenger Überwachung kurz
besuchen. Nach 81 Tagen in illegaler Haft
wird Ai am 22. Juni gegen Kaution freigelassen. Er muss zusichern, ein Jahr lang Peking
nicht zu verlassen, keine Interviews zu geben
und sich aller Kommentare in Medien und
Social Media zu enthalten. Die Firma FAKE
Design wird ohne nähere Begründung zu
einer Steuerstrafe in Höhe von 2,36 Millionen
US-Dollar verurteilt. Die Anwälte des Künstlers legen Berufung beim Finanzamt ein.
Unterstützer spenden 1,8 Millionen US-Dollar
zur Begleichung der Steuerschuld. Zahlreiche
Anerkennungen unterstreichen den internationalen Stellenwert des Künstlers. Die Zeitschrift *ArtReview* wählt Ai zur mächtigsten
Figur der Kunstwelt, und *Time* rechnet ihn
zu den wichtigsten 100 Persönlichkeiten
des Jahres.

2012 Zum Jahrestag seiner Verhaftung startet Ai das Selbstüberwachungsprojekt *Weiwei-
Cam,* das 24 Stunden täglich Live-Feeds aus
seinem Haus und Atelier sendet. Die Webseite
wird nach 46 Stunden von den Behörden
geschlossen. Ais Steuerfall wird unter Aus-

schluss der Öffentlichkeit geprüft. Er selbst
darf nicht an den Verhandlungen teilnehmen.
Nach der Zwangsauflösung von FAKE Design
und der gerichtlichen Bestätigung seiner
Steuerstrafe beginnt Ai im November, die
erhaltenen Spenden rückzuerstatten. Er
besitzt nach wie vor keinen Reisepass. Der
Dokumentarfilm *Ai Weiwei: Never Sorry* der
US-amerikanischen Filmemacherin Alison
Klayman erhält auf dem Sundance Festival
den Special Jury Prize for Spirit of Defiance.
Bei seiner Ausstellung in der Magasin 3
Stockholm Konsthall wird Ai zum Mitglied
der Königlich Schwedischen Akademie der
freien Künste gewählt.

2013 Ai veröffentlicht seine erste Single,
„Dumbass“, auf der er seinen Text zur Musik
des befreundeten Rockmusikers Zuoxiao
Zuzhou singt. Das dazugehörige Video,
gedreht von Christopher Doyle, zeigt surreal
übersteigerte Szenen aus der Haftzeit. Es folgen die EP *The Divine Comedy* und zwei weitere Musikvideos. Auf der Biennale von Venedig ist Ai mit zwei Beiträgen vertreten. Neben
seiner offiziellen Installation im Deutschen
Pavillon zeigt er in der Kirche Sant'Antonin
das Sonderprojekt *S.A.C.R.E.D.,* sechs Eisenkästen, in denen Szenen aus seiner Haftzelle
dioramaartig nachgestellt sind.

2015 wird es Ai gestattet, China zu verlassen,
und er lässt sich in Berlin nieder, wo ihm die
Universität der Künste (UdK) eine Professur
anbietet. Seine Kunst und sein Aktivismus
fokussieren auf das Thema der globalen
Flüchtlingskrise, besonders im Dokumentarfilm *Human Flow,* der **2017** für den Wettbewerb des Filmvestivals von Venedig ausge-
sucht wird. **Heute** lebt und arbeitet Ai Weiwei
in Cambridge, Berlin und überall auf Reisen.

Ai Weiwei : Vie et œuvre

1957 Ai Weiwei naît à Pékin le 28 août. Il est le deuxième fils de Gao Ying et du poète Ai Qing, une célébrité du monde littéraire dans la Chine communiste devenue la cible d'une des campagnes de Mao accusant de nombreux intellectuels d'avoir des opinions « réactionnaires ».

1958 Suite aux purges, la famille d'Ai Qing est envoyée à Beidahuang, dans la province de Heilongjiang, à l'extrême nord-est du pays.

1960 La famille est envoyée à Shihezi, petite ville de la province de Xinjiang, dans le nord-ouest de la Chine, au milieu du désert de Gobi.

1967 La Révolution culturelle, commencée en mai 1966, bat son plein. La famille est contrainte de s'installer dans un village encore plus isolé et vit dans un abri souterrain dans des conditions de vie épouvantables : « Nous étions quatre ou cinq membres de la famille dans 12 m². Nous dormions tous dans le même lit. Le plafond était très bas, il n'y avait pas de lumière. Nous avons dû creuser la terre pour pouvoir nous tenir debout. Le lit se résumait à une grande surface de terre. Lorsque nous avons creusé le sol, nous avons laissé cette surface en guise de lit. La nuit, nous entendions souvent les rats. Le matin, au réveil, j'allais voir mes pièges. Souvent, j'y trouvais plus d'une dizaine de rats. J'ai vécu dans ces conditions pendant cinq ans. » On assigne à Ai Qing des tâches pénibles.

1972 La famille est autorisée à revenir à Shihezi.

1975 En été, première visite d'Ai Weiwei à Pékin, où son père a été autorisé à suivre un traitement médical.

1976 Ai Qing est réhabilité. Ai Weiwei termine en mai sa scolarité au Lycée n°1 de Shihezi, puis la famille revient définitivement à Pékin. Elle arrive deux jours après le terrible séisme de Tangshan. Leur ancien logement ayant été attribué à d'autres gens, ils vivent chez différents amis. Toutes les universités du pays ayant été fermées depuis presque 10 ans, Ai Weiwei prend des cours privés avec des professeurs de l'école des beaux-arts.

1978 Ai Weiwei s'inscrit à la Beijing Film Academy. Il fait partie de la première promotion après la Révolution culturelle. Parmi les autres étudiants, on trouve Zhang Yimou et Chen Kaige, futurs réalisateurs connus dans le monde entier. Il effectue son premier voyage d'études en Chine. Des images de ses travaux paraissent dans le mensuel *Renmin Huabao* (*China Pictorial*).

1979 Ai Weiwei quitte l'école de cinéma pour devenir un des membres fondateurs du groupe d'artistes radicaux des « Stars ». Leurs demandes d'un espace d'exposition n'aboutissant jamais, ils organisent une première exposition collective non autorisée sur le trottoir de la National Art Museum of China. L'exposition, souvent considérée comme la naissance d'une nouvelle avant-garde chinoise, est fermée par la police au bout de trois jours. Le 1ᵉʳ octobre, jour du trentième anniversaire de la République populaire de Chine, les « Stars » manifestent dans le centre de Pékin, renouvelant leur demande d'un lieu d'exposition. On leur accorde 10 jours dans le studio Hua Fang Zhai, dans le parc Beihai. La plupart des œuvres présentées sont des tableaux expressionnistes. Ai Weiwei contribue à cette exposition avec des paysages à l'aquarelle.

1980 Les « Stars » obtiennent une exposition à la National Art Museum de Pékin du 20 août au 7 septembre. Cette première exposition d'art contemporain dans un grand musée fait sensation et attire près de 200 000 visiteurs, selon les chiffres officiels.

1981 Avec sa petite amie, Ai Weiwei quitte la Chine pour les États-Unis. Il étudie brièvement à l'Université de Pennsylvanie à Philadelphie, avant de passer un semestre à Berkeley, en Californie.

1982–1993 La première exposition individuelle d'Ai Weiwei, rassemble à la Asia Foundation Gallery de San Francisco 30 tableaux réalisés en Chine. Il s'installe à New York et s'inscrit à la Parsons School of Design, où il ne restera qu'un semestre. Il survit grâce à divers petits boulots. À son arrivée, il vit dans un studio de Long Island City dans le Queens, puis à Brooklyn, et enfin dans le Lower East Side à Manhattan. Son domicile sert de lieu de rassemblement aux expatriés chinois, parmi lesquels on trouve les artistes Xu Bing et Tehching Hsieh, le musicien Tan Dun et d'autres amis comme le poète de la *beat generation* Allen Ginsberg. Le week-end, Ai Weiwei joue au blackjack à Atlantic City. Il visite tous les musées, assiste à de nombreux vernissages, des classiques modernes à la foisonnante scène artistique contemporaine new-yorkaise. Il dit de son propre travail : « Je n'ai pas fait grand-chose. En 12 ans, j'ai peut-être consacré une année à l'art. Ma situation économique et mon dialogue avec le monde de l'art ne laissaient pas beaucoup de champ à la création. Je suis davantage devenu un artiste en pensée, pas vraiment disposé à produire quoi que ce soit : pour le montrer et le vendre à qui ? Je suis vraiment heureux de ne pas avoir passé trop de temps à penser à tout ça. » Ai Weiwei prend des milliers de photographies qu'il ne développera pas pour la plupart jusqu'à son retour en Chine.

1988 *Old Shoes, Safe Sex*, à la galerie Art Waves/Ethan Cohen, est la seule exposition individuelle d'Ai Weiwei pendant ses années new-yorkaises. L'habitude qu'il a de prendre des photos et son intérêt pour les sujets sociaux le mènent au photoreportage. En août, il travaille sur les émeutes de Tompkins Square Park.

1989 Ai Weiwei participe à une grève de la faim devant le bâtiment des Nations Unies en réponse au massacre de la Place Tiananmen du 4 juin.

1990 Nouvelle série de travaux : des tableaux sont progressivement recouverts jusqu'à disparition totale de leur sujet. Ai Weiwei les entrepose dans des caisses avant son retour en Chine quelques années après ; ces travaux ne seront jamais montrés ni même déballés.

1992 L'appartement souterrain d'Ai Weiwei sur East Seventh Street à New York, sorte d'ambassade officieuse de l'avant-garde en exil, sert de décor au feuilleton télévisé post-Tiananmen *Des Pékinois à New-York*, produit par la chaîne de télévision d'État chinoise CCTV.

1993 Apprenant que son père est atteint d'une maladie cardiaque, Ai Weiwei doit prendre une décision : « Ma famille me disait de revenir en visite, pour le voir, mais je savais que si je rentrais en Chine, ce serait pour toujours, sinon, je resterais définitivement à New York. » Ai Weiwei rentre à Pékin et s'installe chez ses parents. Après avoir exploré l'art occidental, il se penche sur les traditions chinoises, fréquente les antiquaires et se met à collectionner les poteries et les meubles anciens. Sans grande ambition artistique, Ai Weiwei commence des séries de travaux telles que *Still Life* (1993–2000) et *Whitewash* (1993–2000). Il rend souvent visite à un groupe de jeunes artistes installés dans un village en périphérie est de Pékin, parmi lesquels se trouvent Zhang Huan et Rong Rong. Ils organisent des performances et rebaptisent le quartier East Village en référence à New York.

1994 Avec le critique Feng Boyi, Ai Weiwei réalise un livre présentant la toute dernière avant-garde chinoise ainsi que l'art occidental moderne et contemporain, le *Black Cover Book*. Il réalise également l'œuvre intitulée *Han Dynasty Urn with Coca-Cola Logo*. Il rencontre sa future femme, Lu Qing.

1995 Ai Weiwei commence ses *Studies of Perspective*, une série de photographies de sites culturels célèbres derrière son majeur tendu en premier plan. Il édite un deuxième livre d'art, plus politique cette fois, le *White Cover Book*.

1996 Décès de son père, le poète Ai Qing.

1997 Ai Weiwei édite le *Gray Cover Book* avec l'artiste Zhuang Hui. Il travaille sur le mobilier, utilisant des techniques traditionnelles chinoises pour fabriquer des tables aux angles étranges ou des tabourets partageant un pied.

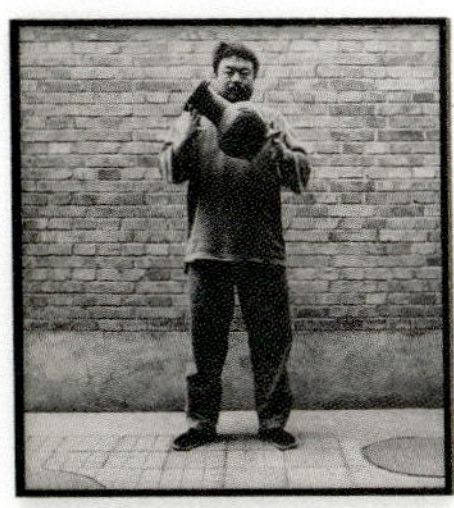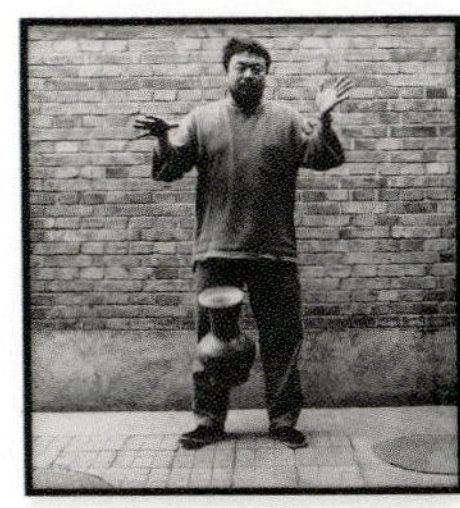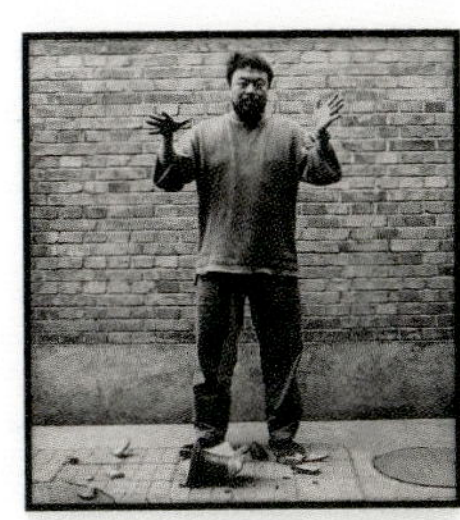

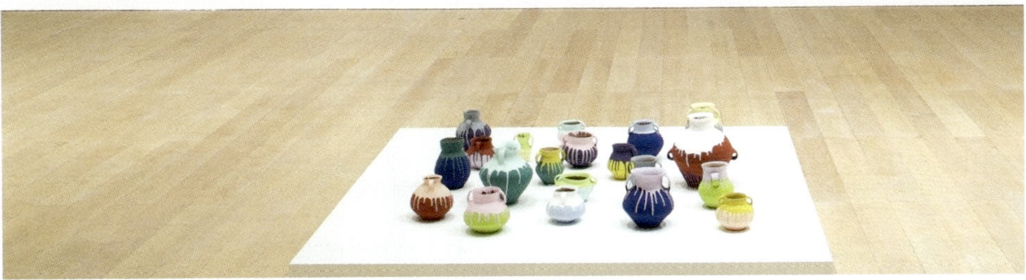

Exhibition view, *Ai Weiwei: According to What?*, Mori Art Museum, Tokyo 2009

1998 Avec l'historien d'art Hans van Dijk et le collectionneur Frank Uytterhaegen, Ai Weiwei crée l'espace à but non lucratif China Art Archives and Warehouse. Il est commissaire d'expositions et édite les catalogues des expositions pour CAAW. Il devient également membre du jury du Chinese Contemporary Art Awards créé par son ami proche, le collectionneur suisse Uli Sigg. Lorsqu'Ai Weiwei envoie *Coca-Cola Vase* (1997) à la Max Protetch Gallery de New York pour une exposition, l'authenticité du vase antique utilisé dans cette œuvre est mise en doute. Une analyse par thermoluminescence lui donne raison.

1999 Ai Weiwei s'installe à Caochangdi, au nordouest de Pékin, où il construit lui-même sa maison et son studio en brique grise. « Le dessin ne m'a pris qu'un après-midi. Nous avons mis 60 jours à construire. 100 jours plus tard, j'y vivais. » D'autres bâtiments suivent bientôt dans le quartier, et c'est le début pour Ai Weiwei d'une carrière internationale d'architecte. À l'automne, Ai Weiwei est invité à participer à la Biennale de Venise organisée sous la direction de Harald Szeemann. Cette première marque de reconnaissance au niveau international l'encourage à poursuivre son travail artistique, même si nombre de ses projets les plus importants dans les années à venir seront d'ordre architectural.

2000 Dans un entrepôt de Shanghai, Ai Weiwei organise, avec Feng Boyi, l'exposition *Fuck Off* (le titre chinois, *Bu hezuo fangshi*, peut être traduit par « comportement non coopératif »), qui restera dans les annales. En opposition avec la très commerciale Biennale de Shanghai, ils y exposent des artistes de l'avant-garde chinoise de toutes les grandes villes du pays. À Caochangdi, Ai Weiwei conçoit le nouveau siège de la CAAW.

2001 Pour l'inauguration du nouveau quartier de Pékin SOHO, un lotissement en préfabriqués d'inspiration occidentale, Ai Weiwei réalise *Tong,* une sculpture en béton massif en forme de C.

2002 Ai Weiwei réalise son premier travail autour du chandelier à près de 6 mètres de hauteur pour la Triennale de Guangzhou.

Il devient commissaire du projet du parc culturel Ai Qing à Jinhua, la ville natale de son père, dans la province de Zhejiang, à l'est du pays. Il y aménage la berge sud du Yang-Tsé-Kiang. Il invite 17 architectes de 7 pays différents à participer au projet et conçoit un mémorial pour son père ainsi qu'un musée de poterie ancienne. Il poursuit également son travail sur le mobilier et sur des sculptures en bois grand format, auxquelles il incorpore des colonnes sauvées lors de la destruction de temples anciens.

2003 Ai Weiwei crée FAKE Design pour gérer ses projets architecturaux. Le nom joue sur les deux syllabes romanisées «fake», qui correspondent à la prononciation habituelle des Chinois du mot «fuck». Les architectes Jacques Herzog et Pierre de Meuron, qu'Ai Weiwei a rencontrés à l'automne précédent dans son studio, l'engagent en tant que consultant pour leur projet de stade pour les Jeux olympiques de 2008 à Pékin. Ensemble, ils révisent entièrement les plans initiaux et envoient leur candidature. Leur projet est retenu et les travaux commencent le 24 décembre.

2004 Le 31 juillet, la construction du «Nid d'oiseau» est interrompue jusqu'en décembre en raison des dépassements de budget. La première grande exposition individuelle d'Ai Weiwei a lieu à la Kunstalle de Berne en Suisse. À Jinhua, les travaux des 17 pavillons du parc architectural, qui ne sera jamais achevé, débutent.

2005 En octobre, Ai Weiwei accepte d'écrire un blog sur le portail Internet chinois Sina. com. Il touche rapidement un très large public. Le contenu varie: textes, photos du quotidien au studio et nombreux chats d'Ai Weiwei, mais aussi articles politiques défendant clairement un point de vue d'opposition.

2006 À côté de ses projets architecturaux et de ses travaux sur le mobilier, Ai Weiwei commence à créer des objets en porcelaine réalisés artisanalement à Jingdezhen, l'ancienne capitale de la porcelaine chinoise.

2007 Ai Weiwei est invité à la Documenta 12 de Cassel et réalise à cette occasion *Fairytale*, œuvre pour laquelle il fait venir en Allemagne 1001 citoyens chinois. Sa deuxième contribution, l'installation en plein air *Template*, s'effondre durant une violente tempête. En août, *The Guardian* publie un article dans lequel Ai Weiwei déclare qu'il boycottera les Jeux olympiques tant que la liberté d'expression ne sera pas garantie dans son pays. Il déclare ensuite que le stade auquel il a contribué n'est plus qu'un «faux sourire», affirmant: «J'aurais honte d'avoir conçu quelque chose juste pour le glamour ou pour donner une fausse image du pays.» Depuis, il est considéré par les médias occidentaux comme un des principaux opposants au gouvernement chinois.

2008 En janvier et en avril, Ai Weiwei préside un congrès international d'architectes à Ordos, en Mongolie intérieure, et FAKE Design invite Herzog et de Meuron à choisir 100 architectes de 27 pays pour y construire chacun une villa de 1000 m². Le projet doit être terminé à la fin de l'année, mais il restera inachevé. À Shanghai, les autorités locales proposent à Ai Weiwei de construire un studio en périphérie de la ville; les travaux commencent. Le 12 mai, un terrible séisme touche la province du Sichuan, faisant 70 000 morts. Ce chiffre s'explique par des défauts de construction dans des écoles où de nombreux enfants ont trouvé la mort. Ai Weiwei se rend dans les régions sinistrées, il parle sur son blog de la situation sur place et du manque d'informations communiquées par les autorités. Il évoque également longuement l'affaire Yang Jia, un homme arrêté pour le meurtre de 6 policiers en juillet et exécuté en novembre. Cette affaire fait l'objet d'une controverse publique: soupçonné d'avoir volé un vélo, Yang avait été arrêté puis maltraité par la police lors de sa détention. Tous ses appels avaient été rejetés.

2009 Les autorités n'ayant toujours pas rendu publique la liste exhaustive des victimes du séisme du Sichuan, Ai Weiwei organise une enquête citoyenne pour collecter les noms des écoliers morts. Avec de nombreux bénévoles, il se rend sur place pour recueillir des informations. En avril, la liste rassemble déjà 5385 noms et le studio d'Ai Weiwei montre deux documentaires vidéo sur leurs recherches. Pour protester contre le projet

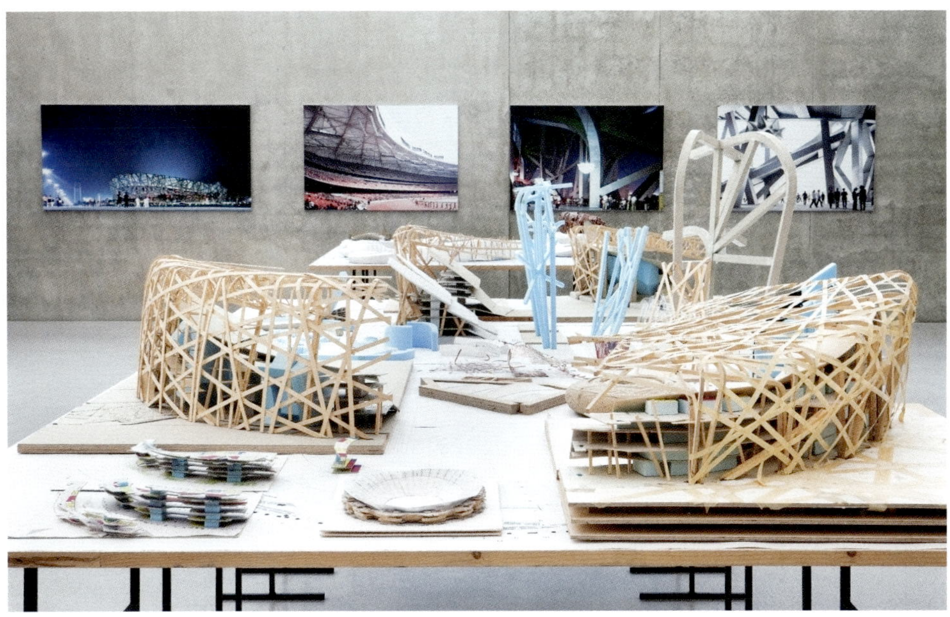

Exhibition view, *Ai Weiwei: Art/Architecture*, Kunsthaus Bregenz, 2011

du gouvernement chinois d'installer le logiciel de censure Green Dam sur tous les ordinateurs vendus en Chine, Ai Weiwei appelle à une journée de boycott d'Internet le 1er juillet. Finalement, le gouvernement renoncera à imposer ce logiciel. Ai Weiwei se rend à Tokyo où se tient la première rétrospective de son œuvre, *According to What?*, au Musée d'Art Mori. À son retour en Chine, il accepte de témoigner au procès de Tan Zuoren, défenseur des droits de l'homme accusé de « subversion du pouvoir de l'État » pour avoir publié les résultats de sa propre enquête sur la mort de 5000 écoliers durant le séisme du Sichuan. Dans la soirée du 12 août, à la veille du procès, Ai Weiwei reçoit la visite de la police dans sa chambre d'hôtel ; il est frappé et ne peut aller témoigner. Quelques semaines plus tard, alors qu'il prépare l'exposition *So Sorry* à la Haus der Kunst à Munich, Ai Weiwei passe un scanner qui décèle une hémorragie interne, probable conséquence des violences policières et pour laquelle Ai Weiwei devra subir une intervention d'urgence. Ai Weiwei rejoint Twitter ; au cours des quatre années suivantes, il publiera plus de 104 000 tweets lus par 234 000 abonnés.

2010 Les *Sunflower Seeds* d'Ai Weiwei, au Turbine Hall de la Tate Modern, sont un succès public et critique. Au début les visiteurs sont autorisés à marcher sur les millions de graines de porcelaine mais après quelques jours leur accès est protégé par un cordon de sécurité. Ai Weiwei est informé par les autorités que le studio qu'il vient de construire à Shanghai va être détruit. Depuis qu'il a ouvertement critiqué le gouvernement, Ai Weiwei n'a plus les faveurs des autorités locales. Il lance l'idée d'une fête avant la démolition, à laquelle il invite tous ses abonnés sur Twitter. La police l'assigne à résidence pour deux jours, l'empêchant de se rendre à Shanghai. Mais plus de 3000 personnes font le déplacement et la fête a lieu sans lui.

2011 Le 11 janvier, le studio de Shanghai est démoli sans préavis. Trois jours plus tard, la rétrospective de son œuvre prévue à l'UCCA de Pékin est annulée. Le 3 avril, Ai Weiwei est retenu à l'aéroport international de Pékin tandis que la police fouille son studio et saisit les disques durs de ses ordinateurs. Ai Weiwei est détenu sans charges officielles dans un endroit secret où il est interrogé et surveillé de près. Personne ne sait où il se trouve. Il s'ensuit une immense vague de solidarité : actions de nombreux artistes, lettres de protestation officielles, manifestations populaires. Pendant sa détention, Ai Weiwei devient membre honorifique de l'Akademie der Künste de Berlin et de la Royal Academy of Arts de Londres, ses œuvres sont exposées dans divers musées et galeries ainsi que, pour la première fois, dans l'espace public : *Circle of Animals* est installé à New York. Le 15 mai, l'épouse d'Ai Weiwei peut lui rendre une brève visite, placée sous haute surveillance. Le 22 juin, après 81 jours de détention illégale, Ai Weiwei est finalement libéré sous caution. Il lui est interdit de quitter Pékin pendant un an et il ne peut plus donner d'interviews ni parler librement à la presse ou sur les réseaux sociaux. Puis, on lui demande de payer 12 millions de yuans (2,36 millions de dollars) d'arriérés d'impôts et d'amendes pour la société FAKE Design, sans que soient fournis ni preuve ni justificatif. Les avocats d'Ai Weiwei font une demande de contrôle administratif auprès des autorités fiscales. Ses sympathisants donnent à l'artiste 9 millions de yuans, cadeaux ou prêts, pour l'aider à payer ces impôts. Ai Weiwei est devenu un personnage public dans le monde entier : en 2011, il occupe la première place de la liste des 100 personnalités les plus influentes du monde de l'art publiée par *ArtReview* et il entre dans le « Time 100 ».

2012 Le jour anniversaire de sa détention, Ai Weiwei lance le projet *WeiweiCam* qui le filme en direct et 24h/24 chez lui et dans son studio. Les autorités chinoises mettent fin à ce projet 46 heures après sa mise en ligne. Le dossier fiscal est réexaminé sans procès public et Ai Weiwei ne peut assister à l'audience à huis clos. FAKE Design est officiellement fermé, les amendes confirmées par le juge. Ai Weiwei commence à rembourser ses créanciers en novembre. Le gouvernement ne lui a toujours pas rendu son passeport. Au festival du film de Sundance, le documentaire *Ai Weiwei : Never Sorry* de la réalisatrice américaine Alison Klayman obtient le prix spécial du jury. À l'occasion d'une exposition à la Magasin 3 Stockholm Konsthall, Ai Weiwei est désigné membre étranger de l'Académie royale des beaux-arts de Suède.

2013 Ai Weiwei sort son premier *single*, « Dumbass ». Il signe les paroles, son ami, le chanteur rock chinois Zuoxiao Zuzhou, compose la musique. Le clip vidéo de la chanson, réalisé par Christopher Doyle, recrée certaines scènes surréalistes de la détention d'Ai Weiwei. Un mini album suit, intitulé *Divine Comedy* ainsi que deux autres clips musicaux. À la Biennale de Venise, Ai Weiwei est présent avec une installation officielle sur le pavillon de l'Allemagne et une installation dans l'église Sant'Antonin, *S.A.C.R.E.D.*, qui retrace, à la façon d'un diorama, six scènes de sa détention en 2011.

2015 Ai est autorisé à quitter la Chine et s'installe à Berlin, où l'université des arts UdK lui propose une chaire. Son art et son activisme thématisent la crise migratoire mondiale, comme c'est notamment le cas dans son documentaire *Human Flow*, réalisé en **2017** et sélectionné pour la Mostra de Venise. **Aujourd'hui,** Ai Weiwei vit et travaille à Cambridge, à Berlin, et partout où le mènent ses voyages.

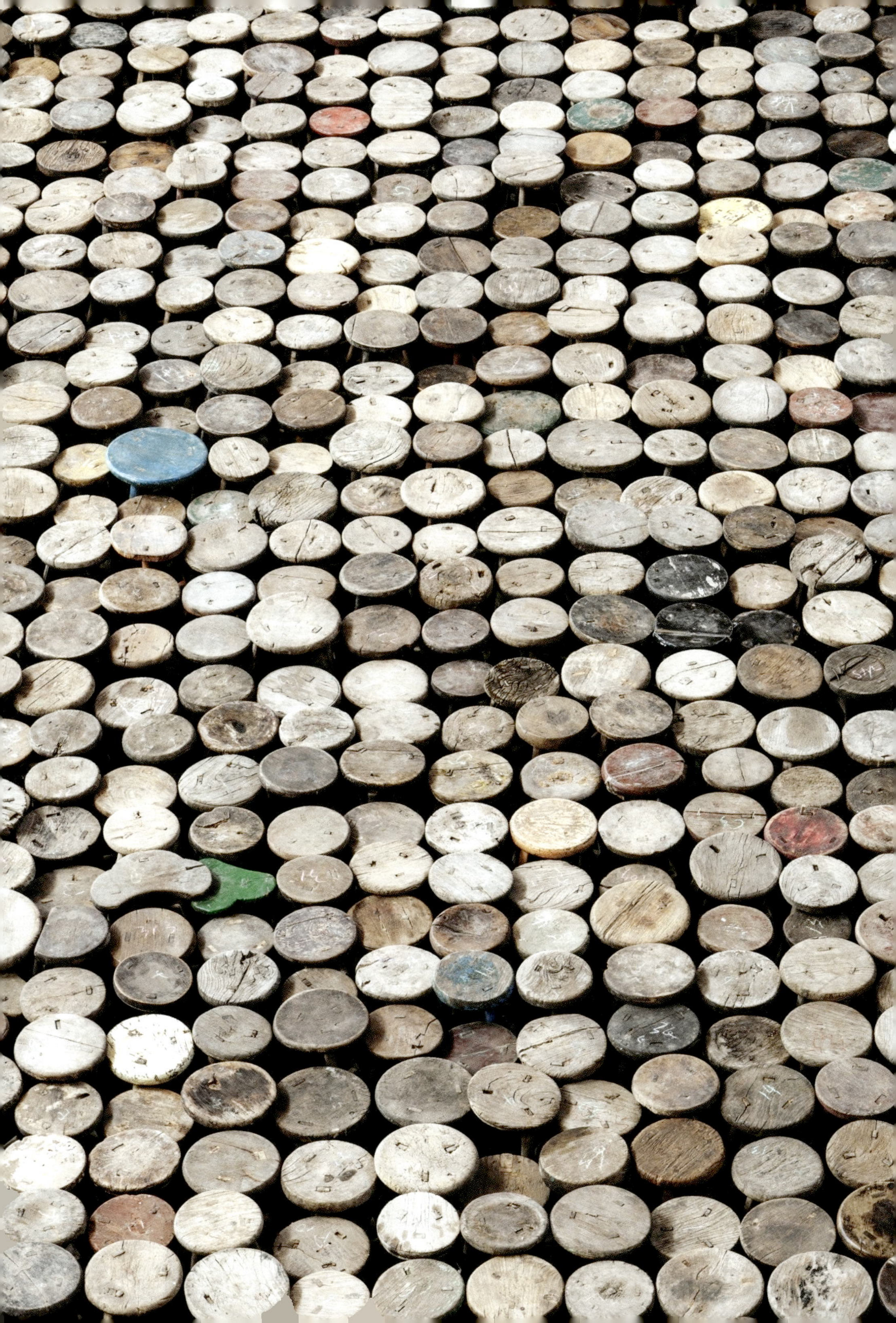

Exhibitions, Books, and Films

1979 *The First Stars Exhibition* (group). Park adjacent to the National Art Museum of China, Beijing (Sep 27–Oct 3); Studio, Beihai Park, Beijing (Nov 23–Dec 2)

1980 *The Second Stars Exhibition* (group). National Art Museum of China, Beijing (Aug 20–Sep 7)

1982 Asia Foundation, San Francisco (Jan)

1986 *Beijing/New York: Avant-Garde Chinese Art* (group). City Gallery, New York (Jul 24–Aug 30); Vassar College Art Gallery, Poughkeepsie (Nov 7–Dec 8); University Art Museum, University at Albany (Mar 10–Apr 10, 1987)

1987 *China's New Expression* (group). Municipal Gallery, New York (Sep 29–Nov 22) | *The Stars at Harvard: Chinese Dissident Art* (group). Fairbank Center for East Asian Research, Harvard University, Cambridge, MA (Oct 2–Nov 26)

1988 *Old Shoes, Safe Sex.* Art Waves/Ethan Cohen, New York (Feb 20–Mar 20)

1990 *The New Generation of Chinese Art* (group). Smith College Museum of Art, Northampton (Jan 12–Feb 21)

1993 *Chinese Contemporary Art: The Stars, 15 Years* (group). Tokyo Gallery, Tokyo

1995 *Change: Chinese Contemporary Art Exhibition* (group). Göteborgs Konsthall, Göteborg (Jan 28–Apr 17)

1996 *Begegnungen mit China* (group). Ludwig Forum für Internationale Kunst, Aachen (Mar 29–Oct 10)

1999 *Innovations Part I* (group). China Art Archives and Warehouse, Beijing (Feb 26–Mar 21) | *Aperto over All* (group). 48. Biennale di Venezia (Jun 12–Nov 7)

2000 *Our Chinese Friends* (group). ACC Galerie and Galerie der Bauhaus-Universität, Weimar (Jun 29–Aug 27) | *Fuck Off* (group). Eastlink, Shanghai, curated by Ai Weiwei and Feng Boyi (Oct 1–10)

2003 Galerie Urs Meile, Lucerne (Nov 8, 2003–Jan 10, 2004)

2004 Kunsthalle Bern (Apr 2–May 30) | *Caermersklooster, Ghent (Apr 30–Jun 13); Robert Miller Gallery, New York (Sep 9–Oct 9)

2006 *Fragments.* Galerie Urs Meile, Beijing (Apr 8–May 20)

2007 *Galerie Urs Meile, Lucerne (Nov 3–Dec 22) | *Traveling Landscapes.* AedesLand, Berlin (Nov 22, 2007–Jan 31, 2008)

2008 *Groninger Museum, Groningen (Mar 2–Nov 23) | *Illumination.* Mary Boone Gallery, New York (Mar 8–Apr 26) | *Under Construction.* Sherman Contemporary Art Foundation, Sydney; Campbelltown Arts Center, Campbelltown (May 1–Jul 26) | *Gallery Hyundai, Seoul (May 7–Jun 1) | *Fairytale.* Institute of Modern Art, Brisbane (Aug 23–Oct 11); Emerson Gallery, Hamilton College, Clinton (Aug 25, 2008–Jan 4, 2009) | Albion Gallery, London (Oct 14–Nov 17)

2009 *New York Photographs 1983–1993.* Three Shadows Photography Art Center, Beijing (Jan 2–Apr 18); Asia Society Museum, New York (Jun 29–Aug 14, 2011); Martin-Gropius-Bau, Berlin (Oct 15, 2011–Mar 18, 2012); Multimedia Art Museum, Moscow (Apr 20–May 31, 2012); Ernst Múzeum, Budapest (Aug 16–Oct 21, 2012) | *Four Movements.* Phillips de Pury, London (Mar 3–28) | Friedman Benda, New York (May 1–Jun 27) | *Ways beyond Art.* Ivory Press Space, Madrid (May 19–Jul 18) | *According to What?* Mori Art Museum, Tokyo (Jul 25–Nov 8); Hirshhorn Museum, Washington, D.C. (Oct 7, 2012–Feb 24, 2013); Indianapolis Museum of Art, Indianapolis (Apr 5–Jul 21, 2013); Art Gallery of Ontario, Toronto (Aug 17–Oct 27, 2013); Perez Art Museum, Miami (Nov 28, 2013–Mar 15, 2014); Brooklyn Museum, New York (Apr 18–Aug 10, 2014) | *World Map.* Galleri Faurschou, Beijing (Sep 5–Dec 20) | *So Sorry.* Haus der Kunst, Munich (Oct 12, 2009–Jan 17, 2010) | *With Milk, Find Something Everybody Can Use.* Mies van der Rohe Pavilion, Barcelona (Dec 10–30)

2010 *Dropping the Urn: Ceramic Works 5000 BCE–2010 CE.* Arcadia University Art Gallery, Glenside (Feb 24–Apr 18); Museum of Contemporary Craft, Portland (Jul 15–Oct 30); Victoria and Albert Museum, London (Oct 15, 2011–Mar 18, 2012) | *Barely Something.* Museum DKM and Galerie DKM, Duisburg (Mar 19–Sep 20) | Haines Gallery, San Francisco (Apr 15–May 29) | *Mermaid Exchange.* Langelinie Pier, Copenhagen (May 1–Oct 31) | *Hurt Feelings.* Christine König Galerie, Vienna (Sep 18–Nov 6) | Galerie Urs Meile, Lucerne (Oct 2–Dec 18) | *The Unilever Series: Ai Weiwei, Sunflower Seeds.* Turbine Hall, Tate Modern, London (Oct 12, 2010–May 2, 2011) | Galleri Faurschou, Copenhagen (Nov 18, 2010–Mar 27, 2011; reopened after Ai Wewei's detention: May 1–June 30, 2011) | *Cube Light.* Misa Shin Gallery, Tokyo (Nov 19, 2010–Feb 19, 2011)

2011 *Teehaus.* Museum für Asiatische Kunst, Berlin (Feb 5, 2011–Jun 7, 2012) | *Circle of Animals/Zodiac Heads.* Pulitzer Fountain, Grand Army Plaza, New York (May 2–Jul 15), and Somerset House, London (May 12–Jun 26); Los Angeles County Museum of Art, Los Angeles (Aug 20, 2011–Feb 12, 2012); Taipei Fine Arts Museum (Oct 29, 2011–Jan 29, 2012); Hermann

Park, Houston (Mar 3–June 3, 2012); Hirshhorn
Museum and Sculpture Garden, Washington, D.C.
(Apr 19, 2012–Feb 24, 2013); Princeton University,
New Jersey (Aug 1, 2012–Aug 1, 2013); Art Gallery of
Ontario, Toronto (Jun 18–Sep 22, 2013); Cleveland
Museum of Art, Cleveland (Jul 24, 2013–Jan 26, 2014);
Miami Art Museum (Dec 3, 2013–Mar 16, 2014);
and many others | neugerriemschneider, Berlin
(Apr 30–Jun 4) | Faurschou Foundation, Copenhagen
(May 1–Jul 1) | *Lisson Gallery, London (May 13–
Jul 16) | *Interlacing. Fotomuseum Winterthur (May
28–Aug 21); Kunsthaus Graz (Sep 17, 2011–Feb 5,
2012); Jeu de Paume, Paris (Feb 21–Apr 29, 2012);
Kistefos-Museet, Jevnaker (May 20–Oct 7, 2012);
Museu da Imagem e do Som, São Paulo (Feb 7–Apr
14, 2013) | *Art/Architecture. Kunsthaus Bregenz
(Jul 16–Oct 16) | Absent. Taipei Fine Arts Museum
(Oct 29, 2011–Jan 29, 2012) | *Louisiana Museum of
Modern Art, Humlebæk (Nov 18, 2011–Feb 12, 2012);
De Pont, Tilburg (Mar 3–Jun 24, 2012)

2012 *Sunflower Seeds.* Mary Boone Gallery, New
York (Jan 7–Feb 4) | Magasin 3 Stockholm Konsthall,
Stockholm (Feb 3–Jun 10) | Lisson Gallery, Milano
(Apr 12–May 25) | *Perspectives: Ai Weiwei.* Arthur M.
Sackler Gallery, Smithsonian Institution, Washing-
ton, D.C. (May 12, 2012–Apr 14, 2013) | *Serpentine
Gallery Pavilion.* Serpentine Gallery, London
(Jun 1–Oct 14) | *Forge.* Mary Boone Gallery, New
York (Oct 13–Dec 21) | *Rebar: Lucerne.* Galerie
Urs Meile, Lucerne (Oct 27, 2012–Jan 12, 2013) |
*Galleria Continua, San Gimignano (Oct 27, 2012–
Jan 26, 2013) | *Apocalypse.* Einzweidrei, Vevey
(Nov 15–Dec 21)

2013 *Resistance and Tradition.* Centro Andaluz
de Arte Contemporáneo, Sevilla (Feb 1–Jun 23) |
Disposition. Zuecca Project Space/Complesso
delle Zitelle, Giudecca and Chiesa di Saint'Antonin,
Venice (Jun 1–Sep 15) | *Baby Formula.* Michael
Janssen, Singapore (Aug 23–Oct 6)

2014 *Evidence.* Martin-Gropius-Bau, Berlin
(Apr 3–Jul 7) | Lisson Gallery, London (May 23–
Jul 19) | *@Large: Ai Weiwei on Alcatraz.*
Alcatraz Island, San Francisco (Sep 27, 2014–
Apr 26, 2015)

2015 *Forever in the City.* Sculpture in the City,
London (Jul 9, 2015–May 2016) | *Royal Academy,
London (Sep 19–Dec 13) | *Helsinki Art Museum
(Sep 25, 2015–Feb 28, 2016) | *Andy Warhol—Ai
Weiwei.* National Gallery of Victoria, Melbourne
(Dec 11, 2015–Apr 24, 2016); The Andy Warhol
Museum, Pittsburgh (Jun 4–Sep 11, 2016)

2016 *The Museum of Cycladic Art, Athens (May
20–Oct 30) | *Translocation—Transformation.* 21er
Haus, Vienna (Jul 14–Nov 20) | Galerie Max Hetzler,
Paris (Sep 3–Oct 8) | *#SafePassage.* foam museum,
Amsterdam (Sep 16–Dec 7) | *Libero.* Palazzo
Strozzi, Florence (Sep 23, 2016–Jan 22, 2017) |
Around Ai Weiwei: Photographs 1983–2016. Camera,

Torino (Oct 28, 2016–Feb 19, 2017) | *Laundromat.*
Jeffrey Deitch, New York (Nov 5–Dec 23) | *Roots
and Branches.* Mary Boone Gallery, New York (Nov 5–
Dec 23) | *Roots and Branches.* Lisson Gallery,
New York (Nov 5–Dec 23)

2017 *Natural State.* Frederik Meijers Gardens &
Sculpture Park, Grand Rapids (Jan 27–Aug 20) |
Tyre. Galerie Forsblom, Stockholm (Feb 5–Mar 26) |
Law of the Journey. National Gallery, Prague (Mar
17, 2017–Jan 7, 2018) | *Mountains and Seas.* Château
La Coste, Le Puy Sainte Réparade (Apr 8–Jun 18) |
#AiWeiwei. Museum of Contemporary Photography,
Columbia College, Chicago (Apr 13–Jul 2) | *Odyssey.*
Zona Arti Contemporanea, Palermo (Apr 23–Jun 20)
| The Contemporary, Austin (opening Jun 3) | *Soleil
Levant.* Kunsthal Charlottenborg, Copenhagen
(Jun 20–Oct 1) | *Trace.* Hirshhorn Museum and
Sculpture Garden, Washington, D.C. (Jul 28, 2017–
Jan 1, 2018) | *On Porcelain.* Sakip Sabanci Museum,
Istanbul (Sep 12, 2017–Apr 15, 2018) | Massimo
de Carlo, Milan (Sep 12–Nov 18) | *D'ailleurs c'est
toujours les autres.* Musée cantonal des beaux-arts,
Lausanne (Sep 22, 2017–Jan 28, 2018) | *Good
Fences Make Good Neighbors.* Public Art Fund, various
locations, New York (Oct 12, 2017– Feb 11, 2018) |
Inoculation. Fundación Proa, Buenos Aires (Nov 25,
2017–Apr 8, 2018); CorpArtes, Santiago (May 18–Sep
9, 2018)

2018 *Laundromat.* Garage Gallery, Fire Station,
Doha (Mar 15–Jun 1) | *Fan-Tan.* Mucem, Marseille
(Jun 20–Nov 12) | *Life Cycle.* Marciano Art Foun-
dation, Los Angeles (Sep 28, 2018–Mar 3, 2019) |
Zodiac. Jeffrey Deitch, Los Angeles (Sep 29, 2018–
Jan 5, 2019) | *Cao/Humanity.* UTA Artist Space,
Beverly Hills (Oct 4–Dec 1) | *Raiz Weiwei.* OCA,
São Paulo (Oct 20–Jan 20, 2019); Centro Cultural
Banco do Brasil, Belo Horizonte (Feb 6–Apr 15, 2019)

2019 *Unbroken.* The Gardiner Museum, Toronto (Feb
28–Jun 9) | *Everything Is Art. Everything Is Politics.*
Kunstsammlung NRW, Düsseldorf (May 17–Sep 1) |
Roots. neugerriemschneider, Berlin (Sep 6–Oct 19) |
Bare Life. Mildred Lane Kemper Art Museum,
Washington University, St. Louis (Sep 28, 2019–Jan 5,
2020) | *Roots.* Lisson Gallery, London (Oct 1–Nov 2) |
*The Mueller Report/Declaration of the Rights of Man
and the Citizen.* Cahiers d'Art, Paris (Oct 17–Dec 21)

SELECTED MONOGRAPHS

2003 *Ai Weiwei: Works, Beijing 1993–2003.*
Beijing, Hong Kong: Timezone 8. Ed. Charles
Merewether

2007 *Ai Weiwei: Works 2004–2007.* Zurich:
JRP Ringier, 2007. Text Charles Merewether,
Peter Pakesch, Philip Tinari

2008 *Ai Weiwei: Under Construction.* Sydney:
University of New South Wales Press. Text Charles

Merewether | *Ai Weiwei/Herzog & de Meuron: Beijing, Venice, London*. London: Albion Gallery; Cologne: Walther König. Ed. Charles Merewether, Matt Price

2009 *Ai Weiwei*. London: Phaidon. Text Bernhard Fibicher, Karen Smith; interview Hans Ulrich Obrist | *Ai Weiwei: According to What?* Tokyo: Mori Art Museum. Text Mami Kataoka, Charles Merewether, et al. | *Ai Weiwei: So Sorry*. Munich: Haus der Kunst; Prestel, 2009. Text Mark Siemons, Karen Smith; interview Mathieu Wellner

2010 *Ai Weiwei: Barely Something*. Duisburg: Stiftung DKM. Text Roger M. Buergel | *Ai Weiwei: Sunflower Seeds*. London: Tate Publishing. Ed. Juliet Bingham

2011 *Ai Weiwei: Art/Architecture*. Bregenz: Kunsthaus Bregenz. Text Yilmaz Dziewior, Andres Lepik, et al. | *Ai Weiwei: Circle of Animals*. Munich, New York: Prestel. Ed. Susan Delson | *Ai Weiwei: Interlacing*. Winterthur: Fotomuseum Winterthur; Göttingen: Steidl. Ed. Daniela Janser, Urs Stahel | *Ai Weiwei's Blog: Writings, Interviews and Digital Rants, 2006–2009*. Cambridge, MA: MIT Press. Ed. and trans. Lee Ambrozy | *Ai Weiwei Speaks with Hans Ulrich Obrist*. London: Penguin Books

2012 *Ai Weiwei: According to What?* Washington, D.C.: Hirshhorn Museum; Tokyo: Mori Art Museum; Munich, New York: Prestel. Text Mami Kataoka, Charles Merewether; interview Kerry Brougher | *Ai Weiwei: Fairytale. A Reader*. Zurich: JRP Ringier. Ed. Lionel Bovier, Salome Schnetz

2013 *Ai Weiwei: Disposition*. Milan: Mousse Publishing, 2013. Text Maurizio Bortolotti, Alessandro Possati | Barnaby Martin, *Hanging Man: The Arrest of Ai Weiwei*. London: Faber and Faber

2014 *Ai Weiwei*. Cologne: Taschen. Ed. Hans Werner Holzwarth; text Roger M. Buergel, William A. Callahan, James J. Lally, Carlos Rojas, Uli Sigg | *Ai Weiwei: Evidence*. Berlin: Martin-Gropius-Bau; Munich, New York: Prestel. Ed. Gereon Sievernich | *@Large: Ai Weiwei on Alcatraz*. San Francisco: Chronicle Books. Ed. David Spalding

2015 *Ai Weiwei*. London: Royal Academy of the Arts. Ed. Tim Marlow, John L. Tancock | *Ai Weiwei @ Helsinki*. Helsinki: HAM. Ed. Erja Pusa, Heli Harni

2016 *Ai Weiwei at Cycladic*. Athens: Museum of Cycladic Art. Ed. Michael Frahm | *Andy Warhol— Ai Weiwei*. Pittsburgh: The Andy Warhol Museum; New Haven: Yale University Press. Ed. Max Delany, Eric Shiner

2017 *#AiWeiwei*. Columbia: Museum of Contemporary Photography. Text Natasha Egan, John Tancock, et al. | *Ai Weiwei: D'ailleurs c'est toujours les autres*. Lausanne: Musée cantonal des beaux-arts; Milan: 5 continents. Text Stefan Banz, Bernhard Fibicher, et al.

2018 *Ai Weiwei: Fan-Tan*. Marseille: Mucem. Ed. Judith Benhamou-Huet | *Ai Weiwei: Yours Truly*. San Francisco: Chronicle Books. Ed. David Spalding

2019 *Ai Weiwei*. Düsseldorf: Kunstsammlung NRW; Munich, New York: Prestel. Ed. Susanne Gaensheimer, Doris Krystof, Falk Wolf | *Ai Weiwei: Bare Life*. St. Louis: Mildred Lane Kemper Art Museum. Text Sabine Eckmann | *Ai Weiwei: Good Fences Make Good Neighbors*. New York: Public Art Fund. Ed. Nicholas Baume

SELECTED FILMS AND VIDEOS

2007 Ai Weiwei, *Fairytale*, 1 h 32 min, English. Beijing: Ai Weiwei Studio. Documentary as part of Documenta 12

2008 Ai Weiwei, *Hua Lian Ba'er (Little Girl's Cheeks)*, 1 h 18 min, Chinese. Beijing: Ai Weiwei Studio. Documentary on the Citizens' Investigation

2011 Ai Weiwei, *So Sorry*, 54 min 28 sec, Chinese with English subtitles. Beijing: Ai Weiwei Studio. Documentary on the conflict with Chinese authorities after the Citizens' Investigation | Alison Klayman, *Ai Weiwei: Never Sorry*, 1 h 31 min, English. New York: Never Sorry, LLC; MUSE Film and Television. Documentary accompanying the artist from 2008 to his 2011 detention

2012 Ai Weiwei, *He Xie Fang Zi (The Crab House)*, video, 1 h 49 min, Chinese with English subtitles. Beijing: Ai Weiwei Studio. Documentary on the Shanghai studio and its destruction in 2011

2013 Andreas Johnsen, *Ai Weiwei: The Fake Case*, 1 h 26 min, Chinese and English. Denmark: DCP. Documentary on the political issues after Ai Weiwei's return from arrest in 2011

2014 Ai Weiwei, *Ai Weiwei's Appeal YEN 5,220,910.50*, video, 2 h 7 min, Chinese with English subtitles. Beijing: Ai Weiwei Studio. Documentary of the FAKE case

2017 Ai Weiwei, *Human Flow*, 2 h 20 min, diverse languages with English subtitles. Germany: AC Films, Participant Media, AWW Germany et al. Documentary on the global refugee crisis

2019 Ai Weiwei, *The Rest*, 1 h 18 min, diverse languages with English subtitles. Germany: AWW Germany. Documentary on the life of global refugees after their arrival in Europe | Cheryl Haines, *Ai Weiwei: Yours Truly*, 1h 16 min, English. USA: FOR-SITE Foundation. Documentary on the aftermath of Ai Weiwei's 2014 Alcatraz exhibition

2020 Ai Weiwei, *Vivos*, 1 h 52 min, English and Spanish. Germany: AWW Germany. Documentary on student abductions in Mexico

QUOTATION SOURCES

All single quote pages from interviews with the artist conducted especially for this book by Angie Baecker, Beijing 2013, except:

56 *Ai Weiwei Speaks with Hans Ulrich Obrist*, London 2011: 81, 83/84 | **64** Ibid.: 79/80, 83 | **70** Ibid.: 82 | **76** Ai Weiwei, "Remembering the Strange Self and Non-Self," *Liu Li Tun: RongRong & inri*, Beijing 2006: 26 | **116** Ai Weiwei with Chin-Chin Yap in *Ai Weiwei: Works, Beijing 1993–2003*, Hong Kong 2003: 51 | **156** Karen Smith, "A Brief History of Light: A Conversation with Ai Weiwei," *Ai Weiwei: Illumination*, New York 2008: 77, 79/80 | **162** Interview Angie Baecker and *Ai Weiwei: According to What?*, Tokyo 2009: 25 | **172** *Ai Weiwei Speaks with Hans Ulrich Obrist*: 98, and "Interview with Ai Weiwei," *Shooting Back*, Vienna 2007: 36 | **262** *Ai Weiwei Speaks with Hans Ulrich Obrist*: 35 | **270** Ibid.: 35, and Adrian Blackwell, "Fragments, Voids, Sections and Rings," *Archinect*, Dec 5, 2006: online | **282** Karen Smith, "A Brief History of Light": 82 | **300** Interview Angie Baecker and Ai Weiwei, "Heartless," *Ai Weiwei's Blog*, Cambridge, MA, 2011: 202 | **384** Ai Weiwei, "On the Bird's Nest," *Ai Weiwei's Blog*: 162, 164 | **386** Ai Weiwei, "China Excluded Its People from the Olympics. London Is Different," *The Guardian*, Jul 26, 2012: G2, 18 | **402** *Ai Weiwei: So Sorry*, Munich: Prestel, 2009: 14; *Ai Weiwei: Never Sorry*, dir. Alison Klayman, video, New York 2011; and interview with Angie Baecker, Beijing 2013 | **406** *Ai Weiwei: Sunflower Seeds*, London 2010: 76–79 | **410** Ai Weiwei, "My Work Is Always a Readymade," *Ai Weiwei: Circle of Animals*, New York 2011: 52

Ai Weiwei Studio, Caochangdi 258, 1999– (pp. 123–139)

All statements by Ai Weiwei from interviews with Angie Baecker, Beijing 2013, except last paragraph first quote from: Bert de Muynck, "I Jumped on the Wrong Train," *Mark* 12, 2008: 74–87
Other sources: Eduard Kögel and Ulf Meyer, *Tu Mu: Young Architecture of China*, Berlin 2001: 18; "Studio in Beijing," *Detail* 1/2, 2002: 79; "Ai Weiwei and His Home," *China Radio International*, Aug 7, 2004: online; Jonathan Napack in *Ai Weiwei: Works, Beijing 1993–2003*, Hong Kong 2003: 38; Arie Chen, "A New Frontier for Chinese Art," *The New York Times,* Apr 1, 2007: 4; and voices from the studio and workshops from interviews conducted for this book by Angie Baecker and Uli Huang Zhiheng, 2013

Fairytale, Documenta 2007 (pp. 315–335)

Aug 7, 2006 Ai Weiwei, "A 'Fairytale' Becomes an Artwork," blog entry from July 20, 2007, *Ai Weiwei's Blog:* 120 | **Feb 22, 2007** Ibid.: 121 | **Feb 26, 2007** Nataline Colonnello, "1=1000," *Artnet*, Aug 10, 2007: online, and "A 'Fairytale' Becomes an Artwork": 120 | **Feb 26–Mar 1, 2007** "A 'Fairytale' Becomes an Artwork": 121/122 | **Mar 7, 2007** Sae-mi Kim, "Realization of Fairytale," *Art in Asia,* May–Jun 2008: 55 | **Mar 16, 2007** Nataline Colonnello, "1=1000" | **Jun 11, 2007** Ulrike Münter, "Märchen mal anders," *taz:* online | **Jun 16, 2007** Nataline Colonnello, "1=1000" | **Jun 20, 2007** "Ai Weiweis Template nach Unwetter eingestürzt," *Frankfurter Allgemeine Zeitung:* online | **Jun 21, 2007** "Documenta-Pannen: Mohn, Reis, Kreuze und ein Sturm," *Focus:* online | **Ai Weiwei** Catherine Hickley, "Ruined Sculpture," *Bloomberg*, Jul 8, 2008: online, and Bert de Muynck, "I Jumped on the Wrong Train": 74–87 | **Fairytale Documentary** *Fairytale*, video, Zurich 2010 | **Sep 1, 2007** Nataline Colonnello, "1=1000"

Sichuan Earthquake and Citizens' Investigation (pp. 345–375)

May 12, 2008 "Thousands Dead in Chinese Quake," *BBC News:* online | **May 13, 2008** Edward Wong, "'No Hope' for Children Buried in Earthquake," *The New York Times:* online | **May 22, 2008** Ai Weiwei, "Grief," *Ai Weiwei's Blog:* 149 | **May 25, 2008** Jim Yardley, "Chinese Are Left to Ask Why Schools Crumbled," *The New York Times:* online | **Jun 1, 2008** Ai Weiwei, "Silent Holiday," *Ai Weiwei's Blog:* 152; Lindsay Beck, Valerie Lee, and Alan Wheatley, "China Breathes More Easily as Quake-Lake Fears Ebb," *Reuters:* online | **Jul 28, 2008** Ai Weiwei, "Does the Nation Have a List?" *Ai Weiwei's Blog:* 177 | **Mar 13, 2009** Ai Weiwei studio records | **Mar 20, 2009** Ai Weiwei, "Citizen Investigation," *Ai Weiwei's Blog:* 209 | **Mar 24, 2009** Ai Weiwei, "Guests from All Corners of the Earth," *Ai Weiwei's Blog:* 211 | **Mar 2009** Interview conducted by Angie Baecker and Uli Huang Zhiheng, 2013 | **Apr 18, 2009** Ai Weiwei studio records | **May 7, 2009** Ai Weiwei, "These Days I Can't Believe Anything You Say," *Ai Weiwei's Blog:* 219/220 | **May 28, 2009** Ai Weiwei, "Don't Harbor Illusions about Me," *Ai Weiwei's Blog:* 228/229 | **Aug 12, 2009** Ai Weiwei studio records; Tania Branigan, "Chinese Police Detain 11 Who Planned to Attend Activist's Trial," *The Guardian:* online | **Sep 16, 2009** "Operation in Munich: Chinese Artist Accuses Government for Injury," *Spiegel:* online | **Oct 11, 2009** Katharina Dorn, "Erinnerung an tote Kinder," *Focus:* online | **Nov 20, 2009** Ai Weiwei, "I Really Can't Believe It," *Ai Weiwei's Blog:* 237 | **Feb 10, 2010** Sky Canaves, "China Sentences Earthquake Activist," *The Wall Street Journal:* online

Detention and the FAKE Case (pp. 435–464)
All tweets from Ai Weiwei studio records, translated from the Chinese

Feb 23, 2011 Peter Foster, "China Facing New Calls for Jasmine Revolution," *The Telegraph:* online | **Mar 7, 2011** Peter Foster, "Ai Wei Wei: 'Growing Force behind Jasmine Revolution Very Strong,'" *The Telegraph:* online | **Apr 3, 2011** "China Artist Ai Weiwei Stopped from Boarding Flight," *BBC News:* online | **Apr 4, 2011** "Police Remain Silent on Ai Weiwei Detention," *AFP:* online; Sharon LaFraniere, "Pressure on China to Release Dissident Artist," *The New York Times:* online | **Apr 5, 2011** Su Yutong, "Ai Weiwei's Mother Says Her Son's Arrest Concerns Everybody," *Deutsche Welle:* online | **Apr 6, 2011** "Law Will Not Concede before Maverick," *Global Times:* online | **Apr 7, 2011** Keith B. Richburg, "China: Ai Weiwei Held for 'Economic Crimes,'" *The Washington Post:* online | **Apr 8, 2011** Carol Vogel, "Museums Press for the Release of Ai Weiwei," *The New York Times:* online | **Apr 10, 2011** "Hong Kong Rallies for Ai Weiwei," *The Wall Street Journal:* online; "Demo für Ai Weiwei in Berlin," *BZ Berlin:* online | **Apr 12, 2011** Tania Branigan, "Chinese Tax Officials Question Ai Weiwei's Wife," *The Guardian:* online | **Apr 17, 2011** Abby d'Arcy Hughes, "Ai Weiwei Arrest Protests at Chinese Embassies Worldwide," *The Guardian:* online | **Apr 19, 2011** Alison Klayman, "Crackdown on Ai Weiwei Extends to Family, Friends and Associates," *PBS:* online | **Apr 20, 2011** "Professur für Ai Weiwei: Dissident wird Dozent in Berlin," *Spiegel:* online | **Apr 23, 2011** James Pomfret, "Thousands March in Hong Kong to Demand Release of China's Ai," *Reuters:* online | **Apr 27, 2011** "China and US Begin Human Rights Talks in Beijing," *BBC News:* online | **May 4, 2011** Roberta Smith, "12 Heads Do the Talking for a Silenced Artist," *The New York Times:* online; **May 15, 2011**: "Detained Chinese Artist Allowed Visit by Wife," *Associated Press*, May 15, 2011: online | **May 20, 2011** "Chinese Artist Ai Weiwei's Company 'Evaded Taxes,'" *BBC News:* online | **Jun 22, 2011** "Ai Weiwei Released on Bail," *Xinhua News Agency:* online; Tania Branigan, "Ai Weiwei Released from Detention," *The Guardian:* online | **Jun 23, 2011** Jeremy Page, "Beijing Releases Detained Artist," *The Wall Street Journal:* online; Tania Branigan, "Ai Weiwei's Cousin Freed But Others from His Circle Still Missing," *The Guardian:* online | **Aug 9, 2011** Chen Liang, "Exclusive: Ai Weiwei Breaks His Silence," *Global Times* | **Nov 1, 2011** "China Artist Ai Weiwei Gets Multi-Million Tax Bill," *AFP:* online; Sui-Lee Wee, "China Orders Ai Weiwei to Pay $2.4 Million for 'Tax Evasion,'" *Reuters:* online | **Nov 4, 2011** Peter Ford, "In Defiant Gesture, Chinese Surge forward to Help Ai Weiwei Pay Tax Bill," *Christian Science Monitor:* online | **Nov 7, 2011** Andrew Jacobs, "Online and by Paper Airplane, Contributions Pour in to Chinese Dissident," *The New York Times:* A4 | **Nov 14, 2011** Jeremy Page, "Ai Weiwei Donations Hit $1.37 Million," *The Wall Street Journal:* online | **Nov 15, 2011** Michael Bristow, "Chinese Artist Ai Weiwei Pays Bond to Appeal Tax Demand," *BBC News:* online | **Jan 6, 2012** "Ai Weiwei Given Hope of Tax Reprieve," *The Guardian:* online | **Mar 29, 2012** Sui-Lee Wee, "China Tells Ai Weiwei No Public Trial for Tax Case," *Reuters:* online | **Apr 13, 2012** Carlos Tejada, "China Dissident Artist Sues over Tax," *The Wall Street Journal:* online | **May 8, 2012** "China Says Artist Ai Weiwei Can Challenge $2.4m Tax Bill," *BBC News:* online | **Jun 20, 2012** Jeremy Page, "Ai Weiwei Blocked from Court," *The Wall Street Journal:* online; Andrew Jacobs, "Chinese Artist Is Barred from His Own Hearing," *The New York Times:* online | **Jun 21, 2012** Sui-Lee Wee, "China's Ai Weiwei Threatened with Bigamy, Pornography Charges," *Reuters:* online | **Jul 20, 2012** Austin Ramzy, "Chinese Activist Ai Weiwei Loses Appeal on Tax Charge," *Time:* online | **Sep 27, 2012** Josh Chin, "Ai Weiwei: I Won't Pay," *The Wall Street Journal:* online | **Oct 1, 2012** Tania Branigan, "Ai Weiwei Firm to Be Closed Down by Chinese Authorities," *The Guardian:* online | **Oct 31, 2012** "Ai Weiwei Returns Money to Supporters," *The Guardian:* online

Life and Work (pp. 487–504)

1967 Ingo Niermann, "The Materials of Ai Weiwei," *China Welcomes You,* Cologne 2007: 32 | **1982–1993** Ibid.: 36 | **1993** Christopher Hawthorne, "At Home with Ai Weiwei," *The New York Times,* Oct 28, 2004: F9 | **1999** Ingo Niermann, "The Materials of Ai Weiwei": 33 | **2007** "China Bird's Nest Designer Rails at Olympic 'Fakeness,'" *Reuters,* Aug 10, 2007: online

ACKNOWLEDGMENTS

The editor would like to thank the authors, who combined their special fields of knowledge to offer us an encompassing study of the artist's work as well as a deeply personal and political portrait. Thanks to Angie Baecker, who extensively interviewed the artist for us, and to Lutz Eitel, who always managed to shape the wealth of material into compelling reading matter. Very special thanks go out to everybody who made me welcome in Beijing, most of all to Chin-Chin Yap and Jeremy Wingfield, who accompanied this project from its inception, Elisabeth Ramsey for being there for us practically every day in transcontinental dialogue, and Uli Huang Zhiheng, Kingson Chan, and Jennifer Ng, who helped with every missing detail. Thanks also to the translators, the editors, and the teams at my studio and at Taschen. Most of all, my deepest gratitude goes out to Ai Weiwei, for his easy hospitality even in personally difficult times, for the incredible energy he brought to our collaboration on this project, and for his generosity in contributing to the design and artwork, making this book an object in line with his work.

ROGER M. BUERGEL is a curator who was artistic director of Documenta 12 (2007) and the Busan Biennale (2012). In 2010 he became the founding director of the Johann Jacobs Museum in Zurich, dedicated to the exploration of global trade routes and their cultural residues.

ULI SIGG is an entrepreneur who established the first joint venture between China and the outside world in 1980. In 1995 he became Swiss ambassador to China, North Korea, and Mongolia for four years, and he has since served as chairman or advisor for several multinational companies and projects. He owned the most substantial collection of Chinese contemporary art worldwide, from which he donated 1,500 works to M+, Hong Kong's new museum for visual culture, in 2012.

IMPRINT

EACH AND EVERY TASCHEN BOOK PLANTS A SEED!
TASCHEN is a carbon neutral publisher. Each year, we offset our annual carbon emissions with carbon credits at the Instituto Terra, a reforestation program in Minas Gerais, Brazil, founded by Lélia and Sebastião Salgado. To find out more about this ecological partnership, please check: www.taschen.com/zerocarbon
Inspiration: unlimited. Carbon footprint: zero.

To stay informed about TASCHEN and our upcoming titles, please subscribe to our free magazine at www.taschen.com/magazine, follow us on Instagram and Facebook, or e-mail your questions to contact@taschen.com.

Edited and designed by Hans Werner Holzwarth
Interviews with the artist: Angie Baecker
Line editing and chronologies: Lutz Eitel
English translation: Christopher Cordy (Buergel), William Wheeler (Sigg)
German translation: Volker Ellerbeck and Bernhard Geyer (chronologies)
French translation: Wolf Fruhtrunk (essays), Stéphanie Lux and Chloé Stein (chronologies)

Page 2: Ai Weiwei, 2012. Photo Gao Yuan; page 4: image from *WeiweiCam*, 2012

© 2024 TASCHEN GmbH
Hohenzollernring 53, D-50672 Köln
www.taschen.com

Original edition: © 2016 TASCHEN GmbH

For all artworks and texts by Ai Weiwei: © Ai Weiwei;
For the texts: the authors; for the photographs: the photographers

Printed in Bosnia-Herzegovina
ISBN 978-3-8365-8195-0